An Introduction to
American Prose

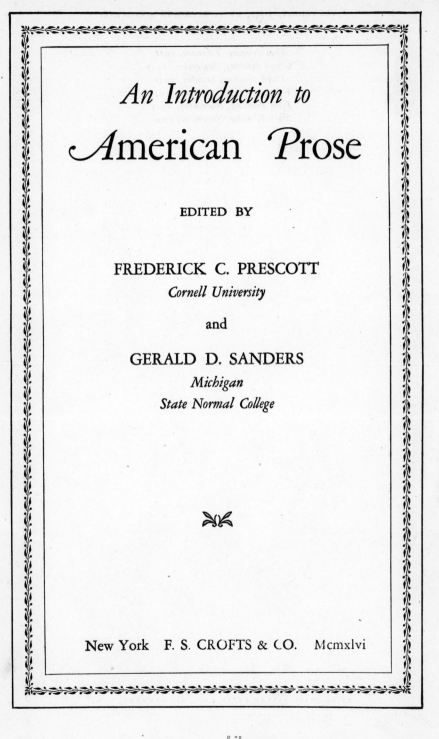

An Introduction to
American Prose

EDITED BY

FREDERICK C. PRESCOTT
Cornell University

and

GERALD D. SANDERS
*Michigan
State Normal College*

New York   F. S. CROFTS & CO.   Mcmxlvi

11705

PREFACE

During the period of two hundred years covered by this book, literature, both in England and in America, has come more and more to find its natural expression in prose. Two centuries ago verse was quite naturally employed not only for stories, but even for essays, treatises, and arguments. It has gradually given way in one field after another, holding its own only in the lyric. Even in fiction and drama prose is now the prevailing and expected form. This trend toward prose, though observable in Europe, has perhaps gone farthest in our modern and practical America. Our prose, compared with our poetry, has probably been, and in spite of an interesting recent revival of poetry, will doubtless continue to be, not merely more cultivated, but more vital and closer to our national life. The present book is intended to represent, as far as space will permit, this valuable and significant portion of our national literature.

Fortunately neglect of this literary heritage is now giving place to interest and appreciation. Students in school and college still read the best in foreign literatures; and will of course continue to do so. But they are no longer, like their predecessors of a generation ago, asked to read English books—De Quincey's *Mail Coach* and Southey's *Life of Nelson*—to the exclusion of their own. We have come to see that it is not the authors of our literature but its depreciators who have been "provincial" and "second-hand"; and that our literature—at any rate in prose, and from the time of the *Sketch-Book* to the present—is not hopelessly inferior to that of England during the same period. We have come to see that it is not obviously "accepting the second-best" to regard Emerson, for example, as a larger figure in world literature than Carlyle; to consider Hawthorne and Poe, Melville and Henry James, as great writers of fiction even when compared to their best English contemporaries; to find Prescott and Parkman the most readable of nineteenth-century historians; to think of Lincoln as a master of prose; or to place *The Education of Henry Adams* among the significant books of our time. And whatever the relative estimate, we have come to see the absolute value of our literature to us, because it is our own; and to feel that our American thought in the future can be sound only if it grows out of the best American thought in the past.

In making the selections the editors have felt an embarrassment of riches. They have omitted many writings, and indeed many writers, very reluctantly, being compelled to select from a great wealth of material only what might be included in one convenient and inexpensive volume. Though the selections are, as far as possible, complete and self-explanatory, they are, as the title suggests, only an *introduction* to American prose—in other words only an introduction to many volumes of good essays, stories, histories, and novels, which will be more interesting when read entire. Similarly the brief sketches and appreciations, prefixed to the extracts from each author, are meant only to let the reader know something of the men whose work he is approaching, and by no means to take the place of fuller accounts. Guides to further reading, both in and about the writers included, may be found in the "Book Lists" at the end of the volume.

This book, as the editors hope, may be fitted to a variety of uses. Readers interested in the historical development of American thought or prose style will find the writers, and also the selections from each, arranged in substantially chronological order, as represented by the first Table of Contents. By following an alternative Table of Contents included for their convenience readers studying the different literary forms may readily turn to the selections illustrating each. Readers of a more general kind may—it is confidently hoped—open the book almost anywhere to find interesting essays, sketches, letters, or stories, and fitting models of style.

For the use of copyright material the editors are indebted to the publishers to whose courtesy specific acknowledgment is made in footnotes.

CONTENTS

JONATHAN EDWARDS

Sarah Pierrepont 3
From Personal Narrative 4

BENJAMIN FRANKLIN

From Autobiography 8
  Books 8
  Entrance into Philadelphia 12
  Whitefield's Preaching 14
To Mrs. Jane Mecom 17
To Miss Mary Stevenson 18
To William Strahan 22
To Benjamin Webb 22
To Ezra Stiles 23
The Whistle: To Madame Brillon 25

ST. JEAN DE CRÈVECŒUR

From Letters from an American Farmer 27
  A System of Felicity 27
  An Artless Countryman 28
  What is an American? 28
  Peculiar Customs of Nantucket 32

GEORGE WASHINGTON

Farewell Address 36

THOMAS JEFFERSON

The Declaration of Independence 50
First Inaugural Address 53
From Notes on the State of Virginia 57
  Slavery 57
From Autobiography 58
  Congress Under the Articles of Confederation 58
To John Adams 59

WASHINGTON IRVING

A History of New York, by Diedrich Knickerbocker, Book III, Chap. I . . 62
Rip Van Winkle 67
Westminster Abbey 81
The Stout Gentleman 88
Palace of the Alhambra 96

CONTENTS

JAMES FENIMORE COOPER

The Last of the Mohicans, Chapter XXIII 106

RALPH WALDO EMERSON

Nature: III. Beauty 118
The American Scholar 122
Self-Reliance 136
Compensation 154
Ezra Ripley, D.D. 168
From English Traits 174
  Wordsworth 174
Thoreau 176
To the Reverend Henry Ware Jr. 190

HENRY DAVID THOREAU

From Walden 193
  Economy 193
  Where I Lived, and What I Lived For 208
  Brute Neighbors 218

NATHANIEL HAWTHORNE

The Minister's Black Veil 222
Legends of the Province House 232
  Lady Eleanore's Mantle 232
The Ambitious Guest 243
A Rill from the Town Pump 250
The Birthmark 254
Young Goodman Brown 267
Ethan Brand 278

EDGAR ALLAN POE

The Assignation 291
Ligeia 301
The Fall of the House of Usher 313
The Purloined Letter 327
The Cask of Amontillado 341
The Philosophy of Composition 347
The Poetic Principle 356
From Marginalia 364
  Marginal Jottings 364
  The Power of Words 366
  Punctuation 368

OLIVER WENDELL HOLMES

From The Autocrat of the Breakfast-Table 370

JAMES RUSSELL LOWELL

On a Certain Condescension in Foreigners 398
My Garden Acquaintance 415
Democracy 429

CONTENTS

DANIEL WEBSTER

From Oration at the Bunker Hill Monument 445
From The Reply to Hayne 447
From The Murder of Captain Joseph White 450

WILLIAM HICKLING PRESCOTT

From The Conquest of Mexico 454
  The March to Mexico City 454
  The Entrance to the City 460
  The Age of Chivalry 464
  The Surrender of Mexico City 464

FRANCIS PARKMAN

From The Conspiracy of Pontiac 480
  The Indian Character 480
  La Salle 484
  Braddock's Defeat 487
  The Siege of Quebec 491

HERMAN MELVILLE

Typee, Chapter XVIII: Marnoo Appears 500
Omoo, Chapter II: Some Account of the Ship 510
Moby Dick, Chapter XXXV: The Mast-Head 513
  Chapter XLVIII: The First Lowering 518
The Encantadas, or the Enchanted Isles 526
  The Isles at Large 526
  Rock Rodondo 530
  A Pisgah View from the Rock 533

ABRAHAM LINCOLN

To John D. Johnston 539
Farewell Address at Springfield 540
Speech in Independence Hall, Philadelphia 541
Gettysburg Address 542
Second Inaugural Address 542
To Horace Greeley 544
To Edward Everett 545
To General Grant 545
To Mrs. Bixby 545

WALT WHITMAN

From Specimen Days 548
  The White House by Moonlight 548
  A New York Soldier 548
  Abraham Lincoln 549

Hours for the Soul 550
The Silent General 551
From November Boughs 551
   A Thought on Shakespeare 551
From Democratic Vistas 553

EDWARD EVERETT HALE

The Man Without a Country 558

MARK TWAIN

Roughing It, Chapter V 578
The Celebrated Jumping Frog of Calaveras County 581
Life on the Mississippi, Chapters IV, XVIII, and XIX 586

BRET HARTE

The Luck of Roaring Camp 597
The Outcasts of Poker Flat 605
Tennessee's Partner 614

HENRY ADAMS

The Education of Henry Adams, Chapter V: Berlin (1858–1859) 622

HENRY JAMES

The Two Faces 632

SARAH ORNE JEWETT

From The Country of the Pointed Firs: Green Island 644

MARY WILKINS FREEMAN

A New England Nun 659

JOEL CHANDLER HARRIS

From Uncle Remus: His Songs and His Sayings 670
   XVI: Old Mr. Rabbit, He's a Good Fisherman 670
   XXXII: "Jacky-My-Lantern" 672

LAFCADIO HEARN

From Glimpses of Unfamiliar Japan 675
   My First Day in the Orient 675
First Impressions 683

PAUL ELMER MORE

The Origins of Hawthorne and Poe 687

O. HENRY

The Whirligig of Life 698
A Municipal Report 703

CONTENTS

EDITH WHARTON

The Debt 716

WILLA CATHER

The Sculptor's Funeral 728

SHERWOOD ANDERSON

I'm a Fool 740

Book Lists 750

CONTENTS

(Arranged by Types)

HISTORY

WILLIAM HICKLING PRESCOTT
From The Conquest of Mexico 454
   The March to Mexico City 454
   The Entrance to the City 460
   The Age of Chivalry 464
   The Surrender of Mexico City 464

FRANCIS PARKMAN
From The Conspiracy of Pontiac 480
   The Indian Character 480
   La Salle 484
   Braddock's Defeat 487
   The Siege of Quebec 491

BIOGRAPHY

JONATHAN EDWARDS
   Sarah Pierrepont 3
   From Personal Narrative 4

BENJAMIN FRANKLIN
   From Autobiography 8
   Books 8
   Entrance into Philadelphia 12
   Whitefield's Preaching 14

THOMAS JEFFERSON
   From Autobiography 58
   Congress Under the Articles of Confederation . . . 58

FRANCIS PARKMAN
   La Salle 484

RALPH WALDO EMERSON
   Ezra Ripley, D.D. 168
   Wordsworth 174
   Thoreau 176

MARK TWAIN
   Life on the Mississippi, Chapters IV, XVIII, and XIX . . . 586

HENRY ADAMS
   The Education of Henry Adams, Chapter V: Berlin (1858–1859) . . 622

LETTERS

BENJAMIN FRANKLIN
   To Mrs. Jane Mecom 17
   To Miss Mary Stevenson 18

CONTENTS

To William Strahan 22
To Benjamin Webb 22
To Ezra Stiles 23
The Whistle: To Madame Brillon 25
THOMAS JEFFERSON
To John Adams 59
RALPH WALDO EMERSON
To the Reverend Henry Ware Jr. 190
ABRAHAM LINCOLN
To John D. Johnston 539
To Horace Greeley 544
To Edward Everett 545
To General Grant 545
To Mrs. Bixby 545

POLITICAL PAPERS AND DISCUSSIONS

GEORGE WASHINGTON
Farewell Address 36
THOMAS JEFFERSON
The Declaration of Independence 50
First Inaugural Address 53
From Notes on the State of Virginia 57
Slavery 57
From Autobiography 58
Congress Under the Articles of Confederation 58
JAMES RUSSELL LOWELL
Democracy 429
DANIEL WEBSTER
From The Reply to Hayne 447
ABRAHAM LINCOLN
Second Inaugural Address 542

ORATIONS AND ADDRESSES

GEORGE WASHINGTON
Farewell Address 36
THOMAS JEFFERSON
First Inaugural Address 53
RALPH WALDO EMERSON
The American Scholar 122
JAMES RUSSELL LOWELL
Democracy 429
DANIEL WEBSTER
From Oration at the Bunker Hill Monument 445
From The Reply to Hayne 447
From The Murder of Captain Joseph White 450
ABRAHAM LINCOLN
Farewell Address at Springfield 540
Speech in Independence Hall, Philadelphia 541
Gettysburg Address 542
Second Inaugural Address 542

CONTENTS

ESSAYS

ST. JEAN DE CRÈVECŒUR
From Letters from an American Farmer 27
    What is an American? 28
WASHINGTON IRVING
    Westminster Abbey 81
    The Stout Gentleman 88
RALPH WALDO EMERSON
    Nature: III. Beauty 118
    The American Scholar 122
    Self-Reliance 136
    Compensation 154
    Thoreau 176
HENRY DAVID THOREAU
From Walden 193
    Economy 193
    Where I Lived, and What I Lived For 208
    Brute Neighbors 218
EDGAR ALLAN POE
From Marginalia 364
    Marginal Jottings 364
    The Power of Words 366
    Punctuation 368
OLIVER WENDELL HOLMES
From The Autocrat of the Breakfast-Table 370
JAMES RUSSELL LOWELL
    On a Certain Condescension in Foreigners 398
    My Garden Acquaintance 415
WALT WHITMAN
From November Boughs 551
    A Thought on Shakespeare 551
From Democratic Vistas 553
LAFCADIO HEARN
    First Impressions 683
PAUL ELMER MORE
    The Origins of Hawthorne and Poe 687

DESCRIPTIONS AND SKETCHES

ST. JEAN DE CRÈVECŒUR
From Letters from an American Farmer 27
    A System of Felicity 27
    An Artless Countryman 28
    Peculiar Customs of Nantucket 32
WASHINGTON IRVING
    A History of New York, by Diedrich Knickerbocker, Book III, Chap. I . 62
    Westminster Abbey 81
    The Stout Gentleman 88
    Palace of the Alhambra 96

CONTENTS

RALPH WALDO EMERSON
  From English Traits 174
    Wordsworth 174
HENRY DAVID THOREAU
  From Walden 193
    Brute Neighbors 218
NATHANIEL HAWTHORNE
  A Rill from the Town Pump 250
HERMAN MELVILLE
  The Encantadas, or the Enchanted Isles 526
    The Isles at Large 526
    Rock Rodondo 530
    A Pisgah View from the Rock 533
WALT WHITMAN
  From Specimen Days 548
    The White House by Moonlight 548
    A New York Soldier 548
    Abraham Lincoln 549
    Hours for the Soul 550
    The Silent General 551
MARK TWAIN
  Roughing It, Chapter V 578
  The Celebrated Jumping Frog of Calaveras County 581
LAFCADIO HEARN
  From Glimpses of Unfamiliar Japan 675
    My First Day in the Orient 675

FICTION

WASHINGTON IRVING
  Rip Van Winkle 67
JAMES FENIMORE COOPER
  The Last of the Mohicans, Chapter XXIII 106
NATHANIEL HAWTHORNE
  The Minister's Black Veil 222
  Lady Eleanore's Mantle 232
  The Ambitious Guest 243
  The Birthmark 254
  Young Goodman Brown 267
  Ethan Brand 278
EDGAR ALLAN POE
  The Assignation 291
  Ligeia 301
  The Fall of the House of Usher 313
  The Purloined Letter 327
  The Cask of Amontillado 341
HERMAN MELVILLE
  Typee, Chapter XVIII: Marnoo Appears 500
  Omoo, Chapter II: Some Account of the Ship 510
  Moby Dick, Chapter XXXV: The Mast-Head 513
    Chapter XLVIII: The First Lowering 518

CONTENTS

Edward Everett Hale
  The Man Without a Country 558
Bret Harte
  The Luck of Roaring Camp 597
  The Outcasts of Poker Flat 605
  Tennessee's Partner 614
Henry James
  The Two Faces 632
Sarah Orne Jewett
  From The Country of the Pointed Firs: Green Island 644
Mary Wilkins Freeman
  A New England Nun 659
Joel Chandler Harris
  From Uncle Remus: His Songs and His Sayings, Sections XVI and XXXII 670
O. Henry
  The Whirligig of Life 698
  A Municipal Report 703
Edith Wharton
  The Debt 716
Willa Cather
  The Sculptor's Funeral 728
Sherwood Anderson
  I'm a Fool 740

An Introduction to
American Prose

JONATHAN EDWARDS

(1703–1758)

Jonathan Edwards, greatest leader of New England Puritanism, was born in East Windsor, Connecticut, in 1703. He was unusually precocious, as is shown by extant papers written when he was about twelve years old. After graduating from Yale in 1720 he studied divinity, and in 1727 became colleague of his grandfather in the church at Northampton, where he spent the next twenty-four years. Here in 1735 he brought about a religious revival which led a few years later to the "Great Awakening," during which in 1741 he preached his most famous sermon, "Sinners in the Hands of an Angry God." His congregation, however, reacted from the rigor of his teaching, and in 1750 voted to dismiss him. On leaving he preached his moving "Farewell Sermon." While serving as missionary to the Indians at the frontier post of Stockbridge he wrote his famous treatise on *The Freedom of the Will*. He was called to the presidency of Princeton, but died soon after his inauguration, in 1758.

In the mental character of Edwards there were two faculties, seldom found together in such high degree: one of keen and powerful thought, the other of high feeling and imagination. The first appears in the logic of his philosophical works in defense of Calvinism; the second, though less conspicuous in his formal works, warms the style of his sermons and glows in his more personal writings. Feeling in duty bound to expound pitilessly the doctrine of eternal damnation in his "imprecatory sermons," he was nevertheless kindly by nature; he led a saintly life, "sweetly conversing with Christ and swallowed up in God." Though, like Cardinal Newman, he devoted himself to religion rather than to literature, he had the true poet's gifts of seeing and singing; he tells in his "Personal Narrative" of being carried away in vision, and of finding it natural to "sing forth his meditations." Though only potentially a poet, he was not only a great theologian and preacher, but also our first prose-writer of true distinction.

SARAH PIERREPONT [1]

THEY say there is a young lady in [New Haven] who is beloved by that Great Being, who made and rules the world, and that there are certain seasons in which this Great Being, in some way or other invisible, comes to her and fills her mind with exceeding sweet delight, and that she hardly cares for anything, except to meditate on him—that she expects after a while to be received up where he is, to be raised up out of the world and caught up into heaven; being assured that he loves her too well to let her remain at a

---

[1] "Written on a blank leaf," probably in 1723, four years before Edwards's marriage to Sarah Pierrepont, when he was twenty and she thirteen. Twenty-seven years later, shortly before his death at Princeton, he sent her the following message: "Tell her that the uncommon union which has so long subsisted between us has been of such a nature as I trust is spiritual, and therefore will continue forever."

distance from him always. There she is to dwell with him, and to be ravished
with his love and delight forever. Therefore, if you present all the world before her, with the richest of its treasures, she disregards and cares not for it,
and is unmindful of any pain or affliction. She has a strange sweetness in
her mind, and singular purity in her affections; is most just and conscientious
in all her conduct; and you could not persuade her to do anything wrong
or sinful, if you would give her all the world, lest she should offend this Great
Being. She is of a wonderful sweetness, calmness, and universal benevolence
of mind; especially after this great God has manifested himself to her mind.
She will sometimes go about from place to place, singing sweetly; and seems
to be always full of joy and pleasure; and no one knows for what. She loves
to be alone, walking in the fields and groves, and seems to have some one
invisible always conversing with her.

From PERSONAL NARRATIVE [2]

FROM my childhood up, my mind has been full of objections against the
doctrine of God's sovereignty, in choosing whom he would to eternal life,
and rejecting whom he pleased; leaving them eternally to perish, and be
everlastingly tormented in hell. It used to appear like a horrible doctrine to
me. But I remember the time very well, when I seemed to be convinced,
and fully satisfied, as to this sovereignty of God, and his justice in thus eternally disposing of men, according to his sovereign pleasure. But I never
could give an account how, or by what means, I was thus convinced, not
in the least imagining at the time, nor a long time after, that there was any
extraordinary influence of God's Spirit in it; but only that now I saw further,
and my reason apprehended the justice and reasonableness of it. However,
my mind rested in it; and it put an end to all those cavils and objections.
And there has been a wonderful alteration in my mind, with respect to the
doctrine of God's sovereignty, from that day to this; so that I scarce ever
have found so much as the rising of an objection against it, in the most absolute sense, in God's showing mercy to whom he will show mercy, and
hardening whom he will. God's absolute sovereignty and justice, with respect to salvation and damnation, is what my mind seems to rest assured
of, as much as of anything that I see with my eyes; at least it is so at times.
But I have often, since that first conviction, had quite another kind of sense
of God's sovereignty than I had then. I have often since had not only
a conviction, but a delightful conviction. The doctrine has very often appeared exceeding pleasant, bright, and sweet. Absolute sovereignty is what
I love to ascribe to God. But my first conviction was not so.

[2] Written at Northampton—as its concluding paragraph shows—after, probably shortly
after, January 1739, when Edwards was thirty-six.

The first instance that I remember of that sort of inward, sweet delight in God and divine things that I have lived much in since, was on reading those words, *1 Tim*. i: 17. *Now unto the King eternal, immortal, invisible, the only wise God, be honor and glory forever and ever, Amen*. As I read the words, there came into my soul, and was as it were diffused through it, a sense of the glory of the Divine Being; a new sense, quite different from anything I ever experienced before. Never any words of Scripture seemed to me as these words did. I thought within myself, how excellent a Being that was, and how happy I should be, if I might enjoy that God, and be rapt up to him in heaven, and be as it were swallowed up in him forever! I kept saying, and as it were singing over these words of Scripture to myself; and went to pray to God that I might enjoy him, and prayed in a manner quite different from what I used to do; with a new sort of affection. But it never came into my thought, that there was anything spiritual, or of a saving nature, in this.

From about that time, I began to have a new kind of apprehensions and ideas of Christ, and the work of redemption, and the glorious way of salvation by him. An inward, sweet sense of these things, at times, came into my heart; and my soul was led away in pleasant views and contemplations of them. And my mind was greatly engaged to spend my time in reading and meditating on Christ, on the beauty and excellency of his person, and the lovely way of salvation by free grace in him. I found no books so delightful to me, as those that treated of these subjects. Those words, *Cant*. ii: 1, used to be abundantly with me, *I am the Rose of Sharon, and the Lily of the valleys*. The words seemed to me sweetly to represent the loveliness and beauty of Jesus Christ. The whole book of *Canticles* used to be pleasant to me, and I used to be much in reading it, about that time; and found, from time to time, an inward sweetness, that would carry me away, in my contemplations. This I know not how to express otherwise, than by a calm, sweet abstraction of soul from all the concerns of this world; and sometimes a kind of vision, or fixed ideas and imaginations, of being alone in the mountains, or some solitary wilderness, far from all mankind, sweetly conversing with Christ, and rapt and swallowed up in God. The sense I had of divine things would often of a sudden kindle up, as it were, a sweet burning in my heart; an ardor of soul that I know not how to express.

Not long after I began to experience these things, I gave an account to my father of some things that had passed in my mind. I was pretty much affected by the discourse we had together; and when the discourse was ended, I walked abroad alone, in a solitary place in my father's pasture, for contemplation. And as I was walking there and looking up on the sky and clouds, there came into my mind so sweet a sense of the glorious *majesty* and *grace* of God, that I know not how to express. I seemed to see them both in a sweet conjunction; majesty and meekness joined together; it was a sweet and gentle, and holy majesty; and also a majestic meekness; an awful sweetness; a high, and great, and holy gentleness.

After this my sense of divine things gradually increased, and became more and more lively, and had more of that inward sweetness. The appearance of everything was altered; there seemed to be, as it were, a calm, sweet cast, or appearance of divine glory, in almost everything. God's excellency, his wisdom, his purity and love, seemed to appear in everything; in the sun, and moon, and stars; in the clouds, and blue sky; in the grass, flowers, trees; in the water, and all nature; which used greatly to fix my mind. I often used to sit and view the moon for continuance; and in the day spent much time in viewing the clouds and sky, to behold the sweet glory of God in these things; in the meantime, singing forth, with a low voice, my contemplations of the Creator and Redeemer. And scarce anything, among all the works of nature, was so sweet to me as thunder and lightning; formerly, nothing had been so terrible to me. Before, I used to be uncommonly terrified with thunder, and to be struck with terror when I saw a thunder storm rising; but now, on the contrary, it rejoiced me. I felt God, so to speak, at the first appearance of a thunder storm; and used to take the opportunity, at such times, to fix myself in order to view the clouds and see the lightnings play, and hear the majestic and awful voice of God's thunder, which oftentimes was exceedingly entertaining, leading me to sweet contemplations of my great and glorious God. While thus engaged, it always seemed natural to me to sing, or chant forth my meditations; or, to speak my thoughts in soliloquies with a singing voice. . . .

I remember the thoughts I used then to have of holiness; and said sometimes to myself, "I do certainly know that I love holiness, such as the gospel prescribes." It appeared to me, that there was nothing in it but what was ravishingly lovely; the highest beauty and amiableness—a *divine* beauty; far purer than anything here upon earth; and that everything else was like mire and defilement, in comparison of it.

Holiness, as I then wrote down some of my contemplations on it, appeared to me to be of a sweet, pleasant, charming, serene, calm nature; which brought an inexpressible purity, brightness, peacefulness and ravishment to the soul. In other words, that it made the soul like a field or garden of God, with all manner of pleasant flowers; all pleasant, delightful, and undisturbed; enjoying a sweet calm, and the gentle vivifying beams of the sun. The soul of a true Christian, as I then wrote my meditations, appeared like such a little white flower as we see in the spring of the year; low and humble on the ground, opening its bosom to receive the pleasant beams of the sun's glory; rejoicing as it were in a calm rapture; diffusing around a sweet fragrancy; standing peacefully and lovingly, in the midst of other flowers round about;

all in like manner opening their bosoms, to drink in the light of the sun. There was no part of creature holiness, that I had so great a sense of its loveliness, as humility, brokenness of heart, and poverty of spirit; and there was nothing that I so earnestly longed for. My heart panted after this, to lie low before God, as in the dust; that I might be nothing, and that God might be ALL, that I might become as a little child.

While at New York, I was sometimes much affected with reflections on my past life, considering how late it was before I began to be truly religious; and how wickedly I had lived till then; and once so as to weep abundantly, and for a considerable time together. . . .

I have sometimes had a sense of the excellent fulness of Christ, and his meetness and suitableness as a Saviour; whereby he has appeared to me, far above all, the chief of ten thousands. His blood and atonement have appeared sweet, and his righteousness sweet; which was always accompanied with ardency of spirit; and inward strugglings and breathings, and groanings that cannot be uttered, to be emptied of myself, and swallowed up in Christ.

Once, as I rode out into the woods for my health, in 1737, having alighted from my horse in a retired place, as my manner commonly has been, to walk for divine contemplation and prayer, I had a view that for me was extraordinary, of the glory of the Son of God, as Mediator between God and man, and his wonderful, great, full, pure and sweet grace and love, and meek and gentle condescension. This grace that appeared so calm and sweet, appeared also great above the heavens. The person of Christ appeared ineffably excellent, with an excellency great enough to swallow up all thought and conception—which continued, as near as I can judge, about an hour; which kept me the greater part of the time in a flood of tears, and weeping aloud. I felt an ardency of soul to be, what I know not otherwise how to express, emptied and annihilated; to lie in the dust, and to be full of Christ alone; to love him with a holy and pure love; to trust in him; to live upon him; to serve and follow him; and to be perfectly sanctified and made pure, with a divine and heavenly purity. I have, several other times, had views very much of the same nature, and which have had the same effects. . . .

BENJAMIN FRANKLIN

(1706–1790)

Benjamin Franklin's life all but covers a century momentous in American affairs. He was born in 1706 in Boston, the seat of a struggling colony; he died in 1790 in Philadelphia, the capital of the new national government. His rise from printer's apprentice to world-honored statesman and philosopher is too well known to be recounted here. From a successful publishing and newspaper business in Philadelphia he soon became financially independent, and having served himself well he devoted the remainder of his life to the service of his country and of mankind. He took part in every public movement in Philadelphia; he made himself famous by his scientific discoveries; he probably did more than any other man save Washington to secure national independence and establish a firm national government. Journalist, scientist, statesman, diplomat, philanthropist, and author, he was indeed the "many-sided Franklin."

Though Franklin was an accomplished writer whose works fill ten volumes he can hardly be called a man of letters. He learned to write because he thought the ability would be useful, and he wrote mainly in the course of business. Even the *Autobiography* he did not intend as a contribution to literature. Often called upon to write, however, he thought it worth while to write well, and merely for his style he stands out among his contemporaries. In a familiar passage he tells how he began by imitating the *Spectator*. Soon, however, he had a style of his own, less formal than Addison's, more simple, democratic—perhaps one may say American. In his writings subsequent to the early Addisonian essays there is perhaps discernible a development of style through three stages: first, that of the Philadelphia period—of *Poor Richard* and *The Way to Wealth*—simple and homespun; secondly, that of his life during some seventeen years in England—a style more cultivated, and sometimes, as in his *Rules by which a Great Empire may be Reduced to a Small One*, Swiftian in its irony; and finally, that of his residence in France—the more mellow manner of the *Bagatelles*, resembling "the familiar, easy manner for which," as he somewhere says, "the French are so remarkable." Throughout his life Franklin wrote letters, all admirably fitted, as letters should be, to the writer, the subject, and the correspondent. The *Autobiography* stands by itself; it is one of the few books appealing to readers of every country, age, and taste; it is our first American classic.

From FRANKLIN'S AUTOBIOGRAPHY [1]

[BOOKS]

FROM a child I was fond of reading, and all the little money that came into my hands was ever laid out in books. Pleased with the *Pilgrim's Progress*, my first collection was of John Bunyan's works in separate little

---

[1] Franklin wrote his *Autobiography* in four installments, beginning it in 1771, in England, in the form of a letter addressed to his son, intended for his family rather than the public;

volumes. I afterward sold them to enable me to buy R. Burton's *Historical Collections;* they were small chapmen's books, and cheap, forty or fifty in all. My father's little library consisted chiefly of books in polemic divinity, most of which I read, and have since often regretted that, at a time when I had such a thirst for knowledge, more proper books had not fallen in my way, since it was now resolved I should not be a clergyman. *Plutarch's Lives* there was in which I read abundantly, and I still think that time spent to great advantage. There was also a book of De Foe's, called an *Essay on Projects,* and another of Dr. Mather's,[2] called *Essays to Do Good,* which perhaps gave me a turn of thinking that had an influence on some of the principal future events of my life.

This bookish inclination at length determined my father to make me a printer, though he had already one son (James) of that profession. In 1717 my brother James returned from England with a press and letters, to set up his business in Boston. I liked it much better than that of my father, but still had a hankering for the sea. To prevent the apprehended effect of such an inclination, my father was impatient to have me bound to my brother. I stood out some time, but at last was persuaded, and signed the indentures when I was yet but twelve years old. I was to serve as an apprentice till I was twenty-one years of age, only I was to be allowed journeyman's wages during the last year. In a little time I made great proficiency in the business, and became a useful hand to my brother. I now had access to better books. An acquaintance with the apprentices of booksellers enabled me sometimes to borrow a small one, which I was careful to return soon and clean. Often I sat up in my room reading the greatest part of the night, when the book was borrowed in the evening and to be returned early in the morning, lest it should be missed or wanted.

And after some time an ingenious tradesman, Mr. Matthew Adams, who had a pretty collection of books, and who frequented our printing-house, took notice of me, invited me to his library, and very kindly lent me such books as I chose to read. I now took a fancy to poetry, and made some little pieces; my brother, thinking it might turn to account, encouraged me, and put me on composing occasional ballads. One was called *The Lighthouse Tragedy,* and contained an account of the drowning of Captain Worthilake,

continuing it in France in 1784, again resuming it in Philadelphia in 1788, and adding a final short passage immediately before his death. It was, however, finally incomplete, covering his life to his arrival in London in 1757, and thereafter very briefly to 1762. Though there were many early editions—the first curiously an incomplete French version of 1791—it was not published correctly and fully until 1868. For the strange fortunes of both manuscript and book see the Everyman edition, Introduction, and A. H. Smyth, *Writings of Franklin,* vol. 1, p. 23.

The *Autobiography* begins with an account of Franklin's ancestry, birth in Boston, and boyhood; from this the first extract above is taken. Then it tells of his leaving Boston, at the age of seventeen, to seek work in Philadelphia; the second extract recounts his journey thither.

[2] Cotton Mather.

with his two daughters; the other was a sailor's song, on the taking of Teach (or Blackbeard), the pirate. They were wretched stuff, in the Grub Street ballad style; and when they were printed he sent me about the town to sell them. The first sold wonderfully, the event being recent, having made a great noise. This flattered my vanity; but my father discouraged me by ridiculing my performances, and telling me verse-makers were generally beggars. So I escaped being a poet, most probably a very bad one; but as prose writing has been of great use to me in the course of my life, and was a principal means of my advancement, I shall tell you how, in such a situation, I acquired what little ability I have in that way.

There was another bookish lad in the town, John Collins by name, with whom I was intimately acquainted. We sometimes disputed, and very fond we were of argument, and very desirous of confuting one another, which disputatious turn, by the way, is apt to become a very bad habit, making people often extremely disagreeable in company by the contradiction that is necessary to bring it into practice; and thence, besides souring and spoiling the conversation, is productive of disgusts and perhaps enmities where you may have occasion for friendship. I had caught it by reading my father's books of dispute about religion. Persons of good sense, I have since observed, seldom fall into it, except lawyers, university men, and men of all sorts that have been bred at Edinburgh.

A question was once, somehow or other, started between Collins and me, of the propriety of educating the female sex in learning, and their abilities for study. He was of the opinion that it was improper, and that they were naturally unequal to it. I took the contrary side, perhaps a little for dispute's sake. He was naturally more eloquent, had a ready plenty of words; and sometimes, as I thought, bore me down more by his fluency than by the strength of his reasons. As we parted without settling the point, and were not to see one another again for some time, I sat down to put my arguments in writing, which I copied fair and sent to him. He answered, and I replied. Three or four letters of a side had passed, when my father happened to find my papers and read them. Without entering into the discussion, he took occasion to talk to me about the manner of my writing; observed that, though I had the advantage of my antagonist in correct spelling and point-ing (which I owed to the printing-house), I fell far short in elegance of expression, in method, and in perspicuity, of which he convinced me by several instances. I saw the justice of his remarks, and thence grew more attentive to the manner in writing, and determined to endeavor at im-provement.

About this time I met with an odd volume of the *Spectator*. It was the third. I had never before seen any of them. I bought it, read it over and over, and was much delighted with it. I thought the writing excellent, and wished, if possible, to imitate it. With this view I took some of the papers, and making short hints of the sentiment in each sentence, laid them by a few days, and then, without looking at the book, tried to complete the papers again, by expressing each hinted sentiment at length, and as fully as it had been expressed before, in any suitable words that should come to hand. Then I compared my *Spectator* with the original, discovered some of my faults, and corrected them. But I found I wanted a stock of words, or a readiness in recollecting and using them, which I thought I should have acquired before that time if I had gone on making verses; since the continual occasion for words of the same import, but of different length, to suit the measure, or of different sound for the rhyme, would have laid me under a constant necessity of searching for variety, and also have tended to fix that variety in my mind, and make me master of it. Therefore I took some of the tales and turned them into verse; and, after a time, when I had pretty well forgotten the prose, turned them back again. I also sometimes jumbled my collections of hints into confusion, and after some weeks endeavored to reduce them into the best order, before I began to form the full sentences and complete the paper. This was to teach me method in the arrangement of thoughts. By comparing my work afterwards with the original, I discovered many faults and amended them; but I sometimes had the pleasure of fancying that, in certain particulars of small import, I had been lucky enough to improve the method or the language, and this encouraged me to think I might possibly in time come to be a tolerable English writer, of which I was extremely ambitious. My time for these exercises and for reading was at night, after work, or before it began in the morning, or on Sundays, when I contrived to be in the printing-house alone, evading as much as I could the common attendance on public worship which my father used to exact of me when I was under his care, and which indeed I still thought a duty, though I could not, as it seemed to me, afford time to practice it.

When about sixteen years of age I happened to meet with a book, written by one Tryon, recommending a vegetable diet. I determined to go into it. My brother, being yet unmarried, did not keep house, but boarded himself and his apprentices in another family. My refusing to eat flesh caused an inconveniency, and I was frequently chid for my singularity. I made myself acquainted with Tryon's manner of preparing some of his dishes, such as boiling potatoes or rice, making hasty pudding, and a few others, and then proposed to my brother that if he would give me, weekly, half the money he paid for my board, I would board myself. He instantly agreed to it, and I presently found I could save half what he paid me. This was an additional fund for buying books. But I had another advantage in it. My brother and the rest going from the printing-house to their meals, I remained there alone, and dispatching presently my light repast, which often was no more than a biscuit or a slice of bread, a handful of raisins or a tart from the pastry-cook's, and a glass of water, had the rest of the time till their return for study, in which I made the greater progress, from that greater clearness of head and quicker apprehension which usually attend temperance in eating and drinking.

And now it was that, being on some occasion made ashamed of my ignorance in figures, which I had twice failed in learning when at school, I took Cocker's book of Arithmetic, and went through the whole by myself with great ease. I also read Seller's and Shermy's books of Navigation, and became acquainted with the little geometry they contain; but never proceeded far in that science. And I read about this time Locke *On Human Understanding* and the *Art of Thinking* by Messrs. du Port Royal.[3]

[ENTRANCE INTO PHILADELPHIA]

IT rained very hard all the day; I was thoroughly soaked, and by noon a good deal tired; so I stopped at a poor inn, where I stayed all night, beginning now to wish that I had never left home. I cut so miserable a figure, too, that I found, by the questions asked me, I was suspected to be some runaway servant, and in danger of being taken up on that suspicion. However, I proceeded the next day, and got in the evening to an inn, within eight or ten miles of Burlington, kept by one Dr. Brown. He entered into conversation with me while I took some refreshment, and, finding I had read a little, became very sociable and friendly. Our acquaintance continued as long as he lived. He had been, I imagine, an itinerant doctor, for there was no town in England, or country in Europe, of which he could not give a very particular account. He had some letters, and was ingenious, but much of an unbeliever, and wickedly undertook, some years after, to travesty the Bible in doggerel verse, as Cotton had done Virgil. By this means he set many of the facts in a very ridiculous light, and might have hurt weak minds if his work had been published; but it never was.

At his house I lay that night, and the next morning reached Burlington, but had the mortification to find that the regular boats were gone a little before my coming, and no other expected to go before Tuesday, this being Saturday; wherefore I returned to an old woman in the town, of whom I had bought gingerbread to eat on the water, and asked her advice. She invited me to lodge at her house till a passage by water should offer; and being tired with my foot traveling, I accepted the invitation. She, understanding I was a printer, would have had me stay at that town and follow my business, being ignorant of the stock necessary to begin with. She was very hospitable,

[3] A book of the Jansenists, of the Abbey of Port Royal, near Paris.

gave me a dinner of ox-cheek with great good will, accepting only a pot of ale in return; and I thought myself fixed till Tuesday should come. However, walking in the evening by the side of the river, a boat came by, which I found was going towards Philadelphia, with several people in her. They took me in, and, as there was no wind, we rowed all the way; and about midnight, not having yet seen the city, some of the company were confident we must have passed it, and would row no farther; the others knew not where we were; so we put toward the shore, got into a creek, landed near an old fence, with the rails of which we made a fire, the night being cold, in October, and there we remained till daylight. Then one of the company knew the place to be Cooper's Creek, a little above Philadelphia, which we saw as soon as we got out of the creek, and arrived there about eight or nine o'clock on the Sunday morning, and landed at the Market Street wharf.

I have been the more particular in this description of my journey, and shall be so of my first entry into that city, that you may in your mind compare such unlikely beginnings with the figure I have since made there. I was in my working dress, my best clothes being to come round by sea. I was dirty from my journey; my pockets were stuffed out with shirts and stockings, and I knew no soul nor where to look for lodging. I was fatigued with traveling, rowing, and want of rest, I was very hungry; and my whole stock of cash consisted of a Dutch dollar, and about a shilling in copper. The latter I gave the people of the boat for my passage, who at first refused it on account of my rowing; but I insisted on their taking it. A man being sometimes more generous when he has but a little money than when he has plenty, perhaps through fear of being thought to have but little.

Then I walked up the street, gazing about, till, near the market-house, I met a boy with bread. I had made many a meal on bread, and, inquiring where he got it, I went immediately to the baker's he directed me to, in Second Street, and asked for biscuit, intending such as we had in Boston; but they, it seems, were not made in Philadelphia. Then I asked for a three-penny loaf, and was told they had none such. So, not considering or knowing the difference of money, and the greater cheapness nor the names of his bread, I bade him give me three-penny worth of any sort. He gave me, accordingly, three great puffy rolls. I was surprised at the quantity, but took it, and, having no room in my pockets, walked off with a roll under each arm, and eating the other. Thus I went up Market Street as far as Fourth Street, passing by the door of Mr. Read, my future wife's father; when she, standing at the door, saw me, and thought I made, as I certainly did, a most awkward, ridiculous appearance. Then I turned and went down Chestnut Street, and part of Walnut Street, eating my roll all the way, and, coming round, found myself again at Market Street wharf, near the boat I came in, to which I went for a draught of the river water; and, being filled with one of my rolls, gave the other two to a woman and her child that came down the river in the boat with us, and were waiting to go farther.

Thus refreshed, I walked again up the street, which by this time had many clean-dressed people in it, who were all walking the same way. I joined them, and thereby was led into the great meeting-house of the Quakers, near the market. I sat down among them, and, after looking round a while and hearing nothing said, being very drowsy through labor and want of rest the preceding night, I fell fast asleep, and continued so till the meeting broke up, when one was kind enough to rouse me. This was, therefore, the first house I was in, or slept in, in Philadelphia.

[WHITEFIELD'S PREACHING]

IN 1739 arrived among us from Ireland the Reverend Mr. Whitefield,[4] who had made himself remarkable there as an itinerant preacher. He was at first permitted to preach in some of our churches; but the clergy, taking a dislike to him, soon refused him their pulpits, and he was obliged to preach in the fields. The multitudes of all sects and denominations that attended his sermons were enormous, and it was matter of speculation to me, who was one of the number, to observe the extraordinary influence of his oratory on his hearers, and how much they admired and respected him, notwithstanding his common abuse of them, by assuring them they were naturally half beasts and half devils. It was wonderful to see the change soon made in the manners of our inhabitants. From being thoughtless or indifferent about religion, it seemed as if all the world were growing religious, so that one could not walk through the town in an evening without hearing psalms sung in different families of every street.

And it being found inconvenient to assemble in the open air, subject to its inclemencies, the building of a house to meet in was no sooner proposed, and persons appointed to receive contributions, but sufficient sums were soon received to procure the ground and erect the building, which was one hundred feet long and seventy broad, about the size of Westminister Hall; and the work was carried on with such spirit as to be finished in a much shorter time than could have been expected. Both house and ground were vested in trustees, expressly for the use of any preacher of any religious persuasion who might desire to say something to the people at Philadelphia; the design in building not being to accommodate any particular sect, but the inhabitants in general; so that even if the Mufti of Constantinople were to send a missionary to preach Mohammedanism to us, he would find a pulpit at his service.

4 George Whitefield, noted English Methodist preacher and evangelist, who in 1739 made his first tour of the Colonies.

Mr. Whitefield, in leaving us, went preaching all the way through the colonies to Georgia. The settlement of that province had lately been begun, but, instead of being made with hardy, industrious husbandmen, accustomed to labor, the only people fit for such an enterprise, it was with families of broken shop-keepers and other insolvent debtors, many of indolent and idle habits, taken out of the jails, who, being set down in the woods, unqualified for clearing land, and unable to endure the hardships of a new settlement, perished in numbers, leaving many helpless children unprovided for. The sight of their miserable situation inspired the benevolent heart of Mr. Whitefield with the idea of building an Orphan House there, in which they might be supported and educated. Returning northward, he preached up this charity, and made large collections, for his eloquence had a wonderful power over the hearts and purses of his hearers, of which I myself was an instance.

I did not disapprove of the design, but, as Georgia was then destitute of materials and workmen, and it was proposed to send them from Philadelphia at a great expense, I thought it would have been better to have built the house here, and brought the children to it. This I advised; but he was resolute in his first project, rejected my counsel, and I therefore refused to contribute. I happened soon after to attend one of his sermons, in the course of which I perceived he intended to finish with a collection, and I silently resolved he should get nothing from me. I had in my pocket a handful of copper money, three or four silver dollars, and five pistoles in gold. As he proceeded I began to soften, and concluded to give the coppers. Another stroke of his oratory made me ashamed of that, and determined me to give the silver; and he finished so admirably, that I emptied my pocket wholly into the collector's dish, gold and all. At this sermon there was also one of our club, who, being of my sentiments respecting the building in Georgia, and suspecting a collection might be intended, had, by precaution, emptied his pockets before he came from home. Towards the conclusion of the discourse, however, he felt a strong desire to give, and applied to a neighbor, who stood near him, to borrow some money for the purpose. The application was unfortunately [made] to perhaps the only man in the company who had the firmness not to be affected by the preacher. His answer was, "At any other time, Friend Hopkinson, I would lend to thee freely; but not now, for thee seems to be out of thy right senses."

Some of Mr. Whitefield's enemies affected to suppose that he would apply these collections to his own private emolument; but I, who was intimately acquainted with him (being employed in printing his Sermons and Journals, etc.), never had the least suspicion of his integrity, but am to this day decidedly of opinion that he was in all his conduct a perfectly honest man; and methinks my testimony in his favor ought to have the more weight, as we had no religious connection. He used, indeed, sometimes to pray for my conversion, but never had the satisfaction of believing that his prayers were heard. Ours was a mere civil friendship, sincere on both sides, and lasted to his death.

The following instance will show something of the terms on which we stood. Upon one of his arrivals from England at Boston, he wrote to me that he should come soon to Philadelphia, but knew not where he could lodge when there, as he understood his old friend and host, Mr. Benezet, was removed to Germantown. My answer was, "You know my house; if you can make shift with its scanty accommodations, you will be most heartily welcome." He replied that if I made that kind offer for Christ's sake, I should not miss of a reward. And I returned, "Don't let me be mistaken; it was not for Christ's sake, but for your sake." One of our common acquaintance jocosely remarked, that, knowing it to be the custom of the saints, when they received any favor, to shift the burden of the obligation from off their own shoulders, and place it in heaven, I had contrived to fix it on earth.

The last time I saw Mr. Whitefield was in London, when he consulted me about his Orphan House concern, and his purpose of appropriating it to the establishment of a college.

He had a loud and clear voice, and articulated his words and sentences so perfectly, that he might be heard and understood at a great distance, especially as his auditories, however numerous, observed the most exact silence. He preached one evening from the top of the Court House steps, which are in the middle of Market Street, and on the west side of Second Street, which crosses it at right angles. Both streets were filled with his hearers to a considerable distance. Being among the hindmost in Market Street, I had the curiosity to learn how far he could be heard, by retiring backwards down the street towards the river; and I found his voice distinct till I came near Front Street, when some noise in that street obscured it. Imagining then a semicircle, of which my distance should be the radius, and that it were filled with auditors, to each of whom I allowed two square feet, I computed that he might well be heard by more than thirty thousand. This reconciled me to the newspaper accounts of his having preached to twenty-five thousand people in the fields, and to the ancient histories of generals haranguing whole armies, of which I had sometimes doubted.

By hearing him often, I came to distinguish easily between sermons newly composed, and those which he had often preached in the course of his travels. His delivery of the latter was so improved by frequent repetitions that every accent, every emphasis, every modulation of voice, was so perfectly well turned and well placed, that, without being interested in the subject, one could not help being pleased with the discourse; a pleasure of much the same kind with that received from an excellent piece of music.

This is an advantage itinerant preachers have over those who are stationary, as the latter cannot well improve their delivery of a sermon by so many rehearsals.

His writing and printing from time to time gave great advantage to his enemies; unguarded expressions, and even erroneous opinions, delivered in preaching, might have been afterwards explained or qualified by supposing others that might have accompanied them, or they might have been denied; but *litera scripta manet*. Critics attacked his writings violently, and with so much appearance of reason as to diminish the number of his votaries and prevent their increase; so that I am of opinion if he had never written anything, he would have left behind him a much more numerous and important sect, and his reputation might in that case have been still growing, even after his death, as there being nothing of his writing on which to found a censure and give him a lower character, his proselytes would be left at liberty to feign for him as great a variety of excellence as their enthusiastic admiration might wish him to have possessed.

TO MRS. JANE MECOM

New York, April 19, 1757.

Dear Sister,

I wrote a few lines to you yesterday, but omitted to answer yours, relating to sister Dowse. As having their own way is one of the greatest comforts of life to old people, I think their friends should endeavor to accommodate them in that, as well as in anything else. When they have long lived in a house, it becomes natural to them; they are almost as closely connected with it, as the tortoise with his shell; they die, if you tear them out of it; old folks and old trees, if you remove them, it is ten to one that you kill them; so let our good old sister be no more importuned on that head. We are growing old fast ourselves, and shall expect the same kind of indulgences; if we give them, we shall have a right to receive them in our turn.

And as to her few fine things, I think she is in the right not to sell them, and for the reasons she gives, that they will fetch but little; when that little is spent, they would be of no further use to her; but perhaps the expectation of possessing them at her death may make that person tender and careful of her, and helpful to her to the amount of ten times their value. If so, they are put to the best use they possibly can be.

I hope you visit sister as often as your affairs will permit, and afford her what assistance and comfort you can in her present situation. Old age, infirmities, and poverty, joined, are afflictions enough. The neglect and slights of friends and near relations should never be added. People in her circumstances are apt to suspect this sometimes without cause; appearances should therefore be attended to, in our conduct towards them, as well as realities. I write by this post to cousin Williams, to continue his care, which I doubt not he will do.

We expect to sail in about a week, so that I can hardly hear from you again on this side the water; but let me have a line from you now and then, while I am in London. I expect to stay there at least a twelvemonth. Direct your letters to be left for me at the Pennsylvania Coffee House, in Birchin Lane, London. My love to all, from, dear sister, your affectionate brother,

B. FRANKLIN

P. S. April 25th. We are still here, and perhaps may be here a week longer. Once more adieu, my dear sister.

TO MISS MARY STEVENSON [5]

Paris, Sept. 14, 1767.

DEAR POLLY,

I am always pleased with a letter from you, and I flatter myself you may be sometimes pleased in receiving one from me, though it should be of little importance, such as this, which is to consist of a few occasional remarks made here, and in my journey hither.

Soon after I left you in that agreeable society at Bromley, I took the resolution of making a trip with Sir John Pringle into France. We set out the 28th past. All the way to Dover we were furnished with post chaises, hung so as to lean forward, the top coming down over one's eyes, like a hood, as if to prevent one's seeing the country; which being one of my great pleasures, I was engaged in perpetual disputes with the inn-keepers, hostlers, and postilions, about getting the straps taken up a hole or two before, and let down as much behind, they insisting that the chaise leaning forward was an ease to the horses, and that the contrary would kill them. I suppose the chaise leaning forward looks to them like a willingness to go forward, and that its hanging back shows a reluctance. They added other reasons, that were no reasons at all, and made me, as upon a hundred other occasions, almost wish that mankind had never been endowed with a reasoning faculty, since they know so little how to make use of it, and so often mislead themselves by it, and that they had been furnished with a good sensible instinct instead of it.

At Dover, the next morning, we embarked for Calais with a number of passengers, who had never been before at sea. They would previously make a hearty breakfast, because, if the wind should fail, we might not get over

---

[5] Daughter of Mrs. Margaret Stevenson, with whom Franklin took lodgings in London in 1757.

till supper time. Doubtless they thought that when they had paid for their breakfast, they had a right to it, and that, when they had swallowed it they were sure of it. But they had scarce been out half an hour, before the sea laid claim to it, and they were obliged to deliver it up. So it seems there are uncertainties, even beyond those between the cup and the lip. If ever you go to sea, take my advice, and live sparingly a day or two beforehand. The sickness, if any, will be lighter and sooner over. We got to Calais that evening.

Various impositions we suffered from boatmen, porters, &c. on both sides the water. I know not which are most rapacious, the English or French, but the latter have, with their knavery, the most politeness.

The roads we found equally good with ours in England, in some places paved with smooth stone, like our new streets, for many miles together, and rows of trees on each side, and yet there are no turnpikes. But then the poor peasants complained to us grievously, that they were obliged to work upon the roads full two months in the year, without being paid for their labor. Whether this is truth, or whether, like Englishmen, they grumble cause or no cause, I have not yet been able fully to inform myself.

The women we saw at Calais, on the road, at Boulogne, and in the inns and villages, were generally of dark complexions; but arriving at Abbeville we found a sudden change, a multitude of both women and men in that place appearing remarkably fair. Whether this is owing to a small colony of spinners, wool-combers, and weavers, brought hither from Holland with the woollen manufacture about sixty years ago; or to their being less exposed to the sun, than in other places, their business keeping them much within doors, I know not. Perhaps as in some other cases, different causes may club in producing the effect, but the effect itself is certain. Never was I in a place of greater industry, wheels and looms going in every house.

As soon as we left Abbeville, the swarthiness returned. I speak generally, for here are some fair women at Paris, who I think are not whitened by art. As to rouge, they don't pretend to imitate nature in laying it on. There is no gradual diminution of the color, from the full bloom in the middle of the cheek to the faint tint near the sides, nor does it show itself differently in different faces. I have not had the honor of being at any lady's toilette to see how it is laid on, but I fancy I can tell you how it is or may be done. Cut a hole of three inches diameter in a piece of paper; place it on the side of your face in such a manner as that the top of the hole may be just under your eye; then with a brush dipped in the color, paint face and paper together; so when the paper is taken off there will remain a round patch of red exactly the form of the hole. This is the mode, from the actresses on the stage upwards through all ranks of ladies to the princesses of the blood, but it stops there, the Queen not using it, having in the serenity, complacence, and benignity that shine so eminently in, or rather through her countenance, sufficient beauty, though now an old woman, to do extremely well without it.

You see I speak of the Queen as if I had seen her, and so I have; for you must know I have been at Court. We went to Versailles last Sunday, and had the honor of being presented to the King; he spoke to both of us very graciously and cheerfully, is a handsome man, has a very lively look, and appears younger than he is. In the evening we were at the *Grand Couvert,* where the family sup in public. The form of their sitting at the table was this:

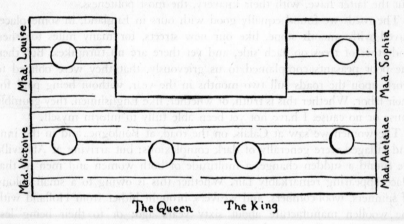

The table was as you see half a hollow square, the service gold. When either made a sign for drink, the word was given by one of the waiters; *A boire pour le Roy,* or, *A boire pour la Reine.* Then two persons within the square approached one with wine, the other with water in caraffes; each drank a little glass of what he brought, and then put both the caraffes with a glass on a salver, and presented it. Their distance from each other was such, as that other chairs might have been placed between any two of them. An officer of the court brought us up through the crowd of spectators, and placed Sir John so as to stand between the King and Madame Adelaide, and me between the Queen and Madame Victoire. The King talked a good deal to Sir John, asking many questions about our royal family; and did me too the honor of taking some notice of me; that's saying enough, for I would not have you think me so much pleased with this King and Queen, as to have a whit less regard than I used to have for ours. No Frenchman shall go beyond me in thinking my own King and Queen the very best in the world, and the most amiable.

Versailles has had infinite sums laid out in building it and supplying it with water. Some say the expenses exceeded eighty millions Sterling.

The range of building is immense; the garden front most magnificent, all of hewn stone; the number of statues, figures, urns, &c., in marble and bronze of exquisite workmanship, is beyond conception. But the water-works are out of repair, and so is great part of the front next the town, looking with its shabby half-brick walls, and broken windows, not much better than the houses in Durham Yard. There is, in short, both at Versailles and Paris, a prodigious mixture of magnificence and negligence, with every kind of elegance except that of cleanliness, and what we call *tidiness*. Though I must do Paris the justice to say, that in two points of cleanliness they exceed us. The water they drink, though from the river, they render as pure as that of the best spring, by filtering it through cisterns filled with sand; and the streets by constant sweeping are fit to walk in, though there is no paved footpath. Accordingly, many well-dressed people are constantly seen walking in them. The crowds of coaches and chairs for this reason is not so great. Men, as well as women, carry umbrellas in their hands, which they extend in case of rain or too much sun; and a man with an umbrella not taking up more than three foot square, or nine square feet of the street, when, if in a coach, he would take up 240 square feet, you can easily conceive that though the streets here are narrower they may be much less encumbered. They are extremely well paved, and the stones, being generally cubes, when worn on one side, may be turned and become new.

The civilities we everywhere receive give us the strongest impressions of the French politeness. It seems to be a point settled here universally, that strangers are to be treated with respect; and one has just the same deference shown one here by being a stranger, as in England by being a lady. The custom-house officers at Port St. Denis, as we entered Paris, were about to seize two dozen of excellent Bordeaux wine given us at Boulogne, and which we brought with us; but, as soon as they found we were strangers, it was immediately remitted on that account. At the Church of Notre Dame, where we went to see a magnificent illumination, with figures, &c., for the deceased Dauphiness, we found an immense crowd, who were kept out by guards; but, the officer being told that we were strangers from England, he immediately admitted us, accompanied and showed us everything. Why don't we practice this urbanity to Frenchmen? Why should they be allowed to outdo us in anything?

Here is an exhibition of paintings like ours in London, to which multitudes flock daily. I am not connoisseur enough to judge which has most merit. Every night, Sundays not excepted, here are plays or operas; and though the weather has been hot, and houses full, one is not incommoded by the heat so much as with us in winter. They must have some way of changing the air, that we are not acquainted with. I shall enquire into it.

Travelling is one way of lengthening life, at least in appearance. It is but about a fortnight since we left London, but the variety of scenes we have gone through makes it seem equal to six months living in one place. Perhaps I have suffered a greater change, too, in my own person, than I could have done in six years at home. I had not been here six days, before my tailor and perruquier had transformed me into a Frenchman. Only think what a figure I make in a little bag-wig and naked ears! They told me I was become twenty years younger, and looked very galante.

So being in Paris where the mode is to be sacredly followed I was once very near making love to my friend's wife.

This letter shall cost you a shilling, and you may consider it cheap, when you reflect, that it has cost me at least fifty guineas to get into the situation, that enables me to write it. Besides, I might, if I had staid at home, have won perhaps two shillings of you at cribbage. By the way, now I mention cards, let me tell you that quadrille is quite out of fashion here, and English whisk all the mode at Paris and the Court.

And pray look upon it as no small matter, that surrounded as I am by the glories of this world, and amusements of all sorts, I remember you and Dolly and all the dear good folks at Bromley. 'Tis true, I can't help it, but must and ever shall remember you all with pleasure.

Need I add that I am particularly, my dear good friend, yours most affectionately,

B. FRANKLIN.

TO WILLIAM STRAHAN [6]

Philada, July 5, 1775.

MR. STRAHAN,

You are a Member of Parliament, and one of that Majority which has doomed my Country to Destruction.—You have begun to burn our Towns, and murder our People.—Look upon your Hands! They are stained with the Blood of your Relations!—You and I were long Friends:—You are now my Enemy,—and I am

Yours,
B. FRANKLIN.

TO BENJAMIN WEBB

Passy, April 22, 1784.

DEAR SIR,

I received yours of the 15th instant, and the memorial it enclosed. The account they give of your situation grieves me. I send you herewith a

[6] A London printer and friend of thirty years standing. This letter was written but never sent.

bill for ten louis d'ors. I do not pretend to *give* such a sum; I only *lend* it to you. When you shall return to your country with a good character, you cannot fail of getting into some business, that will in time enable you to pay all your debts. In that case, when you meet with another honest man in similar distress, you must pay me by lending this sum to him; enjoining him to discharge the debt by a like operation, when he shall be able, and shall meet with such another opportunity. I hope it may thus go through many hands, before it meets with a knave that will stop its progress. This is a trick of mine for doing a deal of good with a little money. I am not rich enough to afford *much* in good works, and so am obliged to be cunning and make the most of a *little*. With best wishes for the success of your memorial, and your future prosperity, I am, dear Sir, your most obedient servant,

B. FRANKLIN.

TO EZRA STILES [7]

Philada, March 9, 1790.

REVEREND AND DEAR SIR,

I received your kind letter of Jan'y 28, and am glad you have at length received the portrait of Gov'r Yale from his family, and deposited it in the College Library. He was a great and good man, and had the merit of doing infinite service to your country by his munificence to that institution. The honor you propose doing me by placing mine in the same room with his, is much too great for my deserts; but you always had a partiality for me, and to that it must be ascribed. I am however too much obliged to Yale College, the first learned society that took notice of me and adorned me with its honors, to refuse a request that comes from it through so esteemed a friend. But I do not think any one of the portraits you mention, as in my possession, worthy of the place and company you propose to place it in. You have an excellent artist lately arrived. If he will undertake to make one for you, I shall cheerfully pay the expense; but he must not delay setting about it, or I may slip through his fingers, for I am now in my eighty-fifth year, and very infirm.

I send with this a very learned work, as it seems to me, on the ancient Samaritan coins, lately printed in Spain, and at least curious for the beauty of the impression. Please to accept it for your College Library. I have subscribed for the Encyclopaedia now printing here, with the intention of presenting it to the College. I shall probably depart before the work is finished, but shall leave directions for its continuance to the end. With this you will receive some of the first numbers.

---

[7] President of Yale, an old friend of Franklin's. Stiles's letter to which this is an answer, may be found in Smyth, *Writings of Franklin*, vol. x, p. 85.

You desire to know something of my religion. It is the first time I have been questioned upon it. But I cannot take your curiosity amiss, and shall endeavor in a few words to gratify it. Here is my creed. I believe in one God, Creator of the Universe. That he governs it by his Providence. That he ought to be worshipped. That the most acceptable service we render to him is doing good to his other children. That the soul of man is immortal, and will be treated with justice in another life respecting its conduct in this. These I take to be the fundamental principles of all sound religion, and I regard them as you do in whatever Sect I meet with them.

As to Jesus of Nazareth, my opinion of whom you particularly desire, I think the system of morals and his religion, as he left them to us, the best the world ever saw or is likely to see; but I apprehend it has received various corrupting changes, and I have, with most of the present dissenters in England, some doubts as to his divinity; though it is a question I do not dogmatize upon, having never studied it, and think it needless to busy myself with it now, when I expect soon an opportunity of knowing the truth with less trouble. I see no harm, however, in its being believed, if that belief has the good consequence, as probably it has, of making his doctrines more respected and better observed; especially as I do not perceive, that the Supreme takes it amiss, by distinguishing the unbelievers in his government of the world with any peculiar marks of his displeasure.

I shall only add, respecting myself, that, having experienced the goodness of that Being in conducting me prosperously through a long life, I have no doubt of its continuance in the next, though without the smallest conceit of meriting such goodness. My sentiments on this head you will see in the copy of an old letter enclosed, which I wrote in answer to one from a zealous religionist, whom I had relieved in a paralytic case by electricity, and who, being afraid I should grow proud upon it, sent me his serious though rather impertinent caution. I send you also the copy of another letter, which will show something of my disposition relating to religion. With great and sincere esteem and affection, I am, your obliged old friend and most obedient humble servant

B. FRANKLIN.

P. S. Had not your College some present of books from the King of France? Please to let me know, if you had an expectation given you of more, and the nature of that expectation? I have a reason for the enquiry.

I confide, that you will not expose me to criticism and censure by publishing any part of this communication to you. I have ever let others enjoy their religious sentiments, without reflecting on them for those that appeared to me unsupportable and even absurd. All sects here, and we have a great variety, have experienced my good will in assisting them with subscriptions for building their new places of worship; and, as I have never opposed any of their doctrines, I hope to go out of the world in peace with them all.

THE WHISTLE

To Madame Brillon

Passy, November 10, 1779.

I RECEIVED my dear friend's two letters, one for Wednesday and one for Saturday. This is again Wednesday. I do not deserve one for to-day, because I have not answered the former. But, indolent as I am, and averse to writing, the fear of having no more of your pleasing epistles, if I do not contribute to the correspondence, obliges me to take up my pen; and as Mr. B. has kindly sent me word, that he sets out to-morrow to see you, instead of spending this Wednesday evening as I have done its namesakes, in your delightful company, I sit down to spend it in thinking of you, in writing to you, and in reading over and over again your letters.

I am charmed with your description of Paradise, and with your plan of living there; and I approve much of your conclusion, that, in the mean time, we should draw all the good we can from this world. In my opinion, we might all draw more good from it than we do, and suffer less evil, if we would take care not to give too much for *whistles*. For to me it seems, that most of the unhappy people we meet with, are become so by neglect of that caution.

You ask what I mean? You love stories, and will excuse my telling one of myself.

When I was a child of seven years old, my friends, on a holiday, filled my pocket with coppers. I went directly to a shop where they sold toys for children; and, being charmed with the sound of a *whistle*, that I met by the way in the hands of another boy, I voluntarily offered and gave all my money for one. I then came home, and went whistling all over the house, much pleased with my *whistle*, but disturbing all the family. My brothers, and sisters, and cousins, understanding the bargain I had made, told me I had given four times as much for it as it was worth; put me in mind what good things I might have bought with the rest of the money; and laughed at me so much for my folly, that I cried with vexation; and the reflection gave me more chagrin than the *whistle* gave me pleasure.

This however was afterwards of use to me, the impression continuing on my mind; so that often, when I was tempted to buy some unnecessary thing, I said to myself, *Don't give too much for the whistle;* and I saved my money.

As I grew up, came into the world, and observed the actions of men, I thought I met with many, very many, who *gave too much for the whistle.*

When I saw one too ambitious of court favor, sacrificing his time in attendance on levees, his repose, his liberty, his virtue, and perhaps his friends, to attain it, I have said to myself, *This man gives too much for his whistle.*

When I saw another fond of popularity, constantly employing himself in political bustles, neglecting his own affairs, and ruining them by that neglect, *He pays, indeed,* said I, *too much for his whistle.*

If I knew a miser, who gave up every kind of comfortable living, all the pleasure of doing good to others, all the esteem of his fellow-citizens, and the joys of benevolent friendship for the sake of accumulating wealth, *Poor man,* said I, *you pay too much for your whistle.*

When I met with a man of pleasure, sacrificing every laudable improvement of the mind, or of his fortune, to mere corporeal sensations, and ruining his health in their pursuit, *Mistaken man,* said I, *you are providing pain for yourself, instead of pleasure; you give too much for your whistle.*

If I see one fond of appearance, or fine clothes, fine houses, fine furniture, fine equipages, all above his fortune, for which he contracts debts, and ends his career in a prison, *Alas!* say I, *he has paid dear, very dear, for his whistle.*

When I see a beautiful, sweet-tempered girl married to an ill-natured brute of a husband, *What a pity,* say I, *that she should pay so much for a whistle!*

In short, I conceive that great part of the miseries of mankind are brought upon them by the false estimates they have made of the value of things, and by their *giving too much for their whistles.*

Yet I ought to have charity for these unhappy people, when I consider, that, with all this wisdom of which I am boasting, there are certain things in the world so tempting, for example, the apples of King John, which happily are not to be bought; for if they were put to sale by auction, I might very easily be led to ruin myself in the purchase, and find that I had once more given too much for the *whistle.*

Adieu, my dear friend, and believe me ever yours very sincerely and with unalterable affection,

B. FRANKLIN.

ST. JEAN DE CRÈVECŒUR

(1735–1813)

Crèvecœur was born from a cultivated family at Caen in Normandy in 1735. Though his early life is obscure he appears to have left France at the age of eighteen, and after spending some time in England to have come to Canada. During several years he made extended journeys, which gave him unusually wide knowledge of the Colonies and the West. In 1765 he became a naturalized citizen of New York, and four years later he married and settled on a farm, which he probably idealizes in his *Letters*—"Pine Hill" in Orange County. His life as a farmer, however, was interrupted by the Revolution, with which he seems not to have sympathized. In 1780 he returned to France, as he came, by way of England; but after the Peace, was again in New York, 1783 to 1790, as French consul. His last years were spent in France, where he died in 1813.

The *Letters from an American Farmer,* on which Crèvecœur's reputation rests, were written in America "for the information of a friend in England." They describe colonial life and nature, in the middle Colonies, in Nantucket, and in Charleston, only the final letter intimating the dismay with which Crèvecœur saw his peaceful life shattered by the upheaval of revolution. But as Hazlitt remarks, they "give not only the objects, but the feelings of a new country." Crèvecœur was an eighteenth-century "man of feeling"; in America he found or fancied man at last living in a "state of nature"; and he was carried away by the enthusiasm natural to a settler on virgin soil. He pictured a colonial Utopia which caught the fancy of Europe and, as Tyler remarks, influenced the youthful fancy of Campbell and Byron, Southey and Coleridge. The simplicity of style is admirably suited to this idyllic conception.

From LETTERS FROM AN AMERICAN FARMER [1]

[A System of Felicity]

I MARRIED, and this perfectly reconciled me to my situation; my wife rendered my house all at once cheerful and pleasing; it no longer appeared gloomy and solitary as before; when I went to work in my fields I worked with more alacrity and sprightliness; I felt that I did not work for myself alone, and this encouraged me much. My wife would often come with her knitting in her hand, and sit under the shady trees, praising the straightness of my furrows, and the docility of my horses; this swelled my heart and made everything light and pleasant, and I regretted that

---

[1] The *Letters* were first published in London in 1782, as by "J. Hector St. John, a Farmer in Pennsylvania." This name Crèvecœur had assumed in America and doubtless thought in war-time better suited to English readers than his own. Though not known to have had a farm in Pennsylvania he was probably familiar with that colony.

I had not married before. I felt myself happy in my new situation, and where is that station which can confer a more substantial system of felicity than that of an American farmer, possessing freedom of action, freedom of thoughts, ruled by a mode of government which requires but little from us? I owe nothing, but a pepper corn to my country, a small tribute to my king, with loyalty and due respect; I know no other landlord than the lord of all land, to whom I owe the most sincere gratitude. My father left me three hundred and seventy-one acres of land, forty-seven of which are good timothy meadow, an excellent orchard, a good house, and a substantial barn. It is my duty to think how happy I am that he lived to build and to pay for all these improvements; what are the labors which I have to undergo, what are my fatigues when compared to his, who had everything to do, from the first tree he felled to the finishing of his house?

[An Artless Countryman]

Pray do not laugh in thus seeing an artless countryman tracing himself through the simple modifications of his life; remember that you have required it, therefore with candor, though with diffidence, I endeavor to follow the thread of my feelings, but I cannot tell you all. Often when I plough my low ground, I place my little boy on a chair which screws to the beam of the plough—its motion and that of the horses please him, he is perfectly happy and begins to chat. As I lean over the handle, various are the thoughts which crowd into my mind. I am now doing for him, I say, what my father formerly did for me; may God enable him to live that he may perform the same operations for the same purposes when I am worn out and old! I relieve his mother of some trouble while I have him with me, the odoriferous furrow exhilarates his spirits, and seems to do the child a great deal of good, for he looks more blooming since I have adopted that practice; can more pleasure, more dignity be added to that primary occupation? The father thus ploughing with his child, and to feed his family, is inferior only to the emperor of China ploughing as an example to his kingdom.

[What Is An American]

I wish I could be acquainted with the feelings and thoughts which must agitate the heart and present themselves to the mind of an enlightened Englishman, when he first lands on this continent. He must greatly rejoice that he lived at a time to see this fair country discovered and settled; he must necessarily feel a share of national pride, when he views the chain of settlements which embellishes these extended shores. When he says to himself, this is the work of my countrymen, who, when convulsed by factions, afflicted by a variety of miseries and wants, restless and impatient, took refuge here. They brought along with them their national genius, to which they principally owe what liberty they enjoy, and what substance they possess. Here he sees the industry of his native country displayed in a new manner, and traces in their works the embrios of all the arts, sciences, and ingenuity which flourish in Europe. Here he beholds fair cities, substantial villages, extensive fields, an immense country filled with decent houses, good roads, orchards, meadows, and bridges, where an hundred years ago all was wild, woody and uncultivated! What a train of pleasing ideas this fair spectacle must suggest; it is a prospect which must inspire a good citizen with the most heartfelt pleasure. The difficulty consists in the manner of viewing so extensive a scene. He is arrived on a new continent; a modern society offers itself to his contemplation, different from what he had hitherto seen. It is not composed, as in Europe, of great lords who possess everything, and of a herd of people who have nothing. Here are no aristocratical families, no courts, no kings, no bishops, no ecclesiastical dominion, no invisible power giving to a few a very visible one; no great manufacturers employing thousands, no great refinements of luxury. The rich and the poor are not so far removed from each other as they are in Europe. Some few towns excepted, we are all tillers of the earth, from Nova Scotia to West Florida. We are a people of cultivators, scattered over an immense territory, communicating with each other by means of good roads and navigable rivers, united by the silken bands of mild government, all respecting the laws, without dreading their power, because they are equitable. We are all animated with the spirit of an industry which is unfettered and unrestrained, because each person works for himself. If he travels through our rural districts he views not the hostile castle, and the haughty mansion, contrasted with the clay-built hut and miserable cabin, where cattle and men help to keep each other warm, and dwell in meanness, smoke, and indigence. A pleasing uniformity of decent competence appears throughout our habitations. The meanest of our log houses is a dry and comfortable habitation. Lawyer or merchant are the fairest titles our towns afford; that of a farmer is the only appellation of the rural inhabitants of our country. It must take some time ere he can reconcile himself to our dictionary, which is but short in words of dignity, and names of honor. There, on a Sunday, he sees a congregation of respectable farmers and their wives, all clad in neat homespun, well mounted, or riding in their own humble wagons. There is not among them an esquire, saving the unlettered magistrate. There he sees a parson as simple as his flock, a farmer who does not riot on the labor of others. We have no princes, for whom we toil, starve, and bleed: we are the most perfect society now existing in the world. Here man is free as he ought to be; nor is this pleasing equality so transitory as many others are. Many

ages will not see the shores of our great lakes replenished with inland
nations, nor the unknown bounds of North America entirely peopled. Who
can tell how far it extends? Who can tell the millions of men whom it
will feed and contain? for no European foot has as yet travelled half the
extent of this mighty continent!

The next wish of this traveller will be to know whence came all these
people? they are a mixture of English, Scotch, Irish, French, Dutch, Germans, and Swedes. From this promiscuous breed, that race now called
Americans have arisen. The eastern provinces must indeed be excepted, as
being the unmixed descendants of Englishmen. I have heard many wish
that they had been more intermixed also: for my part, I am no wisher,
and think it much better as it has happened. They exhibit a most conspicuous figure in this great and variegated picture; they too enter for
a great share in the pleasing perspective displayed in these thirteen provinces. I know it is fashionable to reflect on them, but I respect them for
what they have done; for the accuracy and wisdom with which they have
settled their territory; for the decency of their manners; for their early
love of letters; their ancient college, the first in this hemisphere; for their
industry; which to me who am but a farmer, is the criterion of everything.
There never was a people, situated as they are, who with so ungrateful
a soil have done more in so short a time. Do you think that the monarchical
ingredients which are more prevalent in other governments, have purged
them from all foul stains? Their histories assert the contrary.

In this great American asylum, the poor of Europe have by some means
met together, and in consequence of various causes; to what purpose should
they ask one another what countrymen they are? Alas, two-thirds of them
had no country. Can a wretch who wanders about, who works and starves,
whose life is a continual scene of sore affliction or pinching penury; can
that man call England or any other kingdom his country? A country that
had no bread for him, whose fields procured him no harvest, who met
with nothing but the frowns of the rich, the severity of the laws, with jails
and punishments; who owned not a single foot of the extensive surface
of this planet? No! urged by a variety of motives, here they came. Everything has tended to regenerate them; new laws, a new mode of living, a
new social system; here they are become men: in Europe they were as
so many useless plants, wanting vegetative mould, and refreshing showers;
they withered, and were mowed down by want, hunger, and war; but
now by the power of transplantation, like all other plants they have taken
root and flourished! Formerly they were not numbered in any civil lists
of their country, except in those of the poor; here they rank as citizens.
By what invisible power has this suprising metamorphosis been performed?
By that of the laws and that of their industry. The laws, the indulgent

laws, protect them as they arrive, stamping on them the symbol of adoption; they receive ample rewards for their labors; these accumulated rewards procure them lands; those lands confer on them the title of freemen, and to that title every benefit is affixed which men can possibly require. This is the great operation daily performed by our laws. From whence proceed these laws? From our government. Whence the government? It is derived from the original genius and strong desire of the people ratified and confirmed by the crown. This is the great chain which links us all, this is the picture which every province exhibits, Nova Scotia excepted. There the crown has done all; either there were no people who had genius, or it was not much attended to: the consequence is, that the province is very thinly inhabited indeed; the power of the crown in conjunction with the mosquitoes has prevented men from settling there. Yet some parts of it flourished once, and it contained a mild harmless set of people. But for the fault of a few leaders, the whole were banished. The greatest political error the crown ever committed in America was to cut off men from a country which wanted nothing but men!

What attachment can a poor European emigrant have for a country where he had nothing? The knowledge of the language, the love of a few kindred as poor as himself, were the only cords that tied him: his country is now that which gives him land, bread, protection, and consequence: *Ubi panis ibi patria,* is the motto of all emigrants. What then is the American, this new man? He is either an European, or the descendant of an European, hence that strange mixture of blood, which you will find in no other country. I could point out to you a family whose grandfather was an Englishman, whose wife was Dutch, whose son married a French woman, and whose present four sons have now four wives of different nations. *He* is an American, who leaving behind him all his ancient prejudices and manners, receives new ones from the new mode of life he has embraced, the new government he obeys, and the new rank he holds. He becomes an American by being received in the broad lap of our great *Alma Mater.* Here individuals of all nations are melted into a new race of men, whose labors and posterity will one day cause great changes in the world. Americans are the western pilgrims, who are carrying along with them that great mass of arts, sciences, vigor, and industry which began long since in the east; they will finish the great circle. The Americans were once scattered all over Europe; here they are incorporated into one of the finest systems of population which has ever appeared, and which will hereafter become distinct by the power of the different climates they inhabit. The American ought therefore to love this country much better than that wherein either he or his forefathers were born. Here the rewards of his industry follow with equal steps the progress of his labor;

his labor is founded on the basis of nature, *self-interest;* can it want a stronger allurement? Wives and children, who before in vain demanded of him a morsel of bread, now, fat and frolicsome, gladly help their father to clear those fields whence exuberant crops are to arise to feed and to clothe them all; without any part being claimed, either by a despotic prince, a rich abbot, or a mighty lord. Here religion demands but little of him; a small voluntary salary to the minister, and gratitude to God; can he refuse these? The American is a new man, who acts upon new principles; he must therefore entertain new ideas, and form new opinions. From involuntary idleness, servile dependence, penury, and useless labor, he has passed to toils of a very different nature, rewarded by ample subsistence.—This is an American.

[PECULIAR CUSTOMS AT NANTUCKET]

THE manners of the *Friends* are entirely founded on that simplicity which is their boast, and their most distinguished characteristic; and those manners have acquired the authority of laws. Here they are strongly attached to plainness of dress, as well as to that of language; insomuch that though some part of it may be ungrammatical, yet should any person who was born and brought up here, attempt to speak more correctly, he would be looked upon as a fop or an innovator. On the other hand, should a stranger come here and adopt their idiom in all its purity (as they deem it) this accomplishment would immediately procure him the most cordial reception; and they would cherish him like an ancient member of their society. So many impositions have they suffered on this account, that they begin now indeed to grow more cautious. They are so tenacious of their ancient habits of industry and frugality, that if any of them were to be seen with a long coat made of English cloth, on any other than the *first-day* (Sunday) he would be greatly ridiculed and censured; he would be looked upon as a careless spendthrift, whom it would be unsafe to trust, and in vain to relieve. A few years ago two *single-horse chairs* were imported from Boston, to the great offence of these prudent citizens; nothing appeared to them more culpable than the use of such gaudy painted vehicles, in contempt of the more useful and more simple *single-horse carts* of their fathers. This piece of extravagant and unknown luxury, almost caused a schism, and set every tongue a-going; some predicted the approaching ruin of those families that had imported them; others feared the dangers of example; never since the foundation of the town had there happened anything which so much alarmed this primitive community. One of the possessors of these profane chairs, filled with repentance, wisely sent it back to the continent; the other, more obstinate and perverse, in defiance to all remonstrances, persisted in the use of his chair until by degrees they became more reconciled to it; though I observed that the wealthiest and the most respectable people still go to meeting or to their farms in a *single-horse cart* with a decent awning fixed over it: indeed, if you consider their sandy soil, and the badness of their roads, these appear to be the best contrived vehicles for this island.

Idleness is the most heinous sin that can be committed in Nantucket: an idle man would soon be pointed out as an object of compassion: for idleness is considered as another word for want and hunger. This principle is so thoroughly well understood, and is become so universal, so prevailing a prejudice, that literally speaking, they are never idle. Even if they go to the market place, which is (if I may be allowed the expression) the coffee-house of the town, either to transact business, or to converse with their friends; they always have a piece of cedar in their hands, and while they are talking, they will, as it were instinctively, employ themselves in converting it into something useful, either in making bungs or spiles for their oil casks, or other useful articles. I must confess, that I have never seen more ingenuity in the use of the knife; thus the most idle moments of their lives become usefully employed. In the many hours of leisure which their long cruises afford them, they cut and carve a variety of boxes and pretty toys, in wood, adapted to different uses; which they bring home as testimonies of remembrance to their wives or sweethearts. They have showed me a variety of little bowls and other implements, executed cooper-wise, with the greatest neatness and elegance. You will be pleased to remember they are all brought up to the trade of coopers, be their future intentions or fortunes what they may; therefore almost every man in this island has always two knives in his pocket, one much larger than the other; and though they hold everything that is called *fashion* in the utmost contempt, yet they are as difficult to please, and as extravagant in the choice and price of their knives, as any young buck in Boston would be about his hat, buckles, or coat. As soon as a knife is injured, or superseded by a more convenient one, it is carefully laid up in some corner of their desk. I once saw upwards of fifty thus preserved at Mr. ——'s, one of the worthiest men on this island; and among the whole, there was not one that perfectly resembled another. As the sea excursions were often very long, their wives in their absence, are necessarily obliged to transact business, to settle accounts, and in short, to rule and provide for their·families. These circumstances being often repeated, give women the abilities as well as a taste for that kind of superintendency, to which, by their prudence and good management, they seem to be in general very equal. This employment ripens their judgment, and justly entitles them to a rank superior to that of other wives; and this is the principal reason why those of Nantucket as well as those of Montreal [2] are so fond of society, so affable, and so conversant with the affairs of the world. The men at their return, weary with the fatigues of the sea, full of confidence and love, cheerfully give their consent to every transaction that has happened during their absence, and all is joy and peace. "Wife, thee hast done well," is the general approbation they receive, for their application and industry. What would the men do without the agency of these faithful mates? The absence of so many of them at particular seasons, leaves the town quite desolate; and this mournful situation disposes the women to go to each other's house much oftener than when their husbands are at home: hence the custom of incessant visiting has infected every one, and even those whose husbands do not go abroad. The house is always cleaned before they set out, and with peculiar alacrity they pursue their intended visit, which consists of a social chat, a dish of tea, and an hearty supper. When the good man of the house returns from his labor, he peaceably goes after his wife and brings her home; meanwhile the young fellows, equally vigilant, easily find out which is the most convenient house, and there they assemble with the girls of the neighborhood. Instead of cards, musical instruments, or songs, they relate stories of their whaling voyages, their various sea adventures, and talk of the different coasts and people they have visited. "The island of Catharine in the Brazil," says one, "is a very droll island, it is inhabited by none but men; women are not permitted to come in sight of it; not a woman is there on the whole island. Who among us is not glad it is not so here? The Nantucket girls and boys beat the world." At this innocent sally the titter goes round, they whisper to one another their spontaneous reflections: puddings, pies, and custards never fail to be produced on such occasions; for I believe there never were any people in their circumstances, who live so well, even to superabundance. As inebriation is unknown, and music, singing, and dancing, are held in equal detestation, they never could fill all the vacant hours of their lives without the repast of the table. Thus these young people sit and talk, and divert themselves as well as they can; if any one has lately returned from a cruise, he is generally the speaker of the night; they often all laugh and talk together, but they are happy, and would not exchange their pleasures for those of the most brilliant assemblies in Europe. This lasts until the father and mother return; when all retire to their respective homes, the men reconducting the partners of their affections.

Thus they spend many of the youthful evenings of their lives; no wonder, therefore, that they marry so early. But no sooner have they undergone this ceremony than they cease to appear so cheerful and gay; the new rank they

[2] Most of the merchants and young men of Montreal spend the greatest part of their time in trading with the Indians, at an amazing distance from Canada; and it often happens that they are three years together absent from home.—*Author's note.*

hold in the society impresses them with more serious ideas than were entertained before. The title of master of a family necessarily requires more solid behavior and deportment; the new wife follows in the trammels of Custom, which are as powerful as the tyranny of fashion; she gradually advises and directs; the new husband soon goes to sea, he leaves her to learn and exercise the new government, in which she is entered. Those who stay at home are full as passive in general, at least with regard to the inferior departments of the family. But you must not imagine from this account that the Nantucket wives are turbulent, of high temper, and difficult to be ruled; on the contrary, the wives of Sherburn in so doing, comply only with the prevailing custom of the island: the husbands, equally submissive to the ancient and respectable manners of their country, submit, without ever suspecting that there can be any impropriety. Were they to behave otherwise, they would be afraid of subverting the principles of their society by altering its ancient rules: thus both parties are perfectly satisfied, and all is peace and concord. The richest person now in the island owes all his present prosperity and success to the ingenuity of his wife: this is a known fact which is well recorded; for while he was performing his first cruises, she traded with pins and needles, and kept a school. Afterward she purchased more considerable articles, which she sold with so much judgment, that she laid the foundation of a system of business, that she has ever since prosecuted with equal dexterity and success. She wrote to London, formed connections, and, in short, became the only ostensible instrument of that house, both at home and abroad. Who is he in this country, and who is a citizen of Nantucket or Boston, who does not know *Aunt Kesiah?* I must tell you that she is the wife of Mr. C——n, a very respectable man, who, well pleased with all her schemes, trusts to her judgment, and relies on her sagacity, with so entire a confidence, as to be altogether passive to the concerns of his family. They have the best country seat on the island, at Quayes, where they live with hospitality, and in perfect union. He seems to be altogether the contemplative man.

GEORGE WASHINGTON

(1732–1799)

George Washington, the son of a Virginia landholder, was born February 22, 1732. He received a limited education at private schools, but picked up the elements of surveying by himself, and at sixteen was employed to survey the vast estates of Lord Fairfax. He would have made surveying his profession had not the death of his brother Lawrence in 1752 made it necessary for him to assume management of the family estates. In the same year he was made adjutant of one of Virginia's four military districts, and this paved the way to various military commissions, which in turn led to his being chosen commander-in-chief of the colonial forces at the beginning of the Revolution. After the war he returned home, devoting the next four years to farming, at the same time lending his support to a more perfect union of the states. In 1787 he went as a Virginia delegate to the Constitutional Convention in Philadelphia, and was chosen its president. Later he was elected unanimously as first President of the United States. After serving two terms, he retired to Mt. Vernon, where he died in 1799.

Washington lacked education in any formal sense of the term, and despite the many volumes containing his state papers, diaries, correspondence, and the like, he can lay no claim to the title of man of letters. It is in the combined character of general and statesman that he must live, and in this character he has no peer in modern times. He possessed an integrity, a strength of purpose, a sound good sense, and a dashing impetuosity tempered by iron control, which were perfectly coördinated and gave him poise and strength beyond most men. Loving domesticity and being happiest in caring for his estates, he nevertheless gave himself unstintedly to his country's service, and lived so that he well merited the words of Henry Lee: "First in war, first in peace, and first in the hearts of his countrymen."

FAREWELL ADDRESS

To the People of the United States [1]

FRIENDS AND FELLOW-CITIZENS: The period for a new election of a citizen, to administer the executive government of the United States, being not far distant, and the time actually arrived, when your thoughts must be employed in designating the person who is to be clothed with that important trust, it appears to me proper, especially as it may conduce to a more distinct

---

[1] The Farewell Address was published on September 19, 1796, in Claypoole's *American Daily Advertiser*. Washington, after consultation with James Madison, had prepared the first draft in 1792, towards the end of his first administration; this draft he submitted in 1796 to Alexander Hamilton, who redrafted it. The Address as finally published represents Washington's ideas, and in part his phrasing, but in the composition he was indebted largely to Hamilton, and, to a less degree, to Madison and Jay.

expression of the public voice, that I should now apprise you of the resolution I have formed, to decline being considered among the number of those out of whom a choice is to be made.

I beg you, at the same time, to do me the justice to be assured, that this resolution has not been taken without a strict regard to all the considerations appertaining to the relation which binds a dutiful citizen to his country; and that, in withdrawing the tender of service, which silence in my situation might imply, I am influenced by no diminution of zeal for your future interest; no deficiency of grateful respect for your past kindness; but am supported by a full conviction that the step is compatible with both.

The acceptance of, and continuance hitherto in, the office to which your suffrages have twice called me, have been a uniform sacrifice of inclination to the opinion of duty, and to a deference for what appeared to be your desire. I constantly hoped, that it would have been much earlier in my power, consistently with motives which I was not at liberty to disregard, to return to that retirement from which I had been reluctantly drawn. The strength of my inclination to do this, previous to the last election, had even led to the preparation of an address to declare it to you; but mature reflection on the then perplexed and critical posture of our affairs with foreign nations, and the unanimous advice of persons entitled to my confidence, impelled me to abandon the idea.

I rejoice that the state of your concerns, external as well as internal, no longer renders the pursuit of inclination incompatible with the sentiment of duty or propriety; and am persuaded, whatever partiality may be retained for my services, that, in the present circumstances of our country, you will not disapprove my determination to retire.

The impressions, with which I first undertook the arduous trust, were explained on the proper occasion. In the discharge of this trust, I will only say, that I have, with good intentions, contributed towards the organization and administration of the government the best exertions of which a very fallible judgment was capable. Not unconscious, in the outset, of the inferiority of my qualifications, experience in my own eyes, perhaps still more in the eyes of others, has strengthened the motives to diffidence of myself; and every day the increasing weight of years admonishes me more and more, that the shade of retirement is as necessary to me as it will be welcome. Satisfied that, if any circumstances have given peculiar value to my services, they were temporary, I have the consolation to believe that, while choice and prudence invite me to quit the political scene, patriotism does not forbid it.

In looking forward to the moment which is intended to terminate the career of my public life, my feelings do not permit me to suspend the deep acknowledgment of that debt of gratitude which I owe to my beloved country for the many honors it has conferred upon me; still more for the steadfast confidence with which it has supported me; and for the opportunities I have thence enjoyed of manifesting my inviolable attachment, by services faithful and persevering, though in usefulness unequal to my zeal. If benefits have resulted to our country from these services, let it always be remembered to your praise, and as an instructive example in our annals, that, under circumstances in which the passions, agitated in every direction, were liable to mislead, amidst appearances sometimes dubious, vicissitudes of fortune often discouraging, in situations in which not unfrequently want of success has countenanced the spirit of criticism, the constancy of your support was the essential prop of the efforts, and a guaranty of the plans, by which they were effected. Profoundly penetrated with this idea, I shall carry it with me to the grave, as a strong incitement to unceasing vows that Heaven may continue to you the choicest tokens of its beneficence; that your union and brotherly affection may be perpetual; that the free constitution, which is the work of your hands, may be sacredly maintained; that its administration in every department may be stamped with wisdom and virtue; that, in fine, the happiness of the people of these States, under the auspices of liberty, may be made complete, by so careful a preservation and so prudent a use of this blessing, as will acquire to them the glory of recommending it to the applause, the affection, and adoption of every nation which is yet a stranger to it.

Here, perhaps, I ought to stop. But a solicitude for your welfare, which cannot end but with my life, and the apprehension of danger, natural to that solicitude, urge me, on an occasion like the present, to offer to your solemn contemplation, and to recommend to your frequent review, some sentiments, which are the result of much reflection, of no inconsiderable observation, and which appear to me all important to the permanency of your felicity as a people. These will be offered to you with the more freedom, as you can only see in them the disinterested warnings of a parting friend, who can possibly have no personal motive to bias his counsels. Nor can I forget, as an encouragement to it, your indulgent reception of my sentiments on a former and not dissimilar occasion.

Interwoven as is the love of liberty with every ligament of your hearts, no recommendation of mine is necessary to fortify or confirm the attachment.

The unity of government, which constitutes you one people, is also now dear to you. It is justly so; for it is a main pillar in the edifice of your real independence, the support of your tranquillity at home, your peace abroad; of your safety; of your prosperity in every shape; of that very liberty which you so highly prize. But as it is easy to foresee, that, from different causes and from different quarters, much pains will be taken, many artifices employed, to weaken in your minds the conviction of this truth; as this is the point in your political fortress against which the batteries of internal and external enemies will be most constantly and actively (though often covertly and insidiously) directed, it is of infinite moment, that you should properly estimate the immense value of your national Union to your collective and individual happiness; that you should cherish a cordial, habitual, and immovable attachment to it; accustoming yourselves to think and speak of it as of the palladium of your political safety and prosperity; watching for its preservation with jealous anxiety; discountenancing whatever may suggest even a suspicion that it can in any event be abandoned; and indignantly frowning upon the first dawning of every attempt to alienate any portion of our country from the rest, or to enfeeble the sacred ties which now link together the various parts.

For this you have every inducement of sympathy and interest. Citizens, by birth or choice, of a common country, that country has a right to concentrate your affections. The name of AMERICAN, which belongs to you, in your national capacity, must always exalt the just pride of patriotism, more than any appellation derived from local discriminations. With slight shades of difference, you have the same religion, manners, habits, and political principles. You have in a common cause fought and triumphed together. The independence and liberty you possess are the work of joint counsels, and joint efforts, of common dangers, sufferings, and successes.

But these considerations, however powerfully they address themselves to your sensibility, are greatly outweighed by those which apply more immediately to your interest. Here every portion of our country finds the most commanding motives for carefully guarding and preserving the union of the whole.

The North, in an unrestrained intercourse with the South, protected by the equal laws of a common government, finds in the productions of the latter great additional resources of maritime and commercial enterprise, and precious materials of manufacturing industry. The South, in the same intercourse, benefiting by the agency of the North, sees its agriculture grow and its commerce expand. Turning partly into its own channels the seamen of the North, it finds its particular navigation invigorated; and, while it contributes, in different ways, to nourish and increase the general mass of the national navigation, it looks forward to the protection of a maritime strength to which itself is unequally adapted. The East, in a like intercourse with the West, already finds, and in the progressive improvement of interior communications, by land and water, will more and more find, a valuable vent for the commodities which it brings from abroad, or manufactures at home. The West derives from the East supplies requisite to its growth and comfort, and, what is perhaps of still greater consequence, it must of necessity owe the secure enjoyment of indispensable outlets for its own productions to the weight, influence, and the future maritime strength of the Atlantic side of the Union, directed by an indissoluble community of interest as one *Nation*.

Any other tenure by which the West can hold this essential advantage, whether derived from its own separate strength, or from an apostate and unnatural connection with any foreign power, must be intrinsically precarious.

While, then, every part of our country thus feels an immediate and particular interest in union, all the parts combined in the united mass of means and efforts cannot fail to find greater strength, greater resource, proportionably greater security from external danger, a less frequent interruption of their peace by foreign nations; and, what is of inestimable value! they must derive from union an exemption from those broils and wars between themselves, which so frequently afflict neighboring countries not tied together by the same government, which their own rivalships alone would be sufficient to produce, but which opposite foreign alliances, attachments, and intrigues would stimulate and embitter. Hence, likewise, they will avoid the necessity of those overgrown military establishments, which, under any form of government, are inauspicious to liberty, and which are to be regarded as particularly hostile to republican liberty. In this sense it is, that your union ought to be considered as a main prop of your liberty, and that the love of the one ought to endear to you the preservation of the other.

These considerations speak a persuasive language to every reflecting and virtuous mind, and exhibit the continuance of the Union as a primary object of patriotic desire. Is there a doubt whether a common government can embrace so large a sphere? Let experience solve it. To listen to mere speculation in such a case were criminal. We are authorized to hope that a proper organization of the whole, with the auxiliary agency of governments for the respective subdivisions, will afford a happy issue to the experiment. It is well worth a fair and full experiment. With such powerful and obvious motives to union, affecting all parts of our country, while experience shall not have demonstrated its impracticability, there will always be reason to distrust the patriotism of those who in any quarter may endeavor to weaken its bands.

In contemplating the causes which may disturb our Union, it occurs as a matter of serious concern, that any ground should have been furnished for characterizing parties by geographical discriminations, Northern and Southern, Atlantic and Western; whence designing men may endeavor to excite a belief that there is a real difference of local interests and views. One of the expedients of party to acquire influence, within particular districts, is to misrepresent the opinions and aims of other districts. You cannot shield yourselves too much against the jealousies and heart-burnings which spring from these misrepresentations; they tend to render alien to each other those who ought to be bound together by fraternal affection. The inhabitants of our western country have lately had a useful lesson on this head; they have seen, in the negotiation by the Executive, and in the unanimous ratification by the

Senate, of the treaty with Spain, and in the universal satisfaction at that event throughout the United States, a decisive proof how unfounded were the suspicions propagated among them of a policy in the general government and in the Atlantic States unfriendly to their interests in regard to the Mississippi; they have been witnesses to the formation of two treaties, that with Great Britain and that with Spain, which secure to them everything they could desire, in respect to our foreign relations, towards confirming their prosperity. Will it not be their wisdom to rely for the preservation of these advantages on the Union by which they were procured? Will they not henceforth be deaf to those advisers, if such there are, who would sever them from their brethren, and connect them with aliens?

To the efficacy and permanency of your union, a government for the whole is indispensable. No alliances, however strict, between the parts can be an adequate substitute; they must inevitably experience the infractions and interruptions which all alliances in all times have experienced. Sensible of this momentous truth, you have improved upon your first essay, by the adoption of a constitution of government better calculated than your former for an intimate union, and for the efficacious management of your common concerns. This government, the offspring of our own choice, uninfluenced and unawed, adopted upon full investigation and mature deliberation, completely free in its principles, in the distribution of its powers, uniting security with energy, and containing within itself a provision for its own amendment, has a just claim to your confidence and your support. Respect for its authority, compliance with its laws, acquiescence in its measures, are duties enjoined by the fundamental maxims of true liberty. The basis of our political systems is the right of the people to make and to alter their constitutions of government. But the constitution which at any time exists, till changed by an explicit and authentic act of the whole people, is sacredly obligatory upon all. The very idea of the power and the right of the people to establish government presupposes the duty of every individual to obey the established government.

All obstructions to the execution of the laws, all combinations and associations, under whatever plausible character, with the real design to direct, control, counteract, or awe the regular deliberation and action of the constituted authorities, are destructive of this fundamental principle, and of fatal tendency. They serve to organize faction, to give it an artificial and extraordinary force; to put, in the place of the delegated will of the nation, the will of a party, often a small but artful and enterprising minority of the community; and, according to the alternate triumphs of different parties, to make the public administration the mirror of the ill-concerted and incongruous projects of faction, rather than the organ of consistent and wholesome plans digested by common councils, and modified by mutual interests.

However combinations or associations of the above description may now and then answer popular ends, they are likely, in the course of time and things, to become potent engines, by which cunning, ambitious, and un-principled men will be enabled to subvert the power of the people, and to usurp for themselves the reins of government; destroying afterwards the very engines which have lifted them to unjust dominion.

Towards the preservation of your government, and the permanency of your present happy state, it is requisite, not only that you steadily discountenance irregular oppositions to its acknowledged authority, but also that you resist with care the spirit of innovation upon its principles, however specious the pretexts. One method of assault may be to effect, in the forms of the con-stitution, alterations, which will impair the energy of the system, and thus to undermine what cannot be directly overthrown. In all the changes to which you may be invited, remember that time and habit are at least as necessary to fix the true character of governments as of other human institutions; that experience is the surest standard by which to test the real tendency of the existing constitution of a country; that facility in changes, upon the credit of mere hypothesis and opinion, exposes to perpetual change, from the endless variety of hypothesis and opinion; and remember, especially, that, for the efficient management of your common interests, in a country so extensive as ours, a government of as much vigor as is consistent with the perfect security of liberty is indispensable. Liberty itself will find in such a government, with powers properly distributed and adjusted, its surest guardian. It is, indeed, little else than a name, where the government is too feeble to withstand the enterprises of faction, to confine each member of the society within the limits prescribed by the laws, and to maintain all in the secure and tranquil enjoy-ment of the rights of person and property.

I have already intimated to you the danger of parties in the State, with particular reference to the founding of them on geographical discrimination. Let me now take a more comprehensive view, and warn you in the most solemn manner against the baneful effects of the spirit of party, generally.

This spirit, unfortunately, is inseparable from our nature, having its root in the strongest passions of the human mind. It exists under different shapes in all governments, more or less stifled, controlled, or repressed; but in those of the popular form it is seen in its greatest rankness, and is truly their worst enemy.

The alternate domination of one faction over another, sharpened by the spirit of revenge, natural to party dissension, which in different ages and countries has perpetrated the most horrid enormities, is itself a frightful des-potism. But this leads at length to a more formal and permanent despotism. The disorders and miseries which result, gradually incline the minds of men to seek security and repose in the absolute power of an individual; and sooner or later the chief of some prevailing faction, more able or more fortunate than his competitors, turns this disposition to the purposes of his own elevation, on the ruins of public liberty.

Without looking forward to an extremity of this kind (which nevertheless ought not to be entirely out of sight), the common and continued mischiefs of the spirit of party are sufficient to make it the interest and duty of a wise people to discourage and restrain it.

It serves always to distract the public councils, and enfeeble the public administration. It agitates the community with ill-founded jealousies and false alarms; kindles the animosity of one part against another, foments occasionally riot and insurrection. It opens the doors to foreign influence and corruption, which find a facilitated access to the government itself through the channels of party passions. Thus the policy and the will of one country are subjected to the policy and will of another.

There is an opinion, that parties in free countries are useful checks upon the administration of the government, and serve to keep alive the spirit of liberty. This within certain limits is probably true, and in governments of a monarchical cast, patriotism may look with indulgence, if not with favor, upon the spirit of party. But in those of the popular character, in governments purely elective, it is a spirit not to be encouraged. From their natural tendency, it is certain there will always be enough of that spirit for every salutary purpose; and there being constant danger of excess, the effort ought to be, by force of public opinion to mitigate and assuage it. A fire not to be quenched, it demands a uniform vigilance to prevent its bursting into a flame, lest, instead of warming, it should consume.

It is important, likewise, that the habits of thinking in a free country should inspire caution, in those intrusted with its administration, to confine themselves within their respective constitutional spheres, avoiding in the exercise of the powers of one department to encroach upon another. The spirit of encroachment tends to consolidate the powers of all the departments in one, and thus to create, whatever the form of government, a real despotism. A just estimate of that love of power, and proneness to abuse it, which predominates in the human heart, is sufficient to satisfy us of the truth of this position. The necessity of reciprocal checks in the exercise of political power, by dividing and distributing it into different depositories, and constituting each the guardian of the public weal against invasions by the others, has been evinced by experiments ancient and modern, some of them in our country and under our own eyes. To preserve them must be as necessary as to institute them. If, in the opinion of the people, the distribution or modification of the constitutional powers be in any particular wrong, let it be corrected by an amendment in the way which the Constitution designates. But let there be no change by usurpation; for, though this, in one instance, may be the instrument of good, it is the customary weapon by which free governments are destroyed. The precedent must always greatly overbalance in permanent evil any partial or transient benefit which the use can at any time yield.

Of all the dispositions and habits which lead to political prosperity, religion and morality are indispensable supports. In vain would that man claim the tribute of patriotism, who should labor to subvert these great pillars of human happiness, these firmest props of the duties of men and citizens. The mere politician, equally with the pious man, ought to respect and to cherish them. A volume could not trace all their connections with private and public felicity. Let it simply be asked, Where is the security for property, for reputation, for life, if the sense of religious obligation desert the oaths, which are the instruments of investigation in courts of justice? And let us with caution indulge the supposition, that morality can be maintained without religion. Whatever may be conceded to the influence of refined education on minds of peculiar structure, reason and experience both forbid us to expect, that national morality can prevail in exclusion of religious principle.

It is substantially true that virtue or morality is a necessary spring of popular government. The rule, indeed, extends with more or less force to every species of free government. Who, that is a sincere friend to it, can look with indifference upon attempts to shake the foundation of the fabric?

Promote, then, as an object of primary importance, institutions for the general diffusion of knowledge. In proportion as the structure of a government gives force to public opinion, it is essential that public opinion should be enlightened.

As a very important source of strength and security, cherish public credit. One method of preserving it is, to use it as sparingly as possible; avoiding occasions of expense by cultivating peace, but remembering also that timely disbursements to prepare for danger frequently prevent much greater disbursements to repel it; avoiding likewise the accumulation of debt, not only by shunning occasions of expense, but by vigorous exertions in time of peace to discharge the debts, which unavoidable wars may have occasioned, not ungenerously throwing upon posterity the burden which we ourselves ought to bear. The execution of these maxims belongs to your representatives, but it is necessary that public opinion should coöperate. To facilitate to them the performance of their duty, it is essential that you should practically bear in mind, that towards the payment of debts there must be revenue; that to have revenue there must be taxes; that no taxes can be devised which are not more or less inconvenient and unpleasant; that the intrinsic embarrassment, inseparable from the selection of the proper objects (which is always a choice of difficulties), ought to be a decisive motive for a candid construction of the conduct of the government in making it, and for a spirit of acquiescence in the measures for obtaining revenue which the public exigencies may at any time dictate.

Observe good faith and justice towards all nations. Cultivate peace and harmony with all. Religion and morality enjoin this conduct; and can it be, that good policy does not equally enjoin it? It will be worthy of a free, enlightened, and, at no distant period, a great nation, to give to mankind the magnanimous and too novel example of a people always guided by an exalted justice and benevolence. Who can doubt that, in the course of time and things, the fruits of such a plan would richly repay any temporary advantages, which might be lost by a steady adherence to it? Can it be that Providence has not connected the permanent felicity of a nation with its virtue? The experiment, at least, is recommended by every sentiment which ennobles human nature. Alas! is it rendered impossible by its vices?

In the execution of such a plan, nothing is more essential than that permanent, inveterate antipathies against particular nations, and passionate attachments for others, should be excluded; and that, in place of them, just and amicable feelings towards all should be cultivated. The nation which indulges towards another an habitual hatred, or an habitual fondness, is in some degree a slave. It is a slave to its animosity or to its affection, either of which is sufficient to lead it astray from its duty and its interest. Antipathy in one nation against another disposes each more readily to offer insult and injury, to lay hold of slight causes of umbrage, and to be haughty and intractable, when accidental or trifling occasions of dispute occur. Hence, frequent collisions, obstinate, envenomed, and bloody contests. The nation, prompted by ill will and resentment, sometimes impels to war the government, contrary to the best calculations of policy. The government sometimes participates in the national propensity, and adopts through passion what reason would reject; at other times, it makes the animosity of the nation subservient to projects of hostility instigated by pride, ambition, and other sinister and pernicious motives. The peace often, sometimes perhaps the liberty, of nations has been the victim.

So likewise, a passionate attachment of one nation for another produces a variety of evils. Sympathy for the favorite nation, facilitating the illusion of an imaginary common interest in cases where no real common interest exists, and infusing into one the enmities of the other, betrays the former into a participation in the quarrels and wars of the latter, without adequate inducement or justification. It leads also to concessions to the favorite nation of privileges denied to others, which is apt doubly to injure the nation making the concessions, by unnecessarily parting with what ought to have been retained, and by exciting jealousy, ill will, and a disposition to retaliate, in the parties from whom equal privileges are withheld; and it gives to ambitious, corrupted, or deluded citizens (who devote themselves to the favorite nation), facility to betray or sacrifice the interests of their own country, without odium, sometimes even with popularity; gilding with the appearances of a virtuous sense of obligation, a commendable deference for public opinion, or a laudable zeal for public good, the base or foolish compliances of ambition, corruption, or infatuation.

As avenues to foreign influence in innumerable ways, such attachments are particularly alarming to the truly enlightened and independent patriot. How many opportunities do they afford to tamper with domestic factions, to practise the arts of seduction, to mislead public opinion, to influence or awe the public councils! Such an attachment of a small or weak, towards a great and powerful nation, dooms the former to be the satellite of the latter.

Against the insidious wiles of foreign influence, I conjure you to believe me, fellow-citizens, the jealousy of a free people ought to be constantly awake, since history and experience prove that foreign influence is one of the most baneful foes of republican government. But that jealousy, to be useful, must be impartial; else it becomes the instrument of the very influence to be avoided, instead of a defence against it. Excessive partiality for one foreign nation, and excessive dislike of another, cause those whom they actuate to see danger only on one side, and serve to veil and even second the arts of influence on the other. Real patriots, who may resist the intrigues of the favorite, are liable to become suspected and odious; while its tools and dupes usurp the applause and confidence of the people, to surrender their interests.

The great rule of conduct for us, in regard to foreign nations, is, in extending our commercial relations, to have with them as little *political* connection as possible. So far as we have already formed engagements, let them be fulfilled with perfect good faith. Here let us stop.

Europe has a set of primary interests, which to us have none, or a very remote relation. Hence she must be engaged in frequent controversies, the causes of which are essentially foreign to our concerns. Hence, therefore, it must be unwise in us to implicate ourselves, by artificial ties, in the ordinary vicissitudes of her politics, or the ordinary combinations and collisions of her friendships or enmities.

Our detached and distant situation invites and enables us to pursue a different course. If we remain one people, under an efficient government, the period is not far off, when we may defy material injury from external annoyance; when we may take such an attitude as will cause the neutrality we may at any time resolve upon to be scrupulously respected; when belligerent nations, under the impossibility of making acquisitions upon us, will not lightly hazard the giving us provocation; when we may choose peace or war, as our interest, guided by our justice, shall counsel.

Why forego the advantages of so peculiar a situation? Why quit our own to stand upon foreign ground? Why, by interweaving our destiny with that of any part of Europe, entangle our peace and prosperity in the toils of European ambition, rivalship, interest, humor, or caprice?

It is our true policy to steer clear of permanent alliances with any portion of the foreign world; so far, I mean, as we are now at liberty to do it; for let me not be understood as capable of patronizing infidelity to existing engagements. (I hold the maxim no less applicable to public than to private affairs, that honesty is always the best policy.) I repeat it, therefore, let those engagements be observed in their genuine sense. But, in my opinion, it is unncessary and would be unwise to extend them.

Taking care always to keep ourselves, by suitable establishments, on a respectably defensive posture, we may safely trust to temporary alliances for extraordinary emergencies.

Harmony, liberal intercourse with all nations, are recommended by policy, humanity, and interest. But even our commercial policy should hold an equal and impartial hand; neither seeking nor granting exclusive favors or preferences; consulting the natural course of things; diffusing and diversifying by gentle means the streams of commerce, but forcing nothing; establishing, with powers so disposed, in order to give trade a stable course, to define the rights of our merchants, and to enable the government to support them, conventional rules of intercourse, the best that present circumstances and mutual opinion will permit, but temporary, and liable to be from time to time abandoned or varied, as experience and circumstances shall dictate; constantly keeping in view that it is folly in one nation to look for disinterested favors from another, that it must pay with a portion of its independence for whatever it may accept under that character; that, by such acceptance, it may place itself in the condition of having given equivalents for nominal favors, and yet of being reproached with ingratitude for not giving more. There can be no greater error than to expect or calculate upon real favors from nation to nation. It is an illusion, which experience must cure, which a just pride ought to discard.

In offering to you, my countrymen, these counsels of an old and affectionate friend, I dare not hope they will make the strong and lasting impression I could wish; that they will control the usual current of the passions, or prevent our nation from running the course which has hitherto marked the destiny of nations. But, if I may even flatter myself, that they may be productive of some partial benefit, some occasional good; that they may now and then recur to moderate the fury of party spirit, to warn against the mischiefs of foreign intrigue, to guard against the impostures of pretended patriotism; this hope will be a full recompense for the solicitude for your welfare, by which they have been dictated.

How far in the discharge of my official duties I have been guided by the principles which have been delineated, the public records and other evidences of my conduct must witness to you and to the world. To myself, the assurance of my own conscience is, that I have at least believed myself to be guided by them.

In relation to the still subsisting war in Europe, my proclamation of the 22d of April, 1793, is the index to my plan. Sanctioned by your approving voice, and by that of your Representatives in both Houses of Congress, the spirit of that measure has continually governed me, uninfluenced by any attempts to deter or divert me from it.

After deliberate examination, with the aid of the best lights I could obtain, I was well satisfied that our country, under all the circumstances of the case, had a right to take, and was bound in duty and interest to take, a neutral position. Having taken it, I determined, as far as should depend upon me, to maintain it, with moderation, perseverance, and firmness.

The considerations which respect the right to hold this conduct, it is not necessary on this occasion to detail. I will only observe, that, according to my understanding of the matter, that right, so far from being denied by any of the belligerent powers, has been virtually admitted by all.

The duty of holding a neutral conduct may be inferred, without anything more, from the obligation which justice and humanity impose on every nation, in cases in which it is free to act, to maintain inviolate the relations of peace and amity towards other nations.

The inducements of interest for observing that conduct will best be referred to your own reflections and experience. With me, a predominant motive has been to endeavor to gain time to our country to settle and mature its yet recent institutions, and to progress without interruption to that degree of strength and consistency which is necessary to give it, humanly speaking, the command of its own fortunes.

Though, in reviewing the incidents of my administration, I am unconscious of intentional error, I am nevertheless too sensible of my defects not to think it probable that I may have committed many errors. Whatever they may be, I fervently beseech the Almighty to avert or mitigate the evils to which they may tend. I shall also carry with me the hope that my country will never cease to view them with indulgence; and that, after forty-five years of my life dedicated to its service with an upright zeal, the faults of incompetent abilities will be consigned to oblivion, as myself must soon be to the mansions of rest.

Relying on its kindness in this as in other things, and actuated by that fervent love towards it, which is so natural to a man who views in it the native soil of himself and his progenitors for several generations, I anticipate with pleasing expectation that retreat, in which I promise myself to realize, without alloy, the sweet enjoyment of partaking, in the midst of my fellow-citizens, the benign influence of good laws under a free government, the ever favorite object of my heart, and the happy reward, as I trust, of our mutual cares, labors, and dangers.

UNITED STATES, September 19th, 1796.

THOMAS JEFFERSON

(1743–1826)

Thomas Jefferson, statesman and apostle of democracy, was born in Albemarle County, Virginia, in 1743. His father, a civil engineer and landholder, died when Thomas was 14, leaving him with a fair fortune and the freedom to choose his own vocation. After attending William and Mary College for two years, he spent five years in close application to the study of law, and was admitted to the bar in 1767. He maintained a lucrative practice until 1774, when political conditions, particularly the cause of America against England, induced him to abandon law for politics. The next thirty-five years he spent in the public service, his political career culminating in his election in 1801 to the Presidency, from which office he retired in 1809 to Monticello, his Virginia estate. There during his remaining years he busied himself attending to a vast correspondence, entertaining hosts of visitors, carrying on various experiments, and, to him most important of all, planning the establishment of the University of Virginia. He died on July 4, 1826.

Believing profoundly in rule by the people, Jefferson devoted his best talents to the establishment of democratic institutions in America, and more than any other man he is responsible for the trend which the government of the United States took in its early years. At the beginning of his public career he stood for such reforms as the repeal of the laws of entail, the abolition of primogeniture and unequal division of inheritances, the abolition of taxation for church support, and for a system of state education. In 1800 he wrote, "I have sworn upon the altar of God eternal hostility against every form of tyranny over the mind of man." And at his death he ordered as his epitaph: "Here was buried Thomas Jefferson, author of the Declaration of Independence, of the statute of Virginia for religious freedom, and father of the University of Virginia," thus perpetuating his pride in his contribution to political and religious freedom. He was greater as a statesman than as a writer, but his *Summary View of the Rights of America,* his first Inaugural Address, and other political writings, have had a far-reaching effect upon the thought of his own and subsequent times.

THE DECLARATION OF INDEPENDENCE [1]

In Congress, July 4, 1776

THE UNANIMOUS DECLARATION OF THE THIRTEEN UNITED STATES OF AMERICA

WHEN in the course of human events, it becomes necessary for one people to dissolve the political bands which have connected them with another, and to assume among the powers of the earth, the separate and equal

---

[1] Jefferson as one of a committee appointed to draft the Declaration was designated by the other members for the actual task of composition. Upon finishing his draft, he submitted it

station to which the laws of nature and of nature's God entitle them, a decent respect to the opinions of mankind requires that they should declare the causes which impel them to the separation.

We hold these truths to be self-evident, that all men are created equal, that they are endowed by their Creator with certain unalienable rights, that among these are life, liberty, and the pursuit of happiness. That to secure these rights, governments are instituted among men, deriving their just powers from the consent of the governed. That whenever any form of government becomes destructive of these ends, it is the right of the people to alter or to abolish it, and to institute new government, laying its foundation on such principles, and organizing its powers in such form, as to them shall seem most likely to effect their safety and happiness. Prudence, indeed, will dictate that governments long established should not be changed for light and transient causes; and accordingly all experience hath shown, that mankind are more disposed to suffer, while evils are sufferable, than to right themselves by abolishing the forms to which they are accustomed. But when a long train of abuses and usurpations, pursuing invariably the same object, evinces a design to reduce them under absolute despotism, it is their right, it is their duty, to throw off such government, and to provide new guards for their future security. Such has been the patient sufferance of these Colonies; and such is now the necessity which constrains them to alter their former systems of government. The history of the present King of Great Britain is a history of repeated injuries and usurpations, all having in direct object the establishment of an absolute tyranny over these States. To prove this, let facts be submitted to a candid world.

He has refused his assent to laws, the most wholesome and necessary for the public good.

He has forbidden his governors to pass laws of immediate and pressing importance, unless suspended in their operation till his assent should be obtained; and when so suspended, he has utterly neglected to attend to them.

He has refused to pass other laws for the accommodation of large districts of people, unless those people would relinquish the right of representation in the legislature, a right inestimable to them and formidable to tyrants only.

He has called together legislative bodies at places unusual, uncomfortable, and distant from the depository of their public records, for the sole purpose of fatiguing them into compliance with his measures.

He has dissolved Representative Houses repeatedly, for opposing with manly firmness his invasions on the rights of the people.

He has refused for a long time, after such dissolutions, to cause others

to the committee for revision, and some minor changes were made; later, the Congress made a number of other changes. The present text represents the final form of the Declaration, and therefore departs at various points from Jefferson's wording. For Jefferson's draft, consult *The Writings of Thomas Jefferson*, edited by P. L. Ford, vol. ii, p. 42.

to be elected; whereby the Legislative Powers, incapable of annihilation, have returned to the People at large for their exercise; the State remaining, in the meantime, exposed to all the dangers of invasion from without, and convulsions within.

He has endeavored to prevent the population of these States; for that purpose obstructing the laws for naturalization of foreigners; refusing to pass others to encourage their migration hither, and raising the conditions of new appropriations of lands.

He has obstructed the administration of justice, by refusing his assent to laws for establishing judiciary powers.

He has made judges dependent on his will alone, for the tenure of their offices, and the amount and payment of their salaries.

He has erected a multitude of new offices, and sent hither swarms of officers to harass our people, and eat out their substance.

He has kept among us, in times of peace, standing armies without the consent of our legislature.

He has affected to render the military independent of and superior to the civil power.

He has combined with others to subject us to a jurisdiction foreign to our constitution, and unacknowledged by our laws; giving his assent to their acts of pretended legislation: for quartering large bodies of armed troops among us; for protecting them, by a mock trial, from punishment for any murders which they should commit on the inhabitants of these States; for cutting off our trade with all parts of the world; for imposing taxes on us without our consent; for depriving us in many cases, of the benefits of trial by jury; for transporting us beyond seas to be tried for pretended offenses; for abolishing the free system of English laws in a neighboring province, establishing therein an arbitrary government, and enlarging its boundaries so as to render it at once an example and fit instrument for introducing the same absolute rule into these Colonies; for taking away our charters, abolishing our most valuable laws, and altering fundamentally the forms of our governments; for suspending our own legislatures, and declaring themselves invested with power to legislate for us in all cases whatsoever.

He has abdicated government here, by declaring us out of his protection and waging war against us.

He has plundered our seas, ravaged our coasts, burned our towns, and destroyed the lives of our people.

He is at this time transporting large armies of foreign mercenaries to complete the works of death, desolation, and tyranny, already begun with circumstances of cruelty and perfidy scarcely paralleled in the most barbarous ages, and totally unworthy the head of a civilized nation.

He has constrained our fellow citizens taken captive on the high seas to bear arms against their country, to become the executioners of their friends and brethren, or to fall themselves by their hands.

He has excited domestic insurrections amongst us, and has endeavored to bring on the inhabitants of our frontiers, the merciless Indian savages, whose known rule of warfare, is an undistinguished destruction of all ages, sexes, and conditions.

In every stage of these oppressions we have petitioned for redress in the most humble terms: our repeated petitions have been answered only by repeated injury. A prince, whose character is thus marked by every act which may define a tyrant, is unfit to be the ruler of a free people.

Nor have we been wanting in attention to our British brethren. We have warned them from time to time of attempts by their legislature to extend an unwarrantable jurisdiction over us. We have reminded them of the circumstances of our emigration and settlement here. We have appealed to their native justice and magnanimity, and we have conjured them by the ties of our common kindred to disavow these usurpations, which would inevitably interrupt our connections and correspondence. They too have been deaf to the voice of justice and of consanguinity. We must, therefore, acquiesce in the necessity, which denounces our separation, and hold them, as we hold the rest of mankind, enemies in war, in peace friends.

We, therefore, the Representatives of the united States of America, in General Congress, assembled, appealing to the Supreme Judge of the world for the rectitude of our intentions, do, in the name, and by authority of the good people of these Colonies, solemnly publish and declare, That these United Colonies are, and of right ought to be Free and Independent States; that they are absolved from all allegiance to the British Crown, and that all political connection between them and the State of Great Britain, is and ought to be totally dissolved; and that as Free and Independent States, they have full power to levy war, conclude peace, contract alliances, establish commerce, and to do all other acts and things which independent states may of right do. And for the support of this Declaration, with a firm reliance on the protection of Divine Providence, we mutually pledge to each other our lives, our fortunes, and our sacred Honor.

FIRST INAUGURAL ADDRESS [2]

FRIENDS AND FELLOW-CITIZENS: Called upon to undertake the duties of the first executive office of our country, I avail myself of the presence of that portion of my fellow-citizens which is here assembled to express my grateful

---

[2] Delivered March 4, 1801. Party conflict before the election had embittered many, and it was now Jefferson's hope to rally all parties to the support of the Republic; hence the pacific tone of the message.

thanks for the favor with which they have been pleased to look towards me, to declare a sincere consciousness that the task is above my talents, and that I approach it with those anxious and awful presentiments which the greatness of the charge, and the weakness of my powers, so justly inspire. A rising nation, spread over a wide and fruitful land, traversing all the seas with the rich productions of their industry, engaged in commerce with nations who feel power and forget right, advancing rapidly to destinies beyond the reach of mortal eye; when I contemplate these transcendent objects, and see the honor, the happiness, and the hopes of this beloved country committed to the issue and the auspices of this day, I shrink from the contemplation, and humble myself before the magnitude of the undertaking.

Utterly, indeed, should I despair, did not the presence of many whom I here see, remind me that, in the other high authorities provided by our Constitution, I shall find resources of wisdom, of virtue, and of zeal, on which to rely under all difficulties. To you, then, gentlemen, who are charged with the sovereign functions of legislation, and to those associated with you, I look with encouragement for that guidance and support which may enable us to steer with safety the vessel in which we are all embarked, amidst the conflicting elements of a troubled sea.

During the contest of opinion through which we have passed, the animation of discussions and of exertions has sometimes worn an aspect which might impose on strangers unused to think freely, and to speak and to write what they think; but this being now decided by the voice of the nation, announced according to the rules of the Constitution, all will of course arrange themselves under the will of the law, and unite in common efforts for the common good. All too will bear in mind this sacred principle, that though the will of the majority is in all cases to prevail, that will, to be rightful, must be reasonable; that the minority possess their equal rights, which equal laws must protect, and to violate would be oppression. Let us, then, fellow-citizens, unite with one heart and one mind, let us restore to social intercourse that harmony and affection without which liberty, and even life itself, are but dreary things. And let us reflect that, having banished from our land that religious intolerance under which mankind so long bled and suffered, we have yet gained little, if we countenance a political intolerance, as despotic as wicked, and capable of as bitter and bloody persecutions. During the throes and convulsions of the ancient world, during the agonized spasms of infuriated man, seeking through blood and slaughter his long-lost liberty, it was not wonderful that the agitation of the billows should reach even this distant and peaceful shore; that this should be felt and feared by some, and less by others, and should divide opinions as to measures of safety; but every difference of opinion is not a difference of principle. We have called by different names brethren of the same principle. We are all Republicans; we are all Federalists. If there be any among us who wish to dissolve this Union, or to change its republican form, let them stand undisturbed as monuments of the safety with which error of opinion may be tolerated, where reason is left free to combat it. I know, indeed, that some honest men have feared that a republican government cannot be strong; that this government is not strong enough. But would the honest patriot, in the full tide of successful experiment, abandon a government which has so far kept us free and firm, on the theoretic and visionary fear that this government, the world's best hope, may, by possibility, want energy to preserve itself? I trust not. I believe this, on the contrary, the strongest government on earth. I believe it the only one where every man, at the call of the law, would fly to the standard of the law; would meet the invasions of the public order as his own personal concern. Sometimes it is said that man cannot be trusted with the government of himself. Can he then be trusted with the government of others? Or have we found angels in the form of kings to govern him? Let history answer this question.

Let us, then, pursue with courage and confidence our own Federal and Republican principles; our attachment to union and representative government. Kindly separated by nature and a wide ocean from the exterminating havoc of one-quarter of the globe; too high-minded to endure the degradations of the others; possessing a chosen country, with room enough for our descendants to the thousandth and thousandth generation; entertaining a due sense of our equal right to the use of our own faculties, to the acquisitions of our own industry, to honor and confidence from our fellow-citizens, resulting not from birth, but from our actions and their sense of them; enlightened by a benign religion, professed indeed and practiced in various forms, yet all of them inculcating honesty, truth, temperance, gratitude, and the love of man; acknowledging and adoring an overruling Providence, which, by all its dispensations, proves that it delights in the happiness of man here, and his greater happiness hereafter; with all these blessings, what more is necessary to make us a happy and a prosperous people? Still one thing more, fellow-citizens, a wise and frugal government which shall restrain men from injuring one another, shall leave them otherwise free to regulate their own pursuits of industry and improvement, and shall not take from the mouth of labor the bread it has earned. This is the sum of good government; and this is necessary to close the circle of our felicities.

About to enter, fellow-citizens, on the exercise of duties which comprehend everything dear and valuable to you, it is proper you should understand what I deem the essential principles of this government, and consequently those which ought to shape its administration. I will compress them within the narrowest compass they will bear, stating the general principle, but not all its limitations. Equal and exact justice to all men, of whatever state or persuasion, religious or political; peace, commerce, and honest friend-

ship with all nations, entangling alliances with none; the support of the
State governments in all their rights, as the most competent administrations
for our domestic concerns, and the surest bulwarks against anti-republican
tendencies; the preservation of the general government in its whole constitutional vigor, as the sheet-anchor of our peace at home, and safety abroad;
a jealous care of the right of election by the people, a mild and safe corrective
of abuses which are lopped by the sword of revolution where peaceable remedies are unprovided; absolute acquiescence in the decisions of the majority,
the vital principle of republics, from which is no appeal but to force, the vital
principle and immediate parent of despotism; a well-disciplined militia, our
best reliance in peace, and for the first moments of war, till regulars may relieve them; the supremacy of the civil over the military authority; economy
in the public expense, that labor may be lightly burdened; the honest payment
of our debts and sacred preservation of the public faith; encouragement of
agriculture, and of commerce as its handmaid; the diffusion of information,
and arraignment of all abuses at the bar of the public reason; freedom of
religion; freedom of the press; and freedom of person, under the protection
of the habeas corpus; and trial by juries impartially selected. These principles
form the bright constellation which has gone before us, and guided our steps
through an age of revolution and reformation. The wisdom of our sages, and
blood of our heroes, have been devoted to their attainment; they should
be the creed of our political faith, the text of civic instruction, the touchstone
by which to try the services of those we trust; and should we wander from
them, in moments of error or of alarm, let us hasten to retrace our steps and to
regain the road which alone leads to peace, liberty, and safety.

I repair, then, fellow-citizens, to the post which you have assigned me. With
experience enough in subordinate stations to know the difficulties of this, the
greatest of all, I have learned to expect that it will rarely fall to the lot of imperfect man to retire from this station with the reputation and the favor
which bring him into it. Without pretensions to that high confidence you re-
posed in our first and greatest revolutionary character, whose pre-eminent
services had entitled him to the first place in his country's love, and had
destined for him the fairest page in the volume of faithful history, I ask so
much confidence only as may give firmness and effect to the legal administration of your affairs. I shall often go wrong through defect of judgment. When
right, I shall often be thought wrong by those whose positions will not command a view of the whole ground. I ask your indulgence for my own errors,
which will never be intentional; and your support against the errors of others,
who may condemn what they would not, if seen in all its parts. The approbation implied by your suffrage is a great consolation to me for the past; and
my future solicitude will be to retain the good opinion of those who have
bestowed it in advance, to conciliate that of others, by doing them all the good

in my power, and to be instrumental to the happiness and freedom of all.

Relying, then, on the patronage of your good-will, I advance with obedience to the work, ready to retire from it whenever you become sensible how much better choice it is in your power to make. And may that Infinite Power which rules the destinies of the universe lead our councils to what is best, and give them a favorable issue for your peace and prosperity.

From NOTES ON THE STATE OF VIRGINIA [3]

[SLAVERY]

THERE must doubtless be an unhappy influence on the manners of our people produced by the existence of slavery among us. The whole commerce between master and slave is a perpetual exercise of the most boisterous passions, the most unremitting despotism on the one part, and degrading submissions on the other. Our children see this, and learn to imitate it; for man is an imitative animal. This quality is the germ of all education in him. From his cradle to his grave he is learning to do what he sees others do. If a parent could find no motive, either in his philanthropy or his self-love, for restraining the intemperance of passion towards his slave, it should always be a sufficient one that his child is present. But generally it is not sufficient. The parent storms, the child looks on, catches the lineaments of wrath, puts on the same airs in the circle of smaller slaves, gives a loose to the worst of passions, and thus nursed, educated, and daily exercised in tyranny, cannot but be stamped by it with odious peculiarities. The man must be a prodigy who can retain his manners and morals undepraved by such circumstances. And with what execrations should the statesman be loaded, who, permitting one half the citizens thus to trample on the rights of the other, transforms those into despots, and these into enemies, destroys the morals of the one part, and the *amor patriae* of the other. For if a slave can have a country in this world, it must be any other in preference to that in which he is born to live and labor for another; in which he must lock up the faculties of his nature, contribute as far as depends on his individual endeavors to the evanishment of the human race, or entail his own miserable condition on the endless generations proceeding from him. With the morals of the people, their industry also is destroyed. For in a warm climate, no man will labor for himself who can make another labor for him. This is so true, that of the proprietors of slaves a very small proportion indeed are ever seen to labor.

---

[3] The *Notes* were written in 1781 in response to sets of queries sent by Marbois, as secretary of the French legation in the United States, to leading men in the various states. As governor of Virginia, Jefferson received the set relating to that State, and wrote a careful reply. The first English edition of the work was published in 1787, a French edition having appeared the previous year. The extract here given is in answer to Query XVIII, relating to the customs and manners in the State.

And can the liberties of a nation be thought secure when we have removed their only firm basis, a conviction in the minds of the people that these liberties are of the gift of God? That they are not to be violated but with His wrath? Indeed I tremble for my country when I reflect that God is just; that His justice cannot sleep forever; that considering numbers, nature, and natural means only, a revolution of the wheel of fortune, an exchange of situation, is among possible events; that it may become probable by supernatural inter-ference! The Almighty has no attribute which can take side with us in such a contest. But it is impossible to be temperate and to pursue this subject through the various considerations of policy, of morals, of history natural and civil. We must be contented to hope they will force their way into every one's mind. I think a change already perceptible, since the origin of the present revolution. The spirit of the master is abating, that of the slave rising from the dust, his condition mollifying, the way I hope preparing, under the auspices of heaven, for a total emancipation; and that this is disposed, in the order of events, to be with the consent of the masters, rather than by their extirpation.

From AUTOBIOGRAPHY [4]

[Congress Under the Articles of Confederation]

Our body was little numerous, but very contentious. Day after day was wasted on the most unimportant questions. My colleague Mercer was one of those afflicted with the morbid rage of debate, of an ardent mind, prompt imagination, and copious flow of words; he heard with impatience any logic which was not his own. Sitting near me on some occasion of a trifling but wordy debate, he asked how I could sit in silence hearing so much false reasoning which a word should refute. I observed to him that to refute in-deed was easy, but to silence impossible. That in measures brought forward by myself I took the laboring oar, as was incumbent on me; but that in general I was willing to listen. If every sound argument or objection was used by some one or other of the numerous debaters, it was enough; if not, I thought it sufficient to suggest the omission, without going into a repetition of what had been already said by others. That this was a waste and abuse of the time and patience of the house which could not be justified. And I believe that if the members of deliberative bodies were to observe this course generally, they would do in a day what takes them a week; and it is really more ques-tionable than may at first be thought whether Bonaparte's dumb legislature which said nothing and did much may not be preferable to one which talks

---

[4] At the age of 77, Jefferson wrote a brief account of his life up to 1790, as he said, "for my own more ready reference and for the information of my family." The extract here given deals with the year 1783.

much and does nothing. I served with General Washington in the legislature of Virginia before the Revolution, and during it with Dr. Franklin in Congress. I never heard either of them speak ten minutes at a time, nor to any but the main point which was to decide the question. They laid their shoulders to the great points, knowing that the little ones would follow of themselves. If the present Congress errs in too much talking, how can it be otherwise in a body to which the people send one hundred and fifty lawyers, whose trade it is to question everything, yield nothing, and talk by the hour? That one hundred and fifty lawyers should do business together ought not to be expected.

TO JOHN ADAMS

Monticello, October 12, 1823.

DEAR SIR:

I do not write with the ease which your letter of September the 18th supposes. Crippled wrists and fingers make writing slow and laborious. But while writing to you, I lose the sense of these things in the recollection of ancient times, when youth and health made happiness out of everything. I forget for a while the hoary winter of age, when we can think of nothing but how to keep ourselves warm, and how to get rid of our heavy hours until the friendly hand of death shall rid us of all at once. Against this *tedium vitæ*, however, I am fortunately mounted on a hobby, which, indeed, I should have better managed some thirty or forty years ago; but whose easy amble is still sufficient to give exercise and amusement to an octogenary writer. This is the establishment of a University, on a scale more comprehensive, and in a country more healthy and central than our old William and Mary, which these obstacles have long kept in a state of languor and inefficiency. But the tardiness with which such works proceed may render it doubtful whether I shall live to see it go into action.

Putting aside these things, however, for the present, I write this letter as due to a friendship coeval with our government, and now attempted to be poisoned, when too late in life to be replaced by new affections. I had for sometime observed in the public papers, dark hints and mysterious innuendoes of a correspondence of yours with a friend, to whom you had opened your bosom without reserve, and which was to be made public by that friend or his representative. And now it is said to be actually published. It has not yet reached us, but extracts have been given, and such as seemed most likely to draw a curtain of separation between you and myself. Were there no other motive than that of indignation against the author of this outrage on private confidence, whose shaft seems to have been aimed at yourself more particularly, this would make it the duty of every honorable mind to disappoint that aim, by opposing to its impression a seven-fold shield of apathy and insensibility. With me, however, no such armor is needed. The circumstances of the times in which we have happened to live, and the partiality of our friends at a particular period, placed us in a state of apparent opposition, which some might suppose to be personal also; and there might not be wanting those who wished to make it so, by filling our ears with malignant falsehoods, by dressing up hideous phantoms of their own creation, presenting them to you under my name, to me under yours, and endeavoring to instil into our minds things concerning each other the most destitute of truth. And if there had been, at any time, a moment when we were off our guard, and in a temper to let the whispers of these people make us forget what we had known of each other for so many years, and years of so much trial, yet all men who have attended to the workings of the human mind, who have seen the false colors under which passion sometimes dresses the actions and motives of others, have seen also those passions subsiding with time and reflection, dissipating like mists before the rising sun, and restoring to us the sight of all things in their true shape and colors. It would be strange indeed, if, at our years, we were to go back an age to hunt up imaginary or forgotten facts, to disturb the repose of affections so sweetening to the evening of our lives. Be assured, my dear Sir, that I am incapable of receiving the slightest impression from the effort now made to plant thorns on the pillow of age, worth, and wisdom, and to sow tares between friends who have been such for near half a century. Beseeching you then, not to suffer your mind to be disquieted by this wicked attempt to poison its peace, and praying you to throw it by among the things which have never happened, I add sincere assurances of my unabated and constant attachment, friendship, and respect.

WASHINGTON IRVING

(1783–1859)

The author of "Rip Van Winkle" was born in New York in 1783, the year of the Peace, and named for General Washington. Because of ill health his schooling was desultory. He read law but, like Sir Walter Scott, soon abandoned it for letters. He regretted not going to college, but he was the first of our authors to be widely read in English literature. His boyish *Jonathan Oldstyle* letters (1802) were followed, after a trip abroad, by further imitations of Addison in *Salmagundi* (1807–8), and by his first notable book, the Knickerbocker *History of New York* (1809). So far, however, he was only the gentlemanly amateur in letters; his adoption of literature as a profession came when, during a stay in England, business failure threw him on his own resources. With the *Sketch-Book* (1819) he scored a literary triumph, and followed it with two other similar, though less spontaneous works, *Bracebridge Hall* and *Tales of a Traveller*. In search of new subjects he went to Spain, lived for a time at the Alhambra, and wrote, besides the *Life of Columbus* and the *Conquest of Granada,* the best of his Spanish writings in *The Alhambra* (1832). After having lived abroad seventeen years he returned, full of honors, to New York in 1832. Except for a trip in the West, from which grew *A Tour of the Prairies,* and four years in Spain as American minister, 1842–1846, he spent his remaining years at "Sunnyside" on the Hudson. As he finished his *Life of Washington* his own life ended, in 1859.

Excepting the Knickerbocker *History,* which stands alone, all Irving's best books might be called "sketch-books"; with equal appropriateness all might be called "tales of a traveller." He "was always fond," he says, "of visiting new scenes and observing strange characters and manners." Like Byron, he could draw inspiration from, and in turn confer fresh distinction upon the places to which he travelled— the Hudson River and the Catskills, even Stratford and the Alhambra. Each "new scene" or "strange character," he "sketched" to the lasting delight of American readers. His first pseudonym, "Jonathan Oldstyle," is peculiarly appropriate to him. Spending nearly half of his mature life abroad, he belongs both to the old country and to the new; and living from the eighteenth century well into the nineteenth, he shares the spirit of both. If he is "old style" in his devotion to the manner of Addison and Goldsmith, he is a true "brother Jonathan" not only in his celebration of Manhattan and Sleepy Hollow, but in his new-world response to the romantic appeal of Europe. He is obviously classical in his style; but as obviously romantic in his fondness for past times and far-off places. He has clear limitations; he does not meddle with the "perplexities" of politics and religion; his "only aim is to paint character and manners." He is our first important humorist, biographer, and writer of short stories; our first stylist and literary artist; the first of our writers to be widely recognized abroad; "the first ambassador," as Thackeray said at his death, "whom the New World of letters sent to the Old."

61

WASHINGTON IRVING

A HISTORY OF NEW YORK [1]

BOOK III. CHAPTER I

OF THE RENOWNED WOUTER VAN TWILLER, HIS UNPARALLELED VIRTUES—AS LIKEWISE
HIS UNUTTERABLE WISDOM IN THE LAW-CASE OF WANDLE SCHOONHOVEN AND
BARENT BLEECKER—AND THE GREAT ADMIRATION OF THE PUBLIC THEREAT

GRIEVOUS and very much to be commiserated is the task of the feeling historian, who writes the history of his native land. If it fall to his lot to be the recorder of calamity or crime, the mournful page is watered with his tears; nor can he recall the most prosperous and blissful era, without a melancholy sigh at the reflection that it has passed away forever! I know not whether it be owing to an immoderate love for the simplicity of former times, or to that certain tenderness of heart incident to all sentimental historians; but I candidly confess that I cannot look back on the happier days of our city, which I now describe, without great dejection of spirit. With faltering hand do I withdraw the curtain of oblivion, that veils the modest merit of our venerable ancestors, and as their figures rise to my mental vision, humble myself before their mighty shades.

Such are my feelings when I revisit the family mansion of the Knickerbockers, and spend a lonely hour in the chamber where hang the portraits of my forefathers, shrouded in dust, like the forms they represent. With pious reverence do I gaze on the countenances of those renowned burghers, who have preceded me in the steady march of existence,—whose sober and temperate blood now meanders through my veins, flowing slower and slower in its feeble conduits, until its current shall soon be stopped forever!

These, I say to myself, are but frail memorials of the mighty men who flourished in the days of the patriarchs; but who, alas, have long since mouldered in that tomb towards which my steps are insensibly and irresistibly hastening! As I pace the darkened chamber and lose myself in melancholy musings, the shadowy images around me almost seem to steal once more into existence, —their countenances to assume the animation of life,—their eyes to pursue

---

[1] From *A History of New York, by Diedrich Knickerbocker* (1809). Irving explains the inception and purpose of the book in an amusing "Author's Apology," prefixed to the edition of 1848. Beginning with the idea of a mere parody on a contemporary handbook, he thought next of a "comic history of the city," but finally "resolved to confine it to the period of the Dutch domination." "This then," he says, "broke upon me as the poetic age of our city; poetic from its very obscurity; and open, like the early and obscure days of ancient Rome, to all the embellishments of heroic fiction. . . . The main object of my work had a bearing wide from the sober aim of history; but one which will meet with some indulgence from poetic minds. It was to embody the traditions of the city in an amusing form; to illustrate its local humors, customs, and peculiarities; to clothe home scenes and places and familiar names with those imaginative and whimsical associations so seldom met with in our new country, but which live like charms and spells about the cities of the old world, binding the heart of the native inhabitant to his home." The publication was heralded by clever advertisements in New York papers concerning the disappearance of the supposed author, Diedrich Knickerbocker—a pseudonym which Irving used frequently in later years.

me in every movement! Carried away by the delusions of fancy, I almost imagine myself surrounded by the shades of the departed, and holding sweet
converse with the worthies of antiquity! Ah, hapless Diedrich! born in a degenerate age, abandoned to the buffetings of fortune,—a stranger and a weary
pilgrim in thy native land,—blest with no weeping wife, nor family of helpless
children, but doomed to wander neglected through those crowded streets,
and elbowed by foreign upstarts from those fair abodes where once thine
ancestors held sovereign empire!

Let me not, however, lose the historian in the man, nor suffer the doting
recollections of age to overcome me, while dwelling with fond garrulity on
the virtuous days of the patriarchs,—on those sweet days of simplicity and
ease, which nevermore will dawn on the lovely island of Mannahata.

These melancholy reflections have been forced from me by the growing
wealth and importance of New Amsterdam, which, I plainly perceive, are to
involve it in all kinds of perils and disasters. Already, as I observed at the close
of my last book, they had awakened the attentions of the mother-country.
The usual mark of protection shown by mother-countries to wealthy colonies
was forthwith manifested; a governor being sent out to rule over the province,
and squeeze out of it as much revenue as possible. The arrival of a governor of
course put an end to the protectorate of Oloffe the Dreamer. He appears, however, to have dreamt to some purpose during his sway, as we find him afterwards living as a patroon on a great landed estate on the banks of the Hudson;
having virtually forfeited all right to his ancient appellation of Kortlandt or
Lackland.

It was in the year of our Lord 1629 that Mynheer Wouter Van Twiller was
appointed governor of the province of Nieuw Nederlandts, under the commission and control of their High Mightinesses the Lords States General of
the United Netherlands, and the privileged West India Company.

This renowned old gentleman arrived at New Amsterdam in the merry
month of June, the sweetest month in all the year; when dan Apollo seems
to dance up the transparent firmament,—when the robin, the thrush, and a
thousand other wanton songsters, make the woods to resound with amorous
ditties, and the luxurious little boblincon revels among the clover blossoms of
the meadows,—all which happy coincidence persuaded the old dames of New
Amsterdam, who were skilled in the art of foretelling events, that this was to
be a happy and prosperous administration.

The renowned Wouter (or Walter) Van Twiller was descended from a
long line of Dutch burgomasters, who had successively dozed away their lives,
and grown fat upon the bench of magistracy in Rotterdam; and who had
comported themselves with such singular wisdom and propriety, that they
were never either heard or talked of—which, next to being universally ap-
plauded, should be the object of ambition of all magistrates and rulers. There

are two opposite ways by which some men make a figure in the world: one, by talking faster than they think, and the other, by holding their tongues and not thinking at all. By the first, many a smatterer acquires the reputation of a man of quick parts; by the other, many a dunderpate, like the owl, the stupidest of birds, comes to be considered the very type of wisdom. This, by the way, is a casual remark, which I would not, for the universe, have it thought I apply to Governor Van Twiller. It is true he was a man shut up within himself, like an oyster, and rarely spoke, except in monosyllables; but then it was allowed he seldom said a foolish thing. So invincible was his gravity that he was never known to laugh or even to smile through the whole course of a long and prosperous life. Nay, if a joke were uttered in his presence, that set light-minded hearers in a roar, it was observed to throw him into a state of perplexity. Sometimes he would deign to inquire into the matter, and when, after much explanation, the joke was made as plain as a pikestaff, he would continue to smoke his pipe in silence, and at length, knocking out the ashes, would exclaim, "Well! I see nothing in all that to laugh about."

With all his reflective habits, he never made up his mind on a subject. His adherents accounted for this by the astonishing magnitude of his ideas. He conceived every subject on so grand a scale that he had not room in his head to turn it over and examine both sides of it. Certain it is, that if any matter were propounded to him on which ordinary mortals would rashly determine at first glance, he would put on a vague, mysterious look, shake his capacious head, smoke some time in profound silence, and at length observe, that "he had his doubts about the matter"; which gained him the reputation of a man slow of belief and not easily imposed upon. What is more, it gained him a lasting name; for to this habit of mind has been attributed his surname Twiller; which is said to be a corruption of the original Twijfler, or, in plain English, *Doubter.*

The person of this illustrious old gentleman was formed and proportioned, as though it had been moulded by the hands of some cunning Dutch statuary, as a model of majesty and lordly grandeur. He was exactly five feet six inches in height, and six feet five inches in circumference. His head was a perfect sphere, and of such stupendous dimensions, that dame Nature, with all her sex's ingenuity, would have been puzzled to construct a neck capable of supporting it; wherefore she wisely declined the attempt, and settled it firmly on the top of his backbone, just between the shoulders. His body was oblong and particularly capacious at bottom; which was wisely ordered by Providence, seeing that he was a man of sedentary habits, and very averse to the idle labor of walking. His legs were short, but sturdy in proportion to the weight they had to sustain; so that when erect he had not a little the appearance of a beer-barrel on skids. His face, that infallible index of the mind, presented a vast expanse, unfurrowed by any of those lines and angles which disfigure the human countenance with what is termed expression. Two small gray eyes twinkled feebly in the midst, like two stars of lesser magnitude in a hazy firmament; and his full-fed cheeks, which seemed to have taken toll of everything that went into his mouth, were curiously mottled and streaked with dusky red, like a spitzenberg apple.

His habits were as regular as his person. He daily took his four stated meals, appropriating exactly an hour to each; he smoked and doubted eight hours, and he slept the remaining twelve of the four-and-twenty. Such was the renowned Wouter Van Twiller,—a true philosopher, for his mind was either elevated above, or tranquilly settled below, the cares and perplexities of this world. He had lived in it for years, without feeling the least curiosity to know whether the sun revolved round it, or it round the sun; and he had watched, for at least half a century, the smoke curling from his pipe to the ceiling, without once troubling his head with any of those numerous theories by which a philosopher would have perplexed his brain, in accounting for its rising above the surrounding atmosphere.

In his council he presided with great state and solemnity. He sat in a huge chair of solid oak, hewn in the celebrated forest of the Hague, fabricated by an experienced timmerman of Amsterdam, and curiously carved about the arms and feet, into exact imitations of gigantic eagle's claws. Instead of a sceptre, he swayed a long Turkish pipe, wrought with jasmin and amber, which had been presented to a stadtholder of Holland at the conclusion of a treaty with one of the petty Barbary powers. In this stately chair would he sit, and this magnificent pipe would he smoke, shaking his right knee with a constant motion, and fixing his eye for hours together upon a little print of Amsterdam, which hung in a black frame against the opposite wall of the council-chamber. Nay, it has even been said, that when any deliberation of extraordinary length and intricacy was on the carpet, the renowned Wouter would shut his eyes for full two hours at a time, that he might not be disturbed by external objects; and at such times the internal commotion of his mind was evinced by certain regular guttural sounds, which his admirers declared were merely the noise of conflict, made by his contending doubts and opinions.

It is with infinite difficulty I have been enabled to collect these biographical anecdotes of the great man under consideration. The facts respecting him were so scattered and vague, and divers of them so questionable in point of authenticity, that I have had to give up the search after many, and decline the admission of still more, which would have tended to heighten the coloring of his portrait.

I have been the more anxious to delineate fully the person and habits of Wouter Van Twiller, from the consideration that he was not only the first, but also the best governor that ever presided over this ancient and respectable province; and so tranquil and benevolent was his reign, that I do not find throughout the whole of it a single instance of any offender being brought to punishment,—a most indubitable sign of a merciful governor, and a case unparalleled, excepting in the reign of the illustrious King Log,[2] from whom, it is hinted, the renowned Van Twiller was a lineal descendant.

The very outset of the career of this excellent magistrate was distinguished by an example of legal acumen, that gave flattering presage of a wise and equitable administration. The morning after he had been installed in office, and at the moment that he was making his breakfast from a prodigious earthen dish, filled with milk and Indian pudding, he was interrupted by the appearance of Wandle Schoonhoven, a very important old burgher of New Amsterdam, who complained bitterly of one Barent Bleecker, inasmuch as he refused to come to a settlement of accounts, seeing that there was a heavy balance in favor of the said Wandle. Governor Van Twiller, as I have already observed, was a man of few words; he was likewise a mortal enemy to multiplying writings—or being disturbed at his breakfast. Having listened attentively to the statement of Wandle Schoonhoven, giving an occasional grunt, as he shovelled a spoonful of Indian pudding into his mouth,—either as a sign that he relished the dish, or comprehended the story,—he called unto him his constable, and pulling out of his breeches-pocket a huge jack-knife, dispatched it after the defendant as a summons, accompanied by his tobacco-box as a warrant.

This summary process was as effectual in those simple days as was the sealring of the great Haroun Alraschid among the true believers. The two parties being confronted before him, each produced a book of accounts, written in a language and character that would have puzzled any but a High-Dutch commentator, or a learned decipherer of Egyptian obelisks. The sage Wouter took them one after the other, and having poised them in his hands, and attentively counted over the number of leaves, fell straightway into a very great doubt, and smoked for half an hour without saying a word; at length, laying his finger beside his nose, and shutting his eyes for a moment, with the air of a man who has just caught a subtle idea by the tail, he slowly took his pipe from his mouth, puffed forth a column of tobacco smoke, and with marvellous gravity and solemnity pronounced, that, having carefully counted over the leaves and weighed the books, it was found, that one was just as thick and as heavy as the other: therefore, it was the final opinion of the court that the accounts were equally balanced: therefore, Wandle should give Barent a receipt, and Barent should give Wandle a receipt, and the constable should pay the costs.

This decision, being straightway made known, diffused general joy throughout New Amsterdam, for the people immediately perceived that they had a very wise and equitable magistrate to rule over them. But its happiest

[2] In Æsop the Frogs, wishing a king, were given by Jove a log of wood as king.

effect was, that not another lawsuit took place throughout the whole of his administration; and the office of constable fell into such decay, that there was not one of those losel scouts known in the province for many years. I am the more particular in dwelling on this transaction, not only because I deem it one of the most sage and righteous judgments on record, and well worthy of the attention of modern magistrates, but because it was a miraculous event in the history of the renowned Wouter,—being the only time he was ever known to come to a decision in the whole course of his life.

RIP VAN WINKLE [3]

A POSTHUMOUS WRITING OF DIEDRICH KNICKERBOCKER

[The following Tale was found among the papers of the late Diedrich Knicker-bocker, an old gentleman of New York, who was very curious in the Dutch history of the province, and the manners of the descendants from its primitive settlers. His historical researches, however, did not lie so much among books as among men; for the former are lamentably scanty on his favorite topics; whereas he found the old burghers, and still more their wives, rich in that legendary lore so invaluable to true history. Whenever, therefore, he happened upon a genuine Dutch family, snugly shut up in its low-roofed farmhouse under a spreading sycamore, he looked upon it as a little clasped volume of black-letter, and studied it with the zeal of a book-worm.

The result of all these researches was a history of the province during the reign of the Dutch governors, which he published some years since. There have been various opinions as to the literary character of his work, and, to tell the truth, it is not a whit better than it should be. Its chief merit is its scrupulous accuracy, which indeed was a little questioned on its first appearance, but has since been completely established; and it is now admitted into all historical collections, as a book of unquestionable authority.

The old gentleman died shortly after the publication of his work; and now that he is dead and gone, it cannot do much harm to his memory to say that his time might have been much better employed in weightier labors. He, however, was apt to ride his hobby his own way; and though it did now and then kick up the dust a little in the eyes of his neighbors, and grieve the spirit of some friends, for whom he felt the truest deference and affection, yet his errors and follies are remembered "more in sorrow than in anger," and it begins to be suspected that he never intended to injure or offend. But however his memory may be appreciated by critics, it is still held dear by many folk whose good opinion is well worth having; particularly by certain biscuit-bakers, who have gone so far as to imprint his likeness on their New-Year cakes; and have thus given him a chance for immortality, almost equal to the being stamped on a Waterloo Medal, or a Queen Anne's Farthing.]

WHOEVER has made a voyage up the Hudson must remember the Kaatskill Mountains. They are a dismembered branch of the great Appalachian family, and are seen away to the west of the river, swelling up to a noble

[3] From *The Sketch-Book* (1819).

height, and lording it over the surrounding country. Every change of season, every change of weather, indeed, every hour of the day, produces some change in the magical hues and shapes of these mountains, and they are regarded by all the good wives, far and near, as perfect barometers. When the weather is fair and settled, they are clothed in blue and purple, and print their bold outlines on the clear evening sky; but sometimes, when the rest of the landscape is cloudless, they will gather a hood of gray vapors about their summits, which, in the last rays of the setting sun, will glow and light up like a crown of glory.

At the foot of these fairy mountains, the voyager may have descried the light smoke curling up from a village, whose shingle-roofs gleam among the trees, just where the blue tints of the upland melt away into the fresh green of the nearer landscape. It is a little village, of great antiquity, having been founded by some of the Dutch colonists in the early times of the province, just about the beginning of the government of the good Peter Stuyvesant, (may he rest in peace!) and there were some of the houses of the original settlers standing within a few years, built of small yellow bricks brought from Holland, having latticed windows and gable fronts, surmounted with weathercocks.

In that same village, and in one of these very houses (which, to tell the precise truth, was sadly time-worn and weather-beaten), there lived, many years since, while the country was yet a province of Great Britain, a simple, good-natured fellow, of the name of Rip Van Winkle. He was a descendant of the Van Winkles who figured so gallantly in the chivalrous days of Peter Stuyvesant, and accompanied him to the siege of Fort Christina. He inherited, however, but little of the martial character of his ancestors. I have observed that he was a simple, good-natured man; he was, moreover, a kind neighbor, and an obedient, henpecked husband. Indeed, to the latter circumstance might be owing that meekness of spirit which gained him such universal popularity; for those men are most apt to be obsequious and conciliating abroad, who are under the discipline of shrews at home. Their tempers, doubtless, are rendered pliant and malleable in the fiery furnace of domestic tribulation; and a curtain lecture is worth all the sermons in the world for teaching the virtues of patience and long-suffering. A termagant wife may, therefore, in some respects, be considered a tolerable blessing, and if so, Rip Van Winkle was thrice blessed.

Certain it is, that he was a great favorite among all the good wives of the village, who, as usual with the amiable sex, took his part in all family squabbles; and never failed, whenever they talked those matters over in their evening gossipings, to lay all the blame on Dame Van Winkle. The children of the village, too, would shout with joy whenever he approached. He assisted at their sports, made their playthings, taught them to fly kites and shoot marbles, and told them long stories of ghosts, witches, and Indians. Whenever he went dodging about the village, he was surrounded by a troop of them, hanging on his skirts, clambering on his back, and playing a thousand tricks on him with impunity; and not a dog would bark at him throughout the neighborhood.

The great error in Rip's composition was an insuperable aversion to all kinds of profitable labor. It could not be from the want of assiduity or perseverance; for he would sit on a wet rock, with a rod as long and heavy as a Tartar's lance, and fish all day without a murmur, even though he should not be encouraged by a single nibble. He would carry a fowling-piece on his shoulder for hours together, trudging through woods and swamps, and up hill and down dale, to shoot a few squirrels or wild pigeons. He would never refuse to assist a neighbor, even in the roughest toil, and was a foremost man at all country frolics for husking Indian corn, or building stone fences; the women of the village, too, used to employ him to run their errands, and to do such little odd jobs as their less obliging husbands would not do for them. In a word, Rip was ready to attend to anybody's business but his own; but as to doing family duty, and keeping his farm in order, he found it impossible.

In fact, he declared it was of no use to work on his farm; it was the most pestilent little piece of ground in the whole country; everything about it went wrong, and would go wrong, in spite of him. His fences were continually falling to pieces; his cow would either go astray or get among the cabbages; weeds were sure to grow quicker in his fields than anywhere else; the rain always made a point of setting in just as he had some out-door work to do; so that though his patrimonial estate had dwindled away under his management, acre by acre, until there was little more left than a mere patch of Indian corn and potatoes, yet it was the worst-conditioned farm in the neighborhood.

His children, too, were as ragged and wild as if they belonged to nobody. His son Rip, an urchin begotten in his own likeness, promised to inherit the habits, with the old clothes, of his father. He was generally seen trooping like a colt at his mother's heels, equipped in a pair of his father's cast-off galligaskins, which he had much ado to hold up with one hand, as a fine lady does her train in bad weather.

Rip Van Winkle, however, was one of those happy mortals, of foolish, well-oiled dispositions, who take the world easy, eat white bread or brown, whichever can be got with least thought or trouble, and would rather starve on a penny than work for a pound. If left to himself, he would have whistled life away in perfect contentment; but his wife kept continually dinning in his ears about his idleness, his carelessness, and the ruin he was bringing on his family. Morning, noon, and night her tongue was incessantly going, and everything he said or did was sure to produce a torrent of household eloquence. Rip had but one way of replying to all lectures of the kind, and that, by frequent use, had grown into a habit. He shrugged his shoulders, shook his head, cast up his eyes, but said nothing. This, however, always provoked a fresh volley from his wife; so that he was fain to draw off his forces, and take to the outside of the house—the only side which, in truth, belongs to a henpecked husband.

Rip's sole domestic adherent was his dog Wolf, who was as much henpecked as his master; for Dame Van Winkle regarded them as companions in idleness, and even looked upon Wolf with an evil eye, as the cause of his master's going so often astray. True it is, in all points of spirit befitting an honorable dog, he was as courageous an animal as ever scoured the woods; but what courage can withstand the ever-during and all-besetting terrors of a woman's tongue? The moment Wolf entered the house his crest fell, his tail drooped to the ground, or curled between his legs, he sneaked about with a gallows air, casting many a sidelong glance at Dame Van Winkle, and at the least flourish of a broomstick or ladle he would fly to the door with yelping precipitation.

Times grew worse and worse with Rip Van Winkle as years of matrimony rolled on; a tart temper never mellows with age, and a sharp tongue is the only edged tool that grows keener with constant use. For a long while he used to console himself, when driven from home, by frequenting a kind of perpetual club of the sages, philosophers, and other idle personages of the village, which held its sessions on a bench before a small inn, designated by a rubicund portrait of His Majesty George the Third. Here they used to sit in the shade through a long, lazy summer's day, talking listlessly over village gossip, or telling endless sleepy stories about nothing. But it would have been worth any statesman's money to have heard the profound discussions that sometimes took place, when by chance an old newspaper fell into their hands from some passing traveller. How solemnly they would listen to the contents, as drawled out by Derrick Van Bummel, the schoolmaster, a dapper learned little man, who was not to be daunted by the most gigantic word in the dictionary; and how sagely they would deliberate upon public events some months after they had taken place.

The opinions of this junto were completely controlled by Nicholas Vedder, a patriarch of the village, and landlord of the inn, at the door of which he took his seat from morning till night, just moving sufficiently to avoid the sun and keep in the shade of a large tree; so that the neighbors could tell the hour by his movements as accurately as by a sun-dial. It is true he was rarely heard to speak, but smoked his pipe incessantly. His adherents, however (for every great man has his adherents), perfectly understood him, and knew how to gather his opinions. When anything that was read or related

displeased him, he was observed to smoke his pipe vehemently, and to send
forth short, frequent, and angry puffs; but when pleased, he would inhale
the smoke slowly and tranquilly, and emit it in light and placid clouds; and
sometimes, taking the pipe from his mouth, and letting the fragrant vapor
curl about his nose, would gravely nod his head in token of perfect approbation.

From even this stronghold the unlucky Rip was at length routed by his
termagant wife, who would suddenly break in upon the tranquillity of the
assemblage and call the members all to naught; nor was that august personage, Nicholas Vedder himself, sacred from the daring tongue of this
terrible virago, who charged him outright with encouraging her husband in
habits of idleness.

Poor Rip was at last reduced almost to despair; and his only alternative,
to escape from the labor of the farm and clamor of his wife, was to take
gun in hand and stroll away into the woods. Here he would sometimes seat
himself at the foot of a tree, and share the contents of his wallet with Wolf,
with whom he sympathized as a fellow-sufferer in persecution. "Poor
Wolf," he would say, "thy mistress leads thee a dog's life of it; but never
mind, my lad, whilst I live thou shalt never want a friend to stand by
thee!" Wolf would wag his tail, look wistfully in his master's face, and if
dogs can feel pity I verily believe he reciprocated the sentiment with all
his heart.

In a long ramble of the kind on a fine autumnal day, Rip had unconsciously scrambled to one of the highest parts of the Kaatskill Mountains.
He was after his favorite sport of squirrel-shooting, and the still solitudes
had echoed and reëchoed with the reports of his gun. Panting and fatigued,
he threw himself, late in the afternoon, on a green knoll, covered with mountain herbage, that crowned the brow of a precipice. From an opening between the trees he could overlook all the lower country for many a mile of
rich woodland. He saw at a distance the lordly Hudson, far, far below him,
moving on its silent but majestic course, with the reflection of a purple
cloud, or the sail of a lagging bark, here and there sleeping on its glassy
bosom, and at last losing itself in the blue highlands.

On the other side he looked down into a deep mountain glen, wild,
lonely, and shagged, the bottom filled with fragments from the impending
cliffs, and scarcely lighted by the reflected rays of the setting sun. For some
time Rip lay musing on this scene; evening was gradually advancing; the
mountains began to throw their long blue shadows over the valleys; he saw
that it would be dark long before he could reach the village, and he heaved
a heavy sigh when he thought of encountering the terrors of Dame Van
Winkle.

As he was about to descend, he heard a voice from a distance, hallooing,

"Rip Van Winkle! Rip Van Winkle!" He looked round, but could see nothing but a crow winging its solitary flight across the mountain. He thought his fancy must have deceived him, and turned again to descend, when he heard the same cry ring through the still evening air: "Rip Van Winkle! Rip Van Winkle!"—at the same time Wolf bristled up his back, and giving a low growl, skulked to his master's side, looking fearfully down into the glen. Rip now felt a vague apprehension stealing over him; he looked anxiously in the same direction, and perceived a strange figure slowly toiling up the rocks, and bending under the weight of something he carried on his back. He was surprised to see any human being in this lonely and unfrequented place; but supposing it to be some one of the neighborhood in need of his assistance, he hastened down to yield it.

On nearer approach he was still more surprised at the singularity of the stranger's appearance. He was a short, square-built old fellow, with thick bushy hair, and a grizzled beard. His dress was of the antique Dutch fashion, —a cloth jerkin strapped round the waist—several pair of breeches, the outer one of ample volume, decorated with rows of buttons down the sides, and bunches at the knees. He bore on his shoulder a stout keg, that seemed full of liquor, and made signs for Rip to approach and assist him with the load. Though rather shy and distrustful of this new acquaintance, Rip complied with his usual alacrity; and mutually relieving one another, they clambered up a narrow gully, apparently the dry bed of a mountain torrent. As they ascended, Rip every now and then heard long, rolling peals like distant thunder, that seemed to issue out of a deep ravine, or rather cleft, between lofty rocks, toward which their rugged path conducted. He paused for an instant, but supposing it to be the muttering of one of those transient thunder-showers which often take place in mountain heights, he proceeded. Passing through the ravine, they came to a hollow, like a small amphitheatre, surrounded by perpendicular precipices, over the brinks of which impending trees shot their branches, so that you only caught glimpses of the azure sky and the bright evening cloud. During the whole time Rip and his companion had labored on in silence; for though the former marvelled greatly what could be the object of carrying a keg of liquor up this wild mountain, yet there was something strange and incomprehensible about the unknown, that inspired awe and checked familiarity.

On entering the amphitheatre, new objects of wonder presented themselves. On a level spot in the centre was a company of odd-looking personages playing at ninepins. They were dressed in a quaint, outlandish fashion; some wore short doublets, others jerkins, with long knives in their belts, and most of them had enormous breeches, of similar style with that of the guide's. Their visages, too, were peculiar: one had a large beard, broad face, and small piggish eyes; the face of another seemed to consist entirely of nose, and was surmounted by a white sugar-loaf hat, set off with a little red cock's tail. They all had beards, of various shapes and colors. There was one who seemed to be the commander. He was a stout old gentleman, with a weather-beaten countenance; he wore a laced doublet, broad belt and hanger, high crowned hat and feather, red stockings, and high-heeled shoes, with roses in them. The whole group reminded Rip of the figures in an old Flemish painting, in the parlor of Dominie Van Shaick, the village parson, and which had been brought over from Holland at the time of the settlement.

What seemed particularly odd to Rip was, that though these folks were evidently amusing themselves, yet they maintained the gravest faces, the most mysterious silence, and were, withal, the most melancholy party of pleasure he had ever witnessed. Nothing interrupted the stillness of the scene but the noise of the balls, which, whenever they were rolled, echoed along the mountains like rumbling peals of thunder.

As Rip and his companion approached them, they suddenly desisted from their play, and stared at him with such fixed, statue-like gaze, and such strange, uncouth, lack-lustre countenances, that his heart turned within him, and his knees smote together. His companion now emptied the contents of the keg into large flagons, and made signs to him to wait upon the company. He obeyed with fear and trembling; they quaffed the liquor in profound silence, and then returned to their game.

By degrees Rip's awe and apprehension subsided. He even ventured, when no eye was fixed upon him, to taste the beverage, which he found had much of the flavor of excellent Hollands. He was naturally a thirsty soul, and was soon tempted to repeat the draught. One taste provoked another; and he reiterated his visits to the flagon so often that at length his senses were overpowered, his eyes swam in his head, his head gradually declined, and he fell into a deep sleep.

On waking, he found himself on the green knoll whence he had first seen the old man of the glen. He rubbed his eyes—it was a bright sunny morning. The birds were hopping and twittering among the bushes, and the eagle was wheeling aloft, and breasting the pure mountain breeze. "Surely," thought Rip, "I have not slept here all night." He recalled the occurrences before he fell asleep. The strange man with a keg of liquor—the mountain ravine—the wild retreat among the rocks—the woe-begone party at ninepins—the flagon— "Oh! that flagon! that wicked flagon!" thought Rip,—"what excuse shall I make to Dame Van Winkle?"

He looked round for his gun, but in place of the clean, well-oiled fowling-piece, he found an old firelock lying by him, the barrel incrusted with rust, the lock falling off, and the stock worm-eaten. He now suspected that the grave roisters of the mountain had put a trick upon him, and, having dosed him with liquor, had robbed him of his gun. Wolf, too, had disappeared, but he might have strayed away after a squirrel or partridge. He whistled after him, and shouted his name, but all in vain; the echoes repeated his whistle and shout, but no dog was to be seen.

He determined to revisit the scene of the last evening's gambol, and if he met with any of the party, to demand his dog and gun. As he rose to walk, he found himself stiff in the joints, and wanting in his usual activity. "These mountain beds do not agree with me," thought Rip, "and if this frolic should lay me up with a fit of the rheumatism, I shall have a blessed time with Dame Van Winkle." With some difficulty he got down into the glen; he found the gully up which he and his companion had ascended the preceding evening; but to his astonishment a mountain stream was now foaming down it, leaping from rock to rock, and filling the glen with babbling murmurs. He, however, made shift to scramble up its sides, working his toilsome way through thickets of birch, sassafras, and witch-hazel, and sometimes tripped up or entangled by the wild grapevines that twisted their coils or tendrils from tree to tree, and spread a kind of network in his path.

At length he reached to where the ravine had opened through the cliffs to the amphitheatre; but no traces of such opening remained. The rocks presented a high, impenetrable wall, over which the torrent came tumbling in a sheet of feathery foam, and fell into a broad, deep basin, black from the shadows of the surrounding forest. Here, then, poor Rip was brought to a stand. He again called and whistled after his dog; he was only answered by the cawing of a flock of idle crows, sporting high in air about a dry tree that overhung a sunny precipice; and who, secure in their elevation, seemed to look down and scoff at the poor man's perplexities. What was to be done? the morning was passing away, and Rip felt famished for want of his breakfast. He grieved to give up his dog and gun; he dreaded to meet his wife; but it would not do to starve among the mountains. He shook his head, shouldered the rusty firelock, and, with a heart full of trouble and anxiety, turned his steps homeward.

As he approached the village he met a number of people, but none whom he knew, which somewhat surprised him, for he had thought himself acquainted with every one in the country round. Their dress, too, was of a different fashion from that to which he was accustomed. They all stared at him with equal marks of surprise, and whenever they cast their eyes upon him, invariably stroked their chins. The constant recurrence of this gesture induced Rip, involuntarily, to do the same, when, to his astonishment, he found his beard had grown a foot long!

He had now entered the skirts of the village. A troop of strange children ran at his heels, hooting after him, and pointing at his gray beard. The dogs, too, not one of which he recognized for an old acquaintance, barked at him as he passed. The very village was altered; it was larger and more populous. There were rows of houses which he had never seen before, and those which had been his familiar haunts had disappeared. Strange names were over the doors—strange faces at the windows—everything was strange. His mind now misgave him; he began to doubt whether both he and the world around him were not bewitched. Surely this was his native village, which he had left but the day before. There stood the Kaatskill Mountains—there ran the silver Hudson at a distance—there was every hill and dale precisely as it had always been. Rip was sorely perplexed. "That flagon last night," thought he, "has addled my poor head sadly!"

It was with some difficulty that he found the way to his own house, which he approached with silent awe, expecting every moment to hear the shrill voice of Dame Van Winkle. He found the house gone to decay—the roof fallen in, the windows shattered, and the doors off the hinges. A half-starved dog that looked like Wolf was skulking about it. Rip called him by name, but the cur snarled, showed his teeth, and passed on. This was an unkind cut indeed. "My very dog," sighed poor Rip, "has forgotten me!"

He entered the house, which, to tell the truth, Dame Van Winkle had always kept in neat order. It was empty, forlorn, and apparently abandoned. This desolateness overcame all his connubial fears—he called loudly for his wife and children—the lonely chambers rang for a moment with his voice, and then all again was silence.

He now hurried forth, and hastened to his old resort, the village inn—but it too was gone. A large, rickety wooden building stood in its place, with great gaping windows, some of them broken and mended with old hats and petticoats, and over the door was painted, "The Union Hotel, by Jonathan Doolittle." Instead of the great tree that used to shelter the quiet little Dutch inn of yore, there now was reared a tall naked pole, with something on the top that looked like a red night-cap, and from it was fluttering a flag, on which was a singular assemblage of stars and stripes;—all this was strange and incomprehensible. He recognized on the sign, however, the ruby face of King George, under which he had smoked so many a peaceful pipe; but even this was singularly metamorphosed. The red coat was changed for one of blue and buff, a sword was held in the hand instead of a sceptre, the head was decorated with a cocked hat, and underneath was painted in large characters, GENERAL WASHINGTON.

There was, as usual, a crowd of folk about the door, but none that Rip recollected. The very character of the people seemed changed. There was a busy, bustling, disputatious tone about it, instead of the accustomed phlegm and drowsy tranquillity. He looked in vain for the sage Nicholas Vedder, with his broad face, double chin, and fair long pipe, uttering clouds of tobacco smoke instead of idle speeches; or Van Bummel, the schoolmaster, doling forth the contents of an ancient newspaper. In place of these, a lean, bilious-looking fellow, with his pockets full of handbills, was haranguing vehemently about rights of citizens—elections—members of congress—liberty —Bunker's Hill—heroes of seventy-six—and other words, which were a perfect Babylonish jargon to the bewildered Van Winkle.

The appearance of Rip, with his long, grizzled beard, his rusty fowling-piece, his uncouth dress, and an army of women and children at his heels, soon attracted the attention of the tavern-politicians. They crowded round him, eying him from head to foot with great curiosity. The orator bustled up to him, and, drawing him partly aside, inquired "On which side he voted?" Rip stared in vacant stupidity. Another short but busy little fellow pulled him by the arm, and, rising on tiptoe, inquired in his ear, "Whether he was Federal or Democrat?" Rip was equally at a loss to comprehend the question; when a knowing, self-important old gentleman, in a sharp cocked hat, made his way through the crowd, putting them to the right and left with his elbows as he passed, and planting himself before Van Winkle, with one arm akimbo, the other resting on his cane, his keen eyes and sharp hat penetrating, as it were, into his very soul, demanded, in an austere tone, "What brought him to the election with a gun on his shoulder, and a mob at his heels, and whether he meant to breed a riot in the village?"—"Alas! gentlemen," cried Rip, somewhat dismayed, "I am a poor quiet man, a native of the place, and a loyal subject of the King, God bless him!"

Here a general shout burst from the bystanders— "A tory! a tory! a spy! a refugee! hustle him! away with him!" It was with great difficulty that the self-important man in the cocked hat restored order; and, having assumed a tenfold austerity of brow, demanded again of the unknown culprit, what he came there for, and whom he was seeking? The poor man humbly assured him that he meant no harm, but merely came there in search of some of his neighbors, who used to keep about the tavern.

"Well—who are they?—name them."

Rip bethought himself a moment, and inquired, "Where's Nicholas Vedder?"

There was a silence for a little while, when an old man replied, in a thin piping voice: "Nicholas Vedder! why, he is dead and gone these eighteen years! There was a wooden tombstone in the churchyard that used to tell all about him, but that's rotten and gone too."

"Where's Brom Dutcher?"

"Oh, he went off to the army in the beginning of the war; some say he was killed at the storming of Stony Point—others say he was drowned in a squall at the foot of Antony's Nose. I don't know—he never came back again."

"Where's Van Bummel, the schoolmaster?"

"He went off to the wars too, was a great militia general, and is now in Congress."

Rip's heart died away at hearing of these sad changes in his home and friends, and finding himself thus alone in the world. Every answer puzzled him too, by treating of such enormous lapses of time, and of matters which he could not understand: war—Congress—Stony Point; he had no courage to ask after any more friends, but cried out in despair, "Does nobody here know Rip Van Winkle?"

"Oh, Rip Van Winkle!" exclaimed two or three, "Oh, to be sure! that's Rip Van Winkle yonder, leaning against the tree."

Rip looked, and beheld a precise counterpart of himself, as he went up the mountain: apparently as lazy, and certainly as ragged. The poor fellow was now completely confounded. He doubted his own identity, and whether he was himself or another man. In the midst of his bewilderment, the man in the cocked hat demanded who he was, and what was his name.

"God knows," exclaimed he, at his wit's end; "I'm not myself—I'm somebody else—that's me yonder—no—that's somebody else got into my shoes —I was myself last night, but I fell asleep on the mountain, and they've changed my gun, and everything's changed, and I'm changed, and I can't tell what's my name, or who I am!"

The bystanders began now to look at each other, nod, wink significantly, and tap their fingers against their foreheads. There was a whisper, also, about securing the gun, and keeping the old fellow from doing mischief, at the very suggestion of which the self-important man in the cocked hat retired with some precipitation. At this critical moment a fresh, comely woman pressed through the throng to get a peep at the gray-bearded man. She had a chubby child in her arms, which, frightened at his looks, began to cry. "Hush, Rip," cried she, "hush, you little fool; the old man won't hurt you." The name of the child, the air of the mother, the tone of her voice, all awakened a train of recollections in his mind. "What is your name, my good woman?" asked he.

"Judith Gardenier."

"And your father's name?"

"Ah, poor man, Rip Van Winkle was his name, but it's twenty years since he went away from home with his gun, and never has been heard of since, —his dog came home without him; but whether he shot himself, or was carried away by the Indians, nobody can tell. I was then but a little girl."

Rip had but one question more to ask; but he put it with a faltering voice:

"Where's your mother?"

"Oh, she too had died but a short time since; she broke a blood-vessel in a fit of passion at a New England peddler."

There was a drop of comfort at least, in this intelligence. The honest man could contain himself no longer. He caught his daughter and her child in his arms. "I am your father!" cried he— "Young Rip Van Winkle once—old Rip Van Winkle now!—Does nobody know poor Rip Van Winkle?"

All stood amazed, until an old woman, tottering out from among the crowd, put her hand to her brow, and peering under it in his face for a moment, exclaimed, "Sure enough it is Rip Van Winkle—it is himself! Welcome home again, old neighbor. Why, where have you been these twenty long years?"

Rip's story was soon told, for the whole twenty years had been to him but as one night. The neighbors stared when they heard it; some were seen to wink at each other, and put their tongues in their cheeks; and the self-important man in the cocked hat, who, when the alarm was over, had returned to the field, screwed down the corners of his mouth, and shook his head—upon which there was a general shaking of the head throughout the assemblage.

It was determined, however, to take the opinion of old Peter Vanderdonk, who was seen slowly advancing up the road. He was a descendant of the historian of that name, who wrote one of the earliest accounts of the province. Peter was the most ancient inhabitant of the village, and well versed in all the wonderful events and traditions of the neighborhood. He recollected Rip at once, and corroborated his story in the most satisfactory manner. He assured the company that it was a fact, handed down from his ancestor the historian, that the Kaatskill Mountains had always been haunted by strange beings. That it was affirmed that the great Hendrick Hudson, the first discoverer of the river and country, kept a kind of vigil there every twenty years, with his crew of the Half-moon; being permitted in this way to revisit the scenes of his enterprise, and keep a guardian eye upon the river and the great city called by his name. That his father had once seen them in their old Dutch dresses playing at ninepins in a hollow of the mountain; and that he himself had heard, one summer afternoon, the sound of their balls like distant peals of thunder.

To make a long story short, the company broke up, and returned to the more important concerns of the election. Rip's daughter took him home to live with her; she had a snug, well-furnished house, and a stout, cheery farmer for a husband, whom Rip recollected for one of the urchins that used to climb upon his back. As to Rip's son and heir, who was the ditto of himself, seen leaning against the tree, he was employed to work on the farm; but evinced an hereditary disposition to attend to anything else but his business.

Rip now resumed his old walks and habits; he soon found many of his former cronies, though all rather the worse for the wear and tear of time; and preferred making friends among the rising generation, with whom he soon grew into great favor.

Having nothing to do at home, and being arrived at that happy age when a man can be idle with impunity, he took his place once more on the bench at the inn door, and was reverenced as one of the patriarchs of the village, and a chronicle of the old times "before the war." It was some time before he could get into the regular track of gossip, or could be made to comprehend the strange events that had taken place during his torpor. How that there had been a revolutionary war,—that the country had thrown off the yoke of old England,—and that, instead of being a subject of his Majesty George the Third, he was now a free citizen of the United States. Rip, in fact, was no politician; the changes of states and empires made but little impression on him; but there was one species of despotism under which he had long groaned, and that was—petticoat government. Happily that was at an end; he had got his neck out of the yoke of matrimony, and could go in and out whenever he pleased, without dreading the tyranny of Dame Van Winkle. Whenever her name was mentioned, however, he shook his head, shrugged his shoulders, and cast up his eyes, which might pass either for an expression of resignation to his fate, or joy at his deliverance.

He used to tell his story to every stranger that arrived at Mr. Doolittle's hotel. He was observed, at first, to vary on some points every time he told it, which was, doubtless, owing to his having so recently awaked. It at last settled down precisely to the tale I have related, and not a man, woman, or child in the neighborhood but knew it by heart. Some always pretended to doubt the reality of it, and insisted that Rip had been out of his head, and that this was one point on which he always remained flighty. The old Dutch inhabitants, however, almost universally gave it full credit. Even to this day they never hear a thunderstorm of a summer afternoon about the Kaatskill, but they say Hendrick Hudson and his crew are at their game of ninepins; and it is a common wish of all henpecked husbands in the neighborhood, when life hangs heavy on their hands, that they might have a quieting draught out of Rip Van Winkle's flagon.

NOTE

The foregoing Tale, one would suspect, had been suggested to Mr. Knickerbocker by a little German superstition about the Emperor Frederick *der Rothbart,* and the Kypphaüser mountain; the subjoined note, however, which he had appended to the tale, shows that it is an absolute fact, narrated with his usual fidelity.

"The story of Rip Van Winkle may seem incredible to many, but nevertheless I give it my full belief, for I know the vicinity of our old Dutch settlements to have been very subject to marvellous events and appearances. Indeed, I have heard many stranger stories than this, in the villages along the Hudson; all of which were too well authenticated to admit of a doubt. I have even talked with Rip Van Winkle myself, who, when last I saw him, was a very venerable old man, and so perfectly rational and consistent on every other point, that I think no conscientious person could refuse to take this into the bargain; nay, I have seen a certificate on the subject taken before a country justice and signed with a cross, in the justice's own handwriting. The story, therefore, is beyond the possibility of doubt.

"D. K."

POSTSCRIPT

THE following are travelling notes from a memorandum-book of Mr. Knickerbocker:

The Kaatsberg, or Catskill Mountains, have always been a region full of fable. The Indians considered them the abode of spirits, who influenced the weather, spreading sunshine or clouds over the landscape, and sending good or bad hunting seasons. They were ruled by an old squaw spirit, said to be their mother. She dwelt on the highest peak of the Catskills, and had charge of the doors of day and night to open and shut them at the proper hour. She hung up the new moons in the skies, and cut up the old ones into stars. In times of drought, if properly propitiated, she would spin light summer clouds out of cobwebs and morning dew, and send them off from the crest of the mountain, flake after flake, like flakes of carded cotton, to float in the air; until, dissolved by the heat of the sun, they would fall in gentle showers, causing the grass to spring, the fruits to ripen, and the corn to grow an inch an hour. If displeased, however, she would brew up clouds black as ink, sitting in the midst of them like a bottle-bellied spider in the midst of its web; and when these clouds broke, woe betide the valleys!

In old times, say the Indian traditions, there was a kind of Manitou or Spirit, who kept about the wildest recesses of the Catskill Mountains, and took a mischievous pleasure in wreaking all kinds of evils and vexations upon the red men. Sometimes he would assume the form of a bear, a panther, or a deer, lead the bewildered hunter a weary chase through tangled forests and among ragged rocks; and then spring off with a loud ho! ho! leaving him aghast on the brink of a beetling precipice or raging torrent.

The favorite abode of this Manitou is still shown. It is a great rock or cliff on the loneliest part of the mountains, and from the flowering vines which clamber about it, and the wild flowers which abound in its neighborhood, is known by the name of the Garden Rock. Near the foot of it is a small lake, the haunt of the solitary bittern, with water-snakes basking in the sun on the leaves of the pond-lilies which lie on the surface. This place was held in great awe by the Indians, insomuch that the boldest hunter would not pursue his game within its precincts. Once upon a time, however, a hunter, who had lost his way, penetrated to the Garden Rock, where he beheld a number of gourds placed in the crotches of trees. One of these he seized and made off with it, but in the hurry of his retreat he let it fall among the rocks, when a great stream gushed forth, which washed him away and swept him down precipices, where he was dashed to pieces, and the stream made its way to the Hudson, and continues to flow to the present day; being the identical stream known by the name of the Kaaters-kill.

WESTMINSTER ABBEY [4]

ON one of those sober and rather melancholy days, in the latter part of autumn, when the shadows of morning and evening almost mingle together, and throw a gloom over the decline of the year, I passed several hours in rambling about Westminster Abbey. There was something congenial to the season in the mournful magnificence of the old pile; and, as I passed its threshold, seemed like stepping back into the regions of antiquity, and losing myself among the shades of former ages.

I entered from the inner court of Westminster School, through a long, low, vaulted passage, that had an almost subterranean look, being dimly lighted in one part by circular perforations in the massive walls. Through this dark avenue I had a distant view of the cloisters, with the figure of an old verger, in his black gown, moving along their shadowy vaults, and seeming like a spectre from one of the neighboring tombs. The approach to the abbey through these gloomy monastic remains prepares the mind for its solemn contemplation. The cloisters still retain something of the quiet and seclusion of former days. The gray walls are discolored by damps, and crumbling with age; a coat of hoary moss has gathered over the inscriptions of the mural monuments, and obscured the death's-heads, and other funereal emblems. The sharp touches of the chisel are gone from the rich tracery of the arches; the roses which adorned the keystones have lost their leafy beauty; everything bears marks of the gradual dilapidations of time, which yet has something touching and pleasing in its very decay.

The sun was pouring down a yellow autumnal ray into the square of the cloisters; beaming upon a scanty plot of grass in the centre, and lighting up an angle of the vaulted passage with a kind of dusky splendor. From between the arcades, the eye glanced up to a bit of blue sky or a passing cloud, and beheld the sun-gilt pinnacles of the abbey towering into the azure heaven.

As I paced the cloisters, sometimes contemplating this mingled picture of glory and decay, and sometimes endeavoring to decipher the inscriptions on the tombstones, which formed the pavement beneath my feet, my eye was attracted to three figures, rudely carved in relief, but nearly worn away by the footsteps of many generations. They were the effigies of three of the early abbots; the epitaphs were entirely effaced; the names alone remained, having no doubt been renewed in later times. (Vitalis. Abbas. 1082, and Gislebertus Crispinus. Abbas. 1114, and Laurentius. Abbas. 1176.) I remained some little while, musing over these casual relics of antiquity, thus left like wrecks upon this distant shore of time, telling no tale but that such beings had been, and had perished; teaching no moral but the futility of that

[4] From *The Sketch-Book* (1819).

pride which hopes still to exact homage in its ashes, and to live in an inscription. A little longer, and even these faint records will be obliterated, and
the monument will cease to be a memorial. Whilst I was yet looking down
upon these gravestones, I was roused by the sound of the abbey clock, reverberating from buttress to buttress, and echoing among the cloisters. It is almost startling to hear this warning of departed time sounding among the
tombs, and telling the lapse of the hour, which, like a billow, has rolled
us onward towards the grave. I pursued my walk to an arched door opening to the interior of the abbey. On entering here, the magnitude of the
building breaks fully upon the mind, contrasted with the vaults of the
cloisters. The eyes gaze with wonder at clustered columns of gigantic dimensions, with arches springing from them to such an amazing height; and
man wandering about their bases, shrunk into insignificance in comparison
with his own handiwork. The spaciousness and gloom of this vast edifice
produces a profound and mysterious awe. We step cautiously and softly
about, as if fearful of disturbing the hallowed silence of the tomb; while
every footfall whispers along the walls, and chatters among the sepulchres,
making us more sensible of the quiet we have interrupted.

It seems as if the awful nature of the place presses down upon the soul,
and hushes the beholder into noiseless reverence. We feel that we are surrounded by the congregated bones of the great men of past times, who have
filled history with their deeds, and the earth with their renown.

And yet it almost provokes a smile at the vanity of human ambition, to
see how they are crowded together and jostled in the dust; what parsimony
is observed in doling out a scanty nook, a gloomy corner, a little portion of
earth, to those whom, when alive, kingdoms could not satisfy; and how
many shapes, and forms, and artifices are devised to catch the casual notice
of the passenger, and save from forgetfulness, for a few short years, a name
which once aspired to occupy ages of the world's thought and admiration.

I passed some time in Poets' Corner, which occupies an end of one of the
transepts or cross aisles of the abbey. The monuments are generally simple;
for the lives of literary men afford no striking themes for the sculptor.
Shakespeare and Addison have statues erected to their memories; but the
greater part have busts, medallions, and sometimes mere inscriptions. Notwithstanding the simplicity of these memorials, I have always observed that
the visitors to the abbey remained longest about them. A kinder and fonder
feeling takes place of that cold curiosity or vague admiration with which
they gaze on the splendid monuments of the great and the heroic. They
linger about these as about the tombs of friends and companions; for indeed
there is something of companionship between the author and the reader.
Other men are known to posterity only through the medium of history,
which is continually growing faint and obscure; but the intercourse between

the author and his fellowmen is ever new, active and immediate. He has lived for them more than for himself; he has sacrificed surrounding enjoyments, and shut himself up from the delights of social life, that he might the more intimately commune with distant minds and distant ages. Well may the world cherish his renown; for it has been purchased, not by deeds of violence and blood, but by the diligent dispensation of pleasure. Well may posterity be grateful to his memory; for he has left it an inheritance, not of empty names and sounding actions, but whole treasures of wisdom, bright gems of thought, and golden veins of language.

From Poets' Corner, I continued my stroll towards that part of the abbey which contains the sepulchres of the kings. I wandered among what once were chapels, but which are now occupied by the tombs and monuments of the great. At every turn I met with some illustrious name or the cognizance of some powerful house renowned in history. As the eye darts into these dusky chambers of death, it catches glimpses of quaint effigies; some kneeling in niches, as if in devotion; others stretched upon the tombs, with hands piously pressed together; warriors in armor, as if reposing after battle; prelates with croziers and mitres; and nobles in robes and coronets, lying as it were in state. In glancing over this scene, so strangely populous, yet where every form is so still and silent, it seems almost as if we were treading a mansion of that fabled city where every being had been suddenly transmuted into stone.

I paused to contemplate a tomb on which lay the effigy of a knight in complete armor. A large buckler was on one arm; the hands were pressed together in supplication upon the breast; the face was almost covered by the morion; the legs were crossed in token of the warrior's having been engaged in the holy war. It was the tomb of a Crusader; of one of those military enthusiasts who so strangely mingled religion and romance, and whose exploits form the connecting link between fact and fiction; between the history and the fairy tale. There is something extremely picturesque in the tombs of these adventurers, decorated as they are with rude armorial bearings and Gothic sculpture. They comport with the antiquated chapels in which they are generally found; and in considering them, the imagination is apt to kindle with the legendary associations, the romantic fiction, the chivalrous pomp and pageantry, which poetry has spread over the wars for the sepulchre of Christ. They are the relics of times utterly gone by; of beings passed from recollection; of customs and manners with which ours have no affinity. They are like objects from some strange and distant land, of which we have no certain knowledge, and about which all our conceptions are vague and visionary. There is something extremely solemn and awful in those effigies on Gothic tombs, extended as if in the sleep of death, or in the supplication of the dying hour. They have an effect infinitely more

impressive on my feelings than the fanciful attitudes, the overwrought
conceits, and allegorical groups, which abound on modern monuments. I
have been struck, also, with the superiority of many of the old sepulchral
inscriptions. There was a noble way, in former times, of saying things
simply, and yet saying them proudly; and I do not know an epitaph that
breathes a loftier consciousness of family worth and honorable lineage than
one which affirms, of a noble house, that "all the brothers were brave, and
all the sisters virtuous."

In the opposite transept to Poets' Corner stands a monument which is
among the most renowned achievements of modern art; but which to me
appears horrible rather than sublime. It is the tomb of Mrs. Nightingale, by
Roubillac. The bottom of the monument is represented as throwing open
its marble doors, and a sheeted skeleton is starting forth. The shroud is
falling from his fleshless frame as he launches his dart at his victim. She is
sinking into her affrighted husband's arms, who strives, with vain and frantic
effort, to avert the blow. The whole is executed with terrible truth and
spirit; we almost fancy we hear the gibbering yell of triumph bursting from
the distended jaws of the spectre.—But why should we thus seek to clothe
death with unnecessary terrors, and to spread horrors round the tomb of
those we love? The grave should be surrounded by everything that might
inspire tenderness and veneration for the dead; or that might win the living
to virtue. It is the place, not of disgust and dismay, but of sorrow and meditation.

While wandering about those gloomy vaults and silent aisles, studying the
records of the dead, the sound of busy existence from without occasionally
reaches the ear;—the rumbling of the passing equipage; the murmur of the
multitude; or perhaps the light laugh of pleasure. The contrast is striking
with the deathlike repose around: and it has a strange effect upon the feelings, thus to hear the surges of active life hurrying along, and beating
against the very walls of the sepulchre.

I continued in this way to move from tomb to tomb, and from chapel to
chapel. The day was gradually wearing away; the distant tread of loiterers
about the abbey grew less and less frequent; the sweet-tongued bell was
summoning to evening prayers; and I saw at a distance the choristers, in
their white surplices, crossing the aisle and entering the choir. I stood before
the entrance to Henry the Seventh's chapel. A flight of steps lead up to it,
through a deep and gloomy, but magnificent arch. Great gates of brass, richly
and delicately wrought, turn heavily upon their hinges, as if proudly reluctant to admit the feet of common mortals into this most gorgeous of
sepulchres.

On entering, the eye is astonished by the pomp of architecture, and the elaborate beauty of sculptured detail. The very walls are wrought into universal ornament, incrusted with tracery, and scooped into niches, crowded with the statues of saints and martyrs. Stone seems, by the cunning labor of the chisel, to have been robbed of its weight and density, suspended aloft, as if by magic, and the fretted roof achieved with the wonderful minuteness and airy security of a cobweb.

Along the sides of the chapel are the lofty stalls of the Knights of the Bath, richly carved of oak, though with the grotesque decorations of Gothic architecture. On the pinnacles of the stalls are affixed the helmets and crests of the knights, with their scarfs and swords; and above them are suspended their banners, emblazoned with armorial bearings, and contrasting the splendor of gold and purple and crimson with the cold gray fretwork of the roof. In the midst of this grand mausoleum stands the sepulchre of its founder,—his effigy, with that of his queen, extended on a sumptuous tomb, and the whole surrounded by a superbly wrought brazen railing.

There is a sad dreariness in this magnificence, this strange mixture of tombs and trophies; these emblems of living and aspiring ambition, close beside mementos which show the dust and oblivion in which all must sooner or later terminate. Nothing impresses the mind with a deeper feeling of loneliness than to tread the silent and deserted scene of former throng and pageant. On looking round on the vacant stalls of the knights and their esquires, and on the rows of dusty but gorgeous banners that were once borne before them, my imagination conjured up the scene when this hall was bright with the valor and beauty of the land; glittering with the splendor of jewelled rank and military array; alive with the tread of many feet and the hum of an admiring multitude. All had passed away; the silence of death had settled again upon the place, interrupted only by the casual chirping of birds, which had found their way into the chapel, and built their nests among its friezes and pendants—sure signs of solitariness and desertion.

When I read the names inscribed on the banners, they were those of men scattered far and wide about the world; some tossing upon distant seas; some under arms in distant lands; some mingling in the busy intrigues of courts and cabinets; all seeking to deserve one more distinction in this mansion of shadowy honors: the melancholy reward of a monument.

Two small aisles on each side of this chapel present a touching instance of the equality of the grave; which brings down the oppressor to a level with the oppressed, and mingles the dust of the bitterest enemies together. In one is the sepulchre of the haughty Elizabeth; in the other is that of her victim, the lovely and unfortunate Mary. Not an hour in the day but some ejaculation of pity is uttered over the fate of the latter, mingled with indignation at her oppressor. The walls of Elizabeth's sepulchre continually echo with the sighs of sympathy heaved at the grave of her rival.

A peculiar melancholy reigns over the aisle where Mary lies buried. The light struggles dimly through windows darkened by dust. The greater part of the place is in deep shadow, and the walls are stained and tinted by time and weather. A marble figure of Mary is stretched upon the tomb, round which is an iron railing, much corroded, bearing her national emblem—the thistle. I was weary with wandering, and sat down to rest myself by the monument, revolving in my mind the checkered and disastrous story of poor Mary.

The sound of casual footsteps had ceased from the abbey. I could only hear, now and then, the distant voice of the priest repeating the evening service, and the faint responses of the choir; these paused for a time, and all were hushed. The stillness, the desertion and obscurity that were gradually prevailing around, gave a deeper and more solemn interest to the place.

> For in the silent grave no conversation,
> No joyful tread of friends, no voice of lovers,
> No careful father's counsel—nothing's heard,
> For nothing is, but all oblivion,
> Dust, and an endless darkness.

Suddenly the notes of the deep-laboring organ burst upon the ear, falling with doubled and redoubled intensity, and rolling, as it were, huge billows of sound. How well do their volume and grandeur accord with this mighty building! With what pomp do they swell through its vast vaults, and breathe their awful harmony through these caves of death, and make the silent sepulchre vocal!—And now they rise in triumph and acclamation, heaving higher and higher their accordant notes, and piling sound on sound. —And now they pause, and the soft voices of the choir break out into sweet gushes of melody; they soar aloft, and warble along the roof, and seem to play about these lofty vaults like the pure airs of heaven. Again the pealing organ heaves its thrilling thunders, compressing air into music, and rolling it forth upon the soul. What long-drawn cadences! What solemn sweeping concords! It grows more and more dense and powerful—it fills the vast pile, and seems to jar the very walls—the ear is stunned—the senses are overwhelmed. And now it is winding up in full jubilee—it is rising from the earth to heaven—the very soul seems rapt away and floated upwards on this swelling tide of harmony!

I sat for some time lost in that kind of reverie which a strain of music is apt sometimes to inspire: the shadows of evening were gradually thickening round me; the monuments began to cast deeper and deeper gloom; and the distant clock again gave token of the slowly waning day.

I rose and prepared to leave the abbey. As I descended the flight of steps which lead into the body of the building, my eye was caught by the shrine of Edward the Confessor, and I ascended the small staircase that conducts to it, to take from thence a general survey of this wilderness of tombs. The shrine is elevated upon a kind of platform, and close around it are the sepulchres of various kings and queens. From this eminence the eye looks down between pillars and funeral trophies to the chapels and chambers below, crowded with tombs,—where warriors, prelates, courtiers, and statesmen lie mouldering in their "beds of darkness." Close by me stood the great chair of coronation, rudely carved of oak, in the barbarous taste of a remote and Gothic age. The scene seemed almost as if contrived, with theatrical artifice, to produce an effect upon the beholder. Here was a type of the beginning and the end of human pomp and power; here it was literally but a step from the throne to the sepulchre. Would not one think that these incongruous mementos had been gathered together as a lesson to living greatness? —to show it, even in the moment of its proudest exaltation, the neglect and dishonor to which it must soon arrive; how soon that crown which encircles its brow must pass away, and it must lie down in the dust and disgraces of the tomb, and be trampled upon by the feet of the meanest of the multitude. For, strange to tell, even the grave is here no longer a sanctuary. There is a shocking levity in some natures, which leads them to sport with awful and hallowed things; and there are base minds, which delight to revenge on the illustrious dead the abject homage and grovelling servility which they pay to the living. The coffin of Edward the Confessor has been broken open, and his remains despoiled of their funereal ornaments; the sceptre has been stolen from the hand of the imperious Elizabeth, and the effigy of Henry the Fifth lies headless. Not a royal monument but bears some proof how false and fugitive is the homage of mankind. Some are plundered; some mutilated; some covered with ribaldry and insult,—all more or less outraged and dishonored!

The last beams of day were now faintly streaming through the painted windows in high vaults above me; the lower parts of the abbey were already wrapped in the obscurity of twilight. The chapels and aisles grew darker and darker. The effigies of the kings faded into shadows; the marble figures of the monuments assumed strange shapes in the uncertain light; the evening breeze crept through the aisles like the cold breath of the grave; and even the distant footfall of a verger, traversing the Poet's Corner, had something strange and dreary in its sound. I slowly retraced my morning's walk, and as I passed out at the portal of the cloisters, the door, closing with a jarring noise behind me, filled the whole building with echoes.

I endeavored to form some arrangement in my mind of the objects I had been contemplating, but found they were already fallen into indistinctness and confusion. Names, inscriptions, trophies, had all become confounded in my recollection, though I had scarcely taken my foot from off the threshold. What, thought I, is this vast assemblage of sepulchres but a treasury of humiliation; a huge pile of reiterated homilies on the emptiness of renown, and the certainty of oblivion! It is, indeed, the empire of death—his great shadowy palace, where he sits in state, mocking at the relics of human glory, and spreading dust and forgetfulness on the monuments of princes. How idle a boast, after all, is the immortality of a name! Time is ever silently turning over his pages; we are too much engrosesd by the story of the present, to think of the characters and anecdotes that gave interest to the past; and each age is a volume thrown aside to be speedily forgotten. The idol of to-day pushes the hero of yesterday out of our recollection; and will, in turn, be supplanted by his successor of to-morrow. "Our fathers," says Sir Thomas Browne, "find their graves in our short memories, and sadly tell us how we may be buried in our survivors." History fades into fable; fact becomes clouded with doubt and controversy; the inscription moulders from the tablet; the statue falls from the pedestal. Columns, arches, pyramids, what are they but heaps of sand; and their epitaphs, but characters written in the dust? What is the security of a tomb, or the perpetuity of an embalmment? The remains of Alexander the Great have been scattered to the wind, and his empty sarcophagus is now the mere curiosity of a museum. "The Egyptian mummies, which Cambyses or time hath spared, avarice now consumeth; Mizraim cures wounds, and Pharaoh is sold for balsams."

What then is to insure this pile which now towers above me from sharing the fate of mightier mausoleums? The time must come when its gilded vaults, which now spring so loftily, shall lie in rubbish beneath the feet; when, instead of the sound of melody and praise, the wind shall whistle through the broken arches, and the owl hoot from the shattered tower,— when the garish sunbeam shall break into these gloomy mansions of death, and the ivy twine round the fallen column; and the foxglove hang its blossoms about the nameless urn, as if in mockery of the dead. Thus man passes away; his name perishes from record and recollection; his history is as a tale that is told, and his very monument becomes a ruin.

THE STOUT GENTLEMAN [5]

A STAGE-COACH ROMANCE

IT was a rainy Sunday in the gloomy month of November. I had been detained, in the course of a journey, by a slight indisposition, from which I

[5] From *Bracebridge Hall* (1822).

was recovering; but was still feverish, and obliged to keep within doors all day, in an inn of the small town of Derby. A wet Sunday in a country inn!—whoever has had the luck to experience one can alone judge of my situation. The rain pattered against the casements; the bells tolled for church with a melancholy sound. I went to the windows in quest of something to amuse the eye; but it seemed as if I had been placed completely out of the reach of all amusement. The windows of my bedroom looked out among tiled roofs and stacks of chimneys, while those of my sitting-room commanded a full view of the stable-yard. I know of nothing more calculated to make a man sick of this world than a stable-yard on a rainy day. The place was littered with wet straw that had been kicked about by travelers and stableboys. In one corner was a stagnant pool of water, surrounding an island of muck; there were several half-drowned fowls crowded together under a cart, among which was a miserable, crest-fallen cock, drenched out of all life and spirit; his drooping tail matted, as it were, into a single feather, along which the water trickled from his back; near the cart was a half-dozing cow, chewing the cud, and standing patiently to be rained on, with wreaths of vapor rising from her reeking hide; a wall-eyed horse, tired of the loneliness of the stable, was poking his spectral head out of a window, with the rain dripping on it from the eaves; an unhappy cur, chained to a doghouse hard by, uttered something, every now and then, between a bark and a yelp; a drab of a kitchen-wench tramped backwards and forwards through the yard in pattens, looking as sulky as the weather itself; everything, in short, was comfortless and forlorn, excepting a crew of hardened ducks, assembled like boon companions round a puddle, and making a riotous noise over their liquor.

I was lonely and listless, and wanted amusement. My room soon became insupportable. I abandoned it, and sought what is technically called the travelers'-room. This is a public room set apart at most inns for the accommodation of a class of wayfarers, called travelers, or riders; a kind of commercial knights-errant, who are incessantly scouring the kingdom in gigs, on horseback, or by coach. They are the only successors that I know of at the present day, to the knights-errant of yore. They lead the same kind of roving, adventurous life, only changing the lance for a driving-whip, the buckler for a pattern-card, and the coat of mail for an upper Benjamin. Instead of vindicating the charms of peerless beauty, they rove about, spreading the fame and standing of some substantial tradesman, or manufacturer, and are ready at any time to bargain in his name; it being the fashion nowadays to trade, instead of fight, with one another. As the room of the hostel, in the good old fighting-times, would be hung round at night with the armor of way-worn warriors, such as coats of mail, falchions, and yawning helmets; so the travelers'-room is garnished with the harnessing of their successors, with box-coats, whips of all kinds, spurs, gaiters, and oil-cloth covered hats.

I was in hopes of finding some of these worthies to talk with, but was disappointed. There were, indeed, two or three in the room; but I could make nothing of them. One was just finishing his breakfast, quarreling with his bread and butter, and huffing the waiter; another buttoned on a pair of gaiters, with many execrations at Boots for not having cleaned his shoes well; a third sat drumming on the table with his fingers and looking at the rain as it streamed down the window-glass; they all appeared infected by the weather, and disappeared, one after the other, without exchanging a word.

I sauntered to the window, and stood gazing at the people, picking their way to church, with petticoats hoisted midleg high, and dripping umbrellas. The bell ceased to toll, and the streets became silent. I then amused myself with watching the daughters of a tradesman opposite; who, being confined to the house for fear of wetting their Sunday finery, played off their charms at the front windows, to fascinate the chance tenants of the inn. They at length were summoned away by a vigilant vinegar-faced mother, and I had nothing further from without to amuse me.

What was I to do to pass away the long-lived day? I was sadly nervous and lonely; and everything about an inn seems calculated to make a dull day ten times duller. Old newspapers, smelling of beer and tobacco smoke, and which I had already read half a dozen times. Good-for-nothing books, that were worse than rainy weather. I bored myself to death with an old volume of the "Lady's Magazine." I read all the commonplace names of ambitious travelers scrawled on the panes of glass; the eternal families of the Smiths, and the Browns, and the Jacksons, and the Johnsons, and all the other sons; and I deciphered several scraps of fatiguing inn-window poetry which I have met with in all parts of the world.

The day continued lowering and gloomy; the slovenly, ragged, spongy cloud drifted heavily along; there was no variety even in the rain: it was one dull, continued, monotonous patter—patter—patter, excepting that now and then I was enlivened by the idea of a brisk shower, from the rattling of the drops upon a passing umbrella.

It was quite *refreshing* (if I may be allowed a hackneyed phrase of the day) when, in the course of the morning, a horn blew, and a stage-coach whirled through the street, with outside passengers stuck all over it, cowering under cotton umbrellas, and seethed together, and reeking with the steams of wet box-coats and upper Benjamins.

The sound brought out from their lurking-places a crew of vagabond boys, and vagabond dogs, and the carroty-headed hostler, and that nondescript animal ycleped Boots, and all the other vagabond race that infest the purlieus of an inn; but the bustle was transient; the coach again whirled on its way; and boy and dog, and hostler and Boots, all slunk back again to their holes; the street again became silent, and the rain continued to rain on. In fact, there was no hope of its clearing up; the barometer pointed to rainy weather; mine hostess's tortoise-shell cat sat by the fire washing her face, and rubbing her paws over her ears; and, on referring to the Almanac, I found a direful prediction stretching from the top of the page to the bottom through the whole month, "expect—much—rain—about—this—time!"

I was dreadfully hipped. The hours seemed as if they would never creep by. The very ticking of the clock became irksome. At length the stillness of the house was interrupted by the ringing of a bell. Shortly after I heard the voice of a waiter at the bar: "The stout gentleman in No. 13 wants his breakfast. Tea and bread and butter, with ham and eggs; the eggs not to be too much done."

In such a situation as mine every incident is of importance. Here was a subject of speculation presented to my mind, and ample exercise for my imagination. I am prone to paint pictures to myself, and on this occasion I had some materials to work upon. Had the guest up-stairs been mentioned as Mr. Smith, or Mr. Brown, or Mr. Jackson, or Mr. Johnson, or merely as "the gentleman in No. 13," it would have been a perfect blank to me. I should have thought nothing of it; but "The stout gentleman!"— the very name had something in it of the picturesque. It at once gave the size; it embodied the personage to my mind's eye, and my fancy did the rest.

He was stout, or, as some term it, lusty; in all probability, therefore, he was advanced in life, some people expanding as they grow old. By his breakfasting rather late, and in his own room, he must be a man accustomed to live at his ease, and above the necessity of early rising; no doubt a round, rosy, lusty old gentleman.

There was another violent ringing. The stout gentleman was impatient for his breakfast. He was evidently a man of importance: "well to do in the world"; accustomed to be promptly waited upon; of a keen appetite, and a little cross when hungry; "perhaps," thought I, "he may be some London Alderman; or who knows but he may be a Member of Parliament?" The breakfast was sent up, and there was a short interval of silence; he was, doubtless, making the tea. Presently there was a violent ringing; and before it could be answered, another ringing still more violent. "Bless me! what a choleric old gentleman!" The waiter came down in a huff. The butter was rancid, the eggs were overdone, the ham was too salt;—the stout gentleman was evidently nice in his eating; one of those who eat and growl, and keep the waiter on the trot, and live in a state militant with the household.

The hostess got into a fume. I should observe that she was a brisk, coquettish woman; a little of a shrew, and something of a slammerkin, but very pretty withal; with a nincompoop for a husband, as shrews are apt to have. She rated the servants roundly for their negligence in sending up so bad a breakfast, but said not a word against the stout gentleman; by which I clearly perceived that he must be a man of consequence, entitled to make a noise and to give trouble at a country inn. Other eggs, and ham, and bread and butter were sent up. They appeared to be more graciously received; at least there was no further complaint.

I had not made many turns about the travelers'-room, when there was another ringing. Shortly afterwards there was a stir and an inquest about the house. The stout gentleman wanted the "Times" or the "Chronicle" newspaper. I set him down, therefore, for a Whig; or rather, from his being so absolute and lordly where he had a chance, I suspected him of being a Radical. Hunt, I had heard, was a large man; "who knows," thought I, "but it is Hunt himself!"

My curiosity began to be awakened. I inquired of the waiter who was this stout gentleman that was making all this stir; but I could get no information; nobody seemed to know his name. The landlords of bustling inns seldom trouble their heads about the names or occupations of their transient guests. The color of a coat, the shape or size of the person, is enough to suggest a traveling name. It is either the tall gentleman, or the short gentleman, or the gentleman in black, or the gentleman in snuff-color; or, as in the present instance, the stout gentleman. A designation of the kind once hit on answers every purpose, and saves all further inquiry.

Rain—rain—rain! pitiless, ceaseless rain! No such thing as putting a foot out of doors, and no occupation nor amusement within. By and by I heard some one walking overhead. It was in the stout gentleman's room. He evidently was a large man by the heaviness of his tread; and an old man from his wearing such creaking soles. "He is doubtless," thought I, "some rich old square-toes of regular habits, and is now taking exercise after breakfast."

I now read all the advertisements of coaches and hotels that were stuck about the mantel-piece. The "Lady's Magazine" had become an abomination to me; it was as tedious as the day itself. I wandered out, not knowing what to do, and ascended again to my room. I had not been there long, when there was a squall from a neighboring bedroom. A door opened and slammed violently; a chambermaid, that I had remarked for having a ruddy, good-humored face, went down-stairs in a violent flurry. The stout gentleman had been rude to her!

This sent a whole host of my deductions to the deuce in a moment. This unknown personage could not be an old gentleman; for old gentlemen are not apt to be so obstreperous to chambermaids. He could not be a young gentleman; for young gentlemen are not apt to inspire such indignation. He must be a middle-aged man, and confounded ugly into the bargain, or the girl would not have taken the matter in such terrible dudgeon. I confess I was sorely puzzled.

In a few minutes I heard the voice of my landlady. I caught a glance of her as she came tramping up-stairs,—her face glowing, her cap flaring, her tongue wagging the whole way. "She'd have no such doings in her house, she'd warrant. If gentlemen did spend money freely, it was no rule. She'd have no servant-maids of hers treated in that way, when they were about their work, that's what she wouldn't."

As I hate squabbles, particularly with women, and above all with pretty women, I slunk back into my room, and partly closed the door; but my curiosity was too much excited not to listen. The landlady marched intrepidly to the enemy's citadel, and entered it with a storm: the door closed after her. I heard her voice in high windy clamor for a moment or two. Then it gradually subsided, like a gust of wind in a garret; then there was a laugh; then I heard nothing more.

After a little while my landlady came out with an odd smile on her face, adjusting her cap, which was a little on one side. As she went down-stairs I heard the landlord ask her what was the matter; she said, "Nothing at all, only the girl's a fool."—I was more than ever perplexed what to make of this unaccountable personage, who could put a good-natured chamber-maid in a passion, and send away a termagant landlady in smiles. He could not be so old, nor cross, nor ugly either.

I had to go to work at his picture again, and to paint him entirely different. I now set him down for one of those stout gentlemen that are frequently met with swaggering about the doors of country inns. Moist, merry fellows, in Belcher handkerchiefs, whose bulk is a little assisted by malt-liquors. Men who have seen the world, and been sworn at Highgate; who are used to tavern life; up to all the tricks of tapsters, and knowing in the ways of sinful publicans. Free-livers on a small scale; who are prodigal within the compass of a guinea; who call all the waiters by name, touzle the maids, gossip with the landlady at the bar, and prose over a pint of port, or a glass of negus, after dinner.

The morning wore away in forming these and similar surmises. As fast as I wove one system of belief, some movement of the unknown would completely overturn it, and throw all my thoughts again into confusion. Such are the solitary operations of a feverish mind. I was, as I have said, extremely nervous; and the continual meditation on the concerns of this invisible personage began to have its effect:—I was getting a fit of the fidgets.

Dinner-time came. I hoped the stout gentleman might dine in the travelers'-room, and that I might at length get a view of his person; but no—he had dinner served in his own room. What could be the meaning of this solitude and mystery? He could not be a radical; there was something too aristocratical in thus keeping himself apart from the rest of the world, and condemning himself to his own dull company throughout a rainy day. And then, too, he lived too well for a discontented politician. He seemed to expatiate on a variety of dishes, and to sit over his wine like a jolly friend of good living. Indeed, my doubts on this head were soon at an end; for he could not have finished his first bottle before I could faintly hear him humming a tune; and on listening, I found it to be "God save the King." 'Twas plain, then, he was no radical, but a faithful subject; one who grew loyal over his bottle, and was ready to stand by king and constitution, when he could stand by nothing else. But who could he be? My conjectures began to run wild. Was he not some personage of distinction traveling incog.? "God knows" said I, at my wit's end; "it may be one of the royal family for aught I know, for they are all stout gentlemen!"

The weather continued rainy. The mysterious unknown kept to his room, and, as far as I could judge, his chair, for I did not hear him move. In the meantime, as the day advanced, the travelers'-room began to be frequented. Some, who had just arrived, came in buttoned up in box-coats; others came home who had been dispersed about the town; some took their dinners, and some their tea. Had I been in a different mood, I should have found entertainment in studying this peculiar class of men. There were two especially, who were regular wags of the road, and up to all the standing jokes of travelers. They had a thousand sly things to say to the waiting-maid, whom they called Louisa, and Ethelinda, and a dozen other fine names, changing the name every time, and chuckling amazingly at their own waggery. My mind, however, had become completely engrossed by the stout gentleman. He had kept my fancy in chase during a long day, and it was not now to be diverted from the scent.

The evening gradually wore away. The travelers read the papers two or three times over. Some drew round the fire and told long stories about their horses, about their adventures, their over-turns, and breakings-down. They discussed the credit of different merchants and different inns; and the two wags told several choice anecdotes of pretty chambermaids, and kind landladies. All this passed as they were quietly taking what they called their night-caps, that is to say, strong glasses of brandy and water and sugar, or some other mixture of the kind; after which they one after another rang for "Boots" and the chambermaid, and walked off to bed in old shoes cut down into marvelously uncomfortable slippers.

There was now only one man left: a short-legged, long-bodied, plethoric fellow, with a very large, sandy head. He sat by himself, with a glass of port-wine negus, and a spoon; sipping and stirring, and meditating and sipping, until nothing was left but the spoon. He gradually fell asleep bolt upright in his chair, with the empty glass standing before him; and the candle seemed to fall asleep too, for the wick grew long, and black, and cabbaged at the end, and dimmed the little light that remained in the chamber. The gloom that now prevailed was contagious. Around hung the shapeless, and almost spectral, box-coats of departed travelers, long since buried in deep sleep. I only heard the ticking of the clock, with the deep-drawn breathings of the sleeping topers, and the drippings of the rain, drop—drop—drop, from the eaves of the house. The church-bells chimed midnight. All at once the stout gentleman began to walk overhead, pacing slowly backwards and forwards. There was something extremely awful in all this, especially to one in my state of nerves. These ghastly great-coats, these gutteral breathings, and the creaking footsteps of this mysterious being. His steps grew fainter and fainter, and at length died away. I could bear it no longer. I was wound up to the desperation of a hero of romance. "Be he who or what he may," said I to myself, "I'll have a sight of him!" I seized a chamber-candle, and hurried up to No. 13. The door stood ajar. I hesitated—I entered: the room was deserted. There stood a large, broad-bottomed elbow-chair at a table, on which was an empty tumbler, and a "Times" newspaper, and the room smelt powerfully of Stilton cheese.

The mysterious stranger had evidently but just retired. I turned off, sorely disappointed, to my room, which had been changed to the front of the house. As I went along the corridor, I saw a large pair of boots, with dirty, waxed tops, standing at the door of a bed-chamber. They doubtless belonged to the unknown; but it would not do to disturb so redoubtable a personage in his den; he might discharge a pistol, or something worse, at my head. I went to bed, therefore, and lay awake half the night in a terribly nervous state; and even when I fell asleep, I was still haunted in my dreams by the idea of the stout gentleman and his wax-topped boots.

I slept rather late the next morning, and was awakened by some stir and bustle in the house, which I could not at first comprehend; until getting more awake, I found there was a mail-coach starting from the door. Suddenly there was a cry from below, "The gentleman has forgot his umbrella! look for the gentleman's umbrella in No. 13!" I heard an immediate scampering of a chambermaid along the passage, and a shrill reply as she ran, "Here it is! here's the gentleman's umbrella!"

The mysterious stranger then was on the point of setting off. This was the only chance I should ever have of knowing him. I sprang out of bed, scrambled to the window, snatched aside the curtains, and just caught a glimpse of the rear of a person getting in at the coach-door. The skirts of a brown coat parted behind, and gave me a full view of the broad disk of a pair of drab breeches. The door closed—"all right!" was the word—the coach whirled off;—and that was all I ever saw of the stout gentleman!

PALACE OF THE ALHAMBRA [6]

To the traveler imbued with a feeling for the historical and poetical, so inseparably intertwined in the annals of romantic Spain, the Alhambra is as much an object of devotion as is the Caaba to all true Moslems. How many legends and traditions, true and fabulous,—how many songs and ballads, Arabian and Spanish, of love and war and chivalry, are associated with this Oriental pile! It was the royal abode of the Moorish kings, where, surrounded with the splendors and refinements of Asiatic luxury, they held dominion over what they vaunted as a terrestrial paradise, and made their last stand for empire in Spain. The royal palace forms but a part of a fortress, the walls of which, studded with towers, stretch irregularly round the whole crest of a hill, a spur of the Sierra Nevada or Snowy Mountains, and overlook the city; externally it is a rude congregation of towers and battlements, with no regularity of plan nor grace of architecture, and giving little promise of the grace and beauty which prevail within.

In the time of the Moors the fortress was capable of containing within its outward precincts an army of forty thousand men, and served occasionally as a stronghold of the sovereigns against their rebellious subjects. After the kingdom had passed into the hands of the Christians, the Alhambra continued to be a royal demesne, and was occasionally inhabited by the Castilian monarchs. The emperor Charles V commenced a sumptuous palace within its walls, but was deterred from completing it by repeated shocks of earthquakes. The last royal residents were Philip V and his beautiful queen, Elizabetta of Parma, early in the eighteenth century. Great preparations were made for their reception. The palace and gardens were placed in a state of repair, and a new suite of apartments erected, and decorated by artists brought from Italy. The sojourn of the sovereigns was transient, and after their departure the palace once more became desolate. Still the place was maintained with some military state. The governor held it immediately from the crown, its jurisdiction extended down into the suburbs of the city, and was independent of the captain-general of Granada. A considerable garrison was kept up; the governor had his apartments in the front of the old Moorish palace, and never descended into Granada without some military parade. The fortress, in fact, was a little town of itself, having several streets of houses within its walls, together with a Franciscan convent and a parochial church.

The desertion of the court, however, was a fatal blow to the Alhambra. Its beautiful halls became desolate, and some of them fell to ruin; the gardens were destroyed, and the fountains ceased to play. By degrees the

[6] From *The Alhambra* (1832). "Rough drafts of some of the following tales and essays were actually written during a residence in the Alhambra; others were subsequently added, founded on notes and observations made there."—*Irving's Preface* (1851).

dwellings became filled with a loose and lawless population: *contrabandistas,* who availed themselves of its independent jurisdiction to carry on a wide and daring course of smuggling, and thieves and rogues of all sorts, who made this their place of refuge whence they might depredate upon Granada and its vicinity. The strong arm of government at length interfered; the whole community was thoroughly sifted; none were suffered to remain but such as were of honest character, and had legitimate right to a residence; the greater part of the houses were demolished and a mere hamlet left, with the parochial church and the Franciscan convent. During the recent troubles in Spain, when Granada was in the hands of the French, the Alhambra was garrisoned by their troops, and the palace was occasionally inhabited by the French commander. With that enlightened taste which has ever distinguished the French nation in their conquests, this monument of Moorish elegance and grandeur was rescued from the absolute ruin and desolation that were overwhelming it. The roofs were repaired, the saloons and galleries protected from the weather, the gardens cultivated, the water-courses restored, the fountains once more made to throw up their sparkling showers; and Spain may thank her invaders for having preserved to her the most beautiful and interesting of her historical monuments.

On the departure of the French they blew up several towers of the outer wall, and left the fortifications scarcely tenable. Since that time the military importance of the post is at an end. The garrison is a handful of invalid soldiers, whose principal duty is to guard some of the outer towers, which serve occasionally as a prison of state; and the governor, abandoning the lofty hill of the Alhambra, resides in the center of Granada, for the more convenient dispatch of his official duties. I cannot conclude this brief notice of the state of the fortress without bearing testimony to the honorable exertions of its present commander, Don Francisco de Serna, who is tasking all the limited resources at his command to put the palace in a state of repair, and by his judicious precautions has for some time arrested its too certain decay. Had his predecessors discharged the duties of their station with equal fidelity, the Alhambra might yet have remained in almost its pristine beauty; were government to second him with means equal to his zeal, this relic of it might still be preserved for many generations to adorn the land, and attract the curious and enlightened of every clime.

Our first object, of course, on the morning after our arrival, was a visit to this time-honored edifice; it has been so often, however, and so minutely described by travelers, that I shall not undertake to give a comprehensive and elaborate account of it, but merely occasional sketches of parts, with the incidents and associations connected with them.

Leaving our *posada,* and traversing the renowned square of the Vivarrambla, once the scene of Moorish jousts and tournaments, now a crowded market-place, we proceeded along the Zacatin, the main street of what, in the time of the Moors, was the Great Bazaar, and where small shops and narrow alleys still retain the Oriental character. Crossing an open place in front of the palace of the captain-general, we ascended a confined and winding street, the name of which reminded us of the chivalric days of Granada. It is called the Calle, or street of the Gomeres, from a Moorish family fa-- mous in chronicle and song. This street led up to the Puerta de las Granadas, a massive gateway of Grecian architecture, built by Charles V, forming the entrance to the domains of the Alhambra.

At the gate were two or three ragged superannuated soldiers, dozing on a stone bench, the successors of the Zegris and the Abencerrages; [7] while a tall, meager varlet, whose rusty-brown cloak was evidently intended to conceal the ragged state of his nether garments, was lounging in the sunshine and gossiping with an ancient sentinel on duty. He joined us as we entered the gate, and offered his services to show us the fortress.

I have a traveler's dislike to officious ciceroni, and did not altogether like the garb of the applicant.

"You are well acquainted with the place, I presume?"

"Ninguno mas; pues, señor, soy hijo de la Alhambra."—(Nobody better; in fact, sir, I am a son of the Alhambra!)

The common Spaniards have certainly a most poetic way of expressing themselves. "A son of the Alhambra!"—the appellation caught me at once; the very tattered garb of my new acquaintance assumed a dignity in my eyes. It was emblematic of the fortunes of the place, and befitted the progeny of a ruin.

I put some further questions to him, and found that his title was legitimate. His family had lived in the fortress from generation to generation ever since the time of the Conquest. His name was Mateo Ximenes. "Then, perhaps," said I, "you may be a descendant from the great Cardinal Ximenes?" "Dios sabe! God knows, señor! It may be so. We are the oldest family in the Alhambra,—Christianos viejos, old Christians, without any taint of Moor or Jew. I know we belong to some great family or other, but I forget whom. My father knows all about it; he has the coat-of-arms hanging up in his cottage, up in the fortress." There is not any Spaniard, however poor, but has some claim to high pedigree. The first title of this ragged worthy, however, had completely captivated me; so I gladly accepted the services of the "son of the Alhambra."

We now found ourselves in a deep, narrow ravine, filled with beautiful groves, with a steep avenue, and various footpaths winding through it, bordered with stone seats, and ornamented with fountains. To our left we

---

[7] Two Moorish families, traditionally hostile to each other.

beheld the towers of the Alhambra beetling above us; to our right, on the opposite side of the ravine, we were equally dominated by rival towers on a rocky eminence. These, we were told, were the *torres bermejas,* or vermilion towers, so called from their ruddy hue. No one knows their origin. They are of a date much anterior to the Alhambra: some suppose them to have been built by the Romans; others, by some wandering colony of Phœnicians. Ascending the steep and shady avenue, we arrived at the foot of a huge square Moorish tower, forming a kind of barbican, through which passed the main entrance to the fortress. Within the barbican was another group of veteran invalids, one mounting guard at the portal, while the rest, wrapped in their tattered cloaks, slept on the stone benches. This portal is called the Gate of Justice, from the tribunal held within its porch during the Moslem domination, for the immediate trial of petty causes—a custom common to the Oriental nations, and occasionally alluded to in the sacred Scriptures. "Judges and officers shalt thou make thee *in all thy gates,* and they shall judge the people with just judgment."

The great vestibule, or porch of the gate, is formed by an immense Arabian arch, of the horseshoe form, which springs to half the height of the tower. On the keystone of this arch is engraven a gigantic hand. Within the vestibule, on the keystone of the portal, is sculptured, in like manner, a gigantic key. Those who pretend to some knowledge of Mohammedan symbols affirm that the hand is the emblem of doctrine, the five fingers designating the five principal commandments of the creed of Islam, fasting, pilgrimage, almsgiving, ablution, and war against infidels. The key, say they, is the emblem of the faith or of power; the key of Daoud, or David, transmitted to the prophet. "And the key of the house of David will I lay upon his shoulder; so he shall open and none shall shut, and he shall shut and none shall open." (Isaiah, xxii, 22.) The key we are told was emblazoned on the standard of the Moslems in opposition to the Christian emblem of the cross, when they subdued Spain or Andalusia. It betokened the conquering power invested in the prophet. "He that hath the key of David, he that openeth and no man shutteth; and shutteth and no man openeth." (Revelation, iii, 7.)

A different explanation of these emblems, however, was given by the legitimate son of the Alhambra, and one more in unison with the notions of the common people, who attach something of mystery and magic to everything Moorish, and have all kinds of superstitions connected with this old Moslem fortress. According to Mateo, it was a tradition handed down from the oldest inhabitants, and which he had from his father and grandfather, that the hand and key were magical devices on which the fate of the Alhambra depended. The Moorish king who built it was a great magician, or, as some believed, had sold himself to the devil, and had laid the whole fortress under a magic spell. By this means it had remained standing for several years, in defiance of storms and earthquakes, while almost all other buildings of the Moors had fallen to ruin and disappeared. This spell, the tradition went on to say, would last until the hand on the outer arch should reach down and grasp the key, when the whole pile would tumble to pieces, and all the treasures buried beneath it by the Moors would be revealed.

Notwithstanding this ominous prediction, we ventured to pass through the spellbound gateway, feeling some little assurance against magic art in the protection of the Virgin, a statue of whom we observed above the portal.

After passing through the barbican, we ascended a narrow lane, winding between walls, and came on an open esplanade within the fortress, called the Plaza de los Algibes, or Place of the Cisterns, from great reservoirs which undermine it, cut in the living rock by the Moors to receive the water brought by conduits from the Darro, for the supply of the fortress. Here, also, is a well of immense depth, furnishing the purest and coldest of water, —another monument of the delicate taste of the Moors, who were indefatigable in their exertions to obtain that element in its crystal purity.

In front of this esplanade is the splendid pile commenced by Charles V, and intended, it is said, to eclipse the residence of the Moorish kings. Much of the Oriental edifice intended for the winter season was demolished to make way for this massive pile. The grand entrance was blocked up; so that the present entrance to the Moorish palace is through a simple and almost humble portal in a corner. With all the massive grandeur and architectural merit of the palace of Charles V, we regarded it as an arrogant intruder, and, passing by it with a feeling almost of scorn, rang at the Moslem portal.

While waiting for admittance, our self-imposed cicerone, Mateo Ximenes, informed us that the royal palace was entrusted to the care of a worthy old maiden dame called Doña Antonia-Molina, but who, according to Spanish custom, went by the more neighborly appellation of Tia Antonia (Aunt Antonia), who maintained the Moorish halls and gardens in order and showed them to strangers. While we were talking, the door was opened by a plump little black-eyed Andalusian damsel, whom Mateo addressed as Dolores, but who, from her bright looks and cheerful disposition, evidently merited a merrier name. Mateo informed me in a whisper that she was the niece of Tia Antonia, and I found she was the good fairy who was to conduct us through the enchanted palace. Under her guidance we crossed the threshold, and were at once transported, as if by magic wand, into other times and an Oriental realm, and were treading the scenes of Arabian story. Nothing could be in greater contrast than the unpromising exterior of the pile with the scene now before us. We found ourselves in a vast *patio,* or court, one hundred and fifty feet in length, and upwards of eighty feet in breadth, paved with white marble, and decorated at each end with light Moorish peristyles, one of which supported an elegant gallery of fretted architecture. Along the moldings of the cornices and on various parts of the walls were escutcheons and ciphers, and cufic and Arabic characters in high relief, repeating the pious mottoes of the Moslem monarchs, the builders of the Alhambra, or extolling their grandeur and munificence. Along the center of the court extended an immense basin or tank (*estanque*), a hundred and twenty-four feet in length, twenty-seven in breadth, and five in depth, receiving its water from two marble vases. Hence it is called the Court of the Alberca (from *al beerkah,* the Arabic for a pond or tank). Great numbers of gold-fish were to be seen gleaming through the waters of the basin, and it was bordered by hedges of roses.

Passing from the Court of the Alberca under a Moorish archway, we entered the renowned Court of Lions. No part of the edifice gives a more complete idea of its original beauty than this, for none has suffered so little from the ravages of time. In the center stands the fountain famous in song and story. The alabaster basins still shed their diamond drops; the twelve lions which support them, and give the court its name, still cast forth crystal streams as in the days of Boabdil. The lions, however, are unworthy of their fame, being of miserable sculpture, the work probably of some Christian captive. The court is laid out in flower-beds, instead of its ancient and appropriate pavement of tiles or marble; the alteration, an instance of bad taste, was made by the French when in possession of Granada. Round the four sides of the court are light Arabian arcades of open filigree work, supported by slender pillars of white marble, which it is supposed were originally gilded. The architecture, like that in most parts of the interior of the palace, is characterized by elegance rather than grandeur, bespeaking a delicate and graceful taste, and a disposition to indolent enjoyment. When one looks upon the fairy traces of the peristyles, and the apparently fragile fretwork of the walls, it is difficult to believe that so much has survived the wear and tear of centuries, the shocks of earthquakes, the violence of war, and the quiet, though no less baneful, pilferings of the tasteful traveler: it is almost sufficient to excuse the popular tradition that the whole is protected by a magic charm.

On one side of the court a rich portal opens into the Hall of the Abencerrages: so called from the gallant cavaliers of that illustrious line who were here perfidiously massacred. There are some who doubt the whole story, but our humble cicerone Mateo pointed out the very wicket of the portal through which they were introduced one by one into the Court of Lions, and the white marble fountain in the center of the hall beside which they were beheaded. He showed us also certain broad ruddy stains on the pavement, traces of their blood, which, according to popular belief, can never be effaced.

Finding we listened to him apparently with easy faith, he added that there was often heard at night, in the Court of Lions, a low confused sound, resembling the murmuring of a multitude; and now and then a faint tinkling, like the distant clank of chains. These sounds were made by the spirits of the murdered Abencerrages; who nightly haunt the scene of their suffering and invoke the vengeance of Heaven on their destroyer.

The sounds in question had no doubt been produced, as I had afterwards an opportunity of ascertaining, by the bubbling currents and tinkling falls of water conducted under the pavement through pipes and channels to supply the fountains; but I was too considerate to intimate such an idea to the humble chronicler of the Alhambra.

Encouraged by my easy credulity, Mateo gave me the following as an undoubted fact, which he had from his grandfather:

There was once an invalid soldier, who had charge of the Alhambra to show it to strangers; as he was one evening, about twilight, passing through the Court of Lions, he heard footsteps on the Hall of the Abencerrages; supposing some strangers to be lingering there, he advanced to attend upon them, when to his astonishment he beheld four Moors richly dressed, with gilded cuirasses and scimitars, and poniards glittering with precious stones. They were walking to and fro, with solemn pace; but paused and beckoned to him. The old soldier, however, took to flight, and could never afterwards be prevailed upon to enter the Alhambra. Thus it is that men sometimes turn their backs upon fortune; for it is the firm opinion of Mateo that the Moors intended to reveal the place where their treasures lay buried. A successor to the invalid soldier was more knowing; he came to the Alhambra poor; but at the end of a year went off to Malaga, bought houses, set up a carriage, and still lives there, one of the richest as well as oldest men of the place; all which, Mateo sagely surmised, was in consequence of his finding out the golden secret of these phantom Moors.

I now perceived I had made an invaluable acquaintance in this son of the Alhambra, one who knew all the apocryphal history of the place, and firmly believed in it, and whose memory was stuffed with a kind of knowledge for which I have a lurking fancy, but which is too apt to be considered rubbish by less indulgent philosophers. I determined to cultivate the acquaintance of this learned Theban.

Immediately opposite the Hall of the Abencerrages, a portal, richly adorned, leads into a hall of less tragical associations. It is light and lofty, exquisitely graceful in its architecture, paved with white marble, and bears the suggestive name of the Hall of the Two Sisters. Some destroy the romance of the name by attributing it to two enormous slabs of alabaster which lie side by side, and form a great part of the pavement: an opinion strongly supported by Mateo Ximenes. Others are disposed to give the name a more poetical significance, as the vague memorial of Moorish beauties who once graced this hall, which was evidently a part of the royal harem. This opinion I was happy to find entertained by our little bright-eyed guide, Dolores, who pointed to a balcony over an inner porch; which gallery, she had been told, belonged to the women's apartment. "You see, señor," said she, "it is all grated and latticed, like the gallery in a convent chapel where the nuns hear mass; for the Moorish kings," added she, indignantly, "shut up their wives just like nuns."

The latticed jalousies, in fact, still remain, whence the dark-eyed beauties of the harem might gaze unseen upon the *zambras* and other dances and entertainments of the hall below.

On each side of this hall are recesses or alcoves for ottomans and couches, on which the voluptuous lords of the Alhambra indulged in that dreamy repose so dear to the Orientalists. A cupola or lantern admits a tempered light from above and a free circulation of air; while on one side is heard the refreshing sound of waters from the Fountain of the Lions, and on the other side the soft plash from the basin in the garden of Lindaraxa.

It is impossible to contemplate this scene, so perfectly Oriental, without feeling the early associations of Arabian romance, and almost expecting to see the white arm of some mysterious princess beckoning from the gallery, or some dark eye sparkling through the lattice. The abode of beauty is here as if it had been inhabited but yesterday; but where are the two sisters, where the Zoraydas and Lindaraxas!

An abundant supply of water, brought from the mountains by old Moorish aqueducts, circulates throughout the palace, supplying its baths and fish-pools, sparkling in jets within its halls or murmuring in channels along the marble pavements. When it has paid its tribute to the royal pile, and visited its gardens and parterres, it flows down the long avenue leading to the city, tinkling in rills, gushing in fountains, and maintaining a perpetual verdure in those groves that embower and beautify the whole hill of the Alhambra.

Those only who have sojourned in the ardent climates of the South can appreciate the delights of an abode combining the breezy coolness of the mountain with the freshness and verdure of the valley. While the city below pants with the noontide heat, and the parched Vega trembles to the eye, the delicate airs from the Sierra Nevada play through these lofty halls, bringing with them the sweetness of the surrounding gardens. Everything invites to that indolent repose, the bliss of southern climes; and while the half-shut eye looks out from shaded balconies upon the glittering landscape, the ear is lulled by the rustling of groves and the murmur of running streams.

I forbear for the present, however, to describe the other delightful apartments of the palace. My object is merely to give the reader a general introduction into an abode where, if so disposed, he may linger and loiter with me day by day until we gradually become familiar with all its localities.

JAMES FENIMORE COOPER

THE LAST OF THE MOHICANS

Chapter XXIII

JAMES FENIMORE COOPER

(1789–1851)

Cooper was born in Burlington, New Jersey, in 1789. Fortunately, before he was a year old, his father established himself on a large grant of land in the wilderness of central New York about Lake Otsego; and here, at what became Cooperstown, his boyhood was spent. Like Irving he owed less to his education, which ended at sixteen with his "dismissal" from Yale for "participation in a frolic," than to other and more fortunate experiences. At Cooperstown he saw the frontier. Sailing "before the mast" on a merchant vessel and serving as midshipman in the navy, he saw the sea. Settling after his marriage and retirement from the navy in Westchester County, he grew familiar with a region—the "neutral ground"—hotly contested during the Revolution. Thus unconsciously he prepared himself for writing the three kinds of fiction in which he was to excel. Though drawn accidentally into authorship he was a born story-teller, and he wrote rapidly his first historical novel in *The Spy* (1821), his first romance of the frontier in *The Pioneers* (1823), and his first story of the sea in *The Pilot* (1824). These being unexpectedly successful, he developed Leatherstocking, his first frontier character, in *The Last of the Mohicans* (1826) and *The Prairie* (1827). Late in his life he added the two stories which, probably without much foresight on their author's part, complete the famous "Leatherstocking Series,"—*The Pathfinder* (1840), and *The Deerslayer* (1841). Meanwhile he had written another capital sea story in *The Red Rover* (1828). Though he wrote more than thirty novels, on the eight just mentioned his reputation rests. He died at Cooperstown in 1851.

In each of his three favorite kinds of romance Cooper was a creator. In *The Spy* he wrote the first American novel of lasting interest, and in its hero, Harvey Birch, he drew our first great fictional character. In *The Pilot* he produced a sea story technically correct even from the point of view of Long Tom Coffin, the Nantucket sailor who is its hero, and put into it the very odor of the sea. In the series which covers the life of Leatherstocking from his youth on the shores of Lake Otsego early in the eighteenth century to his death on the western prairies early in the nineteenth, he covers symbolically the life of America during the same period. Cooper's greatest creation, the courageous, unwearied, and resourceful Leatherstocking, typifies the American frontiersman and his conquest of the continent in the face of physical difficulty and Indian hostility. It is a truly epic theme with a worthy hero.

Obviously so large a work cannot be adequately represented in this book. The chapter following, however, is typical of Cooper's style and method.

THE LAST OF THE MOHICANS [1]

CHAPTER XXIII

IT is unusual to find an encampment of the natives, like those of the more instructed whites, guarded by the presence of armed men. Well informed of the approach of every danger, while it is yet at a distance, the Indian generally rests secure under his knowledge of the signs of the forest, and the long and difficult paths that separate him from those he has most reason to dread. But the enemy who, by any lucky concurrence of accidents, has found means to elude the vigilance of the scouts, will seldom meet with sentinels nearer home to sound the alarm. In addition to this general usage, the tribes friendly to the French knew too well the weight of the blow that had just been struck, to apprehend any immediate danger from the hostile nations that were tributary to the crown of Britain.

When Duncan and David, therefore, found themselves in the centre of the children, who played the antics already mentioned, it was without the least previous intimation of their approach. But so soon as they were observed the whole of the juvenile pack raised, by common consent, a shrill and warning whoop; and then sank, as it were, by magic, from before the sight of their visitors. The naked, tawny bodies of the crouching urchins blended so nicely, at that hour, with the withered herbage, that at first it seemed as if the earth had, in truth, swallowed up their forms; though when surprise permitted Duncan to bend his look more curiously about the spot, he found it everywhere met by dark, quick, and rolling eyeballs.

Gathering no encouragement from this startling presage of the nature of the scrutiny he was likely to undergo from the more mature judgments of the men, there was an instant when the young soldier would have retreated. It was, however, too late to appear to hesitate. The cry of the children had drawn a dozen warriors to the door of the nearest lodge, where they stood clustered in a dark and savage group, gravely awaiting the nearer approach of those who had unexpectedly come among them.

David, in some measure familiarized to the scene, led the way with a steadiness that no slight obstacle was likely to disconcert, into this very building. It was the principal edifice of the village, though roughly constructed of the bark and branches of trees; being the lodge in which the tribe held its councils and public meetings during their temporary residence

---

[1] The scene of the story is eastern New York in 1757, during the French and Indian War. Leatherstocking and an English officer, Duncan Heyward, with the friendly Indians Chingachgook and Uncas, have conducted the daughters of Munro, Cora and Alice, through great dangers to their father at Fort William Henry. After the fall of the Fort the girls have been captured and carried off by the hostile Hurons into the Adirondack wilderness. In Chapter XXIII Heyward, who is in love with Alice, enters the Huron village where she is captive, in disguise, accompanied by the witless David; and Uncas, "the last of the Mohicans," is brought in captive.

on the borders of the English province. Duncan found it difficult to assume the necessary appearance of unconcern, as he brushed the dark and powerful frames of the savages who thronged its threshold; but, conscious that his existence depended on his presence of mind, he trusted to the discretion of his companion, whose footsteps he closely followed, endeavoring, as he proceeded, to rally his thoughts for the occasion. His blood curdled when he found himself in absolute contact with such fierce and implacable enemies; but he so far mastered his feelings as to pursue his way into the centre of the lodge, with an exterior that did not betray the weakness. Imitating the example of the deliberate Gamut, he drew a bundle of fragrant brush from beneath a pile that filled the corner of the hut, and seated himself in silence.

So soon as their visitor had passed, the observant warriors fell back from the entrance, and arranging themselves about him, they seemed patiently to await the moment when it might comport with the dignity of the stranger to speak. By far the greater number stood leaning, in lazy, lounging attitudes, against the upright posts that supported the crazy building, while three or four of the oldest and most distinguished of the chiefs placed themselves on the earth a little more in advance.

A flaring torch was burning in the place, and sent its red glare from face to face and figure to figure, as it waved in the currents of air. Duncan profited by its light to read the probable character of his reception, in the countenances of his hosts. But his ingenuity availed him little against the cold artifices of the people he had encountered. The chiefs in front scarce cast a glance at his person, keeping their eyes on the ground, with an air that might have been intended for respect, but which it was quite easy to construe into distrust. The men in shadow were less reserved. Duncan soon detected their searching, but stolen looks, which, in truth, scanned his person and attire inch by inch; leaving no emotion of the countenance, no gesture, no line of the paint, nor even the fashion of a garment, unheeded, and without comment.

At length one whose hair was beginning to be sprinkled with gray, but whose sinewy limbs and firm tread announced that he was still equal to the duties of manhood, advanced out of the gloom of a corner, whither he had probably posted himself to make his observations unseen, and spoke. He used the language of the Wyandots, or Hurons; his words were, consequently, unintelligible to Heyward, though they seemed, by the gestures that accompanied them, to be uttered more in courtesy than anger. The latter shook his head, and made a gesture indicative of his inability to reply.

"Do none of my brothers speak the French or the English?" he said, in the former language, looking about him from countenance to countenance, in hopes of finding a nod of assent.

Though more than one had turned, as if to catch the meaning of his words, they remained unanswered.

"I should be grieved to think," continued Duncan, speaking slowly, and using the simplest French of which he was the master, "to believe that none of this wise and brave nation understand the language that the 'Grand Monarque' uses when he talks to his children. His heart would be heavy did he believe his red warriors paid him so little respect!"

A long and grave pause succeeded, during which no movement of a limb, nor any expression of an eye, betrayed the impression produced by his remark. Duncan, who knew that silence was a virtue among his hosts, gladly had recourse to the custom, in order to arrange his ideas. At length the same warrior who had before addressed him replied, by dryly demanding in the language of the Canadas:

"When our Great Father speaks to his people, is it with the tongue of a Huron?"

"He knows no difference in his children, whether the color of the skin be red, or black, or white," returned Duncan, evasively; "though chiefly is he satisfied with the brave Hurons."

"In what manner will he speak," demanded the wary chief, "when the runners count to him the scalps which five nights ago grew on the heads of the Yengeese?"

"They were his enemies," said Duncan, shuddering involuntarily; "and doubtless, he will say, It is good; my Hurons are very gallant."

"Our Canada father does not think it. Instead of looking forward to reward his Indians, his eyes are turned backward. He sees the dead Yengeese, but no Huron. What can this mean?"

"A great chief, like him, has more thoughts than tongues. He looks to see that no enemies are on his trail."

"The canoe of a dead warrior will not float on the Horican," [2] returned the savage, gloomily. "His ears are open to the Delawares, who are not our friends, and they fill them with lies."

"It cannot be. See; he has bid me, who am a man that knows the art of healing, to go to his children, the red Hurons of the great lakes, and ask if any are sick!"

Another silence succeeded this annunciation of the character Duncan had assumed. Every eye was simultaneously bent on his person, as if to inquire into the truth or falsehood of the declaration, with an intelligence and keenness that caused the subject of their scrutiny to tremble for the result. He was, however, relieved again by the former speaker.

"Do the cunning men of the Canadas paint their skins?" the Huron coldly continued; "we have heard them boast that their faces were pale."

[2] Cooper's "appellation for our finest sheet of water," Lake George.

"When an Indian chief comes among his white fathers," returned Duncan, with great steadiness, "he lays aside his buffalo robe, to carry the shirt that is offered him. My brothers have given me paint, and I wear it."

A low murmur of applause announced that the compliment to the tribe was favorably received. The elderly chief made a gesture of commendation, which was answered by most of his companions, who each threw forth a hand and uttered a brief exclamation of pleasure. Duncan began to breathe more freely, believing that the weight of his examination was past; and as he had already prepared a simple and probable tale to support his pretended occupation, his hopes of ultimate success grew brighter.

After a silence of a few moments, as if adjusting his thoughts, in order to make a suitable answer to the declaration their guest had just given, another warrior arose, and placed himself in an attitude to speak. While his lips were yet in the act of parting, a low but fearful sound arose from the forest, and was immediately succeeded by a high, shrill yell, that was drawn out, until it equalled the longest and most plaintive howl of the wolf. The sudden and terrible interruption caused Duncan to start from his seat, unconscious of everything but the effect produced by so frightful a cry. At the same moment, the warriors glided in a body from the lodge, and the outer air was filled with loud shouts, that nearly drowned those awful sounds, which were still ringing beneath the arches of the woods. Unable to command himself any longer, the youth broke from the place, and presently stood in the centre of a disorderly throng, that included nearly everything having life, within the limits of the encampment. Men, women, and children; the aged, the infirm, the active, and the strong, were alike abroad, some exclaiming aloud, others clapping their hands with a joy that seemed frantic, and all expressing their savage pleasure in some unexpected event. Though astounded, at first, by the uproar, Heyward was soon enabled to find its solution by the scene that followed.

There yet lingered sufficient light in the heavens to exhibit those bright openings among the tree-tops, where different paths left the clearing to enter the depths of the wilderness. Beneath one of them, a line of warriors issued from the woods, and advanced slowly towards the dwellings. One in front bore a short pole, on which, as it afterward appeared, were suspended several human scalps. The startling sounds that Duncan had heard, were what the whites have, not inappropriately, called the "death halloo"; and each repetition of the cry was intended to announce to the tribe the fate of an enemy. Thus far the knowledge of Heyward assisted him in the explanation; and as he now knew that the interruption was caused by the unlooked-for return of a successful war-party, every disagreeable sensation was quieted in inward congratulations, for the opportune relief and insignificance it conferred on himself.

When at the distance of a few hundred feet from the lodges, the newly
arrived warriors halted. Their plaintive and terrific cry, which was intended
to represent equally the wailings of the dead and the triumph of the victors,
had entirely ceased. One of their number now called aloud, in words that
were far from appalling, though not more intelligible to those for whose ears
they were intended, than their expressive yells. It would be difficult to convey a suitable idea of the savage ecstasy with which the news, thus imparted,
was received. The whole encampment, in a moment, became a scene of the
most violent bustle and commotion. The warriors drew their knives, and
flourishing them, they arranged themselves in two lines, forming a lane that
extended from the war-party to the lodges. The squaws seized clubs, axes,
or whatever weapon of offence first offered itself to their hands, and rushed
eagerly to act their part in the cruel game that was at hand. Even the children would not be excluded; but boys, little able to wield the instruments,
tore the tomahawks from the belts of their fathers, and stole into the ranks,
apt imitators of the savage traits exhibited by their parents.

Large piles of brush lay scattered about the clearing, and a wary and aged
squaw was occupied in firing as many as might serve to light the coming
exhibition. As the flame arose, its power exceeded that of the parting day,
and assisted to render objects at the same time more distinct and more hideous. The whole scene formed a striking picture, whose frame was composed
of the dark and tall border of pines. The warriors just arrived were the most
distant figures. A little in advance stood two men, who were apparently
selected from the rest, as the principal actors in what was to follow. The
light was not strong enough to render their features distinct, though it was
quite evident that they were governed by very different emotions. While
one stood erect and firm, prepared to meet his fate like a hero, the other
bowed his head, as if palsied by terror or stricken with shame. The high-
spirited Duncan felt a powerful impulse of admiration and pity towards the
former, though no opportunity could offer to exhibit his generous emotions.
He watched his slightest movement, however, with eager eyes; and as he
traced the fine outline of his admirably proportioned and active frame, he
endeavored to persuade himself that if the powers of man, seconded by such
noble resolution, could bear one harmless through so severe a trial, the youthful captive before him might hope for success in the hazardous race he was
about to run. Insensibly the young man drew nigher to the swarthy lines
of the Hurons, and scarcely breathed, so intense became his interest in the
spectacle. Just then the signal yell was given, and the momentary quiet
which had preceded it was broken by a burst of cries, that far exceeded any
before heard. The most abject of the two victims continued motionless; but
the other bounded from the place at the cry with the activity and swiftness
of a deer. Instead of rushing through the hostile lines, as had been expected,

he just entered the dangerous defile, and before time was given for a single blow, turned short, and leaping the heads of a row of children, he gained at once the exterior and safer side of the formidable array. The artifice was answered by a hundred voices raised in imprecations; and the whole of the excited multitude broke from their order, and spread themselves about the place in wild confusion.

A dozen blazing piles now shed their lurid brightness on the place, which resembled some unhallowed and supernatural arena, in which malicious demons had assembled to act their bloody and lawless rites. The forms in the background looked like unearthly beings, gliding before the eye, and cleaving the air with frantic and unmeaning gestures; while the savage passions of such as passed the flames, were rendered fearfully distinct by the gleams that shot athwart their inflamed visages.

It will easily be understood, that amid such a concourse of vindictive enemies, no breathing time was allowed the fugitive. There was a single moment when it seemed as if he would have reached the forest, but the whole body of his captors threw themselves before him, and drove him back into the centre of his relentless persecutors. Turning like a headed deer, he shot, with the swiftness of an arrow, through a pillar of forked flame, and passing the whole multitude harmless, he appeared on the opposite side of the clearing. Here too he was met and turned by a few of the older and more subtle of the Hurons. Once more he tried the throng, as if seeking safety in its blindness, and then several moments succeeded, during which Duncan believed the active and courageous young stranger was lost.

Nothing could be distinguished but a dark mass of human forms tossed and involved in inexplicable confusion. Arms, gleaming knives, and formidable clubs, appeared above them, but the blows were evidently given at random. The awful effect was heightened by the piercing shrieks of the women and the fierce yells of the warriors. Now and then Duncan caught a glimpse of a light form cleaving the air in some desperate bound, and he rather hoped than believed that the captive yet retained the command of his astonishing powers of activity. Suddenly the multitude rolled backward, and approached the spot where he himself stood. The heavy body in the rear pressed upon the women and children in front, and bore them to the earth. The stranger reappeared in the confusion. Human power could not, however, much longer endure so severe a trial. Of this the captive seemed conscious. Profiting by the momentary opening, he darted from among the warriors, and made a desperate, and what seemed to Duncan a final effort to gain the wood. As if aware that no danger was to be apprehended from the young soldier, the fugitive nearly brushed his person in his flight. A tall and powerful Huron, who had husbanded his forces, pressed close upon his heels, and with an uplifted arm menaced a fatal blow. Duncan thrust forth a foot, and the shock precipitated the eager savage headlong, many feet in advance of his intended victim. Thought itself is not quicker than was the motion with which the latter profited by the advantage; he turned, gleamed like a meteor again before the eyes of Duncan, and at the next moment, when the latter recovered his recollection, and gazed around in quest of the captive, he saw him quietly leaning against a small painted post, which stood before the door of the principal lodge.

Apprehensive that the part he had taken in the escape might prove fatal to himself, Duncan left the place without delay. He followed the crowd, which drew nigh the lodges, gloomy and sullen, like any other multitude that had been disappointed in an execution. Curiosity, or perhaps a better feeling, induced him to approach the stranger. He found him, standing with one arm cast about the protecting post, and breathing thick and hard, after his exertions, but disdaining to permit a single sign of suffering to escape. His person was now protected by immemorial and sacred usage, until the tribe in council had deliberated and determined on his fate. It was not difficult, however, to foretell the result, if any presage could be drawn from the feelings of those who crowded the place.

There was no term of abuse known to the Huron vocabulary that the disappointed women did not lavishly expend on the successful stranger. They flouted at his efforts, and told him, with bitter scoffs, that his feet were better than his hands; and that he merited wings, while he knew not the use of an arrow or a knife. To all this the captive made no reply; but was content to preserve an attitude in which dignity was singularly blended with disdain. Exasperated as much by his composure as by his good-fortune, their words became unintelligible, and were succeeded by shrill, piercing yells. Just then the crafty squaw, who had taken the necessary precaution to fire the piles, made her way through the throng, and cleared a place for herself in front of the captive. The squalid and withered person of this hag might well have obtained for her the character of possessing more than human cunning. Throwing back her light vestment, she stretched forth her long skinny arm, in derision, and using the language of the Lenape, as more intelligible to the subject of her gibes, she commenced aloud:

"Look you, Delaware!" she said, snapping her fingers in his face; "your nation is a race of women, and the hoe is better fitted to your hands than the gun. Your squaws are the mothers of deer; but if a bear, or a wildcat or a serpent were born among you, ye would flee. The Huron girls shall make you petticoats, and we will find you a husband."

A burst of savage laughter succeeded this attack, during which the soft and musical merriment of the younger females strangely chimed with the cracked voice of their older and more malignant companion. But the stranger was superior to all their efforts. His head was immovable; nor did he betray the slightest consciousness that any were present, except when his haughty eye rolled toward the dusky forms of the warriors, who stalked in the background, silent and sullen observers of the scene.

Infuriated at the self-command of the captive, the woman placed her arms akimbo; and throwing herself into a posture of defiance, she broke out anew, in a torrent of words that no art of ours could commit successfully to paper. Her breath was, however, expended in vain; for although distinguished in her nation as a proficient in the art of abuse, she was permitted to work herself into such a fury as actually to foam at the mouth, without causing a muscle to vibrate in the motionless figure of the stranger. The effect of his indifference began to extend itself to the other spectators; and a youngster, who was just quitting the condition of a boy, to enter the state of manhood, attempted to assist the termagant, by flourishing his tomahawk before their victim, and adding his empty boasts to the taunts of the woman. Then, indeed, the captive turned his face towards the light, and looked down on the stripling with an expression that was superior to contempt. At the next moment he resumed his quiet and reclining attitude against the post. But the change of posture had permitted Duncan to exchange glances with the firm and piercing eyes of Uncas.

Breathless with amazement, and heavily oppressed with the critical situation of his friend, Heyward recoiled before the look, trembling lest its meaning might, in some unknown manner, hasten the prisoner's fate. There was not, however, any instant cause for such an apprehension. Just then a warrior forced his way into the exasperated crowd. Motioning the woman and children aside with a stern gesture, he took Uncas by the arm, and led him towards the door of the council lodge. Thither all the chiefs, and most of the distinguished warriors, followed; among whom the anxious Heyward found means to enter without attracting any dangerous attention to himself.

A few minutes were consumed in disposing of those present in a manner suitable to their rank and influence in the tribe. An order very similar to that adopted in the preceding interview was observed; the aged and superior chiefs occupying the area of the spacious apartment, within the powerful light of a glaring torch, while their juniors and inferiors were arranged in the background, presenting a dark outline of swarthy and marked visages. In the very centre of the lodge, immediately under an opening that admitted the twinkling light of one or two stars, stood Uncas, calm, elevated, and collected. His high and haughty carriage was not lost on his captors, who often bent their looks on his person, with eyes which, while they lost none of their inflexibility of purpose, plainly betrayed their admiration of the stranger's daring.

The case was different with the individual whom Duncan had observed to stand forth with his friend, previously to the desperate trial of speed; and who, instead of joining in the chase, had remained, throughout its turbulent uproar, like a cringing statue, expressive of shame and disgrace. Though not a hand had been extended to greet him, nor yet an eye had condescended to watch his movements, he had also entered the lodge, as though impelled by a fate to whose decrees he submitted, seemingly, without a struggle. Heyward profited by the first opportunity to gaze in his face, secretly apprehensive he might find the features of another acquaintance; but they proved to be those of a stranger, and, what was still more inexplicable, of one who bore all the distinctive marks of a Huron warrior. Instead of mingling with his tribe, however, he sat apart, a solitary being in a multitude, his form shrinking into a crouching and abject attitude, as if anxious to fill as little space as possible. When each individual had taken his proper station, and silence reigned in the place, the gray-haired chief already introduced to the reader spoke aloud, in the language of the Lenni Lenape.

"Delaware," he said, "though one of a nation of women, you have proved yourself a man. I would give you food; but he who eats with a Huron should become his friend. Rest in peace till the morning sun, when our last words shall be spoken."

"Seven nights, and as many summer days, have I fasted on the trail of the Hurons," Uncas coldly replied; "the children of the Lenape know how to travel the path of the just without lingering to eat."

"Two of my young men are in pursuit of your companion," resumed the other, without appearing to regard the boast of his captive; "when they get back, then will our wise men say to you,—'live' or 'die.'"

"Has a Huron no ears?" scornfully exclaimed Uncas; "twice, since he has been your prisoner, has the Delaware heard a gun that he knows. Your young men will never come back!"

A short and sullen pause succeeded this bold assertion. Duncan, who understood the Mohican to allude to the fatal rifle of the scout, bent forward in earnest observation of the effect it might produce on the conquerors; but the chief was content with simply retorting:

"If the Lenape are so skilful, why is one of their bravest warriors here?"

"He followed in the steps of a flying coward, and fell into a snare. The cunning beaver may be caught."

As Uncas thus replied, he pointed with his finger toward the solitary Huron, but without deigning to bestow any other notice on so unworthy an object. The words of the answer and the air of the speaker produced a strong sensation among his auditors. Every eye rolled sullenly towards the individual indicated by the simple gesture, and a low, threatening murmur passed through the crowd. The ominous sounds reached the outer door, and the women and children pressing into the throng, no gap had been left, between shoulder and shoulder, that was not now filled with the dark lineaments of some eager and curious human countenance.

In the meantime, the more aged chiefs, in the centre, communed with each other in short and broken sentences. Not a word was uttered that did not convey the meaning of the speaker, in the simplest and most energetic form. Again, a long and deeply solemn pause took place. It was known, by all present, to be the grave precursor of a weighty and important judgment. They who composed the outer circle of faces were on tiptoe to gaze; and even the culprit for an instant forgot his shame in a deeper emotion, and exposed his abject features, in order to cast an anxious and troubled glance at the dark assemblage of chiefs. The silence was finally broken by the aged warrior so often named. He arose from the earth, and moving past the immovable form of Uncas, placed himself in a dignified attitude before the offender. At that moment, the withered squaw already mentioned moved into the circle, in a slow, sidling sort of a dance, holding the torch, and muttering the indistinct words of what might have been a species of incantation. Though her presence was altogether an intrusion, it was unheeded.

Approaching Uncas, she held the blazing brand in such a manner as to cast its red glare on his person, and to expose the slightest emotion of his countenance. The Mohican maintained his firm and haughty attitude; and his eye, so far from deigning to meet her inquisitive look, dwelt steadily on the distance, as though it penetrated the obstacles which impeded the view and looked into futurity. Satisfied with her examination, she left him, with a slight expression of pleasure, and proceeded to practice the same trying experiment on her delinquent countryman.

The young Huron was in his war paint, and very little of a finely moulded form was concealed by his attire. The light rendered every limb and joint discernible, and Duncan turned away in horror when he saw they were writhing in irrepressible agony. The woman was commencing a low and plaintive howl at the sad and shameful spectacle, when the chief put forth his hand and gently pushed her aside.

"Reed-that-bends," he said, addressing the young culprit by name, and in his proper language, "though the Great Spirit has made you pleasant to the eyes, it would have been better that you had not been born. Your tongue is loud in the village, but in battle it is still. None of my young men strike the tomahawk deeper into the war-post—none of them so lightly on the Yengeese. The enemy know the shape of your back, but they have never seen the color of your eyes. Three times have they called on you to come, and as often did you forget to answer. Your name will never be mentioned again in your tribe—it is already forgotten."

As the chief slowly uttered these words, pausing impressively between each sentence, the culprit raised his face, in deference to the other's rank and years. Shame, horror, and pride struggled in its lineaments. His eye, which was contracted with inward anguish, gleamed on the persons of those whose breath was his fame; and the latter emotion for an instant predominated. He arose to his feet, and baring his bosom, looked steadily on the keen, glittering knife, that was already upheld by his inexorable judge. As the weapon passed slowly into his heart he even smiled, as if in joy at having found death less dreadful than he had anticipated, and fell heavily on his face, at the feet of the rigid and unyielding form of Uncas.

The squaw gave a loud and plaintive yell, dashed the torch to the earth, and buried everything in darkness. The whole shuddering group of spectators glided from the lodge like troubled sprites; and Duncan thought that he and the yet throbbing body of the victim of an Indian judgment had now become its only tenants.

RALPH WALDO EMERSON

(1803–1882)

Emerson, descendant from a long line of New England clergymen and scholars, was born in Boston in 1803, and was educated for the calling to which he seemed destined by his inheritance—at the Boston Latin School, Harvard College, and the Harvard Divinity School. Chosen pastor of the old North Church, now become Unitarian, at the age of twenty-six, he seemed to be taking up his life work; but after three years, finding himself too liberal for the liberals, he "cast behind him all conformity," and resigned his pastorate; only, however, to become a lay preacher,—still wearing the black coat, but preaching from the Lyceum platform instead of the pulpit, and to larger audiences, first in New England and later very widely over the country. Except for these lecture journeys and two trips abroad, he spent the rest of his outwardly uneventful life mainly at Concord, reading in his "idle times," meditating much, and recording his meditations in copious "Journals," which were worked up first into his lectures, and then into his famous essays. Thus, excepting his first modest book, *Nature* (1836), which contains most of his later thought in germ, his *Poems,* and his exposition of England in *English Traits,* his important work is found in his lectures, addresses, and essays. He was at first frowned upon for his non-conformity, but before his death, in 1882, he had proved the validity of self-reliance; he had lived to see his "latent conviction" become the "universal sense."

Readers approaching Emerson sometimes find him difficult, either in his thought or in his style. To his thought, however, the key is presently found in a few simple ideas, which run through all his work. He is of course an idealist. Primary in his thought is *mind,* infinite in divinity, but infinite in man also, for in the universal mind or "oversoul" each man is full sharer; he "is an inlet to the same and to all of the same." Quite secondary in Emerson's conception is *nature;* the world of sense is only the creation, externalization, or expression of the active mind. As we come to know mind through its expression, nature indeed has great significance for us; it teaches and ministers to us in countless ways. But it is only apparent and transitory; the soul is real and eternal. Emerson's two cardinal ideas then are succinctly summed in his own words: "The mind is One, and nature is its correlative." From these the other doctrines—of self-reliance, of revelation, of genius— follow with little difficulty. Unless, indeed, they may be at first obscured by his peculiar but very expressive style. His thought is not logical and continuous, but intuitive; it comes in flashes. Hence he must be read with an alert mind, grasping the thought not so much by sentences as by paragraphs. So read he has been found stimulating by countless readers. Not only in America but over the world he has been the "friend and aider of those who would live in the spirit."

NATURE [1]

III. Beauty

A NOBLER want of man is served by nature, namely, the love of Beauty. The ancient Greeks called the world κόσμος, beauty. Such is the constitution of all things, or such the plastic power of the human eye, that the primary forms, as the sky, the mountain, the tree, the animal, give us a delight *in and for themselves;* a pleasure arising from outline, color, motion, and grouping. This seems partly owing to the eye itself. The eye is the best of artists. By the mutual action of its structure and of the laws of light, perspective is produced, which integrates every mass of objects, of what character soever, into a well colored and shaded globe, so that where the particular objects are mean and unaffecting, the landscape which they compose is round and symmetrical. And as the eye is the best composer, so light is the first of painters. There is no object so foul that intense light will not make beautiful. And the stimulus it affords to the sense, and a sort of infinitude which it hath, like space and time, make all matter gay. Even the corpse has its own beauty. But besides this general grace diffused over nature, almost all the individual forms are agreeable to the eye, as is proved by our endless imitations of some of them, as the acorn, the grape, the pine-cone, the wheat-ear, the egg, the wings and forms of most birds, the lion's claw, the serpent, the butterfly, sea-shells, flames, clouds, buds, leaves, and the forms of many trees, as the palm.

For better consideration, we may distribute the aspects of Beauty in a threefold manner.

1. First, the simple perception of natural forms is a delight. The influence of the forms and actions in nature is so needful to man, that, in its lowest functions, it seems to lie on the confines of commodity and beauty. To the body and mind which have been cramped by noxious work or company, nature is medicinal and restores their tone. The tradesman, the attorney comes out of the din and craft of the street and sees the sky and the woods, and is a man again. In their eternal calm, he finds himself. The health of the eye seems to demand a horizon. We are never tired, so long as we can see far enough.

But in other hours, Nature satisfies by its loveliness, and without any mixture of corporeal benefit. I see the spectacle of morning from the hilltop over against my house, from daybreak to sunrise, with emotions which an angel might share. The long slender bars of cloud float like fishes in the sea of crimson light. From the earth, as a shore, I look out into that silent sea. I seem

---

[1] This, Emerson's first book, published anonymously in 1836, contains his main ideas in germ. The uses of nature, he says, "admit of being thrown into one of the following classes: Commodity; Beauty; Language; and Discipline"; section III above deals with "Beauty."

The extracts from Emerson are used by permission of, and by arrangement with, Houghton Mifflin Company, the authorized publishers.

to partake its rapid transformations; the active enchantment reaches my dust, and I dilate and conspire with the morning wind. How does Nature deify us with a few and cheap elements! Give me health and a day, and I will make the pomp of emperors ridiculous. The dawn is my Assyria; the sunset and moonrise my Paphos, and unimaginable realms of faerie; broad noon shall be my England of the senses and the understanding; the night shall be my Germany of mystic philosophy and dreams.

Not less excellent, except for our less susceptibility in the afternoon, was the charm, last evening, of a January sunset. The western clouds divided and subdivided themselves into pink flakes modulated with tints of unspeakable softness, and the air had so much life and sweetness that it was a pain to come within doors. What was it that nature would say? Was there no meaning in the live repose of the valley behind the mill, and which Homer or Shakespeare could not re-form for me in words? The leafless trees become spires of flame in the sunset, with the blue east for their background, and the stars of the dead calices of flowers, and every withered stem and stubble rimed with frost, contribute something to the mute music.

The inhabitants of cities suppose that the country landscape is pleasant only half the year. I please myself with the graces of the winter scenery, and believe that we are as much touched by it as by the genial influences of summer. To the attentive eye, each moment of the year has its own beauty, and in the same field, it beholds, every hour, a picture which was never seen before, and which shall never be seen again. The heavens change every moment, and reflect their glory or gloom on the plains beneath. The state of the crop in the surrounding farms alters the expression of the earth from week to week. The succession of native plants in the pastures and roadsides, which makes the silent clock by which time tells the summer hours, will make even the divisions of the day sensible to a keen observer. The tribes of birds and insects, like the plants punctual to their time, follow each other, and the year has room for all. By water-courses, the variety is greater. In July, the blue pontederia or pickerel-weed blooms in large beds in the shallow parts of our pleasant river, and swarms with yellow butterflies in continual motion. Art cannot rival this pomp of purple and gold. Indeed the river is a perpetual gala, and boasts each month a new ornament.

But this beauty of Nature which is seen and felt as beauty, is the least part. The shows of day, the dewy morning, the rainbow, mountains, orchards in blossom, stars, moonlight, shadows in still water, and the like, if too eagerly hunted, become shows merely, and mock us with their unreality. Go out of the house to see the moon, and 'tis mere tinsel; it will not please as when its light shines upon your necessary journey. The beauty that shimmers in the yellow afternoons of October, who ever could clutch it? Go forth to find it, and it is gone; 'tis only a mirage as you look from the windows of diligence.

2. The presence of a higher, namely, of the spiritual element is essential to its perfection. The high and divine beauty which can be loved without effeminacy, is that which is found in combination with the human will. Beauty is the mark God sets upon virtue. Every natural action is graceful. Every heroic act is also decent, and causes the place and the bystanders to shine. We are taught by great actions that the universe is the property of every individual in it. Every rational creature has all nature for his dowry and estate. It is his, if he will. He may divest himself of it; he may creep into a corner, and abdicate his kingdom, as most men do, but he is entitled to the world by his constitution. In proportion to the energy of his thought and will, he takes up the world into himself. "All those things for which men plough, build, or sail, obey virtue," said Sallust. "The winds and waves," said Gibbon, "are always on the side of the ablest navigators." So are the sun and moon and all the stars of heaven. When a noble act is done,—perchance in a scene of great natural beauty; when Leonidas and his three hundred martyrs consume one day in dying, and the sun and moon come each and look at them once in the steep defile of Thermopylæ; when Arnold Winkelried, in the high Alps, under the shadow of the avalanche, gathers in his side a sheaf of Austrian spears to break the line for his comrades; are not these heroes entitled to add the beauty of the scene to the beauty of the deed? When the bark of Columbus nears the shore of America;—before it the beach lined with savages, fleeing out of all their huts of cane; the sea behind; and the purple mountains of the Indian Archipelago around, can we separate the man from the living picture? Does not the New World clothe his form with her palm-groves and savannahs as fit drapery? Ever does natural beauty steal in like air, and envelop great actions. When Sir Harry Vane was dragged up the Tower-hill, sitting on a sled, to suffer death as the champion of the English laws, one of the multitude cried out to him, "You never sate on so glorious a seat!" Charles II., to intimidate the citizens of London, caused the patriot Lord Russell to be drawn in an open coach through the principal streets of the city on his way to the scaffold. "But," his biographer says, "the multitude imagined they saw liberty and virtue sitting by his side." In private places, among sordid objects, an act of truth or heroism seems at once to draw to itself the sky as its temple, the sun as its candle. Nature stretches out her arms to embrace man, only let his thoughts be of equal greatness. Willingly does she follow his steps with the rose and the violet, and bend her lines of grandeur and grace to the decoration of her darling child. Only let his thoughts be of equal scope, and the frame will suit the picture. A virtuous man is in unison with her works, and makes the central figure of the visible sphere. Homer, Pindar, Socrates, Phocion, associate themselves fitly in our memory with the geography and climate of Greece. The visible heavens and earth sympathize with Jesus. And in common life whosoever has seen a person of powerful character and happy genius,

will have remarked how easily he took all things along with him,—the persons, the opinions, and the day, and nature became ancillary to a man.

3. There is still another aspect under which the beauty of the world may be viewed, namely, as it becomes an object of the intellect. Besides the relation of things to virtue, they have a relation to thought. The intellect searches out the absolute order of things as they stand in the mind of God, and without the colors of affection. The intellectual and the active powers seem to succeed each other, and the exclusive activity of the one generates the exclusive activity of the other. There is something unfriendly in each to the other, but they are like the alternate periods of feeding and working in animals; each prepares and will be followed by the other. Therefore does beauty, which, in relation to actions, as we have seen, comes unsought, and comes because it is unsought, remain for the apprehension and pursuit of the intellect; and then again, in its turn, of the active power. Nothing divine dies. All good is eternally re-productive. The beauty of nature re-forms itself in the mind, and not for barren contemplation, but for new creation.

All men are in some degree impressed by the face of the world; some men even to delight. This love of beauty is Taste. Others have the same love in such excess, that, not content with admiring, they seek to embody it in new forms. The creation of beauty is Art.

The production of a work of art throws a light upon the mystery of humanity. A work of art is an abstract or epitome of the world. It is the result or expression of nature, in miniature. For although the works of nature are innumerable and all different, the result or the expression of them all is similar and single. Nature is a sea of forms radically alike and even unique. A leaf, a sunbeam, a landscape, the ocean, make an analogous impression on the mind. What is common to them all,—that perfectness and harmony, is beauty. The standard of beauty is the entire circuit of natural forms,—the totality of nature; which the Italians expressed by defining beauty "il più nell' uno." Nothing is quite beautiful alone; nothing but is beautiful in the whole. A single object is only so far beautiful as it suggests this universal grace. The poet, the painter, the sculptor, the musician, the architect, seek each to concentrate this radiance of the world on one point, and each in his several work to satisfy the love of beauty which stimulates him to produce. Thus is Art a nature passed through the alembic of man. Thus in art does Nature work through the will of a man filled with the beauty of her first works.

The world thus exists to the soul to satisfy the desire of beauty. This element I call an ultimate end. No reason can be asked or given why the soul seeks beauty. Beauty, in its largest and profoundest sense, is one expression for the universe. God is the all-fair. Truth, and goodness, and beauty, are but different faces of the same All. But beauty in nature is not ultimate. It is the herald of inward and eternal beauty, and is not alone a solid and satisfactory good.

It must stand as a part, and not as yet the last or highest expression of the final cause of Nature.

THE AMERICAN SCHOLAR

AN ORATION DELIVERED BEFORE THE PHI BETA KAPPA SOCIETY, AT CAMBRIDGE, AUGUST 31, 1837

MR. PRESIDENT AND GENTLEMEN: I greet you on the recommencement of our literary year. Our anniversary is one of hope, and, perhaps, not enough of labor. We do not meet for games of strength or skill, for the recitation of histories, tragedies, and odes, like the ancient Greeks; for parliaments of love and poesy, like the Troubadours; nor for the advancement of science, like our contemporaries in the British and European capitals. Thus far, our holiday has been simply a friendly sign of the survival of the love of letters amongst a people too busy to give to letters any more. As such it is precious as the sign of an indestructible instinct. Perhaps the time is already come when it ought to be, and will be, something else; when the sluggard intellect of this continent will look from under its iron lids and fill the postponed expectation of the world with something better than the exertions of mechanical skill. Our day of dependence, our long apprenticeship to the learning of other lands, draws to a close. The millions that around us are rushing into life, cannot always be fed on the sere remains of foreign harvests. Events, actions arise, that must be sung, that will sing themselves. Who can doubt that poetry will revive and lead in a new age, as the star in the constellation Harp, which now flames in our zenith, astronomers announce, shall one day be the polestar for a thousand years?

In this hope I accept the topic which not only usage but the nature of our association seem to prescribe to this day,—the AMERICAN SCHOLAR. Year by year we come up hither to read one more chapter of his biography. Let us inquire what light new days and events have thrown on his character and his hopes.

It is one of those fables which out of an unknown antiquity convey an unlooked-for wisdom, that the gods, in the beginning, divided Man into men, that he might be more helpful to himself; just as the hand was divided into fingers, the better to answer its end.

The old fable covers a doctrine ever new and sublime; that there is One Man,—present to all particular men only partially, or through one faculty; and that you must take the whole society to find the whole man. Man is not a farmer, or a professor, or an engineer, but he is all. Man is priest, and scholar, and statesman, and producer, and soldier. In the *divided* or social state these functions are parcelled out to individuals, each of whom aims to do his stint of the joint work, whilst each other performs his. The fable implies that the individual, to possess himself, must sometimes return from his own labor to embrace all the other laborers. But, unfortunately, this original unit, this fountain of power, has been so distributed to multitudes, has been so minutely subdivided and peddled out, that it is spilled into drops, and cannot be gathered. The state of society is one in which the members have suffered amputation from the trunk, and strut about so many walking monsters,—a good finger, a neck, a stomach, an elbow, but never a man.

Man is thus metamorphosed into a thing, into many things. The planter, who is Man sent out into the field to gather food, is seldom cheered by any idea of the true dignity of his ministry. He sees his bushel and his cart, and nothing beyond, and sinks into the farmer, instead of Man on the farm. The tradesman scarcely ever gives an ideal worth to his work, but is ridden by the routine of his craft, and the soul is subject to dollars. The priest becomes a form; the attorney a statute-book; the mechanic a machine; the sailor a rope of the ship.

In this distribution of functions the scholar is the delegated intellect. In the right state he is *Man Thinking*. In the degenerate state, when the victim of society, he tends to become a mere thinker, or still worse, the parrot of other men's thinking.

In this view of him, as Man Thinking, the theory of his office is contained. Him Nature solicits with all her placid, all her monitory pictures; him the past instructs; him the future invites. Is not indeed every man a student, and do not all things exist for the student's behoof? And, finally, is not the true scholar the only true master? But the old oracle said, "All things have two handles: beware of the wrong one." In life, too often, the scholar errs with mankind and forfeits his privilege. Let us see him in his school, and consider him in reference to the main influences he receives.

I. The first in time and the first in importance of the influences upon the mind is that of nature. Every day, the sun; and, after sunset, Night and her stars. Ever the winds blow; ever the grass grows. Every day, men and women, conversing—beholding and beholden. The scholar is he of all men whom this spectacle most engages. He must settle its value in his mind. What is nature to him? There is never a beginning, there is never an end, to the in-explicable continuity of this web of God, but always circular power returning into itself. Therein it resembles his own spirit, whose beginning, whose ending, he never can find,—so entire, so boundless. Far too as her splendors shine, system on system shooting like rays, upward, downward, without centre, without circumference,—in the mass and in the particle, Nature hastens to render account of herself to the mind. Classification begins. To the young mind every thing is individual, stands by itself. By and by, it finds how to join two things and see in them one nature; then three, then three thousand; and so, tyrannized over by its own unifying instinct, it goes on tying things together, diminishing anomalies, discovering roots running under ground whereby contrary and remote things cohere and flower out from one stem. It presently learns that since the dawn of history there has been a constant accumulation and classifying of facts. But what is classification but the perceiving that these objects are not chaotic, and are not foreign, but have a law which is also a law of the human mind? The astronomer discovers that geometry, a pure abstraction of the human mind, is the measure of planetary motion. The chemist finds proportions and intelligible method throughout matter; and science is nothing but the finding of analogy, identity, in the most remote parts. The ambitious soul sits down before each refractory fact; one after another reduces all strange constitutions, all new powers, to their class and their law, and goes on forever to animate the last fibre of organization, the outskirts of nature, by insight.

Thus to him, to this schoolboy under the bending dome of day, is suggested that he and it proceed from one root; one is leaf and one is flower; relation, sympathy, stirring in every vein. And what is that root? Is not that the soul of his soul? A thought too bold; a dream too wild. Yet when this spiritual light shall have revealed the law of more earthly natures,—when he has learned to worship the soul, and to see that the natural philosophy that now is, is only the first gropings of its gigantic hand, he shall look forward to an ever expanding knowledge as to a becoming creator. He shall see that nature is the opposite of the soul, answering to it part for part. One is seal and one is print. Its beauty is the beauty of his own mind. Its laws are the laws of his own mind. Nature then becomes to him the measure of his attainments. So much of nature as he is ignorant of, so much of his own mind does he not yet possess. And, in fine, the ancient precept, "Know thyself," and the modern precept, "Study nature," become at last one maxim.

II. The next great influence into the spirit of the scholar is the mind of the Past,—in whatever form, whether of literature, of art, of institutions, that mind is inscribed. Books are the best type of the influence of the past, and perhaps we shall get at the truth,—learn the amount of this influence more conveniently,—by considering their value alone.

The theory of books is noble. The scholar of the first age received into him the world around; brooded thereon; gave it the new arrangement of his own mind, and uttered it again. It came into him life; it went out from him truth. It came to him short-lived actions; it went out from him immortal thoughts. It came to him business; it went from him poetry. It was dead fact; now, it is quick thought. It can stand, and it can go. It now endures, it now flies, it now inspires. Precisely in proportion to the depth of mind from which it issued, so high does it soar, so long does it sing.

Or, I might say, it depends on how far the process had gone, of transmuting life into truth. In proportion to the completeness of the distillation, so will the purity and imperishableness of the product be. But none is quite perfect. As no air-pump can by any means make a perfect vacuum, so neither can any artist entirely exclude the conventional, the local, the perishable from his book, or write a book of pure thought, that shall be as efficient, in all respects, to a remote posterity, as to contemporaries, or rather to the second age. Each age, it is found, must write its own books; or rather, each generation for the next succeeding. The books of an older period will not fit this.

Yet hence arises a grave mischief. The sacredness which attaches to the act of creation, the act of thought, is transferred to the record. The poet chanting was felt to be a divine man: henceforth the chant is divine also. The writer was a just and wise spirit: henceforward it is settled the book is perfect; as love of the hero corrupts into worship of his statue. Instantly the book becomes noxious: the guide is a tyrant. The sluggish and perverted mind of the multitude, slow to open to the incursions of Reason, having once so opened, having once received this book, stands upon it, and makes an outcry if it is disparaged. Colleges are built on it. Books are written on it by thinkers, not by Man Thinking; by men of talent, that is, who start wrong, who set out from accepted dogmas, not from their own sight of principles. Meek young men grow up in libraries, believing it their duty to accept the views which Cicero, which Locke, which Bacon, have given; forgetful that Cicero, Locke, and Bacon were only young men in libraries when they wrote these books.

Hence, instead of Man Thinking, we have the bookworm. Hence the book-learned class, who value books, as such; not as related to nature and the human constitution, but as making a sort of Third Estate with the world and the soul. Hence the restorers of readings, the emendators, the bibliomaniacs of all degrees.

Books are the best of things, well used; abused, among the worst. What is the right use? What is the one end which all means go to effect? They are for nothing but to inspire. I had better never see a book than to be warped by its attraction clean out of my own orbit, and made a satellite instead of a system. The one thing in the world, of value, is the active soul. This every man is entitled to; this every man contains within him, although in almost all men obstructed and as yet unborn. The soul active sees absolute truth and utters truth, or creates. In this action it is genius; not the privilege of here and there a favorite, but the sound estate of every man. In its essence it is progressive. The book, the college, the school of art, the institution of any kind, stop with some past utterance of genius. This is good, say they,—let us hold by this. They pin me down. They look backward and not forward. But genius looks forward: the eyes of man are set in his forehead, not in his hind-head: man hopes: genius creates. Whatever talents may be, if the man create not, the pure efflux of the Deity is not his;—cinders and smoke there may be, but not yet flame. There are creative manners, there are creative actions, and creative words; manners, actions, words, that is, indicative of no custom or authority, but springing spontaneous from the mind's own sense of good and fair.

On the other part, instead of being its own seer, let it receive from another mind its truth, though it were in torrents of light, without periods of solitude, inquest, and self-recovery, and a fatal disservice is done. Genius is always sufficiently the enemy of genius by over-influence. The literature of every nation bears me witness. The English dramatic poets have Shakespearized now for two hundred years.

Undoubtedly there is a right way of reading, so it be sternly subordinated. Man Thinking must not be subdued by his instruments. Books are for the scholar's idle times. When he can read God directly, the hour is too precious to be wasted in other men's transcripts of their readings. But when the intervals of darkness come, as come they must,—when the sun is hid and the stars withdraw their shining,—we repair to the lamps which were kindled by their ray, to guide our steps to the East again, where the dawn is. We hear, that we may speak. The Arabian proverb says, "A fig tree, looking on a fig tree, becometh fruitful."

It is remarkable, the character of the pleasure we derive from the best books. They impress us with the conviction that one nature wrote and the same reads. We read the verses of one of the great English poets, of Chaucer, of Marvell, of Dryden, with the most modern joy,—with a pleasure, I mean, which is in great part caused by the abstraction of all *time* from their verses. There is some awe mixed with the joy of our surprise, when this poet, who lived in some past world, two or three hundred years ago, says that which lies close to my own soul, that which I also had well-nigh thought and said. But for the evidence thence afforded to the philosophical doctrine of the identity of all minds, we should suppose some preëstablished harmony, some foresight of souls that were to be, and some preparation of stores for their future wants, like the fact observed in insects, who lay up food before death for the young grub they shall never see.

I would not be hurried by any love of system, by any exaggeration of instincts, to underrate the Book. We all know, that as the human body can be nourished on any food, though it were boiled grass and the broth of shoes, so the human mind can be fed by any knowledge. And great and heroic men have existed who had almost no other information than by the printed page. I only would say that it needs a strong head to bear that diet. One must be an inventor to read well. As the proverb says, "He that would bring home the wealth of the Indies, must carry out the wealth of the Indies." There is then creative reading as well as creative writing. When the mind is braced by labor and invention, the page of whatever book we read becomes luminous with manifold allusion. Every sentence is doubly significant, and the sense of our author is as broad as the world. We then see, what is always true, that as the seer's hour of vision is short and rare among heavy days and months, so is its record, perchance, the least part of his volume. The discerning will read, in his Plato or Shakespeare, only that least part,—only the authentic utterances of the oracle;—all the rest he rejects, were it never so many times Plato's and Shakespeare's.

Of course there is a portion of reading quite indispensable to a wise man. History and exact science he must learn by laborious reading. Colleges, in like manner, have their indispensable office,—to teach elements. But they can only highly serve us when they aim not to drill, but to create; when they gather from far every ray of various genius to their hospitable halls and, by the concentrated fires, set the hearts of their youth on flame. Thought and knowledge are natures in which apparatus and pretension avail nothing. Gowns and pecuniary foundations, though of towns of gold, can never countervail the least sentence or syllable of wit. Forget this, and our American colleges will recede in their public importance, whilst they grow richer every year.

III. There goes in the world a notion that the scholar should be a recluse, a valetudinarian,—as unfit for any handiwork or public labor as a penknife for an axe. The so-called "practical men" sneer at speculative men, as if, because they speculate or *see,* they could do nothing. I have heard it said that the clergy,—who are always, more universally than any other class, the scholars of their day,—are addressed as women; that the rough, spontaneous conversation of men they do not hear, but only a mincing and diluted speech. They are often virtually disfranchised; and indeed there are advocates for their celibacy. As far as this is true of the studious classes, it is not just and wise. Action is with the scholar subordinate, but it is essential. Without it he is not yet man. Without it thought can never ripen into truth. Whilst the world hangs before the eye as a cloud of beauty, we cannot even see its beauty. Inaction is cowardice, but there can be no scholar without the heroic mind. The preamble of thought, the transition through which it passes from the unconscious to the conscious, is action. Only so much do I know, as I have lived. Instantly we know whose words are loaded with life, and whose not.

The world,—this shadow of the soul, or *other me,*—lies wide around. Its attractions are the keys which unlock my thoughts and make me acquainted with myself. I run eagerly into this resounding tumult. I grasp the hands of those next me, and take my place in the ring to suffer and to work, taught by an instinct that so shall the dumb abyss be vocal with speech. I pierce its order; I dissipate its fear; I dispose of it within the circuit of my expanding life. So much only of life as I know by experience, so much of the wilderness have I vanquished and planted, or so far have I extended my being, my dominion. I do not see how any man can afford, for the sake of his nerves and his nap, to spare any action in which he can partake. It is pearls and rubies to his discourse. Drudgery, calamity, exasperation, want, are instructors in eloquence and wisdom. The true scholar grudges every opportunity of action past by, as a loss of power. It is the raw material out of which the intellect moulds her splendid products. A strange process too, this by which experience is converted into thought, as a mulberry leaf is converted into satin. The manufacture goes forward at all hours.

The actions and events of our childhood and youth are now matters of calmest observation. They lie like fair pictures in the air. Not so with our recent actions,—with the business which we now have in hand. On this we are quite unable to speculate. Our affections as yet circulate through it. We no more feel or know it than we feel the feet, or the hand, or the brain of our body. The new deed is yet a part of life,—remains for a time immersed in our unconscious life. In some contemplative hour it detaches itself from the life like a ripe fruit, to become a thought of the mind. Instantly it is raised, transfigured; the corruptible has put on incorruption. Henceforth it is an object of beauty, however base its origin and neighborhood. Observe too the impossibility of antedating this act. In its grub state, it cannot fly, it cannot shine, it is a dull grub. But suddenly, without observation, the selfsame thing unfurls beautiful wings, and is an angel of wisdom. So is there no fact, no event, in our private history, which shall not, sooner or later, lose its adhesive, inert form, and astonish us by soaring from our body into the empyrean. Cradle and infancy, school and playground, the fear of boys, and dogs, and ferules, the love of little maids and berries, and many another fact that once filled the whole sky, are gone already; friend and relative, profession and party, town and country, nation and world, must also soar and sing.

Of course, he who has put forth his total strength in fit actions has the richest return of wisdom. I will not shut myself out of this globe of action, and transplant an oak into a flowerpot, there to hunger and pine; nor trust the revenue of some single faculty, and exhaust one vein of thought, much like those Savoyards, who, getting their livelihood by carving shepherds, shepherdesses, and smoking Dutchmen, for all Europe, went out one day to the mountain to find stock, and discovered that they had whittled up the last of their pine trees. Authors we have, in numbers, who have written out their vein, and who, moved by a commendable prudence, sail for Greece or Palestine, follow the trapper into the prairie, or ramble round Algiers, to replenish their merchantable stock.

If it were only for a vocabulary, the scholar would be covetous of action. Life is our dictionary. Years are well spent in country labors; in town; in the insight into trades and manufactures; in frank intercourse with many men and women; in science; in art; to the one end of mastering in all their facts a language by which to illustrate and embody our perceptions. I learn immediately from any speaker how much he has already lived, through the poverty or the splendor of his speech. Life lies behind us as the quarry from whence we get tiles and copestones for the masonry of to-day. This is the way to learn grammar. Colleges and books only copy the language which the field and the workyard made.

But the final value of action, like that of books, and better than books, is that it is a resource. That great principle of Undulation in nature, that shows itself in the inspiring and expiring of the breath; in desire and satiety; in the ebb and flow of the sea; in day and night; in heat and cold; and, as yet more deeply ingrained in every atom and every fluid, is known to us under the name of Polarity,—these "fits of easy transmission and reflection," as Newton called them, are the law of nature because they are the law of spirit.

The mind now thinks, now acts, and each fit reproduces the other. When the artist has exhausted his materials, when the fancy no longer paints, when thoughts are no longer apprehended and books are a weariness,—he has always the resource *to live*. Character is higher than intellect. Thinking is the function. Living is the functionary. The stream retreats to its source. A great soul will be strong to live, as well as strong to think. Does he lack organ or medium to impart his truths? He can still fall back on this elemental force of living them. This is a total act. Thinking is a partial act. Let the grandeur of justice shine in his affairs. Let the beauty of affection cheer his lowly roof. Those "far from fame," who dwell and act with him, will feel the force of his constitution in the doings and passages of the day better than it can be measured by any public and designed display. Time shall teach him that the scholar loses no hour which the man lives. Herein he unfolds the sacred germ of his instinct, screened from influence. What is lost in seemliness is gained in strength. Not out of those on whom systems of education have exhausted their culture, comes the helpful giant to destroy the old or to build the new, but out of unhandselled savage nature; out of terrible Druids and Berserkers come at last Alfred and Shakespeare.

I hear therefore with joy whatever is beginning to be said of the dignity and necessity of labor to every citizen. There is virtue yet in the hoe and the spade, for learned as well as for unlearned hands. And labor is everywhere welcome; always we are invited to work; only be this limitation observed, that a man shall not for the sake of wider activity sacrifice any opinion to the popular judgments and modes of action.

I have now spoken of the education of the scholar by nature, by books, and by action. It remains to say somewhat of his duties.

They are such as become Man Thinking. They may all be comprised in self-trust. The office of the scholar is to cheer, to raise, and to guide men by showing them facts amidst appearances. He plies the slow, unhonored, and unpaid task of observation. Flamsteed and Herschel, in their glazed observatories, may catalogue the stars with the praise of all men, and the results being splendid and useful, honor is sure. But he, in his private observatory, cataloguing obscure and nebulous stars of the human mind, which as yet no man has thought of as such,—watching days and months sometimes for a few facts; correcting still his old records;—must relinquish display and immediate fame. In the long period of his preparation he must betray often an ignorance and shiftlessness in popular arts, incurring the disdain of the able who shoulder him aside. Long he must stammer in his speech; often forego the living for the dead. Worse yet, he must accept—how often!—poverty and solitude. For the ease and pleasure of treading the old road, accepting the fashions, the education, the religion of society, he takes the cross of making his own, and, of course, the self-accusation, the faint heart, the frequent uncertainty and loss of time, which are the nettles and tangling vines in the way of the self-relying and self-directed; and the state of virtual hostility in which he seems to stand to society, and especially to educated society. For all this loss and scorn, what offset? He is to find consolation in exercising the highest functions of human nature. He is one who raises himself from private considerations and breathes and lives on public and illustrious thoughts. He is the world's eye. He is the world's heart. He is to resist the vulgar prosperity that retrogrades ever to barbarism, by preserving and communicating heroic sentiments, noble biographies, melodious verse, and the conclusions of history. Whatsoever oracles the human heart, in all emergencies, in all solemn hours, has uttered as its commentary on the world of actions,—these he shall receive and impart. And whatsoever new verdict Reason from her inviolable seat pronounces on the passing men and events of to-day,—this he shall hear and promulgate.

These being his functions, it becomes him to feel all confidence in himself, and to defer never to the popular cry. He and he only knows the world. The world of any moment is the merest appearance. Some great decorum, some fetish of a government, some ephemeral trade, or war, or man, is cried up by half mankind and cried down by the other half, as if all depended on this particular up or down. The odds are that the whole question is not worth the poorest thought which the scholar has lost in listening to the controversy. Let him not quit his belief that a popgun is a popgun, though the ancient and honorable of the earth affirm it to be the crack of doom. In silence, in steadiness, in severe abstraction, let him hold by himself; add observation to observation, patient of neglect, patient of reproach, and bide his own time,— happy enough if he can satisfy himself alone that this day he has seen something truly. Success treads on every right step. For the instinct is sure, that prompts him to tell his brother what he thinks. He then learns that in going down into the secrets of his own mind he has descended into the secrets of all minds. He learns that he who has mastered any law in his private thoughts, is master to that extent of all men whose language he speaks, and of all into whose language his own can be translated. The poet, in utter solitude remembering his spontaneous thoughts and recording them, is found to have recorded that which men in crowded cities find true for them also. The orator distrusts at first the fitness of his frank confessions, his want of knowledge of the persons he addresses, until he finds that he is the complement of his hearers;—that they drink his words because he fulfils for them their own nature; the deeper he dives into his privatest, secretest presentiment, to his wonder he finds this is the most acceptable, most public, and universally true. The people delight in it; the better part of every man feels, This is my music; this is myself.

In self-trust all the virtues are comprehended. Free should the scholar be, —free and brave. Free even to the definition of freedom, "without any hindrance that does not arise out of his own constitution." Brave; for fear is a thing which a scholar by his very function puts behind him. Fear always springs from ignorance. It is a shame to him if his tranquillity, amid danger- ous times, arise from the presumption that like children and women his is a protected class; or if he seek a temporary peace by the diversion of his thoughts from politics or vexed questions, hiding his head like an ostrich in the flowering bushes, peeping into microscopes, and turning rhymes, as a boy whistles to keep his courage up. So is the danger a danger still; so is the fear worse. Manlike let him turn and face it. Let him look into its eye and search its nature, inspect its origin,—see the whelping of this lion,—which lies no great way back; he will then find in himself a perfect comprehension of its nature and extent; he will have made his hands meet on the other side, and can henceforth defy it and pass on superior. The world is his who can see through its pretension. What deafness, what stone-blind custom, what over- grown error you behold is there only by sufferance,—by your sufferance. See it to be a lie, and you have already dealt it its mortal blow.

Yes, we are the cowed,—we the trustless. It is a mischievous notion that we are come late into nature; that the world was finished a long time ago. As the world was plastic and fluid in the hands of God, so it is ever to so much of his attributes as we bring to it. To ignorance and sin, it is flint. They adapt themselves to it as they may; but in proportion as a man has anything in him divine, the firmament flows before him and takes his sig- net and form. Not he is great who can alter matter, but he who can alter my state of mind. They are the kings of the world who give the color of their present thought to all nature and all art, and persuade men by the cheerful serenity of their carrying the matter, that this thing which they do is the apple which the ages have desired to pluck, now at last ripe, and inviting

nations to the harvest. The great man makes the great thing. Wherever Macdonald sits, there is the head of the table. Linnæus makes botany the most
alluring of studies, and wins it from the farmer and the herb-woman; Davy,
chemistry; and Cuvier, fossils. The day is always his who works in it with
serenity and great aims. The unstable estimates of men crowd to him whose
mind is filled with a truth, as the heaped waves of the Atlantic follow the
moon.

For this self-trust, the reason is deeper than can be fathomed—darker than
can be enlightened. I might not carry with me the feeling of my audience in
stating my own belief. But I have already shown the ground of my hope,
in adverting to the doctrine that man is one. I believe man has been wronged;
he has wronged himself. He has almost lost the light that can lead him back
to his prerogatives. Men are become of no account. Men in history, men in the
world of to-day, are bugs, are spawn, and are called "the mass" and "the
herd." In a century, in a millennium, one or two men; that is to say, one or
two approximations to the right state of every man. All the rest behold in the
hero or the poet their own green and crude being,—ripened; yes, and are content to be less, so *that* may attain to its full stature. What a testimony, full of
grandeur, full of pity, is borne to the demands of his own nature, by the poor
clansman, the poor partisan, who rejoices in the glory of his chief. The poor
and the low find some amends to their immense moral capacity, for their
acquiescence in a political and social inferiority. They are content to be
brushed like flies from the path of a great person, so that justice shall by done
by him to that common nature which it is the dearest desire of all to see enlarged and glorified. They sun themselves in the great man's light, and feel
it to be their own element. They cast the dignity of man from their down-
trod selves upon the shoulders of a hero, and will perish to add one drop of
blood to make that great heart beat, those giant sinews combat and conquer.
He lives for us, and we live in him.

Men, such as they are, very naturally seek money or power; and power because it is as good as money,—the "spoils," so called, "of office." And why
not? for they aspire to the highest, and this, in their sleep-walking, they
dream is highest. Wake them and they shall quit the false good and leap to the
true, and leave governments to clerks and desks. This revolution is to be
wrought by the gradual domestication of the idea of Culture. The main
enterprise of the world for splendor, for extent, is the upbuilding of a man.
Here are the materials strewn along the ground. The private life of one man
shall be a more illustrious monarchy, more formidable to its enemy, more
sweet and serene in its influence to its friend, than any kingdom in history.
For a man, rightly viewed, comprehendeth the particular natures of all men.
Each philosopher, each bard, each actor has only done for me, as by a delegate, what one day I can do for myself. The books which once we valued

more than the apple of the eye, we have quite exhausted. What is that but saying that we have come up with the point of view which the universal mind took through the eyes of one scribe; we have been that man, and have passed on. First, one, then another, we drain all cisterns, and waxing greater by all these supplies, we crave a better and more abundant food. The man has never lived that can feed us ever. The human mind cannot be enshrined in a person who shall set a barrier on any one side to this unbounded, unboundable empire. It is one central fire, which, flaming now out of the lips of Etna, lightens the capes of Sicily, and now out of the throat of Vesuvius, illuminates the towers and vineyards of Naples. It is one light which beams out of a thousand stars. It is one soul which animates all men.

But I have dwelt perhaps tediously upon this abstraction of the Scholar. I ought not to delay longer to add what I have to say of nearer reference to the time and to this country.

Historically, there is thought to be a difference in the ideas which predominate over successive epochs, and there are data for marking the genius of the Classic, of the Romantic, and now of the Reflective or Philosophical age. With the views I have intimated of the oneness or the identity of the mind through all individuals, I do not much dwell on these differences. In fact, I believe each individual passes through all three. The boy is a Greek; the youth, romantic; the adult, reflective. I deny not, however, that a revolution in the leading idea may be distinctly enough traced.

Our age is bewailed as the age of Introversion. Must that needs be evil? We, it seems, are critical; we are embarrassed with second thoughts; we cannot enjoy anything for hankering to know whereof the pleasure consists; we are lined with eyes; we see with our feet; the time is infected with Hamlet's unhappiness,—

Sicklied o'er with the pale cast of thought.

It is so bad then? Sight is the last thing to be pitied. Would we be blind? Do we fear lest we should outsee nature and God, and drink truth dry? I look upon the discontent of the literary class as a mere announcement of the fact that they find themselves not in the state of mind of their fathers, and regret the coming state as untried; as a boy dreads the water before he has learned that he can swim. If there is any period one would desire to be born in, is it not the age of Revolution; when the old and the new stand side by side and admit of being compared; when the energies of all men are searched by fear and by hope; when the historic glories of the old can be compensated by the rich possibilities of the new era? This time, like all times, is a very good one, if we but know what to do with it.

I read with some joy of the auspicious signs of the coming days, as they glimmer already through poetry and art, through philosophy and science, through church and state.

One of these signs is the fact that the same movement which effected the elevation of what was called the lowest class in the state, assumed in literature a very marked and as benign an aspect. Instead of the sublime and beautiful, the near, the low, the common, was explored and poetized. That which had been negligently trodden under foot by those who were harnessing and provisioning themselves for long journeys into far countries, is suddenly found to be richer than all foreign parts. The literature of the poor, the feelings of the child, the philosophy of the street, the meaning of household life, are the topics of the time. It is a great stride. It is a sign—is it not?—of new vigor when the extremities are made active, when currents of warm life run into the hands and the feet. I ask not for the great, the remote, the romantic; what is doing in Italy or Arabia; what is Greek art, or Provençal minstrelsy; I embrace the common, I explore and sit at the feet of the familiar, the low. Give me insight into to-day, and you may have the antique and future worlds. What would we really know the meaning of? The meal in the firkin; the milk in the pan; the ballad in the street; the news of the boat; the glance of the eye; the form and the gait of the body;—show me the ultimate reason of these matters; show me the sublime presence of the highest spiritual cause lurking, as always it does lurk, in these suburbs and extremities of nature; let me see every trifle bristling with the polarity that ranges it instantly on an eternal law; and the shop, the plough, and the ledger referred to the like cause by which light undulates and poets sing;—and the world lies no longer a dull miscellany and lumber-room, but has form and order; there is no trifle, there is no puzzle, but one design unites and animates the farthest pinnacle and the lowest trench.

This idea has inspired the genius of Goldsmith, Burns, Cowper, and, in a newer time, of Goethe, Wordsworth, and Carlyle. This idea they have differently followed and with various success. In contrast with their writing, the style of Pope, of Johnson, of Gibbon, looks cold and pedantic. This writing is blood-warm. Man is surprised to find that things near are not less beautiful and wondrous than things remote. The near explains the far. The drop is a small ocean. A man is related to all nature. This perception of the worth of the vulgar is fruitful in discoveries. Goethe, in this very thing the most modern of the moderns, has shown us, as none ever did, the genius of the ancients.

There is one man of genius who has done much for this philosophy of life, whose literary value has never yet been rightly estimated;—I mean Emanuel Swedenborg. The most imaginative of men, yet writing with the precision of a mathematician, he endeavored to engraft a purely philosophical Ethics on the popular Christianity of his time. Such an attempt of course must have difficulty which no genius could surmount. But he saw and showed the connection between nature and the affections of the soul. He pierced the emblematic or spiritual character of the visible, audible, tangible world. Especially did his shade-loving muse hover over and interpret the lower parts of nature; he showed the mysterious bond that allies moral evil to the foul material forms, and has given in epical parables a theory of insanity, of beasts, of unclean and fearful things.

Another sign of our times, also marked by an analogous political movement, is the new importance given to the single person. Everything that tends to insulate the individual,—to surround him with barriers of natural respect, so that each man shall feel the world is his, and man shall treat with man as a sovereign state with a sovereign state,—tends to true union as well as greatness. "I learned," said the melancholy Pestalozzi, "that no man in God's wide earth is either willing or able to help any other man." Help must come from the bosom alone. The scholar is that man who must take up into himself all the ability of the time, all the contributions of the past, all the hopes of the future. He must be an university of knowledges. If there be one lesson more than another which should pierce his ear, it is, The world is nothing, the man is all; in yourself is the law of all nature, and you know not yet how a globule of sap ascends; in yourself slumbers the whole of Reason; it is for you to know all; it is for you to dare all. Mr. President and Gentlemen, this confidence in the unsearched might of man belongs, by all motives, by all prophecy, by all preparation, to the American Scholar. We have listened too long to the courtly muses of Europe. The spirit of the American freeman is already suspected to be timid, imitative, tame. Public and private avarice make the air we breathe thick and fat. The scholar is decent, indolent, complaisant. See already the tragic consequence. The mind of this country, taught to aim at low objects, eats upon itself. There is no work for any but the decorous and the complaisant. Young men of the fairest promise, who begin life upon our shores, inflated by the mountain winds, shined upon by all the stars of God, find the earth below not in unison with these, but are hindered from action by the disgust which the principles on which business is managed inspire, and turn drudges, or die of disgust, some of them suicides. What is the remedy? They did not yet see, and thousands of young men as hopeful now crowding to the barriers for the career do not yet see, that if the single man plant himself indomitably on his instincts, and there abide, the huge world will come round to him. Patience,—patience; with the shades of all the good and great for company; and for solace the perspective of your own infinite life; and for work the study and the communication of principles, the making those instincts prevalent, the conversion of the world. Is it not the chief disgrace in the world, not to be an unit;—not to be reckoned one character;— not to yield that peculiar fruit which each man was created to bear, but to be reckoned in the gross, in the hundred, or the thousand, of the party, the section, to which we belong; and our opinion predicted geographically, as the north, or the south? Not so, brothers and friends—please God, ours shall not be so. We will walk on our own feet; we will work with our own hands; we will speak our own minds. The study of letters shall be no longer a name for pity, for doubt, and for sensual indulgence. The dread of man and the love of man shall be a wall of defence and a wreath of joy around all. A nation of men will for the first time exist, because each believes himself inspired by the Divine Soul which also inspires all men.

SELF-RELIANCE [2]

I READ the other day some verses written by an eminent painter which were original and not conventional. The soul always hears an admonition in such lines, let the subject be what it may. The sentiment they instil is of more value than any thought they may contain. To believe your own thought, to believe that what is true for you in your private heart is true for all men,— that is genius. Speak your latent conviction, and it shall be the universal sense; for the inmost in due time becomes the outmost, and our first thought is rendered back to us by the trumpets of the Last Judgment. Familiar as the voice of the mind is to each, the highest merit we ascribe to Moses, Plato and Milton is that they set at naught books and traditions, and spoke not what men, but what *they* thought. A man should learn to detect and watch that gleam of light which flashes across his mind from within, more than the lustre of the firmament of bards and sages. Yet he dismisses without notice his thought, because it is his. In every work of genius we recognize our own rejected thoughts; they come back to us with a certain alienated majesty. Great works of art have no more affecting lesson for us than this. They teach us to abide by our spontaneous impression with good-humored inflexibility then most when the whole cry of voices is on the other side. Else to-morrow a stranger will say with masterly good sense precisely what we have thought and felt all the time, and we shall be forced to take with shame our own opinion from another.

There is a time in every man's education when he arrives at the conviction that envy is ignorance; that imitation is suicide; that he must take himself for better for worse as his portion; that though the wide universe is full of good, no kernel of nourishing corn can come to him but through his toil bestowed on that plot of ground which is given to him to till. The power which resides in him is new in nature, and none but he knows what that is which he can do, nor does he know until he has tried. Not for nothing one face, one character, one fact, makes much impression on him, and another

[2] This and the following essay, "Compensation," are from *Essays, First Series,* (1841).

none. This sculpture in the memory is not without preëstablished harmony. The eye was placed where one ray should fall, that it might testify of that particular ray. We but half express ourselves, and are ashamed of that divine idea which each of us represents. It may be safely trusted as proportionate and of good issues, so it be faithfully imparted, but God will not have his work made manifest by cowards. A man is relieved and gay when he has put his heart into his work and done his best; but what he has said or done otherwise shall give him no peace. It is a deliverance which does not deliver. In the attempt his genius deserts him; no muse befriends; no invention, no hope.

Trust thyself: every heart vibrates to that iron string. Accept the place the divine providence has found for you, the society of your contemporaries, the connection of events. Great men have always done so, and confided themselves childlike to the genius of their age, betraying their perception that the absolutely trustworthy was seated at their heart, working through their hands, predominating in all their being. And we are now men, and must accept in the highest mind the same transcendent destiny; and not minors and invalids in a protected corner nor cowards fleeing before a revolution, but guides, redeemers, and benefactors, obeying the Almighty effort and advancing on Chaos and the Dark.

What pretty oracles nature yields us on this text in the face and behavior of children, babes, and even brutes! That divided and rebel mind, that distrust of a sentiment because our arithmetic has computed the strength and means opposed to our purpose, these have not. Their mind being whole, their eye is as yet unconquered, and when we look in their faces we are disconcerted. Infancy conforms to nobody; all conform to it; so that one babe commonly makes four or five out of the adults who prattle and play to it. So God has armed youth and puberty and manhood no less with its own piquancy and charm, and made it enviable and gracious and its claims not to be put by, if it will stand by itself. Do not think the youth has no force, because he cannot speak to you and me. Hark! in the next room his voice is sufficiently clear and emphatic. It seems he knows how to speak to his contemporaries. Bashful or bold then, he will know how to make us seniors very unnecessary.

The nonchalance of boys who are sure of a dinner, and would disdain as much as a lord to do or say aught to conciliate one, is the healthy attitude of human nature. A boy is in the parlor what the pit is in the playhouse; independent, irresponsible, looking out from his corner on such people and facts as pass by, he tries and sentences them on their merits, in the swift, summary way of boys, as good, bad, interesting, silly, eloquent, troublesome. He cumbers himself never about consequences, about interests; he gives an independent, genuine verdict. You must court him; he does not court you. But the man is as it were clapped into jail by his consciousness. As soon as he has once acted or spoken with *éclat* he is a committed person, watched by the sympathy or the hatred of hundreds, whose affections must now enter into his account. There is no Lethe for this. Ah, that he could pass again into his neutrality! Who can thus avoid all pledges and, having observed, observe again from the same unaffected, unbiased, unbribable, unaffrighted innocence,— must always be formidable. He would utter opinions on all passing affairs, which being seen to be not private but necessary, would sink like darts into the ear of men and put them in fear.

These are the voices which we hear in solitude, but they grow faint and inaudible as we enter into the world. Society everywhere is in conspiracy against the manhood of every one of its members. Society is a joint-stock company, in which the members agree, for the better securing of his bread to each shareholder, to surrender the liberty and culture of the eater. The virtue in most request is conformity. Self-reliance is its aversion. It loves not realities and creators, but names and customs.

Whoso would be a man, must be a nonconformist. He who would gather immortal palms must not be hindered by the name of goodness, but must explore if it be goodness. Nothing is at last sacred but the integrity of your own mind. Absolve you to yourself, and you shall have the suffrage of the world. I remember an answer which when quite young I was prompted to make to a valued adviser who was wont to importune me with the dear old doctrines of the church. On my saying, "What have I to do with the sacredness of traditions, if I live wholly from within?" my friend suggested, —"But these impulses may be from below, not from above." I replied, "They do not seem to me to be such; but if I am the Devil's child, I will live then from the Devil." No law can be sacred to me but that of my nature. Good and bad are but names very readily transferable to that or this; the only right is what is after my constitution; the only wrong what is against it. A man is to carry himself in the presence of all opposition as if everything were titular and ephemeral but he. I am ashamed to think how easily we capitulate to badges and names, to large societies and dead institutions. Every decent and well-spoken individual affects and sways me more than is right. I ought to go upright and vital, and speak the rude truth in all ways. If malice and vanity wear the coat of philanthropy, shall that pass? If an angry bigot assumes this bountiful cause of Abolition, and comes to me with his last news from Barbadoes, why should I not say to him, "Go love thy infant; love thy wood-chopper; be good-natured and modest; have that grace; and never varnish your hard, uncharitable ambition with this incredible tenderness for black folk a thousand miles off. Thy love afar is spite at home." Rough and graceless would be such greeting, but truth is handsomer than the affectation of love. Your goodness must have some edge to it,—else it is none. The doctrine of hatred must be preached, as the counteraction of the doctrine of love, when that pules and whines. I shun father and mother and wife and brother when

my genius calls me. I would write on the lintels of the door-post, *Whim*. I hope
it is somewhat better than whim at last, but we cannot spend the day in explanation. Expect me not to show cause why I seek or why I exclude company. Then again, do not tell me, as a good man did to-day, of my obligation
to put all poor men in good situations. Are they *my* poor? I tell thee, thou
foolish philanthropist, that I grudge the dollar, the dime, the cent I give to
such men as do not belong to me and to whom I do not belong. There is a
class of persons to whom by all spiritual affinity I am bought and sold; for
them I will go to prison if need be; but your miscellaneous popular charities;
the education at college of fools; the building of meeting-houses to the vain
end to which many now stand; alms to sots, and the thousand-fold Relief
Societies;—though I confess with shame I sometimes succumb and give the
dollar, it is a wicked dollar, which by and by I shall have the manhood to
withhold.

Virtues are, in the popular estimate, rather the exception than the rule.
There is the man *and* his virtues. Men do what is called a good action, as some
piece of courage or charity, much as they would pay a fine in expiation of
daily non-appearance on parade. Their works are done as an apology of ex-
tenuation of their living in the world,—as invalids and the insane pay a high
board. Their virtues are penances. I do not wish to expiate, but to live. My
life is for itself and not for a spectacle. I much prefer that it should be of a
lower strain, so it be genuine and equal, than that it should be glittering and
unsteady. I wish it to be sound and sweet, and not to need diet and bleeding.
I ask primary evidence that you are a man, and refuse this appeal from the
man to his actions. I know that for myself it makes no difference whether I
do or forbear those actions which are reckoned excellent. I cannot consent
to pay for a privilege where I have intrinsic right. Few and mean as my gifts
may be, I actually am, and do not need for my own assurance or the assurance
of my fellows any secondary testimony.

What I must do is all that concerns me, not what the people think. This
rule, equally arduous in actual and in intellectual life, may serve for the
whole distinction between greatness and meanness. It is the harder because
you will always find those who think they know what is your duty better than
you know it. It is easy in the world to live after the world's opinion; it is easy
in solitude to live after our own; but the great man is he who in the midst of
the crowd keeps with perfect sweetness the independence of solitude.

The objection to conforming to usages that have become dead to you is that
it scatters your force. It loses your time and blurs the impression of your
character. If you maintain a dead church, contribute to a dead Bible-society,
vote with a great party either for the government or against it, spread your
table like base housekeepers,—under all these screens I have difficulty to detect the precise man you are: and of course so much force is withdrawn from

your proper life. But do your work, and I shall know you. Do your work, and you shall reinforce yourself. A man must consider what a blind-man's-buff is this game of conformity. If I know your sect I anticipate your argument. I hear a preacher announce for his text and topic the expediency of one of the institutions of his church. Do I not know beforehand that not possibly can he say a new and spontaneous word? Do I not know that with all this ostentation of examining the grounds of the institution he will do no such thing? Do I not know that he is pledged to himself not to look but at one side, the permitted side, not as a man, but as a parish minister? He is a retained attorney, and these airs of the bench are the emptiest affectation. Well, most men have bound their eyes with one or another handkerchief, and attached themselves to some one of these communities of opinion. This conformity makes them not false in a few particulars, authors of a few lies, but false in all particulars. Their every truth is not quite true. Their two is not the real two, their four not the real four; so that every word they say chagrins us and we know not where to begin to set them right. Meantime nature is not slow to equip us in the prison-uniform of the party to which we adhere. We come to wear one cut of face and figure, and acquire by degrees the gentlest asinine expression. There is a mortifying experience in particular, which does not fail to wreak itself also in the general history; I mean "the foolish face of praise," the forced smile which we put on in company where we do not feel at ease, in answer to conversation which does not interest us. The muscles, not spontaneously moved but moved by a low usurping wilfulness, grow tight about the outline of the face, with the most disagreeable sensation.

For nonconformity the world whips you with its displeasure. And therefore a man must know how to estimate a sour face. The by-standers look askance on him in the pubic street or in the friend's parlor. If this aversion had its origin in contempt and resistance like his own he might well go home with a sad countenance; but the sour faces of the multitude, like their sweet faces, have no deep cause, but are put on and off as the wind blows and a newspaper directs. Yet is the discontent of the multitude more formidable than that of the senate and the college. It is easy enough for a firm man who knows the world to brook the rage of the cultivated classes. Their rage is decorous and prudent, for they are timid, as being very vulnerable themselves. But when to their feminine rage the indignation of the people is added, when the ignorant and the poor are aroused, when the unintelligent brute force that lies at the bottom of society is made to growl and mow, it needs the habit of magnanimity and religion to treat it godlike as a trifle of no concernment.

The other terror that scares us from self-trust is our consistency; a reverence for our past act or word because the eyes of others have no other data for computing our orbit than our past acts, and we are loth to disappoint them.

But why should you keep your head over your shoulder? Why drag about this corpse of your memory, lest you contradict somewhat you have stated in this or that public place? Suppose you should contradict yourself, what then? It seems to be a rule of wisdom never to rely on your memory alone, scarcely even in acts of pure memory, but to bring the past for judgment into the thousand-eyed present, and live ever in a new day. In your metaphysics you have denied personality to the Deity, yet when the devout motions of the soul come, yield to them heart and life, though they should clothe God with shape and color. Leave your theory, as Joseph his coat in the hand of the harlot, and flee.

A foolish consistency is the hobgoblin of little minds, adored by little statesmen and philosophers and divines. With consistency a great soul has simply nothing to do. He may as well concern himself with his shadow on the wall. Speak what you think now in hard words and to-morrow speak what to-morrow thinks in hard words again, though it contradict everything you said to-day.—"Ah, so you shall be sure to be misunderstood."—Is it so bad then to be misunderstood? Pythagoras was misunderstood, and Socrates, and Jesus, and Luther, and Copernicus, and Galileo, and Newton, and every pure and wise spirit that ever took flesh. To be great is to be misunderstood.

I suppose no man can violate his nature. All the sallies of his will are rounded in by the law of his being, as the inequalities of Andes and Himmaleh are insignificant in the curve of the sphere. Nor does it matter how you gauge and try him. A character is like an acrostic or Alexandrian stanza;— read it forward, backward, or across, it still spells the same thing. In this pleasing contrite wood-life which God allows me, let me record day by day my honest thought without prospect or retrospect, and, I cannot doubt, it will be found symmetrical, though I mean it not and see it not. My book should smell of pines and resound with the hum of insects. The swallow over my window should interweave that thread or straw he carries in his bill into my web also. We pass for what we are. Character teaches above our wills. Men imagine that they communicate their virtue or vice only by overt actions, and do not see that virtue or vice emit a breath every moment.

There will be an agreement in whatever variety of actions, so they be each honest and natural in their hour. For of one will, the actions will be harmonious, however unlike they seem. These varieties are lost sight of at a little distance, at a little height of thought. One tendency unites them all. The voyage of the best ship is a zigzag line of a hundred tacks. See the line from a sufficient distance, and it straightens itself to the average tendency. Your genuine action will explain itself and will explain your other genuine actions. Your conformity explains nothing. Act singly, and what you have already done singly will justify you now. Greatness appeals to the future. If I can be firm enough to-day to do right and scorn eyes, I must have done so much right before as to defend me now. Be it how it will, do right now. Al-

ways scorn appearances and you always may. The force of character is cumulative. All the foregone days of virtue work their health into this. What makes
the majesty of the heroes of the senate and the field, which so fills the imagination? The consciousness of a train of great days and victories behind. They
shed a united light on the advancing actor. He is attended as by a visible escort
of angels. That is it which throws thunder into Chatham's voice, and dignity
into Washington's port, and America into Adams's eye. Honor is venerable
to us because it is no ephemera. It is always ancient virtue. We worship it to-
day because it is not of to-day. We love it and pay it homage because it is not
a trap for our love and homage, but is self-dependent, self-derived, and therefore of an old immaculate pedigree, even if shown in a young person.

I hope in these days we have heard the last of conformity and consistency.
Let the words be gazetted and ridiculous henceforward. Instead of the gong
for dinner, let us hear a whistle from the Spartan fife. Let us never bow and
apologize more. A great man is coming to eat at my house. I do not wish to
please him; I wish that he should wish to please me. I will stand here for
humanity, and though I would make it kind, I would make it true. Let us
affront and reprimand the smooth mediocrity and squalid contentment of
the times, and hurl in the face of custom and trade and office, the fact which
is the upshot of all history, that there is a great responsible Thinker and Actor
working wherever a man works; that a true man belongs to no other time or
place, but is the centre of things. Where he is, there is nature. He measures you
and all men and all events. Ordinarily, every body in society reminds us of
somewhat else, or of some other person. Character, reality, reminds you of nothing else; it takes place of the whole creation. The man must be so much that he
must make all circumstances indifferent. Every true man is a cause, a country,
and an age; requires infinite spaces and numbers and time fully to accomplish
his design;—and posterity seem to follow his steps as a train of clients. A man
Cæsar is born, and for ages after we have a Roman Empire. Christ is born,
and millions of minds so grow and cleave to his genius that he is confounded
with virtue and the possible of man. An institution is the lengthened shadow
of one man; as, Monachism, of the Hermit Antony; the Reformation, of
Luther; Quakerism, of Fox; Methodism, of Wesley; Abolition, of Clarkson.
Scipio, Milton called "the height of Rome"; and all history resolves itself very
easily into the biography of a few stout and earnest persons.

Let a man then know his worth, and keep things under his feet. Let him
not peep or steal, or skulk up and down with the air of a charity-boy, a bastard, or an interloper in the world which exists for him. But the man in the
street, finding no worth in himself which corresponds to the force which
built a tower or sculptured a marble god, feels poor when he looks on these.
To him a palace, a statue, or a costly book have an alien and forbidding air,
much like a gay equipage, and seem to say like that, "Who are you, Sir?" Yet

they all are his, suitors for his notice, petitioners to his faculties that they will come out and take possession. The picture waits for my verdict; it is not to command me, but I am to settle its claims to praise. That popular fable of the sot who was picked up dead-drunk in the street, carried to the duke's house, washed and dressed and laid in the duke's bed, and, on his waking, treated with all obsequious ceremony like the duke, and assured that he had been insane, owes its popularity to the fact that it symbolizes so well the state of man, who is in the world a sort of sot, but now and then wakes up, exercises his reason and finds himself a true prince.

Our reading is mendicant and sycophantic. In history our imagination plays us false. Kingdom and lordship, power and estate, are a gaudier vocabulary than private John and Edward in a small house and common day's work; but the things of life are the same to both; the sum total of both is the same. Why all this deference to Alfred and Scanderbeg and Gustavus? Suppose they were virtuous; did they wear out virtue? As great a stake depends on your private act to-day as followed their public and renowned steps. When private men shall act with original views, the lustre will be transferred from the actions of kings to those of gentlemen.

The world has been instructed by its kings, who have so magnetized the eyes of nations. It has been taught by this colossal symbol the mutual reverence that is due from man to man. The joyful loyalty with which men have everywhere suffered the king, the noble, or the great proprietor to walk among them by a law of his own, make his own scale of men and things and reverse theirs, pay for benefits not with money but with honor, and represent the law in his person, was the hieroglyphic by which they obscurely signified their consciousness of their own right and comeliness, the right of every man.

The magnetism which all original action exerts is explained when we inquire the reason of self-trust. Who is the Trustee? What is the aboriginal Self, on which a universal reliance may be grounded? What is the nature and power of that science-baffling star, without parallax, without calculable elements, which shoots a ray of beauty even into trivial and impure actions, if the least mark of independence appear? The inquiry leads us to that source, at once the essence of genius, of virtue, and of life, which we call Spontaneity or Instinct. We denote this primary wisdom as Intuition, whilst all later teachings are tuitions. In that deep force, the last fact behind which analysis cannot go, all things find their common origin. For the sense of being which in calm hours rises, we know not how, in the soul, is not diverse from things, from space, from light, from time, from man, but one with them and proceeds obviously from the same source whence their life and being also proceed. We first share the life by which things exist and afterwards see them as appearances in nature and forget that we have shared their cause. Here is the fountain of action and of thought. Here are the lungs of that inspiration which

giveth man wisdom and which cannot be denied without impiety and atheism. We lie in the lap of immense intelligence, which makes us receivers of
its truth and organs of its activity. When we discern justice, when we discern
truth, we do nothing of ourselves, but allow a passage to its beams. If we
ask whence this comes, if we seek to pry into the soul that causes, all philosophy
is at fault. Its presence or its absence is all we can affirm. Every man discriminates between the voluntary acts of his mind and his involuntary perceptions, and knows that to his involuntary perceptions a perfect faith is due. He
may err in the expression of them, but he knows that these things are so, like
day and night, not to be disputed. My wilful actions and acquisitions are but
roving;—the idlest reverie, the faintest native emotion, command my curiosity
and respect. Thoughtless people contradict as readily the statement of perceptions as of opinions, or rather much more readily; for they do not distinguish between perception and notion. They fancy that I choose to see this or
that thing. But perception is not whimsical, but fatal. If I see a trait, my children will see it after me, and in course of time all mankind,—although it may
chance that no one has seen it before me. For my perception of it is as much
a fact as the sun.

The relations of the soul to the divine spirit are so pure that it is profane to
seek to interpose helps. It must be that when God speaketh he should communicate, not one thing, but all things; should fill the world with his voice;
should scatter forth light, nature, time, souls, from the centre of the present
thought; and new date and new create the whole. Whenever a mind is simple
and receives a divine wisdom, old things pass away,—means, teachers, texts,
temples fall; it lives now, and absorbs past and future into the present hour.
All things are made sacred by relation to it,—one as much as another. All
things are dissolved to their centre by their cause, and in the universal miracle
petty and particular miracles disappear. If therefore a man claims to know and
speak of God and carries you backward to the phraseology of some old mouldered nation in another country, in another world, believe him not. Is the
acorn better than the oak which is its fulness and completion? Is the parent
better than the child into whom he has cast his ripened being? Whence then
this worship of the past? The centuries are conspirators against the sanity and
authority of the soul. Time and space are but physiological colors which the
eye makes, but the soul is light: where it is, is day; where it was, is night;
and history is an impertinence and an injury if it be anything more than a
cheerful apologue or parable of my being and becoming.

Man is timid and apologetic; he is no longer upright; he dares not say "I
think," "I am," but quotes some saint or sage. He is ashamed before the
blade of grass or the blowing rose. These roses under my window make no
reference to former roses or to better ones; they are for what they are; they
exist with God to-day. There is no time to them. There is simply the rose;

it is perfect in every moment of its existence. Before a leaf-bud has burst, its whole life acts; in the full-blown flower there is no more; in the leafless root there is no less. Its nature is satisfied and it satisfies nature in all moments alike. But man postpones or remembers; he does not live in the present, but with reverted eye laments the past, or, heedless of the riches that surround him, stands on tiptoe to foresee the future. He cannot be happy and strong until he too lives with nature in the present, above time.

This should be plain enough. Yet see what strong intellects dare not yet hear God himself unless he speak the phraseology of I know not what David, or Jeremiah, or Paul. We shall not always set so great a price on a few texts, on a few lives. We are like children who repeat by rote the sentences of grandames and tutors, and, as they grow older, of the men of talents and character they chance to see,—painfully recollecting the exact words they spoke; afterwards, when they come into the point of view which those had who uttered these sayings, they understand them and are willing to let the words go; for at any time they can use words as good when occasion comes. If we live truly, we shall see truly. It is as easy for the strong man to be strong, as it is for the weak to be weak. When we have new perception, we shall gladly disburden the memory of its hoarded treasures as old rubbish. When a man lives with God, his voice shall be as sweet as the murmur of the brook and the rustle of the corn.

And now at last the highest truth on this subject remains unsaid; probably cannot be said; for all that we say is the far-off remembering of the intuition. That thought by what I can now nearest approach to say it, is this. When good is near you, when you have life in yourself, it is not by any known or accustomed way; you shall not discern the footprints of any other; you shall not see the face of man; you shall not hear any name;—the way, the thought, the good, shall be wholly strange and new. It shall exclude example and experience. You take the way from man, not to man. All persons that ever existed are its forgotten ministers. Fear and hope are alike beneath it. There is somewhat low even in hope. In the hour of vision there is nothing that can be called gratitude, nor properly joy. The soul raised over passion beholds identity and eternal causation, perceives the self-existence of Truth and Right, and calms itself with knowing that all things go well. Vast spaces of nature, the Atlantic Ocean, the South Sea; long intervals of time, years, centuries, are of no account. This which I think and feel underlay every former state of life and circumstances, as it does underlie my present, and what is called life and what is called death.

Life only avails, not the having lived. Power ceases in the instant of repose; it resides in the moment of transition from a past to a new state, in the shooting of the gulf, in the darting to an aim. This one fact the world hates; that the soul *becomes;* for that forever degrades the past, turns all riches to poverty, all reputation to a shame, confounds the saint with the rogue, shoves Jesus and Judas equally aside. Why then do we prate of self-reliance? Inasmuch as the soul is present there will be power not confident but agent. To talk of reliance is a poor external way of speaking. Speak rather of that which relies because it works and is. Who has more obedience than I masters me, though he should not raise his finger. Round him I must revolve by the gravitation of spirits. We fancy it rhetoric when we speak of eminent virtue. We do not yet see that virtue is Height, and that a man or a company of men, plastic and permeable to principles, by the law of nature must overpower and ride all cities, nations, kings, rich men, poets, who are not.

This is the ultimate fact which we so quickly reach on this, as on every topic, the resolution of all into the ever-blessed ONE. Self-existence is the attribute of the Supreme Cause, and it constitutes the measure of good by the degree in which it enters into all lower forms. All things real are so by so much virtue as they contain. Commerce, husbandry, hunting, whaling, war, eloquence, personal weight, are somewhat, and engage my respect as examples of its presence and impure action. I see the same law working in nature for conservation and growth. Power is, in nature, the essential measure of right. Nature suffers nothing to remain in her kingdoms which cannot help itself. The genesis and maturation of a planet, its poise and orbit, the bended tree recovering itself from the strong wind, the vital resources of every animal and vegetable, are demonstrations of the self-sufficing and therefore self-relying soul.

Thus all concentrates: let us not rove; let us sit at home with the cause. Let us stun and astonish the intruding rabble of men and books and institutions by a simple declaration of the divine fact. Bid the invaders take the shoes from off their feet, for God is here within. Let our simplicity judge them, and our docility to our own law demonstrate the poverty of nature and fortune beside our native riches.

But now we are a mob. Man does not stand in awe of man, nor is his genius admonished to stay at home, to put itself in communication with the internal ocean, but it goes abroad to beg a cup of water of the urns of other men. We must go alone. I like the silent church before the service begins, better than any preaching. How far off, how cool, how chaste the persons look, begirt each one with a precinct or sanctuary! So let us always sit. Why should we assume the faults of our friend, or wife, or father, or child, because they sit around our hearth or are said to have the same blood? All men have my blood and I all men's. Not for that will I adopt their petulance or folly, even to the extent of being ashamed of it. But your isolation must not be mechanical, but spiritual, that is, must be elevation. At times the whole world seems to be in conspiracy to importune you with emphatic trifles. Friend, client, child, sickness, fear, want, charity, all knock at once at thy closet door and say,—"Come out unto us." But keep thy state; come not into their confusion. The power men possess to annoy me I give them by a weak curiosity. No man can come near me but through my act. "What we love that we have, but by desire we bereave ourselves of the love."

If we cannot at once rise to the sanctities of obedience and faith, let us at least resist our temptations; let us enter into the state of war and wake Thor and Woden, courage and constancy, in our Saxon breasts. This is to be done in our smooth times by speaking the truth. Check this lying hospitality and lying affection. Live no longer to the expectation of these deceived and deceiving people with whom we converse. Say to them, "O father, O mother, O wife, O brother, O friend, I have lived with you after appearances hitherto. Henceforward I am the truth's. Be it known unto you that henceforward I obey no law less than the eternal law. I will have no covenants but proximities. I shall endeavor to nourish my parents, to support my family, to be the chaste husband of one wife,—but these relations I must fill after a new and unprecedented way. I appeal from your customs. I must be myself. I cannot break myself any longer for you, or you. If you can love me for what I am, we shall be the happier. If you cannot, I will still seek to deserve that you should. I will not hide my tastes or aversions. I will so trust that what is deep is holy, that I will do strongly before the sun and moon whatever inly rejoices me and the heart appoints. If you are noble, I will love you; if you are not, I will not hurt you and myself by hypocritical attentions. If you are true, but not in the same truth with me, cleave to your companions; I will seek my own. I do this not selfishly but humbly and truly. It is alike your interest, and mine, and all men's, however long we have dwelt in lies, to live in truth. Does this sound harsh to-day? You will soon love what is dictated by your nature as well as mine, and if we follow the truth it will bring us out safe at last."—But so may you give these friends pain. Yes, but I cannot sell my liberty and my power, to save their sensibility. Besides, all persons have their moments of reason, when they look out into the region of absolute truth; then will they justify me and do the same thing.

The populace think that your rejection of popular standards is a rejection of all standard, and mere antinomianism; and the bold sensualist will use the name of philosophy to gild his crimes. But the law of consciousness abides. There are two confessionals, in one or the other of which we must be shriven. You may fulfil your round of duties by clearing yourself in the *direct,* or in the *reflex* way. Consider whether you have satisfied your relations to father, mother, cousin, neighbor, town, cat, and dog—whether any of these can upbraid you. But I may also neglect this reflex standard and absolve me to myself. I have my own stern claims and perfect circle. It denies the name of duty to many offices that are called duties. But if I can discharge its debts it enables me to dispense with the popular code. If any one imagines that this law is lax, let him keep its commandment one day.

And truly it demands something godlike in him who has cast off the common motives of humanity and has ventured to trust himself for a taskmaster. High be his heart, faithful his will, clear his sight, that he may in good earnest be doctrine, society, law, to himself, that a simple purpose may be to him as strong as iron necessity is to others!

If any man consider the present aspects of what is called by distinction *society,* he will see the need of these ethics. The sinew and heart of man seem to be drawn out, and we are become timorous, desponding whimperers. We are afraid of truth, afraid of fortune, afraid of death, and afraid of each other. Our age yields no great and perfect persons. We want men and women who shall renovate life and our social state, but we see that most natures are insolvent, cannot satisfy their own wants, have an ambition out of all proportion to their practical force and do lean and beg day and night continually. Our housekeeping is mendicant, our arts, our occupations, our marriages, our religion we have not chosen, but society has chosen for us. We are parlor soldiers. We shun the rugged battle of fate, where strength is born.

If our young men miscarry in their first enterprises they lose all heart. If the young merchant fails, men say he is *ruined.* If the finest genius studies at one of our colleges and is not installed in an office within one year afterwards in the cities or suburbs of Boston or New York, it seems to his friends and to himself that he is right in being disheartened and in complaining the rest of his life. A sturdy lad from New Hampshire or Vermont, who in turn tries all the professions, who *teams it, farms it, peddles,* keeps a school, preaches, edits a newspaper, goes to Congress, buys a township, and so forth, in successive years, and always like a cat falls on his feet, is worth a hundred of these city dolls. He walks abreast with his days and feels no shame in not "studying a profession," for he does not postpone his life, but lives already. He has not one chance, but a hundred chances. Let a Stoic open the resources of man and tell men they are not leaning willows, but can and must detach themselves; that with the exercise of self-trust, new powers shall appear; that a man is the word made flesh, born to shed healing to the nations; that he should be ashamed of our compassion, and that the moment he acts from himself, tossing the laws, the books, idolatries and customs out of the window, we pity him no more but thank and revere him;—and that teacher shall restore the life of man to splendor and make his name dear to all history.

It is easy to see that a greater self-reliance must work a revolution in all the offices and relations of men; in their religion; in their education; in their pursuits; their modes of living; their association; in their property; in their speculative views.

1. In what prayers do men allow themselves! That which they call a holy office is not so much as brave and manly. Prayer looks abroad and asks for some foreign addition to come through some foreign virtue, and loses itself in endless mazes of natural and supernatural, and mediatorial and miraculous. Prayer that craves a particular commodity, anything less than all good, is vicious. Prayer is the contemplation of the facts of life from the highest point of view. It is the soliloquy of a beholding and jubilant soul. It is the spirit of God pronouncing his works good. But prayer as a means to effect a private end is meanness and theft. It supposes dualism and not unity in nature and consciousness. As soon as the man is at one with God, he will not beg. He will then see prayer in all action. The prayer of the farmer kneeling in his field to weed it, the prayer of the rower kneeling with the stroke of his oar, are true prayers heard throughout nature, though for cheap ends. Caratach, in Fletcher's *Bonduca,* when admonished to inquire the mind of the god Andate, replies,—

> His hidden meaning lies in our endeavors;
> Our valors are our best gods.

Another sort of false prayers are our regrets. Discontent is the want of self-reliance: it is infirmity of will. Regret calamities if you can thereby help the sufferer; if not, attend your own work and already the evil begins to be repaired. Our sympathy is just as base. We come to them who weep foolishly and sit down and cry for company, instead of imparting to them truth and health in rough electric shocks, putting them once more in communication with their own reason. The secret of fortune is joy in our hands. Welcome evermore to gods and men is the self-helping man. For him all doors are flung wide; him all tongues greet, all honors crown, all eyes follow with desire. Our love goes out to him and embraces him because he did not need it. We solicitously and apologetically caress and celebrate him because he held on his way and scorned our disapprobation. The gods love him because men hated him. "To the persevering mortal," said Zoroaster, "the blessed Immortals are swift."

As men's prayers are a disease of the will, so are their creeds a disease of the intellect. They say with those foolish Israelites, "Let not God speak to us, lest we die. Speak thou, speak any man with us, and we will obey." Everywhere I am hindered of meeting God in my brother, because he has shut his own temple doors and recites fables merely of his brother's, or his brother's brother's God. Every new mind is a new classification. If it prove a mind of uncommon activity and power, a Locke, a Lavoisier, a Hutton, a Bentham, a Fourier, it imposes its classification on other men, and lo! a new system. In proportion to the depth of the thought, and so to the number of the objects it touches and brings within reach of the pupil, is his complacency. But chiefly is this apparent in creeds and churches, which are also classifications of some powerful mind acting on the elemental thought of duty and man's relation to the Highest. Such is Calvinism, Quakerism, Swedenborgism. The pupil takes the same delight in subordinating everything to the new terminology as a girl who has just learned botany in seeing a new earth and new seasons thereby. It will happen for a time that the pupil will find his intellectual power has grown by the study of his master's mind. But in all unbalanced minds the classification is idolized, passes for the end and not for a speedily exhaustible means, so that the walls of the system blend to their eye in the remote horizon with the walls of the universe; the luminaries of heaven seem to them hung on the arch their master built. They cannot imagine how you aliens have any right to see,—how you can see; "It must be somehow that you stole the light from us." They do not yet perceive that light, unsystematic, indomitable, will break into any cabin, even into theirs. Let them chirp awhile and call it their own. If they are honest and do well, presently their neat new pinfold will be too strait and low, will crack, will lean, will rot and vanish, and the immortal light, all young and joyful, million-orbed, million-colored, will beam over the universe as on the first morning.

2. It is for want of self-culture that the superstition of Travelling, whose idols are Italy, England, Egypt, retains its fascination for all educated Americans. They who made England, Italy, or Greece venerable in the imagination, did so by sticking fast where they were, like an axis of the earth. In manly hours we feel that duty is our place. The soul is no traveller; the wise man stays at home, and when his necessities, his duties, on any occasion call him from his house, or into foreign lands, he is at home still and shall make men sensible by the expression of his countenance that he goes, the missionary of wisdom and virtue, and visits cities and men like a sovereign and not like an interloper or a valet.

I have no churlish objection to the circumnavigation of the globe for the purposes of art, of study, and benevolence, so that the man is first domesticated, or does not go abroad with the hope of finding somewhat greater than he knows. He who travels to be amused, or to get somewhat which he does not carry, travels away from himself, and grows old even in youth among old things. In Thebes, in Palmyra, his will and mind have become old and dilapidated as they. He carries ruins to ruins.

Travelling is a fool's paradise. Our first journeys discover to us the indifference of places. At home I dream that at Naples, at Rome, I can be intoxicated with beauty and lose my sadness. I pack my trunk, embrace my friends, embark on the sea, and at last wake up in Naples, and there beside me is the stern fact, the sad self, unrelenting, identical, that I fled from. I seek the Vatican and the palaces. I affect to be intoxicated with sights and suggestions, but I am not intoxicated. My giant goes with me wherever I go.

3. But the rage of travelling is a symptom of a deeper unsoundness affecting the whole intellectual action. The intellect is vagabond, and our system of education fosters restlessness. Our minds travel when our bodies are forced to stay at home. We imitate; and what is imitation but the travelling of the mind? Our houses are built with foreign taste; our shelves are garnished with foreign ornaments; our opinions, our tastes, our faculties, lean, and follow the Past and the Distant. The soul created the arts wherever they have flourished. It was in his own mind that the artist sought his model. It was an application of his own thought to the thing to be done and the conditions to be observed. And why need we copy the Doric or the Gothic model? Beauty, convenience, grandeur of thought and quaint expression are as near to us as to any, and if the American artist will study with hope and love the precise thing to be done by him, considering the climate, the soil, the length of the day, the wants of the people, the habit and form of the government, he will create a house in which all these will find themselves fitted, and taste and sentiment will be satisfied also.

Insist on yourself; never imitate. Your own gift you can present every moment with the cumulative force of a whole life's cultivation; but of the adopted talent of another you have only an extemporaneous half possession. That which each can do best, none but his Maker can teach him. No man yet knows what it is, nor can, till that person has exhibited it. Where is the master who could have taught Shakespeare? Where is the master who could have instructed Franklin, or Washington, or Bacon, or Newton? Every great man is a unique. The Scipionism of Scipio is precisely that part he could not borrow. Shakespeare will never be made by the study of Shakespeare. Do that which is assigned you, and you cannot hope too much or dare too much. There is at this moment for you an utterance brave and grand as that of the colossal chisel of Phidias, or trowel of the Egyptians, or the pen of Moses or Dante, but different from all these. Not possibly will the soul, all rich, all eloquent, with thousand-cloven tongue, deign to repeat itself; but if you can hear what these patriarchs say, surely you can reply to them in the same pitch of voice; for the ear and the tongue are two organs of one nature. Abide in the simple and noble regions of thy life, obey thy heart, and thou shalt reproduce the Foreworld again.

4. As our Religion, our Education, our Art look abroad, so does our spirit of society. All men plume themselves on the improvement of society, and no man improves.

Society never advances. It recedes as fast on one side as it gains on the other. It undergoes continual changes; it is barbarous, it is civilized, it is christianized, it is rich, it is scientific; but this change is not amelioration. For everything that is given something is taken. Society acquires new arts and loses old instincts. What a contrast between the well-clad, reading, writing, thinking American, with a watch, a pencil, and a bill of exchange in his pocket, and the naked New Zealander, whose property is a club, a spear, a mat, and an undivided twentieth of a shed to sleep under! But compare the health of the two men and you shall see that the white man has lost his aboriginal strength. If the traveller tells us truly, strike the savage with a broadaxe and in a day or two the flesh shall unite and heal as if you struck the blow into soft pitch, and the same blow shall send the white to his grave.

The civilized man has built a coach, but has lost the use of his feet. He is supported on crutches, but lacks so much support of muscle. He has a fine Geneva watch, but he fails of the skill to tell the hour by the sun. A Greenwich nautical almanac he has, and so being sure of the information when he wants it, the man in the street does not know a star in the sky. The solstice he does not observe; the equinox he knows as little; and the whole bright calendar of the year is without a dial in his mind. His note-books impair his memory; his libraries overload his wit; the insurance-office increases the number of accidents; and it may be a question whether machinery does not encumber; whether we have not lost by refinement some energy, by a Christianity, entrenched in establishments and forms, some vigor of wild virtue. For every Stoic was a Stoic; but in Christendom where is the Christian?

There is no more deviation in the moral standard than in the standard of height or bulk. No greater men are now than ever were. A singular equality may be observed between the great men of the first and of the last ages; nor can all the science, art, religion, and philosophy of the nineteenth century avail to educate greater men than Plutarch's heroes, three or four and twenty centuries ago. Not in time is the race progressive. Phocion, Socrates, Anaxagoras, Diogenes, are great men, but they leave no class. He who is really of their class will not be called by their name, but will be his own man, and in his turn the founder of a sect. The arts and inventions of each period are only its costume and do not invigorate men. The harm of the improved machinery may compensate its good. Hudson and Behring accomplished so much in their fishing-boats as to astonish Parry and Franklin, whose equipment exhausted the resources of science and art. Galileo, with an opera-glass, discovered a more splendid series of celestial phenomena than any one since. Columbus found the New World in an undecked boat. It is curious to see the periodical disuse and perishing of means and machinery which were introduced with loud laudation a few years or centuries before. The great genius returns to essential man. We reckoned the improvements of the art of war among the triumphs of science, and yet Napoleon conquered Europe by the bivouac, which consisted of falling back on naked valor and disencumbering it of all aids. The Emperor held it impossible to make a perfect army, says Las Cases, "without abolishing our arms, magazines, commissaries and carriages, until, in imitation of the Roman custom, the soldier should receive his supply of corn, grind it in his hand-mill, and bake his bread himself."

Society is a wave. The wave moves onward, but the water of which it is composed does not. The same particle does not rise from the valley to the ridge. Its unity is only phenomenal. The persons who make up a nation to-day, next year die, and their experience dies with them.

And so the reliance on Property, including the reliance on governments which protect it, is the want of self-reliance. Men have looked away from themselves and at things so long that they have come to esteem the religious, learned and civil institutions as guards of property, and they deprecate assaults on these, because they feel them to be assaults on property. They measure their esteem of each other by what each has, and not by what each is. But a cultivated man becomes ashamed of his property, out of new respect for his nature. Especially he hates what he has if he see that it is accidental, —came to him by inheritance, or gift, or crime; then he feels that it is not having; it does not belong to him, has no root in him, and merely lies there because no revolution or no robber takes it away. But that which a man is, does always by necessity acquire; and what the man acquires, is living property, which does not wait the beck of rulers, or mobs, or revolutions, or fire, or storm, or bankruptcies, but perpetually renews itself wherever the man breathes. "Thy lot or portion of life," said the Caliph Ali, "is seeking after thee; therefore be at rest from seeking after it." Our dependence on these foreign goods leads us to our slavish respect for numbers. The political parties meet in numerous conventions; the greater the concourse and with each new uproar of announcement, The delegation from Essex! The Democrats from New Hampshire! The Whigs of Maine! the young patriot feels himself stronger than before by a new thousand of eyes and arms. In like manner the reformers summon conventions and vote and resolve in multitude. Not so, O friends! will the God deign to enter and inhabit you, but by a method precisely the reverse. It is only as a man puts off all foreign support and stands alone that I see him to be strong and to prevail. He is weaker by every recruit to his banner. Is not a man better than a town? Ask nothing of men, and, in the endless mutation, thou only firm column must presently appear the upholder of all that surrounds thee. He who knows that power is inborn, that he is weak because he has looked for good out of him and elsewhere, and, so perceiving, throws himself unhesitatingly on his thought, instantly rights himself, stands in the erect position, commands his limbs, works miracles; just as a man who stands on his feet is stronger than a man who stands on his head.

So use all that is called Fortune. Most men gamble with her, and gain all, and lose all, as her wheel rolls. But do thou leave as unlawful these winnings, and deal with Cause and Effect, the chancellors of God. In the Will work and acquire, and thou hast chained the wheel of Chance, and shall sit hereafter out of fear from her rotations. A political victory, a rise of rents, the recovery of your sick or the return of your absent friend, or some other favorable event raises your spirits, and you think good days are preparing for you. Do not believe it. Nothing can bring you peace but yourself. Nothing can bring you peace but the triumph of principles.

COMPENSATION

EVER since I was a boy I have wished to write a discourse on Compensation; for it seemed to me when very young that on this subject life was ahead of theology and the people knew more than the preachers taught. The documents too from which the doctrine is to be drawn, charmed my fancy by their endless variety, and lay always before me, even in sleep; for they are the tools in our hands, the bread in our basket, the transactions of the street, the farm and the dwelling-house; greetings, relations, debts and credits, the influence of character, the nature and endowment of all men. It seemed to me also that in it might be shown men a ray of divinity, the present action of the soul of this world, clean from all vestige of tradition; and so the heart of man might be bathed by an inundation of eternal love, conversing with that which he knows was always and always must be, because it really is now. It appeared moreover that if this doctrine could be stated in terms with any resemblance to those bright intuitions in which this truth is sometimes revealed to us, it would be a star in many dark hours and crooked passages in our journey, that would not suffer us to lose our way.

I was lately confirmed in these desires by hearing a sermon at church. The preacher, a man esteemed for his orthodoxy, unfolded in the ordinary manner the doctrine of the Last Judgment. He assumed that judgment is not executed in this world; that the wicked are successful; that the good are miserable; and then urged from reason and from Scripture a compensation to be made to both parties in the next life. No offence appeared to be taken by the congregation at this doctrine. As far as I could observe when the meeting broke up they separated without remark on the sermon.

Yet what was the import of this teaching? What did the preacher mean by saying that the good are miserable in the present life? Was it that houses and lands, offices, wine, horses, dress, luxury, are had by unprincipled men, whilst the saints are poor and despised; and that a compensation is to be made to these last hereafter, by giving them the like gratifications another day,— bank-stock and doubloons, venison and champagne? This must be the compensation intended; for what else? Is it that they are to have leave to pray and praise? to love and serve men? Why, that they can do now. The legitimate inference the disciple would draw was,—"We are to have *such* a good time as the sinners have now;"—or, to push it to its extreme import,—"You sin now, we shall sin by and by; we would sin now, if we could; not being successful we expect our revenge to-morrow."

The fallacy lay in the immense concession that the bad are successful; that justice is not done now. The blindness of the preacher consisted in deferring to the base estimate of the market of what constitutes a manly success, instead of confronting and convicting the world from the truth; announcing the presence of the soul; the omnipotence of the will; and so establishing the standard of good and ill, of success and falsehood.

I find a similar base tone in the popular religious works of the day and the same doctrines assumed by the literary men when occasionally they treat the related topics. I think that our popular theology has gained in decorum, and not in principle, over the superstitions it has displaced. But men are better than their theology. Their daily life gives it the lie. Every ingenuous and aspiring soul leaves the doctrine behind him in his own experience, and all men feel sometimes the falsehood which they cannot demonstrate. For men are wiser than they know. That which they hear in schools and pulpits without afterthought, if said in conversation would probably be questioned in silence. If a man dogmatize in a mixed company on Providence and the divine laws, he is answered by a silence which conveys well enough to an observer the dissatisfaction of the hearer, but his incapacity to make his own statement.

I shall attempt in this and the following chapter to record some facts that indicate the path of the law of Compensation; happy beyond my expectation if I shall truly draw the smallest arc of this circle.

Polarity, or action and reaction, we meet in every part of nature; in darkness and light; in heat and cold; in the ebb and flow of waters; in male and female; in the inspiration and expiration of plants and animals; in the equation of quantity and quality in the fluids of the animal body; in the systole and diastole of the heart; in the undulations of fluids and of sound; in the centrifugal and centripetal gravity; in electricity, galvanism, and chemical affinity. Superinduce magnetism at one end of a needle, the opposite magnetism takes place at the other end. If the south attracts, the north repels. To empty here, you must condense there. An inevitable dualism bisects nature, so that each thing is a half, and suggests another thing to make it whole; as, spirit, matter; man, woman; odd, even; subjective, objective; in, out; upper, under; motion, rest; yea, nay.

Whilst the world is thus dual, so is every one of its parts. The entire system of things gets represented in every particle. There is somewhat that resembles the ebb and flow of the sea, day and night, man and woman, in a single needle of the pine, in a kernel of corn, in each individual of every animal tribe. The reaction, so grand in the elements, is repeated within these small boundaries.

For example, in the animal kingdom the physiologist has observed that no creatures are favorites, but a certain compensation balances every gift and every defect. A surplusage given to one part is paid out of a reduction from another part of the same creature. If the head and neck are enlarged, the trunk and extremities are cut short.

The theory of the mechanic forces is another example. What we gain in power is lost in time, and the converse. The periodic or compensating errors of the planets is another instance. The influences of climate and soil in political history is another. The cold climate invigorates. The barren soil does not breed fevers, crocodiles, tigers or scorpions.

The same dualism underlies the nature and condition of man. Every excess causes a defect; every defect an excess. Every sweet hath its sour; every evil its good. Every faculty which is a receiver of pleasure has an equal penalty put on its abuse. It is to answer for its moderation with its life. For every grain of wit there is a grain of folly. For everything you have missed, you have gained something else; and for everything you gain, you lose something. If riches increase, they are increased that use them. If the gatherer gathers too much, Nature takes out of the man what she puts into his chest; swells the estate, but kills the owner. Nature hates monopolies and exceptions. The waves of the sea do not more speedily seek a level from their loftiest tossing than the varieties of condition tend to equalize themselves. There is always some levelling circumstance that puts down the overbearing, the strong, the rich, the fortunate, substantially on the same ground with all others. Is a man too strong and fierce for society and by temper and position a bad citizen,—a morose ruffian, with a dash of the pirate in him?—Nature sends him a troop of pretty sons and daughters who are getting along in the dame's classes at the village school, and love and fear for them smooths his grim scowl to courtesy. Thus she contrives to intenerate the granite and felspar, takes the boar out and puts the lamb in, and keeps her balance true.

The farmer imagines power and place are fine things. But the President has paid dear for his White House. It has commonly cost him all his peace, and the best of his manly attributes. To preserve for a short time so conspicuous an appearance before the world, he is content to eat dust before the real masters who stand erect behind the throne. Or do men desire the more substantial and permanent grandeur of genius? Neither has this an immunity. He who by force of will or of thought is great and overlooks thousands, has the charges of that eminence. With every influx of light comes new danger. Has he light? he must bear witness to the light, and always outrun that sympathy which gives him such keen satisfaction, by his fidelity to new revelations of the incessant soul. He must hate father and mother, wife and child. Has he all that the world loves and admires and covets?—he must cast behind him their admiration and afflict them by faithfulness to his truth and become a by-word and a hissing.

This law writes the laws of cities and nations. It is in vain to build or plot or combine against it. Things refuse to be mismanaged long. *Res nolunt diu male administrari.* Though no checks to a new evil appear, the checks exist, and will appear. If the government is cruel, the governor's life is not safe. If you tax too high, the revenue will yield nothing. If you make the criminal code sanguinary, juries will not convict. If the law is too mild, private vengeance comes in. If the government is a terrific democracy, the pressure is resisted by an over-charge of energy in the citizen, and life glows with a fiercer flame. The true life and satisfactions of man seem to elude the utmost rigors of felicities of condition and to establish themselves with great indifferency under all varieties of circumstances. Under all governments the influence of character remains the same,—in Turkey and in New England about alike. Under the primeval despots of Egypt, history honestly confesses that man must have been as free as culture could make him.

These appearances indicate the fact that the universe is represented in every one of its particles. Everything in nature contains all the powers of nature. Everything is made of one hidden stuff; as the naturalist sees one type under every metamorphosis, and regards a horse as a running man, a fish as a swimming man, a bird as a flying man, a tree as a rooted man. Each new form repeats not only the main character of the type, but part for part all the details, all the aims, furtherances, hindrances, energies and whole system of every other. Every occupation, trade, art, transaction, is a compend of the world and a correlative of every other. Each one is an entire emblem of human life; of its good and ill, its trials, its enemies, its course and its end. And each one must somehow accommodate the whole man and recite all his destiny.

The world globes itself in a drop of dew. The microscope cannot find the animalcule which is less perfect for being little. Eyes, ears, taste, smell, motion, resistance, appetite, and organs of reproduction that take hold on eternity,—all find room to consist in the small creature. So do we put our life into every act. The true doctrine of omnipresence is that God reappears with all his parts in every moss and cobweb. The value of the universe contrives to throw itself into every point. If the good is there, so is the evil; if the affinity, so the repulsion; if the force, so the limitation.

Thus is the universe alive. All things are moral. That soul which within us is a sentiment, outside of us is a law. We feel its inspiration; but there in history we can see its fatal strength. "It is in the world, and the world was made by it." Justice is not postponed. A perfect equity adjusts its balance in all parts of life. Ἀεὶ γὰρ εὖ πίπτουσιν οἱ Διὸς κύβοι,—The dice of God are always loaded. The world looks like a multiplication-table, or a mathematical equation, which, turn it how you will, balances itself. Take what figure you will, its exact value, nor more nor less, still returns to you. Every secret is told, every crime is punished, every virtue rewarded, every wrong redressed, in silence and certainty. What we call retribution is the universal necessity by which the whole appears wherever a part appears. If you see smoke, there must be fire. If you see a hand or a limb, you know that the trunk to which it belongs is there behind.

Every act rewards itself, or in other words integrates itself, in a twofold manner; first in the thing, or in real nature; and secondly in the circumstance, or in apparent nature. Men call the circumstance the retribution. The causal retribution is in the thing and is seen by the soul. The retribution in the circumstance is seen by the understanding; it is inseparable from the thing, but is often spread over a long time and so does not become distinct until after many years. The specific stripes may follow late after the offence, but they follow because they accompany it. Crime and punishment grow out of one stem. Punishment is a fruit that unsuspected ripens within the flower of the pleasure which concealed it. Cause and effect, means and ends, seed and fruit, cannot be severed; for the effect already blooms in the cause, the end preëxists in the means, the fruit in the seed.

Whilst thus the world will be whole and refuses to be disparted, we seek to act partially, to sunder, to appropriate; for example,—to gratify the senses we sever the pleasure of the senses from the needs of the character. The ingenuity of man has always been dedicated to the solution of one problem,— how to detach the sensual sweet, the sensual strong, the sensual bright, etc., from the moral sweet, the moral deep, the moral fair; that is, again, to contrive to cut clean off this upper surface so thin as to leave it bottomless; to get a *one end,* without an *other end.* The soul says, "Eat"; the body would feast. The soul says, "The man and woman shall be one flesh and one soul"; the body would join the flesh only. The soul says, "Have dominion over all things to the ends of virtue"; the body would have the power over things to its own ends.

The soul strives amain to live and work through all things. It would be the only fact. All things shall be added unto it,—power, pleasure, knowledge, beauty. The particular man aims to be somebody; to set up for himself; to truck and higgle for a private good; and, in particulars, to ride that he may ride; to dress that he may be dressed; to eat that he may eat; and to govern, that he may be seen. Men seek to be great; they would have offices, wealth, power, and fame. They think that to be great is to possess one side of nature, —the sweet, without the other side, the bitter.

This dividing and detaching is steadily counteracted. Up to this day it must be owned no projector has had the smallest success. The parted water reunites behind our hand. Pleasure is taken out of pleasant things, profit out of profitable things, power out of strong things, as soon as we seek to separate them from the whole. We can no more halve things and get the sensual good, by itself, than we can get an inside that shall have no outside, or a light without a shadow. "Drive out Nature with a fork, she comes running back."

Life invests itself with inevitable conditions, which the unwise seek to dodge, which one and another brags that he does not know, that they do not touch him;—but the brag is on his lips, the conditions are in his soul. If he escapes them in one part they attack him in another more vital part. If he has escaped them in form and in the appearance, it is because he has resisted his life and fled from himself, and the retribution is so much death. So signal is the failure of all attempts to make this separation of the good from the tax, that the experiment would not be tried,—since to try it is to be mad,—but for the circumstance that when the disease began in the will, of rebellion and separation, the intellect is at once infected, so that the man ceases to see God whole in each object, but is able to see the sensual allurement of an object and not see the sensual hurt; he sees the mermaid's head but not the dragon's tail, and thinks he can cut off that which he would have from that which he would not have. "How secret art thou who dwellest in the highest heavens in silence, O thou only great God, sprinkling with an unwearied providence certain penal blindnesses upon such as have unbridled desires!"

The human soul is true to these facts in the painting of fable, of history, of law, of proverbs, of conversation. It finds a tongue in literature unawares. Thus the Greeks called Jupiter, Supreme Mind; but having traditionally ascribed to him many base actions, they involuntarily made amends to reason by tying up the hands of so bad a god. He is made as helpless as a king of England. Prometheus knows one secret which Jove must bargain for; Minerva, another. He cannot get his own thunders; Minerva keeps the key of them:—

> Of all the gods, I only know the keys
> That ope the solid doors within whose vaults
> His thunders sleep.

A plain confession of the in-working of the All and of its moral aim. The Indian mythology ends in the same ethics; and it would seem impossible for any fable to be invented and get any currency which was not moral. Aurora forgot to ask youth for her lover, and though Tithonus is immortal, he is old. Achilles is not quite invulnerable; the sacred waters did not wash the heel by which Thetis held him. Siegfried, in the Nibelungen, is not quite immortal, for a leaf fell on his back whilst he was bathing in the dragon's blood, and that spot which it covered is mortal. And so it must be. There is a crack in everything God has made. It would seem there is always this vindictive circumstance stealing in at unawares even into the wild poesy in which the human fancy attempted to make bold holiday and to shake itself free of the old laws, —this back-stroke, this kick of the gun, certifying that the law is fatal; that in nature nothing can be given, all things are sold.

This is that ancient doctrine of Nemesis, who keeps watch in the universe and lets no offence go unchastised. The Furies, they said, are attendants on justice, and if the sun in heaven should transgress his path they would punish him. The poets related that stone walls and iron swords and leathern thongs had an occult sympathy with the wrongs of their owners; that the belt which Ajax gave Hector dragged the Trojan hero over the field at the wheels of the car of Achilles, and the sword which Hector gave Ajax was that on whose point Ajax fell. They recorded that when the Thasians erected a statue to Theagenes, a victor in the games, one of his rivals went to it by night and endeavored to throw it down by repeated blows, until at last he moved it from its pedestal and was crushed to death beneath its fall.

This voice of fable has in it somewhat divine. It came from thought above the will of the writer. That is the best part of each writer which has nothing private in it; that which he does not know; that which flowed out of his constitution and not from his too active invention; that which in the study of a single artist you might not easily find, but in the study of many you would abstract as the spirit of them all. Phidias it is not, but the work of man in that early Hellenic world that I would know. The name and circumstance of Phidias, however convenient for history, embarrass when we come to the highest criticism. We are to see that which man was tending to do in a given period, and was hindered, or, if you will, modified in doing, by the interfering volitions of Phidias, of Dante, of Shakespeare, the organ whereby man at the moment wrought.

Still more striking is the expression of this fact in the proverbs of all nations, which are always the literature of reason, or the statements of an absolute truth without qualification. Proverbs, like the sacred books of each nation, are the sanctuary of the intuitions. That which the droning world, chained to appearances, will not allow the realist to say in his own words, it will suffer him to say in proverbs without contradiction. And this law of laws, which the pulpit, the senate and the college deny, is hourly preached in all markets and workshops by flights of proverbs, whose teaching is as true and as omnipresent as that of birds and flies.

All things are double, one against another.—Tit for tat; an eye for an eye; a tooth for a tooth; blood for blood; measure for measure; love for love.— Give, and it shall be given you.—He that watereth shall be watered himself.— What will you have? quoth God; pay for it and take it.—Nothing venture, nothing have.—Thou shalt be paid exactly for what thou hast done, no more, no less.—Who doth not work shall not eat.—Harm watch, harm catch.— Curses always recoil on the head of him who imprecates them.—If you put a chain around the neck of a slave, the other end fastens itself around your own. —Bad counsel confounds the adviser.—The Devil is an ass.

It is thus written, because it is thus in life. Our action is overmastered and characterized above our will by the law of nature. We aim at a petty end quite aside from the public good, but our act arranges itself by irresistible magnetism in a line with the poles of the world.

A man cannot speak but he judges himself. With his will or against his will he draws his portrait to the eye of his companions by every word. Every opinion reacts on him who utters it. It is a thread-ball thrown at a mark, but the other end remains in the thrower's bag. Or rather it is a harpoon hurled at the whale, unwinding, as it flies, a coil of cord in the boat, and, if the harpoon is not good, or not well thrown, it will go nigh to cut the steersman in twain or to sink the boat.

You cannot do wrong without suffering wrong. "No man had ever a point of pride that was not injurious to him," said Burke. The exclusive in fashionable life does not see that he excludes himself from enjoyment, in the attempt to appropriate it. The exclusionist in religion does not see that he shuts the door of heaven on himself, in striving to shut out others. Treat men as pawns and ninepins and you shall suffer as well as they. If you leave out their heart, you shall lose your own. The senses would make things of all persons; of women, of children, of the poor. The vulgar proverb, "I will get it from his purse or get it from his skin," is sound philosophy.

All infractions of love and equity in our social relations are speedily punished. They are punished by fear. Whilst I stand in simple relations to my fellow-man, I have no displeasure in meeting him. We meet as water meets water, or as two currents of air mix, with perfect diffusion and interpenetration of nature. But as soon as there is any departure from simplicity and attempt at halfness, or good for me that is not good for him, my neighbor feels the wrong; he shrinks from me as far as I have shrunk from him; his eyes no longer seek mine; there is war between us; there is hate in him and fear in me.

All the old abuses in society, universal and particular, all unjust accumulations of property and power, are avenged in the same manner. Fear is an instructor of great sagacity and the herald of all revolutions. One thing he teaches that there is rottenness where he appears. He is a carrion crow, and though you see not well what he hovers for, there is death somewhere. Our property is timid, our laws are timid, our cultivated classes are timid. Fear for ages has boded and mowed and gibbered over government and property. That obscene bird is not there for nothing. He indicates great wrongs which must be revised.

Of the like nature is that expectation of change which instantly follows the suspension of our voluntary activity. The terror of cloudless noon, the emerald of Polycrates, the awe of prosperity, the instinct which leads every generous soul to impose on itself tasks of a noble asceticism and vicarious virtue, are the tremblings of the balance of justice through the heart and mind of man.

Experienced men of the world know very well that it is best to pay scot and lot as they go along, and that a man often pays dear for a small frugality. The borrower runs in his own debt. Has a man gained anything who has received a hundred favors and rendered none? Has he gained by borrowing, through indolence or cunning, his neighbor's wares, or horses, or money? There arises on the deed the instant acknowledgment of benefit on the one part and of debt on the other; that is, of superiority and inferiority. The transaction remains in the memory of himself and his neighbor; and every new transaction alters according to its nature their relation to each other. He may soon come to see that he had better have broken his own bones than to have ridden in his neighbor's coach, and that "the highest price he can pay for a thing is to ask for it."

A wise man will extend this lesson to all parts of life, and know that it is the part of prudence to face every claimant and pay every just demand on your time, your talents, or your heart. Always pay; for first or last you must pay your entire debt. Persons and events may stand for a time between you and justice, but it is only a postponement. You must pay at last your own debt. If you are wise you will dread a prosperity which only loads you with more. Benefit is the end of nature. But for every benefit which you receive, a tax is levied. He is great who confers the most benefits. He is base,—and that is the one base thing in the universe,—to receive favors and render none. In the order of nature we cannot render benefits to those from whom we receive them, or only seldom. But the benefit we receive must be rendered again, line for line, deed for deed, cent for cent, to somebody. Beware of too much good staying in your hand. It will fast corrupt and worm worms. Pay it away quickly in some sort.

Labor is watched over by the same pitiless laws. Cheapest, say the prudent, is the dearest labor. What we buy in a broom, a mat, a wagon, a knife, is some application of good sense to a common want. It is best to pay in your land a skilful gardener, or to buy good sense applied to gardening; in your sailor, good sense applied to navigation; in the house, good sense applied to cooking, sewing, serving; in your agent, good sense applied to accounts and affairs. So do you multiply your presence, or spread yourself throughout your estate. But because of the dual constitution of things, in labor as in life there can be no cheating. The thief steals from himself. The swindler swindles himself. For the real price of labor is knowledge and virtue, whereof wealth and credit are signs. These signs, like paper money, may be counterfeited or stolen, but that which they represent, namely, knowledge and virtue, cannot be counterfeited or stolen. These ends of labor cannot be answered but by real exertions of the mind, and in obedience to pure motives. The cheat, the defaulter, the gambler, cannot extort the knowledge of material and moral nature which his honest care and pains yield to the operative. The law of nature is, Do the thing, and you shall have the power; but they who do not the thing have not the power.

Human labor, through all its forms, from the sharpening of a stake to the construction of a city or an epic, is one immense illustration of the perfect compensation of the universe. The absolute balance of Give and Take, the doctrine that everything has its price,—and if that price is not paid, not that thing but something else is obtained, and that it is impossible to get anything without its price,—is not less sublime in the columns of a ledger than in the budgets of states, in the laws of light and darkness, in all the action and re-action of nature. I cannot doubt that the high laws which each man sees implicated in those processes with which he is conversant, the stern ethics which sparkle on his chisel-edge, which are measured out by his plumb and foot-rule, which stand as manifest in the footing of the shop-bill as in the history of a state,—do recommend to him his trade, and though seldom named, exalt his business to his imagination.

The league between virtue and nature engages all things to assume a hostile front to vice. The beautiful laws and substances of the world persecute and whip the traitor. He finds that things are arranged for truth and benefit, but there is no den in the wide world to hide a rogue. Commit a crime, and the earth is made of glass. Commit a crime, and it seems as if a coat of snow fell on the ground, such as reveals in the woods the track of every partridge and fox and squirrel and mole. You cannot recall the spoken word, you cannot wipe out the foot-track, you cannot draw up the ladder, so as to leave no inlet or clew. Some damning circumstance always transpires. The laws and substances of nature,—water, snow, wind, gravitation,—become penalties to the thief.

On the other hand the law holds with equal sureness for all right action. Love, and you shall be loved. All love is mathematically just, as much as the two sides of an algebraic equation. The good man has absolute good, which like fire turns everything to its own nature, so that you cannot do him any harm; but as the royal armies sent against Napoleon, when he approached cast down their colors and from enemies became friends, so disasters of all kinds, as sickness, offence, poverty, prove benefactors:

> Winds blow and waters roll
> Strength to the brave and power and deity,
> Yet in themselves are nothing.

The good are befriended even by weakness and defect. As no man had ever a point of pride that was not injurious to him, so no man had ever a defect that was not somewhere made useful to him. The stag in the fable admired his horns and blamed his feet, but when the hunter came, his feet saved him, and afterwards, caught in the thicket, his horns destroyed him. Every man in his lifetime needs to thank his faults. As no man thoroughly understands a truth until he has contended against it, so no man has a thorough acquaintance with the hindrances or talents of men until he has suffered from the one and seen the triumph of the other over his own want of the same. Has he a defect of temper that unfits him to live in society? Thereby he is driven to entertain himself alone and acquire habits of self-help; and thus, like the wounded oyster, he mends his shell with pearl.

Our strength grows out of our weakness. The indignation which arms itself with secret forces does not awaken until we are pricked and stung and sorely assailed. A great man is always willing to be little. Whilst he sits on the cushion of advantages, he goes to sleep. When he is pushed, tormented, defeated, he has a chance to learn something; he has been put on his wits, on his manhood; he has gained facts; learns his ignorance; is cured of the insanity of conceit; has got moderation and real skill. The wise man throws himself on the side of his assailants. It is more his interest than it is theirs to find his weak point. The wound cicatrizes and falls off from him like a dead skin, and when they would triumph, lo! he has passed on invulnerable. Blame is safer than praise. I hate to be defended in a newspaper. As long as all that is said is said against me, I feel a certain assurance of success. But as soon as honeyed words of praise are spoken for me I feel as one that lies unprotected before his enemies. In general, every evil to which we do not succumb is a benefactor. As the Sandwich Islander believes that the strength and valor of the enemy he kills passes into himself, so we gain the strength of the temptation we resist.

The same guards which protect us from disaster, defect and enmity, defend us, if we will, from selfishness and fraud. Bolts and bars are not the best of our institutions, nor is shrewdness in trade a mark of wisdom. Men suffer all their life long under the foolish superstition that they can be cheated. But it is as impossible for a man to be cheated by any one but himself, as for a thing to be and not to be at the same time. There is a third silent party to all our bargains. The nature and soul of things takes on itself the guaranty of the fulfilment of every contract, so that honest service cannot come to loss. If you serve an ungrateful master, serve him the more. Put God in your debt. Every stroke shall be repaid. The longer the payment is withholden, the better for you; for compound interest on compound interest is the rate and usage of this exchequer.

The history of persecution is a history of endeavors to cheat nature, to make water run up hill, to twist a rope of sand. It makes no difference whether the actors be many or one, a tyrant or a mob. A mob is a society of bodies voluntarily bereaving themselves of reason and traversing its work. The mob is man voluntarily descending to the nature of the beast. Its fit hour of activity is night. Its actions are insane, like its whole constitution. It persecutes a principle; it would whip a right; it would tar and feather justice, by inflicting fire and outrage upon the houses and persons of those who have these. It resembles the prank of boys, who run with fire-engines to put out the ruddy aurora streaming to the stars. The inviolate spirit turns their spite against the wrongdoers. The martyr cannot be dishonored. Every lash inflicted is a tongue of fame; every prison a more illustrious abode; every burned book or house enlightens the world; every suppressed or expunged word reverberates through the earth from side to side. Hours of sanity and consideration are always arriving to communities, as to individuals, when the truth is seen and the martyrs are justified.

Thus do all things preach the indifferency of circumstances. The man is all. Everything has two sides, a good and an evil. Every advantage has its tax. I learn to be content. But the doctrine of compensation is not the doctrine of indifferency. The thoughtless say, on hearing these representations,—What boots it to do well? there is one event to good and evil; if I gain any good I must pay for it; if I lose any good I gain some other; all actions are indifferent.

There is a deeper fact in the soul than compensation, to wit, its own nature. The soul is not a compensation, but a life. The soul *is*. Under all this running sea of circumstance, whose waters ebb and flow with perfect balance, lies the aboriginal abyss of real Being. Essence, or God, is not a relation or a part, but the whole. Being is the vast affirmative, excluding negation, self-balanced, and swallowing up all relations, parts and times within itself. Nature, truth, virtue, are the influx from thence. Vice is the absence or departure of the same. Nothing, Falsehood, may indeed stand as the great Night or shade on which as a background the living universe paints itself forth, but no fact is begotten by it; it cannot work, for it is not. It cannot work any good; it cannot work any harm. It is harm inasmuch as it is worse not to be than to be.

We feel defrauded of the retribution due to evil acts, because the criminal adheres to his vice and contumacy and does not come to a crisis or judgment anywhere in visible nature. There is no stunning confutation of his nonsense before men and angels. Has he therefore outwitted the law? Inasmuch as he carries the malignity and the lie with him he so far deceases from nature. In some manner there will be a demonstration of the wrong to the understanding also; but, should we not see it, this deadly deduction makes square the eternal account.

Neither can it be said, on the other hand, that the gain of rectitude must be bought by any loss. There is no penalty to virtue; no penalty to wisdom; they are proper additions of being. In a virtuous action I properly *am;* in a virtuous act I add to the world; I plant into deserts conquered from Chaos and Nothing and see the darkness receding on the limits of the horizon. There can be no excess to love, none to knowledge, none to beauty, when these attributes are considered in the purest sense. The soul refuses limits, and always affirms an Optimism, never a Pessimism.

His life is a progress, and not a station. His instinct is trust. Our instinct uses "more" and "less" in application to man, of the *presence of the soul,* and not of its absence; the brave man is greater than the coward; the true, the benevolent, the wise, is more a man and not less, than the fool and knave. There is no tax on the good of virtue, for that is the incoming of God himself, or absolute existence, without any comparative. Material good has its tax, and if it came without desert or sweat, has no root in me, and the next wind will blow it away. But all the good of nature is the soul's, and may be had if paid for in nature's lawful coin, that is, by labor which the heart and the head allow. I no longer wish to meet a good I do not earn, for example to find a pot of buried gold, knowing that it brings with it new burdens. I do not wish more external goods,—neither possessions, nor honors, nor powers, nor persons. The gain is apparent; the tax is certain. But there is no tax on the knowledge that the compensation exists and that it is not desirable to dig up treasure. Herein I rejoice with a serene eternal peace. I contract the boundaries of possible mischief. I learn the wisdom of St. Bernard,—"Nothing can work me damage except myself; the harm that I sustain I carry about with me, and never am a real sufferer but by my own fault."

In the nature of the soul is the compensation for the inequalities of condition. The radical tragedy of nature seems to be the distinction of More and Less. How can Less not feel the pain; how not feel indignation or malevolence towards More? Look at those who have less faculty, and one feels sad and knows not well what to make of it. He almost shuns their eye; he fears they will upbraid God. What should they do? It seems a great injustice. But see the facts nearly and these mountainous inequalities vanish. Love reduces them as the sun melts the iceberg in the sea. The heart and soul of all men being one, this bitterness of *His* and *Mine* ceases. His is mine. I am my brother and my brother is me. If I feel overshadowed and outdone by great neighbors, I can yet love; I can still receive; and he that loveth maketh his own the grandeur he loves. Thereby I make the discovery that my brother is my guardian, acting for me with the friendliest designs, and the estate I so admired and envied is my own. It is the nature of the soul to appropriate all things. Jesus and Shakespeare are fragments of the soul, and by love I conquer and incorporate them in my own conscious domain. His virtue,—is not that mine? His wit,—if it cannot be made mine, it is not wit.

Such also is the natural history of calamity. The changes which break up at short intervals the prosperity of men are advertisements of a nature whose law is growth. Every soul is by this intrinsic necessity quitting its whole system of things, its friends and home and laws and faith, as the shell-fish crawls out of its beautiful but stony case, because it no longer admits of its growth, and slowly forms a new house. In proportion to the vigor of the individual these revolutions are frequent, until in some happier mind they are incessant and all worldly relations hang very loosely about him, becoming as it were a transparent fluid membrane through which the living form is seen, and not, as in most men, an indurated heterogeneous fabric of many dates and of no settled character, in which the man is imprisoned. Then there can be enlargement, and the man of to-day scarcely recognizes the man of yesterday. And such should be the outward biography of man in time, a putting off of dead circumstances day by day, as he renews his raiment day by day. But to us, in our lapsed estate, resting, not advancing, resisting, not coöperating with the divine expansion, this growth comes by shocks.

We cannot part with our friends. We cannot let our angels go. We do not see that they only go out that archangels may come in. We are idolaters of the old. We do not believe in the riches of the soul, in its proper eternity and omnipresence. We do not believe there is any force in to-day to rival or recreate that beautiful yesterday. We linger in the ruins of the old tent where once we had bread and shelter and organs, nor believe that the spirit can feed, cover, and nerve us again. We cannot again find aught so dear, so sweet, so graceful. But we sit and weep in vain. The voice of the Almighty saith, "Up and onward for evermore!" We cannot stay amid the ruins. Neither will we rely on the new; and so we walk ever with reverted eyes, like those monsters who look backwards.

And yet the compensations of calamity are made apparent to the understanding also, after long intervals of time. A fever, a mutilation, a cruel disappointment, a loss of wealth, a loss of friends, seems at the moment unpaid loss, and unpayable. But the sure years reveal the deep remedial force that underlies all facts. The death of a dear friend, wife, brother, lover, which seemed nothing but privation, somewhat later assumes the aspect of a guide or genius; for it commonly operates revolutions in our way of life, terminates an epoch of infancy or of youth which was waiting to be closed, breaks up a wonted occupation, or a household, or style of living, and allows the formation of new ones more friendly to the growth of character. It permits or constrains the formation of new acquaintances and the reception of new influences that prove of the first importance to the next years; and the man or woman who would have remained a sunny garden-flower, with no room for its roots and too much sunshine for its head, by the falling of the walls and the neglect of the gardener is made the banian of the forest, yielding shade and fruit to wide neighborhoods of men.

EZRA RIPLEY, D.D.[3]

EZRA RIPLEY was born May 1, 1751 (O.S.), at Woodstock, Connecticut. He was the fifth of the nineteen children of Noah and Lydia (Kent) Ripley. Seventeen of these nineteen children married, and it is stated that the mother died leaving nineteen children, one hundred and two grandchildren and ninety-six great grandchildren. The father was born at Hingham, on the farm purchased by his ancestor, William Ripley, of England, at the first settlement of the town; which farm has been occupied by seven or eight generations. Ezra Ripley followed the business of farming till sixteen years of age, when his father wished him to be qualified to teach a grammar school, not thinking himself able to send one son to college without injury to his other children. With this view, the father agreed with the late Rev. Dr. Forbes of Gloucester, then minister of North Brookfield, to fit Ezra for college by the time he should be twenty-one years of age, and to have him labor during the time sufficiently to pay for his instruction, clothing and books.

But, when fitted for college, the son could not be contented with teaching, which he had tried the preceding winter. He had early manifested a desire for learning, and could not be satisfied without a public education. Always inclined to notice ministers, and frequently attempting, when only five or six years old, to imitate them by preaching, now that he had become a professor of religion he had an ardent desire to be a preacher of the gospel. He had to encounter great difficulties, but, through a kind providence and the patronage of Dr. Forbes, he entered Harvard University, July, 1772. The commencement of the Revolutionary War greatly interrupted his education at college. In 1775, in his senior year, the college was removed from Cambridge to this town. The studies were much broken up. Many of the students entered the army, and the class never returned to Cambridge. There were an unusually large number of distinguished men in this class of 1776: Christopher Gore, Governor of Massachusetts and Senator in Congress; Samuel Sewall, Chief Justice of Massachusetts; George Thacher, Judge of the Supreme Court; Royall Tyler, Chief Justice of Vermont; and the late learned Dr. Prince, of Salem.

Mr. Ripley was ordained minister of Concord November 7, 1778. He married, November 16, 1780, Mrs. Phebe (Bliss) Emerson, then a widow of thirty-nine, with five children. They had three children: Sarah, born August 18, 1781; Samuel, born May 11, 1783; Daniel Bliss, born August 1, 1784. He died September 21, 1841.

To these facts, gathered chiefly from his own diary, and stated nearly in his own words, I can only add a few traits from memory.

---

[3] From *Lectures and Biographical Sketches.* Dr. Ezra Ripley, of Concord, was second husband of Emerson's grandmother. Emerson had known him from childhood.

He was identified with the ideas and forms of the New England Church, which expired about the same time with him, so that he and his coevals seemed the rear guard of the great camp and army of the Puritans, which, however in its last days declining into formalism, in the heyday of its strength had planted and liberated America. It was a pity that his old meeting-house should have been modernized in his time. I am sure all who remember both will associate his form with whatever was grave and droll in the old, cold, unpainted, uncarpeted, square-pewed meeting-house, with its four iron-gray deacons in their little box under the pulpit,—with Watts's hymns, with long prayers, rich with the diction of ages; and not less with the report like musketry from the movable seats. He and his contemporaries, the old New England clergy, were believers in what is called a particular providence,—certainly, as they held it, a very particular providence,—following the narrowness of King David and the Jews, who thought the universe existed only or mainly for their church and congregation. Perhaps I cannot better illustrate this tendency than by citing a record from the diary of the father of his predecessor, the minister of Malden, written in the blank leaves of the almanac for the year 1735. The minister writes against January 31st: "Bought a shay for 27 pounds, 10 shillings. The Lord grant it may be a comfort and blessing to my family." In March following he notes: "Had a safe and comfortable journey to York." But April 24th, we find: "Shay overturned, with my wife and I in it, yet neither of us much hurt. Blessed be our gracious Preserver. Part of the shay, as it lay upon one side, went over my wife, and yet she was scarcely anything hurt. How wonderful the preservation." Then again, May 5th: "Went to the beach with three of the children. The beast, being frightened when we were all out of the shay, overturned and broke it. I desire (I hope I desire it) that the Lord would teach me suitably to resent this Providence, to make suitable remarks on it, and to be suitably affected with it. Have I done well to get me a shay? Have I not been proud or too fond of this convenience? Do I exercise the faith in the Divine care and protection which I ought to do? Should I not be more in my study and less fond of diversion? Do I not withhold more than is meet from pious and charitable uses?" Well, on 15th May we have this: "Shay brought home; mending cost thirty shillings. Favored in this respect beyond expectation." 16th May: "My wife and I rode together to Rumney Marsh. The beast frightened several times." And at last we have this record, June 4th: "Disposed of my shay to Rev. Mr. White."

The same faith made what was strong and what was weak in Dr. Ripley and his associates. He was a perfectly sincere man, punctual, severe, but just and charitable, and if he made his forms a strait-jacket to others, he wore the same himself all his years. Trained in this church, and very well qualified by his natural talent to work in it, it was never out of his mind. He looked at every person and thing from the parochial point of view. I remember, when a boy, driving about Concord with him, and in passing each house he told the story of the family that lived in it, and especially he gave me anecdotes of the nine church members who had made a division in the church in the time of his predecessor, and showed me how every one of the nine had come to bad fortune or to a bad end. His prayers for rain and against the lightning, "that it may not lick up our spirits;" and for good weather; and against sickness and insanity; "that we have not been tossed to and fro until the dawning of the day; that we have not been a terror to ourselves and others,"—are well remembered, and his own entire faith that these petitions were not to be overlooked, and were entitled to a favorable answer. Some of those around me will remember one occasion of severe drought in this vicinity, when the late Rev. Mr. Goodwin offered to relieve the Doctor of the duty of leading in prayer; but the Doctor suddenly remembering the season, rejected his offer with some humor, as with an air that said to all the congregation, "This is no time for you young Cambridge men; the affair, sir, is getting serious. I will pray myself." One August afternoon, when I was in his hayfield helping him with his man to rake up his hay, I well remember his pleading, almost reproachful looks at the sky, when the thundergust was coming up to spoil his hay. He raked very fast, then looked at the cloud, and said, "We are in the Lord's hand; mind your rake, George! We are in the Lord's hand;" and seemed to say, "You know me; this field is mine,—Dr. Ripley's,—thine own servant!"

He used to tell the story of one of his old friends, the minister of Sudbury, who, being at the Thursday lecture in Boston, heard the officiating clergyman praying for rain. As soon as the service was over, he went to the petitioner, and said, "You Boston ministers, as soon as a tulip wilts under your windows, go to church and pray for rain, until all Concord and Sudbury are under water." I once rode with him to a house at Nine Acre Corner to attend the funeral of the father of a family. He mentioned to me on the way his fears that the oldest son, who was now to succeed to the farm, was becoming intemperate. We presently arrived, and the Doctor addressed each of the mourners separately: "Sir, I condole with you." "Madam, I condole with you." "Sir, I knew your great-grandfather. When I came to this town, your great-grandfather was a substantial farmer in this very place, a member of the church, and an excellent citizen. Your grandfather followed him, and was a virtuous man. Now your father is to be carried to his grave, full of labors and virtues. There is none of that large family left but you, and it rests with you to bear up the good name and usefulness of your ancestors. If you fail,— 'Ichabod, the glory is departed.' Let us pray." Right manly he was, and the manly thing he could always say. I can remember a little speech he made to me, when the last tie of blood which held me and my brothers to his house was broken by the death of his daughter. He said, on parting, "I wish you and your brothers to come to this house as you have always done. You will not like to be excluded; I shall not like to be neglected."

When "Put" Merriam, after his release from the state prison, had the effrontery to call on the Doctor as an old acquaintance, in the midst of general conversation Mr. Frost came in, and the Doctor presently said, "Mr. Merriam, my brother and colleague, Mr. Frost, has come to take tea with me. I regret very much the causes (which you know very well) which make it impossible for me to ask you to stay and break bread with us." With the Doctor's views it was a matter of religion to say thus much. He had a reverence and love of society, and the patient, continuing courtesy, carrying out every respectful attention to the end, which marks what is called the manners of the old school. His hospitality obeyed Charles Lamb's rule, and "ran fine to the last." His partiality for ladies was always strong, and was by no means abated by time. He claimed privilege of years, was much addicted to kissing; spared neither maid, wife nor widow, and, as a lady thus favored remarked to me, "seemed as if he was going to make a meal of you."

He was very credulous, and as he was no reader of books or journals, he knew nothing beyond the columns of his weekly religious newspaper, the tracts of his sect, and perhaps the Middlesex Yeoman. He was the easy dupe of any tonguey agent, whether colonizationist or anti-papist, or charlatan of iron combs, or tractors, or phrenology, or magnetism, who went by. At the time when Jack Downing's letters were in every paper, he repeated to me at table some of the particulars of that gentleman's intimacy with General Jackson, in a manner that betrayed to me at once that he took the whole for fact. To undeceive him, I hastened to recall some particulars to show the absurdity of the thing, as the Major and the President going out skating on the Potomac, etc. "Why," said the Doctor with perfect faith, "it was a bright moonlight night"; and I am not sure that he did not die in the belief in the reality of Major Downing. Like other credulous men, he was opinionative, and, as I well remember, a great browbeater of the poor old fathers who still survive from the 19th of April, to the end that they should testify to his history as he had written it.

He was a man so kind and sympathetic, his character was so transparent, and his merits so intelligible to all observers, that he was very justly appreciated in this community. He was a natural gentleman, no dandy, but courtly, hospitable, manly and public-spirited; his nature social, his house open to all men. We remember the remark made by the old farmer who used to travel hither from Maine, that no horse from the Eastern country would go by the Doctor's gate. Travellers from the West and North and South bear the like testimony. His brow was serene and open to his visitor, for he loved men, and he had no studies, no occupations, which company could interrupt. His friends were his study, and to see them loosened his talents and his tongue.

In his house dwelt order and prudence and plenty. There was no waste and no stint. He was open-handed and just and generous. Ingratitude and meanness in his beneficiaries did not wear out his compassion; he bore the insult, and the next day his basket for the beggar, his horse and chaise for the cripple, were at their door. Though he knew the value of a dollar as well as another man, yet he loved to buy dearer and sell cheaper than others. He subscribed to all charities, and it is no reflection on others to say that he was the most public-spirited man in the town. The late Dr. Gardiner, in a funeral sermon on some parishioner whose virtues did not readily come to mind, honestly said, "He was good at fires." Dr. Ripley had many virtues, and yet all will remember that even in his old age, if the firebell was rung, he was instantly on horseback with his buckets, and bag.

He showed even in his fireside discourse traits of that pertinency and judgment, softening ever and anon into elegancy, which make the distinction of the scholar, and which, under better discipline, might have ripened into a Bentley or a Porson. He had a foresight, when he opened his mouth, of all that he would say, and he marched straight to the conclusion. In debate, in the vestry of the Lyceum, the structure of his sentences was admirable; so neat, so natural, so terse, his words fell like stones; and often, though quite unconscious of it, his speech was a satire on the loose, voluminous, draggletail periods of other speakers. He sat down when he had done. A man of anecdote, his talk in the parlor was chiefly narrative. We remember the remark of a gentleman who listened with much delight to his conversation at the time when the Doctor was preparing to go to Baltimore and Washington, that "a man who could tell a story so well was company for kings and John Quincy Adams."

Sage and savage strove harder in him than in any of my acquaintances, each getting the mastery by turns, and pretty sudden turns: "Save us from the extremity of cold and these violent sudden changes." "The society will meet after the Lyceum, as it is difficult to bring people together in the evening, —and no moon." "Mr. N. F. is dead, and I expect to hear of the death of Mr. B. It is cruel to separate old people from their wives in this cold weather."

With a very limited acquaintance with books, his knowledge was an external experience, an Indian wisdom, the observation of such facts as country life for nearly a century could supply. He watched with interest the garden, the field, the orchard, the house and the barn, horse, cow, sheep and dog, and all the common objects that engage the thought of the farmer. He kept his eye on the horizon, and knew the weather like a sea-captain. The usual experiences of men, birth, marriage, sickness, death, burial; the common temptations; the common ambitions;—he studied them all, and sympathized so well in these that he was excellent company and counsel to all, even the most humble and ignorant. With extraordinary states of mind, with states of enthusiasm or enlarged speculation, he had no sympathy, and pretended to none. He was sincere, and kept to his point, and his mark was never remote. His conversation was strictly personal and apt to the party and the occasion. An eminent skill he had in saying difficult and unspeakable things; in delivering to a man or a woman that which all their other friends had abstained from saying, in uncovering the bandage from a sore place, and applying the surgeon's knife with a truly surgical spirit. Was a man a sot, or a spendthrift, or too long time a bachelor, or suspected of some hidden crime, or had he quarrelled with his wife, or collared his father, or was there any cloud or suspicious circumstances in his behavior, the good pastor knew his way straight to that point, believing himself entitled to a full explanation, and whatever relief to the conscience of both parties plain speech could effect was sure to be procured. In all such passages he justified himself to the conscience, and commonly to the love, of the persons concerned. He was the more competent to these searching discourses from his knowledge of family history. He knew everybody's grandfather, and seemed to address each person rather as the representative of his house and name, than as an individual. In him have perished more local and personal anecdotes of this village and vicinity than are possessed by any survivor. This intimate knowledge of families, and this skill of speech, and still more, his sympathy, made him incomparable in his parochial visits, and in his exhortations and prayers. He gave himself up to his feelings, and said on the instant the best things in the world. Many and many a felicity he had in his prayer, now forever lost, which defied all the rules of all the rhetoricians. He did not know when he was good in prayer or sermon, for he had no literature and no art; but he believed, and therefore spoke. He was eminently loyal in his nature, and not fond of adventure or innovation. By education, and still more by temperament, he was engaged to the old forms of the New England Church. Not speculative, but affectionate; devout, but with an extreme love of order, he adopted heartily, though in its mildest form, the creed and catechism of the fathers, and appeared a modern Israelite in his attachment to the Hebrew history and faith. He was a man very easy to read, for his whole life and conversation were consistent. All his opinions and actions might be securely predicted by a good observer on short acquaintance. My classmate at Cambridge, Frederick King, told me from Governor Gore, who was the Doctor's classmate, that in college he was called Holy Ripley.

And now, in his old age, when all the antique Hebraism and its customs are passing away, it is fit that he too should depart,—most fit that in the fall of laws a loyal man should die.

From ENGLISH TRAITS

[WORDSWORTH] [4]

ON the 28th August I went to Rydal Mount, to pay my respects to Mr. Wordsworth. His daughters called in their father, a plain, elderly, white-haired man, not prepossessing, and disfigured by green goggles. He sat down, and talked with great simplicity. He had just returned from a journey. His health was good, but he had broken a tooth by a fall, when walking with two lawyers, and had said that he was glad it did not happen forty years ago; whereupon they had praised his philosophy.

He had much to say of America, the more that it gave occasion for his favorite topic,—that society is being enlightened by a superficial tuition, out of all proportion to its being restrained by moral culture. Schools do no good. Tuition is not education. He thinks more of the education of circumstances than of tuition. 'Tis not question whether there are offences of which the law takes cognizance, but whether there are offences of which the law does not take cognizance. Sin is what he fears,—and how society is to escape without gravest mischiefs from this source. He has even said, what seemed a paradox, that they needed a civil war in America, to teach the necessity of knitting the social ties stronger. "There may be," he said, "in America some vulgarity in manner, but that's not important. That comes of the pioneer state of things. But I fear they are too much given to the making of money; and secondly, to politics; that they make political distinction the end and not the means. And I fear they lack a class of men of leisure,—in short, of gentlemen,—to give a tone of honor to the community. I am told that things are boasted of in the second class of society there, which, in England,—God knows, are done in England every day, but would never be spoken of. In America I wish to know not how many churches or schools but what newspapers? My friend Colonel Hamilton, at the foot of the hill, who was a year in America, assures me that the newspapers are atrocious, and accuse members of Congress of stealing spoons!" He was against taking off the tax on newspapers in England, —which the reformers represent as a tax upon knowledge,—for this reason, that they would be inundated with base prints. He said he talked on political aspects, for he wished to impress on me and all good Americans to cultivate the moral, the conservative, etc., etc., and never to call into action the physical strength of the people, as had just now been done in England, in the Reform Bill,—a thing prophesied by Delolme. He alluded once or twice to his conversation with Dr. Channing who had recently visited him (laying his hand on a particular chair in which the Doctor had sat).

The conversation turned on books. Lucretius he esteems a far higher poet

---

[4] Emerson "paid his respects" to Wordsworth during his first visit to England in 1833; and included this portrait in *English Traits,* chap. i (1856).

than Virgil; not in his system, which is nothing, but in his power of illustration. Faith is necessary to explain anything and to reconcile the foreknowledge of God with human evil. Of Cousin (whose lectures we had all been reading in Boston), he knew only the name.

I inquired if he had read Carlyle's critical articles and translations. He said he thought him sometimes insane. He proceeded to abuse Goethe's Wilhelm Meister heartily. It was full of all manner of fornication. It was like the crossing of flies in the air. He had never gone farther than the first part; so disgusted was he that he threw the book across the room. I deprecated this wrath, and said what I could for the better parts of the book, and he courteously promised to look at it again. Carlyle he said wrote most obscurely. He was clever and deep, but he defied the sympathies of everybody. Even Mr. Coleridge wrote more clearly, though he had always wished Coleridge would write more to be understood. He led me out into his garden, and showed me the gravel walk in which thousands of his lines were composed. His eyes are much inflamed. This is no loss except for reading, because he never writes prose, and of poetry he carries even hundreds of lines in his head before writing them. He had just returned from a visit to Staffa, and within three days had made three sonnets on Fingal's Cave, and was composing a fourth when he was called in to see me. He said, "If you are interested in my verses perhaps you will like to hear these lines." I gladly assented, and he recollected himself for a few moments and then stood forth and repeated, one after the other, the three entire sonnets with great animation. I fancied the second and third more beautiful than his poems are wont to be. The third is addressed to the flowers, which, he said, especially the ox-eye daisy, are very abundant on the top of the rock. The second alludes to the name of the cave, which is "Cave of Music"; the first to the circumstance of its being visited by the promiscuous company of the steamboat.

This recitation was so unlooked for and surprising,—he, the old Wordsworth, standing apart, and reciting to me in a garden-walk, like a school-boy declaiming,—that I at first was near to laugh; but recollecting myself, that I had come thus far to see a poet and he was chanting poems to me, I saw that he was right and I was wrong, and gladly gave myself up to hear. I told him how much the few printed extracts had quickened the desire to possess his unpublished poems. He replied he never was in haste to publish; partly because he corrected a good deal, and every alteration is ungraciously received after printing; but what he had written would be printed, whether he lived or died. I said Tintern Abbey appeared to be the favorite poem with the public, but more contemplative readers preferred the first books of the Excursion, and the Sonnets. He said, "Yes, they are better." He preferred such of his poems as touched the affections, to any others; for whatever is didactic —what theories of society, and so on—might perish quickly; but whatever combined a truth with an affection was κτῆμα ἐς ἀεί, good to-day and good forever. He cited the sonnet, On the feelings of a highminded Spaniard, which he preferred to any other (I so understood him), and the Two Voices; and quoted, with evident pleasure, the verses addressed To the Skylark. In this connection he said of the Newtonian theory that it might yet be superseded and forgotten; and Dalton's atomic theory.

When I prepared to depart he said he wished to show me what a common person in England could do, and he led me into the enclosure of his clerk, a young man to whom he had given this slip of ground, which was laid out, or its natural capabilities shown, with much taste. He then said he would show me a better way towards the inn; and he walked a good part of a mile, talking and ever and anon stopping short to impress the word or the verse, and finally parted from me with great kindness and returned across the fields.

Wordsworth honored himself by his simple adherence to truth, and was very willing not to shine; but he surprised by the hard limits of his thought. To judge from a single conversation, he made the impression of a narrow and very English mind; of one who paid for his rare elevation by general tameness and conformity. Off his own beat, his opinions were of no value. It is not very rare to find persons loving sympathy and ease, who expiate their departure from the common in one direction, by their conformity in every other.

THOREAU [5]

It seemed as if the breezes brought him,
It seemed as if the sparrows taught him,
As if by secret sign he knew
Where in far fields the orchis grew.

HENRY DAVID THOREAU was the last male descendant of a French ancestor who came to this country from the Isle of Guernsey. His character exhibited occasional traits drawn from this blood, in singular combination with a very strong Saxon genius.

He was born in Concord, Massachusetts, on the 12th of July, 1817. He was graduated at Harvard College in 1837, but without any literary distinction. An iconoclast in literature, he seldom thanked colleges for their service to him, holding them in small esteem, whilst yet his debt to them was important. After leaving the University, he joined his brother in teaching a private school, which he soon renounced. His father was a manufacturer of lead-pencils, and Henry applied himself for a time to this craft, believing he could make a better pencil than was then in use. After completing his experiments, he

[5] This portrait, made just after Thoreau's death in 1862, and first published in the *Atlantic Monthly* in that year, is from *Lectures and Biographical Sketches*.

exhibited his work to chemists and artists in Boston, and having obtained their certificates to its excellence and to its equality with the best London manufacture, he returned home contented. His friends congratulated him that he had now opened his way to fortune. But he replied that he should never make another pencil. "Why should I? I would not do again what I have done once." He resumed his endless walks and miscellaneous studies, making every day some new acquaintance with Nature, though as yet never speaking of zoölogy or botany, since, though very studious of natural facts, he was incurious of technical and textual science.

At this time, a strong, healthy youth, fresh from college, whilst all his companions were choosing their profession, or eager to begin some lucrative employment, it was inevitable that his thoughts should be exercised on the same question, and it required rare decision to refuse all the accustomed paths and keep his solitary freedom at the cost of disappointing the natural expectations of his family and friends: all the more difficult that he had a perfect probity, was exact in securing his own independence, and in holding every man to the like duty. But Thoreau never faltered. He was a born protestant. He declined to give up his large ambition of knowledge and action for any narrow craft or profession, aiming at a much more comprehensive calling, the art of living well. If he slighted and defied the opinions of others, it was only that he was more intent to reconcile his practice with his own belief. Never idle or self-indulgent, he preferred, when he wanted money, earning it by some piece of manual labor agreeable to him, as building a boat or a fence, planting, grafting, surveying or other short work, to any long engagements. With his hardy habits and few wants, his skill in wood-craft, and his powerful arithmetic, he was very competent to live in any part of the world. It would cost him less time to supply his wants than another. He was therefore secure of his leisure.

A natural skill for mensuration, growing out of his mathematical knowledge and his habit of ascertaining the measures and distances of objects which interested him, the size of trees, the depth and extent of ponds and rivers, the height of mountains and the air-line distance of his favorite summits,—this, and his intimate knowledge of the territory about Concord, made him drift into the profession of land-surveyor. It had the advantage for him that it led him continually into new and secluded grounds, and helped his studies of Nature. His accuracy and skill in this work were readily appreciated, and he found all the employment he wanted.

He could easily solve the problems of the surveyor, but he was daily beset with graver questions, which he manfully confronted. He interrogated every custom, and wished to settle all his practice on an ideal foundation. He was a protestant *à outrance,* and few lives contain so many renunciations. He was bred to no profession; he never married; he lived alone; he never went to church; he never voted; he refused to pay a tax to the State; he ate no flesh, he drank no wine, he never knew the use of tobacco; and, though a naturalist, he used neither trap nor gun. He chose, wisely no doubt for himself, to be the bachelor of thought and Nature. He had no talent for wealth, and knew how to be poor without the least hint of squalor or inelegance. Perhaps he fell into his way of living without forecasting it much, but approved it with later wisdom. "I am often reminded," he wrote in his journal, "that if I had bestowed on me the wealth of Crœsus, my aims must be still the same, and my means essentially the same." He had no temptations to fight against, —no appetites, no passions, no taste for elegant trifles. A fine house, dress, the manners and talk of highly cultivated people were all thrown away on him. He much preferred a good Indian, and considered these refinements as impediments to conversation, wishing to meet his companion on the simplest terms. He declined invitations to dinner-parties, because there each was in every one's way, and he could not meet the individuals to any purpose. "They make their pride," he said, "in making their dinner cost much; I make my pride in making my dinner cost little." When asked at table what dish he preferred, he answered, "The nearest." He did not like the taste of wine, and never had a vice in his life. He said,—"I have a faint recollection of pleasure derived from smoking dried lily-stems, before I was a man. I had commonly a supply of these. I have never smoked anything more noxious."

He chose to be rich by making his wants few, and supplying them himself. In his travels, he used the railroad only to get over so much country as was unimportant to the present purpose, walking hundreds of miles, avoiding taverns, buying a lodging in farmers' and fishermen's houses, as cheaper, and more agreeable to him, and because there he could better find the men and the information he wanted.

There was somewhat military in his nature, not to be subdued, always manly and able, but rarely tender, as if he did not feel himself except in opposition. He wanted a fallacy to expose, a blunder to pillory, I may say required a little sense of victory, a roll of the drum, to call his powers into full exercise. It cost him nothing to say No; indeed he found it much easier than to say Yes. It seemed as if his first instinct on hearing a proposition was to controvert it, so impatient was he of the limitations of our daily thought. This habit, of course, is a little chilling to the social affections; and though the companion would in the end acquit him of any malice or untruth, yet it mars conversation. Hence, no equal companion stood in affectionate relations with one so pure and guileless. "I love Henry," said one of his friends, "but I cannot like him; and as for taking his arm, I should as soon think of taking the arm of an elm-tree."

Yet, hermit and stoic as he was, he was really fond of sympathy, and threw himself heartily and childlike into the company of young people whom he loved, and whom he delighted to entertain, as he only could, with the varied and endless anecdotes of his experiences by field and river: and he was always ready to lead a huckleberry-party or a search for chestnuts or grapes. Talking, one day, of a public discourse, Henry remarked that whatever succeeded with the audience was bad. I said, "Who would not like to write something which all can read, like Robinson Crusoe? and who does not see with regret that his page is not solid with a right materialistic treatment, which delights everybody?" Henry objected, of course, and vaunted the better lectures which reached only a few persons. But, at supper, a young girl, understanding that he was to lecture at the Lyceum, sharply asked him, "Whether his lecture would be a nice, interesting story, such as she wished to hear, or whether it was one of those old philosophical things that she did not care about." Henry turned to her, and bethought himself, and, I saw, was trying to believe that he had matter that might fit her and her brother, who were to sit up and go to the lecture, if it was a good one for them.

He was a speaker and actor of the truth, born such, and was ever running into dramatic situations from this cause. In any circumstance it interested all bystanders to know what part Henry would take, and what he would say; and he did not disappoint expectation, but used an original judgment on each emergency. In 1845 he built himself a small framed house on the shores of Walden Pond, and lived there two years alone, a life of labor and study. This action was quite native and fit for him. No one who knew him would tax him with affectation. He was more unlike his neighbors in his thought than in his action. As soon as he had exhausted the advantages of that solitude, he abandoned it. In 1847, not approving some uses to which the public expenditure was applied, he refused to pay his town tax, and was put in jail. A friend paid the tax for him, and he was released. The like annoyance was threatened the next year. But as his friends paid the tax, notwithstanding his protest, I believe he ceased to resist. No opposition or ridicule had any weight with him. He coldly and fully stated his opinion without affecting to believe that it was the opinion of the company. It was of no consequence if every one present held the opposite opinion. On one occasion he went to the University Library to procure some books. The librarian refused to lend them. Mr. Thoreau repaired to the President, who stated to him the rules and usages, which permitted the loan of books to resident graduates, to clergymen who were alumni, and to some others resident within a circle of ten miles' radius from the College. Mr. Thoreau explained to the President that the railroad had destroyed the old scale of distances,—that the library was useless, yes, and President and College useless, on the terms of his rules,—that the one benefit he owed to the College was its library,—that, at this moment, not only his want of books was imperative, but he wanted a large number of books, and assured him that he, Thoreau and not the librarian, was the proper custodian of these. In short, the President found the petitioner so formidable, and the rules getting to look so ridiculous, that he ended by giving him a privilege which in his hands proved unlimited thereafter.

No truer American existed than Thoreau. His preference of his country and condition was genuine, and his aversation from English and European manners and tastes almost reached contempt. He listened impatiently to news or *bon mots* gleaned from London circles; and though he tried to be civil, these anecdotes fatigued him. The men were all imitating each other, and on a small mould. Why can they not live as far apart as possible, and each be a man by himself? What he sought was the most energetic nature; and he wished to go to Oregon, not to London. "In every part of Great Britain," he wrote in his diary, "are discovered traces of the Romans, their funereal urns, their camps, their roads, their dwellings. But New England, at least, is not based on any Roman ruins. We have not to lay the foundations of our houses on the ashes of a former civilization."

But idealist as he was, standing for abolition of slavery, abolition of tariffs, almost for abolition of government, it is needless to say he found himself not only unrepresented in actual politics, but almost equally opposed to every class of reformers. Yet he paid the tribute of his uniform respect to the Anti-Slavery party. One man, whose personal acquaintance he had formed, he honored with exceptional regard. Before the first friendly word had been spoken for Captain John Brown, he sent notices to most houses in Concord that he would speak in a public hall on the condition and character of John Brown, on Sunday evening, and invited all people to come. The Republican Committee, the Abolitionist Committee, sent him word that it was premature and not advisable. He replied,—"I did not send to you for advice, but to announce that I am to speak." The hall was filled at an early hour by people of all parties, and his earnest eulogy of the hero was heard by all respectfully, by many with a sympathy that surprised themselves.

It was said of Plotinus that he was ashamed of his body, and 'tis very likely he had good reason for it,—that his body was a bad servant, and he had not skill in dealing with the material world, as happens often to men of abstract intellect. But Mr. Thoreau was equipped with a most adapted and serviceable body. He was of short stature, firmly built, of light complexion, with strong, serious blue eyes, and a grave aspect,—his face covered in the late years with a becoming beard. His senses were acute, his frame well-knit and hardy, his hands strong and skilful in the use of tools. And there was a wonderful fitness of body and mind. He could pace sixteen rods more accurately than another man could measure them with rod and chain. He could find his path in the woods at night, he said, better by his feet than his eyes. He could estimate the measure of a tree very well by his eye; he could estimate the weight of a calf like a dealer. From a box containing a bushel or more of loose pencils, he could take up with his hands fast enough just a dozen pencils at every grasp. He was a good swimmer, runner, skater, boatman, and would probably outwalk most countrymen in a day's journey. And the relation of body to mind was still finer than we have indicated. He said he wanted every stride his legs made. The length of his walk uniformly made the length of his writing. If shut up in the house he did not write at all.

He had a strong common sense, like that which Rose Flammock, the weaver's daughter in Scott's romance, commends in her father, as resembling a yardstick, which whilst it measures dowlas and diaper, can equally well measure tapestry and cloth of gold. He had always a new resource. When I was planting forest trees, and had procured half a peck of acorns, he said that only a small portion of them would be sound, and proceeded to examine them and select the sound ones. But finding this took time, he said, "I think if you put them all into water the good ones will sink;" which experiment we tried with success. He could plan a garden or a house or a barn; would have been competent to lead a "Pacific Exploring Expedition"; could give judicious counsel in the gravest private or public affairs.

He lived for the day, not cumbered and mortified by his memory. If he brought you yesterday a new proposition, he would bring you to-day another not less revolutionary. A very industrious man, and setting, like all highly organized men, a high value on his time, he seemed the only man of leisure in town, always ready for any excursion that promised well, or for conversation prolonged into late hours. His trenchant sense was never stopped by his rules of daily prudence, but was always up to the new occasion. He liked and used the simplest food, yet, when some one urged a vegetable diet, Thoreau thought all diets a very small matter, saying that "the man who shoots the buffalo lives better than the man who boards at the Graham House." He said,—"You can sleep near the railroad, and never be disturbed: Nature knows very well what sounds are worth attending to, and has made up her mind not to hear the railroad-whistle. But things respect the devout mind, and a mental ecstasy was never interrupted." He noted what repeatedly befell him, that, after receiving from a distance a rare plant, he would presently find the same in his own haunts. And those pieces of luck which happen only to good players happened to him. One day, walking with a stranger, who inquired where Indian arrowheads could be found, he replied, "Everywhere," and, stooping forward, picked one on the instant from the ground. At Mount Washington, in Tuckerman's Ravine, Thoreau had a bad fall, and sprained his foot. As he was in the act of getting up from his fall, he saw for the first time the leaves of the *Arnica mollis*.

His robust common sense, armed with stout hands, keen perceptions and strong will, cannot yet account for the superiority which shone in his simple and hidden life. I must add the cardinal fact, that there was an excellent wisdom in him, proper to a rare class of men, which showed him the material world as a means and symbol. This discovery, which sometimes yields to poets a certain casual and interrupted light, serving for the ornament of their writing, was in him an unsleeping insight; and whatever faults or obstructions of temperament might cloud it, he was not disobedient to the heavenly vision. In his youth, he said one day, "The other world is all my art; my pencils will draw no other; my jack-knife will cut nothing else; I do not use it as a means." This was the muse and genius that ruled his opinions, conversation, studies, work and course of life. This made him a searching judge of men. At first glance he measured his companion, and, though insensible to some fine traits of culture, could very well report his weight and calibre. And this made the impression of genius which his conversation sometimes gave.

He understood the matter in hand at a glance, and saw the limitations and poverty of those he talked with, so that nothing seemed concealed from such terrible eyes. I have repeatedly known young men of sensibility converted in a moment to the belief that this was the man they were in search of, the man of men, who could tell them all they should do. His own dealing with them was never affectionate, but superior, didactic, scorning their petty ways,— very slowly conceding, or not conceding at all, the promise of his society at their houses, or even at his own. "Would he not walk with them?" "He did not know. There was nothing so important to him as his walk; he had no walks to throw away on company." Visits were offered him from respectful parties, but he declined them. Admiring friends offered to carry him at their own cost to the Yellowstone River,—to the West Indies,—to South America. But though nothing could be more grave or considered than his refusals, they remind one, in quite new relations, of that fop Brummel's reply to the gentleman who offered him his carriage in a shower, "But where will *you* ride, then?"—and what accusing silences, and what searching and irresistible speeches, battering down all defences, his companions can remember!

Mr. Thoreau dedicated his genius with such entire love to the fields, hills and waters of his native town, that he made them known and interesting to all reading Americans, and to people over the sea. The river on whose banks he was born and died he knew from its springs to its confluence with the Merrimack. He had made summer and winter observations on it for many years, and at every hour of the day and night. The result of the recent survey of the Water Commissioners appointed by the State of Massachusetts he had reached by his private experiments, several years earlier. Every fact which occurs in the bed, on the banks or in the air over it; the fishes, and their spawning and nests, their manners, their food; the shad-flies which fill the air on a certain evening once a year, and which are snapped at by the fishes so ravenously that many of these die of repletion; the conical heaps of small stones on the river-shallows, the huge nests of small fishes, one of which will sometimes overfill a cart; the birds which frequent the stream, heron, duck, sheldrake, loon, osprey; the snake, muskrat, otter, woodchuck and fox, on the banks; the turtle, frog, hyla, and cricket, which make the banks vocal, —were all known to him, and, as it were, townsmen and fellow creatures; so that he felt an absurdity or violence in any narrative of one of these by itself apart, and still more of its dimensions on an inch-rule, or in the exhibition of its skeleton, or the specimen of a squirrel or a bird in brandy. He liked to speak of the manners of the river, as itself a lawful creature, yet with exactness, and always to an observed fact. As he knew the river, so the ponds in this region.

One of the weapons he used, more important to him than microscope or alcohol-receiver to other investigators, was a whim which grew on him by indulgence, yet appeared in gravest statement, namely, of extolling his own town and neighborhood as the most favored centre for natural observation. He remarked that the flora of Massachusetts embraced almost all the important plants of America,—most of the oaks, most of the willows, the best pines, the ash, the maple, the beech, the nuts. He returned Kane's Arctic Voyage to a friend of whom he had borrowed it, with the remark, that "Most of the phenomena noted might be observed in Concord." He seemed a little envious of the Pole, for the coincident sunrise and sunset, or five minutes' day after six months: a splendid fact, which Annursnuc had never afforded him. He found red snow in one of his walks, and told me that he expected to find yet the *Victoria regia* in Concord. He was the attorney of the indigenous plants, and owned to a preference of the weeds to the imported plants, as of the Indian to the civilized man, and noticed, with pleasure, that the willow bean-poles of his neighbor had grown more than his beans. "See these weeds," he said, "which have been hoed at by a million farmers all spring and summer, and yet have prevailed, and just now come out triumphant over all lanes, pastures, fields and gardens, such is their vigor. We have insulted them with low names, too,—as Pigweed, Wormwood, Chickweed, Shad-blossom." He says, "They have brave names, too,—Ambrosia, Stellaria, Amelanchier, Amaranth, etc."

I think his fancy for referring everything to the meridian of Concord did not grow out of any ignorance or depreciation of other longitudes or latitudes, but was rather a playful expression of his conviction of the indifference of all places, and that the best place for each is where he stands. He expressed it once in this wise: "I think nothing is to be hoped from you, if this bit of mould under your feet is not sweeter to you to eat than any other in this world, or in any world."

The other weapon with which he conquered all obstacles in science was patience. He knew how to sit immovable, a part of the rock he rested on, until the bird, the reptile, the fish, which had retired from him, should come back and resume its habits, nay, moved by curiosity, should come to him and watch him.

It was a pleasure and a privilege to walk with him. He knew the country like a fox or a bird, and passed through it as freely by paths of his own. He knew every track in the snow or on the ground, and what creature had taken this path before him. One must submit abjectly to such a guide, and the reward was great. Under his arm he carried an old music-book to press plants; in his pocket, his diary and pencil, a spy-glass for birds, microscope, jack-knife and twine. He wore a straw hat, stout shoes, strong gray trousers, to brave scrub-oaks and smilax, and to climb a tree for a hawk's or a squirrel's nest. He waded into the pool for the waterplants, and his strong legs were no insignificant part of his armor. On the day I speak of he looked for the Menyanthes, detected it across the wide pool, and, on examination of the florets, decided that it had been in flower five days. He drew out of his breast-pocket his diary, and read the names of all the plants that should bloom on this day, whereof he kept account as a banker when his notes fall due. The Cypripedium not due till to-morrow. He thought that, if waked up from a trance, in this swamp, he could tell by the plants what time of the year it was within two days. The redstart was flying about, and presently the fine gros-beaks, whose brilliant scarlet "makes the rash gazer wipe his eye," and whose fine clear note Thoreau compared to that of a tanager which has got rid of its hoarseness. Presently he heard a note which he called that of the night-warbler, a bird he had never identified, had been in search of twelve years, which always, when he saw it, was in the act of diving down into a tree or bush, and which it was vain to seek; the only bird which sings indifferently by night and by day. I told him he must beware of finding and booking it, lest life should have nothing more to show him. He said, "What you seek in vain for, half your life, one day you come full upon, all the family at dinner. You seek it like a dream, and as soon as you find it you become its prey."

His interest in the flower or the bird lay very deep in his mind, was connected with Nature,—and the meaning of Nature was never attempted to be defined by him. He would not offer a memoir of his observations to the Natural History Society. "Why should I? To detach the description from its connections in my mind would make it no longer true or valuable to me: and they do not wish what belongs to it." His power of observation seemed to indicate additional senses. He saw as with microscope, heard as with ear-trumpet, and his memory was a photographic register of all he saw and heard. And yet none knew better than he that it is not the fact that imports, but the impression or effect of the fact on your mind. Every fact lay in glory in his mind, a type of the order and beauty of the whole.

His determination on Natural History was organic. He confessed that he sometimes felt like a hound or a panther, and, if born among Indians, would have been a fell hunter. But, restrained by his Massachusetts culture, he played out the game in this mild form of botany and ichthyology. His intimacy with animals suggested what Thomas Fuller records of Butler the apiologist, that "either he had told the bees things or the bees had told him." Snakes coiled round his legs; the fishes swam into his hand, and he took them out of the water; he pulled the woodchuck out of its hole by the tail, and took the foxes under his protection from the hunters. Our naturalist had perfect magnanimity; he had no secrets: he would carry you to the heron's haunt, or even to his most prized botanical swamp,—possibly knowing that you could never find it again, yet willing to take his risks.

No college ever offered him a diploma, or a professor's chair; no academy made him its corresponding secretary, its discoverer or even its member. Perhaps these learned bodies feared the satire of his presence. Yet so much knowledge of Nature's secret and genius few others possessed; none in a more large and religious synthesis. For not a particle of respect had he to the opinions of any man or body of men, but homage solely to the truth itself; and as he discovered everywhere among doctors some leaning of courtesy, it discredited them. He grew to be revered and admired by his townsmen, who had at first known him only as an oddity. The farmers who employed him as a surveyor soon discovered his rare accuracy and skill, his knowledge of their lands, of trees, of birds, of Indian remains and the like, which enabled him to tell every farmer more than he knew before of his own farm; so that he began to feel a little as if Mr. Thoreau had better rights in his land than he. They felt, too, the superiority of character which addressed all men with a native authority.

Indian relics abound in Concord,—arrowheads, stone chisels, pestles and fragments of pottery; and on the river-bank, large heaps of clam-shells and ashes mark spots which the savages frequented. These, and every circumstance touching the Indian, were important in his eyes. His visits to Maine were chiefly for love of the Indian. He had the satisfaction of seeing the manufacture of the bark canoe, as well as of trying his hand in its management on the rapids. He was inquisitive about the making of the stone arrowhead, and in his last days charged a youth setting out for the Rocky Mountains to find an Indian who could tell him that: "It was well worth a visit to California to learn it." Occasionally, a small party of Penobscot Indians would visit Concord, and pitch their tents for a few weeks in summer on the river-bank. He failed not to make acquaintance with the best of them; though he well knew that asking questions of Indians is like catechizing beavers and rabbits. In his last visit to Maine he had great satisfaction from Joseph Polis, an intelligent Indian of Oldtown, who was his guide for some weeks.

He was equally interested in every natural fact. The depth of his perception found likeness of law throughout Nature, and I know not any genius who so swiftly inferred universal law from the single fact. He was no pedant of a department. His eye was open to beauty, and his ear to music. He found these, not in rare conditions, but wheresoever he went. He thought the best of music was in single strains; and he found poetic suggestion in the humming of the telegraph-wire.

His poetry might be bad or good; he no doubt wanted a lyric facility and technical skill, but he had the source of poetry in his spiritual perception. He was a good reader and critic, and his judgment on poetry was to the ground of it. He could not be deceived as to the presence or absence of the poetic element in any composition, and his thirst for this made him negligent and perhaps scornful of superficial graces. He would pass by many delicate rhythms, but he would have detected every live stanza or line in a volume and knew very well where to find an equal poetic charm in prose. He was so enamored of the spiritual beauty that he held all actual written poems in very light esteem in the comparison. He admired Æschylus and Pindar; but when some one was commending them, he said that Æschylus and the Greeks, in describing Apollo and Orpheus, had given no song, or no good one. "They ought not to have moved trees, but to have chanted to the gods such a hymn as would have sung all their old ideas out of their heads, and new ones in." His own verses are often rude and defective. The gold does not yet run pure, is drossy and crude. The thyme and marjoram are not yet honey. But if he want lyric fineness and technical merits, if he have not the poetic temperament, he never lacks the casual thought, showing that his genius was better than his talent. He knew the worth of the Imagination for the uplifting and consolation of human life, and liked to throw every thought into a symbol. The fact you tell is of no value, but only the impression. For this reason his presence was poetic, always piqued the curiosity to know more deeply the secrets of his mind. He had many reserves, an unwillingness to exhibit to profane eyes what was still sacred in his own, and knew well how to throw a poetic veil over his experience. All readers of Walden will remember his mythical record of his disappointments:

"I long ago lost a hound, a bay horse and a turtle-dove, and am still on their trail. Many are the travellers I have spoken concerning them, describing their tracks, and what calls they answered to. I have met one or two who have heard the hound, and the tramp of the horse, and even seen the dove disappear behind a cloud; and they seemed as anxious to recover them as if they had lost them themselves."

His riddles were worth the reading, and I confide that if at any time I do not understand the expression, it is yet just. Such was the wealth of his truth that it was not worth his while to use words in vain. His poem entitled "Sympathy" reveals the tenderness under that triple steel of stoicism, and the intellectual subtility it could animate. His classic poem on "Smoke" suggests Simonides, but is better than any poem of Simonides. His biography is in his verses. His habitual thought makes all his poetry a hymn to the Cause of causes, the Spirit which vivifies and controls his own:

> I hearing get, who had but ears,
> And sight, who had but eyes before;
> I moments live, who lived but years,
> And truth discern, who knew but learning's lore.

And still more in these religious lines:

> Now chiefly is my natal hour,
> And only now my prime of life;
> I will not doubt the love untold,
> Which not my worth nor want have bought,
> Which wooed me young, and wooes me old,
> And to this evening hath me brought.

Whilst he used in his writings a certain petulance of remark in reference to churches or churchmen, he was a person of a rare, tender and absolute religion, a person incapable of any profanation, by act or by thought. Of course, the same isolation which belonged to his original thinking and living detached him from the social religious forms. This is neither to be censured nor regretted. Aristotle long ago explained it, when he said, "One who surpasses his fellow citizens in virtue is no longer a part of the city. Their law is not for him, since he is a law to himself."

Thoreau was sincerity itself, and might fortify the convictions of prophets in the ethical laws by his holy living. It was an affirmative experience which refused to be set aside. A truth-speaker he, capable of the most deep and strict conversation; a physician to the wounds of any soul; a friend, knowing not only the secret of friendship, but almost worshipped by those few persons who resorted to him as their confessor and prophet, and knew the deep value of his mind and great heart. He thought that without religion or devotion of some kind nothing great was ever accomplished: and he thought that the bigoted sectarian had better bear this in mind.

His virtues, of course, sometimes ran into extremes. It was easy to trace to the inexorable demand on all for exact truth that austerity which made this willing hermit more solitary even than he wished. Himself of a perfect probity, he required not less of others. He had a disgust at crime, and no worldly success would cover it. He detected paltering as readily in dignified and prosperous persons as in beggars, and with equal scorn. Such dangerous frankness was in his dealing that his admirers called him "that terrible Thoreau," as if he spoke when silent, and was still present when he had departed. I think the severity of his ideal interfered to deprive him of a healthy sufficiency of human society.

The habit of a realist to find things the reverse of their appearance inclined him to put every statement in a paradox. A certain habit of antagonism defaced his earlier writings,—a trick of rhetoric not quite outgrown in his later, of substituting for the obvious word and thought its diametrical opposite. He praised wild mountains and winter forests for their domestic air, in snow and ice he would find sultriness, and commended the wilderness for resembling Rome and Paris. "It was so dry, that you might call it wet."

The tendency to magnify the moment, to read all the laws of Nature in the one object or one combination under your eye, is of course comic to those who do not share the philosopher's perception of identity. To him there was no such thing as size. The pond was a small ocean; the Atlantic, a large Walden Pond. He referred every minute fact to cosmical laws. Though he meant to be just, he seemed haunted by a certain chronic assumption that the science of the day pretended completeness, and he had just found out that the *savans* had neglected to discriminate a particular botanical variety, had failed to describe the seeds or count the sepals. "That is to say," we replied, "the blockheads were not born in Concord; but who said they were? It was their unspeakable misfortune to be born in London, or Paris, or Rome; but poor fellows, they did what they could, considering that they never saw Bateman's Pond, or Nine-Acre Corner, or Becky Stow's Swamp; besides, what were you sent into the world for, but to add this observation?"

Had his genius been only contemplative, he had been fitted to his life, but with his energy and practical ability he seemed born for greater enterprise and for command; and I so much regret the loss of his rare powers of action, that I cannot help counting it a fault in him that he had no ambition. Wanting this, instead of engineering for all America, he was the captain of a huckleberry-party. Pounding beans is good to the end of pounding empires one of these days; but if, at the end of years, it is still only beans!

But these foibles, real or apparent, were fast vanishing in the incessant growth of a spirit so robust and wise, and which effaced its defeats with new triumphs. His study of Nature was a perpetual ornament to him, and inspired his friends with curiosity to see the world through his eyes, and to hear his adventures. They possessed every kind of interest.

He had many elegancies of his own, whilst he scoffed at conventional elegance. Thus, he could not bear to hear the sound of his own steps, the grit of gravel; and therefore never willingly walked in the road, but in the grass, on mountains and in woods. His senses were acute, and he remarked that by night every dwelling-house gives out bad air, like a slaughter-house. He liked the pure fragrance of melilot. He honored certain plants with special regard, and, over all, the pond-lily,—then, the gentian, and the *Mikania scandens,* and "life-everlasting," and a bass-tree which he visited every year when it bloomed, in the middle of July. He thought the scent a more oracular inquisition than the sight,—more oracular and trustworthy. The scent, of course, reveals what is concealed from the other senses. By it he detected earthliness. He delighted in echoes, and said they were almost the only kind of kindred voices that he heard. He loved Nature so well, was so happy in her solitude, that he became very jealous of cities and the sad work which their refinements and artifices made with man and his dwelling. The axe was always destroying his forest. "Thank God," he said, "they cannot cut down the clouds!" "All kinds of figures are drawn on the blue ground with this fibrous white paint."

I subjoin a few sentences taken from his unpublished manuscripts, not only as records of his thought and feeling, but for their power of description and literary excellence:

"Some circumstantial evidence is very strong, as when you find a trout in the milk."

"The chub is a soft fish, and tastes like boiled brown paper salted."

"The youth gets together his materials to build a bridge to the moon, or, perchance, a palace or temple on the earth, and, at length the middle-aged man concludes to build a wood-shed with them."

"The locust z-ing."

"Devil's-needles zigzagging along the Nut-Meadow brook."

"Sugar is not so sweet to the palate as sound to the healthy ear."

"I put on some hemlock-boughs, and the rich salt crackling of their leaves was like mustard to the ear, the crackling of uncountable regiments. Dead trees love the fire."

"The bluebird carries the sky on his back."

"The tanager flies through the green foliage as if it would ignite the leaves."

"If I wish for a horse-hair for my compass-sight I must go to the stable; but the hair-bird, with her sharp eyes, goes to the road."

"Immortal water, alive even to the superficies."

"Fire is the most tolerable third party."

"Nature made ferns for pure leaves, to show what she could do in that line."

"No tree has so fair a bole and so handsome an instep as the beech."

"How did these beautiful rainbow-tints get into the shell of the fresh-water clam, buried in the mud at the bottom of our dark river?"

"Hard are the times when the infant's shoes are second-foot."

"We are strictly confined to our men to whom we give liberty."

"Nothing is so much to be feared as fear. Atheism may comparatively be popular with God himself."

"Of what significance the things you can forget? A little thought is sexton to all the world."

"How can we expect a harvest of thought who have not had a seed-time of character?"

"Only he can be trusted with gifts who can present a face of bronze to expectations."

"I ask to be melted. You can only ask of the metals that they be tender to the fire that melts them. To nought else can they be tender."

There is a flower known to botanists, one of the same genus with our summer plant called "Life-Everlasting," a *Gnaphalium* like that, which grows on the most inaccessible cliffs of the Tyrolese mountains, where the chamois dare hardly venture, and which the hunter, tempted by its beauty, and by his love (for it is immensely valued by the Swiss maidens), climbs the cliffs to gather, and is sometimes found dead at the foot, with the flower in his hand. It is called by botanists the *Gnaphalium leontopodium,* but by the Swiss *Edelweisse,* which signifies *Noble Purity.* Thoreau seemed to me living in the hope to gather this plant, which belonged to him of right. The scale on which his studies proceeded was so large as to require longevity, and we were the less prepared for his sudden disappearance. The country knows not yet, or in the least part, how great a son it has lost. It seems an injury that he should leave in the midst his broken task which none else can finish, a kind of indignity to so noble a soul that he should depart out of Nature before yet he has been really shown to his peers for what he is. But he, at least, is content. His soul was made for the noblest society; he had in a short life exhausted the capabilities of this world; wherever there is knowledge, wherever there is virtue, wherever there is beauty, he will find a home.

TO THE REVEREND HENRY WARE, JR.[6]

CONCORD, *October* 8, 1838.

MY DEAR SIR,—I ought sooner to have acknowledged your kind letter of last week, and the Sermon it accompanied. The letter was right manly and noble. The Sermon, too, I have read with attention. If it assails any doctrines of mine, perhaps I am not so quick to see it as writers generally—certainly I did not feel any disposition to depart from my habitual contentment that you should say your thought, whilst I say mine.

I believe I must tell you what I think of my new position. It strikes me very oddly that good and wise men at Cambridge and Boston should think of raising me into an object of criticism. I have always been, from my very incapacity of methodical writing, "a chartered libertine," free to worship and

[6] Henry Ware, a professor at the Harvard Divinity School, wrote Emerson a friendly letter protesting against his Divinity School Address: to this Emerson is here replying.

free to rail; lucky when I could make myself understood, but never esteemed near enough to the institutions and mind of society to deserve the notice of the masters of literature and religion. I have appreciated fully the advantage of my position; for I well know that there is no scholar less willing or less able to be a polemic. I could not give account of myself, if challenged. I could not possibly give you one of the "arguments" you cruelly hint at, on which any doctrine of mine stands. For I do not know what arguments mean in reference to any expression of a thought. I delight in telling what I think, but if you ask how I dare say so, or why it is so, I am the most helpless of mortal men. I do not even see that either of these questions admits of an answer. So that, in the present droll posture of my affairs, when I see myself suddenly raised into the importance of a heretic, I am very uneasy when I advert to the supposed duties of such a personage, who is expected to make good his thesis against all comers.

I certainly shall do no such thing. I shall read what you and other good men write, as I have always done,—glad when you speak my thought, and skipping the page that has nothing for me. I shall go on, just as before, seeing whatever I can, and telling what I see; and, I suppose, with the same fortune that has hitherto attended me,—the joy of finding that my abler and better brothers, who work with the sympathy of society, loving and beloved, do now and then unexpectedly confirm my perceptions, and find my nonsense is only their own thought in motley. And so I am

Your affectionate servant,
R. W. EMERSON

HENRY DAVID THOREAU

(1817–1862)

Thoreau, the only member of the "New England group" not of the old puritan stock, was descended from "a French ancestor who came to this country from the Isle of Guernsey." He was born in Concord, Massachusetts, where his father was a maker of lead pencils, in 1817. At Harvard, where he graduated "without distinction" in 1837, he showed "an unsocial disposition." He adopted no regular profession, "aiming," Emerson says, "at a much more comprehensive calling." "I have as many trades as I have fingers," he writes in *Walden,* and at one or another of these—teaching, surveying, tinkering, lecturing—he worked off and on in Concord, devoting little time to making a living, much to the "art of living well." For two years he lived in the home of Emerson, as something between "hired man" and intellectual companion, and was thought to imitate Emerson—who, however, never had a more original disciple. He assisted at the family business of manufacturing lead pencils, and perfected its product, but thought "his life too valuable to him to put what remained of it into pencils." In 1839 he made the trip described in his first book, *A Week on the Concord and Merrimac Rivers,* which, however, was written later and not published until 1849. From July, 1845, to September, 1847, he lived in a hut built with his own hands on the shore of Walden Pond, in the manner described later in his famous book, *Walden* (1854). Only these two books appeared during his life; but from his graduation in 1837 he had kept "Journals," and from these and other papers came the volumes published after his death, including *The Maine Woods, Cape Cod,* and *A Yankee in Canada.* He died at Concord in 1862.

Thoreau was well read in English, classical, and oriental literatures, and was a literary critic of originality and insight. In spite of his scorn of literary, as of other worldly success, he was clearly determined to write, and trained himself to write well. His style is highly individual, direct but given to reserve and understatement, and often touched with irony or whim—the literary counterpart of the colloquial Yankee speech. Though he read and wrote much he was a very unconventional and out-of-doors man of letters. Emerson's characterization is far better than any other. "He was a born protestant. . . . He was bred to no profession; he never married; he lived alone; he never went to church; he never voted; he refused to pay a tax to the State; he ate no flesh, he drank no wine, he never knew the use of tobacco; and, though a naturalist, he used neither trap nor gun. . . . He knew the country like a fox or a bird, and passed through it as freely by paths of his own." To this character the merits of *Walden* correspond. By criticising shrewdly the surfaces and pretenses of life it leads to quite fresh attitudes and feelings; and it is full of close and sympathetic descriptions of nature. But though he was a pioneer in American "nature study" Thoreau is not finally to be thought of as a scientist or naturalist. "Though very studious of natural facts," says Emerson, "he was incurious of technical or textual science . . . None knew better than he that it is not the fact that imports, but the impression or effect of the fact on your mind." He takes his high place in literature because he was not only a patient but an imaginative observer; not only a naturalist but a poet of nature.

From WALDEN

Economy [1]

NEAR the end of March, 1845, I borrowed an axe and went down to the woods by Walden Pond, nearest to where I intended to build my house, and began to cut down some tall arrowy white pines, still in their youth, for timber. It is difficult to begin without borrowing, but perhaps it is the most generous course thus to permit your fellow-men to have an interest in your enterprise. The owner of the axe, as he released his hold on it, said that it was the apple of his eye; but I returned it sharper than I received it. It was a pleasant hillside where I worked, covered with pine woods, through which I looked out on the pond, and a small open field in the woods where pines and hickories were springing up. The ice in the pond was not yet dissolved, though there were some open spaces, and it was all dark colored and saturated with water. There were some slight flurries of snow during the days that I worked there; but for the most part when I came out on to the railroad, on my way home, its yellow sand heap stretched away gleaming in the hazy atmosphere, and the rails shone in the spring sun, and I heard the lark and pewee and other birds already come to commence another year with us. They were pleasant spring days, in which the winter of man's discontent was thawing as well as the earth, and the life that had lain torpid began to stretch itself. One day, when my axe had come off and I had cut a green hickory for a wedge, driving it with a stone, and had placed the whole to soak in a pond hole in order to swell the wood, I saw a striped snake run into the water, and he lay on the bottom, apparently without inconvenience, as long as I stayed there, or more than a quarter of an hour; perhaps because he had not yet fairly come out of the torpid state. It appeared to me that for a like reason men remain in their present low and primitive condition; but if they should feel the influence of the spring of springs arousing them, they would of necessity rise to a higher and more ethereal life. I had previously seen the snakes in frosty mornings in my path with portions of their bodies still numb and inflexible, waiting for the sun to thaw them. On the 1st of April it rained and melted the ice, and in the early part of the day, which was very foggy, I heard a stray goose groping about over the pond and cackling as if lost, or like the spirit of the fog.

[1] From chap. i.—which begins: "When I wrote the following pages, or rather the bulk of them, I lived alone, in the woods, a mile from any neighbor, in a house I had built myself, on the shore of Walden Pond, in Concord, Massachusetts, and earned my living by the labor of my hands only. I lived there two years and two months. At present I am a sojourner in civilized life again."

The extracts from *Walden* are used by permission of, and by arrangement with, Houghton Mifflin Company, the authorized publishers.

So I went on for some days cutting and hewing timber, and also studs and rafters, all with my narrow axe, not having many communicable or scholar-like thoughts, singing to myself,—

> Men say they know many things,
> But lo! they have taken wings—
> The arts and sciences,
> And a thousand appliances;
> The wind that blows
> Is all that anybody knows.

I hewed the main timbers six inches square, most of the studs on two sides only, and the rafters and floor timbers on one side, leaving the rest of the bark on, so that they were just as straight and much stronger than sawed ones. Each stick was carefully mortised or tenoned by its stump, for I had bor-rowed other tools by this time. My days in the woods were not very long ones; yet I usually carried my dinner of bread and butter, and read the news-paper in which it was wrapped, at noon, sitting amid the green pine boughs which I had cut off, and to my bread was imparted some of their fragrance, for my hands were covered with a thick coat of pitch. Before I had done I was more the friend than the foe of the pine tree, though I had cut down some of them, having become better acquainted with it. Sometimes a rambler in the wood was attracted by the sound of my axe, and we chatted pleasantly over the chips which I had made.

By the middle of April, for I made no haste in my work, but rather made the most of it, my house was framed and ready for the raising. I had already bought the shanty of James Collins, an Irishman who worked on the Fitch-burg Railroad, for boards. James Collins' shanty was considered an uncom-monly fine one. When I called to see it he was not at home. I walked about the outside, at first unobserved from within, the window was so deep and high. It was of small dimensions, with a peaked cottage roof, and not much else to be seen, the dirt being raised five feet all around as if it were a compost heap. The roof was the soundest part, though a good deal warped and made brittle by the sun. Doorsill there was none, but a perennial passage for the hens under the door board. Mrs. C. came to the door and asked me to view it from the inside. The hens were driven in by my approach. It was dark, and had a dirt floor for the most part, dank, clammy, and aguish, only here a board and there a board which would not bear removal. She lighted a lamp to show me the inside of the roof and the walls, and also that the board floor extended under the bed, warning me not to step into the cellar, a sort of dust hole two feet deep. In her own words, they were "good boards overhead, good boards all around, and a good window,"—of two whole squares origi-nally, only the cat had passed out that way lately. There was a stove, a bed, and a place to sit, an infant in the house where it was born, a silk parasol, gilt-framed looking-glass, and a patent new coffee-mill nailed to an oak sapling, all told. The bargain was soon concluded, for James had in the meanwhile returned. I to pay four dollars and twenty-five cents to-night, he to vacate at five to-morrow morning, selling to nobody else meanwhile: I to take possession at six. It were well, he said, to be there early, and anticipate certain indistinct but wholly unjust claims on the score of ground rent and fuel. This he assured me was the only encumbrance. At six I passed him and his family on the road. One large bundle held their all,—bed, coffee-mill, looking-glass, hens,—all but the cat; she took to the woods and became a wild cat, and, as I learned afterward, trod in a trap set for woodchucks, and so became a dead cat at last.

I took down this dwelling the same morning, drawing the nails, and removed it to the pond side by small cartloads, spreading the boards on the grass there to bleach and warp back again in the sun. One early thrush gave me a note or two as I drove along the woodland path. I was informed treacherously by a young Patrick that neighbor Seeley, an Irishman, in the intervals of the carting, transferred the still tolerable, straight, and drivable nails, staples, and spikes to his pocket, and then stood when I came back to pass the time of day, and look freshly up, unconcerned, with spring thoughts, at the devastation; there being a dearth of work, as he said. He was there to represent spectatordom, and help make this seemingly insignificant event one with the removal of the gods of Troy.

I dug my cellar in the side of a hill sloping to the south, where a woodchuck had formerly dug his burrow, down through sumach and blackberry roots, and the lowest stain of vegetation, six feet square by seven deep, to a fine sand where potatoes would not freeze in any winter. The sides were left shelving, and not stoned; but the sun having never shone on them, the sand still keeps its place. It was but two hours' work. I took particular pleasure in this breaking of ground, for in almost all latitudes men dig into the earth for an equable temperature. Under the most splendid house in the city is still to be found the cellar where they store their roots as of old, and long after the superstructure has disappeared posterity remark its dent in the earth. The house is still but a sort of porch at the entrance of a burrow.

At length, in the beginning of May, with the help of some of my acquaintances, rather to improve so good an occasion for neighborliness than from any necessity, I set up the frame of my house. No man was ever more honored in the character of his raisers than I. They are destined, I trust, to assist at the raising of loftier structures one day. I began to occupy my house on the 4th of July, as soon as it was boarded and roofed, for the boards were carefully feather-edged and lapped, so that it was perfectly impervious to rain; but before boarding, I laid the foundation of a chimney at one end, bringing two cartloads of stones up the hill from the pond in my arms. I built the chimney after my hoeing in the fall, before a fire became necessary for warmth, doing my cooking in the meanwhile out of doors on the ground, early in the morning: which mode I still think is in some respects more convenient and agreeable than the usual one. When it stormed before my bread was baked, I fixed a few boards over the fire, and sat under them to watch my loaf, and passed some pleasant hours in that way. In those days, when my hands were much employed, I read but little, but the least scraps of paper which lay on the ground, my holder, or tablecloth, afforded me as much entertainment, in fact answered the same purpose as the Iliad.

It would be worth the while to build still more deliberately than I did, considering, for instance, what foundation a door, a window, a cellar, a garret, have in the nature of man, and perchance never raising any superstructure until we have found a better reason for it than our temporal necessities even. There is some of the same fitness in a man's building his own house that there is in a bird's building its own nest. Who knows but if men constructed their dwellings with their own hands, and provided food for themselves and families simply and honestly enough, the poetic faculty would be universally developed, as birds universally sing when they are so engaged? But alas! we do like cowbirds and cuckoos, which lay their eggs in nests which other birds have built, and cheer no traveller with their chattering and unmusical notes. Shall we forever resign the pleasure of construction to the carpenter? What does architecture amount to in the experience of the mass of men? I never in all my walks came across a man engaged in so simple and natural an occupation as building his house. We belong to the community. It is not the tailor alone who is the ninth part of a man; it is as much the preacher, and the merchant, and the farmer. Where is this division of labor to end? and what object does it finally serve? No doubt another *may* also think for me; but it is not therefore desirable that he should do so to the exclusion of my thinking for myself.

True, there are architects so called in this country, and I have heard of one at least possessed with the idea of making architectural ornaments have a core of truth, a necessity, and hence a beauty, as if it were a revelation to him. All very well perhaps from his point of view, but only a little better than the common dilettantism. A sentimental reformer in architecture, he began at the cornice, not at the foundation. It was only how to put a core of truth within the ornaments, that every sugar plum in fact might have an almond or caraway seed in it,—though I hold that almonds are most wholesome without the sugar,—and not how the inhabitant, the indweller, might build truly within and without, and let the ornaments take care of themselves. What reasonable man ever supposed that ornaments were something outward and in the skin merely,—that the tortoise got his spotted shell, or the shellfish its mother-o'-pearl tints, by such a contract as the inhabitants of Broadway their Trinity Church? But a man has no more to do with the style of architecture of his house than a tortoise with that of its shell: nor need the soldier be so idle as to try to paint the precise *color* of his virtue on his standard. The enemy will find it out. He may turn pale when the trial comes. This man seemed to me to lean over the cornice, and timidly whisper his half truth to the rude occupants, who really knew it better than he. What of architectural beauty I now see, I know has gradually grown from within outward, out of the necessities and character of the indweller, who is the only builder,— out of some unconscious truthfulness, and nobleness, without ever a thought for the appearance; and whatever additional beauty of this kind is destined to be produced will be preceded by a like unconscious beauty of life. The most interesting dwellings in this country, as the painter knows, are the most unpretending, humble log huts and cottages of the poor commonly; it is the life of the inhabitants whose shells they are, and not any peculiarity in their surfaces merely, which makes them *picturesque;* and equally interesting will be the citizen's suburban box, when his life shall be as simple and as agreeable to the imagination, and there is as little straining after effect in the style of his dwelling. A great proportion of architectural ornaments are litterally hollow, and a September gale would strip them off, like borrowed plumes, without injury to the substantials. They can do without *architecture* who have no olives nor wines in the cellar. What if an equal ado were made about the ornaments of style in literature, and the architects of our bibles spent as much time about their cornices as the architects of our churches do? So are made the *belles-lettres* and the *beaux-arts* and their professors. Much it concerns a man, forsooth, how a few sticks are slanted over him or under him, and what colors are daubed upon his box. It would signify somewhat, if, in any earnest sense, *he* slanted them and daubed it; but the spirit having departed out of the tenant, it is of a piece with constructing his own coffin— the architecture of the grave, and "carpenter" is but another name for "coffin-maker." One man says, in his despair or indifference to life, take up a handful of the earth at your feet, and paint your house that color. Is he thinking of his last and narrow house? Toss up a copper for it as well. What an abundance of leisure he must have! Why do you take up a handful of dirt? Better paint your house your own complexion; let it turn pale or blush for you. An enterprise to improve the style of cottage architecture! When you have got my ornaments ready I will wear them.

Before winter, I built a chimney, and shingled the sides of my house, which were already impervious to rain, with imperfect and sappy shingles made of the first slice of the log, whose edges I was obliged to straighten with a plane.

I have thus a tight shingled and plastered house, ten feet wide by fifteen long, and eight-feet posts, with a garret and a closet, a large window on each side, two trap doors, one door at the end, and a brick fireplace opposite. The exact cost of my house, paying the usual price for such materials as I used, but not counting the work, all of which was done by myself, was as follows; and I give the details because very few are able to tell exactly what their houses cost, and fewer still, if any, the separate cost of the various materials which compose them:—

Boards	$8 03½,	mostly shanty boards.
Refuse shingles for roof and sides	4 00	
Laths	1 25	
Two second-hand windows with glass	2 43	
One thousand old brick	4 00	
Two casks of lime	2 40	That was high.
Hair	0 31	More than I needed.
Mantle-tree iron	0 15	
Nails	3 90	
Hinges and screws	0 14	
Latch	0 10	
Chalk	0 01	
Transportation	1 40	{ I carried a good part on my back.
In all	$28 12½	

These are all the materials excepting the timber, stones, and sand, which I claimed by squatter's right. I have also a small wood-shed adjoining, made chiefly of the stuff which was left after building the house.

I intend to build me a house which will surpass any on the main street in Concord in grandeur and luxury, as soon as it pleases me as much and will cost me no more than my present one.

I thus found that the student who wishes for a shelter can obtain one for a lifetime at an expense not greater than the rent which he now pays annually. If I seem to boast more than is becoming, my excuse is that I brag for humanity rather than for myself; and my short-comings and inconsistencies do not affect the truth of my statement. Notwithstanding much cant and hypocrisy,—chaff, which I find it difficult to separate from my wheat, but for which I am as sorry as any man,—I will breathe freely and stretch myself in this respect, it is such a relief to both the moral and physical system; and I am resolved that I will not through humility become the devil's attorney. I will endeavor to speak a good word for the truth. At Cambridge College the mere rent of a student's room, which is only a little larger than my own, is thirty dollars each year, though the corporation had the advantage of building thirty-two side by side and under one roof, and the occupant suffers the inconvenience of many and noisy neighbors, and perhaps a residence in the fourth story. I cannot but think that if we had more true wisdom in these respects, not only less education would be needed, because, forsooth, more would already have been acquired, but the pecuniary expense of getting an education would in a great measure vanish. Those conveniences which the student requires at Cambridge or elsewhere cost him or somebody else ten times as great a sacrifice of life as they would with proper management on both sides. Those things for which the most money is demanded are never the things which the student most wants. Tuition, for instance, is an important item in the term bill, while for the far more valuable education which he gets by associating with the most cultivated of his contemporaries no charge is made. The mode of founding a college is, commonly, to get up a subscription of dollars and cents, and then following blindly the principles of a division of labor to its extreme, a principle which should never be followed but with circumspection,—to call in a contractor who makes this a subject of speculation, and he employs Irishmen or other operatives actually to lay the foundations, while the students that are to be are said to be fitting themselves for it; and for these oversights successive generations have to pay. I think that it would be *better than this,* for the students, or those who desire to be benefited by it, even to lay the foundation themselves. The student who secures his coveted leisure and retirement by systematically shirking any labor necessary to man obtains but an ignoble and unprofitable leisure, defrauding himself of the experience which alone can make leisure fruitful. "But," says one, "you do not mean that the students should go to work with their hands instead of their heads?" I do not mean that exactly, but I mean something which he might think a good deal like that; I mean that they should not *play* life, or *study* it merely, while the community supports them at this expensive game, but earnestly *live* it from beginning to end. How could youths better learn to live than by at once trying the experiment of living? Methinks this would exercise their minds as much as mathematics. If I wished a boy to know something about the arts and sciences, for instance, I would not pursue the common course, which is merely to send him into the neighborhood of some professor, where anything is professed and practised but the art of life;— to survey the world through a telescope, or a microscope, and never with his natural eye; to study chemistry, and not learn how his bread is made, or mechanics, and not learn how it is earned; to discover new satellites to Neptune, and not detect the motes in his eyes, or to what vagabond he is a satellite himself; or to be devoured by the monsters that swarm all around him, while contemplating the monsters in a drop of vinegar. Which would have advanced the most at the end of a month,—the boy who had made his own jackknife from the ore which he had dug and smelted, reading as much as would be necessary for this—or the boy who had attended the lectures on metallurgy at the Institute in the meanwhile, and had received a Rogers' penknife from his father? Which would be most likely to cut his fingers? ... To my astonishment I was informed on leaving college that I had studied navigation!—why, if I had taken one turn down the harbor I should have known more about it. Even the *poor* student studies and is taught only *political* economy, while that economy of living which is synonymous with philosophy is not even sincerely professed in our colleges. The consequence is, that while he is reading Adam Smith, Ricardo, and Say, he runs his father in debt irretrievably.

As with our colleges, so with a hundred "modern improvements"; there is an illusion about them; there is not always a positive advance. The devil goes on exacting compound interest to the last for his early share and numerous succeeding investments in them. Our inventions are wont to be pretty toys, which distract our attention from serious things. They are but improved means to an unimproved end, an end which it was already but too easy to arrive at; as railroads lead to Boston or New York. We are in great haste to construct a magnetic telegraph from Maine to Texas; but Maine and Texas, it may be, have nothing important to communicate. Either is in such a predicament as the man who was earnest to be introduced to a distinguished deaf woman, but when he was presented, and one end of her ear trumpet was put into his hand, had nothing to say. As if the main object were to talk fast and not to talk sensibly. We are eager to tunnel under the Atlantic and bring the old world some weeks nearer to the new; but perchance the first news that will leak through into the broad, flapping American ear will be that the Princess Adelaide has the whooping cough. After all, the man whose horse trots a mile in a minute does not carry the most important messages; he is not an evangelist, nor does he come round eating locusts and wild honey. I doubt if Flying Childers ever carried a peck of corn to mill.

One says to me, "I wonder that you do not lay up money; you love to travel; you might take the cars and go to Fitchburg to-day and see the country." But I am wiser than that. I have learned that the swiftest traveller is he that goes afoot. I say to my friend, Suppose we try who will get there first. The distance is thirty miles; the fare ninety cents. That is almost a day's wages. I remember when wages were sixty cents a day for laborers on this very road. Well, I start now on foot, and get there before night; I have travelled at that rate by the week together. You will in the meanwhile have earned your fare, and arrive there some time to-morrow, or possibly this evening, if you are lucky enough to get a job in season. Instead of going to Fitchburg, you will be working here the greater part of the day. And so, if the railroad reached round the world, I think that I should keep ahead of you; and as for seeing the country and getting experience of that kind, I should have to cut your acquaintance altogether.

Such is the universal law, which no man can ever outwit, and with regard to the railroad even we may say it is as broad as it is long. To make a railroad round the world available to all mankind is equivalent to grading the whole surface of the planet. Men have an indistinct notion that if they keep up this activity of joint stocks and spades long enough all will at length ride somewhere, in next to no time, and for nothing; but though a crowd rushes to the depot, and the conductor shouts "All aboard!" when the smoke is blown away and the vapor condensed, it will be perceived that a few are riding, but the rest are run over,—and it will be called, and will be, "A melancholy accident." No doubt they can ride at last who shall have earned their fare, that is, if they survive so long, but they will probably have lost their elasticity and desire to travel by that time. This spending of the best part of one's life earning money in order to enjoy a questionable liberty during the least valuable part of it, reminds me of the Englishman who went to India to make a fortune first, in order that he might return to England and live the life of a poet. He should have gone up garret at once. "What!" exclaim a million Irishmen starting up from all the shanties in the land, "is not this railroad which we have built a good thing?" Yes, I answer, *comparatively* good, that is, you might have done worse; but I wish, as you are brothers of mine, that you could have spent your time better than digging in this dirt.

Before I had finished my house, wishing to earn ten or twelve dollars by some honest and agreeable method, in order to meet my unusual expenses, I planted about two acres and a half of light and sandy soil near it chiefly with beans, but also a small part with potatoes, corn, peas, and turnips. The whole lot contains eleven acres, mostly growing up to pines and hickories, and was sold the preceding season for eight dollars and eight cents an acre. One farmer said that it was "good for nothing but to raise cheeping squirrels on." I put no manure whatever on this land, not being the owner, but merely a squatter, and not expecting to cultivate so much again, and I did not quite hoe it all once. I got out several cords of stumps in ploughing, which supplied me with fuel for a long time, and left small circles of virgin mould, easily distinguishable through the summer by the greater luxuriance of the beans there. The dead and for the most part unmerchantable wood behind my house, and the driftwood from the pond, have supplied the remainder of my fuel. I was obliged to hire a team and a man for the ploughing, though I held the plough myself. My farm outgoes for the first season were, for implements, seed, work, etc., $14.72½. The seed corn was given me. This never costs anything to speak of, unless you plant more than enough. I got twelve bushels of beans, and eighteen bushels of potatoes, besides some peas and sweet corn. The yellow corn and turnips were too late to come to anything. My whole income from the farm was

	$23 44
Deducting the outgoes	14 72½
There are left	$8 71½

beside produce consumed and on hand at the time this estimate was made of the value of $4.50,—the amount on hand much more than balancing a little grass which I did not raise. All things considered, that is, considering the importance of a man's soul and of to-day, notwithstanding the short time occupied by my experiment, nay, partly even because of its transient character, I believe that that was doing better than any farmer in Concord did that year.

The next year I did better still, for I spaded up all the land which I required, about a third of an acre, and I learned from the experience of both years, not being in the least awed by many celebrated works on husbandry, Arthur Young among the rest, that if one would live simply and eat only the crop which he raised, and raise no more than he ate, and not exchange it for an insufficient quantity of more luxurious and expensive things, he would need to cultivate only a few rods of ground, and that it would be cheaper to spade up that than to use oxen to plough it, and to select a fresh spot from time to time than to manure the old, and he could do all his necessary farm work as it were with his left hand at odd hours in the summer; and thus he would not be tied to an ox, or horse, or cow, or pig, as at present. I desire to speak impartially on this point, and as one not interested in the success or failure of the present economical and social arrangements. I was more independent than any farmer in Concord, for I was not anchored to a house or farm, but could follow the bent of my genius, which is a very crooked one, every moment. Beside being better off than they already, if my house had been burned or my crops had failed, I should have been nearly as well off as before.

I am wont to think that men are not so much the keepers of herds as herds are the keepers of men, the former are so much the freer. Men and oxen exchange work; but if we consider necessary work only, the oxen will be seen to have greatly the advantage, their farm is so much the larger. Man does some of his part of the exchange work in his six weeks of haying, and it is no boy's play. Certainly no nation that lived simply in all respects, that is, no nation of philosophers, would commit so great a blunder as to use the labor of animals. True, there never was and is not likely soon to be a nation of philosophers, nor am I certain it is desirable there should be. However, I should never have broken a horse or bull and taken him to board for any work he might do for me, for fear I should become a horse-man or a herds-man merely; and if society seems to be the gainer by so doing, are we certain that what is one man's gain is not another's loss, and that the stable-boy has equal cause with his master to be satisfied? Granted that some public works would not have been constructed without this aid, and let man share the glory of such with the ox and horse; does it follow that he could not have accomplished works yet more worthy of himself in that case? When men begin to do, not merely unnecessary or artistic, but luxurious and idle work, with their assistance, it is inevitable that a few do all the exchange work with the oxen, or, in other words, become the slaves of the strongest. Man thus not only works for the animal within him, but, for a symbol of this, he works for the animal without him. Though we have many substantial houses of brick or stone, the prosperity of the farmer is still measured by the degree to which the barn overshadows the house. This town is said to have the largest houses for oxen, cows, and horses hereabouts, and it is not behindhand in its public buildings; but there are very few halls for free worship or free speech in this county. It should not be by their architecture, but why not even by their power of abstract thought, that nations should seek to commemorate themselves? How much more admirable the Bhagvat-Geeta than all the ruins of the East! Towers and temples are the luxury of princes. A simple and independent mind does not toil at the bidding of any prince. Genius is not a retainer to any emperor, nor is its material silver, or gold, or marble, except to a trifling extent. To what end, pray, is so much stone hammered? In Arcadia, when I was there, I did not see any hammering stone. Nations are possessed with an insane ambition to perpetuate the memory of themselves by the amount of hammered stone they leave. What if equal pains were taken to smooth and polish their manners? One piece of good sense would be more memorable than a monument as high as the moon. I love better to see stones in place. The grandeur of Thebes was a vulgar grandeur. More sensible is a rod of stone wall that bounds an honest man's field than a hundred-gated Thebes that has wandered farther from the true end of life. The religion and civilization which are barbaric and heathenish build splendid temples; but what you might call Christianity does not. Most of the stone a nation hammers goes toward its tomb only. It buries itself alive. As for the Pyramids, there is nothing to wonder at in them so much as the fact that so many men could be found degraded enough to spend their lives constructing a tomb for some ambitious booby, whom it would have been wiser and manlier to have drowned in the Nile, and then given his body to the dogs. I might possibly invent some excuse for them and him, but I have no time for it. As for the religion and love of art of the builders, it is much the same all the world over, whether the building be an Egyptian temple or the United States Bank. It costs more than it comes to. The mainspring is vanity, assisted by the love of garlic and bread and butter. Mr. Balcom, a promising young architect, designs it on the back of his Vitruvius, with hard pencil and ruler, and the job is let out to Dobson & Sons, stone-cutters. When the thirty centuries begin to look down on it, mankind begins to look up at it. As for your high towers and monuments, there was a crazy fellow once in this town who undertook to dig through to China, and he got so far that, as he said, he heard the Chinese pots and kettles rattle; but I think that I shall not go out of my way to admire the hole which he made. Many are concerned about the monuments of the West and the East,—to know who built them. For my part, I should like to know who in those days did not build them,—who were above such trifling. But to proceed with my statistics.

By surveying, carpentry, and day-labor of various other kinds in the village in the meanwhile, for I have as many trades as fingers, I had earned $13.34. The expense of food for eight months, namely, from July 4th to March 1st, the time when these estimates were made, though I lived there more than two years,—not counting potatoes, a little green corn, and some peas, which I had raised, nor considering the value of what was on hand at the last date, was

Rice	$1 73½	
Molasses	1 73	Cheapest form of the saccharine.
Rye meal	1 04¾	
Indian meal	0 99¾	Cheaper than rye.
Pork	0 22	
Flour	0 88	{ Costs more than Indian meal, both money and trouble.
Sugar	0 80	
Lard	0 65	
Apples	0 25	
Dried apple	0 22	
Sweet potatoes	0 10	
One pumpkin	0 06	
One watermelon	0 02	
Salt	0 03	

(All experiments which failed.)

Yes, I did eat $8.74, all told; but I should not thus unblushingly publish my guilt, if I did not know that most of my readers were equally guilty with myself, and that their deeds would look no better in print. The next year I sometimes caught a mess of fish for my dinner, and once I went so far as to slaughter a woodchuck which ravaged my beanfield,—effect his transmigration, as a Tartar would say,—and devour him, partly for experiment's sake; but though it afforded me a momentary enjoyment, notwithstanding a musky flavor, I saw that the longest use would not make that a good practice, however it might seem to have your woodchucks ready dressed by the village butcher.

Clothing and some incidental expenses within the same dates, though little can be inferred from this item, amounted to

$8 40¾

Oil and some household utensils 2 00

So that all the pecuniary outgoes, excepting for washing and mending, which for the most part were done out of the house, and their bills have not yet been received,—and these are all and more than all the ways by which money necessarily goes out in this part of the world,—were ·

House	$28 12½
Farm, one year	14 72½
Food, eight months	8 74
Clothing, &c., eight months	8 40¾
Oil, &c., eight months	2 00
In all	$61 99¾

I address myself now to those of my readers who have a living to get. And to meet this I have for farm produce sold

	$23 44
Earned by day labor	13 34
In all	$36 78

which subtracted from the sum of the outgoes leaves a balance of $25.21¾ on the one side,—this being very nearly the means with which I started, and the measure of expenses to be incurred,—and on the other, beside the leisure and independence and health thus secured, a comfortable house for me as long as I choose to occupy it.

These statistics, however accidental and therefore uninstructive they may appear, as they have a certain completeness, have a certain value also. Nothing was given me of which I have not rendered some account. It appears from the above estimate that my food alone cost me in money about twenty-seven cents a week. It was, for nearly two years after this, rye and Indian meal without yeast, potatoes, rice, a very little salt pork, molasses, and salt; and my drink, water. It was fit that I should live on rice, mainly, who loved so well the philosophy of India. To meet the objections of some inveterate cavillers, I may as well state, that if I dined out occasionally, as I always had done, and I trust shall have opportunities to do again, it was frequently to the detriment of my domestic arrangements. But the dining out, being, as I have stated, a constant element, does not in the least affect a comparative statement like this.

I learned from my two years' experience that it would cost incredibly little trouble to obtain one's necessary food, even in this latitude; that a man may use as simple a diet as the animals, and yet retain health and strength. I have made a satisfactory dinner, satisfactory on several accounts, simply off a dish of purslane (*Portulaca oleracea*) which I gathered in my cornfield, boiled and salted. I give the Latin on account of the savoriness of the trivial name. And pray what more can a reasonable man desire, in peaceful times, in ordinary noons, than a sufficient number of ears of green sweet-corn boiled, with the addition of salt? Even the little variety which I used was a yielding to the demands of appetite, and not of health. Yet men have come to such a pass that they frequently starve, not for want of necessaries, but for want of luxuries; and I know a good woman who thinks that her son lost his life because he took to drinking water only.

The reader will perceive that I am treating the subject rather from an economic than a dietetic point of view, and he will not venture to put my abstemiousness to the test unless he has a well-stocked larder.

Bread I at first made of pure Indian meal and salt, genuine hoe-cakes, which I baked before my fire out of doors on a shingle or the end of a stick of timber sawed off in building my house; but it was wont to get smoked and to have a piny flavor. I tried flour also; but have at last found a mixture of rye and Indian meal most convenient and agreeable. In cold weather it was no little amusement to bake several small loaves of this in succession, tending and turning them as carefully as an Egyptian his hatching eggs. They were a real cereal fruit which I ripened, and they had to my senses a fragrance like that of other noble fruits, which I kept in as long as possible by wrapping them in cloths. I made a study of the ancient and indispensable art of breadmaking, consulting such authorities as offered, going back to the primitive days and first invention of the unleavened kind, when from the wildness of nuts and meats men first reached the mildness and refinement of this diet, and travelling gradually down in my studies through that accidental souring of the dough which, it is supposed, taught the leavening process, and through the various fermentations thereafter, till I came to "good, sweet, wholesome bread," the staff of life. Leaven, which some deem the soul of bread, the *spiritus* which fills its cellular tissue, which is religiously preserved like the vestal fire,— some precious bottle-full, I suppose, first brought over in the Mayflower, did the business for America, and its influence is still rising, swelling, spreading, in cerealian billows over the land,—this seed I regularly and faithfully procured from the village, till at length one morning I forgot the rules, and scalded my yeast; by which accident I discovered that even this was not indispensable,—for my discoveries were not by the synthetic but analytic process, —and I have gladly omitted it since, though most housewives earnestly assured me that safe and wholesome bread without yeast might not be, and elderly people prophesied a speedy decay of the vital forces. Yet I find it not to be an essential ingredient, and after going without it for a year am still in the land of the living; and I am glad to escape the trivialness of carrying a bottle-full in my pocket, which would sometimes pop and discharge its contents to my discomfiture. It is simpler and more respectable to omit it. Man is an animal who more than any other can adapt himself to all climates and circumstances. Neither did I put any sal soda, or other acid or alkali, into my bread. It would seem that I made it according to the recipe which Marcus Porcius Cato gave about two centuries before Christ. "Panem depsticium sic facito. Manus mortariumque bene lavato. Farinam in mortarium indito, aquæ paulatim addito, subigitoque pulchre. Ubi bene subegeris, defingito, coquitoque sub testu." Which I take to mean—"Make kneaded bread thus. Wash your hands and trough well. Put the meal into the trough, add water gradually, and knead it thoroughly. When you have kneaded it well, mould it, and bake it under a cover," that is, in a baking-kettle. Not a word about leaven. But I did not always use this staff of life. At one time, owing to the emptiness of my purse, I saw none of it for more than a month.

Every New Englander might easily raise all his own breadstuffs in this land of rye and Indian corn, and not depend on distant and fluctuating markets for them. Yet so far are we from simplicity and independence that, in Concord, fresh and sweet meal is rarely sold in the shops, and hominy and corn in a still coarser form are hardly used by any. For the most part the farmer gives to his cattle and hogs the grain of his own producing, and buys flour, which is at least no more wholesome, at a greater cost, at the store. I saw that I could easily raise my bushel or two of rye and Indian corn, for the former will grow on the poorest land, and the latter does not require the best, and grind them in a hand-mill, and so do without rice and pork; and if I must have some concentrated sweet, I found by experiment that I could make a very good molasses either of pumpkins or beets, and I knew that I needed only to set out a few maples to obtain it more easily still, and while these were growing I could use various substitutes beside those which I have named. "For," as the forefathers sang,—

> "we can make liquor to sweeten our lips,
> Of pumpkins and parsnips and walnut-tree chips."

Finally, as for salt, that grossest of groceries, to obtain this might be a fit occasion for a visit to the seashore, or, if I did without it altogether, I should probably drink the less water. I do not learn that the Indians ever troubled themselves to go after it.

Thus I could avoid all trade and barter, so far as my food was concerned, and having a shelter already, it would only remain to get clothing and fuel. The pantaloons which I now wear were woven in a farmer's family,—thank Heaven there is so much virtue still in man; for I think the fall from the farmer to the operative as great and memorable as that from the man to the farmer;—and in a new country fuel is an encumbrance. As for a habitat, if I were not permitted still to squat, I might purchase one acre at the same price for which the land I cultivated was sold—namely, eight dollars and eight cents. But as it was, I considered that I enhanced the value of the land by squatting on it.

There is a certain class of unbelievers who sometimes ask me such questions as, if I think that I can live on vegetable food alone; and to strike at the root of the matter at once,—for the root is faith,—I am accustomed to answer such, that I can live on board nails. If they cannot understand that, they cannot understand much that I have to say. For my part, I am glad to hear of experiments of this kind being tried; as that a young man tried for a fortnight to live on hard, raw corn on the ear, using his teeth for all mortar. The squirrel tribe tried the same and succeeded. The human race is interested in these experiments, though a few old women who are incapacitated for them or who own their thirds in mills, may be alarmed.

Where I Lived, and What I Lived For [2]

At a certain season of our life we are accustomed to consider every spot as the possible site of a house. I have thus surveyed the country on every side within a dozen miles of where I live. In imagination I have bought all the farms in succession, for all were to be bought, and I knew their price. I walked over each farmer's premises, tasted his wild apples, discoursed on husbandry with him, took his farm at his price, at any price, mortgaging it to him in my mind; even put a higher price on it,—took everything but a deed of it,— took his word for his deed, for I dearly love to talk,—cultivated it, and him too to some extent, I trust, and withdrew when I had enjoyed it long enough, leaving him to carry it on. This experience entitled me to be regarded as a sort of real-estate broker by my friends. Wherever I sat, there I might live, and the landscape radiated from me accordingly. What is a house but a *sedes*, a seat?—better if a country seat. I discovered many a site for a house not likely to be soon improved, which some might have thought too far from the village, but to my eyes the village was too far from it. Well, there I might live, I said; and there I did live, for an hour, a summer and a winter life; saw how I could let the years run off, buffet the winter through, and see the spring come in. The future inhabitants of this region, wherever they may place their houses, may be sure that they have been anticipated. An afternoon sufficed to lay out the land into orchard, woodlot, and pasture, and to decide what fine oaks or pines should be left to stand before the door, and whence each blasted tree could be seen to the best advantage; and then I let it lie, fallow perchance, for a man is rich in proportion to the number of things which he can afford to let alone.

My imagination carried me so far that I even had the refusal of several farms,—the refusal was all I wanted,—but I never got my fingers burned by actual possession. The nearest that I came to actual possession was when I bought the Hollowell place, and had begun to sort my seeds, and collected materials with which to make a wheelbarrow to carry it on or off with; but before the owner gave me a deed of it, his wife—every man has such a wife— changed her mind and wished to keep it, and he offered me ten dollars to release him. Now, to speak the truth, I had but ten cents in the world, and it surpassed my arithmetic to tell, if I was that man who had ten cents, or

---

[2] From *Walden*, chap. ii.

who had a farm, or ten dollars, or all together. However, I let him keep the ten dollars and the farm too, for I had carried it far enough; or rather, to be generous, I sold him the farm for just what I gave for it, and, as he was not a rich man, made him a present of ten dollars, and still had my ten cents, and seeds, and materials for a wheelbarrow left. I found thus that I had been a rich man without any damage to my poverty. But I retained the landscape, and I have since annually carried off what it yielded without a wheelbarrow. With respect to landscapes,—

> "I am monarch of all I *survey,*
> My right there is none to dispute."

I have frequently seen a poet withdraw, having enjoyed the most valuable part of a farm, while the crusty farmer supposed that he had got a few wild apples only. Why, the owner does not know it for many years when a poet has put his farm in rhyme, the most admirable kind of invisible fence, has fairly impounded it, milked it, skimmed it, and got all the cream, and left the farmer only the skimmed milk.

The real attractions of the Hollowell farm, to me, were: its complete retirement, being about two miles from the village, half a mile from the nearest neighbor, and separated from the highway by a broad field; its bounding on the river, which the owner said protected it by its fogs from frosts in the spring, though that was nothing to me; the gray color and ruinous state of the house and barn, and the dilapidated fences, which put such an interval between me and the last occupant; the hollow and lichen-covered apple trees, gnawed by rabbits, showing what kind of neighbors I should have; but above all, the recollection I had of it from my earliest voyages up the river, when the house was concealed behind a dense grove of red maples, through which I heard the house-dog bark. I was in haste to buy it, before the proprietor finished getting out some rocks, cutting down the hollow apple trees, and grubbing up some young birches which had sprung up in the pasture, or, in short, had made any more of his improvements. To enjoy these advantages I was ready to carry it on; like Atlas, to take the world on my shoulders, —I never heard what compensation he received for that,—and do all those things which had no other motive or excuse but that I might pay for it and be unmolested in my possession of it; for I knew all the while that it would yield the most abundant crop of the kind I wanted if I could only afford to let it alone. But it turned out as I have said.

All that I could say, then, with respect to farming on a large scale, (I have always cultivated a garden,) was, that I had had my seeds ready. Many think that seeds improve with age. I have no doubt that time discriminates between the good and the bad; and when at last I shall plant, I shall be less likely to be disappointed. But I would say to my fellows, once for all, As long as possible live free and uncommitted. It makes but little difference whether you are committed to a farm or the county jail.

Old Cato, whose *De Re Rusticâ* is my "Cultivator," says, and the only translation I have seen makes sheer nonsense of the passage, "When you think of getting a farm, turn it thus in your mind, not to buy greedily; nor spare your pains to look at it, and do not think it enough to go around it once. The oftener you go there the more it will please you, if it is good." I think I shall not buy greedily, but go round and round it as long as I live, and be buried in it first, that it may please me the more at last.

The present was my next experiment of this kind, which I purpose to describe more at length, for convenience putting the experience of two years into one. As I have said, I do not propose to write an ode to dejection, but to brag as lustily as chanticleer in the morning, standing on his roost, if only to wake my neighbors up.

When first I took up my abode in the woods, that is, began to spend my nights as well as days there, which, by accident, was on Independence Day, or the fourth of July, 1845, my house was not finished for winter, but was merely a defence against the rain, without plastering or chimney, the walls being of rough weather-stained boards, with wide chinks, which made it cool at night. The upright white hewn studs and freshly planed door and window casings gave it a clean and airy look, especially in the morning, when its timbers were saturated with dew, so that I fancied that by noon some sweet gum would exude from them. To my imagination it retained throughout the day more or less of this auroral character, reminding me of a certain house on a mountain which I had visited the year before. This was an airy and unplastered cabin, fit to entertain a travelling god, and where a goddess might trail her garments. The winds which passed over my dwelling were such as sweep over the ridges of mountains, bearing the broken strains, or celestial parts only, of terrestrial music. The morning wind forever blows, the poem of creation is uninterrupted; but few are the ears that hear it. Olympus is but the outside of the earth everywhere.

The only house I had been the owner of before, if I except a boat, was a tent, which I used occasionally when making excursions in the summer, and this is still rolled up in my garret; but the boat, after passing from hand to hand, has gone down the stream of time. With this more substantial shelter about me, I had made some progress towards settling in the world. This frame, so slightly clad, was a sort of crystallization around me, and reacted on the builder. It was suggestive somewhat as a picture in outlines. I did not need to go out doors to take the air, for the atmosphere within had lost none of its freshness. It was not so much within doors as behind a door where I sat, even in the rainiest weather. The Harivansa says, "An abode without birds is like a meat without seasoning." Such was not my abode, for

I found myself suddenly neighbor to the birds; not by having imprisoned one, but having caged myself near them. I was not only nearer to some of those which commonly frequent the garden and the orchard, but to those wilder and more thrilling songsters of the forest which never, or rarely, serenade a villager,—the woodthrush, the veery, the scarlet tanager, the field-sparrow, the whippoorwill, and many others.

I was seated by the shore of a small pond, about a mile and a half south of the village of Concord and somewhat higher than it, in the midst of an extensive wood between that town and Lincoln, and about two miles south of that our only field known to fame, Concord Battle Ground; but I was so low in the woods that the opposite shore, half a mile off, like the rest, covered with wood, was my most distant horizon. For the first week, whenever I looked out on the pond it impressed me like a tarn high up on the side of a mountain, its bottom far above the surface of other lakes, and, as the sun arose, I saw it throwing off its nightly clothing of mist, and here and there, by degrees, its soft ripples or its smooth reflecting surface was revealed, while the mists, like ghosts, were stealthily withdrawing in every direction into the woods, as at the breaking up of some nocturnal conventicle. The very dew seemed to hang upon the trees later into the day than usual, as on the sides of mountains.

This small lake was of most value as a neighbor in the intervals of a gentle rain storm in August, when, both air and water being perfectly still, but the sky overcast, mid-afternoon had all the serenity of evening, and the wood-thrush sang around, and was heard from shore to shore. A lake like this is never smoother than at such a time; and the clear portion of the air above it being shallow and darkened by clouds, the water, full of light and re-flections, becomes a lower heaven itself so much the more important. From a hill top near by, where the wood had been recently cut off, there was a pleasing vista southward across the pond, through a wide indentation in the hills which form the shore there, where their opposite sides sloping toward each other suggested a stream flowing out in that direction through a wooded valley, but stream there was none. That way I looked between and over the near green hills to some distant and higher ones in the horizon, tinged with blue. Indeed, by standing on tiptoe I could catch a glimpse of some of the peaks of the still bluer and more distant mountain ranges in the northwest, those true-blue coins from heaven's own mint, and also of some portion of the village. But in other directions, even from this point, I could not see over or beyond the woods which surrounded me. It is well to have some water in your neighborhood, to give buoyancy to and float the earth. One value even of the smallest well is, that when you look into it you see that earth is not continent but insular. This is as important as that it keeps butter cool. When I looked across the pond from this peak toward the Sudbury meadows, which in time of flood I distinguished elevated perhaps by a mirage in their seething valley, like a coin in a basin, all the earth beyond the pond appeared like a thin crust insulated and floated even by this small sheet of intervening water, and I was reminded that this on which I dwelt was but *dry land*.

Though the view from my door was still more contracted, I did not feel crowded or confined in the least. There was pasture enough for my imagination. The low shrub-oak plateau to which the opposite shore arose, stretched away toward the prairies of the West and the steppes of Tartary, affording ample room for all the roving families of men. "There are none happy in the world but beings who enjoy freely a vast horizon," said Damodara, when his herds required new and larger pastures.

Both place and time were changed, and I dwelt nearer to those parts of the universe and to those eras in history which had most attracted me. Where I lived was as far off as many a region viewed nightly by astronomers. We are wont to imagine rare and delectable places in some remote and more celestial corner of the system, behind the constellation of Cassiopeia's Chair, far from noise and disturbance. I discovered that my house actually had its site in such a withdrawn, but forever new and unprofaned, part of the universe. If it were worth the while to settle in those parts near to the Pleiades or the Hyades, to Aldebaran or Altair, then I was really there, or at an equal remoteness from the life which I had left behind, dwindled and twinkling with as fine a ray to my nearest neighbor, and to be seen only in moonless nights by him. Such was that part of creation where I had squatted:

> "There was a shepherd that did live,
>   And held his thoughts as high
>   As were the mounts whereon his flocks
>   Did hourly feed him by."

What should we think of the shepherd's life if his flocks always wandered to higher pastures than his thoughts?

Every morning was a cheerful invitation to make my life of equal simplicity, and I may say innocence, with Nature herself. I have been as sincere a worshipper of Aurora as the Greeks. I got up early and bathed in the pond; that was a religious exercise, and one of the best things which I did. They say that characters were engraven on the bathing tub of king Tching-thang to this effect: "Renew thyself completely each day; do it again and again, and forever again." I can understand that. Morning brings back the heroic ages. I was as much affected by the faint hum of a mosquito making its invisible and unimaginable tour through my apartments at earliest dawn, when I was sitting with door and windows open, as I could be by any trumpet that ever sang of fame. It was Homer's requiem; itself an Iliad and Odyssey in the air,

singing its own wrath and wanderings. There was something cosmical about
it; a standing advertisement, till forbidden, of the everlasting vigor and fer-
tility of the world. The morning, which is the most memorable season of the
day, is the awakening hour. Then there is least somnolence in us; and for an
hour, at least, some part of us awakes which slumbers all the rest of the day
and night. Little is to be expected of that day, if it can be called a day, to which
we are not awakened by our Genius, but by the mechanical nudgings of some
servitor, are not awakened by our own newly-acquired force and aspirations
from within, accompanied by the undulations of celestial music, instead of
factory bells, and a fragrance filling the air—to a higher life than we fell
asleep from; and thus the darkness bear its fruit, and prove itself to be good,
no less than the light. That man who does not believe that each day contains
an earlier, more sacred, and auroral hour than he has yet profaned, has
despaired of life, and is pursuing a descending and darkening way. After a
partial cessation of his sensuous life, the soul of man, or its organs rather, are
reinvigorated each day, and his Genius tries again what noble life it can
make. All memorable events, I should say, transpire in morning time and in
a morning atmosphere. The Vedas say, "All intelligences awake with the
morning." Poetry and art, and the fairest and most memorable of the actions
of men, date from such an hour. All poets and heroes, like Memnon, are the
children of Aurora, and emit their music at sunrise. To him whose elastic
and vigorous thought keeps pace with the sun, the day is a perpetual morning. It matters not what the clocks say or the attitudes and labors of men.
Morning is when I am awake and there is a dawn in me. Moral reform is the
effort to throw off sleep. Why is it that men give so poor an account of their
day if they have not been slumbering? They are not such poor calculators.
If they had not been overcome with drowsiness they would have performed
something. The millions are awake enough for physical labor; but only one
in a million is awake enough for effective intellectual exertion, only one in a
hundred millions to a poetic or divine life. To be awake is to be alive. I have
never yet met a man who was quite awake. How could I have looked him
in the face?

We must learn to reawaken and keep ourselves awake, not by mechanical
aids, but by an infinite expectation of the dawn, which does not forsake us in
our soundest sleep. I know of no more encouraging fact than the unquestionable ability of man to elevate his life by a conscious endeavor. It is something to be able to paint a particular picture, or to carve a statue, and so to
make a few objects beautiful; but it is far more glorious to carve and paint the
very atmosphere and medium through which we look, which morally we
can do. To affect the quality of the day, that is the highest of arts. Every
man is tasked to make his life, even in its details, worthy of the contempla-

tion of his most elevated and critical hour. If we refused, or rather used up, such paltry information as we get, the oracles would distinctly inform us how this might be done.

I went to the woods because I wished to live deliberately, to front only the essential facts of life, and see if I could not learn what it had to teach, and not, when I came to die, discover that I had not lived. I did not wish to live what was not life, living is so dear; nor did I wish to practise resignation, unless it was quite necessary. I wanted to live deep and suck out all the marrow of life, to live so sturdily and Spartan-like as to put to rout all that was not life, to cut a broad swath and shave close, to drive life into a corner, and reduce it to its lowest terms, and, if it proved to be mean, why then to get the whole and genuine meanness of it, and publish its meanness to the world; or if it were sublime, to know it by experience, and be able to give a true account of it in my next excursion. For most men, it appears to me, are in a strange uncertainty about it, whether it is of the devil or of God, and have *somewhat hastily* concluded that it is the chief end of man here to "glorify God and enjoy him forever."

Still we live meanly, like ants; though the fable tells us that we were long ago changed into men; like pygmies we fight with cranes; it is error upon error, and clout upon clout, and our best virtue has for its occasion a super-fluous and evitable wretchedness. Our life is frittered away by detail. An honest man has hardly need to count more than his ten fingers, or in extreme cases he may add his ten toes, and lump the rest. Simplicity, simplicity, simplicity! I say, let your affairs be as two or three, and not a hundred or a thousand; instead of a million count half a dozen, and keep your accounts on your thumb nail. In the midst of this chopping sea of civilized life, such are the clouds and storms and quicksands and thousand-and-one items to be allowed for, that a man has to live, if he would not founder and go to the bottom and not make his port at all, by dead reckoning, and he must be a great calculator indeed who succeeds. Simplify, simplify. Instead of three meals a day, if it be necessary eat but one; instead of a hundred dishes, five; and reduce other things in proportion. Our life is like a German Confederacy, made up of petty states, with its boundary forever fluctuating, so that even a German cannot tell you how it is bounded at any moment. The nation itself, with all its so-called internal improvements, which, by the way, are all external and superficial, is just such an unwieldy and overgrown establishment, cluttered with furniture and tripped up by its own traps, ruined by luxury and heedless expense, by want of calculation and a worthy aim, as the million households in the land; and the only cure for it as for them is in a rigid economy, a stern and more than Spartan simplicity of life and elevation of purpose. It lives too fast. Men think that it is essential that the *Nation* have commerce, and export ice, and talk through a telegraph, and ride thirty miles an hour, without a doubt, whether *they* do or not; but whether we should live like baboons or like men, is a little uncertain. If we do not get out sleepers, and forge rails, and devote days and nights to the work, but go to tinkering upon our *lives* to improve *them,* who will build railroads? And if railroads are not built, how shall we get to heaven in season? But if we stay at home and mind our business, who will want railroads? We do not ride on the railroad; it rides upon us. Did you ever think what those sleepers are that underlie the railroad? Each one is a man, an Irishman, or a Yankee man. The rails are laid on them, and they are covered with sand, and the cars run smoothly over them. They are sound sleepers, I assure you. And every few years a new lot is laid down and run over; so that, if some have the pleasure of riding on a rail, others have the misfortune to be ridden upon. And when they run over a man that is walking in his sleep, a supernumerary sleeper in the wrong position, and wake him up, they suddenly stop the cars, and make a hue and cry about it, as if this were an exception. I am glad to know that it takes a gang of men for every five miles to keep the sleepers down and level in their beds as it is, for this is a sign that they may sometime get up again.

Why should we live with such hurry and waste of life? We are determined to be starved before we are hungry. Men say that a stitch in time saves nine, and so they take a thousand stitches to-day to save nine to-morrow. As for *work,* we haven't any of any consequence. We have the Saint Vitus' dance, and cannot possibly keep our heads still. If I should only give a few pulls at the parish bell-rope, as for a fire, that is, without setting the bell, there is hardly a man on his farm in the outskirts of Concord, notwithstanding that press of engagements which was his excuse so many times this morning, nor a boy, nor a woman, I might almost say, but would forsake all and follow that sound, not mainly to save property from the flames, but, if we will confess the truth, much more to see it burn, since burn it must, and we, be it known, did not set it on fire,—or to see it put out, and have a hand in it, if that is done as handsomely; yes, even if it were the parish church itself. Hardly a man takes a half hour's nap after dinner but when he wakes he holds up his head and asks, "What's the news?" as if the rest of mankind had stood his sentinels. Some give directions to be waked every half hour, doubtless for no other purpose; and then, to pay for it, they tell what they have dreamed. After a night's sleep the news is as indispensable as the breakfast. "Pray tell me any-thing new that has happened to a man anywhere on this globe,"—and he reads it over his coffee and rolls, that a man has had his eyes gouged out this morning on the Wachito River; never dreaming the while that he lives in the dark unfathomed mammoth cave of this world, and has but the rudiment of an eye himself.

For my part, I could easily do without the post-office. I think that there are very few important communications made through it. To speak critically, I never received more than one or two letters in my life—I wrote this some years ago—that were worth the postage. The penny-post is, commonly, an institution through which you seriously offer a man that penny for his thoughts which is too often safely offered in jest. And I am sure that I never read any memorable news in a newspaper. If we read of one man robbed, or murdered, or killed by accident, or one house burned, or one vessel wrecked, or one steamboat blown up, or one cow run over on the Western Railroad, or one mad dog killed, or one lot of grasshoppers in the winter,—we never need read of another. One is enough. If you are acquainted with the principle, what do you care for a myriad instances and applications? To a philosopher all *news,* as it is called, is gossip, and they who edit and read it are old women over their tea. Yet not a few are greedy after this gossip. There was such a rush, as I hear, the other day at one of the offices to learn the foreign news by the last arrival, that several large squares of plate glass belonging to the establishment were broken by the pressure,—news which I seriously think a ready wit might write a twelvemonth, or twelve years, beforehand with sufficient accuracy. As for Spain, for instance, if you know how to throw in Don Carlos and the Infanta and Don Pedro and Seville and Granada, from time to time in the right proportions,—they may have changed the names a little since I saw the papers,—and serve up a bull-fight when other entertainments fail, it will be true to the letter, and give us as good an idea of the exact state or ruin of things in Spain as the most succinct and lucid reports under this head in the newspapers; and as for England, almost the last significant scrap of news from that quarter was the revolution of 1649; and if you have learned the history of her crops for an average year, you never need attend to that thing again, unless your speculations are of a merely pecuniary character. If one may judge who rarely looks into the newspapers, nothing new does ever happen in foreign parts, a French revolution not excepted.

What news! how much more important to know what that is which was never old! "Kieou-he-yu (great dignitary of the state of Wei) sent a man to Khoung-tseu to know his news. Khoung-tseu caused the messenger to be seated near him, and questioned him in these terms: What is your master doing? The messenger answered with respect: My master desires to diminish the number of his faults, but he cannot come to the end of them. The messenger being gone, the philosopher remarked: What a worthy messenger! What a worthy messenger!" The preacher instead of vexing the ears of drowsy farmers on their day of rest at the end of the week,—for Sunday is the fit conclusion of an ill-spent week, and not the fresh and brave beginning of a new one,—with this one other draggle-tail of a sermon, should shout with thundering voice,—"Pause! Avast! Why so seeming fast, but deadly slow?"

Shams and delusions are esteemed for soundest truths, while reality is fabulous. If men would steadily observe realities only, and not allow themselves to be deluded, life, to compare it with such things as we know, would be like a fairy tale and the Arabian Nights' Entertainments. If we respected only what is inevitable and has a right to be, music and poetry would resound along the streets. When we are unhurried and wise, we perceive that only great and worthy things have any permanent and absolute existence,—that petty fears and petty pleasures are but the shadow of the reality. This is always exhilarating and sublime. By closing the eyes and slumbering, and consenting to be deceived by shows, men establish and confirm their daily life of routine and habit everywhere, which still is built on purely illusory foundations. Children, who play life, discern its true law and relations more clearly than men, who fail to live it worthily, but who think that they are wiser by experience, that is, by failure. I have read in a Hindoo book, that "there was a king's son, who, being expelled in infancy from his native city, was brought up by a forester, and, growing up to maturity in that state, imagined himself to belong to the barbarous race with which he lived. One of his father's ministers having discovered him, revealed to him what he was, and the misconception of his character was removed, and he knew himself to be a prince. So the soul," continues the Hindoo philosopher, "from the circumstances in which it is placed, mistakes its own character, until the truth is revealed to it by some holy teacher, and then it knows itself to be *Brahme*." I perceive that we inhabitants of New England live this mean life that we do because our vision does not penetrate the surface of things. We think that that *is* which *appears* to be. If a man should walk through this town and see only the reality, where, think you, would the "Mill-dam" go to? If he should give us an account of the realities he beheld there, we should not recognize the place in his description. Look at a meeting-house, or a court-house, or a jail, or a shop, or a dwelling-house, and say what that thing really is before a true gaze, and they would all go to pieces in your account of them. Men esteem truth remote, in the outskirts of the system, behind the farthest star, before Adam and after the last man. In eternity there is indeed something true and sublime. But all these times and places and occasions are now and here. God himself culminates in the present moment, and will never be more divine in the lapse of all the ages. And we are enabled to apprehend at all what is sublime and noble only by the perpetual instilling and drenching of the reality that surrounds us. The universe constantly and obediently answers to our conceptions; whether we travel fast or slow, the track is laid for us. Let us spend our lives in conceiving them. The poet or the artist never yet had so fair and noble a design but some of his posterity at least could accomplish it.

Let us spend one day as deliberately as Nature, and not be thrown off the track by every nutshell and mosquito's wing that falls on the rails. Let us rise early and fast, or break fast, gently and without perturbation; let company come and let company go, let the bells ring and the children cry,—determined to make a day of it. Why should we knock under and go with the stream? Let us not be upset and overwhelmed in that terrible rapid and whirlpool called a dinner, situated in the meridian shallows. Weather this danger and you are safe, for the rest of the way is down hill. With unrelaxed nerves, with morning vigor, sail by it, looking another way, tied to the mast like Ulysses. If the engine whistles, let it whistle till it is hoarse for its pains. If the bell rings, why should we run? We will consider what kind of music they are like. Let us settle ourselves, and work and wedge our feet downward through the mud and slush of opinion, and prejudice, and tradition, and delusion, and appearances, that alluvion which covers the globe, through Paris and London, through New York and Boston and Concord, through church and state, through poetry and philosophy and religion, till we come to a hard bottom and rocks in place, which we can call *reality,* and say, This is, and no mistake; and then begin, having a *point d'appui,* below freshet and frost and fire, a place where you might found a wall or a state, or set a lamp-post safely, or perhaps a gauge, not a Nilometer, but a Realometer, that future ages might know how deep a freshet of shams and appearances had gathered from time to time. If you stand right fronting and face to face to a fact, you will see the sun glimmer on both its surfaces, as if it were a cimeter, and feel its sweet edge dividing you through the heart and marrow, and so you will happily conclude your mortal career. Be it life or death, we crave only reality. If we are really dying, let us hear the rattle in our throats and feel cold in the extremities; if we are alive, let us go about our business.

Time is but the stream I go a-fishing in. I drink at it; but while I drink I see the sandy bottom and detect how shallow it is. Its thin current slides away, but eternity remains. I would drink deeper; fish in the sky, whose bottom is pebbly with stars. I cannot count one. I know not the first letter of the alphabet. I have always been regretting that I was not as wise as the day I was born. The intellect is a cleaver; it discerns and rifts its way into the secret of things. I do not wish to be any more busy with my hands than is necessary. My head is hands and feet. I feel all my best faculties concentrated in it. My instinct tells me that my head is an organ for burrowing, as some creatures use their snout and fore-paws, and with it I would mine and burrow my way through these hills. I think that the richest vein is somewhere hereabouts; so by the divining rod and thin rising vapors I judge; and here I will begin to mine.

BRUTE NEIGHBORS [3]

I WAS witness to events of a less peaceful character. One day when I went out to my wood-pile, or rather my pile of stumps, I observed two large ants, the one red, the other much larger, nearly half an inch long, and black, fiercely

[3] From *Walden,* chap. xii.

contending with one another. Having once got hold they never let go, but struggled and wrestled and rolled on the chips incessantly. Looking farther, I was surprised to find that the chips were covered with such combatants, that it was not a *duellum,* but a *bellum,* a war between two races of ants, the red always pitted against the black, and frequently two red ones to one black. The legions of these Myrmidons covered all the hills and vales in my wood-yard, and the ground was already strewn with the dead and dying, both red and black. It was the only battle which I have ever witnessed, the only battle-field I ever trod while the battle was raging; internecine war; the red republicans on the one hand, and the black imperialists on the other. On every side they were engaged in deadly combat, yet without any noise that I could hear, and human soldiers never fought so resolutely. I watched a couple that were fast locked in each other's embraces, in a little sunny valley amid the chips, now at noon-day prepared to fight till the sun went down, or life went out. The smaller red champion had fastened himself like a vice to his adversary's front, and through all the tumblings on that field never for an instant ceased to gnaw at one of his feelers near the root, having already caused the other to go by the board; while the stronger black one dashed him from side to side, and, as I saw on looking nearer, had already divested him of several of his members. They fought with more pertinacity than bull-dogs. Neither manifested the least disposition to retreat. It was evident that their battle-cry was Conquer or die. In the meanwhile there came along a single red ant on the hill-side of this valley, evidently full of excitement, who either had despatched his foe, or had not yet taken part in the battle; probably the latter, for he had lost none of his limbs; whose mother had charged him to return with his shield or upon it. Or perchance he was some Achilles, who had nourished his wrath apart, and had now come to avenge or rescue his Patroclus. He saw this unequal combat from afar,—for the blacks were nearly twice the size of the red,—he drew near with rapid pace till he stood on his guard within half an inch of the combatants; then, watching his opportunity, he sprang upon the black warrior, and commenced his operations near the root of his right foreleg, leaving the foe to select among his own members; and so there were three united for life, as if a new kind of attraction had been invented which put all other locks and cements to shame. I should not have wondered by this time to find they had their respective musical bands stationed on some eminent chip, and playing their national airs the while, to excite the slow and cheer the dying combatants. I was myself excited somewhat even as if they had been men. The more you think of it, the less the difference. And certainly there is not the fight recorded in Concord history, at least, if in the history of America, that will bear a moment's comparison with this, whether for the numbers engaged in it, or for the patriotism and heroism displayed. For numbers and for carnage it was an Austerlitz or

Dresden. Concord Fight! Two killed on the patriots' side, and Luther Blanch-
ard wounded! Why here every ant was a Buttrick,—"Fire! for God's sake
fire!"—and thousands shared the fate of Davis and Hosmer. There was not
one hireling there. I have no doubt that it was a principle they fought for, as
much as our ancestors, and not to avoid a three-penny tax on their tea; and
the results of this battle will be as important and memorable to those whom
it concerns as those of the battle of Bunker Hill at least.

NATHANIEL HAWTHORNE

(1804–1864)

Tradition and inheritance moulded the character and work of Hawthorne. During two centuries his ancestors, like the Pyncheons of the "Seven Gables," had at first prospered and then vegetated in the atmosphere of old Salem, where he was born in 1804, and where his formative years were spent. Leaving Bowdoin, where by his own account he had been an "idle student," he shut himself up in his "chamber under the eaves," at Salem, "seldom going out except at twilight." Here for twelve years he read, wrote, and dreamed, learning both the value and the danger of musing in solitude. He was at last drawn out of his seclusion by the moderate recognition given to his *Twice Told Tales* (1837), by his engagement to Sophia Peabody of Salem, and by an appointment in the Boston Custom House. Losing this place he became one of the proprietors at the transcendental Brook Farm, hoping it would provide "leisure for study with healthful and honest toil," but he soon tired of "providing food for cows and horses." His marriage in 1842 was followed by years of very fruitful creation. He lived first at the Old Manse, Concord, where he produced *Mosses from an Old Manse* (1846); then at Salem, as Surveyor of the Port, where he conceived *The Scarlet Letter* (1850); and afterwards at Lenox, where he wrote *The House of the Seven Gables* (1851), and *The Blithedale Romance* (1852). He returned to Concord, but was soon appointed consul at Liverpool, and spent the next seven years in England and Italy. *The Marble Faun,* product of his Italian visit, was published in 1860. He left three romances unfinished at his death in 1864.

Hawthorne can best be called—though to some the terms may seem contradictory—a puritan artist. Fortunately living at a time when old beliefs had weakened but had not yet disappeared, he could still regard inherited puritan conceptions and superstitions with that "suspension of disbelief which constitutes poetic faith"; he could still find in them food for his imagination. Like all the puritans preoccupied with moral problems,—particularly the problem of sin—he dealt with them not discursively, but imaginatively, not as a preacher, but as an artist. Though he was not a philosopher and thought in stories rather than in essays, he was, like Emerson, an idealist and transcendentalist. With keen eye for the material world he saw in it mainly a symbol of the immaterial one; to him also nature was only "a metaphor of the human mind"; and hence he thought mainly in symbols. Each tale is a "fanciful story, evolving a thoughtful moral." And in general the thought evolved is better worth attention than that of the early puritans. Hampered by no outworn theology and by no distorted notions of the human heart, he dealt with sins that were not fanciful but actual in the puritan character —pride, hypocrisy, greed, moral isolation—and traced instructively their devastating effects. But finally the artist is uppermost, for this thought is embodied in a series of wonderfully beautiful creations, and expressed in a remarkably pure and transparent style. "The puritanism of the past," Lowell rightly says, "found its poet in Nathaniel Hawthorne."

NATHANIEL HAWTHORNE

THE MINISTER'S BLACK VEIL [1]

A PARABLE [2]

THE sexton stood in the porch of Milford meeting-house, pulling busily at the bell-rope. The old people of the village came stooping along the street. Children, with bright faces, tripped merrily beside their parents, or mimicked a graver gait, in the conscious dignity of their Sunday clothes. Spruce bachelors looked sidelong at the pretty maidens, and fancied that the Sabbath sunshine made them prettier than on week days. When the throng had mostly streamed into the porch, the sexton began to toll the bell, keeping his eye on the Reverend Mr. Hooper's door. The first glimpse of the clergyman's figure was the signal for the bell to cease its summons.

"But what has good Parson Hooper got upon his face?" cried the sexton in astonishment.

All within hearing immediately turned about, and beheld the semblance of Mr. Hooper, pacing slowly his meditative way towards the meeting-house. With one accord they started, expressing more wonder than if some strange minister were coming to dust the cushions of Mr. Hooper's pulpit.

"Are you sure it is our parson?" inquired Goodman Gray of the sexton.

"Of a certainty it is good Mr. Hooper," replied the sexton. "He was to have exchanged pulpits with Parson Shute, of Westbury; but Parson Shute sent to excuse himself yesterday, being to preach a funeral sermon."

The cause of so much amazement may appear sufficiently slight. Mr. Hooper, a gentlemanly person, of about thirty, though still a bachelor, was dressed with due clerical neatness, as if a careful wife had starched his band, and brushed the weekly dust from his Sunday's garb. There was but one thing remarkable in his appearance. Swathed about his forehead, and hanging down over his face, so low as to be shaken by his breath, Mr. Hooper had on a black veil. On a nearer view it seemed to consist of two folds of crape, which entirely concealed his features, except the mouth and chin, but probably did not intercept his sight, further than to give a darkened aspect to all living and inanimate things. With this gloomy shade before him, good Mr. Hooper walked onward, at a slow and quiet pace, stooping somewhat, and looking on the ground, as is customary with abstracted men, yet nodding kindly to those of his parishioners who still waited on the meeting-house

---

[1] First published in the *Token*, 1836, and included in *Twice-Told Tales* (1837). This and the following Tales of Hawthorne are reprinted by permission of, and by arrangement with, Houghton Mifflin Company, the authorized publishers.

[2] Another clergyman in New England, Mr. Joseph Moody, of York, Maine, who died about eighty years since, made himself remarkable by the same eccentricity that is here related of the Reverend Mr. Hooper. In his case, however, the symbol had a different import. In early life he had accidentally killed a beloved friend; and from that day till the hour of his own death, he hid his face from men.—*Author's note.*

steps. But so wonder-struck were they that his greeting hardly met with a return.

"I can't really feel as if good Mr. Hooper's face was behind that piece of crape," said the sexton.

"I don't like it," muttered an old woman, as she hobbled into the meeting-house. "He has changed himself into something awful, only by hiding his face."

"Our parson has gone mad!" cried Goodman Gray, following him across the threshold.

A rumor of some unaccountable phenomenon had preceded Mr. Hooper into the meeting-house, and set all the congregation astir. Few could refrain from twisting their heads towards the door; many stood upright, and turned directly about; while several little boys clambered upon the seats, and came down again with a terrible racket. There was a general bustle, a rustling of the women's gowns and shuffling of the men's feet, greatly at variance with that hushed repose which should attend the entrance of the minister. But Mr. Hooper appeared not to notice the perturbation of his people. He entered with an almost noiseless step, bent his head mildly to the pews on each side, and bowed as he passed his oldest parishioner, a white-haired great-grandsire, who occupied an arm-chair in the centre of the aisle. It was strange to observe how slowly this venerable man became conscious of something singular in the appearance of his pastor. He seemed not fully to partake of the prevailing wonder, till Mr. Hooper had ascended the stairs, and showed himself in the pulpit, face to face with his congregation, except for the black veil. That mysterious emblem was never once withdrawn. It shook with his measured breath, as he gave out the psalm; it threw its obscurity between him and the holy page, as he read the Scriptures; and while he prayed, the veil lay heavily on his uplifted countenance. Did he seek to hide it from the dread Being whom he was addressing?

Such was the effect of this simple piece of crape, that more than one woman of delicate nerves was forced to leave the meeting-house. Yet perhaps the pale-faced congregation was almost as fearful a sight to the minister, as his black veil to them.

Mr. Hooper had the reputation of a good preacher, but not an energetic one: he strove to win his people heavenward by mild, persuasive influences, rather than to drive them thither by the thunders of the Word. The sermon which he now delivered was marked by the same characteristics of style and manner as the general series of his pulpit oratory. But there was something, either in the sentiment of the discourse itself, or in the imagination of the auditors, which made it greatly the most powerful effort that they had ever heard from their pastor's lips. It was tinged, rather more darkly than us- with the gentle gloom of Mr. Hooper's temperament. The subject bence to secret sin, and those sad mysteries which we hide from our nearest and dearest, and would fain conceal from our own consciousness, even forgetting that the Omniscient can detect them. A subtle power was breathed into his words. Each member of the congregation, the most innocent girl, and the man of hardened breast, felt as if the preacher had crept upon them, behind his awful veil, and discovered their hoarded iniquity of deed or thought. Many spread their clasped hands on their bosoms. There was nothing terrible in what Mr. Hooper said, at least no violence; and yet, with every tremor of his melancholy voice, the hearers quaked. An unsought pathos came hand in hand with awe. So sensible were the audience of some unwonted attribute in their minister, that they longed for a breath of wind to blow aside the veil, almost believing that a stranger's visage would be discovered, though the form, gesture, and voice were those of Mr. Hooper.

At the close of the services, the people hurried out with indecorous confusion, eager to communicate their pent-up amazement, and conscious of lighter spirits the moment they lost sight of the black veil. Some gathered in little circles, huddled closely together, with their mouths all whispering in the centre; some went homeward alone, wrapt in silent meditation; some talked loudly, and profaned the Sabbath day with ostentatious laughter. A few shook their sagacious heads, intimating that they could penetrate the mystery; while one or two affirmed that there was no mystery at all, but only that Mr. Hooper's eyes were so weakened by the midnight lamp, as to require a shade. After a brief interval, forth came good Mr. Hooper also, in the rear of his flock. Turning his veiled face from one group to another, he paid due reverence to the hoary heads, saluted the middle aged with kind dignity as their friend and spiritual guide, greeted the young with mingled authority and love, and laid his hands on the little children's heads to bless them. Such was always his custom on the Sabbath day. Strange and bewildered looks repaid him for his courtesy. None, as on former occasions, aspired to the honor of walking by their pastor's side. Old Squire Saunders, doubtless by an accidental lapse of memory, neglected to invite Mr. Hooper to his table, where the good clergyman had been wont to bless the food, almost every Sunday since his settlement. He returned, therefore, to the parsonage, and, at the moment of closing the door, was observed to look back upon the people, all of whom had their eyes fixed upon the minister. A sad smile gleamed faintly from beneath the black veil, and flickered about his mouth, glimmering as he disappeared.

"How strange," said a lady, "that a simple black veil, such as any woman might wear on her bonnet, should become such a terrible thing on Mr. Hooper's face!"

"Something must surely be amiss with Mr. Hooper's intellects," observed her husband, the physician of the village. "But the strangest part of the affair is the effect of this vagary, even on a sober-minded man like myself. The black veil, though it covers only our pastor's face, throws its influence over his whole person, and makes him ghostlike from head to foot. Do you not feel it so?"

"Truly do I," replied the lady; "and I would not be alone with him for the world. I wonder he is not afraid to be alone with himself!"

"Men sometimes are so," said her husband.

The afternoon service was attended with similar circumstances. At its conclusion, the bell tolled for the funeral of a young lady. The relatives and friends were assembled in the house, and the more distant acquaintances stood about the door, speaking of the good qualities of the deceased, when their talk was interrupted by the appearance of Mr. Hooper, still covered with his black veil. It was now an appropriate emblem. The clergyman stepped into the room where the corpse was laid, and bent over the coffin, to take a last farewell of his deceased parishioner. As he stooped, the veil hung straight down from his forehead, so that, if her eyelids had not been closed forever, the dead maiden might have seen his face. Could Mr. Hooper be fearful of her glance, that he so hastily caught back the black veil? A person who watched the interview between the dead and living, scrupled not to affirm, that, at the instant when the clergyman's features were disclosed, the corpse had slightly shuddered, rustling the shroud and muslin cap, though the countenance retained the composure of death. A superstitious old woman was the only witness of this prodigy. From the coffin Mr. Hooper passed into the chamber of the mourners, and thence to the head of the staircase, to make the funeral prayer. It was a tender and heart-dissolving prayer, full of sorrow, yet so imbued with celestial hopes, that the music of a heavenly harp, swept by the fingers of the dead, seemed faintly to be heard among the saddest accents of the minister. The people trembled, though they but darkly understood him when he prayed that they, and himself, and all of mortal race, might be ready, as he trusted this young maiden had been, for the dreadful hour that should snatch the veil from their faces. The bearers went heavily forth, and the mourners followed, saddening all the street, with the dead before them, and Mr. Hooper in his black veil behind.

"Why do you look back?" said one in the procession to his partner.

"I had a fancy," replied she, "that the minister and the maiden's spirit were walking hand in hand."

"And so had I, at the same moment," said the other.

That night, the handsomest couple in Milford village were to be joined in wedlock. Though reckoned a melancholy man, Mr. Hooper had a placid cheerfulness for such occasions, which often excited a sympathetic smile where livelier merriment would have been thrown away. There was no quality of his disposition which made him more beloved than this. The company at the wedding awaited his arrival with impatience, trusting that the strange awe, which had gathered over him throughout the day, would now be dispelled. But such was not the result. When Mr. Hooper came, the first thing that their eyes rested on was the same horrible black veil, which had added deeper gloom to the funeral, and could portend nothing but evil to the wedding. Such was its immediate effect on the guests that a cloud seemed to have rolled duskily from beneath the black crape, and dimmed the light of the candles. The bridal pair stood up before the minister. But the bride's cold fingers quivered in the tremulous hand of the bridegroom, and her deathlike paleness caused a whisper that the maiden who had been buried a few hours before was come from her grave to be married. If ever another wedding were so dismal, it was that famous one where they tolled the wedding knell. After performing the ceremony, Mr. Hooper raised a glass of wine to his lips, wishing happiness to the new-married couple in a strain of mild pleasantry that ought to have brightened the features of the guests, like a cheerful gleam from the hearth. At that instant, catching a glimpse of his figure in the looking-glass, the black veil involved his own spirit in the horror with which it overwhelmed all others. His frame shuddered, his lips grew white, he spilt the untasted wine upon the carpet, and rushed forth into the darkness. For the Earth, too, had on her Black Veil.

The next day, the whole village of Milford talked of little else than Parson Hooper's black veil. That, and the mystery concealed behind it, supplied a topic for discussion between acquaintances meeting in the street, and good women gossiping at their open windows. It was the first item of news that the tavern-keeper told to his guests. The children babbled of it on their way to school. One imitative little imp covered his face with an old black handkerchief, thereby so affrighting his playmates that the panic seized himself, and he well-nigh lost his wits by his own waggery.

It was remarkable that of all the busybodies and impertinent people in the parish, not one ventured to put the plain question to Hr. Hooper, wherefore he did this thing. Hitherto, whenever there appeared the slightest call for such interference, he had never lacked advisers, nor shown himself averse to be guided by their judgment. If he erred at all, it was by so painful a degree of self-distrust, that even the mildest censure would lead him to consider an indifferent action as a crime. Yet, though so well acquainted with this amiable weakness, no individual among his parishioners chose to make the black veil a subject of friendly remonstrance. There was a feeling of dread, neither plainly confessed nor carefully concealed, which caused each to shift the responsibility upon another, till at length it was found expedient to send a deputation of the church, in order to deal with Mr. Hooper about the mystery, before it should grow into a scandal. Never did an embassy so ill discharge its duties. The minister received them with friendly courtesy, but became silent, after they were seated, leaving to his visitors the whole burden of introducing their important business. The topic, it might be supposed, was obvious enough. There was the black veil swathed round Mr. Hooper's forehead, and concealing every feature above his placid mouth, on which, at times, they could perceive the glimmering of a melancholy smile. But that piece of crape, to their imagination, seemed to hang down before his heart, the symbol of a fearful secret between him and them. Were the veil but cast aside, they might speak freely of it, but not till then. Thus they sat a considerable time, speechless, confused, and shrinking uneasily from Mr. Hooper's eye, which they felt to be fixed upon them with an invisible glance. Finally, the deputies returned abashed to their constituents, pronouncing the matter too weighty to be handled, except by a council of the churches, if, indeed, it might not require a general synod.

But there was one person in the village unappalled by the awe with which the black veil had impressed all beside herself. When the deputies returned without an explanation, or even venturing to demand one, she, with the calm energy of her character, determined to chase away the strange cloud that appeared to be settling round Mr. Hooper, every moment more darkly than before. As his plighted wife, it should be her privilege to know what the black veil concealed. At the minister's first visit, therefore, she entered upon the subject with a direct simplicity, which made the task easier both for him and her. After he had seated himself, she fixed her eyes steadfastly upon the veil, but could discern nothing of the dreadful gloom that had so overawed the multitude: it was but a double fold of crape, hanging down from his forehead to his mouth, and slightly stirring with his breath.

"No," said she aloud, and smiling, "there is nothing terrible in this piece of crape, except that it hides a face which I am always glad to look upon. Come, good sir, let the sun shine from behind the cloud. First lay aside your black veil: then tell me why you put it on."

Mr. Hooper's smile glimmered faintly.

"There is an hour to come," said he, "when all of us shall cast aside our veils. Take it not amiss, beloved friend, if I wear this piece of crape till then."

"Your words are a mystery, too," returned the young lady. "Take away the veil from them, at least."

"Elizabeth, I will," said he, "so far as my vow may suffer me. Know, then, this veil is a type and a symbol, and I am bound to wear it ever, both in light and darkness, in solitude and before the gaze of multitudes, and as with strangers, so with my familiar friends. No mortal eye will see it withdrawn. This dismal shade must separate me from the world: even you, Elizabeth, can never come behind it!"

"What grievous affliction hath befallen you," she earnestly inquired, "that you should thus darken your eyes forever?"

"If it be a sign of mourning," replied Mr. Hooper, "I, perhaps, like most other mortals, have sorrows dark enough to be typified by a black veil."

"But what if the world will not believe that it is the type of an innocent sorrow?" urged Elizabeth. "Beloved and respected as you are, there may be whispers that you hide your face under the consciousness of secret sin. For the sake of your holy office, do away this scandal!"

The color rose into her cheeks as she intimated the nature of the rumors that were already abroad in the village. But Mr. Hooper's mildness did not forsake him. He even smiled again—that same sad smile, which always appeared like a faint glimmering of light, proceeding from the obscurity beneath the veil.

"If I hide my face for sorrow, there is cause enough," he merely replied; "and if I cover it for secret sin, what mortal might not do the same?"

And with this gentle, but unconquerable obstinacy did he resist all her entreaties. At length Elizabeth sat silent. For a few moments she appeared lost in thought, considering, probably, what new methods might be tried to withdraw her lover from so dark a fantasy, which, if it had no other meaning, was perhaps a symptom of mental disease. Though of a firmer character than his own, the tears rolled down her cheeks. But, in an instant, as it were, a new feeling took the place of sorrow: her eyes were fixed insensibly on the black veil, when, like a sudden twilight in the air, its terrors fell around her. She arose, and stood trembling before him.

"And do you feel it then, at last?" said he mournfully.

She made no reply, but covered her eyes with her hand, and turned to leave the room. He rushed forward and caught her arm.

"Have patience with me, Elizabeth!" cried he, passionately. "Do not desert me, though this veil must be between us here on earth. Be mine, and hereafter there shall be no veil over my face, no darkness between our souls! It is but a mortal veil—it is not for eternity! O! you know not how lonely I am, and how frightened, to be alone behind my black veil. Do not leave me in this miserable obscurity forever!"

"Lift the veil but once, and look me in the face," said she.

"Never! It cannot be!" replied Mr. Hooper.

"Then farewell!" said Elizabeth.

She withdrew her arm from his grasp, and slowly departed, pausing at the door, to give one long shuddering gaze, that seemed almost to penetrate the mystery of the black veil. But, even amid his grief, Mr. Hooper smiled to think that only a material emblem had separated him from happiness, though the horrors, which it shadowed forth, must be drawn darkly between the fondest of lovers.

From that time no attempts were made to remove Mr. Hooper's black veil, or, by a direct appeal, to discover the secret which it was supposed to hide. By persons who claimed a superiority to popular prejudice, it was reckoned merely an eccentric whim, such as often mingles with the sober actions of men otherwise rational, and tinges them all with its own semblance of insanity. But with the multitude, good Mr. Hooper was irreparably a bugbear. He could not walk the street with any peace of mind, so conscious was he that the gentle and timid would turn aside to avoid him, and that others would make it a point of hardihood to throw themselves in his way. The impertinence of the latter class compelled him to give up his customary walk at sunset to the burial ground; for when he leaned pensively over the gate, there would always be faces behind the gravestones, peeping at his black veil. A fable went the rounds that the stare of the dead people drove him thence. It grieved him, to the very depth of his kind heart, to observe how the children fled from his approach, breaking up their merriest sports, while his melancholy figure was yet afar off. Their instinctive dread caused him to feel more strongly than aught else, that a preternatural horror was interwoven with the threads of the black crape. In truth, his own antipathy to the veil was known to be so great, that he never willingly passed before a mirror, nor stooped to drink at a still fountain, lest, in its peaceful bosom, he should be affrighted by himself. This was what gave plausibility to the whispers, that Mr. Hooper's conscience tortured him for some great crime too horrible to be entirely concealed, or otherwise than so obscurely intimated. Thus, from beneath the black veil, there rolled a cloud into the sunshine, an ambiguity of sin or sorrow, which enveloped the poor minister, so that love or sympathy could never reach him. It was said that ghost and fiend consorted with him there. With self-shudderings and outward terrors, he walked continually in its shadow, groping darkly within his own soul, or gazing through a medium that saddened the whole world. Even the lawless wind, it was believed, respected his dreadful secret, and never blew aside the veil. But still good Mr. Hooper sadly smiled at the pale visages of the worldly throng as he passed by.

Among all its bad influences, the black veil had the one desirable effect, of making its wearer a very efficient clergyman. By the aid of his mysterious emblem—for there was no other apparent cause—he became a man of awful power over souls that were in agony for sin. His converts always regarded him with a dread peculiar to themselves, affirming, though but figuratively, that, before he brought them to celestial light, they had been with him behind the black veil. Its gloom, indeed, enabled him to sympathize with all dark affections. Dying sinners cried aloud for Mr. Hooper, and would not yield their breath till he appeared; though ever, as he stooped to whisper consolation, they shuddered at the veiled face so near their own. Such were the terrors of the black veil, even when Death had bared his visage! Strangers came long distances to attend service at his church, with the mere idle purpose of gazing at his figure, because it was forbidden them to behold his face. But many were

made to quake ere they departed! Once, during Governor Belcher's administration, Mr. Hooper was appointed to preach the election sermon. Covered
with his black veil, he stood before the chief magistrate, the council, and the
representatives, and wrought so deep an impression, that the legislative measures of that year were characterized by all the gloom and piety of our earliest
ancestral sway.

In this manner Mr. Hooper spent a long life, irreproachable in outward
act, yet shrouded in dismal suspicions; kind and loving, though unloved, and
dimly feared; a man apart from men, shunned in their health and joy, but
ever summoned to their aid in mortal anguish. As years wore on, shedding
their snows above his sable veil, he acquired a name throughout the New
England churches, and they called him Father Hooper. Nearly all his parishioners, who were of mature age when he was settled, had been borne away by
many a funeral: he had one congregation in the church, and a more crowded
one in the churchyard; and having wrought so late into the evening, and done
his work so well, it was now good Father Hooper's turn to rest.

Several persons were visible by the shaded candlelight, in the death chamber of the old clergyman. Natural connections he had none. But there was the
decorously grave, though unmoved physician, seeking only to mitigate the
last pangs of the patient whom he could not save. There were the deacons, and
other eminently pious members of his church. There, also, was the Reverend
Mr. Clark, of Westbury, a young and zealous divine, who had ridden in haste
to pray by the bedside of the expiring minister. There was the nurse, no hired
handmaiden of death, but one whose calm affection had endured thus long in
secrecy, in solitude, amid the chill of age, and would not perish, even at the
dying hour. Who, but Elizabeth! And there lay the hoary head of good Father
Hooper upon the death pillow, with the black veil still swathed about his
brow, and reaching down over his face, so that each more difficult gasp of his
faint breath caused it to stir. All through life that piece of crape had hung
between him and the world: it had separated him from cheerful brotherhood
and woman's love, and kept him in that saddest of all prisons, his own heart;
and still it lay upon his face, as if to deepen the gloom of his darksome chamber, and shade him from the sunshine of eternity.

For some time previous, his mind had been confused, wavering doubtfully
between the past and the present, and hovering forward, as it were, at intervals, into the indistinctness of the world to come. There had been feverish
turns, which tossed him from side to side, and wore away what little strength
he had. But in his most convulsive struggles, and in the wildest vagaries of
his intellect, when no other thought retained its sober influence, he still
showed an awful solicitude lest the black veil should slip aside. Even if his
bewildered soul could have forgotten, there was a faithful woman at his

pillow, who, with averted eyes, would have covered that aged face, which she had last beheld in the comeliness of manhood. At length the death-stricken old man lay quietly in the torpor of mental and bodily exhaustion, with an imperceptible pulse, and breath that grew fainter and fainter, except when a long, deep, and irregular inspiration seemed to prelude the flight of his spirit.

The minister of Westbury approached the bedside.

"Venerable Father Hooper," said he, "the moment of your release is at hand. Are you ready for the lifting of the veil that shuts in time from eternity?"

Father Hooper at first replied merely by a feeble motion of his head; then, apprehensive, perhaps, that his meaning might be doubtful, he exerted himself to speak.

"Yea," said he, in faint accents, "my soul hath a patient weariness until that veil be lifted."

"And is it fitting," resumed the Reverend Mr. Clark, "that a man so given to prayer, of such a blameless example, holy in deed and thought, so far as mortal judgment may pronounce; is it fitting that a father in the church should leave a shadow on his memory, that may seem to blacken a life so pure? I pray you, my venerable brother, let not this thing be! Suffer us to be gladdened by your triumphant aspect as you go to your reward. Before the veil of eternity be lifted, let me cast aside this black veil from your face!"

And thus speaking, the Reverend Mr. Clark bent forward to reveal the mystery of so many years. But, exerting a sudden energy, that made all the beholders stand aghast, Father Hooper snatched both his hands from beneath the bedclothes, and pressed them strongly on the black veil, resolute to struggle, if the minister of Westbury would contend with a dying man.

"Never!" cried the veiled clergyman. "On earth, never!"

"Dark old man!" exclaimed the affrighted minister, "with what horrible crime upon your soul are you now passing to the judgment?"

Father Hooper's breath heaved; it rattled in his throat; but, with a mighty effort, grasping forward with his hands, he caught hold of life, and held it back till he should speak. He even raised himself in bed; and there he sat, shivering with the arms of death around him, while the black veil hung down, awful, at that last moment, in the gathered terrors of a lifetime. And yet the faint, sad smile, so often there, now seemed to glimmer from its obscurity, and linger on Father Hooper's lips.

"Why do you tremble at me alone?" cried he, turning his veiled face round the circle of pale spectators. "Tremble also at each other! Have men avoided me, and women shown no pity, and children screamed and fled, only for my black veil? What, but the mystery which it obscurely typifies, has made this piece of crape so awful? When the friend shows his inmost heart to his friend; the lover to his best beloved; when man does not vainly shrink from the eye of his Creator, loathsomely treasuring up the secret of his sin; then deem me a monster, for the symbol beneath which I have lived, and die! I look around me, and, lo! on every visage a Black Veil!"

While his auditors shrank from one another, in mutual affright, Father Hooper fell back upon his pillow, a veiled corpse, with a faint smile lingering on the lips. Still veiled, they laid him in his coffin, and a veiled corpse they bore him to the grave. The grass of many years has sprung up and withered on that grave, the burial stone is moss-grown, and good Mr. Hooper's face is dust; but awful is still the thought that it mouldered beneath the Black Veil!

LEGENDS OF THE PROVINCE HOUSE

LADY ELEANORE'S MANTLE [3]

MINE excellent friend, the landlord of the Province House, was pleased, the other evening, to invite Mr. Tiffany and myself to an oyster supper. This slight mark of respect and gratitude, as he handsomely observed, was far less than the ingenious tale-teller, and I, the humble note-taker of his narratives, had fairly earned, by the public notice which our joint lucubrations had attracted to his establishment. Many a cigar had been smoked within his premises—many a glass of wine, or more potent *aqua vitæ,* had been quaffed —many a dinner had been eaten by curious strangers, who, save for the fortunate conjunction of Mr. Tiffany and me, would never have ventured through that darksome avenue which gives access to the historic precincts of the Province House. In short, if any credit be due to the courteous assurances of Mr. Thomas Waite, we had brought his forgotten mansion almost as effectually into public view as if we had thrown down the vulgar range of shoe shops and dry goods stores, which hides its aristocratic front from Washington Street. It may be unadvisable, however, to speak too loudly of the increased custom of the house, lest Mr. Waite should find it difficult to renew the lease on so favorable terms as heretofore.

Being thus welcomed as benefactors, neither Mr. Tiffany nor myself felt any scruple in doing full justice to the good things that were set before us. If the feast were less magnificent than those same panelled walls had witnessed in a by-gone century,—if mine host presided with somewhat less of state than might have befitted a successor of the royal Governors,—if the guests made a less imposing show than the bewigged and powdered and embroidered dignitaries, who erst banqueted at the gubernatorial table, and now sleep, within their armorial tombs on Copp's Hill, or round King's Chapel,—yet never, I may boldly say, did a more comfortable little party assemble in the Province House, from Queen Anne's days to the Revolution. The occasion was ren-

[3] First published in the *Democratic Review,* 1838, and included in *Twice-Told Tales,* second series (1842).

dered more interesting by the presence of a venerable personage, whose own actual reminiscences went back to the epoch of Gage and Howe, and even supplied him with a doubtful anecdote or two of Hutchinson. He was one of that small, and now all but extinguished, class, whose attachment to royalty, and to the colonial institutions and customs that were connected with it, had never yielded to the democratic heresies of after times. The young queen of Britain has not a more loyal subject in her realm—perhaps not one who would kneel before her throne with such reverential love—as this old grandsire, whose head has whitened beneath the mild sway of the Republic, which still, in his mellower moments, he terms a usurpation. Yet prejudices so obstinate have not made him an ungentle or impracticable companion. If the truth must be told, the life of the aged loyalist has been of such a scrambling and unsettled character,—he has had so little choice of friends and been so often destitute of any,—that I doubt whether he would refuse a cup of kindness with either Oliver Cromwell or John Hancock,—to say nothing of any democrat now upon the stage. In another paper of this series I may perhaps give the reader a closer glimpse of his portrait.

Our host, in due season, uncorked a bottle of Madeira, of such exquisite perfume and admirable flavor that he surely must have discovered it in an ancient bin, down deep beneath the deepest cellar, where some jolly old butler stored away the Governor's choicest wine, and forgot to reveal the secret on his death-bed. Peace to his red-nosed ghost, and a libation to his memory! This precious liquor was imbibed by Mr. Tiffany with peculiar zest; and after sipping the third glass, it was his pleasure to give us one of the oddest legends which he had yet raked from the storehouse where he keeps such matters. With some suitable adornments from my own fancy, it ran pretty much as follows.

Not long after Colonel Shute had assumed the government of Massachusetts Bay, now nearly a hundred and twenty years ago, a young lady of rank and fortune arrived from England, to claim his protection as her guardian. He was her distant relative, but the nearest who had survived the gradual extinction of her family; so that no more eligible shelter could be found for the rich and high-born Lady Eleanore Rochcliffe than within the Province House of a transatlantic colony. The consort of Governor Shute, morever, had been as a mother to her childhood, and was now anxious to receive her, in the hope that a beautiful young woman would be exposed to infinitely less peril from the primitive society of New England than amid the artifices and corruptions of a court. If either the Governor or his lady had especially consulted their own comfort, they would probably have sought to devolve the responsibility on other hands; since, with some noble and splendid traits of character, Lady Eleanore was remarkable for a harsh, unyielding pride, a haughty consciousness of her hereditary and personal advantages, which made her almost incapable of control. Judging from many traditionary anecdotes, this peculiar temper was hardly less than a monomania; or, if the acts which it inspired were those of a sane person, it seemed due from Providence that pride so sinful should be followed by as severe a retribution. That tinge of the marvellous, which is thrown over so many of these half-forgotten legends, has probably imparted an additional wildness to the strange story of Lady Eleanore Rochcliffe.

The ship in which she came passenger had arrived at Newport, whence Lady Eleanore was conveyed to Boston in the Governor's coach, attended by a small escort of gentlemen on horseback. The ponderous equipage, with its four black horses, attracted much notice as it rumbled through Cornhill, surrounded by the prancing steeds of half a dozen cavaliers, with swords dangling to their stirrups and pistols at their holsters. Through the large glass windows of the coach, as it rolled along, the people could discern the figure of Lady Eleanore, strangely combining an almost queenly stateliness with the grace and beauty of a maiden in her teens. A singular tale had gone abroad among the ladies of the province, that their fair rival was indebted for much of the irresistible charm of her appearance to a certain article of dress—an embroidered mantle—which had been wrought by the most skilful artist in London, and possessed even magical properties of adornment. On the present occasion, however, she owed nothing to the witchery of dress, being clad in a riding habit of velvet, which would have appeared stiff and ungraceful on any other form.

The coachman reined in his four black steeds, and the whole cavalcade came to a pause in front of the contorted iron balustrade that fenced the Province House from the public street. It was an awkward coincidence that the bell of the Old South was just then tolling for a funeral; so that, instead of a gladsome peal with which it was customary to announce the arrival of distinguished strangers, Lady Eleanore Rochcliffe was ushered by a doleful clang, as if calamity had come embodied in her beautiful person.

"A very great disrespect!" exclaimed Captain Langford, an English officer, who had recently brought dispatches to Governor Shute. "The funeral should have been deferred, lest Lady Eleanore's spirits be affected by such a dismal welcome."

"With your pardon, sir," replied Doctor Clarke, a physician, and a famous champion of the popular party, "whatever the heralds may pretend, a dead beggar must have precedence of a living queen. King Death confers high privileges."

These remarks were interchanged while the speakers waited a passage through the crowd, which had gathered on each side of the gateway, leaving an open avenue to the portal of the Province House. A black slave in livery now leaped from behind the coach, and threw open the door; while at the same moment Governor Shute descended the flight of steps from his mansion, to assist Lady Eleanore in alighting. But the Governor's stately approach was anticipated in a manner that excited general astonishment. A pale young man, with his black hair all in disorder, rushed from the throng, and prostrated himself beside the coach, thus offering his person as a footstool for Lady Eleanore Rochcliffe to tread upon. She held back an instant, yet with an expression as if doubting whether the young man were worthy to bear the weight of her footsteps, rather than dissatisfied to receive such awful reverence from a fellow-mortal.

"Up, sir," said the Governor, sternly, at the same time lifting his cane over the intruder. "What means the Bedlamite by this freak?"

"Nay," answered Lady Eleanore playfully, but with more scorn than pity in her tone, "your Excellency shall not strike him. When men seek only to be trampled upon, it were a pity to deny them a favor so easily granted—and so well deserved!"

Then, though as lightly as a sunbeam on a cloud, she placed her foot upon the cowering form, and extended her hand to meet that of the Governor. There was a brief interval, during which Lady Eleanore retained this attitude; and never, surely, was there an apter emblem of aristocracy and hereditary pride trampling on human sympathies and the kindred of nature, than these two figures presented at that moment. Yet the spectators were so smitten with her beauty, and so essential did pride seem to the existence of such a creature, that they gave a simultaneous acclamation of applause.

"Who is this insolent young fellow?" inquired Captain Langford, who still remained beside Doctor Clarke. "If he be in his senses, his impertinence demands the bastinado. If mad, Lady Eleanore should be secured from further inconvenience, by his confinement."

"His name is Jervase Helwyse," answered the Doctor; "a youth of no birth or fortune, or other advantages, save the mind and soul that nature gave him; and being secretary to our colonial agent in London, it was his misfortune to meet this Lady Eleanore Rochcliffe. He loved her—and her scorn has driven him mad."

"He was mad so to aspire," observed the English officer.

"It may be so," said Doctor Clarke, frowning as he spoke. "But I tell you, sir, I could well-nigh doubt the justice of the Heaven above us if no signal humiliation overtake this lady, who now treads so haughtily into yonder mansion. She seeks to place herself above the sympathies of our common nature, which envelops all human souls. See, if that nature do not assert its claim over her in some mode that shall bring her level with the lowest!"

"Never!" cried Captain Langford indignantly—"neither in life, nor when they lay her with her ancestors."

Not many days afterwards the Governor gave a ball in honor of Lady Eleanore Rochcliffe. The principal gentry of the colony received invitations, which were distributed to their residences, far and near, by messengers on horseback, bearing missives sealed with all the formality of official dispatches. In obedience to the summons, there was a general gathering of rank, wealth, and beauty; and the wide door of the Province House had seldom given admittance to more numerous and honorable guests than on the evening of Lady Eleanore's ball. Without much extravagance of eulogy, the spectacle might even be termed splendid; for, according to the fashion of the times, the ladies shone in rich silks and satins, outspread over wide-projecting hoops; and the gentlemen glittered in gold embroidery, laid unsparingly upon the purple, or scarlet, or sky-blue velvet, which was the material of their coats and waistcoats. The latter article of dress was of great importance, since it enveloped the wearer's body nearly to the knees, and was perhaps bedizened with the amount of his whole year's income, in golden flowers and foliage. The altered taste of the present day—a taste symbolic of a deep change in the whole system of society—would look upon almost any of those gorgeous figures as ridiculous; although that evening the guests sought their reflections in the pier-glasses, and rejoiced to catch their own glitter amid the glittering crowd. What a pity that one of the stately mirrors has not preserved a picture of the scene, which, by the very traits that were so transitory, might have taught us much that would be worth knowing and remembering!

Would, at least, that either painter or mirror could convey to us some faint idea of a garment, already noticed in this legend,—the Lady Eleanore's embroidered mantle,—which the gossips whispered was invested with magic properties, so as to lend a new and untried grace to her figure each time that she put it on! Idle fancy as it is, this mysterious mantle has thrown an awe around my image of her, partly from its fabled virtues, and partly because it was the handiwork of a dying woman, and, perchance, owed the fantastic grace of its conception to the delirium of approaching death.

After the ceremonial greetings had been paid, Lady Eleanore Rochcliffe stood apart from the mob of guests, insulating herself within a small and distinguished circle, to whom she accorded a more cordial favor than to the general throng. The waxen torches threw their radiance vividly over the scene, bringing out its brilliant points in strong relief; but she gazed carelessly, and with now and then an expression of weariness or scorn, tempered with such feminine grace that her auditors scarcely perceived the moral deformity of which it was the utterance. She beheld the spectacle not with vulgar ridicule, as disdaining to be pleased with the provincial mockery of a court festival, but with the deeper scorn of one whose spirit held itself too high to participate in the enjoyment of other human souls. Whether or no the recollections of those who saw her that evening were influenced by the strange events with which she was subsequently connected, so it was that her figure ever after recurred to them as marked by something wild and unnatural,—although, at the time, the general whisper was of her exceeding beauty, and of the indescribable charm which her mantle threw around her. Some close observers, indeed, detected a feverish flush and alternate paleness of countenance, with a corresponding flow and revulsion of spirits, and once or twice a painful and helpless betrayal of lassitude, as if she were on the point of sinking to the ground. Then, with a nervous shudder, she seemed to arouse her energies and threw some bright and playful yet half-wicked sarcasm into the conversation. There was so strange a characteristic in her manners and sentiments that it astonished every right-minded listener; till looking in her face, a lurking and incomprehensible glance and smile perplexed them with doubts both as to her seriousness and sanity. Gradually, Lady Eleanore Rochcliffe's circle grew smaller, till only four gentlemen remained in it. These were Captain Langford, the English officer before mentioned; a Virginian planter, who had come to Massachusetts on some political errand; a young Episcopal clergyman, the grandson of a British earl; and, lastly, the private secretary of Governor Shute, whose obsequiousness had won a sort of tolerance from Lady Eleanore.

At different periods of the evening the liveried servants of the Province House passed among the guests, bearing huge trays of refreshments and French and Spanish wines. Lady Eleanore Rochcliffe, who refused to wet her beautiful lips even with a bubble of Champagne, had sunk back into a large damask chair, apparently overwearied either with the excitement of the scene or its tedium, and while, for an instant, she was unconscious of voices, laughter and music, a young man stole forward, and knelt down at her feet. He bore a salver in his hand, on which was a chased silver goblet, filled to the brim with wine, which he offered as reverentially as to a crowned queen, or rather with the awful devotion of a priest doing sacrifice to his idol. Conscious that some one touched her robe, Lady Eleanore started, and unclosed her eyes upon the pale, wild features and dishevelled hair of Jervase Helwyse.

"Why do you haunt me thus?" said she, in a languid tone, but with a kindlier feeling than she ordinarily permitted herself to express. "They tell me that I have done you harm."

"Heaven knows if that be so," replied the young man solemnly. "But, Lady Eleanore, in requital of that harm, if such there be, and for your own earthly and heavenly welfare, I pray you to take one sip of this holy wine, and then to pass the goblet round among the guests. And this shall be a symbol that you have not sought to withdraw yourself from the chain of human sympathies—which whoso would shake off must keep company with fallen angels."

"Where has this mad fellow stolen that sacramental vessel?" exclaimed the Episcopal clergyman.

This question drew the notice of the guests to the silver cup, which was recognized as appertaining to the communion plate of the Old South Church; and, for aught that could be known, it was brimming over with the consecrated wine.

"Perhaps it is poisoned," half whispered the Governor's secretary.

"Pour it down the villain's throat!" cried the Virginian fiercely.

"Turn him out of the house!" cried Captain Langford, seizing Jervase Helwyse so roughly by the shoulder that the sacramental cup was overturned, and its contents sprinkled upon Lady Eleanore's mantle. "Whether knave, fool, or Bedlamite, it is intolerable that the fellow should go at large."

"Pray, gentleman, do my poor admirer no harm," said Lady Eleanore, with a faint and weary smile. "Take him out of my sight, if such be your pleasure; for I can find in my heart to do nothing but laugh at him; whereas, in all decency and conscience, it would become me to weep for the mischief I have wrought!"

But while the by-standers were attempting to lead away the unfortunate young man, he broke from them, and with a wild, impassioned earnestness, offered a new and equally strange petition to Lady Eleanore. It was no other than that she should throw off the mantle, which, while he pressed the silver cup of wine upon her, she had drawn more closely around her form, so as almost to shroud herself within it.

"Cast it from you!" exclaimed Jervase Helwyse, clasping his hands in an agony of entreaty. "It may not yet be too late! Give the accursed garment to the flames!"

But Lady Eleanore, with a laugh of scorn, drew the rich folds of the embroidered mantle over her head, in such a fashion as to give a completely new aspect to her beautiful face, which—half hidden, half revealed—seemed to belong to some being of mysterious character and purposes.

"Farewell, Jervase Helwyse!" said she. "Keep my image in your remembrance, as you behold it now."

"Alas, lady!" he replied, in a tone no longer wild, but sad as a funeral bell. "We must meet shortly, when your face may wear another aspect—and that shall be the image that must abide within me."

He made no more resistance to the violent efforts of the gentlemen and servants, who almost dragged him out of the apartment, and dismissed him roughly from the iron gate of the Province House. Captain Langford, who had been very active in this affair, was returning to the presence of Lady Eleanore Rochcliffe, when he encountered the physician, Doctor Clarke, with whom he had held some casual talk on the day of her arrival. The Doctor stood apart, separated from Lady Eleanore by the width of the room, but eying her with such keen sagacity that Captain Langford involuntarily gave him credit for the discovery of some deep secret.

"You appear to be smitten, after all, with the charms of this queenly maiden," said he, hoping thus to draw forth the physician's hidden knowledge.

"God forbid!" answered Doctor Clarke, with a grave smile; "and if you be wise you will put up the same prayer for yourself. Woe to those who shall be smitten by this beautiful Lady Eleanore! But yonder stands the Governor— and I have a word or two for his private ear. Good night!"

He accordingly advanced to Governor Shute, and addressed him in so low a tone that none of the by-standers could catch a word of what he said, although the sudden change of his Excellency's hitherto cheerful visage betokened that the communication could be of no agreeable import. A very few moments afterwards it was announced to the guests that an unforeseen circumstance rendered it necessary to put a premature close to the festival.

The ball at the Province House supplied a topic of conversation for the colonial metropolis for some days after its occurrence, and might still longer have been the general theme, only that a subject of all-engrossing interest thrust it, for a time, from the public recollection. This was the appearance of a dreadful epidemic, which, in that age and long before and afterwards, was wont to slay its hundreds and thousands on both sides of the Atlantic. On the occasion of which we speak, it was distinguished by a peculiar virulence, insomuch that it has left its traces—its pit-marks, to use an appropriate figure —on the history of the country, the affairs of which were thrown into confusion by its ravages. At first, unlike its ordinary course, the disease seemed to confine itself to the higher circles of society, selecting its victims from among the proud, the well-born, and the wealthy, entering unabashed into stately chambers, and lying down with the slumberers in silken beds. Some of the most distinguished guests of the Province House—even those whom the haughty Lady Eleanore Rochcliffe had deemed not unworthy of her favor— were stricken by this fatal scourge. It was noticed, with an ungenerous bitterness of feeling, that the four gentlemen—the Virginian, the British officer, the young clergyman, and the Governor's secretary—who had been her most devoted attendants on the evening of the ball, were the foremost on whom the plague stroke fell. But the disease, pursuing its onward progress, soon ceased to be exclusively a prerogative of aristocracy. Its red brand was no longer conferred like a noble's star, or an order of knighthood. It threaded its way through the narrow and crooked streets, and entered the low, mean, darksome dwellings, and laid its hand of death upon the artisans and laboring classes of the town. It compelled rich and poor to feel themselves brethren then; and stalking to and fro across the Three Hills, with a fierceness which made it almost a new pestilence, there was that mighty conquerer—that scourge and horror of our forefathers—the Small-Pox!

We cannot estimate the affright which this plague inspired of yore, by contemplating it as the fangless monster of the present day. We must remember, rather, with what awe we watched the gigantic footsteps of the Asiatic cholera, striding from shore to shore of the Atlantic, and marching like destiny upon cities far remote which flight had already half depopulated. There is no other fear so horrible and unhumanizing as that which makes man dread to breathe heaven's vital air lest it be poison, or to grasp the hand of a brother or friend lest the gripe of the pestilence should clutch him. Such was the dismay that now followed in the track of the disease, or ran before it throughout the town. Graves were hastily dug, and the pestilential relics as hastily covered, because the dead were enemies of the living, and strove to draw them headlong, as it were, into their own dismal pit. The public councils were suspended, as if mortal wisdom might relinquish its devices, now that an unearthly usurper had found his way into the ruler's mansion. Had an enemy's fleet been hovering on the coast, or his armies trampling on our soil, the people would probably have committed their defence to that same direful conqueror who had wrought their own calamity, and would permit no interference with his sway. This conqueror had a symbol of his triumphs. It was a blood-red flag, that fluttered in the tainted air, over the door of every dwelling into which the Small-Pox had entered.

Such a banner was long since waving over the portal of the Province House; for thence, as was proved by tracking its footsteps back, had all this dreadful mischief issued. It had been traced back to a lady's luxurious chamber—to the proudest of the proud—to her that was so delicate, and hardly owned herself of earthly mould—to the haughty one, who took her stand above human sympathies—to Lady Eleanore! There remained no room for doubt that the contagion had lurked in that gorgeous mantle, which threw so strange a grace around her at the festival. Its fantastic splendor had been conceived in the delirious brain of a woman on her death-bed, and was the last toil of her stiffening fingers, which had interwoven fate and misery with its golden threads. This dark tale, whispered at first, was now bruited far and wide. The people raved against the Lady Eleanore, and cried out that her pride and scorn had evoked a fiend, and that, between them both, this monstrous evil had been born. At times, their rage and despair took the semblance of grinning mirth; and whenever the red flag of the pestilence was hoisted over another and yet another door, they clapped their hands and shouted through the streets, in bitter mockery: "Behold a new triumph for the Lady Eleanore!"

One day, in the midst of these dismal times, a wild figure approached the portal of the Province House, and folding his arms, stood contemplating the scarlet banner which a passing breeze shook fitfully, as if to fling abroad the contagion that it typified. At length, climbing one of the pillars by means of the iron balustrade, he took down the flag and entered the mansion, waving it above his head. At the foot of the staircase he met the Governor, booted and spurred, with his cloak drawn around him, evidently on the point of setting forth upon a journey.

"Wretched lunatic, what do you seek here?" exclaimed Shute, extending his cane to guard himself from contact. "There is nothing here but Death. Back—or you will meet him!"

"Death will not touch me, the banner-bearer of the pestilence!" cried Jervase Helwyse, shaking the red flag aloft. "Death, and the Pestilence, who wears the aspect of the Lady Eleanore, will walk through the streets to-night, and I must march before them with his banner!"

"Why do I waste words on the fellow?" muttered the Governor, drawing his cloak across his mouth. "What matters his miserable life, when none of us are sure of twelve hours' breath? On, fool, to your own destruction!"

He made way for Jervase Helwyse, who immediately ascended the staircase, but, on the first landing-place was arrested by the firm grasp of a hand upon his shoulder. Looking fiercely up, with a madman's impulse to struggle with and rend asunder his opponent, he found himself powerless beneath a calm, stern eye, which possessed the mysterious property of quelling frenzy at its height. The person whom he had now encountered was the physician, Doctor Clarke, the duties of whose sad profession had led him to the Province House, where he was an infrequent guest in more prosperous times.

"Young man, what is your purpose?" demanded he.

"I seek the Lady Eleanore," answered Jervase Helwyse, submissively.

"All have fled from her," said the physician. "Why do you seek her now? I tell you, youth, her nurse fell death-stricken on the threshold of that fatal chamber. Know ye not, that never came such a curse to our shores as this lovely Lady Eleanore?—that her breath has filled the air with poison?—that she has shaken pestilence and death upon the land, from the folds of her accursed mantle?"

"Let me look upon her!" rejoined the mad youth, more wildly. "Let me behold her, in her awful beauty, clad in the regal garments of the pestilence! She and Death sit on a throne together. Let me kneel down before them!"

"Poor youth!" said Doctor Clarke; and, moved by a deep sense of human weakness, a smile of caustic humor curled his lip even then. "Wilt thou still worship the destroyer and surround her image with fantasies the more magnificent, the more evil she has wrought? Thus man doth ever to his tyrants. Approach, then! Madness, as I have noted, has that good efficacy, that it will guard you from contagion—and perchance its own cure may be found in yonder chamber."

Ascending another flight of stairs, he threw open a door and signed to Jervase Helwyse that he should enter. The poor lunatic, it seems probable, had cherished a delusion that his haughty mistress sat in state, unharmed herself by the pestilential influence, which, as by enchantment, she scattered round about her. He dreamed, no doubt, that her beauty was not dimmed, but brightened into superhuman splendor. With such anticipations, he stole reverentially to the door at which the physician stood, but paused upon the threshold, gazing fearfully into the gloom of the darkened chamber.

"Where is the Lady Eleanore?" whispered he.

"Call her," replied the physician.

"Lady Eleanore!—Princess!—Queen of Death!" cried Jervase Helwyse, advancing three steps into the chamber. "She is not here! There, on yonder table, I behold the sparkle of a diamond which once she wore upon her bosom. There"—and he shuddered—"there hangs her mantle, on which a dead woman embroidered a spell of dreadful potency. But where is the Lady Eleanore?"

Something stirred within the silken curtains of a canopied bed; and a low moan was uttered, which, listening intently, Jervase Helwyse began to distinguish as a woman's voice, complaining dolefully of thirst. He fancied, even, that he recognized its tones.

"My throat!—my throat is scorched," murmured the voice. "A drop of water!"

"What thing art thou?" said the brain-stricken youth, drawing near the bed and tearing asunder its curtains. "Whose voice hast thou stolen for thy murmurs and miserable petitions, as if Lady Eleanore could be conscious of mortal infirmity? Fie! Heap of diseased mortality, why lurkest thou in my lady's chamber?"

"O Jervase Helwyse," said the voice—and as it spoke the figure contorted itself, struggling to hide its blasted face—"look not now on the woman you once loved! The curse of Heaven hath stricken me, because I would not call man my brother, nor woman sister. I wrapped myself in PRIDE as in a MANTLE, and scorned the sympathies of nature; and therefore has nature made this wretched body the medium of a dreadful sympathy. You are avenged—they are all avenged—Nature is avenged—for I am Eleanore Rochcliffe!"

The malice of his mental disease, the bitterness lurking at the bottom of his heart, mad as he was, for a blighted and ruined life, and love that had been paid with cruel scorn, awoke within the breast of Jervase Helwyse. He shook his finger at the wretched girl, and the chamber echoed, the curtains of the bed were shaken, with his outburst of insane merriment.

"Another triumph for the Lady Eleanore!" he cried. "All have been her victims! Who so worthy to be the final victim as herself?"

Impelled by some new fantasy of his crazed intellect, he snatched the fatal mantle and rushed from the chamber and the house. That night a procession passed, by torchlight, through the streets, bearing in the midst the figure of a woman, enveloped with a richly embroidered mantle; while in advance stalked Jervase Helwyse, waving the red flag of the pestilence. Arriving opposite the Province House, the mob burned the effigy, and a strong wind came and swept away the ashes. It was said that, from that very hour, the pestilence abated, as if its sway had some mysterious connection, from the first plague stroke to the last, with Lady Eleanore's Mantle. A remarkable uncertainty broods over that unhappy lady's fate. There is a belief, however, that in a certain chamber of this mansion a female form may sometimes be duskily discerned, shrinking into the darkest corner and muffling her face within an embroidered mantle. Supposing the legend true, can this be other than the once proud Lady Eleanore?

Mine host and the old loyalist and I bestowed no little warmth of applause upon this narrative, in which we had all been deeply interested; for the reader can scarcely conceive how unspeakably the effect of such a tale is heightened when, as in the present case, we may repose perfect confidence in the veracity of him who tells it. For my own part, knowing how scrupulous is Mr. Tiffany to settle the foundation of his facts, I could not have believed him one whit the more faithfully had he professed himself an eye-witness of the doings and sufferings of poor Lady Eleanore. Some sceptics, it is true, might demand documentary evidence, or even require him to produce the embroidered mantle, forgetting that—Heaven be praised—it was consumed to ashes. But now the old loyalist, whose blood was warmed by the good cheer, began to talk, in his turn, about the traditions of the Province House, and hinted that he, if it were agreeable, might add a few reminiscences to our legendary stock. Mr. Tiffany, having no cause to dread a rival, immediately besought him to favor us with a specimen; my own entreaties, of course, were urged to the same effect; and our venerable guest, well pleased to find willing auditors, awaited only the return of Mr. Thomas Waite, who had been summoned forth to provide accommodations for several new arrivals. Perchance the public—but be this as its own caprice and ours shall settle the matter—may read the result in another Tale of the Province House.

THE AMBITIOUS GUEST [4]

ONE September night, a family had gathered round their hearth, and piled it high with the driftwood of mountain streams, the dry cones of the pine, and the splintered ruins of great trees that had come crashing down the precipice. Up the chimney roared the fire, and brightened the room with its broad blaze. The faces of the father and mother had a sober gladness; the children laughed; the eldest daughter was the image of Happiness at seventeen; and the aged grandmother, who sat knitting in the warmest place, was

[4] First published in the *New England Magazine*, 1835, and included in *Twice-Told Tales* (1842).

the image of Happiness grown old. They had found the "herb, heart's-ease," in the bleakest spot of all New England. This family were situated in the Notch of the White Hills, where the wind was sharp throughout the year, and pitilessly cold in the winter,—giving their cottage all its fresh inclemency before it descended on the valley of the Saco. They dwelt in a cold spot and a dangerous one; for a mountain towered above their heads, so steep, that the stones would often rumble down its sides and startle them at midnight.

The daughter had just uttered some simple jest that filled them all with mirth, when the wind came through the Notch and seemed to pause before their cottage,—rattling the door, with a sound of wailing and lamentation, before it passed into the valley. For a moment it saddened them, though there was nothing unusual in the tones. But the family were glad again when they perceived that the latch was lifted by some traveller, whose footsteps had been unheard amid the dreary blast which heralded his approach, and wailed as he was entering, and went moaning away from the door.

Though they dwelt in such a solitude, these people held daily converse with the world. The romantic pass of the Notch is a great artery, through which the life-blood of internal commerce is continually throbbing, between Maine on one side and the Green Mountains and the shores of the St. Lawrence on the other. The stage-coach always drew up before the door of the cottage. The wayfarer, with no companion but his staff, paused here to exchange a word, that the sense of loneliness might not utterly overcome him ere he could pass through the cleft of the mountain, or reach the first house in the valley. And here the teamster, on his way to Portland market, would put up for the night; and, if a bachelor, might sit an hour beyond the usual bed-time, and steal a kiss from the mountain maid, at parting. It was one of those primitive taverns where the traveller pays only for food and lodging, but meets with a homely kindness beyond all price. When the footsteps were heard, therefore, between the outer door and the inner one, the whole family rose up, grandmother, children, and all, as if about to welcome some one who belonged to them, and whose fate was linked with theirs.

The door was opened by a young man. His face at first wore the melancholy expression, almost despondency, of one who travels a wild and bleak road, at nightfall and alone, but soon brightened up when he saw the kindly warmth of his reception. He felt his heart spring forward to meet them all, from the old woman who wiped a chair with her apron, to the little child that held out its arms to him. One glance and smile placed the stranger on a footing of innocent familiarity with the eldest daughter.

"Ah, this fire is the right thing!" cried he; "especially when there is such a pleasant circle round it. I am quite benumbed; for the Notch is just like the pipe of a great pair of bellows; it has blown a terrible blast in my face all the way from Bartlett."

"Then you are going towards Vermont?" said the master of the house, as he helped to take a light knapsack off the young man's shoulders.

"Yes; to Burlington, and far enough beyond," replied he. "I meant to have been at Ethan Crawford's to-night; but a pedestrian lingers along such a road as this. It is no matter; for, when I saw this good fire, and all your cheerful faces, I felt as if you had kindled it on purpose for me, and were waiting my arrival. So I shall sit down among you, and make myself at home."

The frank-hearted stranger had just drawn his chair to the fire when something like a heavy footstep was heard without, rushing down the steep side of the mountain, as with long and rapid strides, and taking such a leap in passing the cottage as to strike the opposite precipice. The family held their breath, because they knew the sound, and their guest held his by instinct.

"The old mountain has thrown a stone at us, for fear we should forget him," said the landlord, recovering himself. "He sometimes nods his head, and threatens to come down; but we are old neighbors, and agree together pretty well, upon the whole. Besides we have a sure place of refuge hard by if he should be coming in good earnest."

Let us now suppose the stranger to have finished his supper of bear's meat; and, by his natural felicity of manner, to have placed himself on a footing of kindness with the whole family, so that they talked as freely together as if he belonged to their mountain brood. He was of a proud, yet gentle spirit,—haughty and reserved among the rich and great; but ever ready to stoop his head to the lowly cottage door, and be like a brother or a son at the poor man's fireside. In the household of the Notch he found warmth and simplicity of feeling, the pervading intelligence of New England, and a poetry of native growth, which they had gathered when they little thought of it from the mountain peaks and chasms, and at the very threshold of their romantic and dangerous abode. He had travelled far and alone; his whole life, indeed, had been a solitary path; for, with the lofty caution of his nature, he had kept himself apart from those who might otherwise have been his companions. The family, too, though so kind and hospitable, had that consciousness of unity among themselves, and separation from the world at large, which, in every domestic circle, should still keep a holy place where no stranger may intrude. But this evening a prophetic sympathy impelled the refined and educated youth to pour out his heart before the simple mountaineers, and constrained them to answer him with the same free confidence. And thus it should have been. Is not the kindred of a common fate a closer tie than that of birth?

The secret of the young man's character was a high and abstracted ambition. He could have borne to live an undistinguished life, but not to be forgotten in the grave. Yearning desire had been transformed to hope; and hope long cherished, had become like certainty, that, obscurely as he journeyed now, a glory was to beam on all his pathway,—though not, perhaps, while he was treading it. But when posterity should gaze back into the gloom of what was now the present, they would trace the brightness of his footsteps, brightening as meaner glories faded, and confess that a gifted one had passed from his cradle to his tomb with none to recognize him.

"As yet," cried the stranger—his cheek glowing and his eye flashing with enthusiasm—"as yet, I have done nothing. Were I to vanish from the earth to-morrow, none would know so much of me as you; that a nameless youth came up, at nightfall from the valley of the Saco, and opened his heart to you in the evening, and passed through the Notch by sunrise, and was seen no more. Not a soul would ask, 'Who was he? Whither did the wanderer go?' But I cannot die till I have achieved my destiny. Then, let Death come! I shall have built my monument!"

There was a continual flow of natural emotion, gushing forth amid abstracted reverie, which enabled the family to understand this young man's sentiments, though so foreign from their own. With quick sensibility of the ludicrous, he blushed at the ardor into which he had been betrayed.

"You laugh at me," said he, taking the eldest daughter's hand, and laughing himself. "You think my ambition as nonsensical as if I were to freeze myself to death on the top of Mount Washington, only that people might spy at me from the country round about. And truly, that would be a noble pedestal for a man's statue!"

"It is better to sit here by this fire," answered the girl, blushing, "and be comfortable and contented, though nobody thinks about us."

"I suppose," said her father, after a fit of musing, "there is something natural in what the young man says; and if my mind had been turned that way, I might have felt just the same. It is strange, wife, how his talk has set my head running on things that are pretty certain never to come to pass."

"Perhaps they may," observed the wife. "Is the man thinking what he will do when he is a widower?"

"No, no!" cried he, repelling the idea with reproachful kindness. "When I think of your death, Esther, I think of mine, too. But I was wishing we had a good farm in Bartlett, or Bethlehem, or Littleton, or some other township round the White Mountains; but not where they could tumble on our heads. I should want to stand well with my neighbors and be called Squire, and sent to General Court for a term or two; for a plain, honest man may do as much good there as a lawyer. And when I should be grown quite an old man, and you an old woman, so as not to be long apart, I might die happy enough in my bed, and leave you all crying around me. A slate gravestone would suit me as well as a marble one,—with just my name and age, and a verse of a hymn, and something to let people know that I lived an honest man and died a Christian."

"There now!" exclaimed the stranger; "it is our nature to desire a monument, be it slate or marble, or a pillar of granite, or a glorious memory in the universal heart of man."

"We're in a strange way, to-night," said the wife, with tears in her eyes. "They say it's a sign of something, when folks' minds go a wandering so. Hark to the children!"

They listened accordingly. The younger children had been put to bed in another room, but with an open door between, so that they could be heard talking busily among themselves. One and all seemed to have caught the infection from the fireside circle, and were outvying each other in wild wishes, and childish projects of what they would do when they came to be men and women. At length a little boy, instead of addressing his brothers and sisters, called out to his mother.

"I'll tell you what I wish, mother," cried he. "I want you and father and grandma'm, and all of us, and the stranger too, to start right away, and go and take a drink out of the basin of the Flume!"

Nobody could help laughing at the child's notion of leaving a warm bed, and dragging them from a cheerful fire, to visit the basin of the Flume,—a brook which tumbles over the precipice, deep within the Notch. The boy had hardly spoken when a wagon rattled along the road, and stopped a moment before the door. It appeared to contain two or three men, who were cheering their hearts with the rough chorus of a song, which resounded, in broken notes, between the cliffs, while the singers hesitated whether to continue their journey or put up here for the night.

"Father," said the girl, "they are calling you by name."

But the good man doubted whether they had really called him, and was unwilling to show himself too solicitous of gain by inviting people to patronize his house. He therefore did not hurry to the door; and the lash being soon applied, the travellers plunged into the Notch, still singing and laughing, though their music and mirth came back drearily from the heart of the mountain.

"There, mother!" cried the boy, again. "They'd have given us a ride to the Flume."

Again they laughed at the child's pertinacious fancy for a night ramble. But it happened that a light cloud passed over the daughter's spirit; she looked gravely into the fire, and drew a breath that was almost a sigh. It forced its way, in spite of a little struggle to repress it. Then starting and blushing, she looked quickly round the circle, as if they had caught a glimpse into her bosom. The stranger asked what she had been thinking of.

"Nothing," answered she, with a downcast smile. "Only I felt lonesome just then."

"Oh, I have always had a gift of feeling what is in other people's hearts," said he, half seriously. "Shall I tell the secrets of yours? For I know what to think when a young girl shivers by a warm hearth, and complains of lonesomeness at her mother's side. Shall I put these feelings into words?"

"They would not be a girl's feelings any longer if they could be put into words," replied the mountain nymph, laughing, but avoiding his eye.

All this was said apart. Perhaps a germ of love was springing in their hearts, so pure that it might blossom in Paradise, since it could not be matured on earth; for women worship such gentle dignity as his; and the proud, contemplative, yet kindly soul is oftenest captivated by simplicity like hers. But while they spoke softly, and he was watching the happy sadness, the lightsome shadows, the shy yearnings of a maiden's nature, the wind through the Notch took a deeper and drearier sound. It seemed, as the fanciful stranger said, like the choral strain of the spirits of the blast, who in old Indian times had their dwelling among these mountains, and made their heights and recesses a sacred region. There was a wail along the road, as if a funeral were passing. To chase away the gloom, the family threw pine branches on their fire, till the dry leaves crackled and the flame arose, discovering once again a scene of peace and humble happiness. The light hovered about them fondly, and caressed them all. There were the little faces of the children, peeping from their bed apart, and here the father's frame of strength, the mother's subdued and careful mien, the high-browed youth, the budding girl, and the good old grandam, still knitting in the warmest place. The aged woman looked up from her task, and, with fingers ever busy, was the next to speak.

"Old folks have their notions," said she, "as well as young ones. You've been wishing and planning; and letting your heads run on one thing and another, till you've set my mind a wandering too. Now what should an old woman wish for, when she can go but a step or two before she comes to her grave? Children, it will haunt me night and day till I tell you."

"What is it, mother?" cried the husband and wife at once.

Then the old woman, with an air of mystery which drew the circle closer round the fire, informed them that she had provided her grave-clothes some years before,—a nice linen shroud, a cap with a muslin ruff, and everything of a finer sort than she had worn since her wedding-day. But this evening an old superstition had strangely recurred to her. It used to be said, in her younger days, that if anything were amiss with a corpse, if only the ruff were not smooth, or the cap did not set right, the corpse in the coffin and beneath the clods would strive to put up its cold hands and arrange it. The bare thought made her nervous.

"Don't talk so, grandmother!" said the girl, shuddering.

"Now," continued the old woman, with singular earnestness, yet smiling strangely at her own folly, "I want one of you, my children,—when your mother is dressed and in the coffin,—I want one of you to hold a looking-glass over my face. Who knows but I may take a glimpse at myself, and see whether all's right?"

"Old and young, we dream of graves and monuments," murmured the stranger youth. "I wonder how mariners feel when the ship is sinking, and they, unknown and undistinguished, are to be buried together in the ocean,—that wide and nameless sepulchre?"

For a moment, the old woman's ghastly conception so engrossed the minds of her hearers that a sound abroad in the night, rising like the roar of a blast, had grown broad, deep, and terrible, before the fated group were conscious of it. The house and all within it trembled; the foundations of the earth seemed to be shaken, as if this awful sound were the peal of the last trump. Young and old exchanged one wild glance, and remained an instant, pale, affrighted, without utterance, or power to move. Then the same shriek burst simultaneously from all their lips.

"The Slide! The Slide!"

The simplest words must intimate, but not portray, the unutterable horror of the catastrophe. The victims rushed from their cottage, and sought refuge in what they deemed a safer spot,—where, in contemplation of such an emergency, a sort of barrier had been reared. Alas! they had quitted their security, and fled right into the pathway of destruction. Down came the whole side of the mountain, in a cataract of ruin. Just before it reached the house, the stream broke into two branches,—shivered not a window there, but over-whelmed the whole vicinity, blocked up the road, and annihilated everything in its dreadful course. Long ere the thunder of the great Slide had ceased to roar among the mountains, the mortal agony had been endured, and the victims were at peace. Their bodies were never found.

The next morning, the light smoke was seen stealing from the cottage chimney up the mountain-side. Within, the fire was yet smouldering on the hearth, and the chairs in a circle round it, as if the inhabitants had but gone forth to view the devastation of the Slide, and would shortly return, to thank Heaven for their miraculous escape. All had left separate tokens, by which those who had known the family were made to shed a tear for each. Who has not heard their name? The story has been told far and wide, and will forever be a legend of these mountains. Poets have sung their fate.

There were circumstances which led some to suppose that a stranger had been received into the cottage on this awful night, and had shared the catastrophe of all its inmates. Others denied that there were sufficient grounds for such a conjecture. Woe for the high-souled youth, with his dream of Earthly Immortality! His name and person utterly unknown; his history, his way of life, his plans, a mystery never to be solved; his death and his existence equally a doubt! Whose was the agony of that death moment?

A RILL FROM THE TOWN PUMP [5]

(SCENE—*the corner of two principal streets.*[6] *The* TOWN PUMP *talking through its nose.*)

NOON, by the North clock! Noon, by the east! High noon, too, by these hot sunbeams which fall, scarcely aslope, upon my head, and almost make the water bubble and smoke in the trough under my nose. Truly, we public characters have a tough time of it! And, among all the town officers, chosen at March meeting, where is he that sustains, for a single year, the burden of such manifold duties as are imposed, in perpetuity, upon the Town Pump? The title of "town treasurer" is rightfully mine, as guardian of the best treasure that the town has. The overseers of the poor ought to make me their chairman, since I provide bountifully for the pauper, without expense to him that pays taxes. I am at the head of the fire department, and one of the physicians to the board of health. As a keeper of the peace, all water drinkers will confess me equal to the constable. I perform some of the duties of the town clerk, by promulgating public notices, when they are posted on my front. To speak within bounds, I am the chief person of the municipality, and exhibit, moreover, an admirable pattern to my brother officers, by the cool, steady, upright, downright, and impartial discharge of my business, and the constancy with which I stand to my post. Summer or winter, nobody seeks me in vain; for, all day long, I am seen at the busiest corner, just above the market, stretching out my arms to rich and poor alike; and at night, I hold a lantern over my head, both to show where I am, and keep people out of the gutters.

At this sultry noontide, I am cupbearer to the parched populace, for whose benefit an iron goblet is chained to my waist. Like a dram seller on the mall, at muster day, I cry aloud to all and sundry, in my plainest accents, and at the very tiptop of my voice: Here it is, gentlemen! Here is the good liquor! Walk up, walk up, gentlemen, walk up, walk up! Here is the superior stuff! Here is the unadulterated ale of father Adam—better than Cognac, Hollands, Jamaica, strong beer, or wine of any price; here it is, by the hogshead or the single glass, and not a cent to pay! Walk up, gentlemen, walk up, and help yourselves!

It were a pity if all this outcry should draw no customers. Here they come. A hot day, gentlemen! Quaff, and away again, so as to keep yourselves in a

---

[5] First published in the *New England Magazine*, 1835, and included in *Twice-Told Tales* (1837).

[6] Essex and Washington Streets, Salem.—*Author's note.*

nice cool sweat. You, my friend, will need another cupful, to wash the dust out of your throat, if it be as thick there as it is on your cowhide shoes. I see that you have trudged half a score of miles to-day; and, like a wise man, have passed by the taverns, and stopped at the running brooks and well curbs. Otherwise, betwixt heat without and fire within, you would have been burned to a cinder, or melted down to nothing at all, in the fashion of a jelly-fish. Drink, and make room for that other fellow, who seeks my aid to quench the fiery fever of last night's potations, which he drained from no cup of mine. Welcome, most rubicund sir! You and I have been great strangers, hitherto; nor, to confess the truth, will my nose be anxious for a closer intimacy, till the fumes of your breath be a little less potent. Mercy on you, man! the water absolutely hisses down your red-hot gullet, and is converted quite to steam in the miniature tophet which you mistake for a stomach. Fill again, and tell me, on the word of an honest toper, did you ever, in cellar, tavern, or any kind of a dram shop, spend the price of your children's food for a swig half so delicious? Now, for the first time these ten years, you know the flavor of cold water. Good-by; and, whenever you are thirsty, remember that I keep a constant supply at the old stand. Who next? O, my little friend, you are let loose from school, and come hither to scrub your blooming face, and drown the memory of certain taps of the ferule, and other school-boy troubles, in a draught from the Town Pump. Take it, pure as the current of your young life. Take it, and may your heart and tongue never be scorched with a fiercer thirst than now! There, my dear child, put down the cup, and yield your place to this elderly gentleman, who treads so tenderly over the paving-stones, that I suspect he is afraid of breaking them. What! he limps by, without so much as thanking me, as if my hospitable offers were meant only for people who have no wine cellars. Well, well, sir—no harm done, I hope! Go draw the cork, tip the decanter; but, when your great toe shall set you a-roaring, it will be no affair of mine. If gentlemen love the pleasant titillation of the gout, it is all one to the Town Pump. This thirsty dog, with his red tongue lolling out, does not scorn my hospitality, but stands on his hind legs, and laps eagerly out of the trough. See how lightly he capers away again! Jowler, did your worship ever have the gout?

Are you all satisfied? Then wipe your mouths, my good friends; and, while my spout has a moment's leisure, I will delight the town with a few historical reminiscences. In far antiquity, beneath a darksome shadow of venerable boughs, a spring bubbled out of the leaf-strewn earth, in the very spot where you now behold me, on the sunny pavement. The water was as bright and clear, and deemed as precious, as liquid diamonds. The Indian sagamores drank of it from time immemorial, till the fatal deluge of the fire water burst upon the red men, and swept their whole race away from the cold fountains. Endicott and his followers came next, and often knelt down to drink, dipping their long beards in the spring. The richest goblet, then, was of birch bark. Governor Winthrop, after a journey afoot from Boston, drank here, out of the hollow of his hand. The elder Higginson here wet his palm, and laid it on the brow of the first town-born child. For many years it was the watering-place, and, as it were, the washbowl of the vicinity—whither all decent folks resorted, to purify their visages and gaze at them afterwards —at least the pretty maidens did—in the mirror which it made. On Sabbath days, whenever a babe was to be baptized, the sexton filled his basin here, and placed it on the communion table of the humble meeting-house, which partly covered the site of yonder stately brick one. Thus, one generation after another was consecrated to Heaven by its waters, and cast their waxing and waning shadows into its glassy bosom, and vanished from the earth, as if mortal life were but a flitting image in a fountain. Finally, the fountain vanished also. Cellars were dug on all sides, and cartloads of gravel flung upon its source, whence oozed a turbid stream, forming a mud puddle, at the corner of two streets. In the hot months, when its refreshment was most needed, the dust flew in clouds over the forgotten birthplace of the waters, now their grave. But, in the course of time, a Town Pump was sunk into the source of the ancient spring; and when the first decayed, another took its place—and then another, and still another—till here stand I, gentlemen and ladies, to serve you with my iron goblet. Drink, and be refreshed! The water is as pure and cold as that which slaked the thirst of the red sagamore beneath the aged boughs, though now the gem of the wilderness is treasured under these hot stones, where no shadow falls but from the brick buildings. And be it the moral of my story, that, as this wasted and long-lost fountain is now known and prized again, so shall the virtues of cold water, too little valued since your fathers' days, be recognized by all.

Your pardon, good people! I must interrupt my stream of eloquence, and spout forth a stream of water, to replenish the trough for this teamster and his two yoke of oxen, who have come from Topsfield, or somewhere along that way. No part of my business is pleasanter than the watering of cattle. Look! how rapidly they lower the watermark on the sides of the trough, till their capacious stomachs are moistened with a gallon or two apiece, and they can afford time to breathe it in, with sighs of calm enjoyment. Now they roll their quiet eyes around the brim of their monstrous drinking vessel. An ox is your true toper.

But I perceive, my dear auditors, that you are impatient for the remainder of my discourse. Impute it, I beseech you, to no defect of modesty, if I insist a little longer on so fruitful a topic as my own multifarious merits. It is altogether for your good. The better you think of me, the better men and women will you find yourselves. I shall say nothing of my all-important aid on washing days; though, on that account alone, I might call myself the household god of a hundred families. Far be it from me also to hint, my respectable friends, at the show of dirty faces which you would present, without my pains to keep you clean. Nor will I remind you how often, when the midnight bells make you tremble for your combustible town, you have fled to the Town Pump, and found me always at my post, firm amid the confusion, and ready to drain my vital current in your behalf. Neither is it worth while to lay much stress on my claims to a medical diploma, as the physician whose simple rule of practice is preferable to all the nauseous lore which has found men sick or left them so, since the days of Hippocrates. Let us take a broader view of my beneficial influence on mankind.

No; these are trifles compared with the merits which wise men concede to me—if not in my single self, yet as the representative of a class—of being the grand reformer of the age. From my spout, and such spouts as mine, must flow the stream that shall cleanse our earth of the vast portion of its crime and anguish, which has gushed from the fiery fountains of the still. In this mighty enterprise, the cow shall be my great confederate. Milk and water! The TOWN PUMP and the Cow! Such is the glorious copartnership that shall tear down the distilleries and brewhouses, uproot the vineyards, shatter the cider presses, ruin the tea and coffee trade, and, finally, monopolize the whole business of quenching thirst. Blessed consummation! Then, Poverty shall pass away from the land, finding no hovel so wretched where her squalid form may shelter itself. Then Disease, for lack of other victims, shall gnaw its own heart, and die. Then Sin, if she do not die, shall lose half her strength. Until now, the frenzy of hereditary fever has raged in the human blood, transmitted from sire to son, and rekindled, in every generation, by fresh draughts of liquid flame. When that inward fire shall be extinguished, the heat of passion cannot but grow cool, and war—the drunkenness of nations—perhaps will cease. At least, there will be no war of households. The husband and wife, drinking deep of peaceful joy,—a calm bliss of temperate affections,—shall pass hand in hand through life, and lie down, not reluctantly, at its protracted close. To them, the past will be no turmoil of mad dreams, nor the future an eternity of such moments as follow the delirium of the drunkard. Their dead faces shall express what their spirits were, and are to be, by a lingering smile of memory and hope.

Ahem! Dry work, this speechifying; especially to an unpractised orator. I never conceived, till now, what toil the temperance lecturers undergo for my sake. Hereafter, they shall have the business to themselves. Do, some kind Christian, pump a stroke or two, just to wet my whistle. Thank you, sir! My dear hearers, when the world shall have been regenerated by my instrumentality, you will collect your useless vats and liquor casks into one great pile, and make a bonfire in honor of the Town Pump. And, when I shall have decayed, like my predecessors, then, if you revere my memory, let a marble fountain, richly sculptured, take my place upon this spot. Such monuments should be erected everywhere, and inscribed with the names of the distinguished champions of my cause. Now listen, for something very important is to come next.

There are two or three honest friends of mine—and true friends, I know, they are—who nevertheless, by their fiery pugnacity in my behalf, do put me in fearful hazard of a broken nose or even a total overthrow upon the pavement, and the loss of the treasure which I guard. I pray you, gentlemen, let this fault be amended. Is it decent, think you, to get tipsy with zeal for temperance, and take up the honorable cause of the Town Pump in the style of a toper fighting for his brandy bottle? Or, can the excellent qualities of cold water be not otherwise exemplified than by plunging, slapdash, into hot water, and wofully scalding yourselves and other people? Trust me, they may. In the moral warfare which you are to wage—and, indeed, in the whole conduct of your lives—you cannot choose a better example than myself, who have never permitted the dust and sultry atmosphere, the turbulence and manifold disquietudes of the world around me, to reach that deep, calm well of purity, which may be called my soul. And whenever I pour out that soul, it is to cool earth's fever or cleanse its stains.

One o'clock! Nay, then, if the dinner bell begins to speak, I may as well hold my peace. Here comes a pretty young girl of my acquaintance, with a large stone pitcher for me to fill. May she draw a husband, while drawing her water, as Rachel did of old. Hold out your vessel, my dear! There it is, full to the brim; so now run home, peeping at your sweet image in the pitcher as you go; and forget not, in a glass of my own liquor, to drink—"SUCCESS TO THE TOWN PUMP!"

THE BIRTHMARK [7]

IN the latter part of the last century there lived a man of science, an eminent proficient in every branch of natural philosophy, who not long before our story opens had made experience of a spiritual affinity more attractive than any chemical one. He had left his laboratory to the care of an assistant, cleared his fine countenance from the furnace smoke, washed the stain of acids from his fingers, and persuaded a beautiful woman to become his wife. In those days when the comparatively recent discovery of electricity and other kindred mysteries of Nature seemed to open paths into the region of miracle, it was not unusual for the love of science to rival the love of woman in its depth and absorbing energy. The higher intellect, the imagination, the spirit, and even the heart might all find their congenial aliment in pursuits which,

[7] First published in the *Pioneer*, 1843, and included in *Mosses from an Old Manse* (1846).

as some of their ardent votaries believed, would ascend from one step of powerful intelligence to another, until the philosopher should lay his hand on the
secret of creative force and perhaps make new worlds for himself. We know
not whether Aylmer possessed this degree of faith in man's ultimate control
over Nature. He had devoted himself, however, too unreservedly to scientific
studies ever to be weaned from them by any second passion. His love for his
young wife might prove the stronger of the two; but it could only be by inter-
twining itself with his love of science, and uniting the strength of the latter
to his own.

Such a union accordingly took place, and was attended with truly remarkable consequences and a deeply impressive moral. One day, very soon after
their marriage, Aylmer sat gazing at his wife with a trouble in his countenance that grew stronger until he spoke.

"Georgiana," said he, "has it never occurred to you that the mark upon your
cheek might be removed?"

"No, indeed," said she, smiling; but perceiving the seriousness of his manner, she blushed deeply. "To tell you the truth it has been so often called a
charm that I was simple enough to imagine it might be so."

"Ah, upon another face perhaps it might," replied her husband; "but never
on yours. No, dearest Georgiana, you came so nearly perfect from the hand
of Nature that this slightest possible defect, which we hesitate whether to
term a defect or a beauty, shocks me, as being the visible mark of earthly
imperfection."

"Shocks you, my husband!" cried Georgiana, deeply hurt; at first reddening with momentary anger, but then bursting into tears. "Then why did you
take me from my mother's side? You cannot love what shocks you!"

To explain this conversation, it must be mentioned that in the centre of
Georgiana's left cheek there was a singular mark, deeply interwoven, as it
were, with the texture and substance of her face. In the usual state of her
complexion—a healthy though delicate bloom—the mark wore a tint of
deeper crimson, which imperfectly defined its shape amid the surrounding
rosiness. When she blushed it gradually became more indistinct, and finally
vanished amid the triumphant rush of blood that bathed the whole cheek
with its brilliant glow. But if any shifting motion caused her to turn pale
there was the mark again, a crimson stain upon the snow, in what Aylmer
sometimes deemed an almost fearful distinctness. Its shape bore not a little
similarity to the human hand, though of the smallest pygmy size. Georgiana's lovers were wont to say that some fairy at her birth hour had laid her
tiny hand upon the infant's cheek, and left this impress there in token of the
magic endowments that were to give her such sway over all hearts. Many a
desperate swain would have risked life for the privilege of pressing his lips
to the mysterious hand. It must not be concealed, however, that the impres-

sion wrought by this fairy sign manual varied exceedingly, according to the difference of temperament in the beholders. Some fastidious persons—but they were exclusively of her own sex—affirmed that the bloody hand, as they chose to call it, quite destroyed the effect of Georgiana's beauty, and rendered her countenance even hideous. But it would be as reasonable to say that one of those small blue stains which sometimes occur in the purest statuary marble would convert the Eve of Powers to a monster. Masculine observers, if the birthmark did not heighten their admiration, contented themselves with wishing it away, that the world might possess one living specimen of ideal loveliness without the semblance of a flaw. After his marriage,—for he thought little or nothing of the matter before,—Aylmer discovered that this was the case with himself.

Had she been less beautiful,—if Envy's self could have found aught else to sneer at,—he might have felt his affection heightened by the prettiness of this mimic hand, now vaguely portrayed, now lost, now stealing forth again and glimmering to and fro with every pulse of emotion that throbbed within her heart; but seeing her otherwise so perfect, he found this one defect grow more and more intolerable with every moment of their united lives. It was the fatal flaw of humanity which Nature, in one shape or another, stamps ineffaceably on all her productions, either to imply that they are temporary and finite, or that their perfection must be wrought by toil and pain. The crimson hand expressed the ineludible gripe in which mortality clutches the highest and purest of earthly mould, degrading them into kindred with the lowest, and even with the very brutes, like whom their visible frames return to dust. In this manner, selecting it as the symbol of his wife's liability to sin, sorrow, decay, and death, Aylmer's sombre imagination was not long in rendering the birthmark a frightful object, causing him more trouble and horror than ever Georgiana's beauty, whether of soul or sense, had given him delight.

At all the seasons which should have been their happiest, he invariably and without intending it, nay, in spite of a purpose to the contrary, reverted to this one disastrous topic. Trifling as it at first appeared, it so connected itself with innumerable trains of thought and modes of feeling that it became the central point of all. With the morning twilight Aylmer opened his eyes upon his wife's face and recognized the symbol of imperfection; and when they sat together at the evening hearth his eyes wandered stealthily to her cheek, and beheld, flickering with the blaze of the wood fire, the spectral hand that wrote mortality where he would fain have worshipped. Georgiana soon learned to shudder at his gaze. It needed but a glance with the peculiar expression that his face often wore to change the roses of her cheek into a death-like paleness, amid which the crimson hand was brought strongly out, like a bas-relief of ruby on the whitest marble.

Late one night when the lights were growing dim, so as hardly to betray the stain on the poor wife's cheek, she herself, for the first time, voluntarily took up the subject.

"Do you remember, my dear Aylmer," said she, with a feeble attempt at a smile, "have you any recollection of a dream last night about this odious hand?"

"None! none whatever!" replied Aylmer, starting; but then he added, in a dry, cold tone, affected for the sake of concealing the real depth of his emotion, "I might well dream of it; for before I fell asleep it had taken a pretty firm hold of my fancy."

"And you did dream of it," continued Georgiana, hastily; for she dreaded lest a gush of tears should interrupt what she had to say. "A terrible dream! I wonder that you can forget it. Is it possible to forget this one expression?— 'It is in her heart now; we must have it out!' Reflect, my husband; for by all means I would have you recall that dream."

The mind is in a sad state when Sleep, the all-involving, cannot confine her spectres within the dim region of her sway, but suffers them to break forth, affrighting this actual life with secrets that perchance belong to a deeper one. Aylmer now remembered his dream. He had fancied himself with his servant Aminadab, attempting an operation for the removal of the birthmark; but the deeper went the knife, the deeper sank the hand, until at length its tiny grasp appeared to have caught hold of Georgiana's heart; whence, however, her husband was inexorably resolved to cut or wrench it away.

When the dream had shaped itself perfectly in his memory, Aylmer sat in his wife's presence with a guilty feeling. Truth often finds its way to the mind close muffled in robes of sleep, and then speaks with uncompromising directness of matters in regard to which we practise an unconscious self-deception during our waking moments. Until now he had not been aware of the tyrannizing influence acquired by one idea over his mind, and of the lengths which he might find in his heart to go for the sake of giving himself peace.

"Aylmer," resumed Georgiana, solemnly, "I know not what may be the cost to both of us to rid me of this fatal birthmark. Perhaps its removal may cause cureless deformity; or it may be the stain goes as deep as life itself. Again: do we know that there is a possibility, on any terms, of unclasping the firm gripe of this little hand which was laid upon me before I came into the world?"

"Dearest Georgiana, I have spent much thought upon the subject," hastily interrupted Aylmer. "I am convinced of the perfect practicability of its removal."

"If there be the remotest possibility of it," continued Georgiana, "let the attempt be made, at whatever risk. Danger is nothing to me; for life, while this hateful mark makes me the object of your horror and disgust,—life is a burden which I would fling down with joy. Either remove this dreadful hand, or take my wretched life! You have deep science. All the world bears witness of it. You have achieved great wonders. Cannot you remove this little, little mark, which I cover with the tips of two small fingers? Is this beyond your power, for the sake of your own peace, and to save your poor wife from madness?"

"Noblest, dearest, tenderest wife," cried Aylmer, rapturously, "doubt not my power. I have already given this matter the deepest thought,—thought which might almost have enlightened me to create a being less perfect than yourself. Georgiana, you have led me deeper than ever into the heart of science. I feel myself fully competent to render this dear cheek as faultless as its fellow; and then, most beloved, what will be my triumph when I shall have corrected what Nature left imperfect in her fairest work! Even Pygmalion, when his sculptured woman assumed life, felt not greater ecstasy than mine will be."

"It is resolved, then," said Georgiana, faintly smiling. "And, Aylmer, spare me not, though you should find the birthmark take refuge in my heart at last."

Her husband tenderly kissed her cheek,—her right cheek,—not that which bore the impress of the crimson hand.

The next day Aylmer apprised his wife of a plan that he had formed whereby he might have opportunity for the intense thought and constant watchfulness which the proposed operation would require; while Georgiana, likewise, would enjoy the perfect repose essential to its success. They were to seclude themselves in the extensive apartments occupied by Aylmer as a laboratory, and where, during his toilsome youth, he had made discoveries in the elemental powers of nature that had roused the admiration of all the learned societies in Europe. Seated calmly in this laboratory, the pale philosopher had investigated the secrets of the highest cloud region and of the profoundest mines; he had satisfied himself of the causes that kindled and kept alive the fires of the volcano; and had explained the mystery of fountains, and how it is that they gush forth, some so bright and pure, and others with such rich medicinal virtues, from the dark bosom of the earth. Here, too, at an earlier period, he had studied the wonders of the human frame, and attempted to fathom the very process by which Nature assimilates all her precious influences from earth and air, and from the spiritual world, to create and foster man, her masterpiece. The latter pursuit, however, Aylmer had long laid aside in unwilling recognition of the truth—against which all seekers sooner or later stumble—that our great creative Mother, while she amuses us with apparently working in the broadest sunshine, is yet severely careful to keep her own secrets, and, in spite of her pretended openness, shows us nothing but results. She permits us, indeed, to mar, but seldom to mend, and, like a jealous patentee, on no account to make. Now, however, Aylmer resumed these half-forgotten investigations; not, of course, with such hopes or wishes as first suggested them; but because they involved much physiological truth and lay in the path of his proposed scheme for the treatment of Georgiana.

As he led her over the threshold of the laboratory, Georgiana was cold and tremulous. Aylmer looked cheerfully into her face, with intent to reassure her, but was so startled with the intense glow of the birthmark upon the whiteness of her cheek that he could not restrain a strong convulsive shudder. His wife fainted.

"Aminadab! Aminadab!" shouted Aylmer, stamping violently on the floor.

Forthwith there issued from an inner apartment a man of low stature, but bulky frame, with shaggy hair hanging about his visage, which was grimed with the vapors of the furnace. This personage had been Aylmer's underworker during his whole scientific career, and was admirably fitted for that office by his great mechanical readiness, and the skill with which, while incapable of comprehending a single principle, he executed all the details of his master's experiments. With his vast strength, his shaggy hair, his smoky aspect, and the indescribable earthiness that incrusted him, he seemed to represent man's physical nature; while Aylmer's slender figure, and pale, intellectual face, were no less apt a type of the spiritual element.

"Throw open the door of the boudoir, Aminadab," said Aylmer, "and burn a pastil."

"Yes, master," answered Aminadab, looking intently at the lifeless form of Georgiana; and then he muttered to himself, "If she were my wife, I'd never part with that birthmark."

When Georgiana recovered consciousness she found herself breathing an atmosphere of penetrating fragrance, the gentle potency of which had recalled her from her deathlike faintness. The scene around her looked like enchantment. Aylmer had converted those smoky, dingy, sombre rooms, where he had spent his brightest years in recondite pursuits, into a series of beautiful apartments not unfit to be the secluded abode of a lovely woman. The walls were hung with gorgeous curtains, which imparted the combination of grandeur and grace that no other species of adornment can achieve; and, as they fell from the ceiling to the floor, their rich and ponderous folds, concealing all angles and straight lines, appeared to shut in the scene from infinite space. For aught Georgiana knew, it might be a pavilion among the clouds. And Aylmer, excluding the sunshine, which would have interfered with his chemical processes, had supplied its place with perfumed lamps, emitting flames of various hue, but all uniting in a soft, impurpled radiance.

He now knelt by his wife's side, watching her earnestly, but without alarm; for he was confident in his science, and felt that he could draw a magic circle round her within which no evil might intrude.

"Where am I? Ah, I remember," said Georgiana, faintly; and she placed her hand over her cheek to hide the terrible mark from her husband's eyes.

"Fear not, dearest!" exclaimed he. "Do not shrink from me! Believe me, Georgiana, I even rejoice in this single imperfection, since it will be such a rapture to remove it."

"O, spare me!" sadly replied his wife. "Pray do not look at it again. I never can forget that convulsive shudder."

In order to soothe Georgiana, and, as it were, to release her mind from the burden of actual things, Aylmer now put in practice some of the light and playful secrets which science had taught him among its profounder lore. Airy figures, absolutely bodiless ideas, and forms of unsubstantial beauty came and danced before her, imprinting their momentary footsteps on beams of light. Though she had some indistinct idea of the method of these optical phenomena, still the illusion was almost perfect enough to warrant the belief that her husband possessed sway over the spiritual world. Then again, when she felt a wish to look forth from her seclusion, immediately, as if her thoughts were answered, the procession of external existence flitted across a screen. The scenery and the figures of actual life were perfectly represented, but with that bewitching, yet indescribable difference which always makes a picture, an image, or a shadow so much more attractive than the original. When wearied of this, Aylmer bade her cast her eyes upon a vessel containing a quantity of earth. She did so, with little interest at first; but was soon startled to perceive the germ of a plant shooting upward from the soil. Then came the slender stalk; the leaves gradually unfolded themselves; and amid them was a perfect and lovely flower.

"It is magical!" cried Georgiana. "I dare not touch it."

"Nay, pluck it," answered Aylmer,—"pluck it, and inhale its brief perfume while you may. The flower will wither in a few moments and leave nothing save its brown seed-vessels; but thence may be perpetuated a race as ephemeral as itself."

But Georgiana had no sooner touched the flower than the whole plant suffered a blight, its leaves turning coal-black as if by the agency of fire.

"There was too powerful a stimulus," said Aylmer, thoughtfully.

To make up for this abortive experiment, he proposed to take her portrait by a scientific process of his own invention. It was to be effected by rays of light striking upon a polished plate of metal. Georgiana assented; but, on looking at the result, was affrighted to find the features of the portrait blurred and indefinable; while the minute figure of a hand appeared where the cheek should have been. Aylmer snatched the metallic plate and threw it into a jar of corrosive acid.

Soon, however, he forgot these mortifying failures. In the intervals of study and chemical experiment he came to her flushed and exhausted, but seemed invigorated by her presence, and spoke in glowing language of the resources of his art. He gave a history of the long dynasty of the alchemists, who spent so many ages in quest of the universal solvent by which the golden principle might be elicited from all things vile and base. Aylmer appeared to believe that, by the plainest scientific logic, it was altogether within the limits of possibility to discover this long-sought medium; "but," he added, "a philosopher who should go deep enough to acquire the power would attain too lofty a wisdom to stoop to the exercise of it." Not less singular were his opinions in regard to the elixir vitæ. He more than intimated that it was at his option to concoct a liquid that should prolong life for years, perhaps interminably; but that it would produce a discord in nature which all the world, and chiefly the quaffer of the immortal nostrum, would find cause to curse.

"Aylmer, are you in earnest?" asked Georgiana, looking at him with amazement and fear. "It is terrible to possess such power, or even to dream of possessing it."

"Oh, do not tremble, my love," said her husband. "I would not wrong either you or myself by working such inharmonious effects upon our lives; but I would have you consider how trifling, in comparison, is the skill requisite to remove this little hand."

At the mention of the birthmark, Georgiana, as usual, shrank as if a red-hot iron had touched her cheek.

Again Aylmer applied himself to his labors. She could hear his voice in the distant furnace-room giving directions to Aminadab, whose harsh, uncouth, misshapen tones were audible in response, more like the grunt or growl of a brute than human speech. After hours of absence, Aylmer reappeared and proposed that she should now examine his cabinet of chemical products and natural treasures of the earth. Among the former he showed her a small vial, in which, he remarked, was contained a gentle yet most powerful fragrance, capable of impregnating all the breezes that blow across a kingdom. They were of inestimable value, the contents of that little vial; and, as he said so, he threw some of the perfume into the air and filled the room with piercing and invigorating delight.

"And what is this?" asked Georgiana, pointing to a small crystal globe containing a gold-colored liquid. "It is so beautiful to the eye that I could imagine it the elixir of life."

"In one sense it is," replied Aylmer; "or rather, the elixir of immortality. It is the most precious poison that ever was concocted in this world. By its aid I could apportion the lifetime of any mortal at whom you might point your finger. The strength of the dose would determine whether he were to linger out years, or drop dead in the midst of a breath. No king on his guarded throne could keep his life if I, in my private station, should deem that the welfare of millions justified me in depriving him of it."

"Why do you keep such a terrific drug?" inquired Georgiana in horror.

"Do not mistrust me, dearest," said her husband, smiling; "its virtuous potency is yet greater than its harmful one. But see! here is a powerful cosmetic. With a few drops of this in a vase of water, freckles may be washed away as easily as the hands are cleansed. A stronger infusion would take the blood out of the cheek, and leave the rosiest beauty a pale ghost."

"Is it with this lotion that you intend to bathe my cheek?" asked Georgiana, anxiously.

"Oh, no," hastily replied her husband; "this is merely superficial. Your case demands a remedy that shall go deeper."

In his interviews with Georgiana, Aylmer generally made minute inquiries as to her sensations and whether the confinement of the rooms and the temperature of the atmosphere agreed with her. These questions had such a particular drift that Georgiana began to conjecture that she was already subjected to certain physical influences, either breathed in with the fragrant air or taken with her food. She fancied likewise, but it might be altogether fancy, that there was a stirring up of her system,—a strange, indefinite sensation creeping through her veins, and tingling, half painfully, half pleasurably, at her heart. Still, whenever she dared to look into the mirror, there she beheld herself pale as a white rose and with the crimson birthmark stamped upon her cheek. Not even Aylmer now hated it so much as she.

To dispel the tedium of the hours which her husband found it necessary to devote to the processes of combination and analysis, Georgiana turned over the volumes of his scientific library. In many dark old tomes she met with chapters full of romance and poetry. They were the works of the philosophers of the Middle Ages, such as Albertus Magnus, Cornelius Agrippa, Paracelsus, and the famous friar who created the prophetic Brazen Head. All these antique naturalists stood in advance of their centuries, yet were imbued with some of their credulity, and therefore were believed, and perhaps imagined themselves to have acquired from the investigation of nature a power above nature, and from physics a sway over the spiritual world. Hardly less curious and imaginative were the early volumes of the Transactions of the Royal Society, in which the members, knowing little of the limits of natural possibility, were continually recording wonders or proposing methods whereby wonders might be wrought.

But to Georgiana the most engrossing volume was a large folio from her husband's own hand, in which he had recorded every experiment of his scientific career, its original aim, the methods adopted for its development, and its final success or failure, with the circumstances to which either event was attributable. The book, in truth, was both the history and emblem of his ardent, ambitious, imaginative, yet practical and laborious life. He handled physical details as if there were nothing beyond them; yet spiritualized them all, and redeemed himself from materialism by his strong and eager aspiration towards the infinite. In his grasp the veriest clod of earth assumed a soul. Georgiana, as she read, reverenced Aylmer and loved him more profoundly than ever, but with a less entire dependence on his judgment than heretofore. Much as he had accomplished, she could not but observe that his most splendid successes were almost invariably failures, if compared with the ideal at which he aimed. His brightest diamonds were the merest pebbles, and felt to be so by himself, in comparison with the inestimable gems which lay hidden beyond his reach. The volume, rich with achievements that had won renown for its author, was yet as melancholy a record as ever mortal hand had penned. It was the sad confession and continual exemplification of the shortcomings of the composite man, the spirit burdened with clay and working in matter, and of the despair that assails the higher nature at finding itself so miserably thwarted by the earthly part. Perhaps every man of genius in whatever sphere might recognize the image of his own experience in Aylmer's journal.

So deeply did these reflections affect Georgiana that she laid her face upon the open volume and burst into tears. In this situation she was found by her husband.

"It is dangerous to read in a sorcerer's books," said he with a smile, though his countenance was uneasy and displeased. "Georgiana, there are pages in that volume which I can scarcely glance over and keep my senses. Take heed lest it prove as detrimental to you."

"It has made me worship you more than ever," said she.

"Ah, wait for this one success," rejoined he, "then worship me if you will. I shall deem myself hardly unworthy of it. But come, I have sought you for the luxury of your voice. Sing to me, dearest."

So she poured out the liquid music of her voice to quench the thirst of his spirit. He then took his leave with a boyish exuberance of gayety, assuring her that her seclusion would endure but a little longer, and that the result was already certain. Scarcely had he departed when Georgiana felt irresistibly impelled to follow him. She had forgotten to inform Aylmer of a symptom which for two or three hours past had begun to excite her attention. It was a sensation in the fatal birthmark, not painful, but which induced a restlessness throughout her system. Hastening after her husband, she intruded for the first time into the laboratory.

The first thing that struck her eye was the furnace, that hot and feverish worker, with the intense glow of its fire, which by the quantities of soot clustered above it seemed to have been burning for ages. There was a distilling apparatus in full operation. Around the room were retorts, tubes, cylinders, crucibles, and other apparatus of chemical research. An electrical machine stood ready for immediate use. The atmosphere felt oppressively close, and was tainted with gaseous odors which had been tormented forth by the processes of science. The severe and homely simplicity of the apartment, with its naked walls and brick pavement, looked strange, accustomed as Georgiana had become to the fantastic elegance of her boudoir. But what chiefly, indeed almost solely, drew her attention, was the aspect of Aylmer himself.

He was pale as death, anxious and absorbed, and hung over the furnace as if it depended upon his utmost watchfulness whether the liquid which it was distilling should be the draught of immortal happiness or misery. How different from the sanguine and joyous mien that he had assumed for Georgiana's encouragement!

"Carefully now, Aminadab; carefully, thou human machine; carefully, thou man of clay!" muttered Aylmer, more to himself than his assistant. "Now, if there be a thought too much or too little, it is all over."

"Ho! ho!" mumbled Aminadab. "Look, master! look!"

Aylmer raised his eyes hastily, and at first reddened, then grew paler than ever, on beholding Georgiana. He rushed towards her and seized her arm with a gripe that left the print of his fingers upon it.

"Why do you come hither? Have you no trust in your husband?" cried he, impetuously. "Would you throw the blight of that fatal birthmark over my labors? It is not well done. Go, prying woman, go!"

"Nay, Aylmer," said Georgiana with the firmness of which she possessed no stinted endowment, "it is not you that have a right to complain. You mistrust your wife; you have concealed the anxiety with which you watch the development of this experiment. Think not so unworthily of me, my husband. Tell me all the risk we run, and fear not that I shall shrink; for my share in it is far less than your own."

"No, no, Georgiana!" said Aylmer, impatiently; "it must not be."

"I submit," replied she calmly. "And, Aylmer, I shall quaff whatever draught you bring me; but it will be on the same principle that would induce me to take a dose of poison if offered by your hand."

"My noble wife," said Aylmer, deeply moved, "I knew not the height and depth of your nature until now. Nothing shall be concealed. Know, then, that this crimson hand, superficial as it seems, has clutched its grasp into your being with a strength of which I had no previous conception. I have already administered agents powerful enough to do aught except to change your entire physical system. Only one thing remains to be tried. If that fail us we are ruined."

"Why did you hesitate to tell me this?" asked she.

"Because, Georgiana," said Aylmer, in a low voice, "there is danger."

"Danger? There is but one danger,—that this horrible stigma shall be left upon my cheek!" cried Georgiana. "Remove it, remove it, whatever be the cost, or we shall both go mad!"

"Heaven knows your words are too true," said Aylmer, sadly. "And now, dearest, return to your boudoir. In a little while all will be tested."

He conducted her back and took leave of her with a solemn tenderness which spoke far more than his words how much was now at stake. After his departure Georgiana became rapt in musings. She considered the character of Aylmer, and did it completer justice than at any previous moment. Her heart exulted, while it trembled, at his honorable love,—so pure and lofty that it would accept nothing less than perfection nor miserably make itself contented with an earthlier nature than he had dreamed of. She felt how much more precious was such a sentiment than that meaner kind which would have borne with the imperfection for her sake, and have been guilty of treason to holy love by degrading its perfect idea to the level of the actual; and with her whole spirit she prayed that, for a single moment, she might satisfy his highest and deepest conception. Longer than one moment she well knew it could not be; for his spirit was ever on the march, ever ascending, and each instant required something that was beyond the scope of the instant before.

The sound of her husband's footsteps aroused her. He bore a crystal goblet containing a liquor colorless as water, but bright enough to be the draught of immortality. Aylmer was pale; but it seemed rather the consequence of a highly-wrought state of mind and tension of spirit than of fear or doubt.

"The concoction of the draught has been perfect," said he, in answer to Georgiana's look. "Unless all my science have deceived me, it cannot fail."

"Save on your account, my dearest Aylmer," observed his wife, "I might wish to put off this birthmark of mortality by relinquishing mortality itself in preference to any other mode. Life is but a sad possession to those who have attained precisely the degree of moral advancement at which I stand. Were I weaker and blinder, it might be happiness. Were I stronger, it might be endured hopefully. But, being what I find myself, methinks I am of all mortals the most fit to die."

"You are fit for heaven without tasting death!" replied her husband. "But why do we speak of dying? The draught cannot fail. Behold its effect upon this plant."

On the window-seat there stood a geranium diseased with yellow blotches, which had overspread all its leaves. Aylmer poured a small quantity of the liquid upon the soil in which it grew. In a little time, when the roots of the plant had taken up the moisture, the unsightly blotches began to be extinguished in a living verdure.

"There needed no proof," said Georgiana, quietly. "Give me the goblet. I joyfully stake all upon your word."

"Drink, then, thou lofty creature!" exclaimed Aylmer, with fervid admiration. "There is no taint of imperfection on thy spirit. Thy sensible frame, too, shall soon be all perfect."

She quaffed the liquid and returned the goblet to his hand.

"It is grateful," said she with a placid smile. "Methinks it is like water from a heavenly fountain; for it contains I know not what of unobtrusive fragrance and deliciousness. It allays a feverish thirst that had parched me for many days. Now, dearest, let me sleep. My earthly senses are closing over my spirit like the leaves around the heart of a rose at sunset."

She spoke the last words with a gentle reluctance, as if it required almost more energy than she could command to pronounce the faint and lingering syllables. Scarcely had they loitered through her lips ere she was lost in slumber. Aylmer sat by her side, watching her aspect with the emotions proper to a man the whole value of whose existence was involved in the process now to be tested. Mingled with this mood, however, was the philosophic investigation characteristic of the man of science. Not the minutest symptom escaped him. A heightened flush of the cheek, a slight irregularity of breath, a quiver of the eyelid, a hardly perceptible tremor through the frame,—such were the details which, as the moments passed, he wrote down in his folio volume. Intense thought had set its stamp upon every previous page of that volume, but the thoughts of years were all concentrated upon the last.

While thus employed, he failed not to gaze often at the fatal hand, and not without a shudder. Yet once, by a strange and unaccountable impulse, he pressed it with his lips. His spirit recoiled, however, in the very act; and Georgiana, out of the midst of her deep sleep, moved uneasily and murmured as if in remonstrance. Again Aylmer resumed his watch. Nor was it without avail. The crimson hand, which at first had been strongly visible upon the marble paleness of Georgiana's cheek, now grew more faintly outlined. She remained not less pale than ever; but the birthmark, with every breath that came and went, lost somewhat of its former distinctness. Its presence had been awful; its departure was more awful still. Watch the stain of the rainbow fading out of the sky, and you will know how that mysterious symbol passed away.

"By Heaven! it is well-nigh gone!" said Aylmer to himself, in almost irrepressible ecstasy. "I can scarcely trace it now. Success! success! And now it is like the faintest rose color. The lightest flush of blood across her cheek would overcome it. But she is so pale!"

He drew aside the window curtain and suffered the light of natural day to fall into the room and rest upon her cheek. At the same time he heard a gross, hoarse chuckle, which he had long known as his servant Aminadab's expression of delight.

"Ah, clod! ah, earthly mass!" cried Aylmer, laughing in a sort of frenzy, "you have served me well! Matter and spirit—earth and heaven—have both done their part in this! Laugh, thing of the senses! You have earned the right to laugh."

These exclamations broke Georgiana's sleep. She slowly unclosed her eyes and gazed into the mirror which her husband had arranged for that purpose. A faint smile flitted over her lips when she recognized how barely perceptible was now that crimson hand which had once blazed forth with such disastrous brilliancy as to scare away all their happiness. But then her eyes sought Aylmer's face with a trouble and anxiety that he could by no means account for.

"My poor Aylmer!" murmured she.

"Poor? Nay, richest, happiest, most favored!" exclaimed he. "My peerless bride, it is successful! You are perfect!"

"My poor Aylmer," she repeated, with a more than human tenderness, "you have aimed loftily; you have done nobly. Do not repent that, with so high and pure a feeling, you have rejected the best the earth could offer. Aylmer, dearest Aylmer, I am dying!"

Alas! it was too true! The fatal hand had grappled with the mystery of life, and was the bond by which an angelic spirit kept itself in union with a mortal frame. As the last crimson tint of the birthmark—that sole token of human imperfection—faded from her cheek, the parting breath of the now perfect woman passed into the atmosphere, and her soul, lingering a moment near her husband, took its heavenward flight. Then a hoarse, chuckling laugh was heard again! Thus ever does the gross fatality of earth exult in its invariable triumph over the immortal essence which, in this dim sphere of half development, demands the completeness of a higher state. Yet, had Aylmer reached a profounder wisdom, he need not thus have flung away the happiness which would have woven his mortal life of the selfsame texture with the celestial. The momentary circumstance was too strong for him; he failed to look beyond the shadowy scope of time, and, living once for all in eternity, to find the perfect future in the present.

YOUNG GOODMAN BROWN [8]

Young Goodman Brown came forth at sunset into the street of Salem village; but put his head back, after crossing the threshold, to exchange a parting

[8] First published in the *New England Magazine,* 1835, and included in *Mosses from an Old Manse* (1846).

kiss with his young wife. And Faith, as the wife was aptly named, thrust her own pretty head into the street, letting the wind play with the pink ribbons of her cap while she called to Goodman Brown.

"Dearest heart," whispered she, softly and rather sadly, when her lips were close to his ear, "prithee put off your journey until sunrise and sleep in your own bed to-night. A lone woman is troubled with such dreams and such thoughts that she's afeared of herself sometimes. Pray tarry with me this night, dear husband, of all nights in the year."

"My love and my Faith," replied young Goodman Brown, "of all nights in the year, this one night must I tarry away from thee. My journey, as thou callest it, forth and back again, must needs be done 'twixt now and sunrise. What, my sweet, pretty wife, dost thou doubt me already, and we but three months married?"

"Then God bless you!" said Faith, with the pink ribbons; "and may you find all well when you come back."

"Amen!" cried Goodman Brown. "Say thy prayers, dear Faith, and go to bed at dusk, and no harm will come to thee."

So they parted; and the young man pursued his way until, being about to turn the corner by the meeting-house, he looked back and saw the head of Faith still peeping after him with a melancholy air, in spite of her pink ribbons.

"Poor little Faith!" thought he, for his heart smote him. "What a wretch am I to leave her on such an errand! She talks of dreams, too. Methought as she spoke, there was trouble in her face, as if a dream had warned her what work is to be done to-night. But no, no; 't would kill her to think it. Well, she's a blessed angel on earth; and after this one night I'll cling to her skirts and follow her to heaven."

With this excellent resolve for the future, Goodman Brown felt himself justified in making more haste on his present evil purpose. He had taken a dreary road, darkened by all the gloomiest trees of the forest, which barely stood aside to let the narrow path creep through, and closed immediately behind. It was all as lonely as could be; and there is this peculiarity in such a solitude, that the traveller knows not who may be concealed by the innumerable trunks and the thick boughs overhead; so that with lonely footsteps he may yet be passing through an unseen multitude.

"There may be a devilish Indian behind every tree," said Goodman Brown to himself; and he glanced fearfully behind him as he added, "What if the Devil himself should be at my very elbow!"

His head being turned back, he passed a crook of the road, and, looking forward again, beheld the figure of a man, in grave and decent attire, seated at the foot of an old tree. He arose at Goodman Brown's approach and walked onward side by side with him.

"You are late, Goodman Brown," said he. "The clock of the Old South was striking as I came through Boston; and that is full fifteen minutes agone."

"Faith kept me back awhile," replied the young man, with a tremor in his voice, caused by the sudden appearance of his companion, though not wholly unexpected.

It was now deep dusk in the forest, and deepest in that part of it where these two were journeying. As nearly as could be discerned, the second traveller was about fifty years old, apparently in the same rank of life as Goodman Brown, and bearing a considerable resemblance to him, though perhaps more in expression than features. Still they might have been taken for father and son. And yet, though the elder person was as simply clad as the younger, and as simple in manner too, he had an indescribable air of one who knew the world, and who would not have felt abashed at the governor's dinner-table or in King William's court, were it possible that his affairs should call him thither. But the only thing about him that could be fixed upon as remarkable was his staff, which bore the likeness of a great black snake, so curiously wrought that it might almost be seen to twist and wriggle itself like a living serpent. This, of course, must have been an ocular deception, assisted by the uncertain light.

"Come, Goodman Brown," cried his fellow-traveller, "this is a dull pace for the beginning of a journey. Take my staff, if you are so soon weary."

"Friend," said the other, exchanging his slow pace for a full stop, "having kept covenant by meeting thee here, it is my purpose now to return whence I came. I have scruples touching the matter thou wot'st of."

"Sayest thou so?" replied he of the serpent, smiling apart. "Let us walk on, nevertheless, reasoning as we go; and if I convince thee not, thou shalt turn back. We are but a little way in the forest yet."

"Too far! too far!" exclaimed the goodman, unconsciously resuming his walk. "My father never went into the woods on such an errand, nor his father before him. We have been a race of honest men and good Christians since the days of the martyrs; and shall I be the first of the name of Brown that ever took this path and kept"—

"Such company, thou wouldst say," observed the elder person, interpreting his pause. "Well said, Goodman Brown! I have been as well acquainted with your family as with ever a one among the Puritans; and that's no trifle to say. I helped your grandfather, the constable, when he lashed the Quaker woman so smartly through the streets of Salem; and it was I that brought your father a pitch-pine knot, kindled at my own hearth, to set fire to an Indian village, in King Philip's war. They were my good friends, both; and many a pleasant walk have we had along this path, and returned merrily after midnight. I would fain be friends with you for their sake."

"If it be as thou sayest," replied Goodman Brown, "I marvel they never spoke of these matters; or, verily, I marvel not, seeing that the least rumor of the sort would have driven them from New England. We are a people of prayer, and good works to boot, and abide no such wickedness."

"Wickedness or not," said the traveller with the twisted staff, "I have a very general acquaintance here in New England. The deacons of many a church have drunk the communion wine with me; the selectmen of divers towns make me their chairman; and a majority of the Great and General Court are firm supporters of my interest. The governor and I, too— But these are state secrets."

"Can this be so?" cried Goodman Brown, with a stare of amazement at his undisturbed companion. "Howbeit, I have nothing to do with the governor and council; they have their own ways, and are no rule for a simple husbandman like me. But, were I to go on with thee, how should I meet the eye of that good old man, our minister, at Salem village? Oh, his voice would make me tremble both Sabbath day and lecture day."

Thus far the elder traveller had listened with due gravity; but now burst into a fit of irrepressible mirth, shaking himself so violently that his snake-like staff actually seemed to wriggle in sympathy.

"Ha! ha! ha!" shouted he again and again; then composing himself, "Well, go on, Goodman Brown, go on; but, prithee, don't kill me with laughing."

"Well, then, to end the matter at once," said Goodman Brown, considerably nettled, "there is my wife, Faith. It would break her dear little heart; and I'd rather break my own."

"Nay, if that be the case," answered the other, "e'en go thy ways, Goodman Brown. I would not for twenty old women like the one hobbling before us that Faith should come to any harm."

As he spoke, he pointed his staff at a female figure on the path, in whom Goodman Brown recognized a very pious and exemplary dame, who had taught him his catechism in youth, and was still his moral and spiritual adviser, jointly with the minister and Deacon Gookin.

"A marvel, truly, that Goody Cloyse should be so far in the wilderness at nightfall," said he. "But, with your leave, friend, I shall take a cut through the woods until we have left this Christian woman behind. Being a stranger to you, she might ask whom I was consorting with and whither I was going."

"Be it so," said his fellow-traveller. "Betake you to the woods, and let me keep the path."

Accordingly the young man turned aside, but took care to watch his companion, who advanced softly along the road until he had come within a staff's length of the old dame. She, meanwhile, was making the best of her way, with singular speed for so aged a woman, and mumbling some indistinct words—a prayer, doubtless—as she went. The traveller put forth his staff and touched her withered neck with what seemed the serpent's tail.

"The Devil!" screamed the pious old lady.

"Then Goody Cloyse knows her old friend?" observed the traveller, confronting her and leaning on his writhing stick.

"Ah, forsooth, and is it your worship indeed?" cried the good dame. "Yea, truly is it, and in the very image of my old gossip, Goodman Brown, the grandfather of the silly fellow that now is. But—would your worship believe it?—my broomstick hath strangely disappeared, stolen, as I suspect, by that unhanged witch, Goody Cory, and that, too, when I was all anointed with the juice of smallage, and cinquefoil, and wolf's-bane"—

"Mingled with fine wheat and the fat of a new-born babe," said the shape of old Goodman Brown.

"Ah, your worship knows the recipe," cried the old lady, cackling aloud. "So, as I was saying, being all ready for the meeting, and no horse to ride on, I made up my mind to foot it; for they tell me there is a nice young man to be taken into communion to-night. But now your good worship will lend me your arm, and we shall be there in a twinkling."

"That can hardly be," answered her friend. "I may not spare you my arm, Goody Cloyse; but here is my staff, if you will."

So saying, he threw it down at her feet, where, perhaps, it assumed life, being one of the rods which its owner had formerly lent to the Egyptian magi. Of this fact, however, Goodman Brown could not take cognizance. He had cast up his eyes in astonishment, and, looking down again, beheld neither Goody Cloyse nor the serpentine staff, but his fellow-traveller alone, who waited for him as calmly as if nothing had happened.

"That old woman taught me my catechism," said the young man; and there was a world of meaning in this simple comment.

They continued to walk onward, while the elder traveller exhorted his companion to make good speed and persevere in the path, discoursing so aptly that his arguments seemed rather to spring up in the bosom of his auditor than to be suggested by himself. As they went, he plucked a branch of maple to serve for a walking-stick, and began to strip it of the twigs and little boughs, which were wet with evening dew. The moment his fingers touched them they became strangely withered and dried up as with a week's sunshine. Thus the pair proceeded, at a good free pace, until suddenly, in a gloomy hollow of the road, Goodman Brown sat himself down on the stump of a tree and refused to go any farther.

"Friend," said he, stubbornly, "my mind is made up. Not another step will I budge on this errand. What if a wretched old woman do choose to go to the Devil when I thought she was going to heaven: is that any reason why I should quit my dear Faith and go after her?"

"You will think better of this by and by," said his acquaintance, composedly. "Sit here and rest yourself awhile; and when you feel like moving again, there is my staff to help you along."

Without more words, he threw his companion the maple stick, and was as speedily out of sight as if he had vanished into the deepening gloom. The young man sat a few moments by the roadside, applauding himself greatly, and thinking with how clear a conscience he should meet the minister in his morning walk, nor shrink from the eye of good old Deacon Gookin. And what calm sleep would be his that very night, which was to have been spent so wickedly, but so purely and sweetly now, in the arms of Faith! Amidst these pleasant and praiseworthy meditations, Goodman Brown heard the tramp of horses along the road, and deemed it advisable to conceal himself within the verge of the forest, conscious of the guilty purpose that had brought him thither, though now so happily turned from it.

On came the hoof tramps and the voices of the riders, two grave old voices, conversing soberly as they drew near. These mingled sounds appeared to pass along the road, within a few yards of the young man's hiding-place; but, owing doubtless to the depth of the gloom at that particular spot, neither the travellers nor their steeds were visible. Though their figures brushed the small boughs by the wayside, it could not be seen that they intercepted, even for a moment, the faint gleam from the strip of bright sky athwart which they must have passed. Goodman Brown alternately crouched and stood on tiptoe, pulling aside the branches and thrusting forth his head as far as he durst without discerning so much as a shadow. It vexed him the more, because he could have sworn, were such a thing possible, that he recognized the voices of the minister and Deacon Gookin, jogging along quietly, as they were wont to do, when bound to some ordination or ecclesiastical council. While yet within hearing, one of the riders stopped to pluck a switch.

"Of the two, reverend sir," said the voice like the deacon's, "I had rather miss an ordination dinner than to-night's meeting. They tell me that some of our community are to be here from Falmouth and beyond, and others from Connecticut and Rhode Island, besides several of the Indian powwows, who, after their fashion, know almost as much deviltry as the best of us. Moreover, there is a goodly young woman to be taken into communion."

"Mighty well, Deacon Gookin!" replied the solemn old tones of the minister. "Spur up, or we shall be late. Nothing can be done, you know, until I get on the ground."

The hoofs clattered again; and the voices, talking so strangely in the empty air, passed on through the forest, where no church had ever been gathered or solitary Christian prayed. Whither, then, could these holy men be journeying so deep into the heathen wilderness? Young Goodman Brown caught hold of a tree for support, being ready to sink down on the ground, faint and overburdened with the heavy sickness of his heart. He looked up to the sky, doubting whether there really was a heaven above him. Yet there was the blue arch, and the stars brightening in it.

"With heaven above and Faith below, I will yet stand firm against the Devil!" cried Goodman Brown.

While he still gazed upward into the deep arch of the firmament and had lifted his hands to pray, a cloud, though no wind was stirring, hurried across the zenith and hid the brightening stars. The blue sky was still visible, except directly overhead, where this black mass of cloud was sweeping swiftly northward. Aloft in the air, as if from the depths of the cloud, came a confused and doubtful sound of voices. Once the listener fancied that he could distinguish the accents of townspeople of his own, men and women, both pious and ungodly, many of whom he had met at the communion-table, and had seen others rioting at the tavern. The next moment, so indistinct were the sounds, he doubted whether he had heard aught but the murmur of the old forest, whispering without a wind. Then came a stronger swell of those familiar tones, heard daily in the sunshine at Salem village, but never until now from a cloud of night. There was one voice, of a young woman, uttering lamentations, yet with an uncertain sorrow, and entreating for some favor, which, perhaps, it would grieve her to obtain; and all the unseen multitude, both saints and sinners, seemed to encourage her onward.

"Faith!" shouted Goodman Brown, in a voice of agony and desperation; and the echoes of the forest mocked him, crying, "Faith! Faith!" as if bewildered wretches were seeking her all through the wilderness.

The cry of grief, rage, and terror was yet piercing the night, when the unhappy husband held his breath for a response. There was a scream, drowned immediately in a louder murmur of voices, fading into far-off laughter, as the dark cloud swept away, leaving the clear and silent sky above Goodman Brown. But something fluttered lightly down through the air and caught on the branch of a tree. The young man seized it, and beheld a pink ribbon.

"My Faith is gone!" cried he, after one stupefied moment. "There is no good on earth; and sin is but a name. Come, Devil; for to thee is this world given."

And, maddened with despair, so that he laughed loud and long, did Goodman Brown grasp his staff and set forth again, at such rate that he seemed to fly along the forest path rather than to walk or run. The road grew wilder and drearier and more faintly traced, and vanished at length, leaving him in the heart of the dark wilderness, still rushing onward with the instinct that guides mortal man to evil. The whole forest was peopled with frightful sounds,—the creaking of the trees, the howling of wild beasts, and the yell of Indians; while sometimes the wind tolled like a distant churchbell, and sometimes gave a broad roar around the traveller, as if all Nature were laughing him to scorn. But he was himself the chief horror of the scene, and shrank not from its other horrors.

"Ha! ha! ha!" roared Goodman Brown when the wind laughed at him. "Let us hear which will laugh loudest. Think not to frighten me with your deviltry. Come witch, come wizard, come Indian powwow, come Devil himself, and here comes Goodman Brown. You may as well fear him as he fear you."

In truth, all through the haunted forest there could be nothing more frightful than the figure of Goodman Brown. On he flew among the black pines, brandishing his staff with frenzied gestures, now giving vent to an inspiration of horrid blasphemy, and now shouting forth such laughter as set all the echoes of the forest laughing like demons around him. The fiend in his own shape is less hideous than when he rages in the breast of man. Thus sped the demoniac on his course, until, quivering among the trees, he saw a red light before him, as when the felled trunks and branches of a clearing have been set on fire, and throw up their lurid blaze against the sky, at the hour of midnight. He paused, in a lull of the tempest that had driven him onward, and heard the swell of what seemed a hymn rolling solemnly from a distance with the weight of many voices. He knew the tune; it was a familiar one in the choir of the village meeting-house. The verse died heavily away, and was lengthened by a chorus, not of human voices, but of all the sounds of the benighted wilderness pealing in awful harmony together. Goodman Brown cried out, and his cry was lost to his own ear by its unison with the cry of the desert.

In the interval of silence he stole forward until the light glared full upon his eyes. At one extremity of an open space, hemmed in by the dark wall of the forest, arose a rock, bearing some rude, natural resemblance either to an altar or a pulpit, and surrounded by four blazing pines, their tops aflame, their stems untouched, like candles at an evening meeting. The mass of foliage that had overgrown the summit of the rock was all on fire, blazing high into the night and fitfully illuminating the whole field. Each pendent twig and leafy festoon was in a blaze. As the red light arose and fell, a numerous congregation alternately shone forth, then disappeared in shadow, and again grew, as it were, out of the darkness, peopling the heart of the solitary woods at once.

"A grave and dark-clad company," quoth Goodman Brown.

In truth they were such. Among them, quivering to and fro between gloom and splendor, appeared faces that would be seen next day at the council board of the province, and others which, Sabbath after Sabbath, looked devoutly heavenward, and benignantly over the crowded pews, from the holiest pulpits in the land. Some affirm that the lady of the governor was there. At least there were high dames well known to her, and wives of honored husbands, and widows, a great multitude, and ancient maidens, all of excellent repute, and fair young girls, who trembled lest their mothers should espy them. Either the sudden gleams of light flashing over the obscure field bedazzled Goodman Brown, or he recognized a score of the church members of Salem village famous for their especial sanctity. Good old Deacon Gookin had arrived, and waited at the skirts of that venerable saint, his revered pastor. But, irreverently consorting with these grave, reputable, and pious people, these elders of the church, these chaste dames and dewy virgins, there were men of dissolute lives and women of spotted fame, wretches given over to all mean and filthy vice, and suspected even of horrid crimes. It was strange to see that the good shrank not from the wicked, nor were the sinners abashed by the saints. Scattered also among their pale-faced enemies were the Indian priests, or powwows, who had often scared their native forest with more hideous incantations than any known to English witchcraft.

"But where is Faith?" thought Goodman Brown; and, as hope came into his heart, he trembled.

Another verse of the hymn arose, a slow and mournful strain, such as the pious love, but joined to words which expressed all that our nature can conceive of sin, and darkly hinted at far more. Unfathomable to mere mortals is the lore of fiends. Verse after verse was sung; and still the chorus of the desert swelled between like the deepest tone of a mighty organ; and with the final peal of that dreadful anthem there came a sound, as if the roaring wind, the rushing streams, the howling beasts, and every other voice of the unconverted wilderness were mingling and according with the voice of guilty man in homage to the prince of all. The four blazing pines threw up a loftier flame, and obscurely discovered shapes and visages of horror on the smoke wreaths above the impious assembly. At the same moment the fire on the rock shot redly forth and formed a glowing arch above its base, where now appeared a figure. With reverence be it spoken, the figure bore no slight similitude, both in garb and manner, to some grave divine of the New England churches.

"Bring forth the converts!" cried a voice that echoed through the field and rolled into the forest.

At the word, Goodman Brown stepped forth from the shadow of the trees and approached the congregation, with whom he felt a loathful brotherhood by the sympathy of all that was wicked in his heart. He could have wellnigh sworn that the shape of his own dead father beckoned him to advance, looking downward from a smoke wreath, while a woman, with dim features of despair, threw out her hand to warn him back. Was it his mother? But he had no power to retreat one step, nor to resist, even in thought, when the minister and good old Deacon Gookin seized his arms and led him to the blazing rock. Thither came also the slender form of a

veiled female, led between Goody Cloyse, that pious teacher of the catechism, and Martha Carrier, who had received the Devil's promise to be queen
of hell. A rampant hag was she. And there stood the proselytes beneath the
canopy of fire.

"Welcome, my children," said the dark figure, "to the communion of your
race. Ye have found thus young your nature and your destiny. My children, look behind you!"

They turned; and flashing forth, as it were, in a sheet of flame, the fiend
worshippers were seen; the smile of welcome gleamed darkly on every visage.

"There," resumed the sable form, "are all whom ye have reverenced from
youth. Ye deemed them holier than yourselves, and shrank from your own
sin, contrasting it with their lives of righteousness and prayerful aspirations
heavenward. Yet here are they all in my worshipping assembly. This night
it shall be granted you to know their secret deeds; how hoary-bearded elders
of the church have whispered wanton words to the young maids of their
households; how many a woman, eager for widows' weeds, has given her
husband a drink at bedtime and let him sleep his last sleep in her bosom;
how beardless youths have made haste to inherit their fathers' wealth; and
how fair damsels—blush not, sweet ones—have dug little graves in the garden,
and bidden me, the sole guest, to an infant's funeral. By the sympathy of
your human hearts for sin ye shall scent out all the places—whether in
church, bedchamber, street, field, or forest—where crime has been committed,
and shall exult to behold the whole earth one stain of guilt, one mighty blood-
spot. Far more than this. It shall be yours to penetrate, in every bosom, the
deep mystery of sin, the fountain of all wicked arts, and which inexhaustibly
supplies more evil impulses than human power—than my power at its utmost—can make manifest in deeds. And now, my children, look upon each
other."

They did so; and by the blaze of the hell-kindled torches, the wretched
man beheld his Faith, and the wife her husband, trembling before that unhallowed altar.

"Lo, there ye stand, my children," said the figure, in a deep and solemn
tone, almost sad with its despairing awfulness, as if his once angelic nature
could yet mourn for our miserable race. "Depending upon one another's
hearts, ye had still hoped that virtue were not all a dream. Now are ye
undeceived. Evil is the nature of mankind. Evil must be your only happiness. Welcome again, my children, to the communion of your race."

"Welcome," repeated the fiend worshippers, in one cry of despair and
triumph.

And there they stood, the only pair, as it seemed, who were yet hesitating
on the verge of wickedness in this dark world. A basin was hollowed, naturally, in the rock. Did it contain water, reddened by the lurid light? or was

it blood? or, perchance, a liquid flame? Herein did the shape of evil dip his hand and prepare to lay the mark of baptism upon their foreheads, that they might be partakers of the mystery of sin, more conscious of the secret guilt of others, both in deed and thought, than they could now be of their own. The husband cast one look at his pale wife, and Faith at him. What polluted wretches would the next glance show them to each other, shuddering alike at what they disclosed and what they saw!

"Faith! Faith!" cried the husband, "look up to Heaven, and resist the wicked one."

Whether Faith obeyed he knew not. Hardly had he spoken, when he found himself amid calm night and solitude, listening to a roar of the wind which died heavily away through the forest. He staggered against the rock, and felt it chill and damp; while a hanging twig, that had been all on fire, besprinkled his cheek with the coldest dew.

The next morning young Goodman Brown came slowly into the street of Salem village, staring around him like a bewildered man. The good old minister was taking a walk along the graveyard to get an appetite for breakfast and meditate his sermon, and bestowed a blessing, as he passed, on Goodman Brown. He shrank from the venerable saint as if to avoid an anathema. Old Deacon Gookin was at domestic worship, and the holy words of his prayer were heard through the open window. "What God doth the wizard pray to?" quoth Goodman Brown. Goody Cloyse, that excellent old Christian, stood in the early sunshine at her own lattice, catechising a little girl who had brought her a pint of morning's milk. Goodman Brown snatched away the child as from the grasp of the fiend himself. Turning the corner by the meeting-house, he spied the head of Faith, with the pink ribbons, gazing anxiously forth, and bursting into such joy at sight of him that she skipped along the street and almost kissed her husband before the whole village. But Goodman Brown looked sternly and sadly into her face, and passed on without a greeting.

Had Goodman Brown fallen asleep in the forest and only dreamed a wild dream of a witch-meeting?

Be it so if you will; but, alas! it was a dream of evil omen for young Goodman Brown. A stern, a sad, a darkly meditative, a distrustful, if not a desperate man did he become from the night of that fearful dream. On the Sabbath day, when the congregation were singing a holy psalm, he could not listen because an anthem of sin rushed loudly upon his ear and drowned all the blessed strain. When the minister spoke from the pulpit with power and fervid eloquence, and with his hand on the open Bible, of the sacred truths of our religion, and of saint-like lives and triumphant deaths, and of future bliss or misery unutterable, then did Goodman Brown turn pale, dreading lest the roof should thunder down upon the gray blasphemer and his hear-

ers. Often, awakening suddenly at midnight, he shrank from the bosom of
Faith; and at morning or eventide, when the family knelt down at prayer,
he scowled and muttered to himself, and gazed sternly at his wife, and turned
away. And when he had lived long, and was borne to his grave, a hoary
corpse, followed by Faith, an aged woman, and children and grandchildren,
a goodly procession, besides neighbors not a few, they carved no hopeful
verse upon his tombstone, for his dying hour was gloom.

ETHAN BRAND [9]

A Chapter from an Abortive Romance

Bartram the lime-burner, a rough, heavy-looking man, begrimed with
charcoal, sat watching his kiln at nightfall, while his little son played at
building houses with the scattered fragments of marble, when, on the hill-
side below them, they heard a roar of laughter, not mirthful, but slow, and
even solemn, like a wind shaking the boughs of the forest.

"Father, what is that?" asked the little boy, leaving his play, and pressing
betwixt his father's knees.

"Oh, some drunken man, I suppose," answered the lime-burner; "some
merry fellow from the bar-room in the village, who dared not laugh loud
enough within doors lest he should blow the roof of the house off. So here he
is, shaking his jolly sides at the foot of Graylock."

"But, father," said the child, more sensitive than the obtuse, middle-aged
clown, "he does not laugh like a man that is glad. So the noise frightens me!"

"Don't be a fool, child!" cried his father, gruffly. "You will never make a
man, I do believe; there is too much of your mother in you. I have known the
rustling of a leaf startle you. Hark! Here comes the merry fellow now. You
shall see that there is no harm in him."

Bartram and his little son, while they were talking thus, sat watching the
same lime-kiln that had been the scene of Ethan Brand's solitary and meditative life, before he began his search for the Unpardonable Sin. Many years,
as we have seen, had now elapsed, since that portentous night when the Idea
was first developed. The kiln, however, on the mountain-side, stood unimpaired, and was in nothing changed since he had thrown his dark thoughts
into the intense glow of its furnace, and melted them, as it were, into the
one thought that took possession of his life. It was a rude, round, tower-like
structure, about twenty feet high, heavily built of rough stones, and with a
hillock of earth heaped about the larger part of its circumference; so that the
blocks and fragments of marble might be drawn by cart-loads, and thrown
in at the top. There was an opening at the bottom of the tower, like an

[9] First published in the *Dollar Magazine*, 1851, and included in *The Snow Image, and
Other Twice-Told Tales* (1851).

oven-mouth, but large enough to admit a man in a stooping posture, and provided with a massive iron door. With the smoke and jets of flame issuing from the chinks and crevices of this door, which seemed to give admittance into the hill-side, it resembled nothing so much as the private entrance to the infernal regions, which the shepherds of the Delectable Mountains were accustomed to show to pilgrims.

There are many such lime-kilns in that tract of country, for the purpose of burning the white marble which composes a large part of the substance of the hills. Some of them, built years ago, and long deserted, with weeds growing in the vacant round of the interior, which is open to the sky, and grass and wild-flowers rooting themselves into the chinks of the stones, look already like relics of antiquity, and may yet be overspread with the lichens of centuries to come. Others, where the lime-burner still feeds his daily and night-long fire, afford points of interest to the wanderer among the hills, who seats himself on a log of wood or a fragment of marble, to hold a chat with the solitary man. It is a lonesome, and, when the character is inclined to thought, may be an intensely thoughtful occupation; as it proved in the case of Ethan Brand, who had mused to such strange purpose, in days gone by, while the fire in this very kiln was burning.

The man who now watched the fire was of a different order, and troubled himself with no thoughts save the very few that were requisite to his business. At frequent intervals, he flung back the clashing weight of the iron door, and, turning his face from the insufferable glare, thrust in huge logs of oak, or stirred the immense brands with a long pole. Within the furnace were seen the curling and riotous flames, and the burning marble, almost molten with the intensity of heat; while without, the reflection of the fire quivered on the dark intricacy of the surrounding forest, and showed in the foreground a bright and ruddy little picture of the hut, the spring beside its door, the athletic and coal-begrimed figure of the lime-burner, and the half-frightened child, shrinking into the protection of his father's shadow. And when, again, the iron door was closed, then reappeared the tender light of the half-full moon, which vainly strove to trace out the indistinct shapes of the neighboring mountains; and, in the upper sky, there was a flitting congregation of clouds, still faintly tinged with the rosy sunset, though thus far down into the valley the sunshine had vanished long and long ago.

The little boy now crept still closer to his father, as footsteps were heard ascending the hill-side, and a human form thrust aside the bushes that clustered beneath the trees.

"Halloo! who is it?" cried the lime-burner, vexed at his son's timidity, yet half infected by it. "Come forward, and show yourself, like a man, or I'll fling this chunk of marble at your head!"

"You offer me a rough welcome," said a gloomy voice, as the unknown man drew nigh. "Yet I neither claim nor desire a kinder one, even at my own fireside."

To obtain a distincter view, Bartram threw open the iron door of the kiln, whence immediately issued a gush of fierce light, that smote full upon the stranger's face and figure. To a careless eye there appeared nothing very remarkable in his aspect, which was that of a man in a coarse, brown, country-made suit of clothes, tall and thin, with the staff and heavy shoes of a way-farer. As he advanced, he fixed his eyes—which were very bright—intently upon the brightness of the furnace, as if he beheld, or expected to behold, some object worthy of note within it.

"Good evening, stranger," said the lime-burner; "whence come you, so late in the day?"

"I come from my search," answered the wayfarer; "for, at last, it is finished."

"Drunk!—or crazy!" muttered Bartram to himself. "I shall have trouble with the fellow. The sooner I drive him away, the better."

The little boy, all in a tremble, whispered to his father, and begged him to shut the door of the kiln, so that there might not be so much light; for that there was something in the man's face which he was afraid to look at, yet could not look away from. And, indeed, even the lime-burner's dull and torpid sense began to be impressed by an indescribable something in that thin, rugged, thoughtful visage, with the grizzled hair hanging wildly about it, and those deeply sunken eyes, which gleamed like fires within the entrance of a mysterious cavern. But, as he closed the door, the stranger turned towards him, and spoke in a quiet, familiar way, that made Bartram feel as if he were a sane and sensible man, after all.

"Your task draws to an end, I see," said he. "This marble has already been burning three days. A few hours more will convert the stone to lime."

"Why, who are you?" exclaimed the lime-burner. "You seem as well acquainted with my business as I am myself."

"And well I may be," said the stranger; "for I followed the same craft many a long year, and here, too, on this very spot. But you are a new-comer in these parts. Did you never hear of Ethan Brand?"

"The man that went in search of the Unpardonable Sin?" asked Bartram, with a laugh.

"The same," answered the stranger. "He has found what he sought, and therefore he comes back again."

"What! then you are Ethan Brand himself?" cried the lime-burner, in amazement. "I am a new-comer here, as you say, and they call it eighteen years since you left the foot of Graylock. But, I can tell you, the good folks still talk about Ethan Brand, in the village yonder, and what a strange errand took him away from his lime-kiln. Well, and so you have found the Unpardonable Sin?"

"Even so!" said the stranger, calmly.

"If the question is a fair one," proceeded Bartram, "where might it be?"

Ethan Brand laid his finger on his own heart.

"Here!" replied he.

And then, without mirth in his countenance, but as if moved by an involuntary recognition of the infinite absurdity of seeking throughout the world for what was the closest of all things to himself, and looking into every heart, save his own, for what was hidden in no other breast, he broke into a laugh of scorn. It was the same slow, heavy laugh, that had almost appalled the lime-burner when it heralded the wayfarer's approach.

The solitary mountain-side was made dismal by it. Laughter, when out of place, mistimed, or bursting forth from a disordered state of feeling, may be the most terrible modulation of the human voice. The laughter of one asleep, even if it be a little child,—the madman's laugh,—the wild, screaming laugh of a born idiot,—are sounds that we sometimes tremble to hear, and would always willingly forget. Poets have imagined no utterance of fiends or hobgoblins so fearfully appropriate as a laugh. And even the obtuse lime-burner felt his nerves shaken, as this strange man looked inward at his own heart, and burst into laughter that rolled away into the night, and was indistinctly reverberated among the hills.

"Joe," said he to his little son, "scamper down to the tavern in the village, and tell the jolly fellows there that Ethan Brand has come back, and that he has found the Unpardonable Sin!"

The boy darted away on his errand, to which Ethan Brand made no objection, nor seemed hardly to notice it. He sat on a log of wood, looking steadfastly at the iron door of the kiln. When the child was out of sight, and his swift and light footsteps ceased to be heard treading first on the fallen leaves and then on the rocky mountain-path, the lime-burner began to regret his departure. He felt that the little fellow's presence had been a barrier between his guest and himself, and that he must now deal, heart to heart, with a man who, on his own confession, had committed the one only crime for which Heaven could afford no mercy. That crime, in its indistinct blackness, seemed to overshadow him. The lime-burner's own sins rose up within him, and made his memory riotous with a throng of evil shapes that asserted their kindred with the Master Sin, whatever it might be, which it was within the scope of man's corrupted nature to conceive and cherish. They were all of one family; they went to and fro between his breast and Ethan Brand's, and carried dark greetings from one to the other.

Then Bartram remembered the stories which had grown traditionary in reference to this strange man, who had come upon him like a shadow of the night, and was making himself at home in his old place, after so long absence that the dead people, dead and buried for years, would have had more right to be at home, in any familiar spot, than he. Ethan Brand, it was said, had conversed with Satan himself in the lurid blaze of this very kiln. The legend had been matter of mirth heretofore, but looked grisly now. According to this tale, before Ethan Brand departed on his search, he had been accustomed to evoke a fiend from the hot furnace of the lime-kiln, night after night, in order to confer with him about the Unpardonable Sin; the man and the fiend each laboring to frame the image of some mode of guilt which could neither be atoned for nor forgiven. And, with the first gleam of light upon the moun-tain-top, the fiend crept in at the iron door, there to abide the intensest element of fire, until again summoned forth to share in the dreadful task of extending man's possible guilt beyond the scope of Heaven's else infinite mercy.

While the lime-burner was struggling with the horror of these thoughts, Ethan Brand rose from the log, and flung open the door of the kiln. The action was in such accordance with the idea in Bartram's mind, that he almost expected to see the Evil One issue forth, red-hot, from the raging furnace.

"Hold! hold!" cried he, with a tremulous attempt to laugh; for he was ashamed of his fears, although they overmastered him. "Don't, for mercy's sake, bring out your Devil now!"

"Man!" sternly replied Ethan Brand, "what need have I of the Devil? I have left him behind me, on my track. It is with such half-way sinners as you that he busies himself. Fear not, because I open the door. I do but act by old custom, and am going to trim your fire, like a lime-burner, as I was once."

He stirred the vast coals, thrust in more wood, and bent forward to gaze into the hollow prison-house of the fire, regardless of the fierce glow that reddened upon his face. The lime-burner sat watching him, and half sus-pected this strange guest of a purpose, if not to evoke a fiend, at least to plunge bodily into the flames, and thus vanish from the sight of man. Ethan Brand, however, drew quietly back, and closed the door of the kiln.

"I have looked," said he, "into many a human heart that was seven times hotter with sinful passions than yonder furnace is with fire. But I found not there what I sought. No, not the Unpardonable Sin!"

"What is the Unpardonable Sin?" asked the lime-burner; and then he shrank farther from his companion, trembling lest his question should be answered.

"It is a sin that grew within my own breast," replied Ethan Brand, standing erect, with a pride that distinguishes all enthusiasts of his stamp. "A sin that grew nowhere else! The sin of an intellect that triumphed over the sense of brotherhood with man and reverence for God, and sacrificed everything to its own mighty claims! The only sin that deserves a recompense of immortal agony! Freely, were it to do again, would I incur the guilt. Unshrinkingly I accept the retribution!"

"The man's head is turned," muttered the lime-burner to himself. "He may be a sinner like the rest of us,—nothing more likely,—but, I'll be sworn, he is a madman too."

Nevertheless, he felt uncomfortable at his situation, alone with Ethan Brand on the wild mountain-side, and was right glad to hear the rough murmur of tongues, and the footsteps of what seemed a pretty numerous party, stumbling over the stones and rustling through the underbrush. Soon appeared the whole lazy regiment that was wont to infest the village tavern, comprehending three or four individuals who had drunk flip beside the barroom fire through all the winters, and smoked their pipes beneath the stoop through all the summers, since Ethan Brand's departure. Laughing boisterously, and mingling all their voices together in unceremonious talk, they now burst into the moonshine and narrow streaks of firelight that illuminated the open space before the lime-kiln. Bartram set the door ajar again, flooding the spot with light, that the whole company might get a fair view of Ethan Brand, and he of them.

There, among other old acquaintances, was a once ubiquitous man, now almost extinct, but whom we were formerly sure to encounter at the hotel of every thriving village throughout the country. It was the stage-agent. The present specimen of the genus was a wilted and smoke-dried man, wrinkled and red-nosed, in a smartly cut, brown, bob-tailed coat, with brass buttons, who, for a length of time unknown, had kept his desk and corner in the barroom, and was still puffing what seemed to be the same cigar that he had lighted twenty years before. He had great fame as a dry joker, though, perhaps, less on account of any intrinsic humor than from a certain flavor of brandy-toddy and tobacco-smoke, which impregnated all his ideas and expressions, as well as his person. Another well-remembered, though strangely altered, face was that of Lawyer Giles, as people still called him in courtesy; an elderly ragamuffin, in his soiled shirt-sleeves and tow-cloth trousers. This poor fellow had been an attorney, in what he called his better days, a sharp practitioner, and in great vogue among the village litigants; but flip, and sling, and toddy, and cocktails, imbibed at all hours, morning, noon, and night, had caused him to slide from intellectual to various kinds and degrees of bodily labor, till at last, to adopt his own phrase, he slid into a soap-vat. In other words, Giles was now a soap-boiler, in a small way. He had come to be but the fragment of a human being, a part of one foot having been chopped off by an axe, and an entire hand torn away by the devilish grip of a steam-engine. Yet, though the corporeal hand was gone, a spiritual member remained; for, stretching forth the stump, Giles steadfastly averred that he felt an invisible thumb and fingers with as vivid a sensation as before the real ones were amputated. A maimed and miserable wretch he was; but one, nevertheless, whom the world could not trample on, and had no right to scorn, either in this or any previous stage of his misfortunes, since he had still kept up the courage and spirit of a man, asked nothing in charity, and with his one hand—and that the left one—fought a stern battle against want and hostile circumstances.

Among the throng, too, came another personage, who, with certain points of similarity to Lawyer Giles, had many more of difference. It was the village doctor; a man of some fifty years, whom, at an earlier period of his life, we introduced as paying a professional visit to Ethan Brand during the latter's supposed insanity. He was now a purple-visaged, rude, and brutal, yet half-gentlemanly figure, with something wild, ruined, and desperate in his talk, and in all the details of his gesture and manners. Brandy possessed this man like an evil spirit, and made him as surly and savage as a wild beast, and as miserable as a lost soul; but there was supposed to be in him such wonderful skill, such native gifts of healing, beyond any which medical science could impart, that society caught hold of him, and would not let him sink out of its reach. So, swaying to and fro upon his horse, and grumbling thick accents at the bedside, he visited all the sick-chambers for miles about among the mountain towns, and sometimes raised a dying man, as it were, by miracle, or quite as often, no doubt, sent his patient to a grave that was dug many a year too soon. The doctor had an everlasting pipe in his mouth, and, as somebody said, in allusion to his habit of swearing, it was always alight with hell-fire.

These three worthies pressed forward, and greeted Ethan Brand each after his own fashion, earnestly inviting him to partake of the contents of a certain black bottle, in which, as they averred, he would find something far better worth seeking for than the Unpardonable Sin. No mind, which has wrought itself by intense and solitary meditation into a high state of enthusiasm, can endure the kind of contact with low and vulgar modes of thought and feeling to which Ethan Brand was now subjected. It made him doubt—and, strange to say, it was a painful doubt—whether he had indeed found the Unpardonable Sin and found it within himself. The whole question on which he had exhausted life, and more than life, looked like a delusion.

"Leave me," he said bitterly, "ye brute beasts, that have made yourselves so, shrivelling up your souls with fiery liquors! I have done with you. Years and years ago, I groped into your hearts and found nothing there for my purpose. Get ye gone!"

"Why, you uncivil scoundrel," cried the fierce doctor, "is that the way you respond to the kindness of your best friends? Then let me tell you the truth. You have no more found the Unpardonable Sin than yonder boy Joe has. You are but a crazy fellow,—I told you so twenty years ago,—neither better nor worse than a crazy fellow, and the fit companion of old Humphrey, here!"

He pointed to an old man, shabbily dressed, with long white hair, thin visage, and unsteady eyes. For some years past this aged person had been wandering about among the hills, inquiring of all travellers whom he met for his daughter. The girl, it seemed, had gone off with a company of circus-performers; and occasionally tidings of her came to the village, and fine stories were told of her glittering appearance as she rode on horseback in the ring, or performed marvellous feats on the tight-rope.

The white-haired father now approached Ethan Brand, and gazed unsteadily into his face.

"They tell me you have been all over the earth," said he, wringing his hands with earnestness. "You must have seen my daughter, for she makes a grand figure in the world, and everybody goes to see her. Did she send any word to her old father, or say when she was coming back?"

Ethan Brand's eye quailed beneath the old man's. That daughter, from whom he so earnestly desired a word of greeting, was the Esther of our tale, the very girl whom, with such cold and remorseless purpose, Ethan Brand had made the subject of a psychological experiment, and wasted, absorbed, and perhaps annihilated her soul, in the process.

"Yes," murmured he, turning away from the hoary wanderer, "it is no delusion. There is an Unpardonable Sin!"

While these things were passing, a merry scene was going forward in the area of cheerful light, beside the spring and before the door of the hut. A number of the youth of the village, young men and girls, had hurried up the hill-side, impelled by curiosity to see Ethan Brand, the hero of so many a legend familiar to their childhood. Finding nothing, however, very remarkable in his aspect,—nothing but a sunburnt wayfarer, in plain garb and dusty shoes, who sat looking into the fire as if he fancied pictures among the coals,—these young people speedily grew tired of observing him. As it happened, there was other amusement at hand. An old German Jew, travelling with a diorama on his back, was passing down the mountain-road towards the village just as the party turned aside from it, and, in hopes of eking out the profits of the day, the showman had kept them company to the lime-kiln.

"Come, old Dutchman," cried one of the young men, "let us see your pictures, if you can swear they are worth looking at!"

"Oh yes, Captain," answered the Jew,—whether as a matter of courtesy or craft, he styled everybody Captain,—"I shall show you, indeed, some very superb pictures!"

So, placing his box in a proper position, he invited the young men and girls to look through the glass orifices of the machine, and proceeded to exhibit a series of the most outrageous scratchings and daubings, as specimens of the fine arts, that ever an itinerant showman had the face to impose upon his circle of spectators. The pictures were worn out, moreover, tattered, full of cracks and wrinkles, dingy with tobacco-smoke, and otherwise in a most pitiable condition. Some purported to be cities, public edifices, and ruined castles in Europe; others represented Napoleon's battles and Nelson's sea-fights; and in the midst of these would be seen a gigantic, brown, hairy hand, —which might have been mistaken for the Hand of Destiny, though, in truth, it was only the showman's,—pointing its forefinger to various scenes of the conflict, while its owner gave historical illustrations. When, with much merriment at its abominable deficiency of merit, the exhibition was concluded, the German bade little Joe put his head into the box. Viewed through the magnifying-glasses, the boy's round, rosy visage assumed the strangest im-aginable aspect of an immense Titanic child, the mouth grinning broadly, and the eyes and every other feature overflowing with fun at the joke. Sud-denly, however, that merry face turned pale, and its expression changed to horror, for this easily impressed and excitable child had become sensible that the eye of Ethan Brand was fixed upon him through the glass.

"You make the little man to be afraid, Captain," said the German Jew, turning up the dark and strong outline of his visage, from his stooping pos-ture. "But look again, and, by chance, I shall cause you to see somewhat that is very fine, upon my word!"

Ethan Brand gazed into the box for an instant, and then starting back, looked fixedly at the German. What had he seen? Nothing, apparently; for a curious youth, who had peeped in almost at the same moment, beheld only a vacant space of canvas.

"I remember you now," muttered Ethan Brand to the showman.

"Ah, Captain," whispered the Jew of Nuremberg, with a dark smile, "I find it to be a heavy matter in my show-box,—this Unpardonable Sin! By my faith, Captain, it has wearied my shoulders, this long day, to carry it over the mountain."

"Peace," answered Ethan Brand, sternly, "or get thee into the furnace yon-der!"

The Jew's exhibition had scarcely concluded, when a great, elderly dog—who seemed to be his own master, as no person in the company laid claim to him—saw fit to render himself the object of public notice. Hitherto, he had shown himself a very quiet, well-disposed old dog, going round from one to another, and, by way of being sociable, offering his rough head to be patted by any kindly hand that would take so much trouble. But now, all of a sudden, this grave and venerable quadruped, of his own mere motion, and without the slightest suggestion from anybody else, began to run round after his tail, which, to heighten the absurdity of the proceeding, was a great deal shorter than it should have been. Never was seen such headlong eagerness in pursuit of an object that could not possibly be attained; never was heard such a tremendous outbreak of growling, snarling, barking, and snapping,—as if one end of the ridiculous brute's body were at deadly and most unforgivable enmity with the other. Faster and faster, round about went the cur; and faster and still faster fled the unapproachable brevity of his tail; and louder and fiercer grew his yells of rage and animosity; until, utterly exhausted, and as far from the goal as ever, the foolish old dog ceased his performance as suddenly as he had begun it. The next moment he was as mild, quiet, sensible, and respectable in his deportment, as when he first scraped acquaintance with the company.

As may be supposed, the exhibition was greeted with universal laughter, clapping of hands, and shouts of encore, to which the canine performer responded by wagging all that there was to wag of his tail, but appeared totally unable to repeat his very successful effort to amuse the spectators.

Meanwhile, Ethan Brand had resumed his seat upon the log, and moved, it might be, by a perception of some remote analogy between his own case and that of this self-pursuing cur, he broke into the awful laugh, which, more than any other token, expressed the condition of his inward being. From that moment, the merriment of the party was at an end; they stood aghast, dreading lest the inauspicious sound should be reverberated around the horizon, and that mountain would thunder it to mountain, and so the horror be prolonged upon their ears. Then, whispering one to another that it was late,—that the moon was almost down,—that the August night was growing chill,—they hurried homewards, leaving the lime-burner and little Joe to deal as they might with their unwelcome guest. Save for these three human beings, the open space on the hill-side was a solitude, set in a vast gloom of forest. Beyond that darksome verge, the firelight glimmered on the stately trunks and almost black foliage of pines, intermixed with the lighter verdure of sapling oaks, maples, and poplars, while here and there lay the gigantic corpses of dead trees, decaying on the leaf-strewn soil. And it seemed to little Joe—a timorous and imaginative child—that the silent forest was holding its breath until some fearful thing should happen.

Ethan Brand thrust more wood into the fire, and closed the door of the kiln; then looking over his shoulder at the lime-burner and his son, he bade, rather than advised, them to retire to rest.

"For myself, I cannot sleep," said he. "I have matters that it concerns me to meditate upon. I will watch the fire, as I used to do in the old time."

"And call the Devil out of the furnace to keep you company, I suppose," muttered Bartram, who had been making intimate acquaintance with the black bottle above mentioned. "But watch, if you like, and call as many devils as you like! For my part, I shall be all the better for a snooze. Come, Joe!"

As the boy followed his father into the hut, he looked back at the wayfarer, and the tears came into his eyes, for his tender spirit had an intuition of the bleak and terrible loneliness in which this man had enveloped himself.

When they had gone, Ethan Brand sat listening to the crackling of the kindled wood, and looking at the little spirts of fire that issued through the chinks of the door. These trifles, however, once so familiar, had but the slightest hold of his attention, while deep within his mind he was reviewing the gradual but marvellous change that had been wrought upon him by the search to which he had devoted himself. He remembered how the night dew had fallen upon him,—how the dark forest had whispered to him,—how the stars had gleamed upon him,—a simple and loving man, watching his fire in the years gone by, and ever musing as it burned. He remembered with what tenderness, with what love and sympathy for mankind, and what pity for human guilt and woe, he had first begun to contemplate those ideas which afterwards became the inspiration of his life; with what reverence he had then looked into the heart of man, viewing it as a temple originally divine, and, however desecrated, still to be held sacred by a brother; with what awful fear he had deprecated the success of his pursuit, and prayed that the Unpardonable Sin might never be revealed to him. Then ensued that vast intellectual development, which, in its progress, disturbed the counterpoise between his mind and heart. The Idea that possessed his life had operated as a means of education; it had gone on cultivating his powers to the highest point of which they were susceptible; it had raised him from the level of an unlettered laborer to stand on a star-lit eminence, whither the philosophers of the earth, laden with the lore of universities, might vainly strive to clamber after him. So much for the intellect! But where was the heart? That, indeed, had withered,—had contracted,—had hardened,—had perished! It had ceased to partake of the universal throb. He had lost his hold of the magnetic chain of humanity. He was no longer a brother-man, opening the chambers of the dungeons of our common nature by the key of holy sympathy, which gave him a right to share in all its secrets; he was now a cold observer, looking on mankind as the subject of his experiment, and, at length, converting man and woman to be his puppets, and pulling the wires that moved them to such degrees of crime as were demanded for his study.

Thus Ethan Brand became a fiend. He began to be so from the moment that his moral nature had ceased to keep the pace of improvement with his intellect. And now, as his highest effort and inevitable development,—as the bright and gorgeous flower, and rich, delicious fruit of his life's labor,—he had produced the Unpardonable Sin!

"What more have I to seek? what more to achieve?" said Ethan Brand to himself. "My task is done, and well done!"

Starting from the log with a certain alacrity in his gait and ascending the hillock of earth that was raised against the stone circumference of the lime-kiln, he thus reached the top of the structure. It was a space of perhaps ten feet across, from edge to edge, presenting a view of the upper surface of the immense mass of broken marble with which the kiln was heaped. All these innumerable blocks and fragments of marble were red-hot and vividly on fire, sending up great spouts of blue flame, which quivered aloft and danced madly, as within a magic circle, and sank and rose again, with continual and multitudinous activity. As the lonely man bent forward over this terrible body of fire, the blasting heat smote up against his person with a breath that, it might be supposed, would have scorched and shrivelled him up in a moment.

Ethan Brand stood erect, and raised his arms on high. The blue flames played upon his face, and imparted the wild and ghastly light which alone could have suited its expression; it was that of a fiend on the verge of plunging into his gulf of intensest torment.

"O Mother Earth," cried he, "who art no more my Mother, and into whose bosom this frame shall never be resolved! O mankind, whose brotherhood I have cast off, and trampled thy great heart beneath my feet! O stars of heaven, that shone on me of old, as if to light me onward and upward!— farewell all, and forever. Come, deadly element of Fire,—henceforth my familiar friend! Embrace me, as I do thee!"

That night the sound of a fearful peal of laughter rolled heavily through the sleep of the lime-burner and his little son; dim shapes of horror and anguish haunted their dreams, and seemed still present in the rude hovel, when they opened their eyes to the daylight.

"Up, boy, up!" cried the lime-burner, staring about him. "Thank Heaven, the night is gone, at last; and rather than pass such another, I would watch my lime-kiln, wide awake, for a twelvemonth. This Ethan Brand, with his humbug of an Unpardonable Sin, has done me no such mighty favor, in taking my place!"

He issued from the hut, followed by little Joe, who kept fast hold of his father's hand. The early sunshine was already pouring its gold upon the mountain-tops, and though the valleys were still in shadow, they smiled cheerfully in the promise of the bright day that was hastening onward. The village, completely shut in by hills, which swelled away gently about it, looked as if it had rested peacefully in the hollow of the great hand of Providence. Every dwelling was distinctly visible; the little spires of the two churches pointed upwards, and caught a foreglimmering of brightness from the sun-gilt skies upon their gilded weathercocks. The tavern was astir, and the figure of the old, smoke-dried stage-agent, cigar in mouth, was seen beneath the stoop. Old Graylock was glorified with a golden cloud upon his head. Scattered likewise over the breasts of the surrounding mountains, there were heaps of hoary mist, in fantastic shapes, some of them far down into the valley, others high up towards the summits, and still others, of the same family of mist or cloud, hovering in the gold radiance of the upper atmosphere.

Stepping from one to another of the clouds that rested on the hills, and thence to the loftier brotherhood that sailed in air, it seemed almost as if a mortal man might thus ascend into the heavenly regions. Earth was so mingled with sky that it was a day-dream to look at it.

To supply that charm of the familiar and homely, which Nature so readily adopts into a scene like this, the stage-coach was rattling down the mountain-road, and the driver sounded his horn, while Echo caught up the notes, and intertwined them into a rich and varied and elaborate harmony, of which the original performer could lay claim to little share. The great hills played a concert among themselves, each contributing a strain of airy sweetness.

Little Joe's face brightened at once.

"Dear father," cried he, skipping cheerily to and fro, "that strange man is gone, and the sky and the mountains all seem glad of it!"

"Yes," growled the lime-burner, with an oath, "but he has let the fire go down, and no thanks to him if five hundred bushels of lime are not spoiled. If I catch the fellow hereabouts again, I shall feel like tossing him into the furnace!"

With his long pole in his hand, he ascended to the top of the kiln. After a moment's pause, he called to his son.

"Come up here, Joe!" said he.

So little Joe ran up the hillock, and stood by his father's side. The marble was all burnt into perfect, snow-white lime. But on its surface, in the midst of the circle,—snow-white too, and thoroughly converted into lime,—lay a human skeleton, in the attitude of a person who, after long toil, lies down to long repose. Within the ribs—strange to say—was the shape of a human heart.

"Was the fellow's heart made of marble?" cried Bartram, in some perplexity at this phenomenon. "At any rate, it is burnt into what looks like special good lime; and taking all the bones together, my kiln is half a bushel the richer for him."

So saying, the rude lime-burner lifted his pole, and, letting it fall upon the skeleton, the relics of Ethan Brand were crumbled into fragments.

EDGAR ALLAN POE

(1809–1849)

Edgar Poe was born in Boston in 1809, of actor parents. His father, who came of a Baltimore family, and his mother, an Englishwoman, died before he was three years old; and he was taken to be reared by John Allan, a Richmond merchant. He attended private schools in England (1815–20), whither Allan had gone on business, and in Richmond; and in 1826 entered the University of Virginia. During his one year there he showed himself a good student, but incurred large gambling and other debts, the former of which Allan refused to pay. This led to a rupture between the two and to Poe's departure for Boston, where he enlisted in the army, in which he served for more than two years. In 1830 he secured a cadetship at West Point, but tiring of army life, deliberately infringed rules, which brought about his dismissal in the spring of 1831. He now settled in Baltimore as man of letters, living in dire poverty and without recognition until 1835, when he secured a post in Richmond with *The Southern Literary Messenger,* of which he soon became editor. In the years following, he alternated between periods of brilliant literary production and of neglect of business duties, the latter leading to the loss of one position after another and to Poe's fluctuating between Richmond, New York, and Philadelphia in search of work. In 1836 he married his thirteen-year-old cousin, Virginia Clemm, who died in 1847, after an illness beginning six years earlier. Following her death his mental irresponsibilities increased, although he continued writing and produced some of his best work. He died in Baltimore in 1849.

Poe published his first volume of verse, *Tamerlane,* when he was eighteen, and followed this during the next four years with two other volumes, without winning wide recognition as a poet. He wrote the first of his prose tales in 1832, and began as a literary critic in 1835. His power of ratiocination enabled him to create Legrand and Dupin, characters from which grew the detective of modern fiction. With such poems as *The Raven* and *The Bells* he won wide popular acclaim, and although taken as a whole his prose perhaps outranks his poetry, it is probably as a poet that he is best known. He had keen perception as a literary critic, but it is as a master of the short story form and as a melodist in poetry that his fame is most secure.

THE ASSIGNATION [1]

> Stay for me there! I will not fail
> To meet thee in that hollow vale.
> HENRY KING, BISHOP OF CHICHESTER: *The Exequy.*

ILL-FATED and mysterious man! bewildered in the brilliancy of thine own imagination, and fallen in the flames of thine own youth! Again in fancy I behold thee! Once more thy form hath risen before me!—not—oh, not as thou art—in the cold valley and shadow—but as thou *shouldst be*—squander-

[1] First published in *Godey's Lady's Book,* January, 1834, and included in *Tales of the Grotesque and Arabesque* (1840).

ing away a life of magnificent meditation in that city of dim visions, thine own Venice—which is a star-beloved Elysium of the sea, and the wide windows of whose Palladian palaces look down with a deep and bitter meaning upon the secrets of her silent waters. Yes! I repeat it—as thou *shouldst be.* There are surely other worlds than this: other thoughts than the thoughts of the multitude, other speculations than the speculations of the sophist. Who then shall call thy conduct into question? who blame thee for thy visionary hours, or denounce those occupations as a wasting away of life, which were but the overflowings of thine everlasting energies?

It was at Venice, beneath the covered archway there called the *Ponte di Sospiri,* that I met for the third or fourth time the person of whom I speak. It is with a confused recollection that I bring to mind the circumstances of that meeting. Yet I remember—ah! how should I forget?—the deep midnight, the Bridge of Sighs, the beauty of woman, and the Genius of Romance that stalked up and down the narrow canal.

It was a night of unusual gloom. The great clock of the Piazza had sounded the fifth hour of the Italian evening. The square of the Campanile lay silent and deserted, and the lights in the old Ducal Palace were dying fast away. I was returning home from the Piazzetta, by way of the Grand Canal. But as my gondola arrived opposite the mouth of the canal San Marco, a female voice from its recesses broke suddenly upon the night, in one wild, hysterical, and long-continued shriek. Startled at the sound, I sprang upon my feet, while the gondolier, letting slip his single oar, lost it in the pitchy darkness beyond a chance of recovery, and we were consequently left to the guidance of the current which here sets from the greater into the smaller channel. Like some huge and sable-feathered condor, we were slowly drifting down towards the Bridge of Sighs, when a thousand flambeaus flashing from the windows, and down the staircases, of the Ducal Palace, turned all at once that deep gloom into a livid and preternatural day.

A child, slipping from the arms of its own mother, had fallen from an upper window of the lofty structure into the deep and dim canal. The quiet waters had closed placidly over their victim; and, although my own gondola was the only one in sight, many a stout swimmer, already in the stream, was seeking in vain upon the surface the treasure which was to be found, alas! only within the abyss. Upon the broad black marble flagstones at the entrance of the palace, and a few steps above the water, stood a figure which none who then saw can have ever since forgotten. It was the Marchesa Aphrodite—the adoration of all Venice—the gayest of the gay—the most lovely where all were beautiful—but still the young wife of the old and intriguing Mentoni, and the mother of that fair child, her first and only one, who now, deep beneath the murky water, was thinking in bitterness of heart upon her sweet caresses, and exhausting its little life in struggles to call upon her name.

She stood alone. Her small, bare, and silvery feet gleamed in the black mirror of marble beneath her. Her hair, not as yet more than half loosened for the night from its ball-room array, clustered, amid a shower of diamonds, round and round her classical head, in curls like those of the young hyacinth. A snowy-white and gauze-like drapery seemed to be nearly the sole covering to her delicate form; but the midsummer and midnight air was hot, sullen, and still, and no motion in the statue-like form itself stirred even the folds of that raiment of very vapor which hung around it as the heavy marble hangs around the Niobe. Yet, strange to say, her large lustrous eyes were not turned downwards upon that grave wherein her brightest hope lay buried—but riveted in a widely different direction! The prison of the Old Republic, is, I think, the stateliest building in all Venice, but how could that lady gaze so fixedly upon it, when beneath her lay stifling her only child? Yon dark, gloomy niche, too, yawns right opposite her chamber window—what, then, *could* there be in its shadows, in its architecture, in its ivy-wreathed and solemn cornices, that the Marchesa di Mentoni had not wondered at a thousand times before? Nonsense! Who does not remember that, at such a time as this, the eye, like a shattered mirror, multiplies the images of its sorrow, and sees in innumerable far-off places the woe which is close at hand?

Many steps above the Marchesa, and within the arch of the water-gate, stood, in full dress, the satyr-like figure of Mentoni himself. He was occasionally occupied in thrumming a guitar, and seemed *ennuyé* to the very death as at intervals he gave directions for the recovery of his child. Stupefied and aghast, I had myself no power to move from the upright position I had assumed upon first hearing the shriek, and must have presented to the eyes of the agitated group a spectral and ominous appearance, as with pale countenance and rigid limbs I floated down among them in that funereal gondola.

All efforts proved in vain. Many of the most energetic in the search were relaxing their exertions, and yielding to a gloomy sorrow. There seemed but little hope for the child (how much less then for the mother!); but now, from the interior of that dark niche which has been already mentioned as forming a part of the Old Republican prison, and as fronting the lattice of the Marchesa, a figure muffled in a cloak stepped out within reach of the light, and, pausing a moment upon the verge of the giddy descent, plunged headlong into the canal. As in an instant afterwards he stood, with the still living and breathing child within his grasp, upon the marble flagstones by the side of the Marchesa, his cloak, heavy with the drenching water, became unfastened, and, falling in folds about his feet, discovered to the wonder-stricken spectators the graceful person of a very young man, with the sound of whose name the greater part of Europe was then ringing.

No word spoke the deliverer. But the Marchesa! She will now receive her child—she will press it to her heart—she will cling to its little form, and smother it with her caresses. Alas! *another's* arms have taken it from the stranger—*another's* arms have taken it away and borne it afar off, unnoticed, into the palace! And the Marchesa! Her lip—her beautiful lip trembles; tears are gathering in her eyes—those eyes which, like Pliny's acanthus, are "soft and almost liquid." Yes, tears are gathering in those eyes—and see! the entire woman thrills throughout the soul, and the statue has started into life! The pallor of the marble countenance, the swelling of the marble bosom, the very purity of the marble feet, we behold suddenly flushed over with a tide of ungovernable crimson; and a slight shudder quivers about her delicate frame, as a gentle air at Napoli about the rich silver lilies in the grass.

Why *should* that lady blush? To this demand there is no answer—except that, having left, in the eager haste and terror of a mother's heart, the privacy of her own boudoir, she has neglected to enthrall her tiny feet in their slippers, and utterly forgotten to throw over her Venetian shoulders that drapery which is their due. What other possible reason could there have been for her so blushing?—for the glance of those wild appealing eyes? for the unusual tumult of that throbbing bosom? for the convulsive pressure of that trembling hand—that hand which fell, as Mentoni turned into the palace, accidentally upon the hand of the stranger? What reason could there have been for the low—singularly low tone of those unmeaning words which the lady uttered hurriedly in bidding him adieu? "Thou hast conquered," she said, or the murmurs of the water deceived me; "thou hast conquered—one hour after sunrise—we shall meet—so let it be!"

. . . .

The tumult had subsided, the lights had died away within the palace, and the stranger, whom I now recognized, stood alone upon the flags. He shook with inconceivable agitation, and his eye glanced around in search of a gondola. I could not do less than offer him the service of my own; and he accepted the civility. Having obtained an oar at the water-gate, we proceeded together to his residence, while he rapidly recovered his self-possession, and spoke of our former slight acquaintance in terms of great apparent cordiality.

There are some subjects upon which I take pleasure in being minute. The person of the stranger—let me call him by this title, who to all the world was still a stranger—the person of the stranger is one of these subjects. In height he might have been below rather than above the medium size; although there were moments of intense passion when his frame actually *expanded* and belied the assertion. The light, almost slender, symmetry of his figure promised more of that ready activity which he evinced at the Bridge of Sighs, than of that Herculean strength which he has been known to wield without an effort, upon occasions of more dangerous emergency. With the mouth and chin of a deity—singular, wild, full, liquid eyes, whose shadows varied from pure hazel to intense and brilliant jet—and a profusion of curling, black hair, from which a forehead of unusual breadth gleamed forth at intervals all light and ivory—his were features than which I have seen none more classically regular, except, perhaps, the marble ones of the Emperor Commodus. Yet his countenance was, nevertheless, one of those which all men have seen at some period of their lives, and have never afterwards seen again. It had no peculiar—it had no settled predominant expression to be fastened upon the memory; a countenance seen and instantly forgotten, but forgotten with a vague and never-ceasing desire of recalling it to mind. Not that the spirit of each rapid passion failed, at any time, to throw its own distinct image upon the mirror of that face; but that the mirror, mirror-like, retained no vestige of the passion, when the passion had departed.

Upon leaving him on the night of our adventure, he solicited me, in what I thought an urgent manner, to call upon him *very* early the next morning. Shortly after sunrise I found myself accordingly at his Palazzo, one of those huge structures of gloomy, yet fantastic pomp, which tower above the waters of the Grand Canal in the vicinity of the Rialto. I was shown up a broad winding staircase of mosaics into an apartment whose unparalleled splendor burst through the opening door with an actual glare, making me blind and dizzy with luxuriousness.

I knew my acquaintance to be wealthy. Report had spoken of his possessions in terms which I had even ventured to call terms of ridiculous exaggeration. But as I gazed about me, I could not bring myself to believe that the wealth of any subject in Europe could have supplied the princely magnificence which burned and blazed around.

Although, as I say, the sun had arisen, yet the room was still brilliantly lighted up. I judged from this circumstance, as well as from an air of exhaustion in the countenance of my friend, that he had not retired to bed during the whole of the preceding night. In the architecture and embellishments of the chamber the evident design had been to dazzle and astound. Little attention had been paid to the *decora* of what is technically called *keeping,* or to the proprieties of nationality. The eye wandered from object to object, and rested upon none—neither the grotesques of the Greek painters, nor the sculptures of the best Italian days, nor the huge carvings of untutored Egypt. Rich draperies in every part of the room trembled to the vibration of low, melancholy music, whose origin was not to be discovered. The senses were oppressed by mingled and conflicting perfumes, reeking up from strange convolute censers, together with multitudinous flaring and flickering tongues of emerald and violet fire. The rays of the newly risen sun poured in upon the whole, through windows, formed each of a single pane of crimson-tinted glass. Glancing to and fro in a thousand reflections, from curtains which rolled from their cornices like cataracts of molten silver, the beams of natural glory mingled at length fitfully with the artificial light, and lay weltering in subdued masses upon a carpet of rich, liquid-looking cloth of Chili gold.

"Ha! ha! ha!—ha! ha! ha!"—laughed the proprietor, motioning me to a seat as I entered the room, and throwing himself back at full length upon an ottoman. "I see," said he, perceiving that I could not immediately reconcile myself to the *bienséance* of so singular a welcome—"I see you are astonished at my apartment—at my statues—my pictures—my originality of conception in architecture and upholstery! absolutely drunk, eh, with my magnificence? But pardon me, my dear sir" (here his tone of voice dropped to the very spirit of cordiality), "pardon me for my uncharitable laughter. You appeared so *utterly* astonished. Besides, some things are so completely ludicrous that a man *must* laugh, or die. To die laughing must be the most glorious of all glorious deaths! Sir Thomas More—a very fine man was Sir Thomas More—Sir Thomas More died laughing, you remember. Also in the *Absurdities* of Ravisius Textor there is a long list of characters who came to the same magnificent end. Do you know, however," continued he, musingly, "that at Sparta—which is now Palæochori—at Sparta, I say, to the west of the citadel, among a chaos of scarcely visible ruins, is a kind of *socle* upon which are still legible the letters ΛΑΣΜ. They are undoubtedly part of ΓΕΛΑΣΜΑ. Now, at Sparta were a thousand temples and shrines to a thousand different divinities. How exceedingy strange that the altar of Laughter should have survived all the others! But in the present instance," he resumed, with a singular alteration of voice and manner, "I have no right to be merry at your expense. You might well have been amazed. Europe cannot produce anything so fine as this, my little regal cabinet. My other apartments are by no means of the same order—mere *ultras* of fashionable insipidity. This is better than fashion, is it not? Yet this has but to be seen to become the rage—that is, with those who could afford it at the cost of their entire patrimony. I have guarded, however, against any such profanation. With one exception you are the only human being, besides myself and my valet, who has been admitted within the mysteries of these imperial precincts, since they have been bedizened as you see!"

I bowed in acknowledgment: for the overpowering sense of splendor and perfume and music, together with the unexpected eccentricity of his address and manner, prevented me from expressing, in words, my appreciation of what I might have construed into a compliment.

"Here," he resumed, arising and leaning on my arm as he sauntered around the apartment,—"here are paintings from the Greeks to Cimabue, and from Cimabue to the present hour. Many are chosen, as you see, with little deference to the opinions of Virtu. They are all, however, fitting tapestry for a chamber such as this. Here, too, are some *chefs d'œuvre* of the unknown great; and here, unfinished designs by men, celebrated in their day, whose very names the perspicacity of the academies has left to silence and to me. What think you," said he, turning abruptly as he spoke—"what think you of this Madonna della Pietà?"

"It is Guido's own!" I said, with all the enthusiasm of my nature, for I had been poring intently over its surpassing loveliness. "It is Guido's own!—how *could* you have obtained it? she is undoubtedly in painting what the Venus is in sculpture."

"Ha!" said he, thoughtfully, "the Venus—the beautiful Venus?—the Venus of the Medici?—she of the diminutive head and the gilded hair? Part of the left arm," (here his voice dropped so as to be heard with difficulty) "and all the right, are restorations; and in the coquetry of that right arm lies, I think, the quintessence of all affectation. Give *me* the Canova! The Apollo, too, is a copy—there can be no doubt of it—blind fool that I am, who cannot behold the boasted inspiration of the Apollo! I cannot help—pity me!—I cannot help preferring the Antinous. Was it not Socrates who said that the statuary found his statue in the block of marble? Then Michel Angelo was by no means original in his couplet—

> 'Non ha l'ottimo artista alcun concetto
> Chè un marmo solo in se non circonscriva.' "

It has been or should be remarked that, in the manner of the true gentleman, we are always aware of a difference from the bearing of the vulgar, without being at once precisely able to determine in what such difference consists. Allowing the remark to have applied in its full force to the outward demeanor of my acquaintance, I felt it, on that eventful morning, still more fully applicable to his moral temperament and character. Nor can I better define that peculiarity of spirit which seemed to place him so essentially apart from all other human beings, than by calling it a *habit* of intense and continual thought, pervading even his most trivial actions, intruding upon his moments of dalliance, and interweaving itself with his very flashes of merriment, like adders which writhe from out the eyes of the grinning masks in the cornices around the temples of Persepolis.

I could not help, however, repeatedly observing, through the mingled tone of levity and solemnity with which he rapidly descanted upon matters of little importance, a certain air of trepidation—a degree of nervous *unction* in action and in speech—an unquiet excitability of manner which appeared to me at all times unaccountable, and upon some occasions even filled me with alarm. Frequently, too, pausing in the middle of a sentence whose commencement he had apparently forgotten, he seemed to be listening in the deepest attention, as if either in momentary expectation of a visitor, or to sounds which must have had existence in his imagination alone.

It was during one of these reveries or pauses of apparent abstraction, that, in turning over a page of the poet and scholar Politian's beautiful tragedy, the *Orfeo* (the first native Italian tragedy), which lay near me upon an ottoman,· I discovered a passage underlined in pencil. It was a passage towards the end of the third act—a passage of the most heart-stirring excitement— a passage which, although tainted with impurity, no man shall read without a thrill of novel emotion, no woman without a sigh. The whole page was blotted with fresh tears; and upon the opposite interleaf were the following English lines, written in a hand so very different from the peculiar characters of my acquaintance that I had some difficulty in recognizing it as his own:—

> Thou wast all that to me, love,
>   For which my soul did pine:
> A green isle in the sea, love,
>   A fountain and a shrine
> All wreathed with fairy fruits and flowers,
>   And all the flowers were mine.
>
> Ah, dream too bright to last!
>   Ah, starry Hope, that didst arise
> But to be overcast!
>   A voice from out the Future cries,
> "On! On!"—but o'er the Past
>   (Dim gulf!) my spirit hovering lies
> Mute—motionless—aghast.
>
> For alas! alas! with me
>   The light of Life is o'er.
>   "No more—no more—no more;"—
> (Such language holds the solemn sea
>   To the sands upon the shore)
> Shall bloom the thunder-blasted tree,
>   Or the stricken eagle soar.
>
> Now all my hours are trances,
>   And all my nightly dreams
> Are where thy gray eye glances,

And where thy footstep gleams,
In what ethereal dances,
By what Italian streams.

Alas! for that accursed time
They bore thee o'er the billow,
From Love to titled age and crime,
And an unholy pillow:
From me, and from our misty clime
Where weeps the silver willow.

That these lines were written in English, a language with which I had not believed their author acquainted, afforded me little matter for surprise. I was too well aware of the extent of his acquirements, and of the singular pleasure he took in concealing them from observation, to be astonished at any similar discovery; but the place of date, I must confess, occasioned me no little amazement. It had been originally written *London,* and afterwards carefully overscored—not, however, so effectually as to conceal the word from a scrutinizing eye. I say, this occasioned me no little amazement; for I well remember that, in a former conversation with my friend, I particularly inquired if he had at any time met in London the Marchesa di Mentoni (who for some years previous to her marriage had resided in that city), when his answer, if I mistake not, gave me to understand that he had never visited the metropolis of Great Britain. I might as well here mention that I have more than once heard (without, of course, giving credit to a report involving so many improbabilities), that the person of whom I speak was not only by birth, but in education, an *Englishman.*

.   .   .   .

"There is one painting," said he, without being aware of my notice of the tragedy—"there is still one painting which you have not seen." And throwing aside a drapery, he discovered a full-length portrait of the Marchesa Aphrodite.

Human art could have done no more in the delineation of her superhuman beauty. The same ethereal figure which stood before me the preceding night, upon the steps of the Ducal Palace, stood before me once again. But in the expression of the countenance, which was beaming all over with smiles, there still lurked (incomprehensible anomaly!) that fitful stain of melancholy which will ever be found inseparable from the perfection of the beautiful. Her right arm lay folded over her bosom. With her left she pointed downward to a curiously fashioned vase. One small, fairy foot, alone visible, barely touched the earth; and, scarcely discernible in the brilliant atmosphere which seemed to encircle and enshrine her loveliness, floated a pair of the most delicately imagined wings. My glance fell from the painting to the figure of my friend, and the vigorous words of Chapman's *Bussy D'Ambois* quivered instinctively upon my lips:—

> "I am up
> Here like a Roman statue; I will stand
> Till death hath made me marble!"

"Come," he said at length, turning towards a table of richly enamelled and massive silver, upon which were a few goblets fantastically stained, together with two large Etruscan vases, fashioned in the same extraordinary model as that in the foreground of the portrait, and filled with what I supposed to be Johannisberger. "Come," he said abruptly, "let us drink! It is early—but let us drink. It is *indeed* early," he continued musingly, as a cherub with a heavy golden hammer made the apartment ring with the first hour after sunrise: "it is *indeed* early—but what matters it? let us drink! Let us pour out an offering to yon solemn sun which these gaudy lamps and censers are so eager to subdue!" And, having made me pledge him in a bumper, he swallowed in rapid succession several goblets of the wine.

"To dream," he continued, resuming the tone of his desultory conversation, as he held up to the rich light of a censer one of the magnificent vases —"to dream has been the business of my life. I have therefore framed for myself, as you see, a bower of dreams. In the heart of Venice could I have erected a better? You behold around you, it is true, a medley of architectural embellishments. The chastity of Ionia is offended by antediluvian devices, and the sphinxes of Egypt are outstretched upon carpets of gold. Yet the effect is incongruous to the timid alone. Proprieties of place, and especially of time, are the bugbears which terrify mankind from the contemplation of the magnificent. Once I was myself a decorist; but that sublimation of folly has palled upon my soul. All this is now the fitter for my purpose. Like these arabesque censers, my spirit is writhing in fire, and the delirium of this scene is fashioning me for the wilder visions of that land of real dreams whither I am now rapidly departing." He here paused abruptly, bent his head to his bosom, and seemed to listen to a sound which I could not hear. At length, erecting his frame, he looked upwards, and ejaculated the lines of the Bishop of Chichester:—

> *"Stay for me there! I will not fail*
> *To meet thee in that hollow vale."*

In the next instant, confessing the power of the wine, he threw himself at full length upon an ottoman.

A quick step was now heard upon the staircase, and a loud knock at the door rapidly succeeded. I was hastening to anticipate a second disturbance, when a page of Mentoni's household burst into the room, and faltered out, in a voice choking with emotion, the incoherent words, "My mistress!—my mistress!—Poisoned!—poisoned! Oh, beautiful—oh, beautiful Aphrodite!"

Bewildered, I flew to the ottoman, and endeavored to arouse the sleeper to a sense of the startling intelligence. But his limbs were rigid—his lips were livid—his lately beaming eyes were riveted in *death*. I staggered back towards the table—my hand fell upon a cracked and blackened goblet—and a consciousness of the entire and terrible truth flashed suddenly over my soul.

LIGEIA [2]

"And the will therein lieth, which dieth not. Who knoweth the mysteries of the will, with its vigor? For God is but a great will pervading all things by nature of its intentness. Man doth not yield himself to the angels, nor unto death utterly, save only through the weakness of his feeble will."—JOSEPH GLANVILL.

I CANNOT, for my soul, remember how, when, or even precisely where, I first became acquainted with the Lady Ligeia. Long years have since elapsed, and my memory is feeble through much suffering. Or, perhaps, I cannot *now* bring these points to mind, because, in truth, the character of my beloved, her rare learning, her singular yet placid cast of beauty, and the thrilling and enthralling eloquence of her low musical language, made their way into my heart by paces so steadily and stealthily progressive, that they have been unnoticed and unknown. Yet I believe that I met her first and most frequently in some large, old, decaying city near the Rhine. Of her family I have surely heard her speak. That it is of a remotely ancient date cannot be doubted. Ligeia! Ligeia! Buried in studies of a nature more than all else adapted to deaden impressions of the outward world, it is by that sweet word alone—by Ligeia—that I bring before mine eyes in fancy the image of her who is no more. And now, while I write, a recollection flashes upon me that I have *never known* the paternal name of her who was my friend and my betrothed, and who became the partner of my studies, and finally the wife of my bosom. Was it a playful charge on the part of my Ligeia? or was it a test of my strength of affection, that I should institute no inquiries upon this point? or was it rather a caprice of my own—a wildly romantic offering on the shrine of the most passionate devotion? I but indistinctly recall the fact itself—what wonder that I have utterly forgotten the circumstances which originated or attended it? And, indeed, if ever that spirit which is entitled *Romance*—if ever she, the wan and the misty-winged *Ashtophet* of idolatrous Egypt, presided, as they tell, over marriages ill-omened, then most surely she presided over mine.

There is one dear topic, however, on which my memory fails me not. It is the *person* of Ligeia. In stature she was tall, somewhat slender, and, in her

[2] First published in *American Museum*, September, 1838, and included in *Tales of the Grotesque and Arabesque* (1840).

latter days, even emaciated. I would in vain attempt to portray the majesty,
the quiet ease, of her demeanor, or the incomprehensible lightness and elasticity of her footfall. She came and departed as a shadow. I was never made
aware of her entrance into my closed study, save by the dear music of her
low sweet voice, as she placed her marble hand upon my shoulder. In beauty
of face no maiden ever equalled her. It was the radiance of an opium-dream
—an airy and spirit-lifting vision more wildly divine than the fantasies which
hovered about the slumbering souls of the daughters of Delos. Yet her features were not of that regular mould which we have been falsely taught
to worship in the classical labors of the heathen. "There is no exquisite beauty,"
says Bacon, Lord Verulam, speaking truly of all the forms and genera of
beauty, "without some *strangeness* in the proportion." Yet, although I saw
that the features of Ligeia were not of a classic regularity—although I perceived that her loveliness was indeed "exquisite," and felt that there was
much of "strangeness" pervading it, yet I have tried in vain to detect the
irregularity and to trace home my own perception of "the strange." I examined the contour of the lofty and pale forehead: it was faultless—how
cold indeed that word when applied to a majesty so divine!—the skin rivalling
the purest ivory, the commanding extent and repose, the gentle prominence
of the regions above the temples; and then the raven-black, the glossy, the
luxuriant and naturally-curling tresses, setting forth the full force of the
Homeric epithet, "hyacinthine!" I looked at the delicate outlines of the nose
—and nowhere but in the graceful medallions of the Hebrews had I beheld
a similar perfection. There were the same luxurious smoothness of surface,
the same scarcely perceptible tendency to the aquiline, the same harmoniously curved nostrils speaking the free spirit. I regarded the sweet mouth.
Here was indeed the triumph of all things heavenly—the magnificent turn
of the short upper lip—the soft, voluptuous slumber of the under—the dimples
which sported, and the color which spoke—the teeth glancing back, with a
brilliancy almost startling, every ray of the holy light which fell upon them
in her serene and placid, yet most exultingly radiant of all smiles. I scrutinised the formation of the chin—and here, too, I found the gentleness of
breadth, the softness and the majesty, the fulness and the spirituality, of the
Greek—the contour which the god Apollo revealed but in a dream, to Cle-
omenes, the son of the Athenian. And then I peered into the large eyes of
Ligeia.

For eyes we have no models in the remotely antique. It might have been,
too, that in these eyes of my beloved lay the secret to which Lord Verulam
alludes. They were, I must believe, far larger than the ordinary eyes of our
own race. They were even fuller than the fullest of the gazelle eyes of the
tribe of the valley of Nourjahad. Yet it was only at intervals—in moments of
intense excitement—that this peculiarity became more than slightly notice-

able in Ligeia. And at such moments was her beauty—in my heated fancy thus it appeared, perhaps—the beauty of beings either above or apart from the earth—the beauty of the fabulous Houri of the Turk. The hue of the orbs was the most brilliant of black, and, far over them, hung jetty lashes of great length. The brows, slightly irregular in outline, had the same tint. The "strangeness," however, which I found in the eyes, was of a nature distinct from the formation, or the color, or the brilliancy of the features, and must, after all, be referred to the *expression*. Ah, word of no meaning! behind whose vast latitude of mere sound we intrench our ignorance of so much of the spiritual. The expression of the eyes of Ligeia—how for long hours have I pondered upon it! How have I, through the whole of a midsummer night, struggled to fathom it! What was it—that something more profound than the well of Democritus—which lay far within the pupils of my beloved? What *was* it? I was possessed with a passion to discover. Those eyes, those large, those shining, those divine orbs! they became to me twin stars of Leda, and I to them devoutest of astrologers.

There is no point, among the many incomprehensible anomalies of the science of mind, more thrillingly exciting than the fact—never, I believe, noticed in the schools—that in our endeavors to recall to memory something long forgotten, we often find ourselves *upon the very verge* of remembrance, without being able, in the end, to remember. And thus how frequently, in my intense scrutiny of Ligeia's eyes, have I felt approaching the full knowledge of their expression—felt it approaching—yet not quite be mine—and so at length entirely depart! And (strange—oh, strangest mystery of all!) I found in the commonest objects of the universe, a circle of analogies to that expression. I mean to say that, subsequently to the period when Ligeia's beauty passed into my spirit, there dwelling as in a shrine, I derived, from many existences in the material world, a sentiment such as I felt always around, within me, by her large and luminous orbs. Yet not the more could I define that sentiment, or analyze, or even steadily view it. I recognised it, let me repeat, sometimes in the survey of a rapidly growing vine—in the contemplation of a moth, a butterfly, a chrysalis, a stream of running water. I have felt it in the ocean; in the falling of a meteor. I have felt it in the glances of unusually aged people. And there are one or two stars in heaven (one especially, a star of the sixth magnitude, double and changeable, to be found near the large star in Lyra), in a telescopic scrutiny of which I have been made aware of the feeling. I have been filled with it by certain sounds from stringed instruments, and not unfrequently by passages from books. Among innumerable other instances, I well remember something in a volume of Joseph Glanvill, which (perhaps merely from its quaintness—who shall say?) never failed to inspire me with the sentiment: "And the will therein lieth, which dieth not. Who knoweth the mysteries of the will, with its vigor? For God is but a great will pervading all things by nature of its intentness. Man doth not yield him to the angels, nor unto death utterly, save only through the weakness of his feeble will."

Length of years and subsequent reflection have enabled me to trace, indeed, some remote connection between this passage in the English moralist and a portion of the character of Ligeia. An *intensity* in thought, action, or speech, was possibly, in her, a result, or at least an index, of that gigantic volition which, during our long intercourse, failed to give other and more immediate evidence of its existence. Of all the women whom I have ever known, she, the outwardly calm, the ever-placid Ligeia, was the most violently a prey to the tumultuous vultures of stern passion. And of such passion I could form no estimate, save by the miraculous expansion of those eyes which at once so delighted and appalled me—by the almost magical melody, modulation, distinctness, and placidity of her very low voice—and by the fierce energy (rendered doubly effective by contrast with her manner of utterance) of the wild words which she habitually uttered.

I have spoken of the learning of Ligeia: it was immense—such as I have never known in woman. In the classical tongues was she deeply proficient, and, as far as my own acquaintance extended in regard to the modern dialects of Europe, I have never known her at fault. Indeed upon any theme of the most admired, because simply the most abstruse of the boasted erudition of the academy, have I *ever* found Ligeia at fault? How singularly—how thrillingly, this one point in the nature of my wife has forced itself, at this late period only, upon my attention! I said her knowledge was such as I have never known in woman—but where breathes the man who has traversed, and successfully, *all* the wide areas of moral, physical, and mathematical science? I saw not then what I now clearly perceive, that the acquisitions of Ligeia were gigantic, were astounding; yet I was sufficiently aware of her infinite supremacy to resign myself, with a childlike confidence, to her guidance through the chaotic world of metaphysical investigation at which I was most busily occupied during the earlier years of our marriage. With how vast a triumph—with how vivid a delight—with how much of all that is ethereal in hope—did I *feel,* as she bent over me in studies but little sought—but less known—that delicious vista by slow degrees expanding before me, down whose long, gorgeous, and all untrodden path, I might at length pass onward to the goal of a wisdom too divinely precious not to be forbidden!

How poignant, then, must have been the grief with which, after some years, I beheld my well-grounded expectations take wings to themselves and fly away! Without Ligeia I was but as a child groping benighted. Her presence, her readings alone, rendered vividly luminous the many mysteries of the transcendentalism in which we were immersed. Wanting the radiant lustre of her eyes, letters, lambent and golden, grew duller than Saturnian lead. And now those eyes shone less and less frequently upon the pages over which I pored. Ligeia grew ill. The wild eyes blazed with a too—too glorious effulgence; the pale fingers became of the transparent waxen hue of the grave; and the blue veins upon the lofty forehead swelled and sank impetuously with the tides of the most gentle emotion. I saw that she must die—and I struggled desperately in spirit with the grim Azrael. And the struggles of the passionate wife were, to my astonishment, even more energetic than my own. There had been much in her stern nature to impress me with the belief that, to her, death would have come without its terrors; but not so. Words are impotent to convey any just idea of the fierceness of resistance with which she wrestled with the Shadow. I groaned in anguish at the pitiable spectacle. I would have soothed—I would have reasoned; but, in the intensity of her wild desire for life—for life—*but* for life—solace and reason were alike the uttermost of folly. Yet not until the last instance, amid the most convulsive writhings of her fierce spirit, was shaken the external placidity of her demeanor. Her voice grew more gentle—grew more low— yet I would not wish to dwell upon the wild meaning of the quietly uttered words. My brain reeled as I hearkened, entranced, to a melody more than mortal—to assumptions and aspirations which mortality had never before known.

That she loved me I should not have doubted; and I might have been easily aware that, in a bosom such as hers, love would have reigned no ordinary passion. But in death only was I fully impressed with the strength of her affection. For long hours, detaining my hand, would she pour out before me the overflowing of a heart whose more than passionate devotion amounted to idolatry. How had I deserved to be so blessed by such confessions?—how had I deserved to be so cursed with the removal of my beloved in the hour of her making them? But upon this subject I cannot bear to dilate. Let me say only, that in Ligeia's more than womanly abandonment to a love, alas! all unmerited, all unworthily bestowed, I at length recognised the principle of her longing, with so wildly earnest a desire, for the life which was now fleeing so rapidly away. It is this wild longing—it is this eager vehemence of desire for life—*but* for life—that I have no power to portray—no utterance capable of expressing.

At high noon of the day in which she departed, beckoning me, peremptorily, to her side, she bade me repeat certain verses composed by herself not many days before. I obeyed her. They were these:—

> Lo! 'tis a gala night
>   Within the lonesome latter years!
> An angel throng, bewinged, bedight
>   In veils, and drowned in tears,
> Sit in a theatre, to see

A play of hopes and fears,
While the orchestra breathes fitfully
    The music of the spheres.

Mimes, in the form of God on high,
    Mutter and mumble low,
And hither and thither fly;
    Mere puppets they, who come and go
At bidding of vast formless things
    That shift the scenery to and fro,
Flapping from out their condor wings
    Invisible Woe!

That motley drama!—oh, be sure
    It shall not be forgot!
With its Phantom chased for evermore,
    By a crowd that seize it not,
Through a circle that ever returneth in
    To the self-same spot;
And much of Madness, and more of Sin,
    And Horror, the soul of the plot!

But see, amid the mimic rout
    A crawling shape intrude!
A blood-red thing that writhes from out
    The scenic solitude!
It writhes!—it writhes!—with mortal pangs
    The mimes become its food,
And the seraphs sob at vermin fangs
    In human gore imbued.

Out—out are the lights—out all!
    And over each quivering form,
The curtain, a funeral pall,
    Comes down with the rush of a storm—
And the angels, all pallid and wan,
    Uprising, unveiling, affirm
That the play is the tragedy, "Man,"
    And its hero, the Conqueror Worm.

"O God!" half-shrieked Ligeia, leaping to her feet and extending her arms aloft with a spasmodic movement, as I made an end of these lines—"O God! O Divine Father!—shall these things be undeviatingly so?—shall this conqueror be not once conquered? Are we not part and parcel in Thee? Who—who knoweth the mysteries of the will, with its vigor? Man doth not yield him to the angels, *nor unto death utterly,* save only through the weakness of his feeble will."

And now, as if exhausted with emotion, she suffered her white arms to fall, and returned solemnly to her bed of death. And as she breathed her last

sighs, there came mingled with them a low murmur from her lips. I bent
to them my ear, and distinguished again the concluding words of the passage in Glanvill: *"Man doth not yield him to the angels, nor unto death utterly, save only through the weakness of his feeble will."*

She died; and I, crushed into the very dust with sorrow, could no longer
endure the lonely desolation of my dwelling in the dim and decaying city by
the Rhine. I had no lack of what the world calls wealth. Ligeia had brought
me far more, very far more than ordinarily falls to the lot of mortals. After a
few months, therefore, of weary and aimless wandering, I purchased, and
put in some repair, an abbey, which I shall not name, in one of the wildest
and least frequented portions of fair England. The gloomy and dreary
grandeur of the building, the almost savage aspect of the domain, the many
melancholy and time-honored memories connected with both, had much
in unison with the feelings of utter abandonment which had driven me into
that remote and unsocial region of the country. Yet although the external
abbey, with its verdant decay hanging about it, suffered but little alteration, I
gave way, with a child-like perversity, and perchance with a faint hope of
alleviating my sorrows, to a display of more than regal magnificence within.
For such follies, even in childhood, I had imbibed a taste, and now they came
back to me as if in the dotage of grief. Alas, I feel how much even of incipient
madness might have been discovered in the gorgeous and fantastic draperies,
in the solemn carvings of Egypt, in the wild cornices and furniture, in the
Bedlam patterns of the carpets of tufted gold! I had become a bounden slave
in the trammels of opium, and my labors and my orders had taken a coloring from my dreams. But these absurdities I must not pause to detail. Let me
speak only of that one chamber, ever accursed, whither in a moment of
mental alienation, I led from the altar as my bride—as the successor of the
unforgotten Ligeia—the fair-haired and blue-eyed Lady Rowena Trevanion,
of Tremaine.

There is no individual portion of the architecture and decoration of that
bridal chamber which is not now visibly before me. Where were the souls
of the haughty family of the bride, when, through thirst of gold, they permitted to pass the threshold of an apartment *so* bedecked, a maiden and a
daughter so beloved? I have said that I minutely remember the details of
the chamber—yet I am sadly forgetful on topics of deep moment—and here
there was no system, no keeping, in the fantastic display, to take hold upon
the memory. The room lay in a high turret of the castellated abbey, was
pentagonal in shape, and of capacious size. Occupying the whole southern
face of the pentagon was the sole window—an immense sheet of unbroken
glass from Venice—a single pane, and tinted of a leaden hue, so that the
rays of either the sun or moon passing through it, fell with a ghastly lustre
on the objects within. Over the upper portion of this huge window extended

the trellis-work of an aged vine, which clambered up the massy walls of the turret. The ceiling, of gloomy-looking oak, was excessively lofty, vaulted, and elaborately fretted with the wildest and most grotesque specimens of a semi-Gothic, semi-Druidical device. From out the most central recess of this melancholy vaulting, depended, by a single chain of gold with long links, a huge censer of the same metal, Saracenic in pattern, and with many perforations so contrived that there writhed in and out of them, as if endued with a serpent vitality, a continual succession of parti-colored fires.

Some few ottomans and golden candelabra, of Eastern figure, were in various stations about; and there was the couch, too—the bridal couch—of an Indian model, and low, and sculptured of solid ebony, with a pall-like canopy above. In each of the angles of the chamber stood on end a gigantic sarcophagus of black granite, from the tombs of the kings over against Luxor, with their aged lids full of immemorial sculpture. But in the draping of the apartment lay, alas! the chief fantasy of all. The lofty walls, gigantic in height—even unproportionably so—were hung from summit to foot, in vast folds, with a heavy and massive-looking tapestry—tapestry of a material which was found alike as a carpet on the floor, as a covering for the ottomans and the ebony bed, as a canopy for the bed, and as the gorgeous volutes of the curtains which partially shaded the window. The material was the richest cloth of gold. It was spotted all over, at irregular intervals, with arabesque figures, about a foot in diameter, and wrought upon the cloth in patterns of the most jetty black. But these figures partook of the true character of the arabesque only when regarded from a single point of view. By a contrivance now common, and indeed traceable to a very remote period of antiquity, they were made changeable in aspect. To one entering the room, they bore the appearance of simple monstrosities; but upon a farther advance, this appearance gradually departed; and, step by step, as the visitor moved his station in the chamber, he saw himself surrounded by an endless succession of the ghastly forms which belong to the superstition of the Norman, or arise in the guilty slumbers of the monk. The phantasmagoric effect was vastly heightened by the artificial introduction of a strong continual current of wind behind the draperies—giving a hideous and uneasy animation to the whole.

In halls such as these—in a bridal chamber such as this—I passed, with the Lady of Tremaine, the unhallowed hours of the first month of our marriage —passed them with but little disquietude. That my wife dreaded the fierce moodiness of my temper—that she shunned me, and loved me but little—I could not help perceiving; but it gave me rather pleasure than otherwise. I loathed her with a hatred belonging more to demon than to man. My memory flew back (oh, with what intensity of regret!) to Ligeia, the beloved, the august, the beautiful, the entombed. I revelled in recollections of her purity;

of her wisdom; of her lofty, her ethereal nature; of her passionate, her idolatrous love. Now, then, did my spirit fully and freely burn with more than all the fires of her own. In the excitement of my opium dreams (for I was habitually fettered in the shackles of the drug) I would call aloud upon her name, during the silence of the night, or among the sheltered recesses of the glens by day, as if, through the wild eagerness, the solemn passion, the consuming ardor of my longing for the departed, I could restore her to the pathway she had abandoned—ah, *could* it be for ever?—upon the earth.

About the commencement of the second month of the marriage, the Lady Rowena was attacked with sudden illness, from which her recovery was slow. The fever which consumed her rendered her nights uneasy; and in her perturbed state of half-slumber, she spoke of sounds, and of motions, in and about the chamber of the turret, which I concluded had no origin save in the distemper of her fancy, or perhaps in the phantasmagoric influences of the chamber itself. She became at length convalescent—finally, well. Yet but a brief period elapsed ere a second more violent disorder again threw her upon a bed of suffering; and from this attack her frame, at all times feeble, never altogether recovered. Her illnesses were, after this epoch, of alarming character, and of more alarming recurrence, defying alike the knowledge and the great exertions of her physicians. With the increase of the chronic disease, which had thus, apparently, taken too sure hold upon her constitution to be eradicated by human means, I could not fail to observe a similar increase in the nervous irritation of her temperament, and in her excitability by trivial causes of fear. She spoke again, and now more frequently and pertinaciously, of the sounds—of the slight sounds—and of the unusual motions among the tapestries, to which she had formerly alluded.

One night, near the closing in of September, she pressed this distressing subject with more than usual emphasis upon my attention. She had just awakened from an unquiet slumber, and I had been watching, with feelings half of anxiety, half of vague terror, the workings of her emaciated countenance. I sat by the side of her ebony bed, upon one of the ottomans of India. She partly arose, and spoke, in an earnest low whisper, of sounds which she *then* heard, but which I could not hear—of motions which she *then* saw, but which I could not perceive. The wind was rushing hurriedly behind the tapestries, and I wished to show her (what, let me confess it, I could not *all* believe) that those almost inarticulate breathings, and those very gentle variations of the figures upon the wall, were but the natural effects of that customary rushing of the wind. But a deadly pallor, overspreading her face, had proved to me that my exertions to reassure her would be fruitless. She appeared to be fainting, and no attendants were within call. I remembered where was deposited a decanter of light wine which had been ordered by her physicians, and hastened across the chamber to procure it. But, as I stepped beneath the light of the censer, two circumstances of a startling nature attracted my attention. I had felt that some palpable although invisible object had passed lightly by my person; and I saw that there lay upon the golden carpet, in the very middle of the rich lustre thrown from the censer, a shadow —a faint, indefinite shadow of angelic aspect—such as might be fancied for the shadow of a shade. But I was wild with the excitement of an immoderate dose of opium, and heeded these things but little, nor spoke of them to Rowena. Having found the wine, I recrossed the chamber, and poured out a gobletful, which I held to the lips of the fainting lady. She had now partially recovered, however, and took the vessel herself, while I sank upon an ottoman near me, with my eyes fastened upon her person. It was then that I became distinctly aware of a gentle footfall upon the carpet, and near the couch; and in a second thereafter, as Rowena was in the act of raising the wine to her lips, I saw, or may have dreamed that I saw, fall within the goblet, as if from some invisible spring in the atmosphere of the room, three or four large drops of a brilliant and ruby-colored fluid. If this I saw—not so Rowena. She swallowed the wine unhesitatingly, and I forbore to speak to her of a circumstance which must, after all, I considered, have been but the suggestion of a vivid imagination, rendered morbidly active by the terror of the lady, by the opium, and by the hour.

Yet I cannot conceal it from my own perception that, immediately subsequent to the fall of the ruby drops, a rapid change for the worse took place in the disorder of my wife; so that, on the third subsequent night, the hands of her menials prepared her for the tomb, and on the fourth, I sat alone, with her shrouded body, in that fantastic chamber which had received her as my bride. Wild visions, opium-engendered, flitted, shadow-like, before me. I gazed with unquiet eye upon the sarcophagi in the angles of the room, upon the varying figures of the drapery, and upon the writhing of the parti-colored fires in the censer overhead. My eyes then fell, as I called to mind the circumstances of a former night, to the spot beneath the glare of the censer where I had seen the faint traces of the shadow. It was there, however, no longer; and breathing with greater freedom, I turned my glances to the pallid and rigid figure upon the bed. Then rushed upon me a thousand memories of Ligeia—and then came back upon my heart, with the turbulent violence of a flood, the whole of that unutterable woe with which I had regarded *her* thus enshrouded. The night waned; and still, with a bosom full of bitter thoughts of the one only and supremely beloved, I remained gazing upon the body of Rowena.

It might have been midnight, or perhaps earlier, or later, for I had taken no note of time, when a sob, low, gentle, but very distinct, startled me from my reverie. I *felt* that it came from the bed of ebony—the bed of death. I listened in an agony of superstitious terror—but there was no repetition of the sound. I strained my vision to detect any motion in the corpse—but there was not the slightest perceptible. Yet I could not have been deceived. I *had* heard the noise, however faint, and my soul was awakened within me. I resolutely and perseveringly kept my attention riveted upon the body. Many minutes elapsed before any circumstance occurred tending to throw light upon the mystery. At length it became evident that a slight, a very feeble, and barely noticeable tinge of color had flushed up within the cheeks, and along the sunken small veins of the eyelids. Through a species of unutterable horror and awe, for which the language of mortality has no sufficiently energetic expression, I felt my heart cease to beat, my limbs grow rigid where I sat. Yet a sense of duty finally operated to restore my self-possession. I could no longer doubt that we had been precipitate in our preparations—that Rowena still lived. It was necessary that some immediate exertion be made; yet the turret was altogether apart from the portion of the abbey tenanted by the servants—there were none within call—I had no means of summoning them to my aid without leaving the room for many minutes—and this I could not venture to do. I therefore struggled alone in my endeavors to call back the spirit still hovering. In a short period it was certain, however, that a relapse had taken place; the color disappeared from both eyelid and cheek, leaving a wanness even more than that of marble; the lips became doubly shrivelled and pinched up in the ghastly expression of death; a repulsive clamminess and coldness overspread rapidly the surface of the body; and all the usual rigorous stiffness immediately supervened. I fell back with a shudder upon the couch from which I had been so startlingly aroused, and again gave myself up to passionate waking visions of Ligeia.

An hour thus elapsed, when (could it be possible?) I was a second time aware of some vague sound issuing from the region of the bed. I listened—in extremity of horror. The sound came again—it was a sigh. Rushing to the corpse, I saw—distinctly saw—a tremor upon the lips. In a minute afterwards they relaxed, disclosing a bright line of the pearly teeth. Amazement now struggled in my bosom with the profound awe which had hitherto reigned there alone. I felt that my vision grew dim, that my reason wandered; and it was only by a violent effort that I at length succeeded in nerving myself to the task which duty thus once more had pointed out. There was now a partial glow upon the forehead and upon the cheek and throat; a perceptible warmth pervaded the whole frame; there was even a slight pulsation at the heart. The lady *lived;* and with redoubled ardor I betook myself to the task of restoration. I chafed and bathed the temples and the hands, and used every exertion which experience, and no little medical reading, could suggest. But in vain. Suddenly, the color fled, the pulsation ceased, the lips resumed the expression of the dead, and, in an instant afterward, the whole body took upon itself the icy chilliness, the livid hue, the intense rigidity, the sunken outline, and all the loathsome peculiarities of that which has been, for many days, a tenant of the tomb.

And again I sunk into visions of Ligeia—and again (what marvel that I shudder while I write?), *again* there reached my ears a low sob from the region of the ebony bed. But why shall I minutely detail the unspeakable horrors of that night? Why shall I pause to relate how, time after time, until near the period of the grey dawn, this hideous drama of revivification was repeated; how each terrific relapse was only into a sterner and apparently more irredeemable death; how each agony wore the aspect of a struggle with some invisible foe; and how each struggle was succeeded by I know not what of wild change in the personal appearance of the corpse? Let me hurry to a conclusion.

The greater part of the fearful night had worn away, and she who had been dead, once again stirred—and now more vigorously than hitherto, although arousing from a dissolution more appalling in its utter hopelessness than any. I had long ceased to struggle or to move, and remained sitting rigidly upon the ottoman, a helpless prey to a whirl of violent emotions, of which extreme awe was perhaps the least terrible, the least consuming. The corpse, I repeat, stirred, and now more vigorously than before. The hues of life flushed up with unwonted energy into the countenance—the limbs relaxed—and, save that the eyelids were yet pressed heavily together and that the bandages and draperies of the grave still imparted their charnel character to the figure, I might have dreamed that Rowena had indeed shaken off, utterly, the fetters of death. But if this idea was not, even then, altogether adopted, I could at least doubt no longer, when arising from the bed, tottering, with feeble steps, with closed eyes, and with the manner of one bewildered in a dream, the thing that was enshrouded advanced bodily and palpably into the middle of the apartment.

I trembled not—I stirred not—for a crowd of unutterable fancies connected with the air, the stature, the demeanor of the figure, rushing hurriedly through my brain, had paralyzed—had chilled me into stone. I stirred not—but gazed upon the apparition. There was a mad disorder in my thoughts—a tumult unappeasable. Could it, indeed, be the *living* Rowena who confronted me? Could it indeed be Rowena *at all*—the fair-haired, the blue-eyed Lady Rowena Trevanion of Tremaine? Why, *why* should I doubt it? The bandage lay heavily about the mouth—but then might it not be the mouth of the breathing Lady of Tremaine? And the cheeks—there were the roses as in her noon of life—yes, these might indeed be the fair cheeks of the living Lady of Tremaine. And the chin, with its dimples, as in health, might it not be hers?—but *had she then grown taller since her malady?* What inexpressible madness seized me with that thought? One bound, and I had reached her feet! Shrinking from my touch, she let fall from her head, unloosened, the ghastly cerements which had confined it, and there streamed forth, into the rushing atmosphere of the chamber, huge masses of long and dishevelled hair; *it was blacker than the raven wings of midnight!* And now slowly opened *the eyes* of the figure which stood before me. "Here then, at least," I shrieked aloud, "can I never—can I never be mistaken—these are the full, and the black, and the wild eyes—of my lost love—of the Lady—of the LADY LIGEIA."

THE FALL OF THE HOUSE OF USHER [3]

"Son cœur est un luth suspendu;
Sitôt qu'on le touche il résonne."
BÉRANGER.

DURING the whole of a dull, dark, and soundless day in the autumn of the year, when the clouds hung oppressively low in the heavens, I had been passing alone, on horseback, through a singularly dreary tract of country; and at length found myself, as the shades of evening drew on, within view of the melancholy House of Usher. I know not how it was—but, with the first glimpse of the building, a sense of insufferable gloom pervaded my spirit. I say insufferable; for the feeling was unrelieved by any of that half-pleasurable, because poetic, sentiment, with which the mind usually receives even the sternest natural images of the desolate or terrible. I looked upon the scene before me—upon the mere house, and the simple landscape features of the domain—upon the bleak walls, upon the vacant eye-like windows, upon a few rank sedges, and upon a few white trunks of decayed trees—with an utter depression of soul which I can compare to no earthly sensation more properly than to the after-dream of the reveller upon opium: the bitter lapse into everyday life, the hideous dropping off of the veil. There was an iciness, a sinking, a sickening of the heart, an unredeemed dreariness of thought which no goading of the imagination could torture into aught of the sublime. What was it—I paused to think—what was it that so unnerved me in the contemplation of the House of Usher? It was a mystery all insoluble; nor could I grapple with the shadowy fancies that crowded upon me as I pondered. I was forced to fall back upon the unsatisfactory conclusion, that while, beyond doubt, there *are* combinations of very simple natural objects which have the power of thus affecting us, still the analysis of this power lies among considerations beyond our depth. It was possible, I reflected, that a mere different arrangement of the particulars of the scene, of the details of the picture, would be sufficient to modify, or perhaps to annihilate its capacity for sorrowful impression; and, acting upon this idea, I reined my horse to the precipi-

[3] First published in *Burton's Gentleman's Magazine,* September, 1839, and included in *Tales of the Grotesque and Arabesque* (1840) and in *Tales* (1845).

tous brink of a black and lurid tarn that lay in unruffled lustre by the dwelling, and gazed down—but with a shudder even more thrilling than before
—upon the remodelled and inverted images of the grey sedge, and the ghastly
tree-stems, and the vacant and eye-like windows.

Nevertheless, in this mansion of gloom I now proposed to myself a sojourn of some weeks. Its proprietor, Roderick Usher, had been one of my
boon companions in boyhood; but many years had elapsed since our last
meeting. A letter, however, had lately reached me in a distant part of the
country—a letter from him—which, in its wildly importunate nature, had
admitted of no other than the personal reply. The MS. gave evidence of nervous agitation. The writer spoke of acute bodily illness—of a mental disorder
which oppressed him—and of an earnest desire to see me, as his best, and
indeed his only personal friend, with a view of attempting, by the cheerfulness of my society, some alleviation of his malady. It was the manner in which
all this, and much more, was said—it was the apparent *heart* that went with
his request—which allowed me no room for hesitation; and I accordingly
obeyed forthwith what I still considered a very singular summons.

Although, as boys, we had been even intimate associates, yet I really knew
little of my friend. His reserve had been always excessive and habitual. I was
aware, however, that his very ancient family had been noted, time out of
mind, for a peculiar sensibility of temperament, displaying itself, through
long ages, in many works of exalted art, and manifested, of late, in repeated
deeds of munificent yet unobtrusive charity, as well as in a passionate devotion to the intricacies, perhaps even more than to the orthodox and easily
recognisable beauties of musical science. I had learned, too, the very remarkable fact, that the stem of the Usher race, all time-honored as it was, had put
forth, at no period, any enduring branch; in other words, that the entire
family lay in the direct line of descent, and had always, with very trifling
and very temporary variation, so lain. It was this deficiency, I considered, while
running over in thought the perfect keeping of the character of the premises
with the accredited character of the people, and while speculating upon the
possible influence which the one, in the long lapse of centuries, might have
exercised upon the other—it was this deficiency, perhaps, of collateral issue,
and the consequent undeviating transmission, from sire to son, of the patrimony with the name, which had, at length, so identified the two as to merge
the original title of the estate in the quaint and equivocal appellation of the
"House of Usher"—an appellation which seemed to include, in the minds
of the peasantry who used it, both the family and the family mansion.

I have said that the sole effect of my somewhat childish experiment—that
of looking down within the tarn—had been to deepen the first singular impression. There can be no doubt that the consciousness of the rapid increase
of my superstition—for why should I not so term it?—served mainly to ac-

celerate the increase itself. Such, I have long known, is the paradoxical law of all sentiments having terror as a basis. And it might have been for this reason only, that, when I again uplifted my eyes to the house itself, from its image in the pool, there grew in my mind a strange fancy—a fancy so ridiculous, indeed, that I but mention it to show the vivid force of the sensations which oppressed me. I had so worked upon my imagination as really to believe that about the whole mansion and domain there hung an atmosphere peculiar to themselves and their immediate vicinity—an atmosphere which had no affinity with the air of heaven, but which had reeked up from the decayed trees, and the grey wall, and the silent tarn—a pestilent and mystic vapor, dull, sluggish, faintly discernible, and leaden-hued.

Shaking off from my spirit what *must* have been a dream, I scanned more narrowly the real aspect of the building. Its principal feature seemed to be that of an excessive antiquity. The discoloration of ages had been great. Minute fungi overspread the whole exterior, hanging in a fine tangled web-work from the eaves. Yet all this was apart from any extraordinary dilapidation. No portion of the masonry had fallen; and there appeared to be a wild inconsistency between its still perfect adaptation of parts, and the crumbling condition of the individual stones. In this there was much that reminded me of the specious totality of old woodwork which has rotted for long years in some neglected vault, with no disturbance from the breath of the external air. Beyond this indication of extensive decay, however, the fabric gave little token of instability. Perhaps the eye of a scrutinising observer might have discovered a barely perceptible fissure, which, extending from the roof of the building in front, made its way down the wall in a zigzag direction, until it became lost in the sullen waters of the tarn.

Noticing these things, I rode over a short causeway to the house. A servant in waiting took my horse, and I entered the Gothic archway of the hall. A valet, of stealthy step, thence conducted me, in silence, through many dark and intricate passages in my progress to the studio of his master. Much that I encountered on the way contributed, I know not how, to heighten the vague sentiments of which I have already spoken. While the objects around me— while the carvings of the ceilings, the sombre tapestries of the walls, the ebon blackness of the floors, and the phantasmagoric armorial trophies which rattled as I strode, were but matters to which, or to such as which, I had been accustomed from my infancy—while I hesitated not to acknowledge how familiar was all this—I still wondered to find how unfamiliar were the fancies which ordinary images were stirring up. On one of the staircases I met the physician of the family. His countenance, I thought, wore a mingled expression of low cunning and perplexity. He accosted me with trepidation and passed on. The valet now threw open a door and ushered me into the presence of his master.

The room in which I found myself was very large and lofty. The windows were long, narrow, and pointed, and at so vast a distance from the black oaken floor as to be altogether inaccessible from within. Feeble gleams of encrimsoned light made their way through the trellised panes, and served to render sufficiently distinct the more prominent objects around; the eye, however, struggled in vain to reach the remoter angles of the chamber, or the recesses of the vaulted and fretted ceiling. Dark draperies hung upon the walls. The general furniture was profuse, comfortless, antique, and tattered. Many books and musical instruments lay scattered about, but failed to give any vitality to the scene. I felt that I breathed an atmosphere of sorrow. An air of stern, deep, and irredeemable gloom hung over and pervaded all.

Upon my entrance, Usher arose from a sofa on which he had been lying at full length, and greeted me with a vivacious warmth which had much in it, I at first thought, of an overdone cordiality—of the constrained effort of the *ennuyé* man of the world. A glance, however, at his countenance, convinced me of his perfect sincerity. We sat down; and for some moments, while he spoke not, I gazed upon him with a feeling half of pity, half of awe. Surely, man had never before so terribly altered, in so brief a period, as had Roderick Usher! It was with difficulty that I could bring myself to admit the identity of the wan being before me with the companion of my early boyhood. Yet the character of his face had been at all times remarkable. A cadaverousness of complexion; an eye large, liquid, and luminous beyond comparison; lips somewhat thin and very pallid, but of a surpassingly beautiful curve; a nose of a delicate Hebrew model, but with a breadth of nostril unusual in similar formations; a finely moulded chin, speaking, in its want of prominence, of a want of moral energy; hair of a more than weblike softness and tenuity; these features, with an inordinate expansion above the regions of the temple, made up altogether a countenance not easily to be forgotten. And now in the mere exaggeration of the prevailing character of these features, and of the expression they were wont to convey, lay so much of change that I doubted to whom I spoke. The now ghastly pallor of the skin, and the now miraculous lustre of the eye, above all things startled and even awed me. The silken hair, too, had been suffered to grow all unheeded, and as, in its wild gossamer texture, it floated rather than fell about the face, I could not, even with effort, connect its Arabesque expression with any idea of simple humanity.

In the manner of my friend I was at once struck with an incoherence, an inconsistency; and I soon found this to arise from a series of feeble and futile struggles to overcome an habitual trepidancy, an excessive nervous agitation. For something of this nature I had indeed been prepared, no less by his letter, than by reminiscences of certain boyish traits, and by conclusions deduced from his peculiar physical conformation and temperament. His action was alternately vivacious and sullen. His voice varied rapidly from a tremulous indecision (when the animal spirits seemed utterly in abeyance) to that species of energetic concision—that abrupt, weighty, unhurried, and hollow-sounding enunciation—that leaden, self-balanced, and perfectly modulated guttural utterance, which may be observed in the lost drunkard, or the irreclaimable eater of opium, during the periods of his most intense excitement.

It was thus that he spoke of the object of my visit, of his earnest desire to see me, and of the solace he expected me to afford him. He entered, at some length, into what he conceived to be the nature of his malady. It was, he said, a constitutional and a family evil, and one for which he despaired to find a remedy—a mere nervous affection, he immediately added, which would undoubtedly soon pass off. It displayed itself in a host of unnatural sensations. Some of these, as he detailed them, interested and bewildered me; although, perhaps, the terms, and the general manner of the narration had their weight. He suffered much from a morbid acuteness of the senses; the most insipid food was alone endurable; he could wear only garments of certain texture; the odors of all flowers were oppressive; his eyes were tortured by even a faint light; and there were but peculiar sounds, and these from stringed instruments, which did not inspire him with horror.

To an anomalous species of terror I found him a bounden slave. "I shall perish," said he, "I *must* perish in this deplorable folly. Thus, thus, and not otherwise, shall I be lost. I dread the events of the future, not in themselves, but in their results. I shudder at the thought of any, even the most trivial, incident, which may operate upon this intolerable agitation of soul. I have, indeed, no abhorrence of danger, except in its absolute effect—in terror. In this unnerved—in this pitiable condition, I feel that the period will sooner or later arrive when I must abandon life and reason together, in some struggle with the grim phantasm, FEAR."

I learned, moreover, at intervals, and through broken and equivocal hints, another singular feature of his mental condition. He was enchained by certain superstitious impressions in regard to the dwelling which he tenanted, and whence, for many years, he had never ventured forth—in regard to an influence whose supposititious force was conveyed in terms too shadowy here to be restated—an influence which some peculiarities in the mere form and substance of his family mansion, had, by dint of long sufferance, he said, obtained over his spirit—an effect which the physique of the grey walls and turrets, and of the dim tarn into which they all looked down, had at length brought about upon the morale of his existence.

He admitted, however, although with hesitation, that much of the peculiar gloom which thus afflicted him could be traced to a more natural and far more palpable origin—to the severe and long-continued illness, indeed to the evidently approaching dissolution, of a tenderly beloved sister—his sole companion for long years, his last and only relative on earth. "Her decease," he said, with a bitterness which I can never forget, "would leave him (him the hopeless and the frail) the last of the ancient race of the Ushers." While he spoke, the Lady Madeline (for so was she called) passed slowly through a remote portion of the apartment, and, without having noticed my presence, disappeared. I regarded her with an utter astonishment not unmingled with dread, and yet I found it impossible to account for such feelings. A sensation of stupor oppressed me, as my eyes followed her retreating steps. When a door at length closed upon her, my glance sought instinctively and eagerly the countenance of the brother, but he had buried his face in his hands, and I could only perceive that a far more than ordinary wanness had overspread the emaciated fingers through which trickled many passionate tears.

The disease of the Lady Madeline had long baffled the skill of her physicians. A settled apathy, a gradual wasting away of the person, and frequent although transient affections of a partially cataleptical character, were the unusual diagnosis. Hitherto she had steadily borne up against the pressure of her malady, and had not betaken herself finally to bed; but, on the closing in of the evening of my arrival at the house, she succumbed (as her brother told me at night with inexpressible agitation) to the prostrating power of the destroyer; and I learned that the glimpse I had obtained of her person would thus probably be the last I should obtain—that the lady, at least while living, would be seen by me no more.

For several days ensuing, her name was unmentioned by either Usher or myself; and during this period I was busied in earnest endeavors to alleviate the melancholy of my friend. We painted and read together; or I listened, as if in a dream, to the wild improvisations of his speaking guitar. And thus, as a closer and still closer intimacy admitted me more unreservedly into the recesses of his spirit, the more bitterly did I perceive the futility of all attempt at cheering a mind from which darkness, as if in an inherent positive quality, poured forth upon all objects of the moral and physical universe, in one unceasing radiation of gloom.

I shall ever bear about me a memory of the many solemn hours I thus spent alone with the master of the House of Usher. Yet I should fail in any attempt to convey an idea of the exact character of the studies, or of the occupations, in which he involved me, or led me the way. An excited and highly distempered ideality threw a sulphureous lustre over all. His long improvised dirges will ring for ever in my ears. Among other things, I hold painfully in mind a certain singular perversion and amplification of the wild air of the last waltz of Von Weber. From the paintings over which his elaborate fancy brooded, and which grew, touch by touch, into vagueness at which I shuddered the more thrillingly, because I shuddered knowing not why—

from these paintings (vivid as their images now are before me) I would in vain endeavor to educe more than a small portion which should lie within the compass of merely written words. By the utter simplicity, by the nakedness of his designs, he arrested and overawed attention. If ever mortal painted an idea, that mortal was Roderick Usher. For me at least, in the circumstances then surrounding me, there arose out of the pure abstractions which the hypochondriac contrived to throw upon his canvas, an intensity of intolerable awe, no shadow of which felt I ever yet in the contemplation of the certainly glowing yet too concrete reveries of Fuseli.

One of the phantasmagoric conceptions of my friend, partaking not so rigidly of the spirit of abstraction, may be shadowed forth, although feebly, in words. A small picture presented the interior of an immensely long and rectangular vault or tunnel, with low walls, smooth, white, and without interruption or device. Certain accessory points of the design served well to convey the idea that this excavation lay at an exceeding depth below the surface of the earth. No outlet was observed in any portion of its vast extent, and no torch, or other artificial source of light, was discernible; yet a flood of intense rays rolled throughout, and bathed the whole in a ghastly and inappropriate splendor.

I have just spoken of that morbid condition of the auditory nerve which rendered all music intolerable to the sufferer, with the exception of certain effects of stringed instruments. It was, perhaps, the narrow limits to which he thus confined himself upon the guitar, which gave birth, in great measure, to the fantastic character of his performances. But the fervid facility of his impromptus could not be so accounted for. They must have been, and were, in the notes, as well as in the words, of his wild fantasias (for he not unfrequently accompanied himself with rhymed verbal improvisations), the result of that intense mental collectedness and concentration to which I have previously alluded as observable only in particular moments of the highest artificial excitement. The words of one of these rhapsodies I have easily remembered. I was, perhaps, the more forcibly impressed with it, as he gave it, because, in the under or mystic current of its meaning, I fancied that I perceived, and for the first time, a full consciousness on the part of Usher, of the tottering of his lofty reason upon her throne. The verses, which were entitled "The Haunted Palace," ran very nearly, if not accurately, thus:—

I

In the greenest of our valleys,
    By good angels tenanted,
Once a fair and stately palace—
    Radiant palace—reared its head.
In the monarch Thought's dominion—
    It stood there!

Never seraph spread a pinion
        Over fabric half so fair.

II

Banners yellow, glorious, golden,
        On its roof did float and flow
(This—all this—was in the olden
        Time long ago);
And every gentle air that dallied,
        In that sweet day,
Along the ramparts plumed and pallid,
        A wingèd odor went away.

III

Wanderers in that happy valley
        Through two luminous windows saw
Spirits moving musically
        To a lute's well-tunèd law,
Round about a throne, where sitting
        (Porphyrogene!)
In state his glory well befitting,
        The ruler of the realm was seen.

IV

And all with pearl and ruby glowing
        Was the fair palace door,
Through which came flowing, flowing, flowing
        And sparkling evermore,
A troop of Echoes, whose sweet duty
        Was but to sing,
In voices of surpassing beauty,
        The wit and wisdom of their king.

V

But evil things, in robes of sorrow,
        Assailed the monarch's high estate.
(Ah, let us mourn, for never morrow
        Shall dawn upon him, desolate!)
And, round about his home, the glory
        That blushed and bloomed
Is but a dim-remembered story
        Of the old time entombed.

VI

And travellers now within that valley,
        Through the red-litten windows, see
Vast forms that move fantastically
        To a discordant melody;

> While, like a ghastly rapid river,
>   Through the pale door,
> A hideous throng rush out for ever,
>   And laugh—but smile no more.

I well remember that suggestions arising from this ballad led us into a train of thought wherein there became manifest an opinion of Usher's, which I mention not so much on account of its novelty (for other men have thought thus), as on account of the pertinacity with which he maintained it. This opinion, in its general form, was that of the sentience of all vegetable things. But, in his disordered fancy, the idea had assumed a more daring character, and trespassed, under certain conditions, upon the kingdom of inorganisation. I lack words to express the full extent, or the earnest *abandon* of his persuasion. The belief, however, was connected (as I have previously hinted) with the grey stones of the home of his forefathers. The conditions of the sentience had been here, he imagined, fulfilled in the method of collocation of these stones—in the order of their arrangement, as well as in that of the many fungi which overspread them, and of the decayed trees which stood around—above all, in the long undisturbed endurance of this arrangement, and in its reduplication in the still waters of the tarn. Its evidence—the evidence of the sentience—was to be seen, he said (and I here started as he spoke), in the gradual yet certain condensation of an atmosphere of their own about the waters and the walls. The result was discoverable, he added, in that silent, yet importunate and terrible influence which for centuries had moulded the destinies of his family, and which made *him* what I now saw him—what he was. Such opinions need no comment, and I will make none.

Our books—the books which, for years, had formed no small portion of the mental existence of the invalid—were, as might be supposed, in strict keeping with this character of phantasm. We pored together over such works as the *Ververt* and *Chartreuse* of Gresset; the *Belphegor* of Machiavelli; the *Heaven and Hell* of Swedenborg; the *Subterranean Voyage of Nicholas Klimm* by Holberg; the *Chiromancy* of Robert Flud, of Jean D'Indaginé, and of De la Chambre; the *Journey into the Blue Distance* of Tieck; and the *City of the Sun* of Campanella. One favorite volume was a small octavo edition of the *Directorium Inquisitorum*, by the Dominican Eymeric de Gironne; and there were passages in Pomponius Mela, about the old African Satyrs and Ægipans, over which Usher would sit dreaming for hours. His chief delight, however, was found in the perusal of an exceedingly rare and curious book in quarto Gothic—the manual of a forgotten church—the *Vigiliae Mortuorum secundum Chorum Ecclesiae Maguntinae.*

I could not help thinking of the wild ritual of this work, and of its probable influence upon the hypochondriac, when, one evening, having informed me abruptly that the Lady Madeline was no more, he stated his intention of preserving her corpse for a fortnight (previously to its final interment), in one of the numerous vaults within the main walls of the building. The worldly reason, however, assigned for this singular proceeding, was one which I did not feel at liberty to dispute. The brother had been led to his resolution (so he told me) by consideration of the unusual character of the malady of the deceased, of certain obtrusive and eager inquiries on the part of her medical men, and of the remote and exposed situation of the burial-ground of the family. I will not deny that when I called to mind the sinister countenance of the person whom I met upon the staircase, on the day of my arrival at the house, I had no desire to oppose what I regarded as at best but a harmless, and by no means an unnatural, precaution.

At the request of Usher, I personally aided him in the arrangements for the temporary entombment. The body having been encoffined, we two alone bore it to its rest. The vault in which we placed it (and which had been so long unopened that our torches, half smothered in its oppressive atmosphere, gave us little opportunity for investigation) was small, damp, and entirely without means of admission for light; lying, at great depth, immediately beneath that portion of the building in which was my own sleeping apartment. It had been used, apparently, in remote feudal times, for the worst purposes of a donjon-keep, and, in latter days, as a place of deposit for powder, or some other highly combustible substance, as a portion of its floor, and the whole interior of a long archway through which we reached it, were carefully sheathed with copper. The door, of massive iron, had been, also, similarly protected. Its immense weight caused an unusually sharp grating sound, as it moved upon its hinges.

Having deposited our mournful burden upon tressels within this region of horror, we partially turned aside the yet unscrewed lid of the coffin, and looked upon the face of the tenant. A striking similitude between the brother and sister now first arrested my attention; and Usher, divining, perhaps, my thoughts, murmured out some few words from which I learned that the deceased and himself had been twins, and that sympathies of a scarcely intelligible nature had always existed between them. Our glances, however, rested not long upon the dead—for we could not regard her unawed. The disease which had thus entombed the lady in the maturity of youth, had left, as usual in all maladies of a strictly cataleptical character, the mockery of a faint blush upon the bosom and the face, and that suspiciously lingering smile upon the lip which is so terrible in death. We replaced and screwed down the lid, and, having secured the door of iron, made our way, with toil, into the scarcely less gloomy apartments of the upper portion of the house.

And now, some days of bitter grief having elapsed, an observable change came over the features of the mental disorder of my friend. His ordinary manner had vanished. His ordinary occupations were neglected or forgotten.

He roamed from chamber to chamber with hurried, unequal, and objectless step. The pallor of his countenance had assumed, if possible, a more ghastly hue—but the luminousness of his eye had utterly gone out. The more occasional huskiness of his tone was heard no more; and a tremulous quaver, as if of extreme terror, habitually characterised his utterance. There were times, indeed, when I thought his unceasingly agitated mind was laboring with some oppressive secret, to divulge which he struggled for the necessary courage. At times, again, I was obliged to resolve all into the mere inexplicable vagaries of madness, for I beheld him gazing upon vacancy for long hours, in an attitude of the profoundest attention, as if listening to some imaginary sound. It was no wonder that his condition terrified—that it infected me. I felt creeping upon me, by slow yet certain degrees, the wild influences of his own fantastic yet impressive superstitions.

It was, especially, upon retiring to bed late in the night of the seventh or eighth day after the placing of the Lady Madeline within the donjon, that I experienced the full power of such feelings. Sleep came not near my couch, while the hours waned and waned away. I struggled to reason off the nervousness which had dominion over me. I endeavored to believe that much, if not all of what I felt, was due to the bewildering influence of the gloomy furniture of the room—of the dark and tattered draperies, which, tortured into motion by the breath of a rising tempest, swayed fitfully to and fro upon the walls, and rustled uneasily about the decorations of the bed. But my efforts were fruitless. An irrepressible tremor gradually pervaded my frame; and, at length, there sat upon my very heart an incubus of utterly causeless alarm. Shaking this off with a gasp and a struggle, I uplifted myself upon the pillows, and, peering earnestly within the intense darkness of the chamber, hearkened—I know not why, except that an instinctive spirit prompted me —to certain low and indefinite sounds which came, through the pauses of the storm, at long intervals, I knew not whence. Overpowered by an intense sentiment of horror, unaccountable yet unendurable, I threw on my clothes with haste (for I felt that I should sleep no more during the night), and endeavored to arouse myself from the pitiable condition into which I had fallen, by pacing rapidly to and fro through the apartment.

I had taken but few turns in this manner, when a light step on an adjoining staircase arrested my attention. I presently recognised it as that of Usher. In an instant afterward he rapped with a gentle touch, at my door, and entered, bearing a lamp. His countenance was, as usual, cadaverously wan—but, moreover, there was a species of mad hilarity in his eyes—an evidently restrained hysteria in his whole demeanor. His air appalled me—but anything was preferable to the solitude which I had so long endured, and I even welcomed his presence as a relief.

"And you have not seen it?" he said abruptly, after having stared about him for some moments in silence—"you have not then seen it?—but, stay! you shall." Thus speaking, and having carefully shaded his lamp, he hurried to one of the casements, and threw it freely open to the storm.

The impetuous fury of the entering gust nearly lifted us from our feet. It was, indeed, a tempestuous yet sternly beautiful night, and one wildly singular in its terror and its beauty. A whirlwind had apparently collected its force in our vicinity; for there were frequent and violent alterations in the direction of the wind; and the exceeding density of the clouds (which hung so low as to press upon the turrets of the house) did not prevent our perceiving the life-life velocity with which they flew careering from all points against each other, without passing away into the distance. I say that even their exceeding density did not prevent our perceiving this; yet we had no glimpse of the moon or stars, nor was there any flashing forth of the lightning. But the under surfaces of the huge masses of agitated vapor, as well as all terrestrial objects immediately around us, were glowing in the unnatural light of a faintly luminous and distinctly visible gaseous exhalation which hung about and enshrouded the mansion.

"You must not—you shall not behold this!" said I, shudderingly, to Usher, as I led him, with a gentle violence, from the window to a seat. "These appearances, which bewilder you, are merely electrical phenomena not uncommon—or it may be that they have their ghastly origin in the rank miasma of the tarn. Let us close this casement—the air is chilling and dangerous to your frame. Here is one of your favorite romances. I will read, and you shall listen —and so we will pass away this terrible night together."

The antique volume which I had taken up was the *Mad Trist* of Sir Launcelot Canning; but I had called it a favorite of Usher's more in sad jest than in earnest; for, in truth, there is little in its uncouth and unimaginative prolixity which could have had interest for the lofty and spiritual ideality of my friend. It was, however, the only book immediately at hand; and I indulged a vague hope that the excitement which now agitated the hypochondriac, might find relief (for the history of mental disorder is full of similar anomalies) even in the extremeness of the folly which I should read. Could I have judged, indeed, by the wild overstrained air of vivacity with which he hearkened, or apparently hearkened, to the words of the tale, I might well have congratulated myself upon the success of my design.

I had arrived at that well-known portion of the story where Ethelred, the hero of the *Trist,* having sought in vain for peaceable admission into the dwelling of the hermit, proceeds to make good an entrance by force. Here, it will be remembered, the words of the narrative run thus:

"And Ethelred, who was by nature of a doughty heart, and who was now mighty withal, on account of the powerfulness of the wine which he had drunken, waited no longer to hold parley with the hermit, who, in sooth, was of an obstinate and maliceful turn, but, feeling the rain upon his shoulders, and fearing the rising of the tempest, uplifted his mace outright, and, with blows, made quickly room in the plankings of the door for his gauntleted hand; and now pulling therewith sturdily, he so cracked, and ripped, and tore all asunder, that the noise of the dry and hollow-sounding wood alarumed and reverberated throughout the forest."

At the termination of this sentence I started, and for a moment paused; for it appeared to me (although I at once concluded that my excited fancy had deceived me)—it appeared to me that, from some very remote portion of the mansion, there came, indistinctly, to my ears, what might have been, in its exact similarity of character, the echo (but a stifled and dull one certainly) of the very cracking and ripping sound which Sir Launcelot had so particularly described. It was, beyond doubt, the coincidence alone which had arrested my attention; for, amid the rattling of the sashes of the casements, and the ordinary commingled noises of the still increasing storm, the sound, in itself, had nothing, surely, which should have interested or disturbed me. I continued the story:

"But the good champion Ethelred, now entering within the door, was sore enraged and amazed to perceive no signal of the maliceful hermit; but, in the stead thereof, a dragon of a scaly and prodigious demeanor, and of a fiery tongue, which sate in guard before a palace of gold, with a floor of silver; and upon the wall there hung a shield of shining brass with this legend enwritten:

'Who entereth herein, a conqueror hath bin;
Who slayeth the dragon, the shield he shall win.'

And Ethelred uplifted his mace, and struck upon the head of the dragon, which fell before him, and gave up his pesty breath, with a shriek so horrid and harsh, and withal so piercing, that Ethelred had fain to close his ears with his hands against the dreadful noise of it, the like whereof was never before heard."

Here again I paused abruptly, and now with a feeling of wild amazement —for there could be no doubt whatever that, in this instance, I did actually hear (although from what direction it proceeded I found it impossible to say) a low and apparently distant, but harsh, protracted, and most unusual screaming or grating sound—the exact counterpart of what my fancy had already conjured up for the dragon's unnatural shriek as described by the romancer.

Oppressed as I certainly was, upon the occurrence of this second and most extraordinary coincidence, by a thousand conflicting sensations, in which wonder and extreme terror were predominant, I still retained sufficient presence of mind to avoid exciting, by any observation, the sensitive nervousness of my companion. I was by no means certain that he had noticed the sound in question; although, assuredly, a strange alteration had, during the last few minutes, taken place in his demeanor. From a position fronting my own, he had gradually brought round his chair, so as to sit with his face to the door of the chamber; and thus I could but partially perceive his features, although I saw that his lips trembled as if he were murmuring inaudibly. His head had dropped upon his breast—yet I knew that he was not asleep, from the wide and rigid opening of the eye as I caught a glance of it in profile. The motion of his body, too, was at variance with this idea—for he rocked from side to side with a gentle yet constant and uniform sway. Having rapidly taken notice of all this, I resumed the narrative of Sir Launcelot, which thus proceeded:

"And now, the champion, having escaped from the terrible fury of the dragon, bethinking himself of the brazen shield, and of the breaking up of the enchantment which was upon it, removed the carcass from out of the way before him, and approached valorously over the silver pavement of the castle to where the shield was upon the wall; which in sooth tarried not for his full coming, but fell down at his feet upon the silver floor, with a mighty great and terrible ringing sound."

No sooner had these syllables passed my lips, than—as if a shield of brass had indeed, at the moment, fallen heavily upon a floor of silver—I became aware of a distinct, hollow, metallic, and clangorous, yet apparently muffled reverberation. Completely unnerved, I leaped to my feet; but the measured rocking movement of Usher was undisturbed. I rushed to the chair in which he sat. His eyes were bent fixedly before him, and throughout his whole countenance there reigned a stony rigidity. But, as I placed my hand upon his shoulder, there came a strong shudder over his whole person; a sickly smile quivered on his lips; and I saw that he spoke in a low, hurried, and gibbering murmur, as if unconscious of my presence. Bending closely over him, I at length drank in the hideous import of his words.

"Not hear it?—yes, I hear it, and *have* heard it. Long—long—long—many minutes, many hours, many days, have I heard it—yet I dared not—oh, pity me, miserable wretch that I am!—I dared not—I *dared* not speak! *We have put her living in the tomb!* Said I not that my senses were acute? I *now* tell you that I heard her first feeble movements in the hollow coffin. I heard them—many, many days ago—yet I dared not—*I dared not speak!* And now —to-night—Ethelred—ha! ha!—the breaking of the hermit's door, and the death-cry of the dragon, and the clangor of the shield!—say, rather, the rending of her coffin, and the grating of the iron hinges of her prison, and her struggles within the coppered archway of the vault! Oh, whither shall I fly? Will she not be here anon? Is she not hurrying to upbraid me for my haste? Have I not heard her footstep on the stair? Do I not distinguish that heavy and horrible beating of her heart? Madman!"—here he sprang furiously to his feet, and shrieked out his syllables, as if in the effort he were giving up his soul—"*Madman! I tell you that she now stands without the door!*"

As if in the superhuman energy of his utterance there had been found the potency of a spell, the huge antique panels to which the speaker pointed threw slowly back, upon the instant, their ponderous and ebony jaws. It was the work of the rushing gust—but then without those doors there *did* stand the lofty and enshrouded figure of the Lady Madeline of Usher. There was blood upon her white robes, and the evidence of some bitter struggle upon every portion of her emaciated frame. For a moment she remained trembling and reeling to and fro upon the threshold—then, with a low moaning cry, fell heavily inward upon the person of her brother, and in her violent and now final death-agonies, bore him to the floor a corpse, and a victim to the terrors he had anticipated.

From that chamber, and from that mansion, I fled aghast. The storm was still abroad in all its wrath as I found myself crossing the old causeway. Suddenly there shot along the path a wild light, and I turned to see whence a gleam so unusual could have issued; for the vast house and its shadows were alone behind me. The radiance was that of the full, setting, and blood-red moon, which now shone vividly through that once barely-discernible fissure, of which I have before spoken as extending from the roof of the building, in a zigzag direction, to the base. While I gazed, this fissure rapidly widened —there came a fierce breath of the whirlwind—the entire orb of the satellite burst at once upon my sight—my brain reeled as I saw the mighty walls rushing asunder—there was a long tumultuous shouting sound like a voice of a thousand waters—and the deep and dank tarn at my feet closed sullenly and silently over the fragments of the *"House of Usher."*

THE PURLOINED LETTER [4]

"Nil sapientiæ odiosius acumine nimio."—SENECA.

At Paris, just after dark one gusty evening in the autumn of 18—, I was enjoying the twofold luxury of meditation and a meerschaum, in company with my friend, C. Auguste Dupin, in his little back library or book-closet, *au troisième,* No. 33 Rue Dunôt, Faubourg St. Germain. For one hour at least we had maintained a profound silence; while each, to any casual observer, might have seemed intently and exclusively occupied with the curling eddies of smoke that oppressed the atmosphere of the chamber. For myself, however, I was mentally discussing certain topics which had formed matter for conversation between us at an earlier period of the evening; I mean the affair of the Rue Morgue, and the mystery attending the murder of Marie Rogêt. I looked upon it, therefore, as something of a coincidence, when the door of our apartment was thrown open and admitted our old acquaintance, Monsieur G——, the Prefect of the Parisian police.

We gave him a hearty welcome; for there was nearly half as much of the entertaining as of the contemptible about the man, and we had not seen him

[4] First published in *The Gift,* 1845, and included in *Tales* (1845).

for several years. We had been sitting in the dark, and Dupin now arose for the purpose of lighting a lamp, but sat down again, without doing so, upon G.'s saying that he had called to consult us, or rather to ask the opinion of my friend, about some official business which had occasioned a great deal of trouble.

"If it is any point requiring reflection," observed Dupin, as he forbore to enkindle the wick, "we shall examine it to better purpose in the dark."

"That is another of your odd notions," said the Prefect, who had a fashion of calling everything "odd" that was beyond his comprehension, and thus lived amid an absolute legion of "oddities."

"Very true," said Dupin, as he supplied his visitor with a pipe, and rolled towards him a comfortable chair.

"And what is the difficulty now?" I asked. "Nothing more in the assassination way, I hope?"

"Oh, no; nothing of that nature. The fact is, the business is *very* simple indeed, and I make no doubt that we can manage it sufficiently well ourselves; but then I thought Dupin would like to hear the details of it, because it is so excessively *odd*."

"Simple and odd," said Dupin.

"Why, yes; and not exactly that, either. The fact is, we have all been a good deal puzzled because the affair *is* so simple, and yet baffles us altogether."

"Perhaps it is the very simplicity of the thing which puts you at fault," said my friend.

"What nonsense you *do* talk!" replied the Prefect, laughing heartily.

"Perhaps the mystery is a little *too* plain," said Dupin.

"Oh, good heavens! who ever heard of such an idea?"

"A little *too* self-evident."

"Ha! ha! ha!—ha! ha! ha!—ho! ho! ho!" roared our visitor, profoundly amused. "O Dupin, you will be the death of me yet."

"And what, after all, *is* the matter on hand?" I asked.

"Why, I will tell you," replied the Prefect, as he gave a long, steady, and contemplative puff, and settled himself in his chair. "I will tell you in a few words; but, before I begin, let me caution you that this is an affair demanding the greatest secrecy, and that I should most probably lose the position I now hold, were it known that I confided it to any one."

"Proceed," said I.

"Or not," said Dupin.

"Well, then; I have received personal information, from a very high quarter, that a certain document of the last importance has been purloined from the royal apartments. The individual who purloined it is known; this beyond a doubt; he was seen to take it. It is known, also, that it still remains in his possession."

"How is this known?" asked Dupin.

"It is clearly inferred," replied the Prefect, "from the nature of the document, and from the non-appearance of certain results which would at once arise from its passing *out* of the robber's possession—that is to say, from his employing it as he must design in the end to employ it."

"Be a little more explicit," I said.

"Well, I may venture so far as to say that the paper gives its holder a certain power in a certain quarter where such power is immensely valuable." The Prefect was fond of the cant of diplomacy.

"Still I do not quite understand," said Dupin.

"No? Well; the disclosure of the document to a third person, who shall be nameless, would bring in question the honor of a personage of most exalted station; and this fact gives the holder of the document an ascendency over the illustrious personage whose honor and peace are so jeopardised."

"But this ascendency," I interposed, "would depend upon the robber's knowledge of the loser's knowledge of the robber. Who would dare—"

"The thief," said G., "is the Minister D——, who dares all things, those unbecoming as well as those becoming a man. The method of the theft was not less ingenious than bold. The document in question—a letter, to be frank—had been received by the personage robbed while alone in the royal boudoir. During its perusal she was suddenly interrupted by the entrance of the other exalted personage from whom especially it was her wish to conceal it. After a hurried and vain endeavor to thrust it in a drawer, she was forced to place it, open as it was, upon a table. The address, however, was uppermost, and, the contents thus unexposed, the letter escaped notice. At this juncture enters the Minister D——. His lynx eye immediately perceives the paper, recognises the handwriting of the address, observes the confusion of the personage addressed, and fathoms her secret. After some business transactions, hurried through in his ordinary manner, he produces a letter somewhat similar to the one in question, opens it, pretends to read it, and then places it in close juxtaposition to the other. Again he converses, for some fifteen minutes, upon the public affairs. At length, in taking leave, he takes also from the table the letter to which he had no claim. Its rightful owner saw, but, of course, dared not call attention to the act, in the presence of the third personage who stood at her elbow. The Minister decamped, leaving his own letter—one of no importance—upon the table."

"Here, then," said Dupin to me, "you have precisely what you demand to make the ascendency complete—the robber's knowledge of the loser's knowledge of the robber."

"Yes," replied the Prefect; "and the power thus attained has, for some months past, been wielded, for political purposes, to a very dangerous extent. The personage robbed is more thoroughly convinced, every day, of the necessity of reclaiming her letter. But this, of course, cannot be done openly. In fine, driven to despair, she has committed the matter to me."

"Than whom," said Dupin, amid a perfect whirlwind of smoke, "no more sagacious agent could, I suppose, be desired, or even imagined."

"You flatter me," replied the Prefect; "but it is possible that some such opinion may have been entertained."

"It is clear," said I, "as you observe, that the letter is still in the possession of the Minister; since it is this possession, and not any employment of the letter, which bestows the power. With the employment the power departs."

"True," said G.; "and upon this conviction I proceeded. My first care was to make thorough search of the Minister's hotel; and here my chief embarrassment lay in the necessity of searching without his knowledge. Beyond all things, I have been warned of the danger which would result from giving him reason to suspect our design."

"But," said I, "you are quite *au fait* in these investigations. The Parisian police have done this thing often before."

"Oh yes; and for this reason I did not despair. The habits of the Minister gave me, too, a great advantage. He is frequently absent from home all night. His servants are by no means numerous. They sleep at a distance from their master's apartment, and, being chiefly Neapolitans, are readily made drunk. I have keys, as you know, with which I can open any chamber or cabinet in Paris. For three months a night has not passed, during the greater part of which I have not been engaged, personally, in ransacking the D—— Hotel. My honor is interested, and, to mention a great secret, the reward is enormous. So I did not abandon the search until I had become fully satisfied that the thief is a more astute man than myself. I fancy that I have investigated every nook and corner of the premises in which it is possible that the paper can be concealed."

"But is it not possible," I suggested, "that although the letter may be in possession of the Minister, as it unquestionably is, he may have concealed it elsewhere than upon his own premises?"

"This is barely possible," said Dupin. "The present peculiar condition of affairs at court, and especially of those intrigues in which D—— is known to be involved, would render the instant availability of the document—its susceptibility of being produced at a moment's notice—a point of nearly equal importance with its possession."

"Its susceptibility of being produced?" said I.

"That is to say, of being *destroyed*," said Dupin.

"True," I observed; "the paper is clearly then upon the premises. As for its being upon the person of the Minister, we may consider that as out of the question."

"Entirely," said the Prefect. "He has been twice waylaid, as if by footpads, and his person rigorously searched under my own inspection."

"You might have spared yourself this trouble," said Dupin. "D——, I presume, is not altogether a fool, and, if not, must have anticipated these waylayings, as a matter of course."

"Not *altogether* a fool," said G.; "but then he's a poet, which I take to be only one remove from a fool."

"True," said Dupin, after a long and thoughtful whiff from his meerschaum, "although I have been guilty of certain doggerel myself."

"Suppose you detail," said I, "the particulars of your search."

"Why, the fact is we took our time, and we searched *everywhere*. I have had long experience in these affairs. I took the entire building, room by room; devoting the nights of a whole week to each. We examined, first, the furniture of each apartment. We opened every possible drawer; and I presume you know that, to a properly trained police agent, such a thing as a *secret* drawer is impossible. Any man is a dolt who permits a 'secret' drawer to escape him in a search of this kind. The thing is *so* plain. There is a certain amount of bulk—of space—to be accounted for in every cabinet. Then we have accurate rules. The fiftieth part of a line could not escape us. After the cabinets we took the chairs. The cushions we probed with the fine long needles you have seen me employ. From the tables we removed the tops."

"Why so?"

"Sometimes the top of a table, or other similarly arranged piece of furniture, is removed by the person wishing to conceal an article; then the leg is excavated, the article deposited within the cavity, and the top replaced. The bottoms and tops of bedposts are employed in the same way."

"But could not the cavity be detected by sounding?" I asked.

"By no means, if, when the article is deposited, a sufficient wadding of cotton be placed around it. Besides, in our case, we were obliged to proceed without noise."

"But you could not have removed—you could not have taken to pieces *all* articles of furniture in which it would have been possible to make a deposit in the manner you mention. A letter may be compressed into a thin spiral roll, not differing much in shape or bulk from a large knitting-needle, and in this form it might be inserted into the rung of a chair, for example. You did not take to pieces all the chairs?"

"Certainly not; but we did better—we examined the rungs of every chair in the hotel, and, indeed, the jointings of every description of furniture, by the aid of a most powerful microscope. Had there been any traces of recent disturbance we should not have failed to detect it instantly. A single grain of gimlet-dust, for example, would have been as obvious as an apple. Any disorder in the glueing—any unusual gaping in the joints—would have sufficed to ensure detection."

"I presume you looked to the mirrors, between the boards and the plates, and you probed the beds and the bedclothes, as well as the curtains and carpets."

"That of course; and when we had absolutely completed every particle of the furniture in this way, then we examined the house itself. We divided its entire surface into compartments, which we numbered, so that none might be missed; then we scrutinised each individual square inch throughout the premises, including the two houses immediately adjoining, with the microscope, as before."

"The two houses adjoining!" I exclaimed; "you must have had a great deal of trouble."

"We had; but the reward offered is prodigious."

"You include the *grounds* about the houses?"

"All the grounds are paved with brick. They gave us comparatively little trouble. We examined the moss between the bricks, and found it undisturbed."

"You looked among D——'s papers, of course, and into the books of the library?"

"Certainly; we opened every package and parcel; we not only opened every book, but we turned over every leaf in each volume, not contenting ourselves with a mere shake, according to the fashion of some of our police officers. We also measured the thickness of every book-*cover,* with the most accurate admeasurement, and applied to each the most jealous scrutiny of the microscope. Had any of the bindings been recently meddled with, it would have been utterly impossible that the fact should have escaped observation. Some five or six volumes, just from the hands of the binder, we carefully probed longitudinally, with the needles."

"You explored the floors beneath the carpets?"

"Beyond doubt. We removed every carpet, and examined the boards with the microscope."

"And the paper on the walls?"

"Yes."

"You looked into the cellars?"

"We did."

"Then," I said, "you have been making a miscalculation, and the letter is *not* upon the premises, as you suppose."

"I fear you are right there," said the Prefect. "And now, Dupin, what would you advise me to do?"

"To make a thorough research of the premises."

"That is absolutely needless," replied G——. "I am not more sure that I breathe than I am that the letter is not at the hotel."

"I have no better advice to give you," said Dupin. "You have, of course, an accurate description of the letter?"

"Oh yes!" And here the Prefect, producing a memorandum-book, proceeded to read aloud a minute account of the internal, and especially of the external appearance of the missing document. Soon after finishing the perusal of this description, he took his departure more entirely depressed in spirits than I had ever known the good gentleman before.

In about a month afterwards he paid us another visit, and found us occupied very nearly as before. He took a pipe and a chair and entered into some ordinary conversation. At length I said—

"Well, but G——, what of the purloined letter? I presume you have at last made up your mind that there is no such thing as overreaching the Minister?"

"Confound him, say I—yes; I made the re-examination, however, as Dupin suggested—but it was all labor lost, as I knew it would be."

"How much was the reward offered, did you say?" asked Dupin.

"Why, a very great deal—a *very* liberal reward—I don't like to say how much, precisely; but I *will* say, that I wouldn't mind giving my individual cheque for fifty thousand francs to any one who could obtain me that letter. The fact is, it is becoming of more and more importance every day; and the reward has been lately doubled. If it were trebled, however, I could do no more than I have done."

"Why, yes," said Dupin drawlingly, between the whiffs of his meerschaum, "I really—think, G——, you have not exerted yourself—to the utmost—in this matter. You might—do a little more, I think, eh?"

"How?—in what way?"

"Why—puff, puff—you might—puff, puff—employ counsel in the matter, eh?—puff, puff, puff. Do you remember the story they tell of Abernethy?"

"No; hang Abernethy!"

"To be sure! hang him and welcome. But once upon a time, a certain rich miser conceived the design of sponging upon this Abernethy for a medical opinion. Getting up, for this purpose, an ordinary conversation in a private company, he insinuated his case to the physician, as that of an imaginary individual.

" 'We will suppose,' said the miser, 'that his symptoms are such and such; now, doctor, what would *you* have directed him to take?'

" 'Take!' said Abernethy, 'why, take *advice*, to be sure.' "

"But," said the Prefect, a little discomposed, "I am *perfectly* willing to take advice, and to pay for it. I would *really* give fifty thousand francs to any one who would aid me in the matter."

"In that case," replied Dupin, opening a drawer, and producing a cheque-book, "you may as well fill me up a cheque for the amount mentioned. When you have signed it, I will hand you the letter."

I was astounded. The Prefect appeared absolutely thunderstricken. For some minutes he remained speechless and motionless, looking incredulously at my friend with open mouth, and eyes that seemed starting from their sockets; then, apparently recovering himself in some measure, he seized a pen, and after several pauses and vacant stares, finally filled up and signed a cheque for fifty thousand francs, and handed it across the table to Dupin. The latter examined it carefully and deposited it in his pocket-book; then, unlocking an escritoire, took thence a letter and gave it to the Prefect. This functionary grasped it in a perfect agony of joy, opened it with a trembling hand, cast a rapid glance at its contents, and then, scrambling and struggling to the door, rushed at length unceremoniously from the room and from the house, without having uttered a syllable since Dupin had requested him to fill up the cheque.

When he had gone, my friend entered into some explanations.

"The Parisian police," he said, "are exceedingly able in their way. They are persevering, ingenious, cunning, and thoroughly versed in the knowledge which their duties seem chiefly to demand. Thus, when G—— detailed to us his mode of searching the premises at the Hôtel D——, I felt entire confidence in his having made a satisfactory investigation—so far as his labors extended."

"So far as his labors extended?" said I.

"Yes," said Dupin. "The measures adopted were not only the best of their kind, but carried out to absolute perfection. Had the letter been deposited within the range of their search, these fellows would, beyond a question, have found it."

I merely laughed—but he seemed quite serious in all that he said.

"The measures, then," he continued, "were good in their kind, and well executed; their defect lay in their being inapplicable to the case, and to the man. A certain set of highly ingenious resources are, with the Prefect, a sort of Procrustean bed, to which he forcibly adapts his designs. But he perpetually errs by being too deep or too shallow for the matter in hand; and many a schoolboy is a better reasoner than he. I knew one about eight years of age, whose success at guessing in the game of 'even and odd' attracted universal admiration. This game is simple, and is played with marbles. One player holds in his hand a number of these toys, and demands of another whether that number is even or odd. If the guess is right, the guesser wins one; if wrong, he loses one. The boy to whom I allude won all the marbles of the school. Of course he had some principle of guessing; and this lay in mere observation and admeasurement of the astuteness of his opponents. For example, an arrant simpleton is his opponent, and, holding up his closed hand, asks, 'Are they even or odd?' Our schoolboy replies 'Odd,' and loses; but upon the second trial he wins, for he then says to himself, 'The simpleton had them even upon the first trial, and his amount of cunning is just sufficient to make him have them odd upon the second; I will therefore guess odd'—he guesses odd, and wins. Now, with a simpleton a degree above the first, he would have reasoned thus: 'This fellow finds that in the first instance I guessed odd, and, in the second, he will propose to himself, upon the first impulse, a simple variation from even to odd, as did the first simpleton; but then a second thought will suggest that this is too simple a variation, and finally he will decide upon putting it even as before. I will therefore guess even'—he guesses even, and wins. Now this mode of reasoning in the school-boy, whom his fellows termed 'lucky'—what, in its last analysis, is it?"

"It is merely," I said, "an identification of the reasoner's intellect with that of his opponent."

"It is," said Dupin; "and upon inquiring of the boy by what means he effected the *thorough* identification in which his success consisted, I received answer as follows: 'When I wish to find out how wise, or how stupid, or how good, or how wicked is any one, or what are his thoughts at the moment, I fashion the expression of my face, as accurately as possible, in accordance with the expression of his, and then wait to see what thoughts or sentiments arise in my mind or heart, as if to match or correspond with the expression.' This response of the schoolboy lies at the bottom of all the spurious profundity which has been attributed to Rochefoucauld, to La Bruyère, to Machiavelli, and to Campanella."

"And the identification," I said, "of the reasoner's intellect with that of his opponent, depends, if I understand you aright, upon the accuracy with which the opponent's intellect is admeasured."

"For its practical value it depends upon this," replied Dupin; "and the Prefect and his cohort fail so frequently, first, by default of his identification, and, secondly, by ill-admeasurement, or rather through non-admeasurement, of the intellect with which they are engaged. They consider only their *own* ideas of ingenuity; and, in searching for anything hidden, advert only to the modes in which *they* would have hidden it. They are right in this much—that their own ingenuity is a faithful representative of that of *the mass;* but when the cunning of the individual felon is diverse in character from their own, the felon foils them, of course. This always happens when it is above their own, and very usually when it is below. They have no variation of principle in their investigations; at best, when urged by some unusual emergency—by some extraordinary reward—they extend or exaggerate their old modes of *practice,* without touching their principles. What, for example, in the case of D——, has been done to vary the principle of action? What is all this boring, and probing, and sounding, and scrutinising with the microscope, and dividing the surface of the building into registered square inches—what is it all but an exaggeration *of the application* of the one principle or set of principles of search, which are based upon the one set of notions regarding human ingenuity, to which the Prefect, in the long routine of his duty, has been accustomed? Do you not see he has taken it for granted that *all* men proceed to conceal a letter—not exactly in a gimlet-hole bored in a chair-leg—but, at least, in *some* out-of-the-way hole or corner suggested by the same tenor of thought which would urge a man to secrete a letter in a gimlet-hole bored in a chair-leg? And do you not see also, that such *recherchés* nooks for conceal-ment are adapted only for ordinary occasions, and would be adopted only by ordinary intellects; for, in all cases of concealment, a disposal of the article concealed—a disposal of it in this *recherché* manner—is, in the very first instance, presumable and presumed; and thus its discovery depends, not at all upon the acumen, but altogether upon the mere care, patience, and determination of the seekers; and where the case is of im-portance—or, what amounts to the same thing in the policial eyes, when the reward is of magnitude—the qualities in question have *never* been known to fail. You will now understand what I meant in suggesting that, had the purloined letter been hidden anywhere within the limits of the Prefect's ex-amination—in other words, had the principle of its concealment been com-prehended within the principles of the Prefect—its discovery would have been a matter altogether beyond question. This functionary, however, has been thoroughly mystified; and the remote source of his defeat lies in the supposi-tion that the Minister is a fool, because he has acquired renown as a poet. All fools are poets—this the Prefect *feels;* and he is merely guilty of a *non distri-butio medii* in thence inferring that all poets are fools."

"But is this really the poet?" I asked. "There are two brothers, I know; and both have attained reputation in letters. The Minister, I believe, has writ-ten learnedly on the Differential Calculus. He is a mathematician, and no poet."

"You are mistaken; I know him well; he is both. As poet *and* mathemati-cian, he would reason well; as mere mathematician, he could not have rea-soned at all, and thus would have been at the mercy of the Prefect."

"You surprise me," I said, "by these opinions, which have been contra-dicted by the voice of the world. You do not mean to set at naught the well-digested idea of centuries. The mathematical reason has long been regarded as *the* reason *par excellence.*"

" 'Il-y-a à parier,' " replied Dupin, quoting from Chamfort, " '*que toute idée publique, toute convention reçue, est une sottise, car elle a convenue au plus grand nombre.*' The mathematicians, I grant you, have done their best to promulgate the popular error to which you allude, and which is none the less an error for its promulgation as truth. With an art worthy a better cause, for example, they have insinuated the term 'analysis' into application to algebra. The French are the originators of this particular deception; but if a term is of any importance—if words derive any value from applicability—then 'analysis' conveys 'algebra' about as much as, in Latin, *'ambitus'* implies 'ambition,' *'religio'* 'religion,' or *'homines honesti'* a set of *honorable* men."

"You have a quarrel on hand, I see," said I, "with some of the algebraists of Paris; but proceed."

"I dispute the availability, and thus the value, of that reason which is cultivated in any especial form other than the abstractly logical. I dispute, in particular, the reason educed by mathematical study. The mathematics are the science of form and quantity; mathematical reasoning is merely logic applied to observation upon form and quantity. The great error lies in supposing that even the truths of what is called *pure* algebra, are abstract or general truths. And this error is so egregious that I am confounded at the universality with which it has been received. Mathematical axioms are *not* axioms of general truth. What is true of *relation*—of form and quantity—is often grossly false in regard to morals, for example. In this latter science it is very usually *un*true that the aggregated parts are equal to the whole. In chemistry also the axiom fails. In the consideration of motive it fails; for two motives, each of a given value, have not, necessarily, a value when united, equal to the sum of their values apart. There are numerous other mathematical truths which are only truths within the limits of *relation*. But the mathematician argues, from his *finite truths,* through habit, as if they were of an absolutely general applicability—as the world indeed imagines them to be. Bryant, in his very learned 'Mythology,' mentions an analogous source of error, when he says that 'although the Pagan fables are not believed, yet we forget ourselves continually, and make inferences from them as existing realities.' With the algebraists, however, who are Pagans themselves, the 'Pagan fables' *are* believed, and the inferences are made, not so much through lapse of memory, as through an unaccountable addling of the brains. In short, I never yet encountered the mere mathematician who could be trusted out of equal roots, or one who did not clandestinely hold it as a point of his faith that $x^2 + px$ was absolutely and unconditionally equal to q. Say to one of these gentlemen, by way of experiment, if you please, that you believe occasions may occur when $x^2 + px$ is *not* altogether equal to $q,$ and, having made him understand what you mean, get out of his reach as speedily as convenient, for, beyond doubt, he will endeavor to knock you down.

"I mean to say," continued Dupin, while I merely laughed at his last observations, "that if the Minister had been no more than a mathematician, the Prefect would have been under no necessity of giving me this cheque. I knew him, however, as both mathematician and poet, and my measures were adapted to his capacity, with reference to the circumstances by which he was surrounded. I knew him as a courtier, too, and as a bold *intriguant*. Such a man,

I considered, could not fail to be aware of the ordinary policial modes of action. He could not have failed to anticipate—and events have proved that he did not fail to anticipate—the waylayings to which he was subjected. He must have foreseen, I reflected, the secret investigations of his premises. His frequent absences from home at night, which were hailed by the Prefect as certain aids to his success, I regarded only as ruses, to afford opportunity for thorough search to the police, and thus the sooner to impress them with the conviction to which G——, in fact, did finally arrive—the conviction that the letter was not upon the premises. I felt, also, that the whole train of thought, which I was at some pains in detailing to you just now, concerning the invariable principle of policial action in searches for articles concealed—I felt that this whole train of thought would necessarily pass through the mind of the Minister. It would imperatively lead him to despise all the ordinary *nooks* of concealment. *He* could not, I reflected, be so weak as not to see that the most intricate and remote recess of his hotel would be as open as his commonest closets to the eyes, to the probes, to the gimlets, and to the microscopes of the Prefect. I saw, in fine, that he would be driven, as a matter of course, to *simplicity,* if not deliberately induced to it as a matter of choice. You will remember, perhaps, how desperately the Prefect laughed when I suggested, upon our first interview, that it was just possible this mystery troubled him so much on account of its being so *very* self-evident."

"Yes," said I, "I remember his merriment well. I really thought he would have fallen into convulsions."

"The material world," continued Dupin, "abounds with very strict analogies to the immaterial; and thus some color of truth has been given to the rhetorical dogma, that metaphor, or simile, may be made to strengthen an argument, as well as to embellish a description. The principle of the *vis inertiæ,* for example, seems to be identical in physics and metaphysics. It is not more true in the former, that a large body is with more difficulty set in motion than a smaller one, and that its subsequent momentum is commensurate with this difficulty, than it is, in the latter, that intellects of the vaster capacity, while more forcible, more constant, and more eventful in their movements than those of inferior grade, are yet the less readily moved, and more embarrassed and full of hesitation in the first few steps of their progress. Again, have you ever noticed which of the street signs over the shop-doors are the most attractive of attention?"

"I have never given the matter a thought," I said.

"There is a game of puzzles," he resumed, "which is played upon a map. One party playing requires another to find a given word—the name of town, river, state, or empire—any word, in short, upon the motley and perplexed surface of the chart. A novice in the game generally seeks to embarrass his opponents by giving them the most minutely lettered names; but the adept selects such words as stretch, in large characters, from one end of the chart to the other. These, like the over-large lettered signs and placards of the street, escape observation by dint of being excessively obvious; and here the physical oversight is precisely analogous with the moral inapprehension by which the intellect suffers to pass unnoticed those considerations which are too obtrusively and too palpably self-evident. But this is a point, it appears, somewhat above or beneath the understanding of the Prefect. He never once thought it probable, or possible, that the Minister had deposited the letter immediately beneath the nose of the whole world, by way of best preventing any portion of that world from perceiving it.

"But the more I reflected upon the daring, dashing, and discriminating ingenuity of D——; upon the fact that the document must always have been *at hand,* if he intended to use it to good purpose; and upon the decisive evidence, obtained by the Prefect, that it was not hidden within the limits of that dignitary's ordinary search—the more satisfied I became that, to conceal this letter, the Minister had resorted to the comprehensive and sagacious expedient of not attempting to conceal it at all.

"Full of these ideas, I prepared myself with a pair of green spectacles, and called one fine morning, quite by accident, at the Ministerial hotel. I found D—— at home, yawning, lounging, and dawdling, as usual, and pretending to be in the last extremity of ennui. He is, perhaps, the most really energetic human being now alive—but that is only when nobody sees him.

"To be even with him, I complained of my weak eyes, and lamented the necessity of the spectacles, under cover of which I cautiously and thoroughly surveyed the whole apartment, while seemingly intent only upon the conversation of my host.

"I paid especial attention to a large writing-table near which he sat, and upon which lay confusedly some miscellaneous letters and other papers, with one or two musical instruments and a few books. Here, however, after a long and very deliberate scrutiny, I saw nothing to excite particular suspicion.

"At length my eyes, in going the circuit of the room, fell upon a trumpery filigree card-rack of paste-board, that hung dangling by a dirty blue ribbon, from a little brass knob just beneath the middle of the mantelpiece. In this rack, which had three or four compartments, were five or six visiting cards and a solitary letter. This last was much soiled and crumpled. It was torn nearly in two, across the middle—as if a design, in the first instance, to tear it entirely up as worthless, had been altered, or stayed, in the second. It had a large black seal, bearing the D—— cipher *very* conspicuously, and was addressed, in a diminutive female hand, to D——, the Minister, himself. It was thrust carelessly, and even, as it seemed, contemptuously, into one of the uppermost divisions of the rack.

"No sooner had I glanced at this letter, than I concluded it to be that of which I was in search. To be sure, it was, to all appearance, radically different from the one of which the Prefect had read us so minute a description. Here the seal was large and black, with the D—— cipher; there it was small and red, with the ducal arms of the S—— family. Here, the address, to the Minister, was diminutive and feminine; there the superscription, to a certain royal personage, was markedly bold and decided; the size alone formed a point of correspondence. But then the *radicalness* of these differences, which was excessive; the dirt; the soiled and torn condition of the paper, so inconsistent with the *true* methodical habits of D——, and so suggestive of a design to delude the beholder into an idea of the worthlessness of the document; these things, together with the hyper-obtrusive situation of this document, full in the view of every visitor, and thus exactly in accordance with the conclusions to which I had previously arrived; these things, I say, were strongly corroborative of suspicion, in one who came with the intention to suspect.

"I protracted my visit as long as possible, and, while I maintained a most animated discussion with the Minister, upon a topic which I knew well had never failed to interest and excite him, I kept my attention really riveted upon the letter. In this examination, I committed to memory its external appearance and arrangement in the rack; and also fell, at length, upon a discovery, which set at rest whatever trivial doubt I might have entertained. In scrutinising the edges of the paper, I observed them to be more *chafed* than seemed necessary. They presented the *broken* appearance which is manifested when a stiff paper, having been once folded and pressed with a folder, is refolded in a reversed direction, in the same creases or edges which had formed the original fold. This discovery was sufficient. It was clear to me that the letter had been turned, as a glove, inside out, redirected and resealed. I bade the Minister good-morning, and took my departure at once, leaving a gold snuff-box upon the table.

"The next morning I called for the snuff-box, when we resumed, quite eagerly, the conversation of the preceding day. While thus engaged, however, a loud report, as if of a pistol, was heard immediately beneath the windows of the hotel, and was succeeded by a series of fearful screams, and the shoutings of a terrified mob. D—— rushed to a casement, threw it open, and looked out. In the meantime, I stepped to the card-rack, took the letter, put it in my pocket, and replaced it by a fac-simile (so far as regards externals) which I had carefully prepared at my lodgings—imitating the D—— cipher, very readily, by means of a seal formed of bread.

"The disturbance in the street had been occasioned by the frantic behavior of a man with a musket. He had fired it among a crowd of women and children. It proved, however, to have been without ball, and the fellow was suffered to go his way as a lunatic or a drunkard. When he had gone, D—— came from the window, whither I had followed him immediately upon securing the object in view. Soon afterwards I bade him farewell. The pretended lunatic was a man in my own pay."

"But what purpose had you," I asked, "in replacing the letter by a facsimile? Would it not have been better, at the first visit, to have seized it openly, and departed?"

"D——," replied Dupin, "is a desperate man, and a man of nerve. His hotel, too, is not without attendants devoted to his interests. Had I made the wild attempt you suggest, I might never have left the Ministerial presence alive. The good people of Paris might have heard of me no more. But I had an object apart from these considerations. You know my political prepossessions. In this matter, I act as a partisan of the lady concerned. For eighteen months the Minister has had her in his power. She has now him in hers—since, being unaware that the letter is not in his possession, he will proceed with his exactions as if it was. Thus will he inevitably commit himself, at once, to his political destruction. His downfall, too, will not be more precipitate than awkward. It is all very well to talk about the *facilis descensus Averni;* but in all kinds of climbing, as Catalani said of singing, it is far more easy to get up than to come down. In the present instance I have no sympathy—at least no pity—for him who descends. He is that *monstrum horrendum,* an unprincipled man of genius. I confess, however, that I should like very well to know the precise character of his thoughts, when, being defied by her whom the Prefect terms 'a certain personage,' he is reduced to opening the letter which I left for him in the card-rack."

"How? Did you put anything particular in it?"

"Why—it did not seem altogether right to leave the interior blank—that would have been insulting. D——, at Vienna once, did me an evil turn, which I told him, quite good-humoredly, that I should remember. So, as I knew he would feel some curiosity in regard to the identity of the person who had outwitted him, I thought it a pity not to give him a clew. He is well acquainted with my MS., and I just copied into the middle of the blank sheet the words:—

'——Un dessein si funeste,
S'il n'est digne d'Atrée, est digne de Thyeste.'

They are to be found in Crébillon's *Atrée.*"

THE CASK OF AMONTILLADO [5]

THE thousand injuries of Fortunato I had borne as I best could; but when he ventured upon insult, I vowed revenge. You, who so well know the nature of my soul, will not suppose, however, that I gave utterance to a threat. *At*

[5] First published in *Godey's Lady's Book,* November, 1846.

length I would be avenged; this was a point definitely settled—but the very definitiveness with which it was resolved, precluded the idea of risk. I must not only punish, but punish with impunity. A wrong is unredressed when retribution overtakes its redresser. It is equally unredressed when the avenger fails to make himself felt as such to him who has done the wrong.

It must be understood, that neither by word nor deed had I given Fortunato cause to doubt my good-will. I continued, as was my wont, to smile in his face, and he did not perceive that my smile *now* was at the thought of his immolation.

He had a weak point—this Fortunato—although in other regards he was a man to be respected and even feared. He prided himself on his connoisseurship in wine. Few Italians have the true virtuoso spirit. For the most part their enthusiasm is adapted to suit the time and opportunity—to practise imposture upon the British and Austrian millionaires. In painting and gemmary Fortunato, like his countrymen, was a quack—but in the matter of old wines he was sincere. In this respect I did not differ from him materially: I was skilful in the Italian vintages myself, and bought largely whenever I could.

It was about dusk, one evening during the supreme madness of the Carnival season, that I encountered my friend. He accosted me with excessive warmth, for he had been drinking much. The man wore motley. He had on a tight-fitting parti-striped dress, and his head was surmounted by the conical cap and bells. I was so pleased to see him, that I thought I should never have done wringing his hand.

I said to him, "My dear Fortunato, you are luckily met. How remarkably well you are looking to-day! But I have received a pipe of what passes for Amontillado, and I have my doubts."

"How?" said he; "Amontillado? A pipe? Impossible! And in the middle of the Carnival!"

"I have my doubts," I replied; "and I was silly enough to pay the full Amontillado price without consulting you in the matter. You were not to be found, and I was fearful of losing a bargain."

"Amontillado!"

"I have my doubts."

"Amontillado!"

"And I must satisfy them."

"Amontillado!"

"As you are engaged, I am on my way to Luchesi. If any one has a critical turn, it is he. He will tell me—"

"Luchesi cannot tell Amontillado from Sherry."

"And yet some fools will have it that his taste is a match for your own."

"Come, let us go."

"Whither?"

"To your vaults."

"My friend, no; I will not impose upon your good-nature. I perceive you have an engagement. Luchesi—"

"I have no engagement; come."

"My friend, no. It is not the engagement, but the severe cold with which I perceive you are afflicted. The vaults are insufferably damp. They are encrusted with nitre."

"Let us go nevertheless. The cold is merely nothing. Amontillado! You have been imposed upon. And as for Luchesi, he cannot distinguish Sherry from Amontillado."

Thus speaking, Fortunato possessed himself of my arm. Putting on a mask of black silk, and drawing a *roquelaire* closely about my person, I suffered him to hurry me to my palazzo.

There were no attendants at home; they had absconded to make merry in honor of the time. I had told them that I should not return until the morning, and had given them explicit orders not to stir from the house. These orders were sufficient, I well knew, to ensure their immediate disappearance, one and all, as soon as my back was turned.

I took from their sconces two flambeaux, and giving one to Fortunato, bowed him through several suites of rooms to the archway that led into the vaults. I passed down a long and winding staircase, requesting him to be cautious as he followed. We came at length to the foot of the descent, and stood together on the damp ground at the catacombs of the Montresors.

The gait of my friend was unsteady, and the bells upon his cap jingled as he strode.

"The pipe," said he.

"It is farther on," said I; "but observe the white webwork which gleams from these cavern walls."

He turned towards me, and looked into my eyes with two filmy orbs that distilled the rheum of intoxication.

"Nitre?" he asked, at length.

"Nitre," I replied. "How long have you had that cough?"

"Ugh! ugh! ugh!—ugh! ugh! ugh!—ugh! ugh! ugh! —ugh! ugh! ugh!— ugh! ugh! ugh!"

My poor friend found it impossible to reply for many minutes.

"It is nothing," he said, at last.

"Come," I said, with decision, "we will go back; your health is precious. You are rich, respected, admired, beloved; you are happy, as once I was. You are a man to be missed. For me it is no matter. We will go back; you will be ill, and I cannot be responsible. Besides, there is Luchesi—"

"Enough," he said, "the cough is a mere nothing; it will not kill me. I shall not die of a cough."

"True—true," I replied; "and, indeed, I had no intention of alarming you unnecessarily—but you should use all proper caution. A draught of this Medoc will defend us from the damps."

Here I knocked off the neck of a bottle which I drew from a long row of its fellows that lay upon the mould.

"Drink," I said, presenting him the wine.

He raised it to his lips with a leer. He paused and nodded to me familiarly, while his bells jingled.

"I drink," he said, "to the buried that repose around us."

"And I to your long life."

He again took my arm, and we proceeded.

"These vaults," he said, "are extensive."

"The Montresors," I replied, "were a great and numerous family."

"I forget your arms."

"A huge human foot d'or, in a field azure; the foot crushes a serpent rampant whose fangs are embedded in the heel."

"And the motto?"

"Nemo me impune lacessit."

"Good!" he said.

The wine sparkled in his eyes and the bells jingled. My own fancy grew warm with the Medoc. We had passed through walls of piled bones, with casks and puncheons intermingling, into the inmost recesses of the catacombs. I paused again, and this time I made bold to seize Fortunato by an arm above the elbow.

"The nitre!" I said; "see, it increases. It hangs like moss upon the vaults. We are below the river's bed. The drops of moisture trickle among the bones. Come, we will go back ere it is too late. Your cough—"

"It is nothing," he said; "let us go on. But first, another draught of the Medoc."

I broke and reached him a flagon of De Grâve. He emptied it at a breath. His eyes flashed with a fierce light. He laughed and threw the bottle upwards with a gesticulation I did not understand.

I looked at him in surprise. He repeated the movement—a grotesque one.

"You do not comprehend?" he said.

"Not I," I replied.

"Then you are not of the brotherhood."

"How?"

"You are not of the masons."

"Yes, yes," I said; "yes, yes."

"You? Impossible! A mason?"

"A mason," I replied.

"A sign," he said.

"It is this," I answered, producing a trowel from beneath the folds of my *roquelaire*.

"You jest," he exclaimed, recoiling a few paces. "But let us proceed to the Amontillado."

"Be it so," I said, replacing the tool beneath the cloak, and again offering him my arm. He leaned upon it heavily. We continued our route in search of the Amontillado. We passed through a range of low arches, descended, passed on, and descending again, arrived at a deep crypt, in which the foulness of the air caused our flambeaux rather to glow than flame.

At the most remote end of the crypt there appeared another less spacious. Its walls had been lined with human remains, piled to the vault overhead, in the fashion of the great catacombs of Paris. Three sides of this interior crypt were still ornamented in this manner. From the fourth the bones had been thrown down, and lay promiscuously upon the earth, forming at one point a mound of some size. Within the wall thus exposed by the displacing of the bones, we perceived a still interior recess, in depth about four feet, in width three, in height six or seven. It seemed to have been constructed for no especial use within itself, but formed merely the interval between two of the colossal supports of the roof of the catacombs, and was backed by one of their circumscribing walls of solid granite.

It was in vain that Fortunato, uplifting his dull torch, endeavored to pry into the depth of the recess. Its termination the feeble light did not enable us to see.

"Proceed," I said; "herein is the Amontillado. As for Luchesi—"

"He is an ignoramus," interrupted my friend, as he stepped unsteadily forward, while I followed immediately at his heels. In an instant he had reached the extremity of the niche, and finding his progress arrested by the rock, stood stupidly bewildered. A moment more and I had fettered him to the granite. In its surface were two iron staples, distant from each other about two feet, horizontally. From one of these depended a short chain, from the other a padlock. Throwing the links about his waist, it was but the work of a few seconds to secure it. He was too much astounded to resist. Withdrawing the key, I stepped back from the recess.

"Pass your hand," I said, "over the wall; you cannot help feeling the nitre. Indeed it is *very* damp. Once more let me *implore* you to return. No? Then I must positively leave you. But I must first render you all the little attentions in my power."

"The Amontillado!" ejaculated my friend, not yet recovered from his astonishment.

"True," I replied, "the Amontillado."

As I said these words I busied myself among the pile of bones of which I have before spoken. Throwing them aside, I soon uncovered a quantity of building stone and mortar. With these materials, and with the aid of my trowel, I began vigorously to wall up the entrance of the niche.

I had scarcely laid the first tier of the masonry when I discovered that the intoxication of Fortunato had in a great measure worn off. The earliest indication I had of this was a low moaning cry from the depth of the recess. It was *not* the cry of a drunken man. There was then a long and obstinate silence. I laid the second tier, and the third, and the fourth; and then I heard the furious vibrations of the chain. The noise lasted for several minutes, during which, that I might hearken to it with the more satisfaction, I ceased my labors and sat down upon the bones. When at last the clanking subsided, I resumed the trowel, and finished without interruption the fifth, the sixth, and the seventh tier. The wall was now nearly upon a level with my breast. I again paused, and holding the flambeaux over the mason-work, threw a few feeble rays upon the figure within.

A succession of loud and shrill screams, bursting suddenly from the throat of the chained form, seemed to thrust me violently back. For a brief moment I hesitated—I trembled. Unsheathing my rapier, I began to grope with it about the recess; but the thought of an instant reassured me. I placed my hand upon the solid fabric of the catacombs, and felt satisfied. I reapproached the wall. I replied to the yells of him who clamored. I re-echoed—I aided—I surpassed them in volume and in strength. I did this, and the clamorer grew still.

It was now midnight, and my task was drawing to a close. I had completed the eighth, the ninth, and the tenth tier. I had finished a portion of the last and the eleventh; there remained but a single stone to be fitted and plastered in. I struggled with its weight; I placed it partially in its destined position. But now there came from out the niche a low laugh that erected the hairs upon my head. It was succeeded by a sad voice, which I had difficulty in recognising as that of the noble Fortunato. The voice said—

"Ha! ha! ha!—he! he! he!—a very good joke indeed—an excellent jest. We will have many a rich laugh about it at the palazzo—he! he! he!—over our wine—he! he! he!"

"The Amontillado!" I said.

"He! he! he!—he! he! he!—yes, the Amontillado. But is it not getting late? Will not they be awaiting us at the palazzo, the Lady Fortunato and the rest? Let us be gone."

"Yes," I said, "let us be gone."

"For the love of God, Montresor!"

"Yes," I said, "for the love of God!"

But to these words I hearkened in vain for a reply. I grew impatient. I called aloud—

"Fortunato!"

No answer. I called again—

"Fortunato!"

No answer still. I thrust a torch through the remaining aperture and let it fall within. There came forth in return only a jingling of the bells. My heart grew sick—on account of the dampness of the catacombs. I hastened to make an end of my labor. I forced the last stone into its position; I plastered it up. Against the new masonry I re-erected the old rampart of bones. For the half of a century no mortal has disturbed them. *In pace requiescat!*

THE PHILOSOPHY OF COMPOSITION [6]

CHARLES DICKENS, in a note now lying before me, alluding to an examination I once made of the mechanism of *Barnaby Rudge,* says—"By the way, are you aware that Godwin wrote his *Caleb Williams* backwards? He first involved his hero in a web of difficulties, forming the second volume, and then, for the first, cast about him for some mode of accounting for what had been done."

I cannot think this the *precise* mode of procedure on the part of Godwin— and indeed what he himself acknowledges, is not altogether in accordance with Mr. Dickens's idea—but the author of *Caleb Williams* was too good an artist not to perceive the advantage derivable from at least a somewhat similar process. Nothing is more clear than that every plot, worth the name, must be elaborated to its *dénouement* before anything be attempted with the pen. It is only with the *dénouement* constantly in view that we can give a plot its indispensable air of consequence, or causation, by making the incidents, and especially the tone at all points, tend to the development of the intention.

There is a radical error, I think, in the usual mode of constructing a story. Either history affords a thesis—or one is suggested by an incident of the day —or at best, the author sets himself to work in the combination of striking events to form merely the basis of his narrative, designing, generally, to fill in with description, dialogue, or autorial comment, whatever crevices of fact, or action, may, from page to page, render themselves apparent.

I prefer commencing with the consideration of an *effect*. Keeping originality *always* in view—for he is false to himself who ventures to dispense with so obvious and so easily attainable a source of interest—I say to myself, in the first place, "Of the innumerable effects, or impressions, of which the heart, the intellect, or (more generally) the soul is susceptible, what one shall I, on

[6] Published in *Graham's Magazine,* April, 1846.

the present occasion, select?" Having chosen a novel, first, and secondly a vivid effect, I consider whether it can be best wrought by incident or tone—whether by ordinary incidents and peculiar tone, or the converse, or by peculiarity both of incident and tone—afterward looking about me (or rather within) for such combinations of event, or tone, as shall best aid me in the construction of the effect.

I have often thought how interesting a magazine paper might be written by any author who would—that is to say who could—detail, step by step, the processes by which any one of his compositions attained its ultimate point of completion. Why such a paper has never been given to the world, I am much at a loss to say—but, perhaps, the autorial vanity has had more to do with the omission than any one other cause. Most writers—poets in especial—prefer having it understood that they compose by a species of fine frenzy—an ecstatic intuition—and would positively shudder at letting the public take a peep behind the scenes, at the elaborate and vacillating crudities of thought—at the true purposes seized only at the last moment—at the innumerable glimpses of idea that arrived not at the maturity of full view—at the fully matured fancies discarded in despair as unmanageable, at the cautious selections and rejections, at the painful erasures and interpolations—in a word, at the wheels and pinions, the tackle for scene-shifting, the step-ladders and demon-traps, the cock's feathers, the red paint, and the black patches, which, in ninety-nine cases out of the hundred, constitute the properties of the literary *histrio.*

I am aware, on the other hand, that the case is by no means common, in which an author is at all in condition to retrace the steps by which his conclusions have been attained. In general, suggestions, having arisen pell-mell, are pursued and forgotten in a similar manner.

For my own part, I have neither sympathy with the repugnance alluded to, nor at any time the least difficulty in recalling to mind the progressive steps of any of my compositions; and, since the interest of an analysis, or reconstruction, such as I have considered a *desideratum,* is quite independent of any real or fancied interest in the thing analyzed, it will not be regarded as a breach of decorum on my part to show the *modus operandi* by which some one of my own works was put together. I select "The Raven," as most generally known. It is my design to render it manifest that no one point in its composition is referrible either to accident or intuition—that the work proceeded, step by step, to its completion with the precision and rigid consequence of a mathematical problem.

Let us dismiss, as irrelevant to the poem, *per se,* the circumstance—or say the necessity—which, in the first place, gave rise to the intention of composing a poem that should suit at once the popular and the critical taste.

We commence, then, with this intention.

THE PHILOSOPHY OF COMPOSITION

The initial consideration was that of extent. If any literary work is too long to be read at one sitting, we must be content to dispense with the immensely important effect derivable from unity of impression—for, if two sittings be required, the affairs of the world interfere, and everything like totality is at once destroyed. But since, *ceteris paribus,* no poet can afford to dispense with *anything* that may advance his design, it but remains to be seen whether there is, in extent, any advantage to counterbalance the loss of unity which attends it. Here I say no, at once. What we term a long poem is, in fact, merely a succession of brief ones—that is to say, of brief poetical effects. It is needless to demonstrate that a poem is such, only inasmuch as it intensely excites, by elevating, the soul; and all intense excitements are, through a psychal necessity, brief. For this reason, at least one half of the *Paradise Lost* is essentially prose—a succession of poetical excitements interspersed, *inevitably,* with corresponding depressions—the whole being deprived, through the extremeness of its length, of the vastly important artistic element, totality, or unity, of effect.

It appears evident, then, that there is a distinct limit, as regards length, to all works of literary art—the limit of a single sitting—and that, although in certain classes of prose composition, such as *Robinson Crusoe* (demanding no unity) this limit may be advantageously overpassed, it can never properly be overpassed in a poem. Within this limit, the extent of a poem may be made to bear mathematical relation to its merit—in other words, to the excitement or elevation—again in other words, to the degree of the true poetical effect which it is capable of inducing; for it is clear that the brevity must be in direct ratio of the intensity of the intended effect:—this, with one proviso—that a certain degree of duration is absolutely requisite for the production of any effect at all.

Holding in view these considerations, as well as that degree of excitement which I deemed not above the popular, while not below the critical, taste, I reached at once what I conceived the proper *length* for my intended poem—a length of about one hundred lines. It is, in fact, a hundred and eight.

My next thought concerned the choice of an impression, or effect, to be conveyed; and here I may as well observe that, throughout the construction, I kept steadily in view the design of rendering the work *universally* appreciable. I should be carried too far out of my immediate topic were I to demonstrate a point upon which I have repeatedly insisted, and which, with the poetical, stands not in the slightest need of demonstration—the point, I mean, that Beauty is the sole legitimate province of the poem. A few words, however, in elucidation of my real meaning, which some of my friends have evinced a disposition to misrepresent. That pleasure which is at once the most intense, the most elevating, and the most pure, is, I believe, found in the contemplation of the beautiful. When, indeed, men speak of Beauty, they mean, precisely, not a quality, as is supposed, but an effect—they refer, in short, just to that intense and pure elevation of *soul*—*not* of intellect, or of heart—upon which I have commented, and which is experienced in consequence of contemplating "the beautiful." Now I designate Beauty as the province of the poem, merely because it is an obvious rule of Art that effects should be made to spring from direct causes—that objects should be attained through means best adapted for their attainment—no one as yet having been weak enough to deny that the peculiar elevation alluded to is *most readily* attained in the poem. Now the object, Truth, or the satisfaction of the intellect, and the object Passion, or the excitement of the heart, are, although attainable, to a certain extent, in poetry, far more readily attainable in prose. Truth, in fact, demands a precision, and Passion a *homeliness* (the truly passionate will comprehend me) which are absolutely antagonistic to that Beauty which, I maintain, is the excitement, or pleasurable elevation, of the soul. It by no means follows from anything here said, that passion, or even truth, may not be introduced, and even profitably introduced, into a poem—for they may serve in elucidation, or aid the general effect, as do discords in music, by contrast; but the true artist will always contrive, first, to tone them into proper subservience to the predominant aim, and, secondly, to enveil them, as far as possible, in that Beauty which is the atmosphere and the essence of the poem.

Regarding, then, Beauty as my province, my next question referred to the *tone* of its highest manifestation; and all experience has shown that this tone is one of *sadness*. Beauty of whatever kind, in its supreme development, invariably excites the sensitive soul to tears. Melancholy is thus the most legitimate of all the poetical tones.

The length, the province, and the tone, being thus determined, I betook myself to ordinary induction, with the view of obtaining some artistic piquancy which might serve me as a key-note in the construction of the poem—some pivot upon which the whole structure might turn. In carefully thinking over all the usual artistic effects—or more properly *points,* in the theatrical sense—I did not fail to perceive immediately that no one had been so universally employed as that of the *refrain.* The universality of its employment sufficed to assure me of its intrinsic value, and spared me the necessity of submitting it to analysis. I considered it, however, with regard to its susceptibility of improvement, and soon saw it to be in a primitive condition. As commonly used, the *refrain,* or burden, not only is limited to lyric verse, but depends for its impression upon the force of monotone—both in sound and thought. The pleasure is deduced solely from the sense of identity—of repetition. I resolved to diversify, and so heighten, the effect, by adhering, in general, to the monotone of sound, while I continually varied that of thought: that is to say, I determined to produce continuously novel effects, by the variation of the *application* of the refrain—the refrain itself remaining, for the most part, unvaried.

These points being settled, I next bethought me of the *nature* of my refrain. Since its application was to be repeatedly varied, it was clear that the refrain itself must be brief, for there would have been an insurmountable difficulty in frequent variations of application in any sentence of length. In proportion to the brevity of the sentence, would, of course, be the facility of the variation. This led me at once to a single word as the best refrain.

The question now arose as to the *character* of the word. Having made up my mind to a refrain, the division of the poem into stanzas was, of course, a corollary: the refrain forming the close of each stanza. That such a close, to have force, must be sonorous and susceptible of protracted emphasis, admitted no doubt; and these considerations inevitably led me to the long *o* as the most sonorous vowel, in connection with *r* as the most producible consonant.

The sound of the refrain being thus determined, it became necessary to select a word embodying this sound, and at the same time in the fullest possible keeping with that melancholy which I had predetermined as the tone of the poem. In such a search it would have been absolutely impossible to overlook the word "Nevermore." In fact, it was the very first which presented itself.

The next *desideratum* was a pretext for the continuous use of the one word "Nevermore." In observing the difficulty which I at once found in inventing a sufficiently plausible reason for its continuous repetition, I did not fail to perceive that this difficulty arose solely from the pre-assumption that the word was to be so continuously or monotonously spoken by a *human* being— I did not fail to perceive, in short, that the difficulty lay in the reconciliation of this monotony with the exercise of reason on the part of the creature repeating the word. Here, then, immediately arose the idea of a *non-reasoning* creature capable of speech; and, very naturally, a parrot, in the first instance, suggested itself, but was superseded forthwith by a Raven, as equally capable of speech, and infinitely more in keeping with the intended *tone*.

I had now gone so far as the conception of a Raven—the bird of ill omen— monotonously repeating the one word, "Nevermore" at the conclusion of each stanza, in a poem of melancholy tone, and in length about one hundred lines. Now, never losing sight of the object *supremeness,* or perfection, at all points, I asked myself—"Of all melancholy topics, what, according to the *universal* understanding of mankind, is the *most* melancholy?" "Death"— was the obvious reply. "And when," I said, "is this most melancholy of topics most poetical?" From what I have already explained at some length, the answer, here also, is obvious—"When it most closely allies itself to *Beauty.*" The death, then, of a beautiful woman is, unquestionably, the most poetical topic in the world—and equally is it beyond doubt that the lips best suited for such a topic are those of a bereaved lover.

I had now to combine the two ideas, of a lover lamenting his deceased mistress, and a Raven continuously repeating the word "Nevermore." I had to combine these, bearing in mind my design of varying, at every turn, the *application* of the word repeated; but the only intelligible mode of such combination is that of imagining the Raven employing the word in answer to the queries of the lover. And here it was that I saw at once the opportunity afforded for the effect on which I had been depending—that is to say, the effect of the *variation of application*. I saw that I could make the first query propounded by the lover—the first query to which the Raven should reply "Nevermore"—that I could make this first query a commonplace one, the second less so, the third still less, and so on, until at length the lover, startled from his original nonchalance by the melancholy character of the word itself, by its frequent repetition, and by a consideration of the ominous reputation of the fowl that uttered it, is at length excited to superstition, and wildly propounds queries of a far different character—queries whose solution he has passionately at heart—propounds them half in superstition and half in that species of despair which delights in self-torture—propounds them not altogether because he believes in the prophetic or demoniac character of the bird (which, reason assures him, is merely repeating a lesson learned by rote) but because he experiences a frenzied pleasure in so modeling his questions as to receive from the *expected* "Nevermore" the most delicious because the most intolerable of sorrow. Perceiving the opportunity thus afforded me—or, more strictly, thus forced upon me in the progress of the construction—I first established in mind the climax, or concluding query—that query to which "Nevermore" should be in the last place an answer—that query in reply to which this word "Nevermore" should involve the utmost conceivable amount of sorrow and despair.

Here then the poem may be said to have its beginning—at the end, where all works of art should begin; for it was here, at this point of my preconsiderations, that I first put pen to paper in the composition of the stanza:

> "Prophet," said I, "thing of evil! prophet still if bird or devil!
> By that heaven that bends above us—by that God we both adore,
> Tell this soul with sorrow laden, if within the distant Aidenn,
> It shall clasp a sainted maiden whom the angels name Lenore—
> Clasp a rare and radiant maiden whom the angels name Lenore."
> Quoth the Raven "Nevermore."

I composed this stanza, at this point, first, that by establishing the climax, I might the better vary and graduate, as regards seriousness and importance, the preceding queries of the lover; and secondly, that I might definitely settle the rhythm, the metre, and the length and general arrangement of the stanza, —as well as graduate the stanzas which were to precede, so that none of them might surpass this in rhythmical effect. Had I been able, in the subsequent composition, to construct more vigorous stanzas, I should, without scruple, have purposely enfeebled them, so as not to interfere with the climacteric effect.

And here I may as well say a few words of the versification. My first object (as usual) was originality. The extent to which this has been neglected, in versification, is one of the most unaccountable things in the world. Admitting that there is little possibility of variety in mere rhythm, it is still clear that the possible varieties of metre and stanza are absolutely infinite—and yet, *for centuries, no man, in verse, has ever done, or ever seemed to think of doing, an original thing.* The fact is, that originality (unless in minds of very unusual force) is by no means a matter, as some suppose, of impulse or intuition. In general, to be found, it must be elaborately sought, and although a positive merit of the highest class, demands in its attainment less of invention than negation.

Of course, I pretend to no originality in either the rhythm or metre of "The Raven." The former is trochaic, the latter is octameter acatalectic, alternating with heptameter catalectic repeated in the refrain of the fifth verse, and terminating with tetrameter catalectic. Less pedantically—the feet employed throughout (trochees) consist of a long syllable followed by a short: the first line of the stanza consists of eight of these feet, the second of seven and a half (in effect two-thirds), the third of eight, the fourth of seven and a half, the fifth the same, the sixth three and a half. Now, each of these lines, taken individually, has been employed before; and what originality "The Raven" has, is in their *combination into stanza;* nothing even remotely approaching this combination has ever been attempted. The effect of this originality of combination is aided by other unusual, and some altogether novel effects, arising from an extension of the application of the principles of rhyme and alliteration.

The next point to be considered was the mode of bringing together the lover and the Raven, and the first branch of this consideration was the *locale.* For this the most natural suggestion might seem to be a forest, or the fields; but it has always appeared to me that a close *circumscription of space* is absolutely necessary to the effect of insulated incident:—it has the force of a frame to a picture. It has an indisputable moral power in keeping concentrated the attention, and, of course, must not be confounded with mere unity of place.

I determined, then, to place the lover in his chamber—in a chamber rendered sacred to him by memories of her who had frequented it. The room is represented as richly furnished—this in mere pursuance of the ideas I have already explained on the subject of Beauty, as the sole true poetical thesis.

The *locale* being thus determined, I had now to introduce the bird—and the thought of introducing him through the window, was inevitable. The idea of making the lover suppose, in the first instance, that the flapping of the wings of the bird against the shutter, is a "tapping" at the door, originated in a wish to increase, by prolonging, the reader's curiosity, and in a desire to admit the incidental effect arising from the lover's throwing open the door, finding all dark, and thence adopting the half-fancy that it was the spirit of his mistress that knocked.

I made the night tempestuous, first, to account for the Raven's seeking admission, and secondly, for the effect of contrast with the (physical) serenity within the chamber.

I made the bird alight on the bust of Pallas, also for the effect of contrast between the marble and the plumage—it being understood that the bust was absolutely *suggested* by the bird—the bust of *Pallas* being chosen, first, as most in keeping with the scholarship of the lover, and secondly, for the sonorousness of the word, *Pallas,* itself.

About the middle of the poem, also, I have availed myself of the force of contrast, with a view of deepening the ultimate impression. For example, an air of the fantastic—approaching as nearly to the ludicrous as was admissible —is given to the Raven's entrance. He comes in "with many a flirt and flutter."

> Not the *least obeisance made he*—not a moment stopped or stayed he,
> *But with mien of lord or lady,* perched above my chamber door.

In the two stanzas which follow, the design is more obviously carried out:—

> Then this ebony bird beguiling my sad fancy into smiling
> By the *grave and stern decorum of the countenance it wore,*
> "Though thy *crest be shorn and shaven* thou," I said, "art sure no craven,
> Ghastly grim and ancient Raven wandering from the nightly shore—
> Tell me what thy lordly name is on the Night's Plutonian shore?"
> Quoth the Raven, "Nevermore."

> Much I marvelled *this ungainly fowl* to hear discourse so plainly
> Though its answer little meaning—little relevancy bore;
> For we cannot help agreeing that no living human being
> *Ever yet was blessed with seeing bird above his chamber door—*
> *Bird or beast upon the sculptured bust above his chamber door,*
>   With such name as "Nevermore."

The effect of the *dénouement* being thus provided for, I immediately drop the fantastic for a tone of the most profound seriousness—this tone commencing in the stanza directly following the one last quoted, with the line,

> But the Raven, sitting lonely on that placid bust, spoke only, etc.

From this epoch the lover no longer jests—no longer sees anything even of the fantastic in the Raven's demeanor. He speaks of him as a "grim, ungainly, ghastly, gaunt, and ominous bird of yore," and feels the "fiery eyes" burning into his "bosom's core." This revolution of thought, or fancy, on the lover's part, is intended to induce a similar one on the part of the reader—to bring the mind into a proper frame for the *dénouement,* which is now brought about as rapidly and as directly as possible.

With the *dénouement* proper—with the Raven's reply, "Nevermore," to the lover's final demand if he shall meet his mistress in another world—the poem, in its obvious phase, that of a simple narrative, may be said to have its completion. So far, everything is within the limits of the accountable—of the real. A raven, having learned by rote the single word "Nevermore," and having escaped from the custody of its owner, is driven at midnight, through the violence of a storm, to seek admission at a window from which a light still gleams—the chamber-window of a student, occupied half in poring over a volume, half in dreaming of a beloved mistress deceased. The casement being thrown open at the fluttering of the bird's wings, the bird itself perches on the most convenient seat out of the immediate reach of the student, who, amused by the incident and the oddity of the visitor's demeanor, demands of it, in jest and without looking for a reply, its name. The raven addressed, answers with its customary word, "Nevermore"—a word which finds immediate echo in the melancholy heart of the student, who, giving utterance aloud to certain thoughts suggested by the occasion, is again startled by the fowl's repetition of "Nevermore." The student now guesses the state of the case, but is impelled, as I have before explained, by the human thirst for self-torture, and in part by superstition, to propound such queries to the bird as will bring him, the lover, the most of the luxury of sorrow, through the anticipated answer "Nevermore." With the indulgence, to the extreme, of this self-torture, the narration, in what I have termed its first or obvious phase, has a natural termination, and so far there has been no overstepping of the limits of the real.

But in subjects so handled, however skilfully, or with however vivid an array of incident, there is always a certain hardness or nakedness, which repels the artistical eye. Two things are invariably required: first, some amount of complexity, or more properly, adaptation; and, secondly, some amount of suggestiveness, some under-current, however indefinite, of meaning. It is this latter, in especial, which imparts to a work of art so much of that *richness* (to borrow from colloquy a forcible term) which we are too fond of confounding with *the ideal.* It is the *excess* of the suggested meaning—it is the rendering this the upper instead of the under current of the theme—which turns into prose (and that of the very flattest kind) the so-called poetry of the so-called transcendentalists.

Holding these opinions, I added the two concluding stanzas of the poem—their suggestiveness being thus made to pervade all the narrative which has preceded them. The undercurrent of meaning is rendered first apparent in the lines—

"Take thy beak from out *my heart,* and take thy form from off my door!"
Quoth the Raven "Nevermore!"

It will be observed that the words, "from out my heart," involve the first metaphorical expression in the poem. They, with the answer, "Nevermore," dispose the mind to seek a moral in all that has been previously narrated. The reader begins now to regard the Raven as emblematical—but it is not until the very last line of the very last stanza, that the intention of making him emblematical of *Mournful and Never-ending Remembrance* is permitted distinctly to be seen:

And the Raven, never flitting, still is sitting, still is sitting,
On the pallid bust of Pallas, just above my chamber door;
And his eyes have all the seeming of a demon's that is dreaming,
And the lamplight o'er him streaming throws his shadow on the floor;
And my soul *from out that shadow* that lies floating on the floor
Shall be lifted—nevermore.

THE POETIC PRINCIPLE [7]

IN speaking of the Poetic Principle, I have no design to be either thorough or profound. While discussing very much at random the essentiality of what we call Poetry, my principal purpose will be to cite for consideration some few of those minor English or American poems which best suit my own taste, or which, upon my own fancy, have left the most definite impression. By "minor poems" I mean, of course, poems of little length. And here, in the beginning, permit me to say a few words in regard to a somewhat peculiar principle, which, whether rightfully or wrongfully, has always had its influence in my own critical estimate of the poem. I hold that a long poem does not exist. I maintain that the phrase "a long poem" is simply a flat contradiction in terms.

I need scarcely observe that a poem deserves its title only inasmuch as it excites, by elevating the soul. The value of the poem is in the ratio of this elevating excitement. But all excitements are, through a psychal necessity, transient. That degree of excitement which would entitle a poem to be so called at all, can not be sustained throughout a composition of any great length. After the lapse of half an hour, at the very utmost, it flags—fails—a revulsion ensues—and then the poem is, in effect, and in fact, no longer such.

There are, no doubt, many who have found difficulty in reconciling the critical dictum that the *Paradise Lost* is to be devoutly admired throughout, with the absolute impossibility of maintaining for it, during perusal, the

[7] This was a lecture which Poe delivered in Richmond, Providence, and several other cities; it was first published, after his death, in *The Home Journal,* August 31, 1850.

amount of enthusiasm which that critical dictum would demand. This great work, in fact, is to be regarded as poetical only when, losing sight of that vital requisite in all works of Art, Unity, we view it merely as a series of minor poems. If, to preserve its Unity—its totality of effect or impression—we read it (as would be necessary) at a single sitting, the result is but a constant alternation of excitement and depression. After a passage of what we feel to be true poetry, there follows, inevitably, a passage of platitude which no critical prejudgment can force us to admire; but if, upon completing the work, we read it again; omitting the first book—that is to say, commencing with the second —we shall be surprised at now finding that admirable which we before condemned—that damnable which we had previously so much admired. It follows from all this that the ultimate, aggregate, or absolute effect of even the best epic under the sun, is a nullity—and this is precisely the fact.

In regard to the *Iliad,* we have, if not positive proof, at least very good reason, for believing it intended as a series of lyrics; but granting the epic intention, I can say only that the work is based in an imperfect sense of Art. The modern epic is, of the supposititious ancient model, but an inconsiderate and blindfold imitation. But the day of these artistic anomalies is over. If, at any time, any very long poem *were* popular in reality—which I doubt—it is at least clear that no very long poem will ever be popular again.

That the extent of a poetical work is, *ceteris paribus,* the measure of its merit, seems undoubtedly, when we thus state it, a proposition sufficiently absurd—yet we are indebted for it to the Quarterly Reviews. Surely there can be nothing in mere *size,* abstractly considered—there can be nothing in mere *bulk,* so far as a volume is concerned, which has so continuously elicited admiration from these saturnine pamphlets! A mountain, to be sure, by the mere sentiment of physical magnitude which it conveys, *does* impress us with a sense of the sublime—but no man is impressed after *this* fashion by the material grandeur of even *The Columbiad.* Even the Quarterlies have not instructed us to be so impressed by it. *As yet,* they have not *insisted* on our estimating Lamartine by the cubic foot, or Pollock by the pound—but what else are we to *infer* from their continual prating about "sustained effort"? If, by "sustained effort," any little gentleman has accomplished an epic, let us frankly commend him for the effort—if this indeed be a thing commendable— but let us forbear praising the epic on the effort's account. It is to be hoped that common-sense, in the time to come, will prefer deciding upon a work of Art rather by the impression it makes—by the effect it produces—than by the time it took to impress the effect, or by the amount of "sustained effort" which had been found necessary in effecting the impression. The fact is, that perseverance is one thing and genius quite another; nor can all the Quarterlies in Christendom confound them. By and by, this proposition, with many which I have been just urging, will be received as self-evident. In the meantime, by being generally condemned as falsities, they will not be essentially damaged as truths.

On the other hand, it is clear that a poem may be improperly brief. Undue brevity degenerates into mere epigrammatism. A *very* short poem, while now and then producing a brilliant or vivid, never produces a profound or enduring effect. There must be the steady pressing down of the stamp upon the wax.

Béranger has wrought innumerable things, pungent and spirit-stirring, but in general they have been too imponderous to stamp themselves deeply into the public opinion, and thus, as so many feathers of fancy, have been blown aloft only to be whistled down the wind.

A remarkable instance of the effect of undue brevity in depressing a poem, in keeping it out of the popular view, is afforded by the following exquisite little Serenade:—

> I arise from dreams of thee
>   In the first sweet sleep of night
> When the winds are breathing low,
>   And the stars are shining bright.
> I arise from dreams of thee,
>   And a spirit in my feet
> Has led me—who knows how?—
>   To thy chamber-window, sweet!
>
> The wandering airs they faint
>   On the dark, the silent stream—
> The champak odors fail
>   Like sweet thoughts in a dream;
> The nightingale's complaint,
>   It dies upon her heart,
> As I must die on thine,
>   O, beloved as thou art!
>
> O, lift me from the grass!
>   I die, I faint, I fail!
> Let thy love in kisses rain
>   On my lips and eyelids pale.
> My cheek is cold and white, alas!
>   My heart beats loud and fast:
> O, press it close to thine again,
>   Where it will break at last.

Very few perhaps are familiar with these lines, yet no less a poet than Shelley is their author. Their warm, yet delicate and ethereal imagination will be appreciated by all, but by none so thoroughly as by him who has himself arisen from sweet dreams of one beloved to bathe in the aromatic air of a southern mid-summer night.

One of the finest poems by Willis—the very best in my opinion which he has ever written—has no doubt, through this same defect of undue brevity, been kept back from its proper position, not less in the critical than in the popular view:

> The shadows lay along Broadway,
>   'Twas near the twilight-tide—
> And slowly there a lady fair
>   Was walking in her pride.
> Alone walk'd she; but, viewlessly,
>   Walk'd spirits at her side.
>
> Peace charm'd the street beneath her feet,
>   And Honor charm'd the air;
> And all astir looked kind on her,
>   And called her good as fair—
> For all God ever gave to her
>   She kept with chary care.
>
> She kept with care her beauties rare
>   From lovers warm and true—
> For heart was cold to all but gold,
>   And the rich came not to woo—
> But honor'd well are charms to sell,
>   If priests the selling do.
>
> Now walking there was one more fair—
>   A slight girl, lily-pale;
> And she had unseen company
>   To make the spirit quail—
> 'Twixt Want and Scorn she walk'd forlorn,
>   And nothing could avail.
>
> No mercy now can clear her brow
>   From this world's peace to pray,
> For as love's wild prayer dissolved in air,
>   Her woman's heart gave way!—
> But the sin forgiven by Christ in Heaven,
>   By man is cursed alway!

In this composition we find it difficult to recognize the Willis who has written so many mere "verses of society." The lines are not only richly ideal but full of energy, while they breathe an earnestness, an evident sincerity of sentiment, for which we look in vain throughout all the other works of this author.

While the epic mania—while the idea that to merit in poetry prolixity is indispensable—has for some years past been gradually dying out of the public mind, by mere dint of its own absurdity, we find it succeeded by a heresy too palpably false to be long tolerated, but one which, in the brief period it has already endured, may be said to have accomplished more in the corruption of our Poetical Literature than all its other enemies combined. I allude to the heresy of "The Didactic." It has been assumed, tacitly and avowedly, directly and indirectly, that the ultimate object of all Poetry is Truth. Every poem, it is said, should inculcate a moral, and by this moral is the poetical merit of the work to be adjudged. We Americans especially have patronized this happy idea, and we Bostonians very especially have developed it in full. We have taken it into our heads that to write a poem simply for the poem's sake, and to acknowledge such to have been our design, would be to confess ourselves radically wanting in the true poetic dignity and force; but the simple fact is that would we but permit ourselves to look into our own souls we should immediately there discover that under the sun there neither exists nor *can* exist any work more thoroughly dignified, more supremely noble, than this very poem, this poem *per se,* this poem which is a poem and nothing more, this poem written solely for the poem's sake.

With as deep a reverence for the True as ever inspired the bosom of man, I would nevertheless limit, in some measure, its modes of inculcation. I would limit to enforce them. I would not enfeeble them by dissipation. The demands of Truth are severe. She has no sympathy with the myrtles. All *that* which is so indispensable in Song is precisely all *that* with which *she* has nothing whatever to do. It is but making her a flaunting paradox to wreathe her in gems and flowers. In enforcing a truth we need severity rather than efflorescence of language. We must be simple, precise, terse. We must be cool, calm, unimpassioned. In a word, we must be in that mood which, as nearly as possible, is the exact converse of the poetical. *He* must be blind indeed who does not perceive the radical and chasmal difference between the truthful and the poetical modes of inculcation. He must be theory-mad beyond redemption who, in spite of these differences, shall still persist in attempting to reconcile the obstinate oils and waters of Poetry and Truth.

Dividing the world of mind into its three most immediately obvious distinctions, we have the Pure Intellect, Taste, and the Moral Sense. I place Taste in the middle because it is just this position which in the mind it occupies. It holds intimate relations with either extreme; but from the Moral Sense is separated by so faint a difference that Aristotle has not hesitated to place some of its operations among the virtues themselves. Nevertheless we find the *offices* of the trio marked with a sufficient distinction. Just as the intellect concerns itself with Truth, so Taste informs us of the Beautiful, while the Moral Sense is regardful of Duty. Of this latter, while Conscience teaches the obligation, and Reason the expediency, Taste contents herself with displaying the charms, waging war upon Vice solely on the ground of her deformity, her disproportion, her animosity to the fitting, to the appropriate, to the harmonious—in a word, to Beauty.

An immortal instinct deep within the spirit of man is thus plainly a sense of the beautiful. This it is which administers to his delight in the manifold forms, and sounds, and odors, and sentiments amid which he exists. And just as the lily is repeated in the lake, or the eyes of Amaryllis in the mirror, so is the mere oral or written repetition of these forms, and sounds, and colors, and odors, and sentiments a duplicate source of delight. But this mere repetition is not poetry. He who shall simply sing, with however glowing enthusiasm, or with however vivid a truth of description, of the sights, and sounds, and odors, and colors, and sentiments which greet *him* in common with all mankind—he, I say, has yet failed to prove his divine title. There is still a something in the distance which he has been unable to attain. We have still a thirst unquenchable, to allay which he has not shown us the crystal springs. This thirst belongs to the immortality of Man. It is at once a consequence and an indication of his perennial existence. It is the desire of the moth for the star. It is no mere appreciation of the Beauty before us, but a wild effort to reach the Beauty above. Inspired by an ecstatic prescience of the glories beyond the grave, we struggle by multiform combinations among the things and thoughts of Time to attain a portion of that Loveliness whose very elements perhaps appertain to eternity alone. And thus when by Poetry—or when by Music, the most entrancing of the poetic moods—we find ourselves melted into tears, we weep then, not as the Abbaté Gravina supposes, through excess of pleasure, but through a certain petulant, impatient sorrow at our inability to grasp *now,* wholly, here on earth, at once and forever, those divine and rapturous joys of which *through* the poem, or *through* the music, we attain to but brief and indeterminate glimpses.

The struggle to apprehend the supernal Loveliness—this struggle, on the part of souls fittingly constituted—has given to the world all *that* which it (the world) has ever been enabled at once to understand and *to feel* as poetic.

The Poetic Sentiment, of course, may develop itself in various modes—in Painting, in Sculpture, in Architecture, in the Dance—very especially in Music—and very peculiarly, and with a wide field, in the composition of the Landscape Garden. Our present theme, however, has regard only to its manifestation in words. And here let me speak briefly on the topic of rhythm. Contenting myself with the certainty that Music, in its various modes of metre, rhythm, and rhyme, is of so vast a moment in Poetry as never to be wisely rejected—is so vitally important an adjunct, that he is simply silly who declines its assistance, I will not now pause to maintain its absolute essentiality. It is in Music perhaps that the soul most nearly attains the great end for which, when inspired by the Poetic Sentiment, it struggles—the creation of supernal Beauty. It *may* be, indeed, that here this sublime end is, now and then, attained in *fact*. We are often made to feel, with a shivering delight, that from an earthly harp are stricken notes which *can not* have been unfamiliar to the angels. And thus there can be little doubt that in the union of Poetry with Music in its popular sense, we shall find the widest field for the Poetic development. The old Bards and Minnesingers had advantages which we do not possess—and Thomas Moore, singing his own songs, was, in the most legitimate manner, perfecting them as poems.

To recapitulate then:—I would define, in brief, the Poetry of words as "The Rhythmical Creation of Beauty." Its sole arbiter is Taste. With the Intellect or with the Conscience it has only collateral relations. Unless incidentally, it has no concern whatever either with Duty or with Truth.

A few words, however, in explanation. *That* pleasure which is at once the most pure, the most elevating, and the most intense, is derived, I maintain, from the contemplation of the Beautiful. In the contemplation of Beauty we alone find it possible to attain that pleasurable elevation, or excitement *of the soul,* which we recognize as the Poetic Sentiment, and which is so easily distinguished from Truth, which is the satisfaction of the Reason, or from Passion, which is the excitement of the heart. I make Beauty, therefore—using the word as inclusive of the sublime—I make Beauty the province of the poem, simply because it is an obvious rule of Art that effects should be made to spring as directly as possible from their causes:—no one as yet having been weak enough to deny that the peculiar elevation in question is at least *most readily* attainable in the poem. It by no means follows, however, that the incitements of Passion, or the precepts of Duty, or even the lessons of Truth, may not be introduced into a poem, and with advantage; for they may subserve incidentally, in various ways, the general purposes of the work: but the true artist will always contrive to tone them down in proper subjection to that *Beauty* which is the atmosphere and the real essence of the poem. . . .[8]

Thus, although in a very cursory and imperfect manner, I have endeavored to convey to you my conception of the Poetic Principle. It has been my purpose to suggest that, while this Principle itself is strictly and simply the Human Aspiration for Supernal Beauty, the manifestation of the Principle is always found in *an elevating excitement of the soul,* quite independent of that passion which is the intoxication of the Heart, or of that truth which is the satisfaction of the Reason. For in regard to passion, alas! its tendency is to degrade rather than to elevate the Soul. Love, on the contrary—Love—the true, the divine Eros—the Uranian as distinguished from the Dionæan Venus

[8] Poe here proceeds with a discussion of several poems in illustration of his theory, but the poems are of minor significance to-day, and are not necessary in the understanding of Poe's idea.

—is unquestionably the purest and truest of all poetical themes. And in regard to Truth, if, to be sure, through the attainment of a truth we are led to perceive a harmony where none was apparent before, we experience at once the true poetical effect; but this effect is referrible to the harmony alone, and not in the least degree to the truth which merely served to render the harmony manifest.

We shall reach, however, more immediately a distinct conception of what the true Poetry is by mere reference to a few of the simple elements which induce in the Poet himself the true poetical effect. He recognizes the ambrosia which nourishes his soul in the bright orbs that shine in Heaven, in the volutes of the flower, in the clustering of low shrubberies, in the waving of the grain-fields, in the slanting of tall Eastern trees, in the blue distance of mountains, in the grouping of clouds, in the twinkling of half-hidden brooks, in the gleaming of silver rivers, in the repose of sequestered lakes, in the star-mirroring depths of lonely wells. He perceives it in the songs of birds, in the harp of Æolus, in the sighing of the night-wind, in the repining voice of the forest, in the surf that complains to the shore, in the fresh breath of the woods, in the scent of the violet, in the voluptuous perfume of the hyacinth, in the suggestive odor that comes to him at eventide from far-distant undiscovered islands, over dim oceans, illimitable and unexplored. He owns it in all noble thoughts, in all unworldly motives, in all holy impulses, in all chivalrous, generous, and self-sacrificing deeds. He feels it in the beauty of woman, in the grace of her step, in the lustre of her eye, in the melody of her voice, in her soft laughter, in her sigh, in the harmony of the rustling of her robes. He deeply feels it in her winning endearments, in her burning enthusiasms, in her gentle charities, in her meek and devotional endurances, but above all— ah, far above all—he kneels to it, he worships it in the faith, in the purity, in the strength, in the altogether divine majesty of her *love*.

Let me conclude by the recitation of yet another brief poem, one very different in character from any that I have before quoted. It is by Motherwell, and is called "The Song of the Cavalier." With our modern and altogether rational ideas of the absurdity and impiety of warfare, we are not precisely in that frame of mind best adapted to sympathize with the sentiments, and thus to appreciate the real excellence of the poem. To do this fully we must identify ourselves in fancy with the soul of the old cavalier:

> Then mounte! then mounte, brave gallants all,
>   And don your helmes amaine:
> Deathe's couriers, Fame and Honor, call
>   Us to the field againe.
> No shrewish teares shall fill our eye
>   When the sword-hilt's in our hand—
> Heart-whole we'll part, and no whit sighe

For the fayrest of the land;
Let piping swaine, and craven wight,
Thus weepe and puling crye,
Our business is like men to fight,
And hero-like to die!

From MARGINALIA [9]

[Marginal Jottings]

In getting my books, I have been always solicitous of an ample margin; this not so much through any love of the thing in itself, however agreeable, as for the facility it affords me of pencilling suggested thoughts, agreements, and differences of opinion, or brief critical comments in general. Where what I have to note is too much to be included within the narrow limits of a margin, I commit it to a slip of paper, and deposit it between the leaves; taking care to secure it by an imperceptible portion of gum tragacanth paste.

All this may be whim; it may be not only a very hackneyed, but a very idle practice;—yet I persist in it still; and it affords me pleasure; which is profit, in despite of Mr. Bentham, with Mr. Mill on his back.

This making of notes, however, is by no means the making of mere *memoranda*—a custom which has its disadvantages, beyond doubt. *"Ce que je mets sur papier,"* says Bernardin de St. Pierre, *"je remets de ma mémoire et par conséquence je l'oublie";*—and, in fact, if you wish to forget anything upon the spot, make a note that this thing is to be remembered.

But the purely marginal jottings, done with no eye to the Memorandum Book, have a distinct complexion, and not only a distinct purpose, but none at all; this it is which imparts to them a value. They have a rank somewhat above the chance and desultory comments of literary chit-chat—for these latter are not unfrequently "talk for talk's sake," hurried out of the mouth; while the *marginalia* are deliberately pencilled, because the mind of the reader wishes to unburthen itself of a *thought;*—however flippant—however silly—however trivial—still a thought indeed, not merely a thing that might have been a thought in time, and under more favorable circumstances. In the *marginalia,* too, we talk only to ourselves; we therefore talk freshly —boldly—originally—with *abandonnement*—without conceit—much after the fashion of Jeremy Taylor, and Sir Thomas Browne, and Sir William Temple, and the anatomical Burton, and that most logical analogist, Butler, and some other people of the old day, who were too full of their matter to have any room for their manner, which, being thus left out of question, was a capital manner, indeed,—a model of manners, with a richly marginalic air.

[9] Under this and other titles Poe published, between 1836 and 1849, in various magazines, articles made up of short, critical observations, of which those here selected are typical.

The circumscription of space, too, in these pencillings, has in it something more of advantage than of inconvenience. It compels us (whatever diffuseness of idea we may clandestinely entertain), into Montesquieu-ism, into Tacitus-ism (here I leave out of view the concluding portion of the "Annals") —or even into Carlyle-ism—a thing which, I have been told, is not to be confounded with your ordinary affectation and bad grammar. I say "bad grammar," through sheer obstinacy, because the grammarians (who would know better) insist upon it that I should not. But then grammar is not what these grammarians will have it; and, being merely the analysis of language, with the result of this analysis, must be good or bad just as the analyst is sage or silly—just as he is a Horne Tooke or a Cobbett.

But to our sheep. During a rainy afternoon, not long ago, being in a mood too listless for continuous study, I sought relief from *ennui* in dipping here and there, at random, among the volumes of my library—no very large one, certainly, but sufficiently miscellaneous; and, I flatter myself, not a little *recherché*.

Perhaps it was what the Germans call the "brain-scattering" humor of the moment; but, while the picturesqueness of the numerous pencil-scratches arrested my attention, the helter-skelter-iness of commentary amused me. I found myself at length forming a wish that it had been some other hand than my own which had so bedevilled the books, and fancying that, in such case, I might have derived no inconsiderable pleasure from turning them over. From this the transition-thought (as Mr. Lyell, or Mr. Murchison, or Mr. Featherstonhaugh would have it) was natural enough:—there might be something even in my scribblings which, for the mere sake of scribbling, would have interest for others.

The main difficulty respected the mode of transferring the notes from the volumes—the context from the text—without detriment to that exceedingly frail fabric of intelligibility in which the context was imbedded. With all appliances to boot, with the printed pages at their back, the commentaries were too often like Dodona's oracles—or those of Lycophron Tenebrosus— or the essays of the pedant's pupils, in Quintilian, which were "necessarily excellent, since even he (the pedant) found it impossible to comprehend them":—what, then, would become of it—this context—if transferred?—if translated? Would it not rather be *traduit* (traduced) which is the French synonym, or *overzezet* (turned topsy-turvy) which is the Dutch one?

I concluded, at length, to put extensive faith in the acumen and imagination of the reader:—this as a general rule. But, in some instances, where even faith would not remove mountains, there seemed no safer plan than so to re-model the note as to convey at least the ghost of a conception as to what it was all about. Where, for such conception, the text itself was absolutely necessary, I could quote it; where the title of the book commented upon was indispensable, I could name it. In short, like a novel-hero dilemma'd, I made up my mind "to be guided by circumstances," in default of more satisfactory rules of conduct.

As for the multitudinous opinion expressed in the subjoined *farrago*—as for my present assent to all, or dissent from any portion of it—as to the possibility of my having, in some instances, altered my mind—or as to the impossibility of my not having altered it often—these are points upon which I say nothing, because upon these there can be nothing cleverly said. It may be as well to observe, however, that just as the goodness of your true pun is in the direct ratio of its intolerability, so is nonsense the essential sense of the Marginal Note.

[The Power of Words]

Some Frenchman—possibly Montaigne—says: "People talk about thinking, but for my part I never think, except when I sit down to write." It is this never thinking, unless when we sit down to write, which is the cause of so much indifferent composition. But perhaps there is something more involved in the Frenchman's observation than meets the eye. It is certain that the mere act of inditing, tends, in a great degree, to the logicalization of thought. Whenever, on account of its vagueness, I am dissatisfied with a conception of the brain, I resort forthwith to the pen, for the purpose of obtaining, through its aid, the necessary form, consequence, and precision.

How very commonly we hear it remarked, that such and such thoughts are beyond the compass of words! I do not believe that any thought, properly so called, is out of the reach of language. I fancy, rather, that where difficulty in expression is experienced, there is, in the intellect which experiences it, a want either of deliberateness or of method. For my own part, I have never had a thought which I could not set down in words, with even more distinctness than that with which I conceived it:—as I have before observed, the thought is logicalized by the effort at (written) expression.

There is, however, a class of fancies, of exquisite delicacy, which are *not* thoughts, and to which, *as yet,* I have found it absolutely impossible to adapt language. I use the word *fancies* at random, and merely because I must use *some* word; but the idea commonly attached to the term is not even remotely applicable to the shadows of shadows in question. They seem to me rather psychal than intellectual. They arise in the soul (alas, how rarely!) only at its epochs of most intense tranquillity—when the bodily and mental health are in perfection—and at those mere points of time where the confines of the waking world blend with those of the world of dreams. I am aware of these "fancies" only when I am upon the very brink of sleep, with the consciousness that I am so. I have satisfied myself that this condition exists but for an inappreciable *point* of time—yet it is crowded with these "shadows of shadows"; and for absolute *thought* there is demanded time's *endurance*.

These "fancies" have in them a pleasurable ecstasy as far beyond the most pleasurable of the world of wakefulness, or of dreams, as the Heaven of the Northman theology is beyond its Hell. I regard the visions, even as they arise, with an awe which, in some measure, moderates or tranquilizes the ecstasy—I so regard them, through a conviction (which seems a portion of the ecstasy itself) that this ecstasy, in itself, is of a character supernal to the Human Nature—is a glimpse of the spirit's outer world; and I arrive at this conclusion—if this term is at all applicable to instantaneous intuition—by a perception that the delight experienced has, as its element, but *the absoluteness of novelty*. I say the absoluteness—for in these fancies—let me now term them psychal impressions—there is really nothing even approximate in character to impressions ordinarily received. It is as if the five senses were supplanted by five myriad others alien to mortality.

Now, so entire is my faith in the *power of words,* that, at times, I have believed it possible to embody even the evanescence of fancies such as I have attempted to describe. In experiments with this end in view, I have proceeded so far as, first, to control (when the bodily and mental health are good) the existence of the condition:—that is to say, I can now (unless when ill) be sure that the condition will supervene, if I so wish it, at the point of time already described: of its supervention, until lately, I could never be certain, even under the most favorable circumstances. I mean to say, merely, that now I can be sure, when all circumstances are favorable, of the supervention of the condition, and feel even the capacity of inducing or compelling it:—the favorable circumstances, however, are not the less rare—else had I compelled, already, the Heaven into the Earth.

I have proceeded so far, secondly, as to prevent the lapse from *the point* of which I speak—the point of blending between wakefulness and sleep—as to prevent at will, I say, the lapse from this border-ground into the dominion of sleep. Not that I can *continue* the condition—not that I can render the point more than a point—but that I can startle myself from the point into wakefulness—*and thus transfer the point itself into the realm of Memory*—convey its impressions, or more properly their recollections, to a situation where (although still for a very brief period) I can survey them with the eye of analysis.

For these reasons—that is to say, because I have been enabled to accomplish thus much—I do not altogether despair of embodying in words at least enough of the fancies in question to convey, to certain classes of intellect, a shadowy conception of their character.

In saying this I am not to be understood as supposing that the fancies, or psychal impressions, to which I allude, are confined to my individual self—are not, in a word, common to all mankind—for on this point it is quite impossible that I should form an opinion—but nothing can be more certain than that even a partial record of the impressions would startle the universal intellect of mankind, by the *supremeness of the novelty* of the material employed, and of its consequent suggestions. In a word—should I ever write a paper on this topic, the world will be compelled to acknowledge that, at last, I have done an original thing.

[PUNCTUATION]

THAT punctuation is important all agree; but how few comprehend the extent of its importance! The writer who neglects punctuation, or mis-punctuates, is liable to be misunderstood—this, according to the popular idea, is the sum of the evils arising from heedlessness or ignorance. It does not seem to be known that, even where the sense is perfectly clear, a sentence may be deprived of half its force—its spirit—its point—by improper punctuation. For the want of merely a comma, it often occurs that an axiom appears a paradox, or that a sarcasm is converted into a sermonoid.

There is *no* treatise on the topic—and there is no topic on which a treatise is more needed. There seems to exist a vulgar notion that the subject is one of pure conventionality, and cannot be brought within the limits of intelligible and consistent *rule*. And yet, if fairly looked in the face, the whole matter is so plain that its *rationale* may be read as we run. If not anticipated, I shall, hereafter, make an attempt at a magazine paper on "The Philosophy of Point."

In the meantime let me say a word or two of *the dash*. Every writer for the press, who has any sense of the accurate, must have been frequently mortified and vexed at the distortion of his sentences by the printer's now general substitution of a semicolon, or comma, for the dash of the MS. The total or nearly total disuse of the latter point, has been brought about by the revulsion consequent upon its excessive employment about twenty years ago. The Byronic poets were *all* dash. John Neal, in his earlier novels, exaggerated its use into the grossest abuse—although his very error arose from the philosophical and self-dependent spirit which has always distinguished him, and which will even yet lead him, if I am not greatly mistaken in the man, to do something for the literature of the country which the country "will not willingly," and cannot possibly, "let die." Without entering now into the *why*, let me observe that the printer may always ascertain when the dash of the MS. is properly and when improperly employed, by bearing in mind that this point represents *a second thought—an emendation*. In using it just above I have exemplified its use. The words "an emendation" are, speaking with reference to grammatical construction, put in *ap*position with the words "a second thought." Having written these latter words, I reflected whether it would not be possible to render their meaning more distinct by certain other words.

Now, instead of erasing the phrase "a second thought," which is of *some* use—which *partially* conveys the idea intended—which advances me *a step toward* my full purpose—I suffer it to remain, and merely put a dash between it and the phrase "an emendation." The dash gives the reader a choice between two, or among three or more expressions, one of which may be more forcible than another, but all of which help out the idea. It stands, in general, for these words—*"or, to make my meaning more distinct."* This force *it has* —and this force no other point can have; since all other points have well-understood uses quite different from this. Therefore, the dash *can not* be dispensed with.

It has its phases—its variation of the force described; but the one principle—that of second thought or emendation—will be found at the bottom of all.

OLIVER WENDELL HOLMES

(1809–1894)

Oliver Wendell Holmes was born at Cambridge, Massachusetts, in 1809. His father was a clergyman, his grandfather a physician, and he was brought up in a cultured home, in an atmosphere of books, and from childhood delighted in writing verse. He was graduated from Harvard in 1829, and the next year attended the law school; but his interest soon turning to medicine, he went to Paris, where he studied from April, 1833, to October, 1835. In 1836 he took his degree of M.D. and in the same year published his first book of poems. He achieved but moderate success in the practice of medicine, the Bostonians finding it hard to believe that a writer of such gay lyrics and a conversationalist of such wit could be entirely serious in his vocation. Nevertheless, his professional papers were well received, and in 1839 he was made professor of anatomy at Dartmouth College, a position he held but a short time. In 1847, however, he was appointed to the same position in the Harvard Medical School, and retained this professorship till 1882. When in 1857 Lowell undertook the editorship of the *Atlantic Monthly*, it was only on condition that Holmes should become a contributor. In consequence, Holmes began a connection with that magazine that lasted during his lifetime. In the first number appeared the opening chapter of *The Autocrat of the Breakfast-Table*, followed in 1859 by *The Professor at the Breakfast-Table*, and in 1872 by *The Poet at the Breakfast-Table*. These made the fortunes of the *Atlantic*, and in turn the fame of Holmes, for so popular were his writings that he abandoned the practice of medicine to become a man of letters. In addition to several volumes of verse, the "Breakfast-Table" series, and a number of important papers on medical subjects, he wrote three novels, and lives of Motley and of Emerson.

If not a great writer, Holmes is a very felicitous one. With his sense of the value of words, his intermingling of a fine fancy with sparkling wit, the whole being supported by good sense, he contributed to American literature writings of singular charm. Without rancour, and yet sternly, he attacked the dogmas of his puritan forebears, and did much towards the liberalizing of puritan thought. He died in 1894, the last survivor of the "New England Group" of poets.

From THE AUTOCRAT OF THE BREAKFAST-TABLE

I WAS just going to say, when I was interrupted,[1] that one of the many ways of classifying minds is under the heads of arithmetical and algebraical intellects. All economical and practical wisdom is an extension or variation of the

---

[1] The interruption referred to in the first sentence of the first of these papers was just a quarter of a century in duration.

Two articles entitled "The Autocrat of the Breakfast-Table" will be found in *The New England Magazine*, formerly published in Boston by J. T. and E. Buckingham. The date of the first of these articles is November, 1831, and that of the second, February, 1832. When *The Atlantic Monthly* was begun, twenty-five years afterwards, and the author was asked to

following arithmetical formula: $2 + 2 = 4$. Every philosophical proposition has the more general character of the expression $a + b = c$. We are mere operatives, empirics, and egotists, until we learn to think in letters instead of figures.

They all stared. There is a divinity student lately come among us to whom I commonly address remarks like the above, allowing him to take a certain share in the conversation, so far as assent or pertinent questions are involved. He abused his liberty on this occasion by presuming to say that Leibnitz had the same observation.—No, sir, I replied, he has not. But he said a mighty good thing about mathematics, that sounds something like it, and you found it, *not in the original,* but quoted by Dr. Thomas Reid. I will tell the company what he did say, one of these days. . . .

—All generous minds have a horror of what are commonly called "facts." They are the brute beasts of the intellectual domain. Who does not know fellows that always have an ill-conditioned fact or two which they lead after them into decent company like so many bull-dogs, ready to let them slip at every ingenious suggestion, or convenient generalization, or pleasant fancy? I allow no "facts" at this table. What! Because bread is good and wholesome, and necessary and nourishing, shall you thrust a crumb into my windpipe while I am talking? Do not these muscles of mine represent a hundred loaves of bread? and is not my thought the abstract of ten thousand of these crumbs of truth with which you would choke off my speech?

[The above remark must be conditioned and qualified for the vulgar mind. The reader will, of course, understand the precise amount of seasoning which must be added to it before he adopts it as one of the axioms of his life. The speaker disclaims all responsibility for its abuse in incompetent hands.] [2]

This business of conversation is a very serious matter. There are men whom it weakens one to talk with an hour more than a day's fasting would do. Mark this which I am going to say, for it is as good as a working professional man's advice, and costs you nothing: It is better to lose a pint of blood from your veins than to have a nerve tapped. Nobody measures your nervous force as it runs away, nor bandages your brain and marrow after the operation.

There are men of *esprit* who are excessively exhausting to some people. They are the talkers who have what may be called *jerky* minds. Their thoughts do not run in the natural order of sequence. They say bright things on all possible subjects, but their zigzags rack you to death. After a jolting half-

---

write for it, the recollection of these crude products of his uncombed literary boyhood suggested the thought that it would be a curious experiment to shake the same bough again, and see if the ripe fruit were better or worse than the early windfalls.—*Author's note.*

The extracts from *The Autocrat of the Breakfast-Table* are used by permission of, and by arrangement with, Houghton Mifflin Company, the authorized publishers.

[2] The square brackets here and later are Holmes's own.

hour with one of these jerky companions, talking with a dull friend affords great relief. It is like taking the cat in your lap after holding a squirrel.

What a comfort a dull but kindly person is, to be sure, at times! A ground-glass shade over a gas-lamp does not bring more solace to our dazzled eyes than such a one to our minds.

"Do not dull people bore you?" said one of the lady-boarders,—the same that sent me her autograph-book last week with a request for a few original stanzas, not remembering that *The Pactolian* pays me five dollars a line for everything I write in its columns.

"Madam," said I (she and the century were in their teens together), "all men are bores, except when we want them. There never was but one man whom I would trust with my latch-key."

".Who might that favored person be?"

"Zimmermann."

—The men of genius that I fancy most, have erectile heads like the cobra-di-capello. You remember what they tell of William Pinkney, the great pleader; how in his eloquent paroxysms the veins of his neck would swell and his face flush and his eyes glitter, until he seemed on the verge of apoplexy. The hydraulic arrangements for supplying the brain with blood are only second in importance to its own organization. The bulbous-headed fellows who steam well when they are at work are the men that draw big audiences and give us marrowy books and pictures. It is a good sign to have one's feet grow cold when he is writing. A great writer and speaker once told me that he often wrote with his feet in hot water; but for this, *all* his blood would have run into his head, as the mercury sometimes withdraws into the ball of a thermometer.

—You don't suppose that my remarks made at this table are like so many postage-stamps, do you,—each to be only once uttered? If you do, you are mistaken. He must be a poor creature who does not often repeat himself. Imagine the author of the excellent piece of advice, "Know thyself," never alluding to that sentiment again during the course of a protracted existence! Why, the truths a man carries about with him are his tools; and do you think a carpenter is bound to use the same plane but once to smooth a knotty board with, or to hang up his hammer after it has driven its first nail? I shall never repeat a conversation, but an idea often. I shall use the same types when I like, but not commonly the same stereotypes. A thought is often original, though you have uttered it a hundred times. It has come to you over a new route, by a new and express train of associations.

Sometimes, but rarely, one may be caught making the same speech twice over, and yet be held blameless. Thus, a certain lecturer, after performing in an inland city, where dwells a *Littératrice* of note, was invited to meet her and others over the social teacup. She pleasantly referred to his many wanderings in his new occupation. "Yes," he replied, "I am like the Huma, the bird that never lights, being always in the cars, as he is always on the wing."— Years elapsed. The lecturer visited the same place once more for the same purpose. Another social cup after the lecture, and a second meeting with the distinguished lady. "You are constantly going from place to place," she said. —"Yes," he answered, "I am like the Huma,"—and finished the sentence as before.

What horrors, when it flashed over him that he had made this fine speech, word for word, twice over! Yet it was not true, as the lady might perhaps have fairly inferred, that he had embellished his conversation with the Huma daily during that whole interval of years. On the contrary, he had never once thought of the odious fowl until the recurrence of precisely the same circumstances brought up precisely the same idea. He ought to have been proud of the accuracy of his mental adjustments. Given certain factors, and a sound brain should always evolve the same fixed product with the certainty of Babbage's calculating machine.

—What a satire, by the way, is that machine on the mere mathematician! A Frankenstein monster, a thing without brains and without heart, too stupid to make a blunder; which turns out results like a cornsheller, and never grows any wiser or better, though it grind a thousand bushels of them!

I have an immense respect for a man of talents *plus* "the mathematics." But the calculating power alone should seem to be the least human of qualities, and to have the smallest amount of reason in it; since a machine can be made to do the work of three or four calculators, and better than any one of them. Sometimes I have been troubled that I had not a deeper intuitive apprehension of the relations of numbers. But the triumph of the ciphering hand-organ has consoled me. I always fancy I can hear the wheels clicking in a calculator's brain. The power of dealing with numbers is a kind of "detached lever" arrangement, which may be put into a mighty poor watch. I suppose it is about as common as the power of moving the ears voluntarily, which is a moderately rare endowment. . . .

—What are the great faults of conversation? Want of ideas, want of words, want of manners, are the principal ones, I suppose you think. I don't doubt it, but I will tell you what I have found spoil more good talks than anything else;—long arguments on special points between people who differ on the fundamental principles upon which these points depend. No men can have satisfactory relations with each other until they have agreed on certain *ultimata* of belief not to be disturbed in ordinary conversation, and unless they have sense enough to trace the secondary questions depending upon these ultimate beliefs to their source. In short, just as a written constitution is essential to the best social order, so a code of finalities is a necessary condition of profitable talk between two persons. Talking is like playing on the harp; there is as much in laying the hand on the strings to stop their vibrations as in twanging them to bring out their music. . . .

I really believe some people save their bright thoughts as being too precious for conversation. What do you think an admiring friend said the other day to one that was talking good things,—good enough to print? "Why," said he, "you are wasting merchantable literature, a cash article, at the rate, as nearly as I can tell, of fifty dollars an hour." The talker took him to the window and asked him to look out and tell what he saw.

"Nothing but a very dusty street," he said, "and a man driving a sprinkling machine through it."

"Why don't you tell the man he is wasting that water? What would be the state of the highways of life, if we did not drive our *thought-sprinklers* through them with the valves open, sometimes?

"Besides there is another thing about this talking, which you forget. It shapes our thoughts for us;—the waves of conversation roll them as the surf rolls the pebbles on the shore. Let me modify the image a little. I rough out my thoughts in talk as an artist models in clay. Spoken language is so plastic, —you can pat and coax, and spread and shave, and rub out, and fill up, and stick on so easily, when you work that soft material, that there is nothing like it for modelling. Out of it come the shapes which you turn into marble or bronze in your immortal books, if you happen to write such. Or, to use another illustration, writing or printing is like shooting with a rifle; you may hit your reader's mind, or miss it; but talking is like playing at a mark with the pipe of an engine; if it is within reach, and you have time enough, you can't help hitting it." . . .

Sometimes people criticize the poems one sends them, and suggest all sorts of improvements. Who was that silly body that wanted Burns to alter "Scots wha hae," so as to lengthen the last line, thus?—

"Edward! Chains and slavery."

Here is a little poem I sent a short time since to a committee for a certain celebration. I understood that it was to be a festive and convivial occasion, and ordered myself accordingly. It seems the president of the day was what is called a "teetotaller." I received a note from him in the following words, containing the copy subjoined, with the emendations annexed to it.

"Dear Sir,—your poem gives good satisfaction to the committee. The sentiments expressed with reference to liquor are not, however, those generally entertained by this community. I have therefore consulted the clergyman of this place, who has made some slight changes, which he thinks will remove all objections, and keep the valuable portions of the poem. Please to inform me of your charge for said poem. Our means are limited, etc., etc., etc.

"Yours with respect."

Here it is,—with the *slight alterations*.

> Come! fill a fresh bumper,—for why should we go
> While the ~~nectar~~ (logwood) still reddens our cups as they flow!
> Pour out the ~~rich juices~~ (decoction) still bright with the sun,
> Till o'er the brimmed crystal the ~~rubies~~ (dye-stuff) shall run.
> The ~~purple-globed clusters~~ (half-ripened apples) their life-dews have bled;
> How sweet is the ~~breath~~ (taste) of the ~~fragrance they shed~~ (sugar of lead)!
> For summer's ~~last roses~~ (rank poisons) lie hid in the ~~wines~~ (wines! ! !)
> That were garnered by ~~maidens who laughed through the vines~~ (stable boys smoking long-nines.)
> Then a ~~smile~~ (scowl), and a ~~glass~~ (howl), and a ~~toast~~ (scoff), and a ~~cheer~~ (sneer),
> For all ~~the good wine, and we've some of it here~~ (strychnine and whisky, and ratsbane and beer)
> In cellar, in pantry, in attic, in hall,
> ~~Long live the gay servant that laughs for us all!~~ (Down, down with the tyrant that masters us all.)

The company said I had been shabbily treated, and advised me to charge the committee double,—which I did. But as I never got my pay, I don't know that it made much difference. I am a very particular person about having all I write printed as I write it. I require to see a proof, a revise, a re-revise, and a double re-revise, or fourth-proof rectified impression of all my productions, especially verse. A misprint kills a sensitive author. An intentional change of his text murders him. No wonder so many poets die young! . . .

—I never saw an author in my life—saving, perhaps one—that did not purr as audibly as a full-grown domestic cat (*Felis catus* LINN.) on having his fur smoothed in the right way by a skilful hand.

But let me give you a caution. Be very careful how you tell an author he is *droll*. Ten to one he will hate you! and if he does, be sure he can do you a mischief, and very probably will. Say you *cried* over his romance or his verses, and he will love you and send you a copy. You can laugh over that as much as you like,—in private.

—Wonder why authors and actors are ashamed of being funny?—Why, there are obvious reasons, and deep philosophical ones. The clown knows very well that the women are not in love with him, but with Hamlet, the fellow in the black cloak and plumed hat. Passion never laughs. The wit knows that his place is at the tail of a procession.

If you want the deep underlying reason, I must take more time to tell it. There is a perfect consciousness in every form of wit,—using that term in its general sense,—that its essence consists in a partial and incomplete view of whatever it touches. It throws a single ray, separated from the rest,—red, yellow, blue, or any intermediate shade,—upon an object; never white light; that is the province of wisdom. We get beautiful effects from wit,—all the prismatic colors,—but never the object as it is in fair daylight. A pun, which is a kind of wit, is a different and much shallower trick in mental optics; throwing the *shadows* of two objects so that one overlies the other. Poetry uses the rainbow tints for special effects, but always keeps its essential object in the purest white light of truth. . . .

—Don't flatter yourselves that friendship authorizes you to say disagreeable things to your intimates. On the contrary, the nearer you come into relation with a person, the more necessary do tact and courtesy become. Except in cases of necessity, which are rare, leave your friend to learn unpleasant truths from his enemies; they are ready enough to tell them. Good-breeding *never* forgets that *amour-propre* is universal. When you read the story of the Archbishop and Gil Blas,[3] you may laugh, if you will, at the poor old man's delusion; but don't forget that the youth was the greater fool of the two, and that his master served such a booby rightly in turning him out of doors.

—You need not get up a rebellion against what I say, if you find everything in my sayings is not exactly new. You can't possibly mistake a man who means to be honest for a literary pickpocket. I once read an introductory lecture that looked to me too learned for its latitude. On examination, I found all its erudition was taken ready-made from Disraeli. If I had been ill-natured, I should have shown up the little great man, who had once belabored me in his feeble way. But one can generally tell these wholesale thieves easily enough, and they are not worth the trouble of putting them in the pillory. I doubt the entire novelty of my remarks just made on telling unpleasant truths, yet I am not conscious of any larceny.

Neither make too much of flaws and occasional over-statements. Some persons seem to think that absolute truth, in the form of rigidly stated propositions, is all that conversation admits. This is precisely as if a musician should insist on having nothing but perfect chords and simple melodies,—no diminished fifths, no flat sevenths, no flourishes on any account. Now it is fair to say, that, just as music must have all these, so conversation must have its partial truths, its embellished truths, its exaggerated truths. It is in its higher forms an artistic product, and admits the ideal element as much as pictures or statues. One man who is a little too literal can spoil the talk of a whole tableful of men of *esprit.*—"Yes," you say, "but who wants to hear fanciful people's nonsense? Put the facts to it, and then see where it is!"—Certainly, if a man is too fond of paradox,—if he is flighty and empty,—if, instead of striking those fifths and sevenths, those harmonious discords, often so much

[3] *Gil Blas,* by Le Sage (1668–1747).

better than the twinned octaves, in the music of thought,—if, instead of striking these, he jangles the chords, stick a fact into him like a stiletto. But remember that talking is one of the fine arts,—the noblest, the most important,
and the most difficult,—and that its fluent harmonies may be spoiled by the
intrusion of a single harsh note. Therefore conversation which is suggestive
rather than argumentative, which lets out the most of each talker's results of
thought, is commonly the pleasantest and the most profitable. It is not easy,
at the best, for two persons talking together to make the most of each other's
thoughts, there are so many of them.

[The company looked as if they wanted an explanation.]

When John and Thomas, for instance, are talking together, it is natural
enough that among the six there should be more or less confusion and misapprehension.

[Our landlady turned pale:—no doubt she thought there was a screw loose
in my intellects,—and that involved the probable loss of a boarder. A severe-
looking person, who wears a Spanish cloak and a sad cheek, fluted by the
passions of the melodrama, whom I understand to be the professional ruffian
of the neighboring theatre, alluded, with a certain lifting of the brow, drawing down of the corners of the mouth, and somewhat rasping *voce di petto,*
to Falstaff's nine men in buckram. Everybody looked up; I believe the old
gentleman opposite was afraid I should seize the carving-knife; at any rate,
he slid it to one side, as it were carelessly.]

I think, I said, I can make it plain to Benjamin Franklin here that there
are at least six personalities distinctly to be recognized as taking part in that
dialogue between John and Thomas.

Three Johns.
1. The real John; known only to his Maker.
2. John's ideal John; never the real one, and often very unlike him.
3. Thomas's ideal John; never the real John nor John's John, but often very unlike either.

Three Thomases.
1. The real Thomas.
2. Thomas's ideal Thomas.
3. John's ideal Thomas.

Only one of the three Johns is taxed; only one can be weighed on a
platform-balance; but the other two are just as important in the conversation. Let us suppose the real John to be old, dull, and ill-looking. But as the
Higher Powers have not conferred on men the gift of seeing themselves in
the true light, John very possibly conceives himself to be youthful, witty, and
fascinating, and talks from the point of view of this ideal. Thomas, again,
believes him to be an artful rogue, we will say; therefore he *is,* so far as
Thomas's attitude in the conversation is concerned, an artful rogue, though

really simple and stupid. The same conditions apply to the three Thomases. It follows, that, until a man can be found who knows himself as his Maker knows him, or who sees himself as others see him, there must be at least six persons engaged in every dialogue between two. Of these, the least important, philosophically speaking, is the one that we have called the real person. No wonder two disputants often get angry, when there are six of them talking and listening all at the same time.

[A very unphilosophical application of the above remarks was made by a young fellow answering to the name of John, who sits near me at table. A certain basket of peaches, a rare vegetable, little known to boarding-houses, was on its way to me *via* this unlettered Johannes. He appropriated the three that remained in the basket, remarking that there was just one apiece for him. I convinced him that his practical inference was hasty and illogical, but in the meantime he had eaten the peaches.]

—The opinions of relatives as to a man's powers are very commonly of little value; not merely because they sometimes overrate their own flesh and blood, as some may suppose; on the contrary, they are quite as likely to underrate those whom they have grown into the habit of considering like themselves. The advent of genius is like what florists style the *breaking* of a seedling tulip into what we may call high-caste colors—ten thousand dingy flowers, then one with the divine streak; or, if you prefer it, like the coming up in old Jacob's garden of that most gentlemanly little fruit, the seckel pear, which I have sometimes seen in shop-windows. It is a surprise,—there is nothing to account for it. All at once we find that twice two make *five*. Nature is fond of what are called "gift-enterprises." This little book of life which she has given into the hands of its joint possessors is commonly one of the old story-books bound over again. Only once in a great while there is a stately poem in it, or its leaves are illuminated with the glories of art, or they enfold a draft for untold values signed by the million-fold millionaire old mother herself. But strangers are commonly the first to find the "gift" that came with the little book.

It may be questioned whether anything can be conscious of its own flavor. Whether the musk-deer, or the civet-cat, or even a still more eloquently silent animal that might be mentioned, is aware of any personal peculiarity, may well be doubted. No man knows his own voice; many men do not know their own profiles. Every one remembers Carlyle's famous "Characteristics" article; allow for exaggerations, and there is a great deal in his doctrine of the self-unconsciousness of genius. It comes under the great law just stated. This incapacity of knowing its own traits is often found in the family as well as in the individual. . . .

—Here is another of these curiously recurring remarks. I have said it, and heard it many times, and occasionally met with something like it in books,

—somewhere in Bulwer's novels, I think, and in one of the works of Mr. Olmsted, I know.

Memory, imagination, old sentiments and associations, are more readily reached through the sense of SMELL *than by almost any other channel.*

Of course the particular odors which act upon each person's susceptibilities differ.—O, yes! I will tell you some of mine. The smell of *phosphorus* is one of them. During a year or two of adolescence I used to be dabbling in chemistry a good deal, and as about that time I had my little aspirations and passions like another, some of these things got mixed up with each other: orange-colored fumes of nitrous acid, and visions as bright and transient; reddening litmus-paper, and blushing cheeks;—*eheu!*

"Soles occidere et redire possunt,"

but there is no reagent that will redden the faded roses of eighteen hundred and —— spare them! But, as I was saying, phosphorus fires this train of associations in an instant; its luminous vapors with their penetrating odor throw me into a trance; it comes to me in a double sense "trailing clouds of glory." Only the confounded Vienna matches, *ohne phosphorgeruch,* have worn my sensibilities a little.

Then there is the *marigold.* When I was of smallest dimensions, and wont to ride impacted between the knees of fond parental pair, we would sometimes cross the bridge to the next village-town and stop opposite a low, brown, "gambrel-roofed" cottage. Out of it would come one Sally, sister of its swarthy tenant, swarthy herself, shady-lipped, sad-voiced, and, bending over her flower-bed, would gather a "posy," as she called it, for the little boy. Sally lies in the churchyard with a slab of blue slate at her head, lichen-crusted, and leaning a little, within the last few years. Cottage, garden-beds, posies, grenadier-like rows of seedling onions,—stateliest of vegetables,—all are gone, but the breath of a marigold brings them all back to me.

Perhaps the herb *everlasting,* the fragrant *immortelle* of our autumn fields, has the most suggestive odor to me of all those that set me dreaming. I can hardly describe the strange thoughts and emotions which come to me as I inhale the aroma of its pale, dry, rustling flowers. A something it has of sepulchral spicery, as if it had been brought from the core of some great pyramid, where it had lain on the breast of a mummied Pharaoh. Something, too, of immortality in the sad, faint sweetness lingering so long in its lifeless petals. Yet this does not tell why it fills my eyes with tears and carries me in blissful thought to the banks of asphodel that border the River of Life.

—I should not have talked so much about these personal susceptibilities, if I had not a remark to make about them which I believe is a new one. It is this. There may be a physical reason for the strange connection between the sense of smell and the mind. The olfactory nerve,—so my friend, the Professor, tells me,—is the only one directly connected with the hemispheres of the brain, the parts in which, as we have every reason to believe, the intellectual processes are profound. To speak more truly, the olfactory "nerve" is not a nerve at all, he says, but a part of the brain, in intimate connection with its anterior lobes. Whether this anatomical arrangement is at the bottom of the facts I have mentioned, I will not decide, but it is curious enough to be worth remembering. Contrast the sense of taste, as a source of suggestive impressions, with that of smell. Now the Professor assures me that you will find the nerve of taste has no immediate connection with the brain proper, but only with the prolongation of the spinal cord.

[The old gentleman opposite did not pay much attention, I think, to this hypothesis of mine. But while I was speaking about the sense of smell he nestled about in his seat, and presently succeeded in getting out a large red bandanna handkerchief. Then he lurched a little to the other side, and after much tribulation at last extricated an ample round snuff-box. I looked as he opened it and felt for the wonted pugil. Moist rappee, and a Tonka-bean lying therein. I made the manual sign understood of all mankind that use the precious dust, and presently my brain, too, responded to the long unused stimulus.—O boys,—that were,—actual papas and possible grandpapas,— some of you with crowns like billiard-balls,—some in locks of sable silvered, and some of silver sabled,—do you remember, as you doze over this, those after-dinners at the Trois Frères, when the Scotch-plaided snuff-box went round, and the dry Lundy-Foot tickled its way along into our happy sensoria? Then it was that the Chambertin or the Clos Vougeot came in, slumbering in its straw cradle. And one among you,—do you remember how he would sit dreaming over his Burgundy, and tinkle his fork against the sides of the bubble-like glass, saying that he was hearing the cow-bells as he used to hear them, when the deep-breathing kine came home at twilight from the huckleberry pasture, in the old home a thousand leagues towards the sunset?]

Ah me! what strains and strophes of unwritten verse pulsate through my soul when I open a certain closet in the ancient house where I was born! On its shelves used to lie bundles of sweet-marjoram and pennyroyal and lavender and mint and catnip; there apples were stored until their seeds should grow black, which happy period there were sharp little milk-teeth always ready to anticipate; there peaches lay in the dark, thinking of the sunshine they had lost, until, like the hearts of saints who dream of heaven in their sorrow, they grew fragrant as the breath of angels. The odorous echo of a score of dead summers lingers yet in those dim recesses.

—Do I remember Byron's line about "striking the electric chain"?—To be sure I do. I sometimes think the less the hint that stirs the automatic machinery of association, the more easily this moves us. What can be more trivial than that old story of opening the folio Shakespeare that used to lie in some ancient English hall and finding the flakes of Christmas pastry between its leaves, shut up in them perhaps a hundred years ago? And, lo! as one looks on these poor relics of a bygone generation, the universe changes in the twinkling of an eye; old George the Second is back again, and the elder Pitt is coming into power, and General Wolfe is a fine, promising young man, and over the channel they are pulling the Sieur Damiens to pieces with wild horses, and across the Atlantic the Indians are tomahawking Hirams and Jonathans and Jonases at Fort William Henry; all the dead people who have been in the dust so long—even to the stout-armed cook that made the pastry —are alive again; the planet unwinds a hundred of its luminous coils, and the precession of the equinoxes is retraced on the dial of heaven! And all this for a bit of pie-crust!

—I will thank you for that pie,—said the provoking young fellow whom I have named repeatedly. He looked at it for a moment, and put his hands to his eyes as if moved.—I was thinking,—he said indistinctly—

—How? What is't?—said our landlady.

—I was thinking—said he—who was king of England when this old pie was baked,—and it made me feel bad to think how long he must have been dead.

[Our landlady is a decent body, poor, and a widow of course; *cela va sans dire*. She told me her story once; it was as if a grain of corn that had been ground and bolted had tried to individualize itself by a special narrative. There was the wooing and the wedding,—the start in life,—the disappoint- ment,—the children she had buried,—the struggle against fate,—the dis- mantling of life, first of its small luxuries, and then of its comforts,—the broken spirits,—the altered character of the one on whom she leaned,— and at last the death that came and drew the black curtain between her and all her earthly hopes.

I never laughed at my landlady after she had told me her story, but I often cried,—not those pattering tears that run off the eaves upon our neighbors' grounds, the *stillicidium* of self-conscious sentiment, but those which steal noiselessly through their conduits until they reach the cisterns lying round about the heart; those tears that we weep inwardly with unchanging features; —such I did shed for her often when the imps of the boarding-house Inferno tugged at her soul with their red-hot pincers.]

Young man,—I said—the pasty you speak lightly of is not old, but courtesy to those who labor to serve us, especially if they are of the weaker sex, is very old, and yet well worth retaining. May I recommend to you the following caution, as a guide, whenever you are dealing with a woman, or an artist, or a poet,—if you are handling an editor or politician, it is superfluous advice. I take it from the back of one of those little French toys which contain paste- board figures moved by a small running stream of fine sand; Benjamin Franklin will translate it for you: *"Quoi-qu'elle soit très solidement montée, il faut ne pas* BRUTALISER *la machine."*—I will thank you for the pie, if you please.

[I took more of it than was good for me,—as much as 85°, I should think,—and had an indigestion in consequence. While I was suffering from it, I wrote some sadly desponding poems, and a theological essay which took a very melancholy view of creation. When I got better I labelled them all "Pie-crust," and laid them by as scarecrows and solemn warnings. I have a number of books on my shelves which I should like to label with some such title; but, as they have great names on their title-pages,—Doctors of Divinity, some of them,—it wouldn't do.]

—My friend, the Professor, whom I have mentioned to you once or twice, told me yesterday that somebody had been abusing him in some of the journals of his calling. I told him that I didn't doubt he deserved it; that I hoped he did deserve a little abuse occasionally, and would for a number of years to come; that nobody could do anything to make his neighbors wiser or better without being liable to abuse for it; especially that people hated to have their little mistakes made fun of, and perhaps he had been doing something of the kind.—The Professor smiled.—Now, said I, hear what I am going to say. It will not take many years to bring you to the period of life when men, at least the majority of writing and talking men, do nothing but praise. Men, like peaches and pears, grow sweet a little while before they begin to decay. I don't know what it is,—whether a spontaneous change, mental or bodily, or whether it is through experience of the thanklessness of critical honesty,—but it is a fact, that most writers, except sour and unsuccessful ones, get tired of finding fault at about the time when they are beginning to grow old. As a general thing, I would not give a great deal for the fair words of a critic, if he is himself an author, over fifty years of age. At thirty we are all trying to cut our names in big letters upon the walls of this tenement of life; twenty years later we have carved it, or shut up our jack-knives. Then we are ready to help others, and care less to hinder any, because nobody's elbows are in our way. So I am glad you have a little life left; you will be saccharine enough in a few years.

—Some of the softening effects of advancing age have struck me very much in what I have heard or seen here and elsewhere. I just now spoke of the sweetening process that authors undergo. Do you know that in the gradual passage from maturity to helplessness the harshest characters sometimes have a period in which they are gentle and placid as young children? I have heard it said, but I cannot be sponsor for its truth, that the famous chieftain, Lochiel, was rocked in a cradle like a baby, in his old age. An old man, whose studies had been of the severest scholastic kind, used to love to hear little nursery stories read over and over to him. One who saw the Duke of Wellington in his last years describes him as very gentle in his aspect and demeanor. I remember a person of singularly stern and lofty bearing who became remarkably gracious and easy in all his ways in the later period of his life.

And that leads me to say that men often remind me of pears in their way of coming to maturity. Some are ripe at twenty, like human Jargonelles, and must be made the most of, for their day is soon over. Some come into their perfect condition late, like the autumn kinds, and they last better than the summer fruit. And some, that, like the Winter-Nelis, have been hard and uninviting until all the rest have had their season, get their glow and perfume long after the frost and snow have done their worst with the orchards. Beware of rash criticisms; the rough and astringent fruit you condemn may be an autumn or a winter pear, and that which you picked up beneath the same bough in August may have been only its worm-eaten windfalls. Milton was a Saint-Germain with a graft of the roseate Early-Catherine. Rich, juicy, lively, fragrant, russet-skinned old Chaucer was an Easter-Beurré; the buds of a new summer were swelling when he ripened. . . .

—I wonder if anybody ever finds fault with anything I say at this table when it is repeated? I hope they do, I am sure. I should be very certain that I had said nothing of much significance, if they did not.

Did you never, in walking in the fields, come across a large flat stone, which had lain, nobody knows how long, just where you found it, with the grass forming a little hedge, as it were, all round it, close to its edges,—and have you not, in obedience to a kind of feeling that told you it had been lying there long enough, insinuated your stick or your foot or your fingers under its edge and turned it over as a housewife turns a cake, when she says to herself, "It's done brown enough by this time"? What an odd revelation, and what an unforeseen and unpleasant surprise to a small community, the very existence of which you had not suspected, until the sudden dismay and scattering among its members produced by your turning the old stone over! Blades of grass flattened down, colorless, matted together, as if they had been bleached and ironed; hideous crawling creatures, some of them coleopterous or horny-shelled,—turtle-bugs one wants to call them; some of them softer, but cunningly spread out and compressed like Lepine watches; (Nature never loses a crack or a crevice, mind you, or a joint in a tavern bedstead, but she always has one of her flat-pattern live timekeepers to slide into it;) black, glossy crickets, with their long filaments sticking out like the whips of four-horse stage-coaches; motionless, slug-like creatures, young larvæ, perhaps more horrible in their pulpy stillness than even in the infernal wriggle of maturity! But no sooner is the stone turned and the wholesome light of day let upon this compressed and blinded community of creeping things, than all of them which enjoy the luxury of legs—and some of them have a good many—rush round wildly, butting each other and everything in their way, and end in a general stampede for underground retreats from the regions poisoned by sunshine. *Next year* you will find the grass growing tall and green where the stone lay; the ground-bird builds her nest where the beetle had its hole; the dandelion and the butter-cup are growing there, and the broad fans of insect-angels open and shut over their golden disks, as the rhythmic waves of blissful consciousness pulsate through their glorified being.

—The young fellow whom they call John saw fit to say, in his very familiar way,—at which I do not choose to take offence, but which I sometimes think it necessary to repress,—that I was coming it rather strong on the butterflies.

No, I replied; there is meaning in each of those images,—the butterfly as well as the others. The stone is ancient error. The grass is human nature borne down and bleached of all its color by it. The shapes which are found beneath are the crafty beings that thrive in darkness, and the weaker organisms kept helpless by it. He who turns the stone over is whosoever puts the staff of truth to the old lying incubus, no matter whether he do it with a serious face or a laughing one. The next year stands for the coming time. Then shall the nature which had lain blanched and broken rise in its full stature and native hues in the sunshine. Then shall God's minstrels build their nests in the hearts of a new-born humanity. Then shall beauty—Divinity taking outlines and color —light upon the souls of men as the butterfly, image of the beatified spirit rising from the dust, soars from the shell that held a poor grub, which would never have found wings had not the stone been lifted.

You never need think you can turn over any old falsehood without a terrible squirming and scattering of the horrid little population that dwells under it. . . . .

—It is a fine thing to be an oracle to which an appeal is always made in all discussions. The men of facts wait their turn in grim silence, with that slight tension about the nostrils which the consciousness of carrying a "settler" in the form of a fact or a revolver gives the individual thus armed. When a person is really full of information, and does not abuse it to crush conversation, his part is to that of the real talkers what the instrumental accompaniment is in a trio or quartette of vocalists.

—What do I mean by the real talkers?—Why, the people with fresh ideas, of course, and plenty of good warm words to dress them in. Facts always yield the place of honor in conversation, to thoughts about facts; but if a false note is uttered, down comes the finger on the key and the man of facts asserts his true dignity. I have known three of these men of facts, at least, who were always formidable,—and one of them was tyrannical.

—Yes, a man sometimes makes a grand appearance on a particular occasion; but these men knew something about almost everything, and never made mistakes.—He? *Veneers* in first-rate style. The mahogany scales off now and then in spots, and then you see the cheap light stuff.—I found ——

very fine in conversational information, the other day when we were in company. The talk ran upon mountains. He was wonderfully well acquainted with the leading facts about the Andes, the Apennines, and the Appalachians; he had nothing in particular to say about Ararat, Ben Nevis, and various other mountains that were mentioned. By and by some Revolutionary anecdote came up, and he showed singular familiarity with the lives of the Adamses, and gave many details relating to Major André. A point of Natural History being suggested, he gave an excellent account of the air-bladder of fishes. He was very full upon the subject of agriculture, but retired from the conversation when horticulture was introduced in the discussion. So he seemed well acquainted with the geology of anthracite, but did not pretend to know anything of other kinds of coal. There was something so odd about the extent and limitations of his knowledge, that I suspected all at once what might be the meaning of it, and waited until I got an opportunity.—Have you seen the *New American Cyclopædia?* said I.—I have, he replied; I received an early copy.—How far does it go?—He turned red, and answered,—To Araguay.—Oh, said I to myself,—not quite so far as Ararat;—that is the reason he knew nothing about it; but he must have read all the rest straight through, and, if he can remember what is in this volume until he has read all those which are to come, he will know more than I ever thought he would. . . . .

—My friend, the Professor, has been full of eggs lately. [This remark excited a burst of hilarity which I did not allow to interrupt the course of my observations.]. . . Some of the things he has told me have suggested several odd analogies enough.

There are half-a-dozen men, or so, who carry in their brains the *ovarian eggs* of the next generation's or century's civilization. These eggs are not ready to be laid in the form of books as yet; some of them are hardly ready to be put into the form of talk. But as rudimentary ideas or inchoate tendencies, there they are; and these are what must form the future. A man's general notions are not good for much, unless he has a crop of these intellectual ovarian eggs in his own brain, or knows them as they exist in the minds of others. One must be in the *habit* of talking with such persons to get at these rudimentary germs of thought; for their development is necessarily imperfect, and they are moulded on new patterns, which must be long and closely studied. But these are the men to talk with. No fresh truth ever gets into a book.

—A good many fresh lies get in, anyhow,—said one of the company.

I proceeded in spite of the interruption.—All uttered thought, my friend, the Professor, says, is of the nature of an excretion. Its materials have been taken in, and have acted upon the system, and been reacted on by it; it has circulated and done its office in one mind before it is given out for the benefit of others. It may be milk or venom to other minds; but, in either case, it is something which the producer has had the use of and can part with. A man instinctively tries to get rid of his thought in conversation or in print so soon as it is matured; but it is hard to get at it as it lies imbedded, a mere potentiality, the germ of a germ, in his intellect.

—Where are the brains that are fullest of these ovarian eggs of thought?— I decline mentioning individuals. The producers of thought, who are few, the "jobbers" of thought, who are many, and the retailers of thought, who are numberless, are so mixed up in the popular apprehension, that it would be hopeless to try to separate them before opinion has had time to settle. Follow the course of opinion on the great subjects of human interest for a few generations or centuries, get its parallax, map out a small arc of its movement, see where it tends, and then see who is in advance of it or even with it; the world calls him hard names, probably; but if you would find the *ova* of the future, you must look into the folds of his cerebral convolutions. . . .

It is by little things that we know ourselves; a soul would very probably mistake itself for another, when once disembodied, were it not for individual experiences which differ from those of others only in details seemingly trifling. All of us have been thirsty thousands of times, and felt, with Pindar, that water was the best of things. I alone, as I think, of all mankind, remember one particular pailful of water, flavored with the white-pine of which the pail was made, and the brown mug out of which one Edmund, a red-faced and curly-haired boy, was averred to have bitten a fragment in his haste to drink; it being then high summer, and little full-blooded boys feeling very warm and porous in the low-"studded" school-room where Dame Prentiss, dead and gone, ruled over young children, many of whom are old ghosts now, and have known Abraham for twenty or thirty years of our mortal time.

Thirst belongs to humanity, everywhere, in all ages; but that white-pine pail, and that brown mug belong to me in particular; and just so of my special relationships with other things and with my race. One could never remember himself in eternity by the mere fact of having loved or hated any more than by that of having thirsted; love and hate have no more individuality in them than single waves in the ocean;—but the accidents or trivial marks which distinguished those whom we loved or hated make their memory our own forever, and with it that of our own personality also. . . .

—Will you walk out and look at those elms with me after breakfast?—I said to the schoolmistress.

[I am not going to tell lies about it, and say that she blushed,—as I suppose she ought to have done, at such a tremendous piece of gallantry as that was for our boarding-house. On the contrary, she turned a little pale,—but smiled brightly and said,— Yes, with pleasure, but she must walk towards her school.—She went for her bonnet.—The old gentleman opposite followed her with his eyes, and said he wished he was a young fellow. Presently she came down, looking very pretty in her half-mourning bonnet, and carrying a school-book in her hand.]

MY FIRST WALK WITH THE SCHOOLMISTRESS

This is the shortest way,—she said, as we came to a corner.—Then we won't take it,—said I.—The schoolmistress laughed a little, and said she was ten minutes early, so she could go round.

We walked under Mr. Paddock's row of English elms. The gray squirrels were out looking for their breakfasts, and one of them came toward us in light, soft, intermittent leaps, until he was close to the rail of the burial-ground. . . .

We came opposite the head of a place or court running eastward from the main street.—Look down there,—I said,—my friend, the Professor, lived in the house at the left hand, next the further corner, for years and years. He died out of it, the other day.—Died?—said the schoolmistress.—Certainly,— said I.—We die out of houses, just as we die out of our bodies. A commercial smash kills a hundred men's houses for them, as a railroad crash kills their mortal frames and drives out the immortal tenants. Men sicken of houses until at last they quit them, as the soul leaves its body when it is tired of its infirmities. The body has been called "the house we live in"; the house is quite as much the body we live in. Shall I tell you some things the Professor said the other day?—Do!—said the schoolmistress.

A man's body,—said the Professor,—is whatever is occupied by his will and his sensibility. The small room down there, where I wrote those papers you remember reading, was much more a portion of my body than a paralytic's senseless and motionless arm or leg is of his.

The soul of a man has a series of concentric envelopes round it, like the core of an onion, or the innermost of a nest of boxes. First he has his natural garment of flesh and blood. Then, his artificial integuments, with their true skin of solid stuffs, their cuticle of lighter tissues, and their variously-tinted pigments. Thirdly, his domicile, be it a single chamber or a stately mansion. And then, the whole visible world, in which Time buttons him up as in a loose outside wrapper.

You shall observe,—the Professor said,—for, like Mr. John Hunter and other great men, he brings in that *shall* with great effect sometimes,—you shall observe that a man's clothing or series of envelopes does after a certain time mould itself upon his individual nature. We know this of our hats, and are always reminded of it when we happen to put them on wrong side foremost. We soon find that the beaver is a hollow cast of the skull, with all its irregular bumps and depressions. Just so all that clothes a man, even to the blue sky which caps his head,—a little loosely,—shapes itself to fit each particular being beneath it. Farmers, sailors, astronomers, poets, lovers, condemned criminals, all find it different, according to the eyes with which they severally look.

But our houses shape themselves palpably on our inner and outer natures. See a householder breaking up and you will be sure of it. There is a shell-fish which builds all manner of smaller shells into the walls of its own. A house is never a home until we have crusted it with the spoils of a hundred lives besides those of our own past. See what these are and you can tell what the occupant is.

I had no idea,—said the Professor,—until I pulled up my domestic establishment the other day, what an enormous quantity of roots I had been making during the years I was planted there. Why, there wasn't a nook or a corner that some fibre had not worked its way into; and when I gave the last wrench, each of them seemed to shriek like a mandrake as it broke its hold and came away.

There is nothing that happens, you know, which must not inevitably, and which does not actually, photograph itself in every conceivable aspect and in all dimensions. The infinite galleries of the Past await but one brief process and all their pictures will be called out and fixed forever. We had a curious illustration of the great fact on a very humble scale. When a certain bookcase, long standing in one place, for which it was built, was removed, there was the exact image on the wall of the whole, and of many of its portions. But in the midst of this picture was another,—the precise outline of a map which had hung on the wall before the bookcase was built. We had all forgotten everything about the map until we saw its photograph on the wall. Then we remembered it, as some day or other we may remember a sin which has been built over and covered up, when this lower universe is pulled away from before the wall of Infinity, where the wrong-doing stands self-recorded.

The Professor lived in that house a long time—not twenty years, but pretty near it. When he entered that door, two shadows glided over the threshold; five lingered in the doorway when he passed through it for the last time,— and one of the shadows was claimed by its owner to be longer than his own. What changes he saw in that quiet place! Death rained through every roof but his; children came into life, grew to maturity, wedded, faded away, threw themselves away; the whole drama of life was played in that stock company's theatre of a dozen houses, one of which was his, and no deep sorrow or severe calamity ever entered his dwelling. Peace be to those walls, forever,—the Professor said,—for the many pleasant years he has passed within them!

The Professor has a friend, now living at a distance, who has been with him in many of his changes of place, and who follows him in imagination with tender interest wherever he goes.—In that little court, where he lived in gay loneliness so long,—

—in his autumnal sojourn by the Connecticut, where it comes loitering down from its mountain fastnesses like a great lord, swallowing up the small proprietary rivulets very quietly as it goes, until it gets proud and swollen and wantons in huge luxurious oxbows about the fair Northampton meadows, and at last overflows the oldest inhabitant's memory in profligate freshets at Hartford and all along its lower shores,—up in that caravansary on the banks of the stream where Ledyard launched his log canoe, and the jovial old Colonel used to lead the Commencement processions,—where blue Ascutney looked down from the far distance, and the hills of Beulah, as the Professor always called them, rolled up the opposite horizon in soft climbing masses, so suggestive of the Pilgrim's Heavenward Path that he used to look through his old "Dollond" [4] to see if the Shining Ones were not within range of sight,—sweet visions, sweetest in those Sunday walks which carried them by the peaceful Common, through the solemn village lying in cataleptic stillness under the shadow of the rod of Moses, to the terminus of their harmless stroll,—the *patulous fage,* in the Professor's classic dialect,—the spreading beech, in more familiar phrase,—[stop and breathe here a moment, for the sentence is not done yet, and we have another long journey before us,]—

—and again once more up among those other hills that shut in the amber-flowing Housatonic,—dark stream, but clear, like the lucid orbs that shine beneath the lids of auburn-haired, sherry-wine-eyed demi-blondes,—in the home overlooking the winding stream and the smooth, flat meadow; looked down upon by wild hills, where the tracks of bears and catamounts may yet sometimes be seen upon the winter snow; facing the twin summits which rise in the far North, the highest waves of the great land-storm in all this billowy region,—suggestive to mad fancies of the breasts of a half-buried Titaness, stretched out by a stray thunderbolt, and hastily hidden away beneath the leaves of the forest,—in that home where seven blessed summers were passed, which stand in memory like the seven golden candlesticks in the beatific vision of the holy dreamer,—

—in that modest dwelling we were just looking at, not glorious, yet not unlovely in the youth of its drab and mahogany,—full of great and little boys' playthings from top to bottom,—in all these summer or winter nests he was always at home and always welcome.

This long articulated sigh of reminiscences,—this calenture which shows me the maple-shadowed plains of Berkshire and the mountain-circled green of Grafton beneath the salt waves which come feeling their way along the wall at my feet, restless and soft-touching as blind men's busy fingers,—is for

---

[4] Telescope, after John Dollond, the inventor of the achromatic telescope.

that friend of mine [5] who looks into the waters of the Patapsco and sees beneath them the same visions that paint themselves for me in the green depths of the Charles.

—Did I talk all this off to the schoolmistress?—Why, no,—of course not. I have been talking with you, the reader, for the last ten minutes. You don't think I should expect any woman to listen to such a sentence as that long one, without giving her a chance to put in a word?

—What did I say to the schoolmistress?—Permit me one moment. I don't doubt your delicacy and good-breeding; but in this particular case, as I was allowed the privilege of walking alone with a very interesting young woman, you must allow me to remark, in the classic version of a familiar phrase, used by our Master Benjamin Franklin, it is *nullum tui negotii*.

When the schoolmistress and I reached the schoolroom door, the damask roses I spoke of were so much heightened in color by exercise that I felt sure it would be useful to her to take a stroll like this every morning, and made up my mind I would ask her to let me join her again. . . .

MY LAST WALK WITH THE SCHOOLMISTRESS
(A Parenthesis)

I can't say just how many walks she and I had taken together before this one. I found the effect of going out every morning was decidedly favorable on her health. Two pleasing dimples, the places for which were just marked when she came, played, shadowy, in her freshening cheeks when she smiled and nodded good morning to me from the schoolhouse-steps.

I am afraid I did the greater part of the talking. At any rate, if I should try to report all that I said during the first half-dozen walks we took together, I fear that I might receive a gentle hint from my friends the publishers, that a separate volume, at my own risk and expense, would be the proper method of bringing them before the public.

—I would have a woman as true as Death. At the first real lie which works from the heart outward, she should be tenderly chloroformed into a better world, where she can have an angel for a governess, and feed on strange fruits which will make her all over again, even to her bones and marrow.— Whether gifted with the accident of beauty or not, she should have been moulded in the rose-red clay of Love, before the breath of life made a moving mortal of her. Love-capacity is a congenital endowment; and I think, after a while, one gets to know the warm-hued natures it belongs to from the pretty pipe-clay counterfeits of them.—Proud she may be, in the sense of respecting herself; but pride, in the sense of contemning others less gifted than herself, deserves the two lowest circles of a vulgar woman's Inferno, where the punishments are Smallpox and Bankruptcy.—She who nips off the end of a

[5] John Roby, a colleague of Holmes's at Dartmouth.

brittle courtesy, as one breaks the tip of an icicle, to bestow upon those whom she ought cordially and kindly to recognize, proclaims the fact that she comes not merely of low blood, but of bad blood. Consciousness of unquestioned position makes people gracious in proper measure to all; but if a woman put on airs with her real equals, she has something about herself or her family she is ashamed of, or ought to be. Middle, and more than middle-aged people, who know family histories, generally see through it. An official of standing was rude to me once. Oh, that is the maternal grandfather,—said a wise old friend to me,—he was a boor.—Better too few words, from the woman we love, than too many: while she is silent, Nature is working for her; while she talks, she is working for herself. Love is sparingly soluble in the words of men; therefore they speak much of it; but one syllable of a woman's speech can dissolve more of it than a man's heart can hold.

—Whether I said any or all of these things to the schoolmistress, or not,—whether I stole them out of Lord Bacon,—whether I cribbed them from Balzac,—whether I dipped them from the ocean of Tupperian wisdom,—or whether I have just found them in my head, laid there by that solemn fowl, Experience (who, according to my observation, cackles oftener than she drops real live eggs), I cannot say. Wise men have said more foolish things,—and foolish men, I don't doubt, have said as wise things. Anyhow, the schoolmistress and I had pleasant walks and long talks, all of which I do not feel bound to report.

—You are a stranger to me, Ma'am.—I don't doubt you would like to know all I said to the schoolmistress.—I sha'n't do it;—I had rather get the publishers to return the money you have invested in these pages. Besides, I have forgotten a good deal of it. I shall tell only what I like of what I remember.

—My idea was, in the first place, to search out the picturesque spots which the city affords a sight of, to those who have eyes. I know a good many, and it was a pleasure to look at them in company with my young friend. There were the shrubs and flowers in the Franklin-Place front-yards or borders; Commerce is just putting his granite foot upon them. Then there are certain small seraglio-gardens, into which one can get a peep through the crevices of high fences,—one in Myrtle Street, or at the back of it,—here and there one at the North and South ends. Then the great elms in Essex Street. Then the stately horse-chestnuts in that vacant lot in Chambers Street, which hold their outspread hands over your head (as I said in my poem the other day), and look as if they were whispering, "May grace, mercy, and peace be with you!"—and the rest of that benediction. Nay, there are certain patches of ground, which, having lain neglected for a time, Nature, who always has her pockets full of seeds, and holes in all her pockets, has covered with hungry plebeian growths, which fight for life with each other, until some of them get broad-leaved and succulent, and you have a coarse vegetable tapestry which Raphael would not have disdained to spread over the foreground of his masterpiece. The Professor pretends that he found such a one in Charles Street, which, in its dare-devil impudence of rough-and-tumble vegetation, beat the pretty-behaved flower-beds of the Public Garden as ignominiously as a group of young tatterdemalions playing at pitch-and-toss beats a row of Sunday-school boys with their teacher at their head.

But then the Professor has one of his burrows in that region, and puts everything in high colors relating to it. That is his way about everything.—I hold any man cheap,—he said,—of whom nothing stronger can be uttered than that all his geese are swans.—How is that, Professor?—said I;—I should have set you down for one of that sort.—Sir,—said he,—I am proud to say, that Nature has so far enriched me, that I cannot own so much as a *duck* without seeing in it as pretty a swan as ever swam the basin in the garden of the Luxembourg. And the Professor showed the whites of his eyes devoutly, like one returning thanks after a dinner of many courses.

I don't know anything sweeter than this leaking in of Nature through all the cracks in the walls and floors of cities. You heap up a million tons of hewn rocks on a square mile or two of earth which was green once. The trees look down from the hill-sides and ask each other, as they stand on tiptoe,—"What are these people about?" And the small herbs at their feet look up and whisper back,—"We will go and see." So the small herbs pack themselves up in the least possible bundles, and wait until the wind steals to them at night and whispers,—"Come with me." Then they go softly with it into the great city,—one to a cleft in the pavement, one to a spout on the roof, one to a seam in the marbles over a rich gentleman's bones, and one to the grave without a stone where nothing but a man is buried,—and there they grow, looking down on the generations of men from mouldy roofs, looking up from between the less-trodden pavements, looking out through iron cemetery-railings. Listen to them, when there is only a light breath stirring, and you will hear them saying to each other,—"Wait a while!" The words run along the telegraph of those narrow green lines that border the roads leading from the city, until they reach the slope of the hills, and the trees repeat in low murmurs to each other,—"Wait a while!" By-and-by the flow of life in the streets ebbs, and the old leafy inhabitants—the smaller tribes always in front—saunter in, one by one, very careless seemingly, but very tenacious, until they swarm so that the great stones gape from each other with the crowding of their roots, and the feldspar begins to be picked out of the granite to find them food. At last the trees take up their solemn line of march, and never rest until they have encamped in the market-place. Wait long enough and you will find an old doting oak hugging a huge worn block in its yellow underground arms; that was the cornerstone of the State House. Oh, so patient she is, this imperturbable Nature.

—Let us cry!—

But all this has nothing to do with my walks and talks with the school-mistress. I did not say that I would not tell you something about them. Let me alone, and I shall talk to you more than I ought to, probably. We never tell our secrets to people that pump for them.

Books we talked about, and education. It was her duty to know some-thing of these, and of course she did. Perhaps I was somewhat more learned than she, but I found that the difference between her reading and mine was like that of a man's and a woman's dusting a library. The man flaps about with a bunch of feathers; the woman goes to work softly with a cloth. She does not raise half the dust, nor fill her own eyes and mouth with it,—but she goes into all the corners and attends to the leaves as much as to the covers. —Books are the *negative* pictures of thought, and the more sensitive the mind that receives their images, the more nicely the finest lines are reproduced. A woman (of the right kind), reading after a man, follows him as Ruth followed the reapers of Boaz, and her gleanings are often the finest of the wheat.

But it was in talking of Life that we came most nearly together. I thought I knew something about that,—that I could speak or write about it some-what to the purpose.

To take up this fluid earthly being of ours as a sponge sucks up water,— to be steeped and soaked in its realities as a hide fills its pores lying seven years in a tan-pit,—to have winnowed every wave of it as a mill-wheel works up the stream that runs through the flume upon its float-boards,—to have curled up in the keenest spasms and flattened out in the laxest languors of this breathing-sickness, which keeps certain parcels of matter uneasy for three or four score years,—to have fought all the devils and clasped all the angels of its delirium,—and then, just at the point when the white-hot passions have cooled down to cherry-red, plunge our experience into the ice-cold stream of some human language or other, one might think would end in a rhapsody with something of spring and temper in it. All this I thought my power and province.

The schoolmistress had tried life, too. Once in a while one meets with a single soul greater than all the living pageant that passes before it. As the pale astronomer sits in his study with sunken eyes and thin fingers, and weighs Uranus or Neptune as in a balance, so there are meek, slight women who have weighed all that this planetary life can offer, and hold it like a bauble in the palm of their slender hands. This was one of them. Fortune had left her, sorrow had baptized her; the routine of labor and the loneliness of almost friendless city-life were before her. Yet, as I looked upon her tranquil face, gradually regaining a cheerfulness which was often sprightly, as she be-came interested in the various matters we talked about and places we visited,

I saw that eye and lip and every shifting lineament were made for love,—unconscious of their sweet office as yet, and meeting the cold aspect of Duty with the natural graces which were meant for the reward of nothing less than the Great Passion.

—I never addressed one word of love to the schoolmistress in the course of these pleasant walks. It seemed to me that we talked of everything but love on that particular morning. There was, perhaps, a little more timidity and hesitancy on my part than I have commonly shown among our people at the boarding-house. In fact, I considered myself the master at the breakfast-table; but, somehow, I could not command myself just then so well as usual. The truth is, I had secured a passage to Liverpool in the steamer which was to leave at noon,—with the condition, however, of being released in case circumstances occurred to detain me. The schoolmistress knew nothing about all this, of course, as yet.

It was on the Common that we were walking. The *mall,* or boulevard of our Common, you know, has various branches leading from it in different directions. One of these runs down from opposite Joy Street southward across the whole length of the Common to Boylston Street. We called it the "long path," and were fond of it.

I felt very weak indeed (though of a tolerably robust habit) as we came opposite the head of this path on that morning. I think I tried to speak twice without making myself distinctly audible. At last I got out the question,—Will you take the long path with me?—Certainly,—said the schoolmistress,—with much pleasure.—Think,—I said,—before you answer: if you take the long path with me now, I shall interpret it that we are to part no more!—The schoolmistress stepped back with a sudden movement, as if an arrow had struck her.

One of the long granite blocks used as seats was hard by,—the one you may still see close by the Gingko-tree.—Pray, sit down,—I said.—No, no,—she answered, softly.—I will walk the *long path* with you!

—The old gentleman who sits opposite met us walking, arm in arm, about the middle of the long path, and said, very charmingly,—"Good-morning, my dears!" . . .

So the last day of summer came. It was our choice to go to the church, but we had a kind of reception at the boarding-house. The presents were all arranged, and among them none gave more pleasure than the modest tributes of our fellow-boarders,—for there was not one, I believe, who did not send something. The landlady would insist on making an elegant bride-cake with her own hands: to which Master Benjamin Franklin wished to add certain embellishments out of his private funds,—namely, a Cupid in a mouse-trap, done in white sugar, and two miniature flags with the stars and stripes, which had a very pleasing effect, I assure you. The landlady's daughter sent a richly-bound copy of Tupper's Poems. On a blank leaf was the following, written in a very delicate and careful hand:—

> Presented to . . . by . . .
> On the eve ere her union in holy matrimony.
> May sunshine ever beam o'er her!

Even the poor relative thought she must do something, and sent a copy of *The Whole Duty of Man,* bound in very attractive variegated sheepskin, the edges nicely marbled. From the divinity-student came the loveliest English edition of Keble's *Christian Year.* I opened it, when it came, to the "Fourth Sunday in Lent," and read that angelic poem, sweeter than anything I can remember since Xavier's "My God, I love Thee."—I am not a Churchman, —I don't believe in planting oaks in flower-pots,—but such a poem as "The Rosebud" makes one's heart a proselyte to the culture it grows from. Talk about it as much as you like,—one's breeding shows itself nowhere more than in his religion. A man should be a gentleman in his hymns and prayers; the fondness for "scenes," among vulgar saints, contrasts so meanly with that—

> "God only and good angels look
> Behind the blissful scene,"—

and that other,—

> "He could not trust his melting soul
> But in his Maker's sight,"—

that I hope some of them will see this, and read the poem, and profit by it.

My laughing and winking young friend undertook to procure and arrange the flowers for the table, and did it with immense zeal. I never saw him look happier than when he came in, his hat saucily on one side, and a cheroot in his mouth, with a huge bunch of tea-roses, which he said were for "Madam."

One of the last things that came was an old square box, smelling of camphor, tied and sealed. It bore, in faded ink, the marks, "Calcutta, 1805." On opening it, we found a white Cashmere shawl with a very brief note from the dear old gentleman opposite, saying that he had kept this some years thinking he might want it, and many more, not knowing what to do with it,—that he had never seen it unfolded since he was a young supercargo,— and now, if she would spread it on her shoulders, it would make him feel young to look at it.

Poor Bridget, or Biddy, our red-armed maid of all work! What must she do but buy a small copper breast-pin and put it under "Schoolma'am's" plate that morning, at breakfast? And Schoolma'am would wear it,—though I made her cover it, as well as I could, with a tea-rose.

It was my last breakfast as a boarder, and I could not leave them in utter silence.

Good-bye,—I said,—my dear friends, one and all of you! I have been long with you, and I find it hard parting. I have to thank you for a thousand courtesies, and above all for the patience and indulgence with which you have listened to me when I have tried to instruct or amuse you. My friend the Professor (who, as well as my friend the Poet, is unavoidably absent on this interesting occasion) has given me reason to suppose that he would occupy my empty chair about the first of January next. If he comes among you, be kind to him, as you have been to me. May the Lord bless you all!— And we shook hands all round the table.

Half an hour afterwards the breakfast things and the cloth were gone. I looked up and down the length of the bare boards over which I had so often uttered my sentiments and experiences—and— Yes, I am a man like another.

All sadness vanished, as, in the midst of these old friends of mine, whom you know, and others a little more up in the world, perhaps, to whom I have not introduced you, I took the schoolmistress before the altar from the hands of the old gentleman who used to sit opposite, and who would insist on giving her away.

And now we two are walking the long path in peace together. The "schoolmistress" finds her skill in teaching called for again, without going abroad to seek little scholars. Those visions of mine have all come true.

I hope you all love me none the less for anything I have told you. Farewell!

JAMES RUSSELL LOWELL

(1819–1891)

Lowell came from a family distinguished throughout the history of New England. He was born in 1819 in the old colonial house in Cambridge where he spent most of his life, and where he died. He was brought up in an atmosphere of books, and was all his life bookish. At Harvard he "read almost everything except the textbooks," and in his senior year was "rusticated" for "continued neglect of his college duties," but graduated with his class in 1838. As class poet he ridiculed transcendentalism, but presently fell under the influence of its leader, devoted himself to abolition and other reforms, and even late in life called himself Emerson's "liegeman." After studying law he adopted literature as his life work, and, though he had wide interests, great versatility, and many employments, can best be described as a lifelong man of letters. During the first part of his literary career he was chiefly a poet; he was next for the most part a prose writer and critic; and in later years he was a publicist and diplomat. But this division is a rough one, for he wrote both prose and poetry all his life and was always interested in public affairs. After becoming known as a poet, particularly as the author of the *Biglow Papers* (1848), he was appointed in 1854 to the Harvard professorship of literature just vacated by Longfellow; and a little later he was editor first of the *Atlantic Monthly* and then of the *North American Review*. In connection with these employments he wrote critical essays, later collected in *Among My Books* (1870 and 1876), and *My Study Windows* (1871). He served as American minister first to Spain, and later to England, and in the latter country interpreted the new world to the old in addresses on "Democracy," "Abraham Lincoln," and similar subjects, which were collected in *Democracy and Other Addresses* (1887). He had many friends with whom he was an indefatigable correspondent, and his collected *Letters* are among the most interesting this country has produced. He died at "Elmwood" in 1891.

Lowell's work in prose was mainly in the form of essays—literary, political, and miscellaneous. Though his reputation as the greatest of American critics is now a little dimmed, his wide reading, his appreciation, and his enthusiasm, at least in his time served American culture well. And similarly his political essays, which are always thoughtful, serious, and elevated, in his time exercised on political thought a salutary influence. Perhaps the essays now most read are those on lighter subjects, such as the first two that follow. He has faults of style—of pretentiousness, of "smartness," in particular of diffuseness. He was a good talker, and did not remember that turning good talk into good writing requires repression and rejection. But on the whole though he paid the penalty of versatility, doing many things well but nothing best, his wide knowledge, breadth of sympathy, and brilliancy of expression are still admirable.

ON A CERTAIN CONDESCENSION IN FOREIGNERS [1]

WALKING one day toward the Village, as we used to call it in the good
old days, when almost every dweller in the town had been born in it,
I was enjoying that delicious sense of disenthrallment from the actual which
the deepening twilight brings with it, giving as it does a sort of obscure
novelty to things familiar. The coolness, the hush, broken only by the distant
bleat of some belated goat, querulous to be disburthened of her milky load,
the few faint stars, more guessed as yet than seen, the sense that the coming
dark would so soon fold me in the secure privacy of its disguise,—all things
combined in a result as near absolute peace as can be hoped for by a man who
knows that there is a writ out against him in the hands of the printer's devil.
For the moment, I was enjoying the blessed privilege of thinking without
being called on to stand and deliver what I thought to the small public who
are good enough to take any interest therein. I love old ways, and the path I
was walking felt kindly to the feet it had known for almost fifty years. How
many fleeting impressions it had shared with me! How many times I had
lingered to study the shadows of the leaves mezzotinted upon the turf that
edged it by the moon, of the bare boughs etched with a touch beyond Rembrandt by the same unconscious artist on the smooth page of snow! If I turned
round, through dusky tree-gaps came the first twinkle of evening lamps in
the dear old homestead. On Corey's hill I could see these tiny pharoses of love
and home and sweet domestic thoughts flash out one by one across the black-
ening salt-meadow between. How much has not kerosene added to the
cheerfulness of our evening landscape! A pair of night-herons flapped heavily
over me toward the hidden river. The war was ended. I might walk townward without that aching dread of bulletins that had darkened the July sunshine and twice made the scarlet leaves of October seem stained with blood. I
remembered with a pang, half-proud, half-painful, how, so many years ago,
I had walked over the same path and felt round my finger the soft pressure
of a little hand that was one day to harden with faithful grip of saber. On how
many paths, leading to how many homes where proud Memory does all she
can to fill up the fireside gaps with shining shapes, must not men be walking
in just such pensive mood as I? Ah, young heroes, safe in immortal youth as
those of Homer, you at least carried your ideal hence untarnished! It is
locked for you beyond moth or rust in the treasure-chamber of Death.

Is not a country, I thought, that has had such as they in it, that could give
such as they a brave joy in dying for it, worth something, then? And as I felt
more and more the soothing magic of evening's cool palm upon my temples,

[1] Published in the *Atlantic Monthly,* 1869, and in *My Study Windows,* 1871.
The essays of Lowell are used by permission of, and by arrangement with, Houghton Mifflin
Company, the authorized publishers.

as my fancy came home from its reverie, and my senses, with reawakened curiosity, ran to the front windows again from the viewless closet of abstraction, and felt a strange charm in finding the old tree and shabby fence still there under the travesty of falling night, nay, were conscious of an unsuspected newness in familiar stars and the fading outlines of hills my earliest horizon, I was conscious of an immortal soul, and could not but rejoice in the unwaning goodliness of the world into which I had been born without any merit of my own. I thought of dear Henry Vaughan's rainbow, "Still young and fine!" I remembered people who had to go over to the Alps to learn what the divine silence of snow was, who must run to Italy before they were conscious of the miracle wrought every day under their very noses by the sunset, who must call upon the Berkshire hills to teach them what a painter autumn was, while close at hand the Fresh Pond meadows made all oriels cheap with hues that showed as if a sunset-cloud had been wrecked among their maples. One might be worse off than even in America, I thought. There are some things so elastic that even the heavy roller of democracy cannot flatten them altogether down. The mind can weave itself warmly in the cocoon of its own thoughts and dwell a hermit anywhere. A country without traditions, without ennobling associations, a scramble of *parvenus,* with a horrible consciousness of shoddy running through politics, manners, art, literature, nay, religion itself? I confess, it did not seem so to me there in that illimitable quiet, that serene self-possession of nature, where Collins might have brooded his "Ode to Evening," or where those verses on Solitude in Dodsley's Collection, that Hawthorne liked so much, might have been composed. Traditions? Granting that we had none, all that is worth having in them is the common property of the soul,—an estate in gavelkind for all the sons of Adam,—and, moreover, if a man cannot stand on his two feet (the prime quality of whoever has left any tradition behind him), were it not better for him to be honest about it at once, and go down on all fours? And for associations, if one have not the wit to make them for himself out of native earth, no ready-made ones of other men will avail much. Lexington is none the worse to me for not being in Greece, nor Gettysburg that its name is not Marathon. "Blessed old fields," I was just exclaiming to myself, like one of Mrs. Radcliffe's heroes, "dear acres, innocently secure from history, which these eyes first beheld, may you be also those to which they shall at last slowly darken!" when I was interrupted by a voice which asked me in German whether I was the Herr Professor, Doctor, So-and-so? The "Doctor" was by brevet or vaticination, to make the grade easier to my pocket.

One feels so intimately assured that one is made up, in part, of shreds and leavings of the past, in part of the interpolations of other people, that an honest man would be slow in saying *yes* to such a question. But "my name is So-and-so" is a safe answer, and I gave it. While I had been romancing with myself, the street-lamps had been lighted, and it was under one of these detectives that have robbed the Old Road of its privilege of sanctuary after nightfall that I was ambushed by my foe. The inexorable villain had taken my description, it appears, that I might have the less chance to escape him. Dr. Holmes tells us that we change our substance, not every seven years, as was once believed, but with every breath we draw. Why had I not the wit to avail myself of the subterfuge, and, like Peter, to renounce my identity, especially, as in certain moods of mind, I have often more than doubted of it myself? When a man is, as it were, his own front-door, and is thus knocked at, why may he not assume the right of that sacred wood to make every house a castle, by denying himself to all visitations? I was truly not at home when the question was put to me, but had to recall myself from all out-of-doors, and to piece my self-consciousness hastily together as well as I could before I answered it.

I knew perfectly well what was coming. It is seldom that debtors or good Samaritans waylay people under gas-lamps in order to force money upon them, so far as I have seen or heard. I was also aware, from considerable experience, that every foreigner is persuaded that, by doing this country the favor of coming to it, he has laid every native thereof under an obligation, pecuniary or other, as the case may be, whose discharge he is entitled to on demand duly made in person or by letter. Too much learning (of this kind) had made me mad in the provincial sense of the word. I had begun life with the theory of giving something to every beggar that came along, though sure of never finding a native-born countryman among them. In a small way, I was resolved to emulate Hatem Tai's tent, with its three hundred and sixty-five entrances, one for every day in the year,—I know not whether he was astronomer enough to add another for leap-years. The beggars were a kind of German-silver aristocracy; not real plate, to be sure, but better than nothing. Where everybody was overworked, they supplied the comfortable equipoise of absolute leisure, so æsthetically needful. Besides, I was but too conscious of a vagrant fiber in myself, which too often thrilled me in my solitary walks with the temptation to wander on into infinite space, and by a single spasm of resolution to emancipate myself from the drudgery of prosaic serfdom to respectability and the regular course of things. This prompting has been at times my familiar demon, and I could not but feel a kind of respectful sympathy for men who had dared what I had only sketched out to myself as a splendid possibility. For seven years I helped maintain one heroic man on an imaginary journey to Portland,—as fine an example as I have ever known of hopeless loyalty to an ideal. I assisted another so long in a fruitless attempt to reach Mecklenburg-Schwerin, that at last we grinned in each other's faces when we met, like a couple of augurs. He was possessed by this harmless mania as some are by the North Pole, and I shall never forget his look of regretful compassion (as for one who was sacrificing his higher life to the fleshpots of Egypt) when I at last advised him somewhat strenuously to go to the D——, whither the road was so much traveled that he could not miss it. General Banks, in his noble zeal for the honor of his country, would confer on the Secretary of State the power of imprisoning, in case of war, all these seekers of the unattainable, thus by a stroke of the pen annihilating the single poetic element in our humdrum life. Alas! not everybody has the genius to be a Bobbin-Boy, or doubtless all these also would have chosen that more prosperous line of life! But moralists, sociologists, political economists, and taxes have slowly convinced me that my beggarly sympathies were a sin against society. Especially was the Buckle doctrine of averages (so flattering to our free-will) persuasive with me; for as there must be in every year a certain number who would bestow an alms on these abridged editions of the Wandering Jew, the withdrawal of my quota could make no possible difference, since some destined proxy must always step forward to fill my gap. Just so many misdirected letters every year and no more! Would it were as easy to reckon up the number of men on whose backs fate has written the wrong address, so that they arrive by mistake in Congress and other places where they do not belong! May not these wanderers of whom I speak have been sent into the world without any proper address at all? Where is our Dead-Letter Office for such? And if wiser social arrangements should furnish us with something of the sort, fancy (horrible thought!) how many a workingman's friend (a kind of industry in which the labor is light and the wages heavy) would be sent thither because not called for in the office where he at present lies!

But I am leaving my new acquaintance too long under the lamp-post. The same Gano which had betrayed me to him revealed to me a well-set young man of about half my own age, as well dressed, so far as I could see, as I was, and with every natural qualification for getting his own livelihood as good, if not better, than my own. He had been reduced to the painful necessity of calling upon me by a series of crosses beginning with the Baden Revolution (for which, I own, he seemed rather young,—but perhaps he referred to a kind of revolution practiced every season at Baden-Baden), continued by repeated failures in business, for amounts which must convince me of his entire respectability, and ending with our Civil War. During the latter, he had served with distinction as a soldier, taking a main part in every important battle, with a rapid list of which he favored me, and no doubt would have admitted that, impartial as Jonathan Wild's great ancestor, he had been on both sides, had I baited him with a few hints of conservative opinions on a subject so distressing to a gentleman wishing to profit by one's sympathy and unhappily doubtful as to which way it might lean. For all these reasons, and, as he seemed to imply, for his merit in consenting to be born in Germany, he considered himself my natural creditor to the extent of five dollars, which he would handsomely consent to accept in greenbacks, though he preferred specie. The offer was certainly a generous one, and the claim presented with an assurance that carried conviction. But, unhappily, I had been led to remark a curious natural phenomenon. If I was ever weak enough to give anything to a petitioner of whatever nationality, it always rained decayed compatriots of his for a month after. *Post hoc ergo propter hoc* may not always be safe logic, but here I seemed to perceive a natural connection of cause and effect. Now, a few days before I had been so tickled with a paper (professedly written by a benevolent American clergyman) certifying that the bearer, a hard-working German, had long "sofered with rheumatic paints in his limps," that, after copying the passage into my note-book, I thought it but fair to pay a trifling *honorarium* to the author. I had pulled the string of the shower-bath! It had been running shipwrecked sailors for some time but forthwith it began to pour Teutons, redolent of *lager-bier*. I could not help associating the apparition of my new friend with this series of otherwise unaccountable phenomena. I accordingly made up my mind to deny the debt, and modestly did so, pleading a native bias toward impecuniosity to the full as strong as his own. He took a high tone with me at once, such as an honest man would naturally take with a confessed repudiator. He even brought down his proud stomach so far as to join himself to me for the rest of my townward walk, that he might give me his views of the American people, and thus inclusively of myself.

I know not whether it is because I am pigeon-livered and lack gall, or whether it is from an overmastering sense of drollery, but I am apt to submit to such bastings with a patience which afterwards surprises me, being not without my share of warmth in the blood. Perhaps it is because I so often meet with young persons who know vastly more than I do, and especially with so many foreigners whose knowledge of this country is superior to my own. However it may be, I listened for some time with tolerable composure as my self-appointed lecturer gave me in detail his opinions of my country and its people. America, he informed me, was without arts, science, literature, culture, or any native hope of supplying them. We were a people wholly given to money-getting, and who, having got it, knew no other use for it than to hold it fast. I am fain to confess that I felt a sensible itching of the biceps, and that my fingers closed with such a grip as he had just informed me was one of the effects of our unhappy climate. But happening just then to be where I could avoid temptation by dodging down a by-street, I hastily left him to finish his diatribe to the lamp-post, which could stand it better than I. That young man will never know how near he came to being assaulted by a respectable gentleman of middle age, at the corner of Church Street. I have never felt quite satisfied that I did all my duty by him in not knocking him down. But perhaps he might have knocked *me* down, and then?

The capacity of indignation makes an essential part of the outfit of every honest man, but I am inclined to doubt whether he is a wise one who allows himself to act upon its first hints. It should be rather, I suspect, a *latent* heat in the blood, which makes itself felt in character, a steady reserve for the brain, warming the ovum of thought to life, rather than cooking it by a too hasty enthusiasm in reaching the boiling point. As my pulse gradually fell back to its normal beat, I reflected that I had been uncomfortably near making a fool of myself,—a handy salve of euphuism for our vanity, though it does not always make a just allowance to Nature for her share in the business. What possible claim had my Teutonic friend to rob me of my composure? I am not, I think, specially thin-skinned as to other people's opinions of myself, having, as I conceive, later and fuller intelligence on that point than anybody else can give me. Life is continually weighing us in very sensitive scales, and telling every one of us precisely what his real weight is to the last grain of dust. Whoever at fifty does not rate himself quite as low as most of his acquaintance would be likely to put him, must be either a fool or a great man, and I humbly disclaim being either. But if I was not smarting in person from any scattering shot of my late companion's commination, why should I grow hot at any implication of my country therein? Surely *her* shoulders are broad enough, if yours or mine are not, to bear up under a considerable avalanche of this kind. It is the bit of truth in every slander, the hint of likeness in every caricature, that makes us smart. "Art thou *there*, old Truepenny?" How did your blade know its way so well to that one loose rivet in our armor? I wondered whether Americans were over-sensitive in this respect, whether they were more touchy than other folks. On the whole, I thought we were not. Plutarch, who at least had studied philosophy, if he had not mastered it, could not stomach something Herodotus had said of Bœotia, and devoted an essay to showing up the delightful old traveler's malice and ill-breeding. French editors leave out of Montaigne's "Travels," some remarks of his about France, for reasons best known to themselves. Pachydermatous Deutschland, covered with trophies from every field of letters, still winces under that question which Père Bouhours put two centuries ago, *Si un Allemand peut être bel-esprit?* John Bull grew apoplectic with angry amazement at the audacious persiflage of Pückler-Muskau. To be sure, he was a prince,—but that was not all of it, for a chance phrase of gentle Hawthorne sent a spasm through all the journals of England. Then this tenderness is not peculiar to *us?* Console yourself, dear man and brother, whatever else you may be sure of, be sure at least of this, that you are dreadfully like other people. Human nature has a much greater genius for sameness than for originality, or the world would be at a sad pass shortly. The surprising thing is that men have such a taste for this somewhat musty flavor, that an Englishman, for example, should feel himself defrauded, nay, even outraged, when he comes over here and finds a people speaking what he admits to be something like English, and yet so very different from (or, as he would say, to) those he left at home. Nothing, I am sure, equals *my* thankfulness when I meet an Englishman who is *not* like every other, or, I may add, an American of the same odd turn.

Certainly it is no shame to a man that he should be as nice about his country as about his sweetheart, and who ever heard even the friendliest appreciation of that unexpressive she that did not seem to fall infinitely short? Yet it would hardly be wise to hold every one an enemy who could not see her with our own enchanted eyes. It seems to be the common opinion of foreigners that Americans are *too* tender upon this point. Perhaps we are; and if so, there must be a reason for it. Have we had fair play? Could the eyes of what is called Good Society (though it is so seldom true either to the adjective or noun) look upon a nation of democrats with any chance of receiving an undistorted image? Were not those, moreover, who found in the old order of things an earthly paradise, paying them quarterly dividends for the wisdom of their ancestors, with the punctuality of the seasons, unconsciously bribed to misunderstand if not to misrepresent us? Whether at war or at peace, there we were, a standing menace to all earthly paradises of that kind, fatal underminers of the very credit on which the dividends were based, all the more hateful and terrible that our destructive agency was so insidious, working invisible in the elements, as it seemed, active while they slept, and coming upon them in the darkness like an armed man. *Could* Laius have the proper feelings of a father toward Œdipus, announced as his destined destroyer by infallible oracles, and felt to be such by every conscious fiber of his soul? For more than a century the Dutch were the laughing-stock of polite Europe. They were butter-firkins, swillers of beer and schnaps, and their *vrouws* from whom Holbein painted the all-but loveliest of Madonnas, Rembrandt the graceful girl who sits immortal on his knee in Dresden, and Rubens his abounding goddesses, were the synonyms of clumsy vulgarity. Even so late as Irving the ships of the greatest navigators in the world were represented as sailing equally well stern-foremost. That the aristocratic Venetians should have

> Riveted with gigantic piles
> Thorough the centre their new-catchèd miles,

was heroic. But the far more marvelous achievement of the Dutch in the same kind was ludicrous even to republican Marvell. Meanwhile, during that very century of scorn, they were the best artists, sailors, merchants, bankers, printers, scholars, jurisconsults, and statesmen in Europe, and the genius of Motley has revealed them to us, earning a right to themselves by the most heroic struggle in human annals. But, alas! they were not merely simple burghers who had fairly made themselves High Mightinesses, and could treat on equal terms with anointed kings, but their commonwealth carried in its bosom the germs of democracy. They even unmuzzled, at least after dark, that dreadful mastiff, the Press, whose scent is, or ought to be, so keen for wolves in sheep's clothing and for certain other animals in lions' skins. They made fun of Sacred Majesty, and, what was worse, managed uncommonly well without it. In an age when periwigs made so large a part of the natural dignity of man, people with such a turn of mind were dangerous. How could they seem other than vulgar and hateful?

In the natural course of things we succeeded to this unenviable position of general butt. The Dutch had thriven under it pretty well, and there was hope that we could at least contrive to worry along. And we certainly did in a very redoubtable fashion. Perhaps we deserved some of the sarcasm more than our Dutch predecessors in office. We had nothing to boast of in arts or letters, and were given to bragging overmuch of our merely material prosperity, due quite as much to the virtue of our continent as to our own. There was some truth in Carlyle's sneer, after all. Till we had succeeded in some higher way than this, we had only the success of physical growth. Our greatness, like that of enormous Russia, was greatness on the map,—barbarian mass only; but had we gone down, like that other Atlantis, in some vast cataclysm, we should have covered but a pin's point on the chart of memory, compared with those ideal spaces occupied by tiny Attica and cramped England. At the same time, our critics somewhat too easily forgot that material must make ready the foundation for ideal triumphs, that the arts have no chance in poor countries. But it must be allowed that democracy stood for a great deal in our shortcoming. The Edinburgh Review never would have thought of asking, "Who reads a Russian book?" and England was satisfied with iron from Sweden without being impertinently inquisitive after her painters and statuaries. Was it that they expected too much from the mere miracle of Freedom? Is it not the highest art of a Republic to make men of flesh and blood, and not the marble ideals of such? It may be fairly doubted whether we have produced this higher type of man yet. Perhaps it is the collective, not the individual, humanity that is to have a chance of nobler development among us. We shall see. We have a vast amount of imported ignorance, and, still worse, of native ready-made knowledge, to digest before even the preliminaries of such a consummation can be arranged. We have got to learn that statesmanship is the most complicated of all arts, and to come back to the apprenticeship-system too hastily abandoned. At present, we trust a man with making constitutions on less proof of competence than we should demand before we gave him our shoe to patch. We have nearly reached the limit of the reaction from the old notion, which paid too much regard to birth and station as qualifications for office, and have touched the extreme point in the opposite direction, putting the highest of human functions up at auction to be bid for by any creature capable of going upright on two legs. In some places, we have arrived at a point at which civil society is no longer possible, and already another reaction has begun, not backwards to the old system, but toward fitness either from natural aptitude or special training. But will it always be safe to let evils work their own cure by becoming unendurable? Every one of them leaves its taint in the constitution of the bodypolitic, each in itself, perhaps, trifling, yet all together powerful for evil.

But whatever we might do or leave undone, we were not genteel, and it was uncomfortable to be continually reminded that, though we should boast that we were the Great West till we were black in the face, it did not bring us an inch nearer to the world's West-End. That sacred enclosure of respectability was tabooed to us. The Holy Alliance did not inscribe us on its visitinglist. The Old World of wigs and orders and liveries would shop with us, but we must ring at the area-bell, and not venture to awaken the more august clamors of the knocker. Our manners, it must be granted, had none of those graces that stamp the caste of Vere de Vere, in whatever museum of British antiquities they may be hidden. In short, we were vulgar.

This was one of those horribly vague accusations, the victim of which has no defense. An umbrella is of no avail against a Scotch mist. It envelops you, it penetrates at every pore, it wets you through without seeming to wet you at all. Vulgarity is an eighth deadly sin, added to the list in these latter days, and worse than all the others put together, since it perils your salvation in *this* world,—far the more important of the two in the minds of most men. It profits nothing to draw nice distinctions between essential and conventional, for the convention in this case *is* the essence, and you may break every command of the decalogue with perfect good-breeding, nay, if you are adroit, without losing caste. We, indeed, had it not to lose, for we had never gained it. *"How* am I vulgar?" asks the culprit, shudderingly. "Because thou art not like unto Us," answers Lucifer, Son of the Morning, and there is no more to be said. The god of this world may be a fallen angel, but he has us *there!* We were as clean,—so far as my observation goes, I think we were cleaner, morally and physically, than the English, and therefore, of course, than everybody else. But we did not pronounce the diphthong *ou* as they did, and we said *eether* and not *eyther,* following therein the fashion of our ancestors, who unhappily could bring over no English better than Shakespeare's; and we did not stammer as they had learned to do from the courtiers, who in this way flattered the Hanoverian king, a foreigner among the people he had come to reign over. Worse than all, we might have the noblest ideas and the finest sentiments in the world, but we vented them through that organ by

which men are led rather than leaders, though some physiologists would persuade us that Nature furnishes her captains with a fine handle to their faces
that Opportunity may get a good purchase on them for dragging them to the
front.

This state of things was so painful that excellent people were not wanting
who gave their whole genius to reproducing here the original Bull, whether
by gaiters, the cut of their whiskers, by a factitious brutality in their tone, or
by an accent that was forever tripping and falling flat over the tangled roots of
our common tongue. Martyrs to a false ideal, it never occurred to them that
nothing is more hateful to gods and men than a second-rate Englishman, and
for the very reason that this planet never produced a more splendid creature
than the first-rate one, witness Shakespeare and the Indian Mutiny. Witness
that truly sublime self-abnegation of those prisoners lately among the bandits
of Greece, where average men gave an example of quiet fortitude for which
all the stoicism of antiquity can show no match. Witness the wreck of the
Birkenhead, an example of disciplined heroism, perhaps the most precious,
as the rarest, of all. If we could contrive to be not too unobtrusively our simple
selves, we should be the most delightful of human beings, and the most original; whereas, when the plating of Anglicism rubs off, as it always will in
points that come to much wear, we are liable to very unpleasing conjectures
about the quality of the metal underneath. Perhaps one reason why the
average Briton spreads himself here with such an easy air of superiority may
be owing to the fact that he meets with so many bad imitations as to conclude
himself the only real thing in a wilderness of shams. He fancies himself moving through an endless Bloomsbury, where his mere apparition confers honor
as an avatar of the court end of the universe. Not a Bull of them all but is
persuaded he bears Europa upon his back. This is the sort of fellow whose
patronage is so divertingly insufferable. Thank Heaven he is not the only
specimen of cater-cousinship from the dear old Mother Island that is shown
to us! Among genuine things, I know nothing more genuine than the better
men whose limbs were made in England. So manly-tender, so brave, so
true, so warranted to wear, they make us proud to feel that blood is thicker
than water.

But it is not merely the Englishmen; every European candidly admits in
himself some right of primogeniture in respect of us, and pats this shaggy
continent on the back with a lively sense of generous unbending. The German who plays the bass-viol has a well-founded contempt, which he is not
always nice in concealing, for a country so few of whose children ever take
that noble instrument between their knees. His cousin, the Ph.D. from
Göttingen, cannot help despising a people who do not grow loud and red
over Aryans and Turanians, and are indifferent about their descent from
either. The Frenchman feels an easy mastery in speaking his mother tongue,

and attributes it to some native superiority of parts that lifts him high above us barbarians of the West. The Italian *prima donna* sweeps a curtsy of careless pity to the over-facile pit which unsexes her with the *bravo!* innocently meant to show a familiarity with foreign usage. But all without exception make no secret of regarding us as the goose bound to deliver them a golden egg in return for *their* cackle. Such men as Agassiz, Guyot, and Goldwin Smith come with gifts in their hands; but since it is commonly European failures who bring hither their remarkable gifts and acquirements, this view of the case is sometimes just the least bit in the world provoking. To think what a delicious seclusion of contempt we enjoyed till California and our own ostentatious *parvenus,* flinging gold away in Europe that might have endowed libraries at home, gave us the ill repute of riches! What a shabby downfall from the Arcadia which the French officers of our Revolutionary War fancied they saw here through Rousseau-tinted spectacles! Something of Arcadia there really was, something of the Old Age; and that divine provincialism were cheaply repurchased could we have it back again in exchange for the tawdry upholstery that has taken its place.

For some reason or other, the European has rarely been able to see America except in caricature. Would the first Review of the world have printed the *niaiseries* of M. Maurice Sand as a picture of society in any civilized country? M. Sand, to be sure, has inherited nothing of his famous mother's literary outfit, except the pseudonym. But since the conductors of the *Revue* could not have published his story because it was clever, they must have thought it valuable for its truth. As true as the last-century Englishman's picture of Jean Crapaud! We do not ask to be sprinkled with rosewater, but may perhaps fairly protest against being drenched with the rinsings of an unclean imagination. The next time the *Revue* allows such ill-bred persons to throw their slops out of its first-floor windows, let it honestly preface the discharge with a *gare l'eau!* that we may run from under in season. And M. Duvergier de Hauranne, who knows how to be entertaining! I know that *le Français est plutôt indiscret que confiant,* and the pen slides too easily when indiscretions will fetch so much a page; but should we not have been *tant-soit-peu* more cautious had we been writing about people on the other side of the Channel? But then it is a fact in the natural history of the American long familiar to Europeans, that he abhors privacy, knows not the meaning of reserve, lives in hotels because of their greater publicity, and is never so pleased as when his domestic affairs (if he may be said to have any) are paraded in the newspapers. Barnum, it is well known, represents perfectly the average national sentiment in this respect. However it be, we are not treated like other people, or perhaps I should say like people who are ever likely to be met with in society.

Is it in the climate? Either I have a false notion of European manners, or else the atmosphere affects them strangely when exported hither. Perhaps they suffer from the sea-voyage like some of the more delicate wines. During our Civil War an English gentleman of the highest description was kind enough to call upon me, mainly, as it seemed, to inform me how entirely he sympathized with the Confederates, and how sure he felt that we could never subdue them,—"they were the *gentlemen* of the country, you know." Another, the first greetings hardly over, asked me how I accounted for the universal meagerness of my countrymen. To a thinner man than I, or from a stouter man than he, the question *might* have been offensive. The Marquis of Hartington [2] wore a secession badge at a public ball in New York. In a civilized country he might have been roughly handled; but here, where the *bienséances* are not so well understood, of course nobody minded it. A French traveler told me he had been a good deal in the British colonies, and had been astonished to see how soon the people became Americanized. He added, with delightful *bonhomie,* and as if he were sure it would charm me, that "they even began to talk through their noses, just like you!" I was naturally ravished with this testimony to the assimilating power of democracy, and could only reply that I hoped they would never adopt our democratic patent-method of seeming to settle one's honest debts, for they would find it paying through the nose in the long run. I am a man of the New World, and do not know precisely the present fashion of May-Fair, but I have a kind of feeling that if an American (*mutato nomine, de te* is always frightfully possible) were to do this kind of thing under a European roof, it would induce some disagreeable reflections as to the ethical results of democracy. I read the other day in print the remark of a British tourist who had eaten large quantities of our salt, such as it is (I grant it has not the European savor), that the Americans were hospitable, no doubt, but that it was partly because they longed for foreign visitors to relieve the tedium of their dead-level existence, and partly from ostentation. What shall we do? Shall we close our doors? Not I, for one, if I should so have forfeited the friendship of L. S., most lovable of men. He somehow seems to find us human, at least, and so did Clough, whose poetry will one of these days, perhaps, be found to have been the best utterance in verse of this generation. And T. H., the mere grasp of whose manly hand carries with it the pledge of frankness and friendship, of an abiding simplicity of nature as affecting as it is rare!

The fine old Tory aversion of former times was not hard to bear. There

[2] One of Mr. Lincoln's neatest strokes of humor was his treatment of this gentleman when a laudable curiosity induced him to be presented to the President of the Broken Bubble. Mr. Lincoln persisted in calling him Mr. Partington. Surely the refinement of good-breeding could go no further. Giving the young man his real name (already notorious in the newspapers) would have made his visit an insult. Had Henri IV done this, it would have been famous.— *Author's note.*

was something even refreshing in it, as in a northeaster to a hardy temperament. When a British parson, traveling in Newfoundland while the slash
of our separation was still raw, after prophesying a glorious future for an
island that continued to dry its fish under the ægis of Saint George, glances
disdainfully over his spectacles in parting at the U. S. A., and forebodes for
them a "speedy relapse into barbarism," now that they have madly cut
themselves off from the humanizing influences of Britain, I smile with barbarian self-conceit. But this kind of thing became by degrees an unpleasant
anachronism. For meanwhile the young giant was growing, was beginning
indeed to feel tight in his clothes, was obliged to let in a gore here and there
in Texas, in California, in New Mexico, in Alaska, and had the scissors and
needle and thread ready for Canada when the time came. His shadow
loomed like a Brocken specter over against Europe,—the shadow of what
they were coming to, that was the unpleasant part of it. Even in such misty
image as they had of him, it was painfully evident that his clothes were not
of any cut hitherto fashionable, nor conceivable by a Bond Street tailor,—
and this in an age, too, when everything depends upon clothes, when, if we
do not keep up appearances, the seeming-solid frame of this universe, nay,
your very God, would slump into himself, like a mockery king of snow,
being nothing, after all, but a prevailing mode, a make-believe of believing.
From this moment the young giant assumed the respectable aspect of a
phenomenon, to be got rid of if possible, but at any rate as legitimate a
subject of human study as the glacial period or the silurian what-d'ye-call-
ems. If the man of the primeval drift-heaps be so absorbingly interesting,
why not the man of the drift that is just beginning, of the drift into whose
irresistible current we are just being sucked whether we will or no? If I
were in their place, I confess I should not be frightened. Man has survived
so much, and contrived to be comfortable on this planet after surviving so
much! I am something of a protestant in matters of government also, and
am willing to get rid of vestments and ceremonies and to come down to
bare benches, if only faith in God take the place of a general agreement to
profess confidence in ritual and sham. Every mortal man of us holds stock
in the only public debt that is absolutely sure of payment, and that is the
debt of the Maker of this Universe to the Universe he has made. I have no
notion of selling out my shares in a panic.

It was something to have advanced even to the dignity of a phenomenon,
and yet I do not know that the relation of the individual American to the
individual European was bettered by it; and that, after all, must adjust itself
comfortably before there can be a right understanding between the two. We
had been a desert, we became a museum. People came hither for scientific
and not social ends. The very cockney could not complete his education
without taking a vacant stare at us in passing. But the sociologists (I think

they call themselves so) were the hardest to bear. There was no escape. I have even known a professor of this fearful science to come disguised in petticoats. We were cross-examined as a chemist cross-examines a new substance. Human? yes, all the elements are present, though abnormally combined. Civilized? Hm! that needs a stricter assay. No entomologist could take a more friendly interest in a strange bug. After a few such experiences, I, for one, have felt as if I were merely one of those horrid things preserved in spirits (and very bad spirits, too) in a cabinet. I was not the fellow-being of these explorers: I was a curiosity; I was a *specimen*. Hath not an American organs, dimensions, senses, affections, passions even as a European hath? If you prick us, do we not bleed? It you tickle us, do we not laugh? I will not keep on with Shylock to his next question but one.

Till after our Civil War it never seemed to enter the head of any foreigner, especially of any Englishman, that an American had what could be called a country, except as a place to eat, sleep, and trade in. Then it seemed to strike them suddenly. "By Jove, you know, fellahs don't fight like that for a shop-till!" No, I rather think not. To Americans America is something more than a promise and an expectation. It has a past and traditions of its own. A descent from men who sacrificed everything and came hither, not to better their fortunes, but to plant their idea in virgin soil, should be a good pedigree. There was never colony save this that went forth, not to seek gold, but God. Is it not as well to have sprung from such as these as from some burly beggar who came over with Wilhelmus Conquestor, unless, indeed, a line grow better as it runs farther away from stalwart ancestors? And for our history, it is dry enough, no doubt, in the books, but, for all that, is of a kind that tells in the blood. I have admitted that Carlyle's sneer had a show of truth in it. But what does he himself, like a true Scot, admire in the Hohenzollerns? First of all, that they were *canny,* a thrifty, forehanded race. Next, that they made a good fight from generation to generation with the chaos around them. That is precisely the battle which the English race on this continent has been pushing doughtily forward for two centuries and a half. Doughtily and silently, for you cannot hear in Europe "that crash, the death-song of the perfect tree," that has been going on here from sturdy father to sturdy son, and making this continent habitable for the weaker Old World breed that has swarmed to it during the last half-century. If ever men did a good stroke of work on this planet, it was the forefathers of those whom you are wondering whether it would not be prudent to acknowledge as far-off cousins. Alas, man of genius, to whom we owe so much, could you see nothing more than the burning of a foul chimney in that clash of Michael and Satan which flamed up under your very eyes?

Before our war we were to Europe but a huge mob of adventurers and shopkeepers. Leigh Hunt expressed it well enough when he said that he could never think of America without seeing a gigantic counter stretched all along the seaboard. And Leigh Hunt, without knowing it, had been more than half Americanized, too! Feudalism had by degrees made commerce, the great civilizer, contemptible. But a tradesman with sword on thigh and very prompt of stroke was not only redoubtable, he had become respectable also. Few people, I suspect, alluded twice to a needle in Sir John Hawkwood's presence, after that doughty fighter had exchanged it for a more dangerous tool of the same metal. Democracy had been hitherto only a ludicrous effort to reverse the laws of nature by thrusting Cleon into the place of Pericles. But a democracy that could fight for an abstraction, whose members held life and goods cheap compared with that larger life which we call country, was not merely unheard of, but portentous. It was the nightmare of the Old World taking upon itself flesh and blood, turning out to be substance and not dream. Since the Norman crusader clanged down upon the throne of the *porphyro-geniti,* carefully-draped appearances had never received such a shock, had never been so rudely called on to produce their titles to the empire of the world. Authority has had its periods not unlike those of geology, and at last comes Man claiming kingship in right of his mere manhood. The world of the Saurians might be in some respects more picturesque, but the march of events is inexorable, and that world is bygone.

The young giant had certainly got out of long-clothes. He had become the *enfant terrible* of the human household. It was not and will not be easy for the world (especially for our British cousins) to look upon us as grown up. The youngest of nations, its people must also be young and to be treated accordingly, was the syllogism,—as if libraries did not make all nations equally old in all those respects, at least, where age is an advantage and not a defect. Youth, no doubt, has its good qualities, as people feel who are losing it, but boyishness is another thing. We had been somewhat boyish as a nation, a little loud, a little pushing, a little braggart. But might it not partly have been because we felt that we had certain claims to respect that were not admitted? The war which established our position as a vigorous nationality has also sobered us. A nation, like a man, cannot look death in the eye for four years without some strange reflections, without arriving at some clearer consciousness of the stuff it is made of, without some great moral change. Such a change, or the beginning of it, no observant person can fail to see here. Our thought and our politics, our bearing as a people, are assuming a manlier tone. We have been compelled to see what was weak in democracy as well as what was strong. We have begun obscurely to recognize that things do not go of themselves, and that popular government is not in itself a panacea, is no better than any other form except as the virtue and wisdom of the people make it so, and that when men undertake to do their own kingship, they enter upon the dangers and responsibilities as well as the privileges of the function. Above all, it looks as if we were on the way to be persuaded that no government can be carried on by declamation. It is noticeable also that facility of communication has made the best English and French thought far more directly operative here than ever before. Without being Europeanized, our discussion of important questions in statesmanship, in political economy, in æsthetics, is taking a broader scope and a higher tone. It had certainly been provincial, one might almost say local, to a very unpleasant extent. Perhaps our experience in soldiership has taught us to value training more than we have been popularly wont. We may possibly come to the conclusion, one of these days, that self-made men may not be always equally skillful in the manufacture of wisdom, may not be divinely commissioned to fabricate the higher qualities of opinion on all possible topics of human interest.

So long as we continue to be the most common-schooled and the least cultivated people in the world, I suppose we must consent to endure this condescending manner of foreigners toward us. The more friendly they mean to be, the more ludicrously prominent it becomes. They can never appreciate the immense amount of silent work that has been done here, making this continent slowly fit for the abode of man, and which will demonstrate itself, let us hope, in the character of the people. Outsiders can only be expected to judge a nation by the amount it has contributed to the civilization of the world; the amount, that is, that can be seen and handled. A great place in history can only be achieved by competitive examinations, nay, by a long course of them. How much new thought have we contributed to the common stock? Till that question can be triumphantly answered, or needs no answer, we must continue to be simply interesting as an experiment, to be studied as a problem, and not respected as an attained result or an accomplished solution. Perhaps, as I have hinted, their patronizing manner toward us is the fair result of their failing to see here anything more than a poor imitation, a plaster cast of Europe. And are they not partly right? If the tone of the uncultivated American has too often the arrogance of the barbarian, is not that of the cultivated as often vulgarly apologetic? In the America they meet with is there the simplicity, the manliness, the absence of sham, the sincere human nature, the sensitiveness to duty and implied obligation, that in any way distinguishes us from what our orators call "the effete civilization of the Old World"? Is there a politician among us daring enough (except a Dana here and there) to risk his future on the chance of our keeping our word with the exactness of superstitious communities like England? Is it certain that we shall be ashamed of a bankruptcy of honor, if we can only keep the letter of our bond? I hope we shall be able to answer all these questions with a frank *yes*. At any rate, we would advise our visitors that we are not merely curious creatures, but belong to the family of man, and that, as individuals, we are not to be always subjected to the competitive examination above mentioned, even if we acknowledged their competence as an examining board. Above all, we beg them to remember that America is not to us, as to them, a mere object of external interest to be discussed and analyzed, but *in* us, part of our very marrow. Let them not suppose that we conceive of ourselves as exiles from the graces and amenities of an older date than we, though very much at home in a state of things not yet all it might be or should be, but which we mean to make so, and which we find both wholesome and pleasant for men (though perhaps not for *dilettanti*) to live in. "The full tide of human existence" may be felt here as keenly as Johnson felt it at Charing Cross, and in a larger sense. I know one person who is singular enough to think Cambridge the very best spot on the habitable globe. "Doubtless God *could* have made a better, but doubtless he never did."

It will take England a great while to get over her airs of patronage toward us, or even passably to conceal them. She cannot help confounding the people with the country, and regarding us as lusty juveniles. She has a conviction that whatever good there is in us is wholly English, when the truth is that we are worth nothing except so far as we have disinfected ourselves of Anglicism. She is especially condescending just now, and lavishes sugar-plums on us as if we had not outgrown them. I am no believer in sudden conversions, especially in sudden conversions to a favorable opinion of people who have just proved you to be mistaken in judgment and therefore unwise in policy. I never blamed her for not wishing well to democracy,—how should she?—but Alabamas are not wishes. Let her not be too hasty in believing Mr. Reverdy Johnson's pleasant words. Though there is no thoughtful man in America who would not consider a war with England the greatest of calamities, yet the feeling toward her here is very far from cordial, whatever our Minister may say in the effusion that comes after ample dining. Mr. Adams, with his famous "My Lord, this means war," perfectly represented his country. Justly or not, we have a feeling that we have been wronged, not merely insulted. The only sure way of bringing about a healthy relation between the two countries is for Englishmen to clear their minds of the notion that we are always to be treated as a kind of inferior and deported Englishman whose nature they perfectly understand, and whose back they accordingly stroke the wrong way of the fur with amazing perseverance. Let them learn to treat us naturally on our merits as human beings, as they would a German or a Frenchman, and not as if we were a kind of counterfeit Briton whose crime appeared in every shade of difference, and before long there would come that right feeling which we naturally call a good understanding. The common blood, and still more the common language, are fatal instruments of misapprehension. Let them give up *trying* to understand us, still more thinking that they do, and acting in various absurd ways as the necessary consequence, for they will never arrive at that devoutly-to-be-wished consummation, till they learn to look at us as we are and not as they suppose us to be. Dear old long-estranged mother-in-law, it is a great many years since we parted. Since 1660, when you married again, you have been a step-mother to us. Put on your spectacles, dear madam. Yes, we *have* grown, and changed likewise. You would not let us darken your doors, if you could help it. We know that perfectly well. But pray, when we look to be treated as men, don't shake that rattle in our faces, nor talk baby to us any longer.

> Do, child, go to it grandam, child;
> Give grandam kingdom, and it grandam will
> Give it a plum, a cherry, and a fig!

MY GARDEN ACQUAINTANCE [3]

ONE of the most delightful books in my father's library was White's *Natural History of Selborne*. For me it has rather gained in charm with years. I used to read it without knowing the secret of the pleasure I found in it, but as I grow older I begin to detect some of the simple expedients of this natural magic. Open the book where you will, it takes you out of doors. In our broiling July weather one can walk out with this genially garrulous Fellow of Oriel and find refreshment instead of fatigue. You have no trouble in keeping abreast of him as he ambles along on his hobby-horse, now pointing to a pretty view, now stopping to watch the motions of a bird or an insect, or to bag a specimen for the Honorable Daines Barrington or Mr. Pennant. In simplicity of taste and natural refinement he reminds one of Walton; in tenderness toward what he would have called the brute creation, of Cowper. I do not know whether his descriptions of scenery are good or not, but they have made me familiar with his neighborhood. Since I first read him, I have walked over some of his favorite haunts, but I still see them through his eyes rather than by any recollection of actual and personal vision. The book has also the delightfulness of absolute leisure. Mr. White seems never to have had any harder work to do than to study the habits of his feathered fellow-townsfolk, or to watch the ripening of his peaches on the wall. His volumes are the journal of Adam in Paradise,

> "Annihilating all that's made
> To a green thought in a green shade."

It is positive rest only to look into that garden of his. It is vastly better than to

[3] First published in the *Atlantic Almanac* for 1869, and then in *My Study Windows,* 1871.

"See great Diocletian walk
In the Salonian garden's noble shade,"

for thither ambassadors intrude to bring with them the noises of Rome,
while here the world has no entrance. No rumor of the revolt of the American
Colonies seems to have reached him. "The natural term of an hog's life"
has more interest for him than that of an empire. Burgoyne may surrender
and welcome; of what consequence is *that* compared with the fact that we
can explain the odd tumbling of rooks in the air by their turning over "to
scratch themselves with one claw"? All the couriers in Europe spurring
rowel-deep make no stir in Mr. White's little Chartreuse; but the arrival of
the house-martin a day earlier or later than last year is a piece of news worth
sending express to all his correspondents.

Another secret charm of this book is its inadvertent humor, so much the
more delicious because unsuspected by the author. How pleasant is his innocent vanity in adding to the list of the British, and still more of the Selbornian,
fauna! I believe he would gladly have consented to be eaten by a tiger or a
crocodile, if by that means the occasional presence within the parish limits
of either of these anthropophagous brutes could have been established. He
brags of no fine society, but is plainly a little elated by "having considerable
acquaintance with a tame brown owl." Most of us have known our share of
owls, but few can boast of intimacy with a feathered one. The great events
of Mr. White's life, too, have that disproportionate importance which is always humorous. To think of his hands having actually been thought worthy
(as neither Willoughby's nor Ray's were) to hold a stilted plover, the
Charadrius himaniopus, with no back toe, and therefore "liable, in speculation, to perpetual vacillations"! I wonder, by the way, if metaphysicians have
no hind toes. In 1770 he makes the acquaintance in Sussex of "an old family
tortoise," which had then been domesticated for thirty years. It is clear that
he fell in love with it at first sight. We have no means of tracing the growth
of his passion; but in 1780 we find him eloping with its object in a post-
chaise. "The rattle and hurry of the journey so perfectly roused it that, when
I turned it out in a border, it walked twice down to the bottom of my garden." It reads like a Court Journal: "Yesterday morning H. R. H. the Princess
Alice took an airing of half an hour on the terrace of Windsor Castle." This
tortoise might have been a member of the Royal Society, if he could have
condescended to so ignoble an ambition. It had but just been discovered that
a surface inclined at a certain angle with the plane of the horizon took more
of the sun's rays. The tortoise had always known this (though he unostenta-
tiously made no parade of it), and used accordingly to tilt himself up against
the garden-wall in the autumn. He seems to have been more of a philosopher
than even Mr. White himself, caring for nothing but to get under a cabbage-

leaf when it rained, or the sun was too hot, and to bury himself alive before frost,—a four-footed Diogenes, who carried his tub on his back.

There are moods in which this kind of history is infinitely refreshing. These creatures whom we affect to look down upon as the drudges of instinct are members of a commonwealth whose constitution rests on immovable bases. Never any need of reconstruction there! *They* never dream of settling it by vote that eight hours are equal to ten, or that one creature is as clever as another and no more. *They* do not use their poor wits in regulating God's clocks, nor think they cannot go astray so long as they carry their guide-board about with them,—a delusion we often practise upon ourselves with our high and mighty reason, that admirable finger-post which points every way and always right. It is good for us now and then to converse with a world like Mr. White's, where Man is the least important of animals. But one who, like me, has always lived in the country and always on the same spot, is drawn to his book by other occult sympathies. Do we not share his indignation at that stupid Martin who had graduated his thermometer no lower than 4° above zero of Fahrenheit, so that in the coldest weather ever known the mercury basely absconded into the bulb, and left us to see the victory slip through our fingers, just as they were closing upon it? No man, I suspect, ever lived long in the country without being bitten by these meteorological ambitions. He likes to be hotter and colder, to have been more deeply snowed up, to have more trees and larger blow down than his neighbors. With us descendants of the Puritans especially, these weather-competitions supply the abnegated excitement of the race-course. Men learn to value thermometers of the true imaginative temperament, capable of prodigious elations and corresponding dejections. The other day (5th July) I marked 98° in the shade, my high water mark, higher by one degree than I had ever seen it before. I happened to meet a neighbor; as we mopped our brows at each other, he told me that he had just cleared 100°, and I went home a beaten man. I had not felt the heat before, save as a beautiful exaggeration of sunshine; but now it oppressed me with the prosaic vulgarity of an oven. What had been poetic intensity became all at once rhetorical hyperbole. I might suspect his thermometer (as indeed I did, for we Harvard men are apt to think ill of any graduation but our own); but it was a poor consolation. The fact remained that his herald Mercury, standing a tiptoe, could look down on mine. I seem to glimpse something of this familiar weakness in Mr. White. He, too, has shared in these mercurial triumphs and defeats. Nor do I doubt that he had a true country-gentleman's interest in the weather-cock; that his first question on coming down of a morning was, like Barabas's,

"Into what quarter peers my halcyon's bill?"

It is an innocent and healthful employment of the mind, distracting one from too continual study of himself, and leading him to dwell rather upon the indigestions of the elements than his own. "Did the wind back round, or go about with the sun?" is a rational question that bears not remotely on the making of hay and the prosperity of crops. I have little doubt that the regulated observation of the vane in many different places, and the interchange of results by telegraph, would put the weather, as it were, in our power, by betraying its ambushes before it is ready to give the assault. At first sight, nothing seems more drolly trivial than the lives of those whose single achievement is to record the wind and the temperature three times a day. Yet such men are doubtless sent into the world for this special end, and perhaps there is no kind of accurate observation, whatever its object, that has not its final use and value for some one or other. It is even to be hoped that the speculations of our newspaper editors and their myriad correspondence upon the signs of the political atmosphere may also fill their appointed place in a well-regulated universe, if it be only that of supplying so many more jack-o'-lanterns to the future historian. Nay, the observations on finance of an M. C. whose sole knowledge of the subject has been derived from a life-long success in getting a living out of the public without paying any equivalent therefor, will perhaps be of interest hereafter to some explorer of our *cloaca maxima,* whenever it is cleansed.

For many years I have been in the habit of noting down some of the leading events of my embowered solitude, such as the coming of certain birds and the like,—a kind of *mémoires pour servir,* after the fashion of White, rather than properly digested natural history. I thought it not impossible that a few simple stories of my winged acquaintances might be found entertaining by persons of kindred taste.

There is a common notion that animals are better meteorologists than men, and I have little doubt that in immediate weather-wisdom they have the advantage of our sophisticated senses (though I suspect a sailor or shepherd would be their match), but I have seen nothing that leads me to believe their minds capable of erecting the horoscope of a whole season, and letting us know beforehand whether the winter will be severe or the summer rainless. I more than suspect that the clerk of the weather himself does not always know very long in advance whether he is to draw an order for hot or cold, dry or moist, and the musquash is scarce likely to be wiser. I have noted but two days' difference in the coming of the song-sparrow between a very early and a very backward spring. This very year I saw the linnets at work thatching, just before a snow-storm which covered the ground several inches deep for a number of days. They struck work and left us for a while, no doubt in search of food. Birds frequently perish from sudden changes in our whimsical spring weather of which they had no foreboding. More than thirty years ago, a cherry-tree, then in full bloom, near my window, was covered with humming-birds benumbed by a fall of mingled rain and snow, which prob-. ably killed many of them. It should seem that their coming was dated by the height of the sun, which betrays them into unthrifty matrimony;

"So priketh hem Nature in hir corages;"

but their going is another matter. The chimney swallows leave us early, for example, apparently so soon as their latest fledglings are firm enough of wing to attempt the long rowing-match that is before them. On the other hand the wild-geese probably do not leave the North till they are frozen out, for I have heard their bugles sounding southward so late as the middle of December. What may be called local migrations are doubtless dictated by the chances of food. I have once been visited by large flights of cross-bills; and whenever the snow lies long and deep on the ground, a flock of cedar-birds comes in mid-winter to eat the berries on my hawthorns. I have never been quite able to fathom the local, or rather geographical partialities of birds. Never before this summer (1870) have the king-birds, handsomest of fly-catchers, built in my orchard; though I always know where to find them within half a mile. The rose-breasted grosbeak has been a familiar bird in Brookline (three miles away), yet I never saw one here till last July, when I found a female busy among my raspberries and surprisingly bold. I hope she was *prospecting* with a view to settlement in our garden. She seemed, on the whole, to think well of my fruit, and I would gladly plant another bed if it would help to win over so delightful a neighbor.

The return of the robin is commonly announced by the newspapers, like that of eminent or notorious people to a watering-place, as the first authentic notification of spring. And such his appearance in the orchard and garden undoubtedly is. But, in spite of his name of migratory thrush, he stays with us all winter, and I have seen him when the thermometer marked 15 degrees below zero of Fahrenheit, armed impregnably within, like Emerson's Tit-mouse, and as cheerful as he. The robin has a bad reputation among people who do not value themselves less for being fond of cherries. There is, I admit, a spice of vulgarity in him, and his song is rather of the Bloomfield sort, too largely ballasted with prose. His ethics are of the Poor Richard school, and the main chance which calls forth all his energy is altogether of the belly. He never has these fine intervals of lunacy into which his cousins, the cat-bird and the mavis, are apt to fall. But for a' that and twice as muckle 's a' that, I would not exchange him for all the cherries that ever came out of Asia Minor. With whatever faults, he has not wholly forfeited that superiority which belongs to the children of nature. He has a finer taste in fruit than could be distilled from many successive committees of the Horticultural Society, and he eats with a relishing gulp not inferior to Dr. Johnson's. He feels and freely exercises his right of eminent domain. His is the earliest mess of green peas; his all the mulberries I had fancied mine. But if he get also the lion's share of the raspberries, he is a great planter, and sows those wild ones in the woods that solace the pedestrian, and give a momentary calm even to the jaded victims of the White Hills. He keeps a strict eye over one's fruit, and knows to a shade of purple when your grapes have cooked long enough in the sun. During the severe drought a few years ago the robins wholly vanished from my garden. I neither saw nor heard one for three weeks. Meanwhile a small foreign grape-vine, rather shy of bearing, seemed to find the dusty air congenial, and, dreaming, perhaps of its sweet Argos across the sea, decked itself with a score or so of fair bunches. I watched them from day to day till they should have secreted sugar enough from the sunbeams, and at last made up my mind that I would celebrate my vintage the next morning. But the robins, too, had somehow kept note of them. They must have sent out spies, as did the Jews into the promised land, before I was stirring. When I went with my basket at least a dozen of these winged vintagers bustled out from among the leaves, and alighting on the nearest trees interchanged some shrill remarks about me of a derogatory nature. They had fairly sacked the vine. Not Wellington's veterans made cleaner work of a Spanish town; not Federals or Confederates were ever more impartial in the confiscation of neutral chickens. I was keeping my grapes a secret to surprise the fair Fidele with, but the robins made them a profounder secret to her than I had meant. The tattered remnant of a single bunch was all my harvest-home. How paltry it looked at the bottom of my basket,—as if a humming-bird had laid her egg in an eagle's nest! I could not help laughing; and the robins seemed to join heartily in the merriment. There was a native grape-vine close by, blue with its less refined abundance, but my cunning thieves preferred the foreign flavor. Could I tax them with want of taste?

The robins are not good solo singers, but their chorus, as, like primitive fire-worshippers, they hail the return of light and warmth to the world, is unrivalled. There are a hundred singing like one. They are noisy enough then, and sing, as poets should, with no afterthought. But when they come after cherries to the tree near my window, they muffle their voices, and their faint *pip pip pop!* sounds far away at the bottom of the garden, where they know I shall not suspect them of robbing the great black-walnut of its bitter-rinded store.[4] They are feathered Pecksniffs, to be sure, but then how brightly their breasts, that look rather shabby in the sunlight, shine in a rainy day against the dark green of the fringe-tree! After they have pinched and shaken all the life of an earthworm, as Italian cooks pound all the spirit out of a steak, and then gulped him, they stand up in honest self-confidence, expand their red

---

[4] The screech-owl, whose cry, despite his ill name, is one of the sweetest sounds in nature, softens his voice in the same way with the most beguiling mockery of distance.—*Author's note.*

waistcoats with the virtuous air of a lobby member, and outface you with an eye that calmly challenges inquiry. "Do *I* look like a bird that knows the flavor of raw vermin? I throw myself upon a jury of my peers. Ask any robin if he ever ate anything less ascetic than the frugal berry of the juniper, and he will answer that his vow forbids him." Can such an open bosom cover such depravity? Alas, yes! I have no doubt his breast was redder at that very moment with the blood of my raspberries. On the whole, he is a doubtful friend in the garden. He makes his dessert of all kinds of berries, and is not averse from early pears. But when we remember how omnivorous he is, eating his own weight in an incredibly short time, and that Nature seems exhaustless in her invention of new insects hostile to vegetation, perhaps we may reckon that he does more good than harm. For my own part, I would rather have his cheerfulness and kind neighborhood than many berries.

For his cousin, the catbird, I have a still warmer regard. Always a good singer, he sometimes nearly equals the brown thrush, and has the merit of keeping up his music later in the evening than any bird of my familiar acquaintance. Ever since I can remember, a pair of them have built in a gigantic syringa near our front door, and I have known the male to sing almost uninterruptedly during the evenings of early summer till twilight duskened into dark. They differ greatly in vocal talent, but all have a delightful way of crooning over, and, as it were, rehearsing their song in an undertone, which makes their nearness always unobtrusive. Though there is the most trustworthy witness to the imitative propensity of this bird, I have only once, during an intimacy of more than forty years, heard him indulge it. In that case, the imitation was by no means so close as to deceive, but a free reproduction of the notes of some other birds, especially of the oriole, as a kind of variation in his own song. The catbird is as shy as the robin is vulgarly familiar. Only when his nest or his fledglings are approached does he become noisy and almost aggressive. I have known him to station his young in a thick cornel-bush on the edge of the raspberry-bed, after the fruit began to ripen, and feed them there for a week or more. In such cases he shows none of that conscious guilt which makes the robin contemptible. On the contrary, he will maintain his post in the thicket, and sharply scold the intruder who ventures to steal *his* berries. After all, his claim is only for tithes, while the robin will bag your entire crop if he get a chance.

Dr. Watts's statement that "birds in their little nests agree," like too many others intended to form the infant mind, is very far from being true. On the contrary, the most peaceful relation of the different species to each other is that of armed neutrality. They are very jealous of neighbors. A few years ago I was much interested in the housebuilding of a pair of summer yellow-birds. They had chosen a very pretty site near the top of a tall white lilac, within easy eye-shot of a chamber window. A very pleasant thing it was to see their

little home growing with mutual help, to watch their industrious skill interrupted only by little flirts and snatches of endearment, frugally cut short
by the common-sense of the tiny housewife. They had brought their work
nearly to an end, and had already begun to line it with fern-down, the gathering of which demanded more distant journeys and longer absences. But, alas!
the syringa, immemorial manor of the catbirds, was not more than twenty
feet away, and these "giddy neighbors" had, as it appeared, been all along
jealously watchful, though silent, witnesses of what they deemed an intrusion of squatters. No sooner were the pretty mates fairly gone for a new
load of lining, than

> "To their unguarded nest these weasel Scots
> Came stealing."

Silently they flew back and forth, each giving a vengeful dab at the nest in
passing. They did not fall-to and deliberately destroy it, for they might have
been caught at their mischief. As it was, whenever the yellow-birds came
back, their enemies were hidden in their own sight-proof bush. Several times
their unconscious victims repaired damages, but at length, after counsel taken
together, they gave it up. Perhaps, like other unlettered folk, they came to
the conclusion that the Devil was in it, and yielded to the invisible persecution
of witchcraft.

The robins, by constant attacks and annoyances, have succeeded in driving off the blue-jays who used to build in our pines, their gay colors and
quaint, noisy ways making them welcome and amusing neighbors. I once had
the chance of doing a kindness to a household of them, which they received
with very friendly condescension. I had had my eye for some time upon a
nest, and was puzzled by a constant fluttering of what seemed full-grown
wings in it whenever I drew nigh. At last I climbed the tree, in spite of angry
protests from the old birds against my intrusion. The mystery had a very
simple solution. In building the nest, a long piece of packthread had been
somewhat loosely woven in. Three of the young had contrived to entangle
themselves in it, and had become full-grown without being able to launch
themselves upon the air. One was unharmed; another had so tightly twisted
the cord about its shank that one foot was curled up and seemed paralyzed;
the third, in its struggles to escape, had sawn through the flesh of the thigh
and so much harmed itself that I thought it humane to put an end to its misery.
When I took out my knife to cut their hempen bonds, the heads of the family
seemed to divine my friendly intent. Suddenly ceasing their cries and threats,
they perched quietly within reach of my hand, and watched me in my work
of manumission. This, owing to the fluttering terror of the prisoners, was an
affair of some delicacy; but ere long I was rewarded by seeing one of them
fly away to a neighboring tree, while the cripple, making a parachute of

his wings, came lightly to the ground, and hopped off as well as he could with one leg, obsequiously waited on by his elders. A week later I had the satisfaction of meeting him in the pine-walk, in good spirits, and already so far recovered as to be able to balance himself with the lame foot. I have no doubt that in his old age he accounted for his lameness by some handsome story of a wound received at the famous Battle of the Pines, when our tribe, overcome by numbers, was driven from its ancient camping-ground. Of late years the jays have visited us only at intervals; and in winter their bright plumage, set off by the snow, and their cheerful cry, are especially welcome. They would have furnished Æsop with a fable, for the feathered crest in which they seem to take so much satisfaction is often their fatal snare. Country boys make a hole with their finger in the snow-crust just large enough to admit the jay's head, and, hollowing it out somewhat beneath, bait it with a few kernels of corn. The crest slips easily into the trap, but refuses to be pulled out again, and he who came to feast remains a prey.

Twice have the crow-blackbirds attempted a settlement in my pines, and twice have the robins, who claim a right of preëmption, so successfully played the part of border-ruffians as to drive them away,—to my great regret, for they are the best substitute we have for rooks. At Shady Hill [5] (now, alas! empty of its so long-loved household) they build by hundreds, and nothing can be more cheery than their creaking clatter (like a convention of old-fashioned tavern-signs) as they gather at evening to debate in mass meeting their windy politics, or to gossip at their tent-doors over the events of the day. Their port is grave, and their stalk across the turf as martial as that of a second-rate ghost in Hamlet. They never meddled with my corn, so far as I could discover.

For a few years I had crows, but their nests are an irresistible bait for boys, and their settlement was broken up. They grew so wonted as to throw off a great part of their shyness, and to tolerate my near approach. One very hot day I stood for some time within twenty feet of a mother and three children, who sat on an elm bough over my head gasping in the sultry air, and holding their wings half-spread for coolness. All birds during the pairing season become more or less sentimental, and murmur soft nothings in a tone very unlike the grinding-organ repetition and loudness of their habitual song. The crow is very comical as a lover, and to hear him trying to soften his croak to the proper Saint Preux standard has something the effect of a Mississippi boatman quoting Tennyson. Yet there are few things to my ear more melodious than his caw of a clear winter morning as it drops to you filtered through five hundred fathoms of crisp blue air. The hostility of all smaller birds makes the moral character of the crow, for all his deaconlike demeanor and garb, somewhat questionable. He could never sally forth without insult. The

[5] The home of Charles Eliot Norton, in Cambridge, who was at the time of this paper in Europe.

golden robins, especially, would chase him as far as I could follow with my eye, making him duck clumsily to avoid their importunate bills. I do not believe, however, that he robbed any nests hereabouts, for the refuse of the gas-works, which, in our free-and-easy community, is allowed to poison the river, supplied him with dead alewives in abundance. I used to watch him making his periodical visits to the salt-marshes and coming back with a fish in his beak to his young savages, who, no doubt, like it in that condition which makes it savory to the Kanakas and other corvine races of men.

Orioles are in great plenty with me. I have seen seven males flashing about the garden at once. A merry crew of them swing their hammocks from the pendulous boughs. During one of these later years, when the canker-worms stripped our elms as bare as winter, these birds went to the trouble of re-building their unroofed nests, and chose for the purpose trees which are safe from those swarming vandals, such as the ash and the button-wood. One year a pair (disturbed, I suppose, elsewhere) built a second nest in an elm within a few yards of the house. My friend, Edward E. Hale, told me once that the oriole rejected from his web all strands of brilliant color, and I thought it a striking example of that instinct of concealment noticeable in many birds, though it should seem in this instance that the nest was amply protected by its position from all marauders but owls and squirrels. Last year, however, I had the fullest proof that Mr. Hale was mistaken. A pair of orioles built on the lowest trailer of a weeping elm, which hung within ten feet of our drawing-room window, and so low that I could reach it from the ground. The nest was wholly woven and felted with ravellings of woollen carpet in which scarlet predominated. Would the same thing have happened in the woods? Or did the nearness of a human dwelling perhaps give the birds a greater feeling of security? They are very bold, by the way, in quest of cordage, and I have often watched them stripping the fibrous bark from a honeysuckle growing over the very door. But, indeed, all my birds look upon me as if I were a mere tenant at will, and they were landlords. With shame I confess it, I have been bullied even by a humming bird. This spring, as I was cleansing a pear-tree of its lichens, one of these little zigzagging blurs came purring toward me, couching his long bill like a lance, his throat sparkling with angry fire, to warn me off from a Missouri-currant whose honey he was sipping. And many a time he has driven me out of a flower-bed. This summer, by the way, a pair of these winged emeralds fastened their mossy acorn-cup upon a bough of the same elm which the orioles had enlivened the year before. We watched all their proceedings from the window through an opera-glass, and saw their two nestlings grow from black needles with a tuft of down at the lower end, till they whirled away on their first short experimental flights. They became strong of wing in a surprisingly short time, and I never saw them or the male bird after, though the female was regular as usual in her visits to

our petunias and verbenas. I do not think it ground enough for a generalization, but in the many times when I watched the old birds feeding their young,
the mother always alighted, while the father as uniformly remained upon
the wing.

The bobolinks are generally chance visitors, tinkling through the garden
in blossoming-time, but this year, owing to the long rains early in the season,
their favorite meadows were flooded, and they were driven to the upland. So
I had a pair of them domiciled in my grass field. The male used to perch in
an apple-tree, then in full bloom, and, while I stood perfectly still close by, he
would circle away, quivering round the entire field of five acres, with no
break in his song, and settle down again among the blossoms, to be hurried
away almost immediately by a new rapture of music. He had the volubility
of an Italian charlatan at a fair, and, like him, appeared to be proclaiming
the merits of some quack remedy. *Opodeldoc-opodeldoc-try-Doctor-Lincoln's-
opodeldoc!* he seemed to repeat over and over again, with a rapidity that
would have distanced the deftest-tongued Figaro that ever rattled. I remember Count Gurowski saying once, with that easy superiority of knowledge about this country which is the monopoly of foreigners, that we had no
singing-birds! Well, well, Mr. Hepworth Dixon has found the typical America
in Oneida and Salt Lake City. Of course, an intelligent European is the best
judge of these matters. The truth is there are more singing-birds in Europe
because there are fewer forests. These songsters love the neighborhood of man
because hawks and owls are rarer, while their own food is more abundant.
Most people seem to think, the more trees, the more birds. Even Châteaubriand, who first tried the primitive-forest-cure, and whose description of the
wilderness in its imaginative effects is unmatched, fancies the "people of the
air singing their hymns to him." So far as my own observation goes, the farther
one penetrates the sombre solitudes of the woods, the more seldom does he
hear the voice of any singing-bird. In spite of Châteaubriand's minuteness of
detail, in spite of that marvellous reverberation of the decrepit tree falling of
its own weight, which he was the first to notice, I cannot help doubting
whether he made his way very deep into the wilderness. At any rate, in a
letter to Fontanes, written in 1804, he speaks of *mes chevaux paissant à quelque
distance.* To be sure Châteaubriand was apt to mount the high horse, and
this may have been but an afterthought of the *grand seigneur,* but certainly
one would not make much headway on horseback toward the druid fastnesses
of the primæval pine.

The bobolinks build in considerable numbers in a meadow within a quarter of a mile of us. A houseless lane passes through the midst of their camp,
and in clear westerly weather, at the right season, one may hear a score of
them singing at once. When they are breeding, if I chance to pass, one of
the male birds always accompanies me like a constable, flitting from post to

post of the rail-fence, with a short note of reproof continually repeated, till I am fairly out of the neighborhood. Then he will swing away into the air and run down the wind, gurgling music without stint over the unheeding tussocks of meadow-grass and dark clumps of bulrushes that mark his domain.

We have no bird whose song will match the nightingale's in compass, none whose note is so rich as that of the European blackbird; but for mere rapture I have never heard the bobolink's rival. But his opera-season is a short one. The ground and tree sparrows are our most constant performers. It is now late in August, and one of the latter sings every day and all day long in the garden. Till within a fortnight, a pair of indigo-birds would keep up their lively *duo* for an hour together. While I write, I hear an oriole gay as in June, and the plaintive *may-be* of the goldfinch tells me he is stealing my lettuce-seeds. I know not what the experience of others may have been, but the only bird I have ever heard sing in the night has been the chip-bird. I should say he sang about as often during the darkness as cocks crow. One can hardly help fancying that he sings in his dreams.

> "Father of light, what sunnie seed,
> What glance of day hast thou confined
> Into this bird? To all the breed
> This busie ray thou hast assigned;
> Their magnetism works all night,
> And dreams of Paradise and light."

On second thought, I remember to have heard the cuckoo strike the hours nearly all night with the regularity of a Swiss clock.

The dead limbs of our elms, which I spare to that end, bring us the flicker every summer, and almost daily I hear his wild scream and laugh close at hand, himself invisible. He is a shy bird, but a few days ago I had the satisfaction of studying him through the blinds as he sat on a tree within a few feet of me. Seen so near and at rest, he makes good his claim to the title of pigeon-woodpecker. Lumberers have a notion that he is harmful to timber, digging little holes through the bark to encourage the settlement of insects. The regular rings of such perforations which one may see in almost any apple-orchard seem to give some probability to this theory. Almost every season a solitary quail visits us, and, unseen among the currant bushes, calls *Bob White, Bob White,* as if he were playing at hide-and-seek with that imaginary being. A rarer visitant is the turtle-dove, whose pleasant coo (something like the muffled crow of a cock from a coop covered with snow) I have sometimes heard, and whom I once had the good luck to see close by me in the mulberry-tree. The wild-pigeon, once numerous, I have not seen for many years.[6] Of savage birds, a hen-hawk now and then quarters him-

---

[6] They made their appearance again this summer (1870).—*Author's note.*

self upon us for a few days, sitting sluggish in a tree after a surfeit of poultry. One of them once offered me a near shot from my study-window one drizzly day for several hours. But it was Sunday, and I gave him the benefit of its gracious truce of God.

Certain birds have disappeared from our neighborhood within my memory. I remember when the whippoorwill could be heard in Sweet Auburn. The night-hawk, once common, is now rare. The brown thrush has moved farther up country. For years I have not seen or heard any of the larger owls, whose hooting was one of my boyish terrors. The cliff-swallow, strange emigrant, that eastward takes his way, has come and gone again in my time. The bank-swallows, wellnigh innumerable during my boyhood, no longer frequent the crumbly cliff of the gravel-pit by the river. The barn-swallows, which once swarmed in our barn, flashing through the dusty sun-streaks of the mow, have been gone these many years. My father would lead me out to see them gather on the roof, and take counsel before their yearly migration, as Mr. White used to see them at Selborne. *Eheu fugaces!* Thank fortune, the swift still glues his nest, and rolls his distant thunders night and day in the wide-throated chimneys, still sprinkles the evening air with his merry twittering. The populous heronry in Fresh Pond meadows has wellnigh broken up, but still a pair or two haunt the old home, as the gypsies of Ellangowan their ruined huts, and every evening fly over us riverwards, clearing their throats with a hoarse hawk as they go, and, in cloudy weather, scarce higher than the tops of the chimneys. Sometimes I have known one to alight in one of our trees, though for what purpose I never could divine. Kingfishers have sometimes puzzled me in the same way, perched at high noon in a pine, springing their watchman's rattle when they flitted away from my curiosity, and seeming to shove their top-heavy heads along as a man does a wheelbarrow.

Some birds have left us, I suppose, because the country is growing less wild. I once found a summer duck's nest within a quarter of a mile of our house, but such a *trouvaille* would be impossible now as Kidd's treasure. And yet the mere taming of the neighborhood does not quite satisfy me as an explanation. Twenty years ago, on my way to bathe in the river, I saw every day a brace of woodcock, on the miry edge of a spring within a few rods of a house, and constantly visited by thirsty cows. There was no growth of any kind to conceal them, and yet these ordinarily shy birds were almost as indifferent to my passing as common poultry would have been. Since bird-nesting has become scientific, and dignified itself as oölogy, that, no doubt, is partly to blame for some of our losses. But some old friends are constant. Wilson's thrush comes every year to remind me of that most poetic of ornithologists. He flits before me through the pine-walk like the very genius of solitude. A pair of pewees have built immemorially on a jutting brick in the arched entrance to the ice-house; always on the same brick, and never more than a single pair, though two broods of five each are raised there every summer. How do they settle their claim to the homestead? By what right of primogeniture? Once the children of a man employed about the place oölogized the nest, and the pewees left us for a year or two. I felt towards those boys as the messmates of the Ancient Mariner did towards him after he had shot the albatross. But the pewees came back at last, and one of them is now on his wonted perch, so near my window that I can hear the click of his bill as he snaps a fly on the wing with the unerring precision a stately Trasteverina shows in the capture of her smaller deer. The pewee is the first bird to pipe up in the morning; and during the early summer he preludes his matutinal ejaculation of *pewee* with a slender whistle, unheard at any other time. He saddens with the season, and, as summer declines, he changes his note to *eheu, pewee!* as if in lamentation. Had he been an Italian bird, Ovid would have had a plaintive tale to tell about him. He is so familiar as often to pursue a fly through the open window into my library.

There is something inexpressibly dear to me in these old friendships of a lifetime. There is scarce a tree of mine but has had, at some time or other, a happy homestead among its boughs, and to which I cannot say,

> "Many light hearts and wings,
> Which now be dead, lodged in thy living bowers."

My walk under the pines would lose half its summer charm were I to miss that shy anchorite, the Wilson's thrush, nor hear in haying-time the metallic ring of his song, that justifies his rustic name of *scythe-whet*. I protect my game as jealously as an English squire. If anybody had oölogized a certain cuckoo's nest I know of (I have a pair in my garden every year), it would have left me a sore place in my mind for weeks. I love to bring these aborigines back to the mansuetude they showed to the early voyagers, and before (forgive the involuntary pun) they had grown accustomed to man and knew his savage ways. And they repay your kindness with a sweet familiarity too delicate ever to breed contempt. I have made a Penn-treaty with them, preferring that to the Puritan way with the natives, which converted them to a little Hebraism and a great deal of Medford rum. If they will not come near enough to me (as most of them will), I bring them close with an opera-glass,—a much better weapon than a gun. I would not, if I could, convert them from their pretty pagan ways. The only one I sometimes have savage doubts about is the red squirrel. I *think* he oölogizes. I *know* he eats cherries (we counted five of them at one time in a single tree, the stones pattering down like the sparse hail that preludes a storm), and that he gnaws off the small end of pears to get at the seeds. He steals the corn from under the noses of my poultry. But what would you have? He will come down upon the limb of the tree I am lying under till he is within a yard of me. He and his mate will scurry up and down the great black-walnut for my diversion, chattering like monkeys. Can I sign his death-warrant who has tolerated me about his grounds so long? Not I. Let them steal, and welcome. I am sure I should, had I had the same bringing up and the same temptation. As for the birds, I do not believe there is one of them but does more good than harm; and of how many feather-less bipeds can this be said?

DEMOCRACY [7]

HE must be a born leader or misleader of men, or must have been sent into the world unfurnished with that modulating and restraining balance-wheel which we call a sense of humor, who, in old age, has as strong a con-fidence in his opinions and in the necessity of bringing the universe into con-formity with them as he had in youth. In a world the very condition of whose being is that it should be in perpetual flux, where all seems mirage, and the one abiding thing is the effort to distinguish realities from appearances, the elderly man must be indeed of a singularly tough and valid fibre who is cer-tain that he has any clarified residuum of experience, any assured verdict of reflection, that deserves to be called an opinion, or who, even if he had, feels that he is justified in holding mankind by the button while he is expounding it. And in a world of daily—nay, almost hourly—journalism, where every clever man, every man who thinks himself clever, or whom anybody else thinks clever, is called upon to deliver his judgment point-blank and at the word of command on every conceivable subject of human thought, or, on what sometimes seems to him very much the same thing, on every inconceivable display of human want of thought, there is such a spend-thrift waste of all those commonplaces which furnish the permitted staple of public discourse that there is little chance of beguiling a new tune out of the one-stringed instrument on which we have been thrumming so long. In this desperate necessity one is often tempted to think that, if all the words of the dictionary were tumbled down in a heap and then all those fortui-tous juxtapositions and combinations that made tolerable sense were picked out and pieced together, we might find among them some poignant sugges-tions towards novelty of thought or expression. But, alas! it is only the great poets who seem to have this unsolicited profusion of unexpected and incal-culable phrase, this infinite variety of topic. For everybody else everything has been said before, and said over again after. He who has read his Aristotle will be apt to think that observation has on most points of general applicability said its last word, and he who has mounted the tower of Plato to look abroad from it will never hope to climb another with so lofty a vantage of specula-

---

[7] An address Lowell delivered, while American minister to England, at Birmingham, Octo-ber 6, 1884. Published in *Democracy and Other Addresses*, 1887.

tion. Where it is so simple if not so easy a thing to hold one's peace, why add to the general confusion of tongues? There is something disheartening, too, in being expected to fill up not less than a certain measure of time, as if the mind were an hourglass, that need only be shaken and set on one end or the other, as the case may be, to run its allotted sixty minutes with decorous exactitude. I recollect being once told by the late eminent naturalist, Agassiz, that when he was to deliver his first lecture as professor (at Zürich, I believe) he had grave doubts of his ability to occupy the prescribed three quarters of an hour. He was speaking without notes, and glancing anxiously from time to time at the watch that lay before him on the desk. "When I had spoken a half hour," he said, "I had told them everything I knew in the world, everything! Then I began to repeat myself," he added, roguishly, "and I have done nothing else ever since." Beneath the humorous exaggeration of the story I seemed to see the face of a very serious and improving moral. And yet if one were to say only what he had to say and then stopped, his audience would feel defrauded of their honest measure. Let us take courage by the example of the French, whose exportation of Bordeaux wines increases as the area of their land in vineyards is diminished.

To me, somewhat hopelessly revolving these things, the undelayable year has rolled round, and I find myself called upon to say something in this place, where so many wiser men have spoken before me. Precluded, in my quality of national guest, by motives of taste and discretion, from dealing with any question of immediate and domestic concern, it seemed to me wisest, or at any rate most prudent, to choose a topic of comparatively abstract interest, and to ask your indulgence for a few somewhat generalized remarks on a matter concerning which I had some experimental knowledge, derived from the use of such eyes and ears as Nature had been pleased to endow me withal, and such report as I had been able to win from them. The subject which most readily suggested itself was the spirit and the working of those conceptions of life and polity which are lumped together, whether for reproach or commendation, under the name of Democracy. By temperament and education of a conservative turn, I saw the last years of that quaint Arcadia which French travellers saw with delighted amazement a century ago, and have watched the change (to me a sad one) from an agricultural to a proletary population. The testimony of Balaam should carry some conviction. I have grown to manhood and am now growing old with the growth of this system of government in my native land; have watched its advances, or what some would call its encroachments, gradual and irresistible as those of a glacier; have been an ear-witness to the forebodings of wise and good and timid men; and have lived to see those forebodings belied by the course of events, which is apt to show itself humorously careless of the reputation of prophets. I recollect hearing a sagacious old gentleman say in 1840 that the doing away with the property qualification for suffrage twenty years before had been the ruin of the State of Massachusetts; that it had put public credit and private estate alike at the mercy of demagogues. I lived to see that Commonwealth twenty odd years later paying the interest on her bonds in gold, though it cost her sometimes nearly three for one to keep her faith, and that while suffering an unparalleled drain of men and treasure in helping to sustain the unity and self-respect of the nation.

If universal suffrage has worked ill in our larger cities, as it certainly has, this has been mainly because the hands that wielded it were untrained to its use. There the election of a majority of the trustees of the public money is controlled by the most ignorant and vicious of a population which has come to us from abroad, wholly unpracticed in self-government and incapable of assimilation by American habits and methods. But the finances of our towns, where the native tradition is still dominant and whose affairs are discussed and settled in a public assembly of the people, have been in general honestly and prudently administered. Even in manufacturing towns, where a majority of the voters live by their daily wages, it is not so often the recklessness as the moderation of public expenditure that surprises an old-fashioned observer. "The beggar is in the saddle at last," cries Proverbial Wisdom. "Why, in the name of all former experience, doesn't he ride to the Devil?" Because in the very act of mounting he ceased to be a beggar and became part owner of the piece of property he bestrides. The last thing we need be anxious about is property. It always has friends or the means of making them. If riches have wings to fly away from their owner, they have wings also to escape danger.

I hear America sometimes playfully accused of sending you all your storms, and am in the habit of parrying the charge by alleging that we are enabled to do this because, in virtue of our protective system, we can afford to make better bad weather than anybody else. And what wiser use could we make of it than to export it in return for the paupers which some European countries are good enough to send over to us who have not attained to the same skill in the manufacture of them? But bad weather is not the worst thing that is laid at our door. A French gentleman, not long ago, forgetting Burke's monition of how unwise it is to draw an indictment against a whole people, has charged us with the responsibility of whatever he finds disagreeable in the morals or manners of his countrymen. If M. Zola or some other competent witness would only go into the box and tell us what those morals and manners were before our example corrupted them! But I confess that I find little to interest and less to edify me in these international bandyings of "You're another."

I shall address myself to a single point only in the long list of offences of which we are more or less gravely accused, because that really includes all the rest. It is that we are infecting the Old World with what seems to be thought the entirely new disease of Democracy. It is generally people who are in what are called easy circumstances who can afford the leisure to treat themselves to a handsome complaint, and these experience an immediate alleviation when once they have found a sonorous Greek name to abuse it by. There is something consolatory also, something flattering to their sense of personal dignity, and to that conceit of singularity which is the natural recoil from our uneasy consciousness of being commonplace, in thinking ourselves victims of a malady by which no one had ever suffered before. Accordingly they find it simpler to class under one comprehensive heading whatever they find offensive to their nerves, their tastes, their interests, or what they suppose to be their opinions, and christen it Democracy, much as physicians label every obscure disease gout, or as cross-grained fellows lay their ill-temper to the weather. But is it really a new ailment, and, if it be, is America answerable for it? Even if she were, would it account for the phylloxera, and hoof-and-mouth disease, and bad harvests, and bad English, and the German bands, and the Boers, and all the other discomforts with which these later days have vexed the souls of them that go in chariots? Yet I have seen the evil example of Democracy in America cited as the source and origin of things quite as heterogeneous and quite as little connected with it by any sequence of cause and effect. Surely this ferment is nothing new. It has been at work for centuries, and we are more conscious of it only because in this age of publicity, where the newspapers offer a rostrum to whoever has a grievance, or fancies that he has, the bubbles and scum thrown up by it are more noticeable on the surface than in those dumb ages when there was a cover of silence and suppression on the cauldron. Bernardo Navagero, speaking of the Provinces of Lower Austria in 1546, tells us that "in them there are five sorts of persons, Clergy, Barons, Nobles, Burghers, and Peasants. Of these last no account is made, *because they have no voice in the Diet.*"

Nor was it among the people that subversive or mistaken doctrines had their rise. A Father of the Church said that property was theft many centuries before Proudhon was born. Bourdaloue reaffirmed it. Montesquieu was the inventor of national workshops, and of the theory that the State owed every man a living. Nay, was not the Church herself the first organized Democracy? A few centuries ago the chief end of man was to keep his soul alive, and then the little kernel of leaven that sets the gases at work was religious, and produced the Reformation. Even in that, far-sighted persons like the Emperor Charles V saw the germ of political and social revolution. Now that the chief end of man seems to have become the keeping of the body alive, and as comfortably alive as possible, the leaven also has become wholly political and social. But there had also been social upheavals before the Reformation and contemporaneously with it, especially among men of Teutonic race. The Reformation gave outlet and direction to an unrest already existing. Formerly the immense majority of men—our brothers—knew only their sufferings, their wants, and their desires. They are beginning now to know their opportunity and their power. All persons who see deeper than their plates are rather inclined to thank God for it than to bewail it, for the sores of Lazarus have a poison in them against which Dives has no antidote.

There can be no doubt that the spectacle of a great and prosperous Democracy on the other side of the Atlantic must react powerfully on the aspirations and political theories of men in the Old World who do not find things to their mind; but, whether for good or evil, it should not be overlooked that the acorn from which it sprang was ripened on the British oak. Every successive swarm that has gone out from this *officina gentium* has, when left to its own instincts—may I not call them hereditary instincts?—assumed a more or less thoroughly democratic form. This would seem to show, what I believe to be the fact, that the British Constitution, under whatever disguises of prudence or decorum, is essentially democratic. England, indeed, may be called a monarchy with democratic tendencies, the United States a democracy with conservative instincts. People are continually saying that America is in the air, and I am glad to think it is, since this means only that a clearer conception of human claims and human duties is beginning to be prevalent. The discontent with the existing order of things, however, pervaded the atmosphere wherever the conditions were favorable, long before Columbus, seeking the back door of Asia, found himself knocking at the front door of America. I say wherever the conditions were favorable, for it is certain that the germs of disease do not stick or find a prosperous field for their development and noxious activity unless where the simplest sanitary precautions have been neglected. "For this effect defective comes by cause," as Polonius said long ago. It is only by instigation of the wrongs of men that what are called the Rights of Man become turbulent and dangerous. It is then only that they syllogize unwelcome truths. It is not the insurrections of ignorance that are dangerous, but the revolts of intelligence:

> The wicked and the weak rebel in vain,
> Slaves by their own compulsion.

Had the governing classes in France during the last century paid as much heed to their proper business as to their pleasures or manners, the guillotine need never have severed that spinal-marrow of orderly and secular tradition through which in a normally constituted state the brain sympathizes with the extremities and sends will and impulsion thither. It is only when the reasonable and practicable are denied that men demand the unreasonable and impracticable; only when the possible is more difficult that they fancy the impossible to be easy. Fairy tales are made out of the dreams of the poor. No; the sentiment which lies at the root of democracy is nothing new. I am speaking always of a sentiment, a spirit, and not of a form of government; for this was but the outgrowth of the other and not its cause. This sentiment is merely an expression of the natural wish of people to have a hand, if need be a controlling hand, in the management of their own affairs. What is new is that they are more and more gaining that control, and learning more and more how to be worthy of it. What we used to call the tendency or drift— what we are being taught to call more wisely the evolution of things—has for some time been setting steadily in this direction. There is no good in arguing with the inevitable. The only argument available with an east wind is to put on your overcoat. And in this case, also, the prudent will prepare themselves to encounter what they cannot prevent. Some people advise us to put on the brakes, as if the movement of which we are conscious were that of a railway train running down an incline. But a metaphor is no argument, though it be sometimes the gunpowder to drive one home and imbed it in the memory. Our disquiet comes of what nurses and other experienced persons call growing-pains, and need not seriously alarm us. They are what every generation before us—certainly every generation since the invention of printing—has gone through with more or less good fortune. To the door of every generation there comes a knocking, and unless the household, like the Thane of Cawdor and his wife, have been doing some deed without a name, they need not shudder. It turns out at worst to be a poor relation who wishes to come in out of the cold. The porter always grumbles and is slow to open. "Who's there, in the name of Beelzebub?" he mutters. Not a change for the better in our human housekeeping has ever taken place that wise and good men have not opposed it,—have not prophesied with the alderman that the world would wake up to find its throat cut in consequence of it. The world, on the contrary, wakes up, rubs its eyes, yawns, stretches itself, and goes about its business as if nothing had happened. Suppression of the slave trade, abolition of slavery, trade unions,—at all of these excellent people shook their heads despondingly, and murmured "Ichabod." But the trade unions are now debating instead of conspiring, and we all read their discussions with comfort and hope, sure that they are learning the business of citizenship and the difficulties of practical legislation.

One of the most curious of these frenzies of exclusion was that against the emancipation of the Jews. All share in the government of the world was denied for centuries to perhaps the ablest, certainly the most tenacious, race that had ever lived in it—the race to whom we owed our religion and the purest spiritual stimulus and consolation to be found in all literature—a race in which ability seems as natural and hereditary as the curve of their noses, and whose blood, furtively mingling with the bluest bloods in Europe, has quickened them with its own indomitable impulsion. We drove them into a corner, but they had their revenge, as the wronged are always sure to have it sooner or later. They made their corner the counter and banking-house of the world, and thence they rule it and us with the ignobler sceptre of finance. Your grandfathers mobbed Priestley only that you might set up his statue and make Birmingham the headquarters of English Unitarianism. We hear it said sometimes that this is an age of transition, as if that made matters clearer; but can any one point us to an age that was not? If he could, he would show us an age of stagnation. The question for us, as it has been for all before us, is to make the transition gradual and easy, to see that our points are right so that the train may not come to grief. For we should remember that nothing is more natural for people whose education has been neglected than to spell evolution with an initial *"r."* A great man struggling with the storms of fate has been called a sublime spectacle; but surely a great man wrestling with these new forces that have come into the world, mastering them and controlling them to beneficent ends, would be a yet sublimer. Here is not a danger, and if there were it would be only a better school of manhood, a nobler scope for ambition. I have hinted that what people are afraid of in democracy is less the thing itself than what they conceive to be its necessary adjuncts and consequences. It is supposed to reduce all mankind to a dead level of mediocrity in character and culture, to vulgarize men's conceptions of life, and therefore their code of morals, manners, and conduct —to endanger the rights of property and possession. But I believe that the real gravamen of the charges lies in the habit it has of making itself generally disagreeable by asking the Powers that Be at the most inconvenient moment whether they are the powers that ought to be. If the powers that be are in a condition to give a satisfactory answer to this inevitable question, they need feel in no way discomfited by it.

Few people take the trouble of trying to find out what democracy really is. Yet this would be a great help, for it is our lawless and uncertain thoughts, it is the indefiniteness of our impressions, that fill darkness, whether mental or physical, with spectres and hobgoblins. Democracy is nothing more than an experiment in government, more likely to succeed in a new soil, but likely to be tried in all soils, which must stand or fall on its own merits as others have done before it. For there is no trick of perpetual motion in politics any more than in mechanics. President Lincoln defined democracy to be "the government of the people by the people for the people." This is a sufficiently compact statement of it as a political arrangement. Theodore Parker said that "Democracy meant not 'I'm as good as you are,' but 'You're as good as I am.'" And this is the ethical conception of it, necessary as a complement of the other; a conception which, could it be made actual and practical, would easily solve all the riddles that the old sphinx of political and social economy who sits by the roadside has been proposing to mankind from the beginning, and which mankind have shown such a singular talent for answering wrongly.

In this sense Christ was the first true democrat that ever breathed, as the old dramatist Dekker said he was the first true gentleman. The characters may be easily doubled, so strong is the likeness between them. A beautiful and profound parable of the Persian poet Jellaladeen tells us that "One knocked at the Beloved's door, and a voice asked from within 'Who is there?' and he answered 'It is I.' Then the voice said, 'This house will not hold me and thee;' and the door was not opened. Then went the lover into the desert and fasted and prayed in solitude, and after a year he returned and knocked again at the door; and again the voice asked 'Who is there?' and he said 'It is thyself;' and the door was opened to him." But that is idealism, you will say, and this is an only too practical world. I grant it; but I am one of those who believe that the real will never find an irremovable basis till it rests on the ideal. It used to be thought that a democracy was possible only in a small territory, and this is doubtless true of a democracy strictly defined, for in such all the citizens decide directly upon every question of public concern in a general assembly. An example still survives in the tiny Swiss canton of Appenzell. But this immediate intervention of the people in their own affairs is not of the essence of democracy; it is not necessary, nor indeed, in most cases, practicable. Democracies to which Mr. Lincoln's definition would fairly enough apply have existed, and now exist, in which, though the supreme authority reside in the people, yet they can act only indirectly on the national policy. This generation has seen a democracy with an imperial figurehead, and in all that have ever existed the body politic has never embraced all the inhabitants included within its territory: the right to share in the direction of affairs has been confined to citizens, and citizenship has been further restricted by various limitations, sometimes of property, sometimes of nativity, and always of age and sex.

The framers of the American Constitution were far from wishing or intending to found a democracy in the strict sense of the word, though, as was inevitable, every expansion of the scheme of government they elaborated has been in a democratical direction. But this has been generally the slow result of growth, and not the sudden innovation of theory; in fact, they had a profound disbelief in theory, and knew better than to commit the folly of breaking with the past. They were not seduced by the French fallacy that a new system of government could be ordered like a new suit of clothes. They would as soon have thought of ordering a new suit of flesh and skin. It is only on the roaring loom of time that the stuff is woven for such a vesture of their thought and experience as they were meditating. They recognized fully the value of tradition and habit as the great allies of permanence and stability. They all had that distaste for innovation which belonged to their race, and many of them a distrust of human nature derived from their creed. The day of sentiment was over, and no dithyrambic affirmations or fine-drawn analyses

DEMOCRACY   437

of the Rights of Man would serve their present turn. This was a practical question, and they addressed themselves to it as men of knowledge and judgment should. Their problem was how to adapt English principles and precedents to the new conditions of American life, and they solved it with singular discretion. They put as many obstacles as they could contrive, not in the way of the people's will, but of their whim. With few exceptions they probably admitted the logic of the then accepted syllogism,—democracy, anarchy, despotism. But this formula was framed upon the experience of small cities shut up to stew within their narrow walls, where the number of citizens made but an inconsiderable fraction of the inhabitants, where every passion was reverberated from house to house and from man to man with gathering rumor till every impulse became gregarious and therefore inconsiderate, and every popular assembly needed but an infusion of eloquent sophistry to turn it into a mob, all the more dangerous because sanctified with the formality of law.[8]

Fortunately their case was wholly different. They were to legislate for a widely scattered population and for States already practised in the discipline of a partial independence. They had an unequalled opportunity and enormous advantages. The material they had to work upon was already democratical by instinct and habitude. It was tempered to their hands by more than a century's schooling in self-government. They had but to give permanent and conservative form to a ductile mass. In giving impulse and direction to their new institutions, especially in supplying them with checks and balances, they had a great help and safeguard in their federal organization. The different, sometimes conflicting, interests and social systems of the several States made existence as a Union and coalescence into a nation conditional on a constant practice of moderation and compromise. The very elements of disintegration were the best guides in political training. Their children learned the lesson of compromise only too well, and it was the application of it to a question of fundamental morals that cost us our civil war. We learned once for all that compromise makes a good umbrella but a poor roof; that it is a temporary expedient, often wise in party politics, almost sure to be unwise in statesmanship.

Has not the trial of democracy in America proved, on the whole, successful? If it had not, would the Old World be vexed with any fears of its proving contagious? This trial would have been less severe could it have been made with a people homogeneous in race, language, and traditions, whereas the United States have been called on to absorb and assimilate enormous masses of foreign population, heterogeneous in all these respects, and drawn mainly from that class which might fairly say that the world was not their friend, nor the

[8] The effect of the electric telegraph in reproducing this trooping of emotion and perhaps of opinion is yet to be measured. The effect of Darwinism as a disintegrator of humanitarianism is also to be reckoned with.—*Author's note.*

world's law. The previous condition too often justified the traditional Irishman, who, landing in New York and asked what his politics were, inquired if there was a Government there, and on being told that there was, retorted, "Thin I'm agin it!" We have taken from Europe the poorest, the most ignorant, the most turbulent of her people, and have made them over into good citizens, who have added to our wealth, and who are ready to die in defence of a country and of institutions which they know to be worth dying for. The exceptions have been (and they are lamentable exceptions) where these hordes of ignorance and poverty have coagulated in great cities. But the social system is yet to seek which has not to look the same terrible wolf in the eyes. On the other hand, at this very moment Irish peasants are buying up the worn-out farms of Massachusetts, and making them productive again by the same virtues of industry and thrift that once made them profitable to the English ancestors of the men who are deserting them. To have achieved even these prosaic results (if you choose to call them so), and that out of materials the most discordant,—I might say the most recalcitrant,—argues a certain beneficent virtue in the system that could do it, and is not to be accounted for by mere luck. Carlyle said scornfully that America meant only roast turkey every day for everybody. He forgot that States, as Bacon said of wars, go on their bellies. As for the security of property, it should be tolerably well secured in a country where every other man hopes to be rich, even though the only property qualification be the ownership of two hands that add to the general wealth. Is it not the best security for anything to interest the largest possible number of persons in its preservation and the smallest in its division? In point of fact, far-seeing men count the increasing power of wealth and its combinations as one of the chief dangers with which the institutions of the United States are threatened in the not distant future. The right of individual property is no doubt the very corner-stone of civilization as hitherto understood, but I am a little impatient of being told that property is entitled to exceptional consideration because it bears all the burdens of the State. It bears those, indeed, which can most easily be borne, but poverty pays with its person the chief expenses of war, pestilence, and famine. Wealth should not forget this, for poverty is beginning to think of it now and then. Let me not be misunderstood. I see as clearly as any man possibly can, and rate as highly, the value of wealth and of hereditary wealth, as the security of refinement, the feeder of all those arts that ennoble and beautify life, and as making a country worth living in. Many an ancestral hall here in England has been a nursery of that culture which has been of example and benefit to all. Old gold has a civilizing virtue which new gold must grow old to be capable of secreting.

I should not think of coming before you to defend or to criticize any form of government. All have their virtues, all their defects, and all have illustrated one period or another in the history of the race, with signal services to humanity and culture. There is not one that could stand a cynical cross-examination by an experienced criminal lawyer, except that of a perfectly wise and perfectly good despot, such as the world has never seen, except in that white-haired king of Browning's, who

> Lived long ago
> In the morning of the world,
> When Earth was nearer Heaven than now.

The English race, if they did not invent government by discussion, have at least carried it nearest to perfection in practice. It seems a very safe and reasonable contrivance for occupying the attention of the country, and is certainly a better way of settling questions than by push of pike. Yet, if one should ask it why it should not rather be called government by gabble, it would have to fumble in its pocket a good while before it found the change for a convincing reply. As matters stand, too, it is beginning to be doubtful whether Parliament and Congress sit at Westminster and Washington or in the editors' rooms of the leading journals, so thoroughly is everything debated before the authorized and responsible debaters get on their legs. And what shall we say of government by a majority of voices? To a person who in the last century would have called himself an Impartial Observer, a numerical preponderance seems, on the whole, as clumsy a way of arriving at truth as could well be devised, but experience has apparently shown it to be a convenient arrangement for determining what may be expedient or advisable or practicable at any given moment. Truth, after all, wears a different face to everybody, and it would be too tedious to wait till all were agreed. She is said to lie at the bottom of a well, for the very reason, perhaps, that whoever looks down in search of her sees his own image at the bottom, and is persuaded not only that he has seen the goddess, but that she is far better-looking than he had imagined.

The arguments against universal suffrage are equally unanswerable. "What," we exclaim, "shall Tom, Dick, and Harry have as much weight in the scale as I?" Of course, nothing could be more absurd. And yet universal suffrage has not been the instrument of greater unwisdom than contrivances of a more select description. Assemblies could be mentioned composed entirely of Masters of Arts and Doctors in Divinity which have sometimes shown traces of human passion or prejudice in their votes. Have the Serene Highnesses and Enlightened Classes carried on the business of Mankind so well, then, that there is no use in trying a less costly method? The democratic theory is that those Constitutions are likely to prove steadiest which have the broadest base, that the right to vote makes a safety-valve of every voter, and that the best way of teaching a man how to vote is to give him the chance of practice. For the question is no longer the academic one, "Is it wise to give every man the ballot?" but rather the practical one, "Is it prudent to deprive whole classes of it any longer?" It may be conjectured that it is cheaper in the long run to lift men up than to hold them down, and that the ballot in their hands is less dangerous to society than a sense of wrong in their heads. At any rate this is the dilemma to which the drift of opinion has been for some time sweeping us, and in politics a dilemma is a more unmanageable thing to hold by the horns than a wolf by the ears. It is said that the right of suffrage is not valued when it is indiscriminately bestowed, and there may be some truth in this, for I have observed that what men prize most is a privilege, even if it be that of chief mourner at a funeral. But is there not danger that it will be valued at more than its worth if denied, and that some illegitimate way will be sought to make up for the want of it? Men who have a voice in public affairs are at once affiliated with one or other of the great parties between which society is divided, merge their individual hopes and opinions in its safer, because more generalized, hopes and opinions, are disciplined by its tactics, and acquire, to a certain degree, the orderly qualities of an army. They no longer belong to a class, but to a body corporate. Of one thing, at least, we may be certain that, under whatever method of helping things to go wrong man's wit can contrive, those who have the divine right to govern will be found to govern in the end, and that the highest privilege to which the majority of mankind can aspire is that of being governed by those wiser than they. Universal suffrage has in the United States sometimes been made the instrument of inconsiderate changes, under the notion of reform, and this from a misconception of the true meaning of popular government. One of these has been the substitution in many of the States of popular election for official selection in the choice of judges. The same system applied to military officers was the source of much evil during our civil war, and, I believe, had to be abandoned. But it has been also true that on all great questions of national policy a reserve of prudence and discretion has been brought out at the critical moment to turn the scale in favor of a wiser decision. An appeal to the reason of the people has never been known to fail in the long run. It is, perhaps, true that, by effacing the principle of passive obedience, democracy, ill understood, has slackened the spring of that ductility to discipline which is essential to "the unity and married calm of States." But I feel assured that experience and necessity will cure this evil, as they have shown their power to cure others. And under what frame of policy have evils ever been remedied till they became intolerable, and shook men out of their indolent indifference through their fears?

We are told that the inevitable result of democracy is to sap the foundations of personal independence, to weaken the principle of authority, to lessen the respect due to eminence, whether in station, virtue, or genius. If these things were so, society could not hold together. Perhaps the best forcing-house of robust individuality would be where public opinion is inclined to be most overbearing, as he must be of heroic temper who should walk along Piccadilly at the height of the season in a soft hat. As for authority, it is one of the symptoms of the time that the religious reverence for it is declining everywhere, but this is due partly to the fact that statecraft is no longer looked upon as a mystery, but as a business, and partly to the decay of superstition, by which I mean the habit of respecting what we are told to respect rather than what is respectable in itself. There is more rough and tumble in the American democracy than is altogether agreeable to people of sensitive nerves and refined habits, and the people take their political duties lightly and laughingly, as is, perhaps, neither unnatural nor unbecoming in a young giant. Democracies can no more jump away from their own shadows than the rest of us can. They no doubt sometimes make mistakes and pay honor to men who do not deserve it. But they do this because they believe them worthy of it, and though it be true that the idol is the measure of the worshipper, yet the worship has in it the germ of a nobler religion. But is it democracies alone that fall into these errors? I, who have seen it proposed to erect a statue to Hudson, the railway king, and have heard Louis Napoleon hailed as the saviour of society by men who certainly had no democratic associations or leanings, am not ready to think so. But democracies have likewise their finer instincts. I have also seen the wisest statesman and most pregnant speaker of our generation, a man of humble birth and ungainly manners, of little culture beyond what his own genius supplied, become more absolute in power than any monarch of modern times through the reverence of his countrymen for his honesty, his wisdom, his sincerity, his faith in God and man, and the nobly humane simplicity of his character. And I remember another whom popular respect enveloped as with a halo, the least vulgar of men, the most austerely genial, and the most independent of opinion. Wherever he went he never met a stranger, but everywhere neighbors and friends proud of him as their ornament and decoration. Institutions which could bear and breed such men as Lincoln and Emerson had surely some energy for good. No, amid all the fruitless turmoil and miscarriage of the world, if there be one thing steadfast and of favorable omen, one thing to make optimism distrust its own obscure distrust, it is the rooted instinct in men to admire what is better and more beautiful than themselves. The touchstone of political and social institutions is their ability to supply them with worthy objects of this sentiment, which is the very tap-root of civilization and progress. There would seem to be no readier way of feeding it with the elements of growth and vigor than such an organization of society as will enable men to respect themselves, and so to justify them in respecting others.

Such a result is quite possible under other conditions than those of an avowedly democratical Constitution. For I take it that the real essence of democracy was fairly enough defined by the First Napoleon when he said that the French Revolution meant *"la carrière ouverte aux talents"*—a clear pathway for merit of whatever kind. I should be inclined to paraphrase this by calling democracy that form of society, no matter what its political classification, in which every man had a chance and knew that he had it. If a man can climb, and feels himself encouraged to climb, from a coalpit to the highest position for which he is fitted, he can well afford to be indifferent what name is given to the government under which he lives. The Bailli of Mirabeau, uncle of the more famous tribune of that name, wrote in 1771: "The English are, in my opinion, a hundred times more agitated and more unfortunate than the very Algerines themselves, because they do not know and will not know till the destruction of their over-swollen power, which I believe very near, whether they are monarchy, aristocracy, or democracy, and wish to play the part of all three." England has not been obliging enough to fulfil the Bailli's prophecy, and perhaps it was this very carelessness about the name, and concern about the substance of popular government, this skill in getting the best out of things as they are, in utilizing all the motives which influence men, and in giving one direction to many impulses, that has been a principal factor of her greatness and power. Perhaps it is fortunate to have an unwritten Constitution, for men are prone to be tinkering the work of their own hands, whereas they are more willing to let time and circumstance mend or modify what time and circumstance have made. All free governments, whatever their name, are in reality governments by public opinion, and it is on the quality of this public opinion that their prosperity depends. It is, therefore, their first duty to purify the element from which they draw the breath of life. With the growth of democracy grows also the fear, if not the danger, that this atmosphere may be corrupted with poisonous exhalations from lower and more malarious levels, and the question of sanitation becomes more instant and pressing. Democracy in its best sense is merely the letting in of light and air. Lord Sherbrooke, with his usual epigrammatic terseness, bids you educate your future rulers. But would this alone be a sufficient safeguard? To educate the intelligence is to enlarge the horizon of its desires and wants. And it is well that this should be so. But the enterprise must go deeper and prepare the way for satisfying those desires and wants in so far as they are legitimate. What is really ominous of danger to the existing order of things is not democracy (which, properly understood, is a conservative force), but the Socialism which may find a fulcrum in it. If we cannot equalize conditions and fortunes any more than we can equalize the brains of men—and a very sagacious person has said that "where two men ride of a horse one must ride behind"—we can yet, perhaps, do something to correct those methods and influences that lead to enormous inequalities, and to prevent their growing more enormous. It is all very well to pooh-pooh Mr. George and to prove him mistaken in his political economy. I do not believe that land should be divided because the quantity of it is limited by nature. Of what may this not be said? *A fortiori*, we might on the same principle insist on a division of human wit, for I have observed that the quantity of this has been even more inconveniently limited. Mr. George himself has an inequitably large share of it. But he is right in his impelling motive; right, also, I am convinced, in insisting that humanity makes a part, by far the most important part, of political economy; and in thinking man to be of more concern and more convincing than the longest columns of figures in the world. For unless you include human nature in your addition, your total is sure to be wrong and your deductions from it fallacious. Communism means barbarism, but Socialism means, or wishes to mean, coöperation and community of interests, sympathy, the giving to the hands not so large a share as to the brains, but a larger share than hitherto in the wealth they must combine to produce—means, in short, the practical application of Christianity to life, and has in it the secret of an orderly and benign reconstruction. State Socialism would cut off the very roots in personal character—self-help, forethought, and frugality —which nourish and sustain the trunk and branches of every vigorous Commonwealth.

I do not believe in violent changes, nor do I expect them. Things in possession have a very firm grip. One of the strongest cements of society is the conviction of mankind that the state of things into which they are born is a part of the order of the universe, as natural, let us say, as that the sun should go round the earth. It is a conviction that they will not surrender except on compulsion, and a wise society should look to it that this compulsion be not put upon them. For the individual man there is no radical cure, outside of human nature itself, for the evils to which human nature is heir. The rule will always hold good that you must

> Be your own palace or the world's your gaol.

But for artificial evils, for evils that spring from want of thought, thought must find a remedy somewhere. There has been no period of time in which wealth has been more sensible of its duties than now. It builds hospitals, it establishes missions among the poor, it endows schools. It is one of the advantages of accumulated wealth, and of the leisure it renders possible, that people have time to think of the wants and sorrows of their fellows. But all these remedies are partial and palliative merely. It is as if we should apply plasters to a single pustule of the small-pox with a view of driving out the disease. The true way is to discover and to extirpate the germs. As society is now constituted these are in the air it breathes, in the water it drinks, in things that seem, and which it has always believed, to be the most innocent and healthful. The evil elements it neglects corrupt these in their springs and pollute

them in their courses. Let us be of good cheer, however, remembering that
the misfortunes hardest to bear are those which never come. The world has
outlived much, and will outlive a great deal more, and men have contrived to
be happy in it. It has shown the strength of its constitution in nothing more
than in surviving the quack medicines it has tried. In the scales of the destinies brawn will never weigh so much as brain. Our healing is not in the
storm or in the whirlwind, it is not in monarchies, or aristocracies, or democracies, but will be revealed by the still small voice that speaks to the conscience and the heart, prompting us to a wider and wiser humanity.

DANIEL WEBSTER

(1782–1852)

Webster was born on a New Hampshire farm in 1782, and was educated at Dartmouth College. He read law, and practiced in Boston with great ability. He exercised his chief influence, however, in politics, serving for the last twenty-five years of his life as senator from Massachusetts, except during two intervals when he was Secretary of State. Throughout his effort was "to form a more perfect union." Before he died at his summer home at Marshfield in 1852 he was recognized as the ablest lawyer, the strongest supporter of a centralized government, and particularly as the greatest orator that America had produced.

He excelled, Rufus Choate said, "in three forms of public speech,—that of the forum, with its double audience of bench and jury, of the halls of legislation, and of the most thronged and tumultuous assemblies of the people." Each of these is briefly illustrated in the selections which follow. He was a man of great physical strength and dignity, the *"beau ideal* of a republican senator," and his style is correspondingly weighty and massive. "His sentences," an admirer said, "are like shafts hewn from the granite of his own hills." If his Ciceronian manner has now given way to the simpler one of Lincoln, and to modern taste seems somewhat pompous and florid, he amply deserves, both for his thought and his style, inclusion in a volume representing the best American prose.

From ORATION AT THE BUNKER HILL MONUMENT [1]

VENERABLE men! you have come down to us from a former generation. Heaven has bounteously lengthened out your lives, that you might behold this joyous day. You are now where you stood fifty years ago, this very hour, with your brothers and your neighbors, shoulder to shoulder, in the strife for your country. Behold, how altered! The same heavens are indeed over your heads; the same ocean rolls at your feet; but all else how changed! You hear now no roar of hostile cannon, you see no mixed volumes of smoke and flame rising from burning Charlestown. The ground strewed with the dead and the dying; the impetuous charge; the steady and successful repulse; the loud call to repeated assault; the summoning of all that is manly to repeated resistance; a thousand bosoms freely and fearlessly bared in an instant to whatever of terror there may be in war and death;—all these you have witnessed, but you witness them no more. All is peace. The heights of yonder

---

[1] Delivered at the laying of the corner-stone of the Bunker Hill Monument, on the fiftieth anniversary of the battle, June 17, 1825, to a large gathering, including Lafayette and some two hundred veterans of the Revolution, among them forty survivors of the battle. These survivors Webster is here addressing.

metropolis, its towers and roofs, which you then saw filled with wives and children and countrymen in distress and terror, and looking with unutterable emotions for the issue of the combat, have presented you to-day with the sight of its whole happy population, come out to welcome and greet you with a universal jubilee. Yonder proud ships, by a felicity of position appropriately lying at the foot of this mount, and seeming fondly to cling around it, are not means of annoyance to you, but your country's own means of distinction and defense. All is peace; and God has granted you this sight of your country's happiness, ere you slumber in the grave. He has allowed you to behold and to partake the reward of your patriotic toils; and he has allowed us, your sons and countrymen, to meet you here, and in the name of the present generation, in the name of your country, in the name of liberty, to thank you!

But, alas! you are not all here! Time and the sword have thinned your ranks. Prescott, Putnam, Stark, Brooks, Read, Pomeroy, Bridge! our eyes seek for you in vain amid this broken band. You are gathered to your fathers, and live only to your country in her grateful remembrance and your own bright example. But let us not too much grieve, that you have met the common fate of men. You lived at least long enough to know that your work had been nobly and successfully accomplished. You lived to see your country's independence established, and to sheathe your swords from war. On the light of Liberty you saw arise the light of Peace, like

> "another morn,
> Risen on mid-noon;"

and the sky on which you closed your eyes was cloudless.

But, ah! Him! the first great martyr [2] in this great cause! Him! the premature victim of his own self-devoting heart! Him! the head of our civil councils, and the destined leader of our military bands, whom nothing brought hither but the unquenchable fire of his own spirit! Him! cut off by Providence in the hour of overwhelming anxiety and thick gloom; falling ere he saw the star of his country rise; pouring out his generous blood like water, before he knew whether it would fertilize a land of freedom or of bondage!—how shall I struggle with the emotions that stifle the utterance of thy name! Our poor work may perish; but thine shall endure! This monument may moulder away; the solid ground it rests upon may sink down to a level with the sea; but thy memory shall not fail! Wheresoever among men a heart shall be found that beats to the transports of patriotism and liberty, its aspirations shall be to claim kindred with thy spirit.

But the scene amidst which we stand does not permit us to confine our thoughts or our sympathies to those fearless spirits who hazarded or lost their lives on this consecrated spot. We have the happiness to rejoice here in the

[2] Joseph Warren.

presence of a most worthy representation of the survivors of the whole Revolutionary army.

VETERANS! you are the remnant of many a well-fought field. You bring with you marks of honor from Trenton and Monmouth, from Yorktown, Camden, Bennington, and Saratoga. VETERANS OF HALF A CENTURY! when in your youthful days you put everything at hazard in your country's cause, good as that cause was, and sanguine as youth is, still your fondest hopes did not stretch onward to an hour like this! At a period to which you could not reasonably have expected to arrive, at a moment of national prosperity such as you could never have foreseen, you are now met here to enjoy the fellowship of old soldiers, and to receive the overflowings of a universal gratitude.

But your agitated countenances and your heaving breasts inform me that even this is not an unmixed joy. I perceive that a tumult of contending feelings rushes upon you. The images of the dead, as well as the persons of the living, present themselves before you. The scene overwhelms you, and I turn from it. May the Father of all mercies smile upon your declining years, and bless them! And when you shall here have exchanged your embraces, when you shall once more have pressed the hands which have been so often extended to give succor in adversity, or grasped in the exultation of victory, then look abroad upon this lovely land which your young valor defended, and mark the happiness with which it is filled; yea, look abroad upon the whole earth, and see what a name you have contributed to give to your country, and what a praise you have added to freedom, and then rejoice in the sympathy and gratitude which beam upon your last days from the improved condition of mankind!

From THE REPLY TO HAYNE[3]

MR. PRESIDENT, in carrying his warfare, such as it is, into New England, the honorable gentleman all along professes to be acting on the defensive. He chooses to consider me as having assailed South Carolina, and insists that he comes forth only as her champion, and in her defence. Sir, I do not admit that I made any attack whatever on South Carolina. Nothing like it. The honorable member, in his first speech, expressed opinions, in regard to revenue and some other topics, which I heard both with pain and with surprise. I told the gentleman I was aware that such sentiments were entertained *out* of the government, but had not expected to find them advanced in it; that I knew there were persons in the South who speak of our Union with indifference or doubt, taking pains to magnify its evils, and to say nothing

---

[3] The most notable passage in a speech delivered in the United States Senate, January 26, 1830, in reply to a speech of Hayne, a senator from South Carolina, and, in particular, in this passage, to an attack Hayne had made on New England.

of its benefits; that the honorable member himself, I was sure, could never be one of these; and I regretted the expression of such opinions as he had avowed, because I thought their obvious tendency was to encourage feelings of disrespect to the Union, and to impair its strength. This, Sir, is the sum and substance of all I said on the subject. And this constitutes the attack which called on the chivalry of the gentleman, in his own opinion, to harry us with such a foray among the party pamphlets and party proceedings of Massachusetts! If he means that I spoke with dissatisfaction or disrespect of the ebullitions of individuals in South Carolina, it is true. But if he means that I assailed the character of the State, her honor, or patriotism, that I reflected on her history or her conduct, he has not the slightest ground for any such assumption. I did not even refer, I think, in my observations, to any collection of individuals. I said nothing of the recent conventions. I spoke in the most guarded and careful manner, and only expressed my regret for the publication of opinions, which I presumed the honorable member disapproved as much as myself. In this, it seems, I was mistaken. I do not remember that the gentleman has disclaimed any sentiment, or any opinion, of a supposed anti-union tendency, which on all or any of the recent occasions has been expressed. The whole drift of his speech has been rather to prove, that, in divers times and manners, sentiments equally liable to my objection have been avowed in New England. And one would suppose that his object, in this reference to Massachusetts, was to find a precedent to justify proceedings in the South, were it not for the reproach and contumely with which he labors, all along, to load these his own chosen precedents. By way of defending South Carolina from what he chooses to think an attack on her, he first quotes the example of Massachusetts, and then denounces that example in good set terms. This twofold purpose, not very consistent, one would think, with itself, was exhibited more than once in the course of his speech. He referred, for instance, to the Hartford Convention. Did he do this for authority, or for a topic of reproach? Apparently for both, for he told us that he should find no fault with the mere fact of holding such a convention, and considering and discussing such questions as he supposes were then and there discussed; but what rendered it obnoxious was its being held at the time, and under the circumstances of the country then existing. We were in a war, he said, and the country needed all our aid; the hand of government required to be strengthened, not weakened; and patriotism should have postponed such proceedings to another day. The thing itself, then, is a precedent; the time and manner of it only, a subject of censure.

Now, Sir, I go much further, on this point, than the honorable member. Supposing, as the gentleman seems to do, that the Hartford Convention assembled for any such purpose as breaking up the Union, because they thought unconstitutional laws had been passed, or to consult on that subject, or *to calculate the value of the Union;* supposing this to be their purpose, or any part of it, then I say the meeting itself was disloyal, and was obnoxious to censure, whether held in time of peace or time of war, or under whatever cir- cumstances. The material question is the *object.* Is dissolution the *object?* If it be, external circumstances may make it a more or less aggravated case, but cannot affect the principle. I do not hold, therefore, Sir, that the Hartford Convention was pardonable, even to the extent of the gentleman's admission, if its objects were really such as have been imputed to it. Sir, there never was a time, under any degree of excitement, in which the Hartford Convention, or any other convention, could have maintained itself one moment in New England, if assembled for any such purpose as the gentleman says would have been an allowable purpose. To hold conventions to decide constitutional law! To try the binding validity of statutes by votes in a convention! Sir, the Hartford Convention, I presume, would not desire that the honorable gentle- man should be their defender or advocate, if he puts their case upon such untenable and extravagant grounds.

Then, Sir, the gentleman has no fault to find with these recently promul- gated South Carolina opinions. And certainly he need have none; for his own sentiments, as now advanced, and advanced on reflection, as far as I have been able to comprehend them, go the full length of all these opinions. I propose, Sir, to say something on these, and to consider how far they are just and constitutional. Before doing that, however, let me observe that the eulogium pronounced by the honorable gentleman on the character of the State of South Carolina, for her Revolutionary and other merits, meets my hearty concurrence. I shall not acknowledge that the honorable member goes before me in regard for whatever of distinguished talent, or distinguished character, South Carolina has produced. I claim part of the honor, I partake in the pride, of her great names. I claim them for countrymen, one and all, the Laurenses, the Rutledges, the Pinckneys, the Sumpters, the Marions, Americans all, whose fame is no more to be hemmed in by State lines, than their talents and patriotism were capable of being circumscribed within the same narrow limits. In their day and generation, they served and honored the country, and the whole country; and their renown is of the treasures of the whole country. Him whose honored name the gentleman himself bears,— does he esteem me less capable of gratitude for his patriotism, or sympathy for his sufferings, than if his eyes had first opened upon the light of Massa- chusetts, instead of South Carolina? Sir, does he suppose it in his power to exhibit a Carolina name so bright as to produce envy in my bosom? No, Sir, increased gratification and delight, rather. I thank God, that, if I am gifted with little of the spirit which is able to raise mortals to the skies, I have yet none, as I trust, of that other spirit, which would drag angels down. When I shall be found, Sir, in my place here in the Senate, or elsewhere, to sneer at public merit, because it happens to spring up beyond the little limits of my own State or neighborhood; when I refuse, for any such cause, or for any cause, the homage due to American talent, to elevated patriotism, to sincere devotion to liberty and the country; or, if I see an uncommon endowment of Heaven, if I see extraordinary capacity and virtue, in any son of the South, and if, moved by local prejudice or gangrened by State jealousy, I get up here to abate the tithe of a hair from his just character and just fame, may my tongue cleave to the roof of my mouth!

Sir, let me recur to pleasing recollections; let me indulge in refreshing remembrance of the past; let me remind you that, in early times, no States cherished greater harmony, both of principle and feeling, than Massachusetts and South Carolina. Would to God that harmony might again return! Shoulder to shoulder they went through the Revolution, hand in hand they stood round the administration of Washington, and felt his own great arm lean on them for support. Unkind feeling, if it exists, alienation, and distrust are the growth, unnatural to such soils, of false principles since sown. They are weeds, the seeds of which that same great arm never scattered.

Mr. President, I shall enter on no encomium upon Massachusetts; she needs none. There she is. Behold her, and judge for yourselves. There is her history; the world knows it by heart. The past, at least, is secure. There is Boston, and Concord, and Lexington, and Bunker Hill; and there they will remain for ever. The bones of her sons, falling in the great struggle for Independence, now lie mingled with the soil of every State from New England to Georgia; and there they will lie for ever. And, Sir, where American Liberty raised its first voice, and where its youth was nurtured and sustained, there it still lives, in the strength of its manhood and full of its original spirit. If discord and disunion shall wound it, if party strife and blind ambition shall hawk at and tear it, if folly and madness, if uneasiness under salutary and necessary restraint, shall succeed in separating it from that Union, by which alone its existence is made sure, it will stand, in the end, by the side of that cradle in which its infancy was rocked; it will stretch forth its arm with whatever of vigor it may still retain over the friends who gather round it; and it will fall at last, if fall it must, amidst the proudest monuments of its own glory, and on the very spot of its origin.

From THE MURDER OF CAPTAIN JOSEPH WHITE [4]

I AM little accustomed, Gentlemen, to the part which I am now attempting to perform. Hardly more than once or twice has it happened to me to be

[4] From a speech for the prosecution, made at Salem, Mass., August, 1830, to a jury, at the trial of Francis Knapp.

concerned on the side of the government in any criminal prosecution whatever; and never, until the present occasion, in any case affecting life.

But I very much regret that it should have been thought necessary to suggest to you that I am brought here to "hurry you against the law and beyond the evidence." I hope I have too much regard for justice, and too much respect for my own character, to attempt either; and were I to make such attempt, I am sure that in this court nothing can be carried against the law, and that gentlemen, intelligent and just as you are, are not, by any power, to be hurried beyond the evidence. Though I could well have wished to shun this occasion, I have not felt at liberty to withhold my professional assistance, when it is supposed that I may be in some degree useful in investigating and discovering the truth respecting this most extraordinary murder. It has seemed to be a duty incumbent on me, as on every other citizen, to do my best and my utmost to bring to light the perpetrators of this crime. Against the prisoner at the bar, as an individual, I cannot have the slightest prejudice. I would not do him the smallest injury or injustice. But I do not affect to be indifferent to the discovery and the punishment of this deep guilt. I cheerfully share in the opprobrium, how great soever it may be, which is cast on those who feel and manifest an anxious concern that all who had a part in planning, or a hand in executing, this deed of midnight assassination, may be brought to answer for their enormous crime at the bar of public justice.

Gentlemen, it is a most extraordinary case. In some respects, it has hardly a precedent anywhere; certainly none in our New England history. This bloody drama exhibited no suddenly excited, ungovernable rage. The actors in it were not surprised by any lion-like temptation springing upon their virtue, and overcoming it, before resistance could begin. Nor did they do the deed to glut savage vengeance, or satiate long-settled and deadly hate. It was a cool, calculating, money-making murder. It was all "hire and salary, not revenge." It was the weighing of money against life; the counting out of so many pieces of silver against so many ounces of blood.

An aged man, without an enemy in the world, in his own house, and in his own bed, is made the victim of a butcherly murder, for mere pay. Truly, here is a new lesson for painters and poets. Whoever shall hereafter draw the portrait of murder, if he will show it as it has been exhibited, where such example was last to have been looked for, in the very bosom of our New England society, let him not give it the grim visage of Moloch, the brow knitted by revenge, the face black with settled hate, and the bloodshot eye emitting livid fires of malice. Let him draw, rather, a decorous, smooth-faced, bloodless demon; a picture in repose, rather than in action; not so much an example of human nature in its depravity, and in its paroxysms of crime, as an infernal being, a fiend, in the ordinary display and development of his character.

The deed was executed with a degree of self-possession and steadiness equal to the wickedness with which it was planned. The circumstances now clearly in evidence spread out the whole scene before us. Deep sleep had fallen on the destined victim, and on all beneath his roof. A healthful old man, to whom sleep was sweet, the first sound slumbers of the night held him in their soft but strong embrace. The assassin enters, through the window already prepared, into an unoccupied apartment. With noiseless foot he paces the lonely hall, half lighted by the moon; he winds up the ascent of the stairs, and reaches the door of the chamber. Of this, he moves the lock, by soft and continued pressure, till it turns on its hinges without noise; and he enters, and beholds his victim before him. The room is uncommonly open to the admission of light. The face of the innocent sleeper is turned from the murderer, and the beams of the moon, resting on the gray locks of his aged temple, show him where to strike. The fatal blow is given! and the victim passes, without a struggle or a motion, from the repose of sleep to the repose of death! It is the assassin's purpose to make sure work; and he plies the dagger, though it is obvious that life has been destroyed by the blow of the bludgeon. He even raises the aged arm, that he may not fail in his aim at the heart, and replaces it again over the wounds of the poniard! To finish the picture, he explores the wrist for the pulse! He feels for it, and ascertains that it beats no longer! It is accomplished. The deed is done. He retreats, retraces his steps to the window, passes out through it as he came in, and escapes. He has done the murder. No eye has seen him, no ear has heard him. The secret is his own, and it is safe!

Ah! Gentlemen, that was a dreadful mistake. Such a secret can be safe nowhere. The whole creation of God has neither nook nor corner where the guilty can bestow it, and say it is safe. Not to speak of that eye which pierces through all disguises, and beholds everything as in the splendor of noon, such secrets of guilt are never safe from detection, even by men. True it is, generally speaking, that "murder will out." True it is, that Providence hath so ordained, and doth so govern things, that those who break the great law of Heaven by shedding man's blood seldom succeed in avoiding discovery. Especially, in a case exciting so much attention as this, discovery must come, and will come, sooner or later. A thousand eyes turn at once to explore every man, every thing, every circumstance, connected with the time and place; a thousand ears catch every whisper; a thousand excited minds intensely dwell on the scene, shedding all their light, and ready to kindle the slightest circumstance into a blaze of discovery. Meanwhile the guilty soul cannot keep its own secret. It is false to itself; or rather it feels an irresistible impulse of conscience to be true to itself. It labors under its guilty possession, and knows not what to do with it. The human heart was not made for the residence of such an inhabitant. It finds itself preyed on by a torment, which it dares not acknowledge to God or man. A vulture is devouring it, and it can ask no sympathy or assistance, either from heaven or earth. The secret which the murderer possesses soon comes to possess him; and, like the evil spirits of which we read, it overcomes him, and leads him whithersoever it will. He feels it beating at his heart, rising to his throat, and demanding disclosure. He thinks the whole world sees it in his face, reads it in his eyes, and almost hears its workings in the very silence of his thoughts. It has become his master. It betrays his discretion, it breaks down his courage, it conquers his prudence. When suspicions from without begin to embarrass him, and the net of circumstance to entangle him, the fatal secret struggles with still greater violence to burst forth. It must be confessed, it will be confessed; there is no refuge from confession but suicide, and suicide is confession.

WILLIAM HICKLING PRESCOTT

(1796–1859)

Prescott came of a prominent and wealthy Massachusetts family, his grandfather having commanded at the battle of Bunker Hill and his father being an eminent attorney. He was born at Salem in 1796. While in his junior year at Harvard, he was blinded in the left eye by a crust of bread thrown in fun by a fellow-student, and this accident changed the course of his life. Intending to study law and entering his father's office, he was forced to give up this plan when the close application necessary caused inflammation, with the threatened loss, of his other eye. After some years of indecision, he settled upon a career of letters, two influences directing him to the particular field he chose: Gibbon's *Memoirs,* which suggested to him the writing of history, and the study of Spanish, begun at the suggestion of a friend, George Ticknor, which led him to "embrace the gift of the Spanish subject" for a theme. He worked under a severe handicap, it being necessary to have all his source material read to him in a darkened room, while he made notes, which in turn were read by a secretary until he had mastered them and could compose from the mass of details in his memory. In 1829 he began writing the *History of the Reign of Ferdinand and Isabella.* It was published in 1837 and met with such favor that he proceeded to write the *History of the Conquest of Mexico* (1843) and the *Conquest of Peru* (1847). At his death in 1859 of a stroke of apoplexy, he had completed three volumes of a projected five-volume work on *Philip II.*

Although material which has invalidated many details of Prescott's work has appeared since his time, he followed with care the sources at his command, his aims being exactness and historic truth. His power lay in the ability to select the best details from masses of material, and to put these together in such way as to make a vivid and profoundly interesting narrative. He is less a philosophical historian than a reporter of events, yet in the story of events he is never dull, and in the depicting of character and in the judicious selection of elements with which to give a total impression he has few rivals among modern historians.

From THE CONQUEST OF MEXICO

[THE MARCH TO MEXICO CITY] [1]

THEY were now leaving the pleasant champaign country, as the road wound up the bold sierra which separates the great plateaus of Mexico and Puebla. The air, as they ascended, became keen and piercing; and the blasts,

---

[1] *The History of the Conquest of Mexico* is divided into seven "books." The first deals with the Aztec civilization before the arrival of the Europeans; the second with the discovery of Mexico by the Spaniards and the arrival of Cortés; the third with the march to Mexico City; the fourth with the residence of the Spaniards in Mexico; the fifth with their expulsion from the city; the sixth with the siege and conquest of the city by the Spaniards; and the seventh with the subsequent career of Cortés. The extract here given is from Book III, chapter viii, and

sweeping down the frozen sides of the mountains, made the soldiers shiver in their thick harness of cotton, and benumbed the limbs of both men and horses.

They were passing between two of the highest mountains on the North American continent; Popocatepetl, "the hill that smokes," and Iztaccihuatl, or "white woman,"—a name suggested, doubtless, by the bright robe of snow spread over its broad and broken surface. A puerile superstition of the Indians regarded these celebrated mountains as gods, and Iztaccihuatl as the wife of her more formidable neighbor. A tradition of a higher character described the northern volcano, as the abode of the departed spirits of wicked rulers, whose fiery agonies, in their prison-house, caused the fearful bellowings and convulsions in times of eruption. It was the classic fable of antiquity. These superstitious legends had invested the mountain with a mysterious horror, that made the natives shrink from attempting its ascent, which, indeed, was from natural causes a work of incredible difficulty.

The great *volcan,* as Popocatepetl was called, rose to the enormous height of 17,852 feet above the level of the sea; more than 2000 feet above the "monarch of mountains,"—the highest elevation in Europe. During the present century, it has rarely given evidence of its volcanic origin, and "the hill that smokes" has almost forfeited its claim to the appellation. But at the time of the Conquest it was frequently in a state of activity, and raged with uncommon fury while the Spaniards were at Tlascala; an evil omen, it was thought, for the natives of Anahuac. Its head, gathered into a regular cone by the deposit of successive eruptions, wore the usual form of volcanic mountains, when not disturbed by the falling in of the crater. Soaring towards the skies, with its silver sheet of everlasting snow, it was seen far and wide over the broad plains of Mexico and Puebla, the first object which the morning sun greeted in his rising, the last where his evening rays were seen to linger, shedding a glorious effulgence over its head, that contrasted strikingly with the ruinous waste of sand and lava immediately below, and the deep fringe of funereal pines that shrouded its base.

The mysterious terrors which hung over the spot, and the wild love of adventure, made some of the Spanish cavaliers desirous to attempt the ascent, which the natives declared no man could accomplish and live. Cortés encouraged them in the enterprise, willing to show the Indians that no achievement was above the dauntless daring of his followers. One of his captains, accordingly, Diego Ordaz, with nine Spaniards, and several Tlascalans, encouraged by their example, undertook the ascent. It was attended with more difficulty than had been anticipated.

describes the approach of the Spaniards to Mexico City, after subjugating various tribes along the way, and forming an alliance with one of these, the Tlascalans, who were inveterate enemies of the Aztec emperor.

The lower region was clothed with a dense forest, so thickly matted, that in some places it was scarcely possible to penetrate it. It grew thinner, however, as they advanced, dwindling, by degrees, into a straggling, stunted vegetation, till, at the height of somewhat more than thirteen thousand feet, it faded away altogether. The Indians who had held on thus far, intimidated by the strange subterraneous sounds of the volcano, even then in a state of combustion, now left them. The track opened on a black surface of glazed volcanic sand and of lava, the broken fragments of which, arrested in its boiling progress in a thousand fantastic forms, opposed continual impediments to their advance. Amidst these, one huge rock, the *Pico del Fraile,* a conspicuous object from below, rose to the perpendicular height of a hundred and fifty feet, compelling them to take a wide circuit. They soon came to the limits of perpetual snow, where new difficulties presented themselves, as the treacherous ice gave an imperfect footing, and a false step might precipitate them into the frozen chasms that yawned around. To increase their distress, respiration in these aerial regions became so difficult, that every effort was attended with sharp pains in the head and limbs. Still they pressed on, till, drawing nearer the crater, such volumes of smoke, sparks, and cinders were belched forth from its burning entrails, and driven down the sides of the mountain, as nearly suffocated and blinded them. It was too much even for their hardy frames to endure, and, however reluctantly, they were compelled to abandon the attempt on the eve of its completion. They brought back some huge icicles,—a curious sight in these tropical regions,—as a trophy of their achievement, which, however imperfect, was sufficient to strike the minds of the natives with wonder, by showing that with the Spaniards the most appalling and mysterious perils were only as pastimes. The undertaking was eminently characteristic of the bold spirit of the cavalier of that day, who, not content with the dangers that lay in his path, seemed to court them from the mere quixotic love of adventure. A report of the affair was transmitted to the Emperor Charles the Fifth, and the family of Ordaz was allowed to commemorate the exploit by assuming a burning mountain on their escutcheon.

The general was not satisfied with the result. Two years after, he sent up another party, under Francisco Montaño, a cavalier of determined resolution. The object was to obtain sulphur to assist in making gunpowder for the army. The mountain was quiet at this time, and the expedition was attended with better success. The Spaniards, five in number, climbed to the very edge of the crater, which presented an irregular ellipse at its mouth, more than a league in circumference. Its depth might be from eight hundred to a thousand feet. A lurid flame burned gloomily at the bottom, sending up a sulphureous steam, which, cooling as it rose, was precipitated on the sides of the cavity. The party cast lots, and it fell on Montaño himself, to descend in a basket into this hideous abyss, into which he was lowered by his companions to the depth of four hundred feet! This was repeated several times, till the adventurous cavalier had collected a sufficient quantity of sulphur for the wants of the army. This doughty enterprise excited general admiration at the time. Cortés concludes his report of it, to the emperor, with the judicious reflection, that it would be less inconvenient, on the whole, to import their powder from Spain.

But it is time to return from our digression, which may, perhaps, be excused, as illustrating, in a remarkable manner, the chimerical spirit of enterprise,—not inferior to that in his own romances of chivalry,—which glowed in the breast of the Spanish cavalier in the sixteenth century.

The army held on its march through the intricate gorges of the sierra. The route was nearly the same as that pursued at the present day by the courier from the capital to Puebla, by the way of Mecameca. It was not that usually taken by travellers from Vera Cruz, who follow the more circuitous road round the northern base of Iztaccihuatl, as less fatiguing than the other, though inferior in picturesque scenery and romantic points of view. The icy winds, that now swept down the sides of the mountains, brought with them a tempest of arrowy sleet and snow, from which the Christians suffered even more than the Tlascalans, reared from infancy among the wild solitudes of their own native hills. As night came on, their sufferings would have been intolerable, but they luckily found a shelter in the commodious stone buildings which the Mexican government had placed at stated intervals along the roads for the accommodation of the traveller and their own couriers. It little dreamed it was providing a protection for its enemies.

The troops, refreshed by a night's rest, succeeded, early on the following day, in gaining the crest of the sierra of Ahualco, which stretches like a curtain between the two great mountains on the north and south. Their progress was now comparatively easy, and they marched forward with a buoyant step, as they felt they were treading the soil of Montezuma.

They had not advanced far, when, turning an angle of the sierra, they suddenly came on a view which more than compensated the toils of the preceding day. It was that of the Valley of Mexico, or Tenochtitlan, as more commonly called by the natives; which, with its picturesque assemblage of water, woodland, and cultivated plains, its shining cities and shadowy hills, was spread out like some gay and gorgeous panorama before them. In the highly rarefied atmosphere of these upper regions, even remote objects have a brilliancy of coloring and a distinctness of outline which seem to annihilate distance. Stretching far away at their feet, were seen noble forests of oak, sycamore, and cedar, and beyond, yellow fields of maize and the towering maguey, intermingled with orchards and blooming gardens; for flowers, in such demand for their religious festivals, were even more abundant in this populous valley than in other parts of Anahuac. In the centre of the great basin were beheld the lakes, occupying then a much larger portion of its surface than at present; their borders thickly studded with towns and hamlets, and, in the midst,—like some Indian empress with her coronal of pearls,—the fair city of Mexico, with her white towers and pyramidal temples, reposing, as it were, on the bosom of the waters,—the far-famed "Venice of the Aztecs." High over all rose the royal hill of Chapoltepec, the residence of the Mexican monarchs, crowned with the same grove of gigantic cypresses, which at this day fling their broad shadows over the land. In the distance beyond the blue waters of the lake, and nearly screened by intervening foliage, was seen a shining speck, the rival capital of Tezcuco, and, still further on, the dark belt of porphyry, girdling the Valley around, like a rich setting which Nature had devised for the fairest of her jewels.

Such was the beautiful vision which broke on the eyes of the Conquerors. And even now, when so sad a change has come over the scene; when the stately forests have been laid low, and the soil, unsheltered from the fierce radiance of a tropical sun, is in many places abandoned to sterility; when the waters have retired, leaving a broad and ghastly margin white with the incrustation of salts, while the cities and hamlets on their borders have mouldered into ruins;—even now that desolation broods over the landscape, so indestructible are the lines of beauty which Nature has traced on its features, that no traveller, however cold, can gaze on them with any other emotions than those of astonishment and rapture.

What, then, must have been the emotions of the Spaniards, when, after working their toilsome way into the upper air, the cloudy tabernacle parted before their eyes, and they beheld these fair scenes in all their pristine magnificence and beauty! It was like the spectacle which greeted the eyes of Moses from the summit of Pisgah, and, in the warm glow of their feelings, they cried out, "It is the promised land!"

But these feelings of admiration were soon followed by others of a very different complexion; as they saw in all this the evidences of a civilization and power far superior to anything they had yet encountered. The more timid, disheartened by the prospect, shrunk from a contest so unequal, and demanded, as they had done on some former occasions, to be led back again to Vera Cruz. Such was not the effect produced on the sanguine spirit of the general. His avarice was sharpened by the display of the dazzling spoil at his feet; and, if he felt a natural anxiety at the formidable odds, his confidence was renewed, as he gazed on the lines of his veterans, whose weather-beaten visages and battered armor told of battles won and difficulties surmounted, while his bold barbarians, with appetites whetted by the view of their enemies' country, seemed like eagles on the mountains, ready to pounce upon their prey. By argument, entreaty, and menace, he endeavored to restore the faltering courage of the soldiers, urging them not to think of retreat, now that they had reached the goal for which they had panted, and the golden gates were open to receive them. In these efforts, he was well seconded by the brave cavaliers, who held honor as dear to them as fortune; until the dullest spirits caught somewhat of the enthusiasm of their leaders, and the general had the satisfaction to see his hesitating columns, with their usual buoyant step, once more on their march down the slopes of the sierra.

With every step of their progress, the woods became thinner; patches of cultivated land more frequent; and hamlets were seen in the green and sheltered nooks, the inhabitants of which, coming out to meet them, gave the troops a kind reception. Everywhere they heard complaints of Montezuma, especially of the unfeeling manner in which he carried off their young men to recruit his armies, and their maidens for his harem. These symptoms of discontent were noticed with satisfaction by Cortés, who saw that Montezuma's "mountain-throne," as it was called, was, indeed, seated on a volcano, with the elements of combustion so active within, that it seemed as if any hour might witness an explosion. He encouraged the disaffected natives to rely on his protection, as he had come to redress their wrongs. He took advantage, moreover, of their favorable dispositions, to scatter among them such gleams of spiritual light as time and the preaching of father Olmedo could afford.

He advanced by easy stages, somewhat retarded by the crowd of curious inhabitants gathered on the highways to see the strangers, and halting at every spot of interest or importance. On the road, he was met by another embassy from the capital. It consisted of several Aztec lords, freighted, as usual, with a rich largess of gold, and robes of delicate furs and feathers. The message of the emperor was couched in the same deprecatory terms as before. He even condescended to bribe the return of the Spaniards, by promising, in that event, four loads of gold to the general, and one to each of the captains, with a yearly tribute to their sovereign. So effectually had the lofty and naturally courageous spirit of the barbarian monarch been subdued by the influence of superstition!

But the man, whom the hostile array of armies could not daunt, was not to be turned from his purpose by a woman's prayers. He received the embassy with his usual courtesy, declaring, as before, that he could not answer it to his own sovereign, if he were now to return without visiting the emperor in his capital. It would be much easier to arrange matters by a personal interview than by distant negotiation. The Spaniards came in the spirit of peace. Montezuma would so find it, but, should their presence prove burdensome to him, it would be easy for them to relieve him of it.

The Aztec monarch, meanwhile, was a prey to the most dismal apprehensions. It was intended that the embassy above noticed should reach the Spaniards before they crossed the mountains. When he learned that this was accomplished, and that the dread strangers were on their march across the Valley, the very threshold of his capital, the last spark of hope died away in his bosom. Like one who suddenly finds himself on the brink of some dark and yawning gulf, he was too much bewildered to be able to rally his thoughts, or even to comprehend his situation. He was the victim of an absolute destiny; against which no foresight or precautions could have availed. It was as if the strange beings, who had thus invaded his shores, had dropped from some distant planet, so different were they from all he had ever seen in appearance and manners; so superior—though a mere handful in numbers —to the banded nations of Anahuac in strength and science, and all the fearful accompaniments of war! They were now in the Valley. The huge mountain screen, which nature had so kindly drawn around it for its defence had been overleaped. The golden visions of security and repose, in which he had so long indulged, the lordly sway descended from his ancestors, his broad imperial domain, were all to pass away. It seemed like some terrible dream,—from which he was now, alas! to awake to a still more terrible reality.

In a paroxysm of despair, he shut himself up in his palace, refused food, and sought relief in prayer and in sacrifice. But the oracles were dumb. He then adopted the more sensible expedient of calling a council of his principal and oldest nobles. Here was the same division of opinion which had before prevailed. Cacama, the young king of Tezcuco, his nephew, counselled him to receive the Spaniards courteously, as ambassadors, so styled by themselves, of a foreign prince. Cuitlahua, Montezuma's more warlike brother, urged him to muster his forces on the instant, and drive back the invaders from his capital, or die in its defence. But the monarch found it difficult to rally his spirits for this final struggle. With downcast eye and dejected mien, he exclaimed, "Of what avail is resistance, when the gods have declared themselves against us! Yet I mourn most for the old and infirm, the women and children, too feeble to fight or to fly. For myself and the brave men around me, we must bare our breasts to the storm, and meet it as we may!" Such are the sorrowful and sympathetic tones in which the Aztec emperor is said to have uttered the bitterness of his grief. He would have acted a more glorious part, had he put his capital in a posture of defence, and prepared, like the last of the Palæologi, to bury himself under its ruins. . . .

[THE ENTRANCE OF THE CITY] [2]

WITH the first faint streak of dawn, the Spanish general was up, mustering his followers. They gathered, with beating hearts, under their respective banners, as the trumpet sent forth its spirit-stirring sounds across water and woodland, till they died away in distant echoes among the mountains. The sacred flames on the altars of numberless *teocallis*, dimly seen through the

[2] From Book III, chapter ix.

gray mists of morning, indicated the site of the capital, till temple, tower, and palace were fully revealed in the glorious illumination which the sun, as he arose above the eastern barrier, poured over the beautiful Valley. It was the eighth of November, 1519; a conspicuous day in history, as that on which the Europeans first set foot in the capital of the Western World.

Cortés with his little body of horse formed a sort of advance guard to the army. Then came the Spanish infantry, who in a summer's campaign had acquired the discipline, and the weather-beaten aspect, of veterans. The baggage occupied the centre; and the rear was closed by the dark files of Tlascalan warriors. The whole number must have fallen short of seven thousand; of which less than four hundred were Spaniards.

For a short distance, the army kept along the narrow tongue of land that divides the Tezcucan from the Chalcan waters, when it entered on the great dike, which, with the exception of an angle near the commencement, stretches in a perfectly straight line across the salt floods of Tezcuco to the gates of the capital. It was the same causeway, or rather the basis of that, which still forms the great southern avenue of Mexico. The Spaniards had occasion more than ever to admire the mechanical science of the Aztecs, in the geometrical precision with which the work was executed, as well as the solidity of its construction. It was composed of huge stones well laid in cement; and wide enough, throughout its whole extent, for ten horsemen to ride abreast.

They saw, as they passed along, several large towns, resting on piles, and reaching far into the water,—a kind of architecture which found great favor with the Aztecs, being in imitation of that of their metropolis. The busy population obtained a good subsistence from the manufacture of salt, which they extracted from the waters of the great lake. The duties on the traffic in this article were a considerable source of revenue to the crown.

Everywhere the Conquerors beheld the evidence of a crowded and thriving population, exceeding all they had yet seen. The temples and principal buildings of the cities were covered with a hard white stucco, which glistened like enamel in the level beams of the morning. The margin of the great basin was more thickly gemmed than that of Chalco with towns and hamlets. The water was darkened by swarms of canoes filled with Indians, who clambered up the sides of the causeway, and gazed with curious astonishment on the strangers. And here, also, they beheld those fairy islands of flowers, overshadowed occasionally by trees of considerable size, rising and falling with the gentle undulation of the billows. At the distance of half a league from the capital, they encountered a solid work or curtain of stone, which traversed the dike. It was twelve feet high, was strengthened by towers at the extremities, and in the centre was a battlemented gateway, which opened a passage to the troops. It was called the Fort of Xoloc, and became memorable in aftertimes as the position occupied by Cortés in the famous siege of Mexico.

Here they were met by several hundred Aztec chiefs, who came out to announce the approach of Montezuma, and to welcome the Spaniards to his capital. They were dressed in the fanciful gala costume of the country, with the *maxtlatl,* or cotton sash, around their loins, and a broad mantle of the same material, or of the brilliant feather-embroidery, flowing gracefully down their shoulders. On their necks and arms they displayed collars and bracelets of turquoise mosaic, with which delicate plumage was curiously mingled, while their ears, under-lips, and occasionally their noses, were garnished with pendants formed of precious stones, or crescents of fine gold. As each cacique made the usual formal salutation of the country separately to the general, the tedious ceremony delayed the march more than an hour. After this, the army experienced no further interruption till it reached a bridge near the gates of the city. It was built of wood, since replaced by one of stone, and was thrown across an opening of the dike, which furnished an outlet to the waters, when agitated by the winds, or swollen by a sudden influx in the rainy season. It was a drawbridge; and the Spaniards, as they crossed it, felt how truly they were committing themselves to the mercy of Montezuma, who, by thus cutting off their communications with the country, might hold them prisoners in his capital.

In the midst of these unpleasant reflections, they beheld the glittering retinue of the emperor emerging from the great street which led then, as it still does, through the heart of the city. Amidst a crowd of Indian nobles, preceded by three officers of state, bearing golden wands, they saw the royal palanquin blazing with burnished gold. It was borne on the shoulders of nobles, and over it a canopy of gaudy feather-work, powdered with jewels, and fringed with silver, was supported by four attendants of the same rank. They were barefooted, and walked with a slow, measured pace, and with eyes bent on the ground. When the train had come within a convenient distance, it halted, and Montezuma, descending from his litter, came forward leaning on the arms of the lords of Tezcuco and Iztapalapan, his nephew and brother, both of whom, as we have seen, had already been made known to the Spaniards. As the monarch advanced under the canopy, the obsequious attendants strewed the ground with cotton tapestry, that his imperial feet might not be contaminated by the rude soil. His subjects of high and low degree, who lined the sides of the causeway, bent forward with their eyes fastened on the ground as he passed, and some of the humbler class prostrated themselves before him. Such was the homage paid to the Indian despot, showing that the slavish forms of Oriental adulation were to be found among the rude inhabitants of the Western World.

Montezuma wore the girdle and ample square cloak, *tilmatli,* of his nation. It was made of the finest cotton, with the embroidered ends gathered in a knot round his neck. His feet were defended by sandals having soles of gold, and the leathern thongs which bound them to his ankles were embossed with the same metal. Both the cloak and sandals were sprinkled with pearls and precious stones, among which the emerald and the *chalchivitl*—a green stone of higher estimation than any other among the Aztecs—were conspicuous. On his head he wore no other ornament than a *panache* of plumes of the royal green which floated down his back, the badge of military, rather than of regal, rank.

He was at this time about forty years of age. His person was tall and thin, but not ill-made. His hair, which was black and straight, was not very long; to wear it short was considered unbecoming persons of rank. His beard was thin; his complexion somewhat paler than is often found in his dusky, or rather copper-colored race. His features, though serious in their expression, did not wear the look of melancholy, indeed of dejection, which characterizes his portrait, and which may well have settled on them at a later period. He moved with dignity, and his whole demeanor, tempered by an expression of benignity not to have been anticipated from the reports circulated of his character, was worthy of a great prince.—Such is the portrait left to us of the celebrated Indian emperor, in this his first interview with the white men.

The army halted as he drew near. Cortés, dismounting, threw his reins to a page, and, supported by a few of the principal cavaliers, advanced to meet him. The interview must have been one of uncommon interest to both. In Montezuma, Cortés beheld the lord of the broad realms he had traversed, whose magnificence and power had been the burden of every tongue. In the Spaniard, on the other hand, the Aztec prince saw the strange being whose history seemed to be so mysteriously connected with his own; the predicted one of his oracles, whose achievements proclaimed him something more than human. But, whatever may have been the monarch's feelings, he so far suppressed them as to receive his guest with princely courtesy, and to express his satisfaction at personally seeing him in his capital. Cortés responded by the most profound expressions of respect, while he made ample acknowledgments for the substantial proofs which the emperor had given the Spaniards of his munificence. He then hung round Montezuma's neck a sparkling chain of colored crystal, accompanying this with a movement as if to embrace him, when he was restrained by the two Aztec lords, shocked at the menaced profanation of the sacred person of their master. After the interchange of these civilities, Montezuma appointed his brother to conduct the Spaniards to their residence in the capital, and again entering his litter was borne off amidst prostrate crowds in the same state in which he had come. The Spaniards quickly followed, and with colors flying and music playing soon made their entrance into the southern quarter of Tenochtitlan.

[THE AGE OF CHIVALRY] [3]

THE period which we are reviewing was still the age of chivalry; that stirring and adventurous age, of which we can form little conception in the present day of sober, practical reality. The Spaniard, with his nice point of honor, high romance, and proud, vainglorious vaunt, was the true representative of that age. The Europeans, generally, had not yet learned to accommodate themselves to a life of literary toil, or to the drudgery of trade, or the patient tillage of the soil. They left these to the hooded inmate of the cloister, the humble burgher, and the miserable serf. Arms was the only profession worthy of gentle blood,—the only career which the high-mettled cavalier could tread with honor. The New World, with its strange and mysterious perils, afforded a noble theatre for the exercise of his calling; and the Spaniard entered on it with all the enthusiasm of a paladin of romance.

Other nations entered on it also, but with different motives. The French sent forth their missionaries to take up their dwelling among the heathen, who, in the good work of winning souls to Paradise, were content to wear —nay, sometimes seemed to court—the crown of martyrdom. The Dutch, too, had their mission, but it was one of worldly lucre, and they found a recompense for toil and suffering in their gainful traffic with the natives. While our own Puritan fathers, with the true Anglo-Saxon spirit, left their pleasant homes across the waters, and pitched their tents in the howling wilderness, that they might enjoy the sweets of civil and religious freedom. But the Spaniard came over to the New World in the true spirit of a knight-errant, courting adventure however perilous, wooing danger, as it would seem, for its own sake. With sword and lance, he was ever ready to do battle for the Faith; and, as he raised his old war-cry of "St. Jago," he fancied himself fighting under the banner of the military apostle, and felt his single arm a match for more than a hundred infidels!—It was the expiring age of chivalry: and Spain, romantic Spain, was the land where its light lingered longest above the horizon.

[THE SURRENDER OF MEXICO CITY] [4]

THERE was no occasion to resort to artificial means to precipitate the ruin of the Aztecs. It was accelerated every hour by causes more potent than those arising from mere human agency. There they were,—pent up in their close and suffocating quarters, nobles, commoners, and slaves, men, women, and children, some in houses, more frequently in hovels,—for this part of the city was not the best,—others in the open air in canoes, or in the streets, shivering in the cold rains of night, and scorched by the burning heat of day. An old chronicler mentions the fact of two women of rank remaining three

[3] From Book VI, chapter iii.
[4] From Book VI, chapter viii.

days and nights up to their necks in the water among the reeds, with only a handful of maize for their support. The ordinary means of sustaining life were long since gone. They wandered about in search of anything, however unwholesome or revolting, that might mitigate the fierce gnawings of hunger. Some hunted for insects and worms on the borders of the lake, or gathered the salt weeds and moss from its bottom, while at times they might be seen casting a wistful look at the green hills beyond, which many of them had left to share the fate of their brethren in the capital.

To their credit, it is said by the Spanish writers, that they were not driven, in their extremity, to violate the laws of naure by feeding on one another. But unhappily this is contradicted by the Indian authorities, who state that many a mother, in her agony, devoured the offspring which she had no longer the means of supporting. This is recorded of more than one siege in history; and it is the more probable here, where the sensibilities must have been blunted by familiarity with the brutal practices of the national superstition.

But all was not sufficient, and hundreds of famished wretches died every day from extremity of suffering. Some dragged themselves into the houses, and drew their last breath alone, and in silence. Others sank down in the public streets. Wherever they died, there they were left. There was no one to bury, or to remove them. Familiarity with the spectacle made men indifferent to it. They looked on in dumb despair, waiting for their own turn. There was no complaint, no lamentation, but deep, unutterable woe.

If in other quarters of the town the corpses might be seen scattered over the streets, here they were gathered in heaps. "They lay so thick," says Bernal Diaz, "that one could not tread except among the bodies." "A man could not set his foot down," says Cortés, yet more strongly, "unless on the corpse of an Indian!" They were piled one upon another, the living mingled with the dead. They stretched themselves on the bodies of their friends, and lay down to sleep there. Death was everywhere. The city was a vast charnel-house, in which all was hastening to decay and decomposition. A poisonous steam arose from the mass of putrefaction, under the action of alternate rain and heat, which so tainted the whole atmosphere, that the Spaniards, including the general himself, in their brief visits to the quarter, were made ill by it, and it bred a pestilence that swept off even greater numbers than the famine.

Men's minds were unsettled by these strange and accumulated horrors. They resorted to all the superstitious rites prescribed by their religion, to stay the pestilence. They called on their priests to invoke the gods in their behalf. But the oracles were dumb, or gave only gloomy responses. Their deities had deserted them, and in their place they saw signs of celestial wrath, telling of still greater woes in reserve. Many, after the siege, declared, that, among other prodigies, they beheld a stream of light, of a blood-red color, coming from the north in the direction of Tepejacac, with a rushing noise, like that of a whirlwind, which swept round the district of Tlatelolco, darting out sparkles and flakes of fire, till it shot far into the centre of the lake! In the disordered state of their nerves, a mysterious fear took possession of their senses. Prodigies were of familiar occurrence, and the most familiar phenomena of nature were converted into prodigies. Stunned by their calamities, reason was bewildered, and they became the sport of the wildest and most superstitious fancies.

In the midst of these awful scenes, the young emperor of the Aztecs remained, according to all accounts, calm and courageous. With his fair capital laid in ruins before his eyes, his nobles and faithful subjects dying around him, his territory rent away, foot by foot, till scarce enough remained for him to stand on, he rejected every invitation to capitulate, and showed the same indomitable spirit as at the commencement of the siege. When Cortés, in the hope that the extremities of the besieged would incline them to listen to an accommodation, persuaded a noble prisoner to bear to Guatemozin his proposals to that effect; the fierce young monarch, according to the general, ordered him at once to be sacrificed. It is a Spaniard, we must remember, who tells the story.

Cortés, who had suspended hostilities for several days, in the vain hope that the distresses of the Mexicans would bend them to submission, now determined to drive them to it by a general assault. Cooped up, as they were, within a narrow quarter of the city, their position favored such an attempt. He commanded Alvarado to hold himself in readiness, and directed Sandoval—who, besides the causeway, had charge of the fleet, which lay off the Tlatelolcan district—to support the attack by a cannonade on the houses near the water. He then led his forces into the city, or rather across the horrid waste that now encircled it.

On entering the Indian precincts, he was met by several of the chiefs, who, stretching forth their emaciated arms, exclaimed, "You are the children of the Sun. But the Sun is swift in his course. Why are you, then, so tardy? Why do you delay so long to put an end to our miseries? Rather kill us at once, that we may go to our god Huitzilopochtli, who waits for us in heaven to give us rest from our sufferings!"

Cortés was moved by their piteous appeal, and answered, that he desired not their death, but their submission. "Why does your master refuse to treat with me," he said, "when a single hour will suffice for me to crush him and all his people?" He then urged them to request Guatemozin to confer with him, with the assurance that he might do it in safety, as his person should not be molested.

The nobles, after some persuasion, undertook the mission; and it was received by the young monarch in a manner which showed—if the anecdote before related of him be true—that misfortune had, at length, asserted some power over his haughty spirit. He consented to the interview, though not to have it take place on that day, but the following, in the great square of Tlatelolco. Cortés, well satisfied, immediately withdrew from the city, and resumed his position on the causeway.

The next morning he presented himself at the place appointed, having previously stationed Alvarado there with a strong corps of infantry, to guard against treachery. The stone platform in the centre of the square was covered with mats and carpets, and a banquet was prepared to refresh the famished monarch and his nobles. Having made these arrangements, he awaited the hour of the interview.

But Guatemozin, instead of appearing himself, sent his nobles, the same who had brought to him the general's invitation, and who now excused their master's absence on the plea of illness. Cortés, though disappointed, gave a courteous reception to the envoys, considering that it might still afford the means of opening a communication with the emperor. He persuaded them, without much entreaty, to partake of the good cheer spread before them, which they did with a voracity that told how severe had been their abstinence. He then dismissed them with a seasonable supply of provisions for their master, pressing him to consent to an interview, without which it was impossible their differences could be adjusted.

The Indian envoys returned in a short time, bearing with them a present of fine cotton fabrics, of no great value, from Guatemozin, who still declined to meet the Spanish general. Cortés, though deeply chagrined, was unwilling to give up the point. "He will surely come," he said to the envoys, "when he sees that I suffer you to go and come unharmed, you who have been my steady enemies, no less than himself, throughout the war. He has nothing to fear from me." He again parted with them, promising to receive their answer the following day.

On the next morning, the Aztec chiefs, entering the Christian quarters, announced to Cortés that Guatemozin would confer with him at noon in the market place. The general was punctual at the hour; but without success. Neither monarch nor ministers appeared there. It was plain that the Indian prince did not care to trust the promises of his enemy. A thought of Montezuma may have passed across his mind. After he had waited three hours the general's patience was exhausted, and, as he learned that the Mexicans were busy in preparations for defence, he made immediate dispositions for the assault.

The confederates had been left without the walls, for he did not care to bring them in sight of the quarry, before he was ready to slip the leash. He now ordered them to join him; and supported by Alvarado's division, marched at once into the enemy's quarters. He found them prepared to receive him. Their most able-bodied warriors were thrown into the van, covering their feeble and crippled comrades. Women were seen occasionally mingling in the ranks, and, as well as children, thronged the *azoteas,* where, with famine-stricken visages, and haggard eyes, they scowled defiance and hatred on their invaders.

As the Spaniards advanced, the Mexicans set up a fierce war cry, and sent off clouds of arrows with their accustomed spirit, while the women and boys rained down darts and stones from their elevated position on the terraces. But the missiles were sent by hands too feeble to do much damage; and, when the squadrons closed, the loss of strength became still more sensible in the Aztecs. Their blows fell feebly and with doubtful aim, though some, it is true, of stronger constitution, or gathering strength from despair, maintained to the last a desperate fight.

The arquebusiers now poured in a deadly fire. The brigantines replied by successive volleys, in the opposite quarter. The besieged, hemmed in, like deer surrounded by the huntsmen, were brought down on every side. The carnage was horrible. The ground was heaped up with slain, until the maddened combatants were obliged to climb over the human mounds to get at one another. The miry soil was saturated with blood, which ran off like water, and dyed the canals themselves with crimson. All was uproar and terrible confusion. The hideous yells of the barbarians; the oaths and execrations of the Spaniards; the cries of the wounded; the shrieks of women and children; the heavy blows of the Conquerors; the death-struggle of their victims; the rapid, reverberating echoes of musketry; the hissing of innumerable missiles; the crash and crackling of blazing buildings, crushing hundreds in their ruins; the blinding volumes of dust and sulphurous smoke shrouding all in their gloomy canopy,—made a scene appalling even to the soldiers of Cortés, steeled as they were by many a rough passage of war, and by long familiarity with blood and violence. "The piteous cries of the women and children, in particular," says the general, "were enough to break one's heart." He commanded that they should be spared, and that all who asked it should receive quarter. He particularly urged this on the confederates, and placed men among them to restrain their violence. But he had set an engine in motion too terrible to be controlled. It were as easy to curb the hurricane in its fury, as the passions of an infuriated horde of savages. "Never did I see so pitiless a race," he exclaims, "or anything wearing the form of man so destitute of humanity." They made no distinction of sex or age, and in this hour of vengeance seemed to be requiting the hoarded wrongs of a century. At length, sated with slaughter, the Spanish commander sounded a retreat. It was full time, if according to his own statement,—we may hope it is an exaggeration,—forty thousand souls had perished! Yet their fate was to be envied, in comparison with that of those who survived.

Through the long night which followed, no movement was perceptible in the Aztec quarter. No light was seen there, no sound was heard, save the low moaning of some wounded or dying wretch, writhing in his agony. All was dark and silent,—the darkness of the grave. The last blow seemed to have completely stunned them. They had parted with hope, and sat in sullen despair, like men waiting in silence the stroke of the executioner. Yet, for all this, they showed no disposition to submit. Every new injury had sunk deeper into their souls, and filled them with a deeper hatred of their enemy. Fortune, friends, kindred, home,—all were gone. They were content to throw away life itself, now that they had nothing more to live for.

Far different was the scene in the Christian camp, where, elated with their recent successes, all was alive with bustle, and preparation for the morrow. Bonfires were seen blazing along the causeways, lights gleamed from tents and barracks, and the sounds of music and merriment, borne over the waters, proclaimed the joy of the soldiers, at the prospect of so soon terminating their wearisome campaign.

On the following morning the Spanish commander again mustered his forces, having decided to follow up the blow of the preceding day, before the enemy should have time to rally, and, at once, to put an end to the war. He had arranged with Alvarado, on the evening previous, to occupy the market place of Tlatelolco; and the discharge of an arquebuse was to be the signal for a simultaneous assault. Sandoval was to hold the northern causeway, and, with the fleet, to watch the movements of the Indian emperor, and to intercept the flight to the main land, which Cortés knew he meditated. To allow him to effect this would be to leave a formidable enemy in his own neighborhood, who might at any time kindle the flame of insurrection throughout the country. He ordered Sandoval, however, to do no harm to the royal person, and not to fire on the enemy at all, except in self-defence.

It was the memorable 13th of August, 1521, the day of St. Hypolito,—from this circumstance selected as the patron saint of modern Mexico,—that Cortés led his warlike array for the last time across the black and blasted environs which lay around the Indian capital. On entering the Aztec precincts he paused, willing to afford its wretched inmates one more chance of escape, before striking the fatal blow. He obtained an interview with some of the principal chiefs, and expostulated with them on the conduct of their prince. "He surely will not," said the general, "see you all perish, when he can so easily save you." He then urged them to prevail on Guatemozin to hold a conference with him, repeating the assurances of his personal safety.

The messengers went on their mission, and soon returned with the *ci-huacoatl* at their head, a magistrate of high authority among the Mexicans. He said, with a melancholy air, in which his own disappointment was visible, that "Guatemozin was ready to die where he was, but would hold no interview with the Spanish commander"; adding, in a tone of resignation, "it is for you to work your pleasure." "Go, then," replied the stern Conqueror, "and prepare your countrymen for death. Their hour is come."

He still postponed the assault for several hours. But the impatience of his troops at this delay was heightened by the rumor that Guatemozin and his nobles were preparing to escape with their effects in the *piraguas* and canoes which were moored on the margin of the lake. Convinced of the fruitlessness and impolicy of further procrastination, Cortés made his final dispositions for the attack, and took his own station on an *azotea,* which commanded the theatre of operations.

When the assailants came into presence of the enemy, they found them huddled together in the utmost confusion, all ages and sexes, in masses so dense that they nearly forced one another over the brink of the causeways into the water below. Some had climbed on the terraces, others feebly supported themselves against the walls of the buildings. Their squalid and tattered garments gave a wildness to their appearance, which still further heightened the ferocity of their expression, as they glared on their enemy with eyes in which hate was mingled with despair. When the Spaniards had approached within bowshot, the Aztecs let off a flight of impotent missiles, showing, to the last, the resolute spirit, though they had lost the strength, of their better days. The fatal signal was then given by the discharge of an arquebuse,—speedily followed by peals of heavy ordnance, the rattle of firearms, and the hellish shouts of the confederates, as they sprang upon their victims. It is unnecessary to stain the page with a repetition of the horrors of the preceding day. Some of the wretched Aztecs threw themselves into the water, and were picked up by the canoes. Others sunk and were suffocated in the canals. The number of these became so great, that a bridge was made of their dead bodies, over which the assailants could climb to the opposite banks. Others again, especially the women, begged for mercy, which, as the chroniclers assure us, was everywhere granted by the Spaniards, and contrary to the instructions and entreaties of Cortés, everywhere refused by the confederates.

While this work of butchery was going on, numbers were observed pushing off in the barks that lined the shore, and making the best of their way across the lake. They were constantly intercepted by the brigantines, which broke through the flimsy array of boats; sending off their volleys to the right and left, as the crews of the latter hotly assailed them. The battle raged as fiercely on the lake as on the land. Many of the Indian vessels were shattered and overturned. Some few, however, under cover of the smoke, which rolled darkly over the waters, succeeded in clearing themselves of the turmoil, and were fast nearing the opposite shore.

Sandoval had particularly charged his captains to keep an eye on the movements of any vessel in which it was at all probable that Guatemozin might be concealed. At this crisis, three or four of the largest *piraguas* were seen skimming over the water, and making their way rapidly across the lake. A captain, named Garci Holguin, who had command of one of the best sailers in the fleet, instantly gave them chase. The wind was favorable, and, every moment, he gained on the fugitives, who pulled their oars with a vigor that despair alone could have given. But it was in vain; and, after a short race, Holguin, coming alongside of one of the *piraguas,* which, whether from its appearance, or from information he had received, he conjectured might bear the Indian emperor, ordered his men to level their crossbows at the boat. But, before they could discharge them, a cry arose from those in it that their lord was on board. At the same moment, a young warrior, armed with buckler and *maquahuitl,* rose up, as if to beat off the assailants. But, as the Spanish captain ordered his men not to shoot, he dropped his weapons, and exclaimed, "I am Guatemozin; lead me to Malinche, I am his prisoner; but let no harm come to my wife and my followers."

Holguin assured him that his wishes should be respected, and assisted him to get on board the brigantine, followed by his wife and attendants. These were twenty in number, consisting of Coanaco, the deposed lord of Tezcuco, the lord of Tlacopan, and several other caciques and dignitaries, whose rank, probably, had secured them some exemption from the general calamities of the siege. When the captives were seated on the deck of his vessel, Holguin requested the Aztec prince to put an end to the combat by commanding his people in the other canoes to surrender. But, with a dejected air, he replied, "It is not necessary. They will fight no longer, when they see that their . prince is taken." He spoke truth. The news of Guatemozin's capture spread rapidly through the fleet, and on shore, where the Mexicans were still engaged in conflict with their enemies. It ceased, however, at once. They made no further resistance; and those on the water quickly followed the brigantines, which conveyed their captive monarch to land. It seemed as if the fight had been maintained thus long, the better to divert the enemy's attention, and cover their master's retreat.

Meanwhile Sandoval, on receiving tidings of the capture, brought his own brigantine alongside of Holguin's, and demanded the royal prisoner to be surrendered to him. But his captain claimed him as his prize. A dispute arose between the parties, each anxious to have the glory of the deed, and perhaps the privilege of commemorating it on his escutcheon. The controversy continued so long that it reached the ears of Cortés, who, in his station on the *azotea,* had learned, with no little satisfaction, the capture of his enemy. He instantly sent orders to his wrangling officers to bring Guatemozin before him, that he might adjust the difference between them. He charged them, at the same time, to treat their prisoner with respect. He then made preparations for the interview; caused the terrace to be carpeted with crimson cloth and matting, and a table to be spread with provisions, of which the unhappy Aztecs stood so much in need. His lovely Indian mistress, Doña Marina, was present to act as interpreter. She had stood by his side through all the troubled scenes of the Conquest, and she was there now to witness its triumphant termination.

Guatemozin, on landing, was escorted by a company of infantry to the presence of the Spanish commander. He mounted the *azotea* with a calm and steady step, and was easily to be distinguished from his attendant nobles, though his full, dark eye was no longer lighted up with its accustomed fire, and his features wore an expression of passive resignation, that told little of the fierce and fiery spirit that burned within. His head was large, his limbs well proportioned, his complexion fairer than those of his bronze-colored nation, and his whole deportment singularly mild and engaging.

Cortés came forward with a dignified and studied courtesy to receive him. The Aztec monarch probably knew the person of his conqueror, for he first broke silence by saying, "I have done all that I could, to defend myself and my people. I am now reduced to this state. You will deal with me, Malinche, as you list." Then, laying his hand on the hilt of a poniard, stuck in the general's belt, he added, with vehemence, "Better despatch me with this, and rid me of life at once." Cortés was filled with admiration at the proud bearing of the young barbarian, showing in his reverses a spirit worthy of an ancient Roman. "Fear not," he replied, "you shall be treated with all honor. You have defended your capital like a brave warrior. A Spaniard knows how to respect valor even in an enemy." He then inquired of him, where he had left the princess, his wife; and, being informed that she still remained under protection of a Spanish guard on board the brigantine, the general sent to have her escorted to his presence.

She was the youngest daughter of Montezuma, and was hardly yet on the verge of womanhood. On the accession of her cousin, Guatemozin, to the throne, she had been wedded to him as his lawful wife. She is celebrated by her contemporaries for her personal charms; and the beautiful princess, Te-cuichpo, is still commemorated by the Spaniards, since from her, by a subsequent marriage, are descended some of the illustrious families of their own nation. She was kindly received by Cortés, who showed her the respectful attentions suited to her rank. Her birth, no doubt, gave her an additional interest in his eyes, and he may have felt some touch of compunction, as he gazed on the daughter of the unfortunate Montezuma. He invited his royal captives to partake of the refreshments, which their exhausted condition rendered so necessary. Meanwhile the Spanish commander made his dispositions for the night, ordering Sandoval to escort the prisoners to Cojohua-can, whither he proposed, himself immediately to follow. The other captains, Olid and Alvarado, were to draw off their forces to their respective quarters.

It was impossible for them to continue in the capital, where the poisonous effluvia from the unburied carcasses loaded the air with infection. A small guard only was stationed to keep order in the wasted suburbs.—It was the hour of vespers when Guatemozin surrendered, and the siege might be considered as then concluded. The evening set in dark, and the rain began to fall, before the several parties had evacuated the city.

During the night, a tremendous tempest, such as the Spaniards had rarely witnessed, and such as is known only within the tropics, burst over the Mexican Valley. The thunder, reverberating from the rocky amphitheatre of hills, bellowed over the waste of waters, and shook the *teocallis* and crazy tenements of Tenochtitlan—the few that yet survived—to their foundations. The lightning seemed to cleave asunder the vault of heaven, as its vivid flashes wrapped the whole scene in a ghastly glare, for a moment, to be again swallowed up in darkness. The war of elements was in unison with the fortunes of the ruined city. It seemed as if the deities of Anahuac, scared from their ancient abodes, were borne along shrieking and howling in the blast, as they abandoned the fallen capital to its fate!

On the day following the surrender, Guatemozin requested the Spanish commander to allow the Mexicans to leave the city, and to pass unmolested into the open country. To this Cortés readily assented, as, indeed, without it he could take no steps for purifying the capital. He gave his orders, accordingly, for the evacuation of the place, commanding that no one, Spaniard or confederate, should offer violence to the Aztecs, or in any way obstruct their departure. The whole number of these is variously estimated at from thirty to seventy thousand, besides women and children, who had survived the sword, pestilence, and famine. It is certain they were three days in defiling along the several causeways,—a mournful train; husbands and wives, parents and children, the sick and the wounded, leaning on one another for support, as they feebly tottered along, squalid, and but half covered with rags, that disclosed at every step hideous gashes, some recently received, others festering from long neglect, and carrying with them an atmosphere of contagion. Their wasted forms and famine-stricken faces told the whole history of the siege; and, as the straggling files gained the opposite shore, they were observed to pause from time to time, as if to take one more look at the spot so lately crowned by the imperial city, once their pleasant home, and endeared to them by many a glorious recollection.

On the departure of the inhabitants, measures were immediately taken to purify the place, by means of numerous fires kept burning day and night, especially in the infected quarter of Tlatelolco, and by collecting the heaps of dead, which lay mouldering in the streets, and consigning them to the earth. —Of the whole number, who perished in the course of the siege, it is impossible to form any probable computation. The accounts range widely from one hundred and twenty thousand, the lowest estimate, to two hundred and forty thousand. The number of the Spaniards who fell was comparatively small, but that of the allies must have been large, if the historian of Tezcuco is correct in asserting that thirty thousand perished of his own countrymen alone. That the number of those destroyed within the city was immense cannot be doubted, when we consider, that, besides its own redundant population, it was thronged with that of the neighboring towns, who, distrusting their strength to resist the enemy, sought protection within its walls.

The booty found there—that is, the treasures of gold and jewels, the only booty of much value in the eyes of the Spaniards—fell far below their expectations. It did not exceed, according to the general's statement, a hundred and thirty thousand *castellanos* of gold, including the sovereign's share, which, indeed, taking into account many articles of curious and costly workmanship, voluntarily relinquished by the army, greatly exceeded his legitimate fifth. Yet the Aztecs must have been in possession of a much larger treasure, if it were only the wreck of that recovered from the Spaniards on the night of the memorable flight from Mexico. Some of the spoil may have been sent away from the capital; some spent in preparations for defence, and more of it buried in the earth, or sunk in the water of the lake. Their menaces were not without a meaning. They had, at least, the satisfaction of disappointing the avarice of their enemies.

Cortés had no further occasion for the presence of his Indian allies. He assembled the chiefs of the different squadrons, thanked them for their services, noticed their valor in flattering terms, and, after distributing presents among them, with the assurance that his master, the Emperor, would recompense their fidelity yet more largely, dismissed them to their own homes. They carried off a liberal share of the spoils, of which they had plundered the dwellings,—not of a kind to excite the cupidity of the Spaniards,—and returned in triumph, short-sighted triumph! at the success of their expedition, and the downfall of the Aztec dynasty.

Great, also, was the satisfaction of the Spaniards at this brilliant termination of their long and laborious campaign. They were, indeed, disappointed at the small amount of treasure found in the conquered city. But the soldier is usually too much absorbed in the present to give much heed to the future; and, though their discontent showed itself afterwards in a more clamorous form, they now thought only of their triumph, and abandoned themselves to jubilee. Cortés celebrated the event by a banquet, as sumptuous as circumstances would permit, to which all the cavaliers and officers were invited. Loud and long was their revelry, which was carried to such an excess, as provoked the animadversion of father Olmedo, who intimated that this was not the fitting way to testify their sense of the favors shown them by the Almighty. Cortés admitted the justice of the rebuke, but craved some indulgence for a soldier's license in the hour of victory. The following day was appointed for the commemoration of their successes in a more suitable manner.

A procession of the whole army was then formed with father Olmedo at its head. The soiled and tattered banners of Castile, which had waved over many a field of battle, now threw their shadows on the peaceful array of the soldiery, as they slowly moved along, rehearsing the litany, and displaying the image of the Virgin and the blessed symbol of man's redemption. The reverend father pronounced a discourse, in which he briefly reminded the troops of their great cause for thankfulness to Providence for conducting them safe through their long and perilous pilgrimage; and, dwelling on the responsibility incurred by their present position, he besought them not to abuse the rights of conquest, but to treat the unfortunate Indians with humanity. The sacrament was then administered to the commander-in-chief and the principal cavaliers, and the services concluded with a solemn thanksgiving to the God of battles, who had enabled them to carry the banner of the Cross triumphant over this barbaric empire.

Thus, after a siege of nearly three months' duration, unmatched in history for the constancy and courage of the besieged, seldom surpassed for the severity of its sufferings, fell the renowned capital of the Aztecs. Unmatched, it may be truly said, for constancy and courage, when we recollect that the door of capitulation on the most honorable terms was left open to them throughout the whole blockade, and that, sternly rejecting every proposal of their enemy, they, to a man, preferred to die rather than surrender. More than three centuries had elapsed, since the Aztecs, a poor and wandering tribe from the far Northwest had come on the plateau. There they built their miserable collection of huts on the spot—as tradition tells us—prescribed by the oracle. Their conquests, at first confined to their immediate neighborhood, gradually covered the Valley, then crossing the mountains, swept over the broad extent of the table-land, descended its precipitous sides, and rolled onwards to the Mexican Gulf, and the distant confines of Central America. Their wretched capital, meanwhile, keeping pace with the enlargement of territory, had grown into a flourishing city, filled with buildings, monuments of art, and a numerous population, that gave it the first rank among the capitals of the Western World. At this crisis, came over another race from the remote East, strangers like themselves, whose coming had also been predicted by the oracle, and, appearing on the plateau, assailed them in the very zenith of their prosperity, and blotted them out from the map of nations forever! The whole story has the air of fable, rather than of history! a legend of romance,—a tale of the genii!

Yet we cannot regret the fall of an empire which did so little to promote the happiness of its subjects or the real interests of humanity. Notwithstanding the lustre thrown over its latter days by the glorious defence of its capital, by the mild munificence of Montezuma, by the dauntless heroism of Guatemozin, the Aztecs were emphatically a fierce and brutal race, little calculated, in their best aspects, to excite our sympathy and regard. Their civilization, such as it was, was not their own, but reflected, perhaps imperfectly, from a race whom they had succeeded in the land. It was, in respect to the Aztecs, a generous graft on a vicious stock, and could have brought no fruit to perfection. They ruled over their wide domains with a sword, instead of a sceptre. They did nothing to ameliorate the condition, or in any way promote the progress, of their vassals. Their vassals were serfs, used only to minister to their pleasure, held in awe by armed garrisons, ground to the dust by imposts in peace, by military conscriptions in war. They did not, like the Romans, whom they resembled in the nature of their conquests, extend the rights of citizenship to the conquered. They did not amalgamate them into one great nation, with common rights and interests. They held them as aliens, —even those who in the Valley were gathered round the very walls of the capital. The Aztec metropolis, the heart of the monarchy, had not a sympathy, not a pulsation, in common with the rest of the body politic. It was a stranger in its own land.

The Aztecs not only did not advance the condition of their vassals, but, morally speaking, they did much to degrade it. How can a nation, where human sacrifices prevail, and especially when combined with cannibalism, further the march of civilization? How can the interests of humanity be consulted, where man is levelled to the rank of the brutes that perish? The influence of the Aztecs introduced their gloomy superstition into lands before unacquainted with it, or where, at least, it was not established in any great strength. The example of the capital was contagious. As the latter increased in opulence, the religious celebrations were conducted with still more terrible magnificence; in the same manner as the gladiatorial shows of the Romans increased in pomp with the increasing splendor of the capital. Men became familiar with scenes of horror and the most loathsome abominations. Women and children—the whole nation—became familiar with, and assisted at them. The heart was hardened, the manners were made ferocious, the feeble light of civilization, transmitted from a milder race, was growing fainter and fainter, as thousands and thousands of miserable victims, throughout the empire, were yearly fattened in its cages, sacrificed on its altars, dressed and served at its banquets! The whole land was converted into a vast human shambles! The empire of the Aztecs did not fall before its time.

Whether these unparalleled outrages furnish a sufficient plea to the Spaniards for their invasion, whether, with the Protestant, we are content to find a warrant for it in the natural rights and demands of civilization, or, with the Roman Catholic, in the good pleasure of the Pope,—on the one or the other of which grounds, the conquests by most Christian nations in the East and the West have been defended,—it is unnecessary to discuss, as it has already been considered in a former Chapter. It is more material to inquire, whether, assuming the right, the conquest of Mexico was conducted with a proper regard to the claims of humanity. And here we must admit, that, with all allowance for the ferocity of the age and the laxity of its principles, there are passages which every Spaniard, who cherishes the fame of his countrymen, would be glad to see expunged from their history; passages not to be vindicated on the score of self-defence, or of necessity of any kind, and which must forever leave a dark spot on the annals of the Conquest. And yet, taken as a whole, the invasion, up to the capture of the capital, was conducted on principles less revolting to humanity, than most, perhaps than any, of the other conquests of the Castilian crown in the New World.

It may seem slight praise to say that the followers of Cortés used no bloodhounds to hunt down their wretched victims, as in some other parts of the Continent, nor exterminated a peaceful and submissive population in mere wantonness of cruelty, as in the Islands. Yet it is something that they were not so far infected by the spirit of the age, and that their swords were rarely stained with blood, unless it was indispensable to the success of their enterprise. Even in the last siege of the capital, the sufferings of the Aztecs, terrible as they were, do not imply any unusual cruelty in the victors; they were not greater than those inflicted on their own countrymen at home, in many a memorable instance, by the most polished nations, not merely of ancient times, but of our own. They were the inevitable consequences which follow from war, when, instead of being confined to its legitimate field, it is brought home to the hearthstone, to the peaceful community of the city,—its burghers untrained to arms, its women and children yet more defenceless. In the present instance, indeed, the sufferings of the besieged were in a great degree to be charged on themselves,—on their patriotic, but desperate, self-devotion. It was not the desire, as certainly it was not the interest, of the Spaniards, to destroy the capital, or its inhabitants. When any of these fell into their hands, they were kindly entertained, their wants supplied, and every means taken to infuse into them a spirit of conciliation; and this, too, it should be remembered, in despite of the dreadful doom to which they consigned their Christian captives. The gates of a fair capitulation were kept open, though unavailingly, to the last hour.

The right of conquest necessarily implies that of using whatever force may be necessary for overcoming resistance to the assertion of that right. For the Spaniards to have done otherwise than they did would have been to abandon the siege, and, with it, the conquest of the country. To have suffered the inhabitants, with their high-spirited monarch, to escape, would but have prolonged the miseries of war by transferring it to another and more inaccessible quarter. They literally, as far as the success of the expedition was concerned, had no choice. If our imagination is struck with the amount of suffering in this, and in similar scenes of the Conquest, it should be borne in mind, that it is a natural result of the great masses of men engaged in the conflict. The amount of suffering does not of itself show the amount of cruelty which caused it; and it is but justice to the Conquerors of Mexico to say, that the very brilliancy and importance of their exploits have given a melancholy celebrity to their misdeeds, and thrown them into somewhat bolder relief than strictly belongs to them.—It is proper that thus much should be stated, not to excuse their excesses, but that we may be enabled to make a more impartial estimate of their conduct, as compared with that of other nations under similar circumstances, and that we may not visit them with peculiar obloquy for evils which necessarily flow from the condition of war. I have not drawn a veil over these evils; for the historian should not shrink from depicting, in their true colors, the atrocities of a condition, over which success is apt to throw a false halo of glory, but which, bursting asunder the strong bonds of human fellowship, purchases its triumphs by arming the hand of man against his brother, makes a savage of the civilized, and kindles the fires of hell in the bosom of the savage.

Whatever may be thought of the Conquest in a moral view, regarded as a military achievement it must fill us with astonishment. That a handful of adventurers, indifferently armed and equipped, should have landed on the shores of a powerful empire inhabited by a fierce and warlike race, and, in defiance of the reiterated prohibitions of its sovereign, have forced their way into the interior;—that they should have done this, without knowledge of the language or of the land, without chart or compass to guide them, without any idea of the difficulties they were to encounter, totally uncertain whether the next step might bring them on a hostile nation, or on a desert, feeling their way along in the dark, as it were;—that, though nearly overwhelmed by their first encounter with the inhabitants, they should have still pressed on to the capital of the empire, and, having reached it, thrown themselves unhesitatingly into the midst of their enemies;—that, so far from being daunted by the extraordinary spectacle there exhibited of power and civilization, they should have been but the more confirmed in their original design;—that they should have seized the monarch, have executed his ministers before the eyes of his subjects, and, when driven forth with ruin from the gates, have gathered their scattered wreck together, and after a system of operations, pursued with consummate policy and daring, have succeeded in overturning the capital, and establishing their sway over the country;—that all this should have been so effected by a mere handful of indigent adventurers, is a fact little short of the miraculous,—too startling for the probabilities demanded by fiction, and without a parallel in the pages of history.

Yet this must not be understood too literally; for it would be unjust to the Aztecs themselves, at least to their military prowess, to regard the Conquest as directly achieved by the Spaniards alone. This would indeed be to arm the latter with the charmed shield of Ruggiero, and the magic lance of Astolfo, overturning its hundreds at a touch. The Indian empire was in a manner conquered by Indians. The first terrible encounter of the Spaniards with the Tlascalans, which had nearly proved their ruin, did in fact insure their success. It secured to them a strong native support, on which to retreat in the hour of trouble, and round which they could rally the kindred races of the land for one great and overwhelming assault. The Aztec monarchy fell by the hands of its own subjects, under the direction of European sagacity and science. Had it been united, it might have bidden defiance to the invaders. As it was, the capital was dissevered from the rest of the country, and the bolt, which might have passed off comparatively harmless, had the empire been cemented by a common principle of loyalty and patriotism, now found its way into every crack and crevice of the ill-compacted fabric, and buried it in its own ruins. —Its fate may serve as a striking proof, that a government, which does not rest on the sympathies of its subjects, cannot long abide; that human institutions, when not connected with human prosperity and progress, must fall, —if not before the increasing light of civilization, by the hand of violence; by violence from within, if not from without. And who shall lament their fall?

FRANCIS PARKMAN

(1823–1893)

Francis Parkman was born in Boston in 1823. Being delicate, he spent much of his childhood at his grandfather's home on the border of Middlesex Fells, where he came to know the forest and received the bent that determined his career. He entered Harvard in 1840, and the next year while on a vacation trip in the woods of northern New Hampshire, decided to write a history of the last French war in America,—of a period when "the forest drama was most stirring and the forest stage more thronged with appropriate actors than in any other passage of our history." He kept this project secret, and after receiving his academic degree, studied law for two years at Harvard. Still keeping in mind his plan to write, he went west in 1846 to study Indian life at first hand, and out of his experiences wrote *The Oregon Trail* (1849); but the hardships of the trip led to a breakdown in his health, and directly or indirectly brought on diseases which threatened his sanity, kept him in a wheel chair or on crutches, and made him nearly blind; from these he suffered the rest of his life. But despite ill health he persevered in his determination to write, and in 1848 began *The Conspiracy of Pontiac*. Unable to hold his eyes open, he learned to write legibly with them closed; and his method of composition was to listen to the reading of documents while he made notes, and then to memorize the notes as they were read to him, after which he could begin writing. For long periods he could write no more than six lines a day, and once he had to lay his work by for several years; yet having decided in youth that "not happiness, but achievement" is the end of life, he persisted in his self-imposed task in spite of physical suffering, and when he died, in 1893, he had finished the last of the volumes dealing with the English and French conflict in the New World. During the decade in which he could do no literary work, he turned for occupation to horticulture, became adept in this field, originated several new varieties of flowers, afterwards wrote a book on roses that is still standard, and became for a short time professor of horticulture at Harvard.

As a historian Parkman was accurate and impartial. More than any other writer on the subject, he understood the character of the North American Indian, and succeeded admirably in depicting it. He chose an unexploited field, and by assiduous and patient labors, combined with rare knowledge and understanding, left little to future historians in the same field.

From THE CONSPIRACY OF PONTIAC

[THE INDIAN CHARACTER] [1]

THE fireside stories of every primitive people are faithful reflections of the form and coloring of the national mind; and it is no proof of sound philosophy to turn with contempt from the study of a fairy tale. The legendary lore

[1] This extract is from Volume I, chapter i. In his opening chapter, Parkman discusses the general traits and characteristics of the Indian tribes east of the Mississippi; in the part immediately preceding the selection here given he describes the various tribes of the Algonquin family.

of the Iroquois, black as the midnight forests, awful in its gloomy strength, is but another manifestation of that spirit of mastery which uprooted whole tribes from the earth, and deluged the wilderness with blood. The traditionary tales of the Algonquins wear a different aspect. The credulous circle around an Ojibwa lodge-fire listened to wild recitals of necromancy and witchcraft—men transformed to beasts, and beasts transformed to men, animated trees, and birds who spoke with human tongue. They heard of malignant sorcerers dwelling among the lonely islands of spell-bound lakes; of grisly *weendigoes,* and bloodless *geebi;* of evil *manitoes* lurking in the dens and fastnesses of the woods; of pygmy champions, diminutive in stature but mighty in soul, who, by the potency of charm and talisman, subdued the direst monsters of the waste; and of heroes, who not by downright force and open onset, but by subtle strategy, tricks, or magic art, achieved marvellous triumphs over the brute force of their assailants. Sometimes the tale will breathe a different spirit, and tell of orphan children abandoned in the heart of a hideous wilderness, beset with fiends and cannibals. Some enamored maiden, scornful of earthly suitors, plights her troth to the graceful manito of the grove; or bright aerial beings, dwellers of the sky, descend to tantalize the gaze of mortals with evanescent forms of loveliness.

The mighty giant, the God of the Thunder, who made his home among the caverns, beneath the cataract of Niagara, was a characteristic conception of Iroquois imagination. The Algonquins held a simpler faith, and maintained that the thunder was a bird who built his nest on the pinnacle of towering mountains. Two daring boys once scaled the height, and thrust sticks into the eyes of the portentous nestlings; which hereupon flashed forth such wrathful scintillations, that the sticks were shivered to atoms.

The religious belief of the Algonquins—and the remark holds good, not of the Algonquins only, but of all the hunting tribes of America—is a cloudy bewilderment, where we seek in vain for system or coherency. Among a primitive and savage people, there were no poets to vivify its images, and no priests to give distinctness and harmony to its rites and symbols. To the Indian mind, all nature was instinct with deity. A spirit was embodied in every mountain, lake, and cataract; every bird, beast, or reptile, every tree, shrub, or grass blade, was endued with mystic influence; yet this untutored pantheism did not exclude the conception of certain divinities, of incongruous and ever shifting attributes. The sun, too, was a god, and the moon was a goddess. Conflicting powers of good and evil divided the universe: but if, before the arrival of Europeans, the Indian recognized the existence of one, almighty, self-existent Being, the Great Spirit, the Lord of Heaven and Earth, the belief was so vague and dubious as scarcely to deserve the name. His perceptions of moral good and evil were perplexed and shadowy; and the belief in a state of future reward and punishment was by no means universal.

Of the Indian character, much has been written foolishly, and credulously believed. By the rhapsodies of poets, the cant of sentimentalists, and the extravagance of some who should have known better, a counterfeit image has been tricked out, which might seek in vain for its likeness through every corner of the habitable earth; an image bearing no more resemblance to its original, than the monarch of the tragedy and the hero of the epic poem bear to their living prototypes in the palace and the camp. The shadows of his wilderness home, and the darker mantle of his own inscrutable reserve, have made the Indian warrior a wonder and a mystery. Yet to the eye of rational observation there is nothing unintelligible in him. He is full, it is true, of contradiction. He deems himself the centre of greatness and renown; his pride is proof against the fiercest torments of fire and steel; and yet the same man would beg for a dram of whiskey, or pick up a crust of bread thrown to him like a dog, from the tent door of the traveller. At one moment, he is wary and cautious to the verge of cowardice; at the next, he abandons himself to a very insanity of recklessness; and the habitual self-restraint which throws an impenetrable veil over emotion is joined to the unbridled passions of a madman or a beast.

Such inconsistencies, strange as they seem in our eyes, when viewed under a novel aspect, are but the ordinary incidents of humanity. The qualities of the mind are not uniform in their action through all the relations of life. With different men, and different races of men, pride, valor, prudence, have different forms of manifestation, and where in one instance they lie dormant, in another they are keenly awake. The conjunction of greatness and littleness, meanness and pride, is older than the days of the patriarchs; and such antiquated phenomena, displayed under a new form in the unreflecting, undisciplined mind of a savage, call for no special wonder, but should rather be classed with the other enigmas of the fathomless human heart. The dissecting knife of a Rochefoucault might lay bare matters of no less curious observation in the breast of every man.

Nature has stamped the Indian with a hard and stern physiognomy. Ambition, revenge, envy, jealousy, are his ruling passions; and his cold temperament is little exposed to those effeminate vices which are the bane of milder races. With him revenge is an overpowering instinct; nay, more, it is a point of honor and a duty. His pride sets all language at defiance. He loathes the thought of coercion; and few of his race have ever stooped to discharge a menial office. A wild love of liberty, an utter intolerance of control, lie at the basis of his character, and fire his whole existence. Yet, in spite of this haughty independence, he is a devout hero-worshipper; and high achievement in war or policy touches a chord to which his nature never fails to respond. He looks up with admiring reverence to the sages and heroes of his tribe; and it is this principle, joined to the respect for age springing from the patriarchal element in his social system, which, beyond all others, contributes union and harmony to the erratic members of an Indian community. With him the love of glory kindles into a burning passion; and to allay its cravings, he will dare cold and famine, fire, tempest, torture, and death itself.

These generous traits are overcast by much that is dark, cold, and sinister, by sleepless distrust, and rankling jealousy. Treacherous himself, he is always suspicious of treachery in others. Brave as he is,—and few of mankind are braver,—he will vent his passion by a secret stab rather than an open blow. His warfare is full of ambuscade and stratagem; and he never rushes into battle with that joyous self-abandonment, with which the warriors of the Gothic races flung themselves into the ranks of their enemies. In his feasts and his drinking bouts we find none of that robust and full-toned mirth, which reigned at the rude carousals of our barbaric ancestry. He is never jovial in his cups, and maudlin sorrow or maniacal rage is the sole result of his potations.

Over all emotion he throws the veil of an iron self-control, originating in a peculiar form of pride, and fostered by rigorous discipline from childhood upward. He is trained to conceal passion, and not to subdue it. The inscrutable warrior is aptly imaged by the hackneyed figure of a volcano covered with snow; and no man can say when or where the wild-fire will burst forth. This shallow self-mastery serves to give dignity to public deliberation, and harmony to social life. Wrangling and quarrel are strangers to an Indian dwelling; and while an assembly of the ancient Gauls was garrulous as a convocation of magpies, a Roman senate might have taken a lesson from the grave solemnity of an Indian council. In the midst of his family and friends, he hides affections, by nature none of the most tender, under a mask of icy coldness; and in the torturing fires of his enemy, the haughty sufferer maintains to the last his look of grim defiance.

His intellect is as peculiar as his moral organization. Among all savages, the powers of perception preponderate over those of reason and analysis; but this is more especially the case with the Indian. An acute judge of character, at least of such parts of it as his experience enables him to comprehend; keen to a proverb in all exercises of war and the chase, he seldom traces effects to their causes, or follows out actions to their remote results. Though a close observer of external nature, he no sooner attempts to account for her phenomena than he involves himself in the most ridiculous absurdities; and quite content with these puerilities, he has not the least desire to push his inquiries further. His curiosity, abundantly active within its own narrow circle, is dead to all things else; and to attempt rousing it from its torpor is but a bootless task. He seldom takes cognizance of general or abstract ideas; and his language has scarcely the power to express them, except through the medium of figures drawn from the external world, and often highly picturesque and forcible. The absence of reflection makes him grossly improvident, and unfits him for pursuing any complicated scheme of war or policy.

Some races of men seem moulded in wax, soft and melting, at once plastic and feeble. Some races, like some metals, combine the greatest flexibility with the greatest strength. But the Indian is hewn out of a rock. You can rarely change the form without destruction of the substance. Races of inferior energy have possessed a power of expansion and assimilation to which he is a stranger; and it is this fixed and rigid quality which has proved his ruin. He will not learn the arts of civilization, and he and his forest must perish together. The stern, unchanging features of his mind excite our admiration from their very immutability; and we look with deep interest on the fate of this irreclaimable son of the wilderness, the child who will not be weaned from the breast of his rugged mother. And our interest increases when we discern in the unhappy wanderer the germs of heroic virtues mingled among his vices,—a hand bountiful to bestow as it is rapacious to seize, and even in extremest famine, imparting its last morsel to a fellow-sufferer; a heart which, strong in friendship as in hate, thinks it not too much to lay down life for its chosen comrade; a soul true to its own idea of honor, and burning with an unquenchable thirst for greatness and renown.

The imprisoned lion in the showman's cage differs not more widely from the lord of the desert than the beggarly frequenter of frontier garrisons and dramshops differs from the proud denizen of the woods. It is in his native wilds alone that the Indian must be seen and studied. Thus to depict him is the aim of the ensuing History; and if, from the shades of rock and forest, the savage features should look too grimly forth, it is because the clouds of a tempestuous war have cast upon the picture their murky shadows and lurid fires.

[LA SALLE] [2]

CONSPICUOUS in the annals of Canada stands the memorable name of Robert Cavelier de La Salle, the man who, beyond all his compeers, contributed to expand the boundary of French empire in the west. La Salle commanded at Fort Frontenac, erected near the outlet of Lake Ontario, on its northern shore, and then forming the most advanced military outpost of the colony. Here he dwelt among Indians, and half-breeds, traders, voyageurs, bush-rangers, and Franciscan monks, ruling his little empire with absolute sway, enforcing respect by his energy, but offending many by his rigor. Here he brooded upon the grand design which had long engaged his thoughts. He had resolved to complete the achievement of Father Marquette, to trace the unknown Mississippi to its mouth, to plant the standard of his king in the

[2] From vol. i, chap. ii.

newly-discovered regions, and found colonies which should make good the sovereignty of France from the Frozen Ocean to Mexico. Ten years of his early life had passed, it is said, in connection with the Jesuits, and his strong mind had hardened to iron under the discipline of that relentless school. To a sound judgment, and a penetrating sagacity, he joined a boundless enterprise and an adamantine constancy of purpose. But his nature was stern and austere; he was prone to rule by fear rather than by love; he took counsel of no man, and chilled all who approached him by his cold reserve.

At the close of the year 1678, his preparations were complete, and he despatched his attendants to the banks of the river Niagara, whither he soon followed in person. Here he began a little fort of palisades, and was the first military tenant of a spot destined to momentous consequence in future wars. Two leagues above the cataract, on the eastern bank of the river, he built the first vessel which ever explored the waters of the upper lakes. Her name was the Griffin, and her burden was forty-five tons. On the seventh of August, 1679, she began her adventurous voyage amid the speechless wonder of the Indians, who stood amazed, alike at the unwonted size of the wooden canoe, at the flash and roar of the cannon from her decks, and at the carved figure of a griffin, which sat crouched upon her prow. She bore on her course along the virgin waters of Lake Erie, through the beautiful windings of the Detroit, and among the restless billows of Lake Huron, where a furious tempest had well nigh engulfed her. La Salle pursued his voyage along Lake Michigan in birch canoes, and after protracted suffering from famine and exposure reached its southern extremity on the eighteenth of October,

He led his followers to the banks of the river now called the St. Joseph. Here, again, he built a fort; and here, in after years, the Jesuits placed a mission and the government a garrison. Thence he pushed on into the unknown region of the Illinois; and now dangers and difficulties began to thicken about him. Indians threatened hostility; his men lost heart, clamored, grew mutinous, and repeatedly deserted; and worse than all, nothing was heard of the vessel which had been sent back to Canada for necessary supplies. Weeks wore on, and doubt ripened into certainty. She had foundered among the storms of these wilderness oceans; and her loss seemed to involve the ruin of the enterprise, since it was vain to proceed farther without the expected supplies. In this disastrous crisis, La Salle embraced a resolution characteristic of his intrepid temper. Leaving his men in charge of a subordinate at a fort which he had built on the river Illinois, he turned his face again towards Canada. He traversed on foot more than a thousand miles of frozen forest, crossing rivers, toiling through snow-drifts, wading ice-encumbered swamps, sustaining life by the fruits of the chase, and threatened day and night by lurking enemies. He gained his destination, but it was only to encounter a fresh storm of calamities. His enemies had been busy in his absence; a malicious report had gone abroad that he was dead; his creditors had seized his property; and the stores on which he most relied had been wrecked at sea, or lost among the rapids of the St. Lawrence. Still he battled against adversity with his wonted vigor, and in Count Frontenac, the governor of the province,—a spirit kindred to his own,—he found a firm friend. Every difficulty gave way before him; and with fresh supplies of men, stores, and ammunition, he again embarked for the Illinois. Rounding the vast circuit of the lakes, he reached the mouth of the St. Joseph, and hastened with anxious speed to the fort where he had left his followers. The place was empty. Not a man remained. Terrified, despondent, mutinous, and embroiled in Indian wars, they had fled to seek peace and safety, he knew not whither.

Once more the dauntless discoverer turned back towards Canada. Once more he stood before Count Frontenac, and once more bent all his resources and all his credit to gain means for the prosecution of his enterprise. He succeeded. With his little flotilla of canoes, he left his fort, at the outlet of Lake Ontario, and slowly retraced those interminable waters, and lines of forest-bounded shore, which had grown drearily familiar to his eyes. Fate at length seemed tired of the conflict with so stubborn an adversary. All went prosperously with the voyagers. They passed the lakes in safety, crossed the rough portage to the waters of the Illinois, followed its winding channel, and descended the turbid eddies of the Mississippi, received with various welcome by the scattered tribes who dwelt along its banks. Now the waters grew bitter to the taste; now the trampling of the surf was heard; and now the broad ocean opened upon their sight, and their goal was won. On the ninth of April, 1682, with his followers under arms, amid the firing of musketry, the chanting of the *Te Deum,* and shouts of "Vive le roi," La Salle took formal possession of the vast valley of the Mississippi, in the name of Louis the Great, King of France and Navarre.

The first stage of his enterprise was accomplished, but labors no less arduous remained behind. Repairing to the court of France, he was welcomed with richly merited favor, and soon set sail for the mouth of the Mississippi, with a squadron of vessels freighted with men and material for the projected colony. But the folly and obstinacy of a jealous naval commander blighted his fairest hopes. The squadron missed the mouth of the river; and the wreck of one of the vessels, and the desertion of the commander, completed the ruin of the expedition. La Salle landed with a band of half famished followers on the coast of Texas; and, while he was toiling with untired energy for their relief, a few vindictive miscreants conspired against him, and a shot from a traitor's musket closed the career of the iron-hearted discoverer.

[BRADDOCK'S DEFEAT] [3]

THUS began that memorable war which, kindling among the forests of America, scattered its fires over the kingdoms of Europe, and the sultry empire of the Great Mogul; the war made glorious by the heroic death of Wolfe, the victories of Frederic, and the exploits of Clive; the war which controlled the destinies of America, and was first in the chain of events which led on to her Revolution with all its vast and undeveloped consequences. On the old battle-ground of Europe, the contest bore the same familiar features of violence and horror which had marked the strife of former generations— fields ploughed by the cannon ball, and walls shattered by the exploding mine, sacked towns and blazing suburbs, the lamentations of women, and the license of a maddened soldiery. But in America, war assumed a new and striking aspect. A wilderness was its sublime arena. Army met army under the shadows of primeval woods; their cannon resounded over wastes unknown to civilized man. And before the hostile powers could join in battle, endless forests must be traversed, and morasses passed, and everywhere the axe of the pioneer must hew a path for the bayonet of the soldier.

Before the declaration of war, and before the breaking off of negotiations between the courts of France and England, the English ministry formed the plan of assailing the French in America on all sides at once, and repelling them, by one bold push, from all their encroachments. A provincial army was to advance upon Acadia, a second was to attack Crown Point, and a third Niagara; while the two regiments which had lately arrived in Virginia under General Braddock, aided by a strong body of provincials, were to dislodge the French from their newly-built fort Du Quesne. To Braddock was assigned the chief command of all the British forces in America; and a person worse fitted for the office could scarcely have been found. His experience had been ample, and none could doubt his courage; but he was profligate, arrogant, perverse, and a bigot to military rules. On his first arrival in Virginia, he called together the governors of the several provinces, in order to explain his instructions and adjust the details of the projected operations. These ar- rangements complete, Braddock advanced to the borders of Virginia, and formed his camp at Fort Cumberland, where he spent several weeks in training the raw backwoodsmen, who joined him, into such discipline as they seemed capable of; in collecting horses and wagons, which could only be had with the utmost difficulty; in railing at the contractors, who scanda- lously cheated him; and in venting his spleen by copious abuse of the country and the people. All at length was ready, and early in June, 1755, the army left civilization behind, and struck into the broad wilderness as a squadron puts out to sea.

[3] From vol. i, chap. iv.

It was no easy task to force their way over that rugged ground, covered with
an unbroken growth of forest; and the difficulty was increased by the needless load of baggage which encumbered their march. The crash of falling
trees resounded in the front, where a hundred axemen labored with ceaseless
toil to hew a passage for the army. The horses strained their utmost strength
to drag the ponderous wagons over roots and stumps, through gullies and
quagmires; and the regular troops were daunted by the depth and gloom of
the forest which hedged them in on either hand, and closed its leafy arches
above their heads. So tedious was their progress, that, by the advice of Washington, twelve hundred chosen men moved on in advance with the lighter
baggage and artillery, leaving the rest of the army to follow, by slower stages,
with the heavy wagons. On the eighth of July, the advanced body reached
the Monongahela, at a point not far distant from Fort du Quesne. The rocky
and impracticable ground on the eastern side debarred their passage, and the
general resolved to cross the river in search of a smoother path, and recross
it a few miles lower down, in order to gain the fort. The first passage was easily
made, and the troops moved, in glittering array, down the western margin
of the water, rejoicing that their goal was well nigh reached, and the hour of
their expected triumph close at hand.

Scouts and Indian runners had brought the tidings of Braddock's approach
to the French at Fort du Quesne. Their dismay was great, and Contrecœur,
the commander, thought only of retreat, when Beaujeu, a captain in the
garrison, made the bold proposal of leading out a party of French and Indians
to waylay the English in the woods, and harass or interrupt their march. The
offer was accepted, and Beaujeu hastened to the Indian camps.

Around the fort and beneath the adjacent forest were the bark lodges of
savage hordes, whom the French had mustered from far and near; Ojibwas
and Ottawas, Hurons and Caughnawagas, Abenakis and Delawares. Beaujeu called the warriors together, flung a hatchet on the ground before them,
and invited them to follow him out to battle; but the boldest stood aghast
at the peril, and none would accept the challenge. A second interview took
place with no better success; but the Frenchman was resolved to carry his
point. "I am determined to go," he exclaimed. "What, will you suffer your
father to go alone?" His daring proved contagious. The warriors hesitated
no longer; and when, on the morning of the ninth of July, a scout ran in
with the news that the English army was but a few miles distant, the Indian
camps were at once astir with the turmoil of preparation. Chiefs harangued
their yelling followers, braves bedaubed themselves with war-paint, smeared
themselves with grease, hung feathers in their scalp-locks, and whooped and
stamped till they had wrought themselves into a delirium of valor.

That morning, James Smith, an English prisoner recently captured on the
frontier of Pennsylvania, stood on the rampart, and saw the half-frenzied

multitude thronging about the gateway, where kegs of bullets and gunpowder were broken open, that each might help himself at will. Then band after band hastened away towards the forest, followed and supported by nearly two hundred and fifty French and Canadians, commanded by Beaujeu. There were the Ottawas, led on, it is said, by the remarkable man whose name stands on the title-page of this history; there were the Hurons of Lorette under their chief, whom the French called Athanase, and many more, all keen as hounds on the scent of blood. At about nine miles from the fort, they reached a spot where the narrow road descended to the river through deep and gloomy woods, and where two ravines, concealed by trees and bushes, seemed formed by nature for an ambuscade. Beaujeu well knew the ground; and it was here that he had resolved to fight; but he and his followers were well nigh too late; for as they neared the ravines, the woods were resounding with the roll of the British drums.

It was past noon of a day brightened with the clear sunlight of an American midsummer, when the forces of Braddock began, for a second time, to cross the Monongahela, at the fording-place, which to this day bears the name of their ill-fated leader. The scarlet columns of the British regulars, complete in martial appointment, the rude backwoodsmen with shouldered rifles, the trains of artillery and the white-topped wagons, moved on in long procession through the shallow current, and slowly mounted the opposing bank. Men were there whose names have become historic. Gage, who, twenty years later, saw his routed battalions recoil in disorder from before the breastwork on Bunker Hill; Gates, the future conqueror of Burgoyne; and one destined to a higher fame,—George Washington, a boy in years, a man in calm thought and self-ruling wisdom.

With steady and well ordered march, the troops advanced into the great labyrinth of woods which shadowed the eastern borders of the river. Rank after rank vanished from sight. The forest swallowed them up, and the silence of the wilderness sank down once more on the shores and waters of the Monongahela.

Several engineers and guides and six light horsemen led the way; a body of grenadiers under Gage was close behind, and the army followed in such order as the rough ground would permit, along a narrow road, twelve feet wide, tunnelled through the dense and matted foliage. There were flanking parties on either side, but no scouts to scour the woods in front, and with an insane confidence Braddock pressed on to meet his fate. The van had passed the low grounds that bordered the river, and were now ascending a gently rising ground, where, on either hand, hidden by thick trees, by tangled undergrowth and rank grasses, lay the two fatal ravines. Suddenly, Gordon, an engineer in advance, saw the French and Indians bounding forward through the forest and along the narrow track, Beaujeu leading them on, dressed in a fringed hunting-shirt, and wearing a silver gorget on his breast. He stopped, turned, and waved his hat, and his French followers, crowding across the road, opened a murderous fire upon the head of the British column, while, screeching their war-cries, the Indians thronged into the ravines, or crouched behind rocks and trees on both flanks of the advancing troops. The astonished grenadiers returned the fire, and returned it with good effect; for a random shot struck down the brave Beaujeu, and the courage of the assailants was staggered by his fall. Dumas, second in command, rallied them to the attack; and while he, with the French and Canadians, made good the pass in front, the Indians from their lurking places opened a deadly fire on the right and left. In a few moments, all was confusion. The advance guard fell back on the main body, and every trace of subordination vanished. The fire soon extended along the whole length of the army, from front to rear. Scarce an enemy could be seen, though the forest resounded with their yells; though every bush and tree was alive with incessant flashes; though the lead flew like a hailstorm, and the men went down by scores. The regular troops seemed bereft of their senses. They huddled together in the road like flocks of sheep; and happy did he think himself who could wedge his way into the midst of the crowd, and place a barrier of human flesh between his life and the shot of the ambushed marksmen. Many were seen eagerly loading their muskets, and then firing them into the air, or shooting their own comrades in the insanity of their terror. The officers, for the most part, displayed a conspicuous gallantry; but threats and commands were wasted alike on the panic-stricken multitude. It is said that at the outset Braddock showed signs of fear; but he soon recovered his wonted intrepidity. Five horses were shot under him, and five times he mounted afresh. He stormed and shouted, and, while the Virginians were fighting to good purpose, each man behind a tree, like the Indians themselves, he ordered them with furious menace to form in platoons, where the fire of the enemy mowed them down like grass. At length, a mortal shot silenced him, and two provincials bore him off the field. Washington rode through the tumult calm and undaunted. Two horses were killed under him, and four bullets pierced his clothes; but his hour was not come, and he escaped without a wound. Gates was shot through the body, and Gage also was severely wounded. Of eighty-six officers, only twenty-three remained unhurt; and of twelve hundred soldiers who crossed the Monongahela, more than seven hundred were killed and wounded. None suffered more severely than the Virginians, who had displayed throughout a degree of courage and steadiness which put the cowardice of the regulars to shame. The havoc among them was terrible, for of their whole number scarcely one-fifth left the field alive.

The slaughter lasted three hours; when, at length, the survivors, as if impelled by a general impulse, rushed tumultuously from the place of carnage, and with dastardly precipitation fled across the Monongahela. The enemy did not pursue beyond the river, flocking back to the field to collect the plunder, and gather a rich harvest of scalps. The routed troops pursued their flight until they met the rear division of the army, under Colonel Dunbar; and even then their senseless terrors did not abate. Dunbar's soldiers caught the infection. Cannon, baggage, provisions and wagons were destroyed, and all fled together, eager to escape from the shadows of those awful woods, whose horrors haunted their imagination. They passed the defenceless settlements of the border, and hurried on to Philadelphia, leaving the unhappy people to defend themselves as they might against the tomahawk and scalping-knife.

The calamities of this disgraceful rout did not cease with the loss of a few hundred soldiers on the field of battle; for it brought upon the provinces all the miseries of an Indian war. Those among the tribes who had thus far stood neutral, wavering between the French and English, now hesitated no longer. Many of them had been disgusted by the contemptuous behavior of Braddock. All had learned to despise the courage of the English, and to regard their own prowess with unbounded complacency. It is not in Indian nature to stand quiet in the midst of war; and the defeat of Braddock was a signal for the western savages to snatch their tomahawks and assail the Engglish settlements with one accord, murdering and pillaging with ruthless fury, and turning the frontier of Pennsylvania and Virginia into one wide scene of havoc and desolation.

[THE SIEGE OF QUEBEC] [4]

By the plan of this summer's campaign, Canada was to be assailed on three sides at once. Upon the west, General Prideaux was to attack Niagara; upon the south, General Amherst was to advance upon Ticonderoga and Crown Point; while upon the east, General Wolfe was to besiege Quebec; and each of these armies, having accomplished its particular object, was directed to push forward, if possible, until all three had united in the heart of Canada. In pursuance of the plan, General Prideaux moved up Lake Ontario and invested Niagara. This post was one of the greatest importance. Its capture would cut off the French from the whole interior country, and they therefore made every effort to raise the siege. An army of seventeen hundred French and Indians, collected at the distant garrisons of Detroit, Presqu' Isle, Le Bœuf, and Venango, suddenly appeared before Niagara. Sir William Johnson was now in command of the English, Prideaux having been killed by the bursting of a cohorn. Advancing in order of battle, he met the French, charged, routed, and pursued them for five miles through the woods. This success was soon followed by the surrender of the fort.

[4] From vol. i, chap. iv.

In the mean time, Sir Jeffrey Amherst had crossed Lake George, and appeared before Ticonderoga; upon which the French blew up their works, and retired down Lake Champlain to Crown Point. Retreating from this position also, on the approach of the English army, they collected all their forces, amounting to little more than three thousand men, at Isle Aux Noix, where they intrenched themselves, and prepared to resist the farther progress of the invaders. The lateness of the season prevented Amherst from carrying out the plan of advancing into Canada, and compelled him to go into winter-quarters at Crown Point. The same cause had withheld Prideaux's army from descending the St. Lawrence.

While the outposts of Canada were thus successfully attacked, a blow was struck at a more vital part. Early in June, General Wolfe sailed up the St. Lawrence with a force of eight thousand men, and formed his camp immediately below Quebec, on the Island of Orleans. From thence he could discern, at a single glance, how arduous was the task before him. Piles of lofty cliffs rose with sheer ascent on the northern border of the river; and from their summits the boasted citadel of Canada looked down in proud security, with its churches and convents of stone, its ramparts, bastions, and batteries; while over them all, from the brink of the precipice, towered the massive walls of the Castle of St. Louis. Above, for many a league, the bank was guarded by an unbroken range of steep acclivities. Below, the River St. Charles, flowing into the St. Lawrence, washed the base of the rocky promontory on which the city stood. Lower yet lay an army of fourteen thousand men, under an able and renowned commander, the Marquis of Montcalm. His front was covered by intrenchments and batteries, which lined the bank of the St. Lawrence; his right wing rested on the city and the St. Charles; his left, on the cascade and deep gulf of Montmorenci; and thick forests extended along his rear. Opposite Quebec rose the high promontory of Point Levi; and the St. Lawrence, contracted to less than a mile in width, flowed between, with deep and powerful current. To a chief of less resolute temper, it might well have seemed that art and nature were in league to thwart his enterprise; but a mind like that of Wolfe could only have seen in this majestic combination of forest and cataract, mountain and river, a fitting theatre for the great drama about to be enacted there.

Yet nature did not seem to have formed the young English general for the conduct of a doubtful and almost desperate enterprise. His person was slight, and his features by no means of a martial cast. His feeble constitution had been undermined by years of protracted and painful disease. His kind and genial disposition seemed better fitted for the quiet of domestic life than for the stern duties of military command; but to these gentler traits he joined a high enthusiasm, and an unconquerable spirit of daring and endurance, which made him the idol of his soldiers, and bore his slender frame through every hardship and exposure.

The work before him demanded all his courage. How to invest the city, or even bring the army of Montcalm to action, was a problem which might have perplexed a Hannibal. A French fleet lay in the river above, and the precipices along the northern bank were guarded at every accessible point by sentinels and outposts. Wolfe would have crossed the Montmorenci by its upper ford, and attacked the French army on its left and rear; but the plan was thwarted by the nature of the ground and the vigilance of his adversaries. Thus baffled at every other point, he formed the bold design of storming Montcalm's position in front; and on the afternoon of the thirty-first of July, a strong body of troops was embarked in boats, and, covered by a furious cannonade from the English ships and batteries, landed on the beach just above the mouth of the Montmorenci. The grenadiers and Royal Americans were the first on shore, and their ill-timed impetuosity proved the ruin of the plan. Without waiting to receive their orders or form their ranks, they ran pell-mell, across the level ground, and with loud shouts began, each man for himself, to scale the heights which rose in front, crested with intrenchments and bristling with hostile arms. The French at the top threw volley after volley among the hot-headed assailants. The slopes were soon covered with the fallen; and at that instant a storm, which had long been threatening, burst with sudden fury, drenched the combatants on both sides with a deluge of rain, extinguished for a moment the fire of the French, and at the same time made the steeps so slippery that the grenadiers fell repeatedly in their vain attempts to climb. Night was coming on with double darkness. The retreat was sounded, and, as the English re-embarked, troops of Indians came whooping down the heights, and hovered about their rear, to murder the stragglers and the wounded; while exulting cries of *Vive le roi,* from the crowded summits, proclaimed the triumph of the enemy.

With bitter agony of mind, Wolfe beheld the headlong folly of his men, and saw more than four hundred of the flower of his army fall a useless sacrifice. The anxieties of the siege had told severely upon his slender constitution; and not long after this disaster, he felt the first symptoms of a fever, which soon confined him to his couch. Still his mind never wavered from its purpose; and it was while lying helpless in the chamber of a Canadian house, where he had fixed his headquarters, that he embraced the plan of the enterprise which robbed him of life, and gave him immortal fame.

This plan had been first proposed during the height of Wolfe's illness, at a council of his subordinate generals, Monkton, Townshend, and Murray. It was resolved to divide the little army; and, while one portion remained before Quebec to alarm the enemy by false attacks, and distract their attention from the scene of actual operation, the other was to pass above the town, land under cover of darkness on the northern shore, climb the guarded heights, gain the plains above, and force Montcalm to quit his vantage-ground, and perhaps to offer battle. The scheme was daring even to rashness; but its audacity was the secret of its success.

Early in September, a crowd of ships and transports, under Admiral Holmes, passed the city under the hot fire of its batteries; while the troops designed for the expedition, amounting to scarcely five thousand, marched upward along the southern bank, beyond reach of the cannonade. All were then embarked; and on the evening of the twelfth, Holmes's fleet, with the troops on board, lay safe at anchor in the river, several leagues above the town. These operations had not failed to awaken the suspicions of Montcalm; and he had detached M. Bougainville to watch the movements of the English, and prevent their landing on the northern shore.

The eventful night of the twelfth was clear and calm, with no light but that of the stars. Within two hours before daybreak, thirty boats, crowded with sixteen hundred soldiers, cast off from the vessels, and floated downward, in perfect order, with the current of the ebb tide. To the boundless joy of the army, Wolfe's malady had abated, and he was able to command in person. His ruined health, the gloomy prospects of the siege, and the disaster at Montmorenci, had oppressed him with the deepest melancholy, but never impaired for a moment the promptness of his decisions, or the impetuous energy of his action. He sat in the stern of one of the boats, pale and weak, but borne up to a calm height of resolution. Every order had been given, every arrangement made, and it only remained to face the issue. The ebbing tide sufficed to bear the boats along, and nothing broke the silence of the night but the gurgling of the river, and the low voice of Wolfe, as he repeated to the officers about him the stanzas of Gray's "Elegy in a Country Churchyard," which had recently appeared and which he had just received from England. Perhaps, as he uttered those strangely appropriate words,—

> "The paths of glory lead but to the grave,"

the shadows of his own approaching fate stole with mournful prophecy across his mind. "Gentlemen," he said as he closed his recital, "I would rather have written those lines than take Quebec tomorrow."

As they approached the landing-place, the boats edged closer in towards the northern shore, and the woody precipices rose high on their left, like a wall of undistinguished blackness.

"*Qui vive?*" shouted a French sentinel, from out the impervious gloom.

"*La France!*" answered a captain of Fraser's Highlanders, from the foremost boat.

"*A quel régiment?*" demanded the soldier.

"*De la Reine!*" promptly replied the Highland captain, who chanced to know that the regiment so designated formed part of Bougainville's command. As boats were frequently passing down the river with supplies for the garrison, and as a convoy from Bougainville was expected that very night, the sentinel was deceived, and allowed the English to proceed.

A few moments after, they were challenged again, and this time they could discern the soldier running close down to the water's edge, as if all his suspicions were aroused; but the skilful replies of the Highlander once more saved the party from discovery.

They reached the landing-place in safety,—an indentation in the shore, about a league above the city, and now bearing the name of Wolfe's Cove. Here a narrow path led up the face of the heights, and a French guard was posted at the top to defend the pass. By the force of the current, the foremost boats, including that which carried Wolfe himself, were borne a little below the spot. The general was one of the first on shore. He looked upward at the rugged heights which towered above him in the gloom. "You can try it," he coolly observed to an officer near him; "but I don't think you'll get up."

At the point where the Highlanders landed, one of their captains, Donald Macdonald, apparently the same whose presence of mind had just saved the enterprise from ruin, was climbing in advance of his men, when he was challenged by a sentinel. He replied in French, by declaring that he had been sent to relieve the guard, and ordering the soldier to withdraw. Before the latter was undeceived, a crowd of Highlanders were close at hand, while the steeps below were thronged with eager climbers, dragging themselves up by trees, roots, and bushes. The guard turned out, and made a brief though brave resistance. In a moment, they were cut to pieces, dispersed, or made prisoners; while men after men came swarming up the height, and quickly formed upon the plains above. Meanwhile, the vessels had dropped downward with the current, and anchored opposite the landing-place. The remaining troops were disembarked, and, with the dawn of day, the whole were brought in safety to the shore.

The sun rose, and, from the ramparts of Quebec, the astonished people saw the Plains of Abraham glittering with arms, and the dark-red lines of the English forming in array of battle. Breathless messengers had borne the evil tidings to Montcalm, and far and near his wide-extended camp resounded with the rolling of alarm drums and the din of startled preparation. He, too, had had his struggles and his sorrows. The civil power had thwarted him; famine, discontent, and disaffection were rife among his soldiers; and no small portion of the Canadian militia had dispersed from sheer starvation. In spite of all, he had trusted to hold out till the winter frosts should drive the invaders from before the town; when, on that disastrous morning, the news of their successful temerity fell like a cannon shot upon his ear. Still he assumed a tone of confidence. "They have got to the weak side of us at last," he is reported to have said, "and we must crush them with our numbers." With headlong haste, his troops were pouring over the bridge of the St. Charles, and gathering in heavy masses under the western ramparts of the town. Could numbers give assurance of success, their triumph would have been secure; for five French battalions and the armed colonial peasantry amounted in all to more than seven thousand five hundred men. Full in sight before them stretched the long, thin lines of the British forces,—the half-wild Highlanders, the steady soldiery of England, and the hardy levies of the provinces,—less than five thousand in number, but all inured to battle, and strong in the full assurance of success. Yet, could the chiefs of that gallant army have pierced the secrets of the future, could they have foreseen that the victory which they burned to achieve would have robbed England of her proudest boast, that the conquest of Canada would pave the way for the independence of America, their swords would have dropped from their hands, and the heroic fire have gone out within their hearts.

It was nine o'clock, and the adverse armies stood motionless, each gazing on the other. The clouds hung low, and, at intervals, warm light showers descended, besprinkling both alike. The coppice and cornfields in front of the British troops were filled with French sharpshooters, who kept up a distant, spattering fire. Here and there a soldier fell in the ranks, and the gap was filled in silence.

At a little before ten, the British could see that Montcalm was preparing to advance, and, in a few moments, all his troops appeared in rapid motion. They came on in three divisions, shouting after the manner of their nation, and firing heavily as soon as they came within range. In the British ranks, not a trigger was pulled, not a soldier stirred; and their ominous composure seemed to damp the spirits of the assailants. It was not till the French were within forty yards that the fatal word was given, and the British muskets blazed forth at once in one crashing explosion. Like a ship at full career, arrested with sudden ruin on a sunken rock, the ranks of Montcalm staggered, shivered, and broke before that wasting storm of lead. The smoke, rolling along the field, for a moment shut out the view; but when the white wreaths were scattered on the wind, a wretched spectacle was disclosed; men and officers tumbled in heaps, battalions resolved into a mob, order and obedience gone; and when the British muskets were levelled for a second volley, the masses of the militia were seen to cower and shrink with uncontrollable panic. For a few minutes, the French regulars stood their ground, returning a sharp and not ineffectual fire. But now, echoing cheer on cheer, redoubling volley on volley, trampling the dying and the dead and driving the fugitives in crowds, the British troops advanced and swept the field before them. The ardor of the men burst all restraint. They broke into a run, and with unsparing slaughter chased the flying multitude to the gates of Quebec. Foremost of all, the light-footed Highlanders dashed along in furious pursuit, hewing down the Frenchmen with their broadswords, and slaying many in the very ditch of the fortifications. Never was victory more quick or more decisive.

In the short action and pursuit, the French lost fifteen hundred men, killed, wounded, and taken. Of the remainder, some escaped within the city, and others fled across the St. Charles to rejoin their comrades who had been left to guard the camp. The pursuers were recalled by sound of trumpet; the broken ranks were formed afresh, and the English troops withdrawn beyond reach of the cannon of Quebec. Bougainville, with his corps, arrived from the upper country, and, hovering about their rear, threatened an attack; but when he saw what greeting was prepared for him, he abandoned his purpose and withdrew. Townshend and Murray, the only general officers who remained unhurt, passed to the head of every regiment in turn, and thanked the soldiers for the bravery they had shown; yet the triumph of the victors was mingled with sadness, as the tidings went from rank to rank that Wolfe had fallen.

In the heat of the action, as he advanced at the head of the grenadiers of Louisburg, a bullet shattered his wrist; but he wrapped his handkerchief about the wound, and showed no sign of pain. A moment more, and a ball pierced his side. Still he pressed forward, waving his sword and cheering his soldiers to the attack, when a third shot lodged deep within his breast. He paused, reeled, and, staggering to one side, fell to the earth. Brown, a lieutenant of the grenadiers, Henderson, a volunteer, an officer of artillery, and a private soldier, raised him together in their arms, and, bearing him to the rear, laid him softly on the grass. They asked if he would have a surgeon; but he shook his head, and answered that all was over with him. His eyes closed with the torpor of approaching death, and those around sustained his fainting form. Yet they could not withhold their gaze from the wild turmoil before them, and the charging ranks of their companions rushing through fire and smoke. "See how they run," one of the officers exclaimed, as the French fled in confusion before the levelled bayonets. "Who run?" demanded Wolfe, opening his eyes like a man aroused from sleep. "The enemy, sir," was the reply; "they give way everywhere." "Then," said the dying general, "tell Colonel Burton to march Webb's regiment down to Charles River, to cut off their retreat from the bridge. Now, God be praised, I will die in peace," he murmured; and, turning on his side, he calmly breathed his last.

Almost at the same moment fell his great adversary, Montcalm, as he strove, with vain bravery, to rally his shattered ranks. Struck down with a mortal wound, he was placed upon a litter and borne to the General

Hospital on the banks of the St. Charles. The surgeons told him that he could not recover. "I am glad of it," was his calm reply. He then asked how long he might survive, and was told that he had not many hours remaining. "So much the better," he said; "I am happy that I shall not live to see the surrender of Quebec." Officers from the garrison came to his bedside to ask his orders and instructions. "I will give no more orders," replied the defeated soldier; "I have much business that must be attended to, of greater moment than your ruined garrison and this wretched country. My time is very short; therefore, pray leave me." The officers withdrew, and none remained in the chamber but his confessor and the Bishop of Quebec. To the last, he expressed his contempt for his own mutinous and half-famished troops, and his admiration for the disciplined valor of his opponents. He died before midnight, and was buried at his own desire in a cavity of the earth formed by the bursting of a bombshell.

The victorious army encamped before Quebec, and pushed their preparations for the siege with zealous energy; but before a single gun was brought to bear, the white flag was hung out, and the garrison surrendered. On the eighteenth of September, 1759, the rock-built citadel of Canada passed forever from the hands of its ancient masters.

HERMAN MELVILLE

(1819–1891)

For Melville's life the material is scanty, the chief source being his own autobiographic romances. He was born of good family in New York in 1819, and reared in an atmosphere of comfort and cultivation, but his father's business failure and early death brought him hardships and disappointments. He had some schooling at the Albany Academy, but obtained his true education elsewhere; "a whale ship," he says, "was my Yale College and my Harvard." A first voyage across the Atlantic when he was eighteen led to a second and longer one four years later from which most of his literary material was drawn. In 1841 he shipped from New Bedford as a common sailor on the whaler "Acushnet," bound for the Pacific. This life proving intolerable, he deserted at Nukuheva, the chief port of the Marquesas, and plunging into the island wilderness, found himself among the cannibals of Taipi, where he spent four months in "an indulgent captivity." Making his escape to an Australian whaler, he visited Tahiti, sailed thence to Honolulu, and finally returned home by Cape Horn in a ship of war in 1844. After these three years of thrilling adventure he settled down, and the rest of his life was commonplace. During the next half dozen years he made good use of his hardly-won material, writing in rapid succession *Typee,* describing his life among the cannibals (1846); *Omoo,* treating similarly his experience in Tahiti (1847); and other stories of the sea. In 1850 he went to live at Lenox, where he found Hawthorne a neighbor; and there he wrote his greatest work, *Moby Dick* (1851). Leaving stories of adventure he attempted a strange kind of autobiographic romance in *Pierre* (1852), which proved a failure. Lack of recognition and other reverses clouded his remaining years. In 1863 he removed to New York, and there he died, practically forgotten, in 1891.

Typee at first contained scathing comment on the missionaries in the Marquesas, but this, along with other caustic criticism of white civilization, was in later editions mostly censored out. The remainder, based on fact but considerably heightened in the treatment, presents an idyllic picture of life in the South Seas, and is written in an admirably limpid and natural style. *Omoo,* losing something in freshness compared to the first book but gaining in humor, is all but as good. Very different from these—indeed so different not only from these but from all other books that it is difficult to characterize or even to grasp after careful reading—is Melville's great *Moby Dick,* the epic of American whaling. Melville is aptly styled by his biographer "mariner and mystic," and *Moby Dick* is his product in both characters. At first it seems the mariner's vivid story, in some chapters realistically describing a whaling voyage in every minutest detail, in others brooding imaginatively over the sea, and catching, as Masefield says, "all the magic, all the sadness, all the wild joy of many waters." But, long before the end, the voyage is seen to be a mystical one, full of profound, if somewhat cloudy, meanings. The descriptions coming vitally from the author's life at sea, and the meanings from his deep imaginative meditation upon it, taken together make up a very unusual and a very genuine and powerful book.

TYPEE [1]

CHAPTER XVIII

MARNOO APPEARS

RETURNING health and peace of mind gave a new interest to everything around me. I sought to diversify my time by as many enjoyments as lay within reach. Bathing in company with troops of girls formed one of my chief amusements. We sometimes enjoyed the recreation in the waters of a miniature lake, into which the central stream of the valley expanded. This lovely sheet of water was almost circular in figure, and about three hundred yards across. Its beauty was indescribable. All around its banks waved luxuriant masses of tropical foliage, soaring high above which was to be seen, here and there, the symmetrical shaft of the cocoanut tree, surmounted by its tuft of graceful branches, drooping in the air like so many waving ostrich plumes.

The ease and grace with which the maidens of the valley propelled themselves through the water, and their familiarity with the element, were truly astonishing. Sometimes they might be seen gliding along, just under the surface, without apparently moving hand or foot—then throwing themselves on their sides, they darted through the water, revealing glimpses of their forms, as, in the course of their rapid progress, they shot for an instant partly into the air—at one moment they dived deep down into the water and the next they rose bounding to the surface.

I remember upon one occasion plunging in among a parcel of these river-nymphs, and counting vainly upon my superior strength, sought to drag some of them under the water, but I quickly repented my temerity. The amphibious young creatures swarmed about me like a shoal of dolphins, and seizing hold of my devoted limbs, tumbled me about and ducked me under the surface, until from the strange noises which rang in my ears, and the supernatural visions dancing before my eyes, I thought I was in the land of spirits. I stood indeed as little chance among them as a cumbrous whale attacked on all sides by a legion of sword-fish. When at length they relinquished their hold of me, they swam away in every direction, laughing at my clumsy endeavors to reach them.

There was no boat on the lake; but at my solicitation and for my special use, some of the young men attached to Marheyo's household, under the direction of the indefatigable Kory-Kory, brought up a light and tastefully

---

[1] *Typee*, published in 1846, is a heightened account of the author's experiences on an island of the Marquesas in the South Pacific. With a companion, "Toby," he deserts from the whaler "Dolly" at the Marquesan port of Nukuheva, and after a perilous scramble through the mountains, finds himself in the valley of Typee among the cannibals. Here he spends four months, kindly treated but not allowed to escape. The chapter selected describes his diversions in company with his servant-guardian, Kory-Kory, and the island nymph Fayaway; and then the appearance of Marnoo, which leads eventually to his escape.

carved canoe from the sea. It was launched upon the sheet of water, and floated there as gracefully as a swan. But, melancholy to relate, it produced an effect I had not anticipated. The sweet nymphs, who had sported with me before in the lake, now all fled its vicinity. The prohibited craft, guarded by the edicts of the "taboo," extended the prohibition to the waters in which it lay.

For a few days, Kory-Kory, with one or two other youths, accompanied me in my excursions to the lake, and while I paddled about in my light canoe, would swim after me, shouting and gambolling in pursuit. But I was ever partial to what is termed in the "Young Men's Own Book" "the society of virtuous and intelligent young ladies," and in the absence of the mermaids, the amusement became dull and insipid. One morning I expressed to my faithful servitor my desire for the return of the nymphs. The honest fellow looked at me bewildered for a moment, and then shook his head solemnly, and murmured, *"Taboo! taboo!"* giving me to understand that unless the canoe was removed, I could not expect to have the young ladies back again. But to this procedure I was averse; I not only wanted the canoe to stay where it was, but I wanted the beauteous Fayaway to get into it, and paddle with me about the lake. This latter proposition completely horrified Kory-Kory's notions of propriety. He inveighed against it, as something too monstrous to be thought of. It not only shocked their established notions of propriety, but was at variance with all their religious ordinances.

However, although the "taboo" was a ticklish thing to meddle with, I determined to test its capabilities of resisting an attack. I consulted the chief Mehevi, who endeavored to dissuade me from my object; but I was not to be repulsed and accordingly increased the warmth of my solicitations. At last he entered into a long, and I have no doubt a very learned and eloquent exposition of the history and nature of the "taboo" as affecting this particular case, employing a variety of most extraordinary words, which, from their amazing length and sonorousness, I have every reason to believe were of a theological nature. But all that he said failed to convince me—partly, perhaps, because I could not comprehend a word that he uttered, but chiefly that for the life of me I could not understand why a woman should not have as much right to enter a canoe as a man. At last he became a little more rational, and intimated that, out of the abundant love he bore me, he would consult with the priests and see what could be done.

How it was that the priesthood of Typee satisfied the affair with their consciences, I know not; but so it was, and Fayaway's dispensation from this portion of the taboo was at length procured. Such an event I believe never before had occurred in the valley; but it was high time the islanders should be taught a little gallantry, and I trust that the example I set them may produce beneficial effects. Ridiculous, indeed, that the lovely creatures should be obliged to paddle about in the water, like so many ducks, while a parcel of great strapping fellows skimmed over its surface in their canoes.

The first day after Fayaway's emancipation I had a delightful little party on the lake—the damsel, Kory-Kory, and myself. My zealous body-servant brought from the house a calabash of poee-poee, half a dozen young cocoa-nuts—stripped of their husks—three pipes, as many yams, and me on his back a part of the way. Something of a load; but Kory-Kory was a very strong man for his size, and by no means brittle in the spine. We had a very pleasant day; my trusty valet plied the paddle and swept us gently along the margin of the water, beneath the shades of the overhanging thickets. Fayaway and I reclined in the stern of the canoe, on the very best terms possible with one another; the gentle nymph occasionally placing her pipe to her lip, and exhaling mild fumes of the tobacco, to which her rosy breath added a fresh perfume. Strange as it may seem, there is nothing in which a young and beautiful female appears to more advantage than in the act of smoking. How captivating is a Peruvian lady swinging in her gaily woven hammock of grass, extended between two orange trees, and inhaling the fragrance of a choice cigarro! But Fayaway, holding in her delicately formed olive hand the long yellow reed of her pipe, with its quaintly carved bowl, and every few moments languishingly giving forth light wreaths of vapor from her mouth and nostrils, looked still more engaging.

We floated about thus for several hours; when I looked up to the warm, glowing, tropical sky, and then down into the transparent depths below; and when my eye, wandering from the bewitching scenery around, fell upon the grotesquely-tattooed form of Kory-Kory, and finally encountered the pensive gaze of Fayaway, I thought I had been transported to some fairy region, so unreal did everything appear.

This lovely piece of water was the coolest spot in all the valley, and I now made it a place of continual resort during the hottest period of the day. One side of it lay near the termination of a long gradually expanding gorge, which mounted to the heights that environed the vale. The strong trade wind, met in its course by these elevations, circled and eddied about their summits, and was sometimes driven down the steep ravine and swept across the valley, ruffling in its passage the otherwise tranquil surface of the lake.

One day, after we had been paddling about for some time, I disembarked Kory-Kory, and paddled the canoe to the windward side of the lake. As I turned the canoe, Fayaway, who was with me, seemed all at once to be struck with some happy idea. With a wild exclamation of delight, she disengaged from her person the ample robe of tappa which was knotted over her shoulder (for the purpose of shielding her from the sun), and spreading it out like a sail, stood erect with upraised arms in the head of the canoe. We American sailors pride ourselves upon our straight clean spars, but a prettier little mast than Fayaway made was never shipped aboard of any craft.

In a moment the tappa was distended by the breeze—the long brown tresses of Fayaway streamed in the air—and the canoe glided rapidly through the water, and shot towards the shore. Seated in the stern, I directed its course with my paddle until it dashed up the soft sloping bank, and Fayaway, with a light spring, alighted on the ground; whilst Kory-Kory, who had watched our manœuvres with admiration, now clapped his hands in transport, and shouted like a madman. Many a time afterwards was this feat repeated.

If the reader has not observed ere this that I was the declared admirer of Miss Fayaway, all I can say is that he is little conversant with affairs of the heart, and I certainly shall not trouble myself to enlighten him any further. Out of the calico I had brought from the ship I made a dress for this lovely girl. In it she looked, I must confess, something like an opera dancer. The drapery of the latter damsel generally commences a little above the elbows, but my island beauty's began at the waist, and terminated sufficiently far above the ground to reveal the most bewitching ankle in the universe.

The day that Fayaway first wore this robe was rendered memorable by a new acquaintance being introduced to me. In the afternoon I was lying in the house, when I heard a great uproar outside; but being by this time pretty well accustomed to the wild halloos which were almost continually ringing through the valley, I paid little attention to it, until old Marheyo, under the influence of some strange excitement, rushed into my presence and communicated the astounding tidings, "Marnoo pemi!" which being interpreted, implied that an individual by the name of Marnoo was approaching. My worthy old friend evidently expected that this intelligence would produce a great effect upon me, and for a time he stood earnestly regarding me, as if curious to see how I should conduct myself, but as I remained perfectly unmoved, the old gentleman darted out of the house again, in as great a hurry as he had entered it.

"Marnoo, Marnoo," cogitated I, "I have never heard that name before. Some distinguished character, I presume, from the prodigious riot the natives are making;" the tumultuous noise drawing nearer and nearer every moment, while "Marnoo!—Marnoo!" was shouted by every tongue.

I made up my mind that some savage warrior of consequence, who had not yet enjoyed the honor of an audience, was desirous of paying his respects on the present occasion. So vain had I become by the lavish attention to which I had been accustomed that I felt half inclined, as a punishment for such neglect, to give this Marnoo a cold reception, when the excited throng came within view, convoying one of the most striking specimens of humanity that I ever beheld.

The stranger could not have been more than twenty-five years of age, and was a little above the ordinary height; had he been a single hair's breadth taller, the matchless symmetry of his form would have been destroyed. His unclad limbs were beautifully formed; whilst the elegant outline of his figure, together with his beardless cheeks, might have entitled him to the distinction of standing for the statue of the Polynesian Apollo; and indeed the oval of his countenance and the regularity of every feature reminded me of an antique bust. But the marble repose of art was supplied by a warmth and liveliness of expression only to be seen in the South Sea Islander under the most favorable developments of nature. The hair of Marnoo was a rich curling brown, and twined about his temples and neck in little close curling ringlets, which danced up and down continually when he was animated in conversation. His cheek was of a feminine softness, and his face was free from the least blemish of tattooing, although the rest of his body was drawn all over with fanciful figures, which—unlike the unconnected sketching usual among the natives—appeared to have been executed in conformity with some general design.

The tattooing on his back in particular attracted my attention. The artist employed must indeed have excelled in his profession. Traced along the course of the spine was accurately delineated the slender, tapering, and diamond-checkered shaft of the beautiful "artu" tree. Branching from the stem on either side, and disposed alternately, were the graceful branches drooping with leaves all correctly drawn and elaborately finished. Indeed, this piece of tattooing was the best specimen of the fine arts I had yet seen in Typee. A rear view of the stranger might have suggested the idea of a spreading vine tacked against a garden wall. Upon his breast, arms, and legs were exhibited an infinite variety of figures, every one of which, however, appeared to have reference to the general effect sought to be produced. The tattooing I have described was of the brightest blue, and when contrasted with the light olive color of the skin produced an unique and even elegant effect. A slight girdle of white tappa, scarcely two inches in width, but hanging before and behind in spreading tassels, composed the entire costume of the stranger.

He advanced surrounded by the islanders, carrying under one arm a small roll of the native cloth, and grasping in his other hand a long and richly decorated spear. His manner was that of a traveller conscious that he is approaching a comfortable stage in his journey. Every moment he turned good-humoredly to the throng around him, and gave some dashing sort of reply to their incessant queries, which appeared to convulse them with uncontrollable mirth.

Struck by his demeanor and the peculiarity of his appearance, so unlike that of the shaven-crowned and face-tattooed natives in general, I involuntarily rose as he entered the house and proffered him a seat on the mats beside me. But without deigning to notice the civility, or even the more incontrovertible fact of my existence, the stranger passed on, utterly regardless of me, and flung himself down upon the farther end of the long couch that traversed the sole apartment of Marheyo's habitation.

Had the belle of the season, in the pride of her beauty and power, been cut in a place of public resort by some supercilious exquisite, she could not have felt greater indignation than I did at this unexpected slight. I was thrown into utter astonishment. The conduct of the savages had prepared me to anticipate from every newcomer the same extravagant expressions of curiosity and regard. This singularity of his conduct, however, only roused my desire to discover who this remarkable personage might be, who now engrossed the attention of every one.

Tinor placed before him a calabash of poee-poee, from which the stranger regaled himself, alternating every mouthful with some rapid exclamation which was eagerly caught up and echoed by the crowd that completely filled the house. When I observed the striking devotion of the natives to him, and their temporary withdrawal of all attention from myself, I felt not a little piqued. The glory of Tommo is departed, thought I, and the sooner he removes from the valley the better. These were my feelings at the moment, and they were prompted by that glorious principle inherent in all heroic natures—the strong-rooted determination to have the biggest share of the pudding or go without any of it.

Marnoo, this all-attractive personage, having satisfied his hunger, and inhaled a few whiffs from a pipe which was handed to him, launched out into an harangue which completely enchained the attention of his auditors.

Little as I understood of the language, yet from his animated gestures and the varying expressions of his features, reflected as from so many mirrors in the countenances around him, I could easily discover the nature of those passions which he sought to arouse. From the frequent occurrence of the words "Nukuheva" and "Frannee" (French), and some others with the meaning of which I was acquainted, he appeared to be rehearsing to his auditors events which had recently occurred in the neighboring bays. But how he had gained the knowledge of these matters I could not understand, unless it were that he had just come from Nukuheva—a supposition which his travel-stained appearance not a little supported. But, if a native of that region, I could not account for his friendly reception at the hands of the Typees.

Never, certainly, had I beheld so powerful an exhibition of natural eloquence as Marnoo displayed during the course of his oration. The grace of the attitudes into which he threw his flexible figure, the striking gestures of his naked arms, and above all the fire which shot from his brilliant eyes, imparted an effect to the continually changing accents of his voice of which

the most accomplished orator might have been proud. At one moment reclining sideways upon the mat, and leaning calmly upon his bended arm, he
related circumstantially the aggressions of the French—their hostile visits to
the surrounding bays, enumerating each one in succession—Happar, Puerka,
Nukuheva, Tior—and then starting to his feet and precipitating himself forward with clenched hands and a countenance distorted with passion, he poured
out a tide of invectives. Falling back into an attitude of lofty command, he
exhorted the Typees to resist these encroachments, reminding them, with a
fierce glance of exultation, that as yet the terror of their name had preserved
them from attack, and with a scornful sneer he sketched in ironical terms
the wondrous intrepidity of the French, who, with five war-canoes and hundreds of men, had not dared to assail the naked warriors of their valley.

The effect he produced upon his audience was electric; one and all they
stood regarding him with sparkling eyes and trembling limbs, as though they
were listening to the inspired voice of a prophet.

But it soon appeared that Marnoo's powers were as versatile as they were
extraordinary. As soon as he had finished this vehement harangue, he threw
himself again upon the mats, and, singling out individuals in the crowd, addressed them by name, in a sort of bantering style, the humor of which,
though nearly hidden from me, filled the whole assembly with uproarious
delight.

He had a word for everybody; and, turning rapidly from one to another,
gave utterance to some hasty witticism, which was sure to be followed by
peals of laughter. To the females, as well as to the men, he addressed his
discourse. Heaven only knows what he said to them, but he caused smiles
and blushes to mantle their ingenuous faces. I am, indeed, very much inclined to believe that Marnoo, with his handsome person and captivating
manners, was a sad deceiver among the simple maidens of the island.

During all this time he had never, for one moment, deigned to regard me.
He appeared, indeed, to be altogether unconscious of my presence. I was
utterly at a loss how to account for this extraordinary conduct. I easily perceived that he was a man of no little consequence among the islanders—that
he possessed uncommon talents, and was gifted with a higher degree of
knowledge than the inmates of the valley. For these reasons, I therefore
greatly feared lest having, from some cause or other, unfriendly feelings
towards me, he might exert his powerful influence to do me mischief.

It seemed evident that he was not a permanent resident of the vale, and
yet, whence could he have come? On all sides the Typees were girt in by
hostile tribes, and how could he possibly, if belonging to any of these, be
received with so much cordiality?

The personal appearance of the enigmatical stranger suggested additional
perplexities. The face, free from tattooing, and the unshaven crown, were

peculiarities I had never before remarked in any part of the island, and I had always heard that the contrary were considered the indispensable distinctions of a Marquesan warrior. Altogether the matter was perfectly incomprehensible to me, and I awaited its solution with no small degree of anxiety.

At length, from certain indications, I suspected that he was making me the subject of his remarks, although he appeared cautiously to avoid either pronouncing my name, or looking in the direction where I lay. All at once he rose from the mats where he had been reclining, and, still conversing, moved towards me, his eye purposely evading mine, and seated himself within less than a yard of me. I had hardly recovered from my surprise when he suddenly turned round and, with a most benignant countenance, extended his right hand gracefully towards me. Of course, I accepted the courteous challenge, and, as soon as our palms met, he bent towards me, and murmured in musical accents,—"How you do? How long you been in this bay? You like this bay?"

Had I been pierced simultaneously by three Happar spears, I could not have started more than I did at hearing these simple questions! For a moment I was overwhelmed with astonishment, and then answered something, I know not what; but as soon as I regained my self-possession, the thought darted through my mind that from this individual I might obtain that information regarding Toby which I suspected the natives had purposely withheld from me. Accordingly I questioned him concerning the disappearance of my companion, but he denied all knowledge of the matter. I then enquired from whence he had come? He replied, from Nukuheva. When I expressed my surprise, he looked at me for a moment, as if enjoying my perplexity, and then, with his strange vivacity, exclaimed,—"Ah! me taboo—me go Nukuheva—me go Tior—me go Typee—me go everywhere—nobody harm me— me taboo."

This explanation would have been altogether unintelligible to me had it not recalled to my mind something I had previously heard concerning a singular custom among these islanders. Though the country is possessed by various tribes whose mutual hostilities almost wholly preclude any intercourse between them, yet there are instances where a person, having ratified friendly relations with some individual belonging to the valley whose inmates are at war with his own, may, under particular restrictions, venture with impunity into the country of his friend, where, under other circumstances, he would have been treated as an enemy. In this light are personal friendships regarded among them, and the individual so protected is said to be "taboo," and his person, to a certain extent, is held as sacred. Thus the stranger informed me he had access to all the valleys in the island.

Curious to know how he had acquired his knowledge of English, I questioned him on the subject. At first, for some reason or other, he evaded the enquiry, but afterwards told me that, when a boy, he had been carried to sea by the captain of a trading vessel, with whom he had staid three years, living part of the time with him at Sydney, in Australia, and that, at a subsequent visit to the island, the captain had, at his own request, permitted him to remain among his countrymen. The natural quickness of the savage had been wonderfully improved by his intercourse with the white men, and his partial knowledge of a foreign language gave him a great ascendancy over his less accomplished countrymen.

When I asked the now affable Marnoo why it was that he had not previously spoken to me, he eagerly enquired what I had been led to think of him from his conduct in that respect. I replied that I had supposed him to be some great chief or warrior, who had seen plenty of white men before, and did not think it worth while to notice a poor sailor. At this declaration of the exalted opinion I had formed of him, he appeared vastly gratified, and gave me to understand that he had purposely behaved in that manner in order to increase my astonishment as soon as he should see proper to address me.

Marnoo now sought to learn my version of the story as to how I came to be an inmate of the Typee valley. When I related to him the circumstances under which Toby and I had entered it, he listened with evident interest; but as soon as I alluded to the absence, yet unaccounted for, of my comrade, he endeavored to change the subject, as if it were something he desired not to agitate. It seemed, indeed, as if everything connected with Toby was destined to beget distrust and anxiety in my bosom. Notwithstanding Marnoo's denial of any knowledge of his fate, I could not avoid suspecting that he was deceiving me; and this suspicion revived those frightful apprehensions with regard to my own fate which, for a short time past, had subsided in my breast.

Influenced by these feelings, I now felt a strong desire to avail myself of the stranger's protection, and under his safeguard return to Nukuheva. But as soon as I hinted at this, he unhesitatingly pronounced it to be entirely impracticable, assuring me that the Typees would never consent to my leaving the valley. Although what he said merely confirmed the impression which I had before entertained, still it increased my anxiety to escape from a captivity which, however endurable, nay, delightful it might be in some respects, involved in its issues a fate marked by the most frightful contingencies.

I could not conceal from my mind that Toby had been treated in the same friendly manner as I had been, and yet all their kindness had terminated in his mysterious disappearance. Might not the same fate await me?—a fate too dreadful to think of. Stimulated by these considerations, I urged anew my request to Marnoo; but he only set forth in stronger colors the impossibility of my escape, and repeated his previous declarations that the Typees would never be brought to consent to my departure.

When I endeavored to learn from him the motives which prompted them to hold me a prisoner, Marnoo again assumed that mysterious tone which had tormented me with apprehensions when I had questioned him with regard to the fate of my companion.

Thus repulsed, in a manner which only served, by arousing the most dreadful forebodings, to excite me to renewed attempts, I conjured him to intercede for me with the natives and endeavor to procure their consent to my leaving them. To this he appeared strongly averse; but, yielding at last to my importunities, he addressed several of the chiefs, who with the rest had been eying us intently during the whole of our conversation. His petition, however, was at once met with the most violent disapprobation, manifesting itself in angry glances and gestures, and a perfect torrent of passionate words, directed to both him and myself. Marnoo, evidently repenting the step he had taken, earnestly deprecated the resentment of the crowd, and in a few moments succeeded in pacifying to some extent the clamors which had broken out as soon as his proposition had been understood.

With the most intense interest had I watched the reception his intercession might receive; and a bitter pang shot through my heart at the additional evidence, now furnished, of the unchangeable determination of the islanders. Marnoo told me, with evident alarm in his countenance, that although admitted into the bay on a friendly footing with its inhabitants, he could not presume to meddle with their concerns, as such a procedure, if persisted in, would at once absolve the Typees from the restraints of the "taboo," although so long as he refrained from any such conduct, it screened him effectually from the consequences of the enmity they bore his tribe.

At this moment Mehevi, who was present, angrily interrupted him; and the words which he uttered, in a commanding tone, evidently meant that he must at once cease talking to me and withdraw to the other part of the house. Marnoo immediately started up, hurriedly enjoining me not to address him again, and, as I valued my safety, to refrain from all further allusion to the subject of my departure; and then, in compliance with the order of the determined chief, but not before it had been angrily repeated, he withdrew to a distance.

I now perceived, with no small degree of apprehension, the same savage expression in the countenance of the natives which had startled me during the scene at the Ti. They glanced their eyes suspiciously from Marnoo to me, as if distrusting the nature of an intercourse carried on, as it was, in a language they could not understand, and they seemed to harbor the belief that already we had concerted measures calculated to elude their vigilance.

The lively countenances of these people are wonderfully indicative of the emotions of the soul, and the imperfections of their oral language are more than compensated for by the nervous eloquence of their looks and gestures.

I could plainly trace, in every varying expression of their faces, all those passions which had been thus unexpectedly aroused in their bosoms.

It required no reflection to convince me, from what was going on, that the injunction of Marnoo was not to be rashly slighted; and accordingly, great as was the effort to suppress my feelings, I accosted Mehevi in a good-humored tone, and with a view of dissipating any ill impression he might have received. But the ireful, angry chief was not so easily mollified. He rejected my advances with that peculiarly stern expression I have before described, and took care by the whole of his behavior towards me to show the displeasure and resentment which he felt.

Marnoo, at the other extremity of the house, apparently desirous of making a diversion in my favor, exerted himself to amuse with his pleasantries the crowd about him; but his lively attempts were not so successful as they had previously been, and, foiled in his efforts, he rose gravely to depart. No one expressed any regret at this movement, so seizing his roll of tappa, and grasping his spear, he advanced to the front of the pi-pi, and waving his hand in adieu to the now silent throng, cast upon me a glance of mingled pity and reproach, and flung himself into the path which led from the house. I watched his receding figure until it was lost in the obscurity of the grove, and then gave myself up to the most desponding reflections.

OMOO [2]

CHAPTER II

SOME ACCOUNT OF THE SHIP

FIRST and foremost, I must give some account of the Julia herself; or "Little Jule," as the sailors familiarly styled her.

She was a small barque of a beautiful model, something more than two hundred tons, Yankee-built and very old. Fitted for a privateer out of a New England port during the war of 1812, she had been captured at sea by a British cruiser, and, after seeing all sorts of service, was at last employed as a government packet in the Australian seas. Being condemned, however, about two years previous, she was purchased at auction by a house in Sydney, who, after some slight repairs, dispatched her on the present voyage.

Notwithstanding the repairs, she was still in a miserable plight. The lower masts were said to be unsound; the standing rigging was much worn; and, in some places, even the bulwarks were quite rotten. Still, she was tolerably tight, and but little more than the ordinary pumping of a morning served to keep her free.

[2] *Omoo*, published in 1847, recounts the author's experiences after his escape from Typee,—his voyage in the "Julia," the ship described in the chapter here selected, and his subsequent adventures on the island of Tahiti.

But all this had nothing to do with her sailing; at that, brave Little Jule, plump Little Jule, was a witch. Blow high, or blow low, she was always ready for the breeze; and when she dashed the waves from her prow, and pranced, and pawed the sea, you never thought of her patched sails and blistered hull. How the fleet creature would fly before the wind! rolling, now and then, to be sure, but in very playfulness. Sailing to windward, no gale could bow her over; with spars erect, she looked right up into the wind's eye, and so she went.

But after all, Little Jule was not to be confided in. Lively enough, and playful she was, but on that very account the more to be distrusted. Who knew, but that like some vivacious old mortal all at once sinking into a decline, she might, some dark night, spring a leak and carry us all to the bottom. However, she played us no such ugly trick, and therefore, I wrong Little Jule in supposing it.

She had a free, roving commission. According to her papers she might go whither she pleased—whaling, sealing, or anything else. Sperm whaling, however, was what she relied upon; though, as yet, only two fish had been brought alongside.

The day they sailed out of Sydney Heads, the ship's company, all told, numbered some thirty-two souls; now, they mustered about twenty; the rest had deserted. Even the three junior mates who had headed the whale boats were gone; and of the four harpooners, only one was left, a wild New Zealander, or *"Mowree,"* as his countrymen are more commonly called in the Pacific. But this was not all. More than half the seamen remaining were more or less unwell from a long sojourn in a dissipated port; some of them wholly unfit for duty, one or two dangerously ill, and the rest managing to stand their watch though they could do but little.

The captain was a young cockney, who, a few years before, had emigrated to Australia, and, by some favoritism or other, had procured the command of the vessel, though in no wise competent. He was esssentially a landsman, and though a man of education, no more meant for the sea than a hairdresser. Hence everybody made fun of him. They called him "The Cabin Boy," "Paper Jack," and half a dozen other undignified names. In truth, the men made no secret of the derision in which they held him; and as for the slender gentleman himself, he knew it all very well, and bore himself with becoming meekness. Holding as little intercourse with them as possible, he left everything to the chief mate, who, as the story went, had been given his captain in charge. Yet, despite his apparent unobtrusiveness, the silent captain had more to do with the men than they thought. In short, although one of your sheepish-looking fellows, he had a sort of still, timid cunning, which no one would have suspected, and which, for that very reason, was all the more active. So the bluff mate, who always thought he did what he pleased, was occasionally made a tool of; and some obnoxious measures which he carried out, in spite of all growlings, were little thought to originate with the dapper little fellow in nankeen jacket and white canvas pumps. But, to all appearance, at least, the mate had everything his own way; indeed, in most things this was actually the case; and it was quite plain that the captain stood in awe of him.

So far as courage, seamanship, and a natural aptitude for keeping riotous spirits in subjection were concerned, no man was better qualified for his vocation then John Jermin. He was the very beau-ideal of the efficient race of short, thick-set men. His hair curled in little rings of iron gray all over his round, bullet head. As for his countenance, it was strongly marked, deeply pitted with the small-pox. For the rest, there was a fierce little squint out of one eye; the nose had a rakish twist to one side; while his large mouth, and great white teeth, looked absolutely sharkish when he laughed. In a word, no one, after getting a fair look at him, would ever think of improving the shape of his nose, wanting in symmetry if it was. Notwithstanding his pugnacious looks, however, Jermin had a heart as big as a bullock's; that you saw at a glance.

Such was our mate; but he had one failing: he abhorred all weak infusions, and cleaved manfully to strong drink. At all times he was more or less under the influence of it. Taken in moderate quantities, I believe, in my soul, it did a man like him good; brightened his eyes, swept the cobwebs out of his brain, and regulated his pulse. But the worst of it was, that sometimes he drank too much, and a more obstreperous fellow than Jermin in his cups, you seldom came across. He was always for having a fight; but the very men he flogged loved him as a brother, for he had such an irresistibly good-natured way of knocking them down, that no one could find it in his heart to bear malice against him. So much for stout little Jermin.

All English whalemen are bound by law to carry a physician, who, of course, is rated a gentleman, and lives in the cabin, with nothing but his professional duties to attend to; but incidentally he drinks "flip" and plays cards with the captain. There was such a worthy aboard of the Julia; but, curious to tell, he lived in the forecastle with the men. And this was the way it happened.

In the early part of the voyage the doctor and the captain lived together as pleasantly as could be. To say nothing of many a can they drank over the cabin transom, both of them had read books, and one of them had traveled; so their stories never flagged. But once on a time they got into a dispute about politics, and the doctor, moreover, getting into a rage, drove home an argument with his fist, and left the captain on the floor literally silenced. This was carrying it with a high hand; so he was shut up in his stateroom for ten days, and left to meditate on bread and water, and the impropriety of flying into a passion. Smarting under his disgrace, he undertook, a short time after his liberation, to leave the vessel clandestinely at one of the islands, but was brought back ignominiously, and again shut up. Being set at large for the second time, he vowed he would not live any longer with the captain, and went forward with his chests among the sailors, where he was received with open arms, as a good fellow and an injured man.

I must give some further account of him, for he figures largely in the narrative. His early history, like that of many other heroes, was enveloped in the profoundest obscurity; though he threw out hints of a patrimonial estate, a nabob uncle, and an unfortunate affair which sent him a-roving. All that was known, however, was this. He had gone out to Sydney as assistant-surgeon of an emigrant ship. On his arrival there, he went back into the country, and after a few months' wanderings, returned to Sydney penniless, and entered as doctor aboard the Julia.

His personal appearance was remarkable. He was over six feet high— a tower of bones, with a complexion absolutely colorless, fair hair, and a light, unscrupulous gray eye, twinkling occasionally with the very devil of mischief. Among the crew, he went by the name of the Long Doctor, or, more frequently still, Doctor Long Ghost. And from whatever high estate Doctor Long Ghost might have fallen, he had certainly at some time or other spent money, drunk Burgundy, and associated with gentlemen.

As for his learning, he quoted Virgil, and talked of Hobbes of Malmsbury, beside repeating poetry by the canto, especially Hudibras. He was, moreover, a man who had seen the world. In the easiest way imaginable, he could refer to an amour he had in Palermo, his lion hunting before breakfast among the Caffres, and the quality of the coffee to be drunk in Muscat; and about these places, and a hundred others, he had more anecdotes than I can tell of. Then such mellow old songs as he sang, in a voice so round and racy, the real juice of sound. How such notes came forth from his lank body was a constant marvel.

Upon the whole, Long Ghost was as entertaining a companion as one could wish; and to me in the Julia, an absolute godsend.

MOBY DICK [3]

Chapter XXXV

The Mast-Head

It was during the more pleasant weather, that in due rotation with the other seamen my first mast-head came round.

[3] In *Moby Dick or, the White Whale*, published in 1851, the fictitious narrator of the story, Ishmael, sails from Nantucket in the whaler "Pequod," under Captain Ahab, on a cruise to the Pacific, in quest of the "white whale," Moby Dick. The chapters selected recount experiences of this voyage.

In most American whalemen the mast-heads are manned almost simultaneously with the vessel's leaving her port; even though she may have fifteen thousand miles, and more, to sail ere reaching her proper cruising ground. And if, after a three, four, or five years' voyage she is drawing nigh home with anything empty in her—say, an empty vial even—then, her mast-heads are kept manned to the last! and not till her skysail-poles sail in among the spires of the port, does she altogether relinquish the hope of capturing one whale more.

Now, as the business of standing mast-heads, ashore or afloat, is a very ancient and interesting one, let us in some measure expatiate here. I take it, that the earliest standers of mast-heads were the old Egyptians; because, in all my researches, I find none prior to them. For though their progenitors, the builders of Babel, must doubtless, by their tower, have intended to rear the loftiest mast-head in all Asia, or Africa either; yet (ere the final truck was put to it) as that great stone mast of theirs may be said to have gone by the board, in the dread gale of God's wrath; therefore, we cannot give these Babel builders priority over the Egyptians. And that the Egyptians were a nation of mast-head standers, is an assertion based upon the general belief among archæologists, that the first pyramids were founded for astronomical purposes: a theory singularly supported by the peculiar stair-like formation of all four sides of those edifices; whereby, with prodigious long upliftings of their legs, those old astronomers were wont to mount to the apex, and sing out for new stars; even as the look-outs of a modern ship sing out for a sail, or a whale just bearing in sight. In Saint Stylites, the famous Christian hermit of old times, who built him a lofty stone pillar in the desert and spent the whole latter portion of his life on its summit, hoisting his food from the ground with a tackle; in him we have a remarkable instance of a dauntless stander-of-mast-heads; who was not to be driven from his place by fogs or frosts, rain, hail, or sleet; but valiantly facing everything out to the last, literally died at his post. Of modern standers-of-mast-heads we have but a lifeless set; mere stone, iron, and bronze men; who, though well capable of facing out a stiff gale, are still entirely incompetent to the business of singing out upon discovering any strange sight. There is Napoleon; who, upon the top of the column of Vendôme, stands with arms folded, some one hundred and fifty feet in the air; careless, now, who rules the decks below; whether Louis Philippe, Louis Blanc, or Louis the Devil. Great Washington, too, stands high aloft on his towering main-mast in Baltimore, and like one of Hercules' pillars, his column marks that point of human grandeur beyond which few mortals will go. Admiral Nelson, also, on a capstan of gun-metal, stands his mast-head in Trafalgar Square; and even when most obscured by that London smoke, token is yet given that a hidden hero is there; for where there is smoke, must be fire. But neither great Washington, nor Napoleon, nor Nelson, will answer a single hail from below, however madly invoked to befriend by their counsels the distracted decks upon which they gaze; however it may be surmised, that their spirits penetrate through the thick haze of the future, and descry what shoals and what rocks must be shunned.

It may seem unwarrantable to couple in any respect the mast-head standers of the land with those of the sea; but that in truth it is not so, is plainly evinced by an item for which Obed Macy, the sole historian of Nantucket, stands accountable. The worthy Obed tells us, that in the early times of the whale fishery, ere ships were regularly launched in pursuit of the game, the people of that island erected lofty spars along the sea-coast, to which the look-outs ascended by means of nailed cleats, something as fowls go upstairs in a hen-house. A few years ago this same plan was adopted by the Bay whalemen of New Zealand, who, upon descrying the game, gave notice to the ready-manned boats nigh the beach. But this custom has now become obsolete; turn we then to the one proper mast-head, that of a whale-ship at sea. The three mast-heads are kept manned from sun-rise to sun-set; the seamen taking their regular turns (as at the helm), and relieving each other every two hours. In the serene weather of the tropics it is exceedingly pleasant—the mast-head: nay, to a dreamy meditative man it is delightful. There you stand, a hundred feet above the silent decks, striding along the deep, as if the masts were gigantic stilts, while beneath you and between your legs, as it were, swim the hugest monsters of the sea, even as ships once sailed between the boots of the famous Colossus at old Rhodes. There you stand, lost in the infinite series of the sea, with nothing ruffled but the waves. The tranced ship indolently rolls; the drowsy trade winds blow; everything resolves you into languor. For the most part, in this tropic whaling life, a sublime un-eventfulness invests you; you hear no news; read no gazettes; extras with startling accounts of commonplaces never delude you into unnecessary excitements; you hear of no domestic afflictions; bankrupt securities; fall of stocks; are never troubled with the thought of what you shall have for dinner—for all your meals for three years and more are snugly stowed in casks, and your bill of fare is immutable.

In one of those southern whalemen, on a long three or four years' voyage, as often happens, the sum of the various hours you spend at the mast-head would amount to several entire months. And it is much to be deplored that the place to which you devote so considerable a portion of the whole term of your natural life, should be so sadly destitute of anything approaching to a cosy inhabitiveness, or adapted to breed a comfortable localness of feeling, such as pertains to a bed, a hammock, a hearse, a sentry box, a pulpit, a coach, or any other of those small and snug contrivances in which men temporarily isolate themselves. Your most usual point of perch is the head of the t' gallant-mast, where you stand upon two thin parallel sticks (almost peculiar to whalemen) called the t' gallant cross-trees. Here, tossed about by the sea, the beginner feels about as cosy as he would standing on a bull's horns. To be sure, in cold weather you may carry your house aloft with you, in the shape of a watch-coat; but properly speaking the thickest watch-coat is no more of a house than the unclad body; for as the soul is glued inside of its fleshy tabernacle, and cannot freely move about in it, nor even move out of it, without running great risk of perishing (like an ignorant pilgrim crossing the snowy Alps in winter); so a watch-coat is not so much of a house as it is a mere envelope, or additional skin encasing you. You cannot put a shelf or chest of drawers in your body, and no more can you make a convenient closet of your watch-coat.

Concerning all this, it is much to be deplored that the mast-heads of a southern whale-ship are unprovided with those enviable little tents or pulpits, called *crow's-nests,* in which the look-outs of a Greenland whaler are protected from the inclement weather of the frozen seas. In the fireside narrative of Captain Sleet, entitled "A Voyage among the Icebergs, in quest of the Greenland Whale, and incidentally for the re-discovery of the Lost Icelandic Colonies of Old Greenland;" in this admirable volume, all standers of mast-heads are furnished with a charmingly circumstantial account of the then recently invented *crow's-nest* of the Glacier, which was the name of Captain Sleet's good craft. He called it the *Sleet's crow's-nest,* in honor of himself; he being the original inventor and patentee, and free from all ridiculous false delicacy, and holding that if we call our own children after our own names (we fathers being the original inventors and patentees), so likewise should we denominate after ourselves any other apparatus we may beget. In shape, the Sleet's crow's-nest is something like a large tierce or pipe; it is open above, however, where it is furnished with a movable side-screen to keep to windward of your head in a hard gale. Being fixed on the summit of the mast, you ascend into it through a little trap-hatch in the bottom. On the after side, or side next the stern of the ship, is a comfortable seat, with a locker underneath for umbrellas, comforters, and coats. In front is a leather rack, in which to keep your speaking trumpet, pipe, telescope, and other nautical conveniences. When Captain Sleet in person stood his mast-head in this crow's-nest of his, he tells us that he always had a rifle with him (also fixed in the rack), together with a powder flask and shot, for the purpose of popping off the stray narwhales, or vagrant sea unicorns infesting those waters; for you cannot successfully shoot at them from the deck owing to the resistance of the water, but to shoot down upon them is a very different thing. Now, it was plainly a labor of love for Captain Sleet to describe, as he does, all the little detailed conveniences of his crow's-nest; but though he so enlarges upon many of these, and though he treats us to a very scientific account of his experiments in this crow's-nest, with a small compass he kept there

for the purpose of counteracting the errors resulting from what is called the
"local attraction" of all binnacle magnets; an error ascribable to the horizontal vicinity of the iron in the ship's planks, and in the Glacier's case, perhaps,
to there having been so many broken-down blacksmiths among her crew;
I say, that though the Captain is very discreet and scientific here, yet, for all
his learned "binnacle deviations," "azimuth compass observations," and "approximate errors," he knows very well, Captain Sleet, that he was not so
much immersed in those profound magnetic meditations, as to fail being
attracted occasionally towards that well replenished little case-bottle, so nicely
tucked in on one side of his crow's-nest, within easy reach of his hand.
Though, upon the whole, I greatly admire and even love the brave, the honest, and learned Captain; yet I take it very ill of him that he should so utterly
ignore that case-bottle, seeing what a faithful friend and comforter it must
have been, while with mittened fingers and hooded head he was studying
the mathematics aloft there in that bird's-nest within three or four perches
of the pole.

But if we Southern whale-fishers are not so snugly housed aloft as Captain
Sleet and his Greenlandmen were; yet that disadvantage is greatly counter-
balanced by the widely contrasting serenity of those seductive seas in which
we South fishers mostly float. For one, I used to lounge up the rigging very
leisurely, resting in the top to have a chat with Queequeg, or any one else off
duty whom I might find there; then ascending a little way further, and
throwing a lazy leg over the top-sail yard, take a preliminary view of the
watery pastures, and so at last mount to my ultimate destination.

Let me make a clean breast of it here, and frankly admit that I kept but
sorry guard. With the problem of the universe revolving in me, how could
I—being left completely to myself at such a thought-engendering al-
titude—how could I but lightly hold my obligations to observe all whale-
ships' standing orders, "Keep your weather eye open, and sing out every
time."

And let me in this place movingly admonish you, ye ship-owners of Nantucket! Beware of enlisting in your vigilant fisheries any lad with lean brow
and hollow eye; given to unseasonable meditativeness; and who offers to
ship with the Phædon instead of Bowditch in his head. Beware of such an
one, I say: your whales must be seen before they can be killed; and this
sunken-eyed young Platonist will tow you ten wakes round the world, and
never make you one pint of sperm the richer. Nor are these monitions at all
unneeded. For nowadays, the whale-fishery furnishes an asylum for many
romantic, melancholy, and absent-minded young men, disgusted with the
carking cares of earth, and seeking sentiment in tar and blubber. Childe
Harold not unfrequently perches himself upon the mast-head of some luckless
disappointed whale-ship, and in moody phrase ejaculates:—

> "Roll on, thou deep and dark blue ocean, roll!
> Ten thousand blubber-hunters sweep over thee in vain."

Very often do the captains of such ships take those absent-minded young philosophers to task, upbraiding them with not feeling sufficient "interest" in the voyage; half-hinting that they are so hopelessly lost to all honorable ambition, as that in their secret souls they would rather not see whales than otherwise. But all in vain; those young Platonists have a notion that their vision is imperfect; they are short-sighted; what use, then, to strain the visual nerve? They have left their opera-glasses at home.

"Why, thou monkey," said a harpooneer to one of these lads, "we've been cruising now hard upon three years, and thou hast not raised a whale yet. Whales are scarce as hen's teeth whenever thou art up here." Perhaps they were; or perhaps there might have been shoals of them in the far horizon; but lulled into such an opium-like listlessness of vacant, unconscious reverie is this absent-minded youth by the blending cadence of waves with thoughts, that at last he loses his identity; takes the mystic ocean at his feet for the visible image of that deep, blue, bottomless soul, pervading mankind and nature; and every strange, half-seen, gliding, beautiful thing that eludes him; every dimly-discovered, uprising fin of some undiscernible form, seems to him the embodiment of those elusive thoughts that only people the soul by continually flitting through it. In this enchanted mood, thy spirit ebbs away to whence it came; becomes diffused through time and space; like Cranmer's sprinkled Pantheistic ashes, forming at last a part of every shore the round globe over.

There is no life in thee, now, except that rocking life imparted by a gently rolling ship; by her, borrowed from the sea; by the sea, from the inscrutable tides of God. But while this sleep, this dream is on ye, move your foot or hand an inch; slip your hold at all; and your identity comes back in horror. Over Descartian vortices you hover. And perhaps, at mid-day, in the fairest weather, with one half-throttled shriek you drop through that transparent air into the summer sea, no more to rise for ever. Heed it well, ye Pantheists!

CHAPTER XLVIII

THE FIRST LOWERING

THE phantoms, for so they then seemed, were flitting on the other side of the deck, and, with a noiseless celerity, were casting loose the tackles and bands of the boat which swung there. This boat had always been deemed one of the spare boats, though technically called the captain's, on account of its hanging from the starboard quarter. The figure that now stood by its bows was tall and swart, with one white tooth evilly protruding from its steel-like lips. A rumpled Chinese jacket of black cotton funereally invested him, with wide black trowsers of the same dark stuff. But strangely crowning this ebonness was a glistening white plaited turban, the living hair braided and coiled round and round upon his head. Less swart in aspect, the companions of this figure were of that vivid, tiger-yellow complexion peculiar to some of the aboriginal natives of the Manillas;—a race notorious for a certain diabolism of subtilty, and by some honest white mariners supposed to be the paid spies and secret confidential agents on the water of the devil, their lord, whose counting-room they suppose to be elsewhere.

While yet the wondering ship's company were gazing upon these strangers, Ahab cried out to the white-turbaned old man at their head, "All ready there, Fedallah?"

"Ready," was the half-hissed reply.

"Lower away then; d'ye hear?" shouting across the deck. "Lower away there, I say."

Such was the thunder of his voice, that spite of their amazement the men sprang over the rail; the sheaves whirled round in the blocks; with a wallow, the three boats dropped into the sea; while, with a dexterous, off-handed daring, unknown in any other vocation, the sailors, goat-like, leaped down the rolling ship's side into the tossed boats below.

Hardly had they pulled out from under the ship's lee, when a fourth keel, coming from the windward side, pulled round under the stern, and showed the five strangers rowing Ahab, who, standing erect in the stern, loudly hailed Starbuck, Stubb, and Flask, to spread themselves widely, so as to cover a large expanse of water. But with all their eyes again riveted upon the swart Fedallah and his crew, the inmates of the other boats obeyed not the command.

"Captain Ahab?—" said Starbuck.

"Spread yourselves," cried Ahab; "give way, all four boats. Thou, Flask, pull out more to leeward!"

"Aye, aye, sir," cheerily cried little King-Post, sweeping round his great steering oar. "Lay back!" addressing his crew. "There!—there!—there again! There she blows right ahead, boys!—lay back!"

"Never heed yonder yellow boys, Archy."

"Oh, I don't mind 'em, sir," said Archy; "I knew it all before now. Didn't I hear 'em in the hold? And didn't I tell Cabaco here of it? What say ye, Cabaco? They are stowaways, Mr. Flask."

"Pull, pull, my fine hearts-alive; pull, my children; pull, my little ones," drawlingly and soothingly sighed Stubb to his crew, some of whom still showed signs of uneasiness. "Why don't you break your backbones, my boys? What is it you stare at? Those chaps in yonder boat? Tut! They are only five more hands come to help us—never mind from where—the more the merrier. Pull, then, do pull; never mind the brimstone—devils are good fellows enough. So, so; there you are now; that's the stroke for a thousand pounds; that's the stroke to sweep the stakes! Hurrah for the gold cup of sperm oil, my heroes! Three cheers, men—all hearts alive! Easy, easy; don't be in a hurry—don't be in a hurry. Why don't you snap your oars, you rascals? Bite something, you dogs! So, so, so, then;—softly, softly! That's it —that's it! long and strong. Give way there, give way! The devil fetch ye, ye ragamuffin rapscallions; ye are all asleep. Stop snoring, ye sleepers, and pull. Pull, will ye? pull, can't ye? pull, won't ye? Why in the name of gudgeons and ginger-cakes don't ye pull?—pull and break something! pull, and start your eyes out! Here!" whipping out the sharp knife from his girdle; "every mother's son of ye draw his knife, and pull with the blade between his teeth. That's it—that's it. Now ye do something; that looks like it, my steel-bits. Start her—start her, my silver-spoons! Start her, marling-spikes!"

Stubb's exordium to his crew is given here at large, because he had rather a peculiar way of talking to them in general, and especially in inculcating the religion of rowing. But you must not suppose from this specimen of his sermonizings that he ever flew into downright passions with his congregation. Not at all; and therein consisted his chief peculiarity. He would say the most terrific things to his crew, in a tone so strangely compounded of fun and fury, and the fury seemed so calculated merely as a spice to the fun, that no oarsman could hear such queer invocations without pulling for dear life, and yet pulling for the mere joke of the thing. Besides he all the time looked so easy and indolent himself, so loungingly managed his steering-oar, and so broadly gaped—open-mouthed at times—that the mere sight of such a yawning commander, by sheer force of contrast, acted like a charm upon the crew. Then again, Stubb was one of those odd sort of humorists, whose jollity is sometimes so curiously ambiguous, as to put all inferiors on their guard in the matter of obeying them.

In obedience to a sign from Ahab, Starbuck was now pulling obliquely across Stubb's bow; and when for a minute or so the two boats were pretty near to each other, Stubb hailed the mate.

"Mr. Starbuck! larboard boat there, ahoy! a word with ye, sir, if ye please!"

"Halloa!" returned Starbuck, turning round not a single inch as he spoke; still earnestly but whisperingly urging his crew; his face set like a flint from Stubb's.

"What think ye of those yellow boys, sir!"

"Smuggled on board, somehow, before the ship sailed. (Strong, strong, boys!)" in a whisper to his crew, then speaking out loud again: "A sad business, Mr. Stubb! (seethe her, seethe her, my lads!) but never mind, Mr. Stubb, all for the best. Let all your crew pull strong, come what will. (Spring, my men, spring!) There's hogsheads of sperm ahead, Mr. Stubb, and that's what ye came for. (Pull, my boys!) Sperm, sperm's the play! This at least is duty; duty and profit hand in hand!"

"Aye, aye, I thought as much," soliloquized Stubb, when the boats diverged, "as soon as I clapt eye on 'em, I thought so. Aye, and that's what he went into the after hold for, so often, as Dough-Boy long suspected. They were hidden down there. The White Whale's at the bottom of it. Well, well, so be it! Can't be helped! All right! Give way, men! It ain't the White Whale to-day! Give way!"

Now the advent of these outlandish strangers at such a critical instant as the lowering of the boats from the deck, this had not unreasonably awakened a sort of superstitious amazement in some of the ship's company; but Archy's fancied discovery having some time previous got abroad among them, though indeed not credited then, this had in some small measure prepared them for the event. It took off the extreme edge of their wonder; and so what with all this and Stubb's confident way of accounting for their appearance, they were for the time freed from superstitious surmisings; though the affair still left abundant room for all manner of wild conjectures as to dark Ahab's precise agency in the matter from the beginning. For me, I silently recalled the mysterious shadows I had seen creeping on board the Pequod during the dim Nantucket dawn, as well as the enigmatical hintings of the unaccountable Elijah.

Meantime, Ahab, out of hearing of his officers, having sided the furthest to windward, was still ranging ahead of the other boats; a circumstance bespeaking how potent a crew was pulling him. Those tiger-yellow creatures of his seemed all steel and whalebone; like five trip-hammers they rose and fell with regular strokes of strength, which periodically started the boat along the water like a horizontal burst boiler out of a Mississippi steamer. As for Fedallah, who was seen pulling the harpooneer oar, he had thrown aside his black jacket, and displayed his naked chest with the whole part of his body above the gunwale, clearly cut against the alternating depressions of the watery horizon; while at the other end of the boat Ahab, with one arm, like a fencer's, thrown half backward into the air, as if to counterbalance any tendency to trip; Ahab was seen steadily managing his steering oar as in a thousand boat lowerings ere the White Whale had torn him. All at once the outstretched arm gave a peculiar motion and then remained fixed, while the boat's five oars were seen simultaneously peaked. Boat and crew sat motionless on the sea. Instantly the three spread boats in the rear paused on their way. The whales had irregularly settled bodily down into the blue, thus giving no distantly discernible token of the movement, though from his closer vicinity Ahab had observed it.

"Every man look out along his oars!" cried Starbuck. "Thou, Queequeg, stand up!"

Nimbly springing up on the triangular raised box in the bow, the savage stood erect there, and with intensely eager eyes gazed off towards the spot where the chase had last been descried. Likewise upon the extreme stern of the boat where it was also triangularly platformed level with the gunwale, Starbuck himself was seen coolly and adroitly balancing himself to the jerking tossings of his chip of a craft, and silently eyeing the vast blue eye of the sea.

Not very far distant Flask's boat was also lying breathlessly still; its commander recklessly standing upon the top of the loggerhead, a stout sort of post rooted in the keel, and rising some two feet above the level of the stern platform. It is used for catching turns with the whale line. Its top is not more spacious than the palm of a man's hand, and standing upon such a base as that, Flask seemed perched at the mast-head of some ship which had sunk to all but her trucks. But little King-Post was small and short, and at the same time little King-Post was full of a large and tall ambition, to that this loggerhead stand-point of his did by no means satisfy King-Post.

"I can't see three seas off; tip us up an oar there, and let me onto that."

Upon this, Daggoo, with either hand upon the gunwale to steady his way, swiftly slid aft, and then erecting himself volunteered his lofty shoulders for a pedestal.

"Good a mast-head as any, sir. Will you mount?"

"That I will, and thank ye very much, my fine fellow; only I wish you fifty feet taller."

Whereupon planting his feet firmly against two opposite planks of the boat, the gigantic negro, stooping a little, presented his flat palm to Flask's foot, and then putting Flask's hand on his hearse-plumed head and bidding him spring as he himself should toss, with one dexterous fling landed the little man high and dry on his shoulders. And here was Flask now standing, Daggoo with one lifted arm furnishing him with a breastband to lean against and steady himself by.

At any time it is a strange sight to the tyro to see with what wondrous habitude of unconscious skill the whaleman will maintain an erect posture in his boat, even when pitched about by the most riotously perverse and cross-running seas. Still more strange to see him giddily perched upon the loggerhead itself, under such circumstances. But the sight of little Flask mounted upon gigantic Daggoo was yet more curious; for sustaining himself with a cool, indifferent, easy, unthought of, barbaric majesty, the noble negro to every roll of the sea harmoniously rolled his fine form. On his broad back, flaxen-haired Flask seemed a snow-flake. The bearer looked nobler than the rider. Though truly vivacious, tumultuous, ostentatious little Flask would now and then stamp with impatience; but not one added heave did he thereby give to the negro's lordly chest. So have I seen Passion and Vanity stamping the living magnanimous earth, but the earth did not alter her tides and her seasons for that.

Meanwhile Stubb, the third mate, betrayed no such far-gazing solicitudes. The whales might have made one of their regular soundings, not a temporary dive from mere fright; and if that were the case, Stubb, as his wont in such cases, it seems, was resolved to solace the languishing interval with his pipe. He withdrew it from his hatband, where he always wore it aslant like a feather. He loaded it, and rammed home the loading with his thumb-end; but hardly had he ignited his match across the rough sandpaper of his hand, when Tashtego, his harpooneer, whose eyes had been setting to windward like two fixed stars, suddenly dropped like light from his erect attitude to his seat, crying out in a quick phrensy of hurry, "Down, down all, and give way!— there they are!"

To a landsman, no whale, nor any sign of a herring, would have been visible at that moment; nothing but a troubled bit of greenish white water, and thin scattered puffs of vapor hovering over it, and suffusingly blowing off to leeward, like the confused scud from white rolling billows. The air around suddenly vibrated and tingled, as it were, like the air over intensely heated plates of iron. Beneath this atmospheric waving and curling, and partially beneath a thin layer of water, also, the whales were swimming. Seen in advance of all the other indications, the puffs of vapor they spouted, seemed their forerunning couriers and detached flying outriders.

All four boats were now in keen pursuit of that one spot of troubled water and air. But it bade far to outstrip them; it flew on and on, as a mass of interblending bubbles borne down a rapid stream from the hills.

"Pull, pull, my good boys," said Starbuck, in the lowest possible but intensest concentrated whisper to his men; while the sharp fixed glance from his eyes darted straight ahead of the bow, almost seemed as two visible needles in two unerring binnacle compasses. He did not say much to his crew, though, nor did his crew say anything to him. Only the silence of the boat was at intervals startlingly pierced by one of his peculiar whispers, now harsh with command, now soft with entreaty.

How different the loud little King-Post. "Sing out and say something, my hearties. Roar and pull, my thunder-bolts! Beach me, beach me on their black backs, boys; only do that for me, and I'll sign over to you my Martha's Vineyard plantation, boys; including wife and children, boys. Lay me on—lay me on! O Lord, Lord! but I shall go stark, staring mad! See! see that white water!" And so shouting, he pulled his hat from his head, and stamped up and down on it; then picking it up, flirted it far off upon the sea; and finally fell to rearing and plunging in the boat's stern like a crazed colt from the prairie.

"Look at that chap now," philosophically drawled Stubb, who, with his unlighted short pipe, mechanically retained between his teeth, at a short distance, followed after—"He's got fits, that Flask has. Fits? yes, give him fits —that's the very word—pitch fits into 'em. Merrily, merrily, hearts-alive. Pudding for supper, you know;—merry's the word. Pull, babes—pull, sucklings—pull, all. But what the devil are you hurrying about? Softly, softly, and steadily, my men. Only pull, and keep pulling; nothing more. Crack all your backbones, and bite your knives in two—that's all. Take it easy—why don't ye take it easy, I say, and burst all your livers and lungs!"

But what it was that inscrutable Ahab said to that tiger-yellow crew of his—these were words best omitted here; for you live under the blessed light of the evangelical land. Only the infidel sharks in the audacious seas may give ear to such words, when, with tornado brow, and eyes of red murder, and foam-glued lips, Ahab leaped after his prey.

Meanwhile, all the boats tore on. The repeated specific allusions of Flask to "that whale," as he called the fictitious monster which he declared to be incessantly tantalizing his boat's bow with its tail—these allusions of his were at times so vivid and life-like, that they would cause some one or two of his men to snatch a fearful look over his shoulder. But this was against all rule; for the oarsmen must put out their eyes, and ram a skewer through their necks; usage pronouncing that they must have no organs but ears, and no limbs but arms, in these critical moments.

It was a sight full of quick wonder and awe! The vast swells of the omnipotent sea; the surging, hollow roar they made, as they rolled along the eight gunwales, like gigantic bowls in a boundless bowling-green; the brief suspended agony of the boat, as it would tip for an instant on the knife-like edge of the sharper waves, that almost seemed threatening to cut it in two; the sudden profound dip into the watery glens and hollows; the keen spurrings and goadings to gain the top of the opposite hill; the headlong, sled-like slide down its other side;—all these, with the cries of the headsmen and harpooneers, and the shuddering gasps of the oarsmen, with the wondrous sight of the ivory Pequod bearing down upon her boats with outstretched sails, like a wild hen after her screaming brood;—all this was thrilling. Not the raw recruit, marching from the bosom of his wife into the fever heat of his first battle; not the dead man's ghost encountering the first unknown phantom in the other world;—neither of these can feel stranger and stronger emotions than that man does, who for the first time finds himself pulling into the charmed, churned circle of the hunted sperm whale.

The dancing white water made by the chase was now becoming more and more visible, owing to the increasing darkness of the dun cloud-shadows flung upon the sea. The jets of vapor no longer blended, but tilted everywhere to right and left; the whales seemed separating their wakes. The boats were pulled more apart; Starbuck giving chase to three whales running dead to leeward. Our sail was now set, and, with the still rising wind, we rushed along; the boat going with such madness through the water, that the lee oars could scarcely be worked rapidly enough to escape being torn from the row-locks.

Soon we were running through a suffusing wide veil of mist; neither ship nor boat to be seen.

"Give way, men," whispered Starbuck, drawing still further aft the sheet of his sail; "there is time to kill a fish yet before the squall comes. There's white water again!—close to! Spring!"

Soon after, two cries in quick succession on each side of us denoted that the other boats had got fast; but hardly were they overheard, when with a lightning-like hurtling whisper Starbuck said: "Stand up!" and Queequeg, harpoon in hand, sprang to his feet.

Though not one of the oarsmen was then facing the life and death peril so close to them ahead, yet with their eyes on the intense countenance of the mate in the stern of the boat, they knew that the imminent instant had come; they heard, too, an enormous wallowing sound as of fifty elephants stirring in their litter. Meanwhile the boat was still booming through the mist, the waves curling and hissing around us like the erected crests of enraged serpents.

"That's his hump. *There, there,* give it to him!" whispered Starbuck.

A short rushing sound leaped out of the boat; it was the darted iron of Queequeg. Then all in one welded commotion came an invisible push from astern, while forward the boat seemed striking on a ledge; the sail collapsed and exploded; a gush of scalding vapor shot up near by; something rolled and tumbled like an earthquake beneath us. The whole crew were half suffocated as they were tossed helter-skelter into the white curdling cream of the squall. Squall, whale, and harpoon had all blended together; and the whale, merely grazed by the iron, escaped.

Though completely swamped, the boat was nearly unharmed. Swimming round it we picked up the floating oars, and lashing them across the gunwale, tumbled back to our places. There we sat up to our knees in the sea, the water covering every rib and plank, so that to our downward gazing eyes the suspended craft seemed a coral boat grown up to us from the bottom of the ocean.

The wind increased to a howl; the waves dashed their bucklers together; the whole squall roared, forked, and crackled around us like a white fire upon the prairie, in which, unconsumed, we were burning; immortal in these jaws of death! In vain we hailed the other boats; as well roar to the live coals down the chimney of a flaming furnace as hail those boats in that storm. Meanwhile the driving scud, rack, and mist, grew darker with the shadows of night; no sign of the ship could be seen. The rising sea forbade all attempts to bale out the boat. The oars were useless as propellers, performing now the office of life-preservers. So, cutting the lashing of the waterproof match keg, after many failures Starbuck contrived to ignite the lamp in the lantern; then stretching it on a waif pole, handed it to Queequeg as the standard-bearer of this forlorn hope. There, then, he sat, holding up that imbecile candle in the heart of that almighty forlornness. There, then, he sat, the sign and symbol of a man without faith, hopelessly holding up hope in the midst of despair.

Wet, drenched through, and shivering cold, despairing of ship or boat, we lifted up our eyes as the dawn came on. The mist still spread over the sea, the empty lantern lay crushed in the bottom of the boat. Suddenly Queequeg started to his feet, hollowing his hand to his ear. We all heard a faint creaking, as of ropes and yards hitherto muffled by the storm. The sound came nearer and nearer; the thick mists were dimly parted by a huge, vague form. Affrighted, we all sprang into the sea as the ship at last loomed into view, bearing right down upon us within a distance of not much more than its length.

Floating on the waves we saw the abandoned boat, as for one instant it tossed and gaped beneath the ship's bows like a chip at the base of a cataract; and then the vast hull rolled over it, and it was seen no more till it came up weltering astern. Again we swam for it, were dashed against it by the seas, and were at last taken up and safely landed on board. Ere the squall came close to, the other boats had cut loose from their fish and returned to the ship in good time. The ship had given us up, but was still cruising, if haply it might light upon some token of our perishing,—an oar or a lance pole.

THE ENCANTADAS, OR ENCHANTED ISLES [4]

SKETCH THE FIRST

THE ISLES AT LARGE

TAKE five-and-twenty heaps of cinders dumped here and there in an outside city lot; imagine some of them magnified into mountains, and the vacant lot the sea; and you will have a fit idea of the general aspect of the Encantadas, or Enchanted Isles. A group rather of extinct volcanoes than of isles; looking much as the world at large might, after a penal conflagration.

It is to be doubted whether any spot of earth can, in desolateness, furnish a parallel to this group. Abandoned cemeteries of long ago, old cities by piecemeal tumbling to their ruin, these are melancholy enough; but, like all else which has but once been associated with humanity they still awaken in us some thoughts of sympathy, however sad. Hence, even the Dead Sea, along with whatever other emotions it may at times inspire, does not fail to touch in the pilgrim some of his less unpleasurable feelings.

And as for solitariness; the great forests of the north, the expanses of unnavigated waters, the Greenland ice-fields, are the profoundest of solitudes

[4] From *The Piazza Tales,* 1856. The Encantadas, islands lying on the Equator, in the Pacific off the coast of Ecuador, are now called the Galapagos.

to a human observer; still the magic of their changeable tides and seasons mitigates their terror; because, though unvisited by men, those forests are visited by the May; the remotest seas reflect familiar stars even as Lake Erie does; and in the clear air of a fine Polar day, the irradiated, azure ice shows beautifully as malachite.

But the special curse, as one may call it, of the Encantadas, that which exalts them in desolation above Idumea and the Pole, is that to them change never comes; neither the change of seasons nor of sorrows. Cut by the Equator, they know not autumn and they know not spring; while already reduced to the lees of fire, ruin itself can work little more upon them. The showers refresh the deserts, but in these isles, rain never falls. Like split Syrian gourds, left withering in the sun, they are cracked by an everlasting drought beneath a torrid sky. "Have mercy upon me," the wailing spirit of the Encantadas seems to cry, "and send Lazarus that he may dip the tip of his finger in water and cool my tongue, for I am tormented in this flame."

Another feature in these isles is their emphatic uninhabitableness. It is deemed a fit type of all-forsaken overthrow, that the jackal should den in the wastes of weedy Babylon; but the Encantadas refuse to harbor even the outcasts of the beasts. Man and wolf alike disown them. Little but reptile life is here found:—tortoises, lizards, immense spiders, snakes, and the strangest anomaly of outlandish Nature, the *aguano*. No voice, no low, no howl is heard; the chief sound of life here is a hiss.

On most of the isles where vegetation is found at all, it is more ungrateful than the blankness of Aracama. Tangled thickets of wiry bushes, without fruit and without a name, springing up among deep fissures of calcined rock, and treacherously masking them; or a parched growth of distorted cactus trees.

In many places the coast is rock-bound, or more properly, clinker-bound; tumbled masses of blackish or greenish stuff like the dross of an iron-furnace, forming dark clefts and caves here and there, into which a ceaseless sea pours a fury of foam; overhanging them with a swirl of grey, haggard mist, amidst which sail screaming flights of unearthly birds heightening the dismal din. However calm the sea without, there is no rest for these swells and those rocks, they lash and are lashed, even when the outer ocean is most at peace with itself. On the oppressive, clouded days such as are peculiar to this part of the watery Equator, the dark vitrified masses, many of which raise themselves among white whirlpools and breakers in detached and perilous places off the shore, present a most Plutonian sight. In no world but a fallen one could such lands exist.

Those parts of the strand free from the marks of fire stretch away in wide level beaches of multitudinous dead shells, with here and there decayed bits of sugar-cane, bamboos, and cocoanuts, washed upon this other and darker world from the charming palm isles to the westward and southward; all the way from Paradise to Tartarus; while mixed with the relics of distant beauty you will sometimes see fragments of charred wood and mouldering ribs of wrecks. Neither will any one be surprised at meeting these last, after observing the conflicting currents which eddy throughout nearly all the wide channels of the entire group. The capriciousness of the tides of air sympathizes with those of the sea. Nowhere is the wind so light, baffling, and every way unreliable, and so given to perplexing calms, as at the Encantadas. Nigh a month has been spent by a ship going from one isle to another, though but thirty miles between; for owing to the force of the current, the boats employed to tow barely suffice to keep the craft from sweeping upon the cliffs, but do nothing toward accelerating her voyage. Sometimes it is impossible for a vessel from afar to fetch up with the group itself, unless large allowances for prospective lee-way have been made ere its coming in sight. And yet, at other times, there is a mysterious indraft, which irresistibly draws a passing vessel among the isles, though not bound to them.

True, at one period, as to some extent at the present day, large fleets of whalemen cruised for Spermaceti upon what some seamen call the Enchanted Ground. But this, as in due place will be described, was off the great outer isle of Albemarle, away from the intricacies of the smaller isles, where there is plenty of sea room; and hence, to that vicinity, the above remarks do not altogether apply; though even there the current runs at times with singular force, shifting, too, with as singular caprice. Indeed, there are seasons when currents quite unaccountable prevail for a great distance round about the total group, and are so strong and irregular as to change a vessel's course against the helm, though sailing at the rate of four or five miles the hour. The difference in the reckonings of navigators produced by these causes, along with the light and variable winds, long nourished a persuasion that there existed two distinct clusters of isles in the parallel of the Encantadas, about a hundred leagues apart. Such was the idea of their earlier visitors, the Buccaneers; and as late as 1750, the charts of that part of the Pacific accorded with the strange delusion. And this apparent fleetingness and unreality of the locality of the isles was most probably one reason for the Spaniards calling them the Encantada, or Enchanted Group.

But not uninfluenced by their character, as they now confessedly exist, the modern voyager will be inclined to fancy that the bestowal of this name might have in part originated in that air of spell-bound desertness which so significantly invests the isles. Nothing can better suggest the aspect of once living things malignly crumbled from ruddiness into ashes. Apples of Sodom, after touching, seem these isles.

However wavering their place may seem by reason of the currents, they themselves, at least to one upon the shore, appear invariably the same: fixed, cast, glued into the very body of cadaverous death.

Nor would the appellation, enchanted, seem misapplied in still another sense. For concerning the peculiar reptile inhabitant of these wilds—whose presence gives the group its second Spanish name, Gallipagos—concerning the tortoises found here, most mariners have long cherished a superstition, not more frightful than grotesque. They earnestly believe that all wrecked sea-officers, more especially commodores and captains, are at death (and in some cases, before death) transformed into tortoises; thenceforth dwelling upon these hot aridities, sole solitary Lords of Asphaltum.

Doubtless so quaintly dolorous a thought was originally inspired by the woe-begone landscape itself, but more particularly, perhaps, by the tortoises. For apart from their strictly physical features, there is something strangely self-condemned in the appearance of these creatures. Lasting sorrow and penal hopelessness are in no animal form so suppliantly expressed as in theirs; while the thought of their wonderful longevity does not fail to enhance the impression.

Nor even at the risk of meriting the charge of absurdly believing in enchantments, can I restrain the admission that sometimes, even now, when leaving the crowded city to wander out July and August among the Adirondack Mountains, far from the influences of towns and proportionally nigh to the mysterious ones of Nature; when at such times I sit me down in the mossy head of some deep-wooded gorge, surrounded by prostrate trunks of blasted pines, and recall, as in a dream, my other and far-distant rovings in the baked heart of the charmed isles; and remember the sudden glimpses of dusky shells, and long languid necks protruded from the leafless thickets; and again have beheld the vitreous inland rocks worn down and grooved into deep ruts by ages and ages of the slow draggings of tortoises in quest of pools of scanty water; I can hardly resist the feeling that in my time I have indeed slept upon evilly enchanted ground.

Nay, such is the vividness of my memory, or the magic of my fancy, that I know not whether I am not the occasional victim of optical delusion concerning the Gallipagos. For often in scenes of social merriment, and especially at revels held by candle light in old-fashioned mansions—when the shadows are thrown into the further recesses of an angular and spacious room, making them put on a look of haunted undergrowth of lonely woods —I have drawn the attention of my comrades by my fixed gaze and sudden change of air, as I have seemed to see, slowly emerging from those imagined solitudes, and heavily crawling along the floor, the ghost of a gigantic tortoise, with "Memento . . ." burning in live letters upon his back.

SKETCH THE THIRD

Rock Rodondo

To go up into a high stone tower is not only a very fine thing in itself, but the very best mode of gaining a comprehensive view of the region round about. It is all the better if this tower stand solitary and alone, like that mysterious Newport one, or else be sole survivor of some perished castle.

Now, with reference to the Enchanted Isles, we are fortunately supplied with just such a noble point of observation in a remarkable rock, from its peculiar figure called of old by the Spaniards, Rock Rodondo, or Round Rock. Some two hundred and fifty feet high, rising straight from the sea ten miles from land, with the whole mountainous group to the south and east, Rock Rodondo occupies, on a large scale, very much the position which the famous Campanile or detached Bell Tower of Saint Mark does with respect to the tangled group of hoary edifices around it.

Ere ascending, however, to gaze abroad upon the Encantadas, this sea-tower itself claims attention. It is visible at the distance of thirty miles; and, fully participating in that enchantment which pervades the group, when first seen afar invariably is mistaken for a sail. Four leagues away, on a golden, hazy noon, it seems some Spanish Admiral's ship, stacked up with glittering canvas. Sail ho! Sail ho! Sail ho! from all three masts. But coming nigh, the enchanted frigate is transformed apace into a craggy keep.

My first visit to the spot was made in the grey of the morning. With a view of fishing, we had lowered three boats, and pulling some two miles from our vessel found ourselves, just before dawn of day, close under the moon-shadow of Rodondo. Its aspect was heightened, and yet softened, by the strange double twilight of the hour. The great full moon burned in the low west like a half-spent beacon casting a soft mellow tinge upon the sea, like that cast by a waning fire of embers upon a midnight hearth; while along the entire east the invisible sun sent pallid intimations of his coming. The wind was light; the waves languid; the stars twinkled with a faint effulgence; all nature seemed supine with the long night watch, and half-suspended in jaded expectation of the sun. This was the critical hour to catch Rodondo in his perfect mood. The twilight was just enough to reveal every striking point, without tearing away the dim investiture of wonder.

From a broken, stair-like base, washed, as the steps of a water-palace, by the waves, the tower rose in entablatures of strata to a shaven summit. These uniform layers which compose the mass form its most peculiar feature. For at their lines of junction they project flatly into encircling shelves, from top to bottom, rising one above another in graduated series. And as the eaves of any old barn or abbey are alive with swallows, so were all these rocky ledges with unnumbered sea-fowl. Eaves upon eaves, and nests upon nests. Here and there were long birdlime streaks of a ghostly white staining the tower from sea to air, readily accounting for its sail-like look afar. All would have been bewitchingly quiescent, were it not for the demoniac din created by the birds. Not only were the eaves rustling with them, but they flew densely overhead, spreading themselves into a winged and continually shifting canopy. The tower is the resort of aquatic birds for hundreds of leagues around. To the north, to the east, to the west, stretches nothing but eternal ocean; so that the man-of-war hawk coming from the coasts of North America, Polynesia, or Peru, makes his first land at Rodondo. And yet though Rodondo be terra-firma, no land bird ever lighted on it. Fancy a red-robin or a canary there! What a falling into the hands of the Philistines, when the poor warbler should be surrounded by such locust-flights of strong bandit birds, with long bills cruel as daggers.

I know not where one can better study the Natural History of strange sea-fowl than at Rodondo. It is the aviary of Ocean. Birds light here which never touched mast or tree; hermit-birds, which ever fly alone, cloud-birds, familiar with unpierced zones of air.

Let us first glance low down to the lowermost shelf of all, which is the widest too, and but a little space from high-water mark. What outlandish beings are these? Erect as men, but hardly as symmetrical, they stand all round the rock like sculptured caryatides, supporting the next range of eaves above. Their bodies are grotesquely misshapen; their bills short; their feet seemingly legless; while the members at their sides are neither fin, wing, nor arm. And truly neither fish, flesh, nor fowl is the penguin; as an edible, pertaining neither to Carnival nor Lent; without exception the most ambiguous and least lovely creature yet discovered by man. Though dabbling in all three elements, and indeed possessing some rudimental claims to all, the penguin is at home in none. On land it stumps; afloat it sculls; in the air it flops. As if ashamed of her failure Nature keeps this ungainly child hidden away at the ends of the earth, in the Straits of Magellan and on the abased sea-story of Rodondo.

But look, what are yon woe-begone regiments drawn up on the next shelf above? What rank and file of large strange fowl? What sea Friars of Orders Grey? Pelicans. Their elongated bills, and heavy leathern pouches, suspended thereto, give them the most lugubrious expression. A pensive race, they stand for hours together without motion. Their dull, ashy plumage imparts an aspect as if they had been powdered over with cinders. A penitential bird indeed—fitly haunting the shores of the clinkered Encantadas—whereon tormented Job himself might have well sat down and scraped himself with potsherds.

Higher up now we mark the gony, or grey albatross, anomalously so called, an unsightly unpoetic bird, unlike its storied kinsman, which is the snow-white ghost of the haunted Capes of Hope and Horn.

As we still ascend from shelf to shelf we find the tenants of the tower serially disposed in order of their magnitude:—gannets, black and speckled haglets, jays, sea-hens, sperm-whale-birds, gulls of all varieties:—thrones, princedoms, powers, dominating one above another in senatorial array; while sprinkled over all, like an ever-repeated fly in a great piece of broidery, the stormy petrel or Mother Cary's chicken sounds his continual challenge and alarm. That this mysterious humming-bird of ocean, which had it but brilliancy of hue might from its evanescent liveliness be almost called its butterfly, yet whose chirrup under the stern is ominous to mariners as to the peasant the death-tick sounding from behind the chimney-jam—should have its special haunt at the Encantadas, contributes in the seaman's mind not a little to their dreary spell.

As day advances the dissonant din augments. With earsplitting cries the wild birds celebrate their matins. Each moment, flights push from the tower, and join the aerial choir hovering overhead, while their places below are supplied by darting myriads. But down through all this discord of commotion I hear clear silver bugle-like notes unbrokenly falling, like oblique lines of swift slanting rain in a cascading shower. I gaze far up, and behold a snow-white angelic thing, with one long lance-like feather thrust out behind. It is the bright inspiriting chanticleer of ocean, the beauteous bird, from its bestirring whistle of musical invocation, fitly styled the "Boatswain's Mate."

The winged life clouding Rodondo on that well-remembered morning, I saw had its full counterpart in the finny hosts which people the waters at its base. Below the waterline, the rock seemed one honeycomb of grottoes, affording labyrinthine lurking places for swarms of fairy fish. All were strange; many exceedingly beautiful; and would have well graced the costliest glass globes in which goldfish are kept for show. Nothing was more striking than the complete novelty of many individuals of this multitude. Here hues were seen as yet unpainted, and figures which are unengraved.

To show the multitude, avidity, and nameless fearlessness and tameness of these fish, let me say that often, marking through clear spaces of water— temporarily made so by the concentric dartings of the fish above the surface —certain larger and less unwary wights, which swam slow and deep, our anglers would cautiously essay to drop their lines down to these last. But in vain; there was no passing the uppermost zone. No sooner did the hook touch the sea than a hundred infatuates contended for the honor of capture. Poor fish of Rodondo! in your victimized confidence you are of the number of those who inconsiderately trust while they do not understand, human nature

THE ENCANTADAS, OR ENCHANTED ISLES 533

But the dawn is now fairly day. Band after band the sea-fowl sail away to forage the deep for their food. The tower is left solitary, save the fish caves at its base. Its birdlime gleams in the golden rays like the whitewash of a tall lighthouse, or the lofty sails of a cruiser. This moment, doubtless, while we know it to be a dead desert rock, other voyagers are taking oaths it is a glad populous ship.

But ropes now, and let us ascend. Yet soft, this is not so easy.

SKETCH THE FOURTH

A Pisgah View from the Rock

If you seek to ascend Rock Rodondo, take the following prescription. Go three voyages round the world as a main-royalman of the tallest frigate that floats; then serve a year or two apprenticeship to the guides who conduct strangers up the Peak of Teneriffe; and as many more, respectively, to a rope-dancer, an Indian juggler, and a chamois. This done, come and be rewarded by the view from our tower. How we get there, we alone know. If we sought to tell others, what the wiser were they? Suffice it, that here at the summit you and I stand. Does any balloonist, does the outlooking man in the moon, take a broader view of space? Much thus, one fancies, looks the universe from Milton's celestial battlements. A boundless watery Kentucky. Here Daniel Boone would have dwelt content.

Never heed for the present yonder Burnt District of the Enchanted Isles. Look edgeways, as it were, past them, to the south. You see nothing; but permit me to point out the direction, if not the place, of certain interesting objects in the vast sea, which kissing this tower's base, we behold unscrolling itself towards the Antarctic Poles.

We stand now ten miles from the Equator. Yonder, to the east, some six hundred miles, lies the continent; this Rock being just about on the parallel of Quito.

Observe another thing here. We are at one of the three uninhabited clusters, which, at pretty nearly uniform distances from the main, sentinel, at long intervals from each other, the entire coast of South America. In a peculiar manner, also, they terminate the South American character of country. Of the unnumbered Polynesian chains to the westward, not one partakes of the qualities of the Encantadas or Gallipagos, the isles St. Felix and St. Ambrose, the isles Juan Fernandes and Massafuero. Of the first it needs not here to speak. The second lie a little above the Southern Tropic; lofty, inhospitable, and uninhabitable rocks, one of which, presenting two round hummocks connected by a low reef, exactly resembles a huge double-headed shot. The last lie in the latitude of 33°; high, wild, and cloven. Juan Fernandes is sufficiently famous without further description. Massafuero is a Spanish name, expressive of the fact, that the isle so called lies *more without,* that is, further off the main than its neighbor Juan. This isle Massafuero has a very imposing aspect at a distance of eight or ten miles. Approached in one direction, in cloudy weather, its great overhanging height and rugged contour, and more especially a peculiar slope of its broad summits, give it much the air of a vast iceberg drifting in tremendous poise. Its sides are split with dark cavernous recesses, as an old cathedral with its gloomy lateral chapels. Drawing nigh one of these gorges from sea after a long voyage, and beholding some tatterdemalion outlaw, staff in hand, descending its steep rocks towards you, conveys a very queer emotion to a lover of the picturesque.

On fishing parties from ships, at various times, I have chanced to visit each of these groups. The impression they give to the stranger pulling close up in his boat under their grim cliffs is, that surely he must be their first discoverer, such for the most part is the unimpaired . . . silence and solitude. And here, by the way, the mode in which these isles were really first lighted upon by Europeans is not unworthy mention, especially as what is about to be said, likewise applies to the original discovery of our Encantadas.

Prior to the year 1563, the voyages made by Spanish ships from Peru to Chili, were full of difficulty. Along this coast the winds from the south most generally prevail; and it had been an invariable custom to keep close in with the land, from a superstitious conceit on the part of the Spaniards, that were they to lose sight of it, the eternal trade wind would waft them into unending waters, from whence would be no return. Here, involved among tortuous capes and headlands, shoals and reefs, beating too against a continual head wind, often light, and sometimes for days and weeks sunk into utter calm, the provincial vessels, in many cases, suffered the extremest hardships, in passages, which at the present day seem to have been incredibly protracted. There is on record in some collections of nautical disasters, an account of one of these ships, which starting on a voyage whose duration was estimated at ten days, spent four months at sea, and indeed never again entered harbor, for in the end she was cast away. Singular to tell, this craft never encountered a gale, but was the vexed sport of malicious calms and currents. Thrice, out of provisions, she put back to an intermediate port, and started afresh, but only yet again to return. Frequently fogs enveloped her; so that no observation could be had of her place, and once, when all hands were joyously anticipating sight of their destination, lo! the vapors lifted and disclosed the mountains from which they had taken their first departure. In the like deceptive vapors she at last struck upon a reef, whence ensued a long series of calamities too sad to detail.

It was the famous pilot, Juan Fernandes, immortalized by the island named after him, who put an end to these coasting tribulations, by boldly venturing the experiment—as De Gama did before him with respect to Europe—of standing broad out from land. Here he found the winds favorable for getting to the south, and by running westward till beyond the influence of the trades, he regained the coast without difficulty; making the passage which, though in a high degree circuitous, proved far more expeditious than the nominally direct one. Now it was upon these new tracks, and about the year 1670 or thereabouts, that the Enchanted Isles and the rest of the sentinel groups, as they may be called, were discovered. Though I know of no account as to whether any of them were found inhabited or no, it may be reasonably concluded that they have been immemorial solitudes. But let us return to Rodondo.

Southwest from our tower lies all Polynesia, hundreds of leagues away; but straight west, on the precise line of his parallel, no land rises till your keel is beached upon the Kingsmills, a nice little sail of say five thousand miles.

Having thus by such distant references—with Rodondo the only possible ones—settled our relative place on the sea, let us consider objects not quite so remote. Behold the grim and charred Enchanted Isles. This nearest crater-shaped headland is part of Albemarle, the largest of the group, being some sixty miles or more long, and fifteen broad. Did you ever lay eye on the real genuine Equator? Have you ever, in the largest sense, toed the Line? Well, that identical crater-shaped headland there, all yellow lava, is cut by the Equator exactly as a knife cuts straight through the centre of a pumpkin pie. If you could only see so far, just to one side of that same headland, across yon low dykey ground, you would catch sight of the isle of Narborough, the loftiest land of the cluster; no soil whatever; one seamed clinker from top to bottom; abounding in black caves like smithies; its metallic shore ringing under foot like plates of iron; its central volcanoes standing grouped like a gigantic chimney-stack.

Narborough and Albemarle are neighbors after a quite curious fashion. A familiar diagram will illustrate this strange neighborhood.

Cut a channel at the above letter joint, and the middle transverse limb is Narborough, and all the rest is Albemarle. Volcanic Narborough lies in the black jaws of Albemarle like a wolf's red tongue in his open mouth.

If now you desire the population of Albemarle, I will give you, in round numbers, the statistics, according to the most reliable estimates made upon the spot:

Men	none
Ant-eaters	unknown
Man-haters	unknown
Lizards	500,000
Snakes	500,000
Spiders	10,000,000
Salamanders	unknown
Devils	do.
Making a clean total of	11,000,000

Exclusive of an incomputable host of fiends, ant-eaters, man-haters, and sala-manders.

Albemarle opens his mouth towards the setting sun. His distended jaws form a great bay, which Narborough, his tongue, divides into halves, one whereof is called Weather Bay, the other Lee Bay; while the volcanic promon-tories terminating his coasts are styled South Head and North Head. I note this, because these Bays are famous in the annals of the Sperm Whale Fishery. The whales come here at certain seasons to calve. When ships first cruised hereabouts, I am told, they used to blockade the entrance of Lee Bay,—when, their boats going round by Weather Bay, passed through Narborough chan-nel,—and so had the Leviathans very neatly in a pen.

The day after we took fish at the base of this Round Tower, we had a fine wind, and, shooting round the north headland, suddenly descried a fleet of full thirty sail, all beating to windward like a squadron in line. A brave sight as ever man saw. A most harmonious concord of rushing keels. Their thirty kelsons hummed like thirty harp-strings, and looked as straight whilst they left their parallel traces on the sea. But there proved too many hunters for the game. The fleet looked up and went their separate ways out of sight, leaving my own ship and two trim gentlemen of London. These last, finding no luck either, likewise vanished; and Lee Bay, with all its appurtenances, and without a rival, devolved to us.

The way of cruising here is this. You keep hovering about the entrance of the bay, in one beat and out the next. But at times—not always, as in other parts of the group—a race horse of a current sweeps right across its mouth. So, with all sails set, you carefully ply your tacks. How often, standing at the foremast head at sunrise, with our patient prow pointed in between these isles, did I gaze upon that land, not of cakes but of clinkers, not of streams of sparkling water, but arrested torrents of tormented lava.

As the ship runs in from the open sea, Narborough presents its side in one dark craggy mass, soaring up some five or six thousand feet, at which point it hoods itself in heavy clouds, whose lowest level fold is as clearly defined against the rocks, as the snow-line against the Andes. There is dire mischief going on in that upper dark. There toil the demons of fire, who at intervals irradiate the nights with a strange spectral illumination for miles and miles around, but unaccompanied by any further demonstration; or else, suddenly announce themselves by terrific concussions, and the full drama of a volcanic eruption. The blacker that cloud by day, the more may you look for light by night. Often whalemen have found themselves cruising nigh that burning mountain when all aglow with a ball-room blaze. Or, rather, glassworks, you may call this same vitreous isle of Narborough, with its tall chimney-stacks.

Where we still stand, here on Rodondo, we cannot see all the other isles, but it is a good place from which to point out where they lie. Yonder, though, to the E.N.E., I mark a distant dusky ridge. It is Abington Isle, one of the most northerly of the group; so solitary, remote, and blank, it looks like No-Man's Land seen off our northern shore. I doubt whether two human beings ever touched upon that spot. So far as yon Abington Isle is concerned, Adam and his billions of posterity remain uncreated.

Ranging south of Abington, and quite out of sight behind the 'ong spire of Albemarle, lies James's Isle, so called by the early Buccaneers after the luckless Stuart, Duke of York. Observe here, by the way, that, excepting the isles particularized in comparatively recent times, and which mostly received the names of famous Admirals, the Encantadas were first christened by the Spaniards; but these Spanish names were generally effaced on English charts by the subsequent christenings of the Buccaneers, who, in the middle of the seventeenth century, called them after English noblemen and kings. Of these loyal freebooters and the things which associate their name with the Encantadas, we shall hear anon. Nay, for one little item, immediately; for between James's Isle and Albemarle, lies a fantastic islet, strangely known as "Cowley's Enchanted Isle." But as all the group is deemed enchanted, the reason must be given for the spell within a spell involved by this particular designation. The name was bestowed by that excellent Buccaneer himself, on his first visit here. Speaking in his published voyages of this spot, he says— "My fancy led me to call it Cowley's Enchanted Isle, for we having had a sight of it upon several points of the compass, it appeared always in so many different forms; sometimes like a ruined fortification; upon another point like a great city," etc. No wonder though, that among the Encantadas all sorts of ocular deceptions and mirages should be met.

That Cowley linked his name with this self-transforming and bemocking isle, suggests the possibility that it conveyed to him some meditative image of himself. At least, as is not impossible, if he were any relative of the mildly thoughtful, and self-upbraiding poet Cowley, who lived about his time, the conceit might not seem unwarranted; for that sort of thing evinced in the naming of this isle runs in the blood, and may be seen in pirates as in poets.

Still south of James's Isle lie Jervis Isle, Duncan Isle, Crossman's Isle, Brattle Isle, Wood's Isle, Chatham Isle, and various lesser isles, for the most part an archipelago of aridities, without inhabitant, history, or hope of either in all time to come. But not far from these are rather notable isles—Barrington, Charles's, Norfolk, and Hood's. Succeeding chapters will reveal some ground for their notability.

ABRAHAM LINCOLN

(1809–1865)

Lincoln was born into a typical frontiersman's family which moved from Hardin County, Kentucky, where he was born in 1809, first to Indiana, then to Illinois. "The aggregate of all his schooling," he says in an account of his life written for the campaign of 1860, "did not amount to one year. . . . What he has in the way of education he has picked up." Though he had access to few books, among them were Shakespeare and the Bible. He felt the need of improving his mind, and he was given to analysis and introspection; he developed, however, very slowly. As a young man he was fond of people and popular, yet contemplative and reticent. Up to the age of forty-five he was a trustworthy but not specially remarkable country lawyer and politician. "In 1854," he says, "his profession had almost superseded the thought of politics in his mind, when the repeal of the Missouri Compromise aroused him as he had never been before." From this time he had a cause to serve, and his mind grew in depth and strength. How he served this cause is known to every American. At his death, less than six weeks after his second inauguration, he had amply earned "the thanks of the Republic he died to save."

Lincoln had greater influence on American life and thought than any other man of his century, and he exercised this influence largely through his command of words, written or spoken. In his case it is especially true that "the style is the man"; his writing has the strength of his character. He was honest and candid; he was generous and tolerant; he was serene; he was full of understanding and compassion in viewing the ways of men; and he was ready to give to the cause he served "the last full measure of devotion." His speeches and writings from his first election to the presidency until his death—especially his Farewell at Springfield, his Gettysburg Address, and his Letter to Mrs. Bixby—have a simplicity, a sincerity, and an elevation and restraint of feeling that are hard to match elsewhere in English speech. "Deep must be the fountains from which there issues so pure a stream."

TO JOHN D. JOHNSTON

January, 1851.

D EAR JOHNSTON: Your request for eighty dollars I do not think it best to comply with now. At the various times when I have helped you a little you have said to me, "We can get along very well now"; but in a very short time I find you in the same difficulty again. Now this can only happen by some defect in your conduct. What that defect is, I think I know. You are not lazy, and still you are an idler. I doubt whether, since I saw you, you have done a good whole day's work in any one day. You do not very much dislike to work, and still you do not work much, merely because it does not seem to you that you could get much for it. This habit of uselessly wasting time is the whole difficulty; it is vastly important to you, and still more so to your children, that you should break the habit. It is more important to them, because they have longer to live, and can keep out of an idle habit before they are in it, easier than they can get out after they are in.

You are now in need of some money; and what I propose is, that you shall go to work, "tooth and nail," for somebody who will give you money for it. Let father and your boys take charge of your things at home, prepare for a crop, and make a crop, and you go to work for the best money wages, or in discharge for any debt you owe, that you can get; and to secure you a fair reward for your labor, I now promise you, that for every dollar you will, between this and the first of May, get for your own labor, either in money or as your own indebtedness, I will then give you one other dollar. By this, if you hire yourself at ten dollars a month, from me you will get ten more, making twenty dollars a month for your work. In this I do not mean you shall go off to St. Louis, or the lead mines, or the gold mines in California, but I mean for you to go at it for the best wages you can get close to home in Coles County. Now, if you will do this, you will be soon out of debt, and, what is better, you will have a habit that will keep you from getting in debt again. But, if I should now clear you out of debt, next year you would be just as deep in as ever. You say you would almost give your place in heaven for seventy or eighty dollars. Then you value your place in heaven very cheap, for I am sure you can, with the offer I make, get the seventy or eighty dollars for four or five months work. You say if I will furnish you the money you will deed me the land, and, if you don't pay the money back, you will deliver possession. Nonsense! If you can't now live with the land, how will you then live without it? You have always been kind to me, and I do not mean to be unkind to you. On the contrary, if you will but follow my advice, you will find it worth more than eighty times eighty dollars to you.

Affectionately your brother,
A. LINCOLN.

FAREWELL ADDRESS AT SPRINGFIELD [1]

February 11, 1861

MY FRIENDS: No one, not in my situation, can appreciate my feeling of sadness at this parting. To this place, and the kindness of these people, I owe everything. Here I have lived a quarter of a century, and have passed from a young to an old man. Here my children have been born, and one is buried.

---

[1] Spoken to Lincoln's fellow-citizens when he left Springfield for Washington to become President.

I now leave, not knowing when or whether ever I may return, with a task before me greater than that which rested upon Washington. Without the assistance of that Divine Being who ever attended him, I cannot succeed. With that assistance, I cannot fail. Trusting in Him who can go with me, and remain with you, and be everywhere for good, let us confidently hope that all will yet be well. To His care commending you, as I hope in your prayers you will commend me, I bid you an affectionate farewell.

SPEECH IN INDEPENDENCE HALL, PHILADELPHIA [2]

February 22, 1861

MR. CUYLER: I am filled with deep emotion at finding myself standing in this place, where were collected together the wisdom, the patriotism, the devotion to principle, from which sprang the institutions under which we live. You have kindly suggested to me that in my hands is the task of restoring peace to our distracted country. I can say in return, sir, that all the political sentiments I entertain have been drawn, so far as I have been able to draw them, from the sentiments which originated in and were given to the world from this hall. I have never had a feeling, politically, that did not spring from the sentiments embodied in the Declaration of Independence. I have often pondered over the dangers which were incurred by the men who assembled here and framed and adopted that Declaration. I have pondered over the toils that were endured by the officers and soldiers of the army who achieved that independence. I have often inquired of myself what great principle or idea it was that kept this Confederacy so long together. It was not the mere matter of separation of the colonies from the motherland, but that sentiment in the Declaration of Independence which gave liberty not alone to the people of this country, but hope to all the world, for all future time. It was that which gave promise that in due time the weights would be lifted from the shoulders of all men, and that all should have an equal chance. This is the sentiment embodied in the Declaration of Independence. Now, my friends, can this country be saved on that basis? If it can, I will consider myself one of the happiest men in the world if I can help to save it. If it cannot be saved upon that principle, it will be truly awful. But if this country cannot be saved without giving up that principle, I was about to say I would rather be assassinated on this spot than surrender it. Now, in my view of the present aspect of affairs, there is no need of bloodshed and war. There is no necessity for it. I am not in favor of such a course; and I may say in advance that there will be no bloodshed unless it is forced upon the government. The government will not use force, unless force is used against it.

[2] Delivered on Washington's birthday, as Lincoln was on his way to Washington to assume the presidency.

My friends, this is wholly an unprepared speech. I did not expect to be called on to say a word when I came here. I supposed I was merely to do something toward raising a flag. I may, therefore, have said something indiscreet. [Cries of "No, no."] But I have said nothing but what I am willing to live by, and, if it be the pleasure of Almighty God, to die by.

GETTYSBURG ADDRESS

November 19, 1863

Fourscore and seven years ago our fathers brought forth on this continent a new nation, conceived in liberty, and dedicated to the proposition that all men are created equal.

Now we are engaged in a great civil war, testing whether that nation, or any nation so conceived and so dedicated, can long endure. We are met on a great battle-field of that war. We have come to dedicate a portion of that field as a final resting-place for those who here gave their lives that that nation might live. It is altogether fitting and proper that we should do this.

But, in a larger sense, we cannot dedicate—we cannot consecrate—we cannot hallow—this ground. The brave men, living and dead, who struggled here, have consecrated it far above our poor power to add or detract. The world will little note nor long remember what we say here, but it can never forget what they did here. It is for us, the living, rather, to be dedicated here to the unfinished work which they who fought here have thus far so nobly advanced. It is rather for us to be here dedicated to the great task remaining before us—that from these honored dead we take increased devotion to that cause for which they gave the last full measure of devotion; that we here highly resolve that these dead shall not have died in vain; that this nation, under God, shall have a new birth of freedom; and that government of the people, by the people, for the people, shall not perish from the earth.

SECOND INAUGURAL ADDRESS

March 4, 1865

Fellow-Countrymen: At this second appearing to take the oath of the presidential office, there is less occasion for an extended address than there was at the first. Then a statement, somewhat in detail, of a course to be pursued, seemed fitting and proper. Now, at the expiration of four years, during which public declarations have been constantly called forth on every point and phase of the great contest which still absorbs the attention and engrosses the energies of the nation, little that is new could be presented. The progress of our arms, upon which all else chiefly depends, is as well known to the public as to myself; and it is, I trust, reasonably satisfactory and encouraging to all. With high hope for the future, no prediction in regard to it is ventured.

On the occasion corresponding to this four years ago, all thoughts were anxiously directed to an impending civil war. All dreaded it—all sought to avert it. While the inaugural address was being delivered from this place, devoted altogether to saving the Union without war, insurgent agents were in the city seeking to destroy it without war—seeking to dissolve the Union, and divide effects, by negotiation. Both parties deprecated war; but one of them would make war rather than let the nation survive; and the other would accept war rather than let it perish. And the war came.

One-eighth of the whole population were colored slaves, not distributed generally over the Union, but localized in the Southern part of it. These slaves constituted a peculiar and powerful interest. All knew that this interest was, somehow, the cause of the war. To strengthen, perpetuate, and extend this interest was the object for which the insurgents would rend the Union, even by war; while the government claimed no right to do more than to restrict the territorial enlargement of it.

Neither party expected for the war the magnitude or the duration which it has already attained. Neither anticipated that the cause of the conflict might cease with, or even before, the conflict itself should cease. Each looked for an easier triumph, and a result less fundamental and astounding. Both read the same Bible, and pray to the same God; and each invokes his aid against the other. It may seem strange that any men should dare to ask a just God's assistance in wringing their bread from the sweat of other men's faces; but let us judge not, that we be not judged. The prayers of both could not be answered—that of neither has been answered fully.

The Almighty has His own purposes. "Woe unto the world because of offenses! for it must needs be that offenses come; but woe to that man by whom the offense cometh." If we shall suppose that American slavery is one of those offenses which, in the providence of God, must needs come, but which, having continued through His appointed time, He now wills to remove, and that He gives to both North and South this terrible war, as the woe due to those by whom the offense came, shall we discern therein any departure from those divine attributes which the believers in a living God always ascribe to Him? Fondly do we hope—fervently do we pray—that this mighty scourge of war may speedily pass away. Yet, if God wills that it continue until all the wealth piled by the bondman's two hundred and fifty years of unrequited toil shall be sunk, and until every drop of blood drawn with the lash shall be paid by another drawn with the sword, as was said three thousand years ago, so still it must be said, "The judgments of the Lord are true and righteous altogether."

With malice toward none; with charity for all; with firmness in the right, as God gives us to see the right, let us strive on to finish the work we are in; to bind up the nation's wounds; to care for him who shall have borne the battle, and for his widow, and his orphan—to do all which may achieve and cherish a just and lasting peace among ourselves, and with all nations.

TO HORACE GREELEY

Executive Mansion, Washington, August 22, 1862.

HON. HORACE GREELEY:

DEAR SIR: I have just read yours of the 19th, addressed to myself through the New York *Tribune*. If there be in it any statements or assumptions of fact which I may know to be erroneous, I do not, now and here, controvert them. If there be in it any inferences which I may believe to be falsely drawn, I do not, now and here, argue against them. If there be perceptible in it an impatient and dictatorial tone, I waive it in deference to an old friend whose heart I have always supposed to be right.

As to the policy I "seem to be pursuing," as you say, I have not meant to leave any one in doubt.

I would save the Union. I would save it the shortest way under the Constitution. The sooner the national authority can be restored, the nearer the Union will be "the Union as it was." If there be those who would not save the Union unless they could at the same time save slavery, I do not agree with them. If there be those who would not save the Union unless they could at the same time destroy slavery, I do not agree with them. My paramount object in this struggle is to save the Union, and is not either to save or to destroy slavery. If I could save the Union without freeing any slave, I would do it; and if I could save it by freeing all the slaves, I would do it; and if I could save it by freeing some and leaving others alone, I would also do that. What I do about slavery and the colored race, I do because I believe it helps to save the Union; and what I forbear, I forbear because I do not believe it would help to save the Union. I shall do less whenever I shall believe what I am doing hurts the cause, and I shall do more whenever I shall believe doing more will help the cause. I shall try to correct errors when shown to be errors, and I shall adopt new views so fast as they shall appear to be true views.

I have here stated my purpose according to my view of official duty; and I intend no modification of my oft-expressed personal wish that all men everywhere could be free.

Yours,

A. LINCOLN.

TO EDWARD EVERETT

Executive Mansion, Washington, November 20, 1863.

HON. EDWARD EVERETT:

MY DEAR SIR: Your kind note of to-day is received. In our respective parts yesterday, you could not have been excused to make a short address, nor I a long one. I am pleased to know that, in your judgment, the little I did say was not entirely a failure. Of course I knew Mr. Everett would not fail, and yet, while the whole discourse was eminently satisfactory, and will be of great value, there were passages in it which transcended my expectations. The point made against the theory of the General Government being only an agency whose principals are the States, was new to me, and, as I think, is one of the best arguments for the national supremacy. The tribute to our noble women for their angel ministering to the suffering soldiers surpasses in its way, as do the subjects of it, whatever has gone before.

Our sick boy, for whom you kindly inquire, we hope is past the worst.

Your obedient servant,

A. LINCOLN.

TO GENERAL GRANT

Executive Mansion, Washington, April 30, 1864.

LIEUTENANT-GENERAL GRANT:

Not expecting to see you again before the spring campaign opens, I wish to express in this way my entire satisfaction with what you have done up to this time, so far as I understand it. The particulars of your plans I neither know nor seek to know. You are vigilant and self-reliant; and, pleased with this, I wish not to obtrude any constraints or restraints upon you. While I am very anxious that any great disaster or capture of our men in great numbers shall be avoided, I know these points are less likely to escape your attention than they would be mine. If there is anything wanting which is within my power to give, do not fail to let me know it. And now, with a brave army and a just cause, may God sustain you.

Yours very truly,

A. LINCOLN.

TO MRS. BIXBY

Executive Mansion, Washington, November 21, 1864.

MRS. BIXBY, Boston, Massachusetts:

DEAR MADAM: I have been shown in the files of the War Department a statement of the Adjutant-General of Massachusetts that you are the mother of five sons who have died gloriously on the field of battle. I feel how weak and fruitless must be any words of mine which should attempt to beguile you from the grief of a loss so overwhelming. But I cannot refrain from tendering to you the consolation that may be found in the thanks of the Republic they died to save. I pray that our heavenly Father may assuage the anguish of your bereavement, and leave you only the cherished memory of the loved and lost, and the solemn pride that must be yours to have laid so costly a sacrifice upon the altar of freedom.

Yours very sincerely and respectfully,

ABRAHAM LINCOLN.

WALT WHITMAN

(1819–1892)

Whitman, the son of "respectable" but uneducated parents, was born on a Long Island farm near Huntington in 1819. He had only elementary schooling, but learning to set type, he got the education afforded by the old-fashioned printing-office. His literary career began late, but had—to use Emerson's phrase—a "long foreground." Among early influences, he owed much to nature and to books, but most to sympathetic contact with all sorts of people. He spent days "on Long Island's seashores." There he "went over thoroughly the Old and New Testaments," and "absorbed" Shakespeare, Homer, and other first-rate books. He had "a passion for ferries" and for hobnobbing with the omnibus drivers along Broadway. He worked as school-teacher, farmer, carpenter, printer, and editor. Presently he began writing for the papers and magazines. He got wider knowledge of the American people in "a leisurely journey and working expedition" of eight thousand miles which he made, as printer and journalist, through the South and West. After "absorbing," as he says, "a million people, for fifteen years, with an intimacy, an eagerness, an abandon, probably never equalled," he was ready to write his *Leaves of Grass,* the first edition of which appeared in 1855. During the Civil War he spent some time with the Army of the Potomac, and then for three years nursed and befriended the wounded soldiers in the hospitals at Washington, an experience which deepened his sympathy with human nature "in the masses" and gave new feeling to his later work. His poems of the "war years" are on the whole his best. His health was now broken and the rest of his life was a decline. He held a government clerkship in Washington until he became partially paralyzed, when he retired to a very modest home in Camden, New Jersey. He collected his prose works, consisting mainly of notes and sketches, made at various periods, together with his "Democratic Vistas," and his prefaces to *Leaves of Grass,* under the title *Specimen Days and Collect* (1882). He was beginning to be recognized at his true worth when he died at Camden, in 1892.

While Whitman was primarily a poet, he has probably been underestimated as a prose writer. His prose is about equal in extent to his poetry, and though naturally less rhapsodical and more reflective, it has similar character, merit, and interest. It preaches the same gospel of democracy and comradeship; it has the same endless concreteness and vitality; and it shows the same disregard for every convention of grammar and style. It is often turgid and tiresomely diffuse; but often too, when warmed by his emotion and enthusiasm, it becomes electric. Its style, though eccentric, is often extraordinarily expressive.

From SPECIMEN DAYS [1]

The White House by Moonlight

February 24th.—A spell of fine soft weather. I wander about a good deal, sometimes at night under the moon. To-night took a long look at the President's house. The white portico—the palace-like, tall, round columns, spotless as snow—the walls also—the tender and soft moonlight, flooding the pale marble, and making peculiar faint languishing shades, not shadows—everywhere a soft transparent hazy, thin, blue moon-lace, hanging in the air—the brilliant and extra-plentiful clusters of gas, on and around the façade, columns, portico, &c.—everything so white, so marbly pure and dazzling, yet soft—the White House of future poems, and of dreams and dramas, there in the soft and copious moon—the gorgeous front, in the trees, under the lustrous flooding moon, full of reality, full of illusion—the forms of the trees, leafless, silent, in trunk and myriad-angles of branches, under the stars and sky—the White House of the land, and of beauty and night—sentries at the gates, and by the portico, silent, pacing there in blue overcoats—stopping you not at all, but eyeing you with sharp eyes, whichever way you move.

A New York Soldier

This afternoon, July 22d, I have spent a long time with Oscar F. Wilber, company G. 154th New York, low with chronic diarrhœa, and a bad wound also. He asked me to read him a chapter in the New Testament. I complied, and ask'd him what I should read. He said, "Make your own choice." I open'd at the close of one of the first books of the evangelists, and read the chapters describing the latter hours of Christ, and the scenes at the crucifixion. The poor, wasted young man ask'd me to read the following chapter also, how Christ rose again. I read very slowly, for Oscar was feeble. It pleased him very much, yet the tears were in his eyes. He ask'd me if I enjoy'd religion. I said, "Perhaps not, my dear, in the way you mean, and yet, may-be, it is the same thing." He said, "It is my chief reliance." He talk'd of death, and said he did not fear it. I said, "Why, Oscar, don't you think you will get well?" He said, "I may, but it is not probable." He spoke calmly of his condition. The wound was very bad, it discharged much. Then the diarrhœa had prostrated him, and I felt that he was even then the same as dying. He behaved very manly and affectionate. The kiss I gave him as I was about leaving he return'd fourfold. He gave me his mother's address, Mrs. Sally D. Wilber, Alleghany post-office, Cattaraugus county, N. Y. I had several such interviews with him. He died a few days after the one just described.

[1] This and the following selections from Whitman are reprinted by permission from Whitman's *Prose Works*, published by David McKay Company, Philadelphia; copyright 1881, 1888,

Abraham Lincoln

August 12th.—I see the President almost every day, as I happen to live where he passes to or from his lodgings out of town. He never sleeps at the White House during the hot season, but has quarters at a healthy location some three miles north of the city, the Soldiers' home, a United States military establishment. I saw him this morning about 8½ coming in to business, riding on Vermont avenue, near L street. He always has a company of twenty-five or thirty cavalry, with sabres drawn and held upright over their shoulders. They say this guard was against his personal wish, but he let his counsellors have their way. The party makes no great show in uniform or horses. Mr. Lincoln on the saddle generally rides a good-sized, easy-going gray horse, is dress'd in plain black, somewhat rusty and dusty, wears a black stiff hat, and looks about as ordinary in attire, &c., as the commonest man. A lieutenant, with yellow straps, rides at his left, and following behind, two by two, come the cavalry men, in their yellow-striped jackets. They are generally going at a slow trot, as that is the pace set them by the one they wait upon. The sabres and accoutrements clank, and the entirely unornamental *cortège* as it trots toward Lafayette square arouses no sensation, only some curious stranger stops and gazes. I see very plainly ABRAHAM LINCOLN's dark brown face, with the deep-cut lines, the eyes, always to me with a deep latent sadness in the expression. We have got so that we exchange bows, and very cordial ones. Sometimes the President goes and comes in an open barouche. The cavalry always accompany him, with drawn sabres. Often I notice as he goes out evenings—and sometimes in the morning, when he returns early—he turns off and halts at the large and handsome residence of the Secretary of War, on K street, and holds conference there. If in his barouche, I can see from my window he does not alight, but sits in his vehicle, and Mr. Stanton comes out to attend him. Sometimes one of his sons, a boy of ten or twelve, accompanies him, riding at his right on a pony. Earlier in the summer I occasionally saw the President and his wife, toward the latter part of the afternoon, out in a barouche, on a pleasure ride through the city. Mrs. Lincoln was dressed in complete black, with a long crape veil. The equipage is of the plainest kind, only two horses, and they nothing extra. They pass'd me once very close, and I saw the President in the face fully, as they were moving slowly, and his look, though abstracted, happen'd to be directed steadily in my eye. He bow'd and smiled, but far beneath his smile I noticed well the expression I have alluded to. None of the artists or pictures has caught the deep, though subtle and indirect expression of this man's face. There is something else there. One of the great portrait painters of two or three centuries ago is needed.

and 1891 by Walt Whitman. Reprinted by permission of Doubleday, Doran & Company, the authorized publishers.

Hours for the Soul

July 22d, 1878.—Living down in the country again. A wonderful conjunction of all that goes to make those sometimes miracle-hours after sunset—so near and yet so far. Perfect, or nearly perfect days, I notice, are not so very uncommon; but the combinations that make perfect nights are few, even in a lifetime. We have one of those perfections to-night. Sunset left things pretty clear; the larger stars were visible soon as the shades allow'd. A while after 8, three or four great black clouds suddenly rose, seemingly from different points, and sweeping with broad swirls of wind but no thunder, underspread the orbs from view everywhere, and indicated a violent heat-storm. But without storm, clouds, blackness, and all, sped and vanish'd as suddenly as they had risen; and from a little after 9 till 11 the atmosphere and the whole show above were in that state of exceptional clearness and glory just alluded to. In the northwest turned the Great Dipper with its pointers round the Cynosure. A little south of east the constellation of the Scorpion was fully up, with red Antares glowing in its neck; while dominating, majestic Jupiter swam, an hour and a half risen, in the east—(no moon till after 11). A large part of the sky seem'd just laid in great splashes of phosphorus. You could look deeper in, see farther through, than usual; the orbs thick as heads of wheat in a field. Not that there was any special brilliancy either—nothing near as sharp as I have seen of keen winter nights, but a curious general luminousness throughout to sight, sense, and soul. The latter had much to do with it. (I am convinced there are hours of Nature, especially of the atmosphere, mornings and evenings, address'd to the soul. Night transcends, for that purpose, what the proudest day can do.) Now, indeed, if never before, the heavens declared the glory of God. It was to the full the sky of the Bible, of Arabia, of the prophets, and of the oldest poems. There, in abstraction and stillness (I had gone off by myself to absorb the scene, to have the spell unbroken), the copiousness, the removedness, vitality, loose-clear-crowdedness, of that stellar concave spreading overhead, softly absorb'd into me, rising so free, interminably high, stretching east, west, north, south—and I, though but a point in the centre below, embodying all.

As if for the first time, indeed, creation noiselessly sank into and through me its placid and untellable lesson, beyond—O, so infinitely beyond!—anything from art, books, sermons, or from science, old or new. The spirit's hour —religion's hour—the visible suggestion of God in space and time—now once definitely indicated, if never again. The untold pointed at—the heavens all paved with it. The Milky Way, as if some superhuman symphony, some ode of universal vagueness, disdaining syllable and sound—a flashing glance of Deity, address'd to the soul. All silently—the indescribable night and stars— far off and silently.

THE SILENT GENERAL

Sept. 28, '79.—So General Grant, after circumambiating the world, has arrived home again—landed in San Francisco yesterday, from the ship City of Tokio from Japan. What a man he is! what a history! what an illustration —his life—of the capacities of that American individuality common to us all. Cynical critics are wondering "what the people can see in Grant" to make such a hubbub about. They aver (and it is no doubt true) that he has hardly the average of our day's literary and scholastic culture, and absolutely no pronounc'd genius or conventional eminence of any sort. Correct: but he proves how an average western farmer, mechanic, boatman, carried by tides of circumstances, perhaps caprices, into a position of incredible military or civic responsibilities (history has presented none more trying, no born monarch's, no mark more shining for attack or envy), may steer his way fitly and steadily through them all, carrying the country and himself with credit year after year—command over a million armed men—fight more than fifty heavy battles—rule for eight years a land larger than all the kingdoms of Europe combined—and then, retiring, quietly (with a cigar in his mouth) make the promenade of the whole world, through its courts and coteries, and kings and czars and mikados, and splendidest glitters and etiquettes, as phlegmatically as he ever walk'd the portico of a Missouri hotel after dinner. I say this all is what people like—and I am sure I like it. Seems to me it transcends Plutarch. How those old Greeks, indeed, would have seized on him; a mere plain man—no art, no poetry—only practical sense, ability to do, or try his best to do, what devolv'd upon him. A common trader, moneymaker, tanner, farmer of Illinois—general for the republic, in its terrific struggle with itself, in the war of attempted secession—President following (a task of peace, more difficult than the war itself)—nothing heroic, as the authorities put it—and yet the greatest hero. The gods, the destinies, seem to have concentrated upon him.

From NOVEMBER BOUGHS

A THOUGHT ON SHAKESPEARE

THE most distinctive poems—the most permanently rooted and with heartiest reason for being—the copious cycle of Arthurian legends, or the almost equally copious Charlemagne cycle, or the poems of the Cid, or Scandinavian Eddas, or Nibelungen, or Chaucer, or Spenser, or *bona fide* Ossian, or Inferno—probably had their rise in the great historic perturbations, which they came in to sum up and confirm, indirectly embodying results to date. Then however precious to "culture," the grandest of those poems, it may be said, preserve and typify results offensive to the modern spirit, and long past away. To state it briefly, and taking the strongest examples, in Homer lives the ruthless military prowess of Greece, and of its special god-descended dynastic houses; in Shakespeare the dragon-rancors and stormy feudal splendor of mediæval caste.

Poetry, largely consider'd, is an evolution, sending out improved and ever-expanded types—in one sense, the past, even the best of it, necessarily giving place, and dying out. For our existing world, the bases on which all the grand old poems were built have become vacuums—and even those of many comparatively modern ones are broken and half-gone. For us to-day, not their own intrinsic value, vast as that is, backs and maintains those poems—but a mountain-high growth of associations, the layers of successive ages. Everywhere—their own lands included—(is there not something terrible in the tenacity with which the one book out of millions holds its grip?)—the Homeric and Virgilian works, the interminable ballad-romances of the middle ages, the utterances of Dante, Spenser, and others, are upheld by their cumulus-entrenchment in scholarship, and as precious, always welcome, unspeakably valuable reminiscences.

Even the one who at present reigns unquestion'd—of Shakespeare—for all he stands for so much in modern literature, he stands entirely for the mighty æsthetic sceptres of the past, not for the spiritual and democratic, the sceptres of the future. The inward and outward characteristics of Shakespeare are his vast and rich variety of persons and themes, with his wondrous delineation of each and all—not only limitless funds of verbal and pictorial resource, but great excess, superfœtation—mannerism, like a fine, aristocratic perfume, holding a touch of musk (Euphues, his mark)—with boundless sumptuousness and adornment, real velvet and gems, not shoddy nor paste—but a good deal of bombast and fustian—(certainly some terrific mouthing in Shakespeare!).

Superb and inimitable as all is, it is mostly an objective and physiological kind of power and beauty the soul finds in Shakespeare—a style supremely grand of the sort, but in my opinion stopping short of the grandest sort, at any rate for fulfilling and satisfying modern and scientific and democratic American purposes. Think, not of growths as forests primeval, or Yellowstone geysers, or Colorado ravines, but of costly marble palaces, and palace rooms, and the noblest fixings and furniture, and noble owners and occupants to correspond—think of carefully built gardens from the beautiful but sophisticated gardening art at its best, with walks and bowers and artificial lakes, and appropriate statue-groups and the finest cultivated roses and lilies and japonicas in plenty—and you have the tally of Shakespeare. The low characters, mechanics, even the loyal henchmen—all in themselves nothing—serve as capital foils to the aristocracy. The comedies (exquisite as they certainly are) bringing in admirably portray'd common characters, have the unmistakable hue of plays, portraits, made for the divertisement only of the élite of the castle, and from its point of view. The comedies are altogether non-acceptable to America and Democracy.

But to the deepest soul, it seems a shame to pick and choose from the riches Shakespeare has left us—to criticise his infinitely royal, multiform quality—to gauge, with optic glasses, the dazzle of his sun-like beams.

The best poetic utterance, after all, can merely hint, or remind, often very indirectly, or at distant removes. Aught of real perfection, or the solution of any deep problem, or any completed statement of the moral, the true, the beautiful, eludes the greatest, deftest poet—flies away like an always uncaught bird.

From DEMOCRATIC VISTAS

I say that democracy can never prove itself beyond cavil, until it founds and luxuriantly grows its own forms of art, poems, schools, theology, displacing all that exists, or that has been produced anywhere in the past, under opposite influences. It is curious to me that while so many voices, pens, minds, in the press, lecture-rooms, in our Congress, &c., are discussing intellectual topics, pecuniary dangers, legislative problems, the suffrage, tariff and labor questions, and the various business and benevolent needs of America, with propositions, remedies, often worth deep attention, there is one need, a hiatus the profoundest, that no eye seems to perceive, no voice to state. Our fundamental want to-day in the United States, with closest, amplest reference to present conditions, and to the future, is of a class, and the clear idea of a class, of native authors, literatuses, far different, far higher in grade than any yet known, sacerdotal, modern, fit to cope with our occasions, lands, permeating the whole mass of American mentality, taste, belief, breathing into it a new breath of life, giving it decision, affecting politics far more than the popular superficial suffrage, with results inside and underneath the elections of Presidents or Congresses—radiating, begetting appropriate teachers, schools, manners, and, as its grandest result, accomplishing (what neither the schools nor the churches and their clergy have hitherto accomplish'd, and without which this nation will no more stand, permanently, soundly, than a house will stand without a substratum) a religious and moral character beneath the political and productive and intellectual bases of the States. For know you not, dear, earnest reader, that the people of our land may all read and write, and may all possess the right to vote—and yet the main things may be entirely lacking?—(and this to suggest them).

View'd, to-day, from a point of view sufficiently over-arching, the problem of humanity all over the civilized world is social and religious, and is to be finally met and treated by literature. The priest departs, the divine literatus comes. Never was anything more wanted than, to-day, and here in the States, the poet of the modern is wanted, or the great literatus of the modern. At all times, perhaps, the central point in any nation, and that whence it is itself really sway'd the most, and whence it sways others, is its national literature, especially its archetypal poems. Above all previous lands, a great original literature is surely to become the justification and reliance (in some respects the sole reliance) of American democracy.

Few are aware how the great literature penetrates all, gives hue to all, shapes aggregates and individuals, and, after subtle ways, with irresistible power, constructs, sustains, demolishes at will. Why tower, in reminiscence, above all the nations of the earth, two special lands, petty in themselves, yet inexpressibly gigantic, beautiful, columnar? Immortal Judah lives, and Greece immortal lives, in a couple of poems. . . .

I say we had best look our times and lands searchingly in the face, like a physician diagnosing some deep disease. Never was there, perhaps, more hollowness at heart than at present, and here in the United States. Genuine belief seems to have left us. The underlying principles of the States are not honestly believ'd in (for all this hectic glow, and these melodramatic screamings), nor is humanity itself believ'd in. What penetrating eye does not everywhere see through the mask? The spectacle is appalling. We live in an atmosphere of hypocrisy throughout. The men believe not in the women, nor the women in the men. A scornful superciliousness rules in literature. The aim of all the *littérateurs* is to find something to make fun of. A lot of churches, sects, &c., the most dismal phantasms I know, usurp the name of religion. Conversation is a mass of badinage. From deceit in the spirit, the mother of all false deeds, the offspring is already incalculable. An acute and candid person, in the revenue department in Washington, who is led by the course of his employment to regularly visit the cities, north, south and west, to investigate frauds, has talk'd much with me about his discoveries. The depravity of the business classes of our country is not less than has been supposed, but infinitely greater. The official services of America, national, state, and municipal, in all their branches and departments, except the judiciary, are saturated in corruption, bribery, falsehood, and maladministration; and the judiciary is tainted. The great cities reek with respectable as much as non-respectable robbery and scoundrelism. In fashionable life, flippancy, tepid amours, weak infidelism, small aims, or no aims at all, only to kill time. In business (this all-devouring word, business), the one sole object is, by any means, pecuniary gain. The magician's serpent in the fable ate up all the other serpents; the money-making is our magician's serpent, remaining to-day sole master of the field. The best class we show, is but a mob of fashionably dress'd speculators and vulgarians. True, indeed, behind this fantastic farce, enacted on the visible stage of society, solid things and stupendous labors are to be discover'd, existing crudely and going on in the background, to advance and tell themselves in time. Yet the truths are none the less terrible. I say that our New World democracy, however great a success in uplifting of the masses out of their sloughs, in materialistic development, products, and in a certain highly-deceptive superficial popular intellectuality, is, so far, an almost complete failure in its social aspects, and in really grand religious, moral, literary, and esthetic results. In vain do we march with unprecedented strides to empire so colossal, outvying the antique, beyond Alexander's, beyond the proudest sway of Rome. In vain have we annex'd Texas, California, Alaska, and reach north for Canada and south for Cuba. It is as if we were somehow being endow'd with a vast and more and more thoroughly-appointed body, and then left with little or no soul.

Let me illustrate further, as I write, with current observations, localities, &c. The subject is important, and will bear repetition. After an absence, I am now again (September, 1870) in New York city and Brooklyn, on a few weeks' vacation. The splendor, picturesqueness, and oceanic amplitude and rush of these great cities, the unsurpass'd situation, rivers and bay, sparkling sea-tides, costly and lofty new buildings, façades of marble and iron, of original grandeur and elegance of design, with the masses of gay color, the preponderance of white and blue, the flags flying, the endless ships, the tumultuous streets, Broadway, the heavy, low, musical roar, hardly ever intermitted, even at night; the jobbers' houses, the rich shops, the wharves, the great Central Park, and the Brooklyn Park of hills (as I wander among them this beautiful fall weather, musing, watching, absorbing)—the assemblages of the citizens in their groups, conversations, trades, evening amusements, or along the by-quarters—these, I say, and the like of these, completely satisfy my senses of power, fulness, motion, &c., and give me, through such senses and appetites, and through my esthetic conscience, a continued exaltation and absolute fulfilment. Always and more and more, as I cross the East and North rivers, the ferries, or with the pilots in their pilot-houses, or pass an hour in Wall street, or the gold exchange, I realize (if we must admit such partialisms), that not Nature alone is great in her fields of freedom and the open air, in her storms, the shows of night and day, the mountains, forests, seas—but in the artificial, the work of man too is equally great—in this profusion of teeming humanity—in these ingenuities, streets, goods, houses, ships—these hurrying, feverish, electric crowds of men, their complicated business genius (not the last among the geniuses), and all this mighty many-threaded wealth and industry concentrated here.

But sternly discarding, shutting our eyes to the glow and grandeur of the general superficial effect, coming down to what is of the only real importance, Personalities, and examining minutely, we question, we ask, Are there, indeed, *men* here worthy the name? Are there athletes? Are there perfect women, to match the generous material luxuriance? Is there a pervading atmosphere of beautiful manners? Are there crops of fine youths, and majestic old persons? Are there arts worthy freedom and a rich people? Is there a great moral and religious civilization—the only justification of a great material one? Confess that to severe eyes, using the moral microscope upon humanity, a sort of dry and flat Sahara appears, these cities, crowded with petty grotesques, malformations, phantoms, playing meaningless antics. Confess that everywhere, in shop, street, church, theatre, bar-room, official chair, are pervading flippancy and vulgarity, low cunning, infidelity—everywhere the youth puny, impudent, foppish, prematurely ripe—everywhere an abnormal libidinousness, unhealthy forms, male, female, painted, padded, dyed, chignon'd, muddy complexions, bad blood, the capacity for good motherhood deceasing or deceas'd, shallow notions of beauty, with a range of manners, or rather lack of manners (considering the advantages enjoy'd), probably the meanest to be seen in the world.

Of all this, and these lamentable conditions, to breathe into them the breath recuperative of sane and heroic life, I say a new founded literature, not merely to copy and reflect existing surfaces, or pander to what is called taste —not only to amuse, pass away time, celebrate the beautiful, the refined, the past, or exhibit technical, rhythmic, or grammatical dexterity—but a literature underlying life, religious, consistent with science, handling the elements and forces with competent power, teaching and training men—and, as perhaps the most precious of its results, achieving the entire redemption of woman out of these incredible holds and webs of silliness, millinery, and every kind of dyspeptic depletion—and thus insuring to the States a strong and sweet Female Race, a race of perfect Mothers—is what is needed. . . .

Dominion strong is the body's; dominion stronger is the mind's. What has fill'd, and fills to-day our intellect, our fancy, furnishing the standards therein, is yet foreign. The great poems, Shakespeare included, are poisonous to the idea of the pride and dignity of the common people, the life-blood of democracy. The models of our literature, as we get it from other lands, ultra-marine, have had their birth in courts, and bask'd and grown in castle sunshine; all smells of princes' favors. Of workers of a certain sort, we have, indeed, plenty, contributing after their kind; many elegant, many learn'd, all complacent. But touch'd by the national test, or tried by the standards of democratic personality, they wither to ashes. I say I have not seen a single writer, artist, lecturer, or what not, that has confronted the voiceless but ever erect and active, pervading, underlying will and typic aspiration of the land, in a spirit kindred to itself. Do you call those genteel little creatures American poets? Do you term that perpetual, pistareen, paste-pot work, American art, American drama, taste, verse? I think I hear, echoed as from some mountain-top afar in the west, the scornful laugh of the Genius of these States.

Democracy, in silence, biding its time, ponders its own ideals, not of literature and art only—not of men only, but of women. The idea of the women of America (extricated from this daze, this fossil and unhealthy air which hangs about the word *lady*), develop'd, raised to become the robust equals, workers, and, it may be, even practical and political deciders with the men— greater than man, we may admit, through their divine maternity, always their towering, emblematical attribute—but great, at any rate, as man, in all departments; or, rather, capable of being so, soon as they realize it, and can bring themselves to give up toys and fictions, and launch forth, as men do, amid real, independent, stormy life.

Then, as towards our thought's finale (and, in that, overarching the true scholar's lesson), we have to say there can be no complete or epical presentation of democracy in the aggregate, or anything like it, at this day, because its doctrines will only be effectually incarnated in any one branch, when, in all, their spirit is at the root and centre. Far, far, indeed, stretch, in distance, our Vistas! How much is still to be disentangled, freed! How long it takes to make this American world see that it is, in itself, the final authority and reliance! . . .

EDWARD EVERETT HALE

(1822–1909)

Edward Everett Hale was born in Boston in 1822. He came of a distinguished family, his father being proprietor and editor of the Boston *Daily Advertiser;* Edward Everett, the orator and statesman, an uncle; and Nathan Hale, the Revolutionary hero, a great-uncle. He was educated at the Boston Latin School and at Harvard, being graduated from the latter in 1839, following which he taught for a time in the former, while studying theology privately. He began to preach in 1842, and served as pastor of the Church of the Unity, Worcester, from 1846 to 1856. In the latter year he became pastor of the South Congregational Society, a Unitarian church in Boston, remaining there in active charge till 1901, and as pastor emeritus until his death in 1909.

Hale was popular as a preacher and lecturer, and was a great organizer, founding the Harry Wadsworth clubs, the King's Daughters, the Look-Up Legions, and a number of other societies. He was a voluminous writer, being author of over sixty books of fiction, biography, sermons, travel, and history; and was an editor, at first of *Old and New,* and after 1886 of *Lend a Hand,* a journal of organized charity. He was probably at his best in such stories as *The Man without a Country,* where he employed a minute realism that gave to the stories the effect of verisimilitude.

THE MAN WITHOUT A COUNTRY [1]

I SUPPOSE that very few casual readers of the *New York Herald* of August 13th observed, in an obscure corner, among the "Deaths," the announcement:

"NOLAN. Died on board U. S. Corvette *Levant,* Lat. 2° 11′ S., Long. 131° W., on the 11th of May, PHILIP NOLAN."

I happened to observe it, because I was stranded at the old Mission-House in Mackinac, waiting for a Lake Superior steamer which did not choose to come; and I was devouring to the very stubble all the current literature I could get hold of, even down to the deaths and marriages in the *Herald*. My memory for names and people is good, and the reader will see, as he goes on, that I had reason enough to remember Philip Nolan. There are hundreds of readers who would have paused at that announcement, if the officer of the *Levant* who reported it had chosen to make it thus: "Died, May 11th, The Man without a Country." For it was as "The Man without a Country" that poor Philip Nolan had generally been known by the officers who had him in charge dur-

[1] First published in the *Atlantic Monthly,* December, 1863.

ing some fifty years, as, indeed, by all the men who sailed under them. I dare say there is many a man who has taken wine with him once a fortnight, in a three years' cruise, who never knew that his name was "Nolan," or whether the poor wretch had any name at all.

There can now be no possible harm in telling this poor creature's story. Reason enough there has been till now, ever since Madison's administration went out in 1817, for very strict secrecy, the secrecy of honor itself, among the gentlemen of the navy who have had Nolan in successive charge. And certainly it speaks well for the *esprit de corps* of the profession, and the personal honor of its members, that to the press this man's story has been wholly unknown,—and, I think, to the country at large also. I have reason to think, from some investigations I made in the Naval Archives when I was attached to the Bureau of Construction, that every official report relating to him was burned when Ross burned the public buildings at Washington. One of the Tuckers, or possibly one of the Watsons, had Nolan in charge at the end of the war; and when, on returning from his cruise, he reported at Washington to one of the Crowninshields,—who was in the Navy Department when he came home,—he found that the Department ignored the whole business. Whether they really knew nothing about it, or whether it was a *"Non mi ricordo,"* determined on as a piece of policy, I do not know. But this I do know, that since 1817, and possibly before, no naval officer has mentioned Nolan in his report of a cruise.

But, as I say, there is no need for secrecy any longer. And now the poor creature is dead, it seems to me worth while to tell a little of his story, by way of showing young Americans of to-day what it is to be A Man without a Country.

Philip Nolan was as fine a young officer as there was in the "Legion of the West," as the Western division of our army was then called. When Aaron Burr made his first dashing expedition down to New Orleans in 1805, at Fort Massac, or somewhere above on the river, he met, as the Devil would have it, this gay, dashing, bright young fellow, at some dinner-party, I think. Burr marked him, talked to him, walked with him, took him a day or two's voyage in his flat-boat, and, in short, fascinated him. For the next year, barrack-life was very tame to poor Nolan. He occasionally availed himself of the permission the great man had given him to write to him. Long, high-worded, stilted letters the poor boy wrote and rewrote and copied. But never a line did he have in reply from the gay deceiver. The other boys in the garrison sneered at him, because he sacrificed in this unrequited affection for a politician the time which they devoted to Monongahela, sledge, and high-low-jack. Bourbon, euchre, and poker were still unknown. But one day Nolan had his revenge. This time Burr came down the river, not as an attorney seeking a place for his office, but as a disguised conqueror. He had defeated I know not how many district-attorneys; he had dined at I know not how many public dinners; he had been heralded in I know not how many *Weekly Arguses;* and it was rumored that he had an army behind him and an empire before him. It was a great day—his arrival—to poor Nolan. Burr had not been at the fort an hour before he sent for him. That evening he asked Nolan to take him out in his skiff to show him a cane-brake or a cottonwood tree, as he said,—really to seduce him; and by the time the sail was over, Nolan was enlisted body and soul. From that time, though he did not yet know it, he lived as a man without a country.

What Burr meant to do I know no more than you, dear reader. It is none of our business just now. Only, when the grand catastrophe came, and Jefferson and the House of Virginia of that day undertook to break on the wheel all the possible Clarences of the then House of York, by the great treason trial at Richmond, some of the lesser fry in that distant Mississippi Valley, which was farther from us than Puget's Sound is to-day, introduced the like novelty on their provincial stage; and, to while away the monotony of the summer at Fort Adams, got up, for *spectacles,* a string of court-martials on the officers there. One and another of the colonels and majors were tried, and, to fill out the list, little Nolan, against whom, Heaven knows, there was evidence enough,—that he was sick of the service, had been willing to be false to it, and would have obeyed any order to march any-whither with any one who would follow him, had the order only been signed, "By command of His Exc. A. Burr." The courts dragged on. The big flies escaped,—rightly for all I know. Nolan was proved guilty enough, as I say; yet you and I would never have heard of him, reader, but that, when the president of the court asked him at the close whether he wished to say anything to show that he had always been faithful to the United States, he cried out, in a fit of frenzy:

"D—n the United States! I wish I may never hear of the United States again!"

I suppose he did not know how the words shocked old Colonel Morgan, who was holding the court. Half the officers who sat in it had served through the Revolution; and their lives, not to say their necks, had been risked for the very idea which he so cavalierly cursed in his madness. He, on his part, had grown up in the West of those days, in the midst of "Spanish plot," "Orleans plot," and all the rest. He had been educated on a plantation, where the finest company was a Spanish officer or a French merchant from Orleans. His education, such as it was, had been perfected in commercial expeditions to Vera Cruz, and I think he told me his father once hired an Englishman to be a private tutor for a winter on the plantation. He had spent half his youth with an older brother, hunting horses in Texas; and, in a word, to him "United States" was scarcely a reality. Yet he had been fed by "United States" for all the years since he had been in the army. He had sworn on his faith as a Christian to be true to "United States." It was "United States" which gave him the uniform he wore, and the sword by his side. Nay, my poor Nolan, it was only because "United States" had picked you out first as one of her own confidential men of honor that "A. Burr" cared for you a straw more than for the flat-boat men who sailed his ark for him. I do not excuse Nolan; I only explain to the reader why he damned his country, and wished he might never hear her name again.

He never did hear her name but once again. From that moment, September 23, 1807, till the day he died, May 11, 1863, he never heard her name again. For that half century and more he was a man without a country.

Old Morgan, as I said, was terribly shocked. If Nolan had compared George Washington to Benedict Arnold, or had cried, "God save King George," Morgan would not have felt worse. He called the court into his private room, and returned in fifteen minutes, with a face like a sheet, to say,—

"Prisoner, hear the sentence of the Court! The Court decides, subject to the approval of the President, that you never hear the name of the United States again."

Nolan laughed. But nobody else laughed. Old Morgan was too solemn, and the whole room was hushed dead as night for a minute. Even Nolan lost his swagger in a moment. Then Morgan added,—

"Mr. Marshal, take the prisoner to Orleans in an armed boat, and deliver him to the naval commander there."

The marshal gave his orders, and the prisoner was taken out of court.

"Mr. Marshal," continued old Morgan, "see that no one mentions the United States to the prisoner. Mr. Marshal, make my respects to Lieutenant Mitchell at Orleans, and request him to order that no one shall mention the United States to the prisoner while he is on board ship. You will receive your written orders from the officer on duty here this evening. The Court is adjourned without day."

I have always supposed that Colonel Morgan himself took the proceedings of the court to Washington City, and explained them to Mr. Jefferson. Certain it is that the President approved them,—certain, that is, if I may believe the men who say they have seen his signature. Before the *Nautilus* got round from New Orleans to the northern Atlantic coast with the prisoner on board, the sentence had been approved, and he was a man without a country.

The plan then adopted was substantially the same which was necessarily followed ever after. Perhaps it was suggested by the necessity of sending him by water from Fort Adams and Orleans. The Secretary of the Navy—it must have been the first Crowninshield, though he is a man I do not remember—was requested to put Nolan on board a government vessel bound on a long cruise, and to direct that he should be only so far confined there as to make it certain that he never saw or heard of the country. We had few long cruises then, and the navy was very much out of favor; and as almost all of this story is traditional, as I have explained, I do not know certainly what his first cruise was. But the commander to whom he was entrusted,—perhaps it was Tingey or Shaw, though I think it was one of the younger men,—we are all old enough now—regulated the etiquette and the precautions of the affair, and according to his scheme they were carried out, I suppose, till Nolan died.

When I was second officer of the *Intrepid,* some thirty years after, I saw the original paper of instructions. I have been sorry ever since that I did not copy the whole of it. It ran, however, much in this way:—

"Washington (with the date, which must have been late in 1807).

"Sir,—You will receive from Lieutenant Neale the person of Philip Nolan, late a lieutenant in the United States Army.

"This person on his trial by court-martial expressed, with an oath, the wish that he might 'never hear of the United States again.'

"The Court sentenced him to have his wish fulfilled.

"For the present, the execution of the order is entrusted by the President to this Department.

"You will take the prisoner on board your ship, and keep him there with such precautions as shall prevent his escape.

"You will provide him with such quarters, rations, and clothing as would be proper for an officer of his late rank, if he were a passenger on your vessel on the business of his Government.

"The gentlemen on board will make any arrangements agreeable to themselves regarding his society. He is to be exposed to no indignity of any kind, nor is he ever unnecessarily to be reminded that he is a prisoner.

"But under no circumstances is he ever to hear of his country or to see any information regarding it; and you will specially caution all the officers under your command to take care, that, in the various indulgences which may be granted, this rule, in which his punishment is involved, shall not be broken.

"It is the intention of the Government that he shall never again see the country which he has disowned. Before the end of your cruise you will receive orders which will give effect to this intention.

"Respectfully yours,
"W. Southard, for the
"Secretary of the Navy."

If I had only preserved the whole of this paper, there would be no break in the beginning of my sketch of this story. For Captain Shaw, if it was he, handed it to his successor in the charge, and he to his; and I suppose the commander of the *Levant* has it to-day as his authority for keeping this man in this mild custody.

The rule adopted on board the ships on which I have met "the man without a country" was, I think, transmitted from the beginning. No mess liked to have him permanently, because his presence cut off all talk of home or of the prospect of return, of politics or letters, of peace or of war,—cut off more than half the talk men like to have at sea. But it was always thought too hard that he should never meet the rest of us, except to touch hats; and we finally sank into one system. He was not permitted to talk with the men, unless an officer was by. With officers he had unrestrained intercourse, as far as they and he chose. But he grew shy, though he had favorites: I was one. Then the captain always asked him to dinner on Monday. Every mess in succession took up the invitation in its turn. According to the size of the ship, you had him at your mess more or less often at dinner. His breakfast he ate in his own stateroom,—he always had a stateroom,—which was where a sentinel or somebody on the watch could see the door. And whatever else he ate or drank, he ate or drank alone. Sometimes, when the marines or sailors had any special jollification, they were permitted to invite "Plain-Buttons," as they called him. Then Nolan was sent with some officer, and the men were forbidden to speak of home while he was there. I believe the theory was that the sight of his punishment did them good. They called him "Plain-Buttons," because, while he always chose to wear a regulation army uniform, he was not permitted to wear the army button, for the reason that it bore either the initials or the insignia of the country he had disowned.

I remember, soon after I joined the navy, I was on shore with some of the older officers from our ship and from the *Brandywine,* which we had met at Alexandria. We had leave to make a party and go up to Cairo and the Pyramids. As we jogged along (you went on donkeys then), some of the gentlemen (we boys called them "Dons," but the phrase was long since changed) fell to talking about Nolan, and some one told the system which was adopted from the first about his books and other reading. As he was almost never permitted to go on shore, even though the vessel lay in port for months, his time at the best hung heavy; and everybody was permitted to lend him books, if they were not published in America and made no allusion to it. These were common enough in the old days, when people in the other hemisphere talked of the United States as little as we do of Paraguay. He had almost all the foreign papers that came into the ship, sooner or later, only somebody must go over them first, and cut out any advertisement or stray paragraph that alluded to America. This was a little cruel sometimes, when the back of what was cut out might be as innocent as Hesiod. Right in the midst of one of Napoleon's battles, or one of Canning's speeches, poor Nolan would find a great hole, because on the back of the page of that paper there had been an advertisement of a packet for New York, or a scrap from the President's message. I say this was the first time I ever heard of this plan, which afterwards I had enough, and more than enough, to do with. I remember it because poor Phillips, who was of the party, as soon as the allusion to reading was made, told a story of something which happened at the Cape of Good Hope on Nolan's first voyage; and it is the only thing I ever knew of that voyage. They had touched at the Cape, and had done the civil thing with the English Admiral and the fleet; and then, leaving for a long cruise up the Indian Ocean, Phillips had borrowed a lot of English books from an officer, which, in those days, as indeed in these, was quite a windfall. Among them, as the Devil would order, was the *Lay of the Last Minstrel,* which they had all of them heard of, but which most of them had never seen. I think it could not have been published long. Well, nobody thought there could be any risk of anything national in that, though Phillips swore old Shaw had cut out *The Tempest* from Shakespeare before he let Nolan have it, because he said "the Bermudas ought to be ours, and, by Jove, should be one day." So Nolan was permitted to join the circle one afternoon when a lot of them sat on deck smoking and reading aloud. People do not do such things so often now; but when I was young we got rid of a great deal of time so. Well, so it happened that in his turn Nolan took the book and read to the others; and he read very well, as I know. Nobody in the circle knew a line of the poem, only it was all magic and Border chivalry, and was ten thousand years ago. Poor Nolan read steadily through the fifth canto, stopped a minute and drank something, and then began, without a thought of what was coming,—

> Breathes there the man, with soul so dead,
> Who never to himself hath said,—

It seems impossible to us that anybody ever heard this for the first time; but all these fellows did then, and poor Nolan himself went on, still unconsciously or mechanically,—

> This is my own, my native land!

Then they all saw something was to pay; but he expected to get through, I suppose, turned a little pale, but plunged on,—

> Whose heart hath ne'er within him burned,
> As home his footsteps he hath turned
> From wandering on a foreign strand?—
> If such there breathe, go, mark him well,—

By this time the men were all beside themselves, wishing there was any way to make him turn over two pages; but he had not quite presence of mind for that; he gagged a little, colored crimson, and staggered on,—

> For him no minstrel raptures swell;
> High though his titles, proud his name,
> Boundless his wealth as wish can claim,

Despite these titles, power, and pelf,
The wretch, concentered all in self,—

and here the poor fellow choked, could not go on, but started up, swung the book into the sea, vanished into his stateroom, "and by Jove," said Phillips, "we did not see him for two months again. And I had to make up some beggarly story to that English surgeon why I did not return his Walter Scott to him."

That story shows about the time when Nolan's braggadocio must have broken down. At first, they said, he took a very high tone, considered his imprisonment a mere farce, affected to enjoy the voyage, and all that; but Phillips said that after he came out of his stateroom he never was the same man again. He never read aloud again, unless it was the Bible or Shakespeare, or something else he was sure of. But it was not that merely. He never entered in with the other young men exactly as a companion again. He was always shy afterwards, when I knew him,—very seldom spoke, unless he was spoken to, except to a very few friends. He lighted up occasionally,—I remember late in his life hearing him fairly eloquent on something which had been suggested to him by one of Fléchier's sermons,—but generally he had the nervous, tired look of a heart-wounded man.

When Captain Shaw was coming home,—if, as I say, it was Shaw,—rather to the surprise of everybody they made one of the Windward Islands, and lay off and on for nearly a week. The boys said the officers were sick of salt-junk, and meant to have turtle-soup before they came home. But after several days the *Warren* came to the same rendezvous; they exchanged signals; she sent to Phillips and these homewardbound men letters and papers, and told them she was outward-bound, perhaps to the Mediterranean, and took poor Nolan and his traps on the boat back to try his second cruise. He looked very blank when he was told to get ready to join her. He had known enough of the signs of the sky to know that till that moment he was going "home." But this was a distinct evidence of something he had not thought of, perhaps,— that there was no going home for him, even to a prison. And this was the first of some twenty such transfers, which brought him sooner or later into half our best vessels, but which kept him all his life at least some hundred miles from the country he had hoped he might never hear of again.

It may have been on that second cruise,—it was once when he was up the Mediterranean,—that Mrs. Graff, the celebrated Southern beauty of those days, danced with him. They had been lying a long time in the Bay of Naples, and the officers were very intimate in the English fleet, and there had been great festivities, and our men thought they must give a great ball on board the ship. How they ever did it on board the *Warren* I am sure I do not know. Perhaps it was not the *Warren,* or perhaps ladies did not take up so much room as they do now. They wanted to use Nolan's stateroom for something, and they hated to do it without asking him to the ball; so the captain said they might ask him, if they would be responsible that he did not talk with the wrong people, "who would give him intelligence." So the dance went on, the finest party that had ever been known, I dare say; for I never heard of a man-of-war ball that was not. For ladies they had the family of the American consul, one or two travelers who had adventured so far, and a nice bevy of English girls and matrons, perhaps Lady Hamilton herself.

Well, different officers relieved each other in standing and talking with Nolan in a friendly way, so as to be sure that nobody else spoke to him. The dancing went on with spirit, and after a while even the fellows who took this honorary guard of Nolan ceased to fear any *contretemps*. Only when some English lady—Lady Hamilton, as I said, perhaps—called for a set of "American dances," an odd thing happened. Everybody then danced contra-dances. The black band, nothing loath, conferred as to what "American dances" were, and started off with "Virginia Reel," which they followed with "Money-Musk," which, in its turn in those days, should have been followed by "The Old Thirteen." But just as Dick, the leader, tapped for his fiddles to begin, and bent forward, about to say, in true negro state, " 'The Old Thirteen,' gentlemen and ladies!" as he had said " 'Virginny Reel,' if you please!" and " 'Money-Musk,' if you please!" the captain's boy tapped him on the shoulder, whispered to him, and he did not announce the name of the dance; he merely bowed, began on the air, and they all fell to,—the officers teaching the English girls the figure, but not telling them why it had no name.

But that is not the story I started to tell. As the dancing went on, Nolan and our fellows all got at ease, as I said,—so much so, that it seemed quite natural for him to bow to that splendid Mrs. Graff, and say,—

"I hope you have not forgotten me, Miss Rutledge. Shall I have the honor of dancing?"

He did it so quickly, that Fellows, who was by him, could not hinder him. She laughed and said,—

"I am not Miss Rutledge any longer, Mr. Nolan; but I will dance all the same," just nodded to Fellows, as if to say he must leave Mr. Nolan to her, and led him off to the place where the dance was forming.

Nolan thought he had got his chance. He had known her at Philadelphia, and at other places had met her, and this was a godsend. You could not talk in contra-dances, as you do in cotillions, or even in the pauses of waltzing; but there were chances for tongues and sounds, as well as for eyes and blushes. He began with her travels, and Europe, and Vesuvius, and the French; and then, when they had worked down, and had that long talking-time at the bottom of the set, he said boldly,—a little pale, she said, as she told me the story years after,—

"And what do you hear from home, Mrs. Graff?"

And that splendid creature looked through him. Jove! how she must have looked through him!

"Home!! Mr. Nolan!!! I thought you were the man who never wanted to hear of home again!"—and she walked directly up the deck to her husband, and left poor Nolan alone, as he always was.—He did not dance again.

I cannot give any history of him in order; nobody can now: and, indeed, I am not trying to. These are the traditions, which I sort out, as I believe them, from the myths which have been told about this man for forty years. The lies that have been told about him are legion. The fellows used to say he was the "Iron Mask"; and poor George Pons went to his grave in the belief that this was the author of "Junius," who was being punished for his celebrated libel on Thomas Jefferson. Pons was not very strong in the historical line. A happier story than either of these I have told is of the war. That came along soon after. I have heard this affair told in three or four ways,—and, indeed, it may have happened more than once. But which ship it was on I cannot tell. However, in one, at least, of the great frigate-duels with the English, in which the navy was really baptized, it happened that a round-shot from the enemy entered one of our ports square, and took right down the officer of the gun himself, and almost every man of the gun's crew. Now you may say what you choose about courage, but that is not a nice thing to see. But, as the men who were not killed picked themselves up, and as they and the surgeon's people were carrying off the bodies, there appeared Nolan, in his shirt-sleeves, with the rammer in his hand, and, just as if he had been the officer, told them off with authority,—who should go to the cock-pit with the wounded men, who should stay with him,—perfectly cheery, and with that way which makes men feel sure all is right and is going to be right. And he finished loading the gun with his own hands, aimed it, and bade the men fire. And there he stayed, captain of that gun, keeping those fellows in spirits, till the enemy struck,—sitting on the carriage while the gun was cooling, though he was exposed all the time,—showing them easier ways to handle heavy shot,—making the raw hands laugh at their own blunders, —and when the gun cooled again, getting it loaded and fired twice as often as any other gun on the ship. The captain walked forward by way of encouraging the men, and Nolan touched his hat and said,—

"I am showing them how we do this in the artillery, sir."

And this is the part of the story where all the legends agree: that the Commodore said,—

"I see you do, and I thank you, sir; and I shall never forget this day, sir, and you never shall, sir."

And after the whole thing was over, and he had the Englishman's sword, in the midst of the state and ceremony of the quarterdeck, he said,—

"Where is Mr. Nolan? Ask Mr. Nolan to come here."

And when Nolan came, the captain said,—

"Mr. Nolan, we are all very grateful to you to-day; you are one of us to-day; you will be named in the despatches."

And then the old man took off his own sword of ceremony, and gave it to Nolan, and made him put it on. The man told me this who saw it. Nolan cried like a baby, and well he might. He had not worn a sword since that infernal day at Fort Adams. But always afterwards, on occasions of ceremony, he wore that quaint old French sword of the Commodore's.

The captain did mention him in the despatches. It was always said he asked that he might be pardoned. He wrote a special letter to the Secretary of War. But nothing ever came of it. As I said, that was about the time when they began to ignore the whole transaction at Washington, and when Nolan's imprisonment began to carry itself on because there was nobody to stop it without any new orders from home.

I have heard it said that he was with Porter when he took possession of the Nukahiwa Islands. Not this Porter, you know, but old Porter, his father, *Essex* Porter,—that is, the old *Essex* Porter, not this *Essex*. As an artillery officer, who had seen service in the West, Nolan knew more about fortifications, embrasures, ravelins, stockades, and all that, than any of them did; and he worked with a right good-will in fixing that battery all right. I have always thought it was a pity Porter did not leave him in command there with Gamble. That would have settled all the question about his punishment. We should have kept the islands, and at this moment we should have one station in the Pacific Ocean. Our French friends, too, when they wanted this little watering-place, would have found it was preoccupied. But Madison and the Virginians, of course, flung all that away.

All that was near fifty years ago. If Nolan was thirty then, he must have been near eighty when he died. He looked sixty when he was forty. But he never seemed to me to change a hair afterwards. As I imagine his life, from what I have seen and heard of it, he must have been in every sea, and yet almost never on land. He must have known, in a formal way, more officers in our service than any man living knows. He told me once, with a grave smile, that no man in the world lived so methodical a life as he. "You know the boys say I am the Iron Mask, and you know how busy he was." He said it did not do for any one to try to read all the time, more than to do anything else all the time; and that he read just five hours a day. "Then," he said, "I keep up my notebooks, writing in them at such and such hours from what I have been reading; and I include in these my scrap-books." These were very curious indeed. He had six or eight, of different subjects. There was one of History, one of Natural Science, one which he called "Odds and Ends." But they were not merely books of extracts from newspapers. They had bits of plants and ribbons, shells tied on, and carved scraps of bone and wood, which he had taught the men to cut for him, and they were beautifully illustrated. He drew admirably. He had some of the funniest drawings there, and some of the most pathetic, that I have ever seen in my life. I wonder who will have Nolan's scrap-books.

Well, he said his reading and his notes were his profession, and that they took five hours and two hours respectively of each day. "Then," said he, "every man should have a diversion as well as a profession. My Natural History is my diversion." That took two hours a day more. The men used to bring him birds and fish, but on a long cruise he had to satisfy himself with centipedes and cockroaches and such small game. He was the only naturalist I ever met who knew anything about the habits of the house-fly and the mosquito. All those people can tell you whether they are *Lepidoptera* or *Steptopotera;* but as for telling how you can get rid of them, or how they get away from you when you strike them,—why Linnæus knew as little of that as John Foy the idiot did. These nine hours made Nolan's regular daily "occupation." The rest of the time he talked or walked. Till he grew very old, he went aloft a great deal. He always kept up his exercise; and I never heard that he was ill. If any other man was ill, he was the kindest nurse in the world; and he knew more than half the surgeons do. Then if anybody was sick or died, or if the captain wanted him to, on any other occasion, he was always ready to read prayers. I have said that he read beautifully.

My own acquaintance with Philip Nolan began six or eight years after the war, on my first voyage after I was appointed a midshipman. It was in the first days after our Slave-Trade treaty, while the Reigning House, which was still the House of Virginia, had still a sort of sentimentalism about the suppression of the horrors of the Middle Passage, and something was sometimes done that way. We were in the South Atlantic on that business. From the time I joined, I believe I thought Nolan was a sort of lay chaplain,—a chaplain with a blue coat. I never asked about him. Everything in the ship was strange to me. I knew it was green to ask questions, and I suppose I thought there was a "Plain-Buttons" on every ship. We had him to dine in our mess once a week, and the caution was given that on that day nothing was to be said about home. But if they had told us not to say anything about the planet Mars or the Book of Deuteronomy, I should not have asked why; there were a great many things which seemed to me to have as little reason. I first came to understand anything about "the man without a country" one day when we overhauled a dirty little schooner which had slaves on board. An officer was sent to take charge of her, and, after a few minutes, he sent back his boat to ask that some one might be sent him who could speak Portuguese. We were all looking over the rail when the message came, and we all wished we could interpret, when the captain asked who spoke Portuguese. But none of the officers did; and just as the captain was sending forward to ask if any of the people could, Nolan stepped out and said he should be glad to interpret, if the captain wished, as he understood the language. The captain thanked him, fitted out another boat with him, and in this boat it was my luck to go.

When we got there, it was such a scene as you seldom see, and never want to. Nastiness beyond account, and chaos run loose in the midst of the nastiness. There were not a great many of the negroes; but by way of making what there were understand that they were free, Vaughan had had their hand-cuffs and ankle-cuffs knocked off, and, for convenience' sake, was putting them upon the rascals of the schooner's crew. The negroes were, most of them, out of the hold, and swarming all round the dirty deck, with a central throng surrounding Vaughan and addressing him in every dialect, and *patois* of a dialect, from the Zulu "click" up to the Parisian of Beledeljereed.

As we came on deck, Vaughan looked down from a hogshead, on which he had mounted in desperation, and said:

"For God's love, is there anybody who can make these wretches understand something? The men gave them rum, and that did not quiet them. I knocked that big fellow down twice, and that did not soothe him. And then I talked Choctaw to all of them together; and I'll be hanged if they understood that as well as they understood the English."

Nolan said he could speak Portuguese, and one or two fine-looking Kroomen were dragged out, who, as it had been found already, had worked for the Portuguese on the coast of Fernando Po.

"Tell them they are free," said Vaughan; "and tell them that these rascals are to be hanged as soon as we can get rope enough."

Nolan "put that into Spanish,"—that is, he explained it in such Portuguese as the Kroomen could understand, and they in turn to such of the negroes as could understand them. Then there was such a yell of delight, clinching of fists, leaping and dancing, kissing of Nolan's feet, and a general rush made to the hogshead by way of spontaneous worship of Vaughan, as the *deus ex machina* of the occasion.

"Tell them," said Vaughan, well pleased, "that I will take them all to Cape Palmas."

This did not answer so well. Cape Palmas was practically as far from the homes of most of them as New Orleans or Rio Janeiro was; that is, they would be eternally separated from home there. And their interpreters, as we could understand, instantly said, *"Ah, non Palmas,"* and began to propose infinite other expedients in most voluble language. Vaughan was rather disappointed at this result of his liberality, and asked Nolan eagerly what they said. The drops stood on poor Nolan's white forehead, as he hushed the men down, and said:

"He says, 'Not Palmas.' He says, 'Take us home, take us to our own country, take us to our own house, take us to our own pickaninnies and our own women.' He says he has an old father and mother who will die if they do not see him. And this one says he left his people all sick, and paddled down to Fernando to beg the white doctor to come and help them, and that these devils caught him in the bay just in sight of home, and that he has never seen anybody from home since then. And this one says," choked out Nolan, "that he has not heard a word from his home in six months, while he has been locked up in an infernal barracoon."

Vaughan always said he grew gray himself while Nolan struggled through this interpretation. I, who did not understand anything of the passion involved in it, saw that the very elements were melting with fervent heat, and that something was to pay somewhere. Even the negroes themselves stopped howling, as they saw Nolan's agony, and Vaughan's almost equal agony of sympathy. As quick as he could get words, he said:

"Tell them yes, yes, yes; tell them they shall go to the Mountains of the Moon, if they will. If I sail the schooner through the Great White Desert, they shall go home!"

And after some fashion Nolan said so. And then they all fell to kissing him again, and wanted to rub his nose with theirs.

But he could not stand it long; and getting Vaughan to say he might go back, he beckoned me down into our boat. As we lay back in the stern-sheets and the men gave way, he said to me: "Youngster, let that show you what it is to be without a family, without a home, and without a country. And if you are ever tempted to say a word or to do a thing that shall put a bar between you and your family, your home, and your country, pray God in His mercy to take you that instant home to His own heaven. Stick by your family, boy; forget you have a self, while you do everything for them. Think of your home, boy; write, and send, and talk about it. Let it be nearer and nearer to your thought, the farther you have to travel from it; and rush back to it when you are free, as that poor black slave is doing now. And for your country, boy," and the words rattled in his throat, "and for that flag," and he pointed to the ship, "never dream a dream but of serving her as she bids you, though the service carry you through a thousand hells. No matter what happens to you, no matter who flatters you or who abuses you, never look at another flag, never let a night pass but you pray God to bless that flag. Remember, boy, that behind all these men you have to do with, behind officers, and government, and people even, there is the Country Herself, your Country, and that you belong to Her as you belong to your own mother. Stand by Her, boy, as you would stand by your mother, if those devils there had got hold of her to-day!"

I was frightened to death by his calm, hard passion; but I blundered out that I would, by all that was holy, and that I had never thought of doing anything else. He hardly seemed to hear me; but he did, almost in a whisper, say,—"Oh, if anybody had said so to me when I was of your age!"

I think it was this half-confidence of his, which I never abused, for I never told this story till now, which afterward made us great friends. He was very kind to me. Often he sat up, or even got up, at night, to walk the deck with me, when it was my watch. He explained to me a great deal of my mathematics, and I owe to him my taste for mathematics. He lent me books, and helped me about my reading. He never alluded so directly to his story again; but from one and another officer I have learned, in thirty years, what I am telling. When we parted from him in St. Thomas harbor, at the end of our cruise, I was more sorry than I can tell. I was very glad to meet him again in 1830; and later in life, when I thought I had some influence in Washington, I moved heaven and earth to have him discharged. But it was like getting a ghost out of prison. They pretended there was no such man, and never was such a man. They will say so at the Department now! Perhaps they do not know. It will not be the first thing in the service of which the Department appears to know nothing!

There is a story that Nolan met Burr once on one of our vessels, when a party of Americans came on board in the Mediterranean. But this I believe to be a lie; or rather, it is a myth, *ben trovato,* involving a tremendous blowing-up with which he sunk Burr,—asking him how he liked to be "without a country." But it is clear, from Burr's life, that nothing of the sort could have happened; and I mention this only as an illustration of the stories which get a-going where there is the least mystery at bottom. . . .

For him, poor fellow, he repented of his folly; and then, like a man, submitted to the fate he had asked for. He never intentionally added to the difficulty or delicacy of the charge of those who had him in hold. Accidents would happen; but they never happened from his fault. Lieutenant Truxton told me that, when Texas was annexed, there was a careful discussion among the officers, whether they should get hold of Nolan's handsome set of maps and cut Texas out of it,—from the map of the world and the map of Mexico. The United States had been cut out when the atlas was bought for him. But it was voted, rightly enough, that to do this would be virtually to reveal to him what had happened, or, as Harry Cole said, to make him think Old Burr had succeeded. So it was from no fault of Nolan's that a great botch happened at my own table, when, for a short time, I was in command of the *George Washington,* corvette, on the South American station. We were lying in the La Plata; and some of the officers, who had been on shore and had just joined again, were entertaining us with accounts of their misadventures in riding the half-wild horses of Buenos Ayres. Nolan was at table, and was in an unusually bright and talkative mood. Some story of a tumble reminded him of an adventure of his own when he was catching wild horses in Texas with his brother Stephen, at a time when he must have been quite a boy. He told the story with a good deal of spirit,—so much so, that the silence which often follows a good story hung over the table for an instant, to be broken by Nolan himself. For he asked, perfectly unconsciously,—"Pray, what has become of Texas? After the Mexicans got their independence, I thought that province of Texas would come forward very fast. It is really one of the finest regions on earth; it is the Italy of this continent. But I have not seen or heard a word of Texas for near twenty years."

There were two Texan officers at the table. The reason he had never heard of Texas was that Texas and her affairs had been painfully cut out of his newspapers since Austin began his settlements; so that, while he read of Honduras and Tamaulipas, and till quite lately, of California, this virgin province, in which his brother had traveled so far, and, I believe, had died, had ceased to be to him. Waters and Williams, the two Texas men, looked grimly at each other and tried not to laugh. Edward Morris had his attention attracted by the third link in the chain of the captain's chandelier. Watrous was seized with a convulsion of sneezing. Nolan himself saw that something was to pay, he did not know what. And I, as master of the feast, had to say,—

"Texas is out of the map, Mr. Nolan. Have you seen Captain Back's curious account of Sir Thomas Roe's Welcome?"

After that cruise I never saw Nolan again. I wrote to him at least twice a year, for in that voyage we became even confidentially intimate; but he never wrote to me. The other men tell me that in those fifteen years he aged very fast, as well he might indeed; but that he was still the same gentle, uncomplaining, silent sufferer that he ever was, bearing as best he could his self-appointed punishment,—rather less social, perhaps, with new men whom he did not know, but more anxious, apparently, than ever to serve and befriend and teach the boys, some of whom fairly seemed to worship him. And now it seems the dear old fellow is dead. He has found a home at last, and a country.

Since writing this, and while considering whether or no I would print it, as a warning to the young Nolans and Vallandighams and Tatnalls of to-day of what it is to throw away a country, I have received from Danforth, who is on board the *Levant*, a letter which gives an account of Nolan's last hours. It removes all my doubts about telling this story.

To understand the first words of the letter, the non-professional reader should remember that after 1817, the position of every officer who had Nolan in charge was one of the greatest delicacy. The government had failed to renew the order of 1807 regarding him. What was a man to do? Should he let him go? What, then, if he were called to account by the Department for violating the order of 1807? Should he keep him? What, then, if Nolan should be liberated some day, and should bring an action for false imprisonment or kidnapping against every man who had had him in charge? I urged and pressed this upon Southard, and I have reason to think that other officers did the same thing. But the Secretary always said, as they often do at Washington, that there were no special orders to give, and that we must act on our own judgment. That means, "if you succeed, you will be sustained; if you fail, you will be disavowed." Well, as Danforth says, all that is over now, though I do not know but I expose myself to a criminal prosecution on the evidence of the very revelation I am making.

Here is the letter:

"Levant, 2° 2' S. @ 131° W.

"Dear Fred:—I try to find heart and life to tell you that it is all over with dear old Nolan. I have been with him on this voyage more than I ever was, and I can understand wholly now the way in which you used to speak of the dear old fellow. I could see that he was not strong, but I had no idea the end was so near. The doctor had been watching him very carefully, and yesterday morning came to me and told me that Nolan was not so well, and had not left his stateroom,—a thing I never remember before. He had let the doctor come and see him as he lay there,—the first time the doctor had been in the stateroom,—and he said he should like to see me. Oh, dear! do you remember the mysteries we boys used to invent about his room in the old *Intrepid* days? Well, I went in, and there, to be sure, the poor fellow lay in his berth, smiling pleasantly as he gave me his hand, but looking very frail. I could not help a glance round, which showed me what a little shrine he had made of the box he was lying in. The stars and stripes were triced up above and around a picture of Washington, and he had painted a majestic eagle, with lightnings blazing from his beak and his foot just clasping the whole globe, which his wings overshadowed. The dear old boy saw my glance, and said, with a sad smile, 'Here, you see, I have a country!' And then he pointed to the foot of his bed, where I had not seen before a great map of the United States, as he had drawn it from memory, and which he had there to look upon as he lay. Quaint, queer old names were on it, in large letters: 'Indiana Territory,' 'Mississippi Territory,' and 'Louisana Territory,' as I suppose our fathers learned such things: but the old fellow had patched in Texas, too; he had carried his western boundary all the way to the Pacific, but on that shore he had defined nothing.

" 'O Danforth,' he said, 'I know I am dying. I cannot get home. Surely you will tell me something now?—Stop! stop! Do not speak till I say what I am sure you know, that there is not in this ship, that there is not in America,— God bless her!—a more loyal man than I. There cannot be a man who loves the old flag as I do, or prays for it as I do, or hopes for it as I do. There are thirty-four stars in it now, Danforth. I thank God for that, though I do not know what their names are. There has never been one taken away: I thank

God for that. I know by that that there has never been any successful Burr. O Danforth, Danforth,' he sighed out, 'how like a wretched night's dream a boy's idea of personal fame or of separate sovereignty seems, when one looks back on it after such a life as mine! But tell me,—tell me something,—tell me everything, Danforth, before I die!'

"Ingham, I swear to you that I felt like a monster that I had not told him everything before. Danger or no danger, delicacy or no delicacy, who was I, that I should have been acting the tyrant all this time over this dear, sainted old man, who had years ago expiated, in his whole manhood's life, the madness of a boy's treason? 'Mr. Nolan,' said I, 'I will tell you everything you ask about. Only, where shall I begin?'

"Oh, the blessed smile that crept over his white face! and he pressed my hand and said, 'God bless you! Tell me their names,' he said, and he pointed to the stars on the flag. 'The last I know is Ohio. My father lived in Kentucky. But I have guessed Michigan and Indiana and Mississippi,—that was where Fort Adams is,—they make twenty. But where are your other fourteen? You have not cut up any of the old ones, I hope?'

"Well, that was not a bad text, and I told him the names in as good order as I could, and he bade me take down his beautiful map and draw them in as I best could with my pencil. He was wild with delight about Texas, told me how his brother died there—he had marked a gold cross where he supposed his brother's grave was—and he had guessed at Texas. Then he was delighted as he saw California and Oregon;—that, he said, he had suspected partly, because he had never been permitted to land on that shore, though the ships were there so much. 'And the men,' said he, laughing, 'brought off a good deal besides furs.' Then he went back—heavens, how far!—to ask about the *Chesapeake,* and what was done to Barron for surrendering her to the *Leopard,* and whether Burr ever tried again,—and he ground his teeth with the only passion he showed. But in a moment that was over, and he said, 'God forgive me, for I am sure I forgive him.' Then he asked about the old war,—told me the true story of his serving the gun the day we took the *Java,*—asked about dear old David Porter, as he called him. Then he settled down more quietly, and very happily, to hear me tell in an hour the history of fifty years.

"How I wished it had been somebody who knew something! But I did as well as I could. I told him of the English war. I told him about Fulton and the steamboat beginning. I told him about old Scott, and Jackson; told him all I could think about the Mississippi, and New Orleans, and Texas, and his own old Kentucky. And do you think, he asked me who was in command of the 'Legion of the West.' I told him it was a very gallant officer named Grant, and that, by our last news, he was about to establish his headquarters at Vicksburg. Then, 'Where was Vicksburg?' I worked that out on the map; it was about a hundred miles, more or less, above his old Fort Adams; and I thought Fort Adams must be a ruin now. 'It must be at old Vick's plantation,' said he: 'well, that is a change!'

"I tell you, Ingham, it was a hard thing to condense the history of half a century into that talk with a sick man. And I do not now know what I told him,—of emigration, and the means of it,—of steamboats, and railroads, and telegraphs,—of inventions, and books, and literature—of the colleges, and West Point, and the Naval School,—but with the queerest interruptions that ever you heard. You see it was Robinson Crusoe asking all the accumulated questions of fifty-six years.

"I remember he asked, all of a sudden, who was President now; and when I told him, he asked if Old Abe was General Benjamin Lincoln's son. He said he met old General Lincoln, when he was quite a boy himself, at some Indian treaty. I said no, that Old Abe was a Kentuckian like himself, but I could not tell him of what family; he had worked up from the ranks. 'Good for him!' cried Nolan; 'I am glad of that. As I have brooded and wondered, I have thought our danger was in keeping up those regular successions in the first families.' Then I got talking about my visit to Washington. I told him of meeting the Oregon Congressman, Harding; I told him about the Smithsonian, and the Exploring Expedition; I told him about the Capitol and the statues for the pediment, and Crawford's Liberty, and Greenough's Washington. Ingham, I told him everything I could think of that would show the grandeur of his country and its prosperity; but I could not make up my mouth to tell him a word about this infernal Rebellion!

"And he drank it in and enjoyed it as I cannot tell you. He grew more and more silent, yet I never thought he was tired or faint. I gave him a glass of water, but he just wet his lips, and told me not to go away. Then he asked me to bring the Presbyterian 'Book of Public Prayer' which lay there, and said, with a smile, that it would open at the right place,—and so it did. There was his double red mark down the page; and I knelt down and read, and he repeated with me, 'For ourselves and our country, O gracious God, we thank Thee, that, notwithstanding our manifold transgressions of Thy holy laws, Thou hast continued to us Thy marvelous kindness,'—and so to the end of that thanksgiving. Then he turned to the end of the same book, and I read the words more familiar to me: 'Most heartily we beseech Thee with Thy favor to behold and bless Thy servant, the President of the United States, and all others in authority,'—and the rest of the Episcopal collect. 'Danforth,' said he, 'I have repeated those prayers night and morning, it is now fifty-five years.' And then he said he would go to sleep. He bent me down over him and kissed me; and he said, 'Look in my Bible, Danforth, when I am gone.' And I went away.

"But I had no thought it was the end. I thought he was tired and would sleep. I knew he was happy, and I wanted him to be alone.

"But in an hour, when the doctor went in gently, he found Nolan had breathed his life away with a smile. He had something pressed close to his lips. It was his father's badge of the Order of Cincinnati.

"We looked in his Bible, and there was a slip of paper at the place where he had marked the text:

" 'They desire a country, even a heavenly: wherefore God is not ashamed to be called their God: for He hath prepared for them a city.'

"On this slip of paper he had written:

" 'Bury me in the sea; it has been my home, and I love it. But will not some one set up a stone for my memory at Fort Adams or at Orleans, that my disgrace may not be more than I ought to bear? Say on it:

'In Memory of

'PHILIP NOLAN,

'Lieutenant in the Army of the United States.

'He loved his country as no other man has loved her; but no man deserved less at her hands.' "

MARK TWAIN

(1835–1910)

Samuel L. Clemens was born in the village of Florida, Missouri, in 1835, and brought up in the old town he so vividly describes—Hannibal on the Mississippi. He had little schooling, but got practical training in a printing-office. He spent three years—invaluable for his later work—as a Mississippi River pilot. He saw life on the Plains and in the Nevada mining-towns in its "palmy days," and began writing for newspapers in Virginia City and San Francisco. He made his first hit with his *Jumping Frog* in 1867, and travelling in Europe as a reporter, he established himself as a maker of books with *Innocents Abroad* (1869). Through his lectures and writings he soon became known as America's leading "funny man," and proceeded to work his vein for all it was worth, producing one eagerly awaited book after another. No American writer has been more widely read. Belonging in soul to the West he may be said to have expatriated himself in his later life in Hartford and New York, and by so doing he probably cut himself off from the sources of his strength. Perhaps because he was so typically American he was welcomed abroad, and at his death in 1910 he had become a great international figure.

A modicum of ignorance and effrontery mixed—perhaps inseparably—with Mark Twain's priceless genius. Time is beginning to choose among his works, discarding the philosophical lucubrations of his *What is Man?*, the labored excursions into historical romance of his *A Connecticut Yankee in King Arthur's Court,* and the somewhat forced and professionalized humor of his *Following the Equator.* In spite of large claims he is comparatively negligible as a philosopher, satirist, and critic, and also as a historian—even as a humorous one. Though his drollery is often irresistible throughout, his humor is at its best when it is unstudied and incidental, as it is for the most part in his best books. These are generally considered to include *Roughing It, Pudd'nhead Wilson, Tom Sawyer, Huckleberry Finn,* and perhaps above all, the original chapters of *Life on the Mississippi.* In these—all of which draw vitally on his early experiences in the West, especially on the Mississippi—he shows tremendous powers of observation and vivid description—of scenes, characters, and manners. He is that rare thing—a literary artist of a new and genuine kind. The first of our writers to be born in the West, he caught and preserved its features at a time when it was most picturesque, and for this he deserves high place in American literature.

ROUGHING IT [1]

CHAPTER V

A NOTHER night of alternate tranquillity and turmoil. But morning came, by and by. It was another glad awakening to fresh breezes, vast expanses of level greensward, bright sunlight, an impressive solitude utterly without

---

[1] In 1861 Clemens journeyed "overland" with his brother, Orion, who had been appointed Secretary of Nevada Territory, to Carson City. *Roughing It,* published in 1873, records his experiences on this trip and in the mining-camps of Nevada.

The chapter here reprinted is used with the permission of Harper & Brothers, the authorized publishers.

visible human beings or human habitations, and an atmosphere of such amazing magnifying properties that trees that seemed close at hand were more than three miles away. We resumed undress uniform, climbed a-top of the flying coach, dangled our legs over the side, shouted occasionally at our frantic mules, merely to see them lay their ears back and scamper faster, tied our hats on to keep our hair from blowing away, and leveled an outlook over the world-wide carpet about us for things new and strange to gaze at. Even at this day it thrills me through and through to think of the life, the gladness and the wild sense of freedom that used to make the blood dance in my veins on those fine overland mornings!

Along about an hour after breakfast we saw the first prairie-dog villages, the first antelope, and the first wolf. If I remember rightly, this latter was the regular *cayote* (pronounced ky-*o*-te) of the farther deserts. And if it *was,* he was not a pretty creature, or respectable either, for I got well acquainted with his race afterward, and can speak with confidence. The cayote is a long, slim, sick and sorry-looking skeleton, with a gray wolf-skin stretched over it, a tolerably bushy tail that forever sags down with a despairing expression of forsakenness and misery, a furtive and evil eye, and a long, sharp face, with slightly lifted lip and exposed teeth. He has a general slinking expression all over. The cayote is a living, breathing allegory of Want. He is *always* hungry. He is always poor, out of luck and friendless. The meanest creatures despise him, and even the fleas would desert him for a velocipede. He is so spiritless and cowardly that even while his exposed teeth are pretending a threat, the rest of his face is apologizing for it. And he is *so* homely!—so scrawny, and ribby, and coarse-haired, and pitiful. When he sees you he lifts his lip and lets a flash of his teeth out, and then turns a little out of the course he was pursuing, depresses his head a bit, and strikes a long, soft-footed trot through the sage-brush, glancing over his shoulder at you, from time to time, till he is about out of easy pistol range, and then he stops and takes a deliberate survey of you; he will trot fifty yards and stop again;—another fifty and stop again; and finally the gray of his gliding body blends with the gray of the sage-brush, and he disappears. All this is when you make no demonstration against him; but if you do, he develops a livelier interest in his journey, and instantly electrifies his heels and puts such a deal of real estate between himself and your weapon, that by the time you have raised the hammer you see that you need a minie rifle, and by the time you have got him in line you need a rifled cannon, and by the time you have "drawn a bead" on him you see well enough that nothing but an unusually long-winded streak of lightning could reach him where he is now. But if you start a swift-footed dog after him, you will enjoy it ever so much—especially if it is a dog that has a good opinion of himself, and has been brought up to think he knows something about speed. The cayote will go swinging gently off on that deceitful trot of his, and every little while he will smile a fraudful smile over his shoulder that will fill that dog entirely full of encouragement and worldly ambition, and make him lay his head still lower to the ground, and stretch his neck further to the front, and pant more fiercely, and stick his tail out straighter behind, and move his furious legs with a yet wilder frenzy, and leave a broader and broader, and higher and denser cloud of desert sand smoking behind, and marking his long wake across the level plain! And all this time the dog is only a short twenty feet behind the cayote, and to save the soul of him he cannot understand why it is that he cannot get perceptibly closer; and he begins to get aggravated, and it makes him madder and madder to see how gently the cayote glides along and never pants or sweats or ceases to smile; and he grows still more and more incensed to see how shamefully he has been taken in by an entire stranger, and what an ignoble swindle that long, calm, soft-footed trot is; and next he notices that he is getting fagged, and that the cayote actually has to slacken speed a little to keep from running away from him—and *then* that town-dog is mad in earnest, and he begins to strain and weep and swear, and paw the sand higher than ever, and reach for the cayote with concentrated and desperate energy. This "spurt" finds him six feet behind the gliding enemy, and two miles from his friends. And then, in the instant that a wild new hope is lighting up his face, the cayote turns and smiles blandly upon him once more, and with a something about it which seems to say: "Well, I shall have to tear myself away from you, bub—business is business, and it will not do for me to be fooling along this way all day"—and forthwith there is a rushing sound, and the sudden splitting of a long crack through the atmosphere, and behold that dog is solitary and alone in the midst of a vast solitude!

It makes his head swim. He stops, and looks all around; climbs the nearest sand-mound, and gazes into the distance; shakes his head reflectively, and then, without a word, he turns and jogs along back to his train, and takes up a humble position under the hindmost wagon, and feels unspeakably mean, and looks ashamed, and hangs his tail at half-mast for a week. And for as much as a year after that, whenever there is a great hue and cry after a cayote, that dog will merely glance in that direction without emotion, and apparently observe to himself, "I believe I do not wish any of the pie."

The cayote lives chiefly in the most desolate and forbidding deserts, along with the lizard, the jackass-rabbit and the raven, and gets an uncertain and precarious living, and earns it. He seems to subsist almost wholly on the carcasses of oxen, mules, and horses that have dropped out of emigrant trains and died, and upon windfalls of carrion, and occasional legacies of offal bequeathed to him by white men who have been opulent enough to have something better to butcher than condemned army bacon. He will eat anything in the world that his first cousins, the desert-frequenting tribes of Indians, will, and they will eat anything they can bite. It is a curious fact that these latter are the only creatures known to history who will eat nitro-glycerine and ask for more if they survive.

The cayote of the deserts beyond the Rocky Mountains has a peculiarly hard time of it, owing to the fact that his relations, the Indians, are just as apt to be the first to detect a seductive scent on the desert breeze, and follow the fragrance to the late ox it emanated from, as he is himself; and when this occurs he has to content himself with sitting off at a little distance watching those people strip off and dig out everything edible, and walk off with it. Then he and the waiting ravens explore the skeleton and polish the bones. It is considered that the cayote, and the obscene bird, and the Indian of the desert, testify their blood kinship with each other in that they live together in the waste places of the earth on terms of perfect confidence and friendship, while hating all other creatures and yearning to assist at their funerals. He does not mind going a hundred miles to breakfast, and a hundred and fifty to dinner, because he is sure to have three or four days between meals, and he can just as well be traveling and looking at the scenery as lying around doing nothing and adding to the burdens of his parents.

We soon learned to recognize the sharp, vicious bark of the cayote as it came across the murky plain at night to disturb our dreams among the mail-sacks; and remembering his forlorn aspect and his hard fortune, made shift to wish him the blessed novelty of a long day's good luck and a limitless larder the morrow.

THE CELEBRATED JUMPING FROG OF CALAVERAS COUNTY [2]

In compliance with the request of a friend of mine, who wrote me from the East, I called on good-natured, garrulous old Simon Wheeler, and inquired after my friend's friend, *Leonidas W*. Smiley, as requested to do, and I hereunto append the result. I have a lurking suspicion that *Leonidas W*. Smiley is a myth; that my friend never knew such a personage; and that he only conjectured that, if I asked old Wheeler about him, it would remind him of his infamous *Jim* Smiley, and he would go to work and bore me nearly to death with some infernal reminiscence of him as long and tedious as it should be useless to me. If that was the design, it certainly succeeded.

I found Simon Wheeler dozing comfortably by the bar-room stove of the old, dilapidated tavern in the ancient mining camp of Angel's, and I noticed that he was fat and bald-headed, and had an expression of winning gentleness and simplicity upon his tranquil countenance. He roused up and gave me

[2] Published first in the New York *Saturday Press*, November 18, 1865; and in book form in *The Celebrated Jumping Frog of Calaveras County and Other Sketches*, 1867.
This sketch is used by permission of Harper & Brothers, the authorized publishers.

good-day. I told him a friend of mine had commissioned me to make some inquiries about a cherished companion of his boyhood named *Leonidas W. Smiley—Rev. Leonidas W.* Smiley—a young minister of the Gospel, who he had heard was at one time a resident of Angel's Camp. I added that, if Mr. Wheeler could tell me anything about this Rev. Leonidas W. Smiley, I would feel under many obligations to him.

Simon Wheeler backed me into a corner and blockaded me there with his chair, and then sat me down and reeled off the monotonous narrative which follows this paragraph. He never smiled, he never frowned, he never changed his voice from the gentle-flowing key to which he tuned the initial sentence, he never betrayed the slightest suspicion of enthusiasm; but all through the interminable narrative there ran a vein of impressive earnestness and sincerity, which showed me plainly that, so far from his imagining that there was any-thing ridiculous or funny about his story, he regarded it as a really important matter, and admired its two heroes as men of transcendent genius in *finesse*. To me, the spectacle of a man drifting serenely along through such a queer yarn without ever smiling, was exquisitely absurd. As I said before, I asked him to tell me what he knew of Rev. Leonidas W. Smiley, and he replied as follows. I let him go on in his own way, and never interrupted him once:

There was a feller here once by the name of *Jim* Smiley, in the winter of '49 —or may be it was the spring of '50—I don't recollect exactly, somehow, though what makes me think it was one or the other is because I remember the big flume wasn't finished when he first came to the camp; but any way, he was the curiosest man about always betting on anything that turned up you ever see, if he could get any body to bet on the other side; and if he couldn't, he'd change sides. Any way that suited the other man would suit him—any way just so's he got a bet, *he* was satisfied. But still he was lucky, uncommon lucky; he most always come out winner. He was always ready and laying for a chance; there couldn't be no solitary thing mentioned but that feller 'd offer to bet on it, and take any side you please, as I was just telling you. If there was a horse-race, you'd find him flush, or you'd find him busted at the end of it; if there was a dog-fight, he'd bet on it; if there was a cat-fight, he'd bet on it; if there was a chicken-fight, he'd bet on it; why, if there was two birds setting on a fence, he would bet you which one would fly first; or if there was a camp-meeting, he would be there reg'lar, to bet on Parson Walker, which he judged to be the best exhorter about there, and so he was, too, and a good man. If he even seen a straddle-bug start to go anywheres, he would bet you how long it would take him to get wherever he was going to, and if you took him up, he would follow that straddle-bug to Mexico but what he would find out where he was bound for and how long he was on the road. Lots of the boys here has seen that Smiley, and can tell you about him. Why, it never made no difference to *him*—he would bet on *any* thing—the dangdest feller. Parson Walker's wife laid very sick once, for a good while, and it seemed as if they warn't going to save her; but one morning he come in, and Smiley asked how she was, and he said she was considerable better—thank the Lord for his inf'nit mercy—and coming on so smart that, with the blessing of Prov'-dence, she'd get well yet; and Smiley, before he thought, says, "Well, I'll risk two-and-a half that she won't, any way."

Thish-yer Smiley had a mare—the boys called her the fifteen-minute nag, but that was only in fun, you know, because, of course, she was faster than that—and he used to win money on that horse, for all she was so slow and always had the asthma, or the distemper, or the consumption, or something of that kind. They used to give her two or three hundred yards start, and then pass her under way; but always at the fag-end of the race she'd get excited and desperate-like, and come cavorting and straddling up, and scatter-ing her legs around limber, sometimes in the air, and sometimes out to one side amongst the fences, and kicking up m-o-r-e dust, and raising m-o-r-e racket with her coughing and sneezing and blowing her nose—and always fetch up at the stand just about a neck ahead, as near as you could cypher it down.

And he had a little small bull pup, that to look at him you'd think he wa'n't worth a cent, but to set around and look ornery, and lay for a chance to steal something. But as soon as money was up on him, he was a different dog; his underjaw 'd begin to stick out like the fo'castle of a steamboat, and his teeth would uncover, and shine savage like the furnaces. And a dog might tackle him, and bully-rag him, and bite him, and throw him over his shoulder two or three times, and Andrew Jackson—which was the name of the pup—An-drew Jackson would never let on but what *he* was satisfied, and hadn't ex-pected nothing else—and the bets being doubled and doubled on the other side all the time, till the money was all up; and then all of a sudden he would grab that other dog jest by the j'int of his hind leg and freeze to it—not chaw, you understand, but only jest grip and hang on till they throwed up the sponge, if it was a year. Smiley always come out winner on that pup, till he harnessed a dog once that didn't have no hind legs, because they'd been sawed off by a circular saw, and when the thing had gone along far enough, and the money was all up, and he come to make a snatch for his pet holt, he saw in a minute how he'd been imposed on, and how the other dog had him in the door, so to speak, and he 'peared surprised, and then he looked sorter discouraged-like, and didn't try no more to win the fight, and so he got shucked out bad. He give Smiley a look, as much as to say his heart was broke, and it was *his* fault, for putting up a dog that hadn't no hind legs for him to take holt of, which was his main dependence in a fight, and then he limped off a piece and laid down and died. It was a good pup, was that Andrew Jackson, and would have made a name for hisself if he'd lived, for the stuff was in him, and he had genius—I know it, because he hadn't had no opportunity to speak of, and it don't stand to reason that a dog could make such a fight as he could under them circumstances, if he hadn't no talent. It always makes me feel sorry when I think of that last fight of his'n, and the way it turned out.

Well, thish-yer Smiley had rat-tarriers, and chicken cocks, and tom-cats, and all them kind of things, till you couldn't rest, and you couldn't fetch nothing for him to bet on but he'd match you. He ketched a frog one day, and took him home, and said he cal'klated to edercate him; and so he never done nothing for three months but set in his back yard and learn that frog to jump. And you bet he *did* learn him, too. He'd give him a little punch behind, and the next minute you'd see that frog whirling in the air like a doughnut—see him turn one summerset, or may be a couple, if he got a good start, and come down flat-footed and all right, like a cat. He got him up so in the matter of catching flies, and kept him in practice so constant, that he'd nail a fly every time as far as he could see him. Smiley said all a frog wanted was education, and he could do most anything—and I believe him. Why, I've seen him set Dan'l Webster down here on this floor—Dan'l Webster was the name of the frog—and sing out, "Flies, Dan'l, flies!" and quicker'n you could wink, he'd spring straight up, and snake a fly off'n the counter there, and flop down on the floor again as solid as a gob of mud, and fall to scratching the side of his head with his hind foot as indifferent as if he hadn't no idea he'd been doin' any more'n any frog might do. You never see a frog so modest and straightfor'ard as he was, for all he was so gifted. And when it come to fair and square jumping on a dead level, he could get over more ground at one straddle than any animal of his breed you ever see. Jumping on a dead level was his strong suit, you understand; and when it come to that, Smiley would ante up money on him as long as he had a red. Smiley was monstrous proud of his frog, and well he might be, for fellers that had traveled and been everywheres, all said he laid over any frog that ever *they* see.

Well Smiley kept the beast in a little lattice box, and he used to fetch him down town sometimes and lay for a bet. One day a feller—a stranger in the camp, he was—come across him with his box, and says:

"What might it be that you've got in the box?"

And Smiley says, sorter indifferent like, "It might be a parrot, or it might be a canary, may be, but it ain't—it's only just a frog."

And the feller took it, and looked at it careful, and turned it round this way and that, and says, "H'm—so 'tis. Well, what's *he* good for?"

"Well," Smiley says, easy and careless, "He's good enough for *one* thing, I should judge—he can outjump ary frog in Calaveras county."

The feller took the box again, and took another long, particular look, and give it back to Smiley, and says, very deliberate, "Well, I don't see no p'ints about that frog that's any better 'n any other frog."

"May be you don't," Smiley says. "May be you understand frogs, and may be you don't understand 'em; may be you've had experience, and may be you an't only a amature, as it were. Anyways, I've got *my* opinion, and I'll risk forty dollars he can outjump any frog in Calaveras county."

And the feller studied a minute, and then says, kinder sad like, "Well, I'm only a stranger here, and I an't got no frog, but if I had a frog, I'd bet you."

And then Smiley says, "That's all right—that's all right—if you'll hold my box a minute, I'll go and get you a frog." And so the feller took the box, and put up his forty dollars along with Smiley's, and set down to wait.

So he set there a good while thinking and thinking to hisself, and then he got the frog out and prized his mouth open and took a teaspoon and filled him full of quail shot—filled him pretty near up to his chin—and set him on the floor. Smiley he went to the swamp and slopped around in the mud for a long time, and finally he ketched a frog, and fetched him in, and give him to this feller, and says:

"Now, if you're ready, set him alongside of Dan'l, with his fore-paws just even with Dan'l, and I'll give the word." Then he says, "One—two—three—jump!" and him and the feller touched up the frogs from behind, and the new frog hopped off, but Dan'l give a heave, and hysted up his shoulders—so—like a Frenchman, but it want no use—couldn't budge; he was planted as solid as an anvil, and he couldn't no more stir than if he was anchored out. Smiley was a good deal surprised, and he was disgusted too, but he didn't have no idea what the matter was, of course.

The feller took the money and started away; and when he was going out of the door, he sorter jerked his thumb over his shoulders—this way—at Dan'l, and says again, very deliberate, "Well, *I* don't see no p'ints about that frog that's any better'n any other frog."

Smiley he stood scratching his head and looking down at Dan'l a long time, and at last he says, "I do wonder what in the nation that frog throw'd off for—I wonder if there ain't something the matter with him—he 'pears to look mighty baggy, somehow." And he ketched Dan'l by the nap of the neck, and lifted him up and says, "Why, blame my cats, if he don't weigh five pound!" and turned him upside down, and he belched out a double handful of shot. And then he see how it was, and he was the maddest man —he set the frog down and took out after that feller, but he never ketched him. And—

[Here Simon Wheeler heard his name called from the front yard, and got up to see what was wanted.] And turning to me as he moved away, he said: "Just set where you are, stranger, and rest easy—I an't going to be gone a second."

But, by your leave, I did not think that a continuation of the history of the enterprising vagabond *Jim* Smiley would be likely to afford me much information concerning the Rev. *Leonidas* W. Smiley, and so I started away.

At the door I met the sociable Wheeler returning, and he buttonholed me and recommenced:

"Well, thish-yer Smiley had a yaller one-eyed cow that didn't have no tail, only jest a short stump like a bannanner, and—"

"Oh! hang Smiley and his afflicted cow!" I muttered, good-naturedly, and bidding the old gentleman good-day, I departed.

LIFE ON THE MISSISSIPPI [3]

CHAPTER IV

THE BOYS' AMBITION

WHEN I was a boy, there was but one permanent ambition among my comrades in our village [4] on the west bank of the Mississippi River. That was, to be a steamboatman. We had transient ambitions of other sorts, but they were only transient. When a circus came and went, it left us all burning to become clowns; the first negro minstrel show that ever came to our section left us all suffering to try that kind of life; now and then we had a hope that, if we lived and were good, God would permit us to be pirates. These ambitions faded out, each in its turn; but the ambition to be a steamboatman always remained.

Once a day a cheap, gaudy packet arrived upward from St. Louis, and another downward from Keokuk. Before these events, the day was glorious with expectancy; after them, the day was a dead and empty thing. Not only the boys, but the whole village, felt this. After all these years I can picture that old time to myself now, just as it was then: the white town drowsing in the sunshine of a summer's morning; the streets empty, or pretty nearly so; one or two clerks sitting in front of the Water Street stores, with their splint-bottomed chairs tilted back against the walls, chins on breasts, hats slouched over their faces, asleep—with shingle-shavings enough around to show what broke them down; a sow and a litter of pigs loafing along the sidewalk, doing a good business in watermelon rinds and seeds; two or three lonely little freight piles scattered about the "levee"; a pile of "skids" on the slope of the stone-paved wharf, and the fragrant town drunkard asleep in the shadow of them; two or three wood flats at the head of the wharf, but no-

---

[3] The first and better part of this book, chapters i–xx, describing Clemens's early experiences as pilot on the River, appeared in the *Atlantic Monthly* in 1875. Seven years later Clemens revisited the Mississippi and added the forty chapters which complete the present book.

The chapters here reprinted are used with the permission of Harper & Brothers, the authorized publishers.

[4] Hannibal, Missouri.—*Author's note.*

body to listen to the peaceful lapping of the wavelets against them; the great Mississippi, the majestic, the magnificent Mississippi, rolling its mile-wide tide along, shining in the sun; the dense forest away on the other side; the "point" above the town, and the "point" below, bounding the river-glimpse and turning it into a sort of sea, and withal a very still and brilliant and lonely one. Presently a film of dark smoke appears above one of those remote "points"; instantly a negro drayman, famous for his quick eye and prodigious voice, lifts up the cry, "S-t-e-a-m-boat a-comin'!" and the scene changes! The town drunkard stirs, the clerks wake up, a furious clatter of drays follows, every house and store pours out a human contribution, and all in a twinkling the dead town is alive and moving. Drays, carts, men, boys, all go hurrying from many quarters to a common center, the wharf. Assembled there, the people fasten their eyes upon the coming boat as upon a wonder they are seeing for the first time. And the boat *is* rather a handsome sight, too. She is long and sharp and trim and pretty; she has two tall, fancy-topped chimneys, with a gilded device of some kind swung between them; a fanciful pilot-house, all glass and "gingerbread," perched on top of the "texas" deck behind them; the paddle-boxes are gorgeous with a picture or with gilded rays above the boat's name; the boiler-deck, the hurricane-deck, and the texas deck are fenced and ornamented with clean white railings; there is a flag gallantly flying from the jack-staff; the furnace doors are open and the fires glaring bravely; the upper decks are black with passengers; the captain stands by the big bell, calm, imposing, the envy of all; great volumes of the blackest smoke are rolling and tumbling out of the chimneys—a husbanded grandeur created with a bit of pitch-pine just before arriving at a town; the crew are grouped on the forecastle; the broad stage is run far out over the port bow, and an envied deck-hand stands picturesquely on the end of it with a coil of rope in his hand; the pent steam is screaming through the gauge-cocks; the captain lifts his hand, a bell rings, the wheels stop; then they turn back, churning the water to foam, and the steamer is at rest. Then such a scramble as there is to get aboard, and to get ashore, and to take in freight and to discharge freight, all at one and the same time; and such a yelling and cursing as the mates facilitate it all with! Ten minutes later the steamer is under way again, with no flag on the jack-staff and no black smoke issuing from the chimneys. After ten more minutes the town is dead again, and the town drunkard asleep by the skids once more.

My father was a justice of the peace, and I supposed he possessed the power of life and death over all men, and could hang anybody that offended him. This was distinction enough for me as a general thing; but the desire to be a steamboatman kept intruding, nevertheless. I first wanted to be a cabin-boy, so that I could come out with a white apron on and shake a tablecloth over the side, where all my old comrades could see me; later I thought I would rather be the deck-hand who stood on the end of the stage-plank with the coil of rope in his hand, because he was particularly conspicuous. But these were only day-dreams—they were too heavenly to be contemplated as real possibilities. By and by one of our boys went away. He was not heard of for a long time. At last he turned up as apprentice engineer or "striker" on a steamboat. This thing shook the bottom out of all my Sunday-school teachings. That boy had been notoriously worldly, and I just the reverse; yet he was exalted to this eminence, and I left in obscurity and misery. There was nothing generous about this fellow in his greatness. He would always manage to have a rusty bolt to scrub while his boat tarried at our town, and he would sit on the inside guard and scrub it, where we all could see him and envy him and loathe him. And whenever his boat was laid up he would come home and swell around the town in his blackest and greasiest clothes, so that nobody could help remembering that he was a steamboatman; and he used all sorts of steamboat technicalities in his talk, as if he were so used to them that he forgot common people could not understand them. He would speak of the "labboard" side of a horse in an easy, natural way that would make one wish he was dead. And he was always talking about "St. Looy" like an old citizen; he would refer casually to occasions when he was "coming down Fourth Street," or when he was "passing by the Planter's House," or when there was a fire and he took a turn on the brakes of "the old Big Missouri"; and then he would go on and lie about how many towns the size of ours were burned down there that day. Two or three of the boys had long been persons of consideration among us because they had been to St. Louis once and had a vague general knowledge of its wonders, but the day of their glory was over now. They lapsed into a humble silence, and learned to disappear when the ruthless "cub"-engineer approached. This fellow had money, too, and hair-oil. Also an ignorant silver watch and a showy brass watch-chain. He wore a leather belt and used no suspenders. If ever a youth was cordially admired and hated by his comrades, this one was. No girl could withstand his charms. He "cut out" every boy in the village. When his boat blew up at last, it diffused a tranquil contentment among us such as we had not known for months. But when he came home the next week, alive, renowned, and appeared in church all battered up and bandaged, a shining hero, stared at and wondered over by everybody, it seemed to us that the partiality of Providence for an undeserving reptile had reached a point where it was open to criticism.

This creature's career could produce but one result, and it speedily followed. Boy after boy managed to get on the river. The minister's son became an engineer. The doctor's and the postmaster's sons became "mud clerks"; the wholesale liquor dealer's son became a barkeeper on a boat; four sons of the chief merchant, and two sons of the county judge, became pilots. Pilot was the grandest position of all. The pilot, even in those days of trivial wages, had a princely salary—from a hundred and fifty to two hundred and fifty dollars a month, and no board to pay. Two months of his wages would pay a preacher's salary for a year. Now some of us were left disconsolate. We could not get on the river—at least our parents would not let us.

So, by and by, I ran away. I said I would never come home again till I was a pilot and could come in glory. But somehow I could not manage it. I went meekly aboard a few of the boats that lay packed together like sardines at the long St. Louis wharf, and humbly inquired for the pilots, but got only a cold shoulder and short words from mates and clerks. I had to make the best of this sort of treatment for the time being, but I had comforting day-dreams of a future when I should be a great and honored pilot, with plenty of money, and could kill some of these mates and clerks and pay for them.

Chapter XVIII
I Take a Few Extra Lessons

During the two or two and a half years of my apprenticeship I served under many pilots, and had experience of many kinds of steamboatmen and many varieties of steamboats; for it was not always convenient for Mr. Bixby to have me with him, and in such cases he sent me with somebody else. I am to this day profiting somewhat by that experience; for in that brief, sharp schooling, I got personally and familiarly acquainted with about all the different types of human nature that are to be found in fiction, biography, or history. The fact is daily borne in upon me that the average shore-employment requires as much as forty years to equip a man with this sort of an education. When I say I am still profiting by this thing, I do not mean that it has constituted me a judge of men—no, it has not done that, for judges of men are born, not made. My profit is various in kind and degree, but the feature of it which I value most is the zest which that early experience has given to my later reading. When I find a well-drawn character in fiction or biography I generally take a warm personal interest in him, for the reason that I have known him before—met him on the river.

The figure that comes before me oftenest, out of the shadows of that vanished time, is that of Brown, of the steamer *Pennsylvania*—the man referred to in a former chapter, whose memory was so good and tiresome. He was a middle-aged, long, slim, bony, smooth-shaven, horse-faced, ignorant, stingy, malicious, snarling, fault-hunting, mote-magnifying tyrant. I early got the habit of coming on watch with dread at my heart, No matter how good a time I might have been having with the off-watch below, and no matter how high my spirits might be when I started aloft, my soul became lead in my body the moment I approached the pilot-house.

I still remember the first time I ever entered the presence of that man. The boat had backed out from St. Louis and was "straightening down." I ascended to the pilot-house in high feather, and very proud to be semi-officially a member of the executive family of so fast and famous a boat. Brown was at the wheel. I paused in the middle of the room, all fixed to make my bow, but Brown did not look around. I thought he took a furtive glance at me out of the corner of his eye, but as not even this notice was repeated, I judged I had been mistaken. By this time he was picking his way among some dangerous "breaks" abreast the woodyards; therefore it would not be proper to interrupt him; so I stepped softly to the high bench and took a seat.

There was silence for ten minutes; then my new boss turned and inspected me deliberately and painstakingly from head to heel for about—as it seemed to me—a quarter of an hour. After which he removed his countenance and I saw it no more for some seconds; then it came around once more, and this question greeted me:

"Are you Horace Bigsby's cub?"

"Yes, sir."

After this there was a pause and another inspection. Then:

"What's your name?"

I told him. He repeated it after me. It was probably the only thing he ever forgot; for although I was with him many months he never addressed himself to me in any other way than "Here!" and then his command followed.

"Where was you born?"

"In Florida, Missouri."

A pause. Then:

"Dern sight better stayed there!"

By means of a dozen or so of pretty direct questions, he pumped my family history out of me.

The leads were going now in the first crossing. This interrupted the inquest. When the leads had been laid in he resumed:

"How long you been on the river?"

I told him. After a pause:

"Where'd you get them shoes?"

I gave him the information.

"Hold up your foot!"

I did so. He stepped back, examined the shoe minutely and contemptuously, scratching his head thoughtfully, tilting his high sugar-loaf hat well forward to facilitate the operation, then ejaculated, "Well, I'll be dod derned!" and returned to his wheel.

What occasion there was to be dod derned about it is a thing which is still as much of a mystery to me now as it was then. It must have been all of fifteen minutes—fifteen minutes of dull, homesick silence—before that long horse-face swung round upon me again—and then what a change! It was as red as fire, and every muscle in it was working. Now came this shriek:

"Here! You going to set there all day?"

I lit in the middle of the floor, shot there by the electric suddenness of the surprise. As soon as I could get my voice I said apologetically: "I have had no orders, sir."

"You've had no *orders!* My, what a fine bird we are! We must have *orders!* Our father was a *gentleman*—owned slaves—and *we've* been to *school.* Yes, *we* are a gentleman, *too,* and got to have *orders!* ORDERS, is it? ORDERS is what you want! Dod dern my skin, *I'll* learn you to swell yourself up and blow around *here* about your dod-derned *orders!* G'way from the wheel!" (I had approached it without knowing it.)

I moved back a step or two and stood as in a dream, all my senses stupefied by this frantic assault.

"What you standing there for? Take that ice-pitcher down to the texas-tender! Come, move along, and don't you be all day about it!"

The moment I got back to the pilot-house Brown said:

"Here! What was you doing down there all this time?"

"I couldn't find the texas-tender; I had to go all the way to the pantry."

"Derned likely story! Fill up the stove."

I proceeded to do so. He watched me like a cat. Presently he shouted:

"Put down that shovel! Derndest num-skull I ever saw—ain't even got sense enough to load up a stove."

All through the watch this sort of thing went on. Yes, and the subsequent watches were much like it during a stretch of months. As I have said, I soon got the habit of coming on duty with dread. The moment I was in the presence, even in the darkest night, I could feel those yellow eyes upon me, and knew their owner was watching for a pretext to spit out some venom on me. Preliminarily he would say:

"Here! Take the wheel."

Two minutes later:

"*Where* in the nation you going to? Pull her down! pull her down!"

After another moment:

"Say! You going to hold her all day? Let her go—meet her! meet her!"

Then he would jump from the bench, snatch the wheel from me, and meet her himself, pouring out wrath upon me all the time.

George Ritchie was the other pilot's cub. He was having good times now; for his boss, George Ealer, was as kind-hearted as Brown wasn't. Ritchie had steered for Brown the season before; consequently, he knew exactly how to entertain himself and plague me, all by the one operation. Whenever I took the wheel for a moment on Ealer's watch, Ritchie would sit back on the bench

and play Brown, with continual ejaculations of "Snatch her! snatch her!
Derndest mud-cat I ever saw!" "Here! Where are you going *now?* Going to
run over that snag?" "Pull he*r down!* Don't you hear me? Pull her *down!*"
"There she goes! *Just* as I expected! I *told* you not to cramp that reef. G'way
from the wheel!"

So I always had a rough time of it, no matter whose watch it was; and sometimes it seemed to me that Ritchie's good-natured badgering was pretty nearly
as aggravating as Brown's dead-earnest nagging.

I often wanted to kill Brown, but this would not answer. A cub had to take
everything his boss gave, in the way of vigorous comment and criticism; and
we all believed that there was a United States law making it a penitentiary
offense to strike or threaten a pilot who was on duty. However, I could
imagine myself killing Brown; there was no law against that; and that was
the thing I used always to do the moment I was abed. Instead of going over
my river in my mind, as was my duty, I threw business aside for pleasure, and
killed Brown. I killed Brown every night for months; not in old, stale, commonplace ways, but in new and picturesque ones—ways that were sometimes
surprising for freshness of design and ghastliness of situation and environment.

Brown was *always* watching for a pretext to find fault; and if he could find
no plausible pretext, he would invent one. He would scold you for shaving a
shore, and for not shaving it; for hugging a bar, and for not hugging it; for
"pulling down" when not invited, and for *not* pulling down when not invited; for firing up without orders, and for waiting *for* orders. In a word, it
was his invariable rule to find fault with *everything* you did; and another
invariable rule of his was to throw all his remarks (to you) into the form of
an insult.

One day we were approaching New Madrid, bound down and heavily
laden. Brown was at one side of the wheel, steering; I was at the other,
standing by to "pull down" or "shove up." He cast a furtive glance at me
every now and then. I had long ago learned what that meant; *viz.,* he was
trying to invent a trap for me. I wondered what shape it was going to take.
By and by he stepped back from the wheel and said in his usual snarly way:

"Here! See if you've got gumption enough to round her to."

This was simply *bound* to be a success; nothing could prevent it; for he had
never allowed me to round the boat to before; consequently, no matter how
I might do the thing, he could find free fault with it. He stood back there with
his greedy eye on me, and the result was what might have been foreseen: I
lost my head in a quarter of a minute, and didn't know what I was about; I
started too early to bring the boat around, but detected a green gleam of joy
in Brown's eye, and corrected my mistake. I started around once more while
too high up, but corrected myself again in time. I made other false moves,

and still managed to save myself; but at last I grew so confused and anxious that I tumbled into the very worst blunder of all—I got too far *down* before beginning to fetch the boat around. Brown's chance was come.

His face turned red with passion; he made one bound, hurled me across the house with a sweep of his arm, spun the wheel down, and began to pour out a stream of vituperation upon me which lasted till he was out of breath. In the course of this speech he called me all the different kinds of hard names he could think of, and once or twice I thought he was even going to swear— but he had never done that, and he didn't this time. "Dod dern" was the nearest he ventured to the luxury of swearing, for he had been brought up with a wholesome respect for future fire and brimstone.

That was an uncomfortable hour; for there was a big audience on the hurricane-deck. When I went to bed that night, I killed Brown in seventeen different ways—all of them new.

CHAPTER XIX
BROWN AND I EXCHANGE COMPLIMENTS

Two trips later I got into serious trouble. Brown was steering; I was "pulling down." My younger brother appeared on the hurricane-deck, and shouted to Brown to stop at some landing or other, a mile or so below. Brown gave no intimation that he had heard anything. But that was his way: he never condescended to take notice of an under-clerk. The wind was blowing; Brown was deaf (although he always pretended he wasn't), and I very much doubted if he had heard the order. If I had had two heads, I would have spoken; but as I had only one, it seemed judicious to take care of it; so I kept still.

Presently, sure enough, we went sailing by that plantation. Captain Klinefelter appeared on the deck, and said:

"Let her come around, sir, let her come around. Didn't Henry tell you to land here?"

"*No,* sir!"

"I sent him up to do it."

"He *did* come up; and that's all the good it done, the dod-derned fool. He never said anything."

"Didn't *you* hear him?" asked the captain of me.

Of course I didn't want to be mixed up in this business, but there was no way to avoid it; so I said:

"Yes, sir."

I knew what Brown's next remark would be, before he uttered it. It was:

"Shut your mouth! You never heard anything of the kind!"

I closed my mouth, according to instructions. An hour later Henry entered the pilot-house, unaware of what had been going on. He was a thoroughly inoffensive boy, and I was sorry to see him come, for I knew Brown would have no pity on him. Brown began, straightway:

"Here! Why didn't you tell me we'd got to land at that plantation?"

"I did tell you, Mr. Brown."

"It's a lie!"

I said:

"You lie, yourself. He did tell you."

Brown glared at me in unaffected surprise; and for as much as a moment he was entirely speechless; then he shouted to me:

"I'll attend to your case in a half a minute!" then to Henry, "And you leave the pilot-house; out with you!"

It was pilot law, and must be obeyed. The boy started out, and even had his foot on the upper step outside the door, when Brown, with a sudden access of fury, picked up a ten-pound lump of coal and sprang after him; but I was between, with a heavy stool, and I hit Brown a good honest blow which stretched him out.

I had committed the crime of crimes—I had lifted my hand against a pilot on duty! I supposed I was booked for the penitentiary sure, and couldn't be booked any surer if I went on and squared my long account with this person while I had the chance; consequently I stuck to him and pounded him with my fists a considerable time. I do not know how long, the pleasure of it probably made it seem longer than it really was; but in the end he struggled free and jumped up and sprang to the wheel: a very natural solicitude, for, all this time, here was this steamboat tearing down the river at the rate of fifteen miles an hour and nobody at the helm! However, Eagle Bend was two miles wide at this bank-full stage, and correspondingly long and deep: and the boat was steering herself straight down the middle and taking no chances. Still, that was only luck—a body *might* have found her charging into the woods.

Perceiving at a glance that the *Pennsylvania* was in no danger, Brown gathered up the big spy-glass, war-club fashion, and ordered me out of the pilot-house with more than Comanche bluster. But I was not afraid of him now; so, instead of going, I tarried, and criticized his grammar. I reformed his ferocious speeches for him, and put them into good English, calling his attention to the advantage of pure English over the bastard dialect of the Pennsylvania collieries whence he was extracted. He could have done his part to admiration in a cross-fire of mere vituperation, of course; but he was not equipped for this species of controversy; so he presently laid aside his glass and took the wheel, muttering and shaking his head; and I retired to the bench. The racket had brought everybody to the hurricane-deck, and I trembled when I saw the old captain looking up from amid the crowd. I said to myself, "Now I *am* done for!" for although, as a rule, he was so fatherly and indulgent toward the boat's family, and so patient of minor shortcomings, he could be stern enough when the fault was worth it.

I tried to imagine what he *would* do to a cub pilot who had been guilty of such a crime as mine, committed on a boat guard-deep with costly freight and alive with passengers. Our watch was nearly ended. I thought I would go and hide somewhere till I got a chance to slide ashore. So I slipped out of the pilot-house, and down the steps, and around to the texas-door, and was in the act of gliding within, when the captain confronted me! I dropped my head, and he stood over me in silence a moment or two, then said impressively:

"Follow me."

I dropped into his wake; he led the way to his parlor in the forward end of the texas. We were alone, now. He closed the after door; then moved slowly to the forward one and closed that. He sat down; I stood before him. He looked at me some little time, then said:

"So you have been fighting Mr. Brown?"

I answered meekly:

"Yes, sir."

"Do you know that that is a very serious matter?"

"Yes, sir."

"Are you aware that this boat was plowing down the river fully five minutes with no one at the wheel?"

"Yes, sir."

"Did you strike him first?"

"Yes, sir."

"What with?"

"A stool, sir."

"Hard?"

"Middling, sir."

"Did it knock him down?"

"He—he fell, sir."

"Did you follow it up? Did you do anything further?"

"Yes, sir."

"What did you do?"

"Pounded him, sir."

"Pounded him?"

"Yes, sir."

"Did you pound him much? that is, severely?"

"One might call it that, sir, maybe."

"I'm deucèd glad of it! Hark ye, never mention that I said that. You have been guilty of a great crime; and don't you ever be guilty of it again, on this boat. *But*—lay for him ashore! Give him a good sound thrashing, do you hear?

I'll pay the expenses. Now go—and mind you, not a word of this to anybody. Clear out with you! You've been guilty of a great crime, you whelp!"

I slid out, happy with the sense of a close shave and a mighty deliverance; and I heard him laughing to himself and slapping his fat thighs after I had closed his door.

When Brown came off watch he went straight to the captain, who was talking with some passengers on the boiler-deck, and demanded that I be put ashore in New Orleans—and added:

"I'll never turn a wheel on this boat again while that cub stays."

The captain said:

"But he needn't come round when you are on watch, Mr. Brown."

"I won't even stay on the same boat with him. *One* of us has got to go ashore."

"Very well," said the captain, "let it be yourself," and resumed his talk with the passengers.

During the brief remainder of the trip I knew how an emancipated slave feels, for I was an emancipated slave myself. While we lay at landings I listened to George Ealer's flute, or to his readings from his two Bibles, that is to say, Goldsmith and Shakespeare, or I played chess with him—and would have beaten him sometimes, only he always took back his last move and ran the game out differently.

BRET HARTE

(1839–1902)

Francis Bret Harte was born in Albany, in 1839. His parents were English and Dutch, and one grandfather Jewish. His environment in childhood was good, his father being a teacher and accomplished scholar and his mother a woman of culture. He was studious and precocious, partly because ill health prevented his participation in games, and before he was ten had read Shakespeare, Froissart, Dickens, Cervantes, Fielding, and Irving. At thirteen he left school to enter a lawyer's office, later worked for a merchant, and at the age of sixteen was self-supporting. When after his father's death his mother remarried and went to California, he followed her there in 1854, and worked for a time in various capacities—as tutor, school-teacher, clerk in a drug store, express messenger, miner, and typesetter. In 1857 while setting type for The *Golden Era* he began contributing to it, and was soon promoted to the editorial room. His rise after this was rapid, and in 1868 he became editor of The *Overland Monthly,* in which first appeared "The Luck of Roaring Camp" (1868), "The Outcasts of Poker Flat" (1869), and the poem "The Heathen Chinee" (1870). These gave him a national reputation, and receiving an offer of ten thousand dollars a year to write exclusively for the *Atlantic Monthly,* he left California in 1871 to return east. In spite of the large sums he received for his writings he became heavily involved in debt, and for the rest of his life struggled with financial worries. In 1878 he secured an appointment as United States Consul to Crefeld, Germany, and in 1880 was transferred to Glasgow. In 1885 he retired and lived in London till his death in 1902.

In his stories of the Old West Harte broke new ground, and became the first interpreter of a life rich in local color and dramatic situations. His chief attributes as a writer were a keen dramatic instinct, a charitable understanding of the perplexities of struggling and frustrated humanity, a deep sympathy for men dazed by an existence too complex and too likely to be tragic, and a pervasive humor which kept sentiment within bounds. He could portray character, not by long analyses but by incident and dialogue, and this ability together with a power of condensation led to his creation of the modern type of short story. He published a number of volumes of verse, but it is as a writer of short, dramatic prose pieces that he left the deepest imprint on American literature.

THE LUCK OF ROARING CAMP [1]

THERE was commotion in Roaring Camp. It could not have been a fight, for in 1850 that was not novel enough to have called together the entire settlement. The ditches and claims were not only deserted, but "Tuttle's

[1] First published in the *Overland Monthly,* August, 1868, and then in *The Luck of Roaring Camp and Other Sketches,* 1870.

This and the two following stories of Bret Harte are used by permission of, and by arrangement with, Houghton Mifflin Company, the authorized publishers.

grocery" had contributed its gamblers, who, it will be remembered, calmly continued their game the day that French Pete and Kanaka Joe shot each other to death over the bar in the front room. The whole camp was collected before a rude cabin on the outer edge of the clearing. Conversation was carried on in a low tone, but the name of a woman was frequently repeated. It was a name familiar enough in the camp,—"Cherokee Sal."

Perhaps the less said of her the better. She was a coarse, and, it is to be feared, a very sinful woman. But at that time she was the only woman in Roaring Camp, and was just then lying in sore extremity, when she most needed the ministration of her own sex. Dissolute, abandoned and irreclaimable, she was yet suffering a martyrdom hard enough to bear even when veiled by sympathizing womanhood, but now terrible in her loneliness. The primal curse had come to her in that original isolation which must have made the punishment of the first transgression so dreadful. It was, perhaps, part of the expiation of her sin, that, at a moment when she most lacked her sex's intuitive tenderness and care, she met only the half-contemptuous faces of her masculine associates. Yet a few of the spectators were, I think, touched by her sufferings. Sandy Tipton thought it was "rough on Sal," and, in the contemplation of her condition, for a moment rose superior to the fact that he had an ace and two bowers in his sleeve.

It will be seen, also, that the situation was novel. Deaths were by no means uncommon in Roaring Camp, but a birth was a new thing. People had been dismissed from the camp, effectively, finally, and with no possibility of return; but this was the first time that anybody had been introduced *ab initio*. Hence the excitement.

"You go in there, Stumpy," said a prominent citizen known as "Kentuck," addressing one of the loungers. "Go in there, and see what you kin do. You've had experience in them things."

Perhaps there was a fitness in the selection. Stumpy, in other climes, had been the putative head of two families; in fact, it was owing to some legal informality in these proceedings that Roaring Camp—a city of refuge—was indebted to his company. The crowd approved the choice, and Stumpy was wise enough to bow to the majority. The door closed on the extempore surgeon and midwife, and Roaring Camp sat down outside, smoked its pipe, and awaited the issue.

The assemblage numbered about a hundred men. One or two of these were actual fugitives from justice, some were criminal, and all were reckless. Physically, they exhibited no indication of their past lives and character. The greatest scamp had a Raphael face, with a profusion of blond hair; Oakhurst, a gambler, had the melancholy air and intellectual abstraction of a Hamlet; the coolest and most courageous man was scarcely over five feet in height, with a soft voice and an embarrassed, timid manner. The term "roughs" applied to them was a distinction rather than a definition. Perhaps in the minor details of fingers, toes, ears, etc., the camp may have been deficient, but these slight omissions did not detract from their aggregate force. The strongest man had but three fingers on his right hand; the best shot had but one eye.

Such was the physical aspect of the men that were dispersed around the cabin. The camp lay in a triangular valley, between two hills and a river. The only outlet was a steep trail over the summit of a hill that faced the cabin, now illuminated by the rising moon. The suffering woman might have seen it from the rude bunk whereon she lay,—seen it winding like a silver thread until it was lost in the stars above.

A fire of withered pine-boughs added sociability to the gathering. By degrees the natural levity of Roaring Camp returned. Bets were freely offered and taken regarding the result. Three to five that "Sal would get through with it"; even, that the child would survive; side bets as to the sex and complexion of the coming stranger. In the midst of an excited discussion an exclamation came from those nearest the door, and the camp stopped to listen. Above the swaying and moaning of the pines, the swift rush of the river, and the crackling of the fire, rose a sharp, querulous cry,—a cry unlike anything heard before in the camp. The pines stopped moaning, the river ceased to rush, and the fire to crackle. It seemed as if Nature had stopped to listen too.

The camp rose to its feet as one man! It was proposed to explode a barrel of gunpowder, but, in consideration of the situation of the mother, better counsels prevailed, and only a few revolvers were discharged; for, whether owing to the rude surgery of the camp, or some other reason, Cherokee Sal was sinking fast. Within an hour she had climbed, as it were, that rugged road that led to the stars, and so passed out of Roaring Camp, its sin and shame forever. I do not think that the announcement disturbed them much, except in speculation as to the fate of the child. "Can he live now?" was asked of Stumpy. The answer was doubtful. The only other being of Cherokee Sal's sex and maternal condition in the settlement was an ass. There was some conjecture as to fitness, but the experiment was tried. It was less problematical than the ancient treatment of Romulus and Remus, and apparently as successful.

When these details were completed, which exhausted another hour, the door was opened, and the anxious crowd of men who had already formed themselves into a queue, entered in single file. Beside the low bunk or shelf, on which the figure of the mother was starkly outlined below the blankets, stood a pine table. On this a candle-box was placed, and within it, swathed in staring red flannel, lay the last arrival at Roaring Camp. Beside the candle-box was placed a hat. Its use was soon indicated. "Gentlemen," said Stumpy, with a singular mixture of authority and *ex officio* complacency,—

"Gentlemen will please pass in at the front door, round the table, and out at the back door. Them as wishes to contribute anything toward the orphan will find a hat handy." The first man entered with his hat on; he uncovered, however, as he looked about him, and so, unconsciously, set an example to the next. In such communities good and bad actions are catching. As the procession filed in, comments were audible,—criticisms addressed, perhaps, rather to Stumpy, in the character of showman,—"Is that him?" "mighty small specimen"; "hasn't mor'n got the color"; "ain't bigger nor a derringer." The contributions were as characteristic: A silver tobacco box; a doubloon; a navy revolver, silver mounted; a gold specimen; a very beautifully embroidered lady's handkerchief (from Oakhurst the gambler); a diamond breastpin; a diamond ring (suggested by the pin, with the remark from the giver that he "saw that pin and went two diamonds better"); a slung shot; a Bible (contributor not detected); a golden spur; a silver teaspoon (the initials, I regret to say, were not the giver's); a pair of surgeon's shears; a lancet; a Bank of England note for £5; and about $200 in loose gold and silver coin. During these proceedings Stumpy maintained a silence as impassive as the dead on his left, a gravity as inscrutable as that of the newly born on his right. Only one incident occurred to break the monotony of the curious procession. As Kentuck bent over the candle-box half curiously, the child turned, and, in a spasm of pain, caught at his groping finger, and held it fast for a moment. Kentuck looked foolish and embarrassed. Something like a blush tried to assert itself in his weather-beaten cheek. "The d—d little cuss!" he said, as he extricated his finger, with, perhaps, more tenderness and care than he might have been deemed capable of showing. He held that finger a little apart from its fellows as he went out, and examined it curiously. The examination provoked the same original remark in regard to the child. In fact, he seemed to enjoy repeating it. "He rastled with my finger," he remarked to Tipton, holding up the member, "the d—d little cuss!"

It was four o'clock before the camp sought repose. A light burnt in the cabin where the watchers sat, for Stumpy did not go to bed that night. Nor did Kentuck. He drank quite freely, and related with great gusto his experience, invariably ending with his characteristic condemnation of the newcomer. It seemed to relieve him of any unjust implication of sentiment, and Kentuck had the weaknesses of the nobler sex. When everybody else had gone to bed, he walked down to the river, and whistled reflectingly. Then he walked up the gulch, past the cabin, still whistling with demonstrative unconcern. At a large redwood tree he paused and retraced his steps, and again passed the cabin. Half-way down to the river's bank he again paused, and then returned and knocked at the door. It was opened by Stumpy. "How goes it!" said Kentuck, looking past Stumpy toward the candle-box.

"All serene," replied Stumpy. "Anything up?" "Nothing." There was a pause—an embarrassing one—Stumpy still holding the door. Then Kentuck had recourse to his finger, which he held up to Stumpy. "Rastled with it,—the d—d little cuss," he said, and retired.

The next day Cherokee Sal had such rude sepulture as Roaring Camp afforded. After her body had been committed to the hillside, there was a formal meeting of the camp to discuss what should be done with her infant. A resolution to adopt it was unanimous and enthusiastic. But an animated discussion in regard to the manner and feasibility of providing for its wants at once sprung up. It was remarkable that the argument partook of none of those fierce personalities with which discussions were usually conducted at Roaring Camp. Tipton proposed that they should send the child to Red Dog,—a distance of forty miles,—where female attention could be procured. But the unlucky suggestion met with fierce and unanimous opposition. It was evident that no plan which entailed parting from their new acquisition would for a moment be entertained. "Besides," said Tom Ryder, "them fellows at Red Dog would swap it, and ring in somebody else on us." A disbelief in the honesty of other camps prevailed at Roaring Camp as in other places.

The introduction of a female nurse in the camp also met with objection. It was argued that no decent woman could be prevailed to accept Roaring Camp as her home, and the speaker urged that "they didn't want any more of the other kind." This unkind allusion to the defunct mother, harsh as it may seem, was the first spasm of propriety,—the first symptom of the camp's regeneration. Stumpy advanced nothing. Perhaps he felt a certain delicacy in interfering with the selection of a possible successor in office. But when questioned, he averred stoutly that he and "Jinny"—the mammal before alluded to—could manage to rear the child. There was something original, independent, and heroic about the plan that pleased the camp. Stumpy was retained. Certain articles were sent for to Sacramento. "Mind," said the treasurer, as he pressed a bag of gold-dust into the expressman's hand, "the best that can be got,—lace, you know, and filigree-work and frills,—d—n the cost!"

Strange to say, the child thrived. Perhaps the invigorating climate of the mountain camp was compensation for material deficiencies. Nature took the foundling to her broader breast. In that rare atmosphere of the Sierra foot-hills,—that air pungent with balsamic odor, that ethereal cordial at once bracing and exhilarating,—he may have found food and nourishment, or a subtle chemistry that transmuted asses' milk to lime and phosphorus. Stumpy inclined to the belief that it was the latter and good nursing. "Me and that ass," he would say, "has been father and mother to him! Don't you," he would add, apostrophizing the helpless bundle before him, "never go back on us."

By the time he was a month old, the necessity of giving him a name became apparent. He had generally been known as "the Kid," "Stumpy's boy," "the Cayote" (an allusion to his vocal powers), and even by Kentuck's endearing diminutive of "the d—d little cuss." But these were felt to be vague and unsatisfactory, and were at last dismissed under another influence. Gamblers and adventurers are generally superstitious, and Oakhurst one day declared that the baby had brought "the luck" to Roaring Camp. It was certain that of late they had been successful. "Luck" was the name agreed upon, with the prefix of Tommy for greater convenience. No allusion was made to the mother, and the father was unknown. "It's better," said the philosophical Oakhurst, "to take a fresh deal all round. Call him Luck, and start him fair." A day was accordingly set apart for the christening. What was meant by this ceremony the reader may imagine, who has already gathered some idea of the reckless irreverence of Roaring Camp. The master of ceremonies was one "Boston," a noted wag, and the occasion seemed to promise the greatest facetiousness. This ingenious satirist had spent two days in preparing a burlesque of the church service, with pointed local allusions. The choir was properly trained, and Sandy Tipton was to stand godfather. But after the procession had marched to the grove with music and banners, and the child had been deposited before a mock altar, Stumpy stepped before the expectant crowd. "It ain't my style to spoil fun, boys," said the little man, stoutly, eying the faces around him, "but it strikes me that this thing ain't exactly on the squar. It's playing it pretty low down on this yer baby to ring in fun on him that he ain't going to understand. And ef there's going to be any godfathers round, I'd like to see who's got any better rights than me." A silence followed Stumpy's speech. To the credit of all humorists be it said, that the first man to acknowledge its justice was the satirist, thus stopped of his fun. "But," said Stumpy, quickly, following up his advantage, "we're here for a christening, and we'll have it. I proclaim you Thomas Luck, according to the laws of the United States and the State of California, so help me God." It was the first time that the name of the Deity had been uttered otherwise than profanely in the camp. The form of christening was perhaps even more ludicrous than the satirist had conceived; but, strangely enough, nobody saw it and nobody laughed. "Tommy" was christened as seriously as he would have been under a Christian roof, and cried and was comforted in as orthodox fashion.

And so the work of regeneration began in Roaring Camp. Almost imperceptibly a change came over the settlement. The cabin assigned to "Tommy Luck"—or "The Luck," as he was more frequently called—first showed signs of improvement. It was kept scrupulously clean and whitewashed. Then it was boarded, clothed, and papered. The rosewood cradle—packed eighty miles by mule—had, in Stumpy's way of putting it, "sorter killed the rest of the furniture." So the rehabilitation of the cabin became a necessity. The men who were in the habit of lounging in at Stumpy's to see "how The Luck got on" seemed to appreciate the change, and, in self-defence, the rival establishment of "Tuttle's grocery" bestirred itself, and imported a carpet and mirrors. The reflections of the latter on the appearance of Roaring Camp tended to produce stricter habits of personal cleanliness. Again, Stumpy imposed a kind of quarantine upon those who aspired to the honor and privilege of holding "The Luck." It was a cruel mortification to Kentuck—who, in the carelessness of a large nature and the habits of frontier life, had begun to regard all garments as a second cuticle, which, like a snake's, only sloughed off through decay—to be debarred this privilege from certain prudential reasons. Yet such was the subtle influence of innovation that he thereafter appeared regularly every afternoon in a clean shirt, and face still shining from his ablutions. Nor were moral and social sanitary laws neglected. "Tommy," who was supposed to spend his whole existence in a persistent attempt to repose, must not be disturbed by noise. The shouting and yelling which had gained the camp its infelicitous title were not permitted within hearing distance of Stumpy's. The men conversed in whispers, or smoked with Indian gravity. Profanity was tacitly given up in these sacred precincts, and throughout the camp a popular form of expletive, known as "D—n the luck!" and "Curse the luck!" was abandoned, as having a new personal bearing. Vocal music was not interdicted, being supposed to have a soothing, tranquillizing quality, and one song, sung by "Man-o'-War Jack," an English sailor, from her Majesty's Australian colonies, was quite popular as a lullaby. It was a lugubrious recital of the exploits of "the Arethusa, Seventy-four," in a muffled minor, ending with a prolonged dying fall at the burden of each verse, "On b-o-o-o-ard of the Arethusa." It was a fine sight to see Jack holding The Luck, rocking from side to side as if with the motion of a ship, and crooning forth this naval ditty. Either through the peculiar rocking of Jack or the length of his song,—it contained ninety stanzas, and was continued with conscientious deliberation to the bitter end,—the lullaby generally had the desired effect. At such times the men would lie at full length under the trees, in the soft summer twilight, smoking their pipes and drinking in the melodious utterances. An indistinct idea that this was pastoral happiness pervaded the camp. "This 'ere kind o' think," said the Cockney Simmons, meditatively reclining on his elbow, "is 'evingly." It reminded him of Greenwich.

On the long summer days The Luck was usually carried to the gulch, from whence the golden store of Roaring Camp was taken. There, on a blanket spread over pine-boughs, he would lie while the men were working in the ditches below. Latterly, there was a rude attempt to decorate this bower with flowers and sweet-smelling shrubs, and generally some one would bring him a cluster of wild honeysuckles, azaleas, or the painted blossoms of

BRET HARTE

Las Mariposas. The men had suddenly awakened to the fact that there were beauty and significance in these trifles, which they had so long trodden carelessly beneath their feet. A flake of glittering mica, a fragment of variegated quartz, a bright pebble from the bed of the creek, became beautiful to eyes thus cleared and strengthened, and were invariably put aside for "The Luck." It was wonderful how many treasures the woods and hillsides yielded that "would do for Tommy." Surrounded by playthings such as never child out of fairy-land had before, it is to be hoped that Tommy was content. He appeared to be securely happy, albeit there was an infantine gravity about him, a contemplative light in his round gray eyes, that sometimes worried Stumpy. He was always tractable and quiet, and it is recorded that once, having crept beyond his "corral,"—a hedge of tessellated pine-boughs, which surrounded his bed,—he dropped over the bank on his head in the soft earth, and remained with his mottled legs in the air in that position for at least five minutes with unflinching gravity. He was extricated without a murmur. I hesitate to record the many other instances of his sagacity, which rest, unfortunately, upon the statements of prejudiced friends. Some of them were not without a tinge of superstition. "I crep' up the bank just now," said Kentuck one day, in a breathless state of excitement, "and dern my skin if he wasn't a talking to a jaybird as was a sittin' on his lap. There they was, just as free and sociable as anything you please, a jawin' at each other just like two cherry-bums." Howbeit, whether creeping over the pine-boughs or lying lazily on his back blinking at the leaves above him, to him the birds sang, the squirrels chattered, and the flowers bloomed. Nature was his nurse and playfellow. For him she would let slip between the leaves golden shafts of sunlight that fell just within his grasp; she would send wandering breezes to visit him with the balm of bay and resinous gums; to him the tall redwoods nodded familiarly and sleepily, the bumblebees buzzed, and the rooks cawed a slumbrous accompaniment.

Such was the golden summer of Roaring Camp. They were "flush times," —and the Luck was with them. The claims had yielded enormously. The camp was jealous of its privileges and looked suspiciously on strangers. No encouragement was given to immigration, and, to make their seclusion more perfect, the land on either side of the mountain wall that surrounded the camp they duly pre-empted. This, and a reputation for singular proficiency with the revolver, kept the reserve of Roaring Camp inviolate. The expressman—their only connecting link with the surrounding world—sometimes told wonderful stories of the camp. He would say, "They've a street up there in 'Roaring,' that would lay over any street in Red Dog. They've got vines and flowers round their houses, and they wash themselves twice a day. But they're mighty rough on strangers, and they worship an Ingin baby."

With the prosperity of the camp came a desire for further improvement.

It was proposed to build a hotel in the following spring, and to invite one or two decent families to reside there for the sake of "The Luck,"—who might perhaps profit by female companionship. The sacrifice that this concession to the sex cost these men, who were fiercely sceptical in regard to its general virtue and usefulness, can only be accounted for by their affection for Tommy. A few still held out. But the resolve could not be carried into effect for three months, and the minority meekly yielded in the hope that something might turn up to prevent it. And it did.

The winter of 1851 will long be remembered in the foot-hills. The snow lay deep on the Sierras, and every mountain creek became a river, and every river a lake. Each gorge and gulch was transformed into a tumultuous water-course that descended the hillsides, tearing down giant trees and scattering its drift and débris along the plain. Red Dog had been twice under water, and Roaring Camp had been forewarned. "Water put the gold into them gulches," said Stumpy. "It's been here once and will be here again!" And that night the North Fork suddenly leaped over its banks, and swept up the triangular valley of Roaring Camp.

In the confusion of rushing water, crushing trees, and crackling timber, and the darkness which seemed to flow with the water and blot out the fair valley, but little could be done to collect the scattered camp. When the morning broke, the cabin of Stumpy nearest the river-bank was gone. Higher up the gulch they found the body of its unlucky owner; but the pride, the hope, the joy, the Luck of Roaring Camp had disappeared. They were returning with sad hearts, when a shout from the bank recalled them.

It was a relief-boat from down the river. They had picked up, they said, a man and an infant, nearly exhausted, about two miles below. Did anybody know them, and did they belong here?

It needed but a glance to show them Kentuck lying there, cruelly crushed and bruised, but still holding the Luck of Roaring Camp in his arms. As they bent over the strangely assorted pair, they saw that the child was cold and pulseless. "He is dead," said one. Kentuck opened his eyes. "Dead?" he repeated feebly. "Yes, my man, and you are dying too." A smile lit the eyes of the expiring Kentuck. "Dying," he repeated, "he's a taking me with him, —tell the boys I've got the Luck with me now"; and the strong man, clinging to the frail babe as a drowning man is said to cling to a straw, drifted away into the shadowy river that flows forever to the unknown sea.

THE OUTCASTS OF POKER FLAT [2]

As Mr. John Oakhurst, gambler, stepped into the main street of Poker Flat on the morning of the twenty-third of November, 1850, he was conscious of

---

[2] First published in the *Overland Monthly*, January, 1869, and then in *The Luck of Roaring Camp and Other Sketches*, 1870.

a change in its moral atmosphere since the preceding night. Two or three men, conversing earnestly together, ceased as he approached, and exchanged significant glances. There was a Sabbath lull in the air, which, in a settlement unused to Sabbath influences, looked ominous.

Mr. Oakhurst's calm, handsome face betrayed small concern in these indications. Whether he was conscious of any predisposing cause, was another question. "I reckon they're after somebody," he reflected; "likely it's me." He returned to his pocket the handkerchief with which he had been whipping away the red dust of Poker Flat from his neat boots, and quietly discharged his mind of any further conjecture.

In point of fact, Poker Flat was "after somebody." It had lately suffered the loss of several thousand dollars, two valuable horses, and a prominent citizen. It was experiencing a spasm of virtuous reaction, quite as lawless and ungovernable as any of the acts that had provoked it. A secret committee had determined to rid the town of all improper persons. This was done permanently in regard of two men who were then hanging from the boughs of a sycamore in the gulch, and temporarily in the banishment of certain other objectionable characters. I regret to say that some of these were ladies. It is but due to the sex, however, to state that their impropriety was professional, and it was only in such easily established standards of evil that Poker Flat ventured to sit in judgment.

Mr. Oakhurst was right in supposing that he was included in this category. A few of the committee had urged hanging him as a possible example, and a sure method of reimbursing themselves from his pockets of the sums he had won from them. "It's agin justice," said Jim Wheeler, "to let this yer young man from Roaring Camp—an entire stranger—carry away our money." But a crude sentiment of equity residing in the breasts of those who had been fortunate enough to win from Mr. Oakhurst overruled this narrower local prejudice.

Mr. Oakhurst received his sentence with philosophic calmness, none the less coolly, that he was aware of the hesitation of his judges. He was too much of a gambler not to accept Fate. With him life was at best an uncertain game, and he recognized the usual percentage in favor of the dealer.

A body of armed men accompanied the deported wickedness of Poker Flat to the outskirts of the settlement. Besides Mr. Oakhurst, who was known to be a coolly desperate man, and for whose intimidation the armed escort was intended, the expatriated party consisted of a young woman familiarly known as "The Duchess"; another, who had won the title of "Mother Shipton"; and "Uncle Billy," a suspected sluice-robber and confirmed drunkard. The cavalcade provoked no comments from the spectators, nor was any word uttered by the escort. Only, when the gulch which marked the uttermost limit of

Poker Flat was reached, the leader spoke briefly and to the point. The exiles were forbidden to return at the peril of their lives.

As the escort disappeared, their pent-up feelings found vent in a few hysterical tears from the Duchess, some bad language from Mother Shipton, and a Parthian volley of expletives from Uncle Billy. The philosophic Oakhurst alone remained silent. He listened calmly to Mother Shipton's desire to cut somebody's heart out, to the repeated statements of the Duchess that she would die in the road, and to the alarming oaths that seemed to be bumped out of Uncle Billy as he rode forward. With the easy good-humor characteristic of his class, he insisted upon exchanging his own riding-horse, "Five Spot," for the sorry mule which the Duchess rode. But even this act did not draw the party into any closer sympathy. The young woman readjusted her somewhat draggled plumes with a feeble, faded coquetry; Mother Shipton eyed the possessor of "Five Spot" with malevolence, and Uncle Billy included the whole party in one sweeping anathema.

The road to Sandy Bar—a camp that, not having as yet experienced the regenerating influences of Poker Flat, consequently seemed to offer some invitation to the emigrants—lay over a steep mountain range. It was distant a day's severe travel. In that advanced season, the party soon passed out of the moist, temperate regions of the foot-hills into the dry, cold, bracing air of the Sierras. The trail was narrow and difficult. At noon the Duchess, rolling out of her saddle upon the ground, declared her intention of going no farther, and the party halted.

The spot was singularly wild and impressive. A wooded amphitheatre, surrounded on three sides by precipitous cliffs of naked granite, sloped gently toward the crest of another precipice that overlooked the valley. It was, undoubtedly, the most suitable spot for a camp, had camping been advisable. But Mr. Oakhurst knew that scarcely half the journey to Sandy Bar was accomplished, and the party were not equipped or provisioned for delay. This fact he pointed out to his companions curtly, with a philosophic commentary on the folly of "throwing up their hand before the game was played out." But they were furnished with liquor, which in this emergency stood them in place of food, fuel, rest, and prescience. In spite of his remonstrances, it was not long before they were more or less under its influence. Uncle Billy passed rapidly from a bellicose state into one of stupor, the Duchess became maudlin, and Mother Shipton snored. Mr. Oakhurst alone remained erect, leaning against a rock, calmly surveying them.

Mr. Oakhurst did not drink. It interfered with a profession which required coolness, impassiveness, and presence of mind, and, in his own language, he "couldn't afford it." As he gazed at his recumbent fellow-exiles, the loneliness begotten of his pariah-trade, his habits of life, his very vices, for the first time seriously oppressed him. He bestirred himself in dusting his black clothes, washing his hands and face, and other acts characteristic of his studiously neat habits, and for a moment forgot his annoyance. The thought of deserting his weaker and more pitiable companions never perhaps occurred to him. Yet he could not help feeling the want of that excitement which, singularly enough, was most conducive to that calm equanimity for which he was notorious. He looked at the gloomy walls that rose a thousand feet sheer above the circling pines around him; at the sky, ominously clouded; at the valley below, already deepening into shadow. And, doing so, suddenly he heard his own name called.

A horseman slowly ascended the trail. In the fresh, open face of the new-comer Mr. Oakhurst recognized Tom Simson, otherwise known as "The Innocent" of Sandy Bar. He had met him some months before over a "little game," and had, with perfect equanimity, won the entire fortune—amounting to some forty dollars—of that guileless youth. After the game was finished, Mr. Oakhurst drew the youthful speculator behind the door and thus addressed him: "Tommy, you're a good little man, but you can't gamble worth a cent. Don't try it over again." He then handed him his money back, pushed him gently from the room, and so made a devoted slave of Tom Simson.

There was a remembrance of this in his boyish and enthusiastic greeting of Mr. Oakhurst. He had started, he said, to go to Poker Flat to seek his fortune. "Alone?" No, not exactly alone; in fact (a giggle), he had run away with Piney Woods. Didn't Mr. Oakhurst remember Piney? She that used to wait on the table at the Temperance House? They had been engaged a long time, but old Jake Woods had objected, and so they had run away, and were going to Poker Flat to be married, and here they were. And they were tired out, and how lucky it was they had found a place to camp and company. All this the Innocent delivered rapidly, while Piney, a stout, comely damsel of fifteen, emerged from behind the pine tree, where she had been blushing unseen, and rode to the side of her lover.

Mr. Oakhurst seldom troubled himself with sentiment, still less with propriety; but he had a vague idea that the situation was not fortunate. He retained, however, his presence of mind sufficiently to kick Uncle Billy, who was about to say something, and Uncle Billy was sober enough to recognize in Mr. Oakhurst's kick a superior power that would not bear trifling. He then endeavored to dissuade Tom Simson from delaying further, but in vain. He even pointed out the fact that there was no provision, nor means of making a camp. But, unluckily, the Innocent met this objection by assuring the party that he was provided with an extra mule loaded with provisions, and by the discovery of a rude attempt at a log house near the trail. "Piney can stay with Mrs. Oakhurst," said the Innocent, pointing to the Duchess, "and I can shift for myself."

Nothing but Mr. Oakhurst's admonishing foot saved Uncle Billy from bursting into a roar of laughter. As it was, he felt compelled to retire up the cañon until he could recover his gravity. There he confided the joke to the tall pine-trees, with many slaps of his leg, contortions of his face, and the usual profanity. But when he returned to the party, he found them seated by a fire—for the air had grown strangely chill and the sky overcast—in apparently amicable conversation. Piney was actually talking in an impulsive, girlish fashion to the Duchess, who was listening with an interest and animation she had not shown for many days. The Innocent was holding forth, apparently with equal effect, to Mr. Oakhurst and Mother Shipton, who was actually relaxing into amiability. "Is this yer a d—d picnic?" said Uncle Billy, with inward scorn, as he surveyed the sylvan group, the glancing firelight, and the tethered animals in the foreground. Suddenly an idea mingled with the alcoholic fumes that disturbed his brain. It was apparently of a jocular nature, for he felt impelled to slap his leg again and cram his fist into his mouth.

As the shadows crept slowly up the mountain, a slight breeze rocked the tops of the pine-trees, and moaned through their long and gloomy aisles. The ruined cabin, patched and covered with pine-boughs, was set apart for the ladies. As the lovers parted, they unaffectedly exchanged a kiss, so honest and sincere that it might have been heard above the swaying pines. The frail Duchess and the malevolent Mother Shipton were probably too stunned to remark upon this last evidence of simplicity, and so turned without a word to the hut. The fire was replenished, the men lay down before the door, and in a few minutes were asleep.

Mr. Oakhurst was a light sleeper. Toward morning he awoke benumbed and cold. As he stirred the dying fire, the wind, which was now blowing strongly, brought to his cheek that which caused the blood to leave it,—snow!

He started to his feet with the intention of awakening the sleepers, for there was no time to lose. But, turning to where Uncle Billy had been lying, he found him gone. A suspicion leaped to his brain and a curse to his lips. He ran to the spot where the mules had been tethered; they were no longer there. The tracks were already rapidly disappearing in the snow.

The momentary excitement brought Mr. Oakhurst back to the fire with his usual calm. He did not waken the sleepers. The Innocent slumbered peacefully, with a smile on his good-humored, freckled face; the virgin Piney slept beside her frailer sisters as sweetly as though attended by celestial guardians, and Mr. Oakhurst, drawing his blanket over his shoulders, stroked his mustaches and waited for the dawn. It came slowly in a whirling mist of snow-flakes, that dazzled and confused the eye. What could be seen of the landscape appeared magically changed. He looked over the valley, and summed up the present and future in two words,—"snowed in!"

A careful inventory of the provisions, which, fortunately for the party, had been stored within the hut, and so escaped the felonious fingers of Uncle Billy, disclosed the fact that with care and prudence they might last ten days longer. "That is," said Mr. Oakhurst, *sotto voce* to the Innocent, "if you're willing to board us. If you ain't—and perhaps you'd better not—you can wait till Uncle Billy gets back with provisions." For some occult reason, Mr. Oakhurst could not bring himself to disclose Uncle Billy's rascality, and so offered the hypothesis that he had wandered from the camp and had accidentally stampeded the animals. He dropped a warning to the Duchess and Mother Shipton, who of course knew the facts of their associate's defection. "They'll find out the truth about us *all* when they find out anything," he added, significantly, "and there's no good frightening them now."

Tom Simson not only put all his worldly store at the disposal of Mr. Oakhurst, but seemed to enjoy the prospect of their enforced seclusion. "We'll have a good camp for a week, and then the snow'll melt, and we'll all go back together." The cheerful gayety of the young man, and Mr. Oakhurst's calm infected the others. The Innocent, with the aid of pine-boughs, extemporized a thatch for the roofless cabin, and the Duchess directed Piney in the rearrangement of the interior with a taste and tact that opened the blue eyes of that provincial maiden to their fullest extent. "I reckon now you're used to fine things at Poker Flat," said Piney. The Duchess turned away sharply to conceal something that reddened her cheek through its professional tint, and Mother Shipton requested Piney not to "chatter." But when Mr. Oakhurst returned from a weary search for the trail, he heard the sound of happy laughter echoed from the rocks. He stopped in some alarm, and his thoughts first naturally reverted to the whiskey, which he had prudently *cachéd*. "And yet it don't somehow sound like whiskey," said the gambler. It was not until he caught sight of the blazing fire through the still blinding storm and the group around it that he settled to the conviction that it was "square fun."

Whether Mr. Oakhurst had *cachéd* his cards with the whiskey as something debarred the free access of the community, I cannot say. It was certain that, in Mother Shipton's words, he "didn't say cards once" during that evening. Haply the time was beguiled by an accordian, produced somewhat ostentatiously by Tom Simson from his pack. Notwithstanding some difficulties attending the manipulation of this instrument, Piney Woods managed to pluck several reluctant melodies from its keys, to an accompaniment by the Innocent on a pair of bone castinets. But the crowning festivity of the evening was reached in a rude camp-meeting hymn, which the lovers, joining hands, sang with great earnestness and vociferation. I fear that a certain defiant tone and Covenanter's swing to its chorus, rather than any devotional quality, caused it speedily to infect the others, who at last joined in the refrain:

I'm proud to live in the service of the Lord,
And I'm bound to die in His army.

The pines rocked, the storm eddied and whirled above the miserable group, and the flames of their altar leaped heavenward, as if in token of the vow.

At midnight the storm abated, the rolling clouds parted, and the stars glittered keenly above the sleeping camp. Mr. Oakhurst, whose professional habits had enabled him to live on the smallest possible amount of sleep, in dividing the watch with Tom Simson, somehow managed to take upon himself the greater part of that duty. He excused himself to the Innocent, by saying that he had "often been a week without sleep." "Doing what?" asked Tom. "Poker!" replied Oakhurst, sententiously; "when a man gets a streak of luck,—niggerluck,—he don't get tired. The luck gives in first. Luck," continued the gambler, reflectively, "is a mighty queer thing. All you know about it for certain is that it's bound to change. And it's finding out when it's going to change that makes you. We've had a streak of bad luck since we left Poker Flat,—you come along, and slap you get into it, too. If you can hold your cards right along you're all right. For," added the gambler, with cheerful irrelevance,—

> "I'm proud to live in the service of the Lord,
> And I'm bound to die in His army."

The third day came, and the sun, looking through the white-curtained valley, saw the outcasts divide their slowly decreasing store of provisions for the morning meal. It was one of the peculiarities of that mountain climate that its rays diffused a kindly warmth over the wintry landscape, as if in regretful commiseration of the past. But it revealed drift on drift of snow piled high around the hut,—a hopeless, uncharted, trackless sea of white lying below the rocky shores to which the castaways still clung. Through the marvellously clear air the smoke of the pastoral village of Poker Flat rose miles away. Mother Shipton saw it, and from a remote pinnacle of her rocky fastness, hurled in that direction a final malediction. It was her last vituperative attempt, and perhaps for that reason was invested with a certain degree of sublimity. It did her good, she privately informed the Duchess. "Just you go out there and cuss, and see." She then set herself to the task of amusing "the child," as she and the Duchess were pleased to call Piney. Piney was no chicken, but it was a soothing and original theory of the pair thus to account for the fact that she didn't swear and wasn't improper.

When night crept up again through the gorges, the reedy notes of the accordion rose and fell in fitful spasms and long-drawn gasps by the flickering camp-fire. But music failed to fill entirely the aching void left by insufficient food, and a new diversion was proposed by Piney,—story-telling. Neither Mr. Oakhurst nor his female companions caring to relate their personal experiences, this plan would have failed, too, but for the Innocent. Some months before he had chanced upon a stray copy of Mr. Pope's ingenious translation of the Iliad. He now proposed to narrate the principal incidents of that poem—having thoroughly mastered the argument and fairly forgotten the words—in the current vernacular of Sandy Bar. And so for the rest of that night the Homeric demigods again walked the earth. Trojan bully and wily Greek wrestled in the winds, and the great pines in the cañon seemed to bow to the wrath of the son of Peleus. Mr. Oakhurst listened with quiet satisfaction. Most especially was he interested in the fate of "Ash-heels," as the Innocent persisted in denominating the "swift-footed Achilles."

So with small food and much of Homer and the accordion, a week passed over the heads of the outcasts. The sun again forsook them, and again from leaden skies the snow-flakes were sifted over the land. Day by day closer around them drew the snowy circle, until at last they looked from their prison over drifted walls of dazzling white, that towered twenty feet above their heads. It became more and more difficult to replenish their fires, even from the fallen trees beside them, now half hidden in the drifts. And yet no one complained. The lovers turned from the dreary prospect and looked into each other's eyes, and were happy. Mr. Oakhurst settled himself coolly to the losing game before him. The Duchess, more cheerful than she had been, assumed the care of Piney. Only Mother Shipton—once the strongest of the party—seemed to sicken and fade. At midnight on the tenth day she called Oakhurst to her side. "I'm going," she said, in a voice of querulous weakness, "but don't say anything about it. Don't waken the kids. Take the bundle from under my head and open it." Mr. Oakhurst did so. It contained Mother Shipton's rations for the last week, untouched. "Give 'em to the child," she said, pointing to the sleeping Piney. "You've starved yourself," said the gambler. "That's what they call it," said the woman, querulously, as she lay down again, and, turning her face to the wall, passed quietly away.

The accordion and the bones were put aside that day, and Homer was forgotten. When the body of Mother Shipton had been committed to the snow, Mr. Oakhurst took the Innocent aside, and showed him a pair of snow-shoes, which he had fashioned from the old pack-saddle. "There one's chance in a hundred to save her yet," he said, pointing to Piney; "but it's there," he added, pointing toward Poker Flat. "If you can reach there in two days she's safe." "And you?" asked Tom Simson. "I'll stay here," was the curt reply.

The lovers parted with a long embrace. "You are not going, too?" said the Duchess, as she saw Mr. Oakhurst apparently waiting to accompany him. "As far as the cañon," he replied. He turned suddenly, and kissed the Duchess, leaving her pallid face aflame, and her trembling lips rigid with amazement.

Night came, but not Mr. Oakhurst. It brought the storm again and the whirling snow. Then the Duchess, feeding the fire, found that some one had quietly piled beside the hut enough fuel to last a few days longer. The tears rose to her eyes, but she hid them from Piney.

The women slept but little. In the morning, looking into each other's faces, they read their fate. Neither spoke; but Piney, accepting the position of the stronger, drew near and placed her arm around the Duchess's waist. They kept this attitude for the rest of the day. That night the storm reached its greatest fury, and, rending asunder the protecting pines, invaded the very hut.

Toward morning they found themselves unable to feed the fire, which gradually died away. As the embers slowly blackened, the Duchess crept closer to Piney, and broke the silence of many hours: "Piney, can you pray?" "No, dear," said Piney, simply. The Duchess, without knowing exactly why, felt relieved, and, putting her head upon Piney's shoulder, spoke no more. And so reclining, the younger and purer pillowing the head of her soiled sister upon her virgin breast, they fell asleep.

The wind lulled as if it feared to waken them. Feathery drifts of snow, shaken from the long pine-boughs, flew like white-winged birds, and settled about them as they slept. The moon through the rifted clouds looked down upon what had been the camp. But all human stain, all trace of earthly travail, was hidden beneath the spotless mantle mercifully flung from above.

They slept all that day and the next, nor did they waken when voices and footsteps broke the silence of the camp. And when pitying fingers brushed the snow from their wan faces, you could scarcely have told from the equal peace that dwelt upon them, which was she that had sinned. Even the law of Poker Flat recognized this, and turned away, leaving them still locked in each other's arms.

But at the head of the gulch, on one of the largest pine-trees, they found the deuce of clubs pinned to the bark with a bowie-knife. It bore the following, written in pencil, in a firm hand:—

†

BENEATH THIS TREE
LIES THE BODY
OF

JOHN OAKHURST,

WHO STRUCK A STREAK OF BAD LUCK
ON THE 23D OF NOVEMBER, 1850,
AND
HANDED IN HIS CHECKS
ON THE 7TH DECEMBER, 1850.

†

And pulseless and cold, with a Derringer by his side and a bullet in his heart, though still calm as in life, beneath the snow lay he who was at once the strongest and yet the weakest of the outcasts of Poker Flat.

TENNESSEE'S PARTNER [3]

I DO not think that we ever knew his real name. Our ignorance of it certainly never gave us any social inconvenience, for at Sandy Bar in 1854 most men were christened anew. Sometimes these appellatives were derived from some distinctiveness of dress, as in the case of "Dungaree Jack"; or from some peculiarity of habit, as shown in "Saleratus Bill," so called from an undue proportion of that chemical in his daily bread; or from some unlucky slip, as exhibited in "The Iron Pirate," a mild, inoffensive man, who earned that baleful title by his unfortunate mispronunciation of the term "iron pyrites." Perhaps this may have been the beginning of a rude heraldry; but I am constrained to think that it was because a man's real name in that day rested solely upon his own unsupported statement. "Call yourself Clifford, do you?" said Boston, addressing a timid new-comer with infinite scorn; "hell is full of such Cliffords!" He then introduced the unfortunate man, whose name happened to be really Clifford, as "Jay-bird Charley,"—an unhallowed inspiration of the moment that clung to him ever after.

But to return to Tennessee's Partner, whom we never knew by any other than this relative title; that he had ever existed as a separate and distinct individuality we only learned later. It seems that in 1853 he left Poker Flat to go to San Francisco, ostensibly to procure a wife. He never got any farther than Stockton. At that place he was attracted by a young person who waited upon the table at the hotel where he took his meals. One morning he said something to her which caused her to smile not unkindly, to somewhat coquettishly break a plate of toast over his upturned, serious, simple face, and to retreat to the kitchen. He followed her, and emerged a few moments later, covered with more toast and victory. That day week they were married by a Justice of the Peace, and returned to Poker Flat. I am aware that something more might be made of this episode, but I prefer to tell it as it was current at Sandy Bar,—in the gulches and bar-rooms,—where all sentiment was modified by a strong sense of humor.

Of their married felicity but little is known, perhaps for the reason that Tennessee, then living with his partner, one day took occasion to say something to the bride on his own account, at which, it is said, she smiled not unkindly and chastely retreated,—this time as far as Marysville, where Tennessee followed her, and where they went to housekeeping without the aid

[3] First published in the *Overland Monthly*, October, 1869, and then in *The Luck of Roaring Camp and Other Sketches*, 1870.

of a Justice of the Peace. Tennessee's Partner took the loss of his wife simply and seriously, as was his fashion. But to everybody's surprise, when Tennessee one day returned from Marysville, without his partner's wife,—she having smiled and retreated with somebody else,—Tennessee's Partner was the first man to shake his hand and greet him with affection. The boys who had gathered in the cañon to see the shooting were naturally indignant. Their indignation might have found vent in sarcasm but for a certain look in Tennessee's Partner's eye that indicated a lack of humorous appreciation. In fact, he was a grave man, with a steady application to practical detail which was unpleasant in a difficulty.

Meanwhile a popular feeling against Tennessee had grown up on the Bar. He was known to be a gambler; he was suspected to be a thief. In these suspicions Tennessee's Partner was equally compromised; his continued intimacy with Tennessee after the affair above quoted could only be accounted for on the hypothesis of a copartnership of crime. At last Tennessee's guilt became flagrant. One day he overtook a stranger on his way to Red Dog. The stranger afterward related that Tennessee beguiled the time with interesting anecdote and reminiscence, but illogically concluded the intervie v in the following words: "And now, young man, I'll trouble you for your knife, your pistols, and your money. You see your weppings might get you into trouble at Red Dog, and your money's a temptation to the evilly disposed. I think you said your address was San Francisco. I shall endeavor to call." It may be stated here that Tennessee had a fine flow of humor, which no business preoccupation could wholly subdue.

This exploit was his last. Red Dog and Sandy Bar made common cause against the highwayman. Tennessee was hunted in very much the same fashion as his prototype, the grizzly. As the toils closed around him, he made a desperate dash through the Bar, emptying his revolver at the crowd before the Arcade Saloon, and so on up Grizzly Cañon; but at its farther extremity he was stopped by a small man on a gray horse. The men looked at each other a moment in silence. Both were fearless, both self-possessed and independent; and both types of a civilization that in the seventeenth century would have been called heroic, but, in the nineteenth, simply "reckless." "What have you got there?—I call," said Tennessee, quietly. "Two bowers and an ace," said the stranger, as quietly, showing two revolvers and a bowie-knife. "That takes me," returned Tennessee; and with this gamblers' epigram, he threw away his useless pistol, and rode back with his captor.

It was a warm night. The cool breeze which usually sprang up with the going down of the sun behind the *chaparral*-crested mountain was that evening withheld from Sandy Bar. The little cañon was stifling with heated resinous odors, and the decaying drift-wood on the Bar sent forth faint, sickening exhalations. The feverishness of day, and its fierce passions, still filled the camp. Lights moved restlessly along the bank of the river, striking no answering reflection from its tawny current. Against the blackness of the pines the windows of the old loft above the express-office stood out staringly bright; and through their curtainless panes the loungers below could see the forms of those who were even then deciding the fate of Tennessee. And above all this, etched on the dark firmament, rose the Sierra, remote and passionless, crowned with remoter passionless stars.

The trial of Tennessee was conducted as fairly as was consistent with a judge and jury who felt themselves to some extent obliged to justify, in their verdict, the previous irregularities of arrest and indictment. The law of Sandy Bar was implacable, but not vengeful. The excitement and personal feeling of the chase were over; with Tennessee safe in their hands they were ready to listen patiently to any defence, which they were already satisfied was insufficient. There being no doubt in their own minds, they were willing to give the prisoner the benefit of any that might exist. Secure in the hypothesis that he ought to be hanged, on general principles, they indulged him with more latitude of defence than his reckless hardihood seemed to ask. The Judge appeared to be more anxious than the prisoner, who, otherwise unconcerned, evidently took a grim pleasure in the responsibility he had created. "I don't take any hand in this yer game," had been his invariable, but good-humored reply to all questions. The Judge—who was also his captor —for a moment vaguely regretted that he had not shot him "on sight," that morning, but presently dismissed this human weakness as unworthy of the judicial mind. Nevertheless, when there was a tap at the door, and it was said that Tennessee's Partner was there on behalf of the prisoner, he was admitted at once without question. Perhaps the younger members of the jury, to whom the proceedings were becoming irksomely thoughtful, hailed him as a relief.

For he was not, certainly, an imposing figure. Short and stout, with a square face, sunburned into a preternatural redness, clad in a loose duck "jumper," and trousers streaked and splashed with red soil, his aspect under any circumstances would have been quaint, and was now even ridiculous. As he stooped to deposit at his feet a heavy carpet-bag he was carrying, it became obvious, from partially developed legends and inscriptions, that the material with which his trousers had been patched had been originally intended for a less ambitious covering. Yet he advanced with great gravity, and after having shaken the hand of each person in the room with labored cordiality, he wiped his serious, perplexed face on a red bandanna handkerchief, a shade lighter than his complexion, laid his powerful hand upon the table to steady himself, and thus adressed the Judge:—

"I was passin' by," he began, by way of apology, "and I thought I'd just step in and see how things was gittin' on with Tennessee thar,—my pardner. It's a hot night. I disremember any sich weather before on the Bar."

He paused a moment, but nobody volunteering any other meteorological recollection, he again had recourse to his pocket-handkerchief, and for some moments mopped his face diligently.

"Have you anything to say in behalf of the prisoner?" said the Judge, finally.

"Thet's it," said Tennessee's Partner, in a tone of relief. "I come yar as Tennessee's pardner,—knowing him nigh on four year, off and on, wet and dry, in luck and out o' luck. His ways ain't allers my ways, but thar ain't any p'ints in that young man, thar ain't any liveliness as he's been up to, as I don't know. And you sez to me, sez you,—confidential-like, and between man and man,—sez you, 'Do you know anything in his behalf?' and I sez to you, sez I,—confidential-like, as between man and man,—'What should a man know of his pardner?'"

"Is this all you have to say?" asked the Judge, impatiently, feeling, perhaps, that a dangerous sympathy of humor was beginning to humanize the Court.

"Thet's so," continued Tennessee's Partner. "It ain't for me to say anything agin' him. And now, what's the case? Here's Tennessee wants money, wants it bad, and doesn't like to ask it of his old pardner. Well, what does Tennessee do? He lays for a stranger, and he fetches that stranger. And you lays for *him,* and you fetches *him;* and the honors is easy. And I put it to you, bein' a far-minded man, and to you, gentlemen, all, as far-minded men, ef this isn't so."

"Prisoner," said the Judge, interrupting, "have you any questions to ask this man?"

"No! no!" continued Tennessee's Partner, hastily. "I play this yer hand alone. To come down to the bed-rock, it's just this: Tennessee, thar, has played it pretty rough and expensive-like on a stranger, and on this yer camp. And now, what's the fair thing? Some would say more; some would say less. Here's seventeen hundred dollars in coarse gold and a watch,—it's about all my pile,—and call it square!" And before a hand could be raised to prevent him, he had emptied the contents of the carpet-bag upon the table.

For a moment his life was in jeopardy. One or two men sprang to their feet, several hands groped for hidden weapons, and a suggestion to "throw him from the window" was only overridden by a gesture from the Judge. Tennessee laughed. And apparently oblivious of the excitement, Tennessee's Partner improved the opportunity to mop his face again with his hand-kerchief.

When order was restored, and the man was made to understand, by the use of forcible figures and rhetoric, that Tennessee's offence could not be condoned by money, his face took a more serious and sanguinary hue, and those who were nearest to him noticed that his rough hand trembled slightly on the table. He hesitated a moment as he slowly returned the gold to the carpet-bag, as if he had not yet entirely caught the elevated sense of justice which swayed the tribunal, and was perplexed with the belief that he had not offered enough. Then he turned to the Judge, and saying, "This yer is a lone hand, played alone, and without my pardner," he bowed to the jury and was about to withdraw, when the Judge called him back. "If you have anything to say to Tennessee, you had better say it now." For the first time that evening the eyes of the prisoner and his strange advocate met. Tennessee smiled, showed his white teeth, and, saying, "Euchred, old man!" held out his hand. Tennessee's Partner took it in his own, and saying, "I just dropped in as I was passin' to see how things was gettin' on," let the hand passively fall, and adding that "it was a warm night," again mopped his face with his handkerchief, and without another word withdrew.

The two men never again met each other alive. For the unparalleled insult of a bribe offered to Judge Lynch—who, whether bigoted, weak, or narrow, was at least incorruptible—firmly fixed in the mind of that mythical personage any wavering determination of Tennessee's fate; and at the break of day he was marched, closely guarded, to meet it at the top of Marley's Hill.

How he met it, how cool he was, how he refused to say anything, how perfect were the arrangements of the committee, were all duly reported, with the addition of a warning moral and example to all future evil-doers, in the Red Dog Clarion, by its editor, who was present, and to whose vigorous English I cheerfully refer the reader. But the beauty of that midsummer morning, the blessed amity of earth and air and sky, the awakened life of the free woods and hills, the joyous renewal and promise of Nature, and above all, the infinite Serenity that thrilled through each, was not reported, as not being a part of the social lesson. And yet, when the weak and foolish deed was done, and a life, with its possibilities and responsibilities, had passed out of the misshapen thing that dangled between earth and sky, the birds sang, the flowers bloomed, the sun shone, as cheerily as before; and possibly the Red Dog Clarion was right.

Tennessee's Partner was not in the group that surrounded the ominous tree. But as they turned to disperse attention was drawn to the singular appearance of a motionless donkey-cart halted at the side of the road. As they approached, they at once recognized the venerable "Jenny" and the two-wheeled cart as the property of Tennessee's Partner,—used by him in carrying dirt from his claim; and a few paces distant the owner of the equipage himself, sitting under a buckeye-tree, wiping the perspiration from his glowing face. In answer to an inquiry, he said he had come for the body of the "diseased," "if it was all the same to the committee." He didn't wish to "hurry anything"; he could "wait." He was not working that day; and when the gentlemen were done with the "diseased," he would take him. "Ef thar is any present," he added, in his simple, serious way, "as would care to jine in the fun'l, they kin come." Perhaps it was from a sense of humor, which I have already intimated was a feature of Sandy Bar,—perhaps it was from something even better than that; but two thirds of the loungers accepted the invitation at once.

It was noon when the body of Tennessee was delivered into the hands of his partner. As the cart drew up to the fatal tree, we noticed that it contained a rough, oblong box,—apparently made from a section of sluicing,—and half filled with bark and the tassels of pine. The cart was further decorated with slips of willow, and made fragrant with buckeye-blossoms. When the body was deposited in the box, Tennessee's Partner drew over it a piece of tarred canvas, and gravely mounting the narrow seat in front, with his feet upon the shafts, urged the little donkey forward. The equipage moved slowly on, at that decorous pace which was habitual with "Jenny" even under less solemn circumstances. The men—half curiously, half jestingly, but all good-humoredly—strolled along beside the cart; some in advance, some a little in the rear of the homely catafalque. But, whether from the narrowing of the road or some present sense of decorum, as the cart passed on, the company fell to the rear in couples, keeping step, and otherwise assuming the external show of a formal procession. Jack Folinsbee, who had at the outset played a funeral march in dumb show upon an imaginary trombone, desisted, from a lack of sympathy and appreciation,—not having, perhaps, your true humorist's capacity to be content with the enjoyment of his own fun.

The way led through Grizzly Cañon,—by this time clothed in funeral drapery and shadows. The redwoods, burying their moccasined feet in the red soil, stood an Indian-file along the track, trailing an uncouth benediction from their bending boughs upon the passing bier. A hare, surprised into helpless inactivity, sat upright and pulsating in the ferns by the roadside, as the *cortége* went by. Squirrels hastened to gain a secure outlook from higher boughs; and the blue-jays, spreading their wings, fluttered before them like outriders, until the outskirts of Sandy Bar were reached, and the solitary cabin of Tennessee's Partner.

Viewed under more favorable circumstances, it would not have been a cheerful place. The unpicturesque site, the rude and unlovely outlines, the unsavory details, which distinguish the nest-building of the California miner, were all here, with the dreariness of decay superadded. A few paces from the cabin there was a rough enclosure, which, in the brief days of Tennessee's Partner's matrimonial felicity, had been used as a garden, but was now overgrown with fern. As we approached it we were surprised to find that what we had taken for a recent attempt at cultivation was the broken soil about an open grave.

The cart was halted before the enclosure; and rejecting the offers of assistance with the same air of simple self-reliance he had displayed throughout, Tennessee's Partner lifted the rough coffin on his back, and deposited it, unaided, within the shallow grave. He then nailed down the board which served as a lid; and mounting the little mound of earth beside it, took off his hat, and slowly mopped his face with his handkerchief. This the crowd felt was a preliminary to speech; and they disposed themselves variously on stumps and boulders, and sat expectant.

"When a man," began Tennessee's Partner, slowly, "has been running free all day, what's the natural thing for him to do? Why, to come home. And if he ain't in a condition to go home, what can his best friend do? Why, bring him home! And here's Tennessee has been running free, and we brings him home from his wandering." He paused, and picked up a fragment of quartz, rubbed it thoughtfully on his sleeve, and went on: "It ain't the first time that I've packed him on my back, as you see'd me now. It ain't the first time that I brought him to this yer cabin when he couldn't help himself; it ain't the first time that I and 'Jinny' have waited for him on yon hill, and picked him up and so fetched him home, when he couldn't speak, and didn't know me. And now that it's the last time, why—" he paused, and rubbed the quartz gently on his sleeve—"you see it's sort of rough on his pardner. And now, gentlemen," he added, abruptly, picking up his long-handled shovel, "the fun'l's over; and my thanks, and Tennessee's thanks, to you for your trouble."

Resisting any proffers of assistance, he began to fill in the grave, turning his back upon the crowd, that after a few moments' hesitation gradually withdrew. As they crossed the little ridge that hid Sandy Bar from view, some, looking back, thought they could see Tennessee's Partner, his work done, sitting upon the grave, his shovel between his knees, and his face buried in his red bandanna handkerchief. But it was argued by others that you couldn't tell his face from his handkerchief at that distance; and this point remained undecided.

In the reaction that followed the feverish excitement of that day, Tennessee's Partner was not forgotten. A secret investigation had cleared him of any complicity in Tennessee's guilt, and left only a suspicion of his general sanity. Sandy Bar made a point of calling on him, and proffering various uncouth, but well-meant kindnesses. But from that day his rude health and great strength seemed visibly to decline; and when the rainy season fairly set in, and the tiny grass-blades were beginning to peep from the rocky mound above Tennessee's grave, he took to his bed.

One night, when the pines beside the cabin were swaying in the storm, and trailing their slender fingers over the roof, and the roar and rush of the swollen river were heard below, Tennessee's Partner lifted his head from the pillow, saying, "It is time to go for Tennessee; I must put 'Jinny' in the cart"; and would have risen from his bed but for the restraint of his attendant. Struggling, he still pursued his singular fancy: "There, now, steady, 'Jinny,' —steady, old girl. How dark it is! Look out for the ruts,—and look out for him, too, old gal. Sometimes, you know, when he's blind drunk, he drops down right in the trail. Keep on straight up to the pine on the top of the hill. Thar—I told you so!—thar he is,—coming this way, too,—all by himself, sober, and his face a-shining. Tennessee! Pardner!"

And so they met.

HENRY ADAMS

(1838–1918)

Henry Adams brought a new kind of distinction to a most distinguished family. He was descended from the early presidents through his father, Charles Francis Adams, and was born in Boston in 1838. In his well known account he tells how little he learned during four years at Harvard and how through a long life he went on seeking an education which at the end was still incomplete. As he inherited an independent mind and could spend what he liked on his tuition, the education was of course unusual. The two books which seem to assure him a place in literature deal, the first with a particular phase, the second with the whole course, of this life-long pursuit. They are *Mont Saint Michel and Chartres* and *The Education of Henry Adams.* They were written near the end of his life in his greatest maturity, and were at first privately printed, but were later published—the second only after his death, which occurred in 1918.

To the amazement of critics the second of these books became a "best seller," and both have been widely read. Probably very few of their many readers have comprehended their full purpose, which appears only when they are read attentively in the light of the author's historical studies and a wide knowledge of the thought of his time. Even casual readers, however, could find in *Mont Saint Michel* a wonderfully vivid reconstruction of the life and spirit of the Middle Ages, and in *The Education,* regarded merely as autobiography, an absorbing account of a life of unusual opportunity and richness. And further they could find in both books a style of rare quality and distinction. The education of Henry Adams, which he thought of as ending in futility, after all bore rich fruit.

THE EDUCATION OF HENRY ADAMS [1]

CHAPTER V

BERLIN (1858–1859)

A FOURTH child has the strength of his weakness. Being of no great value, he may throw himself away if he likes, and never be missed. Charles Francis Adams, the father, felt no love for Europe, which, as he and all the world agreed, unfitted Americans for America. A captious critic might have replied that all the success he or his father or his grandfather achieved was chiefly due to the field that Europe gave them, and it was more than likely that without the help of Europe they would have all remained local politicians or lawyers, like their neighbors, to the end. Strictly followed, the rule would have obliged them never to quit Quincy; and, in fact, so much more

---

[1] The chapter from *The Education of Henry Adams* is used by permission of, and by arrangement with, Houghton Mifflin Company, the authorized publishers.

timid are parents for their children than for themselves, that Mr. and Mrs. Adams would have been content to see their children remain forever in Mount Vernon Street, unexposed to the temptations of Europe, could they have relied on the moral influences of Boston itself. Although the parents little knew what took place under their eyes, even the mothers saw enough to make them uneasy. Perhaps their dread of vice, haunting past and present, worried them less than their dread of daughters-in-law or sons-in-law who might not fit into the somewhat narrow quarters of home. On all sides were risks. Every year some young person alarmed the parental heart even in Boston, and although the temptations of Europe were irresistible, removal from the temptations of Boston might be imperative. The boy Henry wanted to go to Eroupe; he seemed well behaved when anyone was looking at him; he observed conventions, when he could not escape them; he was never quarrelsome, toward a superior; his morals were apparently good, and his moral principles, if he had any, were not known to be bad. Above all, he was timid and showed a certain sense of self-respect, when in public view. What he was at heart, no one could say; least of all himself; but he was probably human, and no worse than some others. Therefore, when he presented to an exceedingly indulgent father and mother his request to begin at a German university the study of the Civil Law—although neither he nor they knew what the Civil Law was, or any reason for his studying it—the parents dutifully consented, and walked with him down to the railway-station at Quincy to bid him good-bye, with a smile which he almost thought a tear.

Whether the boy deserved such indulgence, or was worth it, he knew no more than they, or than a professor at Harvard College; but whether worthy or not, he began his third or fourth attempt at education in November, 1858, by sailing on the steamer Persia, the pride of Captain Judkins and the Cunard Line; the newest, largest, and fastest steamship afloat. He was not alone. Several of his college companions sailed with him, and the world looked cheerful enough until, on the third day, the world—as far as concerned the young man—ran into a heavy storm. He learned then a lesson that stood by him better than any university teaching ever did—the meaning of a November gale on the mid-Atlantic—which, for mere physical misery, passed endurance. The subject offered him material for none but serious treatment; he could never see the humor of seasickness; but it united itself with a great variety of other impressions which made the first month of travel altogether the rapidest school of education he had yet found. The stride in knowledge seemed gigantic. One began at last to see that a great many impressions were needed to make a very little education, but how many could be crowded into one day without making any education at all, became the *pons asinorum* of tourist mathematics. How many would turn out to be wrong, and whether any could turn out right, was ultimate wisdom.

The ocean, the Persia, Captain Judkins, and Mr. G. P. R. James, the most distinguished passenger, vanished one Sunday morning in a furious gale in the Mersey, to make place for the drearier picture of a Liverpool street as seen from the Adelphi coffee-room in November murk, followed instantly by the passionate delights of Chester and the romance of red-sandstone architecture. Millions of Americans have felt this succession of emotions. Possibly very young and ingenuous tourists feel them still, but in days before tourists, when the romance was a reality, not a picture, they were overwhelming. When the boys went out to Eaton Hall, they were awed, as Thackeray or Dickens would have felt in the presence of a Duke. The very name of Grosvenor struck a note of grandeur. The long suite of lofty, gilded rooms with their gilded furniture; the portraits; the terraces; the gardens, the landscape; the sense of superiority in the England of the fifties, actually set the rich nobleman apart, above Americans and shopkeepers. Aristocracy was real. So was the England of Dickens. Oliver Twist and Little Nell lurked in every churchyard shadow, not as shadow but alive. Even Charles the First was not very shadowy, standing on the tower to see his army defeated. Nothing thereabouts had very much changed since he lost his battle and his head. An eighteenth-century American boy fresh from Boston naturally took it all for education, and was amused at this sort of lesson. At least he thought he felt it.

Then came the journey up to London through Birmingham and the Black District, another lesson, which needed much more to be rightly felt. The plunge into darkness lurid with flames; the sense of unknown horror in this weird gloom which then existed nowhere else, and never had existed before, except in volcanic craters; the violent contrast between this dense, smoky, impenetrable darkness, and the soft green charm that one glided into, as one emerged—the revelation of an unknown society of the pit—made a boy uncomfortable, though he had no idea that Karl Marx was standing there waiting for him, and that sooner or later the process of education would have to deal with Karl Marx much more than with Professor Bowen of Harvard College or his Satanic free-trade majesty John Stuart Mill. The Black District was a practical education, but it was infinitely far in the distance. The boy ran away from it, as he ran away from everything he disliked.

Had he known enough to know where to begin he would have seen something to study, more vital than the Civil Law, in the long, muddy, dirty, sordid, gas-lit dreariness of Oxford Street as his dingy four-wheeler dragged its weary way to Charing Cross. He did notice one peculiarity about it worth remembering. London was still London. A certain style dignified its grime; heavy, clumsy, arrogant, purse-proud, but not cheap; insular but large; barely tolerant of an outside world, and absolutely self-confident. The boys in the streets made such free comments on the American clothes and figures, that the travellers hurried to put on tall hats and long overcoats to escape criticism.

No stranger had rights even in the Strand. The eighteenth century held its own. History muttered down Fleet Street, like Dr. Johnson, in Adams's ear; Vanity Fair was alive on Piccadilly in yellow chariots with coachmen in wigs, on hammer-cloths; footmen with canes, on the footboard, and a shrivelled old woman inside; half the great houses, black with London smoke, bore large funereal hatchments; every one seemed insolent, and the most insolent structures in the world were the Royal Exchange and the Bank of England. In November, 1858, London was still vast, but it was the London of the eighteenth century that an American felt and hated.

Education went backward. Adams, still a boy, could not guess how intensely intimate this London grime was to become to him as a man, but he could still less conceive himself returning to it fifty years afterwards, noting at each turn how the great city grew smaller as it doubled in size; cheaper as it quadrupled its wealth; less imperial as its empire widened; less dignified as it tried to be civil. He liked it best when he hated it. Education began at the end, or perhaps would end at the beginning. Thus far it had remained in the eighteenth century, and the next step took it back to the sixteenth. He crossed to Antwerp. As the Baron Osy steamed up the Scheldt in the morning mists, a travelling band on deck began to play, and groups of peasants, working along the fields, dropped their tools to join in dancing. Ostade and Teniers were as much alive as they ever were, and even the Duke of Alva was still at home. The thirteenth-century cathedral towered above a sixteenth-century mass of tiled roofs, ending abruptly in walls and a landscape that had not changed. The taste of the town was thick, rich, ripe, like a sweet wine; it was mediæval, so that Rubens seemed modern; it was one of the strongest and fullest flavors that ever touched the young man's palate; but he might as well have drunk out his excitement in old Malmsey, for all the education he got from it. Even in art, one can hardly begin with Antwerp Cathedral and the Descent from the Cross. He merely got drunk on his emotions, and had then to get sober as best he could. He was terribly sober when he saw Antwerp half a century afterwards. One lesson he did learn without suspecting that he must immediately lose it. He felt his middle ages and the sixteenth century alive. He was young enough, and the towns were dirty enough—unimproved, unrestored, untouristed—to retain the sense of reality. As a taste or a smell, it was education, especially because it lasted barely ten years longer; but it was education only sensual. He never dreamed of trying to educate himself to the Descent from the Cross. He was only too happy to feel himself kneeling at the foot of the Cross; he learned only to loathe the sordid necessity of getting up again, and going about his stupid business.

This was one of the foreseen dangers of Europe, but it vanished rapidly enough to reassure the most anxious of parents. Dropped into Berlin one morning without guide or direction, the young man in search of education floundered in a mere mess of misunderstandings. He could never recall what he expected to find, but whatever he expected, it had no relation with what it turned out to be. A student at twenty takes easily to anything, even to Berlin, and he would have accepted the thirteenth century pure and simple since his guides assured him that this was his right path; but a week's experience left him dazed and dull. Faith held out, but the paths grew dim. Berlin astonished him, but he had no lack of friends to show him all the amusement it had to offer. Within a day or two he was running about with the rest to beer-cellars and music-halls and dance-rooms, smoking bad tobacco, drinking poor beer, and eating sauerkraut and sausages as though he knew no better. This was easy. One can always descend the social ladder. The trouble came when he asked for the education he was promised. His friends took him to be registered as a student of the university; they selected his professors and courses; they showed him where to buy the Institutes of Gaius and several German works on the Civil Law in numerous volumes; and they led him to his first lecture.

His first lecture was his last. The young man was not very quick, and he had almost religious respect for his guides and advisors; but he needed no more than one hour to satisfy him that he had made another failure in education, and this time a fatal one. That the language would require at least three months' hard work before he could touch the Law was an annoying discovery; but the shock that upset him was the discovery of the university itself. He had thought Harvard College a torpid school, but it was instinct with life compared with all that he could see of the University of Berlin. The German students were strange animals, but their professors were beyond pay. The mental attitude of the university was not of an American world. What sort of instruction prevailed in other branches, or in science, Adams had no occasion to ask, but in the Civil Law he found only the lecture system in its deadliest form as it flourished in the thirteenth century. The professor mumbled his comments; the students made, or seemed to make, notes; they could have learned from books or discussion in a day more than they could learn from him in a month, but they must pay his fees, follow his course, and be his scholars, if they wanted a degree. To an American the result was worthless. He could make no use of the Civil Law without some previous notion of the Common Law; but the student who knew enough of the Common Law to understand what he wanted, had only to read the Pandects or the commentators at his ease in America, and be his own professor. Neither the method nor the matter nor the manner could profit an American education.

This discovery seemed to shock none of the students. They went to the lectures, made notes, and read textbooks, but never pretended to take their professor seriously. They were much more serious in reading Heine. They knew no more than Heine what good they were getting, beyond the Berlin accent—which was bad; and the beer—which was not to compare with Munich; and the dancing—which was better at Vienna. They enjoyed the beer and music, but they refused to be responsible for the education. Anyway, as they defended themselves, they were learning the language.

So the young man fell back on the language, and being slow at languages, he found himself falling behind all his friends, which depressed his spirits, the more because the gloom of a Berlin winter and of Berlin architecture seemed to him a particular sort of gloom never attained elsewhere. One day on the Linden he caught sight of Charles Sumner in a cab, and ran after him. Sumner was then recovering from the blows of the South Carolinian cane or club, and he was pleased to find a young worshipper in the remote Prussian wilderness. They dined together and went to hear "William Tell" at the Opera. Sumner tried to encourage his friend about his difficulties of language: "I came to Berlin," or Rome, or whatever place it was, as he said with his grand air of mastery, "I came to Berlin, unable to say a word in the language; and three months later when I went away, I talked it to my cabman." Adams felt himself quite unable to attain in so short a time such social advantages, and one day complained of his trials to Mr. Robert Apthorp, of Boston, who was passing the winter in Berlin for the sake of its music. Mr. Apthorp told of his own similar struggle, and how he had entered a public school and sat for months with ten-year-old boys, reciting their lessons and catching their phrases. The idea suited Adams's desperate frame of mind. At least it ridded him of the university and the Civil Law and American associations in beer-cellars. Mr. Apthorp took the trouble to negotiate with the headmaster of the Friedrichs-Wilhelm-Werdersches Gymnasium for permission to Henry Adams to attend the school as a member of the Ober-tertia, a class of boys twelve or thirteen years old, and there Adams went for three months as though he had not always avoided high schools with singular antipathy. He never did anything else so foolish, but he was given a bit of education which served him some purpose in life.

It was not merely the language, though three months passed in such fashion would teach a poodle enough to talk with a cabman, and this was all that foreign students could expect to do, for they never by any chance would come in contact with German society, if German society existed, about which they knew nothing. Adams never learned to talk German well, but the same might be said of his English, if he could believe Englishmen. He learned not to annoy himself on this account. His difficulties with the language gradually ceased. He thought himself quite Germanized in 1859. He even deluded himself with the idea that he read it as though it were English, which proved that he knew little about it; but whatever success he had in his own experiment interested him less than his contact with German education.

He had revolted at the American school and university; he had instantly rejected the German university; and as his last experience of education he tried the German high school. The experiment was hazardous. In 1858 Berlin was a poor, keen-witted, provincial town, simple, dirty, uncivilized, and in most respects disgusting. Life was primitive beyond what an American boy could have imagined. Overridden by military methods and bureaucratic pettiness, Prussia was only beginning to free her hands from internal bonds. Apart from discipline, activity scarcely existed. The future Kaiser Wilhelm I, regent for his insane brother King Friedrich Wilhelm IV, seemed to pass his time looking at the passers-by from the window of his modest palace on the Linden. German manners, even at Court, were sometimes brutal, and German thoroughness at school was apt to be routine. Bismarck himself was then struggling to begin a career against the inertia of the German system. The condition of Germany was a scandal and nuisance to every earnest German, all whose energies were turned to reforming it from top to bottom; and Adams walked into a great public school to get educated, at precisely the time when the Germans wanted most to get rid of the education they were forced to follow. As an episode in the search for education, this adventure smacked of Heine.

The school system has doubtless changed, and at all events the school-masters are probably long ago dead; the story has no longer a practical value, and had very little even at the time; one could at least say in defence of the German school that it was neither very brutal nor very immoral. The head-master was excellent in his Prussian way, and the other instructors were not worse than in other schools; it was their system that struck the systemless American with horror. The arbitrary training given to the memory was stupefying; the strain that the memory endured was a form of torture; and the feats that the boys performed, without complaint, were pitiable. No other faculty than the memory seemed to be recognized. Least of all was any use made of reason, either analytic, synthetic, or dogmatic. The German government did not encourage reasoning.

All State education is a sort of dynamo machine for polarizing the popular mind; for turning and holding its lines of force in the direction supposed to be most effective for State purposes. The German machine was terribly efficient. Its effect on the children was pathetic. The Friedrichs-Wilhelm-Werdersches Gymnasium was an old building in the heart of Berlin which served the educational needs of the small tradesman or *bourgeoisie* of the neighborhood; the children were Berliner-kinder if ever there were such, and of a class suspected of sympathy and concern in the troubles of 1848. None was noble or connected with good society. Personally they were rather sympathetic than not, but as the objects of education they were proofs of nearly all the evils that a bad system could give. Apparently Adams, in his rigidly illogical pursuit, had at last reached his ideal of a viciously logical education. The boys' physique showed it first, but their physique could not be wholly charged to the school. German food was bad at best, and a diet of sauerkraut, sausage, and beer could never be good; but it was not the food alone that made their faces white and their flesh flabby. They never breathed fresh air; they had never heard of a playground; in all Berlin not a cubic inch of oxygen was admitted in winter into an inhabited building; in the school every room was tightly closed and had no ventilation; the air was foul beyond all decency; but when the American opened a window in the five minutes between hours, he violated the rules and was invariably rebuked. As long as cold weather lasted, the windows were shut. If the boys had a holiday, they were apt to be taken on long tramps in the Thiergarten or elsewhere, always ending in over-fatigue, tobacco-smoke, sausages, and beer. With this, they were required to prepare daily lessons that would have quickly broken down strong men of a healthy habit, and which they could learn only because their minds were morbid. The German university had seemed a failure, but the German high school was something very near an indictable nuisance.

Before the month of April arrived, the experiment of German education had reached this point. Nothing was left of it except the ghost of the Civil Law shut up in the darkest of closets, never to gibber again before anyone who could repeat the story. The derisive Jew laughter of Heine ran through the university and everything else in Berlin. Of course, when one is twenty years old, life is bound to be full, if only of Berlin beer, although German student life was on the whole the thinnest of beer, as an American looked on it, but though nothing except small fragments remained of the education that had been so promising—or promised—this is only what most often happens in life, when by-products turn out to be more valuable than staples. The German university and German law were failures; German society, in an American sense, did not exist, or if it existed, never showed itself to an American; the German theatre, on the other hand, was excellent, and German opera, with the ballet, was almost worth a journey to Berlin; but the curious and perplexing result of the total failure of German education was that the student's only clear gain—his single step to a higher life—came from time wasted; studies neglected; vices indulged; education reversed;—it came from the despised beer-garden and music-hall; and it was accidental, unintended, unforeseen.

When his companions insisted on passing two or three afternoons in the week at music-halls, drinking beer, smoking German tobacco, and looking at fat German women knitting, while an orchestra played dull music, Adams went with them for the sake of the company, but with no pretence of enjoyment; and when Mr. Apthorp gently protested that he exaggerated his indifference, for of course he enjoyed Beethoven, Adams replied simply that he loathed Beethoven; and felt a slight surprise when Mr. Apthorp and the others laughed as though they thought it humor. He saw no humor in it. He supposed that, except musicians, every one thought Beethoven a bore, as every one except mathematicians thought mathematics a bore. Sitting thus at his beer-table, mentally impassive, he was one day surprised to notice that his mind followed the movement of a Sinfonie. He could not have been more astonished had he suddenly read a new language. Among the marvels of education, this was the most marvellous. A prison-wall that barred his senses on one great side of life, suddenly fell, of its own accord, without so much as his knowing when it happened. Amid the fumes of coarse tobacco and poor beer, surrounded by the commonest of German Haus-frauen, a new sense burst out like a flower in his life, so superior to the old senses, so bewildering, so astonished at its own existence, that he could not credit it, and watched it as something apart, accidental, and not to be trusted. He slowly came to admit that Beethoven had partly become intelligible to him, but he was the more inclined to think that Beethoven must be much overrated as a musician, to be so easily followed. This could not be called education, for he had never so much as listened to the music. He had been thinking of other things. Mere mechanical repetition of certain sounds had stuck to his unconscious mind. Beethoven might have this power, but not Wagner, or at all events not the Wagner later than "Tannhäuser." Near forty years passed before he reached the "Gotterdämmerung."

One might talk of a revival of atrophied sense—the mechanical reaction of a sleeping consciousness—but no other sense awoke. His sense of line and color remained as dull as ever, and as far as ever below the level of an artist. His metaphysical sense did not spring into life, so that his mind could leap the bars of German expression into sympathy with the idealities of Kant and Hegel. Although he insisted that his faith in German thought and literature was exalted, he failed to approach German thought, and he shed never a tear of emotion over the pages of Goethe and Schiller. When his father rashly ventured from time to time to write him a word of common sense, the young man would listen to no sense at all, but insisted that Berlin was the best of educations in the best of Germanies; yet, when, at last, April came, and some genius suggested a tramp in Thüringen, his heart sang like a bird; he realized what a nightmare he had suffered, and he made up his mind that, wherever else he might, in the infinities of space and time, seek for education, it should not be again in Berlin.

HENRY JAMES

(1843-1916)

Henry James was born in New York in 1843 from a family of high intelligence and refinement. His father, a philosopher of independent views, had ample means to give his sons, William, later the famous psychologist, and Henry, an unusual education. They had private tutors, they read foreign books, and they were not allowed to "import shocking bad manners from the street." They were much abroad and were soon "Europeanized." From childhood Henry James was less familiar with the "American scene" than with the refinements of the leisured cosmopolitan society in which his characters move. He read law without intending to become a lawyer, and was clearly destined to become a literary artist. He began contributing stories to the *Atlantic,* in which appeared also his first full-length novel, *Roderick Hudson* (1875). Interested above all in social life, finding that of America thin, and going instinctively where it was richest, he—doubtless wisely—settled permanently in England in 1876. Though he occasionally visited America, his remaining career was substantially that of a conscientious and prolific English author. Loyalty to England during the War led him in 1915 to become an English subject. He died at his English home at Rye in 1916.

James's many novels and short stories are ordinarily divided into two groups. In the earlier—of which *The Portrait of a Lady* is probably the best—he has more movement and incident than in the later, and writes in a more normal style. In these he was moderately popular, *Daisy Miller* (1879), making "a quite extraordinary hit." Those in a second group, in his so-called "later manner"—of which *The Ambassadors* (1903) was considered by him his best—are too subtle in analysis and involved in style to go much beyond confirmed worshippers. Throughout he often, but not always, deals with Americans sojourning in Europe and exhibiting their newness against a background of old-world culture, and is accordingly given credit for creating the "international novel." He is said, with some truth, to be narrow in range and interest. He does not indeed deal with life broadly. He is a confirmed realist, he is a very conscious and intellectual artist, and there are heights and depths in the human soul he does not reach. He lacks warmth, movement, and perhaps vitality. But his true field—the thoughts, motives, feelings, of characters living a life of quick intelligence and high refinement and brought into relations of poignant interest—is after all broad enough, and this field he cultivates with unequalled insight, subtlety, and expressiveness. Few writers, at least in English, could have caught so perfectly the shadings in the characters portrayed in the sketch that follows; and this is one of the simplest in his long gallery of portraits.

THE TWO FACES [1]

I

THE servant, who, in spite of his sealed, stamped look, appeared to have his reasons, stood there for instruction, in a manner not quite usual, after announcing the name. Mrs. Grantham, however, took it up—"Lord Gwyther?"—with a quick surprise that for an instant justified him even to the small scintilla in the glance she gave her companion, which might have had exactly the sense of the butler's hesitation. This companion, a shortish, fairish, youngish man, clean-shaven and keen-eyed, had, with a promptitude that would have struck an observer—which the butler indeed was—sprang to his feet and moved to the chimney-piece, though his hostess herself, meanwhile, managed not otherwise to stir. "Well?" she said, as for the visitor to advance; while she immediately followed with a sharper "He's not there?"

"Shall I show him up, ma'am?"

"But of course!" The point of his doubt made her at last rise for impatience, and Bates, before leaving the room, might still have caught the achieved irony of her appeal to the gentleman into whose communion with her he had broken. "Why in the world not—? What a way—!" she exclaimed, as Sutton felt beside his cheek the passage of her eyes to the glass behind him.

"He wasn't sure you'd see anyone."

"I don't see 'anyone,' but I see individuals."

"That's just it; and sometimes you don't see them."

"Do you mean ever because of *you*?" she asked as she touched into place a tendril of hair. "That's just his impertinence, as to which I shall speak to him."

"Don't," said Shirley Sutton. "Never notice anything."

"That's nice advice from you," she laughed, "who notice everything!"

"Ah, but I speak of nothing."

She looked at him a moment. "You're still more impertinent than Bates. You'll please not budge," she went on.

"Really? I must sit him out?" he continued as, after a minute, she had not again spoken—only glancing about, while she changed her place, partly for another look at the glass and partly to see if she could improve her seat. What she felt was rather more than, clever and charming though she was, she could hide. "If you're wondering how you seem, I can tell you. Awfully cool and easy."

She gave him another stare. She was beautiful and conscious. "And if you're wondering how *you* seem—"

[1] From *The Better Sort* (1903). Copyright, 1903, by Charles Scribner's Sons.

"Oh, I'm not!" he laughed from before the fire; "I always perfectly know."

"How you seem," she retorted, "is as if you didn't!"

Once more for a little he watched her. "You're looking lovely for him —extraordinarily lovely, within the marked limits of your range. But that's enough. Don't be clever."

"Then who *will* be?"

"There you are!" he sighed with amusement.

"Do you know him?" she asked as, through the door left open by Bates, they heard steps on the landing.

Sutton had to think an instant, and produced a "No" just as Lord Gwyther was again announced, which gave an unexpectedness to the greeting offered him a moment later by this personage—a young man, stout and smooth and fresh, but not at all shy, who, after the happiest rapid passage with Mrs. Grantham, put out a hand with a frank, pleasant "How d'ye do?"

"Mr. Shirley Sutton," Mrs. Grantham explained.

"Oh, yes," said her second visitor, quite as if he knew; which, as he couldn't have known, had for her first the interest of confirming a perception that his lordship would be—no, not at all, in general, embarrassed, only was now exceptionally and especially agitated. As it is, for that matter, with Sutton's total impression that we are particularly and almost exclusively concerned, it may be further mentioned that he was not less clear as to the really handsome way in which the young man kept himself together and little by little —though with all proper aid indeed—finally found his feet. All sorts of things, for the twenty minutes, occurred to Sutton, though one of them was certainly not that it would, after all, be better he should go. One of them was that their hostess was doing it in perfection—simply, easily, kindly, yet with something the least bit queer in her wonderful eyes; another was that if he had been recognized without the least ground it was through a tension of nerves on the part of his fellow-guest that produced inconsequent motions; still another was that, even had departure been indicated, he would positively have felt dissuasion in the rare promise of the scene. This was in especial after Lord Gwyther not only had announced that he was now married, but had mentioned that he wished to bring his wife to Mrs. Grantham for the benefit so certain to be derived. It was the passage immediately produced by that speech that provoked in Sutton the intensity, as it were, of his arrest. He already knew of the marriage as well as Mrs. Grantham herself, and as well also as he knew of some other things; and this gave him, doubtless, the better measure of what took place before him and the keener consciousness of the quick look that, at a marked moment—though it was not absolutely meant for him any more than for his companion—Mrs. Grantham let him catch.

She smiled, but it had a gravity. "I think, you know, you ought to have told me before."

"Do you mean when I first got engaged? Well, it all took place so far away, and we really told, at home, so few people."

Oh, there might have been reasons; but it had not been quite right. "You were married at Stuttgart? That wasn't too far for *my* interest, at least, to reach."

"Awfully kind of you—and of course one knew you *would* be kind. But it wasn't at Stuttgart; it was over there but quite in the country. We should have managed it in England but that her mother naturally wished to be present, yet was not in health to come. So it was really, you see, a sort of little hole-and-corner German affair."

This didn't in the least check Mrs. Grantham's claim, but it started a slight anxiety. "Will she be—a, then, German?"

Sutton knew her to know perfectly what Lady Gwyther would "be," but he had by this time, while their friend explained, his independent interest. "Oh dear, no! My father-in-law has never parted with the proud birthright of a Briton. But his wife, you see, holds an estate in Württemberg from *her* mother, Countess Kremnitz, on which, with the awful condition of his English property, you know, they've found it for years a tremendous saving to live. So that though Valda was luckily born at home she has practically spent her life over there."

"Oh, I see." Then, after a slight pause, "Is Valda her pretty name?" Mrs. Grantham asked.

"Well," said the young man, only wishing, in his candor, it was clear, to be drawn out—"well, she has, in the manner of her mother's people, about thirteen; but that's the one we generally use."

Mrs. Grantham hesitated but an instant. "Then may *I* generally use it?"

"It would be too charming of you; and nothing would give her—as, I assure you, nothing would give *me,* greater pleasure." Lord Gwyther quite glowed with the thought.

"Then I think that instead of coming alone you might have brought her to see me."

"It's exactly what," he instantly replied, "I came to ask your leave to do." He explained that for the moment Lady Gwyther was not in town, having as soon as she arrived gone down to Torquay to put in a few days with one of her aunts, also her godmother, to whom she was an object of great interest. She had seen no one yet, and no one—not that *that* mattered—had seen her; she knew nothing whatever of London and was awfully frightened at facing it and at what—however little—might be expected of her. "She wants some one," he said, "some one who knows the whole thing, don't you see? and who's thoroughly kind and clever, as you would be, if I may say so, to take her by the hand." It was at this point and on these words that the eyes of Lord Gwyther's two auditors inevitably and wonderfully met. But there was nothing in the way he kept it up to show that he caught the encounter. "She wants, if I may tell you so, for the great labyrinth, a real friend; and asking myself what I could do to make things ready for her, and who would be absolutely the best woman in London—"

"You thought, naturally, of *me?*" Mrs. Grantham had listened with no sign but the faint flash just noted; now, however, she gave him the full light of her expressive face—which immediately brought Shirley Sutton, looking at his watch, once more to his feet.

"She *is* the best woman in London!" He addressed himself with a laugh to the other visitor, but offered his hand in farewell to their hostess.

"You're going?"

"I must," he said, without scruple.

"Then we do meet at dinner?"

"I hope so." On which, to take leave, he returned with interest to Lord Gwyther the friendly clutch he had a short time before received.

II

They did meet at dinner, and if they were not, as it happened, side by side, they made up afterwards in the happiest angle of a drawing-room that offered both shine and shadow and that was positively much appreciated, in the circle in which they moved, for the favorable "corners" created by its shrewd mistress. Her face, charged with something produced in it by Lord Gwyther's visit, had been with him so constantly for the previous hours that, when she instantly challenged him on his "treatment" of her in the afternoon, he was on the point of naming it as his reason for not having remained with her. Something new had quickly come into her beauty; he couldn't as yet have said what, nor whether on the whole to its advantage or its loss. Till he could make up his mind about that, at any rate, he would say nothing; so that, with sufficient presence of mind, he found a better excuse. If in short he had in defiance of her particular request left her alone with Lord Gwyther, it was simply because the situation had suddenly turned so exciting that he had fairly feared the contagion of it—the temptation of its making him, most improperly, put in his word.

They could now talk of these things at their ease. Other couples, ensconced and scattered, enjoyed the same privilege, and Sutton had more and more the profit, such as it was, of feeling that his interest in Mrs. Grantham had become—what was the luxury of so high a social code—an acknowledged and protected relation. He knew his London well enough to know that he was on the way to be regarded as her main source of consolation for the trick that, several months before, Lord Gwyther had publicly played her. Many persons had not held that, by the high social code in question, his lordship could have "reserved the right" to turn up in that way, from one day to another, engaged. For himself London took, with its short cuts and its cheap psychology, an immense deal for granted. To his own sense he was never—could in the nature of things never be—any man's "successor." Just what had constituted the predecessorship of other men was apparently that they had been able to make up their mind. He, worse luck, was at the mercy of her face, and more than ever at the mercy of it now, which meant, moreover, not that it made a slave of him, but that it made, disconcertingly, a sceptic. It was the absolute perfection of the handsome; but things had a way of coming into it. "I felt," he said, "that you were there together at a point at which you had a right to the ease that the absence of a listener would give. I reflected that when you made me promise to stay you hadn't guessed—"

"That he could possibly have come to me on such an extraordinary errand? No, of course, I hadn't guessed. Who *would*? But didn't you see how little I was upset by it?"

Sutton demurred. Then with a smile, "I think *he* saw how little."

"You yourself didn't, then?"

He again held back, but not, after all, to answer. "He was wonderful, wasn't he?"

"I think he was," she replied after a moment. To which she added: "Why did he pretend that way he knew you?"

"He didn't pretend. He felt on the spot as if we were friends." Sutton had found this afterwards, and found truth in it. "It was an effusion of cheer and hope. He was so glad to see me there, and to find you happy."

"Happy?"

"Happy. Aren't you?"

"Because of *you*?"

"Well—according to the impression he received as he came in."

"That was sudden then," she asked, "and unexpected?"

Her companion thought. "Prepared in some degree, but confirmed by the sight of us, there together, so awfully jolly and sociable over your fire."

Mrs. Grantham turned this round. "If he knew I was 'happy' then—which, by the way, is none of his business, nor of yours either—why in the world did he come?"

"Well, for good manners, and for his idea," said Sutton.

She took it in, appearing to have no hardness of rancor that could bar discussion. "Do you mean by his idea his proposal that I should grandmother his wife? And, if you do, is the proposal your reason for calling him wonderful?"

Sutton laughed. "Pray, what's yours?" As this was a question, however, that she took her time to answer or not to answer—only appearing interested for a moment in a combination that had formed itself on the other side of the room—he presently went on. "What's *his*?—that would seem to be the point. His, I mean, for having decided on the extraordinary step of throwing his little wife, bound hands and feet, into your arms. Intelligent as you are, and with these three or four hours to have thought it over, I yet don't see how that can fail still to mystify you."

She continued to watch their opposite neighbors. "'Little,' you call her. Is she so very small?"

"Tiny, tiny—she *must* be; as different as possible in every way—of necessity —from you. They always *are* the opposite pole, you know," said Shirley Sutton.

She glanced at him now. "You strike me as of an impudence—!"

"No, no. I only like to make it out with you."

She looked away again and, after a little, went on. "I'm sure she's charming, and only hope one isn't to gather that he's already tired of her."

"Not a bit! He's tremendously in love, and he'll remain so."

"So much the better. And if it's a question," said Mrs. Grantham, "of one's doing what one can for her, he has only, as I told him when you had gone, to give me the chance."

"Good! So he *is* to commit her to you?"

"You use extraordinary expressions, but it's settled that he brings her."

"And you'll really and truly help her?"

"Really and truly?" said Mrs. Grantham, with her eyes again upon him. "Why not? For what do you take me?"

"Ah, isn't that just what I still have the discomfort, every day I live, of asking myself?"

She had made, as she spoke, a movement to rise, which, as if she was tired of his tone, his last words seemed to determine. But, also getting up, he held her, when they were on their feet, long enough to hear the rest of what he had to say. "If you do help her, you know, you'll show that you've understood."

"Understood what?"

"Why, his idea—the deep, acute train of reasoning that has led him to take, as one may say, the bull by the horns; to reflect that as you might, as you probably *would,* in any case, get at her, he plays the wise game, as well as the bold one, by assuming your generosity and placing himself publicly under an obligation to you."

Mrs. Grantham showed not only that she had listened, but that she had for an instant considered. "What is it you elegantly describe as my getting 'at' her?"

"He takes his risk, but puts you, you see, on your honor."

She thought a moment more. "What profundities indeed then over the simplest of matters! And if your idea is," she went on, "that if I do help her I shall show him I've understood them, so it will be that if I don't—"

"You'll show him"—Sutton took her up—"that you haven't? Precisely. But in spite of not wanting to appear to have understood *too* much—"

"I may still be depended on to do what I can? Quite certainly. You'll see what I may still be depended on to do." And she moved away.

III

It was not, doubtless, that there had been anything in their rather sharp separation at that moment to sustain or prolong the interruption; yet it definitely befell that, circumstances aiding, they practically failed to meet again before the great party at Burbeck. This occasion was to gather in some thirty persons from a certain Friday to the following Monday, and it was on the Friday that Sutton went down. He had known in advance that Mrs. Grantham was to be there, and this perhaps, during the interval of hindrance, had helped him to be a little patient. He had before him the certitude of a real full cup—two days brimming over with the sight of her. He found, however, on his arrival that she was not yet in the field, and presently learned that her place would be in a small contingent that was to join the party on the morrow. This knowledge he extracted from Miss Banker, who was always the first to present herself at any gathering that was to enjoy her, and whom, moreover—partly on that very account—the wary not less than the speculative were apt to hold themselves well-advised to engage with at as early as possible a stage of the business. She was stout, red, rich, mature, universal—a massive, much-fingered volume, alphabetical, wonderful, indexed, that opened of itself at the right place. She opened for Sutton instinctively at G—, which happened to be remarkably convenient. "What she's really waiting over for is to bring down Lady Gwyther."

"Ah, the Gwythers are coming?"

"Yes; caught, through Mrs. Grantham, just in time. *She'll* be the feature—everyone wants to see her."

Speculation and wariness met and combined at this moment in Shirley Sutton. "Do you mean—a—Mrs. Grantham?"

"Dear no! Poor little Lady Gwyther, who, but just arrived in England, appears now literally for the first time in her life in any society whatever, and whom (don't you know the extraordinary story? you ought to—*you!*) she, of all people, has so wonderfully taken up. It will be quite—here—as if she were 'presenting' her."

Sutton, of course, took in more things than even appeared. "I never know what I ought to know; I only know, inveterately, what I oughtn't. So what *is* the extraordinary story?"

"You really haven't heard—?"

"Really," he replied without winking.

"It happened, indeed, but the other day," said Miss Banker, "yet everyone is already wondering. Gwyther has thrown his wife on her mercy—but I won't believe you if you pretend to me you don't know why he shouldn't."

Sutton asked himself what he *could* pretend. "Do you mean because she's merciless?"

She hesitated. "If you don't know, perhaps I oughtn't to tell you."

He liked Miss Banker, and found just the right tone to plead. *"Do* tell me."

"Well," she sighed, "it will be your own fault—! They had been such friends that there could have been but one name for the crudity of his original *procédé*. When I was a girl we used to call it throwing over. They call it in French to *lâcher*. But I refer not so much to the act itself as to the manner of it, though you may say indeed, of course, that there is in such cases, only one manner. Least said, soonest mended."

Sutton seemed to wonder. "Oh, he said too much?"

"He said nothing. That was it."

Sutton kept it up. "But was *what?*"

"Why, what she must, like any woman in her shoes, have felt to be his perfidy. He simply went and *did* it—took to himself this child, that is, without the preliminary of a scandal or a rupture—before she could turn round."

"I follow you. But it would appear from what you say that she *has* turned round now."

"Well," Miss Banker laughed, "we shall see for ourselves how far. It will be what everyone will try to see."

"Oh, then we've work cut out!" And Sutton certainly felt that he himself had—an impression that lost nothing from a further talk with Miss Banker in the course of a short stroll in the grounds with her the next day. He spoke as one who had now considered many things.

"Did I understand from you yesterday that Lady Gwyther's a 'child'?"

"Nobody knows. It's prodigious the way she has managed."

"The way Lady Gwyther has—?"

"No; the way May Grantham has kept her till this hour in her pocket."

He was quick at his watch. "Do you mean by 'this hour' that they're due now?"

"Not till tea. All the others arrive together in time for that." Miss Banker had clearly, since the previous day, filled in gaps and become, as it were, revised and enlarged. "She'll have kept a cat from seeing her, so as to produce her entirely herself."

"Well," Sutton mused, "that will have been a very noble sort of return—"

"For Gwyther's behavior? Very. Yet I feel creepy."

"Creepy?"

"Because so much depends for the girl—in the way of the right start or the wrong start—on the signs and omens of this first appearance. It's a great house and a great occasion, and we're assembled here, it strikes me, very much as the Roman mob at the circus used to be to see the next Christian maiden brought out to the tigers."

"Oh, if she *is* a Christian maiden—!" Sutton murmured. But he stopped at what his imagination called up.

It perhaps fed that faculty a little that Miss Banker had the effect of making out that Mrs. Grantham might individually be, in any case, something of a Roman matron. "She has kept her in the dark so that we may only take her from her hand. She will have formed her for us."

"In so few days?"

"Well, she will have prepared her—decked her for the sacrifice with ribbons and flowers."

"Ah, if you only mean that she will have taken her to the dressmaker—!" And it came to Sutton, at once as a new light and as a check, almost, to anxiety, that this was all poor Gwyther, mistrustful probably of a taste formed by Stuttgart, might have desired of their friend.

There were usually at Burbeck many things taking place at once; so that wherever else, on such occasions, tea might be served, it went forward with matchless pomp, weather permitting, on a shaded stretch of one of the terraces and in presence of one of the prospects. Shirley Sutton, moving, as the afternoon waned, more restlessly about and mingling in dispersed groups only to find they had nothing to keep him quiet, came upon it as he turned a corner of the house—saw it seated there in all its state. It might be said that at Burbeck it was, like everything else, made the most of. It constituted immediately, with multiplied tables and glittering plate, with rugs and cushions and ices and fruit and wonderful porcelain and beautiful women, a scene of splendor, almost an incident of grand opera. One of the beautiful women might quite have been expected to rise with a gold cup and a celebrated song.

One of them did rise, as it happened, while Sutton drew near, and he found himself a moment later seeing nothing and nobody but Mrs. Grantham. They met on the terrace, just away from the others, and the movement in which he had the effect of arresting her might have been that of withdrawal. He quickly saw, however, that if she had been about to pass into the house it was only on some errand—to get something or to call someone—that would have immediately restored her to the public. It somehow struck him on the spot—and more than ever yet, though the impression was not wholly new to him—that she felt herself a figure for the forefront of the stage and indeed would have been recognized by anyone at a glance as the *prima donna assoluta*. She caused, in fact, during the few minutes he stood talking to her, an extraordinary series of waves to roll extraordinarily fast over his sense, not the least mark of the matter being that the appearance with which it ended was again the one with which it had begun. "The face

—the face," as he kept dumbly repeating; that was at last, as at first, all he could clearly see. She had a perfection resplendent, but what in the world had it done, this perfection, to her beauty? It was her beauty, doubtless, that looked out at him, but it was into something else that, as their eyes met, he strangely found himself looking.

It was as if something had happened in consequence of which she had changed, and there was that in this swift perception that made him glance eagerly about for Lady Gwyther. But as he took in the recruited group— identities of the hour added to those of the previous twenty-four—he saw, among his recognitions, one of which was the husband of the person missing, that Lady Gwyther was not there. Nothing in the whole business was more singular than his consciousness that, as he came back to his interlocutress after the nods and smiles and handwaves he had launched, she knew what had been his thought. She knew for whom he had looked without success; but why should this knowledge visibly have hardened and sharpened her, and precisely at a moment when she was unprecedentedly magnificent? The indefinable apprehension that had somewhat sunk after his second talk with Miss Banker and then had perversely risen again—this nameless anxiety now produced on him, with the sudden sharper pinch, the effect of a great suspense. The action of that, in turn, was to show him that he had not yet fully known how much he had at stake on a final view. It was revealed to him for the first time that he "really cared" whether Mrs. Grantham were a safe nature. It was too ridiculous by what a thread it hung, but something was certainly in the air that would definitely tell him.

What was in the air descended the next moment to earth. He turned round as he caught the expression with which her eyes attached themselves to something that approached. A little person, very young and very much dressed, had come out of the house, and the expression in Mrs. Grantham's eyes was that of the artist confronted with her work and interested, even to impatience, in the judgment of others. The little person drew nearer, and though Sutton's companion, without looking at him now, gave it a name and met it, he had jumped for himself at certitude. He saw many things— too many, and they appeared to be feathers, frills, excrescences of silk and lace—massed together and conflicting, and after a moment also saw struggling out of them a small face that struck him as either scared or sick. Then, with his eyes again returning to Mrs. Grantham, he saw another.

He had no more talk with Miss Banker till late that evening—an evening during which he had felt himself too noticeably silent; but something had passed between this pair, across dinner-table and drawing-room, without speech, and when they at last found words it was in the needed ease of a quiet end of the long, lighted gallery, where she opened again at the very paragraph.

"You were right—that *was* it. She did the only thing that, at such short notice, she *could* do. She took her to her dressmaker."

Sutton, with his back to the reach of the gallery, had, as if to banish a vision, buried his eyes for a minute in his hands. "And oh, the face—the face!"

"Which?" Miss Banker asked.

"Whichever one looks at."

"But May Grantham's glorious. She has turned herself out—"

"With a splendor of taste and a sense of effect, eh? Yes." Sutton showed he saw far.

"She *has* the sense of effect. The sense of effect as exhibited in Lady Gwyther's clothes—!" was something Miss Banker failed of words to express. "Everybody's overwhelmed. Here, you know, that sort of thing's grave. The poor creature's lost."

"Lost?"

"Since on the first impression, as we said, so much depends. The first impression's made—oh, made! I defy her now ever to unmake it. Her husband, who's proud, won't like her the better for it. And I don't see," Miss Banker went on, "that her prettiness *was* enough—a mere little feverish, frightened freshness; what *did* he see in her?—to be so blasted. It has been done with an atrocity of art—"

"That supposes the dressmaker then also a devil?"

"Oh, your London women and their dressmakers!" Miss Banker laughed.

"But the face—the face!" Sutton woefully repeated.

"May's?"

"The little girl's. It's exquisite."

"Exquisite?"

"For unimaginable pathos."

"Oh!" Miss Banker dropped.

"She has at last begun to see." Sutton showed again how far *he* saw. "It glimmers upon her innocence, she makes it dimly out—what has been done with her. She's even worse this evening—the way, my eye, she looked at dinner!—than when she came. Yes"—he was confident—"it has dawned (how couldn't it, out of all of you?) and she knows."

"She ought to have known before!" Miss Banker intelligently sighed.

"No; she wouldn't in that case have been so beautiful."

"Beautiful?" cried Miss Banker; "overloaded like a monkey in a show!"

"The face, yes; which goes to the heart. It's that that makes it," said Shirley Sutton. "And it's that"—he thought it out—"that makes the other."

"I see. Conscious?"

"Horrible!"

"You take it hard," said Miss Banker.

Lord Gwyther, just before she spoke, had come in sight and now was near them. Sutton on this, appearing to wish to avoid him, reached, before answering his companion's observation, a door that opened close at hand. "So hard," he replied from that point, "that I shall be off to-morrow morning."

"And not see the rest?" she called after him.

But he had already gone, and Lord Gwyther, arriving, amiably took up her question. "The rest of what?"

Miss Banker looked him well in the eyes. "Of Mrs. Grantham's clothes."

SARAH ORNE JEWETT

(1849–1909)

Sarah Orne Jewett was born in South Berwick, Maine, in 1849. Delicate health kept her much at home, and except for irregular attendance at the Berwick Academy, her education consisted in wide reading and in observing people and places as she drove about the country with her father, a physician. The reading of Mrs. Stowe's *The Pearl of Orr's Island* opened her eyes to the possibility of writing of the life around her, and while but a girl she began to write,—verse at first, and then prose. Under an assumed name, and with only a sister in the secret, she began contributing to *The Riverside,* and her work being praised by the editor, she had courage to send a sketch to the *Atlantic Monthly.* This too was accepted, and in consequence she determined to make writing her career. From this time she wrote steadily, contributing to the best magazines and publishing volumes with fair frequency till her death in 1909. Early in life she became the intimate friend of Annie Fields, widow of the publisher, James T. Fields, and with her made several trips to Europe, where she met many well-known writers. She also usually spent the winters with Mrs. Fields in Boston, but continued to live part of each year in Berwick among the people of whom she wrote.

Miss Jewett began writing with the purpose of interpreting New England country characters to the outside world, and of preserving in chronicles their ways and speech. Her first book was a series of sketches, *Deephaven* (1877), and this she followed with volumes similar in form; then essaying the novel, she gave in *A Country Doctor* (1884) a portrait of her father. Her first wide success, however, came with the publication of *A White Heron and Other Stories* (1886), a volume of short stories; and although she wrote other novels, a series of children's books, and one book of verse, it is in the short story and in such volumes of loosely knit sketches as *The Country of the Pointed Firs* (1896) that she made her chief contribution to literature. She described inimitably the inhabitants of the small Maine fishing villages and countryside, suppressing the harsher aspects in the people and in their environment, and giving prominence to the warmer and more genial qualities of both.

From THE COUNTRY OF THE POINTED FIRS [1]

[GREEN ISLAND]

ONE morning, very early, I heard Mrs. Todd in the garden outside my window. By the unusual loudness of her remarks to a passer-by, and the notes of a familiar hymn which she sang as she worked among the herbs,

[1] The extract here reprinted is used by permission of, and by arrangement with, Houghton Mifflin Company, the authorized publishers.

and which came as if directed purposely to the sleepy ears of my consciousness, I knew that she wished I would wake up and come and speak to her.

In a few minutes she responded to a morning voice from behind the blinds. "I expect you're goin' up to your schoolhouse to pass all this pleasant day; yes, I expect you're goin' to be dreadful busy," she said despairingly.

"Perhaps not," said I. "Why, what's going to be the matter with you, Mrs. Todd?" For I supposed that she was tempted by the fine weather to take one of her favorite expeditions along the shore pastures to gather herbs and simples, and would like to have me keep the house.

"No; I don't want to go nowhere by land," she answered gayly,—"no, not by land; but I don't know's we shall have a better day all the rest of the summer to go out to Green Island an' see mother. I waked up early thinkin' of her. The wind's light northeast,—'t will take us right straight out; an' this time o' year it's liable to change round southwest an' fetch us home pretty, 'long late in the afternoon. Yes, it's goin' to be a good day."

"Speak to the captain and the Bowden boy, if you see anybody going by toward the landing," said I. "We'll take the big boat."

"Oh, my sakes! now you let me do things my way," said Mrs. Todd scornfully. "No, dear, we won't take no big bo't. I'll just get a handy dory, an' Johnny Bowden an' me, we'll man her ourselves. I don't want no abler bo't than a good dory, an' a nice light breeze ain't goin' to make no sea; an' Johnny's my cousin's son,—mother'll like to have him come; an' he'll be down to the herrin' weirs all the time we're there, anyway; we don't want to carry no men folks havin' to be considered every minute an' takin' up all our time. No, you let me do; we'll just slip out an' see mother by ourselves. I guess what breakfast you'll want's about ready now."

I had become well acquainted with Mrs. Todd as landlady, herb-gatherer, and rustic philosopher; we had been discreet fellow-passengers once or twice when I had sailed up the coast to a larger town than Dunnet Landing to do some shopping; but I was yet to become acquainted with her as a mariner. An hour later we pushed off from the landing in the desired dory. The tide was just on the turn, beginning to fall, and several friends and acquaintances stood along the side of the dilapidated wharf and cheered us by their words and evident interest. Johnny Bowden and I were both rowing in haste to get out where we could catch the breeze and put up the small sail which lay clumsily furled along the gunwale. Mrs. Todd sat aft, a stern and unbending lawgiver.

"You better let her drift; we'll get there 'bout as quick; the tide'll take her right out from under these old buildin's; there's plenty wind outside."

"Your bo't ain't trimmed proper, Mis' Todd!" exclaimed a voice from shore. "You're lo'ded so the bo't 'll drag; you can't git her before the wind,

ma'am. You set 'midships, Mis' Todd, an' let the boy hold the sheet 'n' steer
after he gits the sail up; you won't never git out to Green Island that way.
She's lo'ded bad, your bo't is,—she's heavy behind's she is now!"

Mrs. Todd turned with some difficulty and regarded the anxious adviser,
my right oar flew out of the water, and we seemed about to capsize. "That
you, Asa? Good-mornin'," she said politely. "I al'ays liked the starn seat best.
When 'd you git back from up country?"

This allusion to Asa's origin was not lost upon the rest of the company.
We were some little distance from shore, but we could hear a chuckle of
laughter, and Asa, a person who was too ready with his criticism and advice
on every possible subject, turned and walked indignantly away.

When we caught the wind we were soon on our seaward course, and only
stopped to underrun a trawl, for the floats of which Mrs. Todd looked earnestly, explaining that her mother might not be prepared for three extra to
dinner; it was her brother's trawl, and she meant to just run her eye along
for the right sort of a little haddock. I leaned over the boat's side with great
interest and excitement, while she skilfully handled the long line of hooks,
and made scornful remarks upon worthless, bait-consuming creatures of the
sea as she reviewed them and left them on the trawl or shook them off into
the waves. At last we came to what she pronounced a proper haddock, and
having taken him on board and ended his life resolutely, we went our way.

As we sailed along I listened to an increasingly delightful commentary
upon the islands, some of them barren rocks, or at best giving sparse pasturage for sheep in the early summer. On one of these an eager little flock
ran to the water's edge and bleated at us so affectingly that I would willingly
have stopped; but Mrs. Todd steered away from the rocks, and scolded at
the sheep's mean owner, an acquaintance of hers, who grudged the little
salt and still less care which the patient creatures needed. The hot midsummer sun makes prisons of these small islands that are a paradise in early
June, with their cool springs and short thick-growing grass. On a larger
island, farther out to sea, my entertaining companion showed me with glee
the small houses of two farmers who shared the island between them, and
declared that for three generations the people had not spoken to each other
even in times of sickness or death or birth. "When the news come that the
war was over, one of 'em knew it a week, and never stepped across his wall
to tell the others," she said. "There, they enjoy it: they've got to have somethin' to interest 'em in such a place; 't is a good deal more tryin' to be tied
to folks you don't like than 't is to be alone. Each of 'em tells the neighbors
their wrongs; plenty likes to hear and tell again; them as fetch a bone 'll
carry one, an' so they keep the fight a-goin'. I must say I like variety myself;
some folks washes Monday an' irons Tuesday the whole year round, even
if the circus is goin' by!"

A long time before we landed at Green Island we could see the small white house, standing high like a beacon, where Mrs. Todd was born and where her mother lived, on a green slope above the water, with dark spruce woods still higher. There were crops in the fields, which we presently distinguished from one another. Mrs. Todd examined them while we were still far at sea. "Mother's late potatoes looks backward; ain't had rain enough so far," she pronounced her opinion. "They look weedier than what they call Front Street down to Cowper Centre. I expect brother William is so occupied with his herrin' weirs an' servin' out bait to the schooners that he don't think once a day of the land."

"What's the flag for, up above the spruces there behind the house?" I inquired, with eagerness.

"Oh, that's the sign for herrin'," she explained kindly, while Johnny Bowden regarded me with contemptuous surprise. "When they get enough for schooners they raise that flag; an' when 't is a poor catch in the weir pocket they just fly a little signal down by the shore, an' then the small bo'ts comes and get enough an' over for their trawls. There, look! there she is: mother sees us; she's wavin' somethin' out o' the fore door! She'll be to the landin'-place quick's we are."

I looked, and could see a tiny flutter in the doorway, but a quicker signal had made its way from the heart on shore to the heart on the sea.

"How do you suppose she knows it's me?" said Mrs. Todd, with a tender smile on her broad face. "There, you never get over bein' a child long's you have a mother to go to. Look at the chimney, now; she's gone right in an' brightened up the fire. Well, there, I'm glad mother's well; you'll enjoy seein' her very much."

Mrs. Todd leaned back into her proper position, and the boat trimmed again. She took a firmer grasp of the sheet, and gave an impatient look up at the gaff and the leech of the little sail, and twitched the sheet as if she urged the wind like a horse. There came at once a fresh gust, and we seemed to have doubled our speed. Soon we were near enough to see a tiny figure with handkerchiefed head come down across the field and stand waiting for us at the cove above a curve of pebble beach.

Presently the dory grated on the pebbles, and Johnny Bowden, who had been kept in abeyance during the voyage, sprang out and used manful exertions to haul us up with the next wave, so that Mrs. Todd could make a dry landing.

"You done that very well," she said, mounting to her feet, and coming ashore somewhat stiffly, but with great dignity, refusing our outstretched hands, and returning to possess herself of a bag which had lain at her feet.

"Well, mother, here I be!" she announced with indifference; but they stood and beamed in each other's faces.

"Lookin' pretty well for an old lady, ain't she?" said Mrs. Todd's mother, turning away from her daughter to speak to me. She was a delightful little person herself, with bright eyes and an affectionate air of expectation like a child on a holiday. You felt as if Mrs. Blackett were an old and dear friend before you let go her cordial hand. We all started together up the hill.

"Now don't you haste too fast, mother," said Mrs. Todd warningly; "'t is a far reach o' risin' ground to the fore door, and you won't set an' get your breath when you're once there, but go trotting about. Now don't you go a mite faster than we proceed with this bag an' basket. Johnny, there, 'll fetch up the haddock. I just made one stop to underrun William's trawl till I come to jes' such a fish 's I thought you'd want to make one o' your nice chowders of. I've brought an onion with me that was layin' about on the window-sill at home."

"That's just what I was wantin'," said the hostess. "I give a sigh when you spoke o' chowder, knowin' my onions was out. William forgot to replenish us last time he was to the Landin'. Don't you haste so yourself, Almiry, up this risin' ground. I hear you commencin' to wheeze a'ready."

This mild revenge seemed to afford great pleasure to both giver and receiver. They laughed a little, and looked at each other affectionately, and then at me. Mrs. Todd considerately paused, and faced about to regard the wide sea view. I was glad to stop, being more out of breath than either of my companions, and I prolonged the halt by asking the names of the neighboring islands. There was a fine breeze blowing, which we felt more there on the high land than when we were running before it in the dory.

"Why, this ain't that kitten I saw when I was out last, the one that I said didn't appear likely?" exclaimed Mrs. Todd as we went our way.

"That's the one, Almiry," said her mother. "She always had a likely look to me, an' she's right after her business. I never see such a mouser for one of her age. If 't wan't for William, I never should have housed that other dronin' old thing so long; but he sets by her on account of her havin' a bob tail. I don't deem it advisable to maintain cats just on account of their havin' bob tails; they're like all other curiosities, good for them that wants to see 'em twice. This kitten catches mice for both, an' keeps me respectable as I ain't been for a year. She's a real understandin' little help, this kitten is. I picked her from among five Miss Augusta Pennell had over to Burnt Island," said the old woman, trudging along with the kitten close at her skirts. "Augusta, she says to me, 'Why, Mis' Blackett, you've took the homeliest;' an' says I, 'I've got the smartest; I'm satisfied.'"

"I'd trust nobody sooner'n you to pick out a kitten, mother," said the daughter handsomely, and we went on in peace and harmony.

The house was just before us now, on a green level that looked as if a huge hand had scooped it out of the long green field we had been ascending. A little way above, the dark spruce woods began to climb the top of the hill and cover the seaward slopes of the island. There was just room for the small farm and the forest; we looked down at the fish-house and its rough sheds, and the weirs stretching far out into the water. As we looked upward, the tops of the firs came sharp against the blue sky. There was a great stretch of rough pasture-land round the shoulder of the island to the eastward, and here were all the thick-scattered gray rocks that kept their places, and the gray backs of many sheep that forever wandered and fed on the thin sweet pasturage that fringed the ledges and made soft hollows and strips of green turf like growing velvet. I could see the rich green of bayberry bushes here and there, where the rocks made room. The air was very sweet; one could not help wishing to be a citizen of such a complete and tiny continent and home of fisherfolk.

The house was broad and clean, with a roof that looked heavy on its low walls. It was one of the houses that seem firm-rooted in the ground, as if they were two-thirds below the surface, like icebergs. The front door stood hospitably open in expectation of company, and an orderly vine grew at each side; but our path led to the kitchen door at the house-end, and there grew a mass of gay flowers and greenery, as if they had been swept together by some diligent garden broom into a tangled heap: there were portulacas all along under the lower step and straggling off into the grass, and clustering mallows that crept as near as they dared, like poor relations. I saw the bright eyes and brainless little heads of two half-grown chickens who were snuggled down among the mallows as if they had been chased away from the door more than once, and expected to be again.

"It seems kind o' formal comin' in this way," said Mrs. Todd impulsively, as we passed the flowers and came to the front doorstep; but she was mindful of the proprieties, and walked before us into the best room on the left.

"Why, mother, if you haven't gone an' turned the carpet!" she exclaimed, with something in her voice that spoke of awe and admiration. "When 'd you get to it? I s'pose Mis' Addicks come over an' helped you, from White Island Landing?"

"No, she didn't," answered the old woman, standing proudly erect, and making the most of a great moment. "I done it all myself with William's help. He had a spare day, an' took right holt with me; an' 't was all well beat on the grass, an' turned, an' put down again afore we went to bed. I ripped and sewed over two o' them long breadths. I ain't had such a good night's sleep for two years."

"There, what do you think o' havin' such a mother as that for eighty-six year old?" said Mrs. Todd, standing before us like a large figure of Victory.

As for the mother, she took on a sudden look of youth; you felt as if she promised a great future, and was beginning, not ending, her summers and their happy toils.

"My, my!" exclaimed Mrs. Todd. "I could n't ha' done it myself, I've got to own it."

"I was much pleased to have it off my mind," said Mrs. Blackett, humbly; "the more so because along at the first of the next week I wasn't very well. I suppose it may have been the change of weather."

Mrs. Todd could not resist a significant glance at me, but, with charming sympathy, she forbore to point the lesson or to connect this illness with its apparent cause. She loomed larger than ever in the little old-fashioned best room, with its few pieces of good furniture and pictures of national interest. The green paper curtains were stamped with conventional landscapes of a foreign order,—castles on inaccessible crags, and lovely lakes with steep wooded shores; under-foot the treasured carpet was covered thick with home-made rugs. There were empty glass lamps and crystallized bouquets of grass and some fine shells on the narrow mantelpiece.

"I was married in this room," said Mrs. Todd unexpectedly; and I heard her give a sigh after she had spoken, as if she could not help the touch of regret that would forever come with all her thoughts of happiness.

"We stood right there between the windows," she added, "and the minister stood here. William wouldn't come in. He was always odd about seein' folks, just's as he is now. I run to meet 'em from a child, an' William, he'd take an' run away."

"I've been the gainer," said the old mother cheerfully. "William has been son an' daughter both since you was married off the island. He's been 'most too satisfied to stop at home 'long o' his old mother, but I always tell 'em I'm the gainer."

We were all moving toward the kitchen as if by common instinct. The best room was too suggestive of serious occasions, and the shades were all pulled down to shut out the summer light and air. It was indeed a tribute to Society to find a room set apart for her behests out there on so apparently neighborless and remote an island. Afternoon visits and evening festivals must be few in such a bleak situation at certain seasons of the year, but Mrs. Blackett was of those who do not live to themselves, and who have long since passed the line that divides mere self-concern from a valued share in what-ever Society can give and take. There were those of her neighbors who never had taken the trouble to furnish a best room, but Mrs. Blackett was one who knew the uses of a parlor.

"Yes, do come right out into the old kitchen; I shan't make any stranger of you," she invited us pleasantly, after we had been properly received in the room appointed to formality. "I expect Almiry, here, 'll be driftin' out 'mongst the pasture-weeds quick's she can find a good excuse. 'T is hot now. You'd better content yourselves till you get nice an' rested, an' 'long after dinner the sea-breeze 'll spring up, an' then you can take your walks, an' go up an' see the prospect from the big ledge. Almiry 'll want to show off everything there is. Then I'll get you a good cup o' tea before you start to go home. The days are plenty long now."

While we were talking in the best room the selected fish had been mysteriously brought up from the shore, and lay all cleaned and ready in an earthen crock on the table.

"I think William might have just stopped an' said a word," remarked Mrs. Todd, pouting with high affront as she caught sight of it. "He's friendly enough when he comes ashore, an' was remarkable social the last time, for him."

"He ain't disposed to be very social with the ladies," explained William's mother, with a delightful glance at me, as if she counted upon my friendship and tolerance. "He's very particular, and he's all in his old fishin'-clothes to-day. He'll want me to tell him everything you said and done, after you've gone. William has very deep affections. He'll want to see you, Almiry. Yes, I guess he'll be in by an' by."

"I'll search for him by 'n' by, if he don't," proclaimed Mrs. Todd, with an air of unalterable resolution. "I know all of his burrows down 'long the shore. I'll catch him by hand 'fore he knows it. I've got some business with William, anyway. I brought forty-two cents with me that was due him for them last lobsters he brought in."

"You can leave it with me," suggested the little old mother, who was already stepping about among her pots and pans in the pantry, and preparing to make the chowder.

I became possessed of a sudden unwonted curiosity in regard to William, and felt that half the pleasure of my visit would be lost if I could not make his interesting acquaintance.

Mrs. Todd had taken the onion out of her basket and laid it down upon the kitchen table. "There's Johnny Bowden come with us, you know," she reminded her mother. "He'll be hungry enough to eat his size."

"I've got new doughnuts, dear," said the little old lady. "You don't often catch William 'n' me out o' provisions. I expect you might have chose a somewhat larger fish, but I'll try an' make it do. I shall have to have a few extra potatoes, but there's a field full out there, an' the hoe's leanin' against the well-house, in 'mongst the climbin' beans." She smiled, and gave her daughter a commanding nod.

"Land sakes alive! Le' 's blow the horn for William," insisted Mrs. Todd, with some excitement. "He needn't break his spirit so far's to come in. He'll know you need him for something particular, an' then we can call to him as he comes up the path. I won't put him to no pain."

Mrs. Blackett's old face, for the first time, wore a look of trouble, and I found it necessary to counteract the teasing spirit of Almira. It was too pleasant to stay indoors altogether, even in such rewarding companionship; besides, I might meet William; and, straying out presently, I found the hoe by the well-house and an old splint basket at the woodshed door, and also found my way down to the field where there was a great square patch of rough, weedy potato-tops and tall ragweed. One corner was already dug, and I chose a fat-looking hill where the tops were well withered. There is all the pleasure that one can have in gold-digging in finding one's hopes satisfied in the riches of a good hill of potatoes. I longed to go on; but it did not seem frugal to dig any longer after my basket was full, and at last I took my hoe by the middle and lifted the basket to go back up the hill. I was sure that Mrs. Blackett must be waiting impatiently to slice the potatoes into the chowder, layer after layer, with the fish.

"You let me take holt o' that basket, ma'am," said a pleasant, anxious voice behind me.

I turned, startled in the silence of the wide field, and saw an elderly man, bent in the shoulders as fishermen often are, gray-headed and clean-shaven, and with a timid air. It was William. He looked just like his mother, and I had been imagining that he was large and stout like his sister, Almira Todd; and, strange to say, my fancy had led me to picture him not far from thirty and a little loutish. It was necessary instead to pay William the respect due to age.

I accustomed myself to plain facts on the instant, and we said good-morning like old friends. The basket was really heavy, and I put the hoe through its handle and offered him one end; then we moved easily toward the house together, speaking of the fine weather and of mackerel which were reported to be striking in all about the bay. William had been out since three o'clock, and had taken an extra fare of fish. I could feel that Mrs. Todd's eyes were upon us as we approached the house, and although I fell behind in the narrow path, and let William take the basket alone and precede me at some little distance the rest of the way, I could plainly hear her greet him.

"Got round to comin' in, didn't you?" she inquired, with amusement. "Well, now, that's clever. Didn't know's I should see you to-day, William, an' I wanted to settle an account."

I felt somewhat disturbed and responsible, but when I joined them they were on most simple and friendly terms. It became evident that, with William, it was the first step that cost, and that, having once joined in social interests, he was able to pursue them with more or less pleasure. He was about sixty, and not young-looking for his years, yet so undying is the spirit of youth, and bashfulness has such a power of survival, that I felt all the time as if one must try to make the occasion easy for some one who was young and new to the affairs of social life. He asked politely if I would like to go up to the great ledge while dinner was getting ready; so, not without a deep sense of pleasure, and a delightful look of surprise from the two hostesses, we started, William and I, as if both of us felt much younger than we looked. Such was the innocence and simplicity of the moment that when I heard Mrs. Todd laughing behind us in the kitchen I laughed too, but William did not even blush. I think he was a little deaf, and he stepped along before me most businesslike and intent upon his errand.

We went from the upper edge of the field above the house into a smooth, brown path among the dark spruces. The hot sun brought out the fragrance of the pitchy bark, and the shade was pleasant as we climbed the hill. William stopped once or twice to show me a great wasps'-nest close by, or some fishhawks'-nests below in a bit of swamp. He picked a few sprigs of late-blooming linnæa as we came out upon an open bit of pasture at the top of the island, and gave them to me without speaking, but he knew as well as I that one could not say half he wished about linnæa. Through this piece of rough pasture ran a huge shape of stone like the great backbone of an enormous creature. At the end, near the woods, we could climb up on it and walk along to the highest point; there above the circle of pointed firs we could look down over all the island, and could see the ocean that circled this and a hundred other bits of island-ground, the mainland shore, and all the far horizons. It gave a sudden sense of space, for nothing stopped the eye or hedged one in,—that sense of liberty in space and time which great prospects always give.

"There ain't no such view in the world, I expect," said William proudly, and I hastened to speak my heartfelt tribute of praise; it was impossible not to feel as if an untraveled boy had spoken, and yet one loved to have him value his native heath.

We were a little late to dinner, but Mrs. Blackett and Mrs. Todd were lenient, and we all took our places after William had paused to wash his hands, like a pious Brahmin, at the well, and put on a neat blue coat which he took from a peg behind the kitchen door. Then he resolutely asked a blessing in words that I could not hear, and we ate the chowder and were thankful. The kitten went round and round the table, quite erect, and, holding on by her fierce young claws, she stopped to mew with pathos at each elbow, or darted off to the open door when a song sparrow forgot himself and lit in the grass too near. William did not talk much, but his sister Todd occupied the time and told all the news there was to tell of Dunnet Landing and its coasts, while the old mother listened with delight. Her hospitality was something exquisite; she had the gift which so many women lack, of being able to make themselves and their houses belong entirely to a guest's pleasure,—that charming surrender for the moment of themselves and whatever belongs to them, so that they make a part of one's own life that can never be forgotten. Tact is after all a kind of mind-reading, and my hostess held the golden gift. Sympathy is of the mind as well as the heart, and Mrs. Blackett's world and mine were one from the moment we met. Besides, she had that final, that highest gift of heaven, a perfect self-forgetfulness. Sometimes, as I watched her eager, sweet old face, I wondered why she had been set to shine on this lonely island of the northern coast. It must have been to keep the balance true, and make up to all her scattered and depending neighbors for other things which they may have lacked.

When we had finished clearing away the old blue plates, and the kitten had taken care of her share of the fresh haddock, just as we were putting back the kitchen chairs in their places, Mrs. Todd said briskly that she must go up into the pasture now to gather the desired herbs.

"You can stop here an' rest, or you can accompany me," she announced. "Mother ought to have her nap, and when we come back she an' William 'll sing for you. She admires music," said Mrs. Todd, turning to speak to her mother.

But Mrs. Blackett tried to say that she couldn't sing as she used, and perhaps William wouldn't feel like it. She looked tired, the good old soul, or I should have liked to sit in the peaceful little house while she slept; I had had much pleasant experience of pastures already in her daughter's company. But it seemed best to go with Mrs. Todd, and off we went.

Mrs. Todd carried the gingham bag which she had brought from home, and a small heavy burden in the bottom made it hang straight and slender from her hand. The way was steep, and she soon grew breathless, so that we sat down to rest awhile on a convenient large stone among the bayberry.

"There, I wanted you to see this,—'t is mother's picture," said Mrs. Todd; " 't was taken once when she was up to Portland, soon after she was married. That's me," she added, opening another worn case, and displaying the full face of the cheerful child she looked like still in spite of being past sixty. "And here's William an' father together. I take after father, large and heavy, an' William is like mother's folks, short an' thin. He ought to have made something o' himself, bein' a man an' so like mother; but though he's been very steady to work, an' kept up the farm, an' done his fishin' too right along, he never had mother's snap an' power o' seein' things just as they be. He's got excellent judgment, too," meditated William's sister, but she could not arrive at any satisfactory decision upon what she evidently thought his failure in life. "I think it is well to see any one so happy an' makin' the most of life just as it falls to hand," she said as she began to put the daguerreotypes away again; but I reached out my hand to see her mother's once more, a most flowerlike face of a lovely young woman in quaint dress. There was in the eyes a look of anticipation and joy, a far-off look that sought the horizon; one often sees it in seafaring families, inherited by girls and boys alike from men who spend their lives at sea, and are always watching for distant sails or the first loom of the land. At sea there is nothing to be seen close by, and this has its counterpart in a sailor's character, in the large and brave and patient traits that are developed, the hopeful pleasantness that one loves so in a seafarer.

When the family pictures were wrapped again in a big handkerchief, we set forward in a narrow footpath and made our way to a lonely place that faced northward, where there was more pasturage and fewer bushes, and we went down to the edge of short grass above some rocky cliffs where the deep sea broke with a great noise, though the wind was down and the water looked quiet a little way from shore. Among the grass grew such pennyroyal as the rest of the world could not provide. There was a fine fragrance in the air as we gathered it sprig by sprig and stepped along carefully, and Mrs. Todd pressed her aromatic nosegay between her hands and offered it to me again and again.

"There's nothin' like it," she said; "oh, no, there's no such pennyr'yal as this in the State of Maine. It's the right pattern of the plant, and all the rest I ever see is but an imitation. Don't it do you good?" And I answered with enthusiasm.

"There, dear, I never showed nobody else but mother where to find this place; 't is kind of sainted to me. Nathan, my husband, an' I used to love this place when we was courtin', and"—she hesitated, and then spoke softly —"when he was lost, 't was just off shore tryin' to get in by the short channel out there between Squaw Islands, right in sight o' this headland where we'd set an' made our plans all summer long."

I had never heard her speak of her husband before, but I felt that we were friends now since she had brought me to this place.

" 'T was but a dream with us," Mrs. Todd said. "I knew it when he was gone. I knew it"—and she whispered as if she were at confession—"I knew it afore he started to go to sea. My heart was gone out o' my keepin' before I ever saw Nathan; but he loved me well, and he made me real happy, and he died before he ever knew what he'd had to know if we'd lived long together. 'T is very strange about love. No, Nathan never found out, but my heart was troubled when I knew him first. There's more women likes to be loved than there is of those that loves. I spent some happy hours right here. I always liked Nathan, and he never knew. But this pennyr'yal always reminded me, as I'd sit and gather it and hear him talkin'—it always would remind me of—the other one."

She looked away from me, and presently rose and went on by herself. There was something lonely and solitary about her great determined shape. She might have been Antigone alone on the Theban plain. It is not often given in a noisy world to come to the places of great grief and silence. An absolute, archaic grief possessed this countrywoman; she seemed like a renewal of some historic soul, with her sorrows and the remoteness of a daily life busied with rustic simplicities and the scents of primeval herbs.

I was not incompetent at herb-gathering, and after a while, when I had sat long enough waking myself to new thoughts, and reading a page of remembrance with new pleasure, I gathered some bunches, as I was bound to do, and at last we met again higher up the shore, in the plain every-day world we had left behind when we went down to the pennyroyal plot. As we walked together along the high edge of the field we saw a hundred sails about the bay and farther seaward; it was mid-afternoon or after, and the day was coming to an end.

"Yes, they're all makin' towards the shore,—the small craft an' the lobster smacks an' all," said my companion. "We must spend a little time with mother now, just to have our tea, an' then put for home."

"No matter if we lose the wind at sundown; I can row in with Johnny," said I; and Mrs. Todd nodded reassuringly and kept to her steady plod, not quickening her gait even when we saw William come round the corner of the house as if to look for us, and wave his hand and disappear.

"Why, William's right on deck; I didn't know's we should see any more of him!" exclaimed Mrs. Todd. "Now mother 'll put the kettle right on; she's got a good fire goin'." I too could see the blue smoke thicken, and then we both walked a little faster, while Mrs. Todd groped in her full bag of herbs to find the daguerreotypes and be ready to put them in their places.

William was sitting on the side door step, and the old mother was busy making her tea; she gave into my hand an old flowered-glass tea-caddy.

"William thought you'd like to see this, when he was settin' the table. My father brought it to my mother from the island of Tobago; an' here's a pair of beautiful mugs that came with it." She opened the glass door of a little cupboard beside the chimney. "These I call my best things, dear," she said. "You'd laugh to see how we enjoy 'em Sunday nights in winter: we have a real company tea 'stead o' livin' right along just the same, an' I make somethin' good for a s'prise an' put on some o' my preserves, an' we get a-talkin' together an' have real pleasant times."

Mrs. Todd laughed indulgently, and looked to see what I thought of such childishness.

"I wish I could be here some Sunday evening," said I.

"William an' me'll be talkin' about you an' thinkin' o' this nice day," said Mrs. Blackett affectionately, and she glanced at William, and he looked up bravely and nodded. I began to discover that he and his sister could not speak their deeper feelings before each other.

"Now I want you an' mother to sing," said Mrs. Todd abruptly, with an air of command, and I gave William much sympathy in his evident distress.

"After I've had my cup o' tea, dear," answered the old hostess cheerfully; and so we sat down and took our cups and made merry while they lasted. It was impossible not to wish to stay on forever at Green Island, and I could not help saying so.

"I'm very happy here, both winter an' summer," said old Mrs. Blackett. "William an' I never wish for any other home, do we, William? I'm glad you find it pleasant; I wish you'd come an' stay, dear, whenever you feel inclined. But here's Almiry; I always think Providence was kind to plot an' have her husband leave her a good house where she really belonged. She'd been very restless if she'd had to continue here on Green Island. You wanted more scope, didn't you, Almiry, an' to live in a large place where more things grew? Sometimes folks wonders that we don't live together; perhaps we shall some time," and a shadow of sadness and apprehension flitted across her face. "The time o' sickness an' failin' has got to come to all. But Almiry's got an herb that's good for everything." She smiled as she spoke, and looked bright again.

"There's some herb that's good for everybody, except for them that thinks they 're sick when they ain't," announced Mrs. Todd, with a truly professional air of finality. "Come, William, let's have Sweet Home, an' then mother'll sing Cupid an' the Bee for us."

Then followed a most charming surprise. William mastered his timidity and began to sing. His voice was a little faint and frail, like the family daguerreotypes, but it was a tenor voice, and perfectly true and sweet. I have never heard Home, Sweet Home sung as touchingly and seriously as he sang it; he seemed to make it quite new; and when he paused for a moment at the end of the first line and began the next, the old mother joined him and they sang together, she missing only the higher notes, where he seemed to lend his voice to hers for the moment and carry on her very note and air. It was the silent man's real and only means of expression, and one could have listened forever, and have asked for more and more songs of old Scotch and English inheritance and the best that have lived from the ballad music of the war. Mrs. Todd kept time visibly, and sometimes audibly, with her ample foot. I saw the tears in her eyes sometimes, when I could see beyond the tears in mine. But at last the songs ended and the time came to say good-by; it was the end of a great pleasure.

Mrs. Blackett, the dear old lady, opened the door of her bedroom while Mrs. Todd was tying up the herb bag, and William had gone down to get the boat ready and to blow the horn for Johnny Bowden, who had joined a roving boat party who were off the shore lobstering.

I went to the door of the bedroom, and thought how pleasant it looked, with its pink-and-white patchwork quilt and the brown unpainted paneling of its woodwork.

"Come right in, dear," she said. "I want you to set down in my old quilted rockin'-chair there by the window; you'll say it's the prettiest view in the house. I set there a good deal to rest me and when I want to read."

There was a worn red Bible on the light-stand, and Mrs. Blackett's heavy silver-bowed glasses; her thimble was on the narrow window-ledge, and folded carefully on the table was a thick striped-cotton shirt that she was making for her son. Those dear old fingers and their loving stitches, that heart which had made the most of everything that had needed love! Here was the real home, the heart of the old house on Green Island! I sat in the rocking-chair, and felt that it was a place of peace, the little brown bedroom, and the quiet outlook upon field and sea and sky.

I looked up, and we understood each other without speaking. "I shall like to think o' your settin' here to-day," said Mrs. Blackett. "I want you to come again. It has been so pleasant for William."

The wind served us all the way home, and did not fall or let the sail slacken until we were close to the shore. We had a generous freight of lobsters in the boat, and new potatoes which William had put aboard, and what Mrs. Todd proudly called a full "kag" of prime number one salted mackerel; and when we landed we had to make business arrangements to have these conveyed to her house in a wheelbarrow.

I never shall forget the day at Green Island. The town of Dunnet Landing seemed large and noisy and oppressive as we came ashore. Such is the power of contrast; for the village was so still that I could hear the shy whippoorwills singing that night as I lay awake in my downstairs bedroom, and the scent of Mrs. Todd's herb garden under the window blew in again and again with every gentle rising of the seabreeze.

MARY WILKINS FREEMAN

(1862–1930)

Mary Eleanor Wilkins was born in 1862, at Randolph, Massachusetts, of puritan ancestry. She attended Mount Holyoke Seminary, and was then for some time secretary to Oliver Wendell Holmes. In the early '80's she began contributing poems and stories to magazines, and wrote several children's books. With the publication of *A Humble Romance and Other Stories* (1887), *A New England Nun and Other Stories* (1891), *Jane Field* (1893), and *Pembroke* (1894)—the two latter novels—she took a leading place among the realistic writers of her time. In 1902 she married Dr. Charles Freeman, of Metuchen, New Jersey, and afterwards lived in Metuchen until her death in 1930.

Miss Wilkins was a keen observer of the life in New England villages, where a decadent puritanism, with its inhibitions and repressions, colored the thought and warped the actions of those in whom it survived; and what she saw she set herself to portray with faithful realism in her early stories and novels. Although following her early successes she tried various kinds of fiction—the historical play in *Giles Corey, Yeoman* (1893); the detective story in *The Long Arm* (1895); the purpose novel in *Jerome, a Poor Man* (1897); the problem novel in *The Portion of Labor* (1901); and the eerie ghost tale in *The Wind in the Rose-Bush* (1903)—in quality she never excelled her early work. Many of her novels lack compression, but in the short stories of rural New England she fitted her style admirably to the content, using short, staccato sentences, avoiding rhetorical devices, and compressing rigidly, thus making her very style suggest the barrenness of the life she was attempting to depict.

A NEW ENGLAND NUN [1]

IT was late in the afternoon, and the light was waning. There was a difference in the look of the tree shadows out in the yard. Somewhere in the distance cows were lowing and a little bell was tinkling; now and then a farm-wagon tilted by, and the dust flew; some blue-shirted laborers with shovels over their shoulders plodded past; little swarms of flies were dancing up and down before the people's faces in the soft air. There seemed to be a gentle stir arising over everything for the mere sake of subsidence—a very premonition of rest and hush and night.

This soft diurnal commotion was over Louisa Ellis also. She had been peacefully sewing at her sitting-room window all the afternoon. Now she quilted her needle carefully into her work, which she folded precisely, and

---

[1] From *A New England Nun and Other Stories*. Reprinted with the permission of Harper & Brothers, the authorized publishers.

laid in a basket with her thimble and thread and scissors. Louisa Ellis could
not remember that ever in her life she had mislaid one of these little feminine
appurtenances, which had become, from long use and constant association, a
very part of her personality.

Louisa tied a green apron round her waist, and got out a flat straw hat
with a green ribbon. Then she went into the garden with a little blue crockery bowl, to pick some currants for her tea. After the currants were picked
she sat on the back door-step and stemmed them, collecting the stems carefully in her apron, and afterward throwing them into the hen-coop. She
looked sharply at the grass beside the step to see if any had fallen there.

Louisa was slow and still in her movements; it took her a long time to
prepare her tea; but when ready it was set forth with as much grace as if
she had been a veritable guest to her own self. The little square table stood
exactly in the centre of the kitchen, and was covered with a starched linen
cloth whose border pattern of flowers glistened. Louisa had a damask napkin
on her tea-tray, where were arranged a cut-glass tumbler full of teaspoons,
a silver cream-pitcher, a china sugar-bowl, and one pink china cup and
saucer. Louisa used china every day—something which none of her neighbors did. They whispered about it among themselves. Their daily tables
were laid with common crockery, their sets of best china stayed in the parlor
closet, and Louisa Ellis was no richer nor better bred than they. Still she
would use the china. She had for her supper a glass dish full of sugared currants, a plate of little cakes, and one of light white biscuits. Also a leaf or two
of lettuce, which she cut up daintily. Louisa was very fond of lettuce, which she
raised to perfection in her little garden. She ate quite heartily, though in a
delicate, pecking way; it seemed almost surprising that any considerable
bulk of food should vanish.

After tea she filled a plate with nicely baked thin corn-cakes, and carried
them out into the back-yard.

"Cæsar!" she called. "Cæsar! Cæsar!"

There was a little rush, and the clank of a chain, and a large yellow-and-
white dog appeared at the door of his tiny hut, which was half hidden among
the tall grasses and flowers. Louisa patted him and gave him the corn-cakes.
Then she returned to the house and washed the tea-things, polishing the
china carefully. The twilight had deepened; the chorus of the frogs floated
in at the open window wonderfully loud and shrill, and once in a while a
long sharp drone from a tree-toad pierced it. Louisa took off her green
gingham apron, disclosing a shorter one of pink-and-white print. She lighted
her lamp, and sat down again with her sewing.

In about half an hour Joe Dagget came. She heard his heavy step on the
walk, and rose and took off her pink-and-white apron. Under that was still
another—white linen with a little cambric edging on the bottom; that was

Louisa's company apron. She never wore it without her calico sewing-apron over it unless she had a guest. She had barely folded the pink-and-white one with methodical haste and laid it in a table-drawer when the door opened and Joe Dagget entered.

He seemed to fill up the whole room. A little yellow canary that had been asleep in his green cage at the south window woke up and fluttered wildly, beating his little yellow wings against the wires. He always did so when Joe Dagget came into the room.

"Good-evening," said Louisa. She extended her hand with a kind of solemn cordiality.

"Good-evening, Louisa," returned the man, in a loud voice.

She placed a chair for him, and they sat facing each other, with the table between them. He sat bolt-upright, toeing out his heavy feet squarely, glancing with a good-humored uneasiness around the room. She sat gently erect, folding her slender hands in her white-linen lap.

"Been a pleasant day," remarked Dagget.

"Real pleasant," Louisa assented, softly. "Have you been haying?" she asked, after a little while.

"Yes, I've been haying all day, down in the ten-acre lot. Pretty hot work."

"It must be."

"Yes, it's pretty hot work in the sun."

"Is your mother well to-day?"

"Yes, mother's pretty well."

"I suppose Lily Dyer's with her now?"

Dagget colored. "Yes, she's with her," he answered, slowly.

He was not very young, but there was a boyish look about his large face. Louisa was not quite as old as he, her face was fairer and smoother, but she gave people the impression of being older.

"I suppose she's a good deal of help to your mother," she said, further.

"I guess she is; I don't know how mother 'd get along without her," said Dagget, with a sort of embarrassed warmth.

"She looks like a real capable girl. She's pretty-looking too," remarked Louisa.

"Yes, she is pretty fair-looking."

Presently Dagget began fingering the books on the table. There was a square red autograph album, and a Young Lady's Gift-Book which had belonged to Louisa's mother. He took them up one after the other and opened them; then laid them down again, the album on the Gift-Book.

Louisa kept eying them with mild uneasiness. Finally she rose and changed the position of the books, putting the album underneath. That was the way they had been arranged in the first place.

Dagget gave an awkward little laugh. "Now what difference did it make which book was on top?" said he.

Louisa looked at him with a deprecating smile. "I always keep them that way," murmured she.

"You do beat everything," said Dagget, trying to laugh again. His large face was flushed.

He remained about an hour longer, then rose to take leave. Going out, he stumbled over a rug, and, trying to recover himself, hit Louisa's work-basket on the table, and knocked it on the floor.

He looked at Louisa, then at the rolling spools; he ducked himself awkwardly toward them, but she stopped him. "Never mind," said she; "I'll pick them up after you're gone."

She spoke with a mild stiffness. Either she was a little disturbed, or his nervousness affected her, and made her seem constrained in her effort to reassure him.

When Joe Dagget was outside he drew in the sweet evening air with a sigh, and felt much as an innocent and perfectly well-intentioned bear might after his exit from a china shop.

Louisa, on her part, felt much as the kind-hearted, long-suffering owner of the china shop might have done after the exit of the bear.

She tied on the pink, then the green apron, picked up all the scattered treasures and replaced them in her work-basket, and straightened the rug. Then she set the lamp on the floor, and began sharply examining the carpet. She even rubbed her fingers over it, and looked at them.

"He's tracked in a good deal of dust," she murmured. "I thought he must have."

Louisa got a dust-pan and brush, and swept Joe Dagget's track carefully.

If he could have known it, it would have increased his perplexity and uneasiness, although it would not have disturbed his loyalty in the least. He came twice a week to see Louisa Ellis, and every time, sitting there in her delicately sweet room, he felt as if surrounded by a hedge of lace. He was afraid to stir lest he should put a clumsy foot or hand through the fairy web, and he had always the consciousness that Louisa was watching fearfully lest he should.

Still the lace and Louisa commanded perforce his perfect respect and patience and loyalty. They were to be married in a month, after a singular courtship which had lasted for a matter of fifteen years. For fourteen out of the fifteen years the two had not once seen each other, and they had seldom exchanged letters. Joe had been all those years in Australia, where he had gone to make his fortune, and where he had stayed until he made it. He would have stayed fifty years if it had taken so long, and come home feeble and tottering, or never come home at all, to marry Louisa.

But the fortune had been made in the fourteen years, and he had come home now to marry the woman who had been patiently and unquestioningly waiting for him all that time.

Shortly after they were engaged he had announced to Louisa his determination to strike out into new fields, and secure a competency before they should be married. She had listened and assented with the sweet serenity which never failed her, not even when her lover set forth on that long and uncertain journey. Joe, buoyed up as he was by his sturdy determination, broke down a little at the last, but Louisa kissed him with a mild blush, and said good-bye.

"It won't be for long," poor Joe had said, huskily; but it was for fourteen years.

In that length of time much had happened. Louisa's mother and brother had died, and she was all alone in the world. But greatest happening of all— a subtle happening which both were too simple to understand—Louisa's feet had turned into a path, smooth maybe under a calm, serene sky, but so straight and unswerving that it could only meet a check at her grave, and so narrow that there was no room for any one at her side.

Louisa's first emotion when Joe Dagget came home (he had not apprised her of his coming) was consternation, although she would not admit it to herself, and he never dreamed of it. Fifteen years ago she had been in love with him—at least she considered herself to be. Just at that time, gently acquiescing with and falling into the natural drift of girlhood, she had seen marriage ahead as a reasonable feature and a probable desirability of life. She had listened with calm docility to her mother's views upon the subject. Her mother was remarkable for her cool sense and sweet, even temperament. She talked wisely to her daughter when Joe Dagget presented himself, and Louisa accepted him with no hesitation. He was the first lover she had ever had.

She had been faithful to him all these years. She had never dreamed of the possibility of marrying any one else. Her life, especially for the last seven years, had been full of a pleasant peace, she had never felt discontented nor impatient over her lover's absence; still she had always looked forward to his return and their marriage as the inevitable conclusion of things. However, she had fallen into a way of placing it so far in the future that it was almost equal to placing it over the boundaries of another life.

When Joe came she had been expecting him, and expecting to be married for fourteen years, but she was as much surprised and taken aback as if she had never thought of it.

Joe's consternation came later. He eyed Louisa with an instant confirmation of his old admiration. She had changed but little. She still kept her pretty manner and soft grace, and was, he considered, every whit as attractive as ever. As for himself, his stent was done; he had turned his face away from fortune-seeking, and the old winds of romance whistled as loud and sweet as ever through his ears. All the song which he had been wont to hear in them was Louisa; he had for a long time a loyal belief that he heard it still, but finally it seemed to him that although the winds sang always that one song, it had another name. But for Louisa the wind had never more than murmured; now it had gone down, and everything was still. She listened for a little while with half-wistful attention; then she turned quietly away and went to work on her wedding-clothes.

Joe had made some extensive and quite magnificent alterations in his house. It was the old homestead; the newly married couple would live there, for Joe could not desert his mother, who refused to leave her old home. So Louisa must leave hers. Every morning, rising and going about among her neat maidenly possessions, she felt as one looking her last upon the faces of dear friends. It was true that in a measure she could take them with her, but, robbed of their old environments, they would appear in such new guises that they would almost cease to be themselves. Then there were some peculiar features of her happy solitary life which she would probably be obliged to relinquish altogether. Sterner tasks than these graceful but half-needless ones would probably devolve upon her. There would be a large house to care for; there would be company to entertain; there would be Joe's rigorous and feeble old mother to wait upon; and it would be contrary to all thrifty village traditions for her to keep more than one servant. Louisa had a little still, and she used to occupy herself pleasantly in summer weather with distilling the sweet and aromatic essences from roses and peppermint and spearmint. By-and-by her still must be laid away. Her store of essences was already considerable, and there would be no time for her to distil for the mere pleasure of it. Then Joe's mother would think it foolishness; she had already hinted her opinion in the matter. Louisa dearly loved to sew a linen seam, not always for use, but for the simple, mild pleasure which she took in it. She would have been loath to confess how more than once she had ripped a seam for the mere delight of sewing it together again. Sitting at her window during long sweet afternoons, drawing her needle gently through the dainty fabric, she was peace itself. But there was small chance of such foolish comfort in the future. Joe's mother, domineering, shrewd old matron that she was even in her old age, and very likely even Joe himself, with his honest masculine rudeness, would laugh and frown down all these pretty but senseless old-maiden ways.

Louisa had almost the enthusiasm of an artist over the mere order and cleanliness of her solitary home. She had throbs of genuine triumph at the sight of the window-panes which she had polished until they shone like jewels. She gloated gently over her orderly bureau-drawers, with their exquisitely folded contents redolent with lavender and sweet clover and very purity. Could she be sure of the endurance of even this? She had visions, so startling that she half repudiated them as indelicate, of coarse masculine belongings strewn about in endless litter; of dust and disorder arising necessarily from a coarse masculine presence in the midst of all this delicate harmony.

Among her forebodings of disturbance, not the least was with regard to Cæsar. Cæsar was a veritable hermit of a dog. For the greater part of his life he had dwelt in his secluded hut, shut out from the society of his kind and all innocent canine joys. Never had Cæsar since his early youth watched at a woodchuck's hole; never had he known the delights of a stray bone at a neighbor's kitchen door. And it was all on account of a sin committed when hardly out of his puppyhood. No one knew the possible depth of remorse of which this mild-visaged, altogether innocent-looking old dog might be capable; but whether or not he had encountered remorse, he had encountered a full measure of righteous retribution. Old Cæsar seldom lifted up his voice in a growl or a bark; he was fat and sleepy; there were yellow rings which looked like spectacles around his dim old eyes; but there was a neighbor who bore on his hand the imprint of several of Cæsar's sharp, white, youthful teeth, and for that he had lived at the end of a chain, all alone in a little hut, for fourteen years. The neighbor, who was choleric and smarting with the pain of his wound, had demanded either Cæsar's death or complete ostracism. So Louisa's brother, to whom the dog had belonged, had built him his little kennel and tied him up. It was now fourteen years since, in a flood of youthful spirits, he had inflicted that memorable bite, and with the exception of short excursions, always at the end of the chain, under the strict guardianship of his master or Louisa, the old dog had remained a close prisoner. It is doubtful if, with his limited ambition, he took much pride in the fact, but it is certain that he was possessed of considerable cheap fame. He was regarded by all the children in the village and by many adults as a very monster of ferocity. St. George's dragon could hardly have surpassed in evil repute Louisa Ellis's old yellow dog. Mothers charged their children with solemn emphasis not to go too near to him, and the children listened and believed greedily, with a fascinated appetite for terror, and ran by Louisa's house stealthily, with many sidelong and backward glances at the terrible dog. If perchance he sounded a hoarse bark, there was a panic. Wayfarers chancing into Louisa's yard eyed him with respect, and inquired if the chain were stout. Cæsar at large might have seemed a very ordinary dog, and excited no comment whatever; chained, his reputation overshadowed him, so that he lost his own proper outlines and looked darkly vague and enormous. Joe Dagget, however, with his good-humored sense and shrewdness, saw him as he was. He strode valiantly up to him and patted him on the head, in spite of Louisa's soft clamor of warning, and even attempted to set him loose. Louisa grew so alarmed that he desisted, but kept announcing his opinion in the matter quite forcibly at intervals. "There ain't a better-natured dog in town," he would say, "and it's downright cruel to keep him tied up there. Some day I'm going to take him out."

Louisa had very little hope that he would not, one of these days, when their interests and possessions should be more completely fused in one. She pictured to herself Cæsar on the rampage through the quiet and unguarded village. She saw innocent children bleeding in his path. She was herself very fond of the old dog, because he had belonged to her dead brother, and he was always very gentle with her; still she had great faith in his ferocity. She always warned people not to go too near him. She fed him on ascetic fare of corn-mush and cakes, and never fired his dangerous temper with heating and sanguinary diet of flesh and bones. Louisa looked at the old dog munching his simple fare, and thought of her approaching marriage and trembled. Still no anticipation of disorder and confusion in lieu of sweet peace and harmony, no forebodings of Cæsar on the rampage, no wild fluttering of her little yellow canary, were sufficient to turn her a hair's-breadth. Joe Dagget had been fond of her and working for her all these years. It was not for her, whatever came to pass, to prove untrue and break his heart. She put the exquisite little stitches into her wedding-garments, and the time went on till it was only a week before her wedding-day. It was a Tuesday evening, and the wedding was to be a week from Wednesday.

There was a full moon that night. About nine o'clock Louisa strolled down the road a little way. There were harvest-fields on either hand, bordered by low stone walls. Luxuriant clumps of bushes grew beside the wall, and trees —wild cherry and old apple trees—at intervals. Presently Louisa sat down on the wall and looked about her with mildly sorrowful reflectiveness. Tall shrubs of blueberry and meadow-sweet, all woven together and tangled with blackberry vines and horsebriers, shut her in on either side. She had a little clear space between them. Opposite her, on the other side of the road, was a spreading tree; the moon shone between its boughs, and the leaves twinkled like silver. The road was bespread with a beautiful shifting dapple of silver and shadow; the air was full of a mysterious sweetness. "I wonder if it's wild grapes?" murmured Louisa. She sat there some time. She was just thinking of rising, when she heard footsteps and low voices, and remained quiet. It was a lonely place, and she felt a little timid. She thought she would keep still in the shadow and let the persons, whoever they might be, pass her.

But just before they reached her the voices ceased, and the footsteps. She understood that their owners had also found seats upon the stone wall. She was wondering if she could not steal away unobserved, when the voice broke the stillness. It was Joe Dagget's. She sat still and listened.

The voice was announced by a loud sigh, which was as familiar as itself. "Well," said Dagget, "you've made up your mind, then, I suppose?"

"Yes," returned another voice; "I'm going day after to-morrow."

"That's Lily Dyer," thought Louisa to herself. The voice embodied itself in her mind. She saw a girl tall and full-figured, with a firm, fair face, looking fairer and firmer in the moonlight, her strong yellow hair braided in a close knot. A girl full of a calm rustic strength and bloom, with a masterful way which might have beseemed a princess. Lily Dyer was a favorite with the village folk; she had just the qualities to arouse the admiration. She was good and handsome and smart. Louisa had often heard her praises sounded.

"Well," said Joe Dagget, "I ain't got a word to say."

"I don't know what you could say," returned Lily Dyer.

"Not a word to say," repeated Joe, drawing out the words heavily. Then there was a silence. "I ain't sorry," he began at last, "that that happened yesterday—that we kind of let on how we felt to each other. I guess it's just as well we knew. Of course, I can't do anything any different. I'm going right on an' get married next week. I ain't going back on a woman that's waited for me fourteen years, an' break her heart."

"If you should jilt her to-morrow, I wouldn't have you," spoke up the girl, with sudden vehemence.

"Well, I ain't going to give you the chance," said he; "but I don't believe you would, either."

"You'd see I wouldn't. Honor's honor, an' right's right. An' I'd never think anything of any man that went against 'em for me or any other girl; you'd find that out, Joe Dagget."

"Well, you'll find out fast enough that I ain't going against 'em for you or any other girl," returned he. Their voices sounded almost as if they were angry with each other. Louisa was listening eagerly.

"I'm sorry you feel as if you must go away," said Joe, "but I don't know but it's best."

"Of course it's best. I hope you and I have got common sense."

"Well, I suppose you're right." Suddenly Joe's voice got an undertone of tenderness. "Say, Lily," said he, "I'll get along well enough myself, but I can't bear to think— You don't suppose you're going to fret much over it?"

"I guess you'll find out I sha'n't fret much over a married man."

"Well, I hope you won't—I hope you won't, Lily. God knows I do. And —I hope—one of these days—you'll—come across somebody else—"

"I don't see any reason why I shouldn't." Suddenly her tone changed. She spoke in a sweet, clear voice, so loud that she could have been heard across the street. "No, Joe Dagget," said she, "I'll never marry any other man as long as I live. I've got good sense, an' I ain't going to break my heart nor make a fool of myself; but I'm never going to be married, you can be sure of that. I ain't that sort of a girl to feel this way twice."

Louisa heard an exclamation and a soft commotion behind the bushes; then Lily spoke again—the voice sounded as if she had risen. "This must be put a stop to," said she. "We've stayed here long enough. I'm going home."

Louisa sat there in a daze, listening to their retreating steps. After a while she got up and slunk softly home herself. The next day she did her house-work methodically; that was as much a matter of course as breathing; but she did not sew on her wedding-clothes. She sat at her window and medi-tated. In the evening Joe came. Louisa Ellis had never known that she had any diplomacy in her, but when she came to look for it that night she found it, although meek of its kind, among her little feminine weapons. Even now she could hardly believe that she had heard aright, and that she would not do Joe a terrible injury should she break her troth-plight. She wanted to sound him without betraying too soon her own inclinations in the matter. She did it successfully, and they finally came to an understanding; but it was a difficult thing, for he was as afraid of betraying himself as she.

She never mentioned Lily Dyer. She simply said that while she had no cause of complaint against him, she had lived so long in one way that she shrank from making a change.

"Well, I never shrank, Louisa," said Dagget. "I'm going to be honest enough to say that I think maybe it's better this way; but if you'd wanted to keep on, I'd have stuck to you till my dying day. I hope you know that."

"Yes, I do," said she.

That night she and Joe parted more tenderly than they had done for a long time. Standing in the door, holding each other's hands, a last great wave of regretful memory swept over them.

"Well, this ain't the way we've thought it was all going to end, is it, Louisa?" said Joe.

She shook her head. There was a little quiver on her placid face.

"You let me know if there's ever anything I can do for you," said he. "I ain't ever going to forget you, Louisa." Then he kissed her, and went down the path.

Louisa, all alone by herself that night, wept a little, she hardly knew why; but the next morning, on waking, she felt like a queen who, after fearing lest her domain be wrested away from her, sees it firmly insured in her possession.

Now the tall weeds and grasses might cluster around Cæsar's little hermit hut, the snow might fall on its roof year in and year out, but he never would go on a rampage through the unguarded village. Now the little canary might turn itself into a peaceful yellow ball night after night, and have no need to wake and flutter with wild terror against its bars. Louisa could sew linen seams, and distil roses, and dust and polish and fold away in lavender, as long as she listed. That afternoon she sat with her needle-work at the window, and felt fairly steeped in peace. Lily Dyer, tall and erect and blooming, went past; but she felt no qualm. If Louisa Ellis had sold her birthright she did not know it, the taste of the pottage was so delicious, and had been her sole satisfaction for so long. Serenity and placid narrowness had become to her as the birthright itself. She gazed ahead through a long reach of future days strung together like pearls in a rosary, every one like the others, and all smooth and flawless and innocent, and her heart went up in thankfulness. Outside was the fervid summer afternoon; the air was filled with the sounds of the busy harvest of men and birds and bees; there were halloos, metallic clatterings, sweet calls, and long hummings. Louisa sat, prayerfully numbering her days, like an uncloistered nun.

JOEL CHANDLER HARRIS

(1848–1908)

Joel Chandler Harris was born in Putnam county, Georgia, in 1848. He attended school irregularly till he was fourteen, when he became a typesetter on *The Countryman,* a plantation newspaper published by J. A. Turner. While thus employed he read widely in Turner's excellent library, and began writing poems, sketches, and essays, with Turner as literary guide. When at the close of the war *The Countryman* suspended publication, Harris began a varied newspaper experience, first as printer and then as editorial writer, in Macon, New Orleans, Forsyth, Savannah, and, after 1876, Atlanta. While on the staff of the Atlanta *Constitution,* he began contributing to that newspaper the Uncle Remus stories that won him his greatest fame. He continued here till his death in 1908.

After 1880, when Harris published his first volume, *Uncle Remus: His Songs and His Sayings,* his fame grew steadily. From childhood he had gathered Southern plantation stories and anecdotes, and in the various Uncle Remus volumes he retold these through the medium of an old negro servant, whose never failing humor, kindliness, and shrewd, homely philosophy brought his creator worldwide fame. Harris also wrote several novels, one of which—*On the Plantation* (1892)—is autobiographical; considerable verse; a series of children's books, which began with *Little Mr. Thimblefinger and His Queer Country* (1894); and a number of volumes of short stories about blacks and poor whites, some of which for vividness and dramatic intensity have few rivals in American fiction. Yet it is as author of the Uncle Remus stories that Harris will rightly be remembered longest, for in these he created one of the few indisputably American characters and at the same time made a distinct addition to folklore.

From UNCLE REMUS: HIS SONGS AND HIS SAYINGS [1]

XVI. Old Mr. Rabbit, He's a Good Fisherman

"BRER RABBIT en Brer Fox wuz like some chilluns w'at I knows un," said Uncle Remus, regarding the little boy, who had come to hear another story, with an affectation of great solemnity. "Bofe un um wuz allers atter wunner nudder, a prankin' en a pester'n 'roun', but Brer Rabbit did had some peace, kaze Brer Fox done got skittish 'bout puttin' de clamps on Brer Rabbit.

"One day, w'en Brer Rabbit, en Brer Fox, en Brer Coon, en Brer B'ar, en a whole lot un um wuz clearin' up a new groun' fer ter plant a roas'n'year patch, de sun 'gun ter git sorter hot, en Brer Rabbit he got tired; but he didn't

---

[1] The chapters from *Uncle Remus: His Songs and Sayings* are reprinted with the permission of D. Appleton & Company.

let on, kaze he 'fear'd de balance un um'd call 'im lazy, en he keep on totin' off trash en pilin' up bresh, twel bimeby he holler out dat he gotter brier in his han', en den he take'n slip off, en hunt fer cool place fer ter res'. Atter w'ile he come 'crosst a well wid a bucket hangin' in it.

" 'Dat look cool,' sez Brer Rabbit, sezee, 'en cool I speck she is. I'll des 'bout git in dar en take a nap,' en wid dat in he jump, he did, en he ain't no sooner fix hisse'f dan de bucket 'gun ter go down."

"Wasn't the Rabbit scared, Uncle Remus?" asked the little boy.

"Honey, dey ain't been no wusser skeer'd beas' sence de worril begin dan dish yer same Brer Rabbit. He fa'rly had a ager. He know whar he cum fum, but he dunner whar he gwine. Dreckly he feel de bucket hit de water, en dar she sot, but Brer Rabbit he keep mighty still, kaze he dunner w'at minnit gwineter be de nex'. He des lay dar en shuck en shiver.

"Brer Fox allers got one eye on Brer Rabbit, en w'en he slip off fum de new groun', Brer Fox he sneak atter 'im. He know Brer Rabbit wuz atter some projick er nudder, en he tuck'n crope off, he did, en watch 'im. Brer Fox see Brer Rabbit come to de well en stop, en den he see 'im jump in de bucket, en den, lo en beholes, he see 'im go down outer sight. Brer Fox wuz de mos' 'stonish Fox dat you ever laid eyes on. He sot off dar in de bushes en study en study, but he don't make no head ner tails ter dis kinder bizness. Den he say ter hisse'f, sezee:

" 'Well, ef dis don't bang my times,' sezee, 'den Joe's dead en Sal's a widder. Right down dar in dat well Brer Rabbit keep his money hid, en ef 'tain't dat den he done gone en 'skiver'd a gole-mine, en ef 'tain't dat, den I'm a gwineter see w'at's in dar,' sezee.

"Brer Fox crope up little nigher, he did, en lissen, but he don't year no fuss, en he keep on gittin' nigher, en yit he don't year nuthin'. Bimeby he git up close en peep down, but he don't see nuthin' en he don't year nuthin'. All dis time Brer Rabbit mighty nigh skeer'd outen his skin, en he fear'd fer ter move kaze de bucket might keel over en spill him out in de water. W'ile he sayin' his pra'rs over like a train er kyars runnin', ole Brer Fox holler out:

" 'Heyo, Brer Rabbit! Who you wizzitin' down dar?' sezee.

" 'Who? Me? Oh, I'm des a fishin', Brer Fox,' sez Brer Rabbit, sezee. 'I des say ter myse'f dat I'd sorter sprize you all wid a mess er fishes fer dinner, en so here I is, en dar's de fishes. I'm a fishin' fer suckers, Brer Fox,' sez Brer Rabbit, sezee.

" 'Is dey many un um down dar, Brer Rabbit?' sez Brer Fox, sezee.

" 'Lots un um, Brer Fox; scoze en scoze un um. De water is natally live wid um. Come down en he'p me haul um in, Brer Fox,' sez Brer Rabbit, sezee.

" 'How I gwineter git down, Brer Rabbit?'

" 'Jump inter de bucket, Brer Fox. Hit'll fetch you down all safe en soun'.'

"Brer Rabbit talk so happy en talk so sweet dat Brer Fox he jump in de bucket, he did, en, ez he went down, co'se his weight pull Brer Rabbit up. W'en dey pass one nudder on de half-way groun', Brer Rabbit he sing out:

> "'Good-by, Brer Fox, take keer yo' cloze,
> Fer dis is de way de worril goes;
> Some goes up en some goes down,
> You'll git ter de bottom all safe en soun'.[2]

"W'en Brer Rabbit got out, he gallop off en tole de fokes w'at de well b'long ter dat Brer Fox wuz down in dar muddyin' up de drinkin' water, en den he gallop back ter de well, en holler down ter Brer Fox:

> "'Yer come a man wid a great big gun—
> W'en he haul you up, you jump en run.'"

"What then, Uncle Remus?" asked the little boy, as the old man paused.

"In des 'bout half n'our, honey, bofe un um wuz back in de new groun' wukkin des like dey never heer'd er no well, ceppin' dat eve'y now'n den Brer Rabbit'd bust out in er laff, en ole Brer Fox, he'd git a spell er de dry grins."

XXXII. "JACKY-MY-LANTERN"[3]

Upon his next visit to Uncle Remus, the little boy was exceedingly anxious to know more about witches, but the old man prudently refrained from exciting the youngster's imagination any further in that direction. Uncle Remus had a board across his lap, and, armed with a mallet and a shoe-knife, was engaged in making shoe-pegs.

"W'iles I wuz crossin' de branch des now," he said, endeavoring to change the subject, "I come up wid a Jacky-my-lantern, en she wuz bu'nin' wuss'n a bunch er lightnin'-bugs, mon. I know'd she wuz a fixin' fer ter lead me inter dat quogmire down in de swamp, en I steer'd cle'r un 'er. Yasser. I did dat. You ain't never seed no Jacky-my-lanterns, is you, honey?"

The little boy never had, but he had heard of them, and he wanted to know what they were, and thereupon Uncle Remus proceeded to tell him.

"One time," said the old darkey, transferring his spectacles from his nose to the top of his head and leaning his elbows upon his peg-board, "dere wuz a blacksmif man, en dish yer blacksmif man, he tuck'n stuck closer by his dram dan he did by his bellus. Monday mawnin' he'd git on a spree, en all

[2] As a Northern friend suggests that this story may be somewhat obscure it may be as well to state that the well is supposed to be supplied with a rope over a wheel, or pulley, with a bucket at each end.—*Author's note.*

[3] This story is popular on the coast and among the rice-plantations, and, since the publication of some of the animal-myths in the newspapers, I have received a version of it from a planter in southwest Georgia; but it seems to me to be an intruder among the genuine myth-stories of the negroes. It is a trifle too elaborate. Nevertheless, it is told upon the plantations with great gusto, and there are several versions in circulation.—*Author's note.*

dat week he'd be on a spree, en de nex' Monday mawnin' he'd take a fresh start. Bimeby, one day, atter de blacksmif bin spreein' 'roun' en cussin' might'ly, he hear a sorter rustlin' fuss at de do', en in walk de Bad Man."

"Who, Uncle Remus?" the little boy asked.

"De Bad Man, honey; de Ole Boy hisse'f right fresh from de ridjun w'at you year Miss Sally readin' 'bout. He done hide his hawns, en his tail, en his hoof, en he come dress up like w'ite fokes. He tuck off his hat en he bow, en den he tell de blacksmif who he is, en dat he done come atter 'im. Den blacksmif, he gun ter cry en beg, en he beg so hard en he cry so loud dat de Bad Man say he make a trade wid 'im. At de een' er one year de sperit er de blacksmif wuz to be his'n en endurin' er dat time de blacksmif mus' put in his hottes' licks in de intruss er de Bad Man, en den he put a spell on de cheer de blacksmif was settin' in, en on his sludge-hammer. De man w'at sot in de cheer couldn't git up less'n de blacksmif let 'im, en de man w'at pick up de sludge 'ud hatter keep on knockin' wid it twel de blacksmif say quit; en den he gun 'im money plenty, en off he put.

"De blacksmif, he sail in fer ter have his fun, en he have so much dat he done clean forgot 'bout his contrack, but bimeby, one day he look down de road, en dar he see de Bad Man comin', en den he know'd de year wuz out. W'en de Bad Man got in de do', de blacksmif wuz poundin' 'way at a hoss-shoe, but he wa'n't so bizzy dat he didn't ax 'im in. De Bad Man sorter do like he ain't got no time fer ter tarry, but de blacksmif say he got some little jobs dat he bleedzd ter finish up, en den he ax de Bad Man fer ter set down a minnit; en de Bad Man, he tuck'n sot down, en he sot in dat cheer w'at he done conju'd en, co'se, dar he wuz. Den de blacksmif, he 'gun ter poke fun at de Bad Man, en he ax him don't he want a dram, en won't he hitch his cheer up little nigher de fier, en de Bad Man, he beg en he beg, but 'twan't doin' no good, kase de blacksmif 'low dat he gwinter keep 'im dar twel he promus dat he let 'im off one year mo', en, sho nuff, de Bad Man promus dat ef de blacksmif let 'im up he give 'im a n'er showin'. So den de blacksmif gun de wud, en de Bad Man sa'nter off down de big road, settin' traps en layin' his progance fer ter ketch mo' sinners.

"De nex' year hit pass same like t'er one. At de 'p'inted time yer come de Ole Boy atter de blacksmif, but still de blacksmif had some jobs dat he bleedzd ter finish up, en he ax de Bad Man fer take holt er de sludge en he'p 'im out; en de Bad Man, he 'low dat r'er'n be disperlite, he don't keer ef he do hit 'er a biff er two; en wid dat he grab up de sludge, en dar he wuz 'gin, kase he done conju'd de sludge so dat whosomedever tuck 'er up can't put 'er down less'n de blacksmif say de wud. Dey perlaver'd dar, dey did, twel bimby de Bad Man he up'n let 'im off n'er year.

"Well, den, dat year pass same ez t'er one. Mont' in en mont' out dat man wuz rollin' in dram, en bimeby yer come de Bad Man. De blacksmif cry en he holler, en he rip 'roun' en t'ar his ha'r, but hit des like he didn't, kase de Bad Man grab 'im up en cram 'im in a bag en tote 'im off. W'iles dey wuz gwine 'long dey come up wid a passel er fokes w'at wuz havin' wunner deze yer fote er July bobbycues, en de Ole Boy, he 'low dat maybe he kin git some mo' game, en w'at do he do but jine in wid um. He jines in en he talk politics same like t'er fokes, twel bimeby dinnertime come 'roun', en dey ax 'im up, w'ich 'greed wid his stummuck, en he pozzit his bag underneed de table 'longside de udder bags w'at de hongry fokes'd brung.

"No sooner did de blacksmif git back on de groun' dan he 'gun ter wuk his way outer de bag. He crope out, he did, en den he tuck'n change de bag. He tuck'n tuck a n'er bag en lay it down whar dish yer bag wuz, en den he crope outer de crowd en lay low in de underbresh.

"Las', w'en de time come fer ter go, de Ole Boy up wid his bag en slung her on his shoulder, en off he put fer de Bad Place. W'en he got dar he tuck'n drap de bag off'n his back en call up de imps, en dey des come a squallin' en a caperin', w'ich I speck dey mus' a bin hongry. Leas'ways dey des swawm'd 'roun', hollerin out:

" 'Daddy, w'at you brung—daddy, w'at you brung?'

"So den dey open de bag, en lo en beholes, out jump a big bulldog, en de way he shuck dem little imps wuz a caution, en he kep' on gnyawin' un um twel de Ole Boy open de gate en tu'n 'im out."

"And what became of the blacksmith?" the little boy asked, as Uncle Remus paused to snuff the candle with his fingers.

"I'm drivin' on 'roun', honey. Atter 'long time, de blacksmif he tuck'n die, en w'en he go ter de Good Place de man at de gate dunner who he is, en he can't squeeze in. Den he go down ter de Bad Place, en knock. De Ole Boy, he look out, he did, en he know'd de blacksmif de minnit he laid eyes on 'im; but he shake his head en say, sezee:

" 'You'll hatter skuze me, Brer Blacksmif, kase I dun had 'speunce 'longer you. You'll hatter go some'rs else ef you wanter raise enny racket,' sezee, en wid dat he shet de do'.

"En dey do say," continued Uncle Remus, with unction, "dat sence dat day de blacksmif bin sorter huv'rin' 'roun' 'twix' de heavens en de ye'th, en dark nights he shine out so fokes call 'im Jacky-my-lantun. Dat's w'at dey tells me. Hit may be wrong er't may be right, but dat's w'at I years."

LAFCADIO HEARN

(1850–1904)

Hearn had the strange life and character associated with genius. He was the son of an Irish officer and a Greek mother, and was born in 1850 on the Ionian island, from which he was named, of Lefcada. Brought as a child to Ireland, he was deserted by both father and mother, carried by his great-aunt into Wales, and taught in Roman Catholic schools in France and England. The loss of one eye at school increased a near-sightedness in the other. He was strange-looking, shy, sensitive, moody, and unpractical. Little is known of his later boyhood except that if he had a home he left it and became a wanderer. He was poor and friendless first in London, then in New York. Soon after coming to America in 1869 he found employment as typesetter and later as reporter in Cincinnati. In 1877 he went on, as a reporter, to New Orleans, where he found the atmosphere congenial, developed his style, and published *Chita,* his first original book. He found material in the Windward Islands for his *Two Years in the French West Indies.* Now recognized as a writer, he went in 1890 with a commission from New York publishers to Japan, where, intending to stay for a few months, he spent the rest of his life. He married a Japanese wife, and grew into the life of her country, finally becoming a subject of Japan and adopting the Buddhist religion. He is credited with best interpreting Japanese life to Western readers in a series of books beginning with his first impressions in *Glimpses of Unfamiliar Japan* (1894) and closing with his study, *Japan, an Attempt at Interpretation,* which appeared in 1904, the year of his death.

Hearn is clearly an international figure, who lived indeed for twenty years in America, but is in no sense an American product. He admired and perhaps followed French writers of prose. Like Poe, his nearest American analogue, he is un-American in his indifference to moral considerations and his devotion to literature as an art. His sense of words and eye for suggestive detail make him a master of description. This side of his work, however, has probably been unduly emphasized, for he is much more than a gifted reporter. Though he thought not discursively but imaginatively his ideas are arresting, and he could not only describe the scenes and manners but penetrate to the inner life and thought of Japan.

From GLIMPSES OF UNFAMILIAR JAPAN [1]

My First Day in the Orient

I

It is with the delicious surprise of the first journey through Japanese streets—unable to make one's kuruma-runner understand anything but gestures, frantic gestures to roll on anywhere, everywhere, since all is un-

---

[1] The extract from *Glimpses of Unfamiliar Japan* is used by permission of, and by arrangement with, Houghton Mifflin Company, the authorized publishers.

speakably pleasurable and new—that one first receives the real sensation of being in the Orient, in this Far East so much read of, so long dreamed of, yet, as the eyes bear witness, heretofore all unknown. There is a romance even in the first full consciousness of this rather commonplace fact; but for me this consciousness is transfigured inexpressibly by the divine beauty of the day. There is some charm unutterable in the morning air, cool with the coolness of Japanese spring and wind-waves from the snowy cone of Fuji; a charm perhaps due rather to the softest lucidity than to any positive tone,— an atmospheric limpidity extraordinary, with only a suggestion of blue in it, through which the most distant objects appear focussed with amazing sharpness. The sun is only pleasantly warm; the jinrikisha, or kuruma, is the most cosy little vehicle imaginable; and the street-vistas, as seen above the dancing white mushroom-shaped hat of my sandalled runner, have an allurement of which I fancy that I could never weary.

Elfish everything seems; for everything as well as everybody is small, and queer, and mysterious: the little houses under their blue roofs, the little shop-fronts hung with blue, and the smiling little people in their blue costumes. The illusion is only broken by the occasional passing of a tall foreigner, and by divers shop-signs bearing announcements in absurd attempts at English. Nevertheless such discords only serve to emphasize reality; they never materially lessen the fascination of the funny little streets.

'Tis at first a delightfully odd confusion only, as you look down one of them, through an interminable flutter of flags and swaying of dark blue drapery, all made beautiful and mysterious with Japanese or Chinese lettering. For there are no immediately discernible laws of construction or decoration: each building seems to have a fantastic prettiness of its own; nothing is exactly like anything else, and all is bewilderingly novel. But gradually, after an hour passed in the quarter, the eye begins to recognize in a vague way some general plan in the construction of these low, light, queerly-gabled wooden houses, mostly unpainted, with their first storeys all open to the street, and thin strips of roofing sloping above each shop-front, like awnings, back to the miniature balconies of paper-screened second storeys. You begin to understand the common plan of the tiny shops, with their matted floors well raised above the street level, and the general perpendicular arrangement of sign-lettering, whether undulating on drapery or glimmering on gilded or lacquered sign-boards. You observe that the same rich dark blue which dominates in popular costume rules also in shop draperies, though there is a sprinkling of other tints,—bright blue and white and red (no greens or yellows). And then you note also that the dresses of the laborers are lettered with the same wonderful lettering as the shop draperies. No arabesques could produce such an effect. As modified for decorative purposes, these ideographs have a speaking symmetry which no design without a meaning could possess. As they appear on the back of a workman's frock—pure white on dark blue—and large enough to be read at a great distance (indicating some guild or company of which the wearer is a member or employee), they give to the poor cheap garment a factitious appearance of splendor.

And finally, while you are still puzzling over the mystery of things, there will come to you like a revelation the knowledge that most of the amazing picturesqueness of these streets is simply due to the profusion of Chinese and Japanese characters in white, black, blue, or gold, decorating everything, —even surfaces of doorposts and paper screens. Perhaps, then, for one moment, you will imagine the effect of English lettering substituted for those magical characters; and the mere idea will give to whatever aesthetic sentiment you may possess a brutal shock, and you will become, as I have become, an enemy of the Romaji-Kwai,—that society founded for the ugly utilitarian purpose of introducing the use of English letters in writing Japanese.

II

An ideograph does not make upon the Japanese brain any impression similar to that created in the Occidental brain by a letter or combination of letters,—dull, inanimate symbols of vocal sounds. To the Japanese brain an ideograph is a vivid picture: it lives; it speaks; it gesticulates. And the whole space of a Japanese street is full of such living characters,—figures that cry out to the eyes, words that smile or grimace like faces.

What such lettering is, compared with our own lifeless types, can be understood only by those who have lived in the farther East. For even the printed characters of the Japanese or Chinese imported texts give no suggestion of the possible beauty of the same characters as modified for decorative inscriptions, for sculptural use, or for the commonest advertising purposes. No rigid convention fetters the fancy of the calligrapher or designer: each strives to make his characters more beautiful than any others; and generations upon generations of artists have been toiling from time immemorial with like emulation, so that through centuries and centuries of tireless effort and study, the primitive hieroglyph or ideograph has been evolved into a thing of beauty indescribable. It consists only of a certain number of brush-strokes; but in each stroke there is an undiscoverable secret art of grace, proportion, imperceptible curve, which actually makes it seem alive, and bears witness that even during the lightning-moment of its creation the artist felt with his brush for the ideal shape of the stroke *equally along its entire length,* from head to tail. But the art of the strokes is not all; the art of their combination is that which produces the enchantment, often so as to astonish the Japanese themselves. It is not surprising, indeed, considering the strangely personal, animate, esoteric aspect of Japanese lettering, that there should be wonderful legends of calligraphy, relating how words written by holy experts became incarnate, and descended from their tablets to hold converse with mankind.

My kurumaya calls himself "Cha." He has a white hat which looks like the top of an enormous mushroom; a short blue wide-sleeved jacket; blue drawers, close-fitting as "tights," and reaching to his ankles; and light straw sandals bound upon his bare feet with cords of palmetto-fibre. Doubtless he typifies all the patience, endurance, and insidious coaxing powers of his class. He has already manifested his power to make me give him more than the law allows; and I have been warned against him in vain. For the first sensation of having a human being for a horse, trotting between shafts, unwearyingly bobbing up and down before you for hours, is alone enough to evoke a feeling of compassion. And when this human being, thus trotting between shafts, with all his hopes, memories, sentiments, and comprehensions, happens to have the gentlest smile, and the power to return the least favor by an apparent display of infinite gratitude, this compassion becomes sympathy, and provokes unreasoning impulses to self-sacrifice. I think the sight of the profuse perspiration has also something to do with the feeling, for it makes one think of the cost of heart-beats and muscle-contractions, likewise of chills, congestions, and pleurisy. Cha's clothing is drenched; and he mops his face with a small sky-blue towel, with figures of bamboo-sprays and sparrows in white upon it, which towel he carries wrapped about his wrist as he runs.

That, however, which attracts me in Cha—Cha considered not as a motive power at all, but as a personality—I am rapidly learning to discern in the multitudes of faces turned toward us as we roll through these miniature streets. And perhaps the supremely pleasurable impression of this morning is that produced by the singular gentleness of popular scrutiny. Everybody looks at you curiously; but there is never anything disagreeable, much less hostile in the gaze: most commonly it is accompanied by a smile or half smile. And the ultimate consequence of all these kindly curious looks and smiles is that the stranger finds himself thinking of fairy-land. Hackneyed to the degree of provocation this statement no doubt is: everybody describing the sensations of his first Japanese day talks of the land as fairy-land, and of its people as fairy-folk. Yet there is a natural reason for this unanimity in choice of terms to describe what is almost impossible to describe more accurately at the first essay. To find oneself suddenly in a world where everything is upon a smaller and daintier scale than with us,—a world of lesser and seemingly kindlier beings, all smiling at you as if to wish you well,—a world where all movement is slow and soft, and voices are hushed,—a world where land, life, and sky are unlike all that one has known elsewhere, —this is surely the realization, for imaginations nourished with English folk lore, of the old dream of a World of Elves.

IV

The traveller who enters suddenly into a period of social change—especially a change from a feudal past to a democratic present—is likely to regret the decay of things beautiful and the ugliness of things new. What of both I may yet discover in Japan I know not; but to-day, in these exotic streets, the old and the new mingle so well that one seems to set off the other. The line of tiny white telegraph poles carrying the world's news to papers printed in a mixture of Chinese and Japanese characters; an electric bell in some tea-house with an Oriental riddle of text pasted beside the ivory button; a shop of American sewing-machines next to the shop of a maker of Buddhist images; the establishment of a photograher beside the establishment of a manufacturer of straw sandals: all these present no striking incongruities, for each sample of Occidental innovation is set into an Oriental frame that seems adaptable to any picture. But on the first day, at least, the Old alone is new for the stranger, and suffices to absorb his attention. It then appears to him that everything Japanese is delicate, exquisite, admirable,—even a pair of common wooden chopsticks in a paper bag with a little drawing upon it; even a package of toothpicks of cherry-wood, bound in a paper wonderfully lettered in three different colors; even the little sky-blue towel, with designs of flying sparrows upon it, which the jinrikisha man uses to wipe his face. The bank bills, the commonest copper coins, are things of beauty. Even the piece of pleated colored string used by the shopkeeper in tying up your last purchase is a pretty curiosity. Curiosities and dainty objects bewilder you by their very multitude: on either side of you, wherever you turn your eyes, are countless wonderful things as yet incomprehensible.

But it is perilous to look at them. Every time you dare to look, something obliges you to buy it,—unless, as may often happen, the smiling vendor invites your inspection of so many varieties of one article, each specially and all unspeakably desirable, that you flee away out of mere terror at your own impulses. The shopkeeper never asks you to buy; but his wares are enchanted, and if you once begin buying you are lost. Cheapness means only a temptation to commit bankruptcy; for the resources of irresistible artistic cheapness are inexhaustible. The largest steamer that crosses the Pacific could not contain what you wish to purchase. For, although you may not, perhaps, confess the fact to yourself, what you really want to buy is not the contents of a shop; you want the shop and the shopkeeper, and streets of shops with their draperies and their habitants, the whole city and the bay and the mountains begirdling it, and Fujiyama's white witchery overhanging it in the speckless sky, all Japan, in very truth, with its magical trees and luminous atmosphere, with all its cities and towns and temples, and forty millions of the most lovable people in the universe.

Now there comes to my mind something I once heard said by a practical American on hearing of a great fire in Japan: "Oh! those people can afford fires; their houses are so cheaply built." It is true that the frail wooden houses of the common people can be cheaply and quickly replaced; but that which was within them to make them beautiful cannot,—and every fire is an art tragedy. For this is the land of infinite hand-made variety; machinery has not yet been able to introduce sameness and utilitarian ugliness in cheap production (except in response to foreign demand for bad taste to suit vulgar markets), and each object made by the artist or artisan differs still from all others, even of his own making. And each time something beautiful perishes by fire, it is a something representing an individual idea.

Happily the art impulse itself, in this country of conflagrations, has a vitality which survives each generation of artists, and defies the flame that changes their labor to ashes or melts it to shapelessness. The idea whose symbol has perished will reappear again in other creations,—perhaps after the passing of a century,—modified, indeed, yet recognizably of kin to the thought of the past. And every artist is a ghostly worker. Not by years of groping and sacrifice does he find his highest expression; the sacrificial past is within him; his art is an inheritance; his fingers are guided by the dead in the delineation of a flying bird, of the vapors of mountains, of the colors of the morning and the evening, of the shape of branches and the spring burst of flowers: generations of skilled workmen have given him their cunning, and revive in the wonder of his drawing. What was conscious effort in the beginning became unconscious in later centuries,—becomes almost automatic in the living man,—becomes the art instinctive. Wherefore, one colored print by a Hokusai or Hiroshige, originally sold for less than a cent, may have more real art in it than many a Western painting valued at more than the worth of a whole Japanese street.

v

Here are Hokusai's own figures walking about in straw raincoats, and immense mushroom-shaped hats of straw, and straw sandals,—bare-limbed peasants, deeply tanned by wind and sun; and patient-faced mothers with smiling bald babies on their backs, toddling by upon their geta (high, noisy, wooden clogs), and robed merchants squatting and smoking their little brass pipes among the countless riddles of their shops.

Then I notice how small and shapely the feet of the people are,—whether bare brown feet of peasants, or beautiful feet of children wearing tiny, tiny geta, or the feet of young girls in snowy tabi. The tabi, the white digitated stocking, gives to a small light foot a mythological aspect,—the white cleft grace of a fauness. Clad or bare, the Japanese foot has the antique symmetry: it has not yet been distorted by the infamous foot-gear which has deformed the feet of Occidentals.

. . . Of every pair of Japanese wooden clogs, one makes in walking a slightly different sound from the other, as *kring* to *krang;* so that the echo of the walker's steps has an alternate rhythm of tones. On a pavement, such as that of a railway station, the sound obtains immense sonority; and the crowd will sometimes intentionally fall into step, with the drollest conceivable effect of drawling wooden noise.

VI

"Tera e yuke!"

I have been obliged to return to the European hotel,—not because of the noon-meal, as I really begrudge myself the time necessary to eat it, but because I cannot make Cha understand that I want to visit a Buddhist temple. Now Cha understands; my landlord has uttered the mystical words,—

"Tera e yuke!"

A few minutes of running along broad thoroughfares lined with gardens and costly ugly European buildings; then passing the bridge of a canal stocked with unpainted sharp-prowed craft of extraordinary construction, we again plunge into narrow, low, bright, pretty streets,—into another part of the Japanese city. And Cha runs at the top of his speed between more rows of little ark-shaped houses, narrower above than below; between other unfamiliar lines of little open shops. And always over the shops little strips of blue-tiled roof slope back to the paper-screened chamber of upper floors; and from all the façades hang draperies dark-blue, or white, or crimson,—footbreadths of texture covered with beautiful Japanese lettering, white on blue, red on black, black on white. But all this flies by swiftly as a dream. Once more we cross a canal; we rush up a narrow street rising to meet a hill; and Cha, halting suddenly before an immense flight of broad stone steps, sets the shafts of his vehicle on the ground that I may dismount, and, pointing to the steps, exclaims,—

"Tera!"

I dismount, and ascend them, and, reaching a broad terrace, find myself face to face with a wonderful gate, topped by a tilted, peaked, many-cornered Chinese roof. It is all strangely carven, this gate. Dragons are intertwined in a frieze above its open doors; and the panels of the doors themselves are similarly sculptured; and there are gargoyles—grotesque lion heads—protruding from the eaves. And the whole is gray, stone-colored; to me, nevertheless, the carvings do not seem to have the fixity of sculpture; all the snakeries and dragonries appear to undulate with a swarming motion, elusively, in eddyings as of water.

I turn a moment to look back through the glorious light. Sea and sky mingle in the same beautiful pale clear blue. Below me the billowing of bluish roofs reaches to the verge of the unruffled bay on the right, and to the feet of the green wooded hills flanking the city on two sides. Beyond that semicircle of green hills rises a lofty range of serrated mountains, indigo silhouettes. And enormously high above the line of them towers an apparition indescribably lovely,—one solitary snowy cone, so filmily exquisite, so spiritually white, that but for its immemorially familiar outline, one would surely deem it a shape of cloud. Invisible its base remains, being the same delicious tint as the sky: only above the eternal snow-line its dreamy cone appears, seeming to hang, the ghost of a peak, between the luminous land and the luminous heaven,—the sacred and matchless mountain, Fujiyama.

And suddenly, a singular sensation comes upon me as I stand before this weirdly sculptured portal,—a sensation of dream and doubt. It seems to me that the steps, and the dragon-swarming gate, and the blue sky arching over the roofs of the town, and the ghostly beauty of Fuji, and the shadow of myself there stretching upon the gray masonry, must all vanish presently. Why such a feeling? Doubtless because the forms before me—the curved roofs, the coiling dragons, the Chinese grotesqueries of carving—do not really appear to me as things new, but as things dreamed: the sight of them must have stirred to life forgotten memories of picture-books. A moment, and the delusion vanishes; the romance of reality returns, with freshened consciousness of all that which is truly and deliciously new; the magical transparencies of distance, the wondrous delicacy of the tones of the living picture, the enormous height of the summer blue, and the white soft witchery of the Japanese sun.

VII

I pass on and climb more steps to a second gate with similar gargoyles and swarming of dragons, and enter a court where graceful votive lanterns of stone stand like monuments. On my right and left two great grotesque stone lions are sitting,—the lions of Buddha, male and female. Beyond is a long, low, light building, with curved and gabled roof of blue tiles, and three wooden steps before its entrance. Its sides are simple wooden screens covered with thin white paper. This is the temple.

On the steps I take off my shoes; a young man slides aside the screens closing the entrance, and bows me a gracious welcome. And I go in, feeling under my feet a softness of matting thick as bedding. An immense square apartment is before me, full of an unfamiliar sweet smell—the scent of Japanese incense; but after the full blaze of the sun, the paper-filtered light here is dim as moonshine; for a minute or two I can see nothing but gleams of gilding in a soft gloom. Then, my eyes becoming accustomed to the obscurity, I perceive against the paper-paned screens surrounding the sanctuary on three sides shapes of enormous flowers cutting like silhouettes against the vague white light. I approach and find them to be paper flowers,—symbolic lotus-blossoms beautifully colored, with curling leaves gilded on the upper surface and bright green beneath. At the dark end of the apartment, facing the entrance, is the altar of Buddha, a rich and lofty altar, covered with bronzes and gilded utensils clustered to right and left of the shrine like a tiny gold temple. But I see no statue; only a mystery of unfamiliar shapes of burnished metal, relieved against darkness, a darkness behind the shrine and altar—whether recess or inner sanctuary I cannot distinguish. . . .

FIRST IMPRESSIONS [2]

I

I WONDER why the emblematical significance of the Composite Photograph has been so little considered by the philosophers of evolution. In the blending and coalescing of the shadows that make it, is there no suggestion of that bioplasmic chemistry which, out of the intermingling of innumerable lives, crystallizes the composite of personality? Has the superimposition of images upon the sensitized plate no likeness to those endless superimpositions of heredity out of which every individuality must shape itself? . . . Surely it is a very weird thing, this Composite Photograph,—and hints of things weirder.

Every human face is a living composite of countless faces,—generations and generations of faces superimposed upon the sensitive film of Life for the great cosmic developing process. And any living face, well watched by love or by hate, will reveal the fact. The face of friend or sweetheart has a hundred different aspects; and you know that you want, when his or her "likeness" is taken, to insist upon the reflection of the dearest of these. The face of your enemy,—and no matter what antipathy it may excite,—is not invariably hateful in itself: you must acknowledge, to yourself at least, having observed in it moments of an expression the reverse of unworthy.

Probably the ancestral types that try to reproduce themselves in the modulations of facial expression, are nearly always the more recent;—the very ancient having become metamorphosed, under weight of superimposition, into a blank underlying vagueness,—a mere protoplasmic background out of which, except in rare and monstrous cases, no outline can detach itself. But in every normal face whole generations of types do certainly, by turns of mood,

[2] From *Exotics and Retrospectives*, 1898. Copyright by Little, Brown & Company.

make flitting apparition. Any mother knows this. Studying day by day the features of her child, she finds in them variations not to be explained by simple growth. Sometimes there is a likeness to one parent or grandparent; sometimes a likeness to another, or to remoter kindred; and at rarer intervals may appear peculiarities of expression that no member of the family can account for. (Thus, in darker centuries, the ghastly superstition of the "changeling," was not only possible, but in a certain sense quite natural.) Through youth and manhood and far into old age these mutations continue,—though always more slowly and faintly,—even while the general characteristics steadily accentuate; and death itself may bring into the countenance some strange expression never noticed during life.

II

As a rule we recognize faces by the modes of expression habitually worn,—by the usually prevalent character-tones of them,—rather than by any steady memory of lines. But no face at all moments remains exactly the same; and in cases of exceptional variability the expression does not suffice for recognition: we have to look for some fixed peculiarity, some minute superficial detail independent of physiognomy. All expression has but a relative permanency: even in faces the most strongly marked, its variations may defy estimate. Perhaps the mobility is, within certain limits, in direct ratio to irregularity of feature;—any approach to ideal beauty being also an approach to relative fixity. At all events, the more familiar we become with any common face, the more astonishing the multitude of the transformations we observe in it,—the more indescribable and bewildering its fugitive subtleties of expression. And what are these but the ebb and flow of life ancestral,—under-ripplings in that well-spring unfathomable of personality whose flood is Soul? Perpetually beneath the fluid tissues of flesh the dead are moulding and moving —not singly (for in no phenomenon is there any singleness), but in currents and by surgings. Sometimes there is an eddying of ghosts of love; and the face dawns as if a sunrise lighted it. Sometimes there is a billowing up of ghosts of hate; and the face darkens and distorts like an evil dream,—and we say to the mind behind it, "You are not now *your better self*." But that which we call the self, whether the better or the worse, is a complexity forever shifting the order of its combinations. According to stimulus of hope or fear, of joy or pain, there must vibrate within every being, at differing rhythms, with varying oscillation, incalculable tremulosities of ancestral life. In the calmest normal existence slumber all the psychical tones of the past,—from the lurid red of primal sense-impulse to the violet of spiritual aspiration,—even as all known colors sleep in white light. And over the sensitive living mask, at each strong alteration of the psychical currents, flit shadowy resurrections of dead expression.

Seeing faces and their changes, we learn intuitively the relation to our own selves of the selves that confront us. In very few cases could we even try to explain how this knowledge comes,—how we reach those conclusions called, in common parlance, "first impressions." Faces are not *read*. The impressions they give are only *felt,* and have much of the same vague character as impressions of sound,—making within us mental states either pleasant or unpleasant or somewhat of both,—evoking now a sense of danger, now a melting sympathy, occasionally a gentle sadness. And these impressions, though seldom at fault, cannot be very well explained in words. The reasons of their accuracy are likewise the reasons of their mystery,—reasons not to be discovered in the narrow range of our personal experience,—reasons very, very much older than we. Could we remember our former lives, we should know more exactly the meaning of our likes and our dislikes. For the truth is that they are superindividual. It is not the individual eye that perceives everything perceived in a face. The dead are the real seers. But as they remain unable to guide us otherwise than by touching the chords of mental pleasure or pain, we can feel the relative meaning of faces only in a dim, though powerful way.

Instinctively, at least, superindividuality is commonly recognized. Hence such phrases as "force of character," "moral force," "personal fascination," "personal magnetism," and others showing that the influence exerted by man upon man is known to be independent of mere physical conditions. Very insignificant bodies have that within them by which formidable bodies are mastered and directed. The flesh-and-blood man is only the visible end of an invisible column of force reaching out of the infinite past into the momentary present,—only the material Symbol of an immaterial host. The contest between even two wills is a contest of phantom armies. The domination of many personalities by the simple will of one,—hinting the perception by the compelled of superior viewless powers behind the compeller,—is never to be interpreted by the old hypothesis of soul-equality. Only by scientific psychology can the mystery of certain formidable characters be even partly explained; but any explanation must rest upon the acceptance, in some form or other, of the immense evolutional fact of psychical inheritance. And psychical inheritance signifies the super-individual,—pre-existence revived in compound personality.

Yet, from our ethical standpoint, that super-individuality which we thus unconsciously allow in the very language used to express psychical domination, is a lower manifestation. Though working often for good, the power in itself is of evil; and the recognition of it by the subjugated is not a recognition of higher moral energy, but of a higher *mental* energy signifying larger evolutional experience of wrong, deeper reserves of aggressive ingenuity, heavier capacities for the giving of pain. Called by no matter what euphemistic name, such power is brutal in its origin, and still allied to those malignities and ferocities shared by man with lower predatory creatures. But the beauty of the super-individual is revealed in that rarer power which the dead lend the living to win trust, to inspire ideals, to create love, to brighten whole circles of existence with the charm and wonder of a personality never to be described save in the language of light and music.

III

Now if we could photographically *decompose* a composite photograph so as to separate in order inverse all the impressions interblended to make it, such process would clumsily represent what really happens when the image of a strange face is telegraphed back—like a police-photograph—from the living retina to the mysterious offices of inherited memory. There, with the quickness of an electric flash, the shadow-face is decomposed into all the ancestral types combined in it; and the resulting verdict of the dead, though rendered only by indefinable sensation, is more trustworthy than any written certificate of character could ever be. But its trustworthiness is limited to the *potential* relation of the individual seen to the individual seeing. Upon different minds, according to the delicate balance of personality,—according to the qualitative sum of inherited experience in the psychical composition of the observer,—the same features will make very different impressions. A face that strongly repels one person may not less strongly attract another, and will produce nearly similar impressions only on groups of emotionally homogeneous natures. Certainly the fact of this ability to discern in the composition of faces that indefinable something which welcomes or which warns, does suggest the possibility of deciding some laws of ethical physiognomy; but such laws would necessarily be of a very general and simple kind, and their relative value could never equal that of the uneducated personal intuition.

How, indeed, should it be otherwise? What science could ever hope to measure the infinite possibilities of psychical combination? And the present in every countenance is a recombination of the past;—the living is always a resurrection of the dead. The sympathies and the fears, the hopes and the repulsions that faces inspire, are but revivals and reiterations,—echoes of sentiency created in millions of minds by immeasurable experience operating through immeasurable time. My friend of this hour, though no more identical with his forefathers than any single ripple of a current is identical with all the ripples that ever preceded it, is nevertheless by soul-composition one with myriads known and loved in other lands and in other lives,—in times recorded and in times forgotten,—in cities that still remain and in cities that have ceased to be,—by thousands of my vanished selves.

PAUL ELMER MORE

(1864-   )

Paul Elmer More was born in 1864, in St. Louis. He graduated at Washington University in 1887, and received the Master's degree there in 1892 and at Harvard the following year. He taught Sanskrit at Harvard one year, and Sanskrit and Greek at Bryn Mawr for two years, after which he retired to a hermitage near Shelburne, New Hampshire, where he spent two years in study and meditation, trying to find order and harmony in the seemingly chaotic universe around him, and to come upon the meaning of life. According to his own statement, he returned to civilization as ignorant upon these points as when he left it, but having arrived at a decision to become a literary critic. He became literary editor, first, of *The Independent,* and later of the New York *Evening Post,* and then editor of *The Nation;* but in 1914 he resigned the latter position, and went to live at Princeton, New Jersey, where he has continued to write, and to give each year a course of lectures at Princeton University.

Mr. More's first volumes were of poetry, but after the Shelburne days he abandoned this form. In 1904 appeared his first book of criticism, *Shelburne Essays, First Series,* and he has extended this work to eleven volumes, embodying in them his mature ideas on literature and life. His chief work in recent years, however, has been the preparation of a series of volumes under the title *The Greek Tradition,* in which he seeks to explain and interpret the ideas of Plato as the basis for a present-day philosophy. The balance and moderation of his estimates and the force and clarity of his style give high value to his criticism.

THE ORIGINS OF HAWTHORNE AND POE [1]

WE are credibly told that in years not so very long past young women and even grave men used to read the Gothic tales of Ann Radcliffe with tense brows and trembling lips; and the essays of Carlyle still stand a voluble witness to prove how seriously the grotesque marvels of German romance were once accepted in England. Mrs. Radcliffe is no doubt read occasionally to-day, and the indefatigable Mr. Lang has even attempted to reinstate her in popular favor. But her most generous admirer could hardly aver that she was anything more to him than a curious amusement; the horror of her tales has vanished away like the moonlight she was so fond of describing. And as for Tieck and Wackenroder and all that dim romantic crew of Teuton *Sturm* and *Drang*—not even an Andrew Lang has arisen for them.

[1] From *Shelburne Essays, First Series* (1904)—a review of *Nathaniel Hawthorne,* by George E. Woodberry, in the American Men of Letters Series.

This essay is used by permission of, and arrangement with, Houghton Mifflin Company, the authorized publishers.

It is a matter for reflection, therefore, that in this country a new life of Hawthorne should be something of a literary event and that there should be a sufficient public to warrant the issue of two new and elaborate editions of Poe; for at first thought it might seem that both Hawthorne and Poe fall in the same class with those forgotten weavers of moonlight and mysticism. What is it, indeed, that gives vitality to their work and separates it from the ephemeral product of English and German Gothicism? More than that: Why is it that the only two writers of America who have won almost universal renown as artists are these romancers, each of whom is, after his own manner, a sovereign in that strange region of emotion which we name the weird? Other work they have done, and done well, but when we call to mind their distinguishing productions we think first of such scenes as *The Fall of the House of Usher, The Raven,* and *The Sleeper,* or of such characters as Arthur Dimmesdale with his morbid remorse and unearthly sufferings, the dreamlike existence of Clifford, the hideous unexplained mystery of Miriam's wrong, and the awful search of Ethan Brand—scenes and characters which belong to the real world, for they appeal to a sympathetic chord in our own breasts, but which are yet quite overlaid with some insistent shadow of the fantastic realm of symbolism.

Hawthorne ascribes the superiority of Nature's work over man's to the fact "that the former works from the innermost germ, while the latter works merely superficially," and the same explanation may be given of the genuineness of his own work and Poe's in comparison with the unreality of Mrs. Radcliffe or Tieck; the weird, unearthly substance moulded by their genius is from the innermost core of the national consciousness. Their achievement is not like the Gothic novel introduced into England by Horace Walpole, a mere dilettante; there is in them very little of that recrudescence of mediæval superstition and gloom which marked the rise of romanticism in Europe, little or nothing of the knights and ladies, turrets and dungeons and all that tawdry paraphernalia, and, fortunately for their reputation, no taint of that peculiar form of sentimentalism which pervades the German *Herzensergiessungen* like the odor of Schiller's decaying apples. Their work is the last efflorescence of a tradition handed down to them unbroken from the earliest Colonial days, and that tradition was the voice of a stern and indomitable moral character. The unearthly visions of Poe and Hawthorne are in no wise the result of literary whim or of unbridled individualism, but are deep-rooted in American history. Neither Professor Woodberry in his Life of Hawthorne nor Professor Harrison in his Life of Poe has, it seems to me, brought out with due emphasis these spiritual origins of a school of romance which is so unique in its way as to have made for itself a sure place in the literature of the world.

The name of Hawthorne carries us back at once to those grim days of his ancestor in Salem Village when for a season almost the whole community gave itself up to the frenzy of witch hunting. In the earlier days the superstitions of England were concerned chiefly with the fairy folk of hearth and field, a quaint people commonly, and kindly disposed, if mischievous. But with the advent of Puritanism came a change; the fair and frolicsome play of the fancy was discredited and the starved imagination had its revenge. In place of the elves and goblins of a freer age, instead of "Robin Goodfellow, the spoorn, the man-in-the-oak, the hellwain, the firedrake, the puckle" and all that antic crew, the imagination now evoked the terrific spectre of the Devil and attributed to his personal agency all the mishaps of life. Hence it is that witchcraft became so much more prominent with the Reformation and reached its height where Puritan feelings prevailed. On the one hand it was employed by the Roman Church as an aid in its exterminating fight with the Waldenses and other heretics—the good monks no doubt being easily persuaded, where persuasion was necessary, that the ascetic revolt against the office of the imagination in worship was of diabolic origin—and, on the other hand, the Protestants, and particularly the Puritans with their morbid horror of sin, were quick to accredit to the author of sin every phenomenon they could not understand. Witchcraft, to be sure, is as old as history, and we need go no further abroad than the classic poets for tales of the most abominable night hags. But there is this difference between such monsters as Lucan's Erichtho and the abortions of Christian demonology: Erichtho may haunt the sepulchres and breathe into the cold mouths of the dead the dark secret she would transmit to the Shades, but in the end she is only a product of the imagination brooding on things unclean and hideous; there is in the dread and repugnance she inspires no such added horror as that which the Christian felt at the thought of a soul leagued for infamous ends with the Prince of Hell and doomed as a rebel against God to everlasting tortures.

Considering the history of the Puritan emigrants we shall not be surprised to find these superstitions breaking out with peculiar virulence in the New World. Persecution and insult at home had not tended to soften their temper, nor did flight across a waste of perilous waters to a wilderness where everything was strange and unexplored bring light and cheerfulness to their imagination. In England at least their morbid intensity was to some extent modified by contact with the worldly life about them; in their new home they were completely given up to the working out of their stern purposes. Terrors and difficulties only added fuel to their zeal. "Our faithers were Englishmen which came over this great ocean and were ready to perish in this wilderness," says old Governor Bradford; and "with what difficulties [they] wrastled in going through these things," we may read in all our schoolbooks. It is easy to see how these hardships and these bitterly-won victories increased the sternness and unyieldingness of the New England Puritans, but perhaps we do not often consider the influence exerted on their imaginations by the wild country and wilder "salvages," as they called the red men, that now engaged their attention. They no longer beheld about them the pleasant vales and green hills of Old England, which the long habitation of man had rendered almost human, but the vast and pathless forests of the wilderness, where nature appeared under a new and forbidding aspect. There is at the best something weird and uncanny about the great woods into whose depths the eye cannot penetrate and from whose interwoven shadows, especially when night has fallen and the ear has grown painfully alert, come forth at intervals sounds that seem to indicate the activity of some nameless secret life within the darkness. What then must have been the feelings of the New England farmer as perchance he made his way homeward at sundown along the border of the gloomy forest? The kindly fancy of his ancestors who peopled the woods with mischievous goblins had yielded to his belief in the extended powers of evil. In these deep shadows he knew not but the very enemy of God might be lurking to lure him to destruction. It was no pleasant *waldeinsamkeit* he felt, such as romantic poets love to indulge, but awe and ghostly terror.

And this feeling was exaggerated by the actual savages who inhabited the woods. The settlers were for the most part thoroughly convinced that these poor, brutal denizens of the wilderness were under the special tutelage of Satan. In times of distress the colonists were ready to charge all their calamities to the machinations of an infernal conspiracy.

It was afterward by *them* [the Indians] confessed, [says Cotton Mather in his *Magnalia*], that upon the arrival of the *English* in these parts, the *Indians* employed their *sorcerers*, whom they called *powaws*, like *Balaam*, to curse them, and let loose their *demons* upon them, to shipwreck them, to distract them, to poison them, or any way to ruin them. All the noted *powaws* in the country spent three days together in diabolical *conjurations*, to obtain the assistance of the *devils* against the settlement of these our *English*.

It is not strange, therefore, that when the delusion of withcraft fell upon these people it should have assumed a peculiarly tragic aspect. They were dwelling in the midst of hostile demonic powers, and, feeling themselves attacked, they turned upon the enemy with all the strength and intensity of their souls. And how real and material the phenomena appeared to the bewildered onlookers may be gathered from this sulfurous account written by an eyewitness of the sufferings of one of the victims:

Margaret Rule would sometimes have her jaws forcibly pulled open, whereupon something invisible would be poured down her throat: we all saw her swallow, and yet we saw her try all she could, by spitting, coughing, and shrieking, that she might not swallow; but one time the standers-by plainly saw something of that odd liquor itself on the outside of her neck; she cried out of it, as if scalding brimstone were poured into her, and the whole house would immediately scent so hot of brimstone that we were scarce able to endure it.

Under the stress of this morbid excitement the good people of Salem and the neighborhood were thrown into a frenzy of fear; crops were abandoned, business stood still, and the only matters considered were the horrible persecutions of Satan in their midst. The general feeling of alarm was aggravated to something like desperation when the Rev. Deodat Lawson in the meeting-house of Salem village preached an inflammatory sermon in which he charged the outburst of the infernal powers directly to the sins of the people.

You are therefore to be deeply humbled, [he said,] and sit in the dust, considering the signal hand of God in singling out this place, this poor village, for the first seat of Satan's tyranny, and to make it (as 't were) the rendezvous of devils, where they muster their infernal forces; appearing to the afflicted as coming armed to carry on their malicious designs against the bodies, and, if God in mercy prevent not, against the souls of many in this place.

No wonder that the people did actually believe "that the devils were walking about our streets with lengthened chains, making a dreadful noise in our ears; and brimstone (even without a metaphor) was making a horrid and a hellish stench in our nostrils."

To stop these terrible inroads of Satan a special court was created, before which those previously examined were tried. Those found guilty were hanged on a conspicuous eminence which thus acquired the ominous title of witch-hill; and how awful was the spectacle there presented to the panic-stricken people may be gathered from the pious ejaculation of the Reverend Mr. Noyes, "What a sad thing it is to see eight firebrands of hell hanging there!" The cruelty engendered by this feeling of insecurity is well indicated by the treatment of Giles Corey, who, refusing to plead either guilty or not guilty, was subjected to the *peine dure et forte,* as the tale is related in Longfellow's *New England Tragedy;* but Longfellow does not relate what we are told in a ballad of the period, that when from the oppression of the stone on his chest Corey's tongue protruded it was rudely thrust back by the staff of a bystander.

In due time this "hellish molestation," as one of the persecuted called it, came to a sudden end; but not before twenty victims had suffered death, many had died in jail, hundreds had endured imprisonment in its worst forms, whole families had been impoverished, and a moral impression had been made upon the community which nothing could efface. The modern historian of the delusion tells us that a sort of curse still rests on the immediate scene of these tragic events and that neglect and desertion still brood on the accursed spot.

Were we to go no further than this episode of Salem history we should find it easy to explain by inheritance that mystic brooding over the dark and intricate effects of sin which the descendant of old John Hathorne has made the substance of his romance, or to account for the realism that underlies the wild fantasies of Poe. And we need only to dip into Cotton Mather's voluminous record of the dealings of Providence in America to see how intensely the mind of the Puritans was occupied with unearthly matters and what a legacy of emotions approaching the weird was left by them to posterity. When the faith of these militant saints was untroubled it often assumed a sweetness and fullness of spiritual content that might even pass into rapturous delight. But always this intoxicating joy bordered on the region of awe—the awe of a soul in the presence of the great and ineffable mysteries of holiness; and the life of Thomas Shepard, which Mather calls *"a trembling walk with God,"* may not unfitly be taken to illustrate the peculiar temper of their religion. And if in the wisest and sanest of the Puritan Fathers this trembling solicitude was never far away, there were others in whom the fear of the Lord became a mania of terror. Consider what the impression on the minds of children must have been when in the midst of their innocent sport the awful apparition of the Rev. James Noyes stood before them and rebuked them into silence with these solemn words: "Cousins, I wonder you can be so merry, unless you are sure of your salvation!" Consider the spiritual state of a young man, celebrated for his godliness, who could note down in his diary with curious precision: "I was almost in the *suburbs of hell* all day."

Literature, in the true sense of the word, could not well flourish among a people who saw in the plastic imagination a mere seduction of the senses, and whose intellectual life was thus absorbed in theological speculation. To be sure, a good deal of verse was written and even printed in early Colonial days; but of all the poets of that age only one attained any real celebrity and has in a way lived on into the present. Michael Wigglesworth, the faithful pastor of Malden, where in the odor of sanctity he died in 1705, is described as "a little feeble *shadow* of a *man"*; but his diminutive frame harbored a mighty spirit. His poems breathed the very quintessence of Puritan faith, and as such obtained immediate and extraordinary popularity. Professor Tyler calculates that in the first year of publication his *Day of Doom* was purchased by at least one in every thirty-five persons of New England; printed as a common ballad it was hawked everywhere about the country, and its lugubrious stanzas were even taught to children along with the catechism. As late as the year 1828 an essayist declared that many an aged person of his acquaintance could still repeat the poem, though they might not have seen a copy of it since they were in leading strings; and in his own time Cotton Mather had thought it might "perhaps find our children till the day itself arrives"—which Gold forbid.

The strength of Master Wigglesworth's genius, in this picture of the *Day of Doom,* is, as we should expect, devoted to those who

> void of tears, but fill'd with fears, and dreadful expectation
> Of endless pains and scalding flames, stand waiting for Damnation.

One after another the various kinds of sinners are arraigned at the bar and receive their due reward. Most hideous and most famous of all are the stanzas that describe the pleading and condemnation of unbaptized infants. As an expression of the grotesque in literature they are not without a kind of crude power; as the voice of a real and tremendously earnest faith they elude the grasp of a modern mind, one can only shudder and avert his eyes. We contrast with some curiosity and no little bewilderment the unflinching frankness of this earlier Calvinist with the shifting creed of a recent Calvanistic convention which has attempted to explain away the catechism's abandonment of non-elect infants. Yet Wigglesworth, like the Presbyterians of to-day, had his moment of compunction for the poor souls who

> from the womb unto the tomb
>   Were straightway carriëd;—

he at least allowed to them "the easiest room in hell!" Those simple words have of recent years acquired a certain notoriety through literary handbooks; indeed, for naked and appalling realism of horror, when all is considered, it would not be easy to find a verse to surpass them.

Wigglesworth's rhymes were, as I said, the intellectual food of the young, and some such strong meat would seem necessary to prepare them for the sermons that nourished their manhood. And at least one of these sermons, Jonathan Edwards's famous Enfield discourse of *Sinners in the Hands of an Angry God,* has gained the unenviable reputation of being perhaps the most tremendous and uncompromising enunciation ever made of the gloomier side of Calvinism. His picture of worldly men hanging over the pit of hell "by a slender thread, with the flames of divine wrath flashing about it, and ready every moment to singe it and burn it asunder," has become classical in its own way.

After the death of Edwards, in 1758, the heart of the country became more and more absorbed in the impending conflict of the Revolution. For a while, at least, religion and the terrors of damnation must give place to the more imminent peril of political subjugation. In New England that other phase of Puritanism, the spirit that had led Cromwell and his Ironsides to victory, and had established the liberties of the English constitution, came to the foreground, and for a time the political pamphlet usurped the place of the sermon. But even then literature did not entirely vanish; and at intervals through the rasping cries of revolution one may catch a note of that pensiveness or gloom, that habitual dwelling on the supernatural significance of life, which had come to be the dominant intellectual tone of the country. Indeed, it was this violent wrenching of the national consciousness into new fields which brought about the change from the old supernaturalism of religion to the shadowy symbolism of literature as exemplified in Hawthorne and Poe. We seem to

see the beginning of this new spirit in the haunting pathos that throbs through
the anonymous ballad of *Nathan Hale:*

> The breezes went steadily through the tall pines,
>   A saying, "Oh! hu-ush!" a saying, "Oh! hu-ush!"
> As stilly stole by a bold legion of horse,
>   For Hale in the bush, for Hale in the bush.
>
> "Keep still," said the thrush as she nestled her young,
>   In a nest by the road; in a nest by the road;
> "For the tyrants are near and with them appear
>   What bodes us no good; what bodes us no good."

Of all the gentlemen—and women, too—who wrote verse in those stirring
times only one can lay claim to any genuine poetic inspiration. Philip Freneau, of New Jersey, has even yet a slight hold on the memory of the reading
public, and would be more read and better known were his works subjected
to proper selection and editing. Like all the other versifiers of the period
Freneau was caught in the wild vortex of political affairs, and, against the
protests of his truer nature as he himself avows, gave up the gentler muses
for the raucous voice of satire. But here and there through his works we find
a suggestion of what he might have accomplished had he fallen on better
times. In him we catch perhaps the first note of the weird as it appears in our
later literature, of that transition of overwhelming superstition into shadowy
haunting symbolism. Not unseldom a stanza, or a single line it may be, wakes
an echo in the mind curiously like Poe. Such, for instance, is the spectral
beauty of that stanza of *The Indian Burying Ground,* whose last line, as Poe
once pointed out, was borrowed intact, and never acknowledged, by Campbell:

> By midnight moons, o'er moistening dews,
>   In vestments for the chase arrayed,
> The hunter still the deer pursues,
>   The hunter and the deer—a shade.

A glance at the titles of Freneau's poems would show how persistently,
when relieved from the immediate pressure of politics, his mind reverted to
subjects of decay and quiet dissolution. In one of his longer poems, *The
House of Death,* he has just failed of achieving a work which might have
come from the brain of Poe himself. At the hour of midnight the poet dreams
that he wanders over a desolate country:

> Dark was the sky, and not one friendly star
>   Shone from the zenith or horizon, clear,
> Mist sate upon the woods, and darkness rode
>   In her black chariot, with a wild career.
>
> And from the woods the late resounding note
>   Issued of the loquacious whip-poor-will,

> Hoarse, howling dogs, and nightly roving wolves
> Clamor'd from far off cliffs invisible.

At last he finds himself in the presence of "a noble dome raised fair and high," standing in the midst of "a mournful garden of autumnal hue":

> The poppy there, companion to repose,
> Displayed her blossoms that began to fall,
> And here the purple amaranthus rose
> With mint strong scented, for the funeral.

In this strange spot, which has something of the unearthly qualities of Rappaccini's garden or Poe's spectral landscapes, stands the desolate home of a young man whose beloved consort death has recently snatched away, and who now harbors as a guest the grisly person of Death himself. Death, stretched on the couch and surrounded by ghoulish phantoms, lies dying. Over the conversation that ensues and the blasphemies of the ghastly sufferer we may pass without delaying. At last after Death has composed his own epitaph and described the tomb he is to occupy, in

> A burning-yard of sinners dead, unblest,

the poet flees terror-smitten out of that house into the tempestuous night.

> Nor looked I back, till to a far off wood
> Trembling with fear, my weary feet had sped—
> Dark was the night, but at the enchanted dome
> I saw the infernal windows flaming red.

At last the hour of dissolution arrives:

> Dim burnt the lamp, and now the phantom Death
> Gave his last groans in horror and despair—
> "All hell demands me hence"—he cried, and threw
> The red lamp hissing through the midnight air.

> Trembling, across the plain my course I held,
> And found the grave-yard, loitering through the gloom,
> And, in the midst, a hell-red wandering light,
> Walking in fiery circles round the tomb.

Whereupon with a gruesome picture of Death's interment and a few stanzas of proper exhortation from the author, this remarkable poem comes to an end.

Between the period of the Revolution and the period that may be called the New England renaissance not much was written which has the distinct mark of the American temperament. Yet it is a significant fact that Charles Brockden Brown's *Wieland,* published in 1798, the first novel of the first American novelist, should be built upon a theme as weird and as steeped in "thrilling melancholy," to use Brown's own words, as anything in the later work of Hawthorne or Poe; and in the proper place it would not be uninteresting to show how far, in his imperfect way, Brown anticipates the very methods and tricks of his greater followers. His immediate inspiration comes no doubt from the mystery-mongering novels then so popular in England, but despite the crudeness of a provincial style there does run through the strange unreality of Brown's pages a note of sincerity, the tongue and accents of a man to whom such themes are a native inheritance, lending to his work a sustained interest which I for my part fail to find in the *Castle of Otranto* or the *Mysteries of Udolpho*. Nor is it without significance that even in New York, where if anywhere this world claims her own, Irving in his genial way could fall so easily into brooding on the dead who sleep in Westminster Abbey or relate with such gusto the wild legends of the Hudson. Bryant, too, has kept his fame chiefly on account of his youthful musings on death and the grandiose pomp of those lines that tell how the rock-ribbed hills, the pensive vales, the venerable rivers, brooks,

> and, poured around them all,
> Old Ocean's grey and melancholy waste,—
> Are but the solemn decorations all
> Of the great tomb of man.

Necessarily this age-long contemplation of things unearthly, this divorcing of the imagination from the fair and blithe harmonies of life to fasten upon the sombre effects of guilt and reprobation, this constant meditation on death and decay—necessarily all these exerted a powerful influence on literature when the renaissance appeared in New England and as a sort of reflection in the rest of the country. So, I think, it happened that out of that famous group of men who really created American literature the only two to attain perfection of form in the higher field of the imagination were writers whose minds were absorbed by the weirder phenomena of life. But it must not be inferred thence that the spirit of Hawthorne and Poe was identical with that of Michael Wigglesworth and Jonathan Edwards. With the passage of time the unquestioning, unflinching faith and vision of those heroic men dissolved away. Already in Freneau, himself born of a Huguenot family, a change is noticeable; that which to the earlier Fathers was a matter of infinite concern, that which to them was more real and urgent than the breath of life, becomes now chiefly an intoxicant of the imagination, and in another generation the transition is complete.

It is this precisely that we understand by the term "weird"—not the veritable vision of unearthly things, but the peculiar half vision inherited by the soul when faith has waned and the imagination prolongs the old sensations in a shadowy involuntary life of its own; and herein too lies the field of true and effective symbolism. If Hawthorne and Poe, as we think, possess an element of force and realism such as Tieck and the German school utterly lack, it is because they write from the depths of this profound moral experience of their people.

O. HENRY

(1862–1910)

William Sydney Porter was born in Greensboro, North Carolina, in 1862. He attended a private school till he was fifteen, then for five years was clerk in his uncle's drug store. Going west for his health, he spent two years on a Texas ranch, but in 1884 moved to Austin, where he was in turn bookkeeper, clerk in the General Land Office, and teller in the First National Bank. About 1887 he began contributing humorous paragraphs and sketches to magazines, and after an unsuccessful venture as publisher of a humorous periodical, he joined the staff of the Houston *Post*, where he was working in 1896 when he was indicted on a charge of embezzling funds while employed in the Austin bank. Instead of standing trial, he fled to New Orleans and then to Central America, but returned in 1897 to be near his dying wife. He was arrested and tried on the old charge, and though he maintained his innocence, his flight was against him. He was convicted and sentenced to serve five years in the Ohio penitentiary, a period lessened by good behavior to three years and three months. He was publishing stories by 1897, and during his imprisonment wrote steadily, adopting from this time the pen name of O. Henry. In 1903 he was engaged to write a story a week for the New York *World,* receiving a hundred dollars for each story. This was the beginning of his most productive period. His first book, *Cabbages and Kings,* was published in 1904, and was followed by other volumes in rapid succession. He died in 1910.

O. Henry's stories are often marred by a straining after effect and an overuse of slang and journalese, yet at their best they show a vivid imagination, a keen sense of humor, and a skill in narrative that has been rivalled by few recent writers. He aimed not so much at the delineation of character as at the portrayal of interesting situations. His descriptions of working-girls, clerks, water-front "bums,"—in short of the "four million" in contradistinction to the "four hundred" of New York society,—are racy and endlessly entertaining, and at times have poignancy and a deep sympathy which his wit saves from saccharine sentimentality.

THE WHIRLIGIG OF LIFE [1]

JUSTICE-OF-THE-PEACE Benaja Widdup sat in the door of his office smoking his elder-stem pipe. Halfway to the zenith the Cumberland range rose blue-gray in the afternoon haze. A speckled hen swaggered down the main street of the "settlement," cackling foolishly.

Up the road came a sound of creaking axles, and then a slow cloud of dust, and then a bull-cart bearing Ransie Bilbro and his wife. The cart stopped at the Justice's door, and the two climbed down. Ransie was a

---

[1] From *Whirligigs* (1910). Copyright, 1903, by Doubleday, Doran & Company.

narrow six feet of sallow brown skin and yellow hair. The imperturbabil-
ity of the mountains hung upon him like a suit of armor. The woman
was calicoed, angled, snuff-brushed, and weary with unknown desires.
Through it all gleamed a faint protest of cheated youth unconscious of
its loss.

The Justice of the Peace slipped his feet into his shoes, for the sake of
dignity, and moved to let them enter.

"We-all," said the woman, in a voice like the wind blowing through pine
boughs, "wants a divo'ce." She looked at Ransie to see if he noted any flaw
or ambiguity or evasion or partiality or self-partisanship in her statement of
their business.

"A divo'ce," repeated Ransie, with a solemn nod. "We-all can't git along
together nohow. It's lonesome enough fur to live in the mount'ins when a
man and a woman keers fur one another. But when she's a-spittin' like a
wildcat or a-sullenin' like a hoot-owl in the cabin, a man ain't got no call
to live with her."

"When he's a no-'count varmint," said the woman, without any especial
warmth, "a-traipsin' along of scalawags and moonshiners and a-layin' on his
back pizen 'ith co'n whiskey, and a-pesterin' folks with a pack o' hungry,
triflin' houn's to feed!"

"When she keeps a-throwin' skillet lids," came Ransie's antiphony, "and
slings b'ilin' water on the best coon-dog in the Cumberlands, and sets herself agin' cookin' a man's victuals, and keeps him awake o' nights accusin'
him of a sight of doin's!"

"When he's al'ays a-fightin' the revenues, and gits a hard name in the
mount'ins fur a mean man, who's gwine to be able fur to sleep o' nights?"

The Justice of the Peace stirred deliberately to his duties. He placed his
one chair and a wooden stool for his petitioners. He opened his book of
statutes on the table and scanned the index. Presently he wiped his spectacles
and shifted his inkstand.

"The law and the statutes," said he, "air silent on the subjeck of divo'ce
as fur as the jurisdiction of this co't air concerned. But, accordin' to equity
and the Constitution and the golden rule, it's a bad barg'in that can't run
both ways. If a justice of the peace can marry a couple, it's plain that he
is bound to be able to divo'ce 'em. This here office will issue a decree of
divo'ce and abide by the decision of the Supreme Co't to hold it good."

Ransie Bilbro drew a small tobacco-bag from his trousers pocket. Out
of this he shook upon the table a five-dollar note. "Sold a b'arskin and two
foxes fur that," he remarked. "It's all the money we got."

"The regular price of a divo'ce in this co't," said the Justice, "air five dollars." He stuffed the bill into the pocket of his homespun vest with a deceptive air of indifference. With much bodily toil and mental travail he wrote

the decree upon half a sheet of foolscap, and then copied it upon the other. Ransie Bilbro and his wife listened to his reading of the document that was to give them freedom:

Know all men by these presents that Ransie Bilbro and his wife, Ariela Bilbro, this day personally appeared before me and promises that hereinafter they will neither love, honor, nor obey each other, neither for better nor for worse, being of sound mind and body, and accept summons for divorce according to the peace and dignity of the State. Herein fail not, so help you God. Benaja Widdup, justice of the peace in and for the county of Piedmont, State of Tennessee.

The Justice was about to hand one of the documents to Ransie. The voice of Ariela delayed the transfer. Both men looked at her. Their dull masculinity was confronted by something sudden and unexpected in the woman.

"Judge, don't you give him that air paper yit. 'Tain't all settled, nohow. I got to have my rights first. I got to have my ali-money. 'Tain't no kind of a way to do fur a man to divo'ce his wife 'thout her havin' a cent fur to do with. I'm a-layin' off to be a-goin' up to brother Ed's up on Hogback Mount'in. I'm bound fur to hev a pa'r of shoes and some snuff and things besides. Ef Rance kin affo'd a divo'ce, let him pay me ali-money."

Ransie Bilbro was stricken to dumb perplexity. There had been no previous hint of alimony. Women were always bringing up startling and unlooked-for issues.

Justice Benaja Widdup felt that the point demanded judicial decision. The authorities were also silent on the subject of alimony. But the woman's feet were bare. The trail to Hogback Mountain was steep and flinty.

"Ariela Bilbro," he asked in official tones, "how much did you 'low would be good and sufficient ali-money in the case befo' the co't?"

"I 'lowed," she answered, "fur the shoes and all, to say five dollars. That ain't much fur ali-money, but I reckon that'll git me up to brother Ed's."

"The amount," said the Justice, "air not onreasonable. Ransie Bilbro, you air ordered by the co't to pay the plaintiff the sum of five dollars befo' the decree of divo'ce air issued."

"I hain't no mo' money," breathed Ransie, heavily. "I done paid you all I had."

"Otherwise," said the Justice, looking severely over his spectacles, "you air in contempt of co't."

"I reckon if you gimme till to-morrow," pleaded the husband, "I mout be able to rake or scrape it up somewhars. I never looked for to be a-payin' no ali-money."

"The case air adjourned," said Benaja Widdup, "till to-morrow, when you-all will present yo'selves and obey the order of the co't. Followin' of which the decrees of divo'ce will be delivered." He sat down in the door and began to loosen a shoestring.

"We mout as well go down to Uncle Ziah's," decided Ransie, "and spend the night." He climbed into the cart on one side, and Ariela climbed in on the other. Obeying the flap of his rope, the little red bull slowly came around on a tack, and the cart crawled away in the nimbus arising from its wheels.

Justice-of-the-peace Benaja Widdup smoked his elder-stem pipe. Late in the afternoon he got his weekly paper, and read it till the twilight dimmed its lines. Then he lit the tallow candle on his table, and read until the moon rose, marking the time for supper. He lived in the double log cabin on the slope near the girdled poplar. Going home to supper he crossed a little branch darkened by a laurel thicket. The dark figure of a man stepped from the laurels and pointed a rifle at his breast. His hat was pulled down low, and something covered most of his face.

"I want yo' money," said the figure, " 'thout any talk. I'm gettin' nervous, and my finger's a-wabblin' on this here trigger."

"I've only got f-f-five dollars," said the Justice, producing it from his vest pocket.

"Roll it up," came the order, "and stick it in the end of this here gun-bar'l."

The bill was crisp and new. Even fingers that were clumsy and trembling found little difficulty in making a spill of it and inserting it (this with less ease) into the muzzle of the rifle.

"Now I reckon you can be goin' along," said the robber.

The Justice lingered not on his way.

The next day came the little red bull, drawing the cart to the office door. Justice Benaja Widdup had his shoes on, for he was expecting the visit. In his presence Ransie Bilbro handed to his wife a five-dollar bill. The official's eye sharply viewed it. It seemed to curl up as though it had been rolled and inserted into the end of a gun-barrel. But the Justice refrained from comment. It is true that other bills might be inclined to curl. He handed each one a decree of divorce. Each stood awkwardly silent, slowly folding the guarantee of freedom. The woman cast a shy glance full of constraint at Ransie.

"I reckon you'll be goin' back up to the cabin," she said, "along 'ith the bull-cart. There's bread in the tin box settin' on the shelf. I put the bacon in the b'ilin'-pot to keep the hounds from gettin' it. Don't forget to wind the clock to-night."

"You air a-goin' to your brother Ed's?" asked Ransie, with fine unconcern.

"I was 'lowin' to get along up thar afore night. I ain't sayin' as they'll
pester theyselves any to make me welcome, but I hain't nowhar else fur
to go. It's a right smart ways, and I reckon I better be goin'. I'll be a-sayin'
good-bye, Ranse—that is, if you keer fur to say so."

"I don't know as anybody's a hound dog," said Ransie, in a martyr's
voice, "fur to not want to say good-bye—'less you air so anxious to get away
that you don't want me to say it."

Ariela was silent. She folded the five-dollar bill and her decree carefully,
and placed them in the bosom of her dress. Benaja Widdup watched the
money disappear with mournful eyes behind his spectacles.

And then with his next words he achieved rank (as his thoughts ran)
with either the great crowd of the world's sympathizers or the little crowd
of its great financiers.

"Be kind o' lonesome in the old cabin to-night, Ranse," he said.

Ransie Bilbro stared out at the Cumberlands, clear blue now in the sunlight. He did not look at Ariela.

"I 'low it might be lonesome," he said; "but when folks gets mad and
wants a divo'ce, you can't make folks stay."

"There's others wanted a divo'ce," said Ariela, speaking to the wooden
stool. "Besides, nobody don't want nobody to stay."

"Nobody never said they didn't."

"Nobody never said they did. I reckon I better start on now to brother
Ed's."

"Nobody can't wind that old clock."

"Want me to go back along 'ith you in the cart and wind it fur you,
Ranse?"

The mountaineer's countenance was proof against emotion. But he
reached out a big hand and enclosed Ariela's thin brown one. Her soul
peeped out once through her impassive face, hallowing it.

"Them hounds sha'n't pester you no more," said Ransie. "I reckon I been
mean and low down. You wind that clock, Ariela."

"My heart—hit's in that cabin, Ranse," she whispered, "along 'ith you. I
ain't a-goin' to git mad no more. Le's be startin', Ranse, so's we kin git
home by sundown."

Justice-of-the-peace Benaja Widdup interposed as they started for the
door, forgetting his presence.

"In the name of the State of Tennessee," he said, "I forbid you-all to be
a-defyin' of its laws and statutes. This co't is mo' than willin' and full of
joy to see the clouds of discord and misunderstandin' rollin' away from
two lovin' hearts, but it air the duty of the co't to p'eserve the morals and

integrity of the State. The co't reminds you that you air no longer man and wife, but air divo'ced by regular decree, and as such air not entitled to the benefits and 'purtenances of the mattermonal estate."

Ariela caught Ransie's arm. Did those words mean that she must lose him now when they had just learned the lesson of life?

"But the co't air prepared," went on the Justice, "fur to remove the disabilities set up by the decree of divo'ce. The co't air on hand to perform the solemn ceremony of marri'ge, thus fixin' things up and enablin' the parties in the case to resume the honor'ble and elevatin' state of mattermony which they desires. The fee fur performin' said ceremony will be, in this case, to wit, five dollars."

Ariela caught the gleam of promise in his words. Swiftly her hand went to her bosom. Freely as an alighting dove the bill fluttered to the Justice's table. Her sallow cheek colored as she stood hand in hand with Ransie and listened to the reuniting words.

Ransie helped her into the cart, and climbed in beside her. The little red bull turned once more, and they set out, hand-clasped, for the mountains.

Justice-of-the-peace Benaja Widdup sat in his door and took off his shoes. Once again he fingered the bill tucked down in his vest pocket. Once again he smoked his elder-stem pipe. Once again the speckled hen swaggered down the main street of the "settlement," cackling foolishly.

A MUNICIPAL REPORT [2]

Fancy a novel about Chicago or Buffalo, let us say, or Nashville, Tennessee! There are just three big cities in the United States that are "story cities"—New York, of course, New Orleans, and, best of the lot, San Francisco.—*Frank Norris.*

EAST is East, and West is San Francisco, according to Californians. Californians are a race of people; they are not merely inhabitants of a State. They are the Southerners of the West. Now, Chicagoans are no less loyal to their city; but when you ask them why, they stammer and speak of lake fish and the new Odd Fellows Building. But Californians go into detail.

Of course they have, in the climate, an argument that is good for half an hour while you are thinking of your coal bills and heavy underwear. But as soon as they come to mistake your silence for conviction, madness comes upon them, and they picture the city of the Golden Gate as the Bagdad of the New World. So far, as a matter of opinion, no refutation is necessary. But, dear cousins all (from Adam and Eve descended), it is a rash one who will lay his finger on the map and say: "In this town there

[2] First published in *Hampton's Magazine*, November, 1909, and then in the volume entitled *Strictly Business* (1910). Copyright, 1909, by Doubleday, Doran & Company.

can be no romance—what could happen here?" Yes, it is a bold and a rash deed to challenge in one sentence history, romance, and Rand and McNally.

NASHVILLE.—A city, port of delivery, and the capital of the State of Tennessee, is on the Cumberland River and on the N. C. & St. L. and the L. & N. railroads. This city is regarded as the most important educational center in the South.

I stepped off the train at 8 P. M. Having searched the thesaurus in vain for adjectives, I must, as a substitution, hie me to comparison in the form of a recipe.

Take of London fog 30 parts; malaria 10 parts; gas leaks 20 parts; dewdrops gathered in a brick yard at sunrise, 25 parts; odor of honeysuckle 15 parts. Mix.

The mixture will give you an approximate conception of a Nashville drizzle. It is not so fragrant as a moth-ball nor as thick as pea-soup; but 't is enough—'t will serve.

I went to a hotel in a tumbril. It required strong self-suppression for me to keep from climbing to the top of it and giving an imitation of Sidney Carton. The vehicle was drawn by beasts of a by-gone era and driven by something dark and emancipated.

I was sleepy and tired, so when I got to the hotel I hurriedly paid it the fifty cents it demanded (with approximate lagniappe, I assure you). I knew its habits; and I did not want to hear it prate about its old "marster" or anything that happened "befo' de wah."

The hotel was one of the kind described as "renovated." That means $20,000 worth of new marble pillars, tiling, electric lights and brass cuspidors in the lobby, and a new L. & N. time table and a lithograph of Lookout Mountain in each one of the great rooms above. The management was without reproach, the attention full of exquisite Southern courtesy, the service as slow as the progress of a snail and as good-humored as Rip Van Winkle. The food was worth traveling a thousand miles for. There is no other hotel in the world where you can get such chicken livers *en brochette*.

At dinner I asked a Negro waiter if there was anything doing in town. He pondered gravely for a minute, and then replied: "Well, boss, I don't really reckon there's anything at all doin' after sundown."

Sundown had been accomplished; it had been drowned in the drizzle long before. So that spectacle was denied me. But I went forth upon the streets in the drizzle to see what might be there.

It is built on undulating grounds; and the streets are lighted by electricity at a cost of $32,470 per annum.

As I left the hotel there was a race riot. Down upon me charged a company of freedmen, or Arabs, or Zulus, armed with—no, I saw with relief that they were not rifles, but whips. And I saw dimly a caravan of black, clumsy vehicles; and at the reassuring shouts, "Kyar you anywhere in the town, boss, fuh fifty cents," I reasoned that I was merely a "fare" instead of a victim.

I walked through long streets, all leading uphill. I wondered how those streets ever came down again. Perhaps they didn't until they were "graded." On a few of the "main streets" I saw lights in stores here and there; saw street cars go by conveying worthy burghers hither and yon; saw people pass engaged in the art of conversation, and heard a burst of semi-lively laughter issuing from a soda-water and ice-cream parlor. The streets other than "main" seemed to have enticed upon their borders houses consecrated to peace and domesticity. In many of them lights shone behind discreetly drawn window shades; in a few pianos tinkled orderly and irreproachable music. There was, indeed, little "doing." I wished I had come before sundown. So I returned to my hotel.

In November, 1864, the Confederate General Hood advanced against Nashville, where he shut up a National force under General Thomas. The latter then sallied forth and defeated the Confederates in a terrible conflict.

All my life I have heard of, admired, and witnessed the fine marksmanship of the South in its peaceful conflicts in the tobacco-chewing regions. But in my hotel a surprise awaited me. There were twelve bright, new, imposing, capacious brass cuspidors in the great lobby, tall enough to be called urns and so wide-mouthed that the crack pitcher of a lady baseball team should have been able to throw a ball into one of them at five paces distant. But, although a terrible battle had raged and was still raging, the enemy had not suffered. Bright, new, imposing capacious, untouched, they stood. But, shades of Jefferson Brick! the tile floor—the beautiful tile floor! I could not avoid thinking of the battle of Nashville, and trying to draw, as is my foolish habit, some deductions about hereditary marksmanship.

Here I first saw Major (by misplaced courtesy) Wentworth Caswell. I knew him for a type the moment my eyes suffered from the sight of him. A rat has no geographical habitat. My old friend, A. Tennyson, said, as he so well said almost everything:

> Prophet, curse me the blabbing lip,
> And curse me the British vermin, the rat.

Let us regard the word "British" as interchangeable *ad lib*. A rat is a rat.

This man was hunting about the hotel lobby like a starved dog that had forgotten where he had buried a bone. He had a face of great acreage, red, pulpy, and with a kind of sleepy massiveness like that of Buddha. He possessed one single virtue—he was very smoothly shaven. The mark of the beast is not indelible upon a man until he goes about with a stubble. I think that if he had not used his razor that day I would have repulsed his advances, and the criminal calendar of the world would have been spared the addition of one murder.

I happened to be standing within five feet of a cuspidor when Major Caswell opened fire upon it. I had been observant enough to perceive that the attacking force was using Gatlings instead of squirrel rifles; so I side-stepped so promptly that the major seized the opportunity to apologize to a noncombatant. He had the blabbing lip. In four minutes he had become my friend and had dragged me to the bar.

I desire to interpolate here that I am a Southerner. But I am not one by profession or trade. I eschew the string tie, the slouch hat, the Prince Albert, the number of bales of cotton destroyed by Sherman, and plug chewing. When the orchestra plays "Dixie" I do not cheer. I slide a little lower on the leather-cornered seat and, well, order another Würzburger and wish that Longstreet had—but what's the use?

Major Caswell banged the bar with his fist, and the first gun at Fort Sumter re-echoed. When he fired the last one at Appomattox I began to hope. But then he began on family trees, and demonstrated that Adam was only a third cousin of a collateral branch of the Caswell family. Genealogy disposed of, he took up, to my distaste, his private family matters. He spoke of his wife, traced her descent back to Eve, and profanely denied any possible rumor that she may have had relations in the land of Nod.

By this time I began to suspect that he was trying to obscure by noise the fact that he had ordered the drinks, on the chance that I would be bewildered into paying for them. But when they were down he crashed a silver dollar loudly upon the bar. Then, of course, another serving was obligatory. And when I had paid for that I took leave of him brusquely; for I wanted no more of him. But before I had obtained my release he had prated loudly of an income that his wife received, and showed a handful of silver money.

When I got my key at the desk the clerk said to me courteously: "If that man Caswell has annoyed you, and if you would like to make a complaint, we will have him ejected. He is a nuisance, a loafer, and without any known means of support, although he seems to have some money most the time. But we don't seem to be able to hit upon any means of throwing him out legally."

"Why, no," said I, after some reflection; "I don't see my way clear to making a complaint. But I would like to place myself on record as asserting that I do not care for his company. Your town," I continued, "seems to be a quiet one. What manner of entertainment, adventure, or excitement have you to offer to the stranger within your gates?"

"Well, sir," said the clerk, "there will be a show here next Thursday. It is —I'll look it up and have the announcement sent up to your room with the ice water. Good night."

After I went up to my room I looked out the window. It was only about ten o'clock, but I looked upon a silent town. The drizzle continued, spangled with dim lights, as far apart as currants in a cake sold at the Ladies' Exchange.

"A quiet place," I said to myself, as my first shoe struck the ceiling of the occupant of the room beneath mine. "Nothing of the life here that gives color and variety to the cities in the East and West. Just a good, ordinary, humdrum, business town."

Nashville occupies a foremost place among the manufacturing centers of the country. It is the fifth boot and shoe market in the United States, the largest candy and cracker manufacturing city in the South, and does an enormous wholesale drygoods, grocery, and drug business.

I must tell you how I came to be in Nashville, and I assure you the digression brings as much tedium to me as it does to you. I was traveling elsewhere on my own business, but I had a commission from a Northern literary magazine to stop over there and establish a personal connection between the publication and one of its contributors, Azalea Adair.

Adair (there was no clue to the personality except the handwriting) had sent in some essays (lost art!) and poems that had made the editors swear approvingly over their one o'clock luncheon. So they had commissioned me to round up said Adair and corner by contract his or her output at two cents a word before some other publisher offered her ten or twenty.

At nine o'clock the next morning, after my chicken livers *en brochette* (try them if you can find that hotel), I strayed out into the drizzle, which was still on for an unlimited run. At the first corner I came upon Uncle Cæsar. He was a stalwart Negro, older than the pyramids, with gray wool and a face that reminded me of Brutus, and a second afterwards of the late King Cettiwayo. He wore the most remarkable coat that I ever had seen or expect to see. It reached to his ankles and had once been a Confederate gray in colors. But rain and sun and age had so variegated it that Joseph's coat, beside it, would have faded to a pale monochrome. I must linger with that coat, for it has to do with the story—the story that is so long in coming, because you can hardly expect anything to happen in Nashville.

Once it must have been the military coat of an officer. The cape of it had vanished, but all adown its front it had been frogged and tasseled magnificently. But now the frogs and tassels were gone. In their stead had been patiently stitched (I surmised by some surviving "black mammy") new frogs made of cunningly twisted common hempen twine. This twine was frayed and disheveled. It must have been added to the coat as a substitute for vanished splendors, with tasteless but painstaking devotion, for it followed faithfully the curves of the long-missing frogs. And, to complete the comedy and pathos of the garment, all its buttons were gone save one. The second button from the top alone remained. The coat was fastened by other twine strings tied through the buttonholes and other holes rudely pierced in the opposite side. There was never such a weird garment so fantastically bedecked and of so many mottled hues. The lone button was the size of a half-dollar, made of yellow horn and sewed on with coarse twine.

This Negro stood by a carriage so old that Ham himself might have started a hack line with it after he left the ark with the two animals hitched to it. As I approached he threw open the door, drew out a feather duster, waved it without using it, and said in deep, rumbling tones:

"Step right in, suh; ain't a speck of dust in it—jus' got back from a funeral, suh."

I inferred that on such gala occasions carriages were given an extra cleaning. I looked up and down the street and perceived that there was little choice among the vehicles for hire that lined the curb. I looked in my memorandum book for the address of Azalea Adair.

"I want to go to 861 Jessamine Street," I said, and was about to step into the hack. But for an instant the thick, long, gorilla-like arm of the old Negro barred me. On his massive and saturnine face a look of sudden suspicion and enmity flashed for a moment. Then, with quickly returning conviction, he asked blandishingly, "What are you gwine there for, boss?"

"What is that to you?" I asked, a little sharply.

"Nothin', suh, jus' nothin'. Only it's a lonesome kind of part of town and few folks ever has business out there. Step right in. The seats is clean —jes' got back from a funeral, suh."

A mile and a half it must have been to our journey's end. I could hear nothing but the fearful rattle of the ancient hack over the uneven brick paving; I could smell nothing but the drizzle, now further flavored with coal smoke and something like a mixture of tar and oleander blossoms. All I could see through the streaming windows were two rows of dim houses.

The city has an area of 10 square miles; 181 miles of streets, of which 137 miles are paved; a system of waterworks that cost $2,000,000, with 77 miles of mains.

Eight-sixty-one Jessamine Street was a decayed mansion. Thirty yards back from the street it stood, outmerged in a splendid grove of trees and untrimmed shrubbery. A row of box bushes overflowed and almost hid the paling fence from sight; the gate was kept closed by a rope noose that encircled the gate post and the first paling of the gate. But when you got inside you saw that 861 was a shell, a shadow, a ghost of former grandeur and excellence. But in the story, I have not yet got inside.

When the hack had ceased from rattling and the weary quadrupeds came to a rest I handed my jehu his fifty cents with an additional quarter, feeling a glow of conscious generosity, as I did so. He refused it.

"It's two dollars, suh," he said.

"How's that?" I asked. "I plainly heard you call out at the hotel: 'Fifty cents to any part of the town.'"

"It's two dollars, suh," he repeated obstinately. "It's a long ways from the hotel."

"It is within the city limits and well within them," I argued. "Don't think that you have picked up a greenhorn Yankee. Do you see those hills over there?" I went on, pointing toward the east (I could not see them, myself, for the drizzle); "well, I was born and raised on their other side. You old fool nigger, can't you tell people from other people when you see 'em?"

The grim face of King Cettiwayo softened. "Is you from the South, suh? I reckon it was them shoes of yourn fooled me. They is somethin' sharp in the toes for a Southern gen'l'man to wear."

"Then the charge is fifty cents, I suppose?" said I inexorably.

His former expression, a mingling of cupidity and hostility, returned, remained ten seconds, and vanished.

"Boss," he said, "fifty cents is right; but I *needs* two dollars, suh; I'm *obleeged* to have two dollars. I ain't *demandin'* it now, suh; after I knows whar you's from; I'm jus' sayin' that I *has* to have two dollars to-night, and business is mighty po'."

Peace and confidence settled upon his heavy features. He had been luckier than he had hoped. Instead of having picked up a greenhorn, ignorant of rates, he had come upon an inheritance.

"You confounded old rascal," I said, reaching down to my pocket, "you ought to be turned over to the police."

For the first time I saw him smile. He knew; *he knew;* HE KNEW.

I gave him two one-dollar bills. As I handed them over I noticed that one of them had seen parlous times. Its upper right-hand corner was missing, and it had been torn through in the middle, but joined again. A strip of blue tissue paper, pasted over the split, preserved its negotiability.

Enough of the African bandit for the present: I left him happy, lifted the rope and opened the creaky gate.

The house, as I said, was a shell. A paint brush had not touched it in twenty years. I could not see why a strong wind should not have bowled it over like a house of cards until I looked again at the trees that hugged it close—the trees that saw the battle of Nashville and still drew their protecting branches around it against storm and enemy and cold.

Azalea Adair, fifty years old, white-haired, a descendant of the cavaliers, as thin and frail as the house she lived in, robed in the cheapest and cleanest dress I ever saw, with an air as simple as a queen's, received me.

The reception room seemed a mile square, because there was nothing in it except some rows of books, on unpainted white-pine bookshelves, a cracked marble-top table, a rag rug, a hairless horsehair sofa and two or three chairs. Yes, there was a picture on the wall, a colored crayon drawing of a cluster of pansies. I looked around for the portrait of Andrew Jackson and the pine-cone hanging basket but they were not there.

Azalea Adair and I had conversation, a little of which will be repeated to you. She was a product of the old South, gently nurtured in the sheltered life. Her learning was not broad, but was deep and of splendid originality in its somewhat narrow scope. She had been educated at home, and her knowledge of the world was derived from inference and by inspiration. Of such is the precious, small group of essayists made. While she talked to me I kept brushing my fingers, trying, unconsciously, to rid them guiltily of the absent dust from the half-calf backs of Lamb, Chaucer, Hazlitt, Marcus Aurelius, Montaigne, and Hood. She was exquisite, she was a valuable discovery. Nearly everybody nowadays knows too much—oh, so much too much—of real life.

I could perceive clearly that Azalea Adair was very poor. A house and a dress she had, not much else, I fancied. So, divided between my duty to the magazine and my loyalty to the poets and essayists who fought Thomas in the valley of the Cumberland, I listened to her voice, which was like a harpsichord's, and found that I could not speak of contracts. In the presence of the nine Muses and the three Graces one hesitated to lower the topic to two cents. There would have to be another colloquy after I had regained my commercialism. But I spoke of my mission, and three o'clock of the next afternoon was set for the discussion of the business proposition.

"Your town," I said, as I began to make ready to depart (which is the time for smooth generalities), "seems to be a quiet, sedate place. A home town, I should say, where few things out of the ordinary ever happen."

It carries on an extensive trade in stoves and hollow ware with the West and South, and its flouring mills have a daily capacity of more than 2,000 barrels.

Azalea Adair seemed to reflect.

"I have never thought of it that way," she said, with a kind of sincere intensity that seemed to belong to her. "Isn't it in the still, quiet places that things do happen? I fancy that when God began to create the earth on the first Monday morning one could have leaned out one's window and heard the drops of mud splashing from His trowel as He built up the everlasting hills. What did the noisiest project in the world—I mean the building of the tower of Babel—result in finally? A page and a half of Esperanto in the *North American Review*."

"Of course," said I platitudinously, "human nature is the same everywhere; but there is more color—er—more drama and movement and—er—romance in some cities than in others."

"On the surface," said Azalea Adair. "I have traveled many times around the world in a golden airship wafted on two wings—print and dreams. I have seen (on one of my imaginary tours) the Sultan of Turkey bowstring with his own hands one of his wives who had uncovered her face in public. I have seen a man in Nashville tear up his theater tickets because his wife was going out with her face covered—with rice powder. In San Francisco's Chinatown I saw the slave girl Sing Yee dipped slowly, inch by inch, in boiling almond oil to make her swear she would never see her American lover again. She gave in when the boiling oil had reached three inches above her knee. At a euchre party in East Nashville the other night I saw Kitty Morgan cut dead by seven of her schoolmates and lifelong friends because she had married a house painter. The boiling oil was sizzling as high as her heart; but I wish you could have seen the fine little smile that she carried from table to table. Oh, yes, it is a humdrum town. Just a few miles of red brick houses and mud and stores and lumber yards."

Some one knocked hollowly at the back of the house. Azalea Adair breathed a soft apology and went to investigate the sound. She came back in three minutes with brightened eyes, a faint flush on her cheeks, and ten years lifted from her shoulders.

"You must have a cup of tea before you go," she said, "and a sugar cake."

She reached and shook a little iron bell. In shuffled a small Negro girl about twelve, barefoot, not very tidy, glowering at me with thumb in mouth and bulging eyes.

Azalea Adair opened a tiny, worn purse and drew out a dollar bill, a dollar bill with the upper right-hand corner missing, torn in two pieces and pasted together again with a strip of blue tissue paper. It was one of the bills I had given the piratical Negro—there was no doubt of it.

"Go up to Mr. Baker's store on the corner, Impy," she said, handing the girl the dollar bill, "and get a quarter of a pound of tea—the kind he always sends me—and ten cents worth of sugar cakes. Now, hurry. The supply of tea in the house happens to be exhausted," she explained to me.

Impy left by the back way. Before the scrape of her hard, bare feet had

died away on the back porch, a wild shriek—I was sure it was hers—filled
the hollow house. Then the deep, gruff tones of an angry man's voice
mingled with the girl's further squeals and unintelligible words.

Azalea Adair rose without surprise or emotion and disappeared. For two
minutes I heard the hoarse rumble of the man's voice; then something like
an oath and a slight scuffle, and she returned calmly to her chair.

"This is a roomy house," she said, "and I have a tenant for part of it.
I am sorry to have to rescind my invitation to tea. It was impossible to get
the kind I always use at the store. Perhaps to-morrow Mr. Baker will be
able to supply me."

I was sure that Impy had not had time to leave the house. I inquired
concerning street-car lines and took my leave. After I was well on my
way I remembered that I had not learned Azalea Adair's name. But to-
morrow would do.

That same day I started in on the course of iniquity that this uneventful
city forced upon me. I was in the town only two days, but in that time
I managed to lie shamelessly by telegraph, and to be an accomplice—after
the fact, if that is the correct legal term—to a murder.

As I rounded the corner nearest my hotel the Afrite coachman of the
polychromatic, nonpareil coat seized me, swung open the dungeony door of
his peripatetic sarcophagus, flirted his feather duster, and· began his ritual:
"Step right in, boss. Carriage is clean—jus' got back from a funeral. Fifty
cents to any—"

And then he knew me and grinned broadly. " 'Scuse me, boss; you is
de gen'l'man what rid out with me dis mawnin'. Thank you kindly, suh."

"I am going out to 861 again to-morrow afternoon at three," said I, "and
if you will be here, I'll let you drive me. So you know Miss Adair?" I concluded, thinking of my dollar bill.

"I belonged to her father, Judge Adair, suh," he replied.

"I judge that she is pretty poor," I said. "She hasn't much money to
speak of, has she?"

For an instant I looked again at the fierce countenance of King Cettiwayo, and then he changed back to an extortionate old Negro hack driver.

"She ain't gwine to starve, suh," he said slowly. "She has reso'ces, suh;
she has reso'ces."

"I shall pay you fifty cents for the trip," said I.

"Dat is puffeckly correct, suh," he answered humbly. "I jus' had to have
dat two dollars dis mawnin', boss."

I went to the hotel and lied by electricity. I wired the magazine: "A.
Adair holds out for eight cents a word."

The answer that came back was: "Give it to her quick, you duffer."

Just before dinner "Major" Wentworth Caswell bore down upon me with the greetings of a long-lost friend. I have seen few men whom I have so instantaneously hated, and of whom it was so difficult to be rid. I was standing at the bar when he invaded me; therefore I could not wave the white ribbon in his face. I would have paid gladly for the drinks, hoping, thereby, to escape another; but he was one of those despicable, roaring, advertising bibbers who must have brass bands and fireworks attend upon every cent that they waste in their follies.

With an air of producing millions he drew two one-dollar bills from a pocket and dashed one of them upon the bar. I looked once more at the dollar bill with the upper right-hand corner missing, torn through the middle, and patched with a strip of blue tissue paper. It was my dollar bill again. It could have been no other.

I went up to my room. The drizzle and the monotony of a dreary, eventless Southern town had made me tired and listless. I remembered that just before I went to bed I mentally disposed of the mysterious dollar bill (which might have formed the clue to a tremendously fine detective story of San Francisco) by saying to myself sleepily: "Seems as if a lot of people here own stock in the Hack-Driver's Trust. Pays dividends promptly, too. Wonder if—" Then I fell asleep.

King Cettiwayo was at his post the next day, and rattled my bones over the stones out to 861. He was to wait and rattle me back again when I was ready.

Azalea Adair looked paler and cleaner and frailer than she had looked on the day before. After she had signed the contract at eight cents per word she grew still paler and began to slip out of her chair. Without much trouble I managed to get her up on the antediluvian horsehair sofa and then I ran out to the sidewalk and yelled to the coffee-colored Pirate to bring a doctor. With a wisdom that I had not suspected in him, he abandoned his team and struck off up the street afoot, realizing the value of speed. In ten minutes he returned with a grave, gray-haired and capable man of medicine. In a few words (worth much less than eight cents each) I explained to him my presence in the hollow house of mystery. He bowed with stately understanding, and turned to the old Negro.

"Uncle Cæsar," he said calmly, "run up to my house and ask Miss Lucy to give you a cream pitcher full of fresh milk and half a tumbler of port wine. And hurry back. Don't drive—run. I want you to get back sometime this week."

It occurred to me that Dr. Merriman also felt a distrust as to the speeding powers of the land-pirate's steeds. After Uncle Cæsar was gone, lumberingly, but swiftly, up the street, the doctor looked me over with great politeness and as much careful calculation until he had decided that I might do.

"It is only a case of insufficient nutrition," he said. "In other words, the result of poverty, pride, and starvation. Mrs. Caswell has many devoted friends who would be glad to aid her, but she will accept nothing except from that old Negro, Uncle Cæsar, who was once owned by her family."

"Mrs. Caswell!" said I, in surprise. And then I looked at the contract and saw that she had signed it "Azalea Adair Caswell."

"I thought she was Miss Adair," I said.

"Married to a drunken, worthless loafer, sir," said the doctor. "It is said that he robs her even of the small sums that her old servant contributes toward her support."

When the milk and wine had been brought the doctor soon revived Azalea Adair. She sat up and talked of the beauty of the autumn leaves that were then in season, and their height of color. She referred lightly to her fainting seizure as the outcome of an old palpitation of the heart. Impy fanned her as she lay on the sofa. The doctor was due elsewhere, and I followed him to the door. I told him that it was within my power and intentions to make a reasonable advance of money to Azalea Adair on future contributions to the magazine, and he seemed pleased.

"By the way," he said, "perhaps you would like to know that you have had royalty for a coachman. Old Cæsar's grandfather was a king in Congo. Cæsar himself has royal ways, as you may have observed."

As the doctor was moving off I heard Uncle Cæsar's voice inside: "Did he git bofe of dem two dollars from you, Mis' Zalea?"

"Yes, Cæsar," I heard Azalea Adair answer weakly. And then I went in and concluded business negotiations with our contributor. I assumed the responsibility of advancing fifty dollars, putting it as a necessary formality in binding our bargain. And then Uncle Cæsar drove me back to the hotel.

Here ends all of the story as far as I can testify as a witness. The rest must be only bare statements of facts.

At about six o'clock I went out for a stroll. Uncle Cæsar was at his corner. He threw open the door of his carriage, flourished his duster and began his depressing formula: "Step right in, suh. Fifty cents to anywhere in the city —hack's puffickly clean, suh—jus' got back from a funeral—"

And then he recognized me. I think his eyesight was getting bad. His coat had taken on a few more faded shades of color, the twine strings were more frayed and ragged, the last remaining button—the button of yellow horn—was gone. A motley descendant of kings was Uncle Cæsar!

About two hours later I saw an excited crowd besieging the front of a drug store. In a desert where nothing happens this was manna; so I wedged my way inside. On an extemporized couch of empty boxes and chairs was stretched the mortal corporeality of Major Wentworth Caswell. A doctor was testing him for the mortal ingredient. His decision was that it was conspicuous by its absence.

The erstwhile Major had been found dead on a dark street and brought by curious and ennuied citizens to the drug store. The late human being had been engaged in terrific battle—the details showed that. Loafer and reprobate though he had been, he had been also a warrior. But he had lost. His hands were yet clinched so tightly that his fingers would not be opened. The gentle citizens who had known him stood about and searched their vocabularies to find some good words, if it were possible, to speak of him. One kind-looking man said, after much thought: "When Cas was about fo'teen he was one of the best spellers in school."

While I stood there the fingers of the right hand of "the man that was," which hung down the side of a white pine box, relaxed, and dropped something at my feet. I covered it with one foot quietly, and a little later on I picked it up and pocketed it. I reasoned that in his last struggle his hand must have seized that object unwittingly and held it in a death grip.

At the hotel that night the main topic of conversation, with the possible exception of politics and prohibition, was the demise of Major Caswell. I heard one man say to a group of listeners:

"In my opinion, gentlemen, Caswell was murdered by some of these no-account niggers for his money. He had fifty dollars this afternoon which he showed to several gentlemen in the hotel. When he was found the money was not on his person."

I left the city the next morning at nine, and as the train was crossing the bridge over the Cumberland River I took out of my pocket a yellow horn overcoat button the size of a fifty-cent piece, with frayed ends of coarse twine hanging from it, and cast it out of the window into the slow, muddy waters below.

I wonder what's doing in Buffalo!

EDITH WHARTON

(1862-   )

Edith Newbold Jones was born in New York City in 1862. She was educated by private tutors, and as a girl spent much time in foreign travel. In 1885 she married Edward Wharton, a Boston banker, and a few years later began a literary career by contributing poems and short stories to *Scribner's Magazine*. Her first book, *The Greater Inclination* (1899), a volume of tales, marked her as an accomplished writer, but *The House of Mirth* (1905) first gave her a national reputation. She has lived in recent years for the most part in Italy and France.

Soon after she began publishing, Mrs. Wharton met Henry James, and became to some extent his disciple, employing his "psychological" methods and his technique. One of her early books was an Italian historical novel, *The Valley of Decision* (1902), which led James to say that "she *must* be tethered in native pastures, even if it reduce her to a backyard in New York." Whether through his influence or of her own will, she turned to "native pastures," and it has been her exposition of American life that has won her a secure place in literature. She made society people and their affairs her peculiar province, and in a series of novels portrayed the life of old New York; but in *Ethan Frome* (1911) and *Summer* (1917) she turned for a theme to rural New England, and in the former wrote what is indubitably a classic. In addition to her novels, she has written a number of books of travel; several volumes dealing with the World War; a volume, *The Writing of Fiction* (1925), in which she discusses her own methods as a writer; and several volumes of short stories. Among the latter are a number of ghost stories, in which she manages supernatural effects with great cleverness. She is strongest perhaps as a delineator of character, but the cutting irony with which she attacks stupidity, whether in the individual or in society at large, has made her one of the most effective of contemporary satirists.

THE DEBT [1]

I

You remember—it's not so long ago—the talk there was about Dredge's "Arrival of the Fittest"? The talk has subsided, but the book of course remains: stands up, in fact, as the tallest thing of its kind since—well, I'd almost said since "The Origin of Species."

I'm not wrong, at any rate, in calling it the most important contribution yet made to the development of the Darwinian theory, or rather to the solution of the awkward problem about which that theory has had to make such

---

[1] First published in *Scribner's Magazine*, August, 1909, and in the volume *Tales of Men and Ghosts* (1910). Copyright, 1910, by Charles Scribner's Sons.

a circuit. Dredge's hypothesis will be contested, may one day be disproved; but at least it has swept out of the way all previous conjectures, including of course Lanfear's great attempt; and for our generation of scientific investigators it will serve as the first safe bridge across a murderous black whirlpool.

It's all very interesting—there are few things more stirring to the imagination than that projection of the new hypothesis, light as a cobweb and strong as steel, across the intellectual abyss; but, for an idle observer of human motives, the other, the personal, side of Dredge's case is even more interesting and arresting.

Personal side? You didn't know there was one? Pictured him simply as a thinking machine, a highly specialized instrument of precision, the result of a long series of "adaptations," as his own jargon would put it? Well, I don't wonder—if you've met him. He does give the impression of being something out of his own laboratory: a delicate instrument that reveals wonders to the initiated, but is useless in an ordinary hand.

In his youth it was just the other way. I knew him twenty years ago, as an awkward lad whom young Archie Lanfear had picked up at college, and brought home for a visit. I happened to be staying at the Lanfears' when the boys arrived, and I shall never forget Dredge's first appearance on the scene. You know the Lanfears always lived very simply. That summer they had gone to Buzzard's Bay, in order that Professor Lanfear should be near the Biological Station at Wood's Holl, and they were picnicking in a kind of sketchy bungalow without any attempt at luxury. But Galen Dredge couldn't have been more awe-struck if he'd been suddenly plunged into a Fifth Avenue ball-room. He nearly knocked his head against the low doorway, and in dodging this peril trod heavily on Mabel Lanfear's foot, and became hopelessly entangled in her mother's draperies—though how he managed it I never knew, for Mrs. Lanfear's dowdy muslins ran to no excess of train.

When the Professor himself came in it was ten times worse, and I saw then that Dredge's emotion was a tribute to the great man's presence. That made the boy interesting, and I began to watch. Archie, always enthusiastic but vague, had said: "Oh, he's a tremendous chap—you'll see—" but I hadn't expected to see quite so early. Lanfear's vision, of course, was sharper than mine; and the next morning he had carried Dredge off to the Biological Station. That was the way it began.

Dredge is the son of a Baptist minister. He comes from East Lethe, New York State, and was working his way through college—waiting at White Mountain hotels in summer—when Archie Lanfear ran across him. There were eight children in the family, and the mother was an invalid. Dredge never had a penny from his father after he was fourteen; but his mother wanted him to be a scholar, and "kept at him," as he put it, in the hope of his going back to "teach school" at East Lethe. He developed slowly, as the scientific mind generally does, and was still adrift about himself and his tendencies when Archie took him down to Buzzard's Bay. But he had read Lanfear's "Utility and Variation," and had always been a patient and curious observer of nature. And his first meeting with Lanfear explained him to himself. It didn't, however, enable him to explain himself to others, and for a long time he remained, to all but Lanfear, an object of incredulity and conjecture.

"*Why* my husband wants him about—" poor Mrs. Lanfear, the kindest of women, privately lamented to her friends; for Dredge, at that time—they kept him all summer at the bungalow—had one of the most encumbering personalities you can imagine. He was as inexpressive as he is to-day, and yet oddly obtrusive: one of those uncomfortable presences whose silence is an interruption.

The poor Lanfears almost died of him that summer, and the pity of it was that he never suspected it, but continued to lavish on them a floundering devotion as inconvenient as the endearments of a dripping dog. He was full of all sorts of raw enthusiasms, which he forced on any one who would listen when his first shyness had worn off. You can't see him spouting sentimental poetry, can you? Yet I've known him to petrify a whole group of Mrs. Lanfear's callers by suddenly discharging on them, in the strident drawl of his state, "Barbarie Frietchie" or "The Queen of the May." His taste in literature was uniformly bad, but very definite, and far more dogmatic than his views on biological questions. In his scientific judgments he showed, even then, a temperance remarkable in one so young; but in literature he was a furious propagandist, aggressive, disputatious, and extremely sensitive to adverse opinion.

Lanfear, of course, had been struck from the first by his gift of observation, and by the fact that his eagerness to learn was offset by his reluctance to conclude. I remember Lanfear's telling me that he had never known a lad of Dredge's age who gave such promise of uniting an aptitude for general ideas with the plodding patience of the observer. Of course when Lanfear talked like that of a young biologist his fate was sealed. There could be no question of Dredge's going back to "teach school" at East Lethe. He must take a course in biology at Columbia, spend his vacations at the Wood's Holl laboratory, and then, if possible, go to Germany for a year or two.

All this meant his virtual adoption by the Lanfears. Most of Lanfear's fortune went in helping young students to a start, and he devoted a liberal subsidy to Dredge.

"Dredge will be my biggest dividend—you'll see!" he used to say, in the chrysalis days when poor Galen was known to the world of science only as a slouching presence in Mrs. Lanfear's drawing-room. And Dredge, it must be said, took his obligations simply, with the dignity, and quiet consciousness of his own worth, which in such cases saves the beneficiary from abjectness. He seemed to trust himself as fully as Lanfear trusted him.

The comic part of it was that his only idea of making what is known as "a return" was to devote himself to the Professor's family. When I hear pretty women lamenting that they can't coax Professor Dredge out of his laboratory I remember Mable Lanfear's cry to me: "If Galen would only keep away!" When Mabel fell on the ice and broke her leg, Galen walked seven miles in a blizzard to get a surgeon; but if he did her this service one day in the year, he bored her by being in the way for the other three hundred and sixty-four. One would have imagined at that time that he thought his perpetual presence the greatest gift he could bestow; for, except on the occasion of his fetching the surgeon, I don't remember his taking any other way of expressing his gratitude.

In love with Mabel? Not a bit! But the queer thing was that he *did* have a passion in those days—a blind hopeless passion for Mrs. Lanfear! Yes: I know what I'm saying. I mean Mrs. Lanfear, the Professor's wife, poor Mrs. Lanfear, with her tight hair and her loose shape, her blameless brow and earnest eye-glasses, and her perpetual air of mild misapprehension. I can see Dredge cowering, long and many-jointed, in a small drawing-room chair, one square-toed shoe coiled round an exposed ankle, his knees clasped in a knot of knuckles, and his spectacles perpetually seeking Mrs. Lanfear's eye-glasses. I never knew if the poor lady was aware of the sentiment she inspired, but her children observed it, and it provoked them to irreverent mirth. Galen was the predestined butt of Mabel and Archie; and secure in their mother's obtuseness, and in her worshipper's timidity, they allowed themselves a latitude of banter that sometimes made their audience shiver. Dredge meanwhile was going on obstinately with his work. Now and then he had fits of idleness, when he lapsed into a state of sulky inertia from which even Lanfear's remonstrances could not rouse him. Once, just before an examination, he suddenly went off to the Maine woods for two weeks, came back, and failed to pass. I don't know if his benefactor ever lost hope; but at times his confidence must have been sorely strained. The queer part of it was that when Dredge emerged from these eclipses he seemed keener and more active than ever. His slowly growing intelligence probably needed its periodical pauses of assimilation; and Lanfear was wonderfully patient.

At last Dredge finished his course and went to Germany; and when he came back he was a new man—was, in fact, the Dredge we all know. He seemed to have shed his encumbering personality, and have come to life as a disembodied intelligence. His fidelity to the Lanfears was unchanged; but he showed it negatively, by his discretions and abstentions. I have an idea that Mabel was less disposed to laugh at him, might even have been induced to softer sentiments; but I doubt if Dredge even noticed the change. As for his ex-goddess, he seemed to regard her as a motherly household divinity, the guardian genius of the darning needle; but on Professor Lanfear he looked with a deepening reverence. If the rest of the family had diminished in his eyes, its head had grown even greater.

II

From that day Dredge's progress continued steadily. If not always perceptible to the untrained eye, in Lanfear's sight it never flagged, and the great man began to associate Dredge with his work, and to lean on him more and more. Lanfear's health was already failing, and in my confidential talks with him I saw how he counted on Dredge to continue and develop his teachings. If he did not describe the young man as his predestined Huxley, it was because any such comparison between himself and his great predecessors would have been distasteful to him; but he evidently felt that it would be Dredge's part to reveal him to posterity. And the young man seemed at that time to take the same view. When he was not busy about Lanfear's work he was recording their conversations with the diligence of a biographer and the accuracy of a naturalist. Any attempt to question Lanfear's theories or to minimize his achievement, roused in his disciple the only flashes of wrath I have ever seen a scientific discussion provoke in him. In defending his master he became almost as intemperate as in the early period of his literary passions.

Such filial devotion must have been all the more precious to Lanfear because, about that time, it became evident that Archie would never carry on his father's work. He had begun brilliantly, you may remember, by a little paper on *Limulus Polyphemus* that attracted a good deal of notice when it appeared; but gradually his zoological ardor yielded to a passion for the violin, which was followed by a plunge into physics. At present, after a side-glance at the drama, I understand he's devoting what is left of his father's money to archæological explorations in Asia Minor.

"Archie's got a delightful little mind," Lanfear used to say to me, rather wistfully, "but it's just a highly polished surface held up to the show as it passes. Dredge's mind takes in only a bit at a time, but the bit stays, and other bits are joined to it, in a hard mosaic of fact, of which imagination weaves the pattern. I saw just how it would be years ago, when my boy used to take my meaning in a flash, and answer me with clever objections, while Galen disappeared into one of his fathomless silences, and then came to the surface like a dripping retriever, a long way beyond Archie's objections, and with an answer to them in his mouth."

It was about this time that the crowning satisfaction of Lanfear's career came to him: I mean, of course, John Weyman's gift to Columbia of the Lanfear Laboratory, and the founding, in connection with it, of a chair of

Experimental Evolution. Weyman had always taken an interest in Lanfear's work, but no one had supposed that his interest would express itself so magnificently. The honor came to Lanfear at a time when he was fighting an accumulation of troubles: failing health, the money difficulties resulting from his irrepressible generosity, his disappointment about Archie's career, and perhaps also the persistent attacks of the new school of German zoologists.

"If I hadn't Galen I should feel the game was up," he said to me once, in a fit of half-real, half-mocking despondency. "But he'll do what I haven't time to do myself, and what my boy can't do for me."

That meant that he would answer the critics, and triumphantly reaffirm Lanfear's theory, which had been rudely shaken, but not dislodged.

"A scientific hypothesis lasts till there's something else to put in its place. People who want to get across a river will use the old bridge till the new one's built. And I don't see any one who's particularly anxious, in this case, to take a contract for the new one," Lanfear ended; and I remember answering with a laugh: "Not while Horatius Dredge holds the other."

It was generally known that Lanfear had not long to live, and the Laboratory was hardly opened before the question of his successor in the chair of Experimental Evolution began to be a matter of public discussion. It was conceded that whoever followed him ought to be a man of achieved reputation, some one carrying, as the French say, a considerable "baggage." At the same time, even Lanfear's critics felt that he should be succeeded by a man who held his views and would continue his teaching. This was not in itself a difficulty, for German criticism had so far been mainly negative, and there were plenty of good men who, while they questioned the permanent validity of Lanfear's conclusions, were yet ready to accept them for their provisional usefulness. And then there was the added inducement of the Laboratory! The Columbia Professor of Experimental Evolution has at his disposal the most complete instrument of biological research that modern ingenuity has yet produced; and it's not only in theology or politics *que Paris vaut bien une messe!* There was no trouble about finding a candidate; but the whole thing turned on Lanfear's decision, since it was tacitly understood that, by Weyman's wish, he was to select his successor. And what a cry there was when he selected Galen Dredge!

Not in the scientific world, though. The specialists were beginning to know about Dredge. His remarkable paper on Sexual Dimorphism had been translated into several languages, and a furious polemic had broken out over it. When a young fellow can get the big men fighting over him his future is pretty well assured. But Dredge was only thirty-four, and some people seemed to feel that there was a kind of deflected nepotism in Lanfear's choice.

"If he could choose Dredge he might as well have chosen his own son," I've heard it said; and the irony was that Archie—will you believe it?—

actually thought so himself! But Lanfear had Weyman behind him, and when the end came the Faculty at once appointed Galen Dredge to the chair of Experimental Evolution.

For the first two years things went quietly, along accustomed lines. Dredge simply continued the course which Lanfear's death had interrupted. He lectured well even then, with a persuasive simplicity surprising in the inarticulate creature one knew him for. But haven't you noticed that certain personalities reveal themselves only in the more impersonal relations of life? It's as if they woke only to collective contacts, and the single consciousness were an unmeaning fragment to them.

If there was anything to criticize in that first part of the course, it was the avoidance of general ideas, of those brilliant rockets of conjecture that Lanfear's students were used to seeing him fling across the darkness. I remember once saying this to Archie, who, having forgotten his absurd disappointment, had returned to his old allegiance to Dredge.

"Oh, that's Galen all over. He doesn't want to jump into the ring till he has a big swishing knockdown argument in his fist. He'll wait twenty years if he has to. That's his strength: he's never afraid to wait."

I thought this shrewd of Archie, as well as generous; and I saw the wisdom of Dredge's course. As Lanfear himself had said, his theory was safe enough till somebody found a more attractive one; and before that day Dredge would probably have accumulated sufficient proof to crystallize the fluid hypothesis.

III

The third winter I was off collecting in Central America, and didn't get back till Dredge's course had been going for a couple of months. The very day I turned up in town Archie Lanfear descended on me with a summons from his mother. I was wanted at once at a family council.

I found the Lanfear ladies in a state of explosive distress, which Archie's own indignation hardly made more intelligible. But gradually I put together their fragmentary charges, and learned that Dredge's lectures were turning into an organized assault on his master's doctrine.

"It amounts to just this," Archie said, controlling his women with the masterful gesture of the weak man. "Galen has simply turned round and betrayed my father."

"Just for a handful of silver he left us," Mabel sobbed in parenthesis, while Mrs. Lanfear tearfully cited Hamlet.

Archie silenced them again. "The ugly part of it is that he must have had this up his sleeve for years. He must have known when he was asked to succeed my father what use he meant to make of his opportunity. What he's doing isn't the result of a hasty conclusion: it means years of work and preparation."

Archie broke off to explain himself. He had returned from Europe the week before, and had learned on arriving that Dredge's lectures were stirring the world of science as nothing had stirred it since Lanfear's "Utility and Variation." And the incredible affront was that they owed their success to the fact of being an attempted refutation of Lanfear's great work.

I own that I was staggered: the case looked ugly, as Archie said. And there was a veil of reticence, of secrecy, about Dredge, that always kept his conduct in a half-light of uncertainty. Of some men one would have said offhand: "It's impossible!" But one couldn't affirm it of him.

Archie hadn't seen him as yet; and Mrs. Lanfear had sent for me because she wished me to be present at the interview between the two men. The Lanfear ladies had a touching belief in Archie's violence: they thought him as terrible as a natural force. My own idea was that if there were any broken bones they wouldn't be Dredge's; but I was too curious as to the outcome not to be glad to offer my services as moderator.

First, however, I wanted to hear one of the lectures; and I went the next afternoon. The hall was jammed, and I saw, as soon as Dredge appeared, what increased security and ease the sympathy of his audience had given him. He has been clear the year before, now he was also eloquent. The lecture was a remarkable effort: you'll find the gist of it in Chapter VII of "The Arrival of the Fittest." Archie sat at my side in a white rage; he was too intelligent not to measure the extent of the disaster. And I was almost as indignant as he when we went to see Dredge the next day.

I saw at a glance that the latter suspected nothing; and it was characteristic of him that he began by questioning me about my finds, and only afterward turned to reproach Archie for having been back a week without letting him know.

"You know I'm up to my neck in this job. Why in the world didn't you hunt me up before this?"

The question was exasperating, and I could understand Archie's stammer of wrath.

"Hunt you up? Hunt you up? What the deuce are you made of, to ask me such a question instead of wondering why I'm here now?"

Dredge bent his slow calm scrutiny on his friend's agitated face; then he turned to me.

"What's the matter?" he said simply.

"The matter?" shrieked Archie, his fist hovering excitedly above the desk by which he stood; but Dredge, with unwonted quickness, caught the fist as it descended.

"Careful—I've got a *Kallima* in that jar there." He pushed a chair forward, and added quietly: "Sit down."

Archie, ignoring the gesture, towered pale and avenging in his place; and Dredge, after a moment, took the chair himself.

"The matter?" Archie reiterated. "Are you so lost to all sense of decency and honor that you can put that question in good faith? Don't you really *know* what's the matter?"

Dredge smiled slowly. "There are so few things one really *knows*."

"Oh, damn your scientific hair-splitting! Don't you know you're insulting my father's memory?"

Dredge thoughtfully turned his spectacles from one of us to the other.

"Oh, that's it, is it? Then you'd better sit down. If you don't see at once it'll take some time to make you."

Archie burst into an ironic laugh.

"I rather think it will!" he retorted.

"Sit down, Archie," I said, setting the example; and he obeyed, with a gesture that made his consent a protest.

Dredge seemed to notice nothing beyond the fact that his visitors were seated. He reached for his pipe, and filled it with the care which the habit of delicate manipulations gave to all the motions of his long knotty hands.

"It's about the lectures?" he said.

Archie's answer was a deep scornful breath.

"You've only been back a week, so you've only heard one, I suppose?"

"It was not necessary to hear even that one. You must know the talk they're making. If notoriety is what you're after—"

"Well, I'm not sorry to make a noise," said Dredge, putting a match to his pipe.

Archie bounded in his chair. "There's no easier way of doing it than to attack a man who can't answer you!"

Dredge raised a sobering hand. "Hold on. Perhaps you and I don't mean the same thing. Tell me first what's in your mind."

The question steadied Archie, who turned on Dredge a countenance really eloquent with filial indignation.

"It's an odd question for you to ask; it makes me wonder what's in *yours*. Not much thought of my father, at any rate, or you couldn't stand in his place and use the chance he's given you to push yourself at his expense."

Dredge received this in silence, puffing slowly at his pipe.

"Is that the way it strikes you?" he asked at length.

"God! It's the way it would strike most men."

He turned to me. "You too?"

"I can see how Archie feels," I said.

"That I am attacking his father's memory to glorify myself?"

"Well, not precisely: I think what he really feels is that, if your convictions didn't permit you to continue his father's teaching, you might perhaps have done better to sever your connection with the Lanfear lectureship."

"Then you and he regard the Lanfear lectureship as having been founded to perpetuate a dogma, not to try and get at the truth?"

"Certainly not," Archie broke in. "But there's a question of taste, of delicacy, involved in the case that can't be decided on abstract principles. We know as well as you that my father meant the laboratory and the lectureship to serve the ends of science, at whatever cost to his own special convictions; what we feel—and you don't seem to—it that you're the last man to put them to that particular use; and I don't want to remind you why."

A slight redness rose through Dredge's sallow skin. "You needn't," he said. "It's because he pulled me out of my hole, woke me up, made me, shoved me off from shore. Because he saved me ten or twenty years of muddled effort, and put me where I am at an age when my best working years are still ahead of me. Every one knows that's what your father did for me, but I'm the only person who knows the time and trouble it took."

It was well said, and I glanced quickly at Archie, who was never closed to generous emotions.

"Well, then—?" he said, flushing also.

"Well, then," Dredge continued, his voice deepening and losing its nasal edge, "I had to pay him back, didn't I?"

The sudden drop flung Archie back on his prepared attitude of irony. "It would be the natural inference—with most men."

"Just so. And I'm not so very different. I knew your father wanted a successor—some one who'd try and tie up the loose ends. And I took the lectureship with that object."

"And you're using it to tear the whole fabric to pieces!"

Dredge paused to re-light his pipe. "Looks that way," he conceded. "This year anyhow."

"This year—?" Archie echoed.

"Yes. When I took up the job I saw it just as your father left it. Or rather, I didn't see any other way of going on with it. The change came gradually, as I worked."

"Gradually? So that you had time to look round you, to know where you were, to see that you were fatally committed to undoing the work he had done?"

"Oh, yes—I had time," Dredge conceded.

"And yet you kept the chair and went on with the course?"

Dredge refilled his pipe, and then turned in his seat so that he looked squarely at Archie.

"What would your father have done in my place?" he asked.

"In your place—?"

"Yes: supposing he'd found out the things I've found out in the last year or two. You'll see what they are, and how much they count, if you'll run over the report of the lectures. If your father'd been alive he might have come across the same facts just as easily."

There was a silence which Archie at last broke by saying: "But he didn't, and you did. There's the difference."

"The difference? What difference? Would your father have suppressed the facts if he'd found them? It's *you* who insult his memory by implying it! And if I'd brought them to him, would he have used his hold over me to get me to suppress them?"

"Certainly not. But can't you see it's his death that makes the difference? He's not here to defend his case."

Dredge laughed, but not unkindly. "My dear Archie, your father wasn't one of the kind who bother to defend their case. Men like him are the masters, not the servants, of their theories. They respect an idea only as long as it's of use to them; when its usefulness ends they chuck it out. And that's what your father would have done."

Archie reddened. "Don't you assume a good deal in taking it for granted that he would have had to do so in this particular case?"

Dredge reflected. "Yes: I was going too far. Each of us can only answer for himself. But to my mind your father's theory is refuted."

"And you don't hesitate to be the man to do it?"

"Should I have been of any use if I had? And did your father ever ask anything of me but to be of as much use as I could?"

It was Archie's turn to reflect. "No. That was what he always wanted, of course."

"That's the way I've always felt. The first day he took me away from East Lethe I knew the debt I was piling up against him, and I never had any doubt as to how I'd pay it, or how he'd want it paid. He didn't pick me out and train me for any object but to carry on the light. Do you suppose he'd have wanted me to snuff it out because it happened to light up a fact *he* didn't fancy? I'm using *his* oil to feed my torch with: yes, but it isn't really his torch or mine, or his oil or mine: they belong to each of us till we drop and hand them on."

Archie turned a sobered glance on him. "I see your point. But if the job had to be done I don't see that you need have done it from his chair."

"There's where we differ. If I did it at all I had to do it in the best way, and with all the authority his backing gave me. If I owe your father anything, I owe him that. It would have made him sick to see the job badly done. And don't you see that the way to honor him, and show what he's done for science, was to spare no advantage in my attack on him—that I'm proving the strength of his position by the desperateness of my assault?" Dredge paused and squared his lounging shoulders. "After all," he added, "he's not down yet, and if I leave him standing I guess it'll be some time before anybody else cares to tackle him."

There was a silence between the two men; then Dredge continued in a lighter tone: "There's one thing, though, that we're both in danger of forgetting: and that is how little, in the long run, it all counts either way." He smiled a little at Archie's indignant gesture. "The most we can any of us do —even by such a magnificent effort as your father's—is to turn the great marching army a hair's breadth nearer what seems to us the right direction; if one of us drops out, here and there, the loss of headway's hardly perceptible. And that's what I'm coming to now."

He rose from his seat, and walked across to the hearth; then, cautiously resting his shoulder-blades against the mantel-shelf jammed with miscellaneous specimens, he bent his musing spectacles on Archie.

"Your father would have understood why I've done what I'm doing; but that's no reason why the rest of you should. And I rather think it's the rest of you who've suffered most from me. He always knew what I was *there for,* and that must have been some comfort even when I was most in the way; but I was just an ordinary nuisance to you and your mother and Mabel. You were all too kind to let me see it at the time, but I've seen it since, and it makes me feel that, after all, the settling of this matter lies with you. If it hurts you to have me go on with my examination of your father's theory, I'm ready to drop the lectures to-morrow, and trust to the Lanfear Laboratory to breed up a young chap who'll knock us both out in time. You've only got to say the word."

There was a pause while Dredge turned and laid his extinguished pipe carefully between a jar of embryo sea-urchins and a colony of regenerating planarians.

Then Archie rose and held out his hand.

"No," he said simply; "go on."

WILLA CATHER

(1876–   )

Willa Sibert Cather was born in Winchester, Virginia, in 1876, but as a child of eight or nine was taken to live on a Nebraska ranch. She was graduated at the University of Nebraska in 1895, and then returned east. She taught English at the Allegheny high school, and from 1897 to 1901 was on the staff of the Pittsburgh *Daily Leader*. At first she wrote verse, publishing a volume, *April Twilights,* in 1903, but she soon turned to prose as her best medium. Her first volume of stories, *The Troll Garden* (1905), procured her an associate editorship on *McClure's Magazine,* which she held from 1906 to 1912. In the latter year appeared her first novel, *Alexander's Bridge.* With *O Pioneers!* (1913) she began a period of prolific writing.

Miss Cather has used various themes in her stories and novels, but her peculiar interest is the pioneer life of Western immigrants. Though her realism has not prevented her from showing warm sympathy for her characters, she often writes with a detachment that gives the impression of coldness. Her keen analysis of motives and her sympathetic understanding of human actions and aspirations, combined with a style remarkable for its restraint and balance, have given her a high place among contemporary novelists.

THE SCULPTOR'S FUNERAL [1]

A GROUP of the townspeople stood on the station siding of a little Kansas town, awaiting the coming of the night train, which was already twenty minutes overdue. The snow had fallen thick over everything; in the pale starlight the line of bluffs across the wide, white meadows south of the town made soft, smoke-colored curves against the clear sky. The men on the siding stood first on one foot and then on the other, their hands thrust deep into their trousers pockets, their overcoats open, their shoulders screwed up with the cold; and they glanced from time to time toward the southeast, where the railroad track wound along the river shore. They conversed in low tones and moved about restlessly, seeming uncertain as to what was expected of them. There was but one of the company who looked as if he knew exactly why he was there, and he kept conspicuously apart; walking to the far end of the platform, returning to the station door, then pacing up the track again, his chin sunk in the high collar of his overcoat, his burly shoulders drooping forward, his gait heavy and dogged. Presently he was approached by a tall,

[1] From *Youth and the Bright Medusa,* by permission of Alfred A. Knopf, Inc., the authorized publishers.

spare, grizzled man clad in a faded Grand Army suit, who shuffled out from the group and advanced with a certain deference, craning his neck forward until his back made the angle of a jack-knife three-quarters open.

"I reckon she's a-goin' to be pretty late again tonight, Jim," he remarked in a squeaky falsetto. "S'pose it's the snow?"

"I don't know," responded the other man with a shade of annoyance, speaking from out an astonishing cataract of red beard that grew fiercely and thickly in all directions.

The spare man shifted the quill toothpick he was chewing to the other side of his mouth. "It ain't likely that anybody from the East will come with the corpse, I s'pose," he went on reflectively.

"I don't know," responded the other, more curtly than before.

"It's too bad he didn't belong to some lodge or other. I like an order funeral myself. They seem more appropriate for people of some repytation," the spare man continued, with an ingratiating concession in his shrill voice, as he carefully placed his toothpick in his vest pocket. He always carried the flag at the G. A. R. funerals in the town.

The heavy man turned on his heel, without replying, and walked up the siding. The spare man rejoined the uneasy group. "Jim's ez full ez a tick, ez ushel," he commented commiseratingly.

Just then a distant whistle sounded, and there was a shuffling of feet on the platform. A number of lanky boys, of all ages, appeared as suddenly and slimily as eels wakened by the crack of thunder; some came from the waiting-room, where they had been warming themselves by the red stove, or half asleep on the slat benches; others uncoiled themselves from baggage trucks or slid out of express wagons. Two clambered down from the driver's seat of a hearse that stood backed up against the siding. They straightened their stooping shoulders and lifted their heads, and a flash of momentary animation kindled their dull eyes at that cold, vibrant scream, the world-wide call for men. It stirred them like the note of a trumpet; just as it had often stirred the man who was coming home tonight, in his boyhood.

The night express shot, red as a rocket, from out the eastward marsh lands and wound along the river shore under the long lines of shivering poplars that sentinelled the meadows, the escaping steam hanging in grey masses against the pale sky and blotting out the Milky Way. In a moment the red glare from the headlight streamed up the snow-covered track before the siding and glittered on the wet, black rails. The burly man with the dishevelled red beard walked swiftly up the platform toward the approaching train, uncovering his head as he went. The group of men behind him hesitated, glanced questioningly at one another, and awkwardly followed his example. The train stopped, and the crowd shuffled up to the express car just as the door was thrown open, the man in the G. A. R. suit thrusting his head forward with curiosity. The express messenger appeared in the doorway accompanied by a young man in a long ulster and travelling cap.

"Are Mr. Merrick's friends here?" inquired the young man.

The group on the platform swayed uneasily. Philip Phelps, the banker, responded with dignity: "We have come to take charge of the body. Mr. Merrick's father is very feeble and can't be about."

"Send the agent out here," growled the express messenger, "and tell the operator to lend a hand."

The coffin was got out of its rough-box and down on the snowy platform. The townspeople drew back enough to make room for it and then formed a close semicircle about it, looking curiously at the palm leaf which lay across the black cover. No one said anything. The baggage man stood by his truck, waiting to get at the trunks. The engine panted heavily, and the fireman dodged in and out among the wheels with his yellow torch and long oil-can, snapping the spindle boxes. The young Bostonian, one of the dead sculptor's pupils who had come with the body, looked about him helplessly. He turned to the banker, the only one of that black, uneasy, stoop-shouldered group who seemed enough of an individual to be addressed.

"None of Mr. Merrick's brothers are here?" he asked uncertainly.

The man with the red beard for the first time stepped up and joined the others. "No, they have not come yet; the family is scattered. The body will be taken directly to the house." He stooped and took hold of one of the handles of the coffin.

"Take the long hill road up, Thompson, it will be easier on the horses," called the liveryman as the undertaker snapped the door of the hearse and prepared to mount to the driver's seat.

Laird, the red-bearded lawyer, turned again to the stranger: "We didn't know whether there would be any one with him or not," he explained. "It's a long walk, so you'd better go up in the hack." He pointed to a single battered conveyance, but the young man replied stiffly: "Thank you, but I think I will go up with the hearse. If you don't object," turning to the undertaker, "I'll ride with you."

They clambered up over the wheels and drove off in the starlight up the long, white hill toward the town. The lamps in the still village were shining from under the low, snow-burdened roofs; and beyond, on every side, the plains reached out into emptiness, peaceful and wide as the soft sky itself, and wrapped in a tangible, white silence.

When the hearse backed up to a wooden sidewalk before a naked, weather-beaten frame house, the same composite, ill-defined group that had stood upon the station siding was huddled about the gate. The front yard was an icy swamp, and a couple of warped planks, extending from the sidewalk to the door, made a sort of rickety footbridge. The gate hung on one hinge, and was opened wide with difficulty. Steavens, the young stranger, noticed that something black was tied to the knob of the front door.

The grating sound made by the casket, as it was drawn from the hearse, was answered by a scream from the house; the front door was wrenched open, and a tall, corpulent woman rushed out bareheaded into the snow and flung herself upon the coffin, shrieking: "My boy, my boy! And this is how you've come home to me!"

As Steavens turned away and closed his eyes with a shudder of unutterable repulsion, another woman, also tall, but flat and angular, dressed entirely in black, darted out of the house and caught Mrs. Merrick by the shoulders, crying sharply: "Come, come, mother; you mustn't go on like this!" Her tone changed to one of obsequious solemnity as she turned to the banker: "The parlor is ready, Mr. Phelps."

The bearers carried the coffin along the narrow boards, while the under-taker ran ahead with the coffin-rests. They bore it into a large, unheated room that smelled of dampness and disuse and furniture polish, and set it down under a hanging lamp ornamented with jingling glass prisms and be-fore a "Rogers group" of John Alden and Priscilla, wreathed with smilax. Henry Steavens stared about him with the sickening conviction that there had been a mistake, and that he had somehow arrived at the wrong destina-tion. He looked at the clover-green Brussels, the fat plush upholstery, among the handpainted china plaques and panels and vases, for some mark of identi-fication,—for something that might once conceivably have belonged to Har-vey Merrick. It was not until he recognized his friend in the crayon portrait of a little boy in kilts and curls, hanging above the piano, that he felt willing to let any of these people approach the coffin.

"Take the lid off, Mr. Thompson; let me see my boy's face," wailed the elder woman between her sobs. This time Steavens looked fearfully, almost beseechingly into her face, red and swollen under its masses of strong, black, shiny hair. He flushed, dropped his eyes, and then, almost incredulously, looked again. There was a kind of power about her face—a kind of brutal handsomeness, even; but it was scarred and furrowed by violence, and so colored and coarsened by fiercer passions that grief seemed never to have laid a gentle finger there. The long nose was distended and knobbed at the end, and there were deep lines on either side of it; her heavy, black brows almost met across her forehead, her teeth were large and square, and set far apart— teeth that could tear. She filled the room; the men were obliterated, seemed tossed about like twigs in an angry water, and even Steavens felt himself being drawn into the whirlpool.

The daughter—the tall, raw-boned woman in crêpe, with a mourning comb in her hair which curiously lengthened her long face—sat stiffly upon the sofa, her hands, conspicuous for their large knuckles, folded in her lap, her mouth and eyes drawn down, solemnly awaiting the opening of the coffin. Near the door stood a mulatto woman, evidently a servant in the house, with a timid bearing and an emaciated face pitifully sad and gentle. She was weeping silently, the corner of her calico apron lifted to her eyes, occasionally suppressing a long, quivering sob. Steavens walked over and stood beside her.

Feeble steps were heard on the stairs, and an old man, tall and frail, odorous of pipe smoke, with shaggy, unkempt grey hair and a dingy beard, tobacco stained about the mouth, entered uncertainly. He went slowly up to the coffin and stood rolling a blue cotton handkerchief between his hands, seeming so pained and embarrassed by his wife's orgy of grief that he had no consciousness of anything else.

"There, there, Annie, dear, don't take on so," he quavered timidly, putting out a shaking hand and awkwardly patting her elbow. She turned and sank upon his shoulder with such violence that he tottered a little. He did not even glance toward the coffin, but continued to look at her with a dull, frightened, appealing expression, as a spaniel looks at the whip. His sunken cheeks slowly reddened and burned with miserable shame. When his wife rushed from the room, her daughter strode after her with set lips. The servant stole up to the coffin, bent over it for a moment, and then slipped away to the kitchen, leaving Steavens, the lawyer, and the father to themselves. The old man stood looking down at his dead son's face. The sculptor's splendid head seemed even more noble in its rigid stillness than in life. The dark hair had crept down upon the wide forehead; the face seemed strangely long, but in it there was not that repose we expect to find in the faces of the dead. The brows were so drawn that there were two deep lines above the beaked nose, and the chin was thrust forward defiantly. It was as though the strain of life had been so sharp and bitter that death could not at once relax the tension and smooth the countenance into perfect peace—as though he were still guarding something precious, which might even yet be wrested from him.

The old man's lips were working under his stained beard. He turned to the lawyer with timid deference: "Phelps and the rest are comin' back to set up with Harve, ain't they?" he asked. "Thank 'ee, Jim, thank 'ee." He brushed the hair back gently from his son's forehead. "He was a good boy, Jim; always a good boy. He was ez gentle ez a child and the kindest of 'em all—only we didn't none of us ever onderstand him." The tears trickled slowly down his beard and dropped upon the sculptor's coat.

"Martin, Martin! Oh, Martin! come here," his wife wailed from the top of the stairs. The old man started timorously: "Yes, Annie, I'm coming." He turned away, hesitated, stood for a moment in miserable indecision; then reached back and patted the dead man's hair softly, and stumbled from the room.

"Poor old man, I didn't think he had any tears left. Seems as if his eyes would have gone dry long ago. At his age nothing cuts very deep," remarked the lawyer.

Something in his tone made Steavens glance up. While the mother had been in the room, the young man had scarcely seen any one else; but now, from the moment he first glanced into Jim Laird's florid face and blood-shot eyes, he knew that he had found what he had been heartsick at not finding before—the feeling, the understanding, that must exist in some one, even here.

The man was red as his beard, with features swollen and blurred by dissipation, and a hot, blazing blue eye. His face was strained—that of a man who is controlling himself with difficulty—and he kept plucking at his beard with a sort of fierce resentment. Steavens, sitting by the window, watched him turn down the glaring lamp, still its jangling pendants with an angry gesture, and then stand with his hands locked behind him, staring down into the master's face. He could not help wondering what link there had been between the porcelain vessel and so sooty a lump of potter's clay.

From the kitchen an uproar was sounding; when the dining-room door opened, the import of it was clear. The mother was abusing the maid for having forgotten to make the dressing for the chicken salad which had been prepared for the watchers. Steavens had never heard anything in the least like it; it was injured, emotional, dramatic abuse, unique and masterly in its excruciating cruelty, as violent and unrestrained as had been her grief of twenty minutes before. With a shudder of disgust the lawyer went into the dining-room and closed the door into the kitchen.

"Poor Roxy's getting it now," he remarked when he came back. "The Merricks took her out of the poorhouse years ago; and if her loyalty would let her, I guess the poor old thing could tell tales that would curdle your blood. She's the mulatto woman who was standing in here a while ago, with her apron to her eyes. The old woman is a fury; there never was anybody like her. She made Harvey's life a hell for him when he lived at home; he was so sick ashamed of it. I never could see how he kept himself sweet."

"He was wonderful," said Steavens slowly, "wonderful; but until tonight I have never known how wonderful."

"That is the eternal wonder of it, anyway; that it can come even from such a dung heap as this," the lawyer cried, with a sweeping gesture which seemed to indicate much more than the four walls within which they stood.

"I think I'll see whether I can get a little air. The room is so close I am beginning to feel rather faint," murmured Steavens, struggling with one of the windows. The sash was stuck, however, and would not yield, so he sat down dejectedly and began pulling at his collar. The lawyer came over, loosened the sash with one blow of his red fist and sent the window up a few inches. Steavens thanked him, but the nausea which had been gradually climbing into his throat for the last half hour left him with but one desire—a desperate feeling that he must get away from this place with what was left of Harvey Merrick. Oh, he comprehended well enough now the quiet bitterness of the smile that he had seen so often on his master's lips!

Once when Merrick returned from a visit home, he brought with him a singularly feeling and suggestive bas-relief of a thin, faded old woman, sitting and sewing something pinned to her knee; while a full-lipped, full-blooded little urchin, his trousers held up by a single gallows, stood beside her, impatiently twitching her gown to call her attention to a butterfly he had caught. Steavens, impressed by the tender and delicate modelling of the thin, tired face, had asked him if it were his mother. He remembered the dull flush that had burned up in the sculptor's face.

The lawyer was sitting in a rocking-chair beside the coffin, his head thrown back and his eyes closed. Steavens looked at him earnestly, puzzled at the line of the chin, and wondering why a man should conceal a feature of such distinction under that disfiguring shock of beard. Suddenly, as though he felt the young sculptor's keen glance, Jim Laird opened his eyes.

"Was he always a good deal of an oyster?" he asked abruptly. "He was terribly shy as a boy."

"Yes, he was an oyster, since you put it so," rejoined Steavens. "Although he could be very fond of people, he always gave one the impression of being detached. He disliked violent emotion; he was reflective, and rather distrustful of himself—except, of course, as regarded his work. He was sure enough there. He distrusted men pretty thoroughly and women even more, yet somehow without believing ill of them. He was determined, indeed, to believe the best; but he seemed afraid to investigate."

"A burnt dog dreads the fire," said the lawyer grimly, and closed his eyes.

Steavens went on and on, reconstructing that whole miserable boyhood. All this raw, biting ugliness had been the portion of the man whose mind was to become an exhaustless gallery of beautiful impressions—so sensitive that the mere shadow of a poplar leaf flickering against a sunny wall would be etched and held there for ever. Surely, if ever a man had the magic word in his fingertips, it was Merrick. Whatever he touched, he revealed its holiest secret; liberated it from enchantment and restored it to its pristine loveliness. Upon whatever he had come in contact with, he had left a beautiful record of the experience—a sort of ethereal signature; a scent, a sound, a color that was his own.

Steavens understood now the real tragedy of his master's life; neither love nor wine, as many had conjectured; but a blow which had fallen earlier and cut deeper than anything else could have done—a shame not his, and yet so unescapably his, to hide in his heart from his very boyhood. And without— the frontier warfare; the yearning of a boy, cast ashore upon a desert of newness and ugliness and sordidness, for all that is chastened and old, and noble with traditions.

At eleven o'clock the tall, flat woman in black announced that the watchers were arriving, and asked them to "step into the dining-room." As Steavens rose, the lawyer said dryly: "You go on—it'll be a good experience for you. I'm not equal to that crowd tonight; I've had twenty years of them."

As Steavens closed the door after him he glanced back at the lawyer, sitting by the coffin in the dim light, with his chin resting on his hand.

The same misty group that had stood before the door of the express car shuffled into the dining-room. In the light of the kerosene lamp they separated and became individuals. The minister, a pale, feeble-looking man with white hair and blond chin-whiskers, took his seat beside a small side table and placed his Bible upon it. The Grand Army man sat down behind the stove and tilted his chair back comfortably against the wall, fishing his quill toothpick from his waistcoat pocket. The two bankers, Phelps and Elder, sat off in a corner behind the dinner-table, where they could finish their discussion of the new usury law and its effect on chattel security loans. The real estate agent, an old man with a smiling, hypocritical face, soon joined them. The coal and lumber dealer and the cattle shipper sat on opposite sides of the hard coal-burner, their feet on the nickel-work. Steavens took a book from his pocket and began to read. The talk around him ranged through various topics of local interest while the house was quieting down. When it was clear that the members of the family were in bed, the Grand Army man hitched his shoulders and, untangling his long legs, caught his heels on the rounds of his chair.

"S'pose there'll be a will, Phelps?" he queried in his weak falsetto.

The banker laughed disagreeably, and began trimming his nails with a pearl-handled pocket-knife.

"There'll scarcely be any need for one, will there?" he queried in his turn.

The restless Grand Army man shifted his position again, getting his knees still nearer his chin. "Why, the ole man says Harve's done right well lately," he chirped.

The other banker spoke up. "I reckon he means by that Harve ain't asked him to mortgage any more farms lately, so as he could go on with his education."

"Seems like my mind don't reach back to a time when Harve wasn't bein' edycated," tittered the Grand Army man.

There was a general chuckle. The minister took out his handkerchief and blew his nose sonorously. Banker Phelps closed his knife with a snap. "It's too bad the old man's sons didn't turn out better," he remarked with reflective authority. "They never hung together. He spent money enough on Harve to stock a dozen cattle-farms, and he might as well have poured it into Sand Creek. If Harve had stayed at home and helped nurse what little they had, and gone into stock on the old man's bottom farm, they might all have been well fixed. But the old man had to trust everything to tenants and was cheated right and left."

"Harve never could have handled stock none," interposed the cattleman. "He hadn't it in him to be sharp. Do you remember when he bought Sander's mules for eight-year olds, when everybody in town knew that Sander's father-in-law give 'em to his wife for a wedding present eighteen years before, an' they was full-grown mules then?"

The company laughed discreetly, and the Grand Army man rubbed his knees with a spasm of childish delight.

"Harve never was much account for anything practical, and he shore was never fond of work," began the coal and lumber dealer. "I mind the last time he was home; the day he left, when the old man was out to the barn helpin' his hand hitch up to take Harve to the train, and Cal Moots was patchin' up the fence; Harve, he come out on the step and sings out, in his ladylike voice: 'Cal Moots, Cal Moots! please come cord my trunk.'"

"That's Harve for you," approved the Grand Army man. "I kin hear him howlin' yet, when he was a big feller in long pants and his mother used to whale him with a raw-hide in the barn for lettin' the cows git foundered in the cornfield when he was drivin' 'em home from pasture. He killed a cow of mine that-a-way onct—a pure Jersey and the best milker I had, an' the ole man had to put up for her. Harve, he was watchin' the sun set acrost the marshes when the anamile got away."

"Where the old man made his mistake was in sending the boy East to school," said Phelps, stroking his goatee and speaking in a deliberate, judicial tone. "There was where he got his head full of nonsense. What Harve needed, of all people, was a course in some first-class Kansas City business college."

The letters were swimming before Steavens's eyes. Was it possible that these men did not understand, that the palm on the coffin meant nothing to them? The very name of their town would have remained for ever buried in the postal guide had it not been now and again mentioned in the world in connection with Harvey Merrick's. He remembered what his master had said to him on the day of his death, after the congestion of both lungs had shut off any probability of recovery, and the sculptor had asked his pupil to send his body home. "It's not a pleasant place to be lying while the world is moving and doing and bettering," he had said with a feeble smile, "but it rather seems as though we ought to go back to the place we came from, in the end. The townspeople will come in for a look at me; and after they have had their say, I shan't have much to fear from the judgment of God!"

The cattleman took up the comment. "Forty's young for a Merrick to cash in; they usually hang on pretty well. Probably he helped it along with whiskey."

"His mother's people were not long lived, and Harvey never had a robust constitution," said the minister mildly. He would have liked to say more. He had been the boy's Sunday-school teacher, and had been fond of him; but he felt that he was not in a position to speak. His own sons had turned out badly, and it was not a year since one of them had made his last trip home in the express car, shot in a gambling-house in the Black Hills.

"Nevertheless, there is no disputin' that Harve frequently looked upon the wine when it was red, also variegated, and it shore made an oncommon fool of him," moralized the cattleman.

Just then the door leading into the parlor rattled loudly and everyone started involuntarily, looking relieved when only Jim Laird came out. The Grand Army man ducked his head when he saw the spark in his blue, blood-shot eye. They were all afraid of Jim; he was a drunkard, but he could twist the law to suit his client's needs as no other man in all western Kansas could do, and there were many who tried. The lawyer closed the door behind him, leaned back against it and folded his arms, cocking his head a little to one side. When he assumed this attitude in the court-room, ears were always pricked up, as it usually foretold a flood of withering sarcasm.

"I've been with you gentlemen before," he began in a dry, even tone, "when you've sat by the coffins of boys born and raised in this town; and, if I remember rightly, you were never any too well satisfied when you checked them up. What's the matter, anyhow? Why is it that reputable young men are as scarce as millionaires in Sand City? It might almost seem to a stranger that there was some way something the matter with your progressive town. Why did Ruben Sayer, the brightest young lawyer you ever turned out, after he had come home from the university as straight as a die, take to drinking and forge a check and shoot himself? Why did Bill Merrit's son die of the shakes in a saloon in Omaha? Why was Mr. Thomas's son, here, shot in a gambling-house? Why did young Adams burn his mill to beat the insurance companies and go to the pen?"

The lawyer paused and unfolded his arms, laying one clenched fist quietly on the table. "I'll tell you why. Because you drummed nothing but money and knavery into their ears from the time they wore knickerbockers; because you carped away at them as you've been carping here tonight, holding our friends Phelps and Elder up to them for their models, as our grandfathers held up George Washington and John Adams. But the boys were young, and raw at the business you put them to, and how could they match coppers with such artists as Phelps and Elder? You wanted them to be successful rascals; they were only unsuccessful ones—that's all the difference. There was only one boy ever raised in this borderland between ruffianism and civilization who didn't come to grief, and you hated Harvey Merrick more for winning out than you hated all the other boys who got under the wheels. Lord, Lord, how you did hate him! Phelps, here, is fond of saying that he could buy and sell us all out any time he's a mind to; but he knew Harve wouldn't have given a tinker's damn for his bank and all his cattlefarms put together; and a lack of appreciation, that way, goes hard with Phelps.

"Old Nimrod thinks Harve drank too much; and this from such as Nimrod and me!

"Brother Elder says Harve was too free with the old man's money—fell short in filial consideration, maybe. Well, we can all remember the very tone in which brother Elder swore his own father was a liar, in the county court; and we all know that the old man came out of that partnership with his son as bare as a sheared lamb. But maybe I'm getting personal, and I'd better be driving ahead at what I want to say."

The lawyer paused a moment, squared his heavy shoulders, and went on: "Harvey Merrick and I went to school together, back East. We were dead in earnest, and we wanted you all to be proud of us some day. We meant to be great men. Even I, and I haven't lost my sense of humor, gentlemen, I meant to be a great man. I came back here to practise, and I found you didn't in the least want me to be a great man. You wanted me to be a shrewd lawyer—oh, yes! Our veteran here wanted me to get him an increase of pension, because he had dyspepsia; Phelps wanted a new county survey that would put the widow Wilson's little bottom farm inside his south line; Elder wanted to lend money at 5 per cent a month, and get it collected; and Stark here wanted to wheedle old women up in Vermont into investing their annuities in real-estate mortgages that are not worth the paper they are written on. Oh, you needed me hard enough, and you'll go on needing me!

"Well, I came back here and became the damned shyster you wanted me to be. You pretend to have some sort of respect for me; and yet you'll stand up and throw mud at Harvey Merrick, whose soul you couldn't dirty and whose hands you couldn't tie. Oh, you're a discriminating lot of Christians! There have been times when the sight of Harvey's name in some Eastern paper has made me hang my head like a whipped dog; and, again, times when I liked to think of him off there in the world, away from all this hog-wallow, climbing the big, clean up-grade he'd set for himself.

"And we? Now that we've fought and lied and sweated and stolen, and hated as only the disappointed strugglers in a bitter, dead little Western town know how to do, what have we got to show for it? Harvey Merrick wouldn't have given one sunset over your marshes for all you've got put together, and you know it. It's not for me to say why, in the inscrutable wisdom of God, a genius should ever have been called from this place of hatred and bitter waters; but I want this Boston man to know that the drivel he's been hearing here tonight is the only tribute any truly great man could have from such a lot of sick, side-tracked, burnt-dog, land-poor sharks as the here-present financiers of Sand City—upon which town may God have mercy!"

The lawyer thrust out his hand to Steavens as he passed him, caught up his overcoat in the hall, and had left the house before the Grand Army man had had time to lift his ducked head and crane his long neck about at his fellows.

Next day Jim Laird was drunk and unable to attend the funeral services. Steavens called twice at his office, but was compelled to start East without seeing him. He had a presentiment that he would hear from him again, and left his address on the lawyer's table; but if Laird found it, he never acknowledged it. The thing in him that Harvey Merrick had loved must have gone under ground with Harvey Merrick's coffin; for it never spoke again, and Jim got the cold he died of driving across the Colorado mountains to defend one of Phelps's sons who had got into trouble out there by cutting government timber.

SHERWOOD ANDERSON

(1876–   )

Sherwood Anderson was born in Camden, Ohio, in 1876. His family was poor, and except for a few years in the public schools he received no formal education. As a boy he worked at various jobs—rolling kegs into trucks at a nail factory, assembling parts in a bicycle factory, caring for race horses—but when he had saved a few dollars he would quit work to read in public libraries till he was without funds again. He was a soldier in the Spanish-American war, afterwards operated a small manufacturing business, and when this failed worked at the advertising business in Chicago. In these years he began writing stories, some of which were published in *The Little Review* and in *The Seven Arts,* and in 1916 published his first novel, *Windy McPherson's Son.* Since then he has published at the rate of about a volume a year,—mostly short stories and novels, but among the rest two volumes of verse. Something of the story of his life and of his methods and aims as a writer may be obtained from *A Story-Teller's Story* (1924), *Tar: a Mid-West Childhood* (1926), and *Sherwood Anderson's Notebook* (1926). He now lives in Marion, Virginia, where he owns two weekly newspapers.

Anderson attempts in his work to interpret the life of industrial America, and to express its inarticulate longings. With a strong sense of the value of the individual, however small his apparent consequence, he believes that the conventions of a standardized society tend to fetter men, and that complete personal freedom is the key to "the good life." His writing is independent of literary tradition, and is notable for its vividness of detail, its integrity of purpose, and the skill with which, despite occasional crudities, it reveals character and depicts life.

I'M A FOOL [1]

IT was a hard jolt for me, one of the most bitterest I ever had to face. And it all came about through my own foolishness, too. Even yet sometimes, when I think of it, I want to cry or swear or kick myself. Perhaps, even now, after all this time, there will be a kind of satisfaction in making myself look cheap by telling of it.

It began at three o'clock one October afternoon as I sat in the grand stand at the fall trotting and pacing meet at Sandusky, Ohio.

To tell the truth, I felt a little foolish that I should be sitting in the grand stand at all. During the summer before I had left my home time with Harry Whitehead and, with a nigger named Burt, had taken a job as swipe with one of the two horses Harry was campaigning through the fall race meets that

[1] From *Horses and Men,* New York, The Viking Press, Inc. Copyright, B. W. Huebsch, Inc., 1923.

year. Mother cried and my sister Mildred, who wanted to get a job as a school-teacher in our town that fall, stormed and scolded about the house all during the week before I left. They both thought it something disgraceful that one of our family should take a place as a swipe with race horses. I've an idea Mildred thought my taking the place would stand in the way of her getting the job she'd been working so long for.

But after all I had to work, and there was no other work to be got. A big lumbering fellow of nineteen couldn't just hang around the house and I had got too big to mow people's lawns and sell newspapers. Little chaps who could get next to people's sympathies by their sizes were always getting jobs away from me. There was one fellow who kept saying to every one who wanted a lawn mowed or a cistern cleaned, that he was saving money to work his way through college, and I used to lay awake nights thinking up ways to injure him without being found out. I kept thinking of wagons running over him and bricks falling on his head as he walked along the street. But never mind him.

I got the place with Harry and I liked Burt fine. We got along splendid together. He was a big nigger with a lazy sprawling body and soft, kind eyes, and when it came to a fight he could hit like Jack Johnson. He had Bucephalus, a big black pacing stallion that could do 2.09 or 2.10, if he had to, and I had a little gelding named Doctor Fritz that never lost a race all fall when Harry wanted him to win.

We set out from home late in July, in a box car with the two horses and after that, until late November, we kept moving along to the race meets and the fairs. It was a peachy time for me, I'll say that. Sometimes now I think that boys who are raised regular in houses, and never have a fine nigger like Burt for best friend, and go to high schools and college, and never steal anything, or get drunk a little, or learn to swear from fellows who know how, or come walking up in front of a grand stand in their shirt sleeves and with dirty horsy pants on when the races are going on and the grand stand is full of people all dressed up— What's the use of talking about it? Such fellows don't know nothing at all. They've never had no opportunity.

But I did. Burt taught me how to rub down a horse and put the bandages on after a race and steam a horse out and a lot of valuable things for any man to know. He could wrap a bandage on a horse's leg so smooth that if it had been the same color you would think it was his skin, and I guess he'd have been a big driver, too, and got to the top like Murphy and Walter Cox and the others if he hadn't been black.

Gee whizz, it was fun. You got to a county seat town, maybe say on a Saturday or Sunday, and the fair began the next Tuesday and lasted until Friday afternoon. Doctor Fritz would be, say in the 2.25 trot on Tuesday afternoon and on Thursday afternoon Bucephalus would knock 'em cold in the "free-for-all" pace. It left you a lot of time to hang around and listen to horse talk, and see Burt knock some yap cold that got too gay, and you'd find out about horses and men and pick up a lot of stuff you could use all the rest of your life, if you had some sense and salted down what you heard and felt and saw.

And the end of the week when the race meet was over, and Harry had run home to tend up to his livery stable business, you and Burt hitched the two horses to carts and drove slow and steady across country, to the place for the next meeting, so as to not over-heat the horses, etc., etc., you know.

Gee whizz, Gosh amighty, the nice hickerynut and beechnut and oaks and other kinds of trees along the roads, all brown and red, and the good smells, and Burt singing a song that was called Deep River, and the country girls at the windows of houses and everything. You can stick your colleges up your nose for all me. I guess I know where I got my education.

Why, one of those little burgs of towns you come to on the way, say now on a Saturday afternoon, and Burt says, "Let's lay up here." And you did.

And you took the horses to a livery stable and fed them, and you got your good clothes out of a box and put them on.

And the town was full of farmers gaping, because they could see you were racehorse people, and the kids maybe never see a nigger before and was afraid and run away when the two of us walked down their main street.

And that was before prohibition and all that foolishness, and so you went into a saloon, the two of you, and all the yaps come and stood around, and there was always some one pretended he was horsy and knew things and spoke up and began asking questions, and all you did was to lie and lie all you could about what horses you had, and I said I owned them, and then some fellow said, "Will you have a drink of whiskey" and Burt knocked his eye out the way he could say, off-hand like, "Oh well, all right, I'm agreeable to a little nip. I'll split a quart with you." Gee whizz.

But that isn't what I want to tell my story about. We got home late in November, and I promised mother I'd quit the race horses for good. There's a lot of things you've got to promise a mother because she don't know any better.

And so, there not being any work in our town any more than when I left there to go to the races, I went off to Sandusky and got a pretty good place taking care of horses for a man who owned a teaming and delivery and storage and coal and real estate business there. It was a pretty good place with good eats, and a day off each week, and sleeping on a cot in a big barn, and mostly just shoveling in hay and oats to a lot of big good-enough skates of horses, that couldn't have trotted a race with a toad. I wasn't dissatisfied, and I could send money home.

And then, as I started to tell you, the fall races come to Sandusky and I got the day off and I went. I left the job at noon and had on my good clothes and my new brown derby hat, I'd just bought the Saturday before, and a stand-up collar.

First of all I went down-town and walked about with the dudes. I've always thought to myself, "put up a good front," and so I did it. I had forty dollars in my pocket and so I went into the West House, a big hotel, and walked up to the cigar stand. "Give me three twenty-five cent cigars," I said. There was a lot of horsemen and strangers and dressed-up people from other towns standing around in the lobby and in the bar, and I mingled amongst them. In the bar there was a fellow with a cane and a Windsor tie on, that it made me sick to look at him. I like a man to be a man and dress up but not to put on that kind of airs. So I pushed him aside, kind of rough, and had me a drink of whiskey. And then he looked at me, as though he thought maybe he'd get gay, but he changed his mind and didn't say anything. And then I had another drink of whiskey, just to show him something, and went out and had a hack out to the races, all to myself, and when I got there I bought myself the best seat I could get up in the grand stand, but didn't go in for any of these boxes. That's putting on too many airs.

And so there I was, sitting up in the grand stand as gay as you please and looking down on the swipes coming out with their horses, and with their dirty horsy pants on and the horse blankets swung over their shoulders, same as I had been doing all the year before. I liked one thing about the same as the other, sitting up there and feeling grand and being down there and looking up at the yaps and feeling grander and more important, too. One thing's about as good as another, if you take it just right. I've often said that.

Well, right in front of me, in the grand stand that day, there was a fellow with a couple of girls and they was about my age. The young fellow was a nice guy all right. He was the kind maybe that goes to college and then comes to be a lawyer or maybe a newspaper editor or something like that, but he wasn't stuck on himself. There are some of that kind are all right and he was one of the ones.

He had his sister with him and another girl and the sister looked around over his shoulder, accidental at first, not intending to start anything—she wasn't that kind—and her eyes and mine happened to meet.

You know how it is. Gee, she was a peach! She had on a soft dress, kind of a blue stuff and it looked carelessly made, but was well sewed and made and everything. I knew that much. I blushed when she looked right at me and so did she. She was the nicest girl I've ever seen in my life. She wasn't stuck on herself and she could talk proper grammar without being like a school teacher or something like that. What I mean is, she was O.K. I think maybe her father was well-to-do, but not rich to make her chesty because she was his daughter, as some are. Maybe he owned a drug store or a drygoods store in their home town, or something like that. She never told me and I never asked.

My own people are all O.K. too, when you come to that. My grandfather was Welsh and over in the old country, in Wales he was— But never mind that.

The first heat of the first race come off and the young fellow setting there with the two girls left them and went down to make a bet. I knew what he was up to, but he didn't talk big and noisy and let everyone around know he was a sport, as some do. He wasn't that kind. Well, he come back and I heard him tell the two girls what horse he'd bet on, and when the heat was trotted they all half got to their feet and acted in the excited, sweaty way people do when they've got money down on a race, and the horse they bet on is up there pretty close at the end, and they think maybe he'll come on with a rush, but he never does because he hasn't got the old juice in him, come right down to it.

And then, pretty soon, the horses came out for the 2.18 pace and there was a horse in it I knew. He was a horse Bob French had in his string but Bob didn't own him. He was a horse owned by a Mr. Mathers down at Marietta, Ohio.

This Mr. Mathers had a lot of money and owned some coal mines or something, and he had a swell place out in the country, and he was stuck on race horses, but was a Presbyterian or something, and I think more than likely his wife was one, too, maybe a stiffer one than himself. So he never raced his horses hisself, and the story round the Ohio race tracks was that when one of his horses got ready to go to the races he turned him over to Bob French and pretended to his wife he was sold.

So Bob had the horses and he did pretty much as he pleased and you can't blame Bob, at least, I never did. Sometimes he was out to win and sometimes he wasn't. I never cared much about that when I was swiping a horse. What I did want to know was that my horse had the speed and could go out in front, if you wanted him to.

And, as I'm telling you, there was Bob in this race with one of Mr. Mathers' horses, was named "About Ben Ahem" or something like that, and was fast as a streak. He was a gelding and had a mark of 2.21, but could step in .08 or .09.

Because when Burt and I were out, as I've told you, the year before, there was a nigger, Burt knew, worked for Mr. Mathers and we went out there one day when we didn't have no race on at the Marietta Fair and our boss Harry was gone home.

And so everyone was gone to the fair but just this one nigger and he took us all through Mr. Mathers' swell house and he and Burt tapped a bottle of

wine Mr. Mathers had hid in his bedroom, back in a closet, without his wife
knowing, and he showed us this Ahem horse. Burt was always stuck on being
a driver but didn't have much chance to get to the top, being a nigger, and
he and the other nigger gulped that whole bottle of wine and Burt got a little
lit up.

So the nigger let Burt take this About Ben Ahem and step him a mile on a
track Mr. Mathers had all to himself, right there on the farm. And Mr. Mathers had one child, a daughter, kinda sick and not very good looking, and she
came home and we had to hustle and get About Ben Ahem stuck back in the
barn.

I'm only telling you to get everything straight. At Sandusky, that afternoon
I was at the fair, this young fellow with the two girls was fussed, being with
the girls and losing his bet. You know how a fellow is that way. One of them
was his girl and the other his sister. I had figured that out. "Gee whizz," I
says to myself, "I'm going to give him the dope."

He was mighty nice when I touched him on the shoulder. He and the girls
were nice to me right from the start and clear to the end. I'm not blaming
them.

And so he leaned back and I give him the dope on About Ben Ahem. "Don't
bet a cent on this first heat because he'll go like an oxen hitched to a plow,
but when the first heat is over go right down and lay on your pile." That's
what I told him.

Well, I never saw a fellow treat any one sweller. There was a fat man sitting beside the little girl, that had looked at me twice by this time, and I at her,
and both blushing, and what did he do but have the nerve to turn and ask
the fat man to get up and change places with me so I could set with his crowd.

Gee whizz, craps amighty. There I was. What a chump I was to go and
get gay up there in the West House bar, and just because that dude was
standing there with a cane and that kind of a necktie on, to go and get all
balled up and drink that whiskey, just to show off.

Of course she would know, me setting right beside her and letting her smell
of my breath. I could have kicked myself right down out of that grand stand
and all around that race track and made a faster record than most of the
skates of horses they had there that year.

Because that girl wasn't any mutt of a girl. What wouldn't I have give
right then for a stick of chewing gum to chew, or a lozenger, or some liquorice,
or most anything. I was glad I had those twenty-five cent cigars in my pocket
and right away I give that fellow one and lit one myself. Then that fat man
got up and we changed places and there I was, plunked right down beside
her.

They introduced themselves and the fellow's best girl, he had with him, was named Miss Elinor Woodbury, and her father was a manufacturer of barrels from a place called Tiffin, Ohio. And the fellow himself was named Wilbur Wessen and his sister was Miss Lucy Wessen.

I suppose it was their having such swell names got me off my trolley. A fellow, just because he has been a swipe with a race horse, and works taking care of horses for a man in the teaming, delivery, and storage business, isn't any better or worse than anyone else. I've often thought that, and said it too.

But you know how a feller is. There's something in that kind of nice clothes and the kind of nice eyes she had, and the way she had looked at me, awhile before, over her brother's shoulder, and me looking back at her, and both of us blushing.

I couldn't show her up for a boob, could I?

I made a fool of myself, that's what I did. I said my name was Walter Mathers from Marietta, Ohio, and then I told all three of them the smashingest lie you ever heard. What I said was that my father owned the horse About Ben Ahem and that he had let him out to this Bob French for racing purposes, because our family was proud and had never gone into racing that way, in our own name, I mean. Then I had got started and they were all leaning over and listening, and Miss Lucy Wessen's eyes were shining, and I went the whole hog.

I told about our place down at Marietta, and about the big stables and the grand brick house we had on a hill, up above the Ohio River, but I knew enough not to do it in no bragging way. What I did was to start things and then let them drag the rest out of me. I acted just as reluctant to tell as I could. Our family hasn't got any barrel factory, and since I've known us, we've always been pretty poor, but not asking anything of any one at that, and my grandfather, over in Wales—but never mind that.

We set there talking like we had known each other for years and years, and I went and told them that my father had been expecting maybe this Bob French wasn't on the square, and had sent me up to Sandusky on the sly to find out what I could.

And I bluffed it through I had found out all about the 2.18 pace, in which About Ben Ahem was to start.

I said he would lose the first heat by pacing like a lame cow and then he would come back and skin 'em alive after that. And to back up what I said I took thirty dollars out of my pocket and handed it to Mr. Wilbur Wessen and asked him, would he mind, after the first heat, to go down and place it on About Ben Ahem for whatever odds he could get. What I said was that I didn't want Bob French to see me and none of the swipes.

Sure enough the first heat come off and About Ben Ahem went off his stride, up the back stretch, and looked like a wooden horse or a sick one, and come in to be last. Then this Wilbur Wessen went down to the betting place under the grand stand and there I was with the two girls, and when that Miss Woodbury was looking the other way once, Lucy Wessen kinda, with her shoulder you know, kinda touched me. Not just tucking down, I don't mean. You know how a woman can do. They get close, but not getting gay either. You know what they do. Gee whizz.

And then they give me a jolt. What they had done, when I didn't know, was to get together, and they had decided Wilbur Wessen would bet fifty dollars, and the two girls had gone and put in ten dollars each, of their own money, too. I was sick then, but I was sicker later.

About the gelding, About Ben Ahem, and their winning their money, I wasn't worried a lot about that. It come out O.K. Ahem stepped the next three heats like a bushel of spoiled eggs going to market before they could be found out, and Wilbur Wessen had got nine to two for the money. There was something else eating at me.

Because Wilbur come back, after he had bet the money, and after that he spent most of his time talking to that Miss Woodbury, and Lucy Wessen and I was left alone together like on a desert island. Gee, if I'd only been on the square or if there had been any way of getting myself on the square. There ain't any Walter Mathers, like I said to her and them, and there hasn't ever been one, but if there was, I bet I'd go to Marietta, Ohio, and shoot him to-morrow.

There I was, big boob that I am. Pretty soon the race was over, and Wilbur had gone down and collected our money, and we had a hack down-town, and he stood us a swell supper at the West House, and a bottle of champagne beside.

And I was with that girl and she wasn't saying much, and I wasn't saying much either. One thing I know. She wasn't stuck on me because of the lie about my father being rich and all that. There's a way you know . . . Craps amighty. There's a kind of girl, you see just once in your life, and if you don't get busy and make hay, then you're gone for good and all, and might as well go jump off a bridge. They give you a look from inside of them somewhere, and it ain't no vamping, and what it means is—you want that girl to be your wife, and you want nice things around her like flowers and swell clothes, and you want her to have the kids you're going to have, and you want good music played and no rag time. Gee whizz.

There's a place over near Sandusky, across a kind of bay, and it's called Cedar Point. And after we had supper we went over to it in a launch, all by ourselves. Wilbur and Miss Lucy and that Miss Woodbury had to catch a ten o'clock train back to Tiffin, Ohio, because, when you're out with girls like that you can't get careless and miss any trains and stay out all night, like you can with some kinds of Janes.

And Wilbur blowed himself to the launch and it cost him fifteen cold plunks, but I wouldn't never have knew if I hadn't listened. He wasn't no tin horn kind of a sport.

Over at the Cedar Point place, we didn't stay around where there was a gang of common kind of cattle at all.

There was big dance halls and dining places for yaps, and there was a beach you could walk along and get where it was dark, and we went there.

She didn't talk hardly at all and neither did I, and I was thinking how glad I was my mother was all right, and always made us kids learn to eat with a fork at table, and not swill soup, and not be noisy and rough like a gang you see around a race track that way.

Then Wilbur and his girl went away up the beach and Lucy and I sat down in a dark place, where there was some roots of old trees, the water had washed up, and after that the time, till we had to go back in the launch and they had to catch their trains, wasn't nothing at all. It went like winking your eye.

Here's how it was. The place we were setting in was dark, like I said, and there was the roots from that old stump sticking up like arms, and there was a watery smell, and the night was like—as if you could put your hand out and feel it—so warm and soft and dark and sweet like an orange.

I most cried and I most swore and I most jumped up and danced, I was so mad and happy and sad.

When Wilbur came back from being alone with his girl, and she saw him coming, Lucy she says, "We got to go to the train now," and she was most crying too, but she never knew nothing I knew, and she couldn't be so all busted up. And then, before Wilbur and Miss Woodbury got up to where we was, she put her face up and kissed me quick and put her head up against me and she was all quivering and— Gee whizz.

Sometimes I hope I have cancer and die. I guess you know what I mean. We went in the launch across the bay to the train like that, and it was dark, too. She whispered and said it was like she and I could get out of the boat and walk on the water, and it sounded foolish, but I knew what she meant.

And then quick we were right at the depot, and there was a big gang of yaps, the kind that goes to the fairs, and crowded and milling around like cattle, and how could I tell her? "It won't be long because you'll write and I'll write to you." That's all she said.

I got a chance like a hay barn afire. A swell chance I got.

And maybe she would write me, down at Marietta that way, and the letter would come back, and stamped on the front of it by the U.S.A. "There ain't any such guy," or something like that, whatever they stamp on a letter that way.

And me trying to pass myself off for a bigbug and a swell—to her, as decent a little body as God ever made. Craps amighty—a swell chance I got!

And then the train come in, and she got on, and Wilbur Wessen he come and shook hands with me, and that Miss Woodbury was nice too and bowed to me, and I at her, and the train went and I busted out and cried like a kid.

Gee, I could have run after that train and made Dan Patch look like a freight train after a wreck but, socks amighty, what was the use? Did you ever see such a fool?

I'll bet you what—if I had an arm broke right now or a train had run over my foot—I wouldn't go to no doctor at all. I'd go set down and let her hurt and hurt—that's what I'd do.

I'll bet you what—if I hadn't a drunk that booze I'd a never been such a boob as to go tell such a lie—that couldn't never be made straight to a lady like her.

I wish I had that fellow right here that had on a Windsor tie and carried a cane. I'd smash him for fair. Gosh darn his eyes. He's a big fool—that's what he is.

And if I'm not another you just go find me one and I'll quit working and be a bum and give him my job. I don't care nothing for working, and earning money, and saving it for no such boob as myself.

BOOK LISTS

The following lists are purposely made brief, attempting merely to select from large numbers of books those most helpful and most easily available to students and general readers. Fuller bibliographies may be found in *The Cambridge History of American Literature,* vols. i, ii, and iv, 1917–1921; in S. T. Williams and N. F. Adkins, *Courses of Reading in American Literature with Bibliographies,* 1930; and, for recent writers, in J. M. Manly and E. Rickert, *Contemporary American Literature; Bibliographies and Study Outlines,* 1922.

JONATHAN EDWARDS

For further selections see C. Van Doren, *Benjamin Franklin and Jonathan Edwards* (in the Modern Students Library), 1920, and H. N. Gardiner, *Selected Sermons,* 1904 (with excellent introduction and notes). For Edwards's religious life, A. V. G. Allen, Jonathan Edwards (in American Religious Leaders), 1889. For critical essays, O. W. Holmes, *Pages from an Old Volume of Life,* 1883; Sir Leslie Stephen, *Hours in a Library,* vol. i, 1894; and P. E. More, *Cambridge History,* vol. i, 1917.

BENJAMIN FRANKLIN

The standard edition of Franklin's works is that edited by A. H. Smyth, in 10 volumes, 1905–07. The *Autobiography,* with correct text, is available in Everyman's Library. Fuller selections may be found in C. Van Doren, *Benjamin Franklin and Jonathan Edwards* (Modern Student's Library), 1920. For biography see J. B. Macmaster, *Benjamin Franklin as Man of Letters* (American Men of Letters), 1887; W. C. Bruce, *Franklin Self-Revealed,* 1917; Bernard Faÿ, *Franklin, the Apostle of Modern Times,* 1929. Franklin's activities are interestingly detailed in P. L. Ford, *The Many-Sided Franklin,* 1899. For criticism see S. P. Sherman, *Americans,* 1922; H. S. Canby, *Everyday Americans* ("American Idealism"), 1920.

ST. JEAN DE CRÈVECŒUR

The *Letters from an American Farmer* are well reprinted in an edition by L. Lewisohn, 1904, and also in Everyman's Library. Newly discovered letters may be found in *Sketches of Eighteenth Century America,* edited by H. L. Bourdin and others (with introduction), 1925. For biography see Julia P. Mitchell, *St. Jean de Crèvecœur,* 1916; and S. T. Williams, *Dictionary of American Biography,* vol. iii, 1929.

GEORGE WASHINGTON

An excellent edition of Washington's writings is that edited by W. C. Ford, 1889–93. *The Diaries of George Washington, 1748–1799,* edited by John C.

Fitzpatrick, 4 vols., 1925, will repay perusal. Notable early biographies are by John Marshall, 1801–07, and Washington Irving, 1855–59. Later biographies are numerous; a good recent one is that by Rupert Hughes, *George Washington, the Human Being and the Hero*, 3 vols. (to date), 1926–1930. See also W. P. Trent's article on Washington in *Southern Statesmen of the Old Régime*, 1897.

THOMAS JEFFERSON

The edition of Jefferson's writings edited by P. L. Ford, 10 vols., 1892–99, is perhaps the best. See too *The Best Letters of Thomas Jefferson* edited by J. G. de R. Hamilton, 1926. There are numerous Lives, among which may be mentioned those by B. L. Rayner, 1834; G. Tucker, 1837; H. S. Randall, 1857; J. T. Morse, Jr., 1883; F. W. Hirst, 1926; and the study by Thomas Chinard, *Thomas Jefferson, the Apostle of Americanism*, 1929. For his attitude on foreign affairs, see Henry Adams, *History of the United States*, 1889–91; for an appreciation of his political opinions, C. Beard, *Economic Origins of Jeffersonian Democracy*, 1915; and for the political history between 1790–1800, C. G. Bowers, *Jefferson and Hamilton*, 1925. W. P. Trent's article on Jefferson in *Southern Statesmen of the Old Régime*, 1897, is good. Paul Wilstach, *Jefferson and Monticello*, 1928, deals interestingly with Jefferson's domestic life.

WASHINGTON IRVING

The authorized *Life and Letters of Washington Irving* is by his nephew, P. M. Irving, 4 vols., 1862–64, and other editions. See also C. D. Warner, *Washington Irving* (American Men of Letters), 1881; G. S. Hellman, *Washington Irving, Esquire*, 1925; and W. D. Howells, *My Literary Passions*, 1895. Interesting English notices of Irving may be found in Hazlitt, *Spirit of the Age*, "Elia and Geoffrey Crayon," and in Thackeray, *Roundabout Papers*, "Nil Nisi Bonum."

JAMES FENIMORE COOPER

Before his death Cooper requested that no biography of him should be authorized. His *Correspondence* has, however, been edited by his grandson, J. F. Cooper, 2 vols., 1922. T. R. Lounsbury, *Cooper*, 1882, is one of the best of the American Men of Letters series. For criticism consult: Francis Parkman, *North American Review*, Jan. 1852; J. Erskine, *Leading American Novelists*, 1910; W. C. Brownell, *American Prose Masters*, 1909; and Mark Twain, *How to Tell a Story and Other Essays* (containing an amusing essay on "Cooper's Literary Offenses" in *The Deerslayer*), 1892.

RALPH WALDO EMERSON

The best edition of Emerson's *Complete Works* is the "Centenary Edition," with introduction and notes by E. W. Emerson, 12 vols., 1903–04. His *Journals* are collected in 10 vols., 1909–14; and a good selection made from these in B. Perry, *The Heart of Emerson's Journals*, 1926. The important works are available in Everyman's Library. The standard biography is by J. E. Cabot, *Memoir of Emerson*, 1887; this is supplemented by E. W. Emerson, *Emerson at Concord*, 1889. O. W. Holmes, *Emerson* (American Men of Letters), 1885, is first-hand and personal, but superficial. G. E. Woodberry, *Emerson* (English Men of Letters), 1907, and O. W. Firkins, *Emerson*, 1915, are admirable. The most recent life, P. Russell, *Emerson, the Wisest American*, is mainly personal. The criticism of Emerson is very extensive, including essays in J. R. Lowell, *Literary Essays*, vol. i, 1890, "Emerson the Lecturer"; M. Arnold, *Discourses in America*, 1885; P. E. More, *Shelburne Essays, First Series*, 1904; J. J. Chapman, *Emerson and Other Essays*, 1898; W. C. Brownell, *American Prose Masters*, 1909; H. James, *Partial Portraits*, 1888; and Van Wyck Brooks, *Emerson and Others*, 1927.

HENRY DAVID THOREAU

The best edition is the "Walden Edition," in 20 vols., 1906, of which the last fourteen contain the Journals. From the Journals a good selection is made by O. Shepard, *The Heart of Thoreau's Journals*, 1927. The best life is by F. B. Sanborn, *Thoreau* (American Men of Letters), 1882. L. Bazalgette, *Thoreau, Bachelor of Nature* (translated from the French by Van Wyck Brooks), 1924, and J. B. Atkinson, *Thoreau, The Cosmic Yankee*, 1927, are largely critical. Emerson's essay, "Thoreau," (in this book p. 176) is invaluable. For further criticism: J. R. Lowell, *Literary Essays*, vol. i, 1890 (unsympathetic); R. L. Stevenson, *Familiar Studies of Men and Books*, 1902; J. Burroughs, *Indoor Studies*, 1889; P. E. More, *Shelburne Essays, First* and *Fifth Series*, 1904, 1908; W. C. Brownell, *American Prose Masters*, 1909; and N. Foerster, *Nature in American Literature*, 1923.

NATHANIEL HAWTHORNE

The authoritative life is by Hawthorne's son, Julian Hawthorne, in *Hawthorne and His Wife*. 1885, and in the supplementary *Hawthorne and His Circle*, 1903. The life by H. James (English Men of Letters), 1879, is inferior to that by G. E. Woodberry (American Men of Letters), 1902. N. Arvin, *Hawthorne*, 1929, is an excellent study. Arvin also edits *The Heart of Hawthorne's Journals*, 1929. A brief life may be found in J. Erskine, *Leading American Novelists*, 1910. For criticism: G. P. Lathrop, *A Study of Hawthorne*, 1876; Sir Leslie Stephen, *Hours in a Library*, vol. i, 1894; L. E. Gates, *Studies and Appreciations*, 1900; P. E. More, *Shelburne Essays, First* and *Second Series* (the former on p. 687 of this book), 1904, 1907; and W. C. Brownell, *American Prose Masters*, 1909.

EDGAR ALLAN POE

The standard edition of Poe's works is the "Virginia Edition," edited by J. A. Harrison, 17 vols., 1902, which contains Poe's letters and also a biography; an excellent edition also is that by E. C. Stedman and G. E. Woodberry, 10 vols., 1914, containing a memoir and critical introductions. Good collections of the Tales are edited by K. Campbell, for the American Authors Series, 1927, and by J. S. Wilson for the Modern Student's Library, 1927. *Selections from the Critical Writings of Poe*, edited, with introduction, by F. C. Prescott, 1909, and *Selections from the Literary Criticism of Poe*, edited, with introducton, by J. B. Moore, 1926, contain the best of Poe's critical work. The most complete biographies are by J. A. Harrison, *Life and Letters of Poe*, 2 vols., 1903; by G. E. Woodberry, *The Life of Edgar Allan Poe*, 2 vols., 1909; and by H. Allen, *Israfel*, 2 vols., 1926. For criticism: *The Cambridge History of American Literature*, vol. ii, 1918, *The*

Book of Poe, with an introduction by H. Allen, 1929, and introductions to the collections already cited.

OLIVER WENDELL HOLMES

Good editions of Holmes's works are the "Riverside," 13 vols., 1891; the Standard Library, 15 vols., including Morse's *Life,* 1896; and the "Autocrat," 13 vols., 1904. The *Complete Poetical Works* may be had in the Cambridge Edition, edited by H. E. Scudder, 1895. *The Autocrat of the Breakfast-Table* is included in Everyman's Library. The standard biography is by J. T. Morse, *Life and Letters of Oliver Wendell Holmes,* 2 vols., 1896; but see too, L. W. Townsend, *Oliver Wendell Holmes,* 1909. For criticism see: T. W. Higginson, *Old Cambridge,* 1900; W. D. Howells, *Literary Friends and Acquaintances,* 1900; Andrew Lang, *Adventures Among Books,* 1905; W. L. Schroeder, *Oliver Wendell Holmes, an Appreciation,* 1909; and *The Cambridge History of American Literature,* vol. ii, 1918.

JAMES RUSSELL LOWELL

The best edition is the "Elmwood Edition," in 16 volumes, 1904. The *Letters,* edited by C. E. Norton, 2 vols., 1904, are interesting. The best life is by F. Greenslet, *Lowell* (American Men of Letters), 1905. For criticism: H. James, *Essays in London and Elsewhere,* 1893; W. D. Howells, *My Literary Passions,* 1895; W. C. Brownell, *American Prose Masters,* 1909; and N. Foerster, *Nature in American Literature,* 1923.

DANIEL WEBSTER

The best collection is the "National Edition"—*The Writings and Speeches of Daniel Webster,* 18 vols., 1903. A sympathetic life is that by H. C. Lodge, *Daniel Webster* (American Statesmen), 1884. A good selection from the speeches is made by A. J. George, *Select Speeches of Daniel Webster,* 1893.

WILLIAM HICKLING PRESCOTT

The definitive edition of Prescott's works, with which is included Ticknor's *Life,* is the "Montezuma Edition," edited by W. H. Munro, 22 vols., 1904. *The History of the Conquest of Mexico* and *The Conquest of Peru* are published in Everyman's Library. The standard *Life* is that by George Ticknor, revised edition, 1875; but see also H. T. Peck's biography in the English Men of Letters Series, 1905. For criticism consult *The Cambridge History of American Literature,* vol. ii, 1918.

FRANCIS PARKMAN

Parkman's historical writings were published under the general title, *France and England in North America,* 9 vols., 1865–92. Recent editions of the *Works* are the "Frontenac," 17 vols., 1910, including the *Life* by Farnham, and the "Centenary Edition," 12 vols., 1922. *The Oregon Trail* may be had in the Modern Student's Library and the Lake English Classics; and *The Conspiracy of Pontiac* is included in the Everyman's Library. For biography see C. H. Farnham,

Life of Francis Parkman, 1900, and H. D. Sedgwick, *Francis Parkman,* 1904. For criticism consult H. C. Vedder, *American Writers of To-day,* 1894, and *The Cambridge History of American Literature,* vol. iii, 1921.

HERMAN MELVILLE

The best collected edition, in 16 volumes, London (Constable), 1922–24, is expensive. The more important works, however, are available in various recent editions: *Typee, Omoo,* and *Moby Dick* in Everyman's Library; these also, with *White Jacket,* in "World's Classics" (Oxford Press); *Pierre* in two editions, 1929 and 1930; and the shorter works in *Shorter Novels of Herman Melville,* 1928, edited by R. M. Weaver. The best biographies are by R. M. Weaver, *Herman Melville, Mariner and Mystic,* 1921, and L. Mumford, *Herman Melville,* 1929; the second is largely critical, as is also F. Freeman, *Melville* (English Men of Letters), 1926. For further criticism: A. MacMechan, *Life in a Little College,* 1913, and Van Wyck Brooks, *Emerson and Others,* 1927.

ABRAHAM LINCOLN

The standard edition is edited by J. G. Nicolay and John Hay, 2 vols., 1894, and 12 vols., 1905. The best of Lincoln may be found conveniently in *Selections from Lincoln,* edited, with an introduction, by N. W. Stephenson, 1927. Stephenson writes also the chapter on Lincoln in the *Cambridge History of American Literature.* Among many books on Lincoln may be recommended: Ida Tarbell, *Lincoln,* 2 vols., 1910; Brand Whitlock, *Lincoln,* 1916; Lord Charnwood, *Lincoln,* 1916; and Carl Sandburg, *Lincoln, the Prairie Years,* 2 vols., 1926.

WALT WHITMAN

The Complete Prose Works of Walt Whitman, 1898, though not complete, contains all Whitman's significant prose, except his interesting "Backward-Glance O'er Travel'd Roads," which is appended to many editions of *Leaves of Grass.* A good selection from both poetry and prose may be found in *Leaves of Grass, Abridged Edition,* edited by E. Holloway, 1926. There is no satisfactory biography, but Bliss Perry, *Whitman* (American Men of Letters), 1906, G. R. Carpenter, *Whitman,* 1909, J. Bailey, *Whitman* (English Men of Letters), 1926, and E. Holloway, *Whitman,* 1926, taken together may give adequate idea of Whitman's elusive personality. The best criticism is perhaps to be found in the older works: J. Burroughs, *Whitman, a Study,* 1896, and J. A. Symonds, *Whitman, a Study,* 1897.

EDWARD EVERETT HALE

Hale's *Works* were published in 10 volumes, 1898–1901. *The Life and Letters of Edward Everett Hale,* by his son, E. E. Hale, Jr., 2 vols., 1917, is the authorized life, but this should be supplemented by his own *A New England Boyhood,* 1893, and *Memories of a Hundred Years,* 1902. For criticism see: H. C. Vedder, *American Writers of To-day,* 1894, and *The Cambridge History of American Literature,* vol. ii, 1918.

MARK TWAIN

A good authorized edition is the "Hillcrest," in 25 vols., 1903. *Life on the Mississippi, Tom Sawyer,* and *Huckleberry Finn* are available in Harper's Modern Classics Series. A. B. Paine, *Mark Twain,* is one of the most interesting of American biographies. It appears also, abridged, in one volume. For criticism: S. P. Sherman's chapter in *The Cambridge History of American Literature,* vol. iii, and especially F. L. Pattee's in his *American Literature Since 1870,* 1915; also Van Wyck Brooks, *The Ordeal of Mark Twain,* 1920.

BRET HARTE

Harte's *Works* were published in 20 volumes, 1896–1903. *The Luck of Roaring Camp* is published in the Modern Readers' Series. For biography see H. C. Merwin, *Life of Bret Harte,* 1911, and *Letters of Bret Harte,* 1926. For criticism see: J. Erskine, *Leading American Novelists,* 1910; H. R. Haweis, *American Humorists,* 1883; and F. L. Pattee, *A History of American Literature Since 1870,* 1915.

HENRY ADAMS

The Education of Henry Adams is available in a "Popular Edition," 1927. *Letters of Henry Adams* (1858–1891), are edited by W. C. Ford, 1930. The best account of Adams's life is that in the *Dictionary of American Biography,* vol. i, 1928. See also J. T. Adams, *The Adams Family,* 1930. For criticism: P. E. More, *Shelburne Essays, Eleventh Series,* 1921, and C. Becker, *American Historical Review,* April, 1919.

HENRY JAMES

James made a selection from his writings for the "New York Edition," 26 vols., 1906–1917, and furnished invaluable introductions discussing his aims and methods. His *Letters,* 2 vols., appeared in 1920. The following are autobiographical: *A Small Boy and Others, Notes of a Son and Brother,* and *The Middle Years.* For criticism: Van Wyck Brooks, *The Pilgrimage of Henry James,* 1925; J. W. Beach, *The Method of Henry James* (a good introduction to the novels), 1918; and W. C. Brownell, *American Prose Masters,* 1909.

SARAH ORNE JEWETT

A good selection from Miss Jewett's work is *The Best Stories of Sarah Orne Jewett,* edited by Willa Cather, 1925. No complete biography of her has been written, but the sympathetic but cursory volume, *Sarah Orne Jewett,* by F. O. Matthiessen, 1929, and *The Letters of Sarah Orne Jewett,* edited by Annie Fields, 1911, throw light on her career. See also: M. Thompson, "The Art of Miss Jewett," in *The Atlantic Monthly,* October, 1904, and Martha H. Shackford, "Sarah Orne Jewett," in *The Sewanee Review,* January, 1922.

MARY WILKINS FREEMAN

A good approach to Mrs. Freeman is through *The Best Stories of Mary E. Wilkins Freeman,* edited by H. W. Lanier, 1927. For criticism see: F. L. Pattee,

Side-Lights on American Literature, 1922, and M. Moss, "Representative American Story-Tellers," in *The Bookman,* September, 1906.

JOEL CHANDLER HARRIS

Harris's works have not been collected. The best single volumes perhaps are *Uncle Remus: His Songs and His Sayings,* 1880; *Nights with Uncle Remus,* 1883; *Mingo and Other Sketches in Black and White,* 1884; and *Free Joe, and Other Georgia Sketches,* 1887. A sympathetic biography is *The Life and Letters of Joel Chandler Harris,* 2 vols., 1918, by his daughter-in-law, Julia Collier Harris; but *On the Plantation,* 1892, an autobiographical novel, should also be read. For criticism consult: W. M. Baskerville, *Southern Writers Series,* 1896; L. L. Knight, *Reminiscences of Famous Georgians,* vol. i, 1907; and *The Cambridge History of American Literature,* vol. ii, 1918.

LAFCADIO HEARN

The best edition is *The Writings of Lafcadio Hearn,* 16 vols., 1922. For biography see: Elizabeth Bisland, *The Life and Letters of Lafcadio Hearn,* 1906; G. M. Gould, *Concerning Lafcadio Hearn,* 1908; E. L. Tinker, *Lafcadio Hearn's American Days,* 1924; and O. Lewis, *Hearn and His Biographers,* (which reviews the preceding), 1930. For criticism: P. E. More, *Shelburne Essays, Second Series,* 1905, and F. L. Pattee, *American Literature Since 1870,* 1915.

O. HENRY

O. Henry's *Complete Writings* were published in 12 volumes in 1911, and the "Memorial Edition," 14 vols., was issued in 1917. Perhaps the best of the single volumes are *The Four Million,* 1906; *Options,* 1909; and *Whirligigs,* 1910. For biography see C. A. Smith, *O. Henry,* 1916, and A. J. Jennings, *Through the Shadows with O. Henry,* 1921. For criticism consult: F. T. Cooper, *Some American Story-Tellers,* 1911; Stephen Leacock, *Essays and Literary Studies,* 1916; and F. L. Pattee, *Side-lights on American Literature,* 1922.

EDITH WHARTON

See L. M. Melish, *Bibliography of the Collected Writings of Edith Wharton,* 1927, for a list of her various works and where they may be procured. For criticism consult: J. C. Underwood, *Literature and Insurgency,* 1914; C. Van Doren, *Contemporary American Novelists,* 1922; R. M. Lovett, *Edith Wharton,* 1925 (the most complete study); and Régis Michaud, *The American Novel To-day,* 1928.

WILLA CATHER

Miss Cather's books which will best repay reading are perhaps *O Pioneers!* 1913; *My Antonia,* 1918; *Youth and the Bright Medusa* (short stories), 1920; *A Lost Lady,* 1923; *The Professor's House,* 1925; and *Death Comes for the Archbishop,* 1927. For criticism see: T. K. Whipple, *Spokesmen: Modern Writers and American Life,* 1928; A. Porterfield, *Contemporary American Authors,* 1928, edited by J. C. Squire; and Elizabeth S. Sergeant, *Fire Under the Andes,* 1927.

SHERWOOD ANDERSON

Of Anderson's works, *Poor White* and *Winesburg, Ohio* may be had in the Modern Library. Although *Tar: a Mid-West Childhood,* 1926, and *A Story Teller's Story,* 1924, are fictionized, they are the best sources for material on the author's life. For criticism consult: V. F. Calverton, *The Newer Spirit,* 1925; S. P. Sherman, *Critical Woodcuts,* 1926; P. H. Boynton, *More Contemporary Americans,* 1927; N. B. Fagin, *The Phenomenon of Sherwood Anderson,* 1927; Régis Michaud, *The American Novel To-day,* 1928; and the introduction by Ernest Boyd to *Winesburg, Ohio* in the Modern Library, 1919.